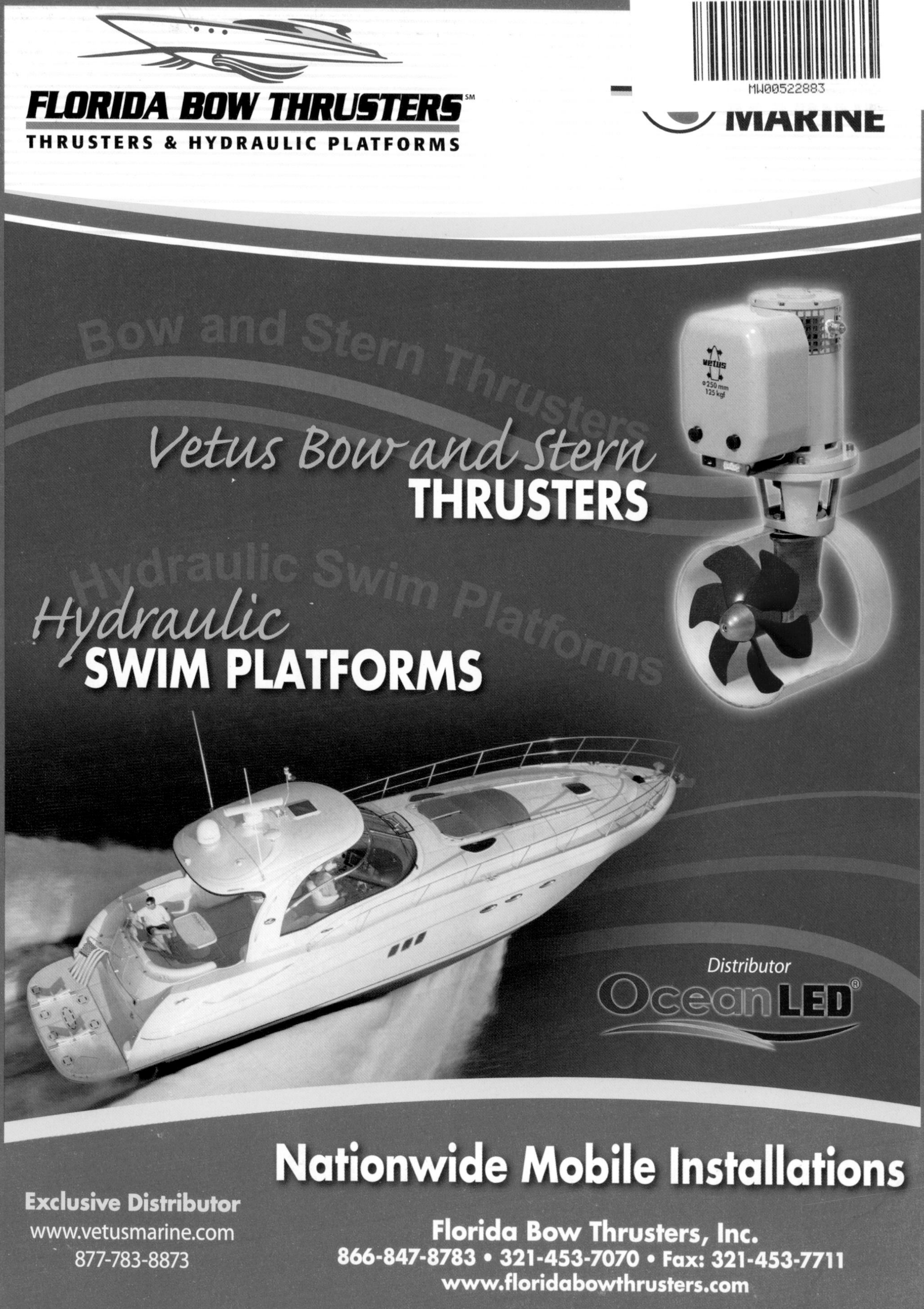

FLORIDA BOW THRUSTERS℠
THRUSTERS & HYDRAULIC PLATFORMS
MARINE
Bow and Stern Thrusters
Vetus Bow and Stern
THRUSTERS
Hydraulic Swim Platforms
Hydraulic
SWIM PLATFORMS
vetus
⌀250 mm
125 kgf
Distributor
OceanLED®
Nationwide Mobile Installations
Exclusive Distributor
www.vetusmarine.com
877-783-8873
Florida Bow Thrusters, Inc.
866-847-8783 • 321-453-7070 • Fax: 321-453-7711
www.floridabowthrusters.com

DOZIER'S

WATERWAY GUIDE®

THE CRUISING AUTHORITY

F O U N D E D I N 1 9 4 7

Publisher **JACK DOZIER**
jdozier@waterwayguide.com

Associate Publisher **CRAIG DOZIER**
cdozier@waterwayguide.com

General Manager **CHUCK BAIER**
cbaier@waterwayguide.com

Editor **SUSAN LANDRY**
slandry@waterwayguide.com

Editorial Assistant **TERRY GRANT**
tgrant@waterwayguide.com

Web & News Editor **TED STEHLE**
tstehle@waterwayguide.com

Director of Marketing **DENIELLE T. D'AMBROSIO**
denielle@waterwayguide.com

Production Artist **REESA KUGLER**
rkugler@waterwayguide.com

Web Coordinator **MIKE SCHWEFLER**

Ad Traffic Manager **TRISH SHARPE**
tsharpe@waterwayguide.com

Book Sales **LESLIE TAYLOR**
ltaylor@waterwayguide.com

Book Sales **DEBI DEAN**
ddean@waterwayguide.com

Accounts Manager **ARTHUR CROWTHER**
accounts@waterwayguide.com

Administrative Assistant **MARGIE MOORE**

Shipping & Receiving **KEVIN GRAVES**

Cover: An aerial view, Lighthouse at Nassau Harbour.
Photo Credit: Robert Linder
Pink House in Hope Town. Photo Credit: Peter Mitchell.
Dock at Compass Point, Nassau. WATERWAY GUIDE PHOTO

Waterway Guide publishers, staff and family enjoy a day on the water to watch the Blue Angels perform over Annapolis.

EDITORIAL OFFICES
York Associates, LLC
326 First Street, Suite 400
Annapolis, MD 21403
Send Correspondence to: P.O. Box 4219
Annapolis, MD 21403, 443-482-9377

BOOK SALES:
www.WaterwayGuide.com
800-233-3359

CORPORATE & ACCOUNTING OFFICES
Waterway Guide/Skipper Bob Publications
Dozier Media Group
P.O. Box 1125, Deltaville, VA 23043

CONTRIBUTORS

• Chris Caldwell • Kay Gibson
• Mark Gonsalves • Pepper Holmes
• Gil Johnson • Carl Jordan
• Rick Kennedy • Robert Linder
• Diane & Michael Marotta
• Peter Mitchell • Alan Pereya
• Kip & Larry Putt • Jim Quince

ADVERTISING SALES
GENERAL ADVERTISING INQUIRIES
CRAIG DOZIER
cdozier@waterwayguide.com

CRUISING EDITORS

CHESAPEAKE BAY EDITION
JACK & CRAIG DOZIER

ATLANTIC ICW EDITION
BUD & ELAINE LLOYD
JACK & CRAIG DOZIER

NORTHERN EDITION
LARRY & RUTH SMITHERS
BUD & ELAINE LLOYD

BAHAMAS EDITION
JANICE BAUER CALLUM
ROBERT WILSON

SOUTHERN EDITION
GEORGE DANNER
BUD & ELAINE LLOYD

GREAT LAKE EDITION
BOB KUNATH
WALLY MORAN
TED & AUDREY STEHLE

Price per copy: $39.95. When ordering by mail or telephone, add shipping and handling charges. Direct all orders to: WATERWAY GUIDE, P.O. Box 4219, Annapolis, MD 21403; or call 800-233-3359, fax 443-482-9422.

York Associates, LLC , the publisher of WATERWAY GUIDE (Guide), makes reasonable efforts to ensure the accuracy of the information in this Guide. However, WATERWAY GUIDE must rely on others over which it has no control for certain information. In addition, no book or guide is a substitute for good judgment, experience and firsthand knowledge. Therefore, WATERWAY GUIDE hereby gives notice that the charts, descriptions, and illustrations in this Guide are not to be used for navigation. The use of any navigational reference or description contained in the Guide is at the user's own risk. Inclusion in the WATERWAY GUIDE of marine facilities, services, restaurants and other information is for informational purposes only; no guarantee is provided as to the accuracy or current status of this information, nor does York Associates, LLC endorse any of the facilities or services described herein.

Because York Associates, LLC cannot and does not guarantee or warrant that the information in the Guide is complete or current, York Associates, LLC disclaims all warranties, express or implied, relating to the information in any manner, including, without limitation, implied warranties of merchantability and fitness for a particular purpose.

York Associates, LLC shall not be liable to the purchaser or any third party for any loss or injury allegedly caused, in whole or in part, by York Associates, LLC and/or WATERWAY GUIDE (or the information contained therein) or for consequential, exemplary, incidental or special damages. Furthermore, in any event, York Associates, LLC's liability, if any, shall never exceed the amount paid by the original purchaser for the directory.

To provide the most complete and accurate information, all facilities have been contacted within the past year. Although facility operators supplied this data, we cannot guarantee accuracy or assume responsibility for errors. Entrance and dockside soundings tend to fluctuate. Always approach marinas carefully. Reference numbers on spotting charts indicate marina locations. Aerial photos are for general overview only and are not to be used for navigation.

Member of National Marine Manufacturers Association – Printed In China

Publisher's Letter

What a reception! Our inaugural 2010 edition of the Bahamas Waterway Guide was widely acclaimed and outsold our projections. Our appreciation goes out to all our dedicated staff and, of course, to all our loyal Waterway Guide followers. Building on the "eyes on" cruising information gathered by our on-site cruising editors and from contributions by cruisers like you, we are proud to present our second Bahamas Edition. Here you will find additional pages of text, updated information and new features throughout the guide.

The positive response to our Bahamas Guide was especially welcome considering forces at work outside of our or anyone's control; namely the challenging economy and the turbulent winter weather. The economy in the Bahamas was hit especially hard by the worldwide recession due to their somewhat isolated location and the nature of their economy. Luxury spending on leisure travel to the islands and funding for a rash of new resorts and marinas was suddenly curtailed, leaving a void in the economic engine of the Bahamas.

The important yachting sector of the Bahamian economy was further hurt by a winter of unusually severe weather patterns, resulting in northerly winds barring crossing of the Gulf Stream and cold fronts that regularly swept through the entire 600 mile length of the islands. For those cruisers who did make it across, there were bargains on slips and secluded anchorages in abundance.

However, in spite of these setbacks, the signature spirit of the Bahamian people has remained upbeat. For them, life in paradise goes on and "een no ting" takes on added meaning. Sure enough, things are turning around. Several of the mega-resorts have new owners, new financing and new life, bringing in tourist dollars that are filtering to the native population. The annual spring and summer influx of Florida boaters is underway. The lure of the Bahamas is as strong as ever.

There is little we can do to control the economy but we can control our passages to and throughout the Bahamas. Proper preparation, planning ahead, but being flexible, coordinating departures around weather systems, being realistic on cruise itineraries, moving with the seasons; all these are necessary for a safe and enjoyable Bahamas experience.

Publisher Jack Dozier and Associate Publisher Craig Dozier, with sons Ned and Skipper.

Inside this guide, you'll find advice and tips covering these and many other points, gathered from many miles and many years of cruising in the Bahamas. Planned properly, you will likely join the veteran cruisers who return over and over, and you'll be offering your own tips to those who follow you. And remember, before you depart and during your cruise, consult our Web site www.waterwayguide.com for the latest navigation updates and cruising news.

See you on the water,

Jack Dozier,
Publisher

Waterway Guide Lady docked at Staniel Cay Yacht Club in the Exumas.

PUBLISHER'S LETTER

A MESSAGE FROM THE MINISTER OF TOURISM & AVIATION

Dear Boating Enthusiasts:

We invite you to visit our breathtaking islands surrounded by miles and miles of sun-kissed beaches. With the closest of our islands located just 55 miles off the coast of Florida, and 700 to choose from, The Islands Of The Bahamas offers a variety of unique cultural experiences all blended together to create one diverse Bahamian palette.

On our islands there is something for everyone. From pristine beaches to sumptuous cuisine and a surprising blend of attractions and activities, we have it all. Added to this, is the warm, inviting hospitality of the Bahamian people.

For centuries, boaters navigating The Bahamas by sea have marveled at our crystal clear waters, secluded anchorages and numerous harbors. Today, our environment remains just as pristine. When you combine that with modern, state-of-the-art facilities and communications, it makes the cruising experience in our country absolutely irresistible.

The Islands Of The Bahamas welcome Waterway Guide, the new publishers of The Bahamas Cruising Guide. We are confident that this new expanded Bahamas guide will continue to serve as a key resource for guiding visiting boaters through the beauty and wonder of our island chain, reaffirming the centuries old cruising fact that nowhere is cruising better than in The Islands Of The Bahamas.

Sincerely,

Sen. Hon. Vincent Vanderpool-Wallace,
Minister of Tourism and Aviation

Bahamas, Turks and Caicos Coverage

DOZIER'S WATERWAY GUIDE
THE CRUISING AUTHORITY

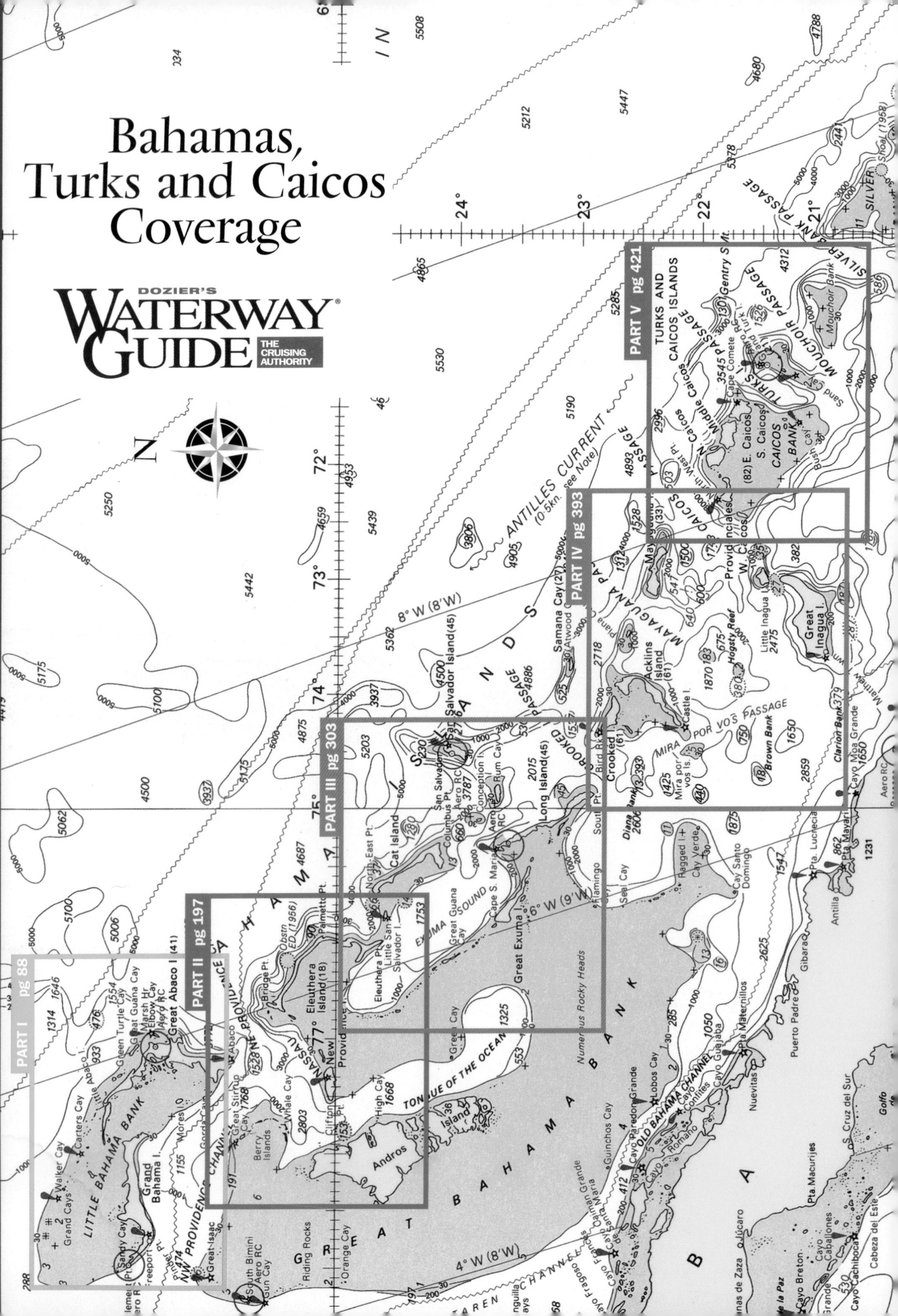

Contents

VOLUME 64, NO.6

Introduction

Skipper's Handbook

Indexes

DOZIER'S WATERWAY GUIDE® THE CRUISING AUTHORITY

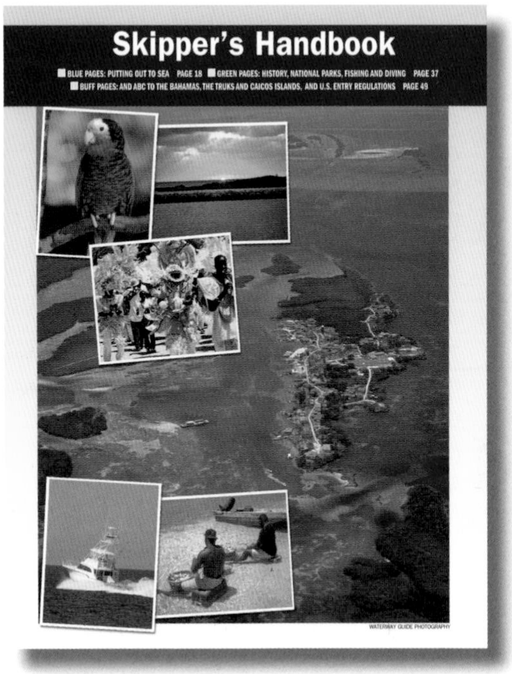

A DOZIER MEDIA GROUP PUBLICATION

INTRODUCTION

PART I. THE NORTHERN CRUISING GROUNDS

PART II. THE CENTRAL CRUISING GROUNDS

PART III. THE SOUTHERN CRUISING GROUNDS

PART IV. FAR HORIZONS

PART V. THE TURKS AND CAICOS ISLANDS

Cruising Editors

Janice Bauer Callum

Janice Bauer Callum

Janice Bauer Callum and her husband, George, have been sailing together for 45 years. George has a much longer sailing history. In his youth, he sailed the eastern seaboard with his family onboard their 8-meter *Gracious,* and crewed for numerous Chicago to Mackinac races, as well as taught sailing for the Michigan City Yacht Club. Over the years, Janice and George have cruised and raced the Great Lakes, the East Coast, the Caribbean and the Bahamas. When they weren't cruising or racing their sloop *Morning Glory* with their three children, Treavor, Heather and Dayne, they were racing windsurfers. Janice was a District Chairperson for the International Windsurfing Class Association for whom she organized races for thousands of sailors and qualified them for the first Olympic sail boarding competition in Los Angeles.

Since their retirement in 2000, Janice and George have been docked on the beaches of Mexico and sailed their Hallberg-Rassy Rasmus, *Calamus,* from the Tennessee-Tombigbee Waterway up and down the eastern seaboard and the ICW to the Bahamas, where they sail several months every year. For the short time that they are not onboard Calamus, they are at their small ranch on Lake Calamus in Burwell, Nebraska—home of the oldest (and only) Windsurfing Rodeo.

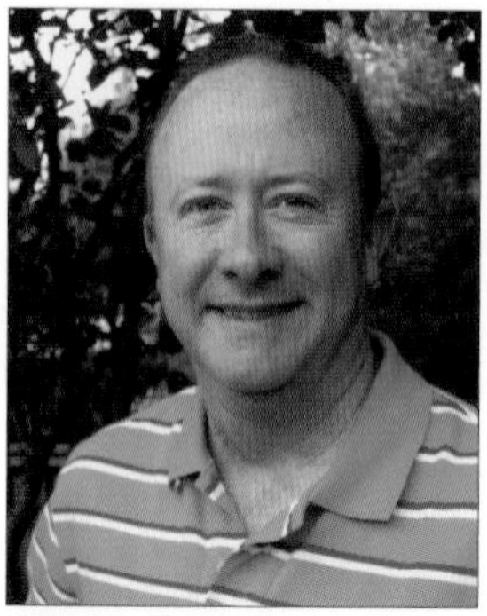

George Danner

George E. Danner

An avid boater whose home port is Galveston Bay, TX, George Danner is WATERWAY GUIDE's cruising editor for the ICW from Mississippi to Brownsville, TX. He began serious cruising several years ago by trailering his 26-foot Monterey express cruiser to Chesapeake Bay, Key West, Destin, FL and the Carolina coast from Charleston to Hilton Head Island. Now with a 2006 Silverton 34C, *La Mariposa*, recently added to the fleet, George focuses on Gulf excursions from Galveston to Mississippi and southern trips to Corpus Christi and South Padre Island. The western Gulf region is home to some of the finest cruising grounds in the country, and the Danner family frequently explores its coastal waters for new land and sea-based adventures. Out of the water, George is president of a corporate strategy consulting firm in Houston.

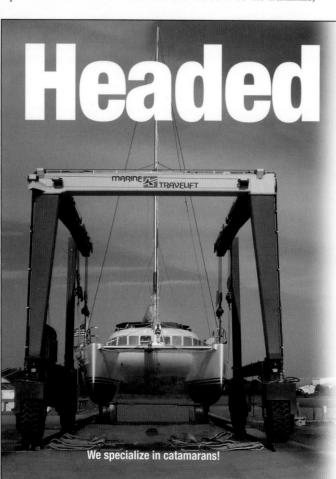

Bob and Carol Kunath

Bob and Carol Kunath

Bob and Carol Kunath have owned about a dozen sail and powerboats over the past 40 years. They've ranged from small-lake open boats to those equipped for offshore shark and tuna fishing, to sail and powerboats on Lake Michigan, where they have been cruising for the past 15 years. During those years they have cruised extensively throughout Lake Michigan and the North Channel of Lake Huron. Both are past commodores of the Bay Shore Yacht Club in Illinois and members of the Waukegan, IL, Sail and Power Squadron, where Bob has served as an officer and instructor. He has also contributed to the U.S. Power Squadron national magazine, Ensign, and holds a U.S. Coast Guard Master's license.

During 2005, Bob and Carol completed a two-year cruise of the Great Loop in their Pacific Seacraft 38T trawler, *Sans Souci,* logging 9,000 miles on the Loop and many of its side trips. Recently they have resumed cruising all of Lake Michigan, but have plans to expand that area, perhaps back into the rivers of the Midwest or canals of Canada. Bob has also been a seminar presenter at Passagemaker Trawler Fests over the past four years, sharing his knowledge of Lake Michigan. For 2011, Bob and Carol cover Lake Michigan for Waterway Guide, including Green Bay and Door County.

Bud and Elaine Lloyd

Bud and Elaine Lloyd

Bud and Elaine Lloyd, are the cruising editors for South Florida, the Keys and Okeechobee Waterway. After being long-time sailors (they had several sailboats over the years), the Lloyds decided that in order to do the type of cruising they dreamed of they needed a trawler. Diamond Girl is a 36-foot 1990 Nova/Heritage East Sundeck. From their home port of Long Beach, California, they cruised all over Southern California and parts of Mexico extensively for over 30 years. After retiring from the printing business in 2005, they decided that it was time to get serious about fulfilling a life-long dream of cruising the Chesapeake Bay and ICW. So in December 2005, they put Diamond Girl on a ship and sent her to Ft. Lauderdale, Florida. They have now been cruising on the East Coast for almost 5 years and have found the experience even more rewarding than they ever imagined. They have made several trips up and down the ICW, have spent the summers cruising on the Chesapeake Bay, and have made numerous crossings of the Okeechobee Waterway. Bud and Elaine are full-time liveaboard cruisers and can't wait to see what awaits them over the next horizon. Now the Waterway Guide has given them the opportunity to write about what they enjoy most...cruising!

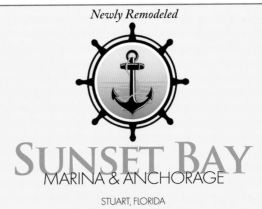

Wally Moran

Wally Moran

Wally Moran, Waterway Guide's cruising editor for Georgian Bay, the North Channel, the St. Marys River and Lake Huron, is a former newspaper publisher who has sailed these favored cruising grounds since honeymooning there in 1978. His more recent travels have taken him from Chesapeake Bay to Tampa Bay, then back to Canada via Lake Huron and Lake Erie, the Erie Barge Canal, the Hudson River, Chesapeake Bay, the Intracoastal Waterway and offshore. Wally's next planned cruise will see his completion of the Great Loop into the Gulf of Mexico and on into the Caribbean, before returning to Canada. Wally sails his Dufour 34 *Gypsy Wind* throughout the Georgian Bay area, which he assures Waterway Guide readers is the "best freshwater boating in the world" and encourages all boaters to visit.

Larry and Ruth Smithers

Larry and Ruth Smithers

Larry and Ruth Smithers are cruising editors for Waterway Guide's Northern edition from Cape Cod through Maine. They have boated in various capacities since the early 1970s. Serious passionate boating gripped them with the acquisition of *Back Dock,* their 56-foot Vantare pilothouse motoryacht. They quickly discovered that work got in the way of boating. Bidding their land life adieu they sold their practice, leased out their home in Wisconsin, packed up and moved aboard to cruise full time in pursuit of high adventure and sunsets worthy of the nightly celebratory conch horn serenade. The Smithers have completed the Great Loop, cruised the Bahamas and, as always, look forward to continue exploring new territories.

Larry spent the first half of his working career in the international corporate world and the last as a chiropractor. He is now retired, a U.S. Coast Guard-licensed captain and can proudly recite the pirate alphabet. Ruth's career was in public accounting. She retired to become a stay-at-home mother, which ultimately evolved into being a professional volunteer and dilettante. She enjoys basket making and her role as "Admiral."

Audrey and Ted Stehle

Audrey and Ted Stehle

Audrey and Ted Stehle are Waterway Guide's cruising editors for the inland rivers and the Tenn-Tom Waterway, from Chicago to Mobile Bay, for the Great Lakes 2011 Guide.

They began boating as sailors in the early 1970s on the Chesapeake Bay, and then switched to power after retirement. In addition to extensive cruising of Chesapeake Bay and its tributaries, they have traveled the ICW to Florida many times, completed the Great Loop, cruised the Ohio, Tennessee and Cumberland rivers and made six trips on the Tenn-Tom Waterway. Their Californian 45 is presently on Chesapeake Bay, but plans call for returning it to Kentucky Lake to resume cruising the Cumberland and Tennessee rivers. When not cruising, the Stehles reside in Cincinnati, OH to be near their children and grandchildren, and engage in volunteer work.

Robert Wilson

Robert Wilson

Robert Wilson has been cruising in the Bahamas from his homeport in Brunswick, GA for the past nine years. He and his wife, Carolyn, began sailing on Lake Lanier, just north of Atlanta, GA, shortly after they met 25 years ago. Robert is a former employee benefits consultant, and is a Past Commodore of the Royal Marsh Harbour Yacht Club in Abaco. Together they have written extensively about their sailing adventures throughout the Bahamas on their 38-foot Island Packet, *Gypsy Common.* Their current boat, *Sea Island Girl,* is a North Pacific 42 pilothouse trawler, which they cruised in the Pacific Northwest along the coast of British Columbia, before shipping the boat to Florida to continue cruising throughout the Bahamas aboard their new trawler.

When not cruising, the Wilsons reside in Atlanta, GA, where Carolyn teaches pre-school, and Robert continues consulting and writing. Robert is Waterway Guide's cruising editor for the northern Bahamas. ■

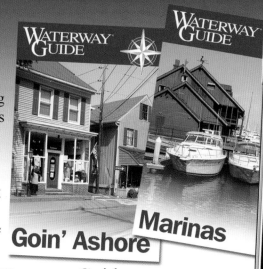

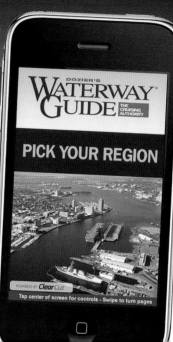

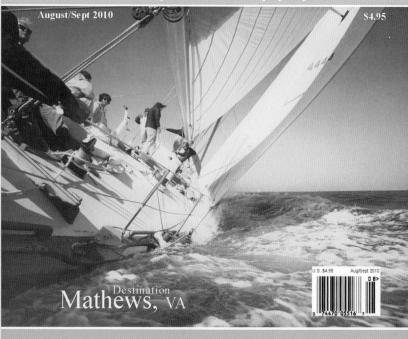

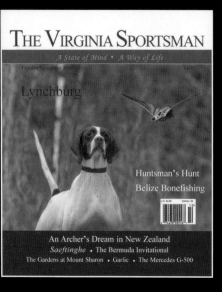

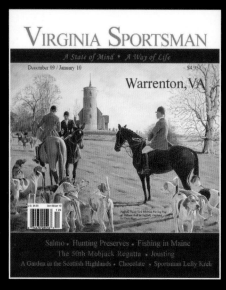

Skipper's Handbook

WATERWAY GUIDE PHOTOGRAPHY

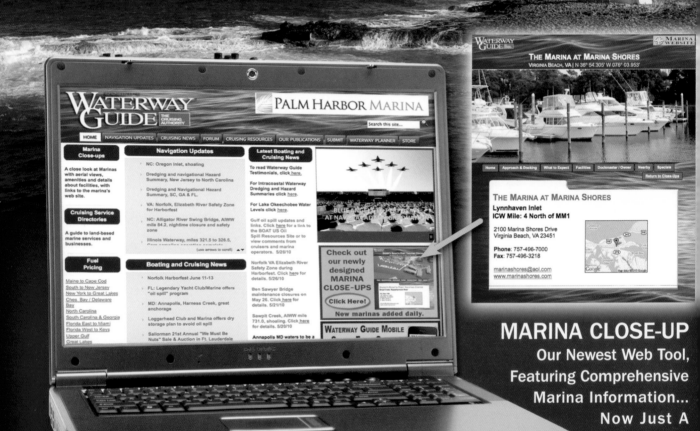

Skipper's Handbook

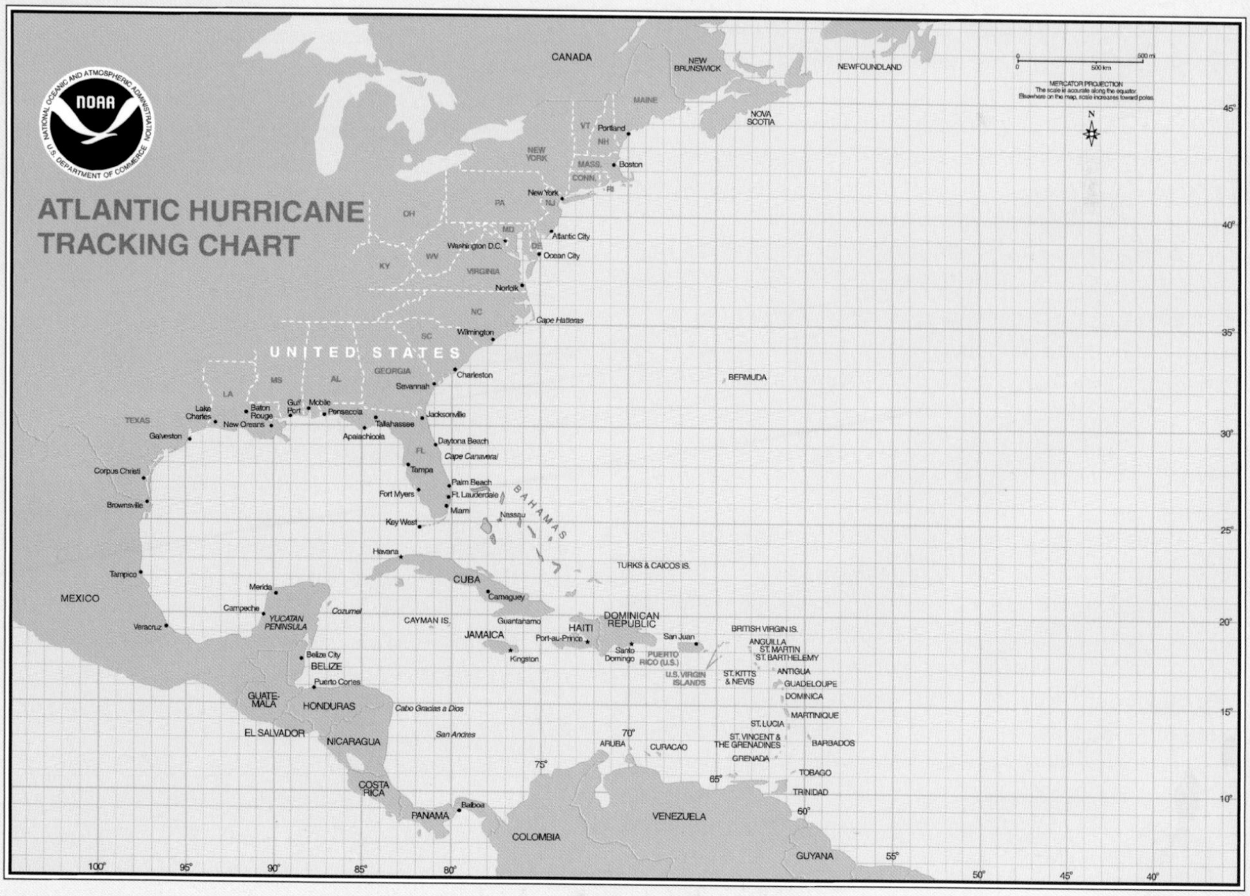

Blue Pages

Putting Out to Sea

Seamanship and Preparation

What is an ideal boat to cruise the islands? Let's agree that it has to meet U.S. Coast Guard minimum requirements, be seaworthy, in good condition and equipped for emergencies. At the most basic, it must be able to cross the Gulf Stream safely, even if the weather does something unexpected and conditions deteriorate. It must have enough bunks to sleep you and your crew comfortably no matter what it's like outside at the helm or on the hook. It has to provide adequate refrigeration to keep fresh food at safe temperatures and cooking facilities to keep even the fussiest of palates happy. A double dish sink is nice, but a bucket will do (just don't throw the silverware overboard). A good complement of electronics – GPS, chartplotter – are good to have on board, but paper charts are a must. A complete set of newer charts with guidebooks is ideal.

A boat's means of propulsion and its length, width and draft have less to do with safety and more to do with how many places it can take you, how fast it can go and what routes it must take to get you there. When crossing the Banks, a deeper draft boat has limitations, but still plenty of options. Options narrow regarding accessible harbors and anchorages with deep draft, however. Sailboats must have good rigging, good sails, good sheets, good lines, good steering, but most importantly, good sailors with good sense. Let's hope that good sense includes reliable auxiliary power. Any boat must have enough fuel capacity, or room for diesel can storage, to make it from the farthest point-to-point refueling spots on your cruising itinerary. The water storage capacity, or the reliability of your watermaker, must match the needs of your crew. For instance, some folks limit the amount of fresh bathing water they use per day to 64 ounces. Then there are others whose family uses the same amount of water showering as if they were on the mainland. Clearly the ideal water capacity on their boats was significantly different. Ideal water capacity is, therefore, relative (like many things).

So is storage - relative that is. If you are cruising from port to port, staying at marinas and eating your meals out or having them served to you by a personal chef, the boat for you needs plenty of space for clothes, shoes and toiletries. If your agenda is more along the lines of getting as far as you can on as little as you can, you will likely need a boat with ample long-term food and supplies storage space. In terms of storage space for "toys" or tools (at least men's toys and tools), there does not seem to be a boat designed with adequate storage space for either. Same story for galley "stuff," it is too tall, too long, too wide, too fragile or the cord is too short.

Janet Wilson

Man-O-War schooner William H. Albury, built in 1963.

Space seems to be relative in regards to sanitary facilities, also. The simple days of a bucket on a line are long gone. We share the seas with boats that have more heads onboard than we do at home. Regardless of the number of heads you want to clean and keep working, make sure the boat has an adequate holding tank and a means to pump it out in deep ocean waters. Pump-out stations are far and few between in the Bahamas. You can make a less-than-ideal situation a bit more "ideal" by not using sea-life harming chemicals and putting toilet tissue in the wastebasket, not the holding tank. Maybe not a "comfortable" practice for your guests, but the environment (and the person who has to unplug the head or unsludge the holding tank) will thank you.

Since we are speaking of comfort, a boat's ventilation system and shade from the sun are high on the list, particularly if there is no air conditioning. No ventilation and no shade in hot climates don't go well together. Ventilation can mean everything from flow-through systems that keep the "down below" areas healthy and dry, to plenty of hatches that open in all directions to keep a breeze flowing no matter which way the bow is pointed. Drop-through-the-hatch, catch-a-breeze kites are a must (the square ones work the best because they don't collapse when the wind shifts or current swings the boat at the anchor), and don't even consider a boat that doesn't have adequate cover over the entire cockpit, steering station or aft deck. For swimming, a platform is a plus, a sturdy ladder a must. And finally, a good tender is essential. Be it an inflatable, a hard dinghy, a T-top or a sea kayak, it is your sea car.

The list of boats that meet these ideals is long. Previous cruising editors have cruised the islands in a sailing catamaran that was just 6.6 meters/22 feet on the waterline and in a 14.7-meter/49-foot motor yacht with three double cabins with heads and every appliance you could find in a house. Did they have anything in common? Let's check the list:

- Seaworthiness
- Sound engines
- Tankage to carry sufficient reserves of fuel and water
- Draft under 1.8 meters/6 feet (you can make most places with 2.4 meters/8 feet)
- Good navigational equipment
- VHF radio, single side band receiver, EPIRB and full safety equipment well beyond the basic U.S. Coast Guard requirements

One time when the cruising editor was in West End, someone was towed in by a Bahamian fishing boat shortly after dawn. The weather had been unsettled and the Gulf Stream had not quieted down, but it was by no means rough out there. The boat being towed in was a 5-meter/17-foot center-console open boat with just one man onboard. He had set out from Palm Beach the evening before for a week in the Abacos. He ran out of fuel during the night, was being thrown around a bit by the seas and fired off the only two flares he had on board. He was lucky. A Coast Guard helicopter passing to the south saw the flares and radioed West End to get help to him. Despite his predicament, he wasn't altogether happy when his rescuer charged him $3,000 for the ride. Asked why he hadn't carried enough fuel to cross the Stream, his reply was, "I didn't think it was that far." You see, it was not the boat's fault at all. It made it! Regardless of the boat you choose, in the end, it is ultimately all up to you.

Pre-Departure Check

- Gas, diesel, outboard fuel, reserve oil, lubricants.
- Engine oil levels, coolant, hoses, belts, bilges.
- Navigation lights, spotlight, deck lights, interior lights Man overboard (MOB) equipment, flares and smoke signals, EPIRB, life raft, survival equipment.
- Dinghy and outboard, snorkeling, fishing, diving gear.
- Check anchors and bitter ends.

Complete Navigation Work

- List waypoints, courses, times and distances, with alternatives for bad weather.
- List lights and tides. Check weather forecast and set barometer.
- Set watch and ship's clock to correct time by GPS satellite.

Other Preparations

- Complete provisioning; list stores and spare parts.
- Yellow Q (quarantine) flag and Bahamas courtesy flag.
- Check that ship's papers are complete: documentation or state registration, insurance, passports, money.
- Check that crew passports or proofs of citizenship are set for entry into the Bahamas; open log and list crew.
- Complete Float Plan
- Prepare first day/night-on-passage food.
- Stow for rough weather and clear decks.
- Secure open ports and hatches.
- Take garbage ashore.
- Obtain marina or (if necessary) port authority departure clearances.
- Turn on radios and navigation instruments.
- Take a head count before sailing.
- Hold a new crew safety briefing, including MOB drill, use of VHF, EPIRB and abandoning ship.

Float Plan

Give your float plan to someone who will keep it handy until you telephone to report your safe arrival. You should set a "fail safe" time. If he or she has not heard from you by then, a call should be made to the U.S. Coast Guard to report that you are overdue. A sample Float Plan is included at the end of this chapter for you to photocopy.

Coming into Port

- Have approach chart, coastal pilot and harbor chart on hand.
- Know the location of your dock or safe anchorage.
- Check on any special timing requirements, bridges for example.
- Know the state of tide, currents and the local wind pattern.
- List navigation aids in order of likely utility: lights, marks, bottom contours and depths.
- Have VHF radio, binoculars, hand-bearing compass, hailer and air horn on hand.
- Prepare anchor, fenders and lines.
- Keep navigation instruments on until log data is recorded.
- Have Q flag or courtesy flag ready to fly after clearance.
- Report to Customs and Immigration if it is your Port of Entry.
- Call and report your safe arrival to the keeper of the float plan.
- After clearance, write up log, check bilges and engines, take garbage ashore, fill water and fuel tanks and wash down decks.

Anchoring and Mooring

- Never anchor over coral.
- Anchor as far off fellow boaters as possible.
- If the shore is covered in vegetation, scrub or mangroves, expect visitors—the kind that bite!
- Be prepared for 180-and 360-degree swings and strong tidal flows, common in Bahamian anchorages. Never use two anchors when one will do. However, if you find yourself in a situation where nothing but two anchors will do, such as a crowded anchorage where everyone is already on two anchors, the easiest solution is to set your first anchor and either dinghy out your second anchor, or drop back to put down the second anchor and then position yourself between them. Remember that current and tidal flow always win over wind.
- Always try to dive to check that your anchor has set or check it using a dive mask or a glass-bottom bucket from your dinghy. Sometimes, if the bottom is hard-packed sand or rocky, you may have to dive to set an anchor by hand.

- Don't run your portable generator unless you are alone - really alone. Sound carries at night. It is rude to run your generator when others are around, and you will spoil the magic of the islands for everyone else.
- Always set an anchor light. Local Bahamian boats go about their business at all hours of the night often at high speed. A conventional masthead light is just too high to warn off someone racing along at sea level. Mount an auxiliary anchor light about 10 feet above the water and see how that looks to you from your dinghy. It could be just the most sensible precaution you ever took.
- Take anchor bearings or get a GPS fix and keep them displayed at the helm station. Check them to ensure that you have not dragged. If the risk is high, make out a roster and keep checking throughout the night. Set an anchor alarm if you have one.

Severe Storm Conditions

If you are unlucky and have to weather a severe storm at anchor, avoid exposed harbors and crowded anchorages. Try to find a hurricane hole or a channel in mangroves where you can secure lines to the sturdy trees. Use every line you have. Make a spider's web of lines allowing 3 meters/10 feet of slack for tidal surge, and use all your anchors fanned out at 90–120 degrees to complement your spider's web.

Use chafe protectors on your lines where they come on board. Reduce your windage. Take down any canvas and sails (if you are a sailboat). Lower your antennas, deflate and store your inflatable below deck, then lash down everything that must remain on deck. Make the hull watertight. Consider plugging your engine and generator exhaust ports, but don't forget that you have done this!

If you can't find a hurricane hole (and there are very few places that are ideal), you can anchor out to face the wind. Set three anchors in a 120-degree fan. Ideally, lead the three rodes to a swivel and then run line from the swivel to the boat. Try for a 10:1 scope. If you use all chain, put a nylon snubber (equal to 10 percent of the chain length) on the chain to absorb shock.

All of these are "last ditch" defensive measures in very severe conditions. Hopefully, you will never need to undertake them. If you are caught out when hurricane or near-hurricane conditions are imminent, remember that your boat is of secondary importance to your life and the lives of those with you. Your action should be to secure the boat if you can do so, but find a better place to take shelter ashore and leave the boat to take what comes.

Ground Tackle

We all dream of idyllic, calm, isolated and uncrowded anchorages. You will definitely find them in the Bahamas. However, you won't have perfection all the time. Your Bahamian anchorage may well turn out to be swept by reversing tidal currents, open to squalls or already crowded with other boats by the time you get there. You need to carry two anchors cruising in the Bahamas (three if you count your tender's anchor):

1. A plow or spade type: Bruce, CQR or Delta
2. A Danforth-style

Fit your anchor to your boat length, and go oversize if in doubt. When it comes to anchors, BIGGER is always better. In addition, make sure you know the safe working load and the breaking point of your ground tackle.

Pull in Pounds: Boat Length and Wind Velocity

LOA (feet)	Wind Speed (knots) 15	30	40	60
25	125	490	980	1960
30	175	700	1400	2800
35	225	900	1800	3600
40	300	1200	2400	4800
50	400	1600	3200	6400
60	500	2000	4000	8000

Bahamian Moor

The Bahamian Moor was used with early types of anchors – the types that did not hold well when twisted or tripped. With the advent of newer-style anchors and the technology to analyze load and force on objects, experts learned that when two anchors are set, the strain on each anchor is increased, especially when wind and current oppose each other. Therefore, it is better to use one anchor, not two, in most anchoring situations, especially in the Bahamas.

Scope

Scope (the length of anchor rode you put out measured from the bow roller into the water to the anchor) helps determine how well your anchor will hold under most conditions. Generally, the greater the scope, the better. With an all-chain rode, 5:1 (that is about 1.5 meters/5 feet of anchor chain for every foot of depth at high tide) is sufficient in sheltered water. With nylon and chain, 7:1 scope is good. If you are working in meters, take that initial 5-foot figure and work it as 1.5 meters. It is simpler and errs on the side of safety.

Anchoring: Depth and Scope

Depth	3:1	4:1	5:1	6:1	7:1	8:1
10 feet	30	40	50	60	70	80
15 feet	45	60	75	90	105	120
20 feet	60	80	100	120	140	160
25 feet	75	100	125	150	175	200
30 feet	90	120	150	180	210	240

Bahamas Dive Site Mooring Buoys

Dive site mooring buoys are in the Green Turtle Cay area in the Central Abacos, along the line of the reef in the Port Lucaya area, throughout the Exuma Land and Sea Park and scattered about the Bimini Islands. Many are maintained by local dive operators. You may tie your dinghy to these mooring buoys for a short time to dive and snorkel however, you must move if a dive operator arrives and needs the mooring.

Turks and Caicos Dive Site Buoys

All recognized dive sites in the Turks and Caicos are marked and numbered. Again, you may take up a dive buoy if a local operator is not using it. These buoys are classified by length overall, and the Turks and Caicos buoyage system is further complicated by private moorings, danger marks with letter IDs (RF for reef, WRK for wreck and BAR for bar), marine park boundaries, anchorage zones (letter A) and channel markers. Refer to the table below:

Large Vessel (24 meters/80 ft LOA) Dive Site	White cylinder, 2 Blue Bands
Standard Dive Site	White Ball, 1 Blue Band
Private Mooring	Red Ball
Danger Mark	Red Ball with a Black Band
Park Boundary Mark	White Post
Anchorage Zone	White Post, 3 Blue Bands
Channel Marker	Red or Green Post

Tides and Currents

Tide is the vertical movement of water. Current is the horizontal movement of water. Both affect you in the Bahamas. Be aware of the state of the tide, particularly when entering and leaving harbors and negotiating passages. Even an inch can make the difference between being afloat or being aground. If your boat draws more than 1.5 meters/5 feet, you will need to pay a lot of attention to tides in the Bahamas.

Bahamian Tides

Bahamas tides are semi-diurnal, which means two high tides and two low tides in 24 hours. You can easily chart the tide without a tide table. Just remember that at full moon and at new moon, high tide comes at 8 a.m. and 8 p.m. local time. High tides then occur roughly an hour later each day. Use the Rule of Twelfths (see Useful Tables and Measurements) to plot the rise and fall.

The mean tidal range in the Bahamas is 2.5 feet. When the moon is full or new, the range increases to around 3 feet 1 inch. At the lowest range, neap tides occur at the first and third quarters of the moon. Then you get the lowest levels, about 6 inches below mean low water. The time of high and low tides throughout the Bahamas varies only 40 minutes or less, except for the west coast of Eleuthera and the bank side of the Grand Lucayan Waterway on Grand Bahama. They are about 2.5 hours behind Nassau. All Bahamian tides are based on Nassau.

Bahamas Tides—Based on Nassau

Northern Cruising Grounds

Marsh Harbour, Abaco	+ 30 minutes
Abaco Cays, North Bar Channel	+ 30 minutes
Memory Rock	+ 30 minutes
Grand Bahama, West End	+ 25 minutes
Grand Bahama, North End Lucayan Waterway	+ 2 hours 30 minutes

Central Cruising Grounds

North Bimini	+ 20 minutes
North Cat Cay	+ 30 minutes
Berry Islands, Whale Cay	+ 40 minutes
Spanish Wells	+ 30 minutes
Eleuthera, Current Mouth	Nassau Time
Eleuthera, East Coast	+ 20 minutes
Eleuthera, Central, West Coast	+ 2 hours 25 minutes
Andros, Fresh Creek	+ 8 minutes

Southern Cruising Grounds

Exuma Cays, Highbourne	+ 20 minutes
Exuma Cays, Warderick Wells	+ 30 minutes
Exuma Bank, Great Exuma Island	– 2 hours
George Town	Nassau time
Cat Island, The Bight	– 25 minutes
San Salvador, Cockburn Town	Nassau time
Long Island, Clarence Town	+ 50 minutes
Long Island, Salt Pond	+ 2 hours 30 minutes

Far Horizons

Acklins Island, Southwest Point	– 10 minutes
Mayaguana, Abrahams Bay	+ 10 minutes
Great Inagua, Matthew Town	+ 20 minutes

Tidal Ranges

North of George Town: height of tide 0.1 meter/0.3 feet below Nassau.
South of George Town: height of tide 0.15 meter/0.5 feet below Nassau.

Neap Tides (first and third quarters of the Moon)	– 0.15 meter/0.5 feet
New and Full Moons	+ 0.15 meter/0.5 feet
Spring Tides	+ 0.15 meter/0.5 feet
Spring Full Moon Tides	+ 0.3 meter/1 foot

Tidal Differences After (+) or Ahead (-) of Nassau

The time differences we quoted are rounded off. For the exact times of high and low water, together with the predicted height and range of each tide, you must refer to full tidal data based on NOAA harmonics and correction tables. In practice, particularly as wind and barometric pressure affect all tides, our figures should serve for all normal cruising and passage-making calculations.

High winds can have a significant impact on tides, particularly in the Bahamas. They will sweep water up much higher than normal in enclosed areas or, conversely, blow the water out to produce much lower tides than normal.

Tide tables are available from sources such as NOAA, the UK Hydrographic Office and Nautical Software's Tides and Currents. Tides are also available online at http://tidesandcurrents.noaa.gov. In the Bahamas, tide tables are published in the newspapers and are often available in pamphlet form in marine stores and dive shops. Bahamas tides are based on Nassau, New Providence Island N25°05.000'/W077°21.000'. You are wise to have tide tables simply for confidence, but without tide tables you are not helpless. You need a known Nassau High and Low as a start point. From then on simply move these times forward by approximately an hour each day. Refer the Tide Difference Table - Bahamas Tides - Based on Nassau - to forecast local highs and lows.

If you tried to produce a "Tidal Atlas of the Bahamas," you might go insane. Perhaps that is why no one has done so. The Banks shed their water in every direction and draw in ocean water from every direction when the flow reverses. How does this work? While this is a far from scientific explanation, here is a simplified view. Imagine the Bank as a great shallow plate with an uneven rim, surrounded by ocean. The high bits of the rim are the islands. On a rising tide, ocean water rises up onto the Bank, over all the low bits of the rim and flows in trying to fill the plate from all directions. On a falling tide, the plate sheds its water in all directions.

You can understand why that tidal atlas could be difficult to draw. When you are on the Banks, you need to know where the nearest low part of the plate rim is; and of course, where the "center" of the plate lies. A line between the two gives you an idea of the current you can expect, in one direction or the other, depending on the state of the tide. In some places, you will find that the current is surprisingly strong and can take you well off course. If you make use of the cross track error capability of your GPS you will see it, can correct it and you will have no problems.

Tide Changes in Passes and Cuts

Do not expect that a slack tide followed by a current reversal will occur at predicted high and low water times in passes and cuts. More often than not, the moment of change will happen after the forecast time. Much depends on bottom contours, depth, width and other factors.

To be safe, plan on a rise and fall of 0.9 meters/3 feet. The Exumas' average is approximately 0.8 meters/2.5 feet. This means that the state of the tide becomes a factor worth taking into account at mid-tide when we are talking about just over 0.3 meter/1 foot. Nevertheless, we hope that no one will calculate their passages so closely that the difference of just 12 inches is critical. However, that 0.8 meters/2.5 feet can make a significant difference when entering say Black Sound in Green Turtle Cay, for example.

Turks and Caicos Tides

Tidal information is based on Hawks Nest anchorage (N 21° 26.000'/W 071° 07.000'), which is the sea area immediately to the southeast of Grand Turk Island. The mean range is 0.9 meter/2 feet 10 inches. The tide set on the Caicos Bank is about 1 knot-plus, running northeast on flood and southwest on ebb. The Turks Island Passage has a strong northerly set. We know of no tidal atlas for the Turks and Caicos Islands.

What Else Should You Know?

Be aware that reef passages and cuts between the islands and cays can produce rip tides that will run from 2.5 to 4 knots and can occasionally reach 6 knots in places. If the wind is against this current, it can produce a narrow millrace of water that you are better off avoiding. Heavy offshore swells can compound the problem and produce the very dangerous seas known as a "Rage." Rages make reef passages out into the ocean, like Whale Cay Passage in the Abacos, impassable. Make transits through restricted waters and choke points only when wind and current are not opposed.

Be cautious approaching an unfamiliar anchorage or harbor. Check the depth it carries and the state of tide before you commit yourself to an approach channel. If in doubt, use your VHF radio and ask for local guidance. If you are off the beaten track on your own, visual piloting and "eyeball" navigation becomes vital. The best procedure is to anchor where you are safe and do your sounding and surveying in the dinghy.

WATERWAY GUIDE PHOTOGRAPHY

Nassau, New Providence Island, Bahamas, 2010

Times and Heights of High and Low Waters

January

Day	Time (h m)	Height (ft)	Height (cm)	Time (h m)	Height (ft)	Height (cm)	Time (h m)	Height (ft)	Height (cm)	Time (h m)	Height (ft)	Height (cm)
1 F	0121	-0.9	-27	0747	3.5	107	0216*	-0.7	-21	0808*	2.7	82
2 Sa	0215	-1.0	-30	0837	3.5	107	0306*	-0.8	-24	0902*	2.8	85
3 Su	0310	-0.9	-27	0928	3.4	104	0355*	-0.8	-24	0956*	2.8	85
4 M	0406	-0.7	-21	1019	3.2	98	0446*	-0.8	-24	1052*	2.8	85
5 Tu	0504	-0.5	-15	1111	2.9	88	0537*	-0.7	-21	1151*	2.8	85
6 W	0605	-0.2	-6	1206*	2.7	82	0630*	-0.6	-18			
7 Th ◑	1251	2.7	82	0709	0.0	0	0104*	2.4	73	0726*	-0.4	-12
8 F	0153	2.7	82	0816	0.2	6	0205*	2.2	67	0823*	-0.3	-9
9 Sa	0256	2.7	82	0923	0.3	9	0307*	2.0	61	0921*	-0.2	-6
10 Su	0355	2.6	79	1026	0.2	6	0408*	1.9	58	1017*	-0.2	-6
11 M	0450	2.7	82	1122	0.2	6	0503*	1.9	58	1109*	-0.2	-6
12 Tu	0540	2.7	82	1211*	0.1	3	0553*	2.0	61	1156*	-0.2	-6
13 W	0625	2.7	82	1254*	0.0	0	0638*	2.0	61			
14 Th	1240	-0.2	-6	0705	2.8	85	0134*	-0.1	-3	0720*	2.1	64
15 F ●	0121	-0.2	-6	0743	2.8	85	0211*	-0.1	-3	0759*	2.2	67
16 Sa	0201	-0.2	-6	0820	2.8	85	0246*	-0.1	-3	0837*	2.2	67
17 Su	0239	-0.2	-6	0855	2.7	82	0320*	-0.1	-3	0915*	2.2	67
18 M	0318	-0.1	-3	0930	2.6	79	0354*	-0.1	-3	0952*	2.3	70
19 Tu	0357	0.1	3	1004	2.5	76	0427*	-0.1	-3	1031*	2.3	70
20 W	0438	0.2	6	1040	2.3	70	0502*	0.0	0	1112*	2.3	70
21 Th	0522	0.3	9	1119	2.2	67	0539*	0.0	0	1157*	2.3	70
22 F	0612	0.4	12	1203*	2.1	64	0622*	0.0	0			
23 Sa ◐	1248	2.3	70	0708	0.5	15	1254*	2.0	61	0712*	0.0	0
24 Su	0145	2.4	73	0811	0.5	15	0153*	1.9	58	0809*	-0.1	-3
25 M	0246	2.6	79	0917	0.4	12	0258*	1.9	58	0910*	-0.2	-6
26 Tu	0348	2.7	82	1021	0.2	6	0403*	2.0	61	1013*	-0.4	-12
27 W	0448	3.0	91	1120	-0.1	-3	0505*	2.2	67	1114*	-0.7	-21
28 Th	0544	3.2	98	1214*	-0.4	-12	0603*	2.5	76			
29 F	1212	-0.9	-27	0638	3.3	101	0105*	-0.7	-21	0659*	2.7	82
30 Sa ○	0108	-1.0	-30	0729	3.4	104	0154*	-0.9	-27	0752*	2.9	88
31 Su	0203	-1.1	-34	0819	3.4	104	0242*	-1.0	-30	0845*	3.0	91

February

Day	Time (h m)	Height (ft)	Height (cm)	Time (h m)	Height (ft)	Height (cm)	Time (h m)	Height (ft)	Height (cm)	Time (h m)	Height (ft)	Height (cm)
1 M	0257	-1.0	-30	0908	3.3	101	0330*	-1.1	-34	0937*	3.1	94
2 Tu	0351	-0.9	-27	0957	3.1	94	0418*	-1.0	-30	1030*	3.0	91
3 W	0447	-0.6	-18	1048	2.8	85	0507*	-0.8	-24	1125*	2.9	88
4 Th	0544	-0.3	-9	1140	2.5	76	0559*	-0.6	-18			
5 F ◑	1222	2.8	85	0645	0.0	0	1236*	2.2	67	0653*	-0.4	-12
6 Sa	0123	2.6	79	0750	0.2	6	0136*	2.0	61	0751*	-0.2	-6
7 Su	0226	2.5	76	0857	0.4	12	0240*	1.9	58	0852*	0.0	0
8 M	0329	2.5	76	1001	0.4	12	0344*	1.8	55	0952*	0.0	0
9 Tu	0426	2.5	76	1059	0.3	9	0442*	1.9	58	1048*	0.0	0
10 W	0517	2.5	76	1147	0.2	6	0532*	2.0	61	1137*	0.0	0
11 Th	0602	2.6	79	1229*	0.1	3	0617*	2.1	64			
12 F	1221	-0.1	-3	0641	2.7	82	0106*	0.0	0	0657*	2.2	67
13 Sa	0102	-0.2	-6	0718	2.7	82	0141*	-0.1	-3	0735*	2.3	70
14 Su ●	0141	-0.2	-6	0753	2.7	82	0214*	-0.2	-6	0811*	2.4	73
15 M	0219	-0.2	-6	0827	2.6	79	0246*	-0.2	-6	0846*	2.5	76
16 Tu	0256	-0.1	-3	0900	2.6	79	0317*	-0.2	-6	0922*	2.5	76
17 W	0333	-0.1	-3	0934	2.4	73	0349*	-0.2	-6	0958*	2.5	76
18 Th	0412	0.0	0	1009	2.3	70	0423*	-0.2	-6	1037*	2.5	76
19 F	0455	0.2	6	1047	2.2	67	0500*	-0.1	-3	1121*	2.5	76
20 Sa	0542	0.3	9	1130	2.1	64	0544*	-0.1	-3			
21 Su	1212	2.5	76	0638	0.4	12	1222*	2.0	61	0636*	0.0	0
22 M ◐	0111	2.5	76	0741	0.4	12	0124*	2.0	61	0738*	0.0	0
23 Tu	0216	2.6	79	0849	0.4	12	0234*	2.0	61	0847*	-0.1	-3
24 W	0323	2.8	85	0955	0.2	6	0343*	2.2	67	0955*	-0.3	-9
25 Th	0426	2.9	88	1056	-0.1	-3	0448*	2.4	73	1100*	-0.5	-15
26 F	0524	3.1	94	1150	-0.4	-12	0547*	2.7	82			
27 Sa	1200	-0.7	-21	0618	3.2	98	1241*	-0.7	-21	0642*	2.9	88
28 Su ○	1256	-0.9	-27	0709	3.3	101	0129*	-0.9	-27	0734*	3.1	94

March

Day	Time (h m)	Height (ft)	Height (cm)	Time (h m)	Height (ft)	Height (cm)	Time (h m)	Height (ft)	Height (cm)	Time (h m)	Height (ft)	Height (cm)
1 M	0150	-1.0	-30	0758	3.2	98	0216*	-1.1	-34	0825*	3.3	101
2 Tu	0243	-1.0	-30	0846	3.1	94	0303*	-1.1	-34	0915*	3.3	101
3 W	0335	-0.8	-24	0934	2.9	88	0349*	-0.9	-27	1005*	3.2	98
4 Th	0427	-0.5	-15	1023	2.7	82	0437*	-0.7	-21	1057*	3.0	91
5 F	0521	-0.2	-6	1114	2.4	73	0526*	-0.4	-12	1151*	2.8	85
6 Sa	0618	0.1	3	1208*	2.2	67	0620*	-0.1	-3			
7 Su ◑	1249	2.6	79	0719	0.3	9	0107*	2.0	61	0718*	0.1	3
8 M	0151	2.5	76	0824	0.5	15	0211*	1.9	58	0821*	0.3	9
9 Tu	0254	2.4	73	0928	0.5	15	0316*	1.9	58	0923*	0.3	9
10 W	0353	2.4	73	1024	0.5	15	0414*	1.9	58	1021*	0.3	9
11 Th	0445	2.4	73	1112	0.4	12	0504*	2.1	64	1112*	0.2	6
12 F	0529	2.5	76	1152	0.2	6	0548*	2.2	67	1157*	0.1	3
13 Sa	0609	2.6	79	1229*	0.1	3	0628*	2.4	73			
14 Su	1239	0.0	0	0747	2.6	79	0203*	0.0	0	0805*	2.5	76
15 M ●	0218	-0.1	-3	0822	2.6	79	0236*	-0.1	-3	0841*	2.6	79
16 Tu	0256	-0.1	-3	0857	2.6	79	0309*	-0.2	-6	0917*	2.7	82
17 W	0334	-0.1	-3	0931	2.5	76	0341*	-0.2	-6	0952*	2.8	85
18 Th	0412	-0.1	-3	1006	2.4	73	0414*	-0.2	-6	1030*	2.8	85
19 F	0451	0.0	0	1043	2.3	70	0450*	-0.2	-6	1110*	2.8	85
20 Sa	0534	0.1	3	1123	2.2	67	0531*	-0.1	-3	1156*	2.7	82
21 Su	0623	0.2	6	1210*	2.1	64	0618*	0.0	0			
22 M	1248	2.7	82	0719	0.3	9	0105*	2.1	64	0715*	0.1	3
23 Tu ◐	0148	2.7	82	0821	0.4	12	0210*	2.1	64	0821*	0.1	3
24 W	0254	2.7	82	0928	0.3	9	0321*	2.2	67	0932*	0.1	3
25 Th	0400	2.8	85	1032	0.1	3	0430*	2.4	73	1042*	-0.1	-3
26 F	0504	2.9	88	1131	-0.1	-3	0533*	2.7	82	1148*	-0.3	-9
27 Sa	0602	3.0	91	1224*	-0.4	-12	0631*	2.9	88			
28 Su	1248	-0.5	-15	0656	3.1	94	0114*	-0.7	-21	0724*	3.2	98
29 M	0143	-0.7	-21	0747	3.1	94	0202*	-0.9	-27	0815*	3.3	101
30 Tu ○	0236	-0.8	-24	0836	3.0	91	0248*	-1.0	-30	0904*	3.4	104
31 W	0327	-0.8	-24	0923	2.9	88	0334*	-0.9	-27	0952*	3.3	101

April

Day	Time (h m)	Height (ft)	Height (cm)	Time (h m)	Height (ft)	Height (cm)	Time (h m)	Height (ft)	Height (cm)	Time (h m)	Height (ft)	Height (cm)
1 Th	0416	-0.6	-18	1011	2.7	82	0420*	-0.7	-21	1040*	3.2	98
2 F	0506	-0.4	-12	1058	2.5	76	0507*	-0.5	-15	1129*	3.0	91
3 Sa	0557	-0.1	-3	1148	2.3	70	0555*	-0.2	-6			
4 Su	1220	2.8	85	0650	0.1	3	1240*	2.1	64	0647*	0.1	3
5 M	0114	2.6	79	0747	0.4	12	0137*	2.0	61	0743*	0.3	9
6 Tu ◑	0212	2.5	76	0846	0.5	15	0238*	1.9	58	0844*	0.5	15
7 W	0311	2.4	73	0944	0.6	18	0341*	2.0	61	0947*	0.6	18
8 Th	0408	2.3	70	1038	0.6	18	0438*	2.1	64	1046*	0.5	15
9 F	0501	2.3	70	1125	0.4	12	0528*	2.2	67	1139*	0.4	12
10 Sa	0547	2.4	73	1206*	0.3	9	0613*	2.4	73			
11 Su	1227	0.3	9	0629	2.4	73	1244*	0.1	3	0653*	2.6	79
12 M	0110	0.1	3	0709	2.4	73	0120*	0.0	0	0732*	2.7	82
13 Tu	0151	0.0	0	0747	2.4	73	0156*	-0.2	-6	0810*	2.8	85
14 W ●	0231	-0.1	-3	0825	2.4	73	0231*	-0.2	-6	0847*	2.9	88
15 Th	0311	-0.2	-6	0902	2.4	73	0307*	-0.3	-9	0926*	3.0	91
16 F	0352	-0.2	-6	0941	2.4	73	0345*	-0.3	-9	1006*	3.0	91
17 Sa	0434	-0.1	-3	1022	2.3	70	0426*	-0.2	-6	1050*	3.0	91
18 Su	0520	0.0	0	1108	2.2	67	0512*	-0.2	-6	1138*	2.9	88
19 M	0610	0.1	3	1159	2.2	67	0604*	0.0	0			
20 Tu	1232	2.9	88	0706	0.2	6	1257*	2.2	67	0704*	0.1	3
21 W ◐	0131	2.8	85	0806	0.2	6	0203*	2.3	70	0811*	0.2	6
22 Th	0234	2.8	85	0907	0.1	3	0311*	2.4	73	0922*	0.2	6
23 F	0339	2.8	85	1007	0.0	0	0417*	2.6	79	1032*	0.0	0
24 Sa	0441	2.8	85	1104	-0.3	-9	0518*	2.8	85	1136*	-0.1	-3
25 Su	0539	2.8	85	1157	-0.5	-15	0614*	3.1	94			
26 M	1235	-0.3	-9	0633	2.8	85	1247*	-0.7	-21	0706*	3.2	98
27 Tu	0130	-0.5	-15	0725	2.7	82	0135*	-0.8	-24	0755*	3.3	101
28 W ○	0221	-0.6	-18	0814	2.7	82	0222*	-0.8	-24	0843*	3.3	101
29 Th	0310	-0.5	-15	0901	2.6	79	0308*	-0.7	-21	0930*	3.3	101
30 F	0358	-0.4	-12	0948	2.5	76	0353*	-0.5	-15	1016*	3.1	94

May

Day	Time (h m)	Height (ft)	Height (cm)	Time (h m)	Height (ft)	Height (cm)	Time (h m)	Height (ft)	Height (cm)	Time (h m)	Height (ft)	Height (cm)
1 Sa	0445	-0.3	-9	1035	2.3	70	0439*	-0.3	-9	1102*	3.0	91
2 Su	0533	0.0	0	1123	2.2	67	0525*	0.0	0	1149*	2.8	85
3 M	0622	0.2	6	1212*	2.1	64	0614*	0.2	6			
4 Tu	1238	2.6	79	0712	0.3	9	0105*	2.0	61	0707*	0.5	15
5 W	0129	2.5	76	0803	0.5	15	0202*	2.0	61	0805*	0.6	18
6 Th ◑	0222	2.4	73	0855	0.5	15	0259*	2.1	64	0905*	0.7	21
7 F	0316	2.3	70	0944	0.5	15	0354*	2.2	67	1004*	0.7	21
8 Sa	0408	2.2	67	1030	0.4	12	0445*	2.3	70	1059*	0.6	18
9 Su	0457	2.2	67	1114	0.3	9	0531*	2.5	76	1150*	0.4	12
10 M	0543	2.2	67	1155	0.1	3	0615*	2.6	79			
11 Tu	1237	0.2	6	0627	2.3	70	1235*	-0.1	-3	0656*	2.8	85
12 W	0122	0.1	3	0710	2.3	70	0116*	-0.2	-6	0738*	3.0	91
13 Th	0205	-0.1	-3	0752	2.3	70	0156*	-0.3	-9	0820*	3.1	94
14 F ●	0248	-0.2	-6	0835	2.3	70	0238*	-0.4	-12	0903*	3.2	98
15 Sa	0333	-0.2	-6	0919	2.4	73	0322*	-0.4	-12	0947*	3.2	98
16 Su	0419	-0.2	-6	1006	2.4	73	0409*	-0.4	-12	1035*	3.2	98
17 M	0507	-0.2	-6	1056	2.4	73	0500*	-0.2	-6	1125*	3.1	94
18 Tu	0558	-0.1	-3	1151	2.4	73	0555*	-0.1	-3			
19 W	1218	3.0	91	0651	-0.1	-3	1251*	2.4	73	0657*	0.1	3
20 Th ◐	0115	2.9	88	0747	-0.1	-3	0154*	2.5	76	0803*	0.2	6
21 F	0215	2.8	85	0845	-0.1	-3	0258*	2.6	79	0912*	0.2	6
22 Sa	0317	2.7	82	0942	-0.2	-6	0402*	2.8	85	1020*	0.2	6
23 Su	0418	2.6	79	1038	-0.3	-9	0501*	3.0	91	1124*	0.0	0
24 M	0516	2.5	76	1131	-0.4	-12	0557*	3.1	94			
25 Tu	1223	-0.1	-3	0612	2.5	76	1222*	-0.5	-15	0649*	3.2	98
26 W	0117	-0.2	-6	0704	2.4	73	0112*	-0.6	-18	0738*	3.2	98
27 Th ○	0207	-0.3	-9	0754	2.4	73	0159*	-0.5	-15	0824*	3.2	98
28 F	0254	-0.3	-9	0841	2.4	73	0244*	-0.4	-12	0909*	3.2	98
29 Sa	0340	-0.2	-6	0927	2.3	70	0329*	-0.3	-9	0953*	3.1	94
30 Su	0424	-0.1	-3	1012	2.3	70	0413*	-0.1	-3	1036*	2.9	88
31 M	0508	0.0	0	1057	2.2	67	0457*	0.1	3	1119*	2.8	85

June

Day	Time (h m)	Height (ft)	Height (cm)	Time (h m)	Height (ft)	Height (cm)	Time (h m)	Height (ft)	Height (cm)	Time (h m)	Height (ft)	Height (cm)
1 Tu	0551	0.2	6	1144	2.2	67	0543*	0.3	9			
2 W	1202	2.7	82	0634	0.3	9	1231*	2.1	64	0632*	0.5	15
3 Th	1247	2.5	76	0718	0.4	12	0121*	2.1	64	0724*	0.7	21
4 F ◑	0133	2.4	73	0803	0.4	12	0213*	2.2	67	0819*	0.8	24
5 Sa	0221	2.3	70	0848	0.4	12	0305*	2.3	70	0917*	0.8	24
6 Su	0312	2.2	67	0934	0.4	12	0357*	2.4	73	1015*	0.7	21
7 M	0403	2.1	64	1020	0.3	9	0446*	2.5	76	1110*	0.6	18
8 Tu	0454	2.1	64	1106	0.1	3	0535*	2.7	82			
9 W	1201	0.4	12	0545	2.2	67	1152	0.0	0	0622*	2.9	88
10 Th	1251	0.2	6	0634	2.2	67	1239*	-0.2	-6	0708*	3.1	94
11 F	0139	0.0	0	0722	2.3	70	0126*	-0.3	-9	0755*	3.2	98
12 Sa ●	0226	-0.1	-3	0811	2.4	73	0214*	-0.4	-12	0842*	3.4	104
13 Su	0313	-0.2	-6	0900	2.5	76	0304*	-0.5	-15	0930*	3.4	104
14 M	0401	-0.3	-9	0951	2.6	79	0356*	-0.4	-12	1019*	3.4	104
15 Tu	0450	-0.3	-9	1044	2.7	82	0450*	-0.3	-9	1110*	3.3	101
16 W	0540	-0.3	-9	1140	2.7	82	0547*	-0.2	-6			
17 Th	1202	3.2	98	0631	-0.3	-9	1238*	2.8	85	0647*	0.0	0
18 F	1257	3.0	91	0725	-0.3	-9	0139*	2.8	85	0752*	0.2	6
19 Sa ◐	0154	2.8	85	0820	-0.2	-6	0241*	2.9	88	0859*	0.3	9
20 Su	0254	2.6	79	0916	-0.2	-6	0343*	2.9	88	1006*	0.3	9
21 M	0355	2.4	73	1013	-0.2	-6	0443*	3.0	91	1110*	0.3	9
22 Tu	0456	2.4	73	1108	-0.2	-6	0540*	3.1	94			
23 W	1210	0.2	6	0553	2.3	70	1202*	-0.2	-6	0633*	3.1	94
24 Th	0103	0.2	6	0647	2.3	70	1252*	-0.2	-6	0721*	3.1	94
25 F	0152	0.1	3	0736	2.3	70	0139*	-0.2	-6	0807*	3.1	94
26 Sa ○	0238	0.1	3	0823	2.3	70	0224*	-0.1	-3	0850*	3.1	94
27 Su	0320	0.1	3	0907	2.3	70	0308*	0.0	0	0931*	3.1	94
28 M	0400	0.1	3	0949	2.4	73	0350*	0.1	3	1010*	3.0	91
29 Tu	0439	0.2	6	1031	2.4	73	0431*	0.3	9	1048*	2.9	88
30 W	0517	0.3	9	1112	2.4	73	0514*	0.4	12	1127*	2.8	85

Heights are referred to mean lower low water which is the chart datum of soundings. All times are local. Daylight Saving Time has been used when needed.

Nassau, New Providence Island, Bahamas, 2010

Times and Heights of High and Low Waters

July

Day	Time (h m)	Height (ft)	Height (cm)	Day	Time (h m)	Height (ft)	Height (cm)
1 Th	0554 1155 0558*	0.3 2.4 0.6	9 73 18	16 F	0606 1219* 0634*	−0.4 3.2 0.1	−12 98 3
2 F	1206 0632 1239* 0645*	2.6 0.4 2.4 0.8	79 12 73 24	17 Sa	1236 0658 0118* 0736*	3.0 −0.2 3.1 0.3	91 −6 94 9
3 Sa	1247 0712 0126* 0735*	2.5 0.4 2.4 0.9	76 12 73 27	18 Su ◐	0132 0753 0219* 0842*	2.8 −0.1 3.1 0.5	85 −3 94 15
4 Su ◑	0131 0754 0215* 0830*	2.3 0.5 2.5 0.9	70 15 76 27	19 M	0232 0850 0322* 0949*	2.6 0.0 3.1 0.6	79 0 94 18
5 M	0219 0839 0308* 0929*	2.2 0.4 2.6 0.9	67 12 79 27	20 Tu	0335 0950 0424* 1055*	2.4 0.1 3.0 0.7	73 3 91 21
6 Tu	0312 0929 0402* 1028*	2.2 0.4 2.7 0.8	67 12 82 24	21 W	0438 1048 0523* 1155*	2.3 0.2 3.1 0.6	70 6 94 18
7 W	0409 1021 0456* 1126*	2.2 0.3 2.9 0.7	67 9 88 21	22 Th	0537 1144 0616*	2.3 0.2 3.1	70 6 94
8 Th	0506 1115 0550*	2.2 0.1 3.1	67 3 94	23 F	1248 0631 1236* 0705*	0.6 2.4 0.3 3.1	18 73 9 94
9 F	1221 0602 1209* 0642*	0.5 2.3 −0.1 3.3	15 70 −3 101	24 Sa	0135 0719 0123* 0748*	0.5 2.4 0.3 3.1	15 73 9 94
10 Sa	0113 0656 0103* 0732*	0.2 2.5 −0.2 3.4	6 76 −6 104	25 Su	0216 0803 0206* 0828*	0.5 2.5 0.3 3.2	15 76 9 98
11 Su ●	0202 0750 0156* 0822*	0.0 2.7 −0.4 3.6	0 82 −12 110	26 M ○	0255 0844 0247* 0906*	0.4 2.6 0.3 3.1	12 79 9 94
12 M	0251 0842 0249* 0912*	−0.2 2.8 −0.4 3.6	−6 85 −12 110	27 Tu	0331 0923 0327* 0942*	0.4 2.6 0.4 3.1	12 79 12 94
13 Tu	0339 0935 0343* 1001*	−0.3 3.0 −0.4 3.6	−9 91 −12 110	28 W	0405 1001 0406* 1017*	0.4 2.7 0.5 3.0	12 82 15 91
14 W	0428 1028 0438* 1051*	−0.4 3.1 −0.3 3.5	−12 94 −9 107	29 Th	0439 1039 0446* 1052*	0.4 2.7 0.6 2.9	12 82 18 88
15 Th	0516 1123 0535* 1142*	−0.4 3.2 −0.1 3.3	−12 98 −3 101	30 F	0513 1118 0526* 1128*	0.5 2.7 0.7 2.7	15 82 21 82
				31 Sa	0547 1158 0609*	0.5 2.7 0.9	15 82 27

August

Day	Time (h m)	Height (ft)	Height (cm)	Day	Time (h m)	Height (ft)	Height (cm)
1 Su	1205 0624 1241* 0656*	2.6 0.6 2.7 1.0	79 18 82 30	16 M ◐	0109 0725 0154* 0821*	2.8 0.2 3.3 0.8	85 6 101 24
2 M	1247 0704 0129* 0749*	2.5 0.7 2.7 1.1	76 21 82 34	17 Tu	0210 0825 0258* 0929*	2.6 0.4 3.1 1.0	79 12 94 30
3 Tu ◑	0135 0751 0223* 0848*	2.3 0.7 2.8 1.2	70 21 85 37	18 W	0315 0927 0402* 1035*	2.5 0.6 3.1 1.0	76 18 94 30
4 W	0230 0845 0322* 0951*	2.3 0.6 2.9 1.1	70 18 88 34	19 Th	0420 1029 0502* 1134*	2.4 0.7 3.1 1.0	73 21 94 30
5 Th	0332 0945 0422* 1054*	2.3 0.6 3.0 1.0	70 18 91 30	20 F	0520 1127 0556*	2.5 0.7 3.1	76 21 94
6 F	0436 1046 0521* 1152*	2.4 0.4 3.2 0.7	73 12 98 21	21 Sa	1225 0613 1219* 0643*	0.9 2.5 0.7 3.1	27 76 21 94
7 Sa	0537 1147 0617*	2.6 0.2 3.5	79 6 107	22 Su	0109 0659 0105* 0724*	0.8 2.7 0.7 3.2	24 82 21 98
8 Su	1246 0635 1245* 0710*	0.4 2.8 0.0 3.6	12 85 0 110	23 M	0148 0740 0147* 0801*	0.7 2.8 0.6 3.2	21 85 18 98
9 M	0137 0730 0141* 0801*	0.2 3.1 −0.2 3.8	6 94 −6 116	24 Tu ○	0223 0819 0226* 0837*	0.7 2.9 0.6 3.2	21 88 18 98
10 Tu ●	0226 0824 0235* 0851*	−0.1 3.3 −0.3 3.8	−3 101 −9 116	25 W	0256 0855 0304* 0911*	0.6 3.0 0.6 3.1	18 91 18 94
11 W	0313 0916 0329* 0940*	−0.3 3.5 −0.3 3.7	−9 107 −9 113	26 Th	0328 0931 0342* 0945*	0.6 3.0 0.6 3.0	18 91 18 91
12 Th	0401 1008 0424* 1029*	−0.4 3.6 −0.2 3.6	−12 110 −6 110	27 F	0400 1006 0419* 1019*	0.6 3.0 0.7 2.9	18 91 21 88
13 F	0449 1101 0519* 1120*	−0.3 3.6 0.0 3.3	−9 110 0 101	28 Sa	0432 1042 0458* 1054*	0.6 3.0 0.8 2.8	18 91 24 85
14 Sa	0538 1156 0616*	−0.2 3.5 0.3	−6 107 9	29 Su	0506 1121 0539* 1130*	0.7 3.0 1.0 2.7	21 91 30 82
15 Su	1213 0630 1253* 0717*	3.1 0.0 3.4 0.5	94 0 104 15	30 M	0542 1203* 0624*	0.8 3.0 1.1	24 91 34
				31 Tu	1212 0623 1251* 0716*	2.5 0.8 3.0 1.2	76 24 91 37

September

Day	Time (h m)	Height (ft)	Height (cm)	Day	Time (h m)	Height (ft)	Height (cm)
1 W ◑	0101 0713 0146* 0816*	2.5 0.9 3.0 1.3	76 27 91 40	16 Th	0253 0902 0333* 1007*	2.5 1.0 3.0 1.2	76 30 91 37
2 Th	0200 0812 0249* 0921*	2.4 0.9 3.1 1.3	73 27 94 40	17 F	0358 1006 0433* 1104*	2.5 1.1 3.0 1.2	76 34 91 37
3 F	0306 0918 0353* 1026*	2.5 0.8 3.2 1.1	76 24 98 34	18 Sa	0458 1105 0526* 1153*	2.6 1.1 3.0 1.1	79 34 91 34
4 Sa	0414 1026 0456* 1125*	2.6 0.7 3.4 0.8	79 21 104 24	19 Su	0549 1157 0612*	2.7 1.0 3.0	82 30 91
5 Su	0518 1130 0553*	2.9 0.4 3.5	88 12 107	20 M	1234 0633 1242* 0652*	1.0 2.8 0.9 3.1	30 85 27 94
6 M	1219 0617 1230* 0647*	0.5 3.2 0.2 3.7	15 98 6 113	21 Tu	0111 0712 0124* 0729*	0.8 3.0 0.8 3.1	24 91 24 94
7 Tu	0110 0712 0127* 0738*	0.2 3.5 0.0 3.8	6 107 0 116	22 W	0145 0749 0203* 0805*	0.7 3.1 0.7 3.1	21 94 21 94
8 W ●	0158 0804 0221* 0828*	−0.1 3.7 −0.2 3.7	−3 113 −6 113	23 Th ○	0218 0825 0241* 0840*	0.6 3.2 0.6 3.0	18 98 18 91
9 Th	0245 0855 0315* 0917*	−0.3 3.9 −0.2 3.6	−9 119 −6 110	24 F	0250 0900 0318* 0914*	0.6 3.2 0.6 2.9	18 98 18 88
10 F	0333 0946 0407* 1007*	−0.3 3.9 −0.1 3.5	−9 119 −3 107	25 Sa	0323 0935 0355* 0949*	0.6 3.2 0.7 2.8	18 98 21 85
11 Sa	0420 1038 0501* 1057*	−0.2 3.8 0.1 3.3	−6 116 3 101	26 Su	0356 1011 0434* 1024*	0.6 3.2 0.8 2.7	18 98 24 82
12 Su	0510 1131 0556* 1149*	0.0 3.7 0.4 3.0	0 113 12 91	27 M	0430 1050 0515* 1103*	0.7 3.2 0.9 2.6	21 98 27 79
13 M	0601 1226* 0654*	0.2 3.5 0.7	6 107 21	28 Tu	0509 1133 0601* 1147*	0.7 3.2 1.0 2.6	21 98 30 79
14 Tu	1246 0657 0126* 0757*	2.8 0.5 3.3 1.0	85 15 101 30	29 W	0554 1223* 0654*	0.8 3.1 1.1	24 94 34
15 W ◐	0147 0757 0229* 0903*	2.6 0.8 3.1 1.1	79 24 94 34	30 Th	1240 0647 0119* 0753*	2.5 0.9 3.1 1.2	76 27 94 37

October

Day	Time (h m)	Height (ft)	Height (cm)	Day	Time (h m)	Height (ft)	Height (cm)
1 F ◑	0142 0750 0222* 0857*	2.5 1.0 3.1 1.1	76 30 94 34	16 Sa	0327 0934 0352* 1022*	2.5 1.2 2.8 1.1	76 37 85 34
2 Sa	0250 0900 0328* 1000*	2.6 0.9 3.2 0.9	79 27 98 27	17 Su	0425 1034 0445* 1109*	2.5 1.1 2.8 1.0	76 34 85 30
3 Su	0358 1011 0431* 1058*	2.8 0.8 3.3 0.7	85 24 101 21	18 M	0515 1127 0531* 1150*	2.7 1.0 2.8 0.8	82 30 85 24
4 M	0502 1116 0529* 1151*	3.1 0.5 3.4 0.3	94 15 104 9	19 Tu	0559 1214* 0614*	2.8 0.9 2.8	85 27 85
5 Tu	0559 1217* 0624*	3.4 0.2 3.5	104 6 107	20 W	1228 0639 1257* 0653*	0.7 3.0 0.7 2.8	21 91 21 85
6 W	1242 0653 0113* 0716*	0.0 3.7 0.0 3.5	0 113 0 107	21 Th	0104 0717 0137* 0731*	0.5 3.1 0.6 2.8	15 94 18 85
7 Th ●	0131 0745 0207* 0806*	−0.2 3.8 −0.1 3.5	−6 116 −3 107	22 F	0139 0754 0216* 0808*	0.4 3.2 0.5 2.7	12 98 15 82
8 F	0218 0835 0259* 0855*	−0.3 3.9 −0.2 3.4	−9 119 −6 104	23 Sa ○	0213 0830 0255* 0844*	0.4 3.3 0.5 2.7	12 101 15 82
9 Sa	0306 0925 0351* 0944*	−0.3 3.9 −0.1 3.2	−9 119 −3 98	24 Su	0248 0908 0334* 0922*	0.3 3.3 0.5 2.6	9 101 15 79
10 Su	0353 1015 0442* 1034*	−0.2 3.8 0.1 3.0	−6 116 3 91	25 M	0325 0946 0415* 1001*	0.3 3.3 0.5 2.6	9 101 15 79
11 M	0442 1105 0535* 1126*	0.0 3.6 0.4 2.8	0 110 12 85	26 Tu	0404 1028 0458* 1044*	0.4 3.3 0.6 2.5	12 101 18 76
12 Tu	0533 1158 0630*	0.3 3.4 0.6	9 104 18	27 W	0446 1113 0545* 1132*	0.5 3.2 0.7 2.5	15 98 21 76
13 W	1221 0627 1254* 0728*	2.6 0.6 3.2 0.9	79 18 98 27	28 Th	0535 1203* 0637*	0.6 3.2 0.8	18 98 24
14 Th ◐	0121 0727 0154* 0829*	2.5 0.9 3.0 1.0	76 27 91 30	29 F	1228 0632 1259* 0734*	2.5 0.7 3.1 0.8	76 21 94 24
15 F	0224 0830 0254* 0928*	2.4 1.1 2.9 1.1	73 34 88 34	30 Sa ◑	0130 0737 0200* 0834*	2.5 0.8 3.1 0.7	76 24 94 21
				31 Su	0237 0847 0303* 0933*	2.7 0.7 3.0 0.5	82 21 91 15

November

Day	Time (h m)	Height (ft)	Height (cm)	Day	Time (h m)	Height (ft)	Height (cm)
1 M	0343 0958 0406* 1030*	2.9 0.6 3.0 0.3	88 18 91 9	16 Tu	0333 0948 0342* 1000*	2.5 0.9 2.4 0.5	76 27 73 15
2 Tu	0445 1104 0505* 1124*	3.1 0.4 3.0 0.0	94 12 91 0	17 W	0419 1039 0429* 1041*	2.7 0.8 2.4 0.4	82 24 73 12
3 W	0542 1204* 0601*	3.4 0.2 3.0	104 6 91	18 Th	0502 1125 0513* 1121*	2.8 0.6 2.4 0.2	85 18 73 6
4 Th	1216 0636 0101* 0654*	−0.2 3.6 0.0 3.0	−6 110 0 91	19 F	0543 1209* 0555*	2.9 0.4 2.4	88 12 73
5 F	0105 0727 0154* 0745*	−0.4 3.7 −0.2 3.0	−12 113 −6 91	20 Sa	1200 0623 1251* 0636*	0.1 3.1 0.3 2.4	3 94 9 73
6 Sa ●	0154 0817 0245* 0835*	−0.5 3.7 −0.2 2.9	−15 113 −6 88	21 Su ○	1239 0704 0132* 0717*	0.0 3.2 0.2 2.4	0 98 6 73
7 Su	0142 0805 0234* 0824*	−0.4 3.7 −0.2 2.8	−12 113 −6 85	22 M	0119 0744 0214* 0759*	−0.1 3.2 0.1 2.4	−3 98 3 73
8 M	0229 0853 0324* 0913*	−0.3 3.6 0.0 2.7	−9 110 0 82	23 Tu	0201 0826 0257* 0843*	−0.1 3.3 0.1 2.4	−3 101 3 73
9 Tu	0317 0942 0413* 1003*	−0.1 3.4 0.2 2.6	−3 104 6 79	24 W	0245 0910 0342* 0930*	−0.1 3.3 0.1 2.5	−3 101 3 76
10 W	0406 1031 0503* 1055*	0.2 3.2 0.4 2.4	6 98 12 73	25 Th	0332 0957 0429* 1021*	0.0 3.2 0.1 2.5	0 98 3 76
11 Th	0458 1121 0555* 1150*	0.5 3.0 0.6 2.3	15 91 18 70	26 F	0424 1047 0520* 1117*	0.1 3.1 0.1 2.5	3 94 3 76
12 F	0552 1213* 0647*	0.7 2.8 0.7	21 85 21	27 Sa	0522 1140 0613*	0.3 3.0 0.1	9 91 3
13 Sa ◐	1248 0651 0106* 0739*	2.3 0.9 2.6 0.8	70 27 79 24	28 Su ◑	1218 0626 1238* 0709*	2.6 0.4 2.9 0.1	79 12 88 3
14 Su	0146 0752 0200* 0829*	2.3 1.0 2.5 0.7	70 30 76 21	29 M	0122 0735 0139* 0806*	2.7 0.4 2.7 0.0	82 12 82 0
15 M	0241 0852 0253* 0916*	2.4 1.0 2.4 0.7	73 30 73 21	30 Tu	0226 0844 0241* 0903*	2.8 0.4 2.6 −0.2	85 12 79 −6

December

Day	Time (h m)	Height (ft)	Height (cm)	Day	Time (h m)	Height (ft)	Height (cm)
1 W	0328 0951 0342* 0959*	3.0 0.2 2.6 −0.3	91 6 79 −9	16 Th	0333 0957 0340* 0952*	2.4 0.6 2.0 0.1	73 18 61 3
2 Th	0426 1052 0441* 1052*	3.2 0.0 2.5 −0.5	98 0 76 −15	17 F	0422 1049 0430* 1038*	2.6 0.5 2.0 0.0	79 15 61 0
3 F	0520 1149 0536* 1144*	3.3 −0.1 2.5 −0.6	101 −3 76 −18	18 Sa	0509 1138 0519* 1124*	2.7 0.3 2.1 −0.2	82 9 64 −6
4 Sa	0612 1242* 0628*	3.4 −0.2 2.5	104 −6 76	19 Su	0554 1224* 0606*	2.9 0.1 2.2	88 3 67
5 Su ●	1234 0701 0132* 0718*	−0.6 3.4 −0.3 2.5	−18 104 −9 76	20 M	1210 0639 0109* 0653*	−0.3 3.0 −0.1 2.3	−9 91 −3 70
6 M	0123 0748 0219* 0806*	−0.5 3.3 −0.3 2.5	−15 101 −9 76	21 Tu ○	1256 0723 0154* 0739*	−0.4 3.2 −0.2 2.4	−12 98 −6 73
7 Tu	0209 0834 0305* 0853*	−0.4 3.2 −0.2 2.4	−12 98 −6 73	22 W	0143 0808 0238* 0827*	−0.5 3.2 −0.3 2.4	−15 98 −9 73
8 W	0255 0918 0349* 0940*	−0.2 3.1 −0.1 2.3	−6 94 −3 70	23 Th	0231 0854 0323* 0917*	−0.5 3.2 −0.4 2.5	−15 98 −12 76
9 Th	0341 1002 0433* 1027*	0.0 2.9 0.0 2.3	0 88 0 70	24 F	0321 0941 0410* 1008*	−0.5 3.2 −0.5 2.6	−15 98 −15 79
10 F	0428 1046 0517* 1115*	0.2 2.8 0.2 2.2	6 85 6 67	25 Sa	0415 1030 0458* 1103*	−0.3 3.1 −0.5 2.7	−9 94 −15 82
11 Sa	0516 1130 0601*	0.4 2.6 0.3	12 79 9	26 Su	0512 1122 0549*	−0.2 2.9 −0.5	−6 88 −15
12 Su	1205 0608 1216* 0645*	2.2 0.6 2.4 0.4	67 18 73 12	27 M	1201 0614 1217* 0642*	2.7 0.0 2.7 −0.4	82 0 82 −12
13 M ◐	1257 0704 0104* 0731*	2.2 0.7 2.2 0.4	67 21 67 12	28 Tu ◑	0103 0720 0116* 0739*	2.7 0.1 2.5 −0.4	82 3 76 −12
14 Tu	0150 0802 0155* 0818*	2.2 0.8 2.1 0.3	67 24 64 9	29 W	0206 0829 0219* 0837*	2.8 0.2 2.3 −0.4	85 6 70 −12
15 W	0242 0901 0247* 0905*	2.3 0.7 2.0 0.3	70 21 61 9	30 Th	0309 0937 0322* 0936*	2.8 0.1 2.2 −0.4	85 3 67 −12
				31 F	0410 1041 0424* 1034*	2.9 0.0 2.2 −0.5	88 0 67 −15

Heights are referred to mean lower low water which is the chart datum of soundings. All times are local. Daylight Saving Time has been used when needed.

Nassau, New Providence Island, Bahamas, 2011

Times and Heights of High and Low Waters

January

Day	Time (h m)	Height (ft)	Height (cm)
1 Sa	0506 1137 0522* 1130*	3.0 –0.1 2.2 –0.5	91 –3 67 –15
2 Su	0559 1229* 0615*	3.0 –0.2 2.2	91 –6 67
3 M	1221 0647 0117* 0704*	–0.5 3.0 –0.3 2.3	–15 91 –9 70
4 Tu ●	0108 0732 0201* 0750*	–0.5 3.0 –0.3 2.3	–15 91 –9 70
5 W	0153 0814 0242* 0834*	–0.5 3.0 –0.3 2.3	–15 91 –9 70
6 Th	0237 0855 0322* 0916*	–0.3 2.9 –0.3 2.3	–9 88 –9 70
7 F	0319 0933 0400* 0957*	–0.2 2.8 –0.2 2.3	–6 85 –6 70
8 Sa	0401 1012 0437* 1039*	0.0 2.6 –0.1 2.3	0 79 –3 70
9 Su	0444 1050 0515* 1122*	0.2 2.4 0.0 2.2	6 73 0 67
10 M	0530 1130 0554*	0.3 2.2 0.0	9 67 0
11 Tu	1208 0619 1214* 0636*	2.2 0.5 2.1 0.1	67 15 64 3
12 W ◐	1258 0713 0102* 0722*	2.2 0.6 1.9 0.1	67 18 58 3
13 Th	0151 0812 0155* 0812*	2.2 0.6 1.8 0.1	67 18 55 3
14 F	0246 0912 0252* 0905*	2.3 0.6 1.8 0.0	70 18 55 0
15 Sa	0341 1011 0350* 1000*	2.5 0.4 1.9 –0.1	76 12 58 –3
16 Su	0434 1105 0446* 1053*	2.6 0.2 2.0 –0.3	79 6 61 –9
17 M	0525 1155 0539* 1145*	2.8 0.0 2.2 –0.5	85 0 67 –15
18 Tu	0613 1242* 0630*	3.0 –0.3 2.3	91 –9 70
19 W ○	1236 0700 0128* 0719*	–0.7 3.2 –0.5 2.5	–21 98 –15 76
20 Th	0127 0747 0213* 0809*	–0.8 3.3 –0.7 2.7	–24 101 –21 82
21 F	0218 0834 0259* 0859*	–0.9 3.3 –0.9 2.8	–27 101 –27 85
22 Sa	0309 0921 0345* 0950*	–0.8 3.2 –0.9 2.9	–24 98 –27 88
23 Su	0403 1010 0433* 1044*	–0.7 3.0 –0.9 2.9	–21 91 –27 88
24 M	0459 1101 0523* 1140*	–0.5 2.8 –0.8 2.9	–15 85 –24 88
25 Tu	0558 1155 0616*	–0.3 2.6 –0.7	–9 79 –21
26 W ◑	1240 0702 1254* 0714*	2.8 –0.1 2.3 –0.5	85 –3 70 –15
27 Th	0144 0811 0159* 0816*	2.7 0.1 2.1 –0.4	82 3 64 –12
28 F	0250 0920 0306* 0919*	2.7 0.2 2.0 –0.3	82 6 61 –9
29 Sa	0354 1026 0411* 1021*	2.7 0.1 2.0 –0.3	82 3 61 –9
30 Su	0453 1124 0510* 1117*	2.7 0.0 2.1 –0.3	82 0 64 –9
31 M	0545 1214* 0602*	2.8 –0.1 2.1	85 –3 64

February

Day	Time (h m)	Height (ft)	Height (cm)
1 Tu	1208 0631 1259* 0649*	–0.3 2.8 –0.2 2.2	–9 85 –6 67
2 W	1254 0713 0138* 0731*	–0.4 2.8 –0.2 2.3	–12 85 –6 70
3 Th ●	0136 0752 0215* 0810*	–0.3 2.8 –0.3 2.4	–9 85 –9 73
4 F	0217 0829 0250* 0848*	–0.3 2.7 –0.3 2.4	–9 82 –9 73
5 Sa	0256 0904 0324* 0926*	–0.2 2.6 –0.3 2.4	–6 79 –9 73
6 Su	0334 0939 0358* 1003*	–0.1 2.5 –0.2 2.4	–3 76 –6 73
7 M	0414 1014 0432* 1042*	0.0 2.4 –0.1 2.4	0 73 –3 73
8 Tu	0455 1051 0507* 1123*	0.2 2.2 0.0 2.3	6 67 0 70
9 W	0539 1130 0546*	0.3 2.0 0.0	9 61 0
10 Th	1209 0629 1216* 0631*	2.3 0.5 1.9 0.1	70 15 58 3
11 F ◐	0101 0726 0108* 0723*	2.3 0.6 1.8 0.1	70 18 55 3
12 Sa	0159 0828 0209* 0822*	2.4 0.6 1.8 0.1	73 18 55 3
13 Su	0300 0931 0313* 0924*	2.5 0.5 1.9 0.0	76 15 58 0
14 M	0359 1029 0415* 1025*	2.6 0.2 2.1 –0.2	79 6 64 –6
15 Tu	0454 1123 0513* 1123*	2.8 0.0 2.3 –0.5	85 0 70 –15
16 W	0547 1212* 0607*	3.0 –0.4 2.6	91 –12 79
17 Th	1218 0636 0100* 0658*	–0.7 3.2 –0.7 2.8	–21 98 –21 85
18 F ○	0111 0725 0146* 0749*	–0.9 3.3 –0.9 3.0	–27 101 –27 91
19 Sa	0203 0813 0232* 0840*	–1.0 3.3 –1.1 3.2	–30 101 –34 98
20 Su	0256 0901 0319* 0931*	–1.0 3.2 –1.1 3.2	–30 98 –34 98
21 M	0349 0950 0407* 1023*	–0.8 3.0 –1.0 3.2	–24 91 –30 98
22 Tu	0444 1042 0458* 1119*	–0.6 2.7 –0.9 3.1	–18 82 –27 94
23 W	0542 1136 0552*	–0.3 2.5 –0.6	–9 76 –18
24 Th ◑	1218 0645 1236* 0651*	2.9 –0.1 2.3 –0.4	88 –3 70 –12
25 F	0122 0752 0141* 0755*	2.7 0.2 2.1 –0.1	82 6 64 –3
26 Sa	0229 0901 0250* 0902*	2.6 0.3 2.0 0.0	79 9 61 0
27 Su	0334 1006 0356* 1006*	2.6 0.3 2.0 0.0	79 9 61 0
28 M	0433 1102 0454* 1103*	2.6 0.2 2.1 0.0	79 6 64 0

March

Day	Time (h m)	Height (ft)	Height (cm)
1 Tu	0524 1150 0544* 1152*	2.6 0.1 2.2 –0.1	79 3 67 –3
2 W	0609 1231* 0628*	2.7 0.0 2.4	82 0 73
3 Th	1237 0649 0108* 0707*	–0.1 2.7 –0.1 2.5	–3 82 –3 76
4 F ●	0117 0725 0142* 0744*	–0.2 2.7 –0.2 2.5	–6 82 –6 76
5 Sa	0156 0800 0215* 0819*	–0.2 2.6 –0.2 2.6	–6 79 –6 79
6 Su	0233 0834 0247* 0855*	–0.2 2.5 –0.2 2.6	–6 76 –6 79
7 M	0310 0908 0320* 0930*	–0.1 2.4 –0.2 2.6	–3 73 –6 79
8 Tu	0347 0942 0353* 1007*	0.0 2.3 –0.1 2.6	0 70 –3 79
9 W	0426 1018 0427* 1046*	0.1 2.2 0.0 2.5	3 67 0 76
10 Th	0508 1057 0506* 1131*	0.3 2.1 0.1 2.5	9 64 3 76
11 F	0555 1141 0551*	0.5 2.0 0.2	15 61 6
12 Sa ◐	1221 0650 1235* 0646*	2.5 0.6 1.9 0.2	76 18 58 6
13 Su	0119 0851 0237* 0849*	2.5 0.6 2.0 0.2	76 18 61 6
14 M	0322 0954 0344* 0956*	2.6 0.5 2.1 0.1	79 15 64 3
15 Tu	0425 1054 0449* 1101*	2.7 0.2 2.3 –0.1	82 6 70 –3
16 W	0524 1149 0549*	2.9 –0.1 2.6	88 –3 79
17 Th	1203 0619 1241* 0644*	–0.4 3.0 –0.4 2.9	–12 91 –12 88
18 F	0100 0711 0130* 0737*	–0.6 3.1 –0.7 3.2	–18 94 –21 98
19 Sa ○	0155 0801 0217* 0828*	–0.8 3.2 –1.0 3.4	–24 98 –30 104
20 Su	0248 0851 0305* 0919*	–1.0 3.1 –1.1 3.5	–30 94 –34 107
21 M	0341 0940 0353* 1010*	–1.0 3.0 –1.1 3.5	–30 91 –34 107
22 Tu	0434 1030 0442* 1103*	–0.8 2.9 –1.0 3.3	–24 88 –30 101
23 W	0528 1122 0534* 1157*	–0.6 2.7 –0.7 3.2	–18 82 –21 98
24 Th	0625 1218* 0629*	–0.3 2.4 –0.4	–9 73 –12
25 F	1255 0725 0118* 0729*	3.0 0.0 2.3 –0.1	91 0 70 –3
26 Sa ◑	0157 0829 0223* 0833*	2.7 0.2 2.1 0.1	82 6 64 3
27 Su	0302 0935 0331* 0940*	2.6 0.3 2.1 0.3	79 9 64 9
28 M	0405 1036 0435* 1044*	2.5 0.4 2.1 0.3	76 12 64 9
29 Tu	0503 1130 0530* 1141*	2.5 0.3 2.2 0.3	76 9 67 9
30 W	0553 1215* 0618*	2.5 0.2 2.4	76 6 73
31 Th	1230 0637 1255* 0700*	0.2 2.5 0.1 2.5	6 76 3 76

April

Day	Time (h m)	Height (ft)	Height (cm)
1 F	0114 0717 0131* 0738*	0.1 2.5 0.0 2.6	3 76 0 79
2 Sa	0154 0754 0205* 0814*	0.0 2.5 –0.1 2.7	0 76 –3 82
3 Su ●	0232 0829 0239* 0850*	–0.1 2.5 –0.2 2.8	–3 76 –6 85
4 M	0310 0904 0312* 0925*	–0.1 2.4 –0.2 2.8	–3 73 –6 85
5 Tu	0347 0939 0345* 1001*	–0.1 2.3 –0.1 2.8	–3 70 –3 85
6 W	0424 1015 0419* 1038*	0.0 2.3 –0.1 2.7	0 70 –3 82
7 Th	0503 1052 0456* 1118*	0.1 2.2 0.0 2.7	3 67 0 82
8 F	0545 1132 0536*	0.3 2.1 0.1	9 64 3
9 Sa	1202 0632 1219* 0624*	2.7 0.4 2.1 0.2	82 12 64 6
10 Su	1252 0724 0114* 0720*	2.6 0.4 2.1 0.3	79 12 64 9
11 M ◐	0149 0822 0216* 0825*	2.6 0.4 2.1 0.3	79 12 64 9
12 Tu	0250 0922 0322* 0934*	2.7 0.3 2.3 0.2	82 9 70 6
13 W	0353 1021 0427* 1041*	2.7 0.1 2.5 0.0	82 3 76 0
14 Th	0453 1116 0527* 1145*	2.8 –0.2 2.8 –0.3	85 –6 85 –9
15 F	0550 1209* 0623*	2.9 –0.5 3.1	88 –15 94
16 Sa	1244 0645 0100* 0716*	–0.5 2.9 –0.8 3.4	–15 88 –24 104
17 Su	0139 0737 0150* 0808*	–0.7 2.9 –1.0 3.5	–21 88 –30 107
18 M ○	0233 0829 0239* 0859*	–0.8 2.9 –1.1 3.6	–24 88 –34 110
19 Tu	0326 0920 0329* 0950*	–0.8 2.8 –1.0 3.5	–24 85 –30 107
20 W	0418 1011 0419* 1042*	–0.7 2.7 –0.8 3.4	–21 82 –24 104
21 Th	0511 1104 0512* 1135*	–0.5 2.6 –0.6 3.2	–15 79 –18 98
22 F	0606 1159 0606*	–0.3 2.4 –0.3	–9 73 –9
23 Sa	1230 0703 1258* 0704*	2.9 0.0 2.3 0.1	88 0 70 3
24 Su	0128 0801 0200* 0807*	2.7 0.2 2.2 0.3	82 6 67 9
25 M ◑	0227 0900 0303* 0911*	2.6 0.3 2.2 0.5	79 9 67 15
26 Tu	0326 0955 0403* 1013*	2.4 0.3 2.2 0.5	73 9 67 15
27 W	0421 1046 0456* 1110*	2.4 0.3 2.3 0.5	73 9 70 15
28 Th	0512 1131 0543*	2.3 0.2 2.4	70 6 73
29 F	1200 0557 1211* 0626*	0.4 2.3 0.1 2.6	12 70 3 79
30 Sa	1245 0639 1249* 0705*	0.2 2.3 0.0 2.7	6 70 0 82

May

Day	Time (h m)	Height (ft)	Height (cm)
1 Su	0127 0719 0126* 0743*	0.1 2.3 –0.1 2.8	3 70 –3 85
2 M	0207 0757 0202* 0820*	0.0 2.3 –0.1 2.8	0 70 –3 85
3 Tu ●	0246 0835 0238* 0858*	0.0 2.3 –0.2 2.9	0 70 –6 88
4 W	0325 0912 0314* 0935*	0.0 2.2 –0.1 2.9	0 67 –3 88
5 Th	0404 0951 0352* 1014*	0.0 2.2 –0.1 2.9	0 67 –3 88
6 F	0444 1031 0432* 1056*	0.1 2.2 0.0 2.9	3 67 0 88
7 Sa	0527 1115 0516* 1140*	0.1 2.2 0.1 2.8	3 67 3 85
8 Su	0613 1204* 0606*	0.2 2.2 0.2	6 67 6
9 M	1230 0703 1259* 0704*	2.8 0.2 2.2 0.3	85 6 67 9
10 Tu ◐	0124 0757 0200* 0809*	2.7 0.1 2.4 0.3	82 3 73 9
11 W	0223 0853 0304* 0917*	2.7 0.0 2.5 0.2	82 0 76 6
12 Th	0324 0950 0406* 1024*	2.7 –0.2 2.7 0.1	82 –6 82 3
13 F	0425 1046 0506* 1128*	2.7 –0.4 3.0 –0.1	82 –12 91 –3
14 Sa	0524 1140 0603*	2.7 –0.6 3.2	82 –18 98
15 Su	1228 0621 1233* 0657*	–0.3 2.7 –0.8 3.4	–9 82 –24 104
16 M	0125 0716 0126* 0750*	–0.5 2.7 –0.9 3.5	–15 82 –27 107
17 Tu ○	0219 0809 0217* 0841*	–0.6 2.7 –0.9 3.5	–18 82 –27 107
18 W	0311 0901 0308* 0932*	–0.6 2.6 –0.8 3.4	–18 79 –24 104
19 Th	0402 0953 0359* 1022*	–0.6 2.6 –0.6 3.3	–18 79 –18 101
20 F	0453 1045 0450* 1112*	–0.4 2.5 –0.4 3.1	–12 76 –12 94
21 Sa	0544 1138 0542*	–0.2 2.4 –0.1	–6 73 –3
22 Su	1203 0635 1233* 0637*	2.9 0.0 2.3 0.2	88 0 70 6
23 M	1254 0726 0129* 0734*	2.7 0.1 2.2 0.4	82 3 67 12
24 Tu ◑	0146 0817 0226* 0833*	2.5 0.3 2.2 0.6	76 9 67 18
25 W	0239 0907 0321* 0932*	2.4 0.3 2.3 0.7	73 9 70 21
26 Th	0331 0954 0414* 1030*	2.2 0.3 2.4 0.6	67 9 73 18
27 F	0422 1040 0502* 1123*	2.2 0.3 2.5 0.6	67 9 76 18
28 Sa	0511 1123 0547*	2.1 0.2 2.6	64 6 79
29 Su	1211 0557 1205* 0630*	0.4 2.1 0.1 2.7	12 64 3 82
30 M	1256 0641 1246* 0711*	0.3 2.1 0.0 2.8	9 64 0 85
31 Tu	0139 0724 0127* 0752*	0.2 2.2 –0.1 2.9	6 67 –3 88

June

Day	Time (h m)	Height (ft)	Height (cm)
1 W ●	0221 0805 0207* 0832*	0.1 2.2 –0.2 3.0	3 67 –6 91
2 Th	0302 0847 0248* 0912*	0.0 2.3 –0.2 3.1	0 70 –6 94
3 F	0343 0929 0330* 0954*	0.0 2.3 –0.1 3.1	0 70 –3 94
4 Sa	0425 1013 0414* 1037*	0.0 2.3 –0.1 3.1	0 70 –3 94
5 Su	0508 1100 0502* 1122*	0.0 2.4 0.0 3.0	0 73 0 91
6 M	0553 1151 0554*	0.0 2.4 0.1	0 73 3
7 Tu	1211 0641 1245* 0652*	2.9 –0.1 2.5 0.2	88 –3 76 6
8 W	0103 0732 0144* 0755*	2.8 –0.1 2.6 0.3	85 –3 79 9
9 Th ◐	0159 0826 0245* 0902*	2.7 –0.2 2.8 0.3	82 –6 85 9
10 F	0259 0922 0347* 1009*	2.6 –0.3 2.9 0.2	79 –9 88 6
11 Sa	0401 1020 0448* 1114*	2.5 –0.4 3.1 0.1	76 –12 94 3
12 Su	0503 1117 0546*	2.5 –0.5 3.2	76 –15 98
13 M	1215 0602 1213* 0642*	–0.1 2.5 –0.6 3.3	–3 76 –18 101
14 Tu	0112 0659 0107* 0735*	–0.2 2.5 –0.6 3.4	–6 76 –18 104
15 W ○	0205 0753 0159* 0826*	–0.3 2.5 –0.6 3.4	–9 76 –18 104
16 Th	0256 0845 0250* 0914*	–0.3 2.6 –0.5 3.4	–9 79 –15 104
17 F	0344 0935 0339* 1001*	–0.3 2.5 –0.4 3.3	–9 76 –12 101
18 Sa	0431 1024 0428* 1047*	–0.2 2.5 –0.2 3.1	–6 76 –6 94
19 Su	0517 1113 0516* 1132*	–0.1 2.5 0.1 2.9	–3 76 3 88
20 M	0601 1202* 0606*	0.0 2.4 0.3	0 73 9
21 Tu	1217 0645 1251* 0656*	2.7 0.2 2.4 0.5	82 6 73 15
22 W	0102 0729 0142* 0750*	2.5 0.3 2.4 0.7	76 9 73 21
23 Th ◑	0149 0814 0233* 0846*	2.4 0.4 2.4 0.8	73 12 73 24
24 F	0239 0900 0325* 0944*	2.2 0.4 2.4 0.8	67 12 73 24
25 Sa	0330 0947 0417* 1040*	2.1 0.4 2.5 0.8	64 12 76 24
26 Su	0423 1035 0506* 1133*	2.1 0.3 2.6 0.7	64 9 79 21
27 M	0514 1123 0554*	2.1 0.2 2.8	64 6 85
28 Tu	1223 0604 1209* 0639*	0.6 2.1 0.1 2.9	18 64 3 88
29 W	0109 0651 1255* 0724*	0.4 2.2 0.0 3.1	12 67 0 94
30 Th	0153 0737 0140* 0807*	0.3 2.3 –0.1 3.2	9 70 –3 98

Heights are referred to mean lower low water which is the chart datum of soundings. All times are local. Daylight Saving Time has been used when needed.

Nassau, New Providence Island, Bahamas, 2011

Times and Heights of High and Low Waters

July

Day	Time (h m)	Height (ft)	Height (cm)	Day	Time (h m)	Height (ft)	Height (cm)
1 F ●	0236 0822 0225* 0850*	0.1 2.5 –0.1 3.3	3 76 –3 101	16 Sa	0323 0915 0320* 0938*	0.0 2.7 0.0 3.3	0 82 0 101
2 Sa	0319 0908 0311* 0933*	0.0 2.6 –0.2 3.3	0 79 –6 101	17 Su	0404 1000 0405* 1019*	0.1 2.7 0.1 3.1	3 82 3 94
3 Su	0401 0955 0359* 1017*	–0.1 2.7 –0.1 3.3	–3 82 –3 101	18 M	0444 1043 0449* 1059*	0.1 2.7 0.3 3.0	3 82 9 91
4 M	0445 1043 0449* 1103*	–0.2 2.8 –0.1 3.2	–6 85 –3 98	19 Tu	0523 1126 0533* 1138*	0.2 2.7 0.5 2.8	6 82 15 85
5 Tu	0530 1134 0543* 1151*	–0.2 2.9 0.1 3.1	–6 88 3 94	20 W	0601 1210* 0619*	0.4 2.6 0.7	12 79 21
6 W	0617 1228* 0640*	–0.2 2.9 0.2	–6 88 6	21 Th	1219 0640 1255* 0707*	2.6 0.5 2.6 0.9	79 15 79 27
7 Th	1243 0708 0126* 0742*	2.9 –0.2 3.0 0.3	88 –6 91 9	22 F	0102 0722 0143* 0759*	2.4 0.6 2.6 1.0	73 18 79 30
8 F ◐	0139 0802 0227* 0848*	2.8 –0.2 3.0 0.4	85 –6 91 12	23 Sa ◑	0148 0807 0235* 0856*	2.3 0.6 2.6 1.1	70 18 79 34
9 Sa	0239 0859 0330* 0956*	2.6 –0.1 3.1 0.5	79 –3 94 15	24 Su	0240 0856 0329* 0955*	2.2 0.7 2.6 1.1	67 21 79 34
10 Su	0343 0959 0433* 1102*	2.5 –0.1 3.2 0.4	76 –3 98 12	25 M	0336 0949 0424* 1053*	2.2 0.6 2.7 1.0	67 18 82 30
11 M	0447 1100 0533*	2.5 –0.1 3.2	76 –3 98	26 Tu	0433 1042 0517* 1147*	2.2 0.6 2.9 0.9	67 18 88 27
12 Tu	1204 0549 1158 0629*	0.3 2.5 –0.2 3.3	9 76 –6 101	27 W	0528 1135 0607*	2.3 0.4 3.1	70 12 94
13 W	0100 0646 1253* 0722*	0.2 2.5 –0.2 3.4	6 76 –6 104	28 Th	1236 0620 1226* 0654*	0.7 2.5 0.3 3.3	21 76 9 101
14 Th	0151 0739 0145* 0810*	0.1 2.6 –0.2 3.4	3 79 –6 104	29 F	0122 0710 0116* 0740*	0.5 2.6 0.1 3.4	15 79 3 104
15 F ○	0239 0829 0234* 0855*	0.0 2.7 –0.1 3.3	0 82 –3 101	30 Sa ●	0207 0758 0205* 0825*	0.2 2.8 0.0 3.5	6 85 0 107
				31 Su	0250 0846 0254* 0910*	0.0 3.0 –0.1 3.6	0 91 –3 110

August

Day	Time (h m)	Height (ft)	Height (cm)	Day	Time (h m)	Height (ft)	Height (cm)
1 M	0333 0934 0344* 0956*	–0.1 3.2 –0.1 3.5	–3 98 –3 107	16 Tu	0407 1011 0421* 1025*	0.4 3.0 0.6 3.0	12 91 18 91
2 Tu	0418 1023 0436* 1042*	–0.2 3.3 –0.1 3.4	–6 101 –3 104	17 W	0442 1049 0502* 1101*	0.5 3.0 0.7 2.9	15 91 21 88
3 W	0504 1114 0529* 1132*	–0.2 3.4 0.1 3.2	–6 104 3 98	18 Th	0517 1128 0543* 1139*	0.6 2.9 0.9 2.7	18 88 27 82
4 Th	0552 1208* 0627*	–0.2 3.4 0.3	–6 104 9	19 F	0554 1210* 0628*	0.7 2.8 1.1	21 85 34
5 F	1224 0643 0106* 0728*	3.0 –0.1 3.3 0.5	91 –3 101 15	20 Sa	1219 0633 1256* 0717*	2.5 0.8 2.8 1.2	76 24 85 37
6 Sa ◐	0121 0739 0208* 0834*	2.8 0.1 3.3 0.7	85 3 101 21	21 Su ◑	0104 0718 0147* 0812*	2.4 0.9 2.8 1.3	73 27 85 40
7 Su	0223 0840 0313* 0943*	2.7 0.2 3.2 0.8	82 6 98 24	22 M	0156 0809 0243* 0912*	2.3 1.0 2.8 1.4	70 30 85 43
8 M	0330 0944 0419* 1050*	2.6 0.3 3.2 0.8	79 9 98 24	23 Tu	0254 0906 0342* 1012*	2.3 1.0 2.9 1.3	70 30 88 40
9 Tu	0437 1048 0521* 1152*	2.5 0.3 3.3 0.7	76 9 101 21	24 W	0356 1006 0439* 1109*	2.4 0.9 3.0 1.1	73 27 91 34
10 W	0539 1149 0617*	2.6 0.3 3.3	79 9 101	25 Th	0456 1105 0533*	2.5 0.7 3.2	76 21 98
11 Th	1246 0635 1243* 0707*	0.6 2.7 0.3 3.3	18 82 9 101	26 F	1201 0551 1201* 0623*	0.9 2.8 0.5 3.4	27 85 15 104
12 F	0133 0725 0133* 0752*	0.5 2.8 0.3 3.3	15 85 9 101	27 Sa	1248 0643 1254* 0712*	0.6 3.0 0.3 3.6	18 91 9 110
13 Sa ○	0216 0811 0218* 0833*	0.4 2.9 0.3 3.3	12 88 9 101	28 Su	0134 0733 0146* 0759*	0.3 3.3 0.1 3.7	9 101 3 113
14 Su	0255 0852 0301* 0912*	0.4 2.9 0.3 3.3	12 88 9 101	29 M ●	0219 0822 0237* 0845*	0.0 3.5 –0.1 3.7	0 107 –3 113
15 M	0332 0932 0341* 0949*	0.4 3.0 0.4 3.1	12 91 12 94	30 Tu	0304 0911 0328* 0933*	–0.2 3.7 –0.1 3.6	–6 113 –3 110
				31 W	0349 1001 0421* 1021*	–0.2 3.8 0.0 3.5	–6 116 0 107

September

Day	Time (h m)	Height (ft)	Height (cm)	Day	Time (h m)	Height (ft)	Height (cm)
1 Th	0437 1053 0515* 1112*	–0.2 3.8 0.1 3.3	–6 116 3 101	16 F	0437 1052 0513* 1104*	0.7 3.1 0.9 2.7	21 94 27 82
2 F	0527 1148 0612*	–0.1 3.7 0.4	–3 113 12	17 Sa	0512 1132 0555* 1144*	0.8 3.0 1.1 2.6	24 91 34 79
3 Sa	1206 0621 1246* 0713*	3.1 0.1 3.5 0.6	94 3 107 18	18 Su	0551 1215* 0642*	0.9 3.0 1.3	27 91 40
4 Su ◐	0105 0719 0149* 0820*	2.9 0.3 3.4 0.8	88 9 104 24	19 M	1228 0636 0105* 0734*	2.5 1.1 2.9 1.4	76 34 88 43
5 M	0210 0824 0256* 0928*	2.7 0.6 3.3 1.0	82 18 101 30	20 Tu ◑	0120 0729 0201* 0833*	2.4 1.1 2.9 1.4	73 34 88 43
6 Tu	0319 0932 0402* 1035*	2.6 0.7 3.2 1.0	79 21 98 30	21 W	0221 0829 0301* 0933*	2.4 1.1 3.0 1.3	73 34 91 40
7 W	0427 1038 0504* 1134*	2.7 0.7 3.2 0.9	82 21 98 27	22 Th	0325 0934 0401* 1031*	2.5 1.1 3.1 1.1	76 34 94 34
8 Th	0528 1138 0558*	2.8 0.7 3.2	85 21 98	23 F	0427 1038 0458* 1124*	2.7 0.9 3.2 0.8	82 27 98 24
9 F	1224 0621 1231* 0646*	0.8 2.9 0.7 3.2	24 88 21 98	24 Sa	0524 1138 0552*	3.0 0.6 3.4	91 18 104
10 Sa	0108 0707 0118* 0728*	0.7 3.0 0.6 3.2	21 91 18 98	25 Su	1213 0618 1234* 0643*	0.5 3.3 0.3 3.5	15 101 9 107
11 Su	0147 0748 0200* 0806*	0.6 3.1 0.6 3.2	18 94 18 98	26 M	0101 0709 0128* 0732*	0.1 3.6 0.0 3.6	3 110 0 110
12 M ○	0223 0826 0240* 0843*	0.6 3.2 0.6 3.1	18 98 18 94	27 Tu ●	0148 0759 0220* 0821*	–0.1 3.8 –0.1 3.6	–3 116 –3 110
13 Tu	0257 0903 0318* 0918*	0.5 3.2 0.6 3.1	15 98 18 94	28 W	0235 0850 0312* 0910*	–0.3 4.0 –0.2 3.5	–9 122 –6 107
14 W	0330 0938 0355* 0953*	0.6 3.2 0.7 2.9	18 98 21 88	29 Th	0323 0940 0405* 1001*	–0.4 4.0 –0.1 3.4	–12 122 –3 104
15 Th	0403 1015 0434* 1028*	0.6 3.2 0.8 2.8	18 98 24 85	30 F	0412 1033 0459* 1053*	–0.3 3.9 0.1 3.2	–9 119 3 98

October

Day	Time (h m)	Height (ft)	Height (cm)	Day	Time (h m)	Height (ft)	Height (cm)
1 Sa	0504 1127 0556* 1149*	–0.1 3.8 0.3 3.0	–3 116 9 91	16 Su	0439 1101 0529* 1116*	0.7 3.1 0.9 2.5	21 94 27 76
2 Su	0559 1226* 0657*	0.2 3.6 0.6	6 110 18	17 M	0518 1143 0614*	0.8 3.0 1.0	24 91 30
3 M	1250 0700 0128* 0801*	2.8 0.5 3.4 0.8	85 15 104 24	18 Tu	1202 0604 1231* 0704*	2.4 0.9 3.0 1.1	73 27 91 34
4 Tu ◐	0156 0806 0233* 0907*	2.7 0.7 3.2 0.9	82 21 98 27	19 W	1254 0658 0125* 0759*	2.4 1.0 2.9 1.1	73 30 88 34
5 W	0305 0915 0338* 1010*	2.7 0.9 3.1 0.9	82 27 94 27	20 Th ◑	0154 0800 0224* 0857*	2.5 1.0 3.0 1.0	76 30 91 30
6 Th	0411 1021 0438* 1106*	2.7 0.9 3.0 0.9	82 27 91 27	21 F	0258 0907 0324* 0953*	2.6 0.9 3.0 0.7	79 27 91 21
7 F	0509 1121 0531* 1153*	2.8 0.9 3.0 0.8	85 27 91 24	22 Sa	0400 1014 0424* 1047*	2.8 0.7 3.1 0.4	85 21 94 12
8 Sa	0559 1212* 0617*	2.9 0.8 3.0	88 24 91	23 Su	0459 1116 0520* 1139*	3.1 0.5 3.1 0.1	94 15 94 3
9 Su	1235 0642 1257* 0658*	0.7 3.0 0.7 3.0	21 91 21 91	24 M	0554 1215* 0615*	3.4 0.2 3.2	104 6 98
10 M	0112 0721 0139* 0736*	0.6 3.1 0.6 2.9	18 94 18 88	25 Tu	1229 0647 0111* 0707*	–0.2 3.7 –0.1 3.2	–6 113 –3 98
11 Tu	0147 0758 0217* 0812*	0.5 3.2 0.6 2.9	15 98 18 88	26 W ●	0119 0739 0204* 0759*	–0.4 3.9 –0.3 3.2	–12 119 –9 98
12 W ○	0221 0833 0255* 0848*	0.5 3.2 0.6 2.8	15 98 18 85	27 Th	0209 0830 0257* 0850*	–0.6 4.0 –0.3 3.2	–18 122 –9 98
13 Th	0254 0909 0332* 0923*	0.5 3.2 0.6 2.7	15 98 18 82	28 F	0259 0922 0350* 0942*	–0.6 4.0 –0.3 3.1	–18 122 –9 94
14 F	0328 0945 0409* 0959*	0.5 3.2 0.7 2.6	15 98 21 79	29 Sa	0350 1014 0444* 1036*	–0.5 3.8 –0.1 3.0	–15 116 –3 91
15 Sa	0402 1022 0448* 1036*	0.6 3.2 0.8 2.5	18 98 24 76	30 Su	0443 1108 0539* 1132*	–0.2 3.7 0.1 2.8	–6 113 3 85
				31 M	0539 1204* 0636*	0.1 3.4 0.3	3 104 9

November

Day	Time (h m)	Height (ft)	Height (cm)	Day	Time (h m)	Height (ft)	Height (cm)
1 Tu	1232 0639 0102* 0736*	2.7 0.4 3.2 0.5	82 12 98 15	16 W	0442 1105 0538* 1134*	0.6 2.9 0.6 2.4	18 88 18 73
2 W ◐	0136 0743 0203* 0836*	2.6 0.7 3.0 0.6	79 21 91 18	17 Th	0536 1155 0629*	0.7 2.9 0.5	21 88 15
3 Th	0241 0849 0303* 0934*	2.6 0.8 2.8 0.7	79 24 85 21	18 F ◑	1232 0638 1251* 0722*	2.5 0.7 2.8 0.4	76 21 85 12
4 F	0343 0954 0401* 1026*	2.6 0.9 2.7 0.6	79 27 82 18	19 Sa	0133 0744 0151* 0818*	2.6 0.6 2.8 0.2	79 18 85 6
5 Sa	0439 1053 0453* 1113*	2.7 0.9 2.6 0.6	82 27 79 18	20 Su	0235 0852 0252* 0913*	2.8 0.5 2.7 0.0	85 15 82 0
6 Su	0428 1045 0441* 1055*	2.8 0.8 2.6 0.5	85 24 79 15	21 M	0335 0957 0352* 1008*	3.1 0.3 2.8 –0.3	94 9 85 –9
7 M	0512 1132 0523* 1133*	2.9 0.7 2.5 0.4	88 21 76 12	22 Tu	0433 1058 0450* 1102*	3.3 0.0 2.8 –0.5	101 0 85 –15
8 Tu	0551 1214* 0603*	3.0 0.5 2.5	91 15 76	23 W	0528 1155 0545* 1155*	3.5 –0.2 2.8 –0.7	107 –6 85 –21
9 W	1210 0629 1253* 0642*	0.3 3.0 0.4 2.5	9 91 12 76	24 Th	0621 1250* 0640*	3.7 –0.4 2.8	113 –12 85
10 Th ○	1246 0706 0132* 0719*	0.2 3.1 0.4 2.5	6 94 12 76	25 F ●	1248 0714 0143* 0733*	–0.8 3.7 –0.5 2.8	–24 113 –15 85
11 F	0122 0743 0210* 0757*	0.2 3.1 0.3 2.4	6 94 9 73	26 Sa	0140 0805 0235* 0826*	–0.8 3.7 –0.5 2.8	–24 113 –15 85
12 Sa	0158 0820 0249* 0835*	0.2 3.1 0.4 2.4	6 94 12 73	27 Su	0232 0856 0327* 0919*	–0.7 3.6 –0.4 2.7	–21 110 –12 82
13 Su	0235 0858 0328* 0914*	0.3 3.1 0.4 2.4	9 94 12 73	28 M	0325 0948 0419* 1013*	–0.4 3.4 –0.2 2.6	–12 104 –6 79
14 M	0314 0937 0408* 0956*	0.4 3.0 0.5 2.3	12 91 15 70	29 Tu	0419 1039 0511* 1109*	–0.2 3.2 –0.1 2.5	–6 98 –3 76
15 Tu	0355 1019 0451* 1042*	0.5 3.0 0.5 2.3	15 91 15 70	30 W	0514 1131 0603*	0.2 2.9 0.1	6 88 3

December

Day	Time (h m)	Height (ft)	Height (cm)	Day	Time (h m)	Height (ft)	Height (cm)
1 Th	1207 0613 1225* 0656*	2.4 0.4 2.7 0.2	73 12 82 6	16 F	0520 1131 0600*	0.2 2.7 –0.1	6 82 –3
2 F ◐	0105 0713 0119* 0747*	2.4 0.6 2.5 0.3	73 18 76 9	17 Sa	1210 0620 1224* 0651*	2.5 0.3 2.6 –0.2	76 9 79 –6
3 Sa	0203 0815 0213* 0837*	2.4 0.7 2.3 0.3	73 21 70 9	18 Su ◑	0110 0725 0122* 0746*	2.6 0.3 2.5 –0.3	79 9 76 –9
4 Su	0258 0915 0306* 0925*	2.4 0.7 2.2 0.3	73 21 67 9	19 M	0212 0833 0224* 0844*	2.8 0.2 2.4 –0.4	85 6 73 –12
5 M	0349 1010 0357* 1010*	2.5 0.7 2.1 0.2	76 21 64 6	20 Tu	0314 0940 0328* 0943*	2.9 0.1 2.4 –0.5	88 3 73 –15
6 Tu	0435 1100 0444* 1053*	2.6 0.5 2.1 0.1	79 15 64 3	21 W	0415 1043 0430* 1041*	3.1 –0.1 2.4 –0.7	94 –3 73 –21
7 W	0519 1146 0529* 1134*	2.7 0.4 2.1 0.0	82 12 64 0	22 Th	0512 1143 0529* 1138*	3.3 –0.3 2.4 –0.8	101 –9 73 –24
8 Th	0600 1228* 0611*	2.8 0.3 2.2	85 9 67	23 F	0608 1238* 0625*	3.4 –0.5 2.5	104 –15 76
9 F	1214 0640 0109* 0653*	0.0 2.9 0.1 2.2	0 88 3 67	24 Sa ●	1233 0700 0130* 0719*	–0.9 3.4 –0.6 2.5	–27 104 –18 76
10 Sa ○	1254 0719 0148* 0733*	–0.1 3.0 0.1 2.2	–3 91 3 67	25 Su	0126 0750 0220* 0811*	–0.9 3.4 –0.6 2.6	–27 104 –18 79
11 Su	0134 0758 0228* 0813*	–0.1 3.0 0.0 2.3	–3 91 0 70	26 M	0217 0839 0308* 0901*	–0.8 3.3 –0.6 2.5	–24 101 –18 76
12 M	0214 0837 0307* 0855*	–0.1 3.0 0.0 2.3	–3 91 0 70	27 Tu	0307 0926 0354* 0951*	–0.6 3.1 –0.5 2.5	–18 94 –15 76
13 Tu	0255 0916 0347* 0938*	–0.1 3.0 0.0 2.3	–3 91 0 70	28 W	0356 1011 0439* 1041*	–0.3 2.9 –0.3 2.4	–9 88 –9 73
14 W	0339 0958 0428* 1024*	0.0 2.9 0.0 2.4	0 88 0 73	29 Th	0446 1057 0524* 1130*	–0.1 2.7 –0.2 2.4	–3 82 –6 73
15 Th	0427 1042 0512* 1115*	0.1 2.9 –0.1 2.4	3 88 –3 73	30 F	0538 1143 0609*	0.2 2.5 –0.1	6 76 –3
				31 Sa	1222 0631 1230* 0655*	2.3 0.4 2.2 0.1	70 12 67 3

Heights are referred to mean lower low water which is the chart datum of soundings. All times are local. Daylight Saving Time has been used when needed.

Distress Calls

VHF Channel 16 is the distress call frequency. The codeword "Mayday" is the international alert signal of a life-threatening situation at sea. After a Mayday message is broadcast, Channel 16 must be kept free of all traffic, other than those directly involved in the rescue situation, until the rescue has been completed. If you hear a Mayday message and no one else is responding, it is your duty to step in to answer the call, relay it to the nearest rescue organization and get to the scene to help.

Remember, a Mayday distress call can only be used when life is threatened. If you have run on the rocks but no one is going to lose their life, that is not a Mayday situation.

Distress Call

Hello All Ships. MAYDAY! MAYDAY! MAYDAY!

This is [give your Vessel name and callsign].

Our position is [read it off the GPS, or give it as something like "two miles southwest of Royal Island." Your rescuers must be able to find you!].

We are [then say what's happening: on fire? have hit a reef and are sinking?].

We have [say how many people there are on board].

At this time we are [say what you're doing about the crisis: abandoning ship?]

For identification we are [say what your boat is: type, length, color, so that your rescuers can identify you at a distance more easily].

We have [say what safety equipment you have: flares? smoke? ocean dye markers? EPIRB?]

We will keep watch on Channel 16 as long as we can.

This is [repeat your vessel name and callsign]. *MAYDAY! MAYDAY! MAYDAY!*

Wait for an answer. If no one responds, keep repeating your distress call until you receive an answer.

VHF Radio

There are international rules governing the use of VHF radio. Monitor Channel 16 the entire time you are at sea. Use Channel 16 for distress calls and hailing. To contact someone on Channel 16, hail the vessel by name twice. Pause and then state your vessel's name once. When the hailed vessel responds, ask them to switch to a designated working channel, preferably a low power channel. Proper communication sounds like this:

"Windsong...Windsong." Pause, "Gypsy."

"Windsong here."

"Channel 17, Windsong?"

"Roger, Gypsy. Channel 17"

Gypsy then switches to Channel 17 and confirms that Windsong is there, too. Sometimes other vessels will be on your chosen channel. If so, return to Channel 16 and start all over again. On any channel, remember that other people are also out there. Refrain from saying anything that you wouldn't want the whole world to hear. Frequently others will purposely listen to your communication. This practice is called "reading your mail." If the eavesdropper wants to add something to your conversation, he will say "Break, break." You respond, "Go ahead, Break." Although this may sound like an impolite practice, many an important update on severe weather or suggestion on how to make a repair comes via a "Break."

Do not use Channel 22 alpha for conversations. It is used by the Coast Guard for vessels in distress. Channels 9 and 13 are frequently used by bridges and commercial traffic. Channel 68 is used in many of the islands as the hailing channel instead of Channel 16. Be aware that you might be broadcasting your conversation in every store in town on Channel 68! Keep your conversation brief and to the point.

VHF in the Bahamas

VHF radio use in the Bahamas is quite different, especially in the Out Islands. Some Bahamians use VHF radios like party-line telephones and take their pick of the channels in the recreational boating frequencies. Almost every house, certainly everyone in business in the Out Islands, has used the VHF as a means of communication. Channel 16 is not "sacred" and carries far more traffic than it should. That's just the way it is in the Bahamas. Yes, there are cellular telephones, just as there is conventional telephone service. But, in some out-of-the-way islands, VHF is more dependable and just the way it has always been done.

Newcomers soon learn that in the main cruising centers, where visiting yachts concentrate (like Marsh Harbour, Staniel Cay, George Town, Salt Pond and Rock Sound), VHF radio can be a lifeline. Cruiser's nets open at a set time each morning to provide weather, local information, social announcements, offers of services or pleas for help with problems. The VHF radio is one piece of equipment every boat has in common, and it is a great communication tool in these areas beyond Channel 16 and 22A (alpha). This said, the International Maritime Organization conventions on VHF channel allocation remain in force, and the "standard" list of channel allocation applies Bahamas-wide.

The primary reserved frequencies are:

Nassau Harbour Control	09
Commercial Communication	13
Distress and Calling	16
U.S. Coast Guard	21–23A
Marine Operator Nassau (radio telephone)	27

Unauthorized Use

In some areas of the Bahamas, notably the Abacos, common usage has resulted in a rash of so-called reserved channels, such as 06 for taxis, 65 for Dolphin Research, 68 as the calling channel, 72 for the Hope Town Fire Brigade and 80 for Trauma One.

SKIPPER'S HANDBOOK

These adoptions of air space are unauthorized. Nonetheless, this is the way it is. Make note of them if you are in waters where local channel designation has become customary.

VHF in the Turks and Caicos

Generally, the international rules apply, and most importantly, VHF Channel 16 is the distress and primary calling frequency. Otherwise channel usage is:

Commercial Vessels.................................... 68
Working Frequencies 09, 12, 14, 65, 69, 74
Taxis 06
Public Bus 70

BTC (Bahamas Telecommunications Company) Towers

Visual navigation in the Bahamas and identifying a landfall after a passage are not always easy. The islands are relatively featureless and low-lying. Cat Island is the place where land rises above 60 meters/200 feet. Just three islands top 45 meters/150 feet. Thirteen islands rise above 30 meters/100 feet, but are less than 45 meters/150 feet in height. The five remaining islands on the list have elevations between 15 meters/50 feet and 30 meters/100 feet. Such problems are considerably alleviated by BTC. BTC's radio towers are, more often than not, the greatest boon to visual navigation. Where there is a tower, there is a settlement nearby.

BTC provided the following information, but they are not responsible for the accuracy of the positions given. Also, we have not taken a hand-held GPS to double check each one.

LOCATION	HEIGHT IN METERS/FEET	POSITION	
ABACOS			
Cherokee	70/235	26°16.48N	77°03.12W
Coopers Town	60/200	26°52.26N	77°30.52W
Crossing Rocks	60/200	26°07.25N	77°11.07W
Fox Town	60/200	26°55.03N	77°47.44W
Grand Cay	82/275	27°14.20N	78°19.30W
Green Turtle Cay	30/100	26°45.25N	77°19.32W
Guana Cay	15/50	26°41.10N	77°08.16W
Hope Town	12/40	26°32.07N	76°57.30W
Man O War Cay	12/40	26°25.44N	77°00.15W
Marsh Harbour (2)	60/200	26°33.35N	77°03.25W
	75/250		
Mores Island	60/200	26°18.51N	77°23.53W
Sandy Point	78/260	26°01.30N	77°23.53W
Treasure Cay (2)	60/200	26°40.08N	77°17.29W
GRAND BAHAMA			
Basset Cove	120/400	26°37.15N	78°19.21W
Eight Mile Rock	60/200	26°32.51N	78°49.17W
Freeport	60/200	26°31.45N	78°41.47W
McLeans Town	60/200	26°39.02N	77°57.24W
South Riding Point	67/225	26°37.44N	78°14.21W
West End	45/150	26°41.44N	78°58.27W
BIMINI			
Bailey Town	79/265	25°21.00N	76°27.20W
BERRY ISLANDS			
Bullocks	70/235	25°49.20N	77°53.20W
Chub Cay	60/200	25°24.39N	77°54.03W

LOCATION	HEIGHT IN METERS/FEET	POSITION	
NEW PROVIDENCE			
Coral Harbour	30/100	25°00.08N	77°28.12W
Delaporte	60/200	25°04.41N	77°31.15W
Lyford Cay	60/200	25°01.43N	77°31.15W
Paradise Island	45/150	25°04.50N	77°19.10W
Perpall Tract (4)	2 x 24/80	25°04.16N	77°21.43W
	2 x 45/150		
Poinciana Drive	60/200	25°03.41N	77°21.41W
Soldier Road	78/260	25°02.47N	77°19.10W
	66/220		
Pinewood	30/100	25°01.25N	77°19.45W
ELEUTHERA			
Current Island	12/40	25°22.53N	76°47.00W
Current	15/50	25°24.28N	76°47.00W
Governors Harbour	54/180	25°11.56N	76°14.30W
Green Castle	72/240	24°46.37N	76°12.54W
Harbour Island	12/40	25°30.01N	76°38.11W
Hatchet Bay	79/265	25°21.18N	76°28.50W
Lower Bogue	60/200	25°26.56N	76°42.56W
Rock Sound	30/100	24°52.00N	76°09.30W
Savannah Sound	60/200	25°05.17N	76°07.58W
Spanish Wells	36/120	25°32.34N	76°44.56W
Tarpum Bay	60/200	24°58.51N	76°11.02W
ANDROS			
Cargill Creek	30/100	24°29.42N	77°43.30W
Fresh Creek	67/225	24°43.44N	77°47.13W
Kemps Bay	54/180	24°05.28N	77°32.58W
Mars Bay	30/100	25°52.06N	77°31.00W
Mastic Point	30/100	25°03.52N	77°58.08W
Nichols Town	67/255	25°08.42N	78°02.40W
Staniard Creek	60/200	24°49.35N	77°54.07W
EXUMA			
Barraterre	45/150	23°41.50N	76°02.55W
Black Point	30/100	24°05.45N	75°24.05W
Farmers Hill	12/40	23°36.56N	75°54.33W
George Town	78/260	23°30.06N	75°46.16W

Highbourne Cay	78/260	24°42.53N	76°49.21W
Little Farmers Cay	78/260	23°57.21N	76°19.13W
Rolle Town	40/12	23°27.54N	75°42.25W
Rolleville	78/260	23°40.28N	75°59.11W
Staniel Cay	78/260	24°10.20N	76°26.30W
Williams Town	60/200	23°25.22N	75°33.36W

LOCATION	HEIGHT IN METERS/FEET	POSITION	
CAT ISLAND			
Arthur Town	60/200	24°37.23N	75°40.31W
The Bight	69/230	24°17.26N	75°24.53W
LONG ISLAND			
Clarence Town	18/60	23°05.50N	74°48.05W
Deadmans	67/225	23°09.36N	75°05.31W
Roses	15/50	22°57.10N	74°52.00W
Simms	69/230	23°29.45N	75°14.02W
Stella Maris	15/50	23°33.40N	75°14.30W
RUM CAY			
Port Nelson	78/260	23°40'00N	78°48.00W
SAN SALVADOR			
Cockburn Town	45/150	24°03.07N	74°31.57W
CROOKED ISLAND			
Cabbage Hill	66/220	22°45.58N	74°12.38W
ACKLINS			
Spring Point	66/220	22°27.43N	73°57.30W
MAYAGUANA			
Abrahams Bay	52/175	22°22.03N	72°58.05W
Betsy Bay	33/110	22°24.52N	73°57.30W
GREAT INAGUA			
Matthew Town	30/100	20°56.04N	73°40.55W

Weather Broadcasts

Florida, Bahamas, and Southwest North Atlantic Ocean South of 32°N and West of 65°W

Radio Bahamas

ZNS-1 is the principal station. ZNS-3 covers the Northern Bahamas (Grand Bahama, Abacos, Berry Islands, Biminis). Radio Bahamas also broadcasts on 107.1 & 107.9 MHz covering Nassau and the

U.S.C.G. High Frequency (Single Side Band) Camslant/Chesapeake, VA. NMN

All times UTC. To convert to local time: EST – 5 hours EDT – 4 hours

Time of Broadcast	Frequency in kHz
0330, 0515, 0930	4426, 6501, 8764
1115, 1530, 1715	6501, 8764, 13089
2130, 2315	6501, 8764, 13089

Color Code: Offshore forecast - BLUE; High Seas forecast - RED

Bahamas AM, FM, HF (SSB) and Marine VHF Weather Forecasts

TIME	FORECAST SERVICE	BAND	FREQUENCY
0600	Nassau Marine Operator	VHF	Channel 27
0615-45	Radio Bahamas ZNS-1	AM	1540 kHz
0615-45	Radio Bahamas ZNS-3	AM	810 kHz
0700	Radio Bahamas Grand Bahama	AM	810 kHz
0700	Bahamas weather	HF (USB)	4003 kHz
0700	4BEH Cap Haitien	AM	1030 kHz
0715	BASRA Nassau	VHF	Channel 16/72
0720	Bahamas offshore weather	HF (LSB)	7096 kHz
0730	Highbourne Cay	VHF	Channel 06
0745	Waterway Net (urgent messages)	HF (LSB)	7268 kHz
0800	Radio Abaco	FM	93.5 MHz
0800	Nassau Marine Operator	VHF	Channel 27
0800	Staniel Cay Cruisers Net	VHF	Channel 14
0800	George Town Cruisers Net	VHF	Channel 68
0815	Abaco Cruisers Net	VHF	Channel 68
1205	Radio Bahamas Grand Bahama	AM	810 kHz
1300	Radio Abaco	FM	93.5 MHz
1800	Radio Abaco	FM	93.5 MHz

Weather By Internet

Abaco Weather	www.oii.net/radioabaco
Buoy Weather	www.buoyweather.com
Disaster Message Service Board	www.viexpo.com/dmstesy/hurricane.html
FEMA Stormwatch	www.fema.gov/fema/weathr.htm
Gulf Stream Information	www.ncep.noaa.gov/MPC
National Hurricane Center	www.nhc.noaa.gov
NOAA National Weather Service	www.weather.gov
NOAA Climatic Data Center	www.ncdc.noaa.gov
NOAA Marine Weather	www.nws.noaa.gov/om/marine
Oceans WeatherNet	www.weathernet.com
Tropical Weather	www.nhc.noaa.gov
U.S. Navy	www.nlmoc.navy.mil
U.S. Weather	www.intellicast.com
Weather Channel	www.weather.com
Weather Channel Marine	www.weather.com/marine (see note)
Weather Underground	www.underground.com/MAR/AM/080.html
Yahoo! Weather	www.yahoo.com

Weather Channel Marine (WCM) is a service that requires hardware and charges a seasonal or annual fee. It offers radar, live reports, forecasts (including wind, wave, and visibility), advisories, sea temperatures and storm tracking over the U.S. and 200 miles offshore.

Turks and Caicos VHF Weather Forecasts

Turks and Caicos Radio 105.9 MHz (Providenciales), 94.9 MHz (Grand Turk).

southeast Bahamas. Weather reports may come up at any time, may occasionally be missed and are not reported on Sundays. Brief weather reports are normally scheduled either before or after the news at noon (1200) and 4 p.m. (1800). The ZNS-1 broadcast at 6:45 a.m. is the best and may give a three-day forecast. If a tropical storm or a hurricane is threatening the islands, full weather reports and warnings are virtually continuous.

Radio Abaco

Radio Abaco does not normally give weather on Saturdays and Sundays.

Nassau Marine Operator

The Nassau Marine Operator will give weather on request on VHF Channel 27.

Weather Plotting Charts

A weather-plotting chart covering the Southwest North Atlantic Ocean, the Caribbean and the Gulf of Mexico is provided at the end of this chapter. The NOAA Atlantic Hurricane Tracking Chart is at the beginning of the chapter. We suggest photocopying the charts for use in following and recording weather reports.

A Pilot House Booklist

In addition to charts, and manuals for your equipment onboard, we also recommend the following reference materials:

Federal Requirements and Safety Tips for Recreational Boaters
NOAA Chart No 1. Nautical Chart Symbols and Abbreviations
Reed's Nautical Almanac East Coast and Bahamas
Reed's Nautical Companion Navigation Rules
Chapman Piloting, Seamanship and Small Boat Handling
Heavy Weather Sailing, Adlard Coles. Revised by Peter Bruce. International Marine. 1996.
Mariners Weather, William P Crawford. W.W. Norton. 1995.
Admiralty List of Radio Signals, Volume 3. United Kingdom Hydrographic Office. NP283 (annual).
Marine Diesel Engines, Nigel Calder. International Marine. 1997.
Boatowner's Electrical and Mechanical Handbook, Nigel Calder. International Marine.
12V Bible, Miner Brotherton. Seven Seas.
Handbook of First Aid and Emergency Care, American Medical Association.
Advanced First Aid Afloat, Peter F Eastman. Cornell Maritime Press. 1995.
Poisonous and Hazardous Marine Life, Sandra Romashko.
Where There Is No Doctor: A Village Health Care Handbook, The Hesperian Foundation.
DAN First Aid for Scuba Diving, Dan Orr.

Day-to-Day Living in the Islands

In the Bahamas, one can buy almost anything that can be had in the U.S. If it is not in stock, someone will order it for you. Sometimes it gets there within twenty-four hours, however, it will cost you. Most things cost more than you would pay in the States—from off the shelf or ordered specially.

You will find fish, yellow bulk cheese, conch, lobster tails, chicken, eggs, bread, beer, rum, soft drinks, Bahamian "spring" water and a seasonal stock of locally grown fruits and vegetables in the groceries. Bahamian bread (even on the smallest of cays) is fresh baked each day and free of artificial preservatives. Most of the bakery ladies offer white, whole wheat and, best of all, coconut breads. Kalik, the beer of the Bahamas, is less expensive than imported beer, but prepare to spend close to $50 for a case of cans. Just about everything else is imported. In the larger cities with American style supermarkets, prices are not that much higher than what you see in the States. On the smaller cays, where food comes in weekly on mailboats, foodstuff is available and not cost prohibitive. The priciest items are non-essentials, such as paper towels, deodorant, salad dressings and such. If you stick to basics, cost is not a big issue. Even frozen meats are affordable. You will not go hungry.

The cost of restaurant meals ranges from inexpensive fish fries and take-away that make you wonder why you would ever bother to cook, to truly outrageous $35 hamburgers at a mega-resort. If in doubt, check it out. Don't be shy to leave a restaurant if the menu doesn't fit your wallet. There is something for everyone's budget in the islands.

You can find accommodations for your visitors from ridiculously high to bargain-basement low. Rates are generally higher in the winter season, but on some of the smaller family islands, the rates never change. Taxi prices are regulated. That doesn't mean you won't meet an unscrupulous driver trying to overcharge for a short ride to or from an airport. Be savvy. Arrange the rides ahead of time, and taxi share whenever you can.

Marine fuel is a bit pricier than at home, but not prohibitively so. Motor vessels practice every fuel conserving trick and sailboats—well, sail! Do utilize your VHF radio to ask fellow cruisers about fuel prices on the different islands. They can vary widely.

Reverse osmosis water is readily available. Although the marinas charge per gallon, there are many settlements where it is available free. Where it is free, please donate to the settlement's schools or churches as a thank you. If you are undertaking extensive cruising farther south, down to the Turks and Caicos and beyond, you will want to have a watermaker onboard. A word of warning about watermakers, they seem to suffer more need for repair than most other things onboard. Have plenty of spare parts in your toolbox.

Major Provisioning Stops

Port Lucaya, Grand Bahama
Nassau, New Providence
Providenciales, Turks and Caicos
Marsh Harbour, Abacos
George Town, Exumas

Re-stocking the Larder

Alice Town, North Bimini
Great Harbour Cay, Berry Islands
Fresh Creek, Andros
Green Turtle, Treasure Cay, Man-O-War and Hope Town, Abacos
Staniel Cay and Blackpoint, Exumas
Spanish Wells and Rock Sound, Eleuthera
New Bight, Cat Island
Cockburn Town, San Salvador
Salt Pond and Clarence Town, Long Island
Matthew Town, Great Inagua
Cockburn Town, Grand Turk Island

Provisioning for Southern Waters

Depart with your fuel tanks, water tanks and jerry cans full. You will be in better shape if a good supply of oil and lubricants are onboard, too. Spare parts are vital. You may be miles away from civilization when something breaks down--bulbs, fuses, belts, impellers, filters, spare pumps, spark plugs, injectors, gaskets, cables for your plotter and electronics and batteries for your Blackberry™. Literally walk through your vessel, make a list and ensure that you have the spares you need to remain self-sufficient. Pay particular attention to the one thing that everyone hopes will never malfunction, the marine sanitation system.

What then of foodstuffs? If you have a freezer, take things you will not find or cannot afford to buy there: steaks, chops and roasts. Chicken, hamburger, hot dogs, lunchmeat and cheese are available. Don't take frozen seafood. You can catch it or buy it fresh. Onions, potatoes, plantains, squash, tomatoes, celery, peppers (sweet and HOT) are usually available, as are oranges, bananas, limes and apples. Stock your refrigerator with a start-out quantity of eggs, cheeses, butter, fresh vegetables and lettuce.

Make sure you have a basket or net hammock in which to hang wrapped fruits and vegetables. Wrap moist fruits and vegetables like bananas or zucchini squash in micro-fiber towels. Wrap less moist fruit and vegetables like onions or apples in cling wrap, and hang them all in your basket or hammock. The wrapping keeps salt air from hastening their demise.

If you drink milk, buy as much shelf-stable milk as you can in the states. Parmalot™ (which costs three to four times more per box in the islands) is a favorite, but any of the soy or rice milk products are good, too. They travel and store well (check the date on the box).

You want to stock up on things that are expensive in the islands. If it is an inexpensive staple in the States, it is an inexpensive staple in the islands. Things to stock up on are: Olive oil, good vinegar (for cooking, not for cleaning and de-crystallizing the head), capers, olives, pickles, mayonnaise, tartar sauce, cocktail sauce, soy sauce, frying oils (including lard for conch fritters), spray oil, coconut milk, curry pastes, couscous, coffee, sugar substitute, boxed cereal, granola bars, shelf-stable tortillas, shelf-stable meat, grated parmesan cheese, deodorant, toothpaste, shampoo, dental floss, wet wipes, dish detergent and laundry detergent (non-petroleum based, not antibacterial), paper towels, heavy mil trash and garbage bags, small propane cans for your grill and the butane clickers to light them, pens, paper, needles and thread, sun screen, bug spray, lotion and lots and lots of batteries. Bring your medications in the original labeled bottles. You can get them refilled at pharmacies, especially in the bigger cities, such as Nassau.

Canned food is worth taking, whatever you eat and enjoy. Be sure to store the cans in plastic bags and mark the ingredients on the can with a permanent marker. Tomatoes, Southern-style squash casserole, greens with bacon and any kind of fruit in its own juice quite versatile. Dry goods like rice, flour, pastas, beans and sugar are readily available in the islands. They take up much needed room and can breed bugs in the hold. Buy smaller quantities as you need them. There are wonderful English teas and biscuits available on the smallest of islands. Do not waste storage space on them.

As for libations, you will have fun trying their mixers like Goombay Punch. However, all the sodas that you find in the States are for sale in the islands. You can literally drink rum free at tasting bars in the liquor stores. Wine can be hard to find; good wine even harder. Remember that there are duties to pay on liquor and wine imported into the Bahamas in excess of one liter each.

You will be invited to many sundowner parties and potlucks. Plan ahead! There are no stores to run to for some chips and dip or a carrot cake. We find that canned mixed nuts are always appreciated and travel well. Stateside liquor stores are a surprisingly good source of canned and jarred tidbits to bring along to sundowners. Everyone has his or her own specialty to bring to potlucks. Banana or mango cream pies are always well received. Some cruisers specialize in chicken wings or hot artichoke dip. Our editor always takes along fresh hot bread. Everyone gets creative and tries to outdo each other! That is part of the fun. Just remember to bring your recipe and your ingredients from home.

What Else Could You Take?

Just remember you can get everything you are likely to need in all the major centers of population, but if you are going off into the Out Islands, you're provisioning on a different scale. We have provided a provisioning checklist that you may want to photocopy for shopping or for checking your onboard stores.

What Should You Take to Them?

Don't arrive empty handed. In the islands, both libraries and schools welcome books. They particularly appreciate art supplies, pens, paper and pencils. Have something just to say, "thank you," especially if you plan to stay in one place for a while. It is very nice to have little gifts representative of your home port.

What about Non-Food Stuff?

If the label says "100% Cotton," you probably don't want to take it onboard. If it says "100% Heavy Weight Cotton," you definitely don't want to take it onboard. This means that you want lightweight, breathable garments in your duffle bag. They are easy to hand wash, take little water to rinse and hang dry quickly on a lifeline. (Cruiser Hint: You can effectively wash clothes in an icebox cooler. Place clothes, water and detergent in a cooler. Secure to the stern and let it agitate during the day's travels. Drain, rinse and wring. Voila! Your own shipboard laundry.)

Cotton/polyester, tee-shirt knit sheets work well on your bunk and dry quickly after a wash. Fiber filled sleeping bags are water and humidity magnets. Instead, look for moisture resistant, polyester blankets that backpackers use. Micro-fiber towels and swimmer's artificial chamois towels are great for drying everything from your hair to your dishes. Use products made for seawater to bathe and clean. For these uses, cruisers have relied upon Campsuds™ (www.campsuds.com) for generations.

Never, ever, bring seawater down below. This means foul-weather gear, footwear, swimming suits and salty towels stay topsides. Perform a fresh water rinse on the deck. If you plan to wash dishes in salt water, use a dish tub or bucket on the deck. Keep in mind that this may rust metal pans. Fresh water rinse before transferring dishes, or anything else, down below. If you don't want to feel sticky, tacky and wet forever, keep salt water topsides.

Useful Tables and Measurements

Distance Equivalents

1 Degree of Latitude	60 nm	111.120 km	69.0 sm
1 Minute of Latitude	1 nm	1.852 km	1.5 sm

Depth

1 fathom = 6 feet = 1.83 meters

1 foot = 0.305 meters   1 meter = 3.281 feet

Weights

Diesel oil	1 US gallon	7.13 lbs
Fresh water	1 US gallon	8.33 lbs
Gasoline	1 US gallon	6.10 lbs
Salt water	1 US gallon	8.56 lbs

Seconds to Thousands (Latitude)

Seconds	Thousands	In Two Figures	Log Count
5	083.33	08	0.083
10	166.66	17	0.166
15	249.99	25	0.249
20	333.32	33	0.333
25	416.65	42	0.416
30	499.98	50	0.500
35	583.31	58	0.583
40	666.64	67	0.666
45	749.97	75	0.750
50	833.30	83	0.833
55	916.63	92	0.916
60	999.99	00	0.999

1 second = 101.33 feet = 33.77 yards = 30.88 meters

Thousands to Seconds divide by 16.6666

Seconds to Thousands multiply by 16.6666

Magnetic Variation

	Variation WEST	Variation EAST
True to Mag:	ADD VARIATION	SUBTRACT VARIATION
Mag to True:	SUBTRACT VARIATION	ADD VARIATION
[Variation West Compass Best]		[Variation East Compass Least]

Nautical Miles to Statute Miles

1 nm = 1.15 mile. 1 mile = 0.86 nm

NMs	Miles	Miles	NMs
1.0	1.15	1.0	0.86
5.0	5.75	5.0	4.30
10.0	11.50	10.0	8.60

Meters–Feet

Meters	Feet	Meters	Feet	Meters	Feet
1	3	9	30	17	56
2	7	10	33	18	59
3	10	11	36	19	62
4	13	12	39	20	66
5	16	13	43	25	82
6	20	14	46	30	98
7	23	15	49	50	164
8	26	16	52	100	328

Hypothermia Chart

Water Temperature °F	Time Until Comatose	Survival Time
60–70	2–7 hours	2–40 hours
70–80	3–12 hours	3 hours–indefinitely
Over 80	Indefinitely	Indefinitely

Tides: Rule of Twelfths

Hour	Rise/Fall	Sum	Hour	Rise/Fall	Sum
1	1/12th	1/12	4	3/12th	9/12
2	2/12th	3/12	5	2/12th	11/12
3	3/12th	6/12	6	1/12th	12/12

GARBAGE SALT WATER DEGRADABILITY RATES

2–4 weeks	paper towels
2 months	apple core
3–14 months	cotton line
1 year	biodegradable diaper
1–3 years	plywood
13 years	painted wood
50 years	tin can
80 years	styrofoam buoy
200 years	aluminum can
400 years	plastic beverage holder
450 years	disposable diaper, plastic bottle
600 years	monofilament line, glass bottle

Bahamas and Turks & Caicos Chart List

British Admiralty Charts

Entire Area of the Guide .... BA 4400

Bahamas: Northern Cruising Grounds

Little Bahama Bank, Abacos,
and Grand Bahama Island .... BA 3910

Freeport .... BA 390, BA 398

Bahamas: Central Cruising Grounds

Berry Islands .... BA 3910, BA 3912

New Providence Island .... BA 3912, BA 1489

Nassau .... BA 1452

Eleuthera, Andros .... BA 3912

Bahamas: Southern Cruising Grounds

Exumas, Out Islands, Long Island .... BA 3912, BA 3913

Bahamas: Far Horizons

Crooked Island Group, Semana .... BA 3914

Plana Cays .... BA 3914, BA 3907

Mira Por Vos Passage .... BA 3914, BA 3908

Mayaguana .... BA 3914, BA 3907

Inaguas .... BA 3907

Turks and Caicos: Providenciales

Providenciales, Caicos Bank .... BA 3907

Fish Cay Channel–Ambergris
Cays, South Caicos .... BA 3907, BA 1450

Turks and Caicos: Grand Turk

Grand Turk Island, Turks Bank .... BA 1450, BA 1441

Defense Mapping Agency Charts

DMA charts covering the area are now outdated. We do not recommend their use.

Waterproof Charts, Inc. (Punta Gorda, Florida)

16	Florida to Puerto Rico & Mona Passage
38	North Bahama Islands
38A	Grand Bahama and the Abacos
38B	Bahama Crossing—Bimini
38C	Central Bahamas
38G	Western Grand Bahama and the Berry Islands
38H	Nassau, Bahamas
120F	Fish/Dive Chart, Bahamas

Wavey Line Publishing Ltd

Turks and Caicos Islands Charts

TC-001C	Turks and Caicos Islands
TC-002C	Providenciales
TC-003	Turks Islands
Bahamas 019	Bahamas
Great Exuma 024	Great Exuma Island

Chart Books and Special to Area Guides

The Cruising Guide to Abaco, Steve Dodge.

Explorer Chart Book Near Bahamas, Fifth Edition (12/2007), Monty and Sara Lewis.

Explorer Chart Book Exumas and Ragged Islands, Fifth Edition, Monty and Sara Lewis.

Explorer Chart Book Far Bahamas, Fourth Edition, Monty and Sara Lewis.

Maptech™ Chart Kit Near Bahamas.

Maptech™ Chart Kit Central Bahamas.

Electronic Charts

British Admiralty

The Bahamas (ARCS portfolio 10 charts)

C-Map NT+™

NAC306 .... Florida East Coast & Bahamas, Turks and Caicos

NAC503 .... Florida South, Bahamas, Turks & Caicos & Cuba North

Garmin BlueCharts™

MUS503L .... South Florida, Bahamas and Turks & Caicos

MUS010RSE .. Florida, Grand Bahama, Abaco, Andros, Eleuthera, Great Exuma, Cat Island

Maptech™

MCP-07 .... The Bahamas (includes the Turks & Caicos)

DCK09 BSB4. The Bahamas

Navionics™

US694XL .... Bahamas including the Turks and Caicos.

1G694XL .... Bahamas including the Turks and Caicos

US906XL3 .... Bahamas including the Turks and Caicos

Nobeltec™

Visual Navigation Suite Visual Series Region 9

These charts and charts on disk are available from Bluewater Books & Charts, Fort Lauderdale, FL 800-942-2583.

Wavey Line charts are available at a number of marinas in the Bahamas (we show this in the maria entry). In the Turks and Caicos, in Providenciales, at the Unicorn Bookstore (in the IGA Plaza on the Leeward Highway) and in Grand Turk, at the Turks and Caicos National Museum (on Front Street in Cockburn Town).

In Canada, Wavey Line charts are available from Nautical Mind Charts & Books, Toronto. In Puerto Rico, from Playa Marine, Salinas. In Antigua, from Lord Jim's Locker, Falmouth Harbour.

WATERWAY GUIDE PHOTOGRAPHY

Provisioning Checklist

FRESH FOOD requiring refrigeration
- ❑ butter or margarine
- ❑ deli meats
- ❑ fresh fish and meat
- ❑ hot dogs
- ❑ milk
- ❑ orange juice
- ❑ prepared salads
- ❑ soft cheeses
- ❑ sour cream
- ❑ yogurt

FOOD that will keep for a short time in a cool place
- ❑ bread
- ❑ hard cheeses
- ❑ eggs
- ❑ cartons fruit juices
- ❑ UHT milk
- ❑ vacuum packed smoked sausages

FRUIT & VEGETABLES needing refrigeration
- ❑ asparagus
- ❑ green beans
- ❑ cut herbs
- ❑ salad, scallions

FRUIT & VEGETABLES that will keep for a short time in a cool place, preferably having never been refrigerated
- ❑ apples
- ❑ avocados
- ❑ green bananas
- ❑ cabbages
- ❑ carrots
- ❑ chili and bell peppers
- ❑ waxed cucumbers
- ❑ dried fruits
- ❑ garlic
- ❑ ginger
- ❑ grapefruit
- ❑ lemons
- ❑ limes
- ❑ mangoes
- ❑ melons
- ❑ onions
- ❑ oranges
- ❑ papaya
- ❑ pineapples
- ❑ potatoes
- ❑ winter squash
- ❑ unripe tomatoes
- ❑ yams
- ❑ zucchini
- ❑ fresh potted herbs
- ❑ Baking potatoes, winter squash and yams, keep longest of all.

FREEZER
- ❑ bacon
- ❑ ground beef
- ❑ chicken pieces
- ❑ fish
- ❑ ice cream
- ❑ shrimp
- ❑ steaks
- ❑ frozen vegetables
- ❑ frozen yogurt

CANS
- ❑ anchovies
- ❑ assorted beans and peas
- ❑ coconut milk
- ❑ corn
- ❑ corned beef
- ❑ corned beef hash
- ❑ ham
- ❑ mushrooms
- ❑ olives
- ❑ salmon
- ❑ soups
- ❑ spaghetti sauce
- ❑ tomatoes
- ❑ tomato paste
- ❑ tuna

DRY GOODS & PASTA
- ❑ bouillon cubes
- ❑ cereals
- ❑ cornstarch
- ❑ flour
- ❑ granola bars
- ❑ dried lentils, beans, peas
- ❑ nuts
- ❑ macaroni and cheese
- ❑ powdered milk
- ❑ variety of pastas
- ❑ popcorn
- ❑ instant mashed potatoes
- ❑ rice varieties
- ❑ sauce mixes
- ❑ dried soups
- ❑ sugar

SAUCES
- ❑ jams, jellies and marmalade
- ❑ mayonnaise
- ❑ mustard
- ❑ variety of oils
- ❑ peanut butter
- ❑ hot pepper sauce
- ❑ soy sauce
- ❑ tomato ketchup
- ❑ vinegars
- ❑ Worcestershire sauce

HERBS & SPICES
- ❑ black pepper
- ❑ cajun spice
- ❑ chili powder
- ❑ curry powder
- ❑ dried basil
- ❑ dried chives
- ❑ dried mint
- ❑ dried parsley
- ❑ Italian seasoning
- ❑ meat tenderizer for jelly fish stings
- ❑ Old Bay seasoning
- ❑ peppercorns and grinder
- ❑ salt

COFFEE, TEAS
- ❑ creamers
- ❑ sugar substitute
- ❑ tea and coffee

SNACKS & CANDY
- ❑ selection of favorites

DRINKS
- ❑ beer, wine or liquor
- ❑ fruit juices
- ❑ lemon juice
- ❑ mixers
- ❑ sodas
- ❑ bottled water

PAPER GOODS
- ❑ foil
- ❑ garbage bags
- ❑ paper towels
- ❑ plastic bags (assorted sizes)
- ❑ plastic wrap
- ❑ tissues
- ❑ toilet paper

CLEANERS
- ❑ air fresheners
- ❑ ant and roach traps
- ❑ bilge cleaner
- ❑ boat soap, fender cleaner
- ❑ bucket with lanyard
- ❑ cleaning cloths and handy wipes
- ❑ clothes hangers
- ❑ clothes pins
- ❑ cold water soap powder, laundry detergent, fabric softener
- ❑ deck swab
- ❑ dust pan and brush, small wet/dry vacuum
- ❑ holding tank biodegradable active agent
- ❑ dishwashing liquid
- ❑ matches or gas lighter
- ❑ mosquito coils
- ❑ Murphy's Oil Soap
- ❑ rubber gloves
- ❑ scouring pads
- ❑ scrubbing brush
- ❑ sewing kit
- ❑ sponges
- ❑ toilet brush and plunger
- ❑ white vinegar for the heads
- ❑ window cleaner
- ❑ wood and brightwork polish

DRUGSTORE
- ❑ after sun lotion
- ❑ antiseptic cream
- ❑ Band Aids
- ❑ dental floss
- ❑ deodorant
- ❑ insect repellent
- ❑ medications
- ❑ mouthwash
- ❑ shampoo
- ❑ soap
- ❑ polarized sunglasses
- ❑ sunscreen
- ❑ toothbrushes
- ❑ toothpaste
- ❑ vitamins

GALLEY EQUIPMENT
- ❑ chopping board
- ❑ fry pan, large, medium and small saucepan, baking tray
- ❑ garbage pail
- ❑ insulated bag, cool box
- ❑ kitchen knives, wooden spoons, ladle, grater, bottle opener, can opener, corkscrew, ice pick
- ❑ kitchen timer
- ❑ knives, forks, spoons
- ❑ measuring cup
- ❑ mixing/serving bowls, sieve
- ❑ plastic food and drink containers
- ❑ pressure cooker
- ❑ tea kettle and/or coffee maker
- ❑ unbreakable mugs, bowls, plates and glasses

LINEN AND BEDDING
- ❑ drying up cloths
- ❑ pillows, blankets, sheets or sleeping bags
- ❑ towels, beach towels

ADMINISTRATION
- ❑ cash and travelers checks
- ❑ credit cards
- ❑ driver's license
- ❑ FCC license
- ❑ health certificates (if going on)
- ❑ log book
- ❑ passports
- ❑ ship's papers
- ❑ veterinary certificates and pet food
- ❑ Bahamas courtesy flag
- ❑ Quarantine flag
- ❑ your national ensign

SWIMMING GEAR
- ❑ masks, snorkels, fins, gloves
- ❑ scuba gear

FISHING GEAR
- ❑ gaff
- ❑ handlines
- ❑ rods, reels, lures
- ❑ spare leaders and hooks

MISCELLANEOUS
- ❑ backpack for carrying groceries
- ❑ books, playing cards
- ❑ camera(s) and film
- ❑ flashlights
- ❑ padlock and chain for tender
- ❑ pump and repair kit for inflatable
- ❑ spare batteries
- ❑ tool kit

ABANDON SHIP PACK
- ❑ Prepared panic bag or pre-list items to take

Float Plan

Boat Name and Port

Year, Type and Model

Radios

Registration #

Call sign

Flag (if not U.S.)

LOA

Engines

Color

Other Means of Propulsion

Port and Date of Departure

Destination and Estimated Date and Time of Arrival

Route Planned

Persons on Board with addresses (note if young children)

(continue list as necessary)

Safety Equipment (list flares, smoke, strobes, EPIRB, life raft, dinghy)

(continue list as necessary)

If a 406 MHz EPIRB

Model

Category

Unique Identifier #

Your name, Home Address, and Telephone Number

Signature

Date

Weather Plotting Chart

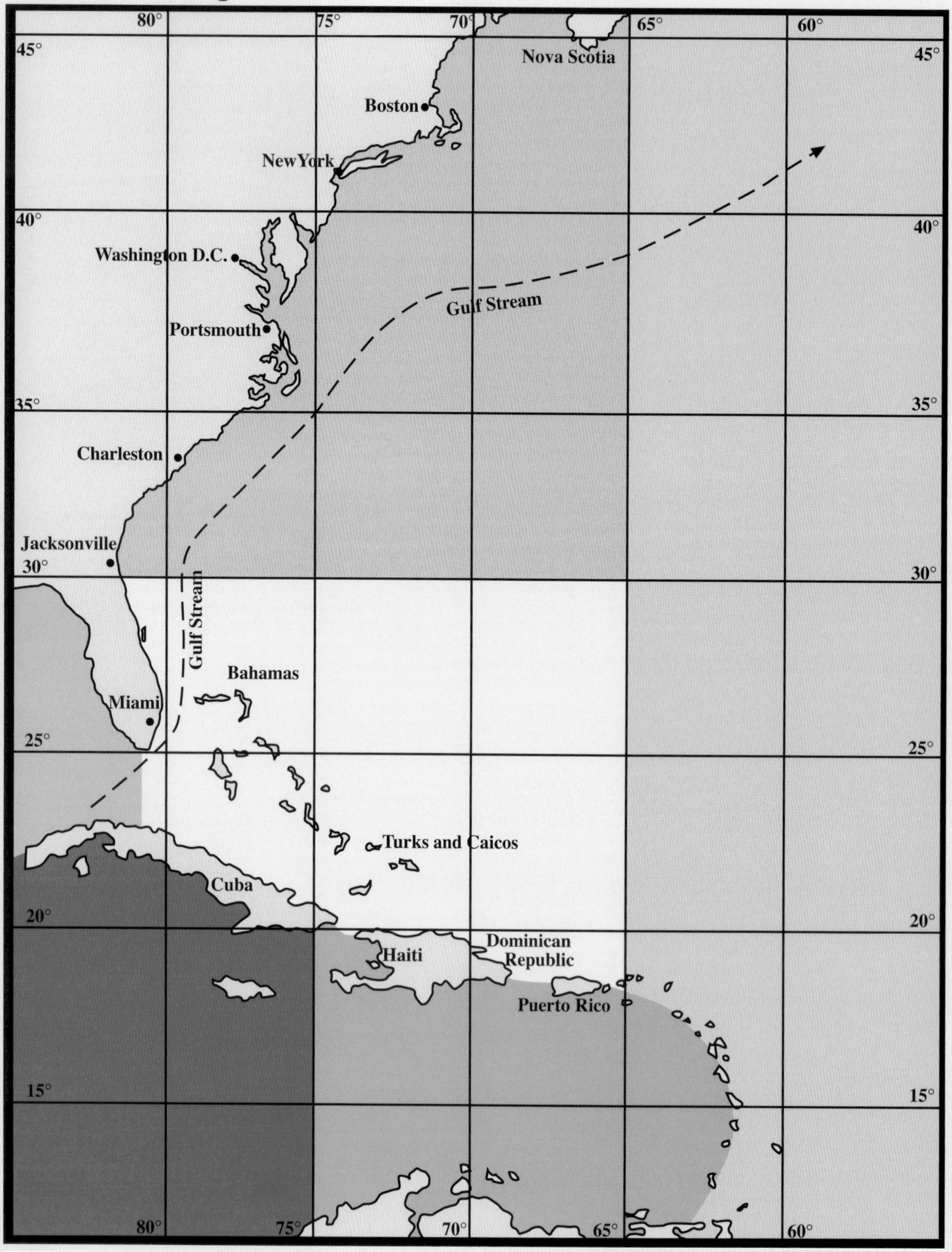

- North Atlantic east of 65° W
- Southwest North Atlantic south of 31°N and west of 65°W
- East Caribbean east of 75°W
- Northwest Caribbean north of 15°N and west of 75°W
- Southwest Caribbean south of 15° N and west of 75°W

Green Pages

History, National Parks, Fishing and Diving

The Story of the Bahamas

"This island is very large and very flat. It is green, with many trees and several bodies of water. There is a very large lagoon in the middle of the island and there are no mountains."

"I was alarmed at seeing that the entire island is surrounded by a large reef. Between the reef and the island it remained deep . . . there are a few shoal spots, to be sure, and the sea moves in it no more than the water in a well."

"I have no desire to sail strange waters at night . . ."

"You must keep your eyes peeled where you wish to anchor and not anchor too near shore. The water is very clear and you can see the bottom during the daylight hours, but a couple of lombard shots offshore there is so much depth that you cannot find bottom."

One could say, "There you have it," in four bites—an introduction to cruising in the Bahamas with all the significant facts laid out: 1. Don't expect any land elevation to guide you. 2. Expect sheltering reefs around the islands with deep water inside. 3. It's fool-hearty to sail Bahamian waters at night. 4. Look for good holding, but anchoring too close to shore can be a mistake. The water is crystal clear. Drop offs run close to land and are extreme. The author? Christopher Columbus. The date? 1492.

> "With 50 men, you could subject everyone and make them do what you wished . . ."
> (Columbus, in the Bahamas, Sunday, October 14, 1492)

Michael Craton and Gail Saunders tell us in *Islanders In The Stream: A History of the Bahamian People* that the Amerindians that Columbus encountered called themselves Lucayans, ("small-island" people). They were an outlying branch of the Arawak-speaking Neo-Indians. Columbus found "handsome" islanders "as naked as their mothers bore them, very simple and honest, and exceedingly liberal with all they have; none of them refusing any thing he may possess when he is asked for it ... they exhibit great love towards all others in preference to themselves; they also give objects of great value for trifles, and content themselves with little or nothing in return..." These simple people lived to regret the attention. The Lucayan dividend from their first contact with European man was extinction within a quarter of a century.

Discovery of America by Christopher Columbus. Salvador Dali.

The Lucayans left petroglyphs, carved wood, stone and pottery artifacts. The pottery scatters suggest that they were open-air dwellers and short-range mariners who lived in small coastal villages and subsisted on natural resources from the sea and manioc-type food from the land. Today, we enjoy the islands much as they were during Lucayan times from the unspoiled landscape to the sea-to-sky waters. Plying the seas quietly and gently as they did, one can assume an affinity with their lifestyle. The daily concerns of their world were much the same as anyone's in the Bahamas today. Theirs was a littoral life, in which boats and fishing were everything. In addition, when they moved about, they were constrained by the size and separation of the islands in relation to the winds and currents, just as we are.

Through mass abduction into slavery, "white-man's" diseases and starvation, the Lucayans disappeared and the Bahamas became a wasteland in Spanish eyes. The islands proved equally disappointing to Ponce de León in his search for the Fountain of Youth, and a trap for treasure galleons lumbering north from Havana on the long haul back to Spain. One hundred and fifty years passed. Then in 1648, the

British landed. The Eleutheran Adventurers, seeking a fresh start and religious freedom, literally hit Eleuthera. One could say their vessel was the first known victim of the Devil's Backbone. From then on, the Bahamas were on the map. By the end of the seventeenth century, the slow re-population of the Bahamas had begun with over a thousand settlers divided between Eleuthera and New Providence Island. It was tough going. The new immigrants soon found that the Bahamas were no self-sustaining Garden of Eden. Their primary needs were imports, and vital imports needed hard cash. Happily, the regular Spanish-galleon runs provided windfall jackpots, as did the wrecks of other ships unfortunate enough to be ill set by wind and current in Bahamian waters. However, there was a downside to this marauding. The "sharks" joined in.

"My name was William Kidd, and so wickedly I did, when I sailed . . ."

(The Ballad of William Kidd)

The sharks were not the kind with triangular dorsal fins, though undoubtedly the shipwrecks attracted them too, but two-legged ones with names like Henry Morgan (of Morgan's Bluff in Andros), Edward Teach (the dreaded Blackbeard), Jack Calico Rackham and a pair of terrifying females, Anne Bonney and Mary Read. Legend has it that they fought naked to the waist. Nassau paid host to enough real pirates and would-be pirates to fill the Bay Street waterfront bars every night. In retaliation, it was hammered by the Spanish four times in just a quarter of a century. The dreams of a simple, peaceful, agricultural God-fearing community had been eclipsed. It got so bad that eventually the British government showed some interest in the territory it had arbitrarily claimed back in 1629. An ex-privateer, Woodes Rogers, was given dispensation and sent to govern the islands and to end piracy. By 1720, he was accomplishing goals–another Spanish attack had been repulsed–and life on shore became quieter, but no easier. The havoc continued.

"If this be treason, make the most of it . . ."

(Patrick Henry, Williamsburg, VA, May 29, 1765)

At the end of the 18th century, watershed events rocked the Bahamas like a succession of tidal waves. In 1776, the American Continental Navy attacked the Bahamas, captured Fort Montague and occupied Nassau. Why? Because it was British. There was little profit from the attack, and the Navy left after two weeks. Two years later, the Americans returned to raise their flag over Nassau. They had second thoughts and left. After four years, the Spanish came back in strength, and the Bahamas became Spanish territory.

Meanwhile, in Versailles, France, important treaties were signed. The British conceded independence to the North American colonies, retained Canada and traded their claim on Florida to the Spanish in exchange for the Bahamas. A wealthy South Carolinian Loyalist's son, Andrew Deveaux, Jr., unaware of the treaties signed in France, led six vessels from St. Augustine, FL to reclaim Nassau for the British. He achieved this goal through a simple, deceptive display of supposed overwhelming strength. More likely, the Spanish officers knew of the treaties signed in Versailles and just let him think he won. The migration of Loyalists, unhappy about living in the newly independent United States, began. They fled the colonies with all their possessions, slaves and sometimes even their house bricks, to start a new life, once again secure under the British flag. Deveaux Jr. returned to England, but his father (who forfeited all his land in South Carolina) and brothers transferred their cattle and slaves to Cat Island. There, Deveaux Sr. built a mansion, the ruins of which can still be seen in Port Howe on the far southern tip of the island. Deveaux Sr. outlasted and outlived them all, dying in 1814, long after the other Loyalists had exhausted the thin soil, freed their slaves and given up.

"Shall be thenceforward and forever free..."

(Abraham Lincoln, Washington, DC, September 22, 1862)

By the early 1830s, permanent settlements existed on seventeen of the islands, and there was precious little land of agricultural value. The black population outnumbered the white, but figures are difficult to establish. A census in the 1820s, when the Abolitionist movement was a ground swell, showed more than 10,000 slaves in the Bahamas. By 1838, slavery had ended, and the Royal Navy added the human cargo they had captured in slave ships to the population of the islands. They joined the newly freed slaves trying to scratch out a living. As the hands of time moved closer to the 20th century, the Bahamas at grassroots level was foundering.

The outbreak of the American Civil War proved to be a shot of adrenaline for the Bahamas. For five years, it was like a Gold Rush boom or a return to the days of Bonney and Read, as Nassau played host and haven to Confederate blockade-runners. Strange, indeed, that the emancipated slaves of the Bahamas would combine in commercial enterprise with the oppressors of the Deep South, but pragmatism wins over the expectations of an empty bowl. When the guns fell silent, the blockade-runners vanished. Even the wrecking

Edward Wilson

Fort Montague, captured by US Marines, 1776

business dried up as rule of law was enforced, lighthouses were built and the islands were finally charted. A market for sponges kept the Bahamians alive, as did relatively productive, easy-to-grow crops, such as pineapples and tomatoes. Unfortunately, a mysterious blight destroyed 99 percent of Bahamian sponges in two months, and stiff tariffs imposed on Bahamian pineapple favored Hawaii to corner the import market. The Bahamian's hopes of a vigorous economy through aquaculture or agriculture were dashed.

"Prohibition comes into force."

U.S. Headline, January 16, 1919

Once again, U.S. internal politics catapulted the Bahamian economy to another all-time high when the manufacture, sale and consumption of alcohol in the U.S. became illegal. Nassau and Bimini returned to the blockade days of the Civil War, this time with powerboats. Nassau boomed, offering new hotel rooms, bars and gambling. Pan American Airways flew in regularly from Miami. In 1933, it all ended with the repeal of Prohibition. Nassau closed down, and Bimini went to sleep.

"Well gentlemen, it amounts to this—if we can't take the liquor to the Americans, we must bring the Americans to the liquor."

Governor BeBe Clifford to the Executive Council on Bahamian Economic Development

Governor Clifford and the Economic Development Board worked hard to improve accommodations and entertainment for tourists, with a transparent preference for the affluent. They hoped the post-war prosperity would increase tourism and benefit their citizenry. Piers built for cruise ships, facilities constructed for seaplanes and a direct phone link arranged between New York and Canada so businessmen could keep in touch, did increase tourism twofold between 1925 and 1935.

However, the racial and sociopolitical tensions created by this vast social division were palpable. At a time when Florida realized that attracting sun-seekers was more lucrative than squeezing oranges, Havana was more exciting than Nassau or anywhere in Florida and airplane tickets were sold almost exclusively to business travelers, the Bahamas was beset with idealists, reformists and general unrest.

"This is my island in the sun..."

Calypso

By the mid-1950s, most of the sociopolitical turmoil in the Bahamas had passed like a summer squall. It was time for another boom. Couple the Freeport Initiative, designed specifically to attract offshore investment, with the development of Freeport, West End, Nassau Harbour and new air services, and the Bahamas were ripe for a boom period. Little cays, once a dime a dozen, became premium property. It seemed there was no holding these islands back. Nevertheless, then the pace slackened. Investors stopped investing. Speculators stopped speculating, and builders stopped building. The momentum worked, but the movement failed. With illegal drug trafficking beckoning at the back door, drug running became a quicker, easier route to riches.

"A sudden demand for cigarette boats and used C-47s..."

Market trends in the 1960s

Memories of piracy, blockade running and rum running resurfaced in the 60s. For the first time, the more remote parts of the Bahamas became hot property. New airstrips spread like a rash over the islands. It became decidedly clear that drug trafficking posed the most serious social problem the Bahamas had yet to face. Not only were drug trafficking profits so vast and easily made that they attracted the "wrong" kind of people to the islands, the drugs themselves became inexpensive and readily available to the local population. It is a sad chapter in the story of the Bahamas, both exacerbated by American citizens trafficking drugs and using these drugs, and partially remedied by Americans who worked closely with the Bahamian police and Defense Forces to slow the drug flow down to a trickle. After two decades, by mid-1990, the corruption and internal problems stemming from drugs had significantly declined.

"I simply do not know where to go next..."

Columbus in the Bahamas, Friday, October 19, 1492

Why did the Freeport initiative stall? Perhaps three prerequisites had to be fulfilled before the dreams of the 1950s initiatives could be achieved. One was the resolution of the political future of the Bahamas. The Bahamas became independent on July 10, 1973. The second was the halting of the drug trade. It was debilitating the nation and distorting the economy. Third was the realization that sponging, wrecking, cotton, sisal, pineapples and agriculture in general were not going to support the populace. What the Bahamas has to offer are two immutable blessings that have come as a package deal with their environment. The first is a maritime tradition dating back three hundred years. The second is the most brilliant waters in the Western Hemisphere.

"Two private sky harbours for executive jets are being developed..."

1997 Bahamas Business Report

Because of their lopsided dependence on the economic conditions in the United States, the Bahamas has broadened its reach. Shrewd business people have positioned the island nation to take the torch from Hong Kong and make a bid to become the banking, shipping and trading epicenter of the western maritime world with links to Europe, North America, South America and throughout the Caribbean and Panama and into the Pacific. Lest you think this an idealized vision, keep an eye on the new generation of educated, self-confident Bahamians whose sense of national purpose and pride is palpable.

An old C-47.

The Columbus Controversy

In November 1986, the National Geographic Society detonated a bomb under conventional theories about the track and landfalls of the First Voyage of Columbus. In a well-argued analysis, "Where Columbus Found the New World" (National Geographic 170, no. 5, pgs. 563-599) by Joseph Judge, based on 1882 writings by Gustavus Fox, Judge presented the argument that Columbus first made landfall on Samana Cay, not San Salvador. The first serious attempt to identify the site of the Columbus landfall in the Americas was published in 1625 and concluded that it was Cat Island. Since then, at least eight islands have been speculated upon for the honor, although Watling's Island, or San Salvador as we know it today, has the most advocates and persuasive arguments.

The Landfall. An Island Called Guanahaní.

As for Columbus, his description of the landfall is insufficiently explicit to identify one single island. The natives called his landfall Guanahaní. Columbus renamed it San Salvador and claimed it for the Queen of Spain. Guanahaní, Columbus said, was surrounded by a large reef that had a narrow entrance, was fairly large, very flat, green, covered in vegetation and had several bodies of water as well as a large central lagoon. The description could fit any number of the 723 islands and cays of the Bahamas. Of the other possibilities (Cat Island, Conception Island, East Caicos Island, Egg Island, Grand Turk Island, Mayaguana and Samana Cay), the spotlight eventually shown on just two places, Watling's Island and Samana Cay.

The San Salvador School

One could say that the official renaming of Watling's Island as San Salvador in 1926 effectively granted it title to "the landfall." Early heavyweight naval historians, later joined by the eminent Harvard historian Samuel Eliot Morison in his book, "Admiral of the Ocean Sea," present evidence that no other landfall fits the description Columbus wrote about in his log quite as completely. Not everyone agreed. A small band of disbelievers said Columbus' recorded routes didn't fit the geography of the Out Islands north of the tropic of Cancer. Everyone accepted that there were translation errors, but some insisted that if Columbus' track is projected after San Salvador, his log does not fit. There are too many fundamental errors in distances and direction.

The Samana School

In 1880, Captain Gustavus Fox, President Abraham Lincoln's Assistant Secretary of the Navy, published an article in which he proposed Samana Cay as the landing site. Despite the fact that the Columbus log fit neatly into the Bahamian map like the long missing piece of a jigsaw puzzle, the Fox theory won little backing, even though, in 1894, the National Geographic Society published an argument reinforcing his observations. The debate continued when, in the hopes of attracting international acclaim, Conception Island, East Caicos and Grand Turk were added to the confusion. In November 1975, the National Geographic Society, after long and careful weighing of the evidence, joined the San Salvador support group.

The Northern Route

Arne B. Molander, a retired engineer, spent thirty years researching this subject. He cruised the Bahamas searching for islands that matched the descriptions in the Columbus Log. He thought that he had identified thirty geographic matches. In the book, "Columbus and His World," Mr. Molander's theories are presented in his chapter, "Egg Island Is the Landfall of Columbus: A Literal Interpretation of His Journal." Mr. Molander writes that Columbus made

The Duke and Duchess of Windsor on his arrival to assume the appointment of Governor of the Bahamas in 1940 (photograph autographed by the Duke and Duchess of Windsor).

a North Eleuthera landfall off Egg Island, then bypassed Nassau to the north and made a second landfall in North Andros. Driven south by a Norther, he made a difficult exit from the Tongue of the Ocean over the Bank and regained ocean water to the southwest of Long Island. After some aimless wandering, he eventually headed southwest and discovered Cuba. Mr. Molander's conclusions have been deemed "outlandish" by some academicians.

The Quincentennial Analysis

The advent of the Quincentennial of the Columbus Landing reawakened interest in the controversy, and the National Geographic Society's senior associate editor, Joseph Judge, took another look at Gustavus Fox and Samana Cay. Mr. Judge assembled a team to compare the San Salvador and Samana Cay theories using computers. Keeping in mind that the information coming out of a computer is only as good as the information going in, their study rested initially on analysis of the Columbus Atlantic log with winds, currents and leeway taken into account. Every one of the team's projections ended at Samana Cay. Mr. Judge and the team continued with analysis of Columbus' America log. They again concluded that Samana Cay fits his landfall description, and that the re-creation of Columbus's track also fit. Upon reading their conclusions, one can only think of NOAA's hurricane computer models and the projected paths and landfalls they produce.

What the National Geographic Society, Mr. Judge and his team did not take into account is that only one island has produced archeological evidence of Columbus' landing–San Salvador. Works by Charles Hoffman in "Columbus and His World," "Archeological Investigations at the Long Bay Site, San Salvador, Bahamas" and "Some Glass Beads Excavated on San Salvador Island in the Bahamas," persuade many academicians to conclude that the site of the finding, a Lucayan village on San Salvador, is almost certain to be the location of Columbus' first landing. Amongst the Spanish artifacts uncovered are a copper coin of Henry IV of Castille (1454-1474), two bronze buckles, several iron nails, fragments of Italian glazed pottery and ten glass beads, just like the ones Columbus describes trading with the natives (see "Islanders in the Stream, A History of the Bahamian People, Volume One").

In three subsequent voyages, Columbus never returned to the Bahamas. Later Spanish expeditions were undertaken to force Lucayan males into slavery in Hispañola (Haiti and

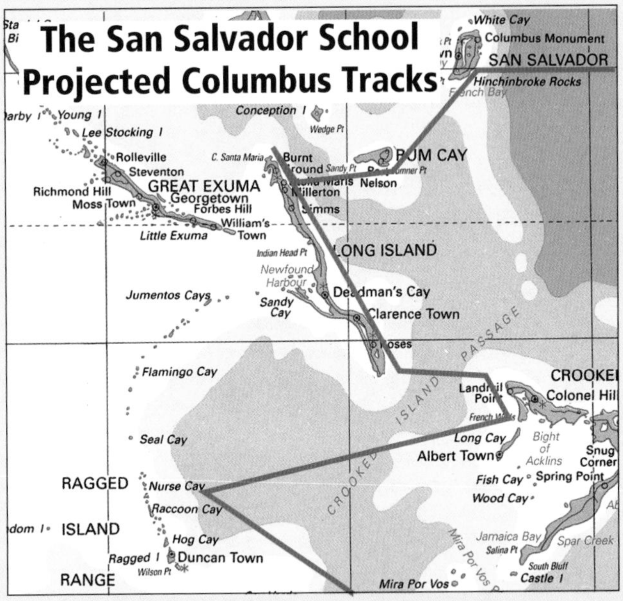

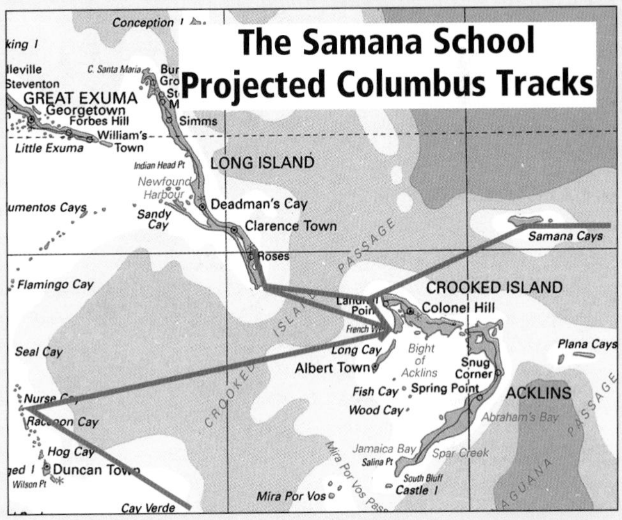

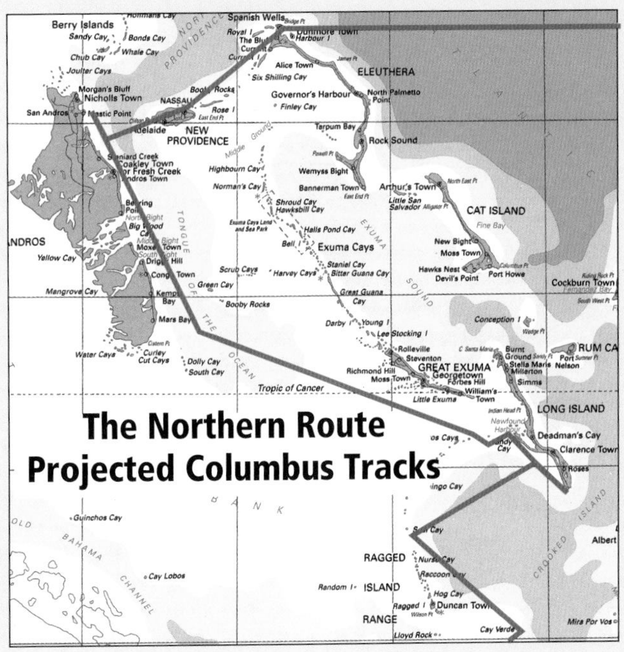

Columbus Naming	Morison's Conventional	Arne Molander	National Geographic
San Salvador	Watling	Eleuthera	Samana Cay
Santa Maria	Rum Cay	New Providence	Crooked-Acklins
Fernandina	Long Island	Andros	Long Island
Isabela	Crooked-Acklins	Long Island	Fortune Island

the Dominican Republic). The islands that had shared, but not enjoyed, the experience of an Italian's discovery of the "New World" for Spain, were then ignored. Within a generation, the Lucayan's were extinct.

Bahamas National Parks

Northern Cruising Grounds

- **Abaco National Park, Great Abaco Island** - A 20,500 acre park between Cherokee Sound and Hole in the Wall. The principal habitat of the endangered Bahamas Parrot.
- **Black Sound Cay National Reserve, Green Turtle Cay** - A two acre, thick stand of mangroves, right in the harbour.
- **Pelican Cays Land and Sea Park, Abacos** - A 2,100 acre park north of Cherokee Sound. The park is noted for its reefs, caves and underwater sea life.
- **Tilloo Cay National Reserve, Abacos** - An 11 acre nesting site for tropical birds, north of Pelican Cay and south of Marsh Harbour.
- **Lucayan National Park, Grand Bahama** - A 42 acre reserve, east of Freeport, with nature trails and boardwalks. The park encompasses one of the world's most extensive underwater cave systems.
- **Peterson Cay National Park, Grand Bahama** - A small cay with a coral reef off the south coast, just east of Port Lucaya. It is the only cay on Grand Bahamas' leeward shore.
- **Rand Nature Center, Freeport** - One hundred acres of pine forest, orchids and wildflower gardens, with flamingos and guided nature walks. The nature center re-creates Grand Bahamas' original ecosystem. It is also the headquarters of the Bahamas National Trust.

Central Cruising Grounds

- **The Retreat, Nassau** - Eleven acres of natural woodlands and the world's largest collection of rare palm trees.
- **Bonefish Pond National Park, New Providence** – An 1,800 acre wetland park serving as an important marine nursery area.
- **Harrold and Wilson Ponds National Park, New Providence** – This 250 acre park is home to 101 different species of birds, including the threatened Bahama Swallow.
- **The Primeval Forest, New Providence** – A 7.5 acre hardwood forest with limestone caverns and sinkholes.
- **Central Andros Park Area** – The park designation is for North Bight, Fresh Creek, Blanket Sound, Young Sound, and Staniard Creek protecting pine forests, blue holes, coral reefs, wetlands and mangroves.

Southern Cruising Grounds

- **Exuma Cays Land and Sea Park** - A well-known and much-visited 112,640 acre protected marine replenishment zone. The park is patrolled and well-managed. Mooring balls at the parks anchorages are available for a fee.

Far Horizons

- **Conception Island National Park** – A 2,100 acre sanctuary for birds and a breeding site for endangered Green Turtles. Additional acres around the island, and its extensive reef, are planned to be added to the preserve.
- **Great Hope House and Marine Farm, Crooked Island** 19th century ruins of a Loyalist plantation one mile northeast of Landrail Point.
- **Inagua National Park** - At 183,740 acres, the park is home to the world's largest breeding colony of West Indian Flamingos—about 60,000. The park is patrolled by two, full-time wardens.
- **Union Creek National Reserve, Great Inagua** - A 4,940 acre reserve on an enclosed tidal creek. It is an important turtle research facility.

The Bahamas continues to allocate additional acres to its National Park system. Currently, 58 additional sites are slated for protection including the Andros Barrier Reef and the Athol/Rose Island area.

Fishing in the Bahamas

Heading the list of the great game fish is marlin. Blue marlin top the list with an average body weight of 250–300 lbs. The chance of catching a fish weighing 800 lbs or more is always a possibility. White marlin is next with an average weight around 100 lbs and makes up for its lesser weight with a fighting stamina that outclasses the blue. Sailfish rank with the marlin, matching the blue marlin in dramatic performance when hooked.

Tuna, and particularly migrating bluefin tuna, are the next on the list. The bluefin pass through the Bahamas on

Columbus landing in the Bahamas. Artist unknown.

their way north each year and can weigh up to 1,000 lbs. Once hooked, you are in for a serious battle that can last for hours. The other varieties of the tuna family - big eye, blackfin, yellowfin and bonito - are Bahamian residents rather than visitors in transit. They do not fight as spectacularly, nor weigh as much, as the bluefin.

Dorado or dolphin-fish (not the Flipper variety, but the fish the Spanish call dorado and Hawaiian's call Maha-Mahi) weigh 10 to 15 lbs. Tough fighters, with iridescent skin colors like a rainbow, the dolphin is prized both for its fighting qualities and its quality as an eating fish. Many consider it to be better than swordfish or tuna. It is often eaten raw, sashimi-style.

The mackerel family is next on the list with Wahoo, the fastest fish in the ocean, and King Mackerel, that come close to 5 feet in length and are never taken without a fight. The fighting list also includes the marauders, barracuda and sharks. We see little point in shark fishing, and we've found barracuda, only too ready to strike at any lure, more of a curse on a line than a blessing. Tarpon, who often take a trolled line and fight fiercely, complete our game fish list

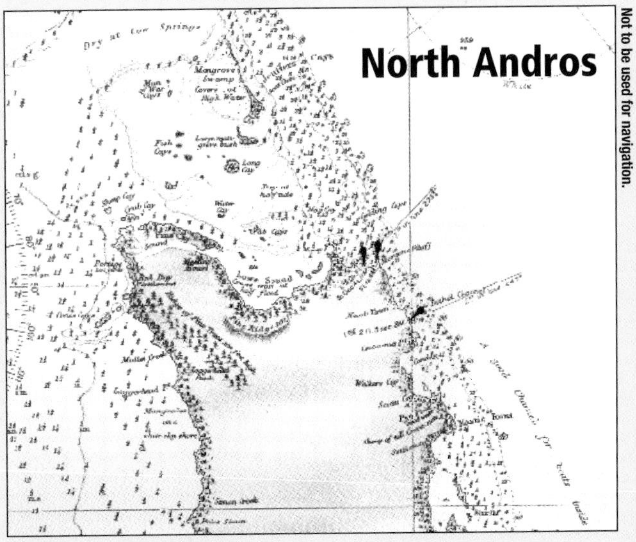

Reproduced from Admirality Chart 1496 (now outdated). Soundings in fathoms and feet.

The Columbus Log

The notes that follow are identifications that will be apparent if you cruise in these waters.

Northeast Acklins Island (never named by Columbus) *The coast that faces San Salvador* [the east coast facing his Guanahani landfall] *lies in a north-south line and extends for 15 miles. The other coast* [the north coast] *which I followed, runs east and west and is more than 30 miles long.*

Crooked Island (Santa María de la Concepción) . . . *the western cape. I anchored at sunset near the cape* [Portland Harbour, probably just southeast of Bird Rock in the deep water inside the reef just off Pittstown Point] *in order to find out if there was gold there.*

Passage to Long Island (Fernandina) *Judged by the clouds and the signs made by the men from San Salvador* [Guanahani men captured to serve as guides] *this large island to the west was about 27 miles distant.*

Long Island *It is very big and about 24 miles due west of Santa María de la Concepción* [Crooked Island]. *This entire part where I am anchored runs NNW-SSE. It appears that this coast runs for 21 miles or more, and I saw 15 miles of it but it did not end there. It is very level without any mountains . . .*

Little Harbour *After I had sailed six miles from the island's cape* [South Point] *where I had been anchored, I discovered a very wonderful harbor* [Little Harbour] *with one entrance, one may say two entrances, for there is an island in the middle. Both passages are very narrow, but once within, the harbor is wide enough for 100 ships. I did not think that either the entrance or the harbor was deep enough, however nor did I feel that the bottom was clear of rocks. It seemed reasonable to me to look it over well and take soundings, so I anchored outside and went in with the small boats. It was fortunate that I did, for there was no depth at all.*

Clarence Town *After taking on water [*at Little Harbour] *I returned to the ship and sailed to the NW until I had explored all that part of the island as far as the coast that runs east-west* [from Booby Cay, just north of Strachan Cay, westward to Longitude 75°N]. The weather turned against Columbus and he was forced to put about and run before the wind. He retraced his track and eventually anchored off French Wells in Crooked Island.

Crooked Island—French Wells (Cabo del Iseo) *Before we had sailed three hours we saw an island to the east for which we steered, and before midday all three ships reach a small island* [Rat Cay] *at the north point* [of Long Cay]. *There is a rocky reef at this island that runs to the north, and between the reef and the large island to the north* [Crooked Island] *there is another island* [Goat Cay]. *To the NE of this small island there is a great bay* [the northwest corner of the Bight of Acklins] . . . *I wanted to anchor in that bay . . . but the water is shallow and I could not anchor.*

Long Cay (Isabela) *The coast trends west for 12 miles from this small island to a cape* [Windsor Point, named Cabo Hermoso]. *It is round, and the water is deep with no shoals offshore.*

The Bight of Acklins *I thought I might sail around the island* [Long Cay] *to the NE and to the east, from the SE and the south . . . but the bottom is so shallow* [the Bight of Acklins] *that I cannot enter or sail . . .*

but, like the marauders, have no place on the food list.

Moving on from trolling to fishing the depths, grouper tops the list of the prize fish for weight and food value. After grouper, come snapper and amberjack; the last respond to live bait and will take your line, when hooked, deep into a wreck or the holes of a reef if they have the chance. The fish of the Bahamian shallows or flats, bonefish and the less widely known permit, are considered by many anglers to be the best prizes of all. You won't feed you family with them, but once you are hooked by bonefishing, you will spend hour after hour fishing the flats.

A New "Gamefish"—The Lionfish

Lionfish are an edible, venomous fish invading Bahamian waters. These fish are voracious eaters of valuable game fish, crustaceans and, perhaps, even coral. Their invasion is of great concern to the Bahamas Department of Marine Resources to the extent that they have introduced a national lionfish response plan. Researchers have discovered that in just five weeks, lionfish can reduce the number of young native fish on a reef by as much as 80 per cent. The ramifications for grouper, lobster, shrimp and similar fishery resources are grave. You can help:

- By reporting lionfish encounters at www.bahamas.gov.bs;
- Asking for and ordering lionfish at restaurants;
- Killing any and all lionfish that you come across;
- Learning how to capture, clean and cook lionfish for great eating.

They have been an Asian cuisine delicacy for centuries.

First, help spread the word that lionfish are venomous, not poisonous. One needs to handle the captured or speared fish carefully. Eating the cooked fish is a gastronome's delight, not a gourmet danger. Second, teach fellow spearfishermen how to safely capture, handle, clean and eat them. Third, pass the word that the lionfish "sting" can be as painful as a string ray's or as mellow as a honey bee's. Just ensure that you wear good, impermeable gloves. If you do get stung, remove the spine if it is stuck in your flesh and immerse the digit in the hottest water that you can possibly stand as soon as possible. The pain does not last as long as a stingray's (nor is there the possibility of an embedded sheath), but it is just as nasty in the immediate sense. Let's just say you don't want your grandkids to ever experience it, and you don't want them to hear your language if you ever do.

Juvenile Lionfish. Photo courtesy of the lionfishhunter.com

Bahamas National Parks Regulations

As you would expect, conservation rules in the park areas are strict. Essentially, you are not allowed to fish or hunt; remove any living or dead animal, fish, vegetation, plant life or coral; or in any way damage, alter or leave a footprint on the environment. Most of the marine parks have moorings that you are required to take up. If you do anchor, you are required to anchor in sand well clear of any reef. You are not allowed to discharge any waste nor dump your garbage.

If you break the rules, not only are you in line for a $500 fine, but your boat may well be confiscated as well.

Lionfish are usually found floating in a stationary position around coral heads, swaying beautifully with their nasty mouths open and ready to feed. Scientists think that they fool prey into thinking they are sea fans, seagrass or seaweed. In the Bahamas, game fish and crustaceans don't even seem to register that they are in danger. These characteristics make the lionfish easy to spear. Although they can be taken by a hook and line, spearing is the easiest technique. Once speared, take them to your dinghy and handle them with great care. Remove the fish from the spear wearing heavy gloves, and drop it into a bucket or cooler. Avoid all spines! If it is still alive, splash a little rum or diluted clove oil into the gills to kill the fish quickly. Lionfish range from bluegill size, all the way to 18 inches long. Please kill all that you encounter. The bigger they are, the easier they are to clean and eat, but even the little ones need to be eliminated.

The obvious dilemma to cleaning lionfish is avoidance of the spines (aka fins). The nastiest spines are the dorsal spines running along the top of the fish. They look so pretty swaying in the water, but they are toxic. They are also very long, some as long as 15 inches. In addition, there are two, lower front spines (they look more like fins) that are venomous pel-

Threatened Whales

A direct correlation between U.S. Navy sonar trials and the death of whales through beaching in the Bahamas has been established (Bahamian waters are home or a transit zone for some twenty-one species of marine mammals). Low-frequency active sonar (LFAS), designed to locate super-quiet submarines, works on 100–500HZ. So do whales. The end result of navy transmissions is damage to a whale's ability to hear and navigate, which affects their ability to communicate and their safe migration.

Whether a ban on the transmission of LFAS in the Bahamas and the Turk and Caicos, were it to be imposed, would remove the threat, particularly to the migration of the humpback whale, has not been assessed to the satisfaction of many marine biologists. The new sonar is sufficiently powerful that four warships could monitor 80 percent of the world's oceans.

vic spines. Lastly, avoid the rear lower fin-like spines - there are three (hard to count because they look like a fin). These are the venomous anal spines.

As the sport of lionfish hunting and lionfish derby prize monies grow, so do the pro's tips for cleaning them. Many hunters suggest that before removing the spines, first sear them with a mini-butane torch (a barbeque grill "clicker" lighter will work, too). Intense heat does, indeed, nullify the venom. Other pros use needle nose pliers to grip the lionfish's jaws, then employ strong kitchen shears to sever the spines and pry them off (to safely dispose of spines, dig a small fire ring and burn them on the beach—even off the fish, they are toxic and nasty). Once the dangerous spines are removed, cut off the non-venomous ventral fins. Lionfish scales are delicate and easily scraped off with a sharp knife blade. One can score the fish and pan-fry it at this point, whole or filleted. For ceviche, sashimi, fried strips, fritters or nuggets, skin and retain as much fish flesh as possible.

In the Bahamian style, local cooks marinate the fish for a while in lime juice or vinegar, then dredge in flour or coat with batter and fry. Cooks less likely to fry are serving lionfish raw as sushi, sashimi and ceviche or lightly grilled or steamed in garlic and lemon butter like lobster. Readers can find a plethora of recipes or schedule a fishing trip in Eleuthera with the lionfish hunter himself at www.lionfishhunter.com. Find useful tips on how to capture and clean them at www.youtube.com/user/lionfishhunterTV. Brochures from the Bahamas Department of Marine Resources are available at fisheries@bahamas.gov.bs.

FISHING REGULATIONS

Fishing Permit

To fish in the Bahamas, you must obtain a fishing permit upon entry. The cost of the fishing permit is included in your Entry Permit Fee. **You must have the Bahamian official endorse your permit declaring that you are allowed to spear fish with a Hawaiian sling.** (Fishing with a spear gun or scuba equipment is illegal.) Fishing regulations are printed on your fishing permit, but they are not necessarily current. In recent years, regulations have changed frequently, but old permits are still being used. When in doubt, ask.

No-Take Zones - Fishing is forbidden in National Parks.

Equipment

- No more than six lines in the water at one time (unless by permit).
- Spear guns of all types are illegal.
- Pole spears and Hawaiian slings only when free diving.
- No fish net may have a gauge less than two inches.
- Scuba activity is limited to photography only.

Seafood Export Limits by Air or Sea (Bag Limits)

- Determine applicable limits at time of entry with the permitting official. Limits are subject to frequent change.

It Is Illegal to:

- Take any turtle or its eggs.
- Shell or spearfish while scuba diving.
- Take a grouper under 3 lbs or any grouper during spawning season ban.
- Use a spear within 200 yards of any Family Island, or within one mile of the coast of New Providence or the southern coast of Grand Bahama.
- Take any live sea fan, coral or starfish.
- Take a conch that does not have a well-formed, fully flared lip.
- Take a crawfish out of season (season runs from August 1 to March 31).
- Take a crawfish with a tail less than 6 inches or a carapace less than 3 3/8 inches.
- Take a female crawfish with eggs.
- Sell fish or crawfish without a license.
- Take stone crab out of season (season runs from October 16 to June 30).
- Take stone crab with a claw length under 4 inches.
- Use firearms or explosives for fishing.
- Use bleach or other noxious substances for fishing.

Restricted Zones: No Fishing, Shelling, Spearing, Conching

- **Guana Cay Northwest Point National Park**
- **Mermaid Reef** (Pelican Shores north Marsh Harbour)
- **Pelican Land and Sea Park** (South Abaco Sea)
- **Peterson Cay National Park** (Grand Bahama)
- **Exuma Land and Sea Park**
- **Conception Island Land and Sea Park**

Under development; may now be restricted zones; check with officials before taking anything from:

- Fowl Cays Land and Sea Park (between Scotland and Man O' War, Abaco)
- West Side National Park including Williams and Billy Islands (Andros)
- Expansion of Conception Island Land and Sea Park

Ciguatera

The possibility always exists of ciguatera poisoning from eating fish you have caught in the Bahamas. See our detailed warning and advice given in the **Buff Pages** under **Medical Facilities and Health Hazards**.

The Best Fishing Months

Blue Marlin	June–July
White Marlin	Winter–Spring
Sailfish	Summer–Fall
Allison Tuna	June–August
Bluefin Tuna	May–June
Blackfin Tuna	May–September
Yellowfin Tuna	June–August
Bonito	May–September
Dolphin	Winter–Spring
Wahoo	November–April
King Mackerel	Mostly winter months
Barracuda, Tarpon, Grouper	Year-round
Amberjack	November–May
Bonefish	Year-round

Crawfish Purchases Out of Season
Do not purchase crawfish out of season. It is forbidden, and you are subject to fines and the confiscation of your vessel.

Grouper Spawning Season
In 2003, the Department of Fisheries declared a total ban on fishing for grouper during the month of January. The grouper spawning season is November to March, and the limited ban was intended to strike a balance between the urgent need to ease pressure on the depleted grouper population and the livelihood of Bahamian fishermen. The penalty for breaking the ban was $3,000 or one year in prison, or both. Later, this ban was extended to include December, January and February. At this writing, the ban is January 1 through February 28. It is imperative that you check current grouper fishing bans before taking them. True sportsmen and conservationists would self-limit and cease catching or spearing grouper during the spawning season.

Tagged Fish
Throughout the Central Bahamas, Nassau grouper have been tagged to study their movements to and from their spawning grounds. Call 242-355-5557 if you catch a tagged fish (this number should also be on the tag), and report the tag color and the letter or code on the tag, the location (a GPS position is quite acceptable) where you caught the fish, the date you caught it and your name and contact address or telephone number.

Keep the tag in case you are asked for it later. Some tagged fish have a transmitter, a plastic orange cylinder a few inches long, which has been inserted in the gut. Report this if it applies to your fish, and keep the transmitter in addition to the tag. Tagged fish are safe to eat.

Diving in the Bahamas

The Bahamas are one of the best destinations for diving in the world. The islands offer everything from shallow reef dives to wall dives with ocean drop-offs, blue holes, drift dives and encounters with dolphins, rays and sharks. The potential dive sites in the Bahamas are endless. Andros alone has the third-largest barrier reef in the world. Above all, not only is the marine life everything you have always dreamed about, but the sea temperature is between 70°F and 80°F, and the visibility is unbelievable. One hundred feet is not uncommon.

Many cruising visitors may prefer to explore and find their own favorite areas for diving, rather than signing on with a dive operator for scheduled dive trips. However, most of us need to touch base at a dive shop sometime to fill tanks, fix equipment if something goes wrong or seek local advice. We have listed some dive operators in the islands to help your planning. For information, see the Goin' Ashore section for that island. However, as usual, the best recommendations and information that you will get are from locals and other divers. Count on them for reliable sources before you count on any Goin' Ashore information. Live-aboard dive boats are not included in our listings.

We would have to write an encyclopedia to list every dive site in the Bahamas. This is beyond our scope. We list two sources of information in our recommended reading list that follows. We suggest, particularly in cases of deep dives (over 80 feet) and specialist dives (such as wrecks), that you seek advice from the local dive operator, and join one of their dive trips to familiarize yourself before setting off on your own.

Dress and Protection

In the winter months, the ocean temperature will drop from the summer 80s to the 70s. A 2mm wetsuit is your best bet for the winter months. During the summer, you hardly need a wetsuit for shallow dives (80 feet or less), but a "skin suit" is sensible to give you some protection in case you accidentally brush against fire coral or encounter sea lice.

Diving Emergencies

All dive operators in the islands have rescue-trained personnel and oxygen. Any island with an airfield or airstrip can provide air evacuation. If you need a recompression chamber, call Lyford Cay Hospital at 242-362-4025 or contact any of the dive operators on VHF Channel 16. The direct line to the hyperbaric chamber is 242-362-5765, but you should contact the hospital first. If you plan to dive in the Bahamas, first read our cautions and notes in the **Buff Pages** under **Medical Facilities and Health Hazards** and the **BASRA** section.

Live-Encounter Diving

We do not encourage you to partake in live-encounter diving, whether it entails shark feeding or porpoise (dolphin) encounters. The effects of such diving distort the patterns of nature and bring predators into waters they did not heretofore frequent. Inevitably, the shark population associates divers with food or divers as food. There are enough encounters of the natural kind to keep you fascinated.

Shark Safety

Shark attacks are rare in the Bahamas and the Turks and Caicos. Nonetheless, there are some basic rules to follow, for the incidence of shark attacks has increased worldwide.

- Don't dive in an area where fish are being fed.
- If you are pole spearing and have a catch, surface with it immediately. Do not swim with your catch.
- Do not dive if you have an open, or even worse, a bleeding wound. For female divers, it is prudent not to dive during menstruation.
- Do not splash on the surface. It is the indication of a fish in trouble.
- Do not wear bright reflective equipment, clothing or jewelry which, catching sunlight, may look like the scales of a fish in trouble twisting and turning.
- Be cautious in locations generally favored by sharks: alleys between sandbars, close to dropoffs, walls at night and cuts and passes at the turn of a tide.

Turks and Caicos National Parks

- **South Caicos, East Harbour Conch and Lobster Reserve**
- **Columbus Landfall Marine National Park, Grand Turk** - Wall diving, swimming, snorkeling, picnicking, shorebirds and raptors.
- **Grand Turk Cays Land and Sea National Park - Gibbs, Penniston, and Martin Alonza Pinzon (East) Cays.** Nesting gulls, terns, Turk's Head cactus, picnicking, swimming and snorkeling.
- **South Creek National Park, Grand Turk** - Wetlands and mangroves; breeding, migrating shorebirds and waders; walks and viewpoints.
- **Admiral Cockburn Land and Sea National Park, South Caicos** - Excellent diving and large marine life.
- **Conch Bar Caves National Park, Middle Caicos** - An extensive cave system with lagoons, bat colonies and Arawak sites.
- **East Bay Islands National Park, North Caicos** - Scenic views, picnic area, coastal flora, shorebirds and waders.
- **Fort George Land and Sea National Park, Pine Cay** - Cannon from the 1790s in 3 feet of water, wall diving, iguanas and ospreys.
- **Chalk Sound National Park, Providenciales** - Small boat sailing, bonefishing and photography opportunities.
- **North West Point Marine National Park, Providenciales** - Spectacular wall diving and deserted beaches.
- **Princess Alexandra Land and Sea National Park, Providenciales** - Reef and wreck diving, all water sports and a spectacular 13-mile beach.
- **West Caicos Marine National Park** - Wall diving from shore and good snorkeling.

TURKS AND CAICOS NATIONAL PARKS REGULATIONS

In the parks, it is prohibited to:

- Remove any land or sea animal or plant, including seabird eggs.
- Damage or destroy any animal or plant.
- Remove animal or plant products including timber, corals, sponges, rocks and sand.
- Remove any man-made artifact.
- Litter or dump on land or sea.

Sanctuaries

- **Big Sand Cay Sanctuary, Grand Turk** - Nesting seabirds, shorebirds and turtles.
- **Long Cay Sanctuary, Grand Turk** - Gulls, terns, iguanas and tropical flora.
- **Three Mary's Cays Sanctuary, North Caicos** - Flamingos, osprey-nesting sites.
- **French, Bush and Seal Cays Sanctuary, Caicos Bank** - Conch, lobster and nurse shark nursery; frigate birds, osprey and nesting seabirds.

Nature Reserves

- **Belle Sound and Admiral Cockburn Cays, South Caicos** - Bonefish, mangroves and tidal flats; shore birds and waders; rare rock iguanas.
- **Vine Point (Man-O-War Bush) and Ocean Hole, Middle Caicos** - Frigate bird breeding colony. Marine sinkhole 70 meters deep by 400 meters wide with turtles, bonefish and sharks.
- **Cottage Pond, North Caicos** - Fresh and salt water, 50-meter-deep sinkhole. Botanical walk, grebes and West Indian whistling duck.
- **Pumpkin Bluff Pond, North Caicos** - Flamingos, Bahamian pintail and waders.
- **Dick Hill Creek and Bellefield Landing Pond, North Caicos** - West Indian whistling duck, flamingos.
- **Northwest Point Pond, Providenciales** - Breeding and migrant wildfowl.
- **Pigeon Pond and Frenchman's Creek, Providenciales** - Tidal flats, mangrove creeks, shorebirds and waders.
- **Princess Alexandra, Little Water Cay, Mangrove Cay, Donna Cay, north of Providenciales** - Iguanas, ospreys and tropical flora.
- **Lake Catherine, West Caicos** - Scenic views, flamingos, ospreys, ducks and waders.

Historic Sites

- **Salt Cay** - Solar, salt industry of 1700s to 1900s, Salinas, windmills, waterfront buildings (including the White House) and an old whaling station.
- **Molasses Reef Wreck** - The earliest known shipwreck in the Western Hemisphere (pre-1509). Excellent museum of artifacts in Grand Turk.
- ***HMS Endymion*** - 1700s British man-o-war ship in 40 feet of water on a reef south of Big Sand Cay.
- **Boiling Hole, South Caicos** - Tidal-powered solar salt works.
- **Ramsar Site Wetlands, on south side of Middle, North and East Caicos** - This reserve of international importance is protected under the International Ramsar Convention. Water birds, intertidal and shallow water flora, lobster, conch and fish nursery.
- **Fort George, Pine Cay** - Late 1790s British fort, north of Pine Cay.
- **Cheshire Hall, Providenciales** - Ruins of 1790s Loyalist plantation.
- **Sapodilla and West Harbour Bluff Rock Carvings, Providenciales** - Rock carvings by shipwrecked sailors.

Anchoring and Mooring in Marine Parks

- No vessel over 18 meters/60 feet length overall (LOA) is allowed to anchor in a national park area except as a permitted large vessel mooring. Contact the local harbormaster or the Department of Environment and Coastal Resources (DECR).
- Anchor only over sand, but not close to reefs, within 100 meters/300 feet of any marked dive site or within 120 meters/400 feet of a nature reserve or sanctuary.

- Damaging coral, either by anchoring over or near coral or by grounding, is an offense. The fines levied in such cases can be substantial.
- Don't drive a boat within 90 meters/100 yards of the shore. No waterskiing, except in designated areas. No personal watercraft or hovercraft.
- You are not allowed to land in a sanctuary without a permit from the Department of Natural Resources.

Diving and Swimming in National Parks

Dive sites are marked by a mooring cylinder or ball with a white background and blue stripes. One blue stripe is for boats up to 15 meters/48 feet. Two blue stripes denote boats up to 33 meters/109 feet. If you use a dive site buoy, secure your own line or bridle (20 to 25 feet in length) to the buoy pickup line. Remember to fly your dive flag.

You may pick up any buoy if it is unused, but you must leave if a dive boat needs it. Peak time for dive site use is 8 a.m. to 3 p.m. Dive sites controlled by the DECR are buoyed. For more detailed information on National Parks and Dive Sites. See Wavey Line charts TC001, TC002 and TC003.

Do not allow your fins, knees or tank to touch the coral. Touching live coral damages its fragile polyps and delicate mucous tissue. Remain 1 meter/3 feet above the reef at all times. A park warden can fine you if you damage anything within the marine park. Be extra cautious not to damage corals when using a camera or video. Wear proper weights and maintain neutral buoyancy at all times. The national parks are for people. Diving, snorkeling, sightseeing and photography are encouraged. Take only pictures and leave only bubbles! It is punishable by law to harass any living creature in the park, including whales, dolphins, turtles and mantas.

Diving Emergencies

Associated Medical Practices on the Leeward Highway in Providenciales has a fully trained staff and a hyperbaric recompression chamber. Call 649-946-4242 in an emergency.

Fishing in the Turks & Caicos

FISHING REGULATIONS

A visitors sport fishing license is valid for 30 days. Permits can be obtained from the Department of the Environment and Coastal Resources Office (649-946-2970/2801), a marina or a sportfishing charter operator.

Lobsters

- The season is August 1 through March 31.
- The minimum size of carapace length is 3 inches.
- Egg-bearing females are prohibited.
- Soft-shell and "tar spotted" lobster (traces of eggs) are prohibited.

Conch

- The shell length must be at least 7 inches and have a fully-developed flared lip.

Fishing

- There are limits on fish for personal consumption. Check the current regulations with the issuer of your permit. Sale is forbidden.
- Special rules may cover sportfishing tournaments. You must check with the operator.
- Spearfishing, fish traps, pole spears and seine nets are banned throughout the islands.

Diving in the Turks & Caicos

- The same regulations apply as in the National Parks.

Bahamas and Turks & Caicos Book List

The Bahamas

Many books have been written about the Bahamas. One novel, which gives you all the flavor of Bahamian history, is Robert Wilder's "Wind From the Carolinas". It is the "Gone With the Wind" of the Bahama Islands and has been re-published by Bluewater Books & Charts.

General Reading

A Family Island. Shaw McCutcheon.
Abaco, History of an Out Island and its Cays. Steve Dodge. White Sound Press.
Bahamas Out Island Odyssey. Nan Jeffrey. Avalon House.
Bahamas Rediscovered. Nicholas Popov. MacMillan Caribbean.
Eleuthera: The Island Called Freedom. Everild Young. Regency Press, London.
Islanders in the Stream: A History of the Bahamian People, Volumes One and Two. Michael Craton and Gail Saunders. University of Georgia Press.
My Castle in the Air. Evans W Cottman. Rehor Publishing.
Mystical Cat Island. Eris Moncur. Available from Balmain Antiques, Nassau.
Out Island Doctor. Evans W Cottman. Landfall Press.
Ready About. Voyages of Life in the Abaco Cays. Dave Gale. Caribe Communications.
The Bahamas, a Family of Islands. Gail Saunders. Caribbean Guides.
The Lyford Legacy. Arthur Hailey.
This Sweet Place; Island Living and Other Adventures. Aileen Vincent-Barwood. Media Publishing, Nassau.
Wind from the Carolinas. Bluewater Books.
Islanders in the Stream: A History of the Bahamian People, Volumes One and Two. Michael Craton and Gail Saunders. University of Georgia Press.

Marine Reference

Diving and Snorkeling Guide to the Bahamas, Family Islands and Grand Bahama. Bob and Charlotte Keller. Pisces.
Fishes of the Atlantic Coast. Gar Goodson. Sanford University.

Guide to Corals and Fishes, Bahamas & Caribbean. Idaz & Jerry Greenberg. Pen & Ink Press.
Reef Coral Identification Guide. Paul Hunan. New World.
Reef Creatures Identification Guide. Paul Hunan. New World.
Reef Fish Identification Guide. Paul Human. New World.
The Dive Sites of the Bahamas. McGraw Hill.

General Reference

Bahamas Handbook and Businessman's Annual. Etienne Dupuch.
Insight Guide to the Bahamas. Insight Guides. Houghton-Mifflin.

The Turks and Caicos

Lonely Planet's Guide to Diving and Snorkeling, Turks and Caicos. Steve Rosenburg.
Olivia Osprey's Tour of the Turks and Caicos Islands. Mark Woodring and Dr. Sam Slattery.
The Birds of the Turks and Caicos Islands. Richard W. Ground, OBE QC.
The Turks and Caicos Islands: Beautiful by Nature. Julia and Phil Davies.
The Turks and Caicos Islands. Lands of Discovery. Amelia Smithers and Anthony Taylor. Macmillan Caribbean.
Turks Islands Landfall, A History of the Turks and Caicos Islands. HE Sadler.

There are not many bookstores, per se, in the islands. But, many of the stores and shops that cater to the tourist trade have books of local interest, even on the smallest islands. In the Abacos, try the shops in Hopetown for unusual book finds (and gorgeous Androsian fabric). On Grand Bahama, both Bahama Tings in Freeport and H&L Bookstore and Cafe in Port Lucaya Market Place have a lot to offer. In New Providence, your best sources are Logos Bookstore in Nassau (in the Harbour Bay Plaza just across the street from Nassau Harbour Club Marina) or take a jitney bus to The Island Book Shop on Bay Street (over 35,000 titles). Exuma Park Headquarters has a good assortment of books, particularly pertaining to island marine life. In Staniel Cay, the little curtained area behind the bar has some interesting reference books and local art work. In George Town, Exuma, The Sandpiper has a remarkable array of island books (you can find "The Little Book of Seabeans" there). In the Turks and Caicos, the best source in Providenciales is the Unicorn Bookstore (in the IGA Plaza on the Leeward Highway). In Grand Turk, check the Turks and Caicos National Museum (on Front Street in Cockburn Town).

Good Wind. Photo Courtesy of Peter Mitchell.

Buff Pages

An ABC to the Bahamas, the Turks and Caicos Islands, and U.S. Entry Regulations

The Bahamas

Airlines

Abaco Air	242-367-2266
Air Ambulance Services	242-362-1606
Air Canada	888-247-2262
Air Gate	386-409-0440
Air Jamaica	800-523-5585
Air Sunshine	800-327-8900
Air Tran	800-247-8726
American Airlines/American Eagle	800-433-7300
Bahamasair	800-222-4262
Bimini Island Air	954-938-8991
British Airways	800-247-9297
Calypso Air	242-365-8660
Cat Island Air	242-377-3318
Chalks Ocean Airways	800-424-2557
Cherokee Air	242-367-2089
Continental Connection (Gulfstream)	800-231-0856
Craig Air	904-641-0300
Delta Air Lines	800-221-1212
Ferg's Air	242-377-3333
Flamingo Air	242-351-4963
Florida Coastal Airlines	888-596-9247
Island Air Charters	800-444-9904
Island Express	954-359-0380
Jet Blue	242-377-1174
Lee Air	242-334-2829
Locair	877-359-4160
Major's Air Services	242-352-5778
Monarch Air	954-958-0485
Pineapple Air	242-377-0140
Reggie's Express (freight, passengers)	954-761-3131
Regional Air	242-352-7121
Stella Maris Resort Aviation	242-338-2051
Southern Air Charter	242-367-2498
Spirit Airlines	800-772-7117
Twin Air	242-367-8677
United	847-700-2957
US Airways	800-622-1015
Watermaker (freight, passengers)	954-467-8920
WestJet	866-884-9188
Vintage Props & Jets	242-367-4852
Yellow Air Taxi	242-367-0032

See local airline numbers in our Goin' Ashore section under Airlines for each location.

Airports

Airports shown in bold type have regular, scheduled flights, with Customs at the airport. Airports shown in normal type are used by charter and private aircraft. Private airstrips are not listed. Departure tax per person is included in the ticket cost.

ABACO: **Marsh Harbour, Sandy Point,** Spanish Cay, **Treasure Cay**
ACKLINS ISLAND: Spring Point
ANDROS: **Andros Town** (Fresh Creek), **Congo Town, San Andros**
BERRY ISLANDS: Chub Cay, **Great Harbour Cay**
BIMINI: **South Bimini,** Cat Cay
CAT ISLAND: **Arthurs Town,** Hawks Nest, **New Bight**
CROOKED ISLAND: **Colonel Hill,** Pittstown Point
ELEUTHERA: **Governors Harbour, North Eleuthera** for Harbour Island and St. George Cay, **Rock Sound**
EXUMAS: Black Point, Farmers Cay, **George Town,** Normans Cay, Sampson Cay, Staniel Cay
GRAND BAHAMA: Deep Water Cay, **Freeport**
GREAT INAGUA: **Matthew Town**
LONG ISLAND: Cape Santa Maria, **Deadmans Cay, Stella Maris**
MAYAGUANA: **Mayaguana**
NEW PROVIDENCE: **Nassau International, Paradise Island** (seaplane only)
RUM CAY: Rum Cay
SAN SALVADOR: **San Salvador**

ATMs, Banks, Credit Cards and Currency

Most banks are open 9:30 a.m. to 3 p.m. Monday through Thursday and until 4:30 p.m. Fridays. Banks in Grand Bahama, Marsh Harbour and Nassau have ATMs. There are ATMs at service stations and shopping areas on the largest islands. Travelers checks can be cashed at banks with a passport. Some banks will give cash against your credit card. In the southern Bahamas, there are no banks between Nassau, New Providence and George Town, Great Exuma or between Long Island and Great Inagua. Many of the smaller islands have no bank.

Visa, MasterCard and American Express are widely accepted, although a credit card surcharge (sometimes as much as 6 percent) may be added, particularly at fuel docks and in the more remote islands. Discover and Diners Club are not widely accepted. The smaller islands may not take credit cards at all, and you should be prepared for this. In general, as the islands go down the scale in size and up the scale in remoteness, the utility of credit cards fades out, then the utility of Travelers checks. Make sure you have adequate cash on hand. If your destination is remote, make sure you have the currency of that country. We have found it difficult to exchange Bahamian dollars in the States and impossible to exchange coins.

Most, if not all, coin operated washers and dryers use U.S. quarters. They are frequently referred to as "tokens." But, these are just quarters, not the rectangular tokens with which you have become familiar in other countries. We have experienced difficulty getting the laundry matrons to exchange Bahamian coins for U.S. quarters. Therefore, we highly recommend that you travel with a good supply of quarters and that you use up coins in the grocery and liquor stores, where you may receive a big sigh and a dirty look, but at least you'll get rid of your Bahamian coins. Or, bring them home and give them to your grandchildren.

Bahamas Air-Sea Rescue Association (BASRA)

A remarkable, all-volunteer group called BASRA—The Bahamas Air-Sea Rescue Association (BASRA)—works 24 hours a day to rescue mariners and pilots in distress. The association works in coordination with the Royal Bahamas Defense Force and the U.S. Coast Guard. Its resources include boats and aircraft supplied and operated by BASRA volunteers. Their only compensation is the reward of doing good works and reimbursement for fuel used during volunteer duty.

BASRA is not a fallback service for those who run out of fuel or run aground, nor is it a towing service for mechanical failure. BASRA responds when lives are in danger and answers hundreds of calls a year. BASRA stands by on single-sideband (SSB) 4125 and 2182, upper sideband, from 9 a.m. to 5 p.m. daily. It also has an emergency repeater station standing by on VHF Channel 22A covering a 100-mile area within range of Nassau on a 24-hour basis. The Royal Bahamas Defense Force keeps a 24-hour watch on SSB 4125 and handles all emergency messages for BASRA after hours. Nassau Harbour Control monitors VHF Channel 16. It has a range of approximately 60 miles and relays emergency calls. Volunteer stations throughout the islands report emergencies to Nassau. BASRA telephone numbers are 242-325-8864 or 242-322-3877.

Memberships and fundraising are BASRA's only source of income. The costs of rescue operations are high. One day your contribution to BASRA may save a life, maybe your own. When you join, you do not have to play an active role in BASRA unless you want to. If you are a part-time resident in the Bahamas and willing to help, BASRA welcomes you. BASRA Headquarters are open 9 a.m. to 5 p.m. daily, except public holidays. You can become a member by stopping in headquarters or downloading a membership application at www.basra.org and mailing the membership fee to:

The Bahamas Air-Sea Rescue Association
P.O. Box SS-6247
Nassau, NP, Bahamas

Since contributions by U.S. citizens to foreign non-profit organizations are not tax-deductible, you may prefer to donate to SEARCH—Search and Rescue Charitable Foundation—based in Ft. Lauderdale, FL. SEARCH assists voluntary search and rescue organizations throughout the Southwest North Atlantic and Caribbean waters. It is a non-profit, tax-exempt foundation that raises funds to provide financial and technical assistance to voluntary search and rescue organizations such as BASRA. Contributors receive a certificate of membership and decal from:

SEARCH, PMB 1313
1811 NW 51st St., Hangar 42D
Fort Lauderdale, FL 33309-7136

More information can be obtained at: 242-362-1574 or http://caribbeansearchandrescue.freeservers.com.

Boating Regulations

- It is illegal to drive a powerboat within 200 feet of the shore of any Bahamian island unless you are approaching or leaving a dock or marina.
- Speed limited to 3 knots within this coastal zone.
- It is illegal to drive a boat in a reckless manner or while under the influence of alcohol or drugs.
- No one under 16 years of age may drive a boat with an engine greater than 10 horsepower.
- Water skiing is forbidden within the 200-foot coastal zone, unless it is taking place in a lane clearly marked with buoys and lines.
- Water skiers are required to use flotation jackets.
- In addition to the driver, a lookout, 16 years of age or older, is required in the boat towing water skiers.
- Water skiing is forbidden at night.

Modes of Respect

The Bahamians are quite formal. You will notice that the businesspersons and employees with whom you have contact treat you very professionally and are dressed accordingly. Although a jacket and tie is rarely required outside Nassau and Grand Bahama for dining, some finer restaurants require a shirt with a collar or a jacket for dinner. Shorts are discouraged. Remember that even though you are on vacation, this is their home. Beach clothes, bikini bras and short cut-offs are not proper attire anywhere but on the beach. Bahamians find our fast-paced, brusque manner of transacting daily activities quite rude. Take the time to greet everyone before requesting service, and you will be rewarded. A simple "good morning" or "good day" does wonders.

Driving

DRIVE ON THE LEFT! Because most vehicles are imported from the United States, the steering wheel is on the left. This makes it more difficult to remember to drive on the left. A "co-pilot" is a big help. It takes work to get used to the "keep left" rule, and it is easy to forget on which side of the road you should be. Speed limits are 25 mph in cities and towns, 30 mph everywhere else, unless specified as 45 mph. There are no seat belt laws, but the rules of common sense tell you to wear yours. Motorcyclists are required to wear helmets. Visitors may drive in the Bahamas for up to three months on their countries driver's license.

Electricity

Electricity supply is single-phase, three wire, 120V, 60-cycle AC, the same as in the United States. Power on the small islands is provided by generators. Expect surges and occasional low voltage. When you are operating sensitive equipment like a computer, use a good surge protector between the computer and the power source. Do not rely on the web cafe's surge protectors. Use your own. Radio Shack sells a reliable, single outlet surge protector with two comforting lights. When lit, you know your computer is both protected and grounded.

Emergencies

Emergency - VHF Channel 16, 2182 single sideband, Ambulance 911
Air Ambulance - 242-362-1606, 800-633-3590, 800-423-3226, 800-327-3710, 800-948-1215
BASRA - 242-322-3877 or 242-325-8864, VHF Channel 16
Divers Recompression Chamber at Lyford Cay Hospital - 242-362-4025, VHF Channel 16
Hospitals:
Doctors Hospital, Nassau - 242-322-8411
Princess Margaret Hospital, Nassau - 242-322-1039
Rand Memorial, Freeport, - 242-352-6735
Med Evac - 242-322-2881
Med Tec - 242-394-3388
Nassau Harbour Control - VHF channel 16, 242-322-1596
Walk-In Clinic - 242-328-0783

Flags and Flag Etiquette

Bahamas National Flag

The Bahamas flag has three equal bands of color. Two aquamarine stripes, at the top and bottom, show the colors of Bahamian skies and waters, and the central yellow stripe represents the shore. The black triangle, superimposed on the left (the staff side), means unity.

Courtesy Flag

This flag is red with a white cross, with the Bahamas national flag superimposed in the upper left quarter. You fly a courtesy flag immediately after you are granted clearance to cruise in national waters and take down your courtesy flag when you are three miles off in international waters bound for another territory.

War Ensign

You may see a variation of the courtesy flag, a white background with a red cross, which also has the national flag superimposed in the upper left quarter. This is the War Ensign, reserved for the Royal Bahamas Defense Force.

The Royal Bahamas Defense Force has the right to board and inspect any vessel in Bahamian waters. They will be armed during such inspections. If you are boarded, you will be asked to sign a certificate at the end of the inspection to state that it was carried out politely, correctly and that the captain of the vessel boarded (or his or her representative) was allowed to be present throughout the inspection.

Q Flag

Remember, it is international law that to fly a yellow Q (quarantine) flag upon entering territorial waters from another country. This applies returning to the United States, regardless of your nationality and registration. You may take down your Q flag when you are granted clearance.

Ferries

The large, high-speed ferry services originate from and return to Potters Cay, Nassau. Reservations and advance ticket purchases are recommended. For The Bahamas Ferries, contact Potters Cay reservation agents at 242-323-2166. Boarding time is one hour prior to departure time. Check-in closes 15 minutes prior to departure. Cruise and stay packages are available to Harbour Island and Andros. Day Away packages are available to Harbour Island, Spanish Wells and Andros. Special events can override the ferry's schedule. Please check with reservations to confirm schedules. Freight services are available to all destinations. The Bahamas Ferries depart Potters Cay to:

- Spanish Wells and Harbour Island - daily
- Governors Harbour, Eleuthera - Wednesday, Friday and Sunday
- Morgans Bluff, Andros - Saturday
- Fresh Creek, Andros - Friday and Sunday
- Current, Eleuthera - Friday and Sunday
- George Town, Exuma - Monday and Wednesday

There are several motor vessels (freighters) that travel to the islands weekly from Potters Cay. One-way tickets on a freighter can be as low as $35.00. There is a complete listing with contact information on these vessels at www.bahamas.com/bahamas-directory/vacation-planning/ferries.

Fuel

Fuel is generally available on the larger islands, but not necessarily on the smaller cays when you want it. Don't let your supplies get too low. There is a credit card surcharge for fuel at most marinas. Fuel is more expensive than in the U.S. Fuel is also subject to contamination. The use of a "Bahamian-type" or "Baja" fuel filter is imperative. Purchase the best one you can buy while you are in the United States (Practical Sailor does comparative tests and makes recommendations on these filters). Do not "go cheap" on this item. Many a skipper has rued the day they skimped on the filter and poured water and other contaminants into the fuel tank.

Trash

Trash is always a problem for the cruising sailor, and the disposal of it is an ongoing and vexing problem for the Bahamians. There is no way for them to excavate landfills. Their solution is fire. Anyone who has spent a miserable day at anchor in Marsh Harbour downwind of the garbage dump knows of what we speak.

So, do your part. Remove all disposable pieces and parts from your food and other items before departing. Even the little things like the boxes around your soap, Jell-O™ and toothpaste helps. Store everything in bulk in reusable containers. If you can buy it in a bag, rather than a can, do! Bags flatten, cans don't. Good examples are drink mixes instead of canned soda, bags of dehydrated soup mix instead of pop-top cans (the mess they make if they accidentally pop is another story), bags of tuna, chicken and hamburger, etc. Beer drinkers, squish your aluminum cans and save them in a separate sack. There are islands that recycle where you can drop them off. Plastic is the big enemy. You will be sick at the sight of it along the shores of what should be pristine beaches fronting the Sound or the Atlantic. For your part, never dump plastic at sea and eliminate the products that come in it to the best of your ability. Refill your own water bottle! Pour six bottles of dish detergent into one reusable container and dump those bottles at home. Use bar soap and shampoo. Use waxed paper and freezer paper instead of plastic wrap and baggies. And, ladies, use tampons without plastic inserters.

Don't even think of burying or burning your trash onshore. Anything that is truly biodegradable can be jettisoned at sea, well-offshore, in deep water. If you must, glass bottles (broken first) may be disposed of in this way. For the rest, you must carry your garbage with you until you can dispose of it, properly bagged (this is not the time to recycle grocery bags) wherever there is a disposal site. There may be a small charge for disposal, pay it! If a bin in a settlement is full, walk on to another. Moreover, do not dispose of waste oil in any refuse can or bin.

Language

Bahamians speak the Queen's English. Their accents are musical and play lovely on the ears. There are also local dialects and colloquialisms indigenous to an area. It will take you some time to get used to the lilt, catch phrases and inflection of their speech. A gracious smile and warm, "Excuse me?" will get you through the rough spots.

Liquor Laws

The legal drinking age is 18.

Mail

You must use Bahamian stamps (which are pretty and make wonderful souvenirs). A one-half-ounce letter to the U.S. and Canada costs 65¢; to Europe and Central and South America 70¢; to the rest of the world (Africa, Asia, Australia, etc.) 80¢. Postcards to all destinations are 50¢. Post offices are usually open 9 a.m. to 4 p.m. Monday through Friday.

Marriage

Weddings in the Bahamas are becoming more and more popular. For the cost of a license, you need only be over the age of 18 (or under 18 if both parents consent), have been in the Bahamas one day at the time of application and received the approved license the day after application. If either person has never been married before, a declaration, obtained from an attorney or notary public, must certify this fact. Divorced or widowed persons must have the original or certified copies of final decree or death. Both parties must present a valid passport, birth certificate and photo ID. You also must present evidence of your arrival in the Bahamas. No blood test is necessary. Marriage licenses are issued at the office of the Registrar General in Nassau or at the Administrator's Office on any other island. To facilitate the procedures and save money, make copies of all the required documents before you leave home.

Pets and Vets

Dogs and cats over the age of six months may accompany you to the Bahamas. Apply to import your pet two months in advance by contacting:

> The Director of Agriculture
> P.O. Box N-3704
> Nassau, NP, Bahamas
> (Tel: 242-325-7413 or Fax: 242-325-3960)

Return the application form with a $10 fee (use an international money order or postal order). There is no fee for service dogs, such as seeing-eye dogs. To expedite the process and have your permit Faxed, enclose an additional $5 (separate check) along with the appropriate FAX number for them to send the forms. In addition, you need a veterinary health certificate (including parasite tests) issued by a veterinarian within 48 hours of your embarkation for the Bahamas and a valid rabies vaccination certificate for either a one or three-year duration. The rabies certificate, if issued with one-year validity, should be valid from not less than one month and not more than ten months before your entry to the Bahamas. If the validity of your rabies certificate covers three years, it is acceptable if it is not less than one month prior to entry and not more than 34 months. Dogs and cats from rabies-free countries many enter without a rabies vaccination if accompanied by a veterinary health certificate and a certificate stating there have been no cases of rabies in that country of origin for the two years immediately prior to date of embarkation and that the animal has been in that country for six months. To facilitate the importation of pet procedures at clearance, have copies of all the required documents ready to hand to the Customs and Immigration officers. Keep additional copies onboard at all times.

Prepare a first-aid and medical kit with the help of your pet's regular veterinarian. Veterinarian services are not widely available in the islands. Your pet's kit should include, at the bare minimum, powder or gel to stop bleeding, an acetic cleaning and drying solution for ears and skin, prescription eye ointment, blistering wound care (such as Silvadene), anti-bacterial ointment, bandages and tapes that don't stick to fur, a de-wormer, sterile syringes to aspirate abscesses and all other items of daily, weekly or monthly care, such as heartworm medication. Pet food is hard to come by. Be sure to bring adequate amounts with you.

Veterinarians

Abacos – Marsh Harbour

Caribbean Veterinary Health 242-367-3551
Community Animal Hospital 242-367-3647

Great Exuma – George Town

Exuma Veterinary Clinic 242-336-2806
VHF Channel 16, "Dr. DeYoung"

Grand Bahama – Freeport

Community Animal Hospital.....................242-352-3647
Dr. Owen Hanna 242-351-2103
Freeport Animal Clinic 242-352-6521

New Providence

Central Animal Hospital 242-325-1288

SKIPPER'S HANDBOOK

Eastern Veterinary Clinic 242-393-3818
Palmdale Veterinary Clinic........................ 242-325-1354
Veterinary Outpatient Care........................ 242-328-5635

Turks & Caicos Islands

Animal House 649-231-0685
Turks and Caicos Veterinary Associates ...649-946-4353

Population

At the start of the 20th century, there were just over 50,000 Bahamians living in the islands. Since then, the population has increased to at least 307,451, the huge majority settling in Nassau. The 2000 census showed:

New Providence	210,832
Grand Bahama	46,994
Abaco	13,170
Eleuthera	7,779
Andros	7,686
Exumas	3,571
Long Island	2,992
Cat Island	1,647
Biminis	1,717
San Salvador & Rum Cay	1,050
Great Inagua	969
Berry Islands	709
Acklins Island	428
Crooked Island	350
Mayaguana	259
Ragged Islands	72

We will surely be seeing a dramatic increase in these numbers after the 2010 census is completed.

Taxes and Tipping

Room and accommodation rentals are subject to service charges and government taxes. Some resorts add other fees and charges as high as 20 percent. Make sure these are itemized and perfectly clear before making any commitments or giving a credit card number. Restaurant meals are subject to government taxes. This is usually stated on the menu. The standard rate for tipping is 15 to 20 percent. Be aware that gratuity may be added automatically to your restaurant bill or to your hotel bill for room cleaning service. Always double check for this.

If you are paying by credit card, a surcharge is often added, especially at fuel docks and in small stores and marinas, less frequently in restaurants. When you can, pay in cash. We have had our credit card double charged a few times in the islands. We like to think this is more likely due to poor connections with the credit card machines than the folks handling the card. Just be aware of it, and keep scrupulous records of your charges to check against your activity statements.

Telephones

Bahamas area code is 242
Directory Assistance is 916
International direct access numbers:
AT&T USA.................. 800-CALLATT/800-872-2881
AT&T Canada..800-389-0004
MCI Call USA..800-888-8000
Sprint Express..800-389-2111
UK Direct 800-389-4444

Card phones have replaced coin-operated public telephones, and BTC telephone cards ($5, $10 or $20) are available at any BTC office and many stores, restaurants, resorts and marinas. There are also foreign direct lines, using special cards available in the bigger marinas.

For calls within the Bahamas, dial seven digits in the same island group, or 1-242 plus the seven-digit number to call outside the area. International calls are expensive and can be frustrating, and some 800 calls to the U.S. are not toll free.

International Direct Dial phones, at some of the bigger marinas, use a credit card, but they are pricey. Increasingly, local people have cell phones. Cellular telephone service is available in the Bahamas, however, you must first register with BTC. If your current cellular service provider does not have an established agreement with BTC, you will need a SIM card from BTC to use your phone in the Bahamas. The phone must be unlocked and dual band, not tri-band. You can buy an inexpensive phone that meets these requirements in the U.S. For instance, Nokia sells an unlocked dual band GSM phone. The $10, $20, $50 and $100 prepaid cell phone cards are available at many marinas, stores, BTC and at EZ Top Up BTC online. The cards are good for 90 days. The per minute rates vary by time of day. The least expensive time to call per minute is from 7 p.m. to 7 a.m. when incoming is $0.15 per minute and outgoing is $0.44 per minute. You can significantly reduce the per minute charges by using a call back system such as Globaltel (www.globaltel-callback.com). You will need to register your Bahamas phone number with Globaltel and give them credit card billing information. They assign you a U.S. phone number to activate their call back system. To call the U.S., dial the Globaltel number assigned to you, let it ring twice and disconnect. A few seconds later, Globaltel calls your phone and prompts you to enter the phone number you want to call in the U.S. This is considered an incoming call and you will only be charged $0.15 per minute off the BTC prepaid card. Globaltel will charge an additional $0.14 minute. The $0.29 total charge per minute is a nice savings compared to $0.44 outgoing on BTC. Alternatively, you can rent a phone by contacting BTC at any branch in a major city or calling 242-225-5282 or emailing customercare@btcbahamas.com.

Tourist Offices

Abaco Tourist Office, Marsh Harbour 242-367-3067
Bimini Tourist Office, Alice Town 242-347-3529
Eleuthera Tourist Office,
Governors Harbour...................................242-333-2142
Exuma Tourist Office, George Town....... 242-336-2430
Freeport, Grand Bahama, Ministry
of Tourism 242-352-8044
Harbour Island Tourist Office,
Harbour Island..3242-33-2621
Nassau, Ministry of Tourism.....................242-322-7501
Bahamas Tourist Board, Miami 800-224-2627
....305-932-0051

Weights and Measures

Weights and measures for linear, dry and liquid measurement used in the Bahamas are the same as in the United States. Fuel is sold in U.S. gallons.

Customs and Immigration, Cruising and Fishing Permits

Bahamas Customs and Immigration

MAKE COPIES OF ALL DOCUMENTATION AND REQUIRED PAPERS AND PASSPORTS BEFORE YOU LEAVE THE STATES. You will need to leave the copies with the Customs and Immigration officers who do not have copy machines at their disposal. Working hours are 9 a.m. to 5:30 p.m. Monday through Friday. You may be charged additional attendance fees on weekends and public holidays. In some instances, the officer may come to the boat, but passengers and crew may not leave the boat until it has been cleared. Forms that you and your crew need to complete and sign are available at marina offices.

Passports: The captain of the vessel must take originals and copies of all valid passports for everyone on board, and all the ship's documentation papers, to the customs officer. U.S. citizens need a valid passport. Non-U.S. citizens need a valid passport. Additionally, if any member of your ship's company is planning to leave while you are still cruising in the Bahamas, they must have a valid air ticket for the return journey, which should be included with their documents.

You will be required to complete an Inward Report – Pleasure Vessels, an Inward Passenger and Crew Manifest, a Maritime Declaration of Health and an application for a Fishing Permit. Individual immigration cards are mandatory for everyone on board.

Boat Papers: You are required to produce a copy of your state registration or U.S. Documentation Certificate, which will be retained by the customs officer. The document must show your name, the name of the vessel and its length overall.

Entry Fees: Vessels up to 35 feet, $150; vessels over 35 feet, $300. Regular hours for Bahamas Customs and Immigration officers are 9 a.m. to 5 p.m. weekdays. Officers are on-call weekends and holidays. There is no overtime charge. Entry fees cover a vessel with four persons or fewer and include: the cruising permit, fishing permit, Customs and Immigration charges and the $15 departure tax up to four persons. There is a $15 departure tax charge for each additional person on board over six years of age. These fees cover two visits to the islands within a 90-day period. You can check with the Bahamas Tourist Office in Miami or visit http://www.bahamas.com/bahamas/regulations-0 to update this information.

Extension of Cruising Permits: Customs and stamp duty are not payable on foreign-registered, foreign-owned pleasure boats that remain in the Bahamas up to one year after arriving under their own power. After that, written application for an extension of a cruising permit must be made to the Comptroller of Customs, and once approved; an annual fee of $500 per year will be applicable. The vessel may then remain in the Bahamas provided it is not used for commercial purposes or for hire, for up to three years, at which point full customs duty must be paid. Questions on current regulations and entry charges should be made to the Comptroller of Customs office (242-326-4401).

Fishing Permit: Fishing permit fees are included in the cost of your cruising permit.

Drugs: Drugs that are illegal in the United States (marijuana, LSD, cocaine, morphine, opium, etc.) are also illegal in the Bahamas. Fines and punishment for possession start at $100,000 and five years in prison. Under U.S. law, the boat may be confiscated with no appeal possible.

Duty Free

Alcohol and Tobacco: Each person may enter the Bahamas with one quart of alcoholic beverage, one quart of wine, one pound of tobacco or 200 cigarettes or 50 cigars.

Bicycles and Motorcycles: Both are subject to import duty, but a bond in lieu may serve. Ask the Customs officer or rent locally.

Boat Spares: The 2008 Customs duty, payable on replacement parts for pleasure vessels, has been rescinded as of this writing. There is no longer a duty on replacement parts. There is a $10 stamp tax on each shipment. For more information, call the Comptroller of Customs (242-326-4401).

Food: You are allowed to bring in food for your own consumption.

Firearms: You may import firearms (rifles, shotguns and handguns) and ammunition if they are declared and kept on board under lock and key. Automatic weapons are banned. If your cruise extends over three months, you must obtain a firearms certificate from the police. Firearms may not be used in Bahamian waters, nor taken ashore.

Ports of Entry

ABACOS: Green Turtle Cay, Marsh Harbour, Spanish Cay, Treasure Cay Marina, Walkers Cay
ANDROS: Congo Town; Fresh Creek, Andros Town; San Andros Airport for Nicholls Town or Morgans Bluff
BERRY ISLANDS: Chub Cay Club Marina, Great Harbour Cay Marina
NORTH BIMINI: Alice Town
SOUTH BIMINI: Bimini Sands Marina
CAT CAY: Cat Cay Club
CAT ISLAND: Smith Bay
ELEUTHERA: Governors Harbour, Harbour Island, Rock Sound, Spanish Wells
EXUMAS: George Town
GRAND BAHAMA: Freeport Harbour*, Port Lucaya Marina, Grand Bahama Yacht Club, Old Bahama Bay
GREAT INAGUA: Matthew Town
LONG ISLAND: Clarence Town, Stella Maris Marina
MAYAGUANA: Abrahams Bay
NEW PROVIDENCE/NASSAU: Clifton Pier*, John Alfred Dock*, Kelly's Dock*, Lyford Cay Club, Nassau Harbour Dock West*, Nassau Harbour Club, Nassau Yacht Haven, Union Dock*

NEW PROVIDENCE/PARADISE ISLAND: The Marina at Atlantis, Hurricane Hole Marina

SAN SALVADOR: Riding Rock Inn Marina. (*commercial shipping only)

Departing the Bahamas

You don't have to report to Customs and Immigration to clear out of the Bahamas. If your last port is an entry port, you may hand in your cruising permit and the immigration departure cards of everyone on board, just before you leave. However, if you have to return for any reason, you may have created a problem with your premature surrender of these vital forms. Alternatively, you can mail your cruising permit and the immigration cards back to the Bahamas government from the U.S. (or your next landfall). The address to use is on the reverse of the cruising permit.

Useful Telephone Numbers

CBP Public Affairs Office 305-810-5120/5135
Bahamas Tourist Board, Miami.. 305-932-0051/800-224-3681

U.S. National Saltwater Angler Registry

In January 2010, the United States implemented a new law requiring recreational fishermen to register with the National Saltwater Angler Registry if they do not hold a saltwater license from a state along the eastern coastline and fish in the Federal waters more than three miles from the ocean shore. Within in the three-mile limit, you must obtain the applicable state saltwater fishing license. Since many boaters troll off their sterns on the voyage to and from the Bahamas, this new Federal law applies. At the time of this writing, registration is free. You can register through www.countmyfish.noaa.gov or call 888-MRIP-411, daily from 4 a.m. to midnight (EST). You need to provide name, date of birth, address and telephone number for each person onboard who fishes. In approximately 30 days, you will receive a registration card in the mail. Exceptions include anglers who are under the age of 16.

U.S. Entry Regulations

Operators of small pleasure vessels, arriving in the United States from a foreign port are required to report their arrival to Customs and Border Patrol (CBP) immediately. The master of the vessel should report their arrival at the nearest Customs facility or as otherwise authorized by regulations.

To eliminate potential problems or questions regarding any items of value that you have on board, obtain a U.S. Customs Form 4457, Certificate of Registration for Personal Effects Taken Abroad, before you depart for the islands. You will need to visit a U.S. Customs Office and bring the items with you. There is no fee for obtaining this form.

Arrival in the United States

The Department of Homeland Security's Bureau of Customs and Border Protection, in tightening defenses against terrorism, have changed the procedures required for pleasure craft clearing into the U.S. The goal is to task one officer at each port of entry to check in recreational boats. At this time, you are required to call 800 CUSTOMS (800-287-8667) on arrival in the U.S. and await instructions. Current regulations require separate visits to Customs and to Immigration. This may mean that you have to rent a car or take a cab to the nearest airport or federal office several miles away. These offices are often closed on weekends. If your arrival is after working hours, you are required to stay on board and clear in the next morning. You must clear in within 24 hours of your arrival.

Everyone on board, regardless of nationality, has to report in person (see Local Boaters Option below for the exception). U.S. nationals must take their passports or passport cards. All non-U.S. nationals should take their passports with valid visas and a Green Card, if held. Take your boat papers, either U.S. documentation or state registration with state decal number. You will need to show:

- Registered name of vessel and the declared home port
- Your FCC call sign
- Your hull identification number
- LOA, LWL, beam and draft

Additionally, have a list of firearms and ammunition on board and your U.S. Customs decal number if required. U.S. Customs decals are required for any boat over 30 feet long. For information regarding CBP Decal, visit www.cbp.gov. Decals are not required for non-U.S. boats and one-time entries from the Bahamas or elsewhere. Decals must be renewed annually.

U.S. Customs and Border Control Ports of Entry

FLORIDA NORTH, CENTRAL AND SOUTH: Port Canaveral, 321-783-2066; Fernandina Beach, 904-261-6154; Jacksonville, 904-360-5020; Manatee, 813-634-1369; Panama City, 850-785-4688; Pensacola, 850-476-0117; Key West, 305-296-5411; Port of Miami, 305-536-4758 (6 a.m. to 10 p.m.); Port Everglades, 954-761-2000 (5 a.m. to midnight); West Palm Beach (Riviera Beach), 561-848-6922 (8 a.m. to 4 p.m., Monday through Friday); Ft. Pierce/St. Lucie Airport 772-461-1733 (10 a.m. to 6 p.m.).

GEORGIA: Port of Savannah, 912-232-7507; Port of Brunswick, 912-262-6692.

SOUTH CAROLINA: Charleston, 843-579-6513.

NORTH CAROLINA: Beaufort/Morehead City, 252-726-5845; Wilmington, 910-772-5900.

VIRGINIA: Newport News, 757-245-6470; Norfolk, 757-533-4211; Richmond, 804-226-9675.

LOCAL BOATER OPTION

Local Boater Option (LBO) is a voluntary effort that allows eligible pleasure boat operators and passengers, who are U.S. Citizens or Lawful Permanent Residents of the U.S., to register themselves and their vessel with Customs and Border Patrol (CBP). LBO facilitates customs and immigration clearance for recreational boaters at time of arrival. LBO satisfies the vessel operator's legal requirement to report to a port-of-entry instead of a face-to-face inspection. Operators must still phone 800-432-1216 or 800-451-0393 and provide the following information.

- LBO number, name, date of birth, citizenship and passport number of all persons on board
- Name of the boat, documentation or boat registration number
- CBP user fee decal number (if 30 feet or longer)
- Homeport and current location
- Return contact phone number

When you have been given your clearance number, record it in your ship's log. Everyone is now free to go ashore, and you may take down your Q flag.

Advance Notice of Arrival

If you are a U.S. vessel greater than 300 gross tons or a non-U.S. vessel regardless of the size, you are required to report an Advance Notice of Arrival (ANOA) with the National Vessel Movement Center. So that there is no misunderstanding about this requirement, here is the United States Coast Guard (USCG) regulation verbatim:

Advance Notice of Arrival Regulations – Effective immediately, the USCG will be enforcing regulations requiring vessels entering U.S. waters from a foreign port to give a 96-Hour Advance Notice of Arrival. Although this regulation is not new, the USCG has recently begun enforcing this law in conjunction with the increased security requirements established by the Homeland Security Regulations. Who is affected? Any foreign recreational vessel, commercial vessel or U.S. vessel in excess of 300 gross tons entering a U.S. port from a foreign destination.

The USCG advises that there are no exceptions regardless of the size of the foreign vessel. You must file an ANOA electronically with the appropriate Captain of the Port (COTP). The Miami COTP area encompasses Malabar to Cape Romano, Florida and includes the Florida Keys. If you have questions, their contact information is: Phone 305-535-8701, Fax 305-535-8761.

How to File Your Electronic Notice of Arrival (eNOA/D):

If you must file an eNOA with the National Vessel Movement Center (NVMC), it must be done at least 96 hours prior to arriving at a US port. Go to the NVMC website at https://enoad.nvmc.uscg.gov/ and click on the eNOA/D tab. The form can be completed and sent to the NVMC from that link. The NVMC can also be contacted at 800-708-9823. (NOTE: When you file an eNOA, it increases the likelihood that your vessel will be boarded and inspected by the U.S. Department of Agriculture. Many foods returning from a foreign port are considered to be contaminated even if they were originally purchased in the U.S.)

What about spontaneous or short day trips to the Bahamas?

The USCG understands that due to Florida's close proximity to the Bahamas, recreational boaters frequently visit foreign ports spontaneously or for short durations of time. The intent of this regulation is to enhance the security of U.S. ports by monitoring who is entering territorial waters. For boaters who are departing from a foreign port with a cruise duration of less than 96 hours, but greater than 24 hours, the appropriate U.S. authorities must be notified prior to leaving the foreign port. If the duration of the cruise is less than 24 hours, the appropriate U.S. authorities must be notified 24 hours in advance of arrival at the first U.S. port. It is also recommended that recreational boaters emphasize in their eNOA that they will be following the reported trip itinerary, weather permitting. In the event that weather conditions prevent boaters from adhering to their proposed schedule, they should notify the appropriate authority within the time limits specified above.

What do you do if your estimated time of arrival changes?

All boaters must notify the appropriate authority of any modifications to their itinerary within the time limits specified in the previous section. Changes to the estimated time of arrival that are less than 6 hours do not need to be reported. If they are greater than 6 hours, you must email your itinerary changes to the NVMC.

What happens if you do not file an eNOA with the appropriate authority?

The vessel is required to remain outside U.S. waters until the required information is provided and processed, addressing appropriate notification and any security issues that would prevent the vessel from entering the port. This may include USCG officers boarding and searching your vessel. First time offenders may be issued a Letter of Warning. Those vessels found to be in violation of the eNOA procedures a second time will be subject to civil penalty action seeking the maximum allowable penalty. Continual offenders (three or more failures) will be required to remain outside U.S. territorial waters for the appropriate 24- or 96-hour time period depending on the last port of call.

For boats outward bound for the Bahamas and the Turks & Caicos, it is a good idea to check (before leaving the U.S.) with the nearest office of the Bureau of Customs and Border Protection at your intended port of return to find out exactly what they will require from you as you clear in.

Medical Facilities and Health Hazards

Medical Facilities

Hardly surprising, the best medical facilities are found in the centers of population. On New Providence in Nassau, there are two main hospitals; the government-owned Princess Margaret Hospital and the ever-expanding privately owned Doctors Hospital, with 72 beds and 100 physicians. There are plans to open a hospital in Marsh Harbour. See our listings in the Goin' Ashore section under individual places. The only hyperbaric chamber in the Bahamas as of spring 2010, is at Lyford Cay hospital, together with the Bahamas Heart Institute. In Freeport, is the Rand Memorial Hospital, and in Marsh Harbour, a large government clinic and the excellent Abaco Family Medicine practice. In the Turks and Caicos, there is a hospital on Grand Turk and excellent facilities on Providenciales, including a hyperbaric chamber.

As a non-resident in the Bahamas, you will be charged $30 for a routine visit to see a nurse or doctor at any of the government clinics. You will be asked for your insurance in the Turks and Caicos. The Bahamian clinics generally have full-time nurses with a doctor on-call, two bed wards, a dispensary, X-ray equipment and a morgue. A few have their own ambulance. It remains that if you are not in New Providence, Grand Bahama, Grand Turk or Providenciales, and someone needs urgent attention in the event of a serious medical condition or injury, they will probably have to be flown to Nassau or back to the U.S. This might not be the first step in their medical evacuation. The patient may have to be taken first by boat (it could be in your boat) to the nearest island or cay with a clinic, and from there, after stabilizing treatment, by boat once again to the nearest airfield or airport and then moved by air to a hospital.

Two broad conclusions can be drawn from this: You should carry the fullest possible medical pack on board, together with first aid manuals, so that you (or your crew) are able to respond with effective, immediate first aid after any accident or medical crisis. Consult your family physician and ensure that everyone on board has an adequate stock of prescription medication to last the voyage. Your aim, even before you set out on your cruise, is to be capable of delivering someone, in an emergency, in a no-worse state to the nearest clinic or health center from wherever you might be, or to an airfield with a waiting air ambulance.

If the patient is in serious danger, rather than risk the trauma of repeated inter-island moves, it may be better to seek direct air evacuation from the nearest airport (such as Marsh Harbour or Treasure Cay in the Abacos, George Town in the Exumas) straight to a hospital in Florida. To this end, the Divers Alert Network (DAN) and other organizations offer insurance with emergency air evacuation included, which is well worth considering. Emergency Hotline: 919-684-8111 or 919-684-4326 (collect). Failing this coverage, it would be sensible to travel with an air evacuation service contact number listed in your Log Book. Take care of this before you set out for the Bahamas. The health centers on all the major islands have access to air evacuation services.

Dental offices are listed in the Goin' Ashore sections, where they exist, although there are few outside the main towns. For this reason, always carry a dental first-aid kit and hope never to have to use it.

Health

You should have no particular health problems in the islands. There are four health hazards, all marine related, which we will deal with separately. In general, the islands are a healthy environment. More and more islands and cays have their own desalination plants, so water is generally potable. There are plentiful supplies of bottled drinking water in the larger towns and settlements, but it is not always easy to find in the remote islands. Stock up wherever you can. Food generally is good and wholesome, and there are no issues there. Both daytime and nighttime temperatures, and humidity, are normally well within your comfort zone.

Those Strange Bahamian Names

Have you ever wondered where those oddball names, Junkanoo and Goombay, came from? There are many theories and explanations. Our preferences are these. The word *Junkanoo* came from Haiti. In French (spoken in Haiti) it was the festival of the *Gens Inconnus*, the "Unknown or Disguised People" from the masks the dancers wore and wear today. *Goombay* seems firmly African. It is a kind of drum, and we have been told, the Bantu word for rhythm.

Are there any areas for concern? Yes, wear a hat. Too many people are sunburned, needlessly. Whatever sun lotion, cream, or gel you use, it should have an SPF of at least 15 and it should be waterproof. If your skin is sensitive or your complexion is fair, chances are that you should use a PABA-free product to prevent blistering. Bring long sleeved shirts and pants with SPF protection. They will provide much-needed sun and insect protection. In the evenings and at night, particularly if you fall into that "fair skin and attractive to insects" category, protect yourself against mosquitoes and No-See-Ums.

Is there anything else to watch? Yes, watch your water intake. Plan to drink at least one gallon of drinking water per person per day, just to keep normally hydrated; 4 ounces of water every 20 minutes is recommended.

Health Hazards

Ciguatera

Also known as poisoning by eating seafood, the name ciguatera comes from the Spanish "cigua," a marine snail that the early Spanish settlers in Cuba tried to add to their diet and found poisonous. That particular snail is no longer a part of our diet, but fish carrying ciguatoxin may well be part of your catch. It is a naturally occurring toxin that passes along the food chain and, if it reaches you, will cause nausea, vomiting and vertigo at best (after an initial tingling and numbness), and paralysis at worst. The most suspect species are reef fish: barracuda, eels, red snapper, amberjack, sea bass and large grouper. Since grouper is a staple Bahamian food - every menu features fried grouper, grilled grouper and grouper fingers - this sounds like bad news. The key is to go for the smaller fish (5 lbs or less), and don't eat the internal organs. Does cooking neutralize it? The answer is no. Neither cooking, freezing, marinating or pickling kills the ciguatera toxin.

If you do get ciguatera, what can you expect? Symptoms usually being within two to 12 hours after eating the affected fish. Drink ample fluids. Seek help at a clinic, or call the DAN Ciguatera Hotline in the states. You have two points of contact: 305-661-0774 or fax 305-667-2270 (Dr. Donna Blythe), or 305-361-4619 (Dr. Donald da Sylva). Rest assured, however bad it is, ciguatera is rarely fatal.

Decompression Sickness

The deep dives of places like the Abaco Barrier Reef (where regular dives to 185 feet are offered by local dive operators) can produce, at best, narcosis with all its dangers and at worst, decompression sickness. If you are not in training, and not experienced in deep diving, do not attempt it. If you do go along for the ride, pay particular attention to your safety stops on your ascent, and keep it slow, slow, slow. Don't neglect to have that extra tank, with a regulator hooked up, hanging on a line at your last stop, so that anyone low on air can stay there until your degassing is complete. Just in case you need it, the only working hyperbaric chamber in the Bahamas is at Lyford Cay Hospital on New Providence at 242-362-4025. There is another at Associated Medical Practices on Providenciales in the Turks and Caicos at 649-946-4242.

Jellyfish & Portuguese Man-of-War Stings

Although these are not common in the islands, there is always risk of being stung by jellyfish. Painful lesions form on the skin unless swift action is taken. Muscle spasms can develop in the affected limb, and there may even be nausea, vomiting, dizziness, headaches or irregular heart rate. Treatment starts with immediate removal of any tentacles that are still sticking to the skin. Lift them off (don't scrape with a knife) using a stick or something to prevent them stinging your hand. Rinse the area with seawater and then apply vinegar gently, if you have it. Male urine can be used if there is no vinegar handy in preference to female urine that could introduce a bacterial infection, if the woman, unknowingly, has a urinary tract infection. Then treat the affected area with a topical anesthetic or use a sunburn preparation containing Lidocaine or Benzocaine. If the pain continues, apply Hydrocortisone 0.5% cream. Go to a doctor or the nearest clinic if an infection sets in or muscle spasms continue.

Sea Lice

Sea lice or jellyfish larvae can "bloom" in sea areas at times on a very local basis. Often the larvae come from seagrass that has been kicked up or disturbed, bringing the larvae to the surface. In contact with the human skin, both sea lice and jellyfish larvae parasites burrow into the upper layers of the skin causing a rash, sometimes tenderness, sometimes small pimples, but always irritation and itching. Wash thoroughly in fresh water as soon as possible. Watch for infection. Sometimes the smallest pimple can become infected easily in the saltwater environment.

Swimmer's Ear

Often overlooked, swimmer's ear can be a very painful malady. Anyone who snorkels or free dives, especially without head gear, is susceptible. The trick to avoiding it is to dry out your ears, not with a towel, but a good soak in a drying solution. There is a product called Swimmer's Ear™ in a little blue and white squeeze bottle. Or you can make your own solution of 50 percent white vinegar and 50 percent rubbing alcohol. The trick is to leave the solution in your ear canal. When you return to the boat, lie down, put the drops in your ears and let it soak in each ear a full five minutes. It is actually quite relaxing spread out on the warm deck, soaking your ears. Do this each time you get in the water. Not taking care of your ears can lead to infections or worse, hearing can be impaired and future diving can be jeopardized. For divers, a visit to your physician to have earwax removed before you depart for the islands is a wise idea. Earwax removers like Debrox™ can be helpful between doctors visits.

Bahamian Holidays and Special Events

Public Holidays

New Years Day January 1
Good Friday, Easter, Easter Monday March or April
Labour Day The first Friday in June
Whit Monday The first Monday seven weeks after Easter
Independence Day July 10
Emancipation Day The first Monday in August
Discovery Day October 12
Christmas Day December 25
Boxing Day December 26
If a public holiday falls on a Saturday or a Sunday, it will be switched to the Friday before or the following Monday.

Special Events

January: *Junkanoo.* Just before dawn on New Year's Day, the Bahamian Junkanoo Festival kicks off. It is the party of the year over most of the islands. Nassau and Freeport–Port Lucaya, as the centers of population, stage the largest events, but you can be swept up into Junkanoo just about anywhere. It is a carnival time with extravagant costumes, parades, wild dancing and all that goes with it, and has its roots in a mix of African drumming, Mardi Gras, Carnival in Rio and Haitian frenzy - just about anything you care to name in that line, rolled into one wild celebration.
Exumas (Staniel Cay). New Year's Day Cruising Regatta.
Spring Break: The spring break vacation, wherever it falls, sometime between February and April, has the Bahamas as a premier destination, at least for east coast colleges. The Bahamas, in turn, does much to attract this influx of visitors bent on celebration. Charter boats are a favored means of reaching the islands, but time and distance dictate that the Biminis, the northern Abacos, Chub Cay in the southern Berrys and Nassau, are about as far as this traffic will reach. Dock space along these routes, and popular anchorages such as Honeymoon Cove in the Biminis, may well be crowded.
February: *Exumas.* Annual 5-F's Little Farmers Cay Festival (First Friday in February Little Farmers Cay Festival).
March: *Exumas* (George Town). Annual Cruising Regatta.
April: *Exumas* (George Town). Annual Family Island Regatta.
May: *Long Island* (Salt Pond). Long Island Regatta.
June: *Goombay Summer Festival.* A kind of summertime Junkanoo, the Goombay Summer Festival starts in June, but continues through the summer months generating parades, street festivals and whatever may be decided to whet the appetite of the locals or tempt the tourists.

Eleuthera (Gregory Town). Pineapple Festival.

July: *Independence Day* (July 10). Celebrated by a week of events. Parades, fireworks, regattas and parties with Kalik and Goombay Smashes, mark the remembrance of the ending of 300 years of British rule.

Abacos (Marsh Harbour). Regatta Time, with a series of races starting from Marsh Harbour, Green Turtle Cay, Man-O-War Cay, Great Guana Cay and Elbow Cay.

Andros (Morgans Bluff). Independence Day Regatta.

Cat Island Regatta, held the last weekend in July.

August: *Emancipation Day* (the first Monday in August). Emancipation Day marks the setting free of all slaves in 1834, and is celebrated with a Junkanoo Rushout that starts at 4 a.m. from Fox Hill Village in Nassau and continues all day.

Exumas Regattas at Black Point and Rolleville.

September: *Abaco.* All Abaco Sailing Regatta from Treasure Cay.

October: *Discovery Day* (October 12). The date in 1492 when Christopher Columbus made his landfall in the Bahamas. It is still disputed which island was his initial landing, but San Salvador holds the official title at this time.

Eleuthera. North Eleuthera Sailing Regatta (held between Harbour Island and Three-Island Bay).

November: *Guy Fawkes Day* (November 5). As a curious link with their one-time British overlordship, the Bahamas celebrates Guy Fawkes Day. Guy Fawkes, the leader of a "Gunpowder Plot" to blow up the British Houses of Parliament in 1605, failed and was cruelly executed. The anniversary is commemorated in a macabre but traditional form with firework displays and the burning of a Guy Fawkes effigy.

December: *Christmas Day* (December 25) and *Boxing Day* (December 26) are celebrated throughout the island during December, with tree lightings, concerts with Christmas music under the stars, carol singing and a Masked Ball, together with a Junkanoo Rehearsal for New Year's Day, on Boxing Day morning.

Nassau, Bahamas International Film Festival.

Bahamas Tourist Office Summer Boating Flings

In June, July and August, regular Summer Boating Flings take off from Florida for the Bahamas. These are flotillas of small boats (not less than 24 feet LOA, or for the Biminis, a 22-foot minimum is permitted) guided by a lead boat, which set out from the Radisson Bahia Mar Marina in Fort Lauderdale or the Harborage Yacht Club and Marina in Stuart for either the Biminis or Freeport–Port Lucaya in Grand Bahama, and may extend their range to include either the Abacos, Eleuthera or the Southern Berry Islands. The purpose is to encourage those who might not otherwise dare to cross the Gulf Stream alone, but have always wanted to cruise in the Bahamas. Departures are scheduled almost weekly through the summer. There is a $75.00 non-refundable registration fee per boat, per fling. For information contact the Bahamas Sports and Aviation Center at 800-327-7678, 305-932-0051 or www.bahamas.com/bahamas/boating-fling-schedule.

Fishing Tournaments

Fishing tournaments are held throughout the Bahamas during the year. For information, call local Tourist offices or contact the individual marinas that host the tournaments. Most have their own Web sites.

Further Information and Firm Dates

As this Guide is updated yearly, and at the time of going to print, the dates of many Bahamian annual fixtures may not been set. We show the events that normally fall in each calendar month, giving guidance on the places where you may want to be, or perhaps, if you don't like the crowd scene, places you will want to avoid. Detailed calendars covering the regattas, fishing tournaments, Summer Boating Flings and holidays are obtainable from:

Bahamas Tourist Board, One Turnberry Place, Suite 809, 19495 Biscayne Boulevard, Aventura, Florida 33180 (305-932-0051);

Bahamas Out Islands Promotion Board, 1100 Lee Wagener Boulevard, Suite 206, Fort Lauderdale, Florida 33315 (954-359-8099); or

The Bahamas Sports and Aviation Center, 255 Alhambra Circle, Suite 415, Coral Gables, Florida 33314 (800-327-7678 or 305-932-0051).

Call one of the Tourist Offices for their local information about special events. For additional information, including weather, airline information, diving and marina and restaurant guides, visit www.bahamas.com.

THE TURKS AND CAICOS ISLANDS

Airlines

American	800-433-7300
Air Canada	800-247-2262
Air Jamaica	800-523-5585
Air Turks & Caicos	649-946-4999
Bahamas Air	800-222-4262
British Airways	800-247-9297
Continental	800-231-0586
Delta	800-241-4141
Tortug Air	866-211-1554
US Airways	800-428-4322
WestJet	877-937-8538

Airports

Grand Turk, North Caicos, Providenciales International Airport, Salt Cay and South Caicos have regular scheduled services. Big Ambergris, West Caicos and Pine Cay have private airstrips. Customs and Immigration are at Providenciales airport, Grand Turk and South Caicos. There is an airport departure tax of $23 per person, except for children under two years of age.

ATMs, Banks, Credit Cards and Currency

Banks are open from 9 a.m. to 3 p.m., Monday through Thursday, and until 4:30 p.m. on Fridays. First Caribbean International Bank and ScotiaBank have offices on Grand Turk and Providenciales.

First Caribbean International Bank has a branch on South Caicos that opens on Thursdays. ATMs are located on Providenciales and Grand Turk. Visa and MasterCard are usually accepted; American Express much less so. You need cash outside tourist areas. U.S. dollars are accepted at par.

Boating Regulations

On the face of it, the regulations governing boating in the Turks and Caicos are essentially what you would expect. They are in accord with the North American standard, the Bahamas and, where international regulations apply, the world at large. However, very strict rules are in force with respect to anchoring in the Turks and Caicos, and particularly in the many protected areas designated as National Parks, Nature Reserves, Sanctuaries and Historic Sites. A significant part of the coastal sea area of the Turks and Caicos is protected and, for this reason alone, it is sensible to review the regulatory side of the more important aspects of cruising there.

- No vessel over 60 feet length overall is allowed to anchor in a National Park area except at a permitted large vessel mooring. For this, you must first contact the local harbormaster or the Department of the Environment.
- Anchor only over sand.
- You are not permitted to anchor close to reefs, within 300 feet of any marked dive site or within 400 feet of a nature reserve or sanctuary.
- Damaging coral, either by anchoring over or near coral or by grounding, is an offense. The fines levied in such cases can be substantial.
- Dive sites controlled by the Turks and Caicos Department of the Environment are buoyed. You may pick up one of these buoys if it is unused, but if it is required by a dive boat, you must leave at once. (The peak period for dive site use is 8 a.m. to 3 p.m.). When using a dive site buoy, secure your own line or bridle, about 20 to 25 feet in length, to the buoy penant.
- You are not allowed to land in a sanctuary without a permit from the Department of Natural Resources.

Customs and Immigration, Cruising and Fishing Permits

Customs: Working hours are 8 a.m. to 4:30 p.m., Monday through Thursday; and until 4 p.m. on Fridays. Weekend and holiday rates apply after 4:30 p.m. weekdays, after 4 p.m. Fridays and all day weekends and holidays.

- Boarding and Clearance In: $26 weekdays, $28 weekends.
- Boarding and Clearance Out: $21 weekdays; $23 weekends.
- Boarding and Clearance In and Out; $41 weekdays; $43 weekends.
- Boarding Fee $5. Boarding Fee overtime $6 an hour weekdays; $8 an hour weekends.
- Pre-clearance (before 8 am) $21 weekdays, $23 weekends.

Customs officials prefer a printed crew list if possible. It cuts out some of the paperwork and time.

Cruising Permits: Two per year at no charge, issued when clearing in. Must be shown to harbormasters when moving between islands. Departure Tax $15 per person.

Duty Free Allowance: 200 cigarettes, 1 liter of spirits and $50 personal goods.

Entry Requirements: U.S. and Canadian citizens require current passports, or an original or notarized copy of a birth certificate, together with a government-issued photo ID. Commonwealth countries require a passport and visa obtainable from the British Consulate. Onward return tickets are required.

Firearms: Must have written approval from the Commissioner of Police. Spear guns and Hawaiian slings are illegal.

Fishing Permits: A visitor's sportfishing license, valid for 30 days, costs $15 per person on board. They must be obtained from a Department of the Environment and Coastal Resources (DECR) Office (649-946-2970/2801), or from a marina or a sport fishing charter operator.

Immigration Extensions: $50 per person every 30 days.

Ports of Entry: GRAND TURK: Freighter Dock at South Base.

PROVIDENCIALES: South Dock, Leeward Marina, Turtle Cove Marina, Caicos Marina and Boatyard.

SOUTH CAICOS: Government Dock, Shell Dock at the Seaview Marina.

SALT CAY: the duty police officer has the authority to clear you in.

Re-entering the U.S.

See details under Bahamas Customs and Immigration.

Dress Code

Dress is generally informal, except for fine dining establishments, first-class resorts and some restaurants. Nude and topless sunbathing and swimming are discouraged.

Driving

DRIVE ON THE LEFT! These islands are still a British Crown Colony. Visitors can drive for 30 days with a valid driver's license from their own country. After that, a three-month permit can be issued for $30. Government stamp duty of $15 is payable on each rental car agreement. Liability insurance is charged at $4 per day, and collision damage waiver from $10 per day, plus nine percent airport charge if you pick up a car at the airport. Gasoline is more expensive than in the U.S.

Electricity

120V/60 cycle, the same as the U.S. Outlets fit all U.S. appliances.

Fuel

Grand Turk: Government Dock, Flamingo Cove Marina (diesel only).

Providenciales: Turtle Cove Marina, South Side Marina, Leeward Marina, Caicos Marina and Boatyard.

South Caicos: Seaview Marina

Propane Gas: TC Gas in Grand Turk (649-946-2532), North Caicos (649-946-7243) and Providenciales (649-941-3585).

Language

Although English is the first language, you may hear French, German, Italian, Spanish, Norwegian, Swedish or French Creole spoken by residents from all over the world.

Liquor Laws

The drinking age is 18.

Mail

Post offices open between 8 a.m. to 4 p.m. and to 3 p.m. on Fridays. A one-half-ounce letter to the U.S. costs 60¢, to Canada and the UK 80¢ and to Europe $1. Postcards cost 50¢ to the U.S., 60¢ to Canada and the UK and 80¢ to Europe.

Marriages

The islands are a popular marriage destination. You need to spend 72 hours on island to establish residency, pay a $50 license fee, provide an original birth certificate, passport and proof of marital status. Contact the Registry of Births, Death and Marriages for details at 649-926-2800.

Medical Facilities

See our Goin' Ashore sections for the individual islands. Serious emergencies should go directly to Grand Turk or Providenciales.

Pets and Vets

A valid health certificate is required, stating that the pet is in good health and has a current rabies vaccination. Your pet will be examined by a public health inspector on arrival.

Veterinarians are on Providenciales
Animal House, Dr. Mark Woodring, 649-231-0685.
Turks and Caicos Veterinary Associates, Ltd., 649-946-4353.
Turks and Caicos SPCA, 649-231-3052..

Taxes and Tipping

A 10 percent government tax is added to restaurant and hotel bills; it is customary to tip 15 percent for good service.

Telephones

The area code for the Turks and Caicos Islands is 649. Cable and Wireless provide communication services throughout the Turks and Caicos Islands. Almost all public telephones take a phone card, widely available for sale in $5, $10 and $20 denominations, usually from a store or restaurant near the telephone, or from the Cable and Wireless offices on Leeward Highway, Providenciales or Duke Street in Cockburn Town, Grand Turk. Calling within the islands dial only seven digits, e.g. 946-2200. International calls using American Express, MasterCard or Visa are expensive.

Telephones will accept AT&T, BT and C&W Communications dialing. Local people mostly use cell phones, which are reasonably inexpensive from Cable and Wireless or from the IGA in Providenciales and use with Pay-as-You-Go cards for $20, $50 and $75. In addition, you can take your own personal mobile phone to a Cable and Wireless office and buy a SIM card to be connected. Email cwtci@tciway.tc for more information. Internet and fax services are at Cable and Wireless offices and Internet cafes in Providenciales. The Internet gateway is www.turksandcaicos.tc.

Time Zone

Eastern Standard Time, or five hours behind Greenwich Mean Time. The islands change to and from Daylight Savings Time the same days as the U.S.

Tourist Offices

Old Dock, Grand Turk 649-946-2321
Stubbs Diamond Plaza, Providenciales............ 649-946-4970
provo@turksandcaicostourism.com

Turks and Caicos Holidays

New Year's Day ....January 1
Commonwealth Day ....2nd Monday in March
Good Friday, Easter and Easter Monday .... March/April
National Heroes Day ....4th Monday in May
HM The Queen's Official Birthday ....
.................................Monday after the 2nd Saturday in June
Emancipation Day .... 1st Monday in August
National Youth Day ....4th Friday in September
Columbus Day .... 2nd Monday in October
International Human Rights Day .... 4th October Monday
Christmas Day, Boxing Day .... December 25 and 26

Bahama Waters. Waterway Guide Photography

SKIPPER'S HANDBOOK

Introduction

WATERWAY GUIDE PHOTOGRAPHY

Chapter 1
Stop Dreaming . . . Start Planning

What Are These Islands?

Looking down at the Bahamas Islands from space, one can see an orb of brilliant colors—shimmering seas of cobalt-blue, opalescent sand banks and, extending southeast from the East Coast of Florida, a scattering of shimmering islands and cays united into contiguous groups by dark tongues of deep water. Each large island may stretch 100 miles long, but most of the cays are sparkling, tiny gemstones, linked like precious jewelry, strung together and begging to be treasured.

Islands, Cays, Keys and the Gulf Stream

Let's get these Bahamian names correct right at the start. A cay, pronounced "key," is a small, low-lying island, probably coral fringed, mostly sand on a limestone-coral base. The word comes from the Spanish *cayo* (with the same meaning), which the early Spanish explorers took from Taino, language of the Arawaks, the indigenous island people whose extinction they brought about. It joins many other words, like barbecue (*barbacoa*), canoe (*canoa*) and hammock (*hammaca*), with the same origins. In the United States the word cay still survives today (misspelled) in the name Key West (Cayo Oeste, the westernmost cay).

As for an island, well, that is an island. Something bigger. You could say so big that if you are on one of the cays, it seems like a continental shore. Great Abaco Island, in the cays, is often referred to as "the mainland."

All around this magical area, save for one side, there is the deep water of the southwestern North Atlantic Ocean. It is some of the deepest ocean water in the northern hemisphere. A narrow piece of water, the Straits of Forida, separates the area from the East Coast of Florida. Just 65 miles wide, the Straits of Forida is far more than the continuance of the ocean around the islands. It is the mainstream course of one of the greatest maritime rivers in the world: the Gulf Stream. Immensely powerful, the Gulf Stream flows north at 2.5 knots or more with the dynamic and thermal energy to create nightmarish seas from contrary north winds and, distantly, gives the fortunate shores of its European landfalls exotic plants and mild winters—a climatic imitation of lands 1,000 miles to their south.

A Vast Cruising Ground

If you draw lines around the Bahamas Islands and the Turks and Caicos, you will find you have drawn a northwest–southeast slanting box running from N 27° 25.000' to N 20° 50.000', bounded by W 072° 30.000' in the east and W 079° 20.000' in the west. Try to count the islands in your box and you will lose count after passing the 700 mark. If you try to work out the area contained within your square you will settle for something like 90,000 square miles. Most of it is water. Perhaps it is simpler to say the islands are spread over something like 700 miles of ocean and circled with 900 square miles of coral reefs. The surrounding ocean is deep. Within sight of land it plunges to 3,000 meters/10,000 feet. The land, by contrast, is no more than 62 meters/203 feet at its highest.

The Spanish Nightmare

Is it all ocean? No way. The Spanish called the area the *gran bahamar,* the "great shallow sea." There is nothing like it. The Bahamas, and the Turks and Caicos, are great tablelands of limestone, coral and sand, much like reef-fringed platforms perched on the edge of the Atlantic Ocean. Depths average 3 to 9 meters/10 to 30 feet over much of the Bahamas and Turks and Caicos Banks, but on all sides the ocean drop-offs plunge to depths your depth sounder will never register.

The waters of the shallow seas are something else, offering both clear sailing and a maze of reefs, coral heads and isolated rocks with sand bores too complex and too subject to seasonal changes to be recorded accurately on a chart.

The islands are low-lying and average no more than 30 meters/98 feet in elevation. This could present some identification problems. However, landmarks, antennas, buildings and distinctive vegetation provide welcome signposts, and the cays are relatively easy to recognize when within deck-level sight range.

In the Bahamas and Turks and Caicos, safe navigation depends vitally on colors: the cobalt to turquoise-blue waters, the silver to iridescent-white sands, the coffee brown reefs to shadowy, olive-green sea grasses. And, it also depends on the no-less-vital illumination from the sun. The Spanish, after losing 17 treasure ships off the coast of Abaco in 1595, wisely avoided the sea that they had named. It was certainly no place for lumbering galleons, especially in the late summer and early fall when hurricanes could mean certain death, or in the winter when fierce northers wreaked havoc on the open water.

It is not a bad thing to carry a sense of history as you cruise these waters, but with prudent planning, it is no longer the perilous area dreaded by the Spanish. The Bahamas Islands rate with the Virgin Islands, the Aegean Sea and Polynesia as one of the top boating destinations in the world. And, hardly surprising, thousands of boats cruise the Bahamas each year. What more could be added to a cruiser's wish list than 27°C/81°F water so crystal clear you can count the starfish on the bottom 9 meters/30 feet below your keel, more places to explore than you can find time to visit and more stars in a soft, black-velvet night sky than you have ever seen?

Where to Go In the Bahamas? A Cruising Ground Analysis

The geography of the islands profoundly affects the cruising opportunities for boaters. Where there are strings of cays (e.g. the Abacos, Berrys and Exumas), boaters find diverse cruising grounds with infinite possibilities whatever the prevailing wind. There are isolated beaches to comb, trails and caves to explore and snug anchorages in which to seek shelter or simply hang on the hook watching the clouds drift by. In addition, there are marinas to serve you, secluded resorts to spoil you, bougainvillea-covered restaurants to offer you local cuisine and lively beach bars to pour your goombay punch.

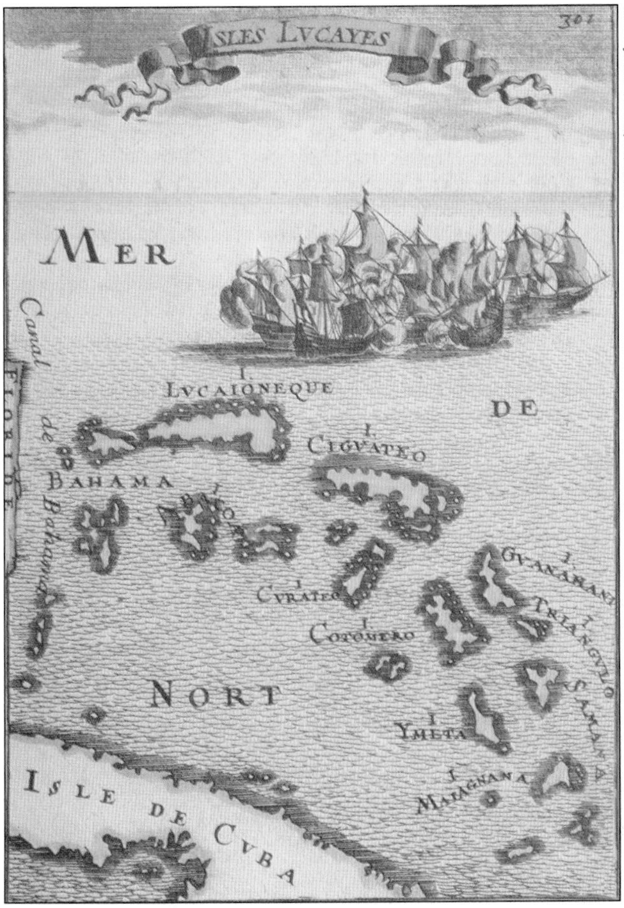

Courtesy Balmain Antiques, Nassau

Ocean Approaches. One of the first charts of the Bahamas, drawn by the French map maker Alain Manesson Mallet (1630–1706). The shape of Cuba had been fairly accurately established by the Spanish by 1650, but the Bahamas were still unexplored, uncharted and a high-risk area.

The bigger islands—Grand Bahama, Nassau, Eleuthera and Long Island—are no less versatile, just a bit more urbanized. Navigating them can entail straight runs along open coasts. There are more marinas, but fewer safe anchorages in which to duck should adverse weather arise unexpectedly. And, with so much territory, walking to see all the sights may be more exercise than you had in mind. However, rental carts or cars are plentiful, and their helpful owners are encyclopedias of local lore. Taxis are readily available, and their friendly drivers are veritable tour guides.

Full-service marinas extend their welcome mats to megayachts and pocket cruisers, alike. At resorts, you are as likely to swim in million-gallon pools with movie moguls or dolphins. Food options range from fresh cooked "take-away" served under colorful umbrellas on the beach to elegant, haute cuisine presented by white-gloved waiters on a mezzanine overlooking a casino. Nightlife options are plentiful from black tie and piano lounges to blue jeans and "rake n' scrape" jams.

Andros Island, the largest of the Bahamian islands at over 100 miles long and 40 miles wide, boasts the third-largest barrier reef in the world. At first glance, it appears to offer the most promising cruising grounds one could imagine, but it deserves due caution. Much of Andros is wilderness—a maze of mahogany and pine forests, scrub brush, marshes, tidal inlets and flats. The barrier reef truly is a barrier, and navigation inside the reef requires care and expertise. For many, these considerations are the whole point of going there! For others, it is too great a challenge.

When choosing where to venture in the cruising grounds of the Bahamas, preparedness and ability, as well as seaworthiness of the vessel, are the critical concerns. In addition, time

Where You Could Go

Where Everyone Goes

- Marsh Harbour and Hope Town, Abaco
- Port Lucaya, Grand Bahama
- Nassau, New Providence Island
- George Town, Exuma

Where the Sailboats Get Together

- Marsh Harbour, Abaco
- Staniel Cay, Exuma
- George Town, Exuma
- Thompson Bay, Long Island
- Black Point, Great Guana Cay
- Round Sound, Eleuthera

Where the Cruise Ships Go

- Gorda Cay (re-named Castaway Island), Abaco
- Freeport/Lucaya, Grand Bahama
- Nassau, New Providence Island
- Little Stirrup and Great Stirrup Cays, Berry Islands
- Princess Cay (Bannerman Town), Eleuthera
- West Bay (Half Moon Bay), Little San Salvador

Where to be Street Wise

- Nassau, New Providence Island
- George Town, Exuma
- Freeport, Grand Bahama

What About the Time Factor?

Time governs two factors, one under your control and the other out of your control. The first is the passage speed and cruising range. The second is weather. If you are unlucky, you might get holed up somewhere for eight days or so. It can happen. Let us assume you have a boat that will average 8 knots on passage. From the east coast of Florida, your target area, from the time factor, works something like this:

A Week to 10 Days: Northern Abacos, Bimini Islands, Grand Bahama, Berry Islands

At Least Two Weeks: Abacos, Bimini Islands and the Berry Islands

A Month: Anywhere in the Northern or Central Cruising Grounds

Over a Month: You can reach the Far Horizons, but if the weather factor is not in your favor, you may find that just one month is not long enough.

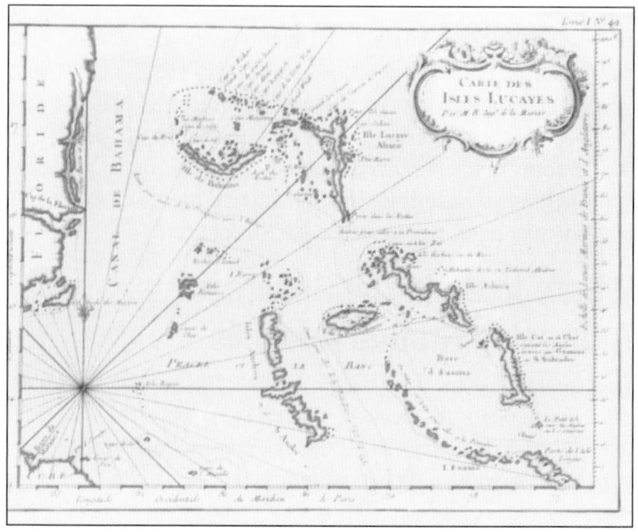

Courtesy Balmain Antiques, Nassau

A chart of the Bahamas by Jacques Nicholas Bellin, 1751.

constraints, fuel and water capacities and airport availability may define your limits. With these factors in mind, the direction in which to point your bow most definitely depends upon your starting point. The following section discusses the different approaches to the Bahamas based on that consideration.

Ocean Approaches

For the ocean voyager, there are as many routes to the Bahamas as there are navigable passes through the fringing reefs and gaps between the islands. On the shorter approaches from the Florida coast, your departure port, crossing route and entry port are determined by your destination cruising ground. Those vessels coming from the south after a long blue-water passage often choose a port of entry based on proximity or on the weather and appropriate shelter. Approaches from the south offer both commercial-like port facilities and smaller, less formal Out Island customs and immigration offices. Base your decision on safety, weather and personal preference. To help maintain low stress on your approach voyage:

- Use daylight to your advantage. Plan your arrival after dawn or before nightfall.
- Time your voyage to transit shallow water when the sun is overhead.
- Simplify your navigation. Double check all waypoints. Use your eyes.

Climate, weather and navigation are critical to safe passage making—particularly eyeball navigation. These are covered in Chapter 2.

Coming From the West: Florida

Bound for the Abacos, the primary routes run to Mantanilla Shoal or Memory Rock and West End or Port Lucaya on Grand Bahama. If you are bound for the Berry Islands, Nassau, the Exumas or Eleuthera, the favored routes are to Great Isaac Light, North Rock Light, Alice Town on North Bimini or Gun Cay Cut.

Departing from Florida entails a Gulf Stream crossing. In general, the farther south you make your departure, the better lift you will get from the Gulf Stream. If you try to fight the current, your crossing will become an unsuccessful, crablike crawl across the Straits of Florida. See Crossing the Gulf Stream in Chapter 2.

Place Names

Bahamian and Turks and Caicos names can be confusing on two counts. The first is repetition. One day we will do a count and see how many Crab Cays, Sandy Cays, Sandy Points and the like we can list. Some doubles can come up far too close to each other, such as the Crab Cay off the northeastern tip of Little Abaco Island and the Crab Cay just north of Green Turtle Cay, but mostly you can figure out which one to focus on.

The spelling of names is another minefield of confusion. Over the last 350 years, place names have been spelled one way, then another, then maybe even a third way. This knock-on effect still shows in our charts today. Is it Man of War or Man-O-War? Powel or Powell? Generally we have tried to use the "newspaper" spelling of place names as it is right now. So from time to time our text names and our chart names will be slightly different versions.

Finally, where variants in naming exist, we call them their charted name. In the Turks and Caicos, the pass we now call Sandbore Channel was once known as Caicos Creek. Big Sand Cay is often known as Sand Cay. And so it goes. Just bear with us.

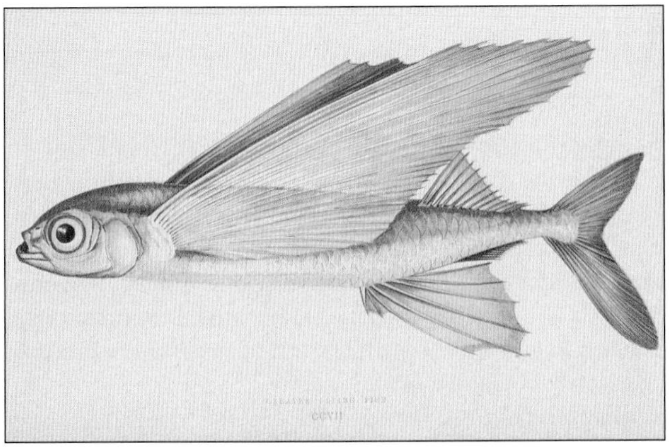

Courtesy Balmain Antiques, Nassau

Antique Print. A Flying Fish.

Coming From the Southeast: The Caribbean

The Turks and Caicos Islands lay squarely in your path to the Bahamas from the Virgin Islands, Puerto Rico or the Dominican Republic. Providenciales makes an ideal stopping point en route. Thereafter you will most likely traverse the deep water to the east of Acklins, Crooked and Long Island before you turn west toward George Town on Great Exuma.

Coming From the Southwest: Havana and the Gulf of Mexico

Perhaps the southwestern approach is the easiest of them all. Just ride with the Gulf Stream as if you were a Spanish galleon and turn to the east when you reach the right latitude to make your chosen landfall.

Charts

A full list of charts covering both the Bahamas and the Turks and Caicos, including electronic charts, is given in the Blue Pages. These are obtainable from Bluewater Books and Charts in Fort Lauderdale, Boat U.S. and West Marine, as well as marine stores specializing as suppliers of marine charts. Small marine stores often carry charts of their local areas.

The Tropic of Cancer

The line of latitude running along N 23°30.000' marks the limit of the sun's summer migration into the Northern Hemisphere (the tropic of Capricorn sets the reverse limit in the south). Cross these lines and you are in the Tropics. In other words, coming from North America, you have gone south. Real south. But more of this later under The Far Horizons.

What Are You Looking For?

Closest to the United States Abacos, Andros, Berry Islands, Bimini Islands, Grand Bahama

Best Air Services to the United States Abacos (Marsh Harbour and Treasure Cay), Bimini Islands (South Bimini), Grand Bahama (Freeport), New Providence (Nassau), Eleuthera (North Eleuthera and Rock Sound), Exuma Cays (Staniel Cay and George Town), Turks and Caicos (Providenciales)

Many Islands and Short Cruise Legs Abacos, Exumas

High Life Grand Bahama (West End, Lucaya), New Providence (Nassau, Paradise Island, Cable Beach, Lyford Cay) Turks and Caicos (Providenciales)

Pretty Towns Abacos (Hopetown), Harbour Island (Dunmore Town)

Best Diving Andros, Bimini Islands, Out Islands, Turks and Caicos, Cat Cay, Eleuthera, Grand Bahama, Long Island, Rum Cay

Sportfishing Abacos, Andros, Bimini Islands, Eleuthera, Cat Island, Rum Cay, San Salvador

Exploring Everywhere!

Real Adventuring Andros, Bight of Abacos, Berry Islands, Little San Salvador, Grand Turk, Ragged Islands

NASA

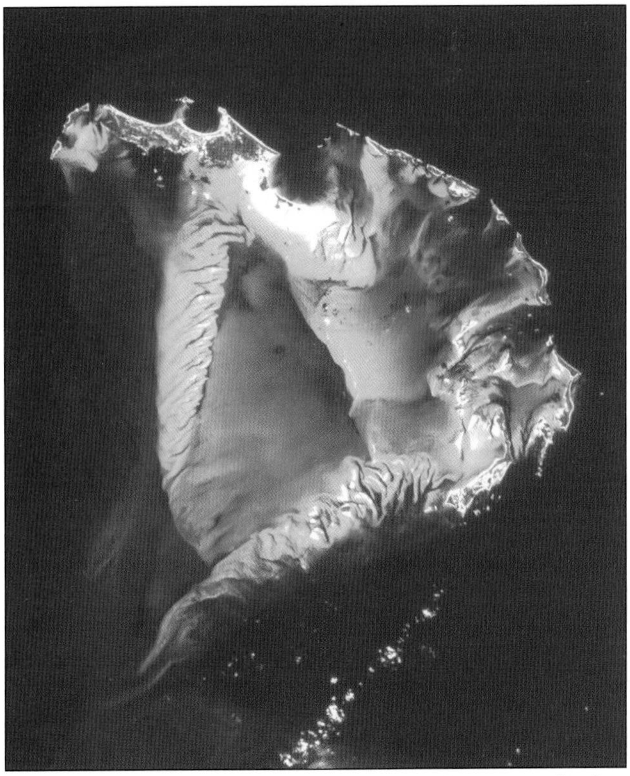

Berry Islands. Photograph taken at an altitude of 234 nautical miles, N 25°08.000' / W 77°09.000.' Skylab, Mission 4.

Bahamas Weather

by Chris Parker

Weather will play a large part in your safety and enjoyment as you explore the Bahamas, so it's worth your time and energy to gain a basic understanding of weather patterns, have tools to obtain weather forecasts and examine forecasts intelligently.

Weather patterns and seasons: In the following discussions, I use abbreviations and capital letters seen in weather forecasts. FRONT = cold front; HI = high pressure system; LO = low pressure system; TROF = Trough; WAVE = tropical wave, etc.

In general, trade winds generated by the Azores-Bermuda HI pressure system are often light and from E to SE in direction during summer (May-October), and E to NE at a stronger velocity in winter (November-April). Size, shape, orientation and strength of HI vary greatly, often in a pattern lasting one to two months. FRONTs are strongest mid-winter (December-March), moving predictably through the area. During fall and spring, FRONTs are often weaker and slower moving, but are more difficult to predict. The following describes each season's typical weather in more detail.

Winter and cold FRONTs: From December through most of March moderate conditions with 15- to 25-knot E-NE winds driven by the Azores-Bermuda HI can last days or weeks, and are typically stronger the farther south you lie in the Bahamas. When an approaching Cold FRONT shoves HI eastward, wind becomes lighter E-SE. Pattern of wind velocity and clocking from NE-E-SE-S-SW can help you gauge strength of an approaching FRONT. Generally, wind clocking NE-E-SE-S-SW over a short time (12 hours), with steady or increasing wind speed, suggests a strong and fast-moving FRONT, maybe accompanied by strong gusty wind and violent squalls. Gradual clocking wind of a decreasing velocity suggests a weaker FRONT. Wind direction may be the best signal of an approaching FRONT – if wind clocks NE-E-SE-S then hesitates, pay careful attention to what happens next. Continued clocking to SW suggests FRONT will pass you, while backing to SE suggests FRONT will stall before reaching you. Warm Bahamian waters tend to modify most FRONTs, so southeast Bahamas see fewer and weaker FRONTs than northwest Bahamas. Weather in northwest Bahamas is similar to Florida Keys, even though the north Bahamas lies over 100 miles farther north.

Spring: In spring (late March into May), systems move more slowly, fewer FRONTs reach the Bahamas, and some of them become stationary, then either dissipate or linger as a TROF. These TROFs tend to occur on a smaller regional scale than HIs and FRONTs, and are often not mentioned sufficiently in forecasts, but they can produce nasty, squally weather over an area up to a couple hundred miles across, and can persist for days. Worst weather often occurs near the north end of TROF, along its axis, where strongest convergence (wind blowing from various directions toward a point) lies. Late spring brings warmer, calmer weather with fewer FRONTs, weaker HI pressure, occasional TROFs, but also more moisture resulting in more squalls. Even in the absence of significant weather features, scattered afternoon thunderstorms become common. Azores-Bermuda HI is frequently shoved south into Bahamas in spring, resulting in longer periods of light and often variable wind, with west wind not unusual in the Northern Bahamas.

Summer: Azores-Bermuda HI is a more moderate player in summer, supplying long periods of warm, humid air, with 10- to 15-knot wind from E-SE. In May and June, FRONTs seldom get past NW Bahamas. Eventually West-to-East progression of FRONTs shifts sufficiently far N to allow tropical weather (which moves from East-to-West) into the Bahamas. Instead of looking to the N and W for approaching weather, begin looking S and E for approaching WAVEs, which can create an environment favorable for eventual development of more significant tropical weather, such as tropical storms and hurricanes. Hurricanes do impact the Bahamas. Some forecasts are good at anticipating significant tropical weather, but forecast language is subtle – if you are cruising the Bahamas in summer, you should get weather information firsthand or from a trusted source so subtle wording is not filtered out along the way. If you trust someone else's translation of the weather, you may be letting them make your decisions.

Fall: The progression of summer into fall usually occurs in October and November, as waters begin to cool, and FRONTs begin to move into the region. Weather can be similar to spring, but the risk for Tropical weather continues through December. Those who accept this risk are rewarded with uncrowded anchorages and often good weather.

In addition to a basic understanding of the weather, you should arm yourself with the tools to obtain good weather forecasts. Once in the Bahamas, your communications capabilities often dictate which weather products you can access. You should consider communications and weather-gathering options carefully, and work with a trusted dealer or consultant before you commit to a large initial and in some cases ongoing investment of money and time purchasing, learning and using this gear. Ask specifically to see an example of the weather products offered for your intended destinations in the Bahamas, and consider carefully whether these products will allow you to make intelligent tactical decisions.

Chris Parker is well-known in the cruising community for his accurate and timely weather forecasts for the Bahamas and Caribbean. He is the author of "Coastal and Offshore Weather: The Essential Handbook" and the chief forecaster for the Caribbean Weather Center, Ltd.

Chapter 2
The Lessons of 500 Years of Voyaging in Bahamian Waters

Climate and Weather

The Bahamas Islands can be divided into three zones by climate: north, central and south. The climatic line between north and central dips southward to include both North Andros and New Providence Island with the Biminis, the Berrys, Grand Bahama Island and the Abacos in the northern zone. The dividing line between central and south runs almost due east-west just below the southern point of Long Island, placing the Crooked–Acklins archipelago, and everything on the same latitude and to the south, in the southern zone. When referring to the Bahamas, this Guide includes the Turks and Caicos. Because of climate and weather, they are included in the southern zone. When there are differences, notably in the hurricane season, it is noted.

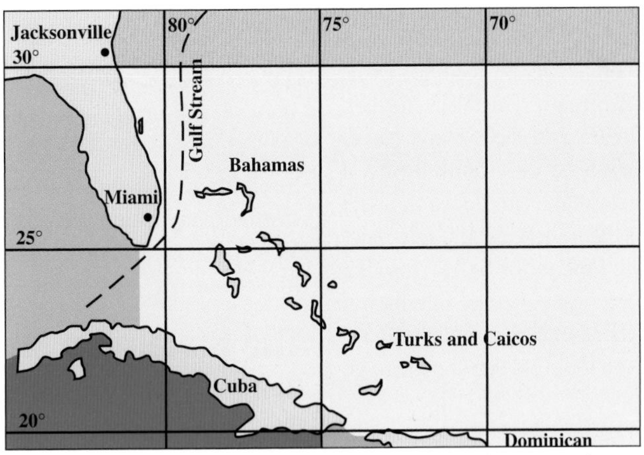

NOAA North Atlantic Weather Forecast Area. Southwest North Atlantic south of N 31° and west of W 65°.

The Northern Zone: In the north, expect colder winters, more wind and marginally more rain. These islands are close to the North American continent and are affected by its weather. Temperatures can fall to as low as 10°C/50°F. The good news is that these blasts of cold continental air never last for long. In the summer, the northern zone enjoys much the same climate as the rest of the Bahamas. Overall, the north has the highest rainfall in the Bahamas, an average of 115 days per year. The summer months are the primary rainfall producers.

The Central Zone: Farther south, one can look forward to a warmer average temperature in winter. In addition, if a norther comes, it will be milder than in the north. Generally, the temperature in winter will not fall below 21°C/70°F. The summers are the Bahamian standard. Hot, tempered by the trade winds and wet at times, for these are the rainfall months. This zone averages 95 days of rain each year.

The Southern Zone: The south is rarely affected by continental weather, except possibly by the whip end of higher winds if the weather is bad up north. Winter temperatures are higher, 24 to 28°C/75 to 80°F. In summer, add 10°F to that. The south has less rainfall annually than the two more northern zones, averaging around 90 rain days per year. Most of this rain falls in the spring and fall.

To simplify things, figure that the northern islands are sub-tropical with a Palm Beach County, FL climate. The central zone, still sub-tropical, is more like the Florida Keys. The south is low-island, similar to the northern Caribbean.

The Hurricane Zone: What about hurricanes? The Bahamas, like the East Coast of the United States and the islands of the Caribbean from Barbados northward, lie in a hurricane zone. June through November is hurricane season. August, September and October are the high-risk months. Does this count the Bahamas out for summer cruising? The answer is no. The islanders expect two to three bad storms a year. This said, winter or summer, hurricane season or not, it makes sense to study Bahamian weather patterns before you sally forth.

The Bahamian Winter

The North American mainland is the driving force behind Bahamian winter weather. What happens in Canada and the continental United States inevitably affects the Bahamas—sometimes a day or two later, sometimes almost at once. If an Alberta Clipper brings sub-zero temperatures right down across the Eastern States, it will be chilly as far south as George Town in the Exumas. If winter storms driving down from the northern quadrants blast Florida, the prevailing southeast Bahamian winds lose and the North American "norther" takes over, dominating weather from the Abacos to Nassau and as far south as the out islands. Sometimes the effects of a norther are felt as far south as Puerto Rico.

Northers

The change from autumnal to winter weather patterns starts around mid-November. The winter-pattern wind cycles are relatively predictable. In the Bahamas, as on the east coast of Florida, the wind first veers to the south and then to the southwest as a cold front starts driving down from the north. As the cold front nears, the winds shift to the northwest, then to the north and finally to the northeast. The strongest winds usually come just ahead of the cold front. Prepare for sustained 15- to 25-knot winds with stronger gusts and fast moving, sometimes violent, squalls. Following a front, winds typically become north, then northeast. The strength of the high-pressure system will determine wind velocity and how long it takes them to moderate.

A norther can last for days or blow through within 24 hours. Sometimes a second norther follows on the heels of the first so fast that the winds shift from northeast or east to northwest, and there is no break in the action. Other times, just about when the norther seems blown out, it recharges itself and blows another two days. As the norther works itself out, the wind moves around to the east and then stabilizes from the southeast, its favored direction.

Northers are never surprises. Just pay attention to North American weather. Eastern United States weather forecasts and Nassau Radio provide ample warning. In the Bahamas, the wind shifts are obvious, and the dark clouds build up conspicuously. However, wind velocity can increase surprisingly fast and the rainfall can be torrential.

These factors command careful note of the weather cycle before attempting to cross the Gulf Stream. During a norther, there are wild seas in the Gulf Stream and steep waves over the banks. Once placid anchorages can become boiling pits of dragging anchors. The prudent cruiser makes all decisions with a watchful eye on the weather. Northers increase the necessity to identify appropriate shelter where you are or before moving on. A norther does not necessarily keep you penned in a harbor or captive in an anchorage. Sailboats can take advantage of the wind direction, and powerboats, given the right sea state, can go largely where they desire.

Northers can make the winter sound like no season for cruising in the Bahamas, but that is just not true. Normal winter conditions are 21 to 27°C/70 to 80°F temperatures, 7- to 16-knot southeast winds, daily sunshine and occasional squalls to wash the salt off your decks. The famous colors of the water are always there. The water temperature is around 23 to 24°C/73 to 75°F. And, on average, winter water visibility is 18 to 30 meters/60 to 100 feet.

Northers bring cooler weather and give you days when you are holed up, anxious to move on. But, when they pass, the northers also leave behind a greater appreciation of the exceptional air and water clarity that transforms these islands into living works of art. If the northers get you down and seem to be stacked one after the other like airplanes trying to land at a busy hub, work your way south. The farther south you go, the less you will be troubled by the tail ends of the storms that plague the commuters of the Mid-Atlantic States and the citrus growers of Florida in the winter months.

Rages

Incredibly rough seas can build up astonishingly fast on the barrier reefs fringing the islands. Normally navigable cuts through the reefs become virtually impassable. This is the sea state the Bahamians call a "rage." Any risk of rage conditions must be taken very seriously. It is prudent to seek local advice before attempting a passage through the reefs at any time.

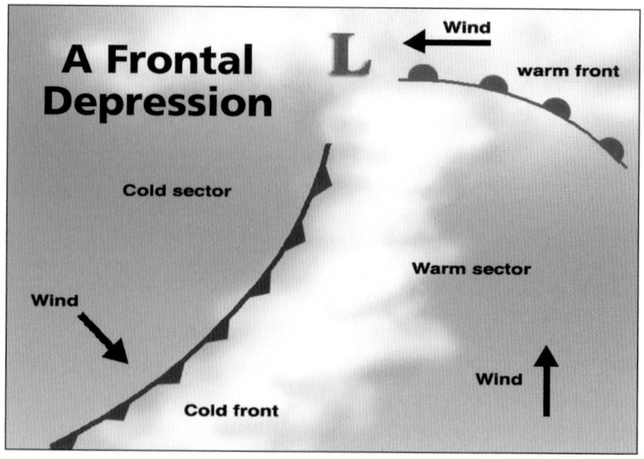

Janet Wilson

The trigger of change is a depression. Here, in a cold front, a counterclockwise flow of air around low pressure, a spiral marked by clouds and rain. Cold air comes in from the northwest. Warm air is sucked in from the south, which rises above the cold air, causing wind sheer and rain. The wind veers. A falling barometer is one of the warnings of a developing front.

In addition to wind, current and tide, distant North Atlantic storms can create swells that produce rage phenomena. You will not survive to relate the experience if you attempt to force your way through a reef passage during a rage.

The Bahamian Summer

By summer, wind patterns settle, influenced by the trade winds that provide breezes from the southern quadrants for most of the time. The wind strength moderates to around 5 to 12 knots, just enough to fill a sail. Calm nights are more frequent than in the winter. Water temperatures rise to 29°C/85°F, and water visibility drops slightly to 15 to 21 meters/50 to 70 feet.

Thunderstorms

Summer months feature thunderstorms. Anvil-headed cumulonimbus clouds build up over super-heated land and shallows, and everything that goes with a thunderstorm when they let loose occurs—rain as heavy as lead pellets, hail, lightning, thunder and violent (60-knot) downdrafts. Microbursts, with winds exceeding 100 knots, are not unheard of, but are very rare events.

The towering summer anvil heads are one-off, one-cloud dramas. These isolated thunderstorms are always observable. They are one-hour affairs for the most part and normally develop and hit their point of discharge in the late afternoon. Out in the ocean, on a blue water passage, thunderstorms "go critical" during the night hours. When on passage, stay well clear of a developing thunderstorm. Radar is a great aid for thunderstorm avoidance. If the thunderstorm's direction of movement can be determined—this is where radar really helps—alter course to pass it on the side, away from the direction of its motion (i.e., go where it has been, not where it is going). If you are at risk, shorten sail, batten down and be prepared to heave-to.

Deborah Spanton

An approaching front, the clear sign of a marked imminent change. Expect temperature change, an immediate increase in wind, the wind to veer and low visibility. As the marked edge of the front passes through, the weather will settle into a new pattern (depending on whether it is a warm front or a cold front). If it is only a weak front, the disturbance in the more normal regular weather pattern may be brief, perhaps a matter of hours, or even less.

The darkening weather of a rain squall. At best just rain, but never take it on trust. The front-like line of rain may carry high wind, sudden changes of wind direction and gusts that are surprisingly strong. Rain in subtropic and tropic waters is rarely just a gentle shower.

Towering, turbulent clouds, a highly visible danger signal. Expect thunder and lightning, heavy rain, visibility of less than 300 feet, a marked drop in temperature and wind that at worst could hit gusts of between 40 and 60 knots. It will not last, but unless you are in safe, deep water, well clear of land and reefs, it is a threat to be taken seriously. Take precautionary action early (anchor somewhere safe and batten down). Your warning is the clouds. The accompanying fall in barometric pressure usually comes as it hits.

Cherokee Sound, approaching storm. WATERWAY GUIDE PHOTOGRAPHY

Lightning Strikes

How likely is it that you might be struck by lightning? The marine insurance division of Boat U.S. gives these figures (the base being any given year):

Auxiliary Sail	0.6%	6 out of 1,000
Multi-hull Sail	0.5%	5 out of 1,000
Trawlers	0.3%	3 out of 1,000
Sail only	0.2%	2 out of 1,000
Cruisers	0.1%	1 out of 1,000
Runabouts	0.02%	2 out of 10,000

You always hope it will never happen to you. The chances are, statistically, that it never will. Our cruising editor has been hit once, in the Bahamas. They had left their boat secured in the inner harbor of Sampson Cay for a week to fly back to the States. When they returned, they found the induced surge of a near-miss lightning strike had taken out their electronics and "fried" their gel-cell batteries. Just carry insurance, and have faith in those statistics.

Waterspouts

In the summer months you will also see waterspouts that, although they may move erratically, can usually be avoided. Do not be tempted to sail through one. A waterspout is a marine tornado, short-lived normally, but still dangerous.

There is a reasonably reliable way to predict in the morning whether there will be scattered thunderstorms later in the day. About mid-morning, say 10:00, check the sky for small puffy white cumulus clouds. Around noon, look again to see if the clouds have thinned out somewhat by appearing to stack themselves on top of each other so that they look like tall lumpy cylinders. If they have, you may expect them to continue to scatter, but a few of them will grow into thunderstorms by late afternoon. As they develop, they will be visible for many miles, so observe their positions and direction of motion and be ready to take evasive action if necessary. Usually, it is wiser to start your course deviation sooner rather than later, not only from a safety standpoint, but also to minimize the total distance to be sailed in the diversion.

Don't Be Surprised by the Weather

Bahamian weather never ceases to surprise. Yes, there are patterns to the winter months and patterns to the summer months, but folks have crossed the Little Bahama Bank in early March in dead calm, literally counting starfish on the bottom as they passed. Later, when the summer pattern should have been established, there has been seven inches of rain in 24 hours at Man-O-War Cay along with 45-knot winds; and this "nasty" came as part of a three-day package of unrelenting gray skies and rainstorm after rainstorm with winds flicking round the clock like a cow's tail in the black fly season.

Overall, the Bahamas have a weather factor that still rates them as one of the best cruising areas one can find. Have faith. Bad weather never lasts forever, and the good days and the good weeks are magic.

Calling the Shots Whatever the Weather

The Critical Sea Areas

As you come to know the Bahamas, you will realize that there are certain sea areas, the ones we call the critical sea areas, where you will get no farther if conditions are not right. None of these areas is impassable, but there are bad weather systems (particularly in winter) that will require waiting for a weather window before you can continue. It is like a board game with squares marked "THROW A SIX TO MOVE ON." You will have to wait until you get that "six."

It is understood that bad weather can discourage you from setting out on just about every leg of every passage, wherever you are going. But you would be foolish to not take account of what is going on out there in the dark blue or across the long stretches of green bank every day, wherever you are. The seven areas we have named are major potential problem zones. Keep them in mind.

One rule of thumb is to take a wind state of 15 to 20 knots as a small craft advisory. This is an upper limit for many passages, particularly the longer runs across the banks; but so much depends upon your vessel. How small is small? There is a vast difference between a vessel over 50 feet with significant weight and two turbo-charged engines and a vessel under 26 feet with a mast and nine horsepower outboard as auxiliary power.

But, what if you are throwing dice, and there is no way that "six" is going to come up in the near future? You are stuck on the wrong side of one of the critical sea areas, and things aren't going your way? Just read on...

The Throw-a-Six Squares

Crossing from or to Florida
The Gulf Stream

Between the Northern and Southern Abacos
Whale Cay Passage

Between the Northern and Central Cruising Grounds
The Chub Cay – North Andros – Nassau Triangle
The Hole in the Wall (South Abaco) sea area

The Central Cruising Grounds
The Devil's Backbone Passage

The Southern Cruising Grounds
The Cape Santa Maria offshore area

Far Horizons
The Crooked Island and Mayaguana Passages

The Turks and Caicos Islands
The Caicos and Turks Island Passages

The Cure for Cabin Fever

Twenty-four hours of bad weather with 6 to 12-foot seas can spoil anyone's day. Four to five days is enough to develop cabin fever. Acute cases of cabin fever, while not fatal, are serious. The results—crew desertions, threats of divorce, resolutions to sell the boat, disorientation and the kind of depression that makes jumping ship seem a good option. Bad news! But, the good news is it can be prevented. There are cures.

Some folks actually enjoy the experience. Overcoming the elements is seen as a worthwhile challenge to crew and boat, as well as the perfect opportunity to catch up on reading, small chores or sleep. It is a great time to pop the top on the potted meat, get out the crackers and eat off paper plates. If you and your crew are not from this mold, read on.

For those who find the prospect of being stuck down below for several days of high winds and high seas disheartening, here are some ideas:

- Be prepared! Plan ahead! Travel sooner, rather than later or stay put. Don't get caught in an isolated anchorage, no matter how secure.
- Choose a "big" island haven where there is a good marina with secure berths, an airport, rental cars, resorts and territory to explore. Or, choose a small cay with ferry service or air links to all of the above.
- If there is any possibility you might want to leave your boat for a while, factor that in. Choose a good, safe place - one fellow travelers recommend and trust.

Hurricane Categorization

CATEGORY	PRESSURE	WIND SPEED	SURGE
1	Above 980 mb (Above 28.91 in.)	64-82 knots (74-95 mph)	4-5 ft. (1-1.5 m)
Visibility much reduced. Maneuvering under engines just possible. Open anchorages untenable. Danger of poorly secured boats torn loose in protected anchorages.			
2	965-979 mb (28.50-28.91 in.)	83-95 knots (96-110 mph)	6-8 ft. (1.5-2.5 m)
Visibility close to zero. Boats in protected anchorages at risk, particularly from boats torn loose. Severe damage to unprotected boats and boats poorly secured and prepared.			
3	945-964 mb (27.91-28.50 in.)	96-113 knots (111-130 mph)	9-12 ft. (2.5-3.5 m)
Deck fittings at risk and may tear loose, anchor links can fail and unprotected lines will chafe through. Extensive severe damage.			
4	920-944 mb (27.17-27.91 in.)	114-135 knots (131-155 mph)	13-18 ft. (3.5-5.4 m)
Very severe damage and loss of life.			
5	Below 920 mb (Below 27.17 in.)	Above 135 knots (Above 155 mph)	Above 18 ft. (Above 5.4 m)
Catastrophic conditions with catastrophic damage.			

Hurricane Season

The North Atlantic–Caribbean hurricane season runs June 1 to November 30. August, September and October are the worst months. Seasonally, an average of ten depressions or tropical waves develop into tropical storms and reach "named" status. On average, eight of these will become severe storms and ultimately reach hurricane status.

Our research suggests that since 1492, the Bahamas have been hit by 72 hurricanes and the Turks and Caicos by 13. These figures give you an idea of the statistical risk of cruising in the hurricane season.

Perhaps greater caution than long-term statistical analysis comes with NOAA's short-term analysis. Since 1995, seven out of nine hurricane seasons have resulted in high severe storm activity. We are, like it or not, in the most active period for Atlantic Ocean hurricanes since our records started.

No one would wish to risk being caught by a hurricane, but in many ways the hurricane months offer the best cruising in the Bahamas, and are not necessarily ruled out of your voyaging calendar as a high-risk period. Hurricane forecasting is accurate and will give you, from the first warnings of the development of a tropical wave, plenty of time to think ahead. When the warnings move up a notch into a tropical depression you should really focus on the weather and your planning moves into an active phase. It follows that to understand the dynamics of hurricane development and learn the rules of hurricane avoidance, you must first be familiar with the language of the hurricane season.

Tropical Waves

A tropical wave is a trough of low pressure. A wave shows itself with falling barometric pressure, overcast skies and the arrival of a succession of mini-fronts, high wind, rain and thunderstorms, with periods of relative calm and rain in between. A tropical wave is born in the Atlantic Ocean, and its movement is always westward. The trough can pass through quickly or linger, nearly stationary, for days. You could say that a wave is an embryonic hurricane. If the pressure dropped dramatically, and the winds started to revolve around the center of low pressure, that is exactly what you would have.

The forecast of a wave may persuade you to sit out its passing in comfort rather than set out on your next passage, and it will interrupt your sunbathing. If you are at sea, a wave is no severe threat to your safety, but it does bring with it all the characteristics of a succession of line squalls, which means reefing if you are under sail, closing hatches and concern for the dinghy you may be towing.

Tropical Depressions

A tropical depression is the next stage. It is the development of the wave into a system of clouds and thunderstorms with a definite circulation, always counterclockwise in the Northern Hemisphere. Top sustained winds are no more than Force 7 (28–33 knots), but gusts will be stronger.

Tropical Storms

A tropical storm is the next step in the evolution of a hurricane. By now it is getting serious. At the outset, sustained winds are up to Force 9 (41–47 knots), and gusts will be stronger. The counterclockwise rotation continues, and the storm will have a recognizable center. It is important to realize that the rotation of the storm is not simply circular but takes the form of a spiral, with the wind working inward toward the eye of the storm. This understanding plays a part in your storm evasion tactics if you are caught out at sea. A severe tropical storm moves into the Force 10 or Force 11 field with wind strength increasing to 63 knots.

The forward speed of a storm usually averages around 10 knots in its early days, and its course, which can be erratic, usually holds west and north. Warm water generally gives a tropical storm the energy burst it needs, and the Gulf Stream often becomes a hurricane interstate highway for this reason.

Hurricanes

When the sustained wind speed of a tropical storm exceeds 63 knots, you are in the Force 12 bracket and you have a hurricane. From then on, although hurricanes are classed in order of magnitude as the wind speed goes up, from a cruiser's point of view, it hardly matters. The highest recorded gusts have hit 175 knots, but the start point, 64-knot winds, is bad enough. The forward speed of a hurricane is likely to average 20 to 25 knots. The message is that you cannot outrun a hurricane.

Wind and waves are the commonly understood lethal agents of a hurricane. What may not be known by many is that a doubling in wind speed results in four times the increase in wind pressure. Take a baseline of 0.1 pound force per square foot for a 5-mph (4.3-knot) wind and, quite apart from wave action, the devastating force of a hurricane or major storm in terms of pure punch can be understood.

Above high winds and waves, hurricanes carry with them a third agent of destruction called storm surge. A dome of water up to 20 feet high is "vacuumed" skyward by the spiral rotation of the hurricane. This massive pile-up of water may have as much as a 100-mile diameter. When the hurricane hits land, particularly if this coincides with high tide, storm surge is often the principal cause of hurricane death and damage.

Storm Warnings

Hurricane forecasts are issued giving a five-day lead time, with a margin of error of some 350 miles. You should start taking an active interest in weather forecasts when you hear that a tropical depression has developed, and from then on plot its progress until it is no longer a threat. Long before you might find yourself listening to a tropical storm watch (or even worse a hurricane watch), you should have anticipated the weather, and be out of the danger area.

The final countdown goes in stages:

Tropical Storm Watch	**36 hrs**
Tropical Storm Warning or Alert	**24 hrs**
Hurricane Watch	**36 hrs**
Hurricane Warning or Alert	**24 hrs**

Playing it Safe in the Hurricane Season

If you are cruising through the islands during the hurricane months, the rules you must follow are:

- Plot the location of every hurricane harbor or potential hurricane hole along your route.
- Set out with the extra ground tackle and extra dock lines on board to secure your boat against a severe storm, be it at anchor, in mangroves or whatever location you select.
- Listen to a reliable weather forecast service at least once every day. Remote as it may seem, you must know what is happening in the North Atlantic Ocean and in the southwest Caribbean Sea between N 7° and N 20°.

Securing Your Boat

The guidelines are straightforward common sense.

- Mangroves are ideal. Canals are good. Any landlocked water is better than open water. Try to get away from other boats. Their lines may not hold.
- Secure your boat. Use every line you have and all your ground tackle. Allow for storm surge.
- Reduce windage. No canvas or curtains of any kind should be above deck.
- Batten down, and leave the boat. Find shelter ashore. Consider flying out of the Bahamas. Your life counts. The boat can take care of itself; and you should have insurance.

In the Worst Case

If you are caught at sea, your survival tactics are totally dependent on accurately plotting the position and course of the hurricane, and plotting radial distances from its center (the eye of the hurricane) to establish estimated danger zones:

Distance from Eye	Wind Speed	
150 miles	Force 8	(34–40 knots)
100 miles	Force 11	(56–63 knots)
75 miles	Force 12	(over 64 knots)

Every hurricane develops its own unique intensity and footprint. These figures are no more than a generalization, but indicative of the wind speed and sea state you can expect. It is also vital to know your position in relation to the eye, and the predicted track of the hurricane, so you can decide which way to turn. The one vital question is this: Are you in the dangerous semicircle or the navigable semicircle?

If you don't know where the center of the hurricane is and can't plot it, if the wind is veering, you are in the dangerous semicircle. If the wind seems steady, or starts to back, you are in the navigable semicircle.

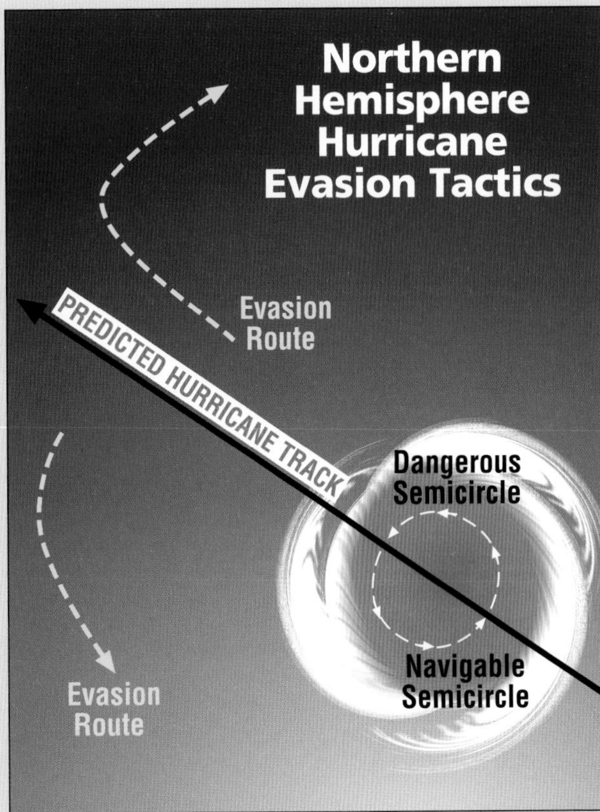

The Dangerous Semicircle

The most dangerous half of the storm is the northern semicircle, the part that lies to the north of the path of the hurricane. It is called the dangerous semicircle because if you are caught in this area, you are in the path of the hurricane and its spiral rotation will take you deeper into its center. Your only hope is to try to break away to the north, and then get behind the worst of it.

Your immediate evasive action is to get away with all the speed you can make, keeping the wind 10 to 45 degrees on your starboard bow, and keep altering to starboard to take you above and eastward away from the storm.

The Navigable Semicircle

The southern semicircle is known as the navigable semicircle, simply because your chances are better there. The hurricane will be moving away from you rather than toward you, and the direction of the wind will blow you away from the storm.

Your immediate evasive action is to turn to bring the wind on your starboard quarter, make all possible speed, and keep turning to port to pass below and eastward away from the storm.

Hurricane Tracker

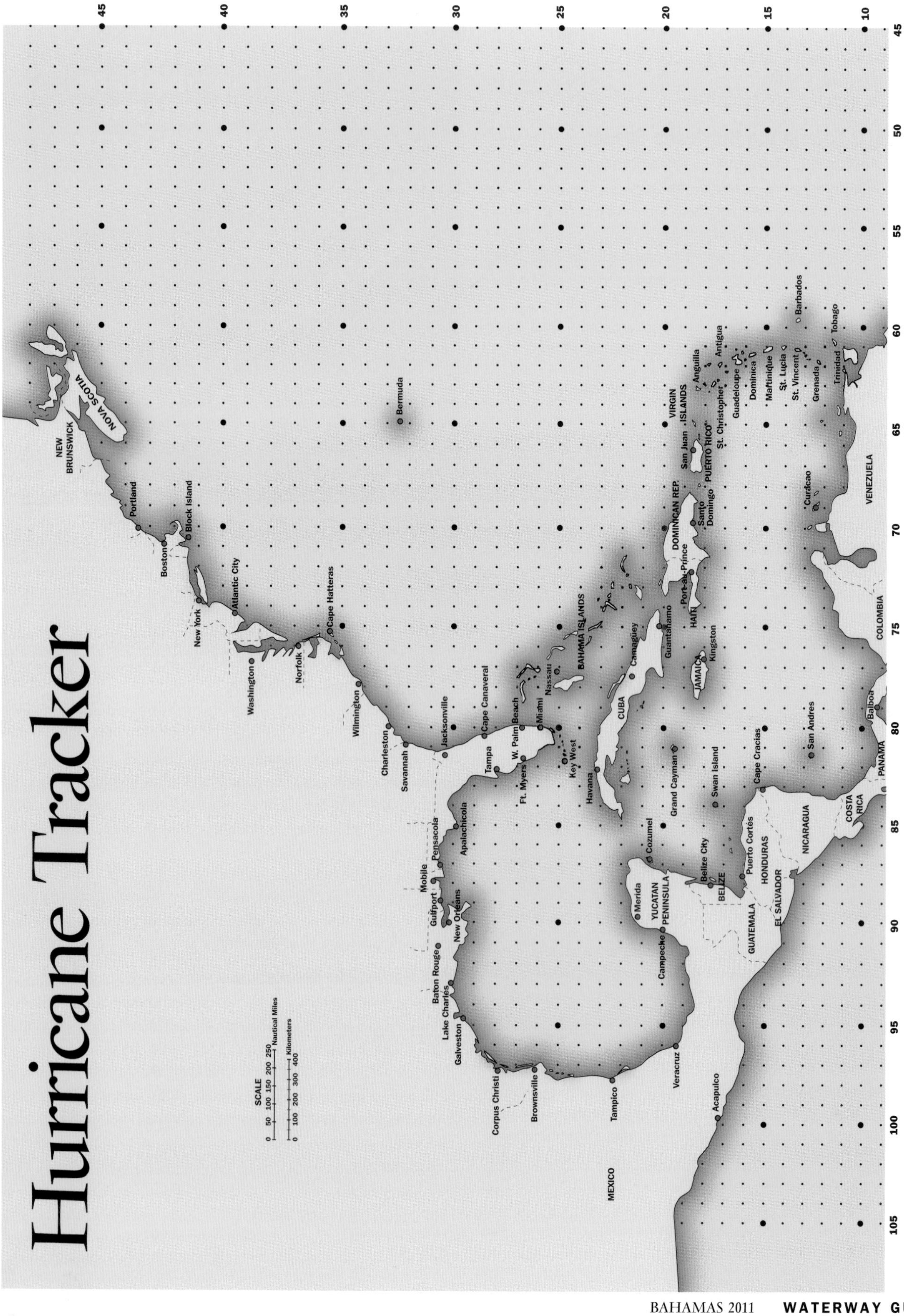

You get the idea. Once you have decided to stay put or made it to a snug place, the world is your oyster. For those who need action, these are better alternatives to just accepting that you are walled in by 30-knot winds and a horizon of piling whitecaps. Do rent that car, venture forth and explore! Or, take the ferry or flight to the bigger neighboring island, and do the same. Maybe it is March; fly back to the States and file your tax return. Don't like that idea? Fly to some islands you can't reach when you cruise. Cat Island, Long Island, maybe Provo? Most flights between islands are affordable. Go for two or three nights and savor the ambience. Then, dream and make plans to take the boat there someday, too. You might begin to look forward to being "weathered in."

Closing Thoughts on the Weather

Hurricanes are the most destructive island weather hazards, but such storms are the exception, not the rule. In addition, they are predicted quite accurately and tracked hour-by-hour. For today's cruisers, lack of attention, forethought, preparation and other oversights or miscalculations cause most of the lost boats and lives. Alcohol and arrogance, sometimes in deadly combination, can act in concert with bad weather, leading to tragedy. Sitting out a thunderstorm in the lee of an island or returning to port early because of freshening unfavorable winds may seem overly cautious. But, you can still enjoy "being there," and you will live to enjoy another day!

Crossing the Gulf Stream

For vessels crossing to the Bahamas from the east coast of Florida or returning to Florida, the Gulf Stream is the dominant navigational consideration. Don't just think of the Gulf Stream as a current. It is a 45-mile-wide river, more powerful than you can imagine. You can't see the speed of its wash like standing on a river bank; but it is there, flowing northward at an average speed of 2.5 knots, day and night, in every season. It is hard to believe at first that it even exists when you look east out over the ocean from a Florida beach.

In winter, you can sometimes mark the Gulf Stream by the steam rising from its warm waters, many degrees warmer than the colder coastal water. In winter too, and whenever a norther is blowing, the sea horizon is often jagged and saw-toothed. That is when there are "elephants" out there, giant square waves; high seas kicked up by the Stream's determination to win its way north against the wind, come what may.

In summer, you can identify the Gulf Stream by a color change to an ultramarine deep blue in which sometimes, if the sun is right, you will see light dancing in its depths. You can guess you are in the Stream when you see blond patches of Sargasso weed drifting northward. You know you are there when the water temperature clicks up something like two degrees above the shore-side ocean temperature, and your GPS reveals that you are moving 2 to 5 knots faster to the north than your knot meter indicates. Anglers, in tune with the rhythm of ocean life, can fix the boundaries of the Gulf Stream by the run of pelagic gamefish.

Planning to Cross the Gulf Stream

Crossing the Gulf Stream in any kind of vessel can best be compared to the progress of an ant trying to traverse an airport's moving walkway. The ant might well have wanted to make a direct crossing. But, inevitably during its transit, it will be taken beyond its target. For every hour a vessel is in the Stream, it will be pushed about 2.5 nautical miles to the north. Like it or not. If a vessel is crossing from a departure point, more or less on an equal latitude to its destination, its first concern is to minimize the time it will be in the Gulf Stream. If the vessel is departing south of its destination, then it is a different story. Then the goal is to stay on that walkway for as long as possible to enjoy the free ride north before turning toward the destination.

NOAA weather broadcasts give daily information about the Stream—its width, speed, distance offshore at different points and its temperature. But, for navigation, it is sensible to assume that the entire distance you have to run from departure point to a destination lying anywhere along the W 79°15.000' line of longitude will be subject to a 2.5-knot, north-flowing current.

If your powered craft averages 12 knots or more, the drift effect of the Gulf Stream is of less concern. A relatively small initial offset, around 10 nautical miles or so, or continual on-course adjustments can take care of it. If your vessel is slower, you must figure compensation more accurately, and ensure that your departure port is far enough south. The goal is to use the Gulf Stream to your advantage, not fight it all the way across. There are various ways to calculate crossing tactics to minimize the negative effect and maximize the positive lift of the Gulf Stream. The simplest way is three easy steps:

- Take your distance to run, and divide it by your average speed to get your passage time.
- Multiply the passage time by 2.5, the average speed of flow of the Stream.
- The result is the distance the Gulf Stream will take you north off a direct course. Factor in an offset heading to take care of that, and the Gulf Stream will bring you to your destination.

There are as many opinions on when to depart Florida and at what time to arrive at your Bahamian waypoint as there are vessels crossing the Gulf Stream. Night crossings are still done, but they present the danger of traveling amidst the ever-growing number of freighters and cruise ships in very busy shipping lanes to and from Florida. Dawn departures provide safer passage in the shipping lanes and arrival in Bahamian waters with the sun behind you. If you decide to continue travel across the banks, night passage will be calmer and safer there than in the Gulf Stream.

It all boils down to how fast you can travel, where you are headed, what conditions would be best to find when you get there and when you plan to stop. A vessel departing for and planning to visit North Bimini will have a much different crossing schedule than one headed non-stop to Nassau. Regardless, pay attention to the weather and don't develop forward-only

Crossing the Gulf Stream

One of the problems the mariner encounters when crossing the Gulf Stream is how to allow for the set of the current. Fast boats have little trouble correcting the effect of the Gulf Stream, but boats with operating speeds of between 5 and 10 knots must make major corrections. Here are some corrected courses and estimated elapsed times at varying speeds under normal sea conditions.

This table should be used only as a guide, not as a reference. Varying wind and weather conditions will influence your passage.

This table should give a general idea of how long your crossing might take under normal conditions. The chart below depicts those rhumb line crossings noted in the tables and can be used in conjunction with your LORAN or GPS headings.

- The Gulf Stream was arbitrarily figured at 001 degrees true, 2.5 knots for runs to Lake Worth Inlet and at 002 degrees true, 2.6 knots, for all other runs.
- Variation used was 004.5 degrees west.
- Crossings to Lucaya extend beyond the Gulf Stream's effect. Thus, the rhumb line distance shown is that used in calculations for the current, followed by the rhumb line distance to complete the run without current to offset.
- Some routes to Lucaya could not be a single, direct run. They were computed to a point off Southwest Point on Grand Bahama Island, then to the buoy off Bell Channel.
- All runs are not the reverse of others. Miami to West End is calculated, but not West End to Miami because the Gulf Stream would be too much "on the nose." Lake Worth Inlet to Bimini is not calculated for the same reason.

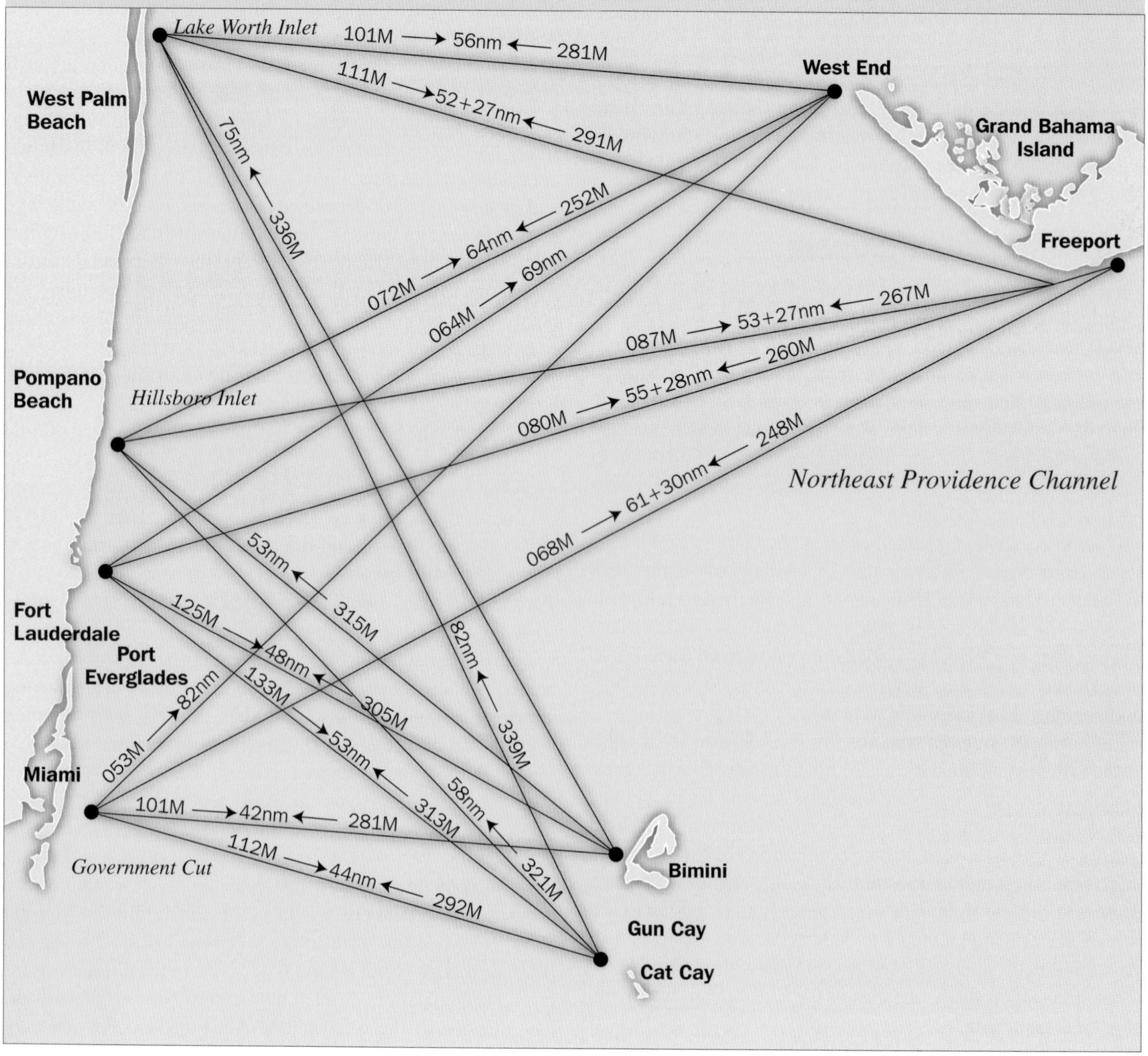

Eastbound to the Bahamas

RLC RLD	From To	Speed 5 CS EET	6 CS EET	8 CS EET	10 CS EET	12 CS EET	15 CS EET	20 CS EET
101	Lake Worth Inlet	131	126	119	115	113	111	108
56	West End	13/20	10/31	7/30	5/52	4/49	3/49	2/50
111	Lake Worth Inlet	140	135	129	125	123	120	118
52	Lucaya	19/04	15/04	10/45	8/23	6/54	5/27	4/02
+27	(via SW Point)							
72	Hillsboro Inlet	100	95	89	85	83	81	79
64	West End	11/24	9/32	7/15	5/52	4/56	4/00	3/02
87	Hillsboro Inlet	118	112	106	102	99	97	94
53	Lucaya	16/20	13/22	9/54	7/53	6/34	5/16	3/57
+27	(via SW Point)							
64	Port Everglades	89	85	79	76	74	72	70
69	West End	11/28	9/43	7/30	6/08	5/11	4/13	3/14
80	Port Everglades	109	104	98	94	92	89	87
55	Lucaya	16/10	13/22	10/00	8/01	6/42	5/23	4/03
+28								
125	Port Everglades	154	148	142	139	136	134	132
48	Bimini	14/38	10/57	7/22	5/36	4/31	3/31	2/34
133	Port Everglades	159	154	149	145	143	141	139
53	Gun Cay	17/20	12/47	8/29	6/23	5/07	3/57	2/53
53	Miami	74	71	66	63	62	60	58
82	West End	12/33	10/48	8/29	7/00	5/58	4/54	3/46
68	Miami	94	90	84	81	79	77	74
61	Lucaya	16/29	13/50	10/31	8/30	7/09	5/46	4/23
+30								
101	Miami	132	127	120	116	114	111	108
42	Bimini	10/03	8/28	5/37	4/23	3/37	2/52	2/08
112	Miami	142	137	130	127	124	122	119
44	Gun Cay	11/49	9/04	6/17	4/50	3/57	3/06	2/17

Westbound to Florida

RLC RLD	From To	Speed 5 CS EET	6 CS EET	8 CS EET	10 CS EET	12 CS EET	15 CS EET	20 CS EET
281	West End	251	256	263	267	269	271	274
56	Lake Worth Inlet	12/33	10/01	7/15	5/42	4/43	3/45	2/48
252	West End	224	229	235	239	241	243	245
64	Hillsboro Inlet	19/41	14/42	9/53	7/29	6/02	4/42	3/26
291	Lucaya	262	267	273	277	279	282	284
52	Lake Worth Inlet	15/57	13/06	9/44	7/46	6/28	5/11	3/54
+27	(via SW Point)							
267	Lucaya	236	242	248	252	255	257	260
53	Hillsboro Inlet	19/29	15/20	10/54	8/30	6/59	5/31	4/06
+27	(via SW Point)							
260	Lucaya	231	236	242	246	248	251	253
55	Port Everglades	21/17	16/33	11/38	9/01	7/23	5/09	4/18
+28								
248	Lucaya	222	226	232	235	237	239	242
61	Miami	25/27	19/25	13/10	10/15	8/20	6/31	4/47
+30								
336	Bimini	320	322	326	328	329	331	332
75	Lake Worth Inlet	10/45	9/22	7/28	6/13	5/19	4/23	3/23
315	Bimini	290	294	300	303	305	307	309
53	Hillsboro Inlet	8/44	7/25	5/44	4/41	3/58	3/14	2/28
305	Bimini	277	282	288	291	294	296	298
48	Port Everglades	8/38	7/12	5/28	4/25	3/43	3/00	2/17
281	Bimini	250	255	262	266	268	271	273
42	Miami	9/38	7/38	6/16	4/55	4/04	3/14	2/25
339	Gun Cay	324	326	330	332	333	334	335
82	Lake Worth Inlet	11/35	10/07	8/05	6/44	5/47	4/46	3/42
321	Gun Cay	298	302	307	310	312	314	315
58	Hillsboro Inlet	9/08	7/49	6/06	5/01	4/16	3/29	2/41
313	Gun Cay	287	292	297	301	302	305	307
53	Port Everglades	8/53	7/31	5/47	4/43	4/00	3/15	2/29
292	Gun Cay	262	267	274	277	280	282	285
44	Miami	8/59	7/18	5/23	4/17	3/34	2/52	2/09

KEY. RLC: Rhumb line Course (degrees magnetic); RLD: Rhumb line Distance (nautical miles): CS: Course Steered (degrees magnetic); EET: Estimated Elapsed Time (hours/minutes)

EXAMPLE. The Rhumb line Course from Lake Worth Inlet to West End is 099 degrees magnetic, over the Rhumb line distance of 56 nautical miles. At 5 knots, you would steer a magnetic course of 129 degrees to offset the effects of the Gulf Stream. The passage would take roughly 13 hours and 20 minutes.

vision. Be vigilant about frequent checks for other vessels to starboard, port and behind you! Don't become another victim rundown by an inattentive skipper traveling on autopilot. And, don't forget that float plan.

Weather

The Gulf Stream is a constant, reckonable force. The weather is not. Listen to the forecasts. Believe the bad ones. Don't trust the good ones! Go to the beach and look out over the ocean. What is happening out there?

The Gulf Stream Rules

To make a successful Gulf Stream crossing:

- Never set out in adverse weather, or risk outrunning the onset of bad weather. Be especially wary of winds from the north. You want pussycat conditions, not a wildcat!
- Always time your arrival in the Bahamas for daylight. Preferably between dawn and noon.
- Don't single-hand. If something happens to you, Murphy's Law will take over. Self-preservation is the name of the game, not macho image-making. The Florida Straits is no place to be when you are in real trouble.
- If you are crossing in a small boat, go in convoy with similar boats or with another boat whose cruising speed matches your achievable speed, which, depending on the sea state, may be very different from the speed you can achieve in calm water.
- If you are making the crossing for the first time, or you are anxious about it (you may have reservations about the competence of your crew if something happened to you), team up and make your passage in company with another of your kind. Then get together for a celebration meal after your safe arrival!
- Always have enough fuel (even on a sailboat) to motor the full distance against head seas and arrive with not less than 20 percent of your fuel remaining.
- Always have a working VHF radio with a backup (hand-held?) VHF.
- Check that you have a working depth sounder, working lights, a flashlight, an air horn, charts, binoculars, distress and smoke flares and a Type I lifejacket for every person on board.
- If you are on a sailboat or an open boat, have a safety harness or fitted tether for every person on board with a secure anchor point.
- If you can afford an EPIRB (Emergency Position-Indicating Radio Beacon), have one, or rent one for the crossing.
- Let a friend know when you are leaving. Call when you arrive. If you don't call after your forecast arrival within a time equal to one third of your anticipated passage time, the friend should contact the Coast Guard. Leave them your float plan with the make, length, color and callsign of your boat, your route, your time of departure and how many people you have on board.

The most difficult and dangerous time for any vessel to cross the Gulf Stream is when the wind is from the north, including the northeast and the northwest. Whether you are running a 180-foot motor yacht or skippering an 18-foot sailboat doesn't matter—northerly conditions are definitely not the ones in which to cross. Remember that the Gulf Stream is flowing north, at 2.5 knots. When the wind blows from the north, it is like rubbing a cat the wrong way; all the fur kicks up and the results are the "elephants" we mentioned earlier. High, ugly waves as closely spaced as elephants holding each other's tails in a circus parade. In those conditions, the Gulf Stream is not where you want to be.

Wait until the weather forecasts sound good and look good, too. Even then, be prepared for unexpected weather. If uncertain, don't take a chance on the weather and try to grab what seems to be a window if you haven't got the speed to get there quickly and safely. We all know the pressure of deadlines—you only have "X number of days" for your holiday, or you have a flight to meet somewhere. However, safety must be the priority. Because of the Gulf Stream, the Florida Straits is a very hazardous stretch of water when the weather turns against you. In adverse conditions, it can be a killer.

Landfalls and Warnings

To the north of West End, the tall casuarina trees of Sandy Cay (nine nautical miles south of Memory Rock and seven nautical miles north of West End) are a useful landmark. There is a light on Indian Cay, immediately north of West End, but it is often hard to pick up and unreliable. West End's water tower is prominent, and the approach to Old Bahama Bay Marina is straightforward. Freeport has approach buoys, as do the marinas between Freeport and Port Lucaya.

To the south, tiny, uninhabited Great Isaac Island has a reliable 23-nautical-mile range light. Gun Cay has a lighthouse that works some of the time. But, it remains that your arrival in Bahamian waters, unless you are taking the Northwest Providence Channel route on to Nassau, is best timed for daylight. It is safer because lights can fail or be obscured in rain, and it is less stressful. More detailed navigational advice is given in the separate island group sections of this Guide.

Returning to Florida

Navigation on the return passage to Florida poses no landfall problems. You will pick up the loom of the lights of the East Coast up to 50 nautical miles away at night and condominium and office tower blocks around 10 nautical miles out on a clear day. It all depends on your height above the water. You can't miss Florida. There is 360 miles of it right in front of you.

Navigation in the Islands

The Global Positioning System (GPS)

When the U.S. Department of Defense first released GPS into civilian service, Selective Availability (SA), which deliberately introduced errors affecting all civilian-received

The colors of Bahamian water. (Not to be used for navigation.) Waterway Guide Photography.

GPS signals, was imposed on grounds of national security. Under SA, GPS positions were somewhere within a 984-foot radius circle of your true position. You had no way of knowing what the error was. It was constantly changing as the timing sequence of satellite signals varied.

Selective Availability was discontinued in 2000, and today only atmospheric distortion and the limitations of your own GPS receiver will affect the accuracy of your read-out. The Wide Area Augmentation System (WAAS), initially designed for aviation use, is now the standard in marine service. WAAS is accurate to within 3 meters/9.8 feet.

Now the cautions! All of our navigation systems depend on charts, be they paper or electronic. The charts are as good as the surveys that produced them. In areas not frequented by a high volume of commercial traffic, the U.S. National Hydrographic Office rates chart updating as less than high priority. NOAA has a massive backlog in re-charting prime commercial traffic areas alone. In the Bahamas and Turks and Caicos, despite the United Kingdom Hydrographic Office's updating and reprinting of charts, base surveys in many areas date back to the days of sail alone and its accompanying technology. Your GPS position may be "spot on" in fixing your location on this planet, but the chart you see on your screen or on your table is probably not remotely as accurate. Be aware of this.

BTC towers, George Town, Great Exuma.
Waterway Guide Photography.

GPS Datum

The GPS Datum used in this Guide is WGS84. This is compatible with the National Oceanic and Atmospheric Administration (NOAA) NAD83 Chart Datum.

Courses: True or Magnetic?

This Guide's courses and headings are given in true rather than magnetic simply for fundamental accuracy. You can convert true to magnetic as you wish. Whichever way you elect to go, take care to set your GPS and electronic navigation programs accordingly.

Navigation Marks

The nature of their world dictated that Bahamians would be very competent seaman. Born and raised within sight of the sea, nurtured on a diet of conch, spiny lobster and fish and more often than not transported by boat to work, worship or celebrate, the establishment of navigation marks has never been a high priority to the residents. They know the reefs, channels and cuts from childhood and can read the waters as if the colors were a map spread before them.

In the past, navigation marks erected by British overlords were regarded with suspicion and at times destroyed or deliberately misplaced. The only source of income for many islanders came from recovering wrecks and profiting from salvage. There are navigation marks in the islands today, but their maintenance is spotty and reliability questionable.

Essentially chart, compass, depth and eyesight are the only navigational tools that can be counted on. Radar can help, particularly with landfall identification, but your own eyes are vital. In the Bahamas, the best rule to follow is if you can't see, don't move. In other words, don't risk running inshore passages at night or in bad weather. In particular, don't move if all the Bahamian colors are lost, and you can't read the water.

BTC Towers

The similarity of low-lying Bahamian cays and islands make identification difficult and sometimes really confusing. There are few natural land features prominent enough to help fix a position. Time and time again, it is the man-made features that help. The greatest aides are the radio towers erected by the Bahamas Telephone Corporation. The BTC towers, faint against the sky at a distance, are the certain indicator of a settlement. Once you have picked up your BTC tower, you have it made.

The Effects of Wind and Wave

Coral is so slow growing that a reef will hardly gain visible height in a thousand years, but sand and sandbars move with currents and swells and, especially, storms. Just as the bars and shoals of the Florida East Coast inlets are never constant, so the underwater profile of much of the Bahamas is always changing.

Be aware that no chart can serve as more than a warning that shoal waters exist in a general area and can never show you the passes through the shoals in the year in which you are cruising. Severe storms and hurricanes rearrange the contours of the seabed, eliminate navigation marks that may not be replaced for years and destroy dwellings and uproot trees, completely changing the profile and appearance of the islands and the cays.

Waypoints and Units of Measurement

We have greatly simplified our waypoint system, which originally covered both pre-GPS and post-GPS position fixing. We have now gone entirely for GPS. Our waypoints are shown in degrees and minutes north of the Equator (22°19), and latitude west of Greenwich (73°03), followed by hundredths of a mile (.30), separated by an oblique stroke (N 22°19.300' / W 073°03.300').

Before the advent of GPS, the terminal measurement for fixing a position was seconds: 1 second = 30.88 meters/101.33 feet. On your GPS log count this equates to 0.083. If you want to switch between the two systems, it is more simply put: 30 seconds = .50. Celestial navigation is still worked on degrees, minutes and seconds.

In our **Useful Tables and Measurements**, in the front of this Guide, we provide you with a bridge between both systems. We have run both in tandem, and have had no problems switching between them.

Our waypoints are intended to help you set your routes. In some places, a waypoint may appear to be set unnecessarily far off the apparent course. If this strikes you as strange, look forward or back along our suggested track. What we've tried to do is simplify navigation by reducing waypoints to a minimum, in other words going for longer single legs rather than short legs with endless changes of heading to work around no-go areas.

We take no responsibility for the accuracy of our waypoints, nor can we guarantee that a course line drawn between any two waypoints will give you safe, navigable, obstruction-free water. The ultimate responsibility for pilotage is yours.

Lady Mathilda on Hogsty Reef. WATERWAY GUIDE PHOTOGRAPHY.

Eyeball Navigation

Most of us have heard about eyeball navigation. It is the learned art of reading depth contours by color—the way you have to do it while you are there, otherwise you will be on the reefs. As a first timer, it sounds like the kind of skill that can only be acquired after many seasons, or maybe after you have left at least three keels lying on Bahamian reefs. The reality is very different.

Eyeball navigation is no more than using one's eyes to pick your way forward, rather than taking a course off the chart and panicking when your depth sounder shows 1.2 meters/4 feet of water. Navigating the Bahamas is eyeball stuff. There is nothing tricky. The dangers are color-coded. All you have to know is the code.

The colors to learn are blue, green, yellow, brown, black, white and some shades in between turquoise and aquamarine. The last, in-between shades, are the colors that make Bahamian waters seem like nowhere else on earth—a transparent green with a touch of blue that looks like it is being floodlit from below. Estimating depth in ocean water with the clarity of a Florida spring seems impossible at first. Are you in 1.5 meters/5 feet, or is that starfish 5.4 meters/18 feet down? But you soon learn that color is the give-away.

First, you need polarized sunglasses. They reduce glare, thereby enhancing your ability to read water and protect your eyes from harmful UV radiation. Gray tints, which minimally distort color, reduce brightness and protect against glare. Reflective coatings reflect about 50 percent of the light that strikes them. With proper sunglasses, surface reflection is reduced, and you can see into the water. But, most importantly, the colors are enhanced.

Sunlight

The position of the sun is key to eyeball navigation. You need the sun to bring the colors of the water alive, and you need the sun as a searchlight working to your advantage rather than as a blinding light in front of you. The optimum is to have the sun fairly high in the sky and behind you. The worst situation is to find yourself making your way through unknown waters into a rising or a setting sun.

Overcast days and rain make eyeball navigation difficult. If you have a tricky passage immediately ahead, and you are caught by a rain squall, hold off until you can read the water. Even on sunny days, the shadows of moving clouds can suddenly confuse the underwater map you are reading. If those dark patches are in motion, they are clouds. Again, you may have to hold back until you can see what the cloud's shadow has been concealing.

The Colors

Let's take the underwater color sequence shade by shade, explaining the variations you will experience from your cockpit:

- Dark blue is deep ocean water.
- Light blue is around 9 meters/30 feet, the depth found at the edge of the banks. You are safe, however surprised you may

1. Safe, deep ocean water (San Salvador).

2. Going from ocean to shore or bank (Samana Cay).

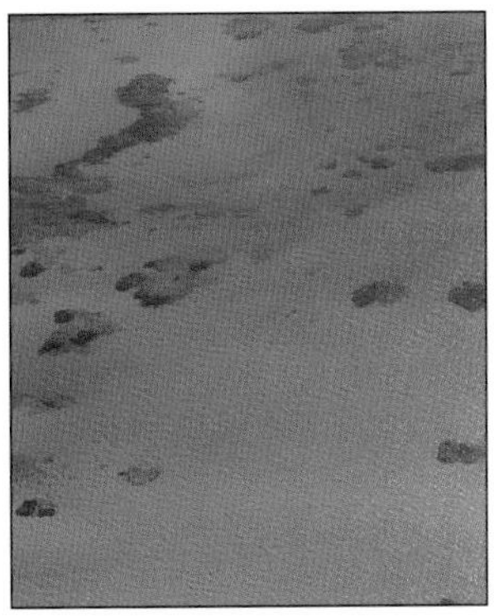

3. Ocean shoaling to reef (Samana Cay).

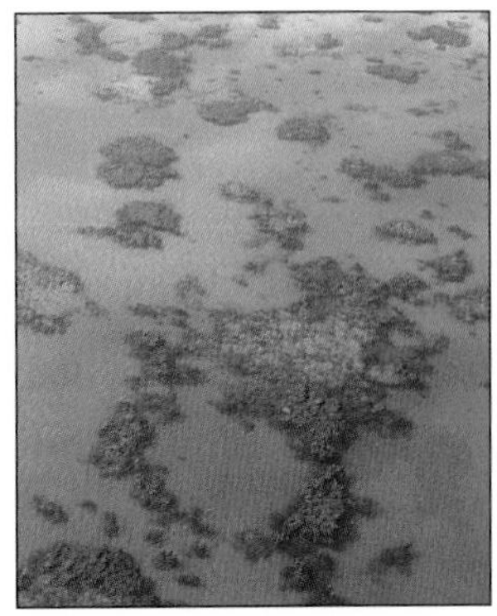

4. Broken coral, 2.7 meters/ 9 feet.

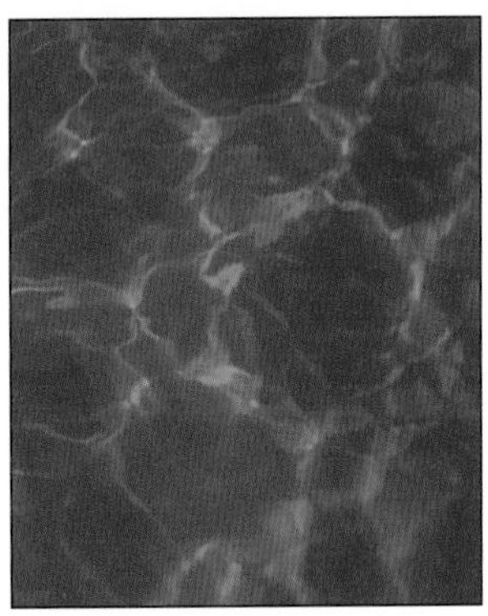

5. Bank water, 9 meters/ 30 feet or more.

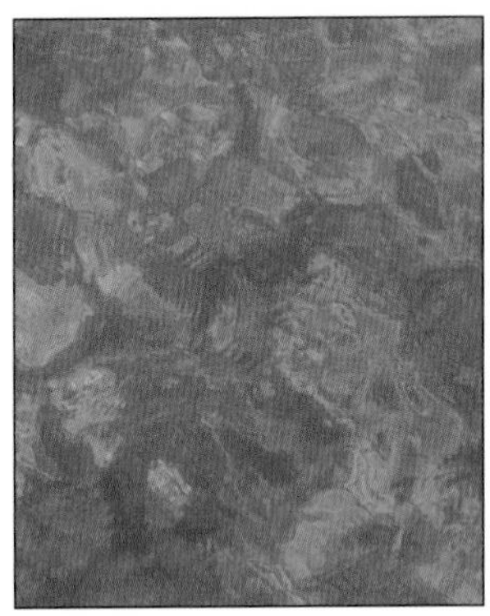

6. Bank water, 3.6–4.5 meters/ 12–15 feet.

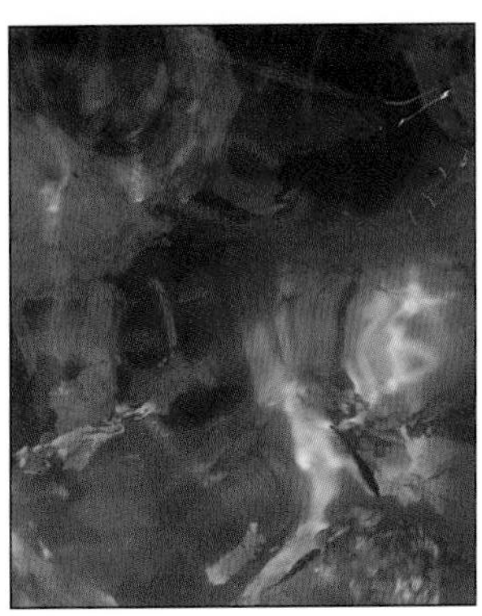

7. A small coral head.

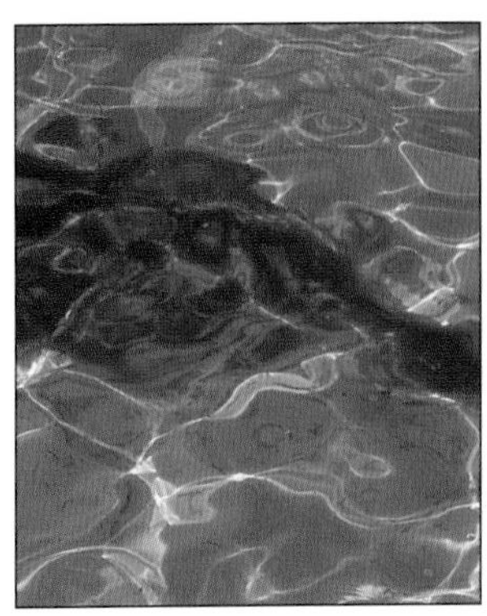

8. Coral or limestone rock just under the surface.

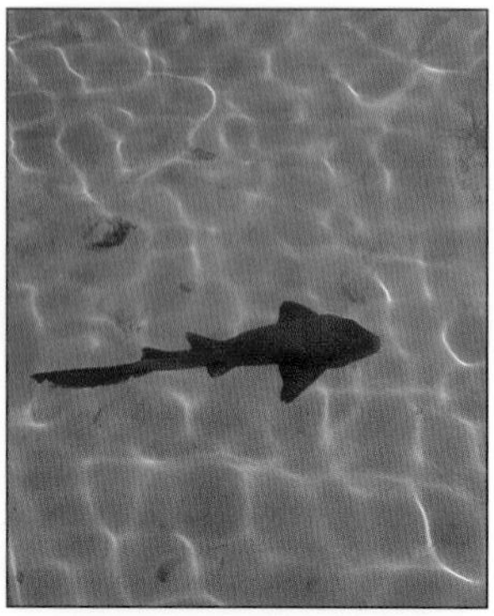

9. 1.5–1.8 meters/5–6 feet (and a nurse shark).

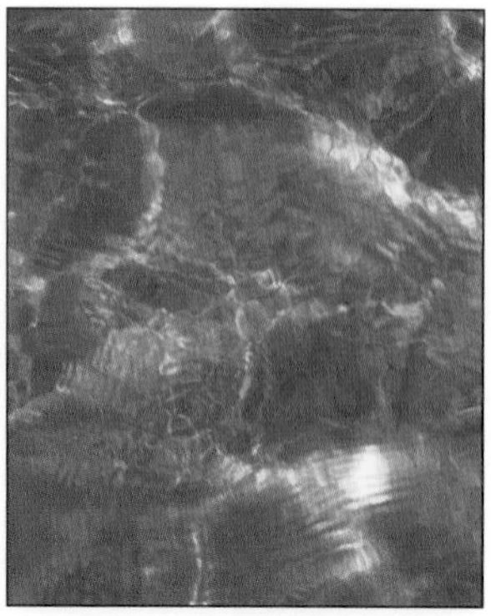

10. Warning color of reef or grass (most likely grass).

11. Grass (under 0.9–1.2 meters/3–4 feet of water).

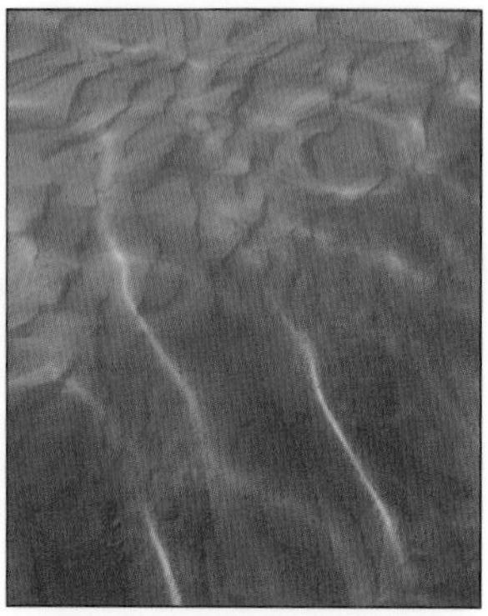

12. Upper left, 0.3–0.6 meter/1–2 feet; lower right, 0.9–1.2 meter/3–4 feet.

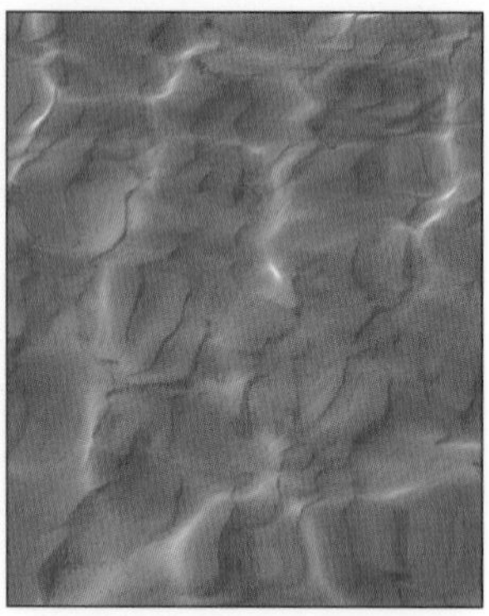

13. 0.9–1.2 meters/3–4 feet.

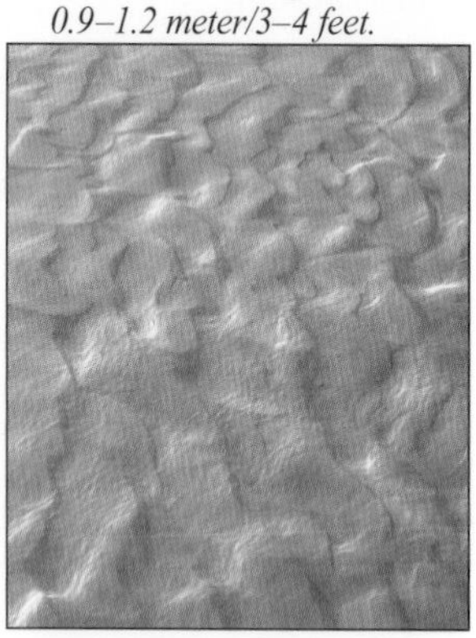

14. 0.3 meter/1 foot.

15. Sand exposed at low water.

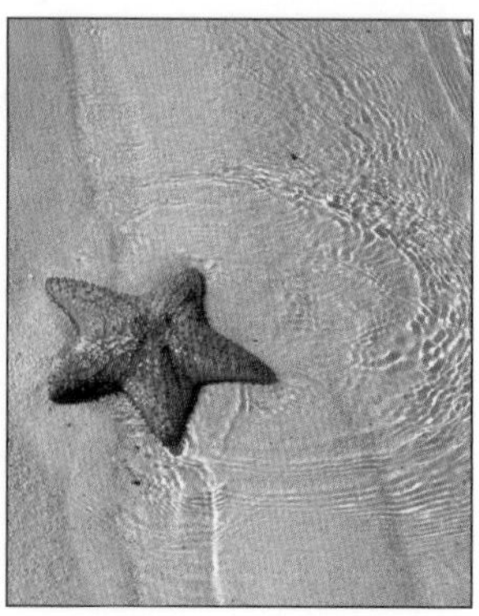

16. The very edge of the beach.

be to suddenly see everything on the bottom as clearly as if there were just 0.9 meter/3 feet of water under your keel.

- Green water is starting to become shallow, the colors changing from dark to light as the depth decreases. Green is banks water, decreasing from 9 meters/30 feet to 4.5 meters/15 feet to 3.6 meters/12 feet. The paler the shade of green, the shallower the water is.
- Yellow, running into white, is shoal water. Figure it to be 1.5 meters/5 feet or less. Proceed slowly if you are deliberately going to beach your boat. Otherwise, avoid water that looks more yellow or white than green.
- Pale aquamarine is your warning color. This color makes the prettiest photographs when set against a distant strip of darker-blue, deep water or the sand and palms of a Bahamian beach.
- Brown starts alarm bells. It could be grass, but it could just as well be a coral reef. Avoid it or slow down. If it is grass, you will learn that the edge of the brown is not as sharp as if it is a coral reef. Grass can be your greatest confusion factor, until you get used to it and can second guess where grass should be, could be or will be.
- Dark brown or black urgently rings alarm bells. That is the color of a coral reef. Upon approach, and as you get nearer, a reef will show sharp edges closer to the surface, but deeper features remain less distinct. Dark brown or black is also the color of an isolated coral head. It is always a tough shot to guess whether it is 0.6 meter/2 feet under the surface or 3 meters/10 feet down. It is best to consider, unless you are in good deep water, that each coral head is a threat and avoid it. As you get closer to a coral head, if the surrounding bottom is grass, you may see a white ring of sand around it where foraging fish have scoured the bottom.
- White also rings alarm bells. It is sand. Generally, white will turn out to be a sand bore, but it can be a shelving beach. Sometimes in shoal water, the aquamarine tint of the water makes it hard to see a sand bore that has built up close to the surface. If you are lucky, a sand bore will show a dry white spine. But, like an iceberg, there is more under water than what is visible on top. Stay well clear. Cloudy white may also signal a "fish mud," an area of sand stirred up by a school of fish rooting around. But, don't guess that it is a fish mud because sand bores aren't shown on the chart in that area. Avoid it or proceed cautiously.

Pulling the Navigation Package Together

Except for vessels and crew equipped for deep-water passages, don't sail at night in the Bahamas. You need your eyes, and you need your skill at reading the water. GPS is useful only for marking the waypoints along deep-water passages. Once you get into shallow water, or near shallow water, forget GPS.

What can help you? Proper sunglasses plus height above water. You don't have to have a tuna tower. But, the higher you are, the better you will be able to see. An aft cockpit sailboat is not necessarily disadvantaged. A lookout on the bow can help pilot the skipper through the shallows. Some sailboats with sturdy spreaders can even post a lookout half way up the mast.

Our final advice is to always plot your waypoints well off the magenta line courses found in electronic navigation software and some chart books. Magenta line courses have become virtual autopilot super highways with more than a few vessels not watching out for others in their path. In addition, island freighters use these courses to ply their way from island to island overloaded with everything from fresh produce to cement trucks. Many are so overloaded that they have no forward visibility and rely on watching out for other vessels from side to side in the pilothouse; or more honestly, other vessels watching out for them! Be especially aware of these "magenta line" dangers when anchoring on the Great Bahama Bank or near approaches to settlements. Always anchor far off the magenta line, in as shallow water as possible, to avoid costly, if not deadly, encounters. ■

Waterway Guide is always open to your observations from the helm. E-mail your comments on any navigation information in the guide to: editor@waterwayguide.com.

Florida Departure Waypoints

Stuart	LUCIE	N 27°10.000 / W 80°08.000
Jupiter	JUPTR	N 26°56.500 / W 80°03.250
Palm Beach	PPALM	N 26°46.000 / W 80°00.000
Hillsboro	HLSBG	N 26°13.000 / W 80°00.500
Fort Lauderdale	LDALE	N 26°05.500 / W 80°05.250
Miami	MIAMI	N 25°46.000 / W 80°05.000

Cruising, note the water's colors. WATERWAY GUIDE PHOTOGRAPHY

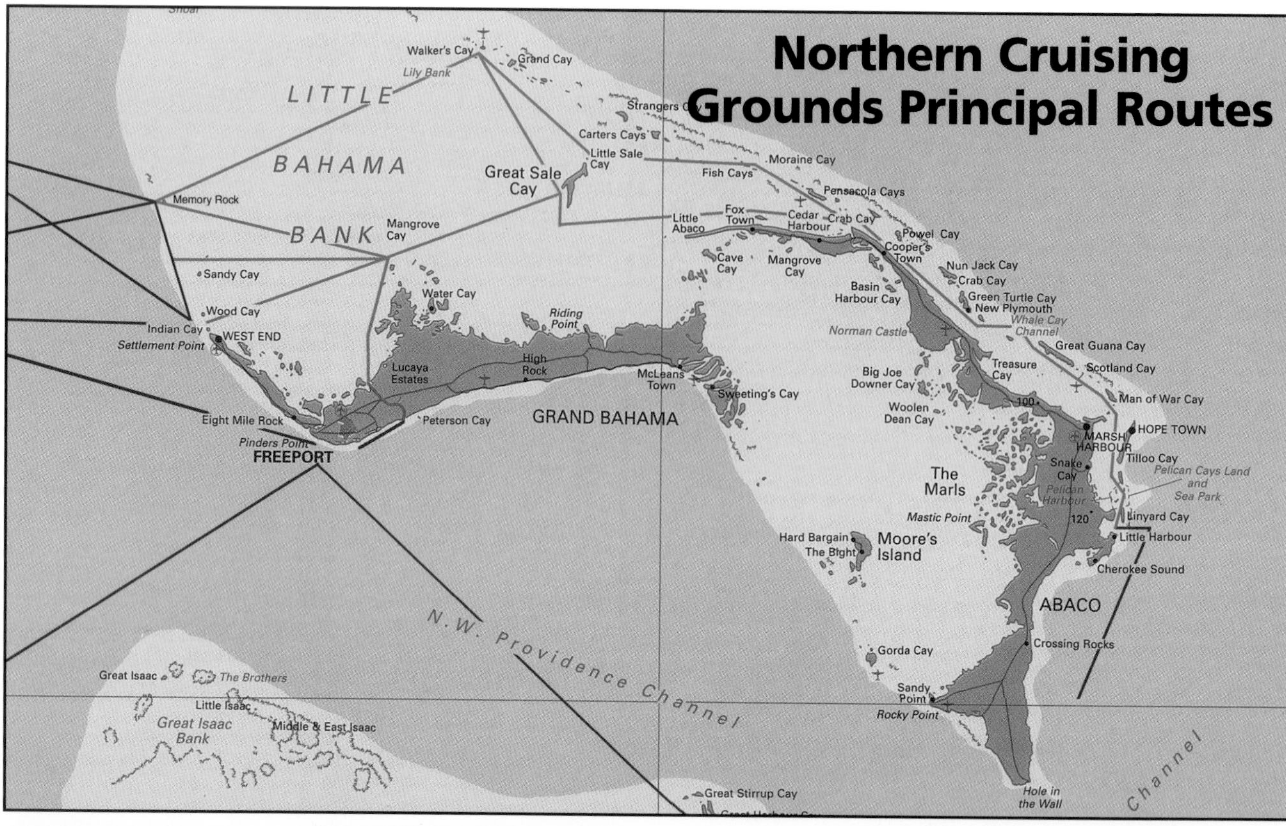

Not to be used for navigation.

Route From	To	Headings	Distance	Passage
Stuart, Florida	Memory Rock North	101/281°T	55 nm	Gulf Stream Crossing
Palm Beach	Memory Rock South	079/259°T	49 nm	Gulf Stream Crossing
Palm Beach	West End	094/274°T	53 nm	Gulf Stream Crossing
Palm Beach	Freeport	104/284°T	67 nm	Gulf Stream Crossing
Fort Lauderdale	Port Lucaya	072/252°T	83 nm	Gulf Stream Crossing
Port Lucaya	Mangrove Cay	see text	33 nm	Lucayan Waterway
Port Lucaya	Little Stirrup (Berry Island)	138/318°T	55 nm	NW Providence Channel
Memory Rock North	Walkers Cay	070/250°T	41 nm	Little Bahama Bank
Memory Rock South	Mangrove Cay	086/266°T	27 nm	Little Bahama Bank
Mangrove Cay	Great Sale Cay	085/265°T	21 nm	Little Bahama Bank
West End	Walkers Cay	see text	45 nm	Little Bahama Bank
West End	Mangrove Cay	see text	28 nm	Little Bahama Bank
Walkers Cay	Great Sale Cay	see text	20 nm	Little Bahama Bank
Great Sale Cay	Crab Cay	see text	41 nm	Little Bahama Bank
Crab Cay Green Turtle Cay	see text		16 nm	Sea of Abaco
Crab Cay Treasure Cay	see text		30 nm	Sea of Abaco
Treasure Cay	Marsh Harbour	see text	12 nm	Sea of Abaco
Green Turtle Cay	Hope Town	see text	23 nm	Sea of Abaco
Hope Town	Little Harbour	see text	15 nm	Sea of Abaco
Ocean Point	Hole-in-the-Wall	197/017°T	29 nm	Atlantic Coastal
Ocean Point	Little Egg Island Northwest	176/356°T	46 nm	NE Providence Channel
Hole-in-the-Wall	Great Stirrup Cay	270/090°T	40 nm	NE Providence Channel

Color Coding

Blue	Ocean or deep water passages
Green	Bank or shallow water passages
Red	Intricate passages or passes requiring Visual Navigation

Distances exclude inshore close approaches at the start and end of a passage. The notation "see text" indicates multi-leg passages that are fully covered in the text.

Part I
Northern Cruising Grounds

Photography Courtesy of Leslie Taylor and Waterway Guide

Chapter 3
The Little Bahama Bank

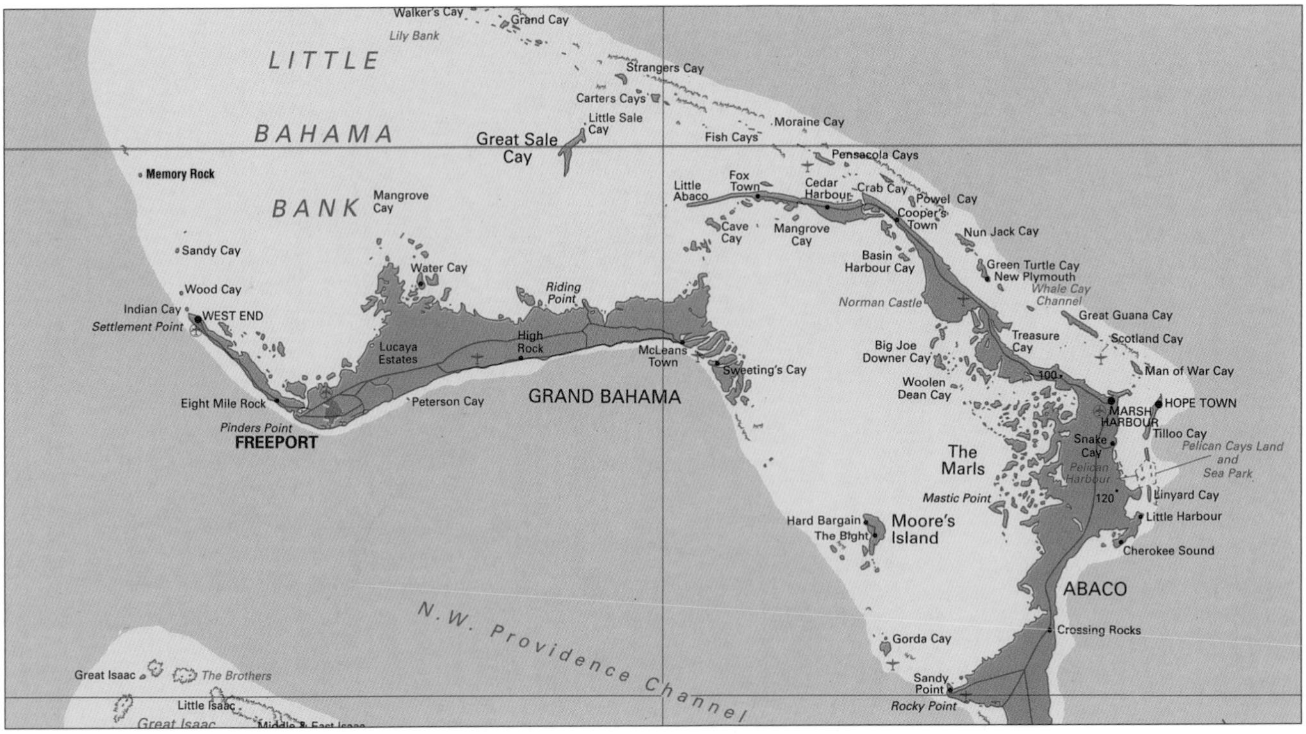

Not to be used for navigation.

Looking At the Charts

The Little Bahama Bank is the northernmost of the shallow seas that lend the Bahamas their unique character. Measured from west to east along north latitude 27 degrees, just north of Memory Rock to the barrier reef east of the Abacos, it is some 85 nautical miles wide. Measured from north to south, dropping down the line of W 078° 30.000', just west of Walkers Cay to the shoals off the north coast of Grand Bahama, it is about 35 nautical miles long. If the Sea of Abaco (which runs between Great Abaco Island and the Abaco Cays) is added, that is an additional 55 nautical miles.

The shallows between the east end of Grand Bahama and Little Abaco Island, the area lying south of Little Abaco Island and west of The Marls, are also part of the Little Bahama Bank. This sector of the Little Bahama Bank, a mess of mud banks, sand ridges and shoals, is no cruising ground. Other than taking a circuitous ocean route, the only way to reach the Abaco Cays is to traverse the Little Bahama Bank.

Depths on most routes over the Little Bahama Bank average 4 to 6 meters/13 to 19 feet. And, provided you keep to the proven routes, offer no particular navigation problems. The primary concern is to be somewhere secure by last light. It is possible to transit the Little Bahama Bank at night, but the cays are low lying with outlying reefs and shoals. There are uncharted rocks and sandbars. The effects of tidal currents are guessable, but not predictable, and there are few navigation lights. Unless you want to get in touch with your insurance agent early in your cruise, give night passage making across the Little Bahama Bank a pass.

Without enough speed to cross the bank and reach a final destination during daylight, one must anchor out. Not "out" in the middle of nowhere, however. Thankfully, there are two uninhabited islands on the way across where it is lawful to anchor even though you haven't yet cleared in—Mangrove Cay and Great Sale Cay. Mangrove Cay is less protected and more suitable for a settled weather stay, but many a boat has ridden out a blow at Great Sale. So your decision-making hinges, as ever, on your departure place and time, your boat and the weather and your final destination. Whatever these may be, the Little Bahama Bank offers options.

From the west, there are many ways to access the Little Bahama Bank. Just north of West End, there is the Indian Rock Channel to Church Bank, Barracuda Shoal and on to Mangrove Cay. Memory Rock, 50 nautical miles east of Palm Beach, FL, and 16 nautical miles north of West End, offers routes both north and south of the rock to Walkers Cay or Mangrove Cay. Even farther north, right up to the Matanilla Shoal area on the northwest edge of the bank, boats can pick an entry point and "read" their way in from ocean water to the green waters of the bank. From the east, a barrier line of coral reefs and cays limits access to the Little Bahama Bank from the Atlantic Ocean. There are some cuts into the bank from the east, but passage is intricate, subject to strong tides and unpredictable currents. Passage can be hazardous even with local pilots.

For the most direct route across the Little Bahama Bank, enter the shallower bank waters at Memory Rock. Then you can overnight at Mangrove Cay, bypass Great Sale and head to the northern cays; or bypass Mangrove, anchor at Great Sale and proceed east. Whichever way you go, Crab Cay will be your point of entry into the Sea of Abaco. If you have the speed and the endurance, you can make it across the bank by any route and continue to places like Spanish Cay or Green Turtle Cay without stopping.

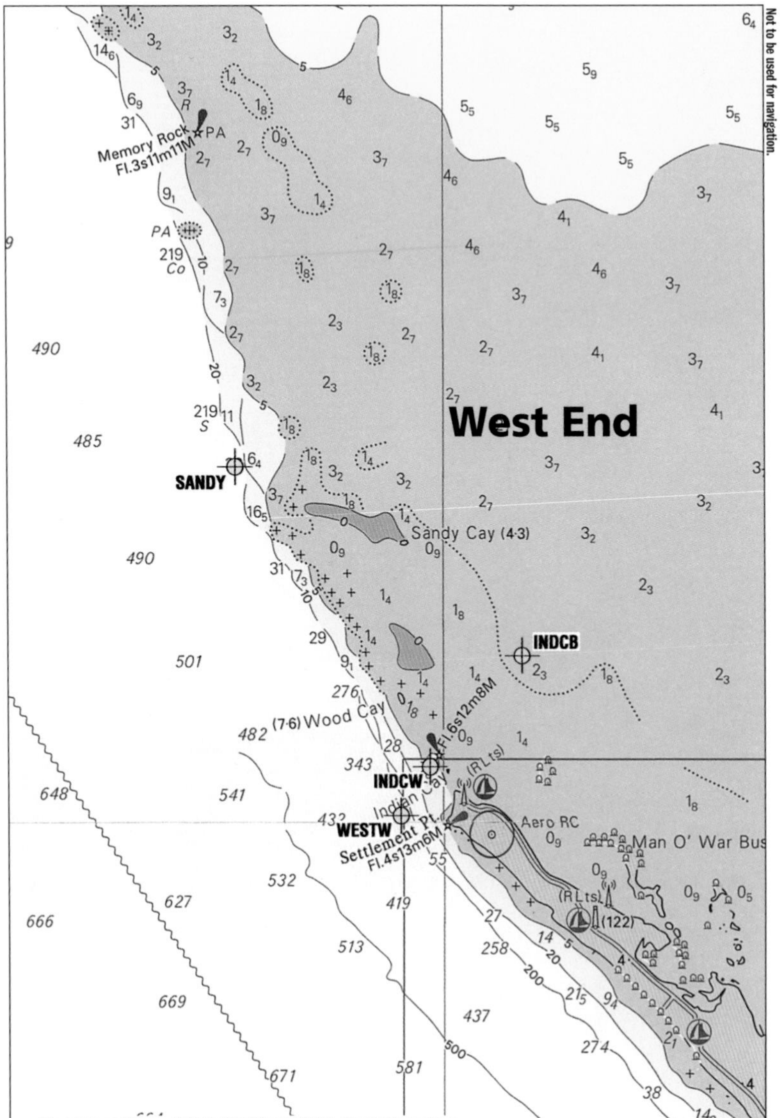

Reproduced from Admiralty Chart 3910. Depth in meters.

In the Spotlight. West End, Grand Bahama

West End is on Grand Bahama, and logically, we should cover it in the chapter dealing with that island. We don't. Why? Let's look at the chart. West End occupies a strategic position. One could say that it is the Bahamian gateway on the Florida–Abaco route. Sure there are alternatives, for instance the Freeport to Lucaya marinas in Grand Bahama or the Grand Lucayan Waterway. The Waterway is not mainstream for most boaters and certainly not those for whom a bridge clearance of 8.2 meters/27 feet at high water is a barrier (the Waterway is crossed by one road, and the bridge is fixed). So if you are one of the many who elect to go by way of West End you have three options: 1. Stage in West End before crossing the Little Bahama Bank, 2. Carry on and anchor somewhere en route, or 3. Make a straight run across the bank.

Measure the distances and look at the courses, and you will see that West End is a convenient arrival or departure point for Gulf Stream crossings. For many, it is just right. After the crossing, you and the crew may well want to rest for a day before setting off across the Bank. Old Bahama Bay, tucked behind West End Settlement Point, beckons you. It is a luxurious marina as well as an entry port, right where you want it.

What's There? The Little Bahama Bank

West End. Old Bahama Bay Marina (Grand Bahama)

Old Bahama Bay exceeds all expectations for well-appointed facilities as well as an ideal geographic position. With ample dockage, fuel, Customs and Immigration, restaurants, hotel and villa accommodations, it offers just about everything you are likely to desire. A favorite with movie stars and boaters alike, it provides solitude in lush surroundings. For those who seek a little more action, downtown Freeport, as well as the Grand Bahama International Airport, are only 25 miles away.

The entrance to Old Bahama Bay Marina is straightforward. The entry channel is marked and obvious. It is shoal close inshore, so don't hug the coastline. In addition, remember that a reef extends southward from Indian Cay. Stay in the blue water, and you will be fine. After negotiating the channel, the fuel dock comes up on starboard just before the port jog into the main marina basin. See more detailed notes under Pilotage and Marina information in Goin' Ashore.

Indian Cay Channel

Indian Cay Channel, to the north of West End, is a challenging pass on or off the Little Bahama Bank. It is a shallow, narrow channel with some patches around 1.6 meters/5.5 feet deep at low water, although 2.1 meters/7 feet is the more common depth. It is a partially marked channel, and its markers can

Old Bahama Bay, from the south. (Not to be used for navigation.) WATERWAY GUIDE PHOTOGRAPHY.

Grand Bahama

WEST END		Largest Vessel Accommodated	VHF Channel Monitored	Transient Berths / Total Berths	Approach / Dockside Depth (reported)	Floating Docks	Gas / Diesel	Groceries, Ice, Marine Supplies, Snacks	Repairs: Hull, Engine, Propeller	Lift (tonnage), Crane, Rail	1=110V, 2=220V, B=Both, Max Amps	Laundry, Pool, Showers	Pump-Out Station	Nearby: Grocery Store, Motel, Restaurant
		Dockage					Supplies				Services			
1. Old Bahama Bay Marina 💻	877-949-4466	120	16/10	72/72	13/8		GD	IS			B/100	LPS	P	GMR

Corresponding chart(s) not to be used for navigation. 💻 Internet Access (WiFi) Wireless Internet Access

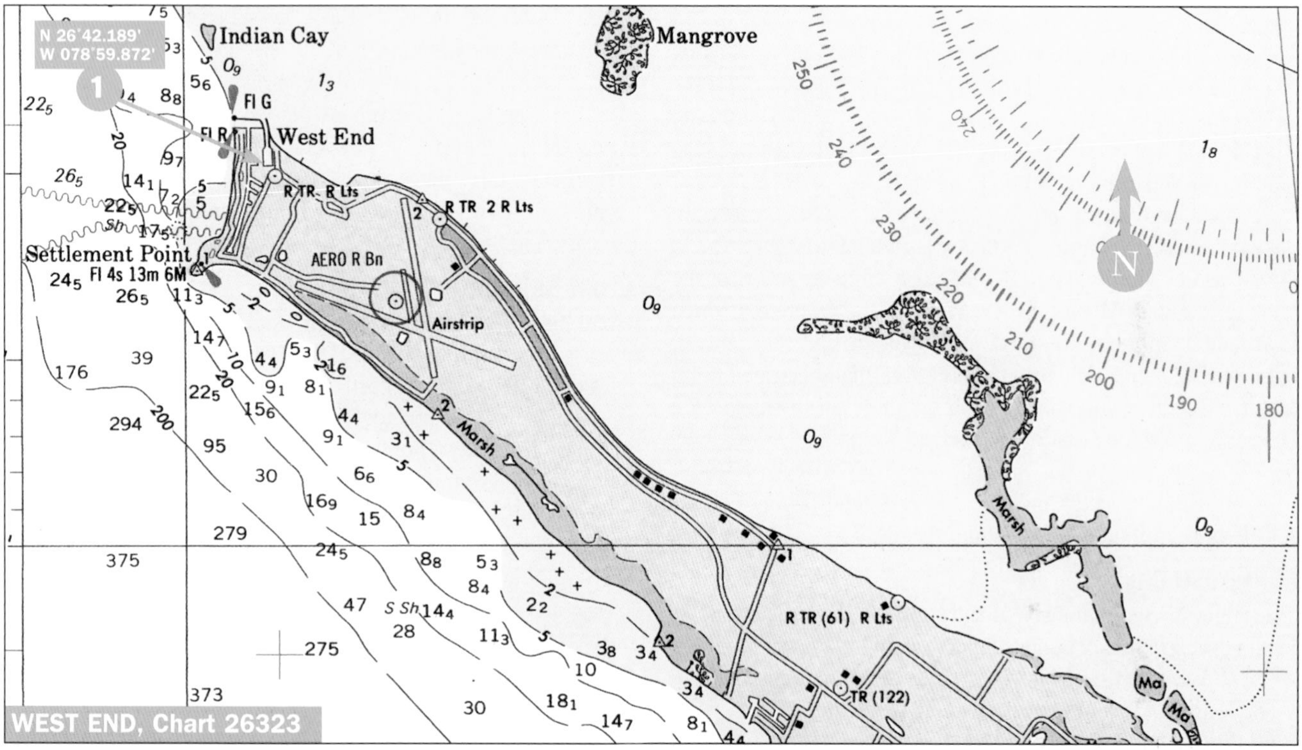

WEST END, Chart 26323

Old Bahama Bay, from the west. (Not to be used for navigation.) Waterway Guide Photography.

come and go. Its strong crosscurrents can push you out of the channel and run you aground if you are not very careful. Don't attempt this passage at night. See our more detailed notes under Pilotage.

Memory Rock

Memory Rock, 16 nautical miles north of West End, is an isolated plug of rock hardly big enough to support a shack, but there is a light on it. It is a stake light, not a lighthouse. And it may, or may not, be working. There is a shipwreck on the reefs to the south and another two wrecks some six miles to the north. None of these are visible. Within a hand span, sometimes two miles, sometimes less, the depth contours along the edge of the ocean-bank interface change from the deep, thousand-foot midnight blue of the Florida Straits to the pale green of 20 feet or less over the Little Bahama Bank. Memory Rock is not only a significant landmark, but also offers arguably the best area for entering or departing the Little Bahama Bank.

For safety reasons, our two Memory Rock waypoints are approximately two miles north and south of Memory Rock. Given good visibility, you can read your way onto or off of the bank far closer to Memory Rock. Virtually little more than three boat lengths to the north, there are depths of 6 meters/20 feet. While to the south, similarly close in, it is shallower, about 3.6 meters/12 feet. If you wish to hang out there for a while, there is a sandy patch due east of the rock at N 26° 57.190'/W 079° 06.000'. One can anchor there in 6 meters/20 feet of water. Memory Rock, its reefs and drop-off, is a good fishing ground for offshore trolling and for bottom fishing.

Mangrove Cay

Though low lying, uninhabited and barely 0.75 nautical mile in length, Mangrove Cay is, nonetheless, an important waypoint, 20 nautical miles northeast of West End. It is featured on six Little Bahama Bank transit routes connecting to Memory Rock, West End, the Lucayan Waterway, Great Sale Cay and the southern route that bypasses Great Sale Cay. The cay has a marker stake just north of it (N 26° 56.250'/W 078° 36.750') on rocky bars.

Dolphin in the Bahamas. Photo Courtesy of Gavin Spencer

Clearing In — Options in the Northern Bahamas

If you have put in to West End, obviously you will clear in there, as it is an entry port. You get the formalities over and done with right at the start of your cruise. However, if you decide to bypass West End, anchoring at uninhabited cays, such as Mangrove or Great Sale, or indeed anchoring anywhere is permitted. Just don't land on the cays, and keep your Q flag flying until you have cleared in. Other ports of entry for you to consider are Port Lucaya on Grand Bahama and Spanish Cay, Green Turtle Cay, Treasure Cay and Marsh Harbour in the Abacos. Walkers Cay is still a port of entry even though the marina is not operational.

A shoal area extends south of the cay for slightly more than twice the length of the visible land. Mangrove Cay can provide a short-stay, fair weather anchorage, but approach the area with caution. Shallows extend farther from shore on the west than on the east, and there are isolated coral heads all around.

Great Sale Cay

Great Sale Cay and its Northwest Harbour are the central point of the Little Bahama Bank. Eventually, most voyagers pass this way. Running north to south for seven nautical miles (including its southern reef), Great Sale Cay is barely a mile broad at its widest point. It is uninhabited. There is a long tongue of reef, coral heads and shoals extending four nautical miles south from the cay's Southeast Point. They are a definite hazard to navigation and are difficult to see until it is too late. Stay well clear.

Great Sale Cay is low lying and heavily protected by mangroves, home to a variety of fish and sea life and is a delight to visit by dinghy. Row in quietly and gently to enjoy the best underwater show. There are nice sandy beaches to land a dinghy and swim, or just jump off the boat. Swimming in the anchorages is fine. Tom Johnson Sound, on the east side of the cay, offers protection from westerly winds, but excellent visual navigation and piloting is required. North of Great Sale Cay is Little Sale Cay, marked with a light, and Sale Cay Rocks, all of which are obvious. Little Sale Cay and Sale Cay Rocks are landmarks on the Little Bahama Bank transit from Walkers Cay to Crab Cay.

The Tom Johnson Sound anchorage runs from north to south along the east coast for nearly a mile. There, you will find 2 to 2.4 meters/7 to 8 feet of water over sand and grass. The holding is good to adequate over mud, sand or marl. Dive to check your anchor. The northern coast of the harbour shoals quickly to the west and is nearly dry at low water. Truly shoal-draft boats can tuck into great protection in 1.2 meters/4 feet of water or less. Look for sandy spots within the grassy bottom.

The Northwest Harbour anchorage, on the west side of the cay, is probably the most commonly used of the two. It does not require rounding numerous waypoints guarding dangerous rocks and reefs. It also carries decent depths of around 12 feet.

Great Sale Cay's anchorages offer some protection from all directions other than the southerly quadrant, but in high winds there can be quite a chop. Set that anchor well, or you

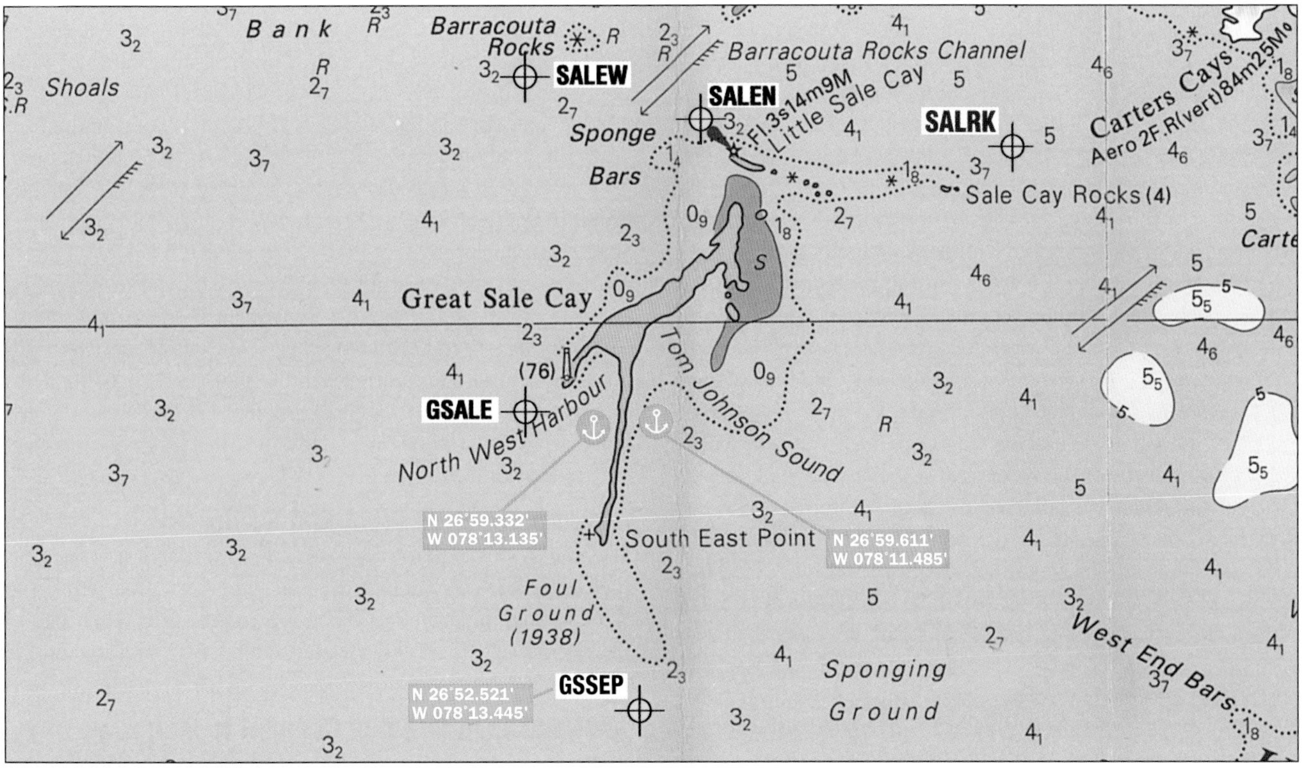

may find yourself dragging in the middle of a blow. During the height of the cruising season, you will find plenty of company here for many consider it the first or last stop when crossing the Little Bahama Bank.

For the truly adventurous, Great Sale Cay is the jumping off point to cruise the southern waters of the Little Bahama Bank in the Bight of Abaco. The Bight is a magical, secluded area where the only other soul you may encounter will be a bonefisherman. For those who want to get away from the crowds in the Sea of Abaco, this is the place. The Bight is also a great short cut to the Northwest Providence Channel and the protected anchorages in between Great Stirrup, Goat and Great Harbour Cays in the Berry Islands.

Hawksbill Cays

Hawksbill Cays run west to east on a line just about one nautical mile north of Fox Town on Little Abaco Island. They act as a barrier to north winds if you nestle under their south side. The anchorage just south of the westernmost beach on Hawksbill Cay has adequate to poor holding, mostly in grass over hard ground with 1.8 meters/6 feet of water. The Hawksbill waypoint is safely off the west end of Hawksbill Cay. When you get there, swing westward in a lazy half circle to pass well away from a rock with a marker on it and come in to the anchorage on the N 26° 56.000' line to anchor under the westernmost end of Hawksbill Cay. It may take several tries before your anchor sets. Although open to the east and west, if the wind stays below 15 knots, you will be okay.

Little Abaco Island, Fox Town and Crown Haven

Fox Town is the first refueling opportunity after West End. It is an easy dinghy ride from the Hawksbill Cay anchorage. Because there is barely 1.2 meters/4 feet of depth at the local docks and the approach winds through a chain of inshore islets and rocks that parallel the coast, it is suitable for dinghies or very shoal-draft craft only. You are welcome to tie up your dinghy at Corner Texaco. Fox Town and neighboring Crown Haven offer an old Bahamas ambience plus restaurants, fuel, water, ice and groceries.

Crab Cay

Crab Cay is a thin isle off the northern end of Great Abaco Island. Crab Cay marks the entry point into the Sea of Abaco. It is barely a mile in length with a light on its northwestern tip. The exit route from the main part of the Little Bahama Bank lies through the pass to the north of that light. Don't try to cut between Crab Cay and Angelfish Point, the northernmost hook of Great Abaco Island. There is a sill of rock there that would radically change your underwater profile. There is a magnificent, isolated anchorage in the lee of Crab Cay, just southwest of the Angelfish Point hook. Be sure to give the shoal south of Crab Cay wide berth.

Here you will find good holding in 2 meters/6 feet of water with palm trees swaying on a pristine beach and rocky crags and channels south of the anchorage begging for exploration. Rumors abound that Angelfish Point development plans are on the board, so enjoy this little piece of paradise while you can.

Allans-Pensacola Cay

Lying northwest to southeast across latitude N 26° 59.000', Allans-Pensacola was once two distinct cays. A hurricane had other ideas and filled in the narrow breach between them. Today, they remain joined and form another one of the

Bahamian cruising destinations where location triumphs. It is at the right spot on the chart, and sooner or later most people go there after crossing or before setting out across the Little Bahama Bank. The unified cay is about three nautical miles long, and the popular anchorage is easy to access. It is deep with good holding and effectively protected. There are ruins of a one-time U.S. missile-tracking station on the northeast tip of Allans as well as a signing tree midway on the trail to the ruins where visiting voyager's leave a message and note their stay at this lovely break in their journey. The beaches on the ocean side are pleasant, and the waters between Allans-Pensacola and Guineamans Cay to the north and Big Hog Cay to the south offer good gunkholing and snorkeling.

Enter the Allans-Pensacola Cay anchorage from the northwest, staying well off the westernmost rocks. The anchorage is nearly a mile in length, but it shoals about two-thirds of the way in at the southeast end. Favor the inshore side at all times. Don't take your boat farther south than the headland by Allans Cay Rocks unless you have very shoal draft. It is a good anchorage, protected from everything but the west and northwest with 1.8 to 2.4 meters/6 to 8 feet of water and decent holding. It can be crowded in the cruising season. Choose your spot cautiously, set your anchor carefully and dive on it to guarantee its hold.

On the eastern end of Pensacola, there is a narrow, mangrove-lined entrance to a landlocked harbor. It appears on charts as a hurricane hole; and you may well be able to creep into it on a high tide if you don't draw more than 1.2 meters/4 feet, and you stick to the south side of the channel. From the looks of it, arm yourself with screens and a lot of bug spray.

Pilotage. Talking Captain to Captain

Memory Rock to Walkers Cay

Our approach waypoint WLKRA places you 1.5 nautical miles off the entrance to the entry channel. One of the Walkers Cay landmarks was its radio tower (which was dwarfed by a taller BTC tower on Grand Cay to the south). In the past, you may have seen the gleam of white hulls in the marina, which would have given you a line to take up. With the marina closed, there are no hulls and no Walkers Cay destination for the foreseeable future. The island is up for sale and no word on its future at press time in summer 2010. It is, however, still a point of entry.

When and if the marina reopens, navigate visually from WLKRA to the WLKRS waypoint, which is fixed just plus of the entry channel. Your heading will be around 045 degrees true.

Ocean Approach to West End and Indian Cay Channel

West End is an easy landfall. Its water tower (situated between the marina and the airfield) is prominent, and its radio mast also shows, perhaps more clearly at night with its red lights. If you are making a night landfall, the light on Settlement Point may show; but it has failed in the past, and you should not rely on it. As standard practice, stand off until daylight before closing any coast in the islands. To the north, Sandy Cay's tall casuarina trees will show up early on your horizon, but don't be seduced by this landfall. Sandy Cay is eight nautical miles north of West End. It is a useful safety net, and folks have been grateful for it more than once in bad weather. If you miss your landfall off West End, remember that a boat-eating reef line extends north from West End along the western edge of the Little Bahama Bank. In daylight, that water abruptly changes from deep blue ocean color to green. Stay in the blue water.

If you navigate carefully, the West End approach waypoint (WESTW) places you just off Settlement Point ready to make a gentle curve in to Old Bahama Bay Marina. If you are heading straight across the Little Bahama Bank and bypassing West End by way of Indian Cay Channel, your landfall should be the Indian Cay West waypoint (INDCW), just over one nautical mile to the north of West End.

Bank Approach to West End Settlement

The shoal areas off West End set absolute limits on your approach route options to West End settlement. Boats have run aground attempting it, and it is not recommended other than in a shoal draft vessel, at high water, with good visibility and the skills to read your way in.

West End to Indian Cay Channel to Mangrove Cay

Indian Cay Channel can be risky and is best left to the experienced skipper and boats with good auxiliary power. If you are eastbound, incoming from the Gulf Stream, Indian Cay Channel can be approached either directly from the Florida Straits or from West End. If you are incoming from the Atlantic Ocean, you can ignore the West End waypoint (WESTW) and simply head for the Indian Cay Channel West (INDCW) waypoint.

From West End, after leaving the marina, turn west into blue water for about 0.5 nautical miles to gain a safe distance off Indian Cay and its reefs. Then head for the Indian Cay Channel West waypoint (INDCW), around 356 degrees true, with just under one nautical mile to run. After half a mile or so, you will see Indian Cay Rock with its light.

Indian Cay Channel opens up to the north of the rock. There is a piling standing in the channel with an arrow shaped board pointing north to indicate that you should pass north of the mark. We recommend passing a safe distance from Indian Cay. If you try to shortcut and run too closely, particularly if something goes wrong, you can find yourself set on the reef.

The pass opening into the channel is marked with the Indian Cay Channel (INDCP) waypoint, which is a quarter of a mile on a course of 045 degrees true from INDCW. The channel marker is the first of three similar pilings marking the south side of the channel. Leave it to starboard as you enter onto the bank. At your entry point, a reef, which is often hard to see, extends south from Wood Cay for well over one nautical mile. Don't assume you have all the distance between that first piling and Wood Cay as your channel. As it is, the shallowest water in the area is around Wood Cay.

If they are there, there are four Indian Cay Channel markers. The first entry mark is by Indian Cay Rock. Then look for

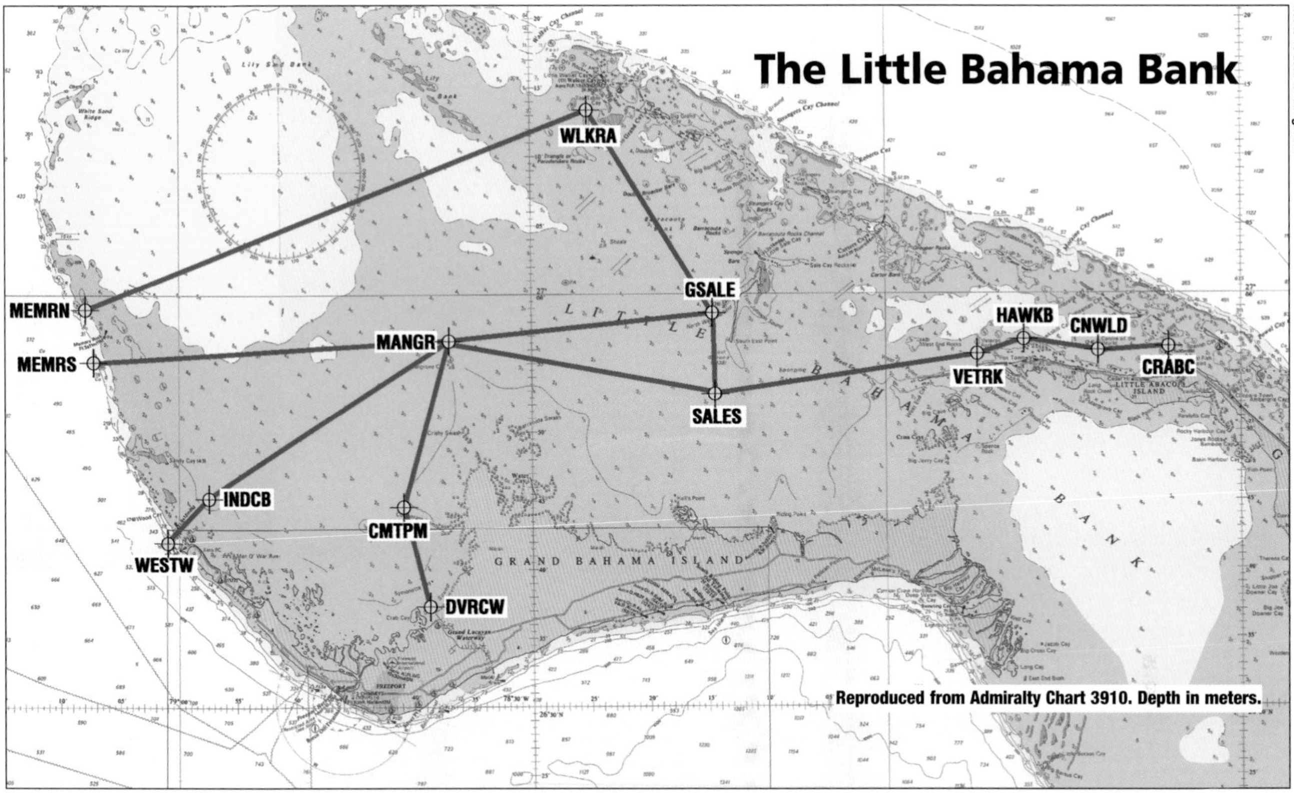

Reproduced from Admiralty Chart 3910. Depth in meters.

Not to be used for navigation.

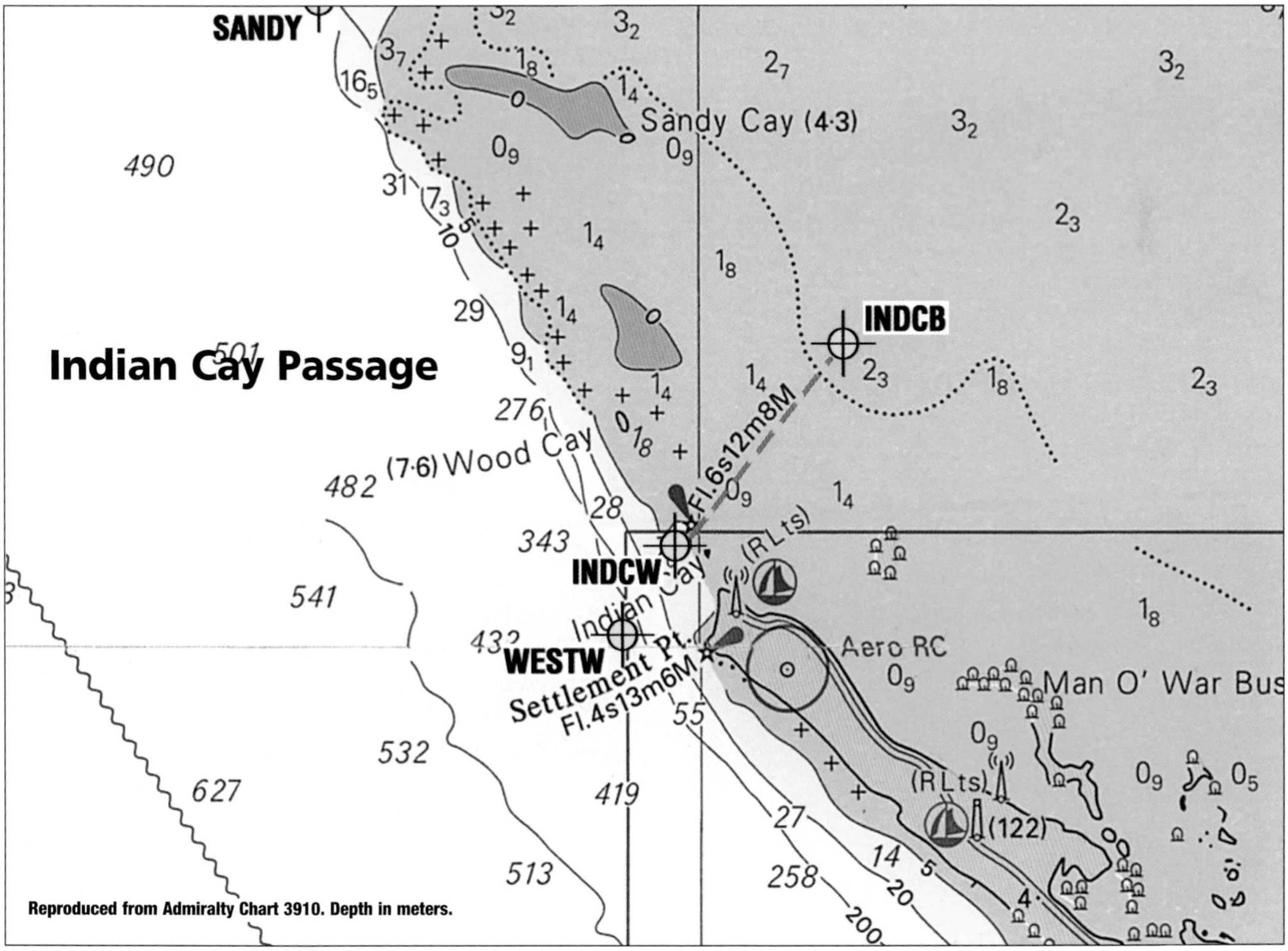

Reproduced from Admiralty Chart 3910. Depth in meters.

Not to be used for navigation.

Grand Lucayan Waterway, north entry. (Not to be used for navigation.) WATERWAY GUIDE PHOTOGRAPHY.

Fish Muds

The Little Bahama Bank has one natural phenomenon that can get you over-excited about sandbars and shoal water, and that is a fish mud. Hundreds of bonefish take it into their collective heads to go shoveling up the sand moving across the bank in search of delicacies, and the end result is water the color of green-tinged milk. From any distance off you could swear that it is a sandbar.

You will come across fish muds just east of Mangrove Cay almost as a routine occurrence. Maybe there is something particularly good on the bottom down there. Now, with great confidence, regulars carry straight on. But, if you don't know the area, just be wise. If you think it is sand, slow down. Inch up close to it. Check it out, and be safe.

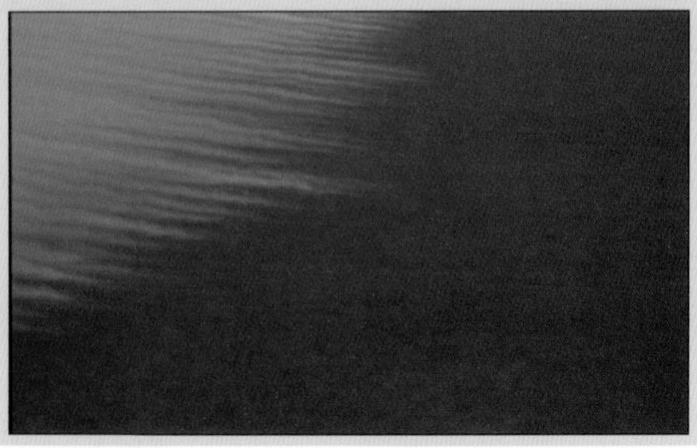

two more channel marks, all of which are left to starboard. The third mark, INDC3, may be missing. One final marker is on Barracuda Shoal. Keep this marker about 0.5 miles to port as you are making your way on to the Bank. If you are in doubt, steer 045 degrees true from the third Indian Cay Channel mark for 1.5 nautical miles. This will keep you in the channel and safely off the shoal.

Although waypoints are listed, do not rely on them to negotiate Indian Cay Channel. The only way is to visually pilot. If you fool around trying to navigate by GPS, you may well run aground. Keep close to the marks all the way and steer by them, taking them one-by-one, rather than setting courses. The tidal flow runs across this channel. At mid-tide, you will probably find yourself being carried to the right or left, so navigate by keeping your eyes on the marker astern as well as the marker ahead. This advice is very important.

When you pass the Barracuda Shoal marker, you can alter course for Mangrove Cay and use GPS. You will have some 22 nautical miles to run to the Mangrove Cay (MANGR) waypoint.

Mangrove Cay to Grand Lucayan Waterway

Westbound from the Abacos, you may consider heading for Port Lucaya on Grand Bahama Island by way of the Grand Lucayan Waterway. Before you commit to take the Grand Lucayan Waterway, we suggest you check with Old Bahama Bay Marina, the Port Lucaya Marina or the Lucayan Marina to get an update on the state of the Dover Channel and the Waterway.

Should you decide to try it, a lone piling well off Cormorant Point (CMTPM), 12 nautical miles south of Mangrove Cay, can give you the reassurance that you are on a transit route.

The shallow bight you cross extends from West End to the Cormorant Point peninsula with Crishy Swash and Mangrove Cay to its immediate north. Closer in to Grand Bahama Island, it is known as Dover Sound. The north-running hook of land, of which Cormorant Point is a western outlier, is the widest part of Grand Bahama. The shore is low-lying, broken up by swamp, mudflats and small islands and barely shows for much of the time. The entrance to the Grand Lucayan Waterway is another eight nautical miles farther south, masked by Crab Cay to the west and Sandy Cay to the east. It is not evident until you are right there. The mean low water depth over much of this area can be 1.8 meters/6 feet, but keep at least three to four nautical miles offshore, as there is a definite shoal depth contour running parallel to the coast. Another lone piling, the Dover Channel Mark (DVRCM), if it is there, provides landfall reassurance. Do not rely on seeing it.

Unfortunately, the Dover Channel marks are taken out by weather and are haphazardly replaced. Without the marks, it is difficult to pick up the channel as you approach from the north, and a number of boats have suffered damage trying to find the channel to enter. Above all, remember you must have high water to use the Dover Channel. **The time of high water in the Dover Channel is two hours 30 minutes after Nassau, and there is a two-hour difference between high water at the northern and southern ends of the Lucayan Waterway.**

Navigating the Dover Channel

From DVRCM, head 144/324 degrees true for 1.8 nautical miles to the posts marking the west entrance to the channel. The half-mile-long Dover Channel runs close to west-east (110/290 degrees true) and is sometimes marked by seven pairs of marker poles with the first pair at each end lighted (red right returning, incoming from the west). It is narrow, open to wind from the north and shallow—as little as 1.8 meters/6 feet at best, and maybe 1.2 meters/4 feet at worst. You can't hammer through it with speed to counter a side wind. You will simply dig your stern in too deeply and potentially drag the bottom with your keel or props. Go for the best compromise speed if you have a side wind, but keep moving. Notice that there is a prominent sandy spoil ledge on the south side of the channel.

After the last pair of posts, upon entry, turn to starboard by two concrete posts, and you are in the Grand Lucayan Waterway. Before navigating the Waterway, read our advice under Pilotage in Chapter 7, Grand Bahama. In addition to the Casuarina Bridge with its limiting 27-foot vertical clearance, there is a new four-lane bridge under construction. The bridge will begin at the intersection of Grand Bahama

Little Bahama Bank Waypoints

LITTLE BAHAMA BANK WEST

Memory Rock North	MEMRN	26°59.25N / 79°08.00W
Memory Rock Light	MEMRK	26°57.00N / 79°07.00W
Memory Rock South	MEMRS (B1)	26°55.00N / 79°07.00W
Sandy Cay	SNDCY	26°49.50N / 79°05.50W
West End	WESTW (B2)	26°42.00N / 79°01.50W
Harbour Hotel Marina Dock	HARBH	26°41.36N / 78°57.96W
Indian Cay Passage West	INDCW	26°43.00N / 79°00.43W
Indian Cay Pass	INDCP	26°43.16N / 79°00.25W
	INDC2	26°43.76N / 78°59.79W
Turn for West End	WESTP	26°44.43N / 78°59.35W
	INDC3	26°44.75N / 78°59.17W
Barracuda Shoal	INDCB	26°45.84N / 78°58.00W
Mangrove Cay	MANGR	26°57.00N / 78°37.00W

LITTLE BAHAMA BANK CENTRAL

Cormorant Point Mark	CMTPM	26°44.63N / 78°40.81W
Sale Cay West	SALEW	27°01.48N / 78°14.50W
Sale Cay North	SALEN (A2)	27°03.50N / 78°12.00W
Sale Rocks	SALRK	27°02.88N / 78°05.59W
Great Sale Cay	GSALE	26°58.75N / 78°14.50W
Great Sale Anchorage	GSANC	26°58.97N / 78°13.53W
Sale Cay South	SALES	26°52.82N / 78°14.50W
Great Sale South East Point	GSSEP	26°52.52N / 78°13.44W
See Grand Bahama for Dover Channel/Grand Lucayan Waterway.		

NORTHERN ABACOS

Walkers Approach	WLKRA	27°12.91N / 78°25.45W
Walkers Cay	WLKRS (A1)	27°14.00N / 78°24.20W
Walkers Cay Channel North	WLKCN	27°19.08N / 78°29.69W
Walkers Cay Channel South	WLKCS	27°13.79N / 78°29.17W
Gully Rocks Channel South	GLRKS	27°15.21N / 78°23.46W
Seal Cay Channel North	SELCN	27°16.00N / 78°21.75W
Seal Cay Channel South	SELCS	27°15.34N / 78°21.75W
Triangle Rocks	TRIRK	27°11.00N / 78°25.00W
Grand Cays	GRAND	27°12.16N / 78°19.29W
Grand Cays Anchorage	GCANC	27°13.16N / 78°19.29W
Double Breasted Cays	DBRST	27°10.86N / 78°16.73W
South Carters Cay	SCRTR	27°01.24N / 78°01.00W
Mid-Carters Cay	MCRTR	27°03.00N / 78°01.00W
Carters Cay	CRTRS	27°04.00N / 78°01.00W
Carters Cay Anchorage	CTANC	27°05.05N / 78°00.11W
Fish Cays	FISHC	27°01.32N / 77°49.00W
Moraine Cay Approach	MORAP	27°01.04N / 77°46.12W
Moraine Cay	MORAI	27°02.10N / 77°46.12W
Moraine Cay Channel North	MORCN	27°03.88N / 77°44.82W
Moraine Cay Channel South	MORCS	27°02.10N / 77°44.82W

LITTLE BAHAMA BANK EAST

Veteran Rock	VETRK	26°55.75N / 77°52.27W
Hawksbill Cays	HAWKB	26°56.80N / 77°48.50W
Center of the World Rock	CNWLD	26°56.09N / 77°41.67W
Allans-Pensacola Cay	ALPEN	26°59.25N / 77°42.25W
Crab Cay	CRABC	26°56.03N / 77°36.31W

Our position format is latitude and longitude in degrees and minutes (hddd°mm.mm). Waypoints in RED are NOT for autopilot navigation. Codes in parenthesis are Wavey Line waypoints marked on the charts. If you have programmed waypoints we listed in a previous edition of this guide, check carefully to ensure the coordinates you have recorded match the list. If a waypoint is no longer on our list we may have changed its code or deleted it.

Highway and Fortune Bay Drive, and span the channel opening with a 30-foot fixed vertical clearance. The bridge is expected to spurn rapid development of housing allotments that line the channels along the Waterway.

Mangrove Cay, Great Sale Cay to Crab Cay

You must run south for just about six nautical miles, before setting your transit course, to avoid the reef extending south from Great Sale Cay. Don't be tempted to cut corners, and turn early for your next waypoint, Veteran Rock (nor attempt the reverse if you are heading from east to west). You should not see Veteran Rock, which is barely awash. Don't look for it. Stay on course. Don't run too close inshore when you reach the Hawksbill Cays, for rocks and shoal lie immediately to the north of them. The Center of the World, a great doughnut of an isolated rock in the middle of nowhere, is a fine landmark. No problems here. Do not attempt to pass between Crab Cay and Angelfish Point, the northernmost tip of Great Abaco Island.

Hawksbill Cays to Moraine Cay

Use this route at high water. The final mile or so of this leg is shoal, reducing it to depths of 1.2 meters/4 feet at mean low water. ■

Waterway Guide is always open to your observations from the helm. E-mail your comments on any navigation information in the guide to: editor@waterwayguide.com.

Waterway Guide Photography

GOIN' ASHORE:

WEST END

customs & immigration • fuel • marina • medical • police
post office • restaurant • telephone • water

MARINA

OLD BAHAMA BAY MARINA

Tel: 242-350-6500, 877-949-4466, 888-800-8959 • Fax: 242-346-6546 • VHF 16, then VHF 10 "Old Bahama Bay" • info@oldbahamabay.com • www.oldbahamabay.com

The strategic position of West End has always made it a safe haven en route to the rest of the Bahamas after a Gulf Stream crossing. Excellent docks with hotel and restaurants, a swimming pool and an attentive staff who will help you clear in to the Bahamas at *Old Bahama Bay*, a five-star resort owned and operated by the Ginn Company. The company is also developing the major resort complex adjacent to *Old Bahama Bay*. Several of the homes are owned by entertainment celebrities including the actor, John Travolta. You may even be tempted to build on one of the canal-side homesites, or spend a vacation at the *Old Bahama Bay Inn*. The settlement itself is close by and steeped in rum running history. The marina has bicycles you can use to get to the settlement.

Customs and Immigration are on site.

Slips 72. **Max LOA** Up to 120 ft. **MLW at Dock** 8 ft. (13-ft. depth in channel). **Dockage** $3.05 per ft. per day; 25% discount for hotel guests. **Fuel** Diesel, gasoline and oils. **Facilities & Services** Power 100A, 50A, 30A; $0.25 per kWh, or $0.80 per ft. monthly. Water $15 per day (mandatory). Showers with hairdryers. Laundry. Phone cards from the marina office. Cable TV included with electricity charges. Ice. Tennis courts and 5 miles of marked nature trails for jogging and biking. The front desk has maps for use on the snorkel trails off Old Bahama Bay North Beach, Indian Cay, Settlement Point and Sandy Cay. Diving with UNEXSO at Port Lucaya. Bicycle, sailfish, windsurfer, glass-bottom paddle boat and kayak rentals. Gift shop. Bonefishing at Bootle Bay (242-349-4010). Rental cars from Freeport, 40 minutes by road. Public bus at 10 a.m. and 3 p.m. daily. New York Times fax, and daily weather fax at 7:30 a.m. from the front office. Faxes $5 per page. For marine repairs, propane, electronic problems, ask the dockmaster. Pump out $25. **Restaurants & Bar** Dockside Grille open for breakfast, lunch and dinner, with the Aqua Restaurant for fine dining. **Accommodations** Old Bahama Bay Inn 49 suites from $250 per night in low season, plus 12% government tax and $12 service charge daily. Credit Cards Visa, MasterCard and AMEX. **Security** 24-hour marina security.

Airport *Freeport International Airport* is a $50 taxi ride away. The airfield at *Old Bahama Bay* is not open to air traffic.

Churches *Church of God of Prophecy, St. Michael's Catholic Church and St. Mary Magdalene Church*

Medical *Clinic* • 242-343-6463/6464 • Open 8 a.m. to 5 p.m. weekdays.

Police In the turquoise building by BTC.

Post Office Open 9 a.m. to 4:30 p.m. weekdays.

Provisions *J & M Grocery* • 242-346-6222

Restaurants *Paradise Cove at Deadmans Reef* • 242-349-2677 • Hamburgers, hot dogs and snacks. Secluded beach, snorkel rental and beachfront accommodations.

EMERGENCIES

BASRA Grand Bahama 242-352-2628 or VHF 16

THINGS TO DO IN WEST END

- Borrow one of the excellent snorkeling maps from *Old Bahama Bay*, and follow their snorkel trails.
- Rent a car and explore Grand Bahama.
- Walk, jog or bicycle the marked nature trails.
- Laze on the beach, or rent some of the fun watersports equipment at *Old Bahama Bay*.

Sponges drying in the sun, Fox Town.

The Sea of Abaco

One explanation may help those new to the Bahamas and to the Abacos. Properly speaking, the Little Bahama Bank is the area of shallow sea that runs to the north of Great Bahama Island and surrounds the entire Abacos, that is the two large islands, Great Abaco and Little Abaco, and the Abaco Cays. In practice, we talk about the Bank as the area to the north of Grand Bahama and Little Abaco, and in this definition the Northern Abacos form an eastern front for the Little Bahama Bank.

It is very different when you reach the central and southern Abacos. There, the Bank water between Great Abaco Island on the west and the cays to the east forms an inland sea, which is known as the Sea of Abaco, or sometimes as Abaco Sound. The Sea of Abaco offers a far greater degree of protection than the "open" waters of the Little Bahama Bank, and apart from one necessary diversion around Whale Cay (the well-known Whale Cay Passage), all your Abaco cruising can take place in sheltered water.

Chapter 4
The Northern Abaco Cays
Walkers Cay to Allans-Pensacola Cay

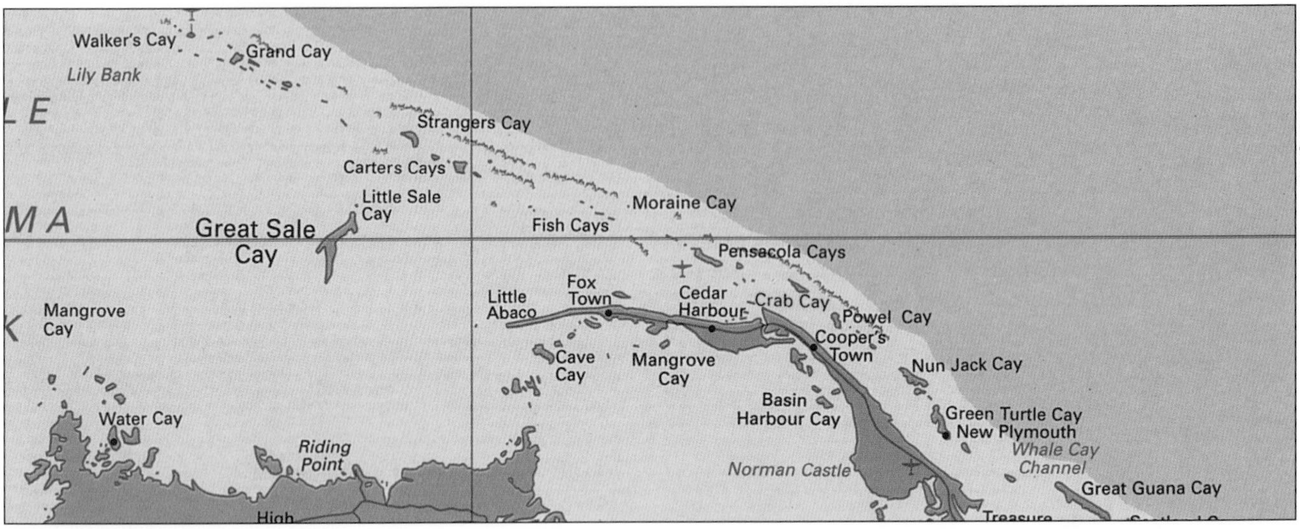

Not to be used for navigation.

Looking At the Charts

The Northern Abaco Cays form a shielding barrier between the Little Bahama Bank and the Atlantic Ocean. They cover some 50 nautical miles and run diagonally (roughly 115/295 degrees true) from northwest to southeast. Look at the chart and you will see that a line of small islands, rock and coral reefs that extends from Walkers Cay at N 27° 12.000'/W 078° 25.000', to Crab Cay at N 26° 56.000'/W 077° 36.000'.

Within a narrow breadth of three nautical miles, this inviting ocean and bank interface zone includes seven pristine cays you will want to visit. Five are uninhabited and alluringly secluded. In addition, there are four deep-water ocean passes into the Atlantic Ocean. Three are in the Walkers Cay area. The fourth is the Moraine Cay Channel. Walkers and Grand Cay are the only inhabited cays in the Northern Abacos. The better-known, uninhabited cays are Moraine Cay, which looks just about the way most people imagine a cay should be, and Allans-Pensacola, with its ever-popular anchorage. Walkers Cay and Allans-Pensacola are also featured in Chapter 3 as Little Bahama Bank transit points.

Glancing at the chart, one might conclude that an ideal cruise would start in Walkers Cay and consist of island hopping all the way to Crab Cay. However, two areas of questionably charted reefs, rock and shoals make this plan as good as impossible, unless you are keen on imitating the cruise of the African Queen. The first is the Big Romers Cay–Rhoda Rocks–Strangers Cay area. The other is the Grouper Rocks–Paw Paw area. Most vessels elect to bypass these hazards by diverting south and west towards Little Sale Cay, staying a good mile off Little Sale. Alternatively, you can cut out into the ocean, going from Walkers Cay to Moraine Cay. But in so doing, you will miss the Grand Cays, Double Breasted Cay and the Carters Cays. That is nearly half of the Northern Abaco destinations that you won't want to miss.

What do the Northern Abacos have to offer? The answer is ocean fishing and the chance to explore the cays. You could say that it is the best of both worlds, and, if you are escaping from population pressures, for much of the time you will be on your own. Later, as you travel farther south in the Abacos, it will be different. There you will find that it is another world entirely and you will rarely be short of company.

In the Spotlight. Walkers Cay

In years past, Walkers Cay Marina and Hotel were bustling operations where barely an empty berth was to be found. The ravages of hurricanes took their toll, however, and since 2004, all commercial establishments on Walkers have been closed. The only inhabitants of Walkers Cay are the Customs and Immigrations officers and a security guard. However, a mere seven miles away, over in the Grand Cays, there is a very sheltered harbor (albeit somewhat tricky to enter) and a charming settlement to explore. The settlement is called Grand Cay, but it is on Little Grand Cay. Big Grand Cay, with a 60-foot dock and its prominent "Edelweiss House," is private, but available for rent. Richard Nixon used to stay in the Edelweiss House when he was president, and you are welcome to visit.

Clearing In—Your Options in the Northern Abacos

At Walkers Cay, the Customs and Immigration facilities are located on the site of the now-closed marina, making it one of the most convenient locations in the Bahamas to clear in.

Walkers Cay, from the east, pre-hurricane. (Not to be used for navigation.) Waterway Guide Photography.

The Grand Cays, from the north.(Not to be used for navigation.) Waterway Guide Photography.

Walkers Cay's loss has been Grand Cay's gain—especially at Rosie's Place. If you don't want to anchor in the cozy harbor, Rosie's marina slips accommodate boats up to 25 feet wide and provide gasoline, diesel and water. Rosie's serves some of the best native cuisine in all the islands. You don't want to miss the cracked conch and potato salad. The pool table is particularly popular here, so plan on being talked into at least one game. For guests, Rosie's has exceptionally nice cottages overlooking the marina. Twice daily flights from Freeport to Walkers Cay are available via Regional Air.

You will enjoy visiting this pleasant settlement. There are plenty of places to poke around, and the residents are very friendly. Don't let the sign "Be Quite (sic), Be Good, Be Gone" deter your explorations. If it is lobstering season, there are not too many men-folk at home. If you are lucky enough to be there when they come back laden with lobster, you are in for a real feast!

Provisioning in the grocery store at Rosie's, and the small shops in town, is good, particularly on mailboat days. Fresh bread is waiting for you at a bakery; and should you need it, there is a clinic in town. Be sure to make plans for lunch at one of the take-aways. Look for one of the lean-to "salad bars," where the conch, crab, lobster, but especially the combo salads, are addictive! You will be back for more. But, don't ask for "hot" unless you are prepared.

The Northern Abacos have long been known for their exceptional dive sites. Walkers Cay was home to one of the first "dive with the sharks" operations. Fortunately, that is gone and with it, humans feeding sea creatures. Today, there are several dependable guides in the settlement to take you for a snorkel or dive of a lifetime. Along with blue hole, cave, wall and reef dives, you will want to look for buried treasure at Money Point - site of the booty laden, sunken ship the *HMS Mermaid*, that met its demise way back in 1760.

Although most of the keel-eating rocks on the approach to the harbor are visible, you may want to enlist the help of a guide or a friendly local fisherman on your first visit to Grand Cay. A call for guidance on VHF Channel 16 will be answered by one of many cheerful folks who monitor the radio and welcome your visit.

What's There? Northern Abaco Cays

Walkers Cay Channel

The northernmost ocean pass in the Walkers Cay area is the old Walkers Cay Channel between the Atlantic Ocean and the Little Bahama Bank. This offers deep water to within some 3.4 nautical miles of the Walkers Cay Approach waypoint, and no particular problems in the final stage. It should be navigated visually, as sandbores in this part of the bank shift with storm action.

Walkers Cay Marina

The entry to the former marina was via a narrow entry channel. Although some entry stakes may still be in place, the channel has not been maintained in years. Underwater hazards left from hurricane damage pose a real threat.

Double Breasted Cay, from the north. (Not to be used for navigation.) WATERWAY GUIDE PHOTOGRAPHY.

A second ocean pass, to the east of Walkers Cay between Walkers Cay and Gully rocks, can be reached directly through deeper water around the southeast point of Walkers Cay, without having to go though the entry channel. This alternative also serves as a route to the Grand Gays and Double Breasted Cay, from which a third ocean pass, between Gully Rocks and Tom Browns Cay, opens.

Gully Rocks–Seal Cay Channel

The shortest route out to the ocean from Walkers Cay is to turn east, parallel Walkers Cay for a short distance, and then head out to the open ocean. Alternatively, take the reverse course coming in. This route avoids the comparative shallows to the west of the Walkers Cay Approach waypoint and bypasses the Walkers Cay entry channel.

Seal Cay Channel

The Seal Cay route involves turning east out of Walkers Cay, passing south of Gully Rocks and Tom Browns Cay, and then swinging northward between Tom Browns Cay and Seal Cay. This pass primarily serves the Grand Cays and Double Breasted Cay, rather than Walkers Cay.

Elephant Rock

Elephant Rock, as you might guess, is a prominent rock south of Seal Cay Cut and east of the chain of rocks (Burying Piece Rocks) that run west from Grand Cay's southwestern point. At one time, deeper water offered an inshore route between Walkers Cay and Grand Cay. We can no longer recommend this as an alternative route.

The Grand Cays

The Grand Cay group consists of five main islands - Grand, Big Grand, Little Grand, Rat and Felix cays. The Grand Cays settlement is on Little Grand Cay. There is a prominent BTC tower on Little Grand's western tip. The waters and cays around the five-cay group are irresistibly gorgeous, but shallow - a mix of bonefish flats, mangrove channels and white sand beaches. It is dinghy country. Since the demise of Walkers Cay, the Grand Cays region has deservedly captured the hearts of anglers and snowbird cruisers. The harbor itself is entered at the far southeastern end of the cays. Begin your entry off the western tip of Felix Cay and favor the eastern shoreline of Rat Cay. Want help? Call VHF Channel 16 for "Love Train's" assistance. There is a tidal current in the harbor, and the bottom is mostly marl.

Double Breasted Cays

Double Breasted Cay is one of the all-time favorite cruiser stops in the Bahamas. It is a place to gunkhole, beach comb, swim, snorkel, fish a little and be amazed at the colors and clarity of the water. The actual Double Breasted Cays lie on the Atlantic Ocean side, shielded from the Bank by two parallel lines of rock. Caught between these two lines of rocky islets is one small plug of rock, Sand Cay, which takes it name from the amazing white sand. You can, with care, work your way into an anchorage here with protection from all but southerly winds.

Moraine Cay, from the northeast. (Not to be used for navigation.) Waterway Guide Photography.

Allans-Pensacola anchorage, from the south. (Not to be used for navigation.) Waterway Guide Photography.

Grand Cays

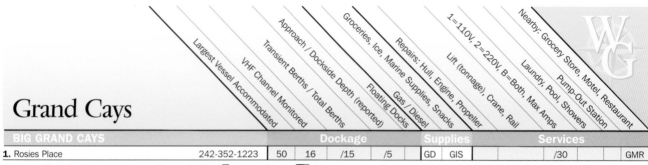

BIG GRAND CAYS		Largest Vessel Accommodated	VHF Channel Monitored	Transient Berths / Total Berths	Approach / Dockside Depth (reported)	Floating Docks	Gas / Diesel	Groceries, Ice, Marine Supplies, Snacks	Repairs: Hull, Engine, Propeller	Lift (tonnage), Crane, Rail	1=110V, 2=220V, B=Both, Max Amps	Laundry, Pool, Showers	Pump-Out Station	Nearby: Grocery Store, Motel, Restaurant
		Dockage					Supplies		Services					
1. Rosies Place	242-352-1223	50	16	/15	/5		GD	GIS			/30			GMR

Corresponding chart(s) not to be used for navigation. Internet Access Wireless Internet Access

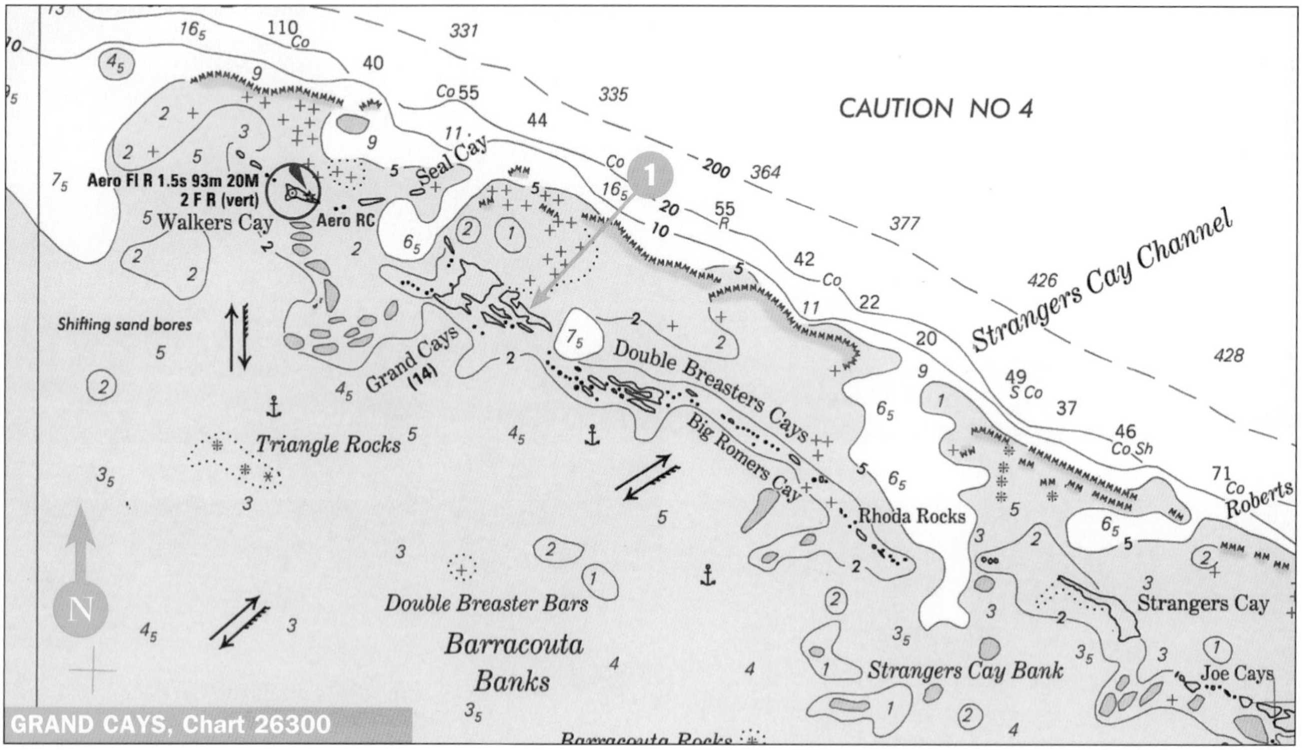

GRAND CAYS, Chart 26300

Big Romers, Rhoda Rocks, Stranger and Joe Cays

Big Romers Cay, Rhoda Rocks, Strangers Cay and Joe Cays are a difficult area of banks, shoals, rocks and reefs. It could well be a gunkhole fanatic's idea of heaven, but for the cruising boat, it is unrewarding. Best to go on to Carters Cay and stay afloat.

Little Sale Cay

Little Sale Cay, with Sale Cay Rocks, presents a four-nautical mile line of rock running east to west about three quarters of a mile north of Great Sale Cay along latitude N 27° 02.000'. Little Sale itself is a large, standing rock. The light on its west headland makes it an unmistakable landmark. It is one of the best Little Bahama Bank landfall waypoints, but don't forget those four miles of rocks and shoals extending eastward.

Carters Cay

If you like offbeat, forgotten places, Carters Cay is for you. Once a U.S. missile-tracking station, Carters Cay has nothing in terms of civilization, but it does have ruins you can explore. No one lives there, but Bahamian fishermen sometimes come to camp. With generators to give them light and charcoal grills as their kitchens, they will use the abandoned barrack blocks and a set of shacks as their base. They are hard working, friendly men who welcome your company and small talk. You may even be able to acquire some cleaned conch or lobster from the big boat's freezers for a small price.

Carters has a magic that captivates - its fantastic, deep-water anchorage, the ease of access by dinghy to the ocean reefs on one side and the bank rocks on the other, the colors of the water and the sense of peace and isolation. If you find any of these things appealing, go there.

Grouper Rocks, Pawpaw Cays and Pawpaw Rocks

You cannot safely take a direct track from Carters Cay to the Fish Cays and Moraine Cay. The shallows of the Carters Cays Bank, with Grouper Rocks, the Pawpaw Cays and Pawpaw Rocks, dictates that you must drop south from Carters Cay to gain deeper water before continuing on your travels.

Moving on from Carters Cay, there are three choices. First, boats can run south of the Carters Bank to the Fish Cays, and then head for Moraine Cay or Allans-Pensacola. Second, you can drop southeast to the Hawksbill Cays (and Fox Town). The

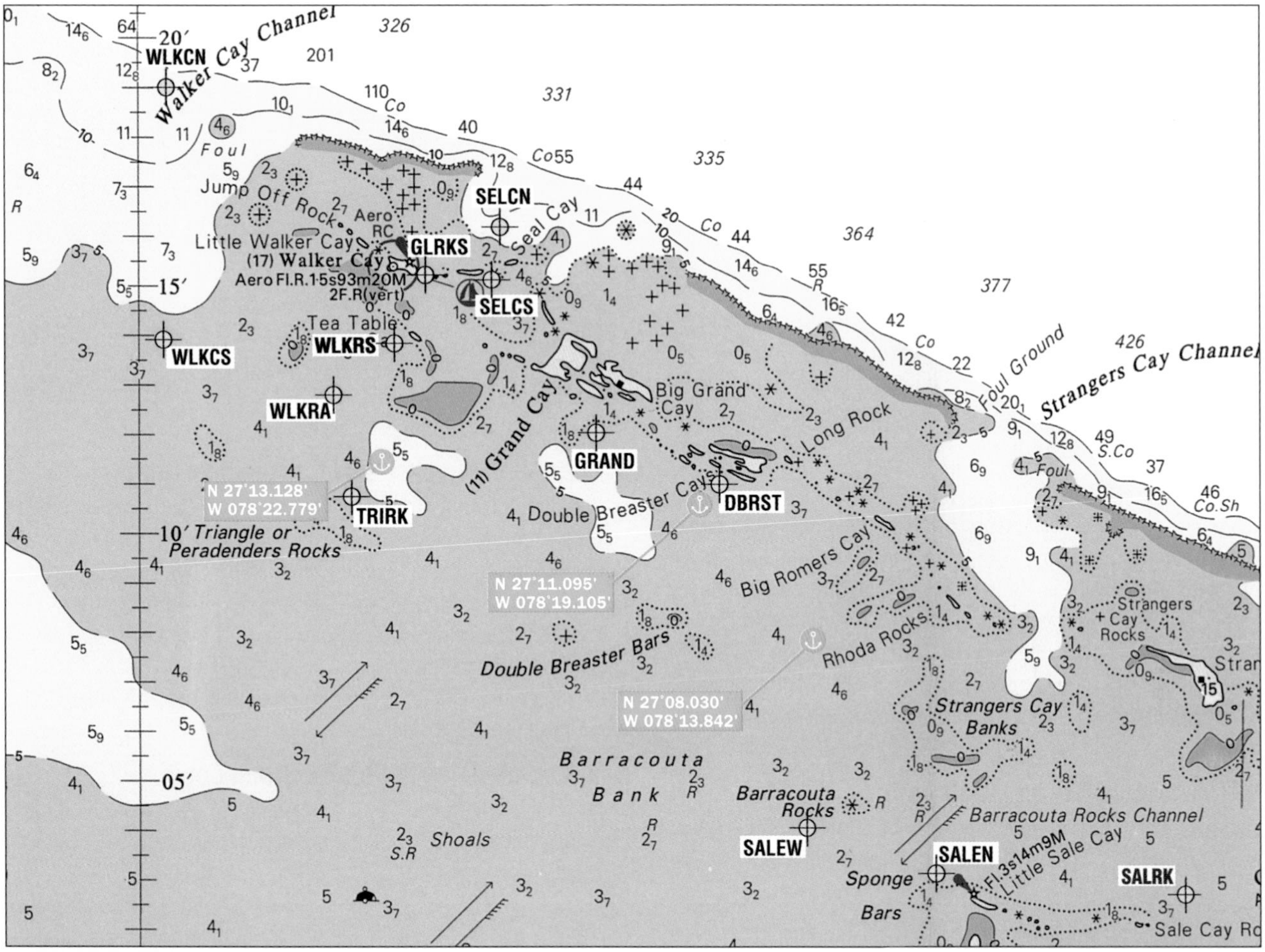

Not to be used for navigation.

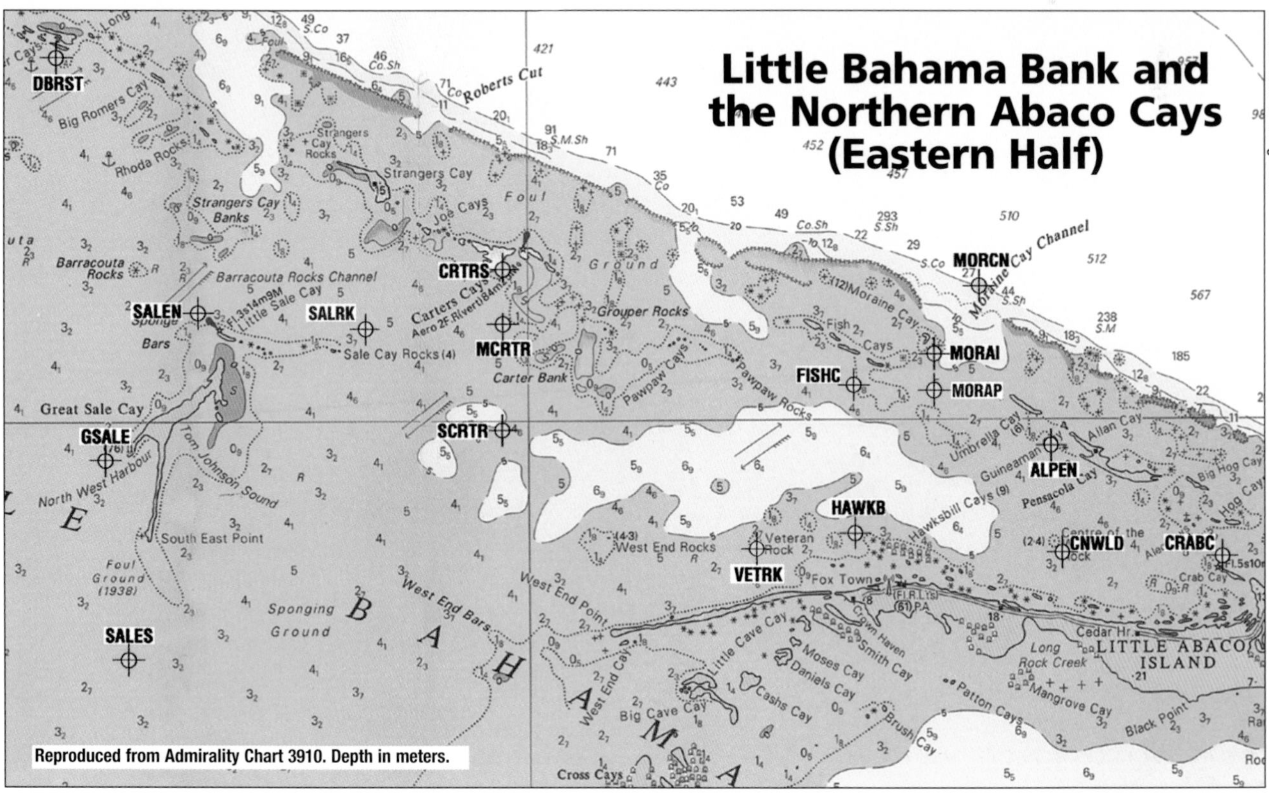

Not to be used for navigation.

third is to make for Crab Cay and head south into the Sea of Abaco. It all hinges on what you fancy doing, and probably on wind and weather, too.

Moraine Cay

Moraine Cay, privately owned but still open to visitors, is a prime, must-see day stop in this part of the Abacos. The beach on the west side, which you reach from your anchorage by dinghy, is postcard material. There, you will find beautiful sand, a 180-degree panorama that encompasses ocean reef, every color of Bahamian water and a horizon that sometimes just merges limitless into the sky. Behind you, there is nothing but one small island, white sand and some palms. Please maintain our welcome—no pets, no garbage burning, pick up plastic refuse and leave only your footprints.

Moraine Cay Channel

There is a good, clear and wide pass out into the ocean to the northeast of Moraine Cay. From the Moraine Approach waypoint, head northeast for about 1.5 nautical miles to reach the Moraine Channel South waypoint. Then, head due north for just under two miles to clear the reef line. Incoming from MORCN, you will be coming in due south, and can either turn for Moraine Cay, or join the main Abaco Cays course line running northwest–southeast to the west of Allans-Pensacola.

Allans-Pensacola Cay and Crab Cay

We covered both places in Chapter 3, The Little Bahama Bank, for they are focal points on the main bank transit routes.

Pilotage. Talking Captain to Captain

Walkers Channel–Walkers Cay (Marina Closed, Customs Only)

From Walkers Channel North (WLKCN), head south on a course of 175/355 degrees true for 5.3 nautical miles to Walkers Channel South (WLKCS). Then, turn on to a course of 105/285 degrees true for 3.4 nautical miles to the Walkers Approach waypoint (WLKRA), which places you 1.5 nautical miles off the entrance to the entry channel. You will need to navigate visually from WLKRA. Your heading will be about 045 degrees true. You may see some stakes that used to mark the marina entry channel. THE MARINA AND FACILITIES ARE NOT OPEN OR OPERATIONAL.

Walkers–Gully Rocks–Seal Cay Channel North

The shortest route out to the ocean from Walkers Cay is to ignore the entry channel, turn east and parallel Walkers Cay for barely 0.2 nautical miles on a course of 115/295 degrees true to the Gully Rocks waypoint (GLRKS). From there, run a course of 063/243 degrees true for 1.7 nautical miles. The route passes between Walkers Cay and Gully Rocks to the Seal Cay Channel North waypoint (SELCN), which serves both the Gully Rocks ocean pass and Seal Cay Channel.

Walkers Cay–Triangle Rocks–Grand Cays

Because the Elephant Rock route from Walkers to the Grand Cays has shoaled, a dogleg out into deeper water is the best

Carters Cays, from the east. (Not to be used for navigation.) WATERWAY GUIDE PHOTOGRAPHY.

way to go. Follow the channel from the marina to the WLKRS waypoint, then navigate visually to WLKRA (1.5 nautical miles on a course of 227/047 degrees true). From there, run 1.9 nautical miles on a course of 168/348 degrees true to Triangle Rocks (TRIRK), then 5.2 nautical miles on a course of 077/257 degrees true to the Grand Cays waypoint (GRAND). The Grand Cays anchorage entrance lies just 0.5 nautical mile on a course of 030/210 degrees true from that last waypoint.

The Grand Cays Anchorage

Don't be tempted to pass between Sandy Cay and Little Grand Cay. Even at high water, one may find depths of 1.2 meters/ 4 feet or less there. You will see that just level with the north end of Sandy Cay, there is an opening between Grand Cay and Little Grand Cay (the BTC tower is there as well as a prominent blue water tank with a white top that looks like a silo). Ignore the opening, and continue your heading. Watch for the rocks south of Sandy Cay, until you pass the W 078° 19.000' line. Then, you will see two more openings lying between Little Grand Cay and Felix Cay. Don't take the first. Go for the second. There is a marker on the starboard side with a prominent white house on Big Grand Cay behind it. Richard Nixon used to stay there to unwind while he was president.

Go carefully into the Little Grand Cay anchorage. Off the settlement, you will find 1.8 to 2.1 meters/6 to 7 feet of water with deeper patches of 2.4 meters/8 feet over sand and grass. Don't be tempted to work your way farther inshore without checking it out first in your dinghy. Your distance run from Walkers Cay to Grand Cay will be just over nine nautical miles going by way of Triangle Rocks.

It is a good anchorage, but open to wind and fetch from the northwest and southeast. Wind and current can chase you round 360 degrees. Make sure you have plenty of space to swing, and don't be surprised if you drag when the tide changes. Stay clear of the fairway in to the settlement (the deeper water on the starboard side as you enter) despite its attractive depths. Use your anchor light at or near deck level, so that it can be seen by someone in a small, fast-running boat. (This advice holds for the Bahamas at large, and the preferred anchor lighting is to use both a conventional masthead light and a light at deck level).

To reach the Double Breasted Cays, continue on a course of 120/300 degrees true for 2.6 nautical miles to reach DBRST. The entrance to the potential anchorages there also lies 0.5 nautical mile on a course of 030/210 degrees true from that last waypoint.

Cracking conch in Carters Cay. Waterway Guide Photography.

The Double Breasted Cays Anchorages

Many are wary of moving in too close to the Double Breasted Cays right at the start and prefer to stand off, use the dinghy to explore, decide where to go and take account of the tide. This last factor is important. There is a strong tidal flow between the gaps in the line of barrier rocks, and there is not much room to maneuver in the inshore channels; certainly not enough to accommodate being swept sideways.

Coming in from the DBRST waypoint on a course of around 030 degrees true, keep about 100 yards to the east of the reef off the southeast end of the first run of rocks. The reef is covered by 0.6-meter/2-foot depths at mean low water. You can drop your hook almost anywhere there, maybe 200 yards off the rocky islets ahead. There is good depth. You will have protection from the west through the north. The downside is that you are not protected from the prevailing winds, and it can be rough. The holding is fair, gravelly sand with some grass and rock.

The Inner Anchorages

Run parallel to the second line of rocks bearing northwest, and follow the dark water (1.8 to 2.1 meters/6 to 7 feet at mean low water) all the way in. Pass midway between the first sandbar to port and the rocks to starboard. An isolated submerged rock has been logged at N 27°11.650'/W 078°16.980'. Pass midway between Sand Cay to port and more rock to starboard. After Sand Cay, you will come to a second sandbar on your port side. You can anchor on the north side of Sand Cay or the north side of this second sandbank, in depths of 1.8 to 2 meters/6 to 6.5 feet. If you want to tuck yourself in on the south side of Sand Cay, round the sandbar turning to port. At that point, briefly, you are exposed to open ocean. That gap carries a strong tidal flow, but it is fine at slack water.

Alternatively, you might want to work your way eastward around the southeastern tip of the second line of rocks, and find yourself a patch to drop your anchor in between the main cays and that line of rock.

South Carters–Carters Cay

At SCRTR, head north (000/180 degrees true for 1.7 nautical miles) to reach Mid-Carters (MCRTR). Then visually navigate, still heading north, for the remaining one nautical mile to Carters Cay.

From the Carters waypoint, feel your way in past the very obvious sandbars, leaving them to port. Head for the center of Gully Cay, and then turn to port. Head toward the mark on the little rock that will be on your bow. Keep about one to two boat lengths off Gully Cay. Then round the end of Gully Cay, not too close inshore, and anchor between Gully Cay and the remains of some kind of military camp on Big Carters Cay. You will have the luxury of 6 meters/20 feet of water there. Don't go in too far to the east as it shoals, and don't opt for mid-channel because the tide rips through there. You are safe where you are. Only a norther will give you a rough time.

Time your arrival for as close to high tide as you can, and that goes for your departure, too. Despite allowing for depths, folks have grounded at mid-tide. The sandbanks and the shoal areas change. No air photograph, chart or guide book can really help you. In the Bahamas, in many places, you are on your own.

South Carters–Moraine Cay

For Moraine Cay, you must bypass Carters Bank, Grouper Rocks and the Pawpaws. Drop south, reversing your entry route, to SCRTR. Turn for the Fish Cays waypoint (FISHC), and then alter for the Moraine Approach waypoint (MORAP). Moraine Cay (MORAI) is due north, one mile off, at that point and visual navigation is required. Moraine Cay is not an overnight stop unless you are certain of your weather, for it is exposed and would be no fun in winds from southeast through southwest. As for the north side, protected though it may be, you would not want to be there in a norther.

Moraine Cay Channel–Moraine Cay

From Moraine Channel South (MORCS) a course of 227/047 degrees true for 1.5 nautical miles brings you to the MORAP waypoint.

Hawksbill Cays–Moraine Cay

A course of 027/207 degrees true from the Hawksbill Cays (HAWKB) will take you to the Moraine Cay Approach waypoint (MORAP). Use this route at high water. The final mile or so of this leg is shoal, reducing to depths of 1.2 meters/4 feet at mean low water.

The Northern Abacos Waypoints

Walkers Approach	WLKRA	27°12.91N / 78°25.45W
Walkers Cay	WLKRS (A1)	27°14.00N / 78°24.20W
Walkers Cay Channel North	WLKCN	27°19.08N / 78°29.69W
Walkers Cay Channel South	WLKCS	27°13.79N / 78°29.17W
Gully Rocks Channel South	GLRKS	27°15.21N / 78°23.46W
Seal Cay Channel North	SELCN	27°16.00N / 78°21.75W
Seal Cay Channel South	SELCS	27°15.34N / 78°21.75W
Triangle Rocks	TRIRK	27°11.00N / 78°25.00W
Grand Cays	GRAND	27°12.16N / 78°19.29W
Grand Cays Anchorage	GCANC	27°13.16N / 78°19.29W
Double Breasted Cays	DBRST	27°10.86N / 78°16.73W
South Carters Cay	SCRTR	27°01.24N / 78°01.00W
Mid-Carters Cay	MCRTR	27°03.00N / 78°01.00W
Carters Cay	CRTRS	27°04.00N / 78°01.00W
Carters Cay Anchorage	CTANC	27°05.05N / 78°00.11W
Fish Cays	FISHC	27°01.32N / 77°49.00W
Moraine Cay Approach	MORAP	27°01.04N / 77°46.12W
Moraine Cay	MORAI	27°02.10N / 77°46.12W
Moraine Cay Channel North	MORCN	27°03.88N / 77°44.82W
Moraine Cay Channel South	MORCS	27°02.10N / 77°44.82W
Allans-Pensacola Cay	ALPEN	26°59.25N / 77°42.25W
Crab Cay	CRABC	26°56.03N / 77°36.31W

Our position format is latitude and longitude in degrees and minutes (hddd°mm.mm). Waypoints in RED are NOT for autopilot navigation. Codes in parenthesis are Wavey Line waypoints marked on the charts. If you have programmed waypoints we listed in a previous edition of this guide, check carefully to ensure the coordinates you have recorded match the list. If a waypoint is no longer on our list we may have changed its code or deleted it.

GOIN' ASHORE:

WALKERS CAY

airport • customs & immigration

The northernmost island in the Bahamas, Walkers Cay provides a northern port of entry into the Bahamas and jumping-off point for the Abacos. Customs and Immigration are here, but the marina is closed.

EMERGENCIES

VHF 16 or VHF 68 Walkers Cay

THINGS TO DO IN WALKERS CAY

- Go deep-sea fishing.
- Spend a day gunkholing around Grand Cay.

LITTLE GRAND CAY

fuel • groceries • restaurant • telephone

Little Grand Cay and the settlement of Grand Cay are easily identified by the tall BTC tower and big, blue water tank. You can anchor in the deep water in front of Rosie's Place or dock there. You can take your dinghy to Walkers Cay to clear customs. The beaches on the Atlantic side of these cays are particularly beautiful, and the bonefishing in these waters is superb.

MARINA

ROSIES PLACE GRAND CAY
Tel: 242-353-1223/1355 - 772-419-8154 - 242-727-4477
VHF Channel 16 or 68 "Love Train"
www.rosiesplace.com - rosie@rosiesplace.com
Slips 15. **MLW at Dock** 5 ft. **Max LOA** 50 ft. **Dockage** $0.75 per ft. per day. **Fuel** Gas and Diesel **Facilities & Services** Power, water, TV and nearby beach. **Restaurant and Bar** *Rosies Place,* Bahamian food with a bar, pool table and televisions. Open 7 a.m. to 5 p.m. for breakfast, lunch and dinner. **Accommodations** *Rosies Island Bay Front Hotel.* Apartments, rooms and efficiencies from $60.

PORT DIRECTORY

Church - *Shilo Baptist*
Fuel - Diesel and gasoline.
Hardware - Small store.
Provisions - *Ena's Bakery* - Fresh bread daily. *Father and Son Grocery and Drug Store* - Fresh bread, cakes, and canned food. *Rosie's Place and Grocery.*
Telephones - Outside *Rosie's Place.*

EMERGENCIES

VHF 16 or VHF 68 "Love Train"

THINGS TO DO IN GRAND CAY

- Go bonefishing on the flats.
- Don't miss Rosie's cracked conch; it gets better and better.
- Count the sting rays and starfish in the anchorage.

FOX TOWN

fuel • groceries • medical • police • post office • restaurant • telephone

You will find a friendly welcome in this quiet community. There is less than 3 feet of water at low tide at the fuel docks, so call ahead if you need help coming in.

EMERGENCIES

Marine • VHF Channel 16 **Medical Clinic** • 242-365-2172
Open daily; the doctor visits on Tuesdays.

Churches - *St. Chad's Anglican Church, Zion Baptist*
Ferry - *Pinder's Ferry* • 242-365-2356 • Runs from Crown Haven, 2 miles west of Fox Town, to Macleans Town on Grand Bahama, daily at 7 a.m. and 2:30 p.m. $40 one way.
Fuel - *Foxtown Shell* • 242-365-2046 • VHF 16 • Diesel, gasoline and propane. Credit cards accepted, 4% surcharge. Ice.
Foxtown Starport • 242-365-2021 • Filling station and a small store run by Daniel and Lilian Parker.
Marine Repairs - 242-365-2021 • VHF 16 • Roy McIntosh through Judy Mae Russell at 242-365-2046
Motel - *Millie's Guest House* • 242-365-2046 • 10 new rooms overlooking the waterfront next to *Foxtown Shell*, with sleeping lofts for extra guests or kids, $65 to $75 per night.
Police - Next door to the post office.
Post Office - Open weekdays 9 a.m. to 5 p.m.
Propane - From *Foxtown Shell.*
Provisions - *M & M Grocery Store; G & J Convenience Store*
Restaurant - 242-365-2046 • Dockside, at *Foxtown Shell.* Re-opened in April 2004 by Judy Mae Russell and her sister Maria Edgecombe; open from 7 a.m. Serves Bahamian fish, chicken, pizza, and burgers, with cracked conch a specialty.
Telephones - At *Starport* and *Shell* fuel docks.

Selling Whatever in the Bahamas. Photo Courtesy of Sebastian Danon

Chapter 5
The Central Abaco Cays and the North of Great Abaco Island

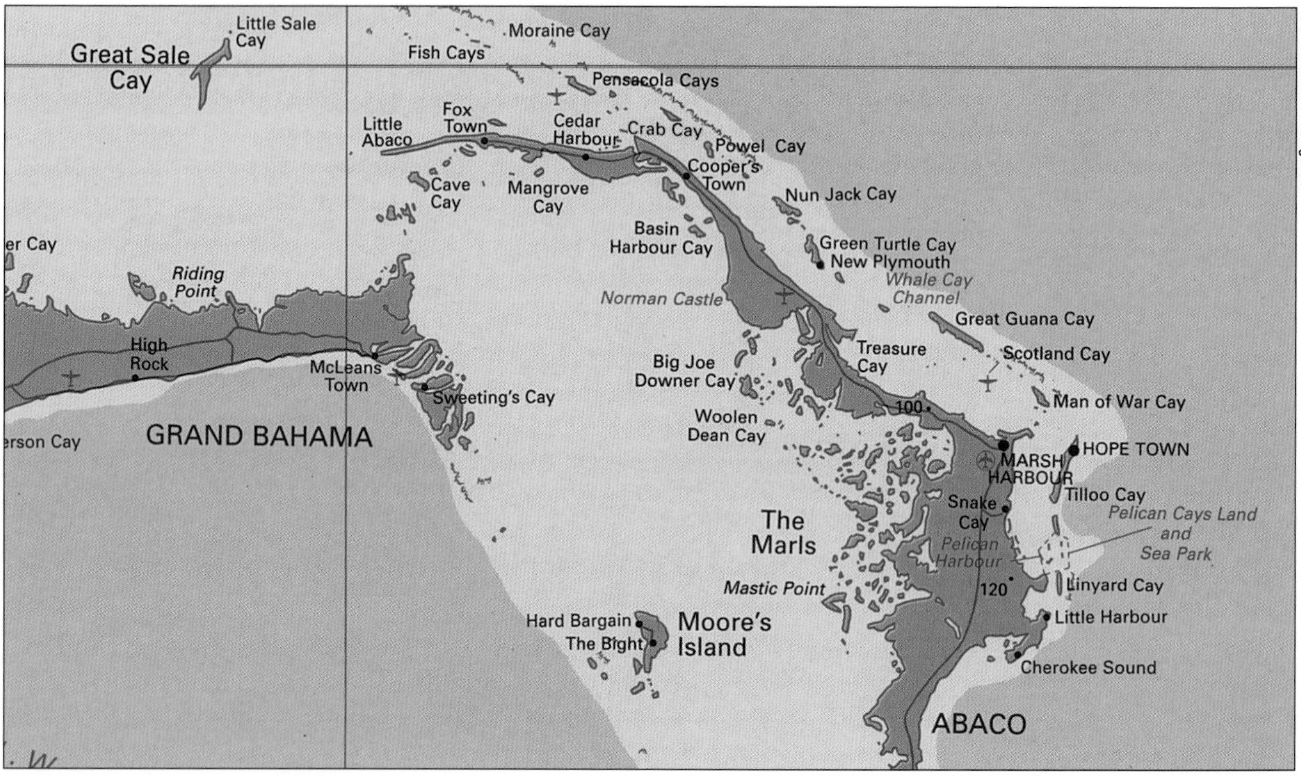

Not to be used for navigation.

Looking At the Charts

From secluded anchorages off uninhabited cays to luxury resorts, The Central Abacos offer just about everything you could wish to find in a cruising ground. Green Turtle Cay and Treasure Cay are by any standard "calendar-page" destinations.

The central section of the Abacos spans about 35 nautical miles, running from Allans-Pensacola to Great Guana Cay. It includes much of Great Abaco Island and some seven "destination" cays. The central section of the Abacos attracts the majority of cruising visitors to the islands. It is here that the reefs and cays lying off the eastern coast of Great Abaco form a barrier, shielding the three-nautical-mile-wide, shallow, largely protected water of the "Sea of Abaco." Note that there are a series of shallow banks that lie in the Sea of Abaco off the southwestern tip of Spanish Cay, the southwest of Powell Cay, the Ambergris Cays, the north end of Manjack Cay and the southwest of Green Turtle Cay. These shoal areas dictate two options as you head south. The first is to stay on the western side of the Sea of Abaco and run along the coast of Great Abaco Island. The second is to stay on the eastern side, running parallel to the cays.

A more extensive area of sand, running from the Treasure Cay peninsula eastward to Whale Cay, effectively blocks the entire width of the Sea of Abaco. Here, vessels continuing southward down the Sea of Abaco (or returning northward), must make a diversion into the Atlantic Ocean (or take a gamble on "Dont Rock") before continuing on their way. Whale Cay Passage "rages" are legend. Whale Cay Passage is a total no-go in bad weather! Along with Whale Cay Passage, there are two other passes out into the Atlantic - Powell Cay and Nunjack channels. Powell Cay Channel is in between Spanish and Powell Cays. Nunjack Channel is in between Ambergris and Manjack Cays. Both are frequently used by anglers and divers, infrequently by cruising vessels.

Because of the shoal areas, your first decision is the route you wish to take in the Central Abacos. The route along the easter side Great Abaco Island is the most direct. It has the safe, deeper water to travel to Green Turtle Cay, Whale Cay Passage and destinations farther south, such as Treasure Cay and Hope Town. However, traveling this route bypasses many beautiful destinations. The outer cays, and Spanish, Powell and Manjack Cays, are popular stops, well worth a visit. The good news is you can switch from side to side as you wish. Just be mindful of the shoals. Isn't that what cruising is all about? Using the freedom of water to go where you want to go.

Treasure Cay, from the northeast. (Not to be used for navigation.) WATERWAY GUIDE PHOTOGRAPHY.

In the Spotlight. Green Turtle Cay

Green Turtle Cay, roughly at the halfway point down the Sea of Abaco, is a little three-mile long island that beckons cruisers. The Atlantic Ocean side of Green Turtle presents a gorgeous stretch of coastline, fringed with reefs and coral heads, and is good for diving. The island is named for the numerous coves along this coast, long ago the major breeding grounds for green turtles. Recently, this area has become a breeding ground for the venomous invader—the lionfish. If you are visiting the island in June, you can partake in the Green Turtle Annual Lionfish Derby. Over 1,000 lionfish were harvested in 2009. More and more restaurants are offering the beautiful, but pesky, lionfish as an appetizer. Folks who have tried them say they taste like grouper, hogfish or snapper. Look for them on local menus or go catch some yourself! You can read about how to catch and clean lionfish under Fishing Regulations in the Skipper's Handbook.

The Sea of Abaco side of the island has two bays in the north and two deeply indented sounds opening to the west. White Sound to the north offers two resorts and great anchorages. Black Sound to the south, with the Leeward Yacht Club, two marinas and a small mooring field, is close to New Plymouth, the main settlement on the southwest tip of the island. If you are here in May, don't miss the Island Roots Festival complete with a Maypole dance, talent contest and unbelievably delicious food. The festival celebrates the island's roots with its sister island, Key West. In the mid 1800s, residents of Green Turtle dismantled their houses in New Providence, put them on barges and sailed to the isolated island of Key West. There, they reassembled their houses and sought fame and fortune in the United States. William Curry left New Providence with his family at the young age of 15 went on to become Florida's first millionaire. To learn more about the loyalists and islanders migration to Key West, be sure to visit the Albert Lowe Museum in a lovely Victorian building. It is a rich source of historical potpourri. Albert Lowe was a model boat builder; and his son, Alton, is a local artist. You can also learn more about the New Providence/Key West architectural connection at the Leeward Yacht Club marina. The developers are building houses there in the traditional architectural style of the 1800s. In addition, don't miss visiting the Sculpture Gardens to learn the loyalist sir names that are still represented on the island.

At the southeast corner of the island, you will find pretty Gillam Bay. The bay is perfect for beachcombing. Don't be surprised if you see cruisers doing the "twist" out in the shallow bay waters. They are using their feet to hunt for sand dollars. The bay is famous for producing the largest sand dollars in the islands. Just spray the dried sand dollars with craft glue, sprinkle on some pink Bahamas' sand, and tie on a velvet ribbon for a souvenir ornament for your landlubber friends back home.

After all that fun diving, beachcombing and visiting of historical spots, you will need some food and spirits. New Providence has plenty of restaurants and bars from which to choose - from dinner-jacket dining rooms at the resorts, to flip-flop take-aways in the settlement. Do not miss a visit with Violet at Miss Emily's Blue Bee Bar. Violet's mother, Miss Emily, started the Goombay Punch mania in the Bahamas with her famous rum punch recipe. Also in town, find Laura's Kitchen for real home-

Flame trees in Spanish Cay.

style, Bahamian fare. Rooster's is another great place for fresh fish and real island chow. If you have never had homemade chicken souse, try The Wreckin' Tree Bar & Restaurant.

The two White Sound resorts, Bluff House and the Green Turtle Club, offer accommodations and great beaches, and the two sounds have some of the safest anchorages in the Abacos. Better yet, they are also wonderful spots to partake of local cuisine and drink. You will want to try a Tipsy Turtle (based on Miss Emily's famous recipe) at the Green Turtle Club bar—that is a drink that makes most cruisers' "don't miss" lists. If you are lucky, the Gully Rooster's band might be there on a Monday, Wednesday or Friday night. Like so many Bahamian destinations, Green Turtle is a magical place that you want to make sure to visit.

In the Spotlight. Treasure Cay, Great Abaco Island

Treasure Cay is not a cay at all, but very much a part of mainland Great Abaco Island. It is a resort community with modern marinas and a convenient, full-service airport. Way back in the 1950s, a pilot named Captain Leonard Thompson dreamed of building a resort on the shores charted as Sand Banks Cay. He partnered with investors and developed the area. Today, the 1,500 acre piece of paradise is home to the Treasure Cay Hotel Resort & Marina. This beautiful property is located in a well-protected basin and is only a short walk to the white sand beach. Here, you will find everything you could want or need from fuel, groceries and duty-free shopping, to a pool and a restaurant and bar. They also host championship fishing tournaments annually.

If you are into fishing, you will certainly have Treasure Cay on your "must visit" list, but it is likely you will want to venture there for other reasons as well. It is a good place to change crew or pick up guests. The airport is close by, and taxi cabs are easy to come by. There is just about every facility one can name - grocery stores, coin laundry, post office, good restaurants and fun bars, rental accommodations and even a golf course, if you want to take an on-shore break. Perhaps most importantly, Treasure Cay boasts a National Geographic's "best beach" nod (it was on a cover). It is truly drop dead gorgeous! For beach lovers, the three and a half mile long walk along the half-moon sugar sands is a once in a lifetime experience. After your stroll, get a drink at the beachside bar. Ask for a gin and coconut water to sound like a "local."

ABACO VHF CHANNELS

The large number of cruising visitors calling on VHF Channel 68 has resulted in an Abaco convention (different from the normal rules) that you name the called party twice, and follow with your own call sign used only once. In addition to this local rule, VHF channel use in the Central and South Abacos differs from the standard international convention, and channel allocation is as follows:

01-05	NOAA Weather (if receivable)
06	Marsh Harbour taxis
16	Distress, BASRA, Calling (All marinas stand by on VHF Channel 16)
22A	BASRA and USCG working
65	Dolphin Reseach
66	Port Operations
68	Cruisers Hailing Channel (All marinas stand by on VHF Channel 16) At 8:15 a.m. VHF 68 is reserved for the Marsh Harbour Cruisers Net
70	Digital Comms only
72	Hope Town Fire Brigade
74	Florida Yacht Charters
80	Trauma One (ambulance)
82	Moorings Yacht Charters

Channels available for cruiser traffic are: 60-61-62-63-64-67-71-73-77-78-79-81-83-84-85-86-87-88

The circular harbor, just before Treasure Cay Marina, is a popular, protected anchorage. Unfortunately, mooring balls have appeared and disappeared in the anchorage over the years, so do use a trip line when anchoring here. For a small fee, you can anchor, tie up your dinghy and use the showers and facilities at the Treasure Cay Marina. Pineapple Point Resort also provides dockage. Truly, you don't want to miss goin' ashore here!

If severe weather is heading your way, seriously consider Treasure Cay as a hurricane hole. If the anchorage and canals of Treasure Cay are full, move to the canals of Leisure Lee to the south. Cruisers (and the Mooring's rental boats out of Marsh Harbour) have ridden out hurricanes in these protected harborages. Secure your vessel with many lines to natural shore fortifications and utilize all of your anchors. Do not endanger other's docks, vessels or property.

Clearing In—Your Options in the Central Abacos

If you bypassed West End and Walkers Cay, your entry port options in the Central Abacos are Spanish Cay, Green Turtle Cay and Treasure Cay. Green Turtle Cay's Customs and Immigration office is in New Plymouth. Call Treasure Cay Marina ahead, as Customs and Immigration officers come from the airport seven miles up the road.

Central Abaco Islands

SPANISH CAY		Largest Vessel Accommodated	VHF Channel Monitored	Transient Berths / Total Berths	Approach / Dockside Depth (reported)	Floating Docks	Gas / Diesel	Groceries, Ice, Marine Supplies, Snacks	Repairs: Hull, Engine, Propeller	Lift (tonnage), Crane, Rail	1=110V, 2=220V, B=Both, Max Amps	Laundry, Pool, Showers	Pump-Out Station	Nearby: Grocery Store, Motel, Restaurant
		Dockage					Supplies			Services				
1. Spanish Cay Marina & Point House Rest. 💻 WiFi	242-365-0083	200	16	81/81	9/7		GD	GIMS			B/100	LPS		GMR

Corresponding chart(s) not to be used for navigation. 💻 Internet Access WiFi Wireless Internet Access

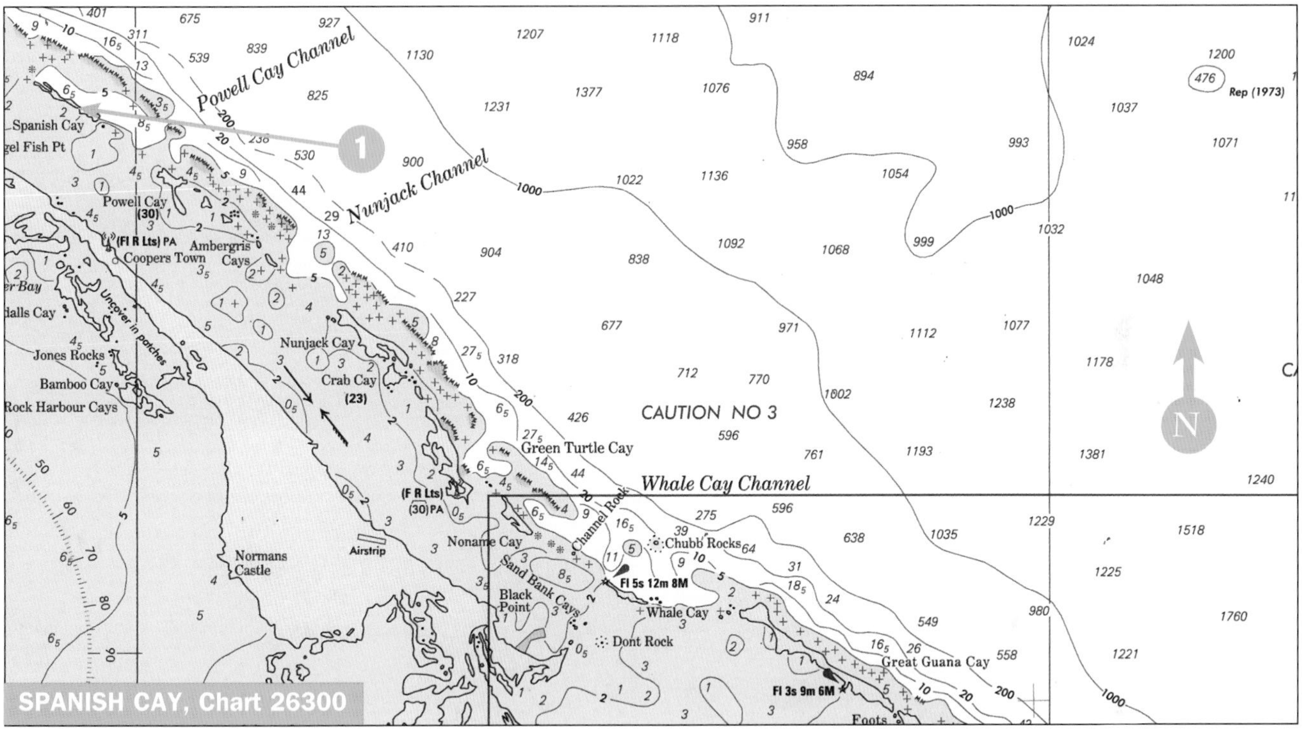

SPANISH CAY, Chart 26300

What's There? The Central Abacos

The Hog Cays

The Hog Cays, which you pass on your way from Allans-Pensacola to Crab and Spanish cays, are grounds for dinghy expeditions and picnics, but not an area where you are likely to anchor for any length of time. This said, Big Hog Cay has some tempting beaches. Explore them and enjoy, but look for and respect the Department of Fisheries signs that prohibit entry.

The Northern Spanish Cay Channel

Boats have been known to suffer serious damage by hitting coral heads as they were running from the ocean into the Sea of Abaco through the northern (Squances Cay) Spanish Cay pass. It is narrow, and we do not recommend using this pass, other than as a small boat passage. Use the Powell Cay Channel to the south of Spanish Cay. Note that it, too, has hazards.

Coopers Town, Great Abaco Island

Look for Coopers Town's 200-foot tall BTC tower. Coopers Town's anchorage is limited especially when the wind is from the north, east and southeast. Be careful. It shoals close to the shore. That is why the length of the Coopers Town docks is limited. Coopers Town has fuel at the Shell Dock and is close to the Treasure Cay airport. Coopers Town is where the Administrator of northern Abaco maintains an office, amid other government offices. There is also a small medical clinic. If you are staying at Spanish Cay, or anchored off Powell Cay, you can fetch an airport taxi to or from the Coopers Town dock.

Spanish Cay

Spanish Cay, just three miles in length, boasts a hard surface, 5,000-foot-long airstrip at its northern end. There is an idyllic, beyond-beautiful marina and resort to the south. Spanish Cay has always been a private paradise, and its grounds are a subtropical heaven of flowering shrubs and trees. The resort's cottages, restaurant and Spanish Cay Marina are top notch, but not cost prohibitive. You can meet your friends and family here, and they can afford to stay. Dinner at the restaurant will not break the bank. This is a great place to tie up, clear in and greet and meet the Abacos. There is a secluded little half-moon beach within a short walk of the marina that is worthy of the best Hollywood backdrops. Bring your towels and your camera—maybe some wine, brie and bread?

Powell Cay, from the east. (Not to be used for navigation.) Waterway Guide Photography.

Quick to respond, the polite, on-site Customs and Immigration personnel make clearing in a breeze at Spanish Cay. The folks here are so accommodating that they have run out to meet an airplane that carried a forgotten purse and tote, filled with imported cheese, for a megayacht. (You have got to love that sort of thing when you are down to beans and rice.)

This is a major spot for sportfishermen and first-class tournaments. Get your camera ready for spectacular shots of sharks circling the fish cleaning stations when those guys come back. Keep a short lead and a steady hand on your dog's leash as you walk the docks. At low tide, expect a big step as slips are built very high to accommodate megayachts. Then, again, those megayachts provide great wind coverage at the slips and wonderful photos to send back home! You will enjoy a stay here.

Powell Cay Channel

Although there are passes through the reefs, both north and south of Spanish Cay, the only one recommended for is the pass between Spanish Cay and Powell Cay, known as the Powell Cay Channel.

Powell Cay

Powell Cay, about 1.5 nautical miles in length. Powell is uninhabited, but far from unfrequented. It is a popular stop with cruising visitors and also within easy reach of Coopers Town, just two nautical miles away across the Sea of Abaco. The northern stretch of beach is divided by the first real elevation in land height that you will have seen in the Abaco Cays, a seemingly great rock headland. There is a trail to the top of the bluff that offers a panoramic view of the anchorage.

Central Abaco Islands

GREEN TURTLE CAY		Largest Vessel Accommodated	VHF Channel Monitored	Transient Berths / Total Berths	Approach / Dockside Depth (reported)	Floating Docks	Gas / Diesel	Groceries, Ice, Marine Supplies, Snacks	Repairs: Hull, Engine, Propeller	Lift (tonnage), Crane, Rail	1=110V, 2=220V, B=Both, Max Amps	Laundry, Pool, Showers	Pump-Out Station	Nearby: Grocery Store, Motel, Restaurant
		Dockage					Supplies		Services					
1. Green Turtle Club & Marina 🖳 WiFi	242-365-4271	130	16	40/40	4.5/8		GD	GIS			B/100	LPS		GMR
2. Bluff House Marina & Resort 🖳 WiFi	**242-365-4247**	**135**	**16**	**20/38**	**5/8**		**GD**	**GIS**			**B/50**	**LPS**		**GMR**
3. Abaco Yacht Services	**242-365-4033**			**/3**				**IM**	**H**	**L40**		**LS**		**GMR**
4. Other Shore Club	242-365-4338	100	16	7/15	4.5/6		GD	GIS			B/50	S		GMR
5. Black Sound Marina WiFi	242-365-4531	55	16	/15	4.5/7			I			/50	LS		
6. Leeward Yacht Club & Marina WiFi	**242-365-4191**	**100**	**16**	**28/28**	**4.5/7**			**IMS**			**B/100**	**LPS**		**GMR**

Corresponding chart(s) not to be used for navigation. 🖳 Internet Access WiFi Wireless Internet Access

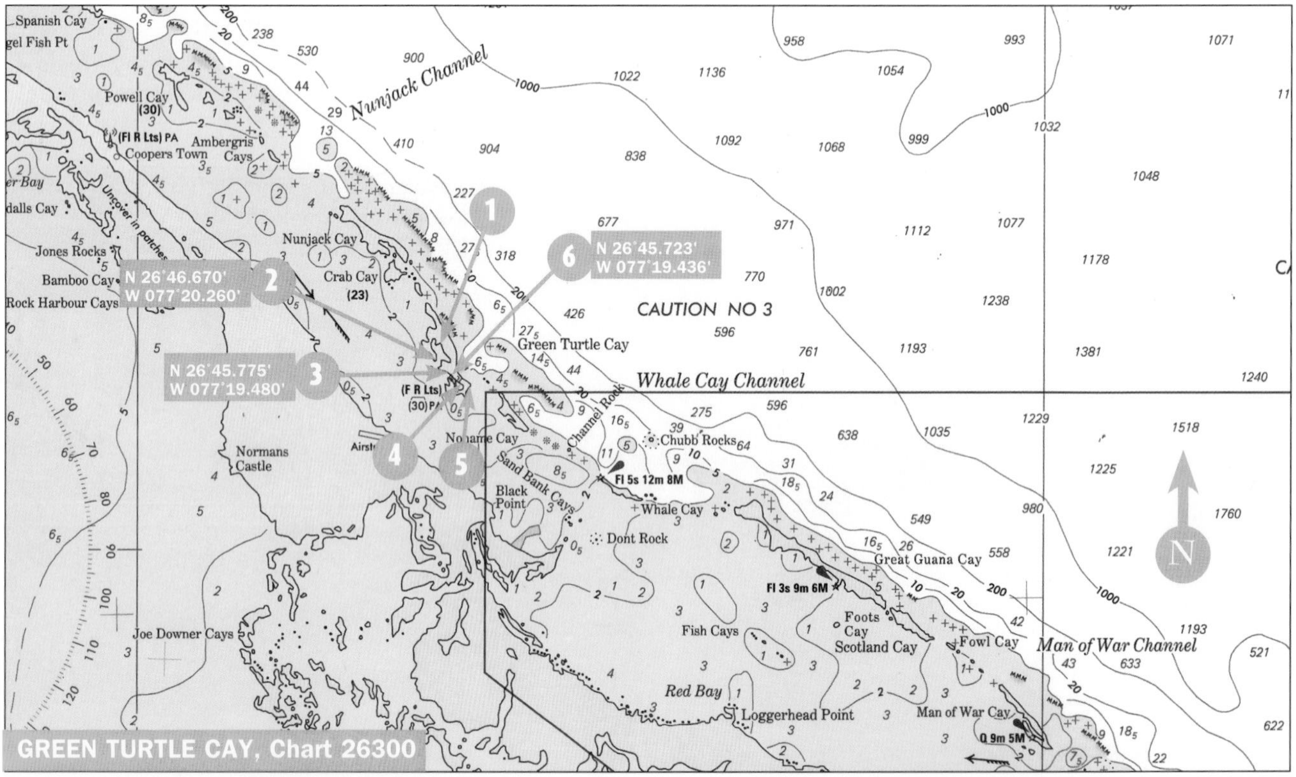

GREEN TURTLE CAY, Chart 26300

Green Turtle Cay Area Atlantic Inshore Reef Buoys

A total of 18 reef dive buoys parallel the line of inshore reef area between the north of Manjack Cay and the south of No Name Cay. These buoys are free for the use of all visitors interested in snorkeling and shallow diving the reefs. The depths between the cays, and in the inshore reef area, set a limit of 0.9 meter/3 feet of draft. Unless you have a shoal-draft vessel, your access to this area is going to be by dinghy or inflatable. Prudence dictates that you do not attempt it in other than settled, calm weather (for you are open to the Atlantic Ocean), ideally at low tide (when the outer barrier reefs partially shield you from any swell) and in good light with the sun in your favor.

The buoys are available on a "first-come, first-served" basis. Do not haul the buoy on board or fix it to your craft. Use a line or a painter as a shock-absorbing rode between you and the buoy. You may also anchor in clear sand, well clear of both reef and grass, or trail your dinghy behind you as you explore the beautiful reefs and coral heads. It goes without saying, but we will say it: do not take any souvenirs away, do not touch the coral or damage the ecosystem in any way, and do not fish. You are there as a visitor. Remove trash if you find it, do not flush your head into the ocean, and help keep one part of the world's precious reef system as it has been since before humans came on the scene.

New Plymouth, from the southwest, with Black Sound at the top of the photograph. (Not to be used for navigation.) WATERWAY GUIDE PHOTOGRAPHY.

Shelling is good on the beautiful southern beaches. A considerable area of shoal lies off the southern end of Powell Cay, which extends to and includes Bonefish Cay. There is an airplane wreck off Bonefish Cay's southwestern tip. It offers great snorkeling. The Ambergris Cays are a three-mile dinghy ride away.

When leaving Powell Cay, head southwest to avoid the shoal area that extends into the Sea of Abaco from its southern end. If you are heading south down the eastern side, stay well off the two Ambergris Cays. The whole area is rock and reef. It is dinghy territory, not a place for big boats.

The Powell Cay Anchorage

Powell Cay attracts many visitors. When choosing your spot, remember that the water is deeper to the north. There is good holding with penetrable sand and some grass, along with protection from the north through southeast. Do not attempt to anchor here in westerly winds. Powell Cay beaches and the snorkeling on the Atlantic Ocean side reefs are memorable. If there are a number of boats anchored off Powell Cay in high season, an opportunistic mobile snack bar from Coopers Town sets up near the pier. Go have some fun and enjoy their local fare.

Bonefish Cay

Bonefish Cay has an airplane wreck to its southwest in 1.5 meters/5 feet of water, little of which shows. It is a fun dinghy destination for exploring and snorkeling.

The Ambergris Cays

When you reach Little Ambergris Cay, you will have run some 8.6 nautical miles from Spanish Cay. Both Ambergris cays have lovely beaches which beckon a visit, but landing is only possible on Little Ambergris Cay. Ambergris Cay is a private estate.

Nunjack Channel

There is a wide ocean pass north of Manjack Cay, just south of the Ambergris Cays. While you have 6 meters/20 feet of depth and almost a mile wide passage going through the reefs, there is one isolated rock south of Ambergris Cay. Favor the Manjack side of the passage.

Piloting in the Central Abacos

Navigation in the Sea of Abaco, apart from one or two straightforward runs, must be done in the old way, using your eyes and common sense. In other words, navigate visually. We will give headings for guidance and distances, too. It is not that there are life-threatening hazards out there, but that the bedrock and barrier reefs of the cays, and sand built up by ocean wave action in the sound, require recognition and avoidance. In particular, the shoals can never be charted, other than as existing in a general area. Do not, save for the few exceptions we show as straightline courses, run on autopilot, and be aware that the routes connecting the cays are in no way suited to high-speed navigation.

Not to be used for navigation.

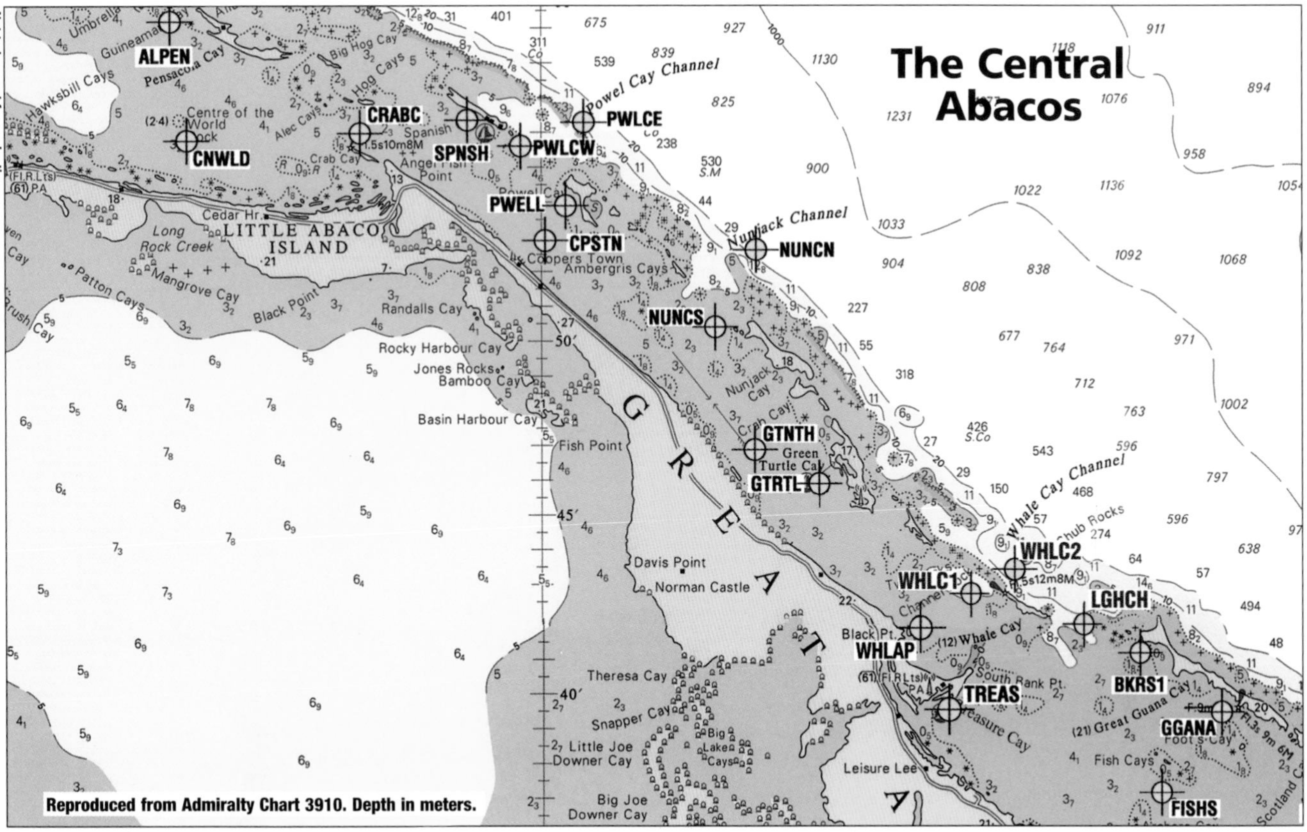

Reproduced from Admiralty Chart 3910. Depth in meters.

Manjack Cay and Crab Cay

Manjack and Crab cays are joined by sand at low water. There is an anchorage at Manjack's northern end with good protection from the south, but it is exposed to the sea. A second anchorage lies in the charted bubble of deeper water off the cay's beach. A third is called Coconut Tree by the locals. It is dead center on Manjack. Despite difficulty with holding there, it is very popular. The best anchorage is in the bight formed by Manjack and Crab cays. There, boats find good protection from the northeast through the south and around 2.4 meters/8 feet of water. Despite the look of a very white bar upon approach to the bight anchorage, it is deep water all around. Shoal draft boats can go past Rat Cay to drop the hook. There is a nature walk on Manjack Cay in the mangrove swamp. Bring along the bug spray.

Green Turtle Cay

About three nautical miles southeast of the Manjack–Crab Cay bight anchorage, you will find the entrance to White Sound in Green Turtle Cay. The entrance to Black Sound is a bit farther south, and the anchorage off New Plymouth is in front of the settlement's shallow harbor, north of the Government Dock. The entrances into the sounds are well-marked, but not deep. Boats that draw more than 1.5 meters/4.5 feet will have to time their passage on a rising tide.

Green Turtle Cay Anchorages and Marinas

There are three anchorages in the Green Turtle Cay vicinity. They include White Sound, Black Sound and New Plymouth. White Sound has resident mooring balls, but there is usually plenty of room to anchor. There are mooring balls available from The Other Shore Club in Black Sound, but anchorage room is scarce. If you choose to anchor off New Plymouth there are no problems in settled weather from the east and southeast, but you are exposed to the north and the west.

The New Plymouth anchorage lies off and outside the entrance markers to the settlement's harbor. When dropping the hook, stay clear of the approach channel to the New Plymouth waterfront and the ferries running to and from Black Sound, White Sound and mainland Great Abaco. When going to New Plymouth by dinghy, use the town dock to the right of the ferry dock or "beach it." The government dock, used by commercial shipping, lies on the west side of New Plymouth. Quite apart from the fact that this quadrant is a commercial route, you wouldn't want to anchor here, for you would be exposed to the southeast.

You have several choices of marinas in the Sounds. Consider the Bluff House in White Sound. The Bluff House Beach Hotel and Yacht Club offers visitors to Green Turtle Cay everything they are looking for in their Bahamas experience. From the 40-slip marina decked with Brazilian teak, giving each slip their little private deck, to the outdoor dining overlooking tranquil White Sound, The Bluff House makes each guest feel they have arrived at their home away from home.

Abaco Yacht Services and the Leeward Yacht Club are located in Black Sound. Abaco Yacht Services is a full-service yard. Many folks wait and have all of their boat projects done here during the winter. Leeward Yacht Club, a 28-slip marina, offers complimentary wireless Internet, a fresh water pool, showers and laundry. From here, you will be able to visit New Plymouth as well as the nearby beaches.

Central Abaco Islands

TREASURE CAY, GREAT GUANA CAY		Largest Vessel Accommodated	VHF Channel Monitored	Transient Berths / Total Berths	Approach / Dockside Depth (reported)	Floating Docks	Gas / Diesel	Groceries, Ice, Marine Supplies, Snacks	Repairs: Hull, Engine, Propeller	Lift (tonnage), Crane, Rail	1=110V, 2=220V, B=Both, Max Amps	Laundry, Pool, Showers	Pump-Out Station	Nearby: Grocery Store, Motel, Restaurant
		Dockage					Supplies				Services			
1. Treasure Cay Hotel Resort & Marina (WiFi)	**242-365-8250**	**155**	**16**	**150/150**	**6/10**		**GD**	**GIMS**			**B/50**	**LPS**	**P**	**GMR**
2. Pineapple Point Resort	242-475-7464			/150							/50			
3. Orchid Bay Yacht Club & Marina (Internet) (WiFi)	**242-365-5175**	**120**	**16**	**/66**	**9/9**		**GD**	**I**			**B/100**	**LS**		**GMR**
4. Guana Hideaways Marina (Internet) (WiFi)	242-366-0224	100	16	40/40	10/10	F		GIS			/100	LPS		GMR
5. Bakers Bay Club and Marina	242-365-5280	250	16	/151	/12.5		GD	GIMS			/200	LS	P	GMR

Corresponding chart(s) not to be used for navigation. (Internet) Internet Access (WiFi) Wireless Internet Access

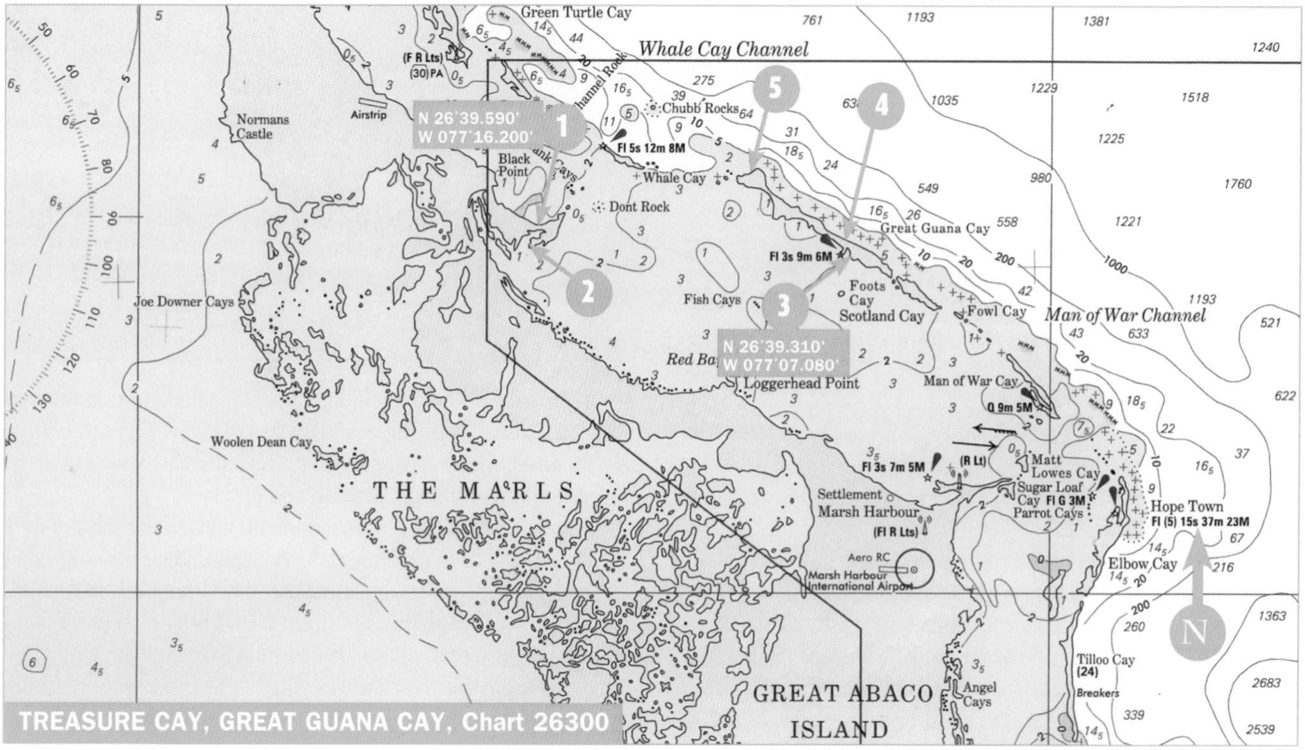

TREASURE CAY, GREAT GUANA CAY, Chart 26300

No Name Cay

No Name Cay, immediately southeast of Green Turtle Cay, is uninhabited. It offers a secure anchorage, nearby coral heads and an offshore reef. It is barely a stone's throw off Gillam Point, the famous sand dollar hunting spot. The cay's beach is pretty and, at low tide, the beach combing is fine. It is a wonderful spot to bring some "litter buckets" and a sturdy trash bag to do a little environmental clean-up. For some reason, there is a tremendous amount of garbage left in the casuarinas by the beach. Pick it up and haul it out as a "thank you" to the islands. Beware, there are shoals extending southeast from Green Turtle Cay. In addition, there are shoals running southwest from the southern tip of No Name Cay. Some vessels purposely ground their boats here at low tide to clean their bottoms. Keep a sharp eye when navigating the area. It is worth the effort to stop here.

Whale Cay and Whale Cay Passage

Whale Cay, two nautical miles south of No Name Cay, is famous for its passage out into the ocean rather than the island itself. This uninhabited cay runs for 1.5 nautical miles and occupies a strategic position, in navigational terms, for it lies at the very point that the Sea of Abaco becomes too shallow, due to sandbanks, for most cruising boats to negotiate.

Whale Cay Passage is probably the best-known ocean pass in the Abacos, simply because everyone has to go that way. This diversion out into Atlantic Ocean water is often dreaded, for it has a fearsome reputation. However, its potential perils are entirely avoidable. In heavy weather it is impassable, and it would be suicidal to attempt to brave the conditions known locally as a "rage."

To the north of Whale Cay, the passage is wide enough to cause no anxiety; but there are rocks to be spotted and it is relatively shallow, some 3.6 meters/12 feet deep. To the south, the apparently wide pass between Whale Cay and Great Guana Cay is partially obstructed by the Loggerhead Bars (one of the

Gumelemi Cay, from the south. (Not to be used for navigation.) WATERWAY GUIDE PHOTOGRAPHY.

factors that contribute to rage conditions). However, between the Loggerhead Bars and Great Guana Cay, it was deep enough to take cruise ships to Bakers Bay, where passengers were brought for day excursions. The cruise ship's approach channel and turning basin are there to this day. The safe transit of Whale Cay Passage demands no more than assessing local conditions before you set out, and matching what is going on there to your boat and your skills. Once around Whale Cay, cruisers can choose to explore the shores of Great Abaco Island, or meander down Great Guana Cay to Man-O-War Cay, with almost all boats ending up at Marsh Harbour at some point.

Treasure Cay

Treasure Cay, highlighted in the Spotlight feature, is only a 6.8 nautical mile run from Whale Cay Passage. Located on mainland Great Abaco, the Treasure Cay entry channel is not easy to pick up from a distance, and the area is shoal. Use caution, your plotter and your eyes, and there won't be any problems.

Treasure Cay provides it all - entry port status, air links, services and great facilities. For sportfishermen, Treasure Cay, Spanish Cay and Boat Harbour Marina in Marsh Harbour are bound to be featured on their tournament calendars. From Treasure Cay to Marsh Harbour, the route is straightforward. The Great Abaco coastline is very pretty and rarely cruised. There are lovely little nooks to duck in and explore by dinghy or shoal draft vessel, as well as the protective canals (7 to 8 feet deep) at Leisure Lee where boats can ride out any kind of bad weather. Travel to the very end of the canals to anchor. Traveling south, just west of Water Cay, you have to dogleg north to avoid the rocks and shoals that extend into the Sea of Abaco. From there, it is a straight 6.5 nautical mile shot into Marsh Harbour.

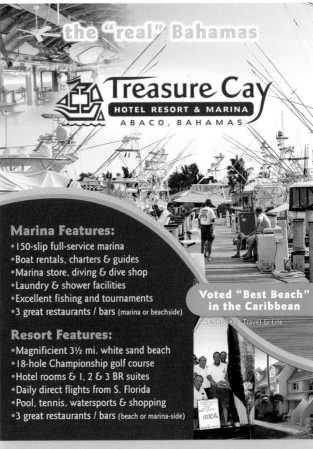

Great Guana Settlement Harbour. (Not to be used for navigation.) WATERWAY GUIDE PHOTOGRAPHY.

Great Guana Cay Northern Anchorages

Bakers Bay, on the southwest side of the north end of Great Guana Cay, owes its unusually deep approach channel to cruise ships that used to anchor here. Bakers had long been a popular destination, and a much-favored anchorage, for those who had completed the Whale Cay Passage. After a vigorous fight put up by the Great Guana Cay natives, Bakers Bay Marina and its developer, Discovery Land Company, were permitted to construct Bakers Bay Marina. The developer has gone to great lengths to meet the islander's environmental concerns, including building the Abacos' first sewage treatment plant.

You can still anchor off Bakers Bay, but the wonderful walks along the half-moon beach, the sundowners at the cruiser's "yacht club" under the big tree and the jungle trail to the Atlantic Ocean side are now just memories, unless you stay at the marina, patronize its restaurant or live in the marina village. The bay is wide open from south through to northeast, shallows quickly as you approach shore and offers varied holding. Don't count on anchoring here while a front is clocking through the first stages of its cycle.

The Spoil Banks (dumped spoil from the excavation of the cruise ship approach channel and turning basin) are a popular stop, known for their shelling. If nothing else, it is an encouraging example of how nature, once given a free hand, can reclaim and make good the toils of mankind. The best anchorage is in the lee of the main spoil bank, one nautical mile west of Bakers Bay. This is a fair weather stop.

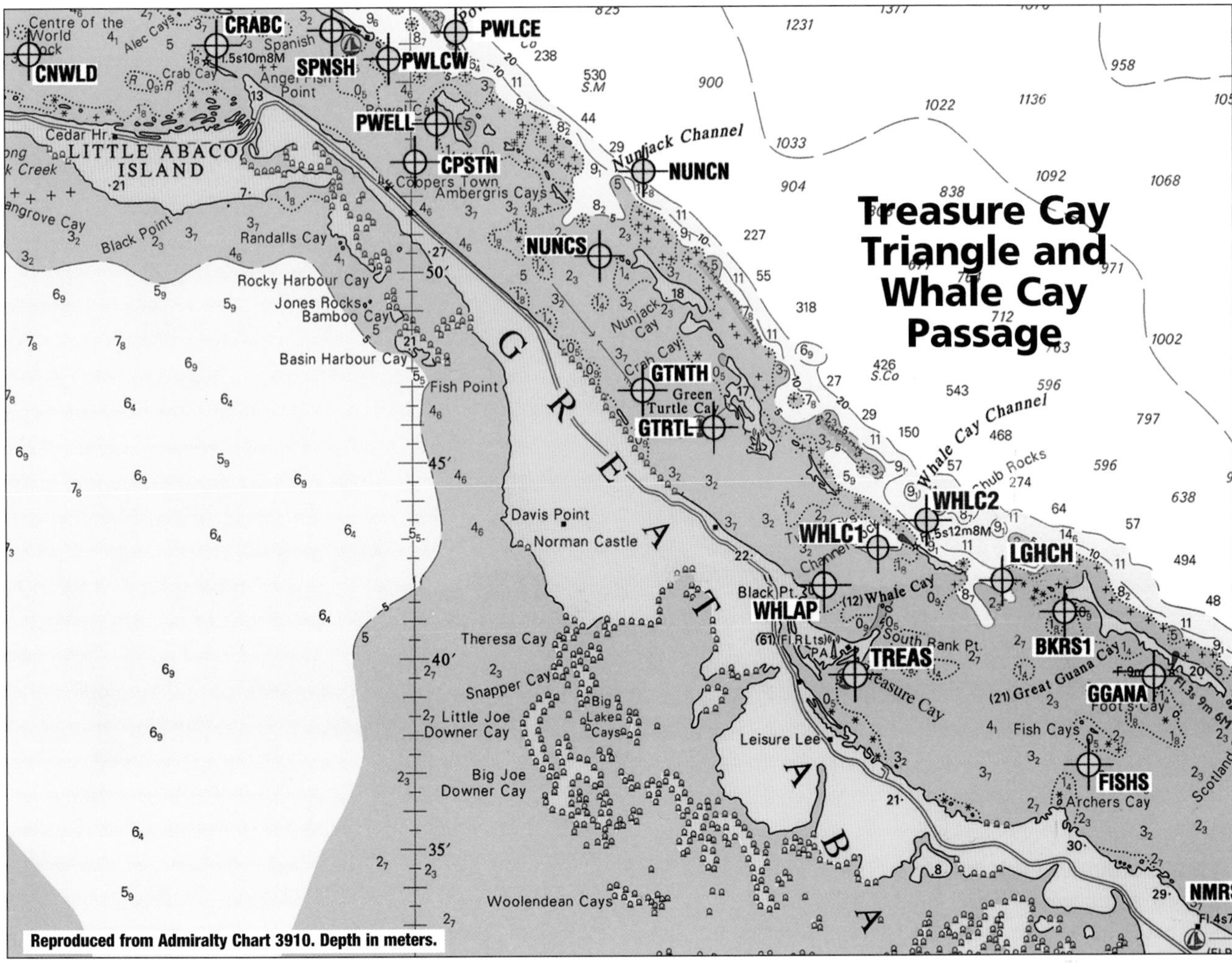

Reproduced from Admiralty Chart 3910. Depth in meters.

Great Guana Cay

Great Guana Cay is higher than the average Abaco cay. A rolling island, it is 5.5 nautical miles in length with a nearly continuous Atlantic Ocean beach. Great Guana's superb beaches, good marinas and great party bars make it one attractive destination.

The Guana Seaside Village on Crossing Bay, just south of Bakers Bay, may have a few mooring balls. Work your way into shore while aiming at the tall antenna. Farther south, toward the settlement, you can anchor in between the obvious mini-island, Delia's Cay, and the coastline. Work your way toward Fishers Bay as depths will allow. There is a dinghy dock to the east. Dive Guana has moorings in Fishers Bay and in Settlement Harbour. Anchoring is permitted in Settlement Harbour, but finding space out of the way can be a challenge and the holding is miserable.

The magnet for cruising visitors, and ferry-borne tourists, is Guana's Settlement Harbour, which is the center of the island population. Grab your camera and hike to the barrier dune east of Settlement Harbour to find Nipper's Beach Bar, with a glorious ocean view and great reef snorkeling below. Nipper's Sunday Pig Roasts are famous, and its rum punch—infamous! On the well-signed trail to Nippers, note the difference between a Poison Tree and its non-poisonous look-alike. Remember which is which on your return to the harbour after a few drinks at Nippers. If you just can't make the hike, Nippers will send the Nipmobile to fetch you from the dock.

There are two first-rate marinas that offer easy access to the settlement (and superb protection in bad weather)—Orchid Bay Yacht Club Marina and Guana Hideaways Marina. Combined, they offer over 100 slips to visiting cruisers, as well as fuel and water. Orchid Bay Yacht Club and Marina is protected by a half circlet of white stone breakwater. Its entry is obvious, as is its Texaco fuel dock at the head of the first dock. The marina is the flag bearer of fast-selling development on a site extending from the Sea of Abaco to the ocean front. A significant parcel of central land has been set aside as a nature reserve. Orchid Bay has well-built slips, fuel, power, water and showers ashore. It boasts a restaurant and swimming pool. The marina itself is removed from the music emanating from the beachside bars and is a sheltered place to stop over in Settlement Harbour.

Guana Harbour (the proper name for the settlement) offers supplies, shops and services on a small-island scale. You will find everything you need along the waterfront road and enjoy good provisioning at Guana Harbour Grocery. To replenish your "spirits," find the Fig Tree. Look for the fresh vegetable stand as you walk around the settlement. Its owner grows and markets his own produce, and he shares a wealth of island his-

White Sound, Green Turtle Cay, from the north. (Not to be used for navigation.) WATERWAY GUIDE PHOTOGRAPHY.

tory. For a special treat, stop into P & J's Variety for homemade coconut ice cream before you leave.

Guana Settlement Anchorages

The best anchorage is in the bay behind Delias Cay and the small point that shields the Great Guana settlement area from view as you come down from the north. On your approach, look out for the submerged rock at N 26° 40.080'/ W 077° 07.330', usually marked by a stake, but don't rely on the stake being there. Don't cut between the rock and Delias Cay, for a submerged reef (with good diving) connects them. There is a shark that is very territorial around that reef, so keep the dinghy close by when in the water.

In the anchorage, you will find reasonably good holding in 2.4 to 3 meters/8 to 10 feet of water. Perhaps a better bet is to take up one of the Dive Guana moorings there. You are well protected from the east and southeast, although you may get some surge. The bay is untenable in a north wind.

On the other side of the point, the holding in Settlement Harbour is not good. Anchoring there is not recommended. There are moorings in the harbor run by Dive Guana. Use one of these if you don't want to take a slip.

Continuing South

The Fish Cays are about three miles southwest of Settlement Harbour. There are fair weather anchorages on either side of them in about 3 meters/9 feet of water. Foots Cay, to their east, is privately owned. Scotland Cay is heavily developed with every nature of cottage and beach house. Many of the big partiers at Nipper's come from Scotland Cay. There is nothing "native" to visit on Scotland Cay, but you can anchor off its shores and dive off its reef. Fowl Cay is just southeast of Scotland Cay. It is a land and water preserve. Cruisers can enjoy exploring the cay and snorkel its protected waters. Watch where you drop your hook and, of course, take nothing and leave only footprints.

Pilotage. Talking Captain to Captain

Spanish Cay–Coopers Town

Getting to Coopers Town from Spanish Cay requires a dogleg because of the bank off the southwest tip of Spanish Cay. On leaving the Spanish Cay Marina, use visual piloting to head for Great Abaco Island on a course of 210/030 degrees true for two nautical miles, straight across the Sea of Abaco. Then turn southeast for Coopers Town, again using your eyes, keeping a comfortable distance offshore on around 118/298 degrees true for three nautical miles to reach the Coopers Town waypoint.

Spanish Cay–Powell Cay

After leaving Spanish Cay Marina, proceed south cautiously, as there are both reefs and sand bores in the area. Use a heading of 123/303 degrees true toward the Powell Cay Channel West waypoint (PWLCW), for about one nautical mile. Pass south of Goat Cay and the shoal on your starboard side. After that first mile, travel an additional 1.6 nautical miles on a slight alteration, around 139/319 degrees true. This will take you to the Powell Cay waypoint (PWELL). Watch out for the reef off the northwest tip of Powell Cay. The first potential anchorages come up along the run of Powell Cay's sweep of beaches facing the Sea of Abaco. You will find 1.8 to 2.4 meters/6 to 8 feet of water there.

Powell Cay Channel

Although there are passes through the reefs both north and south of Spanish Cay, the only one recommended is the pass between Spanish Cay and Powell Cay, commonly known as Powell Cay Channel. This pass has also been known as South Spanish Cay Channel.

Powell Cay–Manjack Cay

Watch out for the shoal area off the southern end of Powell Cay. Initially head 175/355 degrees true for a mile to clear this shoal and the reefs around and south of Bonefish Cay. Then alter for the Ambergris Cays on a course of 125/305 degrees true for 3.4 nautical miles. Be aware of the shoal and rocks that run out for nearly half a mile southwest from the southern end of Ambergris Cay. There should be a warning stake on one of the outermost rocks. Its position is approximately N 26° 51.580'/W 077° 25.830'. The AMSTK waypoint marks the safety zone.

After Ambergris, cross the Nunjack Channel. Another shoal area, extending about a mile and half southwest off the north end of Manjack Cay, dictates running offshore for another 2.5 nautical miles from the AMSTK area on a course of 150/330 degrees true before you reach the turning point for Manjack Cay. From here, if you want to go straight on to Green Turtle (GTRTL), it is just over four nautical miles on a course of 135/315 degrees true.

Nunjack Channel

Nunjack? Yet another confusing Bahamian name. The cay called Manjack was Nunjack at one time. Somehow, the cays name changed, but the channel kept its original moniker. The Nunjack Channel is a good, wide ocean pass between Ambergris and Manjack cays, with 6-meter/20-foot depths and close to a mile in width through the reefs. There is one isolated rock on the northern side, just south of Ambergris Cay. You will see it.

Manjack–Crab Cay Anchorage

The Manjack–Crab Cay anchorage is a little more than a mile due east from the turning point after running south from the Ambergris stake. You will find two secluded anchorages on the southern end with good protection. A turn for Green Turtle, directly from the doorstep of the anchorage, will give you just over a three nautical mile run to GTRTL on a course of 157/337 degrees true.

Green Turtle Cay. White Sound

As you approach White Sound, you will notice Bluff House Resort to port as you come from the north. A landmark is the tower-like observation deck built above the ridgeline house to the north of Bluff House. The dock you see on the Sea of Abaco was built to accommodate the fuel tanker, but is not a fuel dock.

Rages

It is the "shelf effect" of heavy weather that can close down Whale Cay Passage. High seas, particularly northeasters and distant Atlantic storms, generate heavy swells that produce dangerously rough conditions as the water piles up on the shoals. These "rages" - powerful, turbulent and lethal seas - are a characteristic of all similar ocean passes.

In unfavorable weather, under no circumstances should you even think of poking your nose out to check what it might be like out there. If someone has a deadline, a flight from Marsh Harbour or something like that, change it to Treasure Cay. Or take the ferry to Treasure Cay and a taxi on to Marsh Harbour. The reverse applies, of course, if you are on the other side of Whale Cay heading north.

Black Sound,Green Turtle Cay, from the southeast. (Not to be used for navigation.) WATERWAY GUIDE PHOTOGRAPHY.

The dredged channel leading into White Sound is well-marked, and you will have no problems. It has 1.5-meter/5-foot depths at mean low water. The channel is maintained at a 30-foot width and leads to the Green Turtle Club Marina (to starboard), and the Bluff House Marina (to port). Between the two sets of docks there is an anchorage in between and around the moorings balls.

Don't be tempted to poke your way into the east extension of White Sound when you see it open up to starboard about halfway up the entrance channel. There may be mooring buoys there, and perhaps 1.8-meter/6-foot depths inside, but the threshold carries barely 0.9-meter/3-foot depths.

Green Turtle Cay. Black Sound

The entry to Black Sound is clearly marked with pilings. A reef runs across three-quarters of the apparent entrance to the Sound, between the starboard piling as you enter and the promontory. You can use it as a depth gauge. If you can't see the reef to starboard as you enter Black Sound, you will have some 1.5-meter/5-foot depths in the channel. If you can see the reef, the channel depth will reduce to 0.9-meter/3-foot depths at mean low water.

A line of pilings leads you in to Black Sound, but the deeper water is obvious. Take a gentle curving course to starboard to settle on the center line to run up the sound. Abaco Yacht Services and The Leeward Yacht Club are to port. To starboard, is the Other Shore Club (with a fuel dock). Farther on, are the Black Sound Marina and Robert's Marine. There are some moorings in Black Sound. Free anchoring is permitted, but space is limited and the holding is not good. Many have dragged there.

Moving on South or Coming from the South

If you are heading for Whale Cay Passage, or coming from there, take note that there is a shoal area immediately south and southwest of the point on which New Plymouth sits. Stand well out into the Sea of Abaco to stay clear of this.

Farther south, the shoal area between No Name Cay and Two Rocks (north of Whale Cay) has extended even more into the Sea of Abaco. Use the Whale Cay Approach waypoint

A Brief History of The Abacos

Despite the Abacos distinct British ambiance, the first settlers in the islands were French. In the mid 1500s, the French Huguenots actively colonized lands close to Spanish settlements and trading routes. Their first big attempt was in the Abacos. They named their fledgling settlement Lucayoneque. Lucayoneque had first-rate harbors, fresh water sources, valuable saltpans and wild boar in the woodlands. Unfortunately, the French let the settlement languish, and it did not prosper. Despite Lucayoneque's failure, French interest in the Bahamas and surrounding islands remained keen. During the 17th century, the French crown colonized Abaco, Inaugua, Mariguana and Gilatur (the spelling of that time). Later, they focused their attention on the Turks and Caicos because they are closer to the Windward Passage. As French interest in the Bahamas waned, unhappy British subjects from Bermuda, who sought religious freedom from the monarchy, foresaw their future in the Bahamas.

The first British émigrés from Bermuda settled on the island of Segatoo. They renamed it "Eleutheria"--the Greek word for "freedom." The settlers used Bermuda as the model for their new Bahamian settlement. The strong link between Bermuda and Great Britain is apparent to this day in the Bahamas. By the late 1600s, approximately 1000 Bermudians had settled in Eleutheria. Unfortunately, their demand for housing materials was detrimental to the once abundant pine and cedar woodlands of the Abacos.

The Abacos remained relatively unpopulated until after the American Revolutionary War. In the war's aftermath, the Abacos were forever changed by the resettlement of Loyalists and freed slaves who had fought alongside the British and against the Revolutionaries. The freed slaves were not of African descent. Most had ties to Bermuda, Jamaica, Haiti and Barbados. The first large relocation of Loyalists and freed slaves was in the summer and fall of 1783. The British offered them resettlement in Canada or the Abacos. Unscrupulous promoters foresaw vast profits in sailing the refugees to the Abacos and promoted the islands without shame. Grossly exaggerated advertisements in leading New York newspapers attested to the Abacos' near perfect climate, astonishing fertile land and bountiful timber stands.

Problems in the Abacos soon followed because the islands did not live up to the over-embellished promises. Some of the Caucasian settlers, dubbed "Conchy Joes," left for Key West, Florida. Many of the freed slaves fled to Cuba or New Providence. In Cuba, they were welcomed warmly and assimilated easily into that society. Others who went to New Providence fared less well because they were vastly out-numbered by criminal elements. So many freed slaves fled the Abacos, the islands became predominantly populated by Caucasian Loyalists. Only one or two families settled some islands. Their surnames are in abundant evidence today.

Since boats were essential to living in this sea of stepping stone islands, the ability to build, maintain and repair them was vital to the newcomers. Males had to learn how to fell trees, build boats, sail and fish. Fortunately, a wide variety of boat building timber grows on the islands. Through trial and error, the Loyalists learned to use pine for masts and planking, cotton for caulking and naturally crooked hardwoods like mahogany and lignum vitae for ribs, keels and rudders. Sisal plants were braided into ropes and lines. The settlers became great boatbuilders and skilled sailors. Abaconian boatbuilding and sailing skills remain much admired throughout the islands, and boatbuilding continues to be an important part of the islands' heritage.

As time passed, the British firmly re-established themselves in the Bahamas and imperially ruled the islands until 1973 when independence was achieved. Since then, the political scene has remained publically vigorous and sometimes turbulent. Political policy plays an integral role in determining the growth and advancement of the Bahamas. Along with Freeport on Grand Bahama, the Abacos have been fervently developed as a cultural and demographic extension of Florida. Those folks who enjoy the lifestyle of southern Florida and the Keys love the Abacos and feel right "at home." Coupled with the gorgeous turquoise waters, modern marinas, lovely anchorages, charming Bermudian-inspired cottages and the residents' lilting British accents, the Abacos are a cruising destination not to be missed.

(WHLAP), favoring the Great Abaco side, to keep away from these two shoal areas and in the deeper water off the mainland. This waypoint serves equally well if you are bypassing Green Turtle Cay coming down from Coopers Town.

Whale Cay Passage

Whale Cay Passage is a simple two-leg diversion around Whale Cay, followed by two additional legs that take you through the Loggerhead Pass and into the discontinued cruise ship channel to Bakers Bay on the northwest tip of Great Guana Cay. Check the weather the day you intend to do the Whale Cay Passage, listen to the Marsh Harbour Cruisers Net, talk to the locals, talk to other boats and call anyone in the area and ask what Whale Cay conditions are like. If it is calm, go for it.

Coming from the north, the Whale Cay Approach point is the turning mark for Whale Cay Channel. The line from this point, through the first Whale Cay Channel waypoint to the second Whale Cay Channel point, is one common bearing, 066/246 degrees true held for 2.9 nautical miles. For clarity in navigation, keep the two channel waypoints identified, and this definition also helps mark the pass when coming up from the south.

The Whale Cay Channel

The first two waypoints (WHLC1 and 2) will take you in or out through Whale Cay Pass. In the pass itself, you have depths of 3.6 meters/12 feet at mean low water, which is sufficiently shoal to produce a wicked sea state if anything significant is happening out in the Atlantic Ocean. Chub Rocks lie about a mile ahead, on the edge of the ocean drop-off, and are easily identifiable. Channel Rock, to port if you are outgoing, is also easy to pick up. Whale Cay with its light is unmistakable.

The Loggerhead Pass

This leg takes you well clear of the Loggerhead Bar, which lies roughly midway between Whale Cay and Great Guana Cay's northwestern tip, into the old cruise ship channel to the Bakers Bay (BKRS1) waypoint. You can see the line of posts along the deep water channel (don't be fooled by some markers off to starboard), the sand of Bakers Bay on your port bow and the main spoil island on your starboard bow. Here you have two options. Turn for Treasure Cay, or continue down the line of the Abaco Cays.

Whale Cay Passage. An Inshore Route?

We have all been attracted by the thought of an inside route past Whale Cay. There is a high-water shoal route there, close inshore, but with depths of 0.9 meter/3 feet at the most. It is only suitable for shoal-draft craft, skiffs, inflatables or dinghies. There is also the Dont Rock passage. Both passages move around year-by-year as the sand moves, so even if you explore these options for fun, each trip requires prior exploration. There is a serious risk of grounding.

That said, the fundamental truth is when the offshore passage becomes impassable, so do the inshore routes. Rage conditions in Whale Cay Channel and seas piling up on the Loggerhead Bars take out all your options, because the whole mid-section of the Sea of Abaco, coast to coast, becomes impassable.

Whale Cay Passage–Great Guana Cay

At BKRS2, you are at the end of the cruise ship channel, at the turning basin. Continuing on the straight-line course takes you from Bakers Bay to the entrance to Great Guana Cay's Settlement Harbour.

Whale Cay Passage–Treasure Cay

The outlying bars of the mid-Abaco Sea sands that obliged you to divert around Whale Cay dictate that your course to Treasure Cay is best taken in two legs from the Loggerhead Pass. First of all, to get safely clear of the Loggerhead Bars, run past the LGHCH waypoint for about 0.4 miles. Then, turn on to a course of 205/025 degrees true for three miles, which will take you safely southeast of Dont Rock (easy to see) and east of a shallow bank (not obvious) that lies less than a mile southeast of Dont Rock.

Having run that three-mile diversion, you can turn directly for the Treasure Cay waypoint (TREAS) on a course of about 279/099 degrees true with about 3.5 nautical miles to run. When you get close to TREAS, you will see the entry channel stakes, just 0.5 nautical mile off your starboard bow. Go slowly, take it easy and get it right, going in between the correct markers. There is a sandbar on your starboard side and another sandbar, which may or may not show, to port. Stay between the markers, and you will have 2.1 meters/7 feet of water all the way into the marina. On your way in, you pass the Treasure Cay fuel dock to port, which is separate from the marina.

Treasure Cay Approach from the South

Approaching Treasure Cay from the south, the Fish Cays waypoint is the way to go, unless you elect to go by way of Great Guana Cay and the route just outlined.

The Central Abacos Waypoints

Crab Cay	CRABC	26°56.03N / 77°36.31W
Spanish Cay	SPNSH	26°56.19N / 77°32.00W
Powell Cay Channel East	PWLCE	26°56.53N / 77°28.76W
Powel Cat Channel West	PWLCW	26°55.50N / 77°30.41W
Powell Cay	PWELL	26°54.25N / 77°29.20W
Cooperstown	CPSTN	26°53.00N / 77°30.00W
Ambergris Warning Stake	AMSTK	26°51.58N / 77°25.83W
Nun/Manjack Channel	NUNCN	26°52.86N / 77°23.09W
Nun/Manjack Channel	NUNCS	26°50.87N / 77°24.37W
Manjack Anchorage	MANCR	26°49.05N / 77°21.78W
Green Turtle North	GTNTH	26°47.20N / 77°23.46W
Green Turtle Cay	GTRTL	26°46.00N / 77°21.00W
Whale Cay Approach	WHLAP	26°42.16N / 77°17.58W
Whale Cay Channel	WHLC1	26°42.84N / 77°15.85W
Whale Cay Channel	WHLC2	26°43.37N / 77°14.51W
Loggerhead Channel	LGHCH	26°42.00N / 77°12.00W
Loggerhead Entry Mark	LGHCM	26°41.86N / 77°11.88W
Bakers Bay	BKRS1	26°41.41N / 77°10.16W
Bakers Bay	BKRS2	26°41.08N / 77°10.08W
Great Guana Cay	GGANA	26°39.51N / 77°07.37W
Treasure Cay	TREAS	26°39.61N / 77°16.83W

Our position format is latitude and longitude in degrees and minutes (hddd°mm.mm). Waypoints in RED are NOT for autopilot navigation. Codes in parenthesis are Wavey Line waypoints marked on the charts. If you have programmed waypoints we listed in a previous edition of this guide, check carefully to ensure the coordinates you have recorded match the list. If a waypoint is no longer on our list we may have changed its code or deleted it.

GOIN' ASHORE:

SPANISH CAY

private airstrip • customs & immigration • fuel • groceries • marina • restaurant • telephone • water

This three-mile-long cay has two miles of beautiful beaches, scattered private homes, rare and exotic birds and some of the best tropical plantings in the Abacos. The marina offers an excellent restaurant and bar and a small grocery. Accommodations overlooking the marina or the ocean are available. Fishing tournaments are big attractions. Spanish Cay is the gateway marina to the Sea of Abaco. Here, you can clear in with Customs and Immigration, refuel and dine ashore while making your Abaco plans.

MARINA

SPANISH CAY MARINA

Tel: 242-365-0083 or 888-722-6474 • Fax: 242-365-0453 • VHF 16 • spanishcay@aol.com • www.spanishcay.com

Slips 81. **Max LOA** Over 200 ft. **MLW at Dock** 7 ft. **Dockage** $2.75 per ft. per day. **Fuel** Diesel and gasoline; 5% surcharge on credit cards. The Fuel dock is inside the marina on your port side as you turn toward the marina office and restaurant. Tie Up For Customs only, $50 fee (when not docking overnight) **Facilities** Power $20 for 30A, $50 per day for 50A, $95 for 100A. Water $0.20 per gallon. Showers, laundry, telephone, ice and WiFi. Small grocery store with fresh produce, liquor. Fresh-water pool with pool bar and hot tub. Golf cart rentals $65 per day. Private and chartered aircraft only use the 5,000-ft. runway. **Restaurant & Bar** *Point House* Open for breakfast, lunch, dinner overlooking the Sea of Abaco. Dinner reservations preferred. *Wreckers Bar* on the ocean side. **Accommodations** hotel rooms overlooking the marina; 12 beachfront rooms. **Credit Cards** Visa and MasterCard. **Dockmasters** Felix Johnson and Don Rolle.

THINGS TO DO IN SPANISH CAY

- Swim and snorkel off one of their fabulous beaches.
- Take your dinghy and explore the passes to the north and south of Spanish Cay, where in settled weather, the inshore reefs offer fine sites for snorkeling and shallow-water diving.
- Watch for the rare albino white owls at dusk.

GREEN TURTLE CAY

bank • customs & immigration • fuel • groceries • marinas • marine sevices • medical • police • post office • restaurants • telephone water

One of the best-loved cays and a favorite Abaco destination, Green Turtle remains a joy and a delight. The historic settlement of New Plymouth retains an old-world charm, with restaurants, well-stocked stores and a thriving community of friendly people who welcome visiting boaters. Both White Sound and Black Sound provide sheltered moorings and marinas, with abundant rental properties for families wishing to stay ashore. Good anchorages, good beaches, good friends and a warm "welcome back" complete the idyllic scene.

Green Turtle Cay is a port of entry for the Bahamas; Customs and Immigration (242-365-4077) is on Parliament Street in New Plymouth, next to the Post Office, open weekdays 9 a.m. to 5 p.m., weekends if specially requested.

EMERGENCIES

BASRA 242-366-0500 or VHF 16
Marine • VHF 16
Medical *Clinic* • 242-365-4028 • Open weekdays 9–3, doctor on Tuesday and Thursday. Nurse in emergency 242-365-4148.
Or call Dr. John Shedd at the *Corbett Medical Centre* in Treasure Cay, 242-365-8288 days, 242-477-5892 in emergency.

MARINAS IN WHITE SOUND

GREEN TURTLE CLUB AND MARINA

Tel: 242-365-4271 • Fax: 242-365-4272 • 866-528-0539 U.S. • VHF 16 • info@greenturtleclub.com • www.greenturtleclub.com

This is a well-maintained, well-run marina in a lovely, sheltered position at the head of White Sound, with all the facilities that the *Green Turtle Club* offers. Fabulous beaches within walking distance and the *Club's* outstanding reputation for fine dining and accommodation make it one of the most attractive marinas in the Abaco cays.

Slips 40. **Max LOA** 130 ft. **MLW at Dock** 8 ft.; 5 ft. in the clearly marked entry channel into White Sound at low water. **Dockage** $2.00 per ft. per day. Nov.-Mar. food and beverage charges offset dockage. **Fuel** Diesel and gasoline, 8 a.m. to 6 p.m. **Facilities & Services** Power unlimited. Water $0.25 per gallon. Showers for marina guests only, $40 deposit. Laundry $4.25 - uses tokens, telephones at the clubhouse and marina store. Cable TV $5 per day. Free WiFi, fax machine, copier at the *Clubhouse*, where mail can be sent or held for you. Garbage receptacles behind the washhouse. Ice, beverages, fresh homemade bread and snacks in marina store. Freshwater pool with bar. Beaches. Diving, sailing, kayaking, windsurfing with *Brendal's Dive Center* next door. Boutique, bicycles available, golf carts. **Restaurants** Breakfast, lunch and dinner served daily with fine dining in elegant air-conditioned dining room. Reservations required by 4 p.m. or a la carte dinner options 6:30 p.m. until 8:30 p.m. on the screened patio at the water's edge; resort casual dress, complimentary hors d'oeuvres 6:45 p.m. Gully Roosters play from 9 p.m. to midnight on Wednesdays. $$$ **Accommodations** Green Turtle Club Deluxe rooms and villas, from $180 to $329 per night. **Credit Cards** Visa, MasterCard, Discover, AMEX.

BLUFF HOUSE MARINA AND RESORT

Tel: 242-365-4247 • 800-747-4911 • Fax: 242-365-4248 • VHF 16 contact@bluffhouse.com • www.BluffHouse.com

This friendly resort and marina, with secluded coves and beaches, features a restaurant, pool, tennis courts and private beach overlooking the Sea of Abaco. There are good entry channel markers as you come into White Sound directing you to the full service *Bluff House Marina* on your port side; Call the dockmaster on VHF 16 as you enter the channel.

Slips 38, **MLW at dock** from 5 to 8 ft., with 5ft. in the approach channel to White Sound. **Fuel** dock on White Sound, open daily 8 a.m. to 5 p.m. **Dockage** $1.75 per ft per day, long-term and winter rates available. **Facilities** Power $25 per day for 50A, $12.50 per day for 30A. Water 1st 100 gallons free, then $0.20 per gallon, showers free to marina guests, $5 for visitors. Laundry uses tokens $4, free trash removal for marina guests. Internet access available. Golf carts available to rent on the island, $50 per day. **Restaurants** Breakfast, lunch and dinner is served a la carte at the Jolly Roger Bar and Bistro daily. Boutique gift shop and commissary dockside, with a few provisions, groceries and Wavey Line charts. **Credit cards** Visa, Mastercard and AMEX. **Manager** Tracey Russell. **Accommodations** Rental Villas adjacent to Bluff House available through Barefoot Homes: www.greenturtleabacohomesforrent.com

MARINAS IN BLACK SOUND

THE OTHER SHORE CLUB
Tel: 242-365-4338/4226 • VHF 16
othershoreclub@cocotels.net

For some cruising visitors, the *Other Shore Club* is a rare find—the Bahamas as it used to be. If you do not want cable TV, gift shops or a sportfishing fraternity, you may find this suits you perfectly. It has fuel, water and a warm welcome from Babs and her family. The dockmaster Kevin McIntosh of Gully Rooster fame. You needn't feed the dogs or the chickens who greet you on land, but remember to save some bread for the ducks who visit every day. It is a pleasant walk through the property to New Plymouth.

Moorings Four at $10 per night. **Slips** 15. **Max LOA** 65ft. (100 ft. on the fuel dock). **MLW at Dock** 6 ft. (only 4.5 ft. in the entry channel at low water). **Dockage** $0.85 per ft. per day. **Fuel** Diesel and gasoline, 7:30 a.m. to 4 p.m. daily. **Facilities** Power $25 per day for 50A, $15 for 30A. Water $0.30 per gallon. Showers $3. Telephone at the dockmaster's office. Ice. Golf carts available from T & A Rentals (242-365-4259) at Black Sound. **Restaurant** *Pineapples Bar and Grill*, open daily from 11 a.m., serving lunch and dinner poolside. **Accommodations** House, cottage, apartment for rent. **Credit Cards** Visa, MasterCard, AMEX (5% surcharge).

BLACK SOUND MARINA
Tel: 242-365-4531 • VHF 16

This small, quiet marina is tucked away past The *Other Shore Club* on the west side of Black Sound. It offers an attractive setting with picnic tables and barbecue grills for guests out under the trees, only a few minutes' walk into New Plymouth.

Slips 15. **Transient Slips** 8 **Max LOA** 55 ft. (85 ft. on the T-dock). **MLW at Dock** 7 ft. (4.0 ft. in the entry channel at low water). **Dockage** $1.00 per ft. per day. **Facilities** Power $20 per day for 50A, $15 for 30A. Water $0.30 per gallon. Showers $3 (only one, but clean). Laundry $8 for the one washer, $4 for dryer. Ice, monthly storage. Golf carts from *T&A Rentals* (242-365-4259) behind the marina. **Restaurants** in town, or *Pineapples at the Other Shore Club.* **Credit Cards** Visa and MasterCard. **Dockmaster** Caroll Sawyer is at the marina between 8 and 10 a.m. weekdays, 9–10 a.m. Sundays.

LEEWARD YACHT CLUB & MARINA
TEL: 242-365-4191• FAX: 242-365-4174 • Cell: 242-577-4111 • VHF 16
leewardyachtclub@hotmail.com • www.leewardyachtclub.com

Leeward Yacht Club docks are for the primary enjoyment and use of the home owners with some outside rentals, space permitting. Well landscaped Key West styled property with fresh water pool.

Slips 28 **Max LOA** 100 ft. MLW at Dock 7 ft., 4.5 ft. in entry channel at mean low water. **Dockage** $1.00/day, weekly and monthly rates. **Facilities & Services** Power/electrical hook-ups are available at 30, 50 and 100 amps at $0.40/kw. Water at $0.25 per gallon. Laundry $4 wash/$4 dry. Showers – free with dockage, otherwise $3. Free WiFi

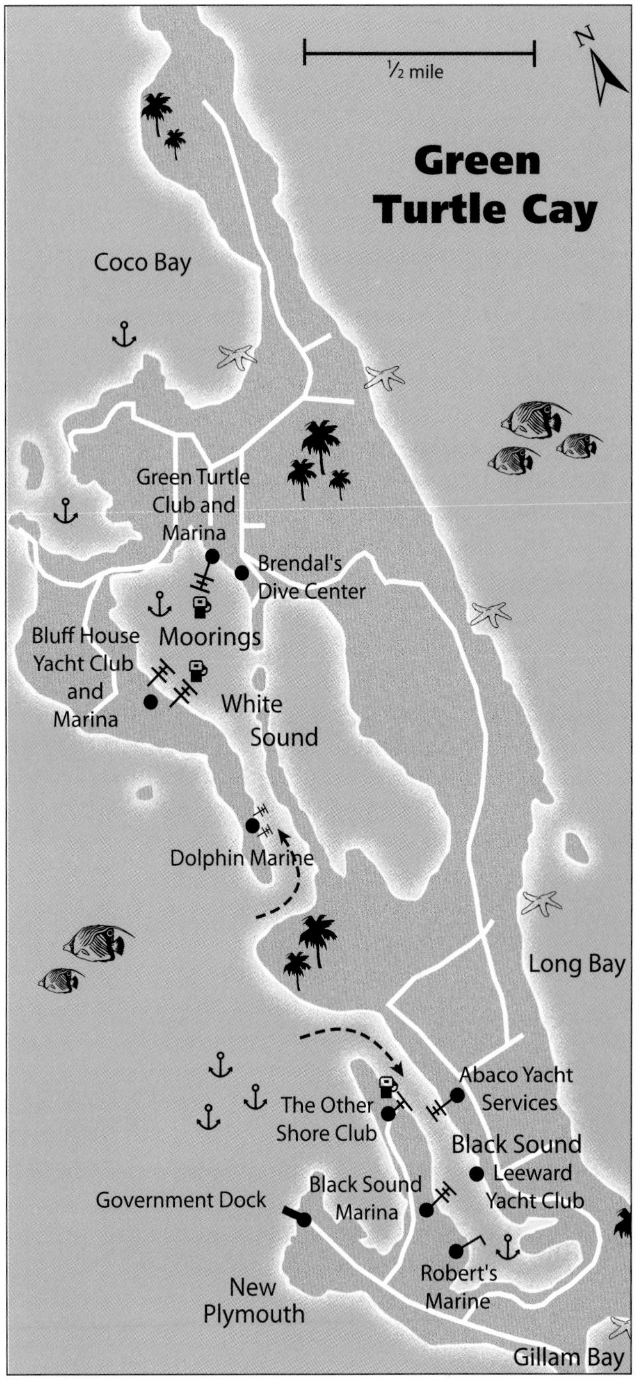

with dockage. A half mile to beach. Tiki bar/grill and marina store coming soon. **Credit Cards** Visa, MasterCard, Discover and AMEX. **Dockmaster** Adrian Lowe.

MARINE SERVICES & SUPPLIES

In White Sound:

DOLPHIN MARINE Tel: 242-365-4262 • VHF 16
Evinrude and Johnson sales, service and parts; dry boat storage.

In Black Sound:

ABACO YACHT SERVICES
Tel: 242-365-4033 • Fax 242-365-4216 • VHF 16 • ays@oii.net
This is a full-service yard with good mechanics, a lift, forklift, small-

boat hoist and long-term dry dockage. Reserve space ahead of time. Sea Hawk Islands 44 tin-based paint is available. Yamaha sales and repairs on site. Marine parts and equipment. The yard is closed weekends. **Dockage** $0.55 per ft. per day, $0.65 with power. **Facilities** Water $0.25 per gallon. Showers $3. Ice. Laundry uses tokens. **Marine Services** Painting, Yamaha mechanics, 50-ton Acme lift, pressure cleaning, and blocking boats up to 45 ft. Small boat hoist up to 25 ft., catamaran haul and storage up to 20-ft. beam, 30-ft. length. **Accommodations** House sleeps 6, $1,250 per week.

ROBERTS MARINE Tel: 242-365-4249 • VHF 16
Boat sales, parts and service, batteries, ice, Evinrude and Johnson dealer; diesel repair.

In New Plymouth:
ROBERTS HARDWARE & MARINE
Tel: 242-365-4122 • VHF 16
Very well-stocked with paints, charts, marine hardware, rope, ice, charts, fishing tackle and diving supplies.

NEW PLYMOUTH PORT DIRECTORY

Bank *First Caribbean International Bank* • 242-365-4144 • Open Monday and Thursday, 10 to 2. No ATM.
Churches *Methodist Church, New Plymouth Gospel Chapel, St. Peter's Anglican Church* (dates from 1786).
Couriers *Fedex* Packages can be sent from or delivered to *Bahamas Outpost Mail and Business Center* (242-365-4695) next to *Curry's Food Store*, open weekdays 9 to 5. Deliveries via Marsh Harbour.
Email and Internet *Bahamas Outpost Mail and Business Center* • 242-365-4695 • Next to *Curry's Food Store*, open weekdays 9 to 5. $5 for 10 minutes. Also fax, copying and house rentals.
Marinas Green Turtle Cay Marina • Bluff House Beach Hotel and Yacht Club • Leeward Yacht Club & Marina
Library Open Mon, Wed, Fri 2 to 5, Sat 9 to 12; has internet access.
Sid's Food Store • 242-365-4055 • harmony@batelnet.bs • Open to 5:30 p.m. Monday through Friday, to 6:30 p.m. Saturdays. $5 connection charge, and $1 per minute after that.
Ferries *Green Turtle Ferry* • 242-365-4151/4166/4128 • VHF 16 • Bolo ferries leave at 8, 9 and 11 a.m., 12:15, 1:30, 3, and 4:30 p.m. for

New Plymouth waterfront. WATERWAY GUIDE PHOTOGRAPHY.

Treasure Cay airport on Great Abaco. Alternative timings and destinations available. $8 one way or $12 round trip from New Plymouth, extra to Black Sound, White Sound and Coco Beach.
Galleries *Alton Lowe Art Gallery* • 242-365-4624/4094 • Alton Lowe's paintings and carved Bahamian boat models by Ventrum Lowe, as well as sculptures and paintings by James Mastin, at the head of Black Sound, with their own dock and Theatre Garden. Call for an appointment.
Captain Roland Roberts House - 242-365-4014 - Historic environmental center - Open Monday through Saturday - Operated by Reef Relief.
Ocean Blue Gallery • 242-365-4234 • Kathy Bethell features many local and island artists, in *Plymouth Rock Liquors*.
Gifts and Souvenirs *Golden Reef, Native Creations, Shavon's, Shell Hut, Tropic Topics Variety Store and Straw Market, Vert's Model Ship Shoppe*.
Gifts and Souvenirs *Golden Reef, Native Creations, Shavon's, Shell Hut, Tropic Topics Variety Store and Straw Market, Vert's Model Ship Shoppe*.
Hardware *New Plymouth Paint and Hardware* • 242-365-4305 • Fax: 242-365-4372 • VHF 16 • npphgtc@hotmail.com • Kevin Roberts is well stocked with paints and household hardware, and some marine goods. Closed Saturday p.m. and Sunday. No credit cards.
Hotel & Cottages Both *Bluff House* and the *Green Turtle Club* have their own hotel accommodation. See **MARINAS** for details.
Coco Bay Cottages • 242-365-5464 • Fax: 242-365-5465 • Overlooking Coco Bay.
Golden Reef Apartments • 242-365-4055/4283 • Above the *Golden Reef Boutique*. Two spacious apartments overlooking the harbor.
Green Turtle Rentals • 242-365-4120/4055 • www.greenturtlerentals.com • Cottages and apartments.
Island Property Management • 242-365-4047, 561-202-8333 • www.go-abacos.com/ipm • With 67 vacation rentals from $650 to $6,500 per week.
Lintons Cottages • 242-365-4003 • Fax: 242-365-4002 • On Long Bay Beach.
New Plymouth Inn • 242-365-4161 • Fax: 242-365-4138
Roberts Cottages • 242-365-4105 • VHF 16 • Three cottages on Black Sound, including dockage for boats. From $600 per week.
Jewelry and Fashions *Golden Reef* • 242-365-4511 • Resort wear and 14K gold jewelry, good selection of children's clothes.
Laundry There is no Laundromat, but *Green Turtle Club*, *Bluff House Yacht Club, Black Sound Marina* and *Abaco Yacht Services* all have washers and dryers.
Library Open Mon, Wed, Fri 2 to 5, Sat 9 to 12, now with internet access and paperback exchange; book donations always welcome.
Liquor *Plymouth Rock Liquors and Ocean Blue Gallery* • 242-365-4055 • Open 9 to 6 weekdays. Wide selection of wines and liquors, with counter service for breakfast and lunch from 9 to 3:30, and art gallery, closed Sundays.
Museums *Albert Lowe Museum* • 242-365-1494 • Open daily 9 to 11:45 a.m. and 1 to 4 p.m., closed Sunday. Admission $5; newly restored kitchen and the *Schooner Gallery* in the cellar of this 200-year-old house. A must-visit. • *New Plymouth Town Jail* Recently restored; currently uninhabited.
Police • 242-365-4450 • In the Administrative building, on Parliament Street.
Post Office • 242-365-4242 • Next to Customs on Parliament Street open 9 a.m. to 5 p.m. weekdays.
Propane From Marsh Harbour. Ask dockmasters or Scott at *Sid's Food Store* for help.

Provisions *Curry's Sunset Grocery* • 242-365-4171 • VHF 16 • Open on the waterfront with their own dinghy dock, from 8 to 5 weekdays, to 7 p.m. on Saturdays. Groceries, frozen foods, meat, produce, some pharmacy, wonderful fresh bread, ice.

Lowe's Food Store • 242-365-4243 • Open 7 a.m. to 7 p.m. weekdays with fresh pastries and bread, sodas, baby clothes, newspapers and magazines, gifts and souvenirs.

Sid's Food Store • 242-365-4055 • Fax: 365-4612 • Open 7 to 6 p.m., to 7 p.m. Sat. Very well stocked with fresh fruit and vegetables, frozen meats, dry and canned goods, homemade breads, household items, some pharmacy and lots more. Scott Lowe, and his sister Martha, give a warm welcome to boaters and let you use their email.

Restaurants & Bars *Bluff House Yacht Club* and *Green Turtle Club* have their own restaurants, see MARINAS in White Sound for details.

Harvey's Island Grill • Bahamian and American style food in a casual atmosphere.

Laura's Kitchen • 242-365-4287 • VHF 16 • On King Street. Open for lunch and dinner daily. Good home cooking, and wine or beer. $$

McIntosh Restaurant and Bakery • 242-365-4625 • VHF 16 • On Parliament Street. Open daily from 8 a.m. to 9 p.m. for breakfast, lunch and dinner; delivery, take-away or dine right there. Good Bahamian food, with seafood a specialty—delicious cakes and breads as well. Bar available. $$

Miss Emily's Blue Bee Bar • 242-365-4181 • Famous! Since Miss Emily died in 1997, the *Blue Bee Bar* has been run by Violet Smith who knows Miss Emily's secret recipe for a Goombay Smash.

Pineapples Bar and Grill • 242-365-4039 • VHF 16 • www.othershoreclub.com • Open from 11 a.m. until everyone is gone, for lunch and dinner around the pool, overlooking New Plymouth and the Sea of Abaco. Fresh fish, fantastic conch, live music, sunfish races and sunsets. Run by Sarah and her mother Babs, at the *Other Shore Club*. $$

Plymouth Rock Liquors & Cafe • 242-365-4234 • Deli counter for breakfast and lunch daily till 3:30 p.m. $ Liquor 9 a.m. to 7 p.m.

Sundowners On the waterfront. Open 7 days a week, with happy hour from 5 to 6 p.m., lunch and dinner. Karaoke nights, pool table and dinghy dock. $

The Wreckin' Tree • 242-365-4263 • VHF 16 • On the southwest corner of New Plymouth harbor, overlooking the water. Local seafood, conch and fish, fresh pies and pastries and drinks during the day. Specialty house drink is a well-named Wrecker. $

Rest Rooms Next to the post office and customs.

Taxis *McIntosh Taxi Service* • 242-365-4309 • VHF 16 or 06.

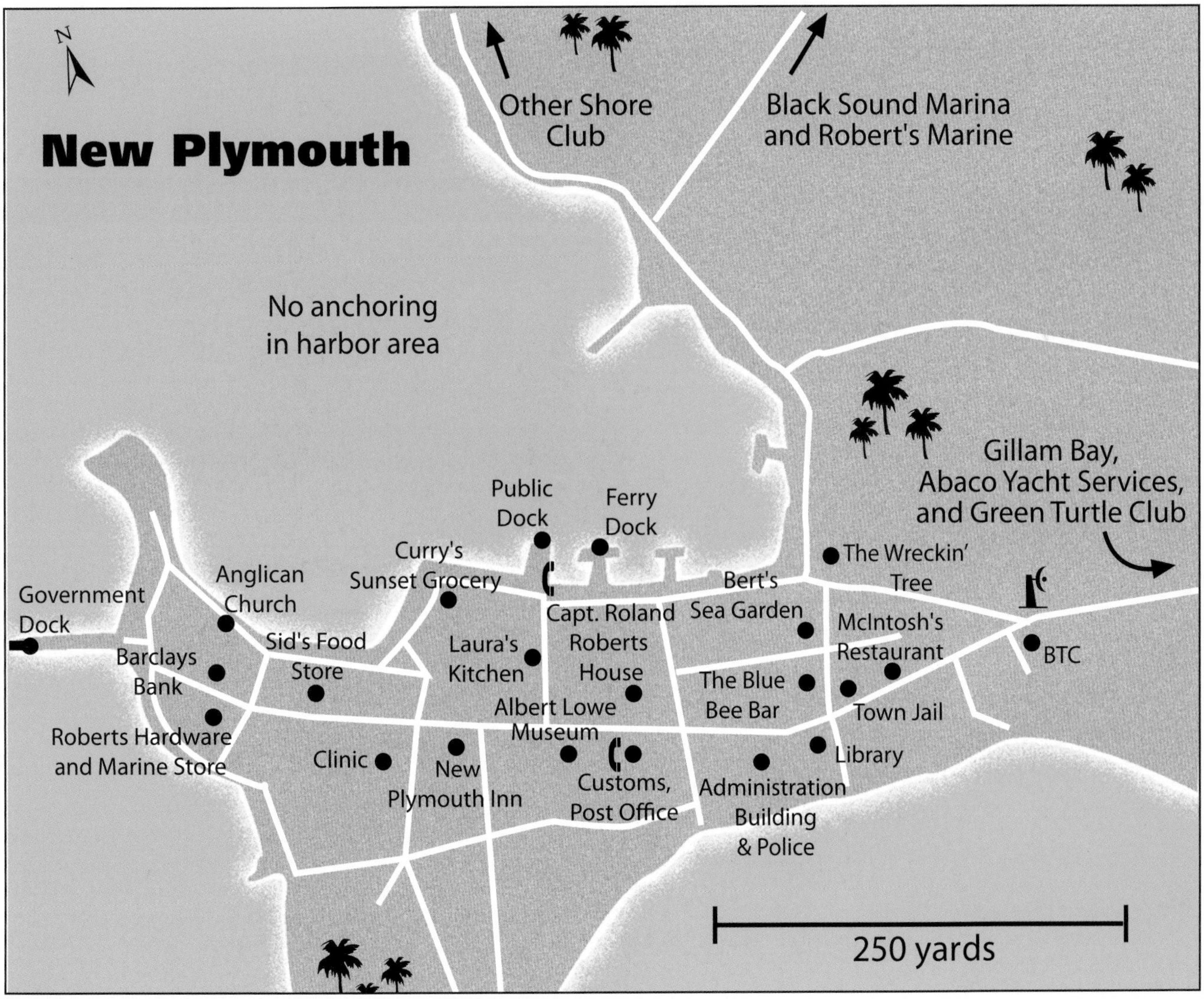

Telephones On the public dock; by the post office on Parliament Street; outside the *BTC* office at the top of the hill leading out of New Plymouth. Quik Cell cards from *McIntosh's* restaurant at weekends, *BTC* and *Sid's Food Store* weekdays.

Travel Agent *A and W Travel Service* • 242-365-4230/4171 • Agent Debbie Lowe.

RENTALS

Bicycles *Brendal's Dive Center* • 242-365-4411 • In White Sound $12 per day.

Boats *Donny's Boat Rentals* • 242-365-4271/4073 • VHF 16 • In Black Sound.

Reef Rentals • 242-365-4145 • Fax: 242-365-4581 • rentals@batelnet.bs

Carts *Island Road Rentals* (242-365-4070, VHF 16 "Island Road Rentals"); *D & P Rentals* at *Green Turtle Club* (242-365-4656) *Sea Side Carts* (242-477-5497); *T & A Rentals* (242-365-4259) at Black Sound; *Mom's Kool Kart's* (242-365-4188). Golf carts rent from $45 per day.

Kayaks *Brendals Dive Center* • 242-365-4411 • $12 an hour for double kayaks. At *Green Turtle Club.*

Scooters *D&P rentals* • 242-365-4656

SPORTS & RECREATION

Diving *Brendal's Dive Center* • 242-365-4411 • VHF 16 • brendal@brendal.com • www.brendal.com • Brendal and his wife Mary have been running an extensive dive operation next to the *Green Turtle Club* in White Sound for over 25 years. Snorkeling, reef trips with beach picnic lunches, sailboat and kayak tours, Wild Dolphin encounters, bicycle and kayak rentals, and instruction in 11 specialist scuba courses for PADI, NAUI and SSI qualification. Daily and multi-day packages available. Moorings available for long or short term.

Reef Mooring Buoys 18 buoys off Munjack Cay, Crab Cay, Green Turtle Cay and No Name Cay. Sailboats are encouraged to avoid these buoys because of the shallow water in the area. The buoys are located to provide access to small dinghies, inflatables and open fishing boats. Pick up a leaflet from *Roland Roberts House Environmental Centre* to give GPS locations of buoys and description of the sites, or go to www.reefrelief.org. Occasionally some of the buoys may be missing.

Bonefishing *Eddie Bodie* (242-365-4069), *Ronnie Sawyer* (242-365-4070, Cell 242-357-6667).

Ocean and Reef Fishing *Joe Sawyer* (242-365-4173, VHF 16), *Rick Sawyer* (242-365-4261).

Fishing Tournaments & Regattas *Annual Green Turtle Classic Fishing Tournament* in June, hosted by *Bluff House Yacht Club and Marina*. Call 242-365-4247 for details.

Regatta Time in Abaco • 242-367-2677 • davralph@batelnet.bs • www.rtia.net • Held the first week in July. Races form up at Green Turtle Cay, Great Guana Cay, Hope Town, Man-O-War and Marsh Harbour. Contact Dave or Kathy Ralph.

All Abaco Sailing Regatta, a Bahamian workboat regatta, is held the first weekend in November.

THINGS TO DO IN GREEN TURTLE CAY

- Visit the Albert Lowe Museum for a fascinating look at the history of Green Turtle Cay.
- Walk over the hill to Gillam Bay and search for sand dollars at low tide.
- Stock up on fresh food and provisions at the excellent grocery stores.
- Have your boat hauled for a bottom job in Black Sound, or have your outboard motor fixed while you have experts on hand.
- Enjoy a cool drink in town at Miss Emily's Blue Bee Bar or the Wreckin' Tree.
- Jump up with Kevin and the Gully Roosters one evening.
- Take your dinghy over to Manjack Cay for some brilliant snorkeling.
- Visit the Capt. Roland Roberts House Environmental Center and learn more about turtles and the ecology of reefs. Open from 10 to 2, Tuesday, Wednesday, Thursday and from 1 to 5 Friday, and Saturdays 9 to 12, with enthusiastic volunteers and charming displays by schoolchildren. Did you know that elkhorn coral that has broken off, can be wired back on to a reef and starts to regenerate after a few months? This is a scientific first, discovered on an Abaco reef.
- Make your dinner reservations at one of the restaurants by 5 p.m. and enjoy fresh island food.

COOPERS TOWN

bank • fuel • groceries • medical • police • post office
restaurant • telephone

Coopers Town, like neighboring Fox Town, was devastated during series of hurricanes, the latest being Frances and Jeanne in 2004. A new sea wall now runs the length of Bay Street and houses have been rebuilt. Coopers Town is the seat for the commissioner for Northern Abaco and boasts several government offices. It is an easy walk to find services and supplies in town. At the north end of Bay Street, around the curve where it meets Bootle Highway, there is a community gazebo with wireless Internet access.

EMERGENCIES

Marine • VHF 16

Medical *Clinic* • 242-365-0300/0301 • Ambulance and fully equipped clinic a short walk south of town. Nurses are there weekdays; doctor on Monday, Wednesday, and Friday from 9:30 a.m. to 1 p.m. After hours, call the clinic number for the duty nurse.

Police • 242-367-0002

Bank *ScotiaBank* Open 9 to 2, Tuesday and Thursday.

Churches *Church of God's Cathedral, Friendship Mission, Pentecostal Church.*

Fuel *Edgecombe's* About a mile southeast of Coopers Town, with diesel and gasoline and a few groceries and ice, but very shallow water. *Diamond 7* diesel, gas, groceries close to town.

Hotel & Lodging *M & M's Guest House* • 242-365-0142

Tangelo Hotel • 242-365-2222

Marine Services *Mc Intosh Underwater Services* • 242-365-0216
Post Office In the administration building, open 9 to 5 weekdays.
Restaurant *M & M Restaurant and Bar* • 242-365-0142 • Breakfast, lunch, dinner.
Telephones At the administration building. *BTC* office is closed.

GREAT GUANA CAY

fuel • groceries • marina • moorings • post office • restaurants • telephone • water

Great Guana Cay is being developed faster than any other Abaco cay, with multiple new homes and the recently opened Bakers Bay Resort on the north end. There are good beaches on both sides of the cay, so you can nearly always find a sheltered spot; there is easy snorkeling right off the beach at Nippers. It is one of the larger Abaco cays, with a small settlement, good restaurants and a newly paved road. There is no Customs and Immigration here, so you cannot clear in if this is your first stop in the Bahamas.

MARINA

BAKERS BAY CLUB AND MARINA
Tel: 242-365-5280 • VHF 16 • www.bakersbayclub.com • info@bakersbayclub.com

A private oasis with public access to the marina, restaurant and bar. State-of-the-art docking facilities include extra-wide piers and the ability to accommodate even the largest of luxury vessels. Access Marina Village via the marked deep-water channel providing megayacht access. The majority of slips are available for purchase by residents of the community.
Slips 151. **Max LOA** Up to 250 ft. MLW at Dock 12.5 ft. **Dockage** $3.00 per ft. per night. **Facilities & Services** Power 50A and 100A (1 phase), 100A and 200A (3 phase). Telephone and cable, WiFi, in-slip sanitary pump out. **Fuel,** ship store and on-island shower and laundry facilities. **Restaurant** and Bar in Marina Village (Will's Island). **Credit Cards** Visa. MasterCard. **Harbormaster** Cecil Ingraham.

ORCHID BAY YACHT CLUB AND MARINA
Tel: 242-365-5175 • Fax: 242-365-5166 • VHF 16 • JAlbury@orchidbaybahamas.com • www.orchidbay.net

This state-of-the-art marina, with its protective sea wall at the southern point of the harbor. Its development has been a big boon to Great Guana Cay. Cruising boats enjoy the benefits of good docks behind a breakwater, with wonderful, clean shore side amenities and a fine restaurant overlooking the Sea of Abaco. Call ahead on VHF 16 before 2 p.m. to reserve a slip. Orchid Bay participates with other Stay and See Abaco marinas.
Slips 66. **Max LOA** Up to 120 ft. at the T-heads. **MLW at Dock** From 9 ft. on the outside dock to 4 ft. on the inner docks, with a 9 ft. approach. **Dockage** $1.95 per ft. per night, minimum charge $35 per day, on the T. Day visit - $25 for 4 hours. Winter rates available. Vessels with more than 4 crew, additional charge of $5 per person. **Fuel** Texaco fuel dock with diesel, gasoline, oil and lubricants; open 8 to 5 daily. **Facilities & Services** Power $0.30 per kWh, 30A and 50A. Water $.30 per gallon. Showers, free to marina guests, $5 for visitors. Laundry for guests only, $5 tokens. WiFi, telephone, ice, complimentary morning coffee in the marina office. Freshwater pool, golf cart rentals. Free trash removal

Great Guana Cay, from the northeast. (Not to be used for navigation.) WATERWAY GUIDE PHOTOGRAPHY.

for guests, $1 per bag to visitors. Ferries to and from Marsh Harbour will stop at Orchid Bay on request. **Restaurant** Open for lunch and dinner. **Credit Cards** Visa, MasterCard. **Resort Managers** Jimmy and Melonie Albury.

GUANA HIDEAWAYS MARINA
TEL: 242-366-0224 FAX: 242-366-0434 • VHF 16 • www.guanacay.com

The old Guana Beach Resort has been redeveloped by Chris and Peggy Thompson. There are brand new docks and a rollicking bar with rum punches to rival Nippers. A long-time favorite spot, the new full-service marina is a welcomed addition to the area.

Slips: 40 **Max LOA** 100 on the T-head **MLW** 10 ft. **Facilities & Services:** Power 30A and 50A. Water. Through an arrangement with neighboring *Guana Grabbers*, laundry, pool and showers available. **Fuel** Both Diesel and Gas are planned. **Credit Cards** Visa, MasterCard.

MOORINGS There are 8 moorings in Settlement Harbour and 10 in Fishers Bay for $15 a night. Call Troy at *Dive Guana* on VHF 16. Three moorings for day use are off *Guana Seaside Village* in Crossing Bay.

ANCHORAGES Off Big Point, Crossing Bay or farther north in popular Bakers Bay.

EMERGENCIES

BASRA 242-366-0500 or VHF 16
Marine • VHF 16.
Medical There is no clinic on Great Guana Cay. Call Marsh Harbour emergency numbers.

PORT DIRECTORY

Accommodations *Dolphin Beach Resort* • 242-365-5137 or 800-222-2646 • VHF 16 • www.dolphinbeachresort.com • On a spectacular Atlantic beach a short distance from the settlement, brightly painted beach-front cottages and a small hotel nestle among the trees. Rooms from $180 per night, cottages from $240 per night. Call Becky Lightbourne or Victoria for details.
Great Guana Cay Villas • 242-365-5028 • reservations@guanacayvillas.com • www.guanacayvillas.com • Seashore villas, *Harbour View Haven* and *Sunrise Cottage*, all air-conditioned with access to the pool at *Sea Shore Villas*.
Ocean Frontier Hideaways, next to *Nippers*. 242-365-5178 - Six villas available just minutes from the Settlement.
Seaside Villas • 242-365-5006
Church *Sea Side Gospel Church*
Ferries *Albury's Ferries* • 242-367-3147, 242-365-6010 • VHF 16 • Leaves Great Guana Government Dock at 8 and 11:30 a.m., 2:30 and 4:45 p.m.; 40 minutes to the Union Jack Dock and the *Conch Inn* in Marsh Harbour. $15 one way, $25 same-day round trip. Will drop you off at *Orchid Bay* on request.
Gifts and Snacks *Seashore Gifts and Villas* • 242-365-5028 • Beach fashions, ice cream, souvenirs, light meals to eat on their harbor-front deck, villa rentals.
Guana Drug Store - 242-365-5050 - Sundries, Cuban cigars and souvenirs. 10 a.m. to 5 p.m. daily.
Hardware Store *Guana Lumber and Supplies* • 242-365-5130, Lumber, hardware and boating supplies.
Laundry *Sea Shore Villas Gift Shop* • 242-365-5006
Post Office. In the pink building on Front Street, open Monday, Wednesday, Friday from 11:30 to 3.
Provisions *Guana Harbour Grocery* • 242-365-5067 • VHF 16 • Open 8 to 5:30, to 6 on Saturday. Closed Sundays. Well stocked and very helpful with some fresh produce. *Milo's Fruit Stand*-Fresh produce and shells on Front Street.
Fig Tree Wines and Spirits • 242-365-5058 • Closed Sundays, ice.
Restaurants *The Art Café*. Coffee, pastries and more. Located at the Government Dock.
Hang Ten At the Crossroads • 242-365-5006. Tiki Bar Food. Ice cream. Closed Wednesdays.
Docksiders • 242-365-5230 • VHF 16 Fine dining. Seafood and steaks. Dinner only. $$$ Dinghy dock.
Nippers Bar and Grill • 242-365-5143 • On the Atlantic side, across from the harbor. Junkanoo colors, very casual dining overlooking a glorious beach, with a 2-level swimming pool and tiki bar. Famous for their Sunday Pig Roasts and live music, when people come in from all over Abaco. $$
Orchid Bay Restaurant • 242-365-5175 • Overlooking Abaco Sound, open for very pleasant lunch and dinner daily. $$$
Grabbers Bar and Grill - 242-365-5133 - Overlooking Fishers Bay, better known as Grabbers pool bar open for food and drinks from morning 'til... $$ Nine hotel rooms available.
Pirates Cove - Snack food and bar overlooking Settlement Harbour.
Telephones By the school and at *Guana Harbour Grocery*.

RENTALS

Bicycles and Carts *Donna Sands* • 242-365-5195
Boats, Bicycles and Kayaks *Dive Guana* • 242-365-5178 • Bicycles $12 per day, kayaks $12 an hour, paddleboats $12 an hour. Day or weekly rental for 23-ft. Robalo and 21-ft. Angler.

SPORTS & RECREATION

Diving *Dive Guana* • 242-365-5178 • VHF 16 • diveguana@yahoo.com • www.diveguana.com • With Troy and Maria Albury. Half- and full-day excursions, 2-tank dive $95. Half-day novice divers lessons and gear $165; snorkeling lessons and gear $45. PADI instruction, rental equipment, daily trips except Sunday. Moorings, boat rentals, bicycles, kayaks and paddleboats.
Fishing *Henry Sands* • 242-365-5140 • VHF 16 "PDQ" • www.h-scharters.com • Full- or half-day, deep sea or bottom fishing.
Gym *Guana Gym* • 242-365-5195 • Open Monday to Friday, 7 to 12 daily. $10 per day.
Regatta *Regatta Time in Abaco* • 242-367-2677 • davralph@batelnet.bs • www.rtia.net • Held the first week in July. Races form up at Green Turtle Cay, Great Guana Cay, Hope Town, Man-O-War and Marsh Harbour. Contact Dave or Kathy Ralph.

THINGS TO DO IN GREAT GUANA CAY

- Walk on the seven-mile beach and snorkel the reef. It is close to shore and good for beginners.
- Take the dinghy around to Guana Seaside Village for lunch or dinner.
- Stroll over to Nippers for an island feast set among the sand dunes. What about trying the pig roast one Sunday?
- Relax on the beach or enjoy lunch or dinner at Grabbers overlooking Fishers Bay.

TREASURE CAY

airport • bank • church • customs & immigration • fuel • groceries • marina • medical • police • post office • restaurant • telephone • water

Treasure Cay is a first-class cruising destination with all the amenities you would expect from a Florida resort. It is also home to a great many winter residents and hotel guests who come for golf, tennis, the beach, fishing and sailing. The marinas are pleasant and well-organized, and everything is within walking distance. It is a good place for a crew change, or to meet friends flying in, with frequent flights to and from the United States. Treasure Cay is a port of entry, and the dock staff will call Customs and Immigration for you.

MARINA

TREASURE CAY HOTEL RESORT & MARINA
Tel: 242-365-8250 • 800-327-1584 • Fax: 242-365-8847 • VHF 16 • www.treasurecay.com • info@treasurecay.com
Moorings 8, first-come, first-served, $12 per day. Anchorage $8 per day includes use of showers and facilities. **Slips** 150. **Max LOA** 155 ft. on the T-docks. **MLW** Newly dredged entrance channel gives 6 ft. at low water from the fuel dock into the marina at normal low tide. **Dockage** $1.30 to $1.95 per ft. per day transient, depending on LOA and time of year. Long-term $0.55 to $0.75 per ft. Minimum $40 per day. During June and July, an additional $0.55 per ft. per day is charged. Treasure Cay is a participating Stay and See Abaco marina. **Fuel** Diesel and gasoline; fuel dock open 8 to 5 daily, port side as you enter the channel to the marina. **Facilities & Services** Power 30A and 50A from $12 to $32 per day, according to boat length. Boats using two 50A shore power cords will be charged double. Water $5 to $12 per day according to boat length. Showers and laundry; cable TV hookup $5 per day, $30 deposit required. Barbecue pits located at the entrances of docks L, T, N and S. No barbecuing or open flame on boats or docks is permitted. Marina guests are welcome to use the freshwater pool by the Tipsy Seagull. Or walk over and and swim off the crescent white sand beach. **Credit Cards** All major credit cards. **Security** VHF 19. **Marina Manager** Michael Sawyer. **Dockmaster** Audrick McKenzie.

PINEAPPLE POINT RESORT AT TREASURE CAY
Tel: 800-545-0395 • 242-475-7464 • www.pineapplepointresort.com • info@pineapplepointresort.com
The newest marina at Treasure Cay. All bolt heads in pilings are recessed to prevent damage. Unique "dock cam" lets you monitor your boat live from anywhere in the world over the Internet. The docks are primarily for condominium owners, but transients are welcome with special summer and winter rates.
Slips Dockage and dolphin tie up for yachts. **Max LOA** up to 70'; beams to 36'. **MLW** 6' approach. **Facilities & Services** Power 50 amp, Fresh water.

EMERGENCIES

BASRA 242-366-0500 or VHF 16
Marine • VHF 16
Medical *Corbett Medical Centre* • 242-365-8288 • Dr. John Shedd, MD. For after-hour emergencies call 242-477-5892. Leave a message, and your call will be returned.
Police • 242-365-8048

PORT DIRECTORY

Airport *Treasure Cay International Airport* 7 miles from the resort, with a 6,500-foot paved runway. Taxis are $14 for 2 people from the marina. Small snackbar at the airport.
Airlines *Bahamasair* (242-365-8601 or 242-377-5505) Fly 3 days a week to Nassau. *Continental* Gulf Stream (242-365-8615 or 800-231-0856) Daily flights to Miami (2:40 p.m.) and Fort Lauderdale (1:45 p.m.). *Island Express* (242-357-6684) To Fort Lauderdale. *US Air Express* (365-8686 or 800-428-4322) To West Palm Beach daily at 2:05 p.m. *Calypso Air* (242-365-8660) Fly daily to Fort Lauderdale and West Palm Beach. *Yellow Air Taxi* (242-367-0032) Fly to Fort Lauderdale and West Palm Beach, and throughout the Bahamas.
Bank *Royal Bank of Canada* Open 9:30 to 2, Monday, Tuesday and Thursday.
Churches *Saints Mary and Andrew Catholic Church, Church of St Simon by the Sea, Treasure Cay Community Church.*
Customs • 242-365-8602 • **Immigration** • 242-365-8604
Email and Faxes Faxes can be received at Treasure Cay Hotel Reception at 242-365-8847. Outgoing faxes $12 for the first page, $1.50 per page thereafter to the U.S. Ask for email access.
Ferries *Bolo* ferries daily to Green Turtle Cay from the *Treasure Cay Airport Dock* at 8:30, 10:30, 11:30 a.m.; 1:30, 2:30, 3:30, 4:30, 5 p.m. Fares $10 one way, $15 round trip.
Abaco Adventure ferries to Great Guana Cay from the Treasure Cay Marina • 242-365-8749 • VHF 16 • Leaves Treasure Cay Sundays at noon, returns 4:45 p.m. $25 round trip. To Man-O-War/Hopetown, leaves Treasure Cay at 9:30 a.m. on Wednesdays, returns at 4:30 p.m. $35 round trip.
Shopping *Abaco Ceramics* • 242-365-8489 • Attractive ceramic gifts made in the pottery.
Bill's Canvas Bags • 242-365-8318 • Marine upholstery renewed or replaced. Canvas bags, cards and gifts.
Harbor Shoppe Open daily at the Marina with logo sportswear and souvenirs.
Tripple J Boutique has a variety of gifts and home accessories.
Hardware *Treasure Cay Home Center* Open 8 to 4 daily, closed Sundays.
Hotels & Lodging *Bahama Beach Club*. 242-365-8500. Two, three, four and five bedroom beachfront rentals.
Banyan Beach Club • 242-365-8111 or 888-625-3060 • Fax: 242-365-8112 • Rental condominiums.
Brigantine Bay Villas • 242-365-8033. Tie up and step into your luxury 2-bedroom villa.
Mark's Beach View Bungalow. 242-365-8506 or 242-365-8582.
Treasure Cay Hotel Resort and Marina • 954-525-7711, 800-327-1584, 242-365-8578 • Fax: 954-525-1699 • info@treasurecay.com • Harbor side hotel rooms from $170, one, two and three bedroom suites from $355 in high season. MAP available. Golf and fishing packages, private air charters.
Laundry *Annie's Laundry* Sells fish and conch, too.
Liquor *Bristol Wines and Spirits* Open 9 to 6 daily, closed Sundays.
Marine Services *Edgecombe's Marine Services* • 242-365-8454 • VHF 16 • Engine repairs and boat delivery.
Prop Pullers, Inc. • VHF 16 "Ice Man" • Colin Albury offers yacht maintenance, management, propeller repairs.
Medical *The Corbett Medical Centre* • 242-365-8288 • With John Shedd, MD Open 9 to noon and 2 to 4 p.m., Monday, Tuesday, Thursday and Friday. Receptionist only on Wednesdays. For after-hour emergencies, call 242-477-5892. Leave a message and your call will be returned.
Post Office Open 9 to 4 weekdays.
Provisions *Treasure Cay Mini-Market* • 242-365-8350 • Fax: 242-365-8352 • VHF 16 • Well stocked. Open 8 to 6 daily, 9 to 1 Sunday.
G & M Variety Store Convenience store, open from 7 a.m. to 10 p.m. daily.

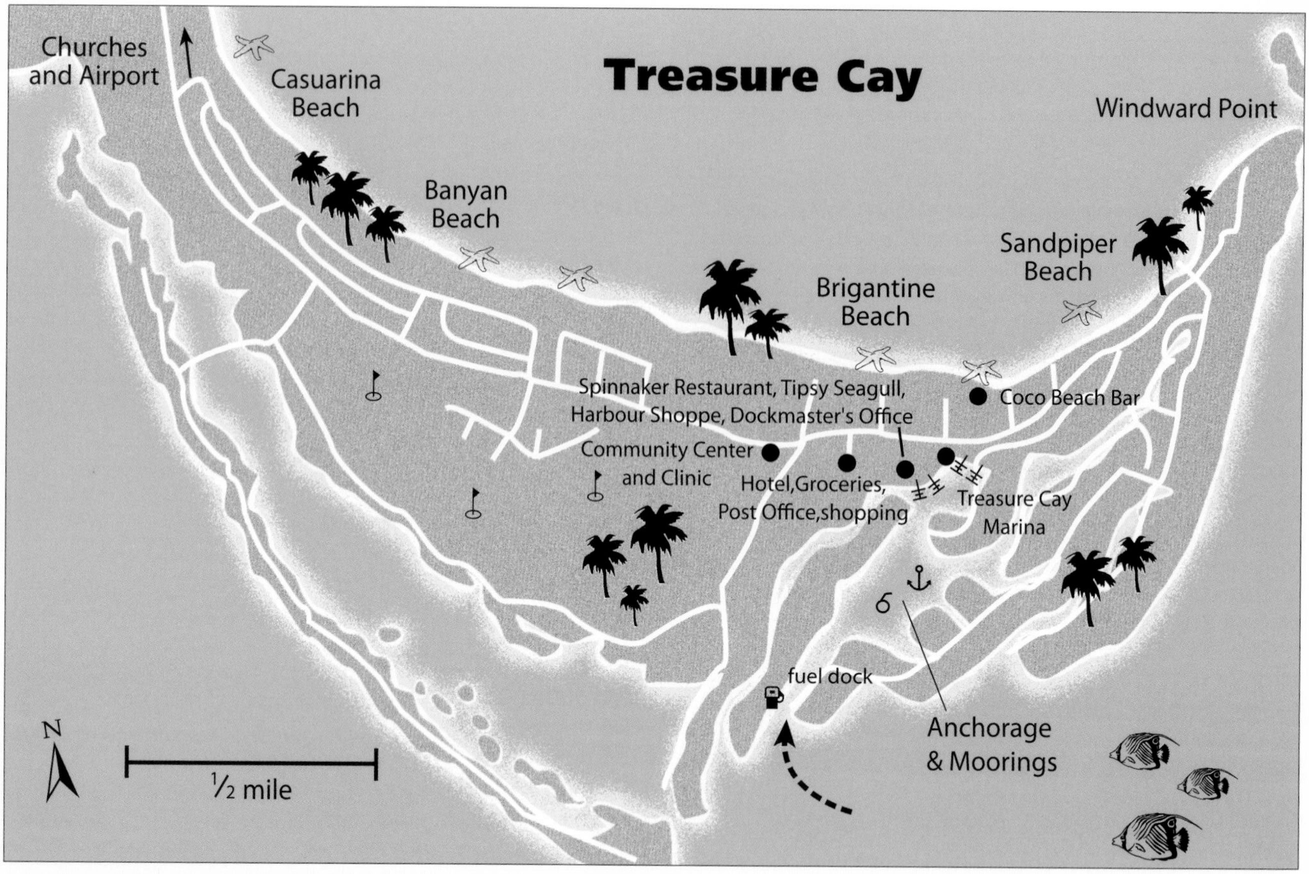

Restaurants *Cafe La Florence* Open daily 7 a.m. to 9 p.m., with delicious pastries and fresh bread too.

Coco Beach Bar Open 11 to 4 daily, with special barbecue nights.

Spinnaker Restaurant and Bar • 242-365-8469 • Open for breakfast, lunch, and dinner daily. Dinner reservations requested.

Tipsy Seagull Bar and Grill Open from 11 a.m. with live entertainment Wednesday, barbecue and pizza evenings in high season.

Taxis Call VHF 06. There are usually taxis waiting outside the shops at Treasure Cay.

Treasure Cay Shuttle • 242-357-6794 or 242-365-8801 • From the hotel to Marsh Harbour Ferry Dock and *Boat Harbour Marina*. $65 per person round trip.

RENTALS

Bicycles *Wendell's Bicycles* • 242-365-8687

Boats *JIC Rentals* • 242-365-8465 • VHF 16 or 79 • Call John Cash. Captains and guides available. Trips to Shell Island and Guana Cay, Green Turtle Cay, Marsh Harbour, Man-O-War and Hope Town. 24-ft. Angels, 26-ft. Intrepid.

Rich's Rentals • 242-367-8582 • VHF 16 • Dusky offshore 20–27-foot boats, sunfish, hobie cats, windsurfers, scuba & snorkel gear, spear fishing, island tours, picnics and scooters.

Cars *Bodie's Car Rental* (242-359-6681), *Cornish Rentals* (242-365-8623), *Tripple J Car Rental & Gift Shop* (242-365-0161, VHF 6). From $75 per day.

Golf Carts $40 per day, $245 per week. *Blue Marlin* (242-365-8687), *Cash's Carts* (242-365-8465, VHF 16 or 79, jic@oii.net).

Scooters *R & A Scooter Rental* • 242-365-8475 • VHF 16

Telephones At the marina and the shops; the *BTC* office has phone cards.

SPORTS & RECREATION

Diving *Treasure Divers* • 242-365-8571 • Fax: 242-365-8508 • VHF 16 • dive@treasuredivers.com • 2-tank dive $80, night and blue hole dives, snorkeling, air fills, Scuba instruction, rentals. PADI certification.

Fishing Guides *Claud Burrows, Odonald McIntosh, Edward Rolle* or *Shelton Gardiner*. Ask at the marina office to find them.

Fishing Tournaments Contact *Treasure Cay Marina*

Golf • 242-365-8045 • 18-hole course, the first on Great Abaco.

Jogging Beach, roads and walkways set in 1,500 acres.

Kayaking *Abaco Adventures* • 242-367-5358 • Marsh Harbour.

Tennis Hard and clay courts. Racket rentals, lessons.

THINGS TO DO IN TREASURE CAY

- Take a short walk over to the beach from the marina, where you will find miles of powdery white sand set in a magnificent, crescent bay. The swimming is glorious. Enjoy lunch at the *Coco Beach Bar* while you are there.
- Play a round of golf—or have a tennis game with friends.
- Explore the network of canals in your dinghy. These canals, incidentally, offer good hurricane protection.
- Explore New Plymouth, and discover the charm of Green Turtle Cay, by taking a taxi to the *Green Turtle Ferry* dock and going across for lunch. Or take your own boat around the Whale, and stay awhile.
- Treat your crew to dinner at the *Spinnaker Restaurant*.
- Enjoy world-class fishing.

Chapter 6 The Southern Abaco Cays, The South of Great Abaco Island and The Bight of Abaco

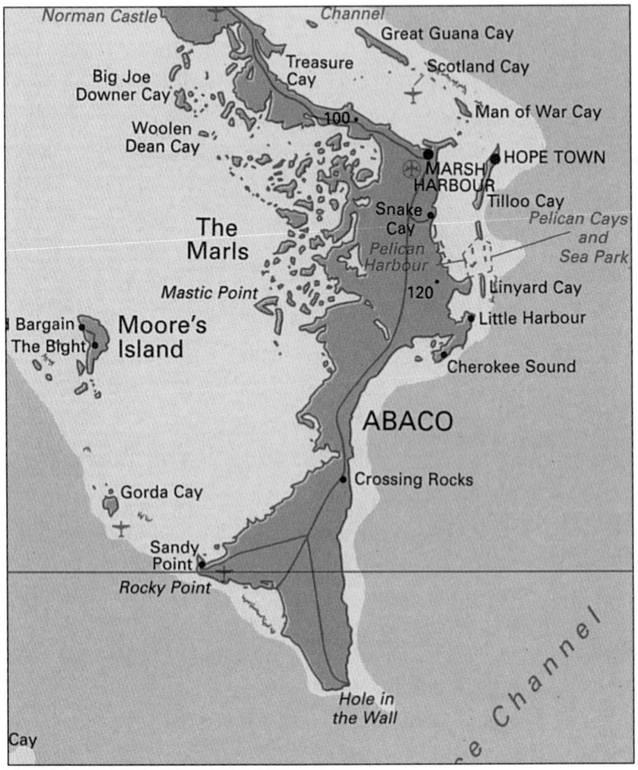

Not to be used for navigation.

Looking At the Charts

The southern cruising waters of the Abacos run south 48 nautical miles from Great Guana and Treasure cays to Hole-in-the-Wall, at the southern end of Great Abaco Island, then northwest to Sandy Point and Moores Island. A large portion of this area encompasses the southern end of Great Abaco Island, which is virtually uninhabited except for Little Harbour, Cherokee Sound, Sandy Point and Mores Island. These remote cruising grounds are of interest to those who enjoy contact with local folks and adventure in shallow waters. Many boaters prefer to visit the more populated spots with lots of other cruisers, modern facilities, fine restaurants and maybe a little nightlife. They are more likely to spend time in Man-O-War and Elbow Cay (that is Hope Town), and Marsh Harbour.

Just as shoal areas in the Central Abacos force you to decide on which side to run - the mainland side or the cay side - so it is in the southern part of the Sea of Abaco. Either way, the travel is essentially hazard free. The southern waters are served by several good passes out into the Atlantic: Man-O-War Channel, north of Man-O-War Cay; Tilloo Cut, north of Tilloo Cay is suitable for most vessel's draft; North Bar Channel, north of Lynyard Cay; and Little Harbour Channel, north of Little Harbour. North Bar Channel and Little Harbour Channel are the exit choices if you are southward bound for Royal Island and Eleuthera (an open water passage of just under 50 nautical miles) or The Berry Islands (a longer passage that commits vessels to traverse along the weather coast of Great Abaco Island and offers scant shelter before crossing the New Providence Channel). The prudent mariner will take careful stock of the weather before exiting from the shelter of the Sea of Abaco. With the right vessel, you do have another option to get to the Berries. Use the Spence Rock Passage into the Bight of Abaco, and enter the Northwest Providence channel at Channel Rock or Sandy Point. That option cuts the passage to the northern Berries down to less than 30 nautical miles from the Abacos.

In the Spotlight. Marsh Harbour

Marsh Harbour is the principal city on Great Abaco Island and the third largest city in the Bahamas. It is the commercial center of the Abacos, as well as the hub of tourist activity. Marsh Harbour International Airport provides daily commercial and frequent charter flights from the United States and Nassau. There are a variety of marine services available and several boat charter operations.

Clearing In—Your Options in the Southern Abacos

At Marsh Harbour, the Customs dock, with the Customs and Immigration Office, is on the south side of the main harbor. However, they will come to you, on your arrival, at any one of the Marsh Harbour marinas.

In addition to medical and dental clinics, pharmacies, a modern coin laundry, a veterinarian, banks, a UPS store and some duty free shopping, you will find well-stocked grocery stores with familiar products at moderate cost. It can be said that Marsh Harbour has something for everyone, especially the uninitiated, first-time cruiser.

Along with the Abacos' only radio station – 93.3 FM - make sure to listen each morning at 8:15 a.m. for the Cruiser's Net on VHF Channel 68. The Net welcomes visiting cruisers, acquaints folks with Marsh Harbour's many restaurants and services, announces forthcoming events and provides up-to-date weather forecasts. A chat session helps answer questions and address problems and concerns. This is a very friendly place with plenty of Americans and Canadians who winter here every year. They are not only a treasure trove of information, but also a wonderful source of camaraderie. Who needs a tour guide when you have a seasoned cruiser to show you around?

Fortunately, everything worth finding is within easy walking distance of the harbor and the marinas. Most ladies put Iggy Biggy's Boutique near the top of their "must do" list. From unique flip-flops to gorgeous resort wear, Iggy Biggy's is the place to shop. If you have never seen conch pearls, visit the Conch Pearl Gallery or any jewelry store, and ask to see some.

The jeweler will spread them out on a velvet cloth for you to admire; or better yet, they will set one in a ring of your own choosing or design. Bahama Dawn Designs offers a large selection of Androsia fabric items, as well as the colorful, batik fabric by the yard. Use the fabric to make stunning sarongs and one-of-a-kind items like pillows, tablecloths and napkins. Just imagine how much your friends and family would love those for souvenirs from your travels. The John Bull duty-free shop may be of more interest to the male crewmembers with its Submariner Rolex watches and cigar humidors, but there is enough leather, perfume and cosmetics in there to keep shoppers of any gender happy. And, don't forget to visit the Corner Value Store where males are hard to get to leave. It is on the corner at the stoplight downtown and a great place to get local advice on fishing tackle and to purchase a couple of handmade "Topwater" plugs. "Topwater" plugs look like a wooden cigar and, it is said, "walk the dog on the water like a spook-type bait." Translation – they are sure to catch fish for even the least experienced angler if you are in the right water.

Worked up an appetite, yet? You can satisfy your hunger pangs in Marsh Harbour from the downright funky, to the need for the Admiral to don a dress and the Captain, a jacket and a tie. On the funky side, walk to the one stoplight on the island. Next door to Corner Value is a small grocery/Internet hotspot called Bahamas Family Market. As you enter, look on top of the glass counter for a wide array of homemade, Bahamian take-out food. How about the tightly wrapped squares of macaroni and cheese washed down

Hope Town Harbour, from the east. WATERWAY GUIDE PHOTOGRAPHY.

with a cold bottle of carrot juice. Want something hot from the cooker? Turn left at Corner Value and head down Don MacKay Blvd. towards the pharmacies, and look for the white panel truck under the big spreading tree. It will be surrounded by a long line of local Bahamians getting their supper. About the only place you will find a longer line is at the Island Bakery in the morning for cinnamon rolls. Hankering for the best sidewalk conch salad? Ask for directions to Show Bo's Conch stand. No guarantee that Bo will show, but if he is there, you are in for a treat. Other great casual eateries in Marsh Harbour include Sapodilly's Tropical Bar & Lookout (which suffered a major fire, and hopefully will have reopened by the time you arrive), Mangoes, Snappa's and Curly Tails. For something a bit less touristy, enjoy the luncheonette, the Golden Grouper or the Hummingbird Restaurant, which is popular with local groups of artisans and civic clubs. If you have had your fill of conch and grouper, the Chinese food at Mandarin Fine Dining on Don MacKay Blvd. is not to be missed. Just want some coffee and a light lunch while you catch up on your email? Cafe La Florence will meet your needs. Celebrating something special? Then visit the island's "voted best," Wally's Restaurant, where you will be more comfortable in less casual dress and with an advance reservation.

If you are bound and determined to dirty up the galley while you are in Marsh Harbour, one finds the best selection of fresh or frozen fish and seafood at Kenny Long's Seafood Landing. Kenny is usually there and can tell you how to fix the catch "i'lan style." For unusual items to complement your dinner, try Bahamas Family Market for fresh, local pastries or locate M & R Market for an interesting variety of Haitian foodstuffs. For the usual fare, go to Price Rite and Maxwell's. Check out both of them - then plan your menu and make your list. In general, Price Rite may offer better prices on staples, paper towels and bulk items. (Don't pass by their amazing array of Jerk sauces.) Maxwell's may offer a better fresh produce selection and stock more high-end items like imported cheese or prosciutto. Thankfully, there is such variety from which to choose. In all cases, keep in mind that fresh wares for the stores arrive by boat on Tuesdays (weather and other island t'ings permitting). Most shelves are not fully restocked until Wednesday, but fresh produce and dairy products can fly off the shelves on Tuesdays, just before closing. If you enjoy adult beverages, the Bristol Wine Cellar and Spirits shop has what you are looking for to complete your Marsh Harbour meal extraordinaire.

In the Spotlight. Hope Town

How perfect can an island settlement be? Visit Hope Town on Elbow Cay to find out. From pastel cottages adorned with murals of twining floral vines and posies, to spectacular sugar-sand beaches with easy to reach reefs, to a protected harbor watched over by a candy-cane striped historic lighthouse. That is Hope Town - perfection realized.

Other than on the waterfront, streets are narrow, concrete paths set between houses painted every color on a palette - pink, lime, turquoise, peach, maize, violet, periwinkle, gray, white

Hope Town Harbour, from the east. (Not to be used for navigation.) Waterway Guide Photography.

and more are all here - together with gingerbread eaves and picket fences festooned with hearts, whales and pineapples. Flowers and bushes bloom as if they are hell bent on staking claim to the prettiest colors, in competition with the houses. Beyond and behind this cacophony of color, the Atlantic Ocean beckons. It is a deep, dark blue on the far horizon and a brilliant green closer to shore, with nearby reefs the color of a well-worn boat shoe. The sand is very nearly pink, especially at sunset. The beaches are gorgeous, wide and go on forever.

Here in Hope Town, you can wander at will, watch the sun go down, and dine on the harbor front as the lighthouse starts its nightly cycle. You will share Hope Town with many others - visiting cruisers like yourselves, cottage renters, hotel dwellers, daytrippers from other islands and locals whose families have lived here for generations.

Oddly enough, Hope Town was founded by a South Carolinian loyalist woman, Wyannie Malone. She and her three stalwart sons founded the settlement in the late 1700s. The settlement relied on fishing, shipbuilding and shipwreck "salvaging" for its livelihood. The residents intentionally misled ships onto reefs to reap the treasures in their holds. Artifacts and relics of the "Wrecker Days" are housed in the Wyannie Malone Historical Museum in Hope Town. It was the salvaging of shipwrecks that spurred great opposition to the famous candy-cane striped lighthouse that the British built in the 1860s. It actually took years to build the 120-foot high lighthouse, because opponents routinely vandalized the project.

Fast forward a hundred years, and tourism was far more lucrative for the island's economy. The Hope Town Harbour Lodge was built way back in the 1950s to capitalize on this phenomenon. In addition, developers made foreigners' dreams of island getaways a reality. Despite its small size and large seasonal population, Hope Town embraces everyone without feeling the need for elbow room on Elbow Cay. You will love it here.

The "must-do's" in Hope Town include a stop by the museum (hours are sporadic), a boat trip to the lighthouse (where the million-dollar view and the exercise climbing steps are free), a somber visit to the old cholera cemetery and long strolls along the Atlantic-side beaches. It wouldn't be a proper visit to Hope Town without picking up a Key Lime pie at Vernon's Grocery & Bakery. (While you are at it, pick up some whipping cream to put on top.) And, if you are itching to get hitched to your honey, Vernon moonlights as the Justice of the Peace. He has married hundreds of cruisers. Have one of the many ladies who plait palms make you wedding crowns intertwined with flowers. It will be a truly a memorable wedding. Already married? Reaffirm your vows. You can have the kids and grandkids stay dockside at the Hope Town Harbour Lodge or The Abaco Inn.

For food and fun, there are plenty of options in Hope Town. Captain Jack's has been here for years. Although it seems to be perennially for sale, it keeps on offering good, inexpensive victuals and entertaining visitors with rowdy Trivia competitions and boisterous Bingo games. You are most likely to find live music with your meal at the Harbour's Edge. For an amazing aromatic experience, stop by the Hope Town Coffee House at Lover's Lane and Front Street, the first Bahamas' "micro-roastery." In the tradition of their grandmothers, who used to roast raw green beans over an open fire in a cast iron skillet, the owners choose select beans to micro-roast and mix into superb coffee blends right in the Coffee

Southern Abacos

MAN-O-WAR CAY		Largest Vessel Accommodated	VHF Channel Monitored	Transient Berths / Total Berths	Approach / Dockside Depth (reported)	Floating Docks	Gas / Diesel	Groceries, Ice, Marine Supplies, Snacks	Repairs: Hull, Engine, Propeller	Lift (tonnage), Crane, Rail	1=110V, 2=220V, B=Both, Max Amps	Laundry, Pool, Showers	Pump-Out Station	Nearby: Grocery Store, Motel, Restaurant
		Dockage					Supplies		Services					
1. Man-O-War Marina (WiFi)	242-365-6008	70	16	10/26	5/8		GD	GIMS	HEP	R	B/50	LPS		GR
2. **Edwin's Boat Yard**	**242-365-6006**	**65**	**16**		**3.5/5**			**M**	**HEP**	**L**				**GMR**

Corresponding chart(s) not to be used for navigation. Internet Access (WiFi) Wireless Internet Access

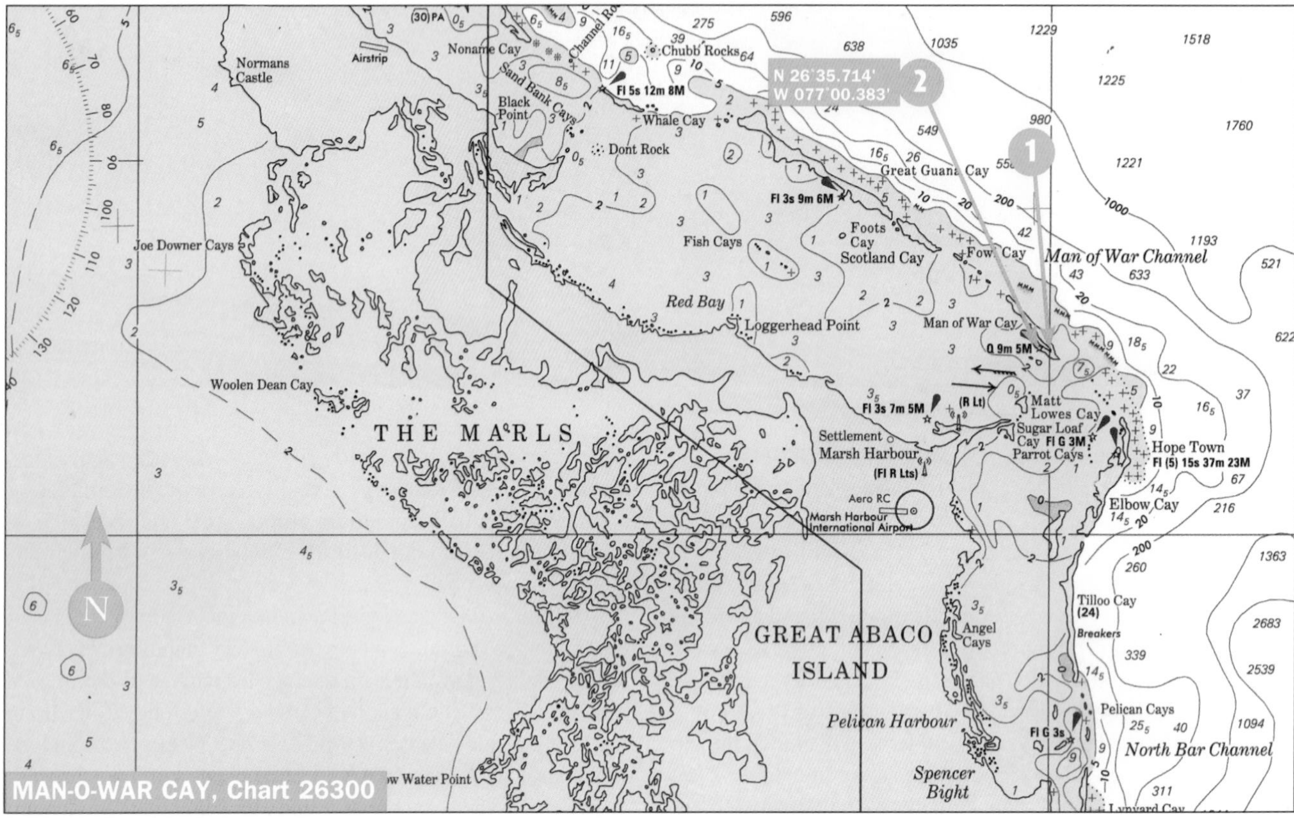

MAN-O-WAR CAY, Chart 26300

House. If you feel like a hike, take a 20-minute walk south of town to the On Da' Beach Bar, Restaurant and Rotisserie. The rotisserie chicken just melts off the bones and into your mouth. At evening cocktail time, don't miss the view at Hopetown Harbour Lodge with their signature drink, the Reef Wreck. Fair warning. It comes by its name honestly if you over imbibe. Also visit the LHL Wine Bar for your evening libation. "Wine down and sip sip."

In the Spotlight. Sandy Point

In the Abacos, Sandy Point provides the only opportunity to experience the ambiance of the Family and Out Islands without doing the mileage. Modest, stoic and devout folks live here. Please don't land your dinghy clad in a string bikini and racer's Speedo™. Walter Lightbourne will welcome you to his marina and Texaco fuel dock. If he has been able to dredge out the sand that the fast ferry ramp deposits under his docks, he might even be able to offer you a berth if your vessel is 12 meters/40 feet or less and your draft is slight. Regardless, you can tie up your dinghy at his dock and start you settlement tour with plenty of friendly help from the folks at Lightbourne.

Man-O-War Cay, from the southeast. (Not to be used for navigation.) Waterway Guide Photography.

The island is home to several restaurants where "just caught" seafood is the standard fare. You will find bars with pool tables and karaoke, too. All are locally owned, run on cash and welcome visitors. Near the government dock, look for Pete & Gay's Guest House and Enza's Place. At Pete & Gay's, the walls are plastered with photos of successful bonefish anglers who have enjoyed a stay at their inn. It is a lot of fun to peruse the pictures with a good rum punch in your hand and a hearty plate of fresh fish or lobster on its way. Enza's Place has been serving up the very best of Bahamian cuisine for well over 35 years. Enza's is very popular with the locals, which should tell you something about their food. Enza's is a liquor free establishment.

Nancy's Sea Side Inn, Restaurant and Bar is the place to be on Friday nights for a Sandy Point Smash and grilled conch. You can recover from the Smashes on Saturday, and head back on Sunday for a stewed fish breakfast. Forget the pancake house flapjacks, sausage, cheese grits and every-which-way hash browns. You will crave fresh stewed fish for breakfast forever more. Nancy's is above the fast ferry ramp.

Hike north along the beach to find the Seaside Inn Restaurant and Bar. There you will find good food and great fun. Then head up the creek a ways and look for the Beach Inn. It has a large bar and restaurant and the liveliest pool table competition in the Abacos. (Don't bet against Basil!) Still farther up the creek is Big J's. It offers a small, island bar atmosphere with a couple of tables and memorable take away food. Big J's serves seafood so fresh it almost jumps onto your plate.

If you have been "lunchin' and munchin'" and need to walk off all these incredible edibles, go shelling. The shelling at Sandy Point is superb. The confluence of deep, deep waters to the south and the shallows around the island equal unparalleled opportunities for the rare find. You may even find treasure. The Spanish galleon, *San Pedro*, sank in the waters between Gorda Cay and Sandy Point in the mid 1600s. It was laden with coins, gold chains, jewels and artifacts that have, from time to time, been found here. Both the Lightbourne and Thompson families can tell you tales of treasure finds.

Every male in the settlement is a boatbuilder. Wander along the many paths that weave through the almost Mormon-like street layout (north, south, east, west grid) and look for a fellow working on a boat. He will share his boating tales (and those of his friends and family) that will captivate you. If you can, visit Sandy Point around the first of June. That is when the annual Homecoming and Conch Festival happens. Along with boat races and general settlement merriment, Sandy Point's conch cleaning contest is legend. No one in the islands can clean more conchs faster than the men of Sandy Point. Bring your camera. Your jaws will ache after you watch them cleaning the conch with their teeth, but you will enjoy the bounty of conch dishes that the locals serve up later.

What's There? The Southern Abacos

Foots Cay, Fish Cays and Scotland Cay

Foots Cay is private and the Fish Cays have little to offer. Scotland Cay is a private resort with an airstrip.

Fowl Cays and Fish Hawk Cay

The Fowl Cays and Fish Hawk Cay are a land and sea preserve. You may visit the park area, but use the mooring buoys provided. You are not allowed to take anything from either land, beach or water, and that includes fish.

Man-O-War Ocean Passes

Man-O-War has two passes through the barrier reef to the ocean, which primarily serve the sportfishermen of Treasure Cay and Marsh Harbour. The southern pass is narrow and not a straight run. With sand and reef to avoid, one can run into trouble. The northern pass is preferred because it is a straightforward shot through a reasonably wide cut, between Fish Hawk Cay and the northern tip of Man-O-War, with 4.8-meter/16-foot depths at mean low water.

Man-O-War Cay and Dickies Cay

Man-O-War Cay is famed for its boatbuilding and safe harbor. The settlement itself, kept as clean as a new pin, reflects an industrious community in the Bahamas, whose interests are primarily boatbuilding, boat repairing and sail making. Inevitably, Man-O-War has long been featured on the tourist "must visit" lists - a port-of-call for every cruising boat passing that way - but Man-O-War maintains its integrity and keeps its unique character. Part of the reason is the residents' strong spiritual commitment, which keeps the little community somewhat apart from the ways of the outside world, including the total ban on the sale of alcohol. There is also a long, strong ancestral heritage—seventy per cent of the residents can trace their ancestry to the first Albury settler.

While you are here, visit the busy boatbuilding shops. Your "looking" at all the work going on is tolerated. If you are lucky, you might even get to share a tale or two. The ladies at Albury's canvas shop have been sewing bags and hats out of canvas for years and years. They don't mind you watching their toils, either. You can grab a bit to eat and drink at the Hibiscus Cafe. Island Treats is an ice cream parlor worth its lick. The Dock and Dine restaurant has a wonderful lunch and dinner menu. If you have family or friends looking for a cottage, try Schooner's Landing or Water Way Rentals (they have boats, too). There is usually an entrepreneurial Man-O-War lady or two who supplements the family income with goodies for sale from her home kitchen oven. Ask around and you are sure to find some fresh bread, pies or biscuits (shortbread cookies) to hoard onboard.

Man-O-War Cay owes its northern, most protected harbor to its little sibling, Dickies Cay. Dickies parallels the western side of Man-O-War for a quarter of its length. With Dickies help, those waters are well-sheltered, but shallow quickly past

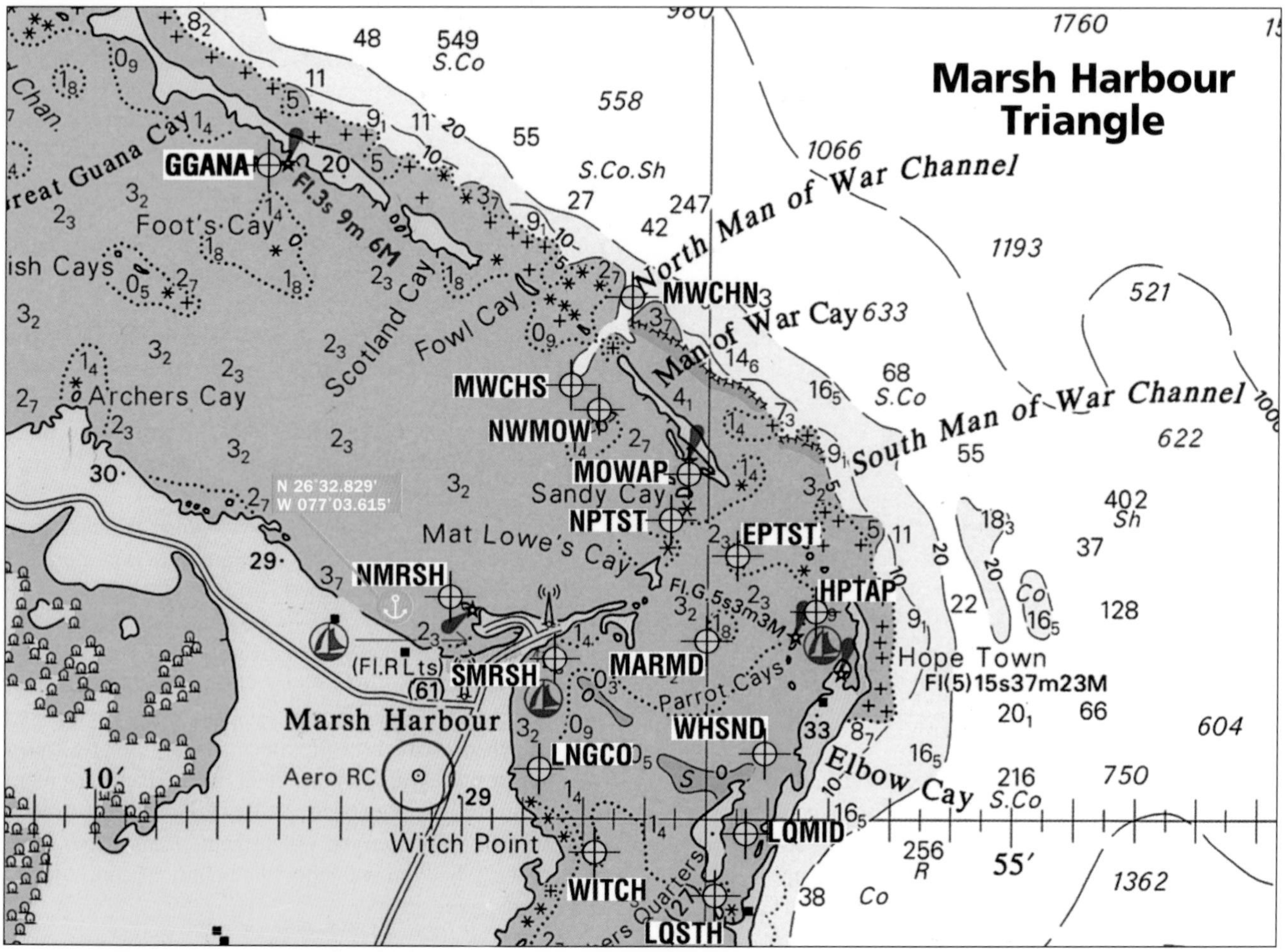

Not to be used for navigation.

Man-O-War Marina. The southern harbor, mysteriously called Eastern Harbour, lies wholly within Man-O-War territory. Although there is deep water to be found there, beware the shallow hump that must be crossed to enter. Both Man-O-War Harbour and its marina are almost always crowded. If you want to be assured of dock space, you must reserve it ahead of time. Before you leave this charmed place, don't forget to get your picture taken at the British royal red, original Royal Telephone Call Box and Postal Box. The signs at the banks, announcing their once-a-week opening day, make for great shots, too. Folks back home can't quite grasp that banking concept.

Garden Cay and Sandy Cay

Both Garden Cay and Sandy Cay are private. For anchoring, boats that draw less than 3 feet can find meager protection from north winds on their western sides, but use visual piloting, and a keen eye on the depth sounder, while working your way in. After a blow, there can be excellent shelling at low tide off Sandy Cay.

Point Set Rock

Cruising vessels can't miss Point Set Rock. Whichever way you go, you pass it. As an extra landmark, Point Set has built on it what appears to be a concrete shed. It is a junction point on the underwater power cable that runs across to Elbow Cay from Marsh Harbour.

Marsh Harbour

We have already introduced Marsh Harbour. You are likely to go there at some time or another. Let's cover the marina options. Within the geographical area of the marina district, the Conch Inn Marina is the base for a chartering operation (The

Making Wake. Photo courtesy of Peter Mitchell.

Southern Abacos

MARSH HARBOUR		Largest Vessel Accommodated	VHF Channel Monitored	Transient Berths / Total Berths	Approach / Dockside Depth (reported)	Floating Docks	Gas / Diesel	Groceries, Ice, Marine Supplies, Snacks	Repairs: Hull, Engine, Propeller	Lift (tonnage), Crane, Rail	1=110V, 2=220V, B=Both, Max Amps	Laundry, Pool, Showers	Pump-Out Station	Nearby: Grocery Store, Motel, Restaurant
		Dockage					Supplies				Services			
1. Marsh Harbour Marina	242-367-2700	70	16	/62	7/6		GD	IM			B/50	LPS		GMR
2. Harbour View Marina (Internet Access) (Wireless Internet Access)	242-367-3910	100	16	25/36	6/7		GD	IS			B/50	LPS		GMR
3. Mangoes Marina (Internet Access) (Wireless Internet Access)	242-367-4255	60	16	31/31	5.5/6	F		I	HEP		B/50	LPS		GMR
4. Conch Inn Resort & Marina	242-367-4000	200	16	/80	7/6		GD	IS			B/100	PS		GMR
5. Abaco Beach Resort At Boat Harbour (Wireless Internet Access)	**242-367-2158**	**200**	**16**	**192/192**	**/10**		**GD**	**IS**			**B/100**	**LPS**		**GMR**
6. Marsh Harbour Boatyards	242-367-5205		16				GD	IMS	HEP	L85				

Corresponding chart(s) not to be used for navigation. ☐ Internet Access (WiFi) Wireless Internet Access

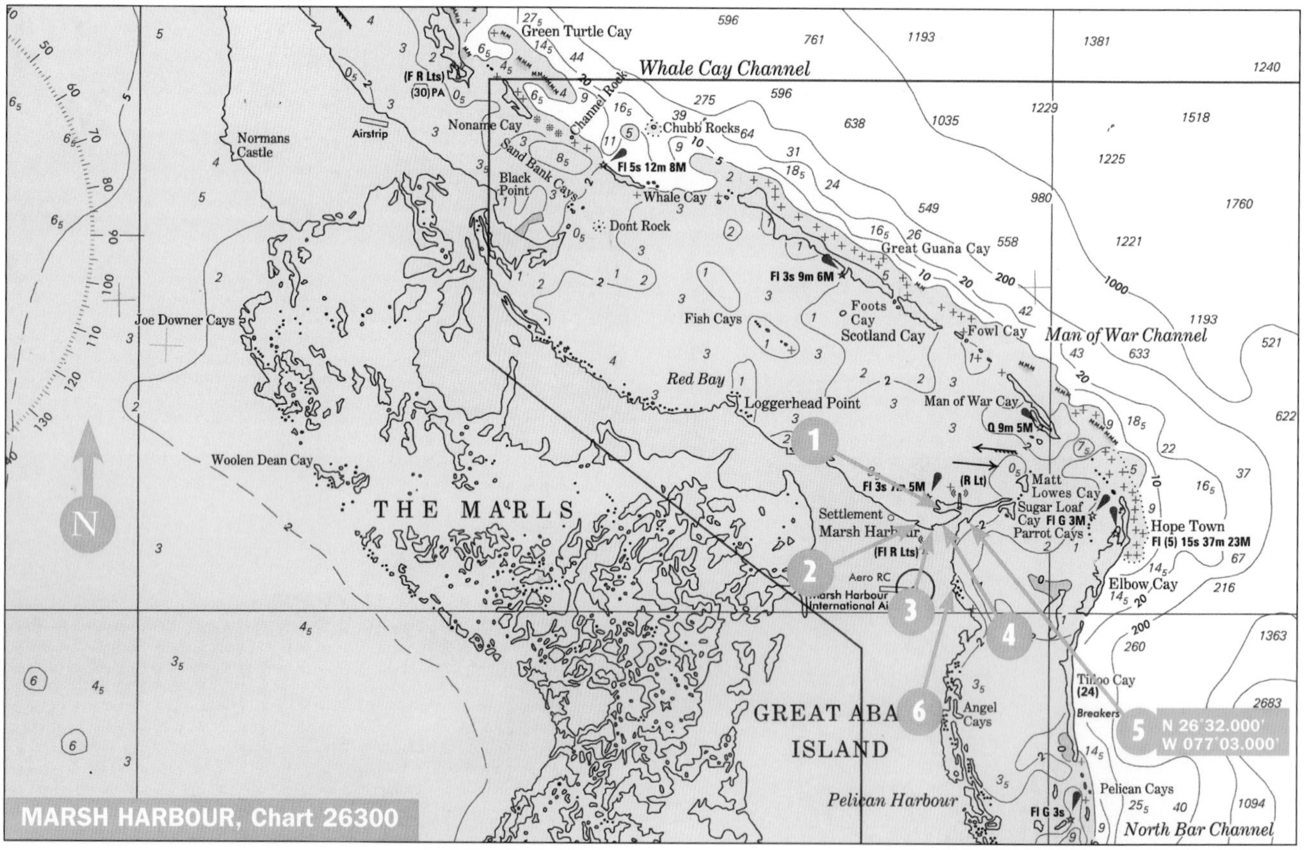

MARSH HARBOUR, Chart 26300

Routes in the Marsh Harbour Triangle

Providing you stay clear of the shoals extending to the west from Johnnies Cay and Lubbers Bank to the south, as well as the obvious inshore shoal areas, there are no navigational problem areas in the Marsh Harbour Triangle. We define this area by placing the apex of the triangle at the northwest approach to Man-O-War Cay, then drawing one line down to hit Great Abaco Island southwest of Marsh Harbour, and another line to hit Elbow Cay south of Hope Town. If both of these points are on latitude N 26° 32.000' that is about right. Join them and there is your triangle.

Within this triangle you have a web of routes, all short runs of a few nautical miles, linking Marsh Harbour to Man-O-War Cay and to Hope Town, and Hope Town to Man-O-War Cay, Marsh Harbour, and the Boat Harbour Marina, and so it goes. The network has Point Set Rock as its hub, and you could hardly wish for a better landmark. Though you should to take note of bearings and distances, as well as the principal coordinates, you visually pilot for every trip in this area.

WEST PALM
165 MILES
FORT LAUDERDALE
185 MILES
MIAMI
200 MILES
KEY LARGO
BOAT HARBOUR
ABACO

Marsh Harbour, from the southeast. (Not to be used for navigation.) WATERWAY GUIDE PHOTOGRAPHY.

Moorings). The marina offers fuel, nice shoreside facilities and a lot of activity with charters arriving and departing. Mangoes is cozy, offers a great restaurant and fabulous boutique. Its shoreside setting is attractive. There is no fuel dock. Harbour View Marina is intimate and offers a fun bar with casual dining and a fuel dock.

The Marsh Harbour Marina, on the north shore, wins points for protection from northers in winter and exposure to the cooling southeast trade winds in summer. It has a fuel dock and a restaurant. It is quite a hike into the town, so it is either a dinghy trip across the harbor or a cab ride around it; that is if you don't get a rental car.

As for anchoring, the Marsh Harbour fairway has yet to be clearly defined, although the Royal Marsh Harbour Yacht Club maintains a set of approach buoys to divert yachtsmen from following a more prominent shipping channel to the Customs dock. Use the recreational traffic buoys to try to determine where the fairway should run, and avoid anchoring there. If you keep your VHF radio up as you circle the harbor looking for a spot to drop the hook, you will get lots of free advice. If you are being told, "Don't drop the hook! The holding is bad there," heed it! Many boats have dragged in Marsh Harbour. In most places, you should find at least 2.4-meter/8-foot depths at mean low water. The harbor is reasonably well-protected, but under threat of a severe storm, you may want to find somewhere better shielded and less crowded.

The well-protected Abaco Beach Resort at Boat Harbour Marina, tucked up under the southeast hook of the Marsh Harbour promontory, is not located in the harbor. It is the largest marina and has first-rate facilities. Once you are there, you are by no means marooned or separated from

Marsh Harbour town, which is within walking distance or a short taxi ride, but you will not want to leave! Pretty much anything you could want is right there.

Great Abaco Western Coast - Marsh Harbour to Spencer Bight

The western coast along Great Abaco, between Marsh Harbour and Spencer Bight just north of the Bight of Old Robinson, is not chronicled as cruising territory. That does not mean that there are not areas worthy of exploration, or that there aren't anchorages and gunkholes worth finding, but you will have to do your own soundings beyond the deep-water channels. Snake Cay, in the middle of this stretch, offers a day anchorage with poor holding, but an interesting dinghy exploration into the interior. Avoid the deteriorating commercial pier. There could be underwater hazards aplenty! A better anchorage lies to the north of Snake Cay off the southern tip of Cormorant Cay. There is deep water in which to navigate off the shoreline here, but be ever vigilant for uncharted hazards and unexpected rocky bars. In southerly winds, you can anchor north of Black Point Cay in 2 meters/6 feet of water. Again, there is good dinghy exploration along the west coast. From there, it is best to head east toward the Pelican Cays, because the waters south of Black Point Cay are just too shallow, and what looks like navigable water ends at a shifting sand bar. For some folks who don't enjoy the hubbub of restaurants, bars and packed marina docks, this is just the sort of cruise they dreamed of taking. If that is your thing, go for it – cautiously.

Matt Lowes Cay and Sugar Loaf Cay

Matt Lowes Cay is named after the 18th century turtler, wrecker and sometime pirate. The love story of Matt Lowe and Miss Ruby is one of Bahamian legend. The cay is 100 percent private. High water mark laws do not apply here. If you would like to visit, $2000 will get you a week at the cottage and a spot on one of the three docks in the inland harbor for boats up to 25 feet. The island, with its five beaches, tiny harbor and house, is reportedly up for sale at press time. There is a nice little anchorage in the nook east of John Cash Point and west of Matt Lowes Cay. Just don't go to shore.

Sugar Loaf Cay has private houses and rental properties with their own docks.

Johnnies Cay and Annas Cay

Johnnies Cay is private. Annas Cay is the tiny islet off the west side of the northern peninsula of Elbow Cay.

Parrot Cays

The Parrot Cays are the chain of five cays running down the west coast of Elbow Cay from the latitude of the approach to Hope Town Harbour. North Parrot Cay, the initial landmark on the approach to Hope Town, has what appears to be an incomplete dock on it (six pilings with no decking) and a light. The

Southern Abacos

ELBOW CAY & HOPE TOWN		Largest Vessel Accommodated	VHF Channel Monitored	Transient Berths / Total Berths	Approach / Dockside Depth (reported)	Floating Docks	Gas / Diesel	Groceries, Ice, Marine Supplies, Snacks	Repairs: Hull, Engine, Propeller	Lift (tonnage), Crane, Rail	1=110V, 2=220V, B=Both, Max Amps	Laundry, Pool, Showers	Pump-Out Station	Nearby: Grocery Store, Motel, Restaurant
		Dockage					Supplies				Services			
1. Sea Spray Resort & Marina 💻 WiFi	**242-366-0065**	**84**	**16**	**38/60**	**5.5/5.5**		**GD**	**IMS**			**B/50**	**LPS**		**GMR**
2. Hope Town Hideaways Marina 💻 WiFi	242-366-0224	65	16/63	12/12	/4			I			B/50	LP		GMR
3. Hope Town Marina & Club Soleil Resort 💻 WiFi	242-366-0003	125	16	12/12	5/6			GIS			B/50	LPS		GMR
4. Lighthouse Marina	242-366-0154	60	16	/6	6/6		GD	IMS	HE		B/50	LS		GMR

Corresponding chart(s) not to be used for navigation. 💻 Internet Access WiFi Wireless Internet Access

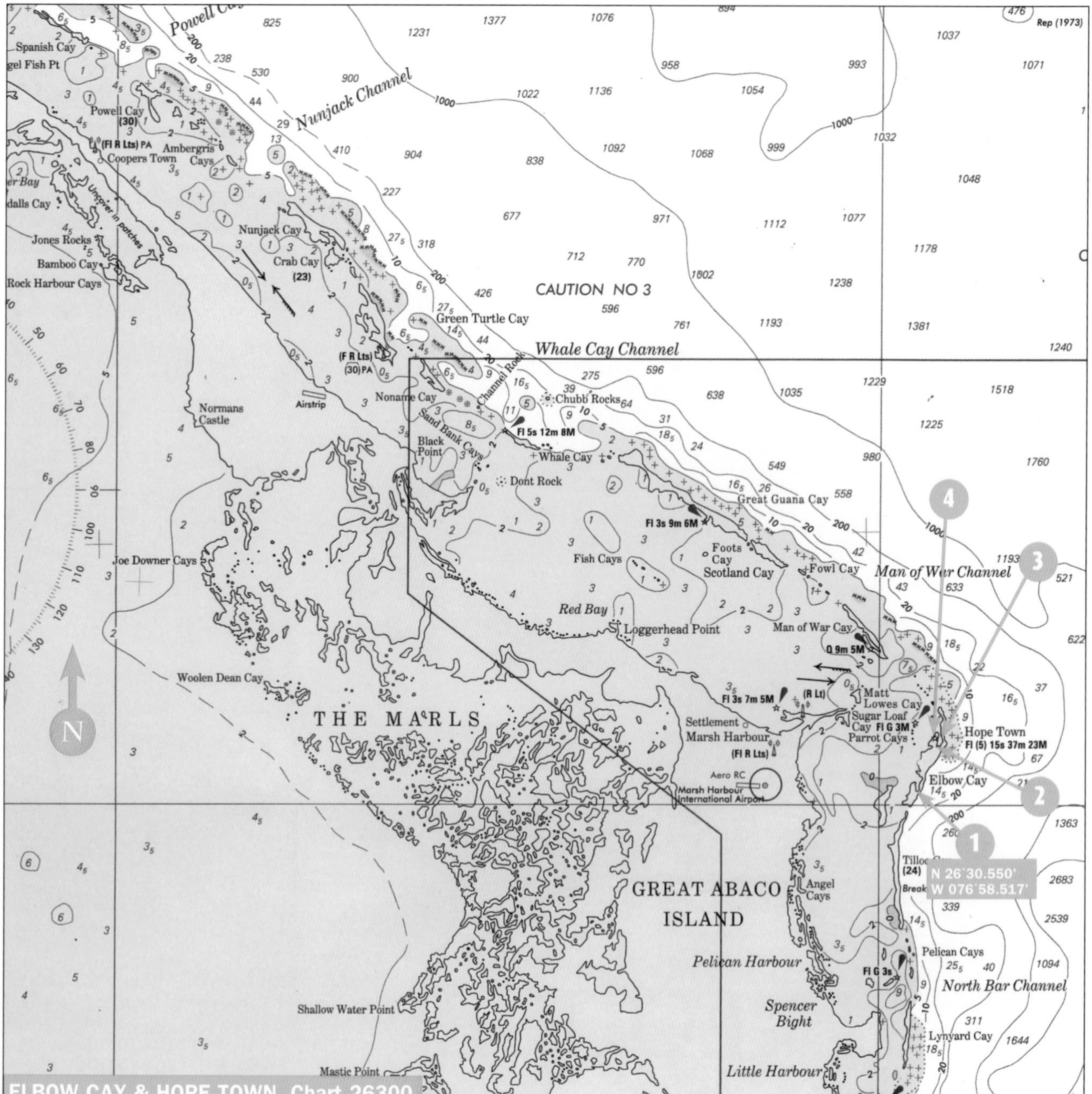

ELBOW CAY & HOPE TOWN, Chart 26300

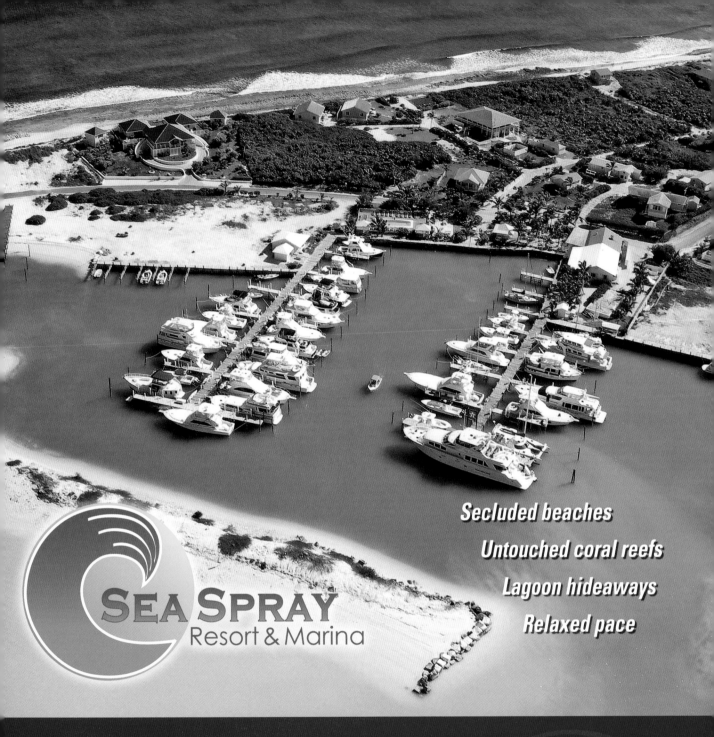

Elbow Cay's White Sound, from the east. (Not to be used for navigation.) WATERWAY GUIDE PHOTOGRAPHY.

fourth cay (counting from north to south) is the base of the Gale family's Island Marine Boat Rentals. They will collect you from wherever you are, take you to Parrot Cay, rent you an Albury 20, Boston Whaler or an Aquasport, and at the end of your rental period, deliver you back to wherever you started. Call them on VHF Channel 16. Many cruisers anchor in the Parrot Cays vicinity and dinghy back and forth to Hope Town to enjoy its facilities. There are several docks in the harbour that will let you tie up your dinghy. There is good conching in the shallow, grassy waters off the northern tip of Elbow Cay.

Elbow Cay. Hope Town

Hope Town was introduced in the Spotlight feature. There are few who cruise in the Northern Bahamas that do not have Hope Town on their visit list. Even if you had never heard of it, it is likely that its red and white candy-striped lighthouse would draw you in. Perhaps you should go there for the lighthouse alone. It is one of the world's last working kerosene-fueled lighthouses.

The Elbow Cay Lighthouse

The Elbow Cay Lighthouse (aka the Hope Town Lighthouse) is one of the last three, continuously operated, kerosene-fueled, hand-wound rotation lighthouses in the world. All three are in the Bahamas. When the lighthouse was first built, it was, well...just a light. It did not flash. By the mid 1930s, the need for a light that was more readily identifiable was evident. Thus, the lighthouse underwent its first major refit since the 1860s. The lenses and turning equipment, that had been at the old Gun Cay Lighthouse (south of the Biminis), were installed in the Elbow Cay Lighthouse. The group of rotating Fresnel lenses—called "bull's eyes"—produces five white flashes every fifteen seconds, 120 feet above sea level with 15 nautical mile visibility. The lighting source is a 325,000 candlepower vapor burner. A hand pump is used to pressurize kerosene stored in containers that lie below the lantern room. The pressurized kerosene travels up a tube to a vaporizer. The vaporizer sprays the fuel onto a pre-heated mantle that is known as the "soul" of the lighthouse (the soul analogy is quixotic; but instead, visualize a very large Coleman™ camping lantern with its sock-like mantles). The Fresnel lenses concentrate the mantle's light into a laser-like beam that shoots towards the horizon. To reduce friction, the four-ton Fresnel lenses float in a circular vat of lubricating mercury to reduce friction. Every two hours, the lighthouse keeper has to raise weights with a hand winch—700 pounds of weights—to the top of the tower (think of a Black Forest cuckoo clock's, pinecone shaped lead weights being pulled up). As the weights descend, they operate a meticulously timed series of bronze gears (picture the insides of the cuckoo clock). The gears rotate the four-ton lenses once around every fifteen seconds. It is just an amazing feat of very simple "engineering." The lighthouse tower itself is 89 feet high and has a 101-step climb to the lens room. The previously smooth, tapered lighthouse tower was reinforced in 1954, when British engineers poured concentric steps around the tower. Clearly, there is more to this candy-cane than meets the eye. Now, you must make the dinghy trip to go climb it, right? Yes, it is still in service. You can and should visit it.

Hope Town Marinas and Anchorages

After traversing the narrow, and somewhat shallow, entrance into the harbor, Lighthouse Marina lies immediately to starboard. Moving counter clockwise, past a mini-headland of mangroves, next is the Hope Town Marina and Club Soleil, then Hope Town Hideaways Marina. The mooring field is to port as you enter. It is, for all but the smallest of craft, a non-anchoring zone. Moorings effectively dominate the harbor, and it would be wise to call ahead to reserve one.

If you can't get a mooring in Hope Town Harbour, anchor off outside between the Parrot Cays and Elbow Cay. Just stay clear of the Albury ferry routes on their runs between Hope Town and Marsh Harbour and up to Man-O-War. You have about 1.8 meters/6 feet there and reasonably good holding, but no wind protection from the north and the south. You will need to seek another, less open anchorage if bad weather is in the forecast.

Elbow Cay. White Sound

Yes, there is a lot more to Elbow Cay than Hope Town. Hope Town so dominates Elbow Cay that it is easy to forget that the cay continues for over 2.5 nautical miles south–southwest from Hope Town Harbour. Just under two nautical miles to the south of Hope Town, Elbow Cay's White Sound opens up into the Sea of Abaco. White Sound offers a Sea of Abaco approach to the Abaco Inn, at the narrowest point of Elbow Cay. Here, but for its rocky spine, Elbow Cay might well have been carved by the ocean into two separate islands.

There is no space for anchoring in Elbow Cay's White Sound, and the depths outside the channel is just 0.6 meters/2 feet in places. The best anchorage, if the wind is right, is just south of the White Sound entry point, well clear of the convergence zone, for boats are constantly entering or leaving White Sound.

The Abaco Inn dock, at the end of the straight west–east approach channel leading into White Sound, has 1.8-meter/ 6-foot depths at mean low water (1.5 meters/5 feet in some spots) and limited space for visitors. You must throw a stern anchor out as you come in and secure bow-to (or come in astern, if you wish) but don't lie alongside. After all that work getting the boat secured, take the Admiral and crew to the Abaco Inn bar and treat them to their signature drinks: the Bahama Breeze, Yellow Bird and Conch Pearl.

Sea Spray Resort, at the end of the southern branch of White Sound, is a well-found, all-weather marina, but not a hurricane hole, for the ocean is just too close. Sea Spray offers 1.8-meter/6-foot depths at their docks, fuel and a pleasant bar and nice restaurant with service outside on the deck or indoors. The Hope Town Islanders provide live music at the Sea Spray restaurant and bar. Your guests that fly in can stay at one of seven villas.

Elbow Cay. Tahiti Beach

All the way at the south end of Elbow Cay is Tahiti Beach (N 26° 30.100'/W 076° 59.260'), famed for its sandbar that virtually dries at low water. It is a very popular picnic spot for small craft and for partiers. It is also one of the very best places to shell in the Abacos. The docks to the north of Tahiti Beach, partly shielded by Bakers Rock, are private. South of Elbow Cay lies the Tilloo Cut with Tilloo Cay, and to the west is Lubbers Quarters with the shallows of the Lubbers Quarters Bank.

The South of the Sea of Abaco and South Great Abaco Island

For many people, the end of Elbow Cay is the turn-around point for their cruise in the Abacos. If you started by crossing the Little Bahama Bank, you may well think of retracing your route when you get to Hope Town. If you have chartered out of Marsh Harbour, the more immediate destinations of Hope Town, Man-O-War Cay, and perhaps Green Turtle Cay, will satisfy a cruise itinerary.

However, should you consider continuing south from Hope Town, you may be asking yourself, what's there? It is the last 10 miles of the Sea of Abaco (measured as a brown pelican might fly) but it more like 15 nautical miles when you add up the legs of the courses down to Little Harbour. Great Abaco Island has another 30 plus nautical miles to run before it ends, forbiddingly, at South West Point with its lonely lighthouse, and Hole-in-the-Wall, which may sound like a cruisers' refuge, but is no safe haven. Unless you have the appropriate vessel and the curiosity to visit Cherokee Sound, Sandy Point and Moores Island, your Abaco cruising grounds end, as does the Sea of Abaco, at Little Harbour.

If you are bent on leaving the Abacos and carrying on south across the Northeast Providence Channel, the North Bar Channel or the Little Harbour Bar will be your point of departure for the Berry Islands, Royal Island or Spanish Wells or Nassau. From those destinations, you can travel on south to Andros, the Exumas and beyond. If you are arriving from one of these cruising grounds, you are most likely to choose one of these ocean passes to gain the Sea of Abaco, rather than work your way offshore farther north up the Abaco chain. These considerations aside, why head for Little Harbour? The answer is because of Little Harbour itself, the Pelican Cays Land and Sea Park and the anchorages of Lynyard Cay.

In the central Abacos, the shoals off Spanish Cay, south of Green Turtle Cay, off Treasure Cay and past Whale Cay and the Loggerhead Bar, govern your options on which courses to run. Similarly, south of Elbow Cay, Lubbers Bank and the Tilloo Bank, shoals dictate that you either set off south running about one nautical mile off the coast of Great Abaco Island, or thread your way between Elbow Cay and Lubbers Quarters Cay, and around the Tilloo Bank. Whichever route you choose, keep the tide in mind. It is comforting to be within three hours of high water, on a rising tide, on the passage to enter Little Harbour.

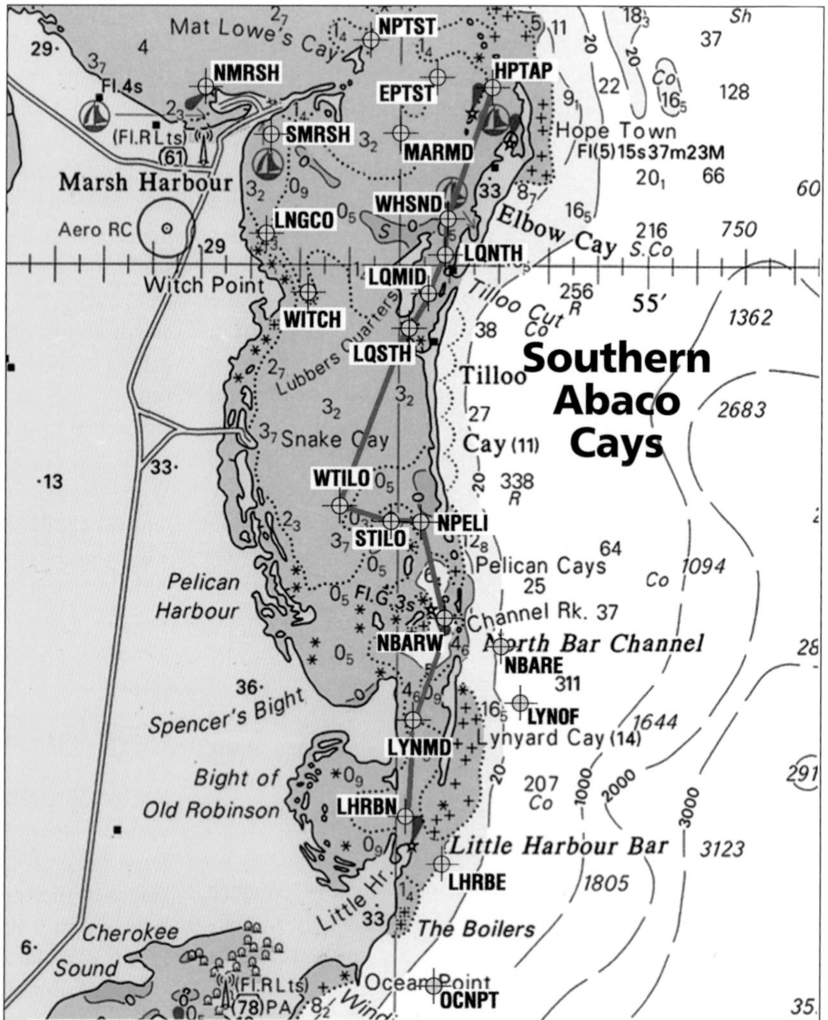

Reproduced from Admiralty Chart 3910. Depth in meters.

Great Abaco Coast. Marsh Harbour to Spencer Bight

Our cruising editors have found little of interest on the Great Abaco coast between Marsh Harbour and Spencer Bight (just north of the Bight of Old Robinson) to tempt the cruising boat to stay awhile and explore, but the possibility remains that there may well be gunkholes worth visiting. Snake Cay, in the middle of this stretch, whose rusting fuel tanks are conspicuous, has poor holding.

Lubbers Quarters Cay

Lubbers Quarters Cay has a small community of homes on the south end of the island with homes for a few full-time residents and some small, owner operated cottage rental operations (www.abacoseaside.com or www.watercolourscottages.com). There is a small, well-protected, private marina on the southeast end of Lubbers, with a dredged channel leading to a community dock that has 6 feet at low water and about 20 private slips.

There is a road system on the south end of the island. CruiseAbaco (www.cruiseabaco.com), a bareboat and captained charter operation, is based north of Cracker P's on the east side of the island and has a mooring field off of their dock. The west side of the island is sparsely inhabited and very shallow in most areas, however, it does have some great secluded beaches and bonefish as well. There are about 25 full-time residents (and some wild boar) who call Lubbers Quarters home. The shallow sand bank, charted going west off the northwest end of the island, shifts some and is a bit shallower than shown at times. Most of the island monitors VHF Channel 09.

Tilloo Cay

Tilloo Cay, which seems to stretch on forever (its length is just over four nautical miles) has good beaches on its southwest tip, and you can work your way in there just north of Tilloo Bank. There is an inshore route south you can take over the bank if you hug the shore, but you will only find little more than 0.6 meter/2 feet of water, so it is dinghy territory unless you have very shoal draft. Tilloo Pond is private. There are beautiful anchorages all along the western shore with great easterly protection and some northerly protection just east of the charted turret, south of Tavern Cay, a private island. When our cruising editor anchored off Tilloo Pond, they saw their one and only Bahamas boa constrictor swimming off the rocks. These are truly enchanting waters in which to dive and snorkel.

Channel Cay

Channel Cay is private. Its waters along the eastern shore offer some good holding in 3 meters/9 feet of water, and you are out of the North Bar Channel swells. This makes the cay an attractive alternative to day anchoring the big boat off Sandy Cay, and it is a manageable dinghy ride to the Pelican Cays Land and Sea Park for snorkeling.

The Pelican Cays and Sandy Cay

The Pelican and Sandy cays, and the adjacent sea area, form the Bahamian National Trust's Pelican Cays Land and Sea Park, which extends south to include the waters of North Bar Channel. You are allowed to anchor here, but not over coral. Holding on the east side of the Sandy Cay reef is not good.

Swells coming in through North Bar Channel can make the Pelican Park sea area bumpy, to say the least. If it is going to be rough there, forget it. Small boat moorings are provided by the Bahamas National Trust. Fishing, shell collecting, the taking of coral or any predatory action is forbidden. Just snorkel and enjoy the pretty fish playing tag on the reefs.

Cornish Cay

Cornish Cay is private and surrounded by very shallow water. Boats with a shallow draft can work their way west toward the cay from the north to day anchor, and avoid the swells off Sandy Cay, to visit the Land and Sea Park.

North Bar Channel

North Bar Channel is the preferred entry channel of the two South Abaco passes. It runs between the northern tip of Lynyard Cay, where the reef extends offshore for a short distance, and the Pelican Cays to the north. There is a reef all the way from the south end of Tilloo Cay, linking the Pelican Cays like a daisy chain, so don't mistake the wide gap immediately east of Channel Cay as the pass. Immediately south of the southernmost Pelican cay, there is more reef and one isolated rock, Channel Rock. Leave Channel Rock to the north.

Lynyard and Goole Cays

Lynyard Cay has good anchorages on its western shore. They start about mid-way down and extend south. Work your way towards shore for waters in the 4- to 6-meter/12- to 18-foot depth range. There are private houses on Lynyard, but you can land your dinghy there. The anchorages are relatively well-protected from the ocean swell. The reason for this may be that Goole Cay to the south and the extensive reef extending 0.75 nautical miles farther south from Goole Cay act as a breakwater. This reef, which does not always show (other than by an upheaval in swell pattern), together with the reef extending north from Little Harbour's Lighthouse Point, sets your limits for passing safely through Little Harbour Bar.

Bridges Cay

Bridges Cay is private property. The house on it is a useful landmark, particularly if you are entering Little Harbour Bar from the ocean. Shallow draft boats can seek shelter from northerly winds south of Bridge's Cay and work their way north toward the big island.

The Bight of Old Robinson

The Bight of Old Robinson, to the west of Little Harbour, is entered at any point between Bridges Cay and Tom Curry Point. It has 2.1 meters/7 feet of water in its central arc, but otherwise is a maze of shallows with extraordinary blue holes and subterranean connections to the ocean. This is why, it is said, that ocean fish like grouper may be found far from their normal habitat. It is truly unsurveyed territory. Explore it by dinghy and hand-held sounder to find some shallow-draft paradise anchorages that none of the rest of us have seen.

Little Harbour. A Bahamian Dream

Little Harbour probably comes close to anyone's dream of a Bahamian hideaway. It certainly met the critical demands of the extraordinarily dynamic, eccentric run-away Smith College professor, Randolph Johnston, one of the great sculptors of the 20th century. Johnston and his wife, Margot, daughter, Marina and three sons, Bill, Pete and Denny, left Northampton, MA on their schooner *Langosta* to escape the maddening rush of civilization and live out their lives in sight of no man, in the pursuit of a free life and devotion to art. With no particular place in mind, *Langosta* sailed to Little

Pelican Cays. (Not to be used for navigation.)
WATERWAY GUIDE PHOTOGRAPHY.

Harbour. The family, in true Swiss Family Robinson-style, lived in caves, built thatched huts and eventually a foundry for Randolph's work. Johnston, who died in 1992 in his late 80s, spent the last 40 years of his life in Little Harbour, pursuing his dream of living free to sculpt in an unspoiled natural environment remote from the fetters, constraints and pollution of life in the developed world.

Today, much of Little Harbour remains in the hands of his three sons. Only Pete maintains a relatively high profile with a gallery devoted to his father's work and his own, as well as that of other local artists. Remote refuge it may well have once been, but the world has found Little Harbour. There are many cottages here, road access has been improved, and weekend pig-roasts and bronze castings draw visitors in droves to Pete's Pub. Its signature drink is the Blaster—a nod to the foundry where sculptures are still cast. There is also a new spot in town called Wine Down, Sip Sip in which to imbibe less explosive beverages and enjoy the ambiance of Little Harbour. Despite a focus on attracting the world to the doorstep, remember there are no facilities for visiting boats other than moorings and maybe some room to anchor. There are no stores, no fuel, no water and no place to leave garbage.

The harbor itself is almost completely enclosed, protected from virtually all wind and surge. It has all the depth one is looking for, once you are inside. Remember that this entrance channel, for most boats, is a no-go until at least half tide. There are buoys to guide you through the entrance that holds a scant 1 meter/3 feet at low tide. It is worth all the effort to get in here. You won't be disappointed.

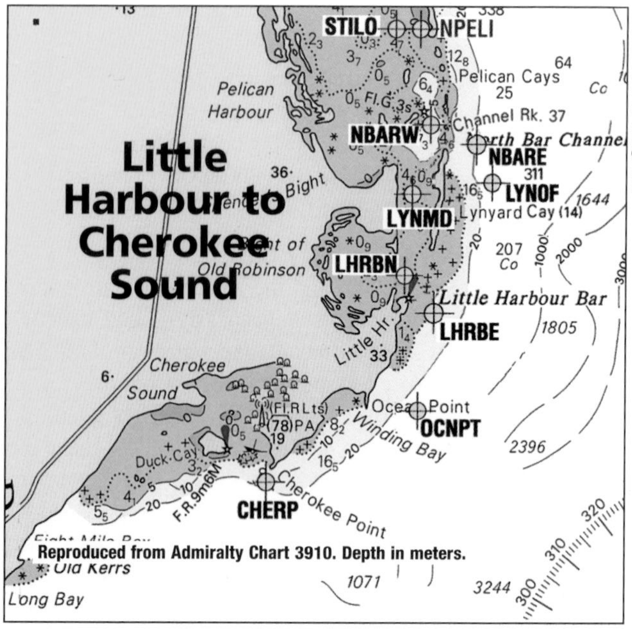

Little Harbour

The harbor itself has a good beach, and there is another good beach on the north side. There is a small reef that is worth snorkeling, and the remains of the old lighthouse on Lighthouse Point (together with a modern light on the old rusty light tower) create a good photo op. The caves on the east side of the harbor are where the Johnston family, when they first migrated to a nearly deserted Little Harbour, found shelter while building

Little Harbour. (Not to be used for navigation.) WATERWAY GUIDE PHOTOGRAPHY.

Cherokee Sound, from the southeast. (Not to be used for navigation.) WATERWAY GUIDE PHOTOGRAPHY.

their home. The waters in and around Little Harbour, as well as the reefs, are dedicated to the Bahamas National Trust and, as such, are protected. You may well see turtles swimming in the harbor, so again, keep the camera handy.

Little Harbour Passage

Little Harbour Passage has 4.2-meters/14-foot depths at mean low water, but there is one report of 3.3-meters/11-foot depths. If you are in this unlikely bracket of depth sensitivity, take note. This apart, it is fairly straightforward. Goole Cay to the north has a reef running south from its southern tip, and Little Harbour Point has a reef running northward. Despite these potential hazards, this passage is the one you are likely to choose if you decide to visit Cherokee Sound and points south.

South of Little Harbour

The Abaco Club on Winding Bay is the next apparent "bay" to the immediate south of Little Harbour. The facilities are gated and managed by Ritz-Carlton. There is no indication that this may one day offer a marina facility open to cruising boats, although consideration has been given to building a marina for Winding Bay residents and guests in Little Harbour.

Cherokee and Cherokee Sound

First, let's make one point clear. A trip to Cherokee Point should only be done in the very best of conditions. If there is a hint of any weather from any direction, this is not a destination for a cruiser, except by rental car. That said, as soon as you round Cherokee Point, the colors of the waters that lead to Little Bay will take your breath away. The snow-white beach and its backdrop are equally breathtaking. You can work your way surprisingly close to shore and still find 2 meters/6 to 8 feet of water. Even in the calmest conditions, there will be surge, however. You can reach the settlement by dinghy. The long pier running out from the beach, in line with the BTC tower, is the pride of the community, but don't tie up your dinghy there. There are some tie-ups at the jetty right at the settlement. The residents you will meet could not be friendlier. The area was renowned for building offshore fishing smacks like the ones seen in Spanish Wells. Near the post office, there is a memorial to fishermen lost at sea and to the art of boat building. There is a good grocery store in town that carries a lot more than just food. Some of the local ladies bake fresh bread and, if the season is right, you might find fresh produce. If you want to stay awhile, and your boat draws less than four feet, you can consider getting a pilot to take you across Cherokee Sound and into the anchorage west of Riding Cay. Your best bet is to go into town, ask for advice about tides and find a pilot. Unless you are paddling a kayak, this is not a harbor entrance you want to try on your own.

South of Cherokee Sound

Casuarina Point, immediately south of Cherokee Sound, is a housing development with homes and lots for sale. There are no plans to construct a marina there.

Farther south, on the way to Hole-in-the-Wall and Sandy Point, other housing developments have materialized, some already settled, others breaking ground and others planned. None of these, given the characteristics of the final southern

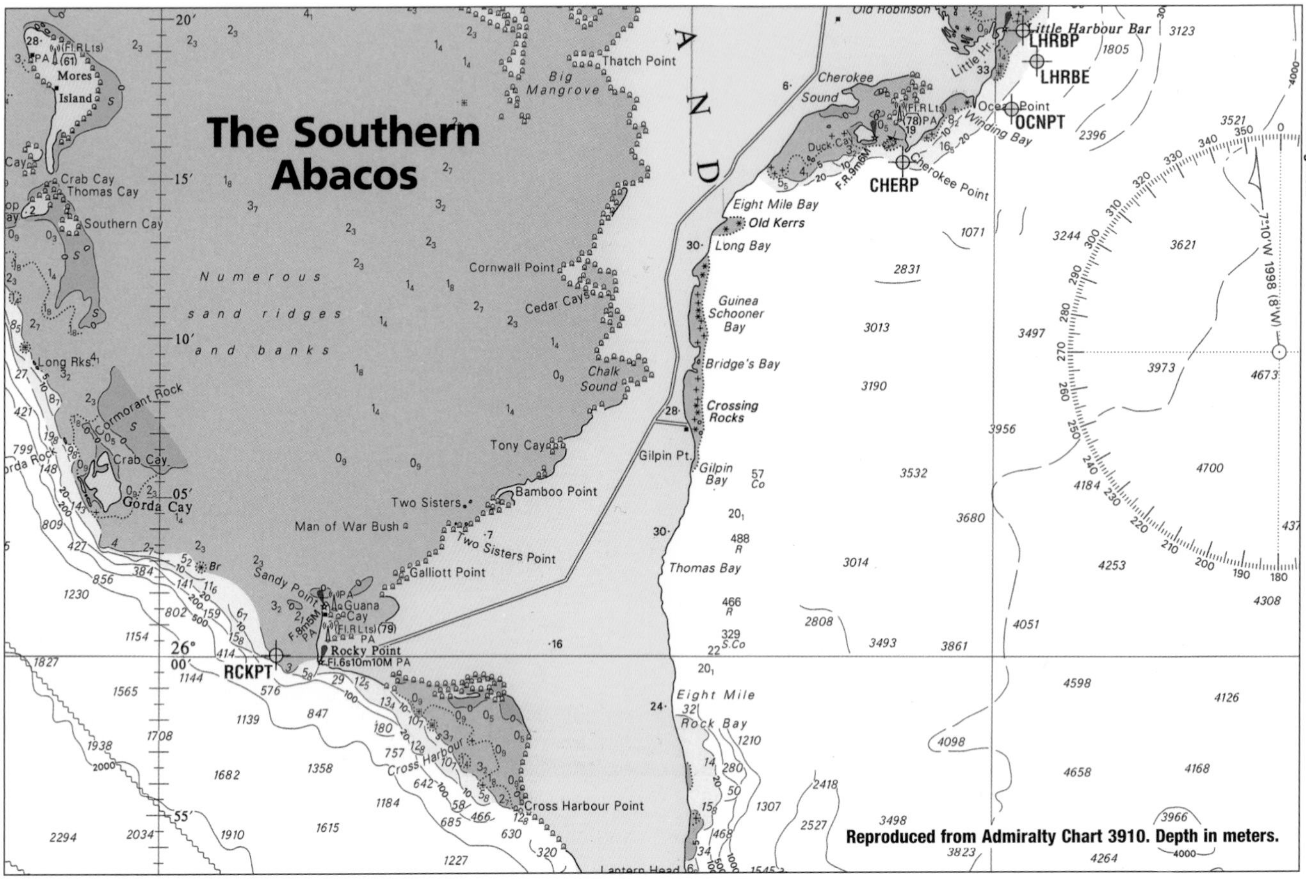

span of the east coast of Great Abaco, are ever likely to offer a marina.

Hole-in-the-Wall

The steep coast from Cherokee Point to Hole-in-the-Wall offers no true shelter. There are shoals along the coast that necessitate giving the shoreline wide berth. The Hole-in-the-Wall peninsula, which is south of the lighthouse, is a wall of rock with the "hole in the wall" punched through it like an eye in a needle. You can tuck yourself behind the point of land on the western side to anchor, in an emergency, only if the winds are light to zero, from the east or southeast. Don't let the name Cross Harbour, whose location lies north of Hole-in-the-Wall, fool you. It is a misnomer. It is a shallow, reef-filled bight. Don't even think of it as a potential refuge. Sandy Point, around the southwest tip (Rocky Point) of Great Abaco, does have an anchoring option. For this reason, we covered Sandy Point in our Spotlight section. If you are going past Hole-in-the-Wall, get the weather right and you will be fine. It is not a route for a quick sprint regardless of the weather.

The Bight of Abaco

Sandy Point

Sandy Point is well-named. It is a low-lying sandy hook running about two miles north from Rocky Point, the extreme southwestern point of Great Abaco Island. It is a shoal area, bordered on the west by the dark blue Northwest Providence Channel, but distanced from it by the sea green and brown of its shoals. To the north and east there are mangrove flats. To the west, also on the edge of the Northwest Providence Channel, lies Gorda Cay (now renamed Castaway Island) the playground of the Disney Cruise Line.

Sandy Point has a BTC office (the tower, as ever, is a landmark), a clinic, basic stores, bars, restaurants and a government dock, and is served by a twice-weekly fast ferry from Nassau and an airstrip. It would seem at first sight that there is nothing there for the cruising visitor, but this is not true. The Texaco Starport station has a dock with slips that serves as a small, basic marina. There are anchorages off the settlement, and after several tries, one can find good holding. Sandy Point creek offers storm shelter to shoal draft vessels. It remains one very remote place, situated 50 miles from Marsh Harbour with very little in between, but the connecting road is good.

Castaway Island

The Disney ships in Nassau run down the Northwest Providence Channel to offer the castaway experience of a day on Gorda Cay to ships passengers. Sandy Point, which had at one time hoped that some benefit from this golden tide might come their way, has not seen that dividend materialize. The Texaco Starport, with its one pump, has been called on to refuel the Disney playcraft, but that is all.

Hole-in-the-Wall, from the southeast. (Not to be used for navigation.) Waterway Guide Photography.

The Bight of Abaco - Little Abaco Island, Great Abaco Island, Gorda Gay, Moores Island

Although most cruisers think of the Bight of Abaco as forbidden territory for vessels with a 4-foot plus draft, cruisers who draw as much as 2.1 meters/7 feet have plied these waters. Our cruising editors never run out of navigable waters with their 1.5 meter/5-foot draft here. You do want to have a favorable, long-term weather forecast before venturing into the Bight (thunderstorms can be swift and vicious). If you draw more than 5 feet, you have to time your trip with the highest, high tides possible. Plan your visit with a new or full moon on the calendar. It is imperative to enter the Spence Rock passage (from the north) on a rising tide. You can "guesstimate" that tides are about three hours later than Nassau tables, but you definitely need to use personal observation and a tide diary. A useful rule of thumb when observing tides is to expect six hours, twelve and a half minutes between high and low tide. With a good antenna, you will get NOAA weather reports from the United States on your VHF radio; and in some spots, you will hear the Marsh Harbour Cruiser's Net in the morning.

You may choose to explore the Bight of Abaco either coming from the north from Great Sale, or the south from Sandy Point, after rounding the tip of Abaco at Hole in the Wall. Since the southern approach is more direct, we will discuss coming from the north. Getting to the Bight from Great Sale is quite straightforward. You will find the route marked in your Explorer Chartbook™ or on your plotter with magenta navigation lines. Depart the Great Sale, Northwest Harbour anchorage on a southwesterly course to avoid the sand bars off its far southern tip. In a little less than seven nautical miles, turn east and slightly south towards Little Cave Cay. Be careful to avoid the shallow bars and mud banks that lie southwest of West End Cay. Little Cave Cay is an attractive spot to anchor, with good holding and good protection from all but the south. There is great gunkholing at Little and Big Cave Cays and the surrounding smaller cays. The underwater displays of sea fans east of Big Cave Cay are spectacular. There are many places to explore here while you wait for a rising high tide and your subsequent careful creep past Spence Rock. You might also want to run the passage in your dinghy, taking some soundings and plotting some waypoints before you take the "big boat." The passage goes down to about 1.2 meters/4 feet at low tide at the shallowest spot.

The water in the passage to Spence Rock is not difficult to read in good light. The deeper water is obvious—the shallows are quite white and the rocky spots are apparent. There are underwater rocks extending south from Spence Rock. Therefore, maintain your southerly course into the deeper water for a good distance before heading east towards the next anchorages that trickle down the coastlines of Little and Great Abaco. Don't plan to make big hops in the Bight. These are lazy day anchorages with little distance between them. Plan on lots of time to relax on the deck and float in the pristine water. Also, expect surprises – like some of the best fishing and lobstering to be found in the islands.

If you plan to stay awhile, head east towards the Little Abaco coastline. Give a wide berth to Breast Cay and the myriad rocks and bars, staying off at least a half mile. Boats that draw 1.5 meters/5 feet or less can carefully approach Mangrove Cay to anchor in front of a beautiful stretch of sugar sand beach. Head north around the western side of Mangrove Cay and then east, into the protected water between Little Abaco and the reef that runs east from Mangrove.

There is plenty of water (at least 3 meters/10 feet) from Mangrove Cay to Black Point and into Cooling Temper Bay. The Little Abaco shoreline is high enough here to provide protection from north winds, and you can work your way towards shore, in between Little Abaco and Randalls Cay, to anchor in Cooling Temper Bay in about 1.8 meters/6 feet of water. Alternatively, you can proceed farther south along Randalls Cay and work your way into the protected water east of Jones Rocks and north of Rocky Harbour Cay.

A bit farther south, the water gets quite deep for the Bight (over 4.5 meters/15 feet) on the approach to Basin Harbour Cay. You can't miss Basin Harbour Cay. It gives the White Cliffs of Dover a run for their money. You can anchor at Basin Harbour Cay, but the nooks and crannies shallow quickly and the bottom is marl with poor holding. It is a great day anchorage, though, and offers excellent fishing and snorkeling opportunities.

Meandering south, you will traverse 3 meters/10 to 12 feet of water to Normans Castle. Normans Castle has an interesting history. In the 1920s and '30s, it was a thriving lumber camp complete with a mill. Horses and mules were used to move timber from all over the island to the mill. It was a thriving business; and as such, it was one of the first settlements on Great Abaco to get a telegraph. By the 1940s, the lumber operations had depleted the forests and killed their own business. By 1941, the last remaining residents of Normans Castle were resettled at Murphy Town, where they were given five acres and a 200-square-foot house. The government leased the land for agriculture. It was clear-cut and planted with citrus trees. The citrus groves struggled there up until 2005, when citrus canker finally took its toll. If you explore Normans Castle, look for wild horses, feral pigs and maybe an orange still managing to hang from an old tree. For anchoring, avoid the water south of the second point of land. There are dangerous, just-under-the-water obstructions there. You will find 1.8 meters/6 to 8 feet of water in front of the low bluffs in between the two points of land that are obvious on the chart.

Starfish. Waterway Guide Photography

True shoal draft boats can wiggle their way from Normans Castle to Big Joe Downer, but it is safer to take a course west before heading south to those cays. The shallow waters off the Joe Downer Cays are truly shallow—dry at low water. There are many unspoiled beaches and sandy stretches to trek. In settled weather, you can drop your hook anywhere along the western shores of the cays. The best protection, deepest water and chance of good holding can be found just north of Amos Bight or tucked up on the eastern side of Ballast Shoal. Our cruising editors particularly love to anchor in between shallow sand bars like Ballast Shoal, but make note of the tide before you drop the hook or find yourself high, dry and at a tilt at low tide. This is a good jump off point for a visit to Sandy Point or a trip over to Hard Bargain on Moores Island. Wind and weather conditions may dictate your destination.

You can make the short hop to an anchorage off the northern tip of Woolendean Cay. There is a picture perfect beach along the western shore, but be mindful of shifting sandbars as you travel and anchor in these waters. From Woolendean, you can travel in 3.5 meters/12 feet of water or more to Mastic Point. There are places to anchor in the Marls closer to shore with good protection from the north and east. However, these are uncharted waters, and anchors will not find a place to dig in here. From Mastic Point, you must cope with the Sarah Wood Bar fraught with ever shifting sand ridges, bars and banks. The water is easy to read, but requires constant vigilance. Fish muds occur here, so beware.

Once you have navigated the Sarah Wood, it is a straight shot to Sandy Point in not less than 1.8 meters/6 feet of water. Depending on your draft, wiggle in as close as you can to anchor off the northern tip and western shore of Sandy Point settlement. You can't miss the swaying coconut palms in this idyllic spot. Be aware that the fast ferry passenger ramp off the government dock affects sand deposits off Sandy Point. You may find that you need to anchor farther west off the settlement than noted on your charts or plotter. Holding is good in the sand, but avoid the grassy areas. Fuel and water are available at the Texaco dock, albeit probably by jerry can. In town, you will find groceries, a bakery, post office, a clinic, telephone, propane, plenty of restaurants and trash bins. Be sure to have your picture taken at the settlement's sign that welcomes you to a "Quaint Place of Friendly People at Land's End."

From Sandy Point, you can head out across the Northwest Providence Channel to the Berry Islands, and anchor in the popular, safe harbor off Goat Cay. Better yet, stay in the Bight and hop to Gorda Cay (called Castaway Cay by the Disney Cruise Line) and then to Moores Island for a visit to Hard Bargain. It is a straight shot from Hard Bargain to the Channel Rock passage into the Northwest Providence Channel. If you are headed to Great Harbour in the Berries, this is a better hopping off point than Sandy Point.

Gorda Cay used to be the vegetable garden for Sandy Point. You might meet some residents of Sandy Point who were born in Pumpkin Harbour and raised on Gorda Cay. Because of a feral pig problem on Abaco, the crafty folks from Sandy Point leased land from the government to farm on Gorda Cay. Gorda, which means "fat," has a beer-belly profile that consists of deep, rich, rock-free soil. Sandy Pointers would row or sail their handcrafted boats seven miles to Gorda Cay, where the women would harvest the gardens, and gather the wild coco plums and sea grapes. The men folk would catch spiny lobsters in the mangroves and land crabs at night by spotlight. The two islands were almost as one, joined by sand bars and shallow water.

However, Gorda Cay's isolation attracted the drug runners of the '70s and '80s. A multi-millionaire from Delray Beach, FL bought the island, established a runway and posted an ex-con with a rifle and several Dobermans to establish his domain and keep any Sandy Pointers off the cay. A few Sandy Pointers, who tried to maintain their rights to Gorda Cay, were rumored to have been taken out to sea and pushed off the boat. From the first marijuana bust in 1977, valued at $30 million, to the last in 1983, that yielded $100 million in cocaine, Sandy Pointers had to tolerate more than their fair share of small aircraft landing and taking off from Gorda Cay and jet-fast, dark-gray speed boats loitering in Pumpkin Harbour.

Today, much of the habitable land and manmade beaches on the cay are owned by Disney for their cruise ship visitors use. Disney does not give Sandy Pointers deferential treatment. The locals are not permitted to ply the mangroves, trap lobsters or catch crabs as they traditionally did for hundreds of years. The Disney guards have not yet interfered with cruisers anchoring off the lovely beach on the north side. The waters off the northern shore are prone to shallow, shifting sand bars, so proceed with visual piloting and drop the hook in 2.1 meters/6 to 8 feet of water. The anchorage is fine in fair weather. Do not try to anchor anywhere near the cruise ship's dock or the Disney facilities. If there is no cruise ship at the dock, a dinghy trip to see the re-created island village is tolerated by the caretakers, but don't breech the orange buoy line. From Gorda Cay, it is an easy trip to the Berry Islands. However, you will miss Mores Island and the interesting settlement of Hard Bargain.

If you opted to go to Moores Island from Woolendean, it is a peril free, 17 nautical mile trip to anchorages off the north coast or the northern most beach on the east coast of Moores. If you have been enjoying a visit to Sandy Point, you will have to back track to the bars of Sarah Wood, navigate uncharted waters to Moores, or exit your anchorage southward into the Northwest Providence Channel, head north and use the Channel Rock passage to Hard Bargain. The anchorage off Hard Bargain is directly off the settlement in front of the enormous pile of conch shells. If the men aren't out fishing, there will be fishing boats in the anchorage. For a perfect picture of a Bahamian fishing boat, look for the *Bushmaster*. It is owned by a retired Hard Bargain fisherman named Thomas and is clearly his pride and joy.

The residents of Hard Bargain are particularly nice to visit. They don't get too many cruisers here, so they are thrilled to have you stop by. The unofficial "mayor" of the town is Mrs. Walker. She will give you a "hallo" and invite you to share the shade on her porch. The children are especially engaging—it is

Secluded Beach. WATERWAY GUIDE PHOTOGRAPHY

a great place to have a load of crayons and coloring books to pass around. Our cruising editors once brought beach paddle-ball sets to the kids, and they could hear everyone laughing way into the night out at anchor. If you want to be regarded as royalty, bring a new basketball or soccer ball for the older kids. These children are rich in love and inventiveness, but a "real" toy is truly appreciated.

You will probably notice that Hard Bargain is devoid of young men. They are gone for months and months at a time. Hard Bargain's entire existence is tied to their success lobstering, crabbing, conching and fishing. Every old man you meet will be retired from those endeavors of the sea. Each has wonderful tales that you will enjoy about building his boat and plying the waters. If you want to learn how to fish with a traditional hand line, go stand along the shoreline with the kids. They are the true pros, and they will have a jolly laugh at your clumsy efforts.

There are roads and paths that you can hike around the island. The most traveled road runs to The Bahamas Electric generator plant. There are some nearby caves to for you to explore. Nigel, the generator plant manager and all round great guy, has been clearing land to build a restaurant and bar at the caves' entrance. Do make sure to patronize his place if his efforts have materialized. Reverse osmosis water is available free in the settlement, but a donation is appreciated.

From Moores Island, you can exit via Channel Rock passage into the Northwest Providence Channel and point your bow to your next destination and island adventures.

Pilotage. Talking Captain to Captain

Man-O-War Cay Approaches and Anchorages

The northern entrance to Man-O-War harbor is for small or shoal-draft boats only. The main entrance lies at the southern tip of Dickies Cay. Enter in between this point of land and the headland of Man-O-War cove to the south. As we talk of two cays, Man-O-War Cay and Dickies Cay, you may need reassurance. It is difficult to identify two separate cays from any distance out, as Dickies Cay lies so close to Man-O-War that it might be a part of it. To starboard, you will have no problems picking up Garden Cay and Sandy Cay.

The Man-O-War entrance is narrow, marked by a prominent light on Dickies Cay. You will have 1.5-meter/5-foot depths at mean low water there. Expect tidal flow. As soon as you clear the entrance, you can turn to starboard to go on into the southern Man-O-War cove, named Eastern Harbour, and anchor there, or turn to port to go into the main harbor that lies between Dickies Cay and Man-O-War Cay. There, you may anchor, pick up a mooring, or go to Man-O-War Marina.

Approach to Marsh Harbour

There are no problems in entering Marsh Harbour. Outer Point Cay has shoals extending out in a hook to the northeast, so stay sensibly clear of it—about 200 yards or so. It has a light, which may or may not work. If nothing else, the light stake helps your identification. You also want to give Inner Point a wide berth, also with a light and stake on its outer most islet. The large red and green buoys that mark the dredged channel southward to the commercial Port of Marsh Harbour are obvious. Follow the channel until you have enough water to proceed southeast. The Inner Point islets and northern shoreline that forms Marsh Harbour will be to port. The anchorage is to starboard. There will be so many boats at anchor there you can not miss the anchorage. The marinas and fuel docks are well-marked. Going from west to east on the southern shoreline, the marinas are in order: Port of Call, Harbour View, Mangoes and Conch Inn. Marsh Harbour Marina is on the northern shore about mid-way.

North Marsh Harbour to South Marsh Harbour

Use waypoints NMRSH-NPTST-MARMD-SMRSH as your stepping stones to get around, but as you do this dogleg around the Marsh Harbour peninsula, you can cut corners. Use your eyes and your judgment.

Marsh Harbour. Approach to Boat Harbour Marina

Boat Harbour Marina is on the southwest side of the Marsh Harbour peninsula. It is most easily reached from the cay side of the Sea of Abaco. The most direct approach is from Hope Town. The entrance to the marina is east of the obvious Abaco Beach Resort buildings.

Man-O-War Cay to Hope Town

To resume your course for Hope Town, head southeast leaving Sandy Cay and Point Set Rock to starboard (the EPTST waypoint serves here). Note the shoal area extending for a mile west from Johnnies Cay. Enter Hope Town harbor (HPTAP), a run of 10 nautical miles from Great Guana Cay.

The Approach to Hope Town Harbour

The approach to Hope Town isn't difficult, but you must negotiate with a 90-degree turn to starboard to enter the protected harbor. This channel carries some 1.5-meter/5-foot depths at mean low water and is marked.

When you are just off the northernmost Parrot Cay, head slightly north of the famous lighthouse marking Hope Town, aiming to clear the headland on which the lighthouse is built, by at least 100 yards. The entrance channel to Hope Town harbor isn't immediately apparent.

There is a conspicuous house on Eagle Rock. Use the house as an approach marker. It will be left to port and the lighthouse headland will be to starboard. The entry channel red and green buoys will appear as you get closer, as will two range marks.

As you line up for the channel, you will see a concrete road that ends abruptly at the water's edge. The alignment of the road itself is as good a leading mark as any, but to make it easier, there are two red triangle range marks. Get the two marks in line and you are right in the channel.

You will see the turn open up to starboard and then you are in Hope Town harbor.

Hope Town to White Sound

Stand off 0.5 nautical miles from the Elbow Cay shoreline after passing the last of the Parrot Cays. Shoal water extends offshore

Sandy Point Creek entrance.

Lightborne Marina

Peter Johnston sculpture, Little Harbour.

at the entrance to White Sound, which has 0.3-meter/1-foot depths at mean low water. Don't cut inside the northern outer channel buoy, as you will hit that shoal, as others have done. The White Sound entrance channel is well-marked and is maintained at 5 feet mean low water. There are red disk range markers on the eastern shore to assist you. Proceed eastward for the Abaco Inn.

Turn due south into the marked channel that leads to the Sea Spray Marina. Their dock, if you want to plot it, is N 26° 30.560'/W 076° 58.550'. Both White Sound channels have 1.5-meter/5-foot depths at mean low water.

White Sound to Pelican Cays

The route is from White Sound to Pelican Cays is fairly straightforward with a few "detours" around clearly charted sandy shoals and bars.

From White Sound (WHSND), hold 187/070 degrees true for 0.6 nautical miles to reach Lubbers Quarters North (LQNTH). This heading places Bakers Rock on your bow.

At LQNTH, turn onto a course of 222/042 degrees true for 0.5 nautical miles to Lubbers Quarters midpoint (LQMID).

From LQMID, take a course of 195/015 degrees true for 0.8 nautical miles to reach Lubbers Quarters South (LQSTH).

At LQSTH, alter course to 201/021 degrees true. Hold this course for 3.3 nautical miles until you reach Tilloo Bank West (WTILO).

At WTILO, turn on a course of 126/306 degrees true for 0.9 nautical miles, which places you at Tilloo Bank South (STILO).

At STILO, turn to head 090/270 degrees true for 0.7 nautical miles, which places you off the north end of Pelican Cay (NPELI). The Pelican Cay park area is right ahead as you turn south.

South Marsh Harbour to Pelican Cays

From SMRSH, head on a course of 180/000 degrees true for 1.6 nautical miles to reach the Long Cay waypoint (LNGCO). Continue south to Witch Point (WITCH) on a course of 144/324 degrees true for 1.3 nautical miles. Then turn for WTILO on a course of 172/352 degrees true for 3.7 nautical miles. At WTILO, you have joined the eastern route south.

North Pelican to North Bar Channel

Once you have reached Pelican Cay, it is plain sailing. You hardly need waypoints and courses to follow. From NPELI, a course of 172/352 degrees true held for 1.8 nautical miles will place you right by North Bar Channel West (NBARW). On this leg, you will see that Channel Cay, which at first sight looks uninhabited, has a house on it. Gaulding Cay becomes visible, as does Cornish Cay. All of this is on your starboard side, as is Sandy Cay with its small boat moorings for snorkelers. To port, you have the north–south run of the Pelican Cays and reefs. The whole area you are transiting is the Pelican Cays Land and Sea Park. Why not stop and go snorkeling?

North Bar Channel

North Bar Channel, just north of Lynyard Cay, has range marks set on Sandy Cay and Cornish Cay, with comfortable 4.8-meter/16-foot depths. The range marks are not easy to see with the naked eye, but the lay of the cays themselves, and the obviousness of North Bar Channel, makes navigation relatively easy. To the north is Channel Rock, and there are the rocks off the north tip of Lynyard Cay. A heading of 103/283 degrees true to North Bar Channel East (NBARE) will keep you clear of hazards through the one nautical mile you have to run. This pass is used by the mailboats, and is a better bet than the Little Harbour Bar pass in less than ideal conditions.

From North Bar Channel to Little Harbour Bar North

If you are bound for Little Harbour from North Bar Channel, parallel the northern half of Lynyard Cay. Favor the Great Abaco side, as the water is deeper there. Around the mid-Lynyard waypoint (LYNMD), switch to the Lynyard Cay side for the southern half where the water depths are reversed. The strange, axe-like headland protruding out from Great Abaco Island was the site of Wilson City, a one time mega-forestry concern that is now derelict.

The anchorages (LYNAN) are not perfectly shielded, but do offer relief from the ocean swell coming in through the Little Harbour pass. At the south end of the cay, Bridges Cay will be to starboard and Little Harbour Bar opens up to port. The entry channel into Little Harbour will be off your starboard bow.

Little Harbour Approach and Anchorage

Tom Curry Point on the west and a beautiful white beach on the east, beckon you into Little Harbour. Pause and check the state of the tide. The entry channel is shallow, but well-marked. If you need more than 1-meter/3.6-foot depths, a rising half-tide state is critical. Upon entering, you will see a rough stone breakwater to port, but your route remains straight in until you curve to port to find a mooring buoy.

There are 25 mooring buoys there, all owned by Pete's Pub and all available on a first-come, first-served basis. There are many private docks, and there may even be available dock space. There is, however, little to no free space for anchoring. The fee for the mooring will be collected sometime during your visit. Inside the harbor, there is a hearty 3.6 meters/12 feet of water at high tide and a good 3 meters/10 feet at low. The distance run from White Sound? Just over 12 nautical miles.

Little Harbour Channel

From LHRBN, a heading of 154/334 degrees true for 1.2 nautical miles to LHRBE takes you through the pass. Little Harbour Channel presents no particular problems. It has 4.2-meter/14-foot depths at mean low water. There is a spot with 3.3-meter/11-foot depths, so take note. To the north, a reef runs south from Goole Cay for 0.75 nautical miles toward the cut. To the south, a reef runs north from Little Harbour Point for 0.25 nautical miles. Both reefs are visible in any kind of weather, as waves will break over them. In between these reefs is the passage itself.

Little Harbour to Cherokee Sound

If you want to visit Cherokee, it is an easy run from Little Harbour, but not one that you should undertake if the ocean is kicking up. In short, if you don't fancy going out over Little Harbour Bar, Cherokee would be no fun trip. The first stages are simple. From LHRBN, head on a course of 154/334 degrees true for 1.2 nautical miles to LHRBE, which takes you through the pass. At LHRBE, turn for Ocean Point (OCNPT) on a course of 186/006 degrees true with 2.3 nautical miles to run. On this leg, keep at least 0.75 nautical miles offshore to maintain a safe distance from the coastal reef known as the Boilers, which lies off the Great Abaco coast between Little Harbour and Ocean Point.

From OCNPT, run on a course of 249/069 degrees true for 3.7 nautical miles to the Cherokee Point waypoint (CHERP). Now it is pure visual piloting. Once you are around Cherokee Point, steer initially for the 250-foot BTC tower. You can't miss it. You will see waves breaking on the reef and shallows to port. To starboard, a beach will open up behind Cherokee Point with a small but precipitous cliff behind it. The water just off that beach is an anchorage, where you will find a clean sand bottom with good holding in 2.4–3 meters/8–10 feet of water. The anchorage is open to the south and southwest and will get surge around the point if swells are running. This said, if the weather is right, it is one of the most pleasant places to visit. The beach is great, and the water is fabulous. You may be tempted by the sight of the old dock. You can get there by dinghy, but if you want to get your own boat as close in to the settlement as possible, call Cherokee Auto and Boat Haven on VHF Channel 16. They are willing to get someone to guide you if the tide is right, and they have gasoline and diesel, as well as auto and boat spares.

Cherokee to Hole-in-the-Wall

From Ocean Point, you have 28.5 nautical miles to go on a course of 197/017 degrees true down the last stretch of the eastern coast of Great Abaco to reach Hole-in-the-Wall, the southernmost headland. There is no shelter on this run and no place where you would wish to stop. The Hole-in-the-Wall waypoint (HOLEW) places you just outside of the 100-fathom line, 2.6 nautical miles off Hole-in-the-Wall and ready to continue across the Northwest Providence Channel to the Berry Islands, or to North Eleuthera.

Hole-in-the-Wall

Quite apart from the lighthouse on its spine of rock with the famous "hole" in the wall, this is one dramatic place. From a 1,000-fathom depth, the ocean bed shelves to 100 fathoms within a hand span and, closer in, around Hole-in-the-Wall, to 3 fathoms. Here, the kind of conditions that make us all start closing and locking ports and hatches - wind above 15 knots, waves of 4 feet plus and distant storm swell coming in from the open Atlantic Ocean - will produce nightmare seas in no time. This is one of the critical seas areas. Like the Gulf Stream, it requires weather analysis before setting out, particularly because there is nowhere to run for shelter once you are out there.

Hole-in-the-Wall to Sandy Point

From HOLEW, turn due west for four miles to clear Southwest Point, then turn for the Rock Point waypoint (RCKPT) on an approximate course of 312/132 degrees true with 15 nautical miles to run. Cross Harbour, which lies to starboard on this transit, is not a harbor. Be aware that reefs run out to the southwest from Rock Point, which is rightly named.

Sandy Point Approaches and Anchorage

Sandy Point settlement is not hard to pick out. Far off to port on the horizon, you may just see the tufts of the palms on Gorda Cay, and the puffs of smoke from the stacks on a Disney Line cruise ship. More immediately to starboard is the tell-tale BTC tower, and at Sandy Cay settlement, the long pier.

The dock with the Texaco sign on the beach behind it is the Lightbourne Marina and the Texaco Starport. You can get fuel there, both gas and diesel, and get in to the outer head dock with 1.5-meter/5-foot depths at mean low water (coming in south of the white buoy that marks a wreck). If the fast ferry hasn't swept sand under their docks, you can enjoy the same depths at their slips. Call ahead or dinghy in to investigate. Keep in mind, it is no safe haven in bad weather. The government dock is the terminal for the fast ferry. At the outer end, it will carry 1.5-meter/5-foot depths at mean low water. It, too, is no safe haven. The mailboat approaches the dock on a course of 047/227 degrees true and enters at half tide if lightly laden.

If you are seeking shelter, you have to work your way around Sandy Point into the creek on the eastern side. You will find the local fishing boats based there on three short docks, one of which is the main fishing boat dock. There is room to anchor farther up the creek. On the initial approach, take an apparent shoal water course over "brown" water to gain the deeper entry channel to the creek. If the seas are rough, expect to have breaking seas to port at one point. Once, there were depths of 1.5 meters/5 feet at mean low water all the way around Sandy Point, but Walter Lightbourne, the owner of the Texaco station, warns that the sand moves in each storm. It is rated as a high-water-only approach and at that, you should have a pilot assist you to wind your way in there. Call Lightbourne Marina on VHF Channel 16 and they will advise you.

Inside the creek, there are generally 1.8-meter/6-foot depths mid-stream, with some deeper patches. Where the creek splits into two branches, either may be taken. In bad weather, the mangroves can offer safety in all but severe high winds.

Moving On to the Central Cruising Grounds

Whether you have exited the Sea of Abaco through the North Bar Channel or through the Little Harbour Channel, Ocean Point (OCNPT) is the departure waypoint. A straight run to Little Egg Island Northwest (EGGNW), the North Eleuthera Approach waypoint, coming from the north, is 45.6 nautical miles on 176/356 degrees true.

If you are bound for the Berry Islands, you must run down to Hole-in-the-Wall first (28.5 nautical miles on 197/017 degrees true), then turn for Great Stirrup Cay (GSTRP), the Northern Berry Eastern Approach waypoint, which is 30.2 nautical miles on a course of 270/090 degrees true. All told, that makes it 58.7 nautical miles to run from Ocean Point.

Waterway Guide is always open to your observations from the helm. E-mail your comments on any navigation information in the guide to: editor@waterwayguide.com.

The Southern Abacos Waypoints

Fish Cays South	FISHS	26°37.23N / 77°09.27W
Man-O-War Channel North	MWCHN	26°37.84N / 77°01.27W
Man-O-War Channel South	MWCHS	26°36.81N / 77°01.92W
Man-O-War Approach	MOWAP	26°35.32N / 77°00.26W
Point Set Rock North	NPTST	26°34.31N / 77°00.64W
Point Set Rock East	EPTST	26°33.81N / 76°59.77W
Marsh Harbour Entrance	NMRSH	26°33.46N / 77°04.20W
Hope Town Approach	HPTAP	26°33.00N / 76°58.50W
Marsh Triangle Mid-Point	MARMD	26°32.97N / 76°59.52W
Marsh Harbour South	SMRSH	26°32.37N / 77°02.53W
Long Cay	LNGCO	26°30.72N / 77°02.53W
White Sound	WHSND	26°31.19N / 76°58.92W
Lubbers Quarters North	LQNTH	26°30.35N / 76°59.10W
Lubbers Quarters Mid-Point	LQMID	26°29.95N / 76°59.48W
Witch Point	WITCH	26°29.66N / 77°01.66W
Lubbers Quarters South	LQSTH	26°29.07N / 76°59.68W
Tilloo Bank West	WTILO	26°25.29N / 77°01.48W
North Pelican Cay	NPELI	26°25.31N / 76°59.33W
North Bar Channel West	NBARW	26°23.61N / 76°58.97W
North Bar Channel East	NBARE (A4)	26°23.30N / 76°58.00W
Wilson City	WCITY	26°22.87N / 76°59.63W
Lynyard Offshore	LYNOF	26°22.26N / 76°57.46W
Lynyard Anchorages	LYNAN	26°21.33N / 76°59.17W
Little Harbour Bar North	LHRBN	26°20.43N / 76°59.67W
Little Harbour Bar East	LHRBE	26°19.34N / 76°59.08W
Ocean Point	OCNPT	26°17.03N / 76°59.34W
Cherokee Point	CHERP	26°15.66N / 77°03.25W
Hole-in-the-Wall	HOLEW	25°49.71N / 77°08.66W
Rock Point	RCKPT (A5)	25°59.50N / 77°26.00W

Our position format is latitude and longitude in degrees and minutes (hddd°mm.mm). Waypoints in RED are NOT for autopilot navigation. Codes in parenthesis are Wavey Line waypoints marked on the charts. If you have programmed waypoints we listed in a previous edition of this guide, check carefully to ensure the coordinates you have recorded match the list. If a waypoint is no longer on our list we may have changed its code or deleted it.

GOIN' ASHORE:

MAN-O-WAR CAY

bank • fuel • groceries • marina • marine services • post office • restaurant • telephone • water

This classic Abaco cay, justifiably proud of its 200-year boat-building and sailmaking traditions, welcomes visitors to its tidy, pristine, alcohol free little piece of historic paradise. Man-O-War has much to offer cruising boats, with its good, sheltered Eastern Harbour moorings and anchorage, and an excellent marina where boats may be safely left for extended periods. Most mooring balls in Man-O-War harbor have a name and VHF call sign on them. You can pick up any that are not marked Private or Reserved. The charge is usually $15 per night. The frequent ferry service to and from Marsh Harbor makes it readily accessible to the Marsh Harbour or Treasure Cay airports. Plan on most places to close promptly at 5 p.m. and remain closed on Sundays. It is not the place for bright lights and night clubs. The island's permanent population is small, but Snowbird cottage owners and visiting boats increase the activity in winter. A special delight is the children who march around in their uniforms to and from their schools.

MARINA

MAN-O-WAR MARINA
Tel: 242-365-6008 • Fax: 242-365-6151 • VHF 16 •
mowmarina@hotmail.com

Man-O-War Marina is a Stay and See Abaco participating marina. **Slips** 26. **Max LOA** 70 ft. **MLW at Dock** 8 ft. (5 ft. in the harbor entrance). **Dockage** $1.75 per ft. per day for transients, $0.90 monthly. Dinghy storage, $20 monthly. **Moorings** (5) $17 per night **Fuel** Diesel, gasoline, oils; open 7 a.m. to 5 p.m. daily, 8 a.m. to 12 noon Sunday. **Facilities & Services** Power $0.45 per kWh. Water $0.20 per gallon. Showers free to marina guests, otherwise $5. Key necessary in the evenings. Laundry open 24 hrs; $3.50 for marina guests, $5 for visitors; tokens from the office. Pool for marina guests. Telephones outside the Dive Shop. Free 40-channel cable TV and telephone hookup at each slip. Trash disposal free to marina guests, otherwise $1 per bag. Gas grill is available. The marina will provision your boat if you give them a list ahead of time. Ice (block or cubes); propane refills take 48 hours. Landscaped pool, good beaches across the island on the Atlantic. Cart and kayak rentals. Mail can be held and sent out. FedEx and UPS via Marsh Harbour. Fax and copy machine; free to receive a fax, appropriate charge per page to send. $0.50 per page for copies. Internet connection $5 per 15 minutes in the marina office. Book exchange, video rental. Complimentary morning coffee. Boat services include bright work, varnishing, painting and wash down. Interior boat cleaning services. Boat checks $25 per check, every two weeks recommended. Dive shop. **Restaurant** Dock n' Dine, closed Sundays. **Credit Cards** Visa and MasterCard, 5% surcharge on AMEX. **Owners/Managers** Tommy and Chris Albury.

PORT DIRECTORY

Bakery *Lola's Bakery*. Lola will track you down on her golf cart offering fresh sweet rolls and bread. If you are lucky enough to visit her home she has jams, jellies and conch fritter mix for sale.

Banks *First Caribbean Bank* 10 a.m. to 2 p.m. Wednesdays. On Bay Street. No ATM.

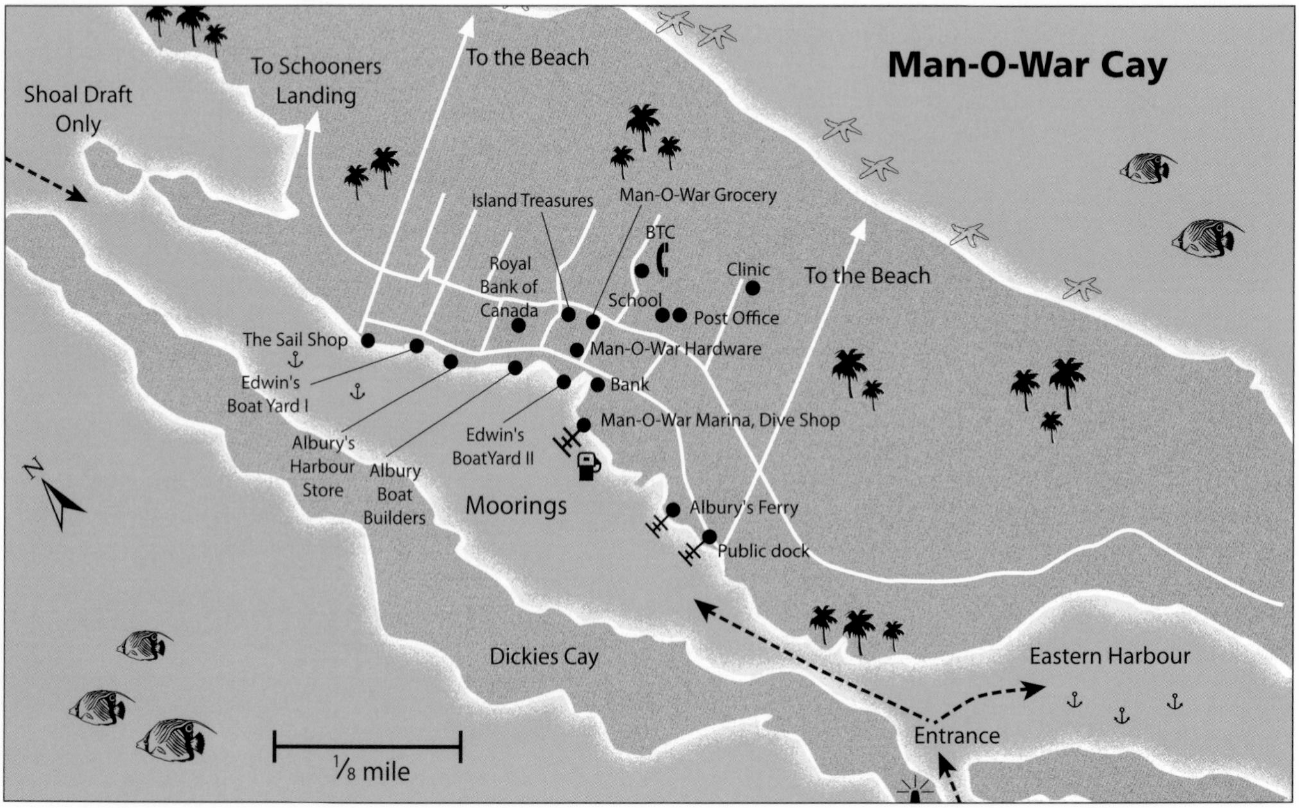

EMERGENCIES

Marine • VHF 16
Medical *Clinic* • 242-365-6081 • The doctor from Marsh Harbour visits on Thursdays. Call *Marsh Harbour Government Clinic* (242-367-2510) or one of the Marsh Harbour doctors or *Trauma One* on VHF 80 in case of serious emergency.

Ferries *Albury's Ferry Service* • 242-365-6010 • Fax: 242-365-6487 • VHF 16 • Leaves for Marsh Harbour at 8 and 11:30 a.m., 1:30 and 3:15 p.m. daily; 8 a.m. and 1:30 p.m. Sundays; $15 same-day round trip for the 20-minute trip.
Hardware *Man-O-War Hardware* • 242-365-6011 • VHF 69 • Interisland delivery service for lumber, marine hardware and paints.
Lodging *Schooners Landing Ocean Club* • 242-365-6072 or 242-367-4469 • Six beachfront units.
Marine Services *Albury Brothers Boats* • 242-365-6086 • Open weekdays. See first hand how these one of a kind deep-V fiberglass boats are constructed. Now also being built in U.S. 561-863-7006.
Edwin's Boat Yard • 242-365-6006 • 242-365-6007 • Hauling up to 65 ft. or 50 tons. Painting, welding, carpentry, mechanical work. Extensive marine parts and supplies.
Jay Manni • 242-365-6171 • Sailmaker.
Provisions *Albury's Harbour Store* • 242-365-6004 • On the waterfront with a good selection neatly displayed; free delivery.
Man-O-War Grocery • 242-365-6016 • VHF 16 • A comprehensive grocery with fresh produce on Queen's Highway; free delivery to dock or house.
Post Office Weekdays 9 a.m. to noon and 2 p.m. to 5 p.m.

RENTALS

Boats *Man O War Marina* • 242-365-6008 • VHF 16
Water Ways • 242-365-6143 • cell: 242-357-6540 • VHF 16 • rentals@waterwaysrentals.com • www.waterwaysrentals.com
Boat rentals, fishing rods, snorkel gear, tackle and bait.
Conch Pearl Rentals. 242-365-6059. VHF 16
Bicycles & Carts *Island Treasures* • 242-365-6072
Ria-Mar • 242-365-6240 • At the Ferry Dock.

Restaurants *Dips Sips & Wishes* • 242-365-6380 • Barnie's coffee, ice cream and take-out food. 9:30 a.m. to 9:30 p.m. Tuesday through Saturday. Closed Sunday and Monday. Free WiFi. $
Dock n' Dine Sandwiches, hamburgers, fried dishes, local fish, chicken and conch. Lunch and dinner. Good homemade pies and cake too. BYOB permitted. $$
Island Treats. 242-365-6501 Take out sandwiches and a variety of ice cream–try the coconut!
Shopping *The Dive Shop at Man-O-War Marina* • 242-365-6013 • Fanny Albury has an attractive selection of beach fashions and accessories, Abaco books and charts, dive gear and boat supplies.
Joe's Studio • 242-365-6082 • Locally carved native woodcrafts, beautiful half models, books, gifts. One of the best gift shops in Abaco. On Bay Street.
Sail Shop • 242-365-6014 • VHF 16 • World-famous canvas bags and accessories made by the Albury family.
Sally's Seaside Boutique • 242-365-6044 • Sally makes enchanting pillows and clothing to order for all ages using Androsia fabrics.
Local artwork and hand-made gifts.
Sammie Boy's Gift Shop - 242-365-6058 - Souvenirs, gifts and shells. 10 a.m. to 4 p.m. Monday through Saturday.
The Shirt Shop • 242-365-6077 • Gifts, household, clothing.
Telephones Outside the *Dive Shop* at the marina.
Trash Leave in the bins beyond the *Sail Shop* if you are not a marina guest.
Travel Agent *A & W Travel Service* • 242-365-6048 • Denise MacDonald.

SPORTS

Diving *The Dive Shop at Man-O-War Marina* • 242-365-6013 • Open 9 a.m. to 5 p.m. daily, closed Sundays. Dive gear rental, tank refills to 3000 psi. Marine repair and maintenance supplies, Abaco books and charts; clothing and beach accessories. Ask for local dive boat operators.
Regattas *Regatta Time in Abaco* • 242-367-2677 • davralph@batelnet.bs • www.rtia.net • Held the first week in July. Races form up at Green Turtle Cay, Great Guana Cay, Hope Town, Man-O-War, and Marsh Harbour. Contact Dave or Kathy Ralph.

THINGS TO DO IN MAN-O-WAR CAY

- Have your boat repairs expertly and efficiently done.
- Stroll through town or swim off North Beach. A "must-see" is the oceanside ball field.
- Visit the Sail Shop and watch how beautifully the Albury family make their canvas bags.
- Visit Andy Albury's woodworking shop and see how half models are crafted.
- Enjoy good home cooking at the *Dock n' Dine*.
- Reprovision with groceries and baked goods.
- Relax and enjoy this quiet and hospitable island, where time seems—almost—to stand still.

HOPE TOWN

bank • fuel • groceries • marinas • marine services • medical • police • post office • propane • restaurant • telephone • water

With its famous red-and-white-striped lighthouse beckoning you into the sheltered harbor on Elbow Cay, Hope Town can justifiably claim to be the Jewel of Abaco. It is the dream come true for every cruising boat. It is picturesque and photogenic, with good facilities, well-stocked stores and excellent restaurants with scenic vistas. Cars and golf carts are not allowed in the village where the cottages are painted the colors of Neapolitan ice cream and run alongside glorious eastern beaches with a safe reef to snorkel within easy reach of swimmers. Fishing and diving in the surrounding waters will make you wish you could stay here forever. As the welcoming sign says, "Slow Down, You're In Hope Town."

MOORINGS AND DINGHY DOCKS

Moorings For boats under 44 ft. *Hope Town Marina* (VHF 16) has 18 numbered, red cylindrical mooring buoys, marked HT Marina. *Abaco Bahamas Charters* (VHF 16) offers 15 numbered mooring buoys, white with blue band. Truman Major (VHF 16 "Lucky Strike") provides green mooring buoys. Moorings cost $15 per night and need daily renewal.
Dinghy Docks *Cap'n Jacks* and *Harbour's Edge* have their own dinghy docks if you are going for meals. *Harbour View Grocery* dock for groceries. *Hope Town Harbour Lodge* for meals or accommodation. Throw out a stern anchor from your dinghy, and tie up to their dock. Use *Hope Town Sailing Club* dock during the day if your dinghy is under 24 ft., but tie away from the ladders. *Lighthouse Marina* for fuel or the liquor store.

EMERGENCIES

Ambulance *Trauma One* • 242-367-2911 • VHF 80 • In Marsh Harbour.

Emergency Email Sent to cruisers@oii.net will be read at 8:15 a.m. on VHF 68 during the Cruisers Net from Marsh Harbour. Have your name or your boat name written in the subject line.

Fire and Rescue • 242-366-0086/0363/0023/0143 • VHF 16, then VHF 22A.

Marine • VHF 16 BASRA

Medical Nurse Sands • 242-366-0108 • On island.

Dr Boyce • 242-367-2295, or 242-357-6569 • At *Abaco Family Medicine* • 242-367-3933 • In Marsh Harbour.

RESTAURANTS & BARS

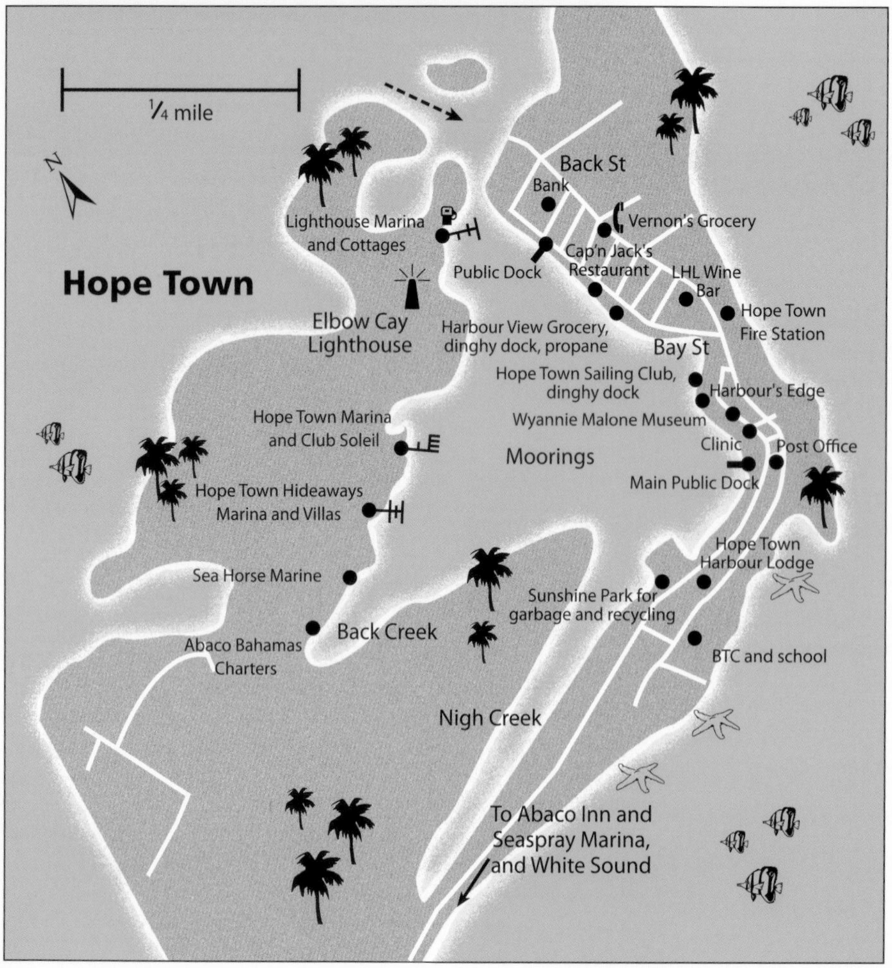

MARINAS IN HOPE TOWN HARBOUR

As they appear to starboard, entering the harbor:

LIGHTHOUSE MARINA

Tel: 242-366-0154 • Fax: 242-366-0171 • VHF 16 • email info@htlighthousemarina.com, www.htlighthousemarina.com

Craig and Linda Knowles welcome you to *Lighthouse Marina*. Nothing is too much trouble for these two to meet the needs of their guests and customers in this cozy marina beneath the famous *Elbow Reef Lighthouse*. The marina has the only fuel dock in town, a well-stocked gift and ships store, coin laundry, accommodations and a boat yard with a 10-ton travel lift. The wine and liquor store boasts a fine collection of select wines, an interesting variety of rum and a good selection of beer. *Lighthouse* is happy to deliver wine and spirits to your boat, with ice. **Slips** 5. **Max LOA** 60 ft. **MLW at Dock** 6 ft. **Dockage** $1.00 per ft. per day. **Fuel** Dock open daily 8 to 5; to 1 p.m. on Sundays. Ice, lubricants, oils. 3% surcharge on credit cards. **Facilities & Services** Power $10 per day for 30A, $12 for 50A. Water $0.25 per gallon. Showers $4, laundry uses tokens. Liquor store, marine supplies. Boat yard services include haul and launch, dry storage, pressure cleaning, fiberglass repair, carpentry and general repairs, bottom painting and bright work. Yamaha sales and service. **Accommodations** *Lighthouse Rentals* • 242-366-0154 • lighthouse@oii.net • Apartment, cottage and two very attractive houses available, well-appointed and fully equipped, from $1,000 per week. **Credit Cards** Visa and MasterCard. **Dockmasters** Paul McDonald and Richard Cunningham.

HOPE TOWN MARINA

Tel: 242-366-0003 or 888-291-5428 • Fax: 242-366-0254 • VHF 16 • info@clubsoleil.com, www.clubsoleil.com

Hope Town Marina is hard to miss with what was formerly the pink and purple *Club Soleil Restaurant* behind it. There is a pool at the hotel that is pleasant for marina and hotel guests. A newly remodeled restaurant and expanded dockage are underway. **Slips** 12 to 14. **Max LOA** 125 ft. **MLW at Dock** 6 ft. **Dockage** $1.00 per ft. per day. Monthly rates available. **Facilities** Power $15 per day for 30A, $20 for 50A. Water $0.25 per gallon. Showers $3.50. Laundry $4. Swimming pool. **Restaurant** Currently closed. **Accommodations** Six rooms ranging from $130-150. **Credit Cards** Visa, MasterCard, AMEX.

HOPE TOWN HIDEAWAYS MARINA

Tel: 242-366-0224 • Fax: 242-366-0434 • VHF 16 and 63 • info@hopetown.com

The Hideaway Villas live up to their name, almost hidden among 11 acres of lush plantings that run down to the pool and the marina. This is a very pretty, small marina and a good place to put up friends or family on shore. Villas from $300 to $400 per night, depending on season.

Slips 12. **Max LOA** 65 ft. **MLW at Dock** 4 to 5 ft. **Dockage** $1.25 per ft. per day. Long-term rates. **Facilities** Power $15 per day for 30A, $20 for 50A. Water $0.25 per gallon. Laundry uses tokens. Harbor front swimming pool. **Credit Cards** Visa, MasterCard, Discover **Accommodations** *Hope Town Hideaway Villas* In the gardens, from $250 per night. *Hope Town Hideaways* has more rental accommodations on Elbow Cay. **Owners** Peggy and Chris Thompson.

MARINA IN WHITE SOUND

SEA SPRAY RESORT & MARINA

Tel: 242-366-0065/0359 • Fax: 242-366-0383 • VHF 16
info@seasprayresort.com, • www.seasprayresort.com

Only a few minutes north of Tahiti Beach, within steps of the surf on Garbanzo Reef, and a mere 3.5 miles from Hope Town (with complimentary transportation to town), this first-class, protected marina lets you enjoy everything that Elbow Cay has to offer, without the crowds of Hope Town harbor. A Stay and See Abaco participating marina offering an excellent restaurant and shore side villa accommodations, as well as close proximity to the private homes of Doros Cove, *Sea Spray* offers excellent winter rates for long-term boats.

Slips 60. **Max LOA** 84 ft. **MLW at Dock** 5.5 ft. **Dockage** Seasonally based. $1.90 per ft. per day off-season, $2.25 in season. 30 days or more is $0.80 off-season, $1.75 in season per foot per day. Monthly rates available. **Fuel** Diesel and gasoline, open 8 a.m. to 5 p.m. daily. **Facilities & Services** Power $0.65 per kWh. Water $0.45 per gallon; showers; wash, dry and fold laundry service, $15 per load. Telephones, charcoal grill near the pool for guest use, ice. Groceries at Sweetings - 242-366-0391, open 7:30 a.m. to 6 p.m., closed Sundays. Beaches and a well-fenced pool, good for children. Deep sea, reef and bonefishing. Surfing off Garbanzo Reef. Snorkeling. Bicycles. Complimentary shuttle to and from Hope Town. Fax and Internet in the gift store, Internet $5 for 15 minutes. Wireless Internet available. Wet storage and maintenance. **Restaurant** *Boat House Restaurant* Breakfast, lunch and dinner daily. Happy hour daily at the Garbanzo Reef Bar. **Accommodations** 1 three-bedroom villa, 2 two-bedroom villas and 3 one-bedroom villas, with full kitchens from $950 per week. **Credit Cards** Visa, MasterCard, AMEX. **Manager** Wally Myers. **Dockmaster** Junior Mernard, one of the friendliest in the Bahamas.

PORT DIRECTORY

Bank *First Caribbean International Bank* • 242-367-0296 • 10 a.m. to 2 p.m. Tuesday.
Boat Charter & Rentals *Abaco Bahamas Charters* 242-366-0151 • 1-800-626-5690 www.abacocharters.com *Cat's Paw Boat Rentals* 242-366-0380 • VHF 16 • located in Hope Town Harbour. *Cruise Abaco* 242-577-0148 • Sailboat charters. *Island Marine Boat Rentals* 242-366-0282 • VHF 16 • Albury Brothers and Boston Whalers. *Maine Cat* Bareboat charter a Maine Cat 30 or 41. www.mecat.com
Churches *Assembly of God, St. James Methodist Church.* Catholic mass Sundays at noon under the cork tree or in the Library.
Clothing, Gifts & Souvenirs *Ebb Tide Gift Shop* • 242-366-0088 • Abaco gold handcrafted jewelry, Androsia clothing and original local art work. *Edith's Straw Shop* Hair braiding and straw work. *El Mercado Gifts* • 242-366-0053. *Iggy Biggy Boutique* • 242-366-0354 Resort fashions and accessories for the home. *Kemp's Gift Shop* • 242-366-0423. *Sun-Dried T's* • 242-366-0616 . Locally printed T-shirts, beach wear and gifts.
Ferries *Albury's Ferry Service* • 242-367-3147/242-365-6010 • VHF 16 • Ferries will pick you up from, or deliver you to, docks in the harbor or from White Sound on request. To Marsh Harbour at 8, 9:45, 11:30 a.m., and 1:30, 3, 4, 5 p.m., Monday to Friday. No 5 p.m. ferry on Sundays or holidays. One way, $10. Same day round trip, $15 .
Fishing Charters *A Salt Weapon* • 242-366-0245. *Lucky Strike* • VHF 16 • Truman Major. • *Sea Gull Deep Sea Fishing.* • 242-366-0266 • VHF 16 • Captain Robert Lowe.
Fishing Tackle *Lighthouse Marina Store* • 242-366-0154
Hotels & Lodging ***Abaco Inn*** • 242-366-0133/0333 • Fax: 242-366-0113 abacoinn@oii.net • www.abacoinn.com • 20 rooms and villas from $140 to $240 per night. Restaurant overlooking the Atlantic beach, swimming pool, complimentary snorkeling gear, bicycles, transfers from Hope Town, rental boat dockage, water sports.
Hope Town Harbour Lodge • 242-366-0095 • Fax: 242-366-0286 • harbourlodge@abacoinet • www.harbourlodge.com • Rooms from $175 to $195 per night; suites from $225, house from $3,000 a week; minimum 3-night stays. Two restaurants and bars, fabulous beach with snorkeling on the reef, and swimming pool.
Hope Town Hideaways • 242-366-0224 • www.hopetown.com • Chris and Peggy Thompson have a selection of 63 rental accommodations, from $300 per night in low season.
Lighthouse Marina and Rentals • 242-366-0154 • lighthousemarina@abacoinet.com • Bungalow, two cottages and one very attractive house available, well-appointed and fully equipped, from $1,200 per week.
Sea Spray Resort. • 242-365-0065 1-,2-,3-bedroom villas with full kitchens from $950 per week.
Turtle Hill Resort • 242-366-0557 • www.TurtleHill.com • 4 villas with swimming pool, private beach access, boat dockage, golf carts, "On Da Beach" bar and grill open from ll:30 a.m. with daily happy hours, closed Mondays. Villas from $1,850 per week.
Laundry *Suds Ahoy Laundromat* • 242-366-0399 • Same day wash, dry, fold service. In by 12 p.m., last pickup at 5 p.m. Closed Sundays.
Liquor *Hope Town Wines and Spirits at Lighthouse Marina* • 242-366-0525 • VHF 16 • Open 8 to 5, Monday to Saturday. Free delivery to boats. *Lighthouse Liquor* • 242-366-0567 • On Back Street. Nice selection of wines and liquors.

RENTALS

Bicycles *The Bike Shop at Harbour's Edge* • 242-366-0292
Boats *Abaco Bahamas Charters* • 800-626-5690 • VHF 16 • www.abacocharters.com • 6 bareboat charters, 15 moorings in Hope Town Harbour, base in Back Creek.
Abaco Multihull Charters • 242-366-0552 • info@mecat.com, www.abacomultihull.com. Sailing charters, rentals and sailing lessons. MainCat 31-ft. and 41-ft. catamaran charters. Visit Web site for pricing or see Captain Ron Engle.
Cat's Paw Boat Rentals • 242-366-0380 • VHF 66 • catspaw@batelnet.bs • Paramounts from $110 daily.
Island Marine Boat Rentals • 242-366-0282 • Fax: 366-0281 • VHF 16 • imarine@oii.net • Boston Whalers, Aquasports, and Albury's on Parrot Cay. Complimentary delivery. Visa and MasterCard.
Sea Horse Boat Rentals • 242-366-0023 • VHF 16 • www.seahorseboatrentals.com • From Marsh Harbour. Boston Whalers, Paramounts, Privateers. Prices start at $630 per week; rates do not include gas.
Golf Carts Carts are not allowed to drive through Hope Town! *Hope Town Cart Rentals* (242-366-0064), *JR's Cart Rentals* (242-366-0361, VHF 16, info@juniorscartrentals.com), *Kevin Albury's Island Cart Rentals* (242-366-0448, VHF 16), *T & N Cart Rentals* (242-366-0069, wand@oii.net). Carts from $50 per day, scarce at peak holiday times.

Marine Hardware *Lighthouse Marina Store* • 242-366-0154
Medical Hope Town Clinic • 242-366-0108 (24 hours) • Nurse Sands is at the clinic (low pink building at the head of the town dock) from 9 to 2 weekdays, to 1:30 p.m. Fridays. Doctor visits every other Friday.
Museum *Wyannie Malone Historical Museum* • VHF 16 "Museum" • Across from Jarrett Park, in two linked buildings; fascinating, well worth a visit. Usually open 10 to 3 weekdays. Donations are gratefully accepted.
Police By the post office.
Post Office Upstairs in the green building at the head of the Government Dock. Open 9 to 12, 1 to 5 weekdays.
Provisions *Albury's Fish Market* • 242-366-0050 • Between *Iggy Biggy* and *Vernon's Grocery*.
Harbour View Grocery • 242-366-0033 • With their own dinghy dock. Closed Sundays and 1 to 2 p.m. daily. A good selection of groceries, fresh produce and bread, water, sodas, dairy, frozen foods, some pharmacy, propane and batteries. Propane tanks go to Marsh Harbour on Tuesdays; same day return.
Salty Sky's Market • 242-366-0245 • Fresh seafood and produce. Closed Sundays and Monday, open 10 a.m. to 4 p.m. daily.
Vernon's Grocery & Upper Crust Bakery • 242-366-0037 • VHF 16 On Back Street. Closed Sundays and 1 to 2 p.m. Impressive choice of groceries, fresh fruit and vegetables, imported meats and cheeses and all the news. Vernon bakes his own fresh bread and pies and officiates at weddings too. The Key Lime pie is legend.
Public Restrooms To the right of the post office.

Restaurants & Bars in Hope Town

Cap'n Jack's • 242-366-0247 • VHF 16 • Breakfast, lunch and dinner overlooking the harbor. Casual atmosphere, great food and live music Fridays. Satellite sports TV. Ice for sale. Closed Sundays. Visa and MasterCard. Tie up at their dock. $$
Harbour's Edge • 242-366-0087 • VHF 16 • Lunch and dinner on the waterfront. Happy hour 5 to 6 p.m., appetizers served all day. Bahamian cuisine. Closed Tuesdays. Ice for sale, pool table and sports TV. Noisy and fun. Tie up at their dock. $$
Hope Town Harbour Lodge • 242-366-0095 • VHF 16 • Breakfast and dinner in their terrace dining room; lunch and happy hour poolside daily from 11 a.m. Fine dining, using fresh local ingredients. Complimentary dinghy dock for guests. Dinner nightly except Monday: reservations appreciated. $$$
LHL Wine Bar is located next to *Lighthouse Liquors* near the Fire station on Back St. Stop in and visit for a cooling cocktail after shopping or visiting the beach. "Wine down and sip, sip."
Munchies • 242-366-0423 • On Back Street. Open from 11 a.m. with limited seating and take-away service. Snacks, sandwiches, pizza and ice cream. $
Reef Bar and Grill . 242-366-0095. Hope Town Harbour Lodge overlooking the Atlantic. Daily lunch 11:30 a.m. to 3 p.m. Bar open 8:00 a.m. to 6:00 p.m. Casual poolside dining. $$

Restaurants & Bars in White Sound

Abaco Inn • 242-366-0133/0333 • VHF 16 • 2.5 miles from Hope Town. Open daily for breakfast, lunch and dinner, serving gourmet Bahamian and International food in the dining room, or outside on their ocean-view terrace. Dinner reservations required; call for transportation. Complimentary dinghy dock. $$$
Boat House Restaurant at Sea Spray Resort • 242-366-0065 • VHF 16 • Open daily for breakfast, lunch and dinner; champagne brunch on Sundays, closed Sunday nights. Dinghy dock, or transport from town. $$

Hope Town Sailing Club.

THINGS TO DO ON ELBOW CAY

- Visit the famous Elbow Reef lighthouse. Built in 1864, this is one of only three remaining lighthouses in the Bahamas that are hand wound by the lighthouse keepers every two hours during the night, using a vapor burner and unique Fresnel "bull's eyes" lenses that concentrate the light so that it is visible for 15 miles. There are 101 steps to the top, but it is well worth the climb, not only to learn how the lighthouse works, but also to take in the stunning views over the harbor and neighboring cays. Why not leave a small donation to the *Bahamas Lighthouse Preservation Society* while you are there, to help maintain this historic landmark and the similar lighthouses on Great Inagua and San Salvador?
- Swim and snorkel off that fabulous long beach running down the east side of Elbow Cay (keep to the marked paths; please don't walk on the replanted dunes), or take your dinghy down to Tahiti Beach for more good swimming. Maybe surf's up on Garbonzo Reef?
- Take advantage of *Froggies* local diving knowledge to explore some of the fascinating underwater sites nearby.
- Walk through town and take lots of photographs of the pastel-painted homes surrounded by colorful flower gardens, or the harbor with the lighthouse in the background.
- Visit the recently enlarged *Wyannie Malone Museum* to find out more about this historic cay.
- Take the dinghy over to Lubbers Quarters, opposite Tahiti Beach, and join the fun at *Cracker P's* for lunch or dinner.
- Succumb to temptation at one of the gift shops and take home a memento of a happy visit.

Restaurant & Bar on Lubbers Quarters

Cracker P's • 242-366-3139 • VHF 16 "Cracker P's" • Open noon to sundown on Sunday, Monday and Thursday, dinner by reservation on Friday and Saturday. Look for the flags at their dock. $$
Telephones Across from *Vernon's Grocery* or outside the *BTC* office next to the school; two more in the office. *BTC* can receive and send faxes at 242-366-0366.
Trash Boats at anchor or on moorings in the harbor, should take garbage in on Monday, Wednesday and Friday, between 9:30 and 10:30 a.m., to Sunshine Park, just south of the public dock. Recycling for aluminum cans only in the big container.

SPORTS

Diving *Froggies Out Island Adventure* • 242-366-0431 • VHF 16 • Froggies@mail.batelnet.bs • www.froggiesabaco.com • Lambert and Theresa Albury run scuba and snorkel trips daily; half day to Fowl Cay Preserve sites, all-day trips to Guana Cay for drinks and lunch at *Nippers* or south to Little Harbour for drinks and lunch at *Pete's Pub*, with a stop to snorkel and dive en route. 2-tank dive $100 including gear, $80 for certified divers, tanks and weights provided. Snorkelers welcome, $50 for full day excursion.

Dive Sites *Johnnies Cay, Fowl Cay* and *Sandy Cay* reefs. Sandy Cay is part of the *Pelican Cay Land and Sea Park*, and Fowl Cay is part of the *Fowl Cay Bahamas National Trust Preserve*. Do not take any shells or coral from them; fishing is prohibited. You can pick up one of the 15 small boat moorings, marked by a colored ball and reflective tape, at *Sandy Cay Reef* and 19 moorings at *Fowl Cay Reef*. The reef buoys are intended only for boats less than 25 ft. Never anchor on any reef as you could damage the coral; anchor in sand or grassy areas away from the reef.

Fishing Guides *JR Albury* • 242-366-3058 • www.fishabaco.com • for bonefishing. *Day's Catch Charters* Will Key • 242-366-0059 • VHF 16 "Fox Chase" • *Lucky Strike* Truman Major • 242-366-0101• VHF 16 "Lucky Strike" • *Rudy Malone* • 242-366-0003 • VHF 16 • *Seagull Deep Sea Charters* Robert Lowe • 242-366-0266 • VHF 16 "Seagull" • *Wild Pigeon Charters* Maitland Lowe • 242-366-0461 • VHF 16 • *Ira Key II* • 242-366-0245 • VHF 16 "A Salt Weapon".

Fishing Tournaments and Regattas *Regatta Time in Abaco* • 242-367-2677 • davralph@batelnet.bs • www.rtia.net • Held the first week in July. Races form up at Green Turtle Cay, Great Guana Cay, Hope Town, Man-O-War and Marsh Harbour. Contact Dave or Kathy Ralph. *Annual Family Fishing Tournament* • 242-366-0065 •

Surfing Sites Northern tip of Elbow Cay, Atlantic side • Four Rocks, exposed beach break, best in W-SW winds and swell direction from NE, beach breaks off left and right, strong rips here • Indicas, exposed reef break, best in W wind and swell direction from NE, left hand break • Rush Reef, exposed reef break, best in W wind and swell direction from NE, a right hand break reef. White Sound, Elbow Cay, Atlantic side • Garbanzo Reef, exposed reef break, best in N-NW winds and swell direction from NE, left hand reef break is better than right hand. Tilloo Cay, Atlantic side • Tilloo Cut, exposed reef break, best in W-NW winds and swell direction from NE. Break is a left hand point.

MARSH HARBOUR

airport • bank • church • customs & immigration • fuel • groceries • marine services • marinas • medical • police • post office • propane • restaurants • telephone • water

Marsh Harbour is the third-largest town in the Bahamas with good roads leading north and south to the rest of the island and an international airport close to town. It is perfectly suited to cruising boats needing stores or spare parts, with a wide choice of marinas, good shopping and medical facilities, as well as frequent ferries to the smaller cays and settlements in Abaco. Marsh Harbour is a port of entry. Customs and Immigration to come to your dock for clearance. Don't anchor in the freight dock channel or its approaches; anchor east of the channel markers. Cruising boats all have a favorite "spot" in the Bahamas, nowhere more so than in Marsh Harbour, where people return year after year to "their" marina or "their" position in the harbor.

MARINAS

To port:

MARSH HARBOUR MARINA

Tel: 242-367-2700 • Fax: 242-367-2033 • VHF 16 • jibroom@hotmail.com

Tom and Boo Lefler operate this popular marina on the north side of the harbor, with its own *Jib Room Restaurant*, swimming pool and social events. It has a charming, peaceful atmosphere, a feeling of being slightly apart from the noise and busy world of Marsh Harbour, and the friendly staff welcomes returning boaters year after year. The Jib Room still offers an outstanding rib night on Wednesdays and steak barbecue on Saturday nights with music and dancing. Make time to snorkel the famous Mermaid Reef, which is right across the road.

Slips 62. **Max LOA** 70 ft. **MLW at Dock** 6 ft. **Dockage** $1.40 per ft. per day, $1.05 with a BoatU.S. discount. Winter rates available. **Fuel** Diesel and gasoline; 8 to 4 daily. **Facilities & Services** Power. Water $4/day, $50 per month. Showers, laundry, telephone, ice, pool. **Restaurant** Open for lunch Wednesday through Saturday, and bar is open seven nights per week. **Credit Cards** Visa and MasterCard, 5% surcharge. **Dockmaster** Jason Davis will greet you with a smiling face when you arrive.

HARBOUR VIEW MARINA

Tel: 242-367-3910 • Fax: 242-367-3911 • VHF 16 • tc@bluewaverentals.com

Shoreside facilities include the popular *Snappa's Bar and Grill*, new swimming pool, showers and toilets. The marina is completely private from the street, with a high wall along the road. Friendly staff, close to grocery stores in town, fresh conch salad outside the wall and more restaurants nearby. If you are worried about crossing the Gulf Stream, Troy Cornea, the owner, can arrange for pickup or delivery of your boat. Ask about their "Stay and See Abaco" program, and you would be wise to call ahead for reservations.

Slips 36. **Max LOA** 100 ft. (24 ft. beam). **MLW at Dock** 7 ft. Dockage $1.90 per ft. per day overnight, $1.00 per ft. monthly, $0.85 per ft. over three months; 35-ft. minimum. (March-August), lower winter rates and special long-term rates available. **Fuel** Diesel and gasoline; 8 to 5 daily. **Facilities & Services** Power $18 per day for 30A, $30 for 50A. Water $15 minimum, $0.20 per gallon. Ice. Showers free to marina guests. Laundry uses $4 tokens; telephone. Cable TV $5.00 per day, phone and wireless Internet at slips, free Internet access in the office for marina guests. Attentive and accommodating staff. *Blue Wave Boat Rentals* on site. **Credit Cards** Visa, MasterCard, AMEX (5% surcharge). **Owner** Troy Cornea. **Dockmasters** Barbara Bethell and Marcel Murry.

MANGOES MARINA

Tel: 242-367-4255 • Fax: 242-367-3336 • VHF 16 "Mangoes" • mangoes@mangoesrestaurant.com

A very pleasant small marina, with well-landscaped shore facilities, boutique, jewelry store and popular restaurant. *Lofty Fig Villas* are just across the street, if you need accommodations.

Slips 31. **Max LOA** 60 ft. **MLW at Dock** 6 ft. **Dockage** $1.00 per ft. per day, $0.75 per ft. per day monthly. 35-ft. minimum rate. Summer rates slightly higher, long-term rates available. **Facilities & Services** Power metered, water $5 per day or $30 per month mandatory. Showers, laundry for guests $3.50. Cable TV hookup. Barbecue grill, ice, swimming pool, complimentary Internet and phone access at every slip. **Restaurant** *Mangoes* Lunch and dinner daily, Sunday buffet, 8 a.m. coffee for marina guests. **Credit Cards** Visa, MasterCard, AMEX. **Owners** Jimmy and Penny Vaughan. **Manager** Lisa Scott. **Dockmaster** Rae Guitchie.

⚓ *Goin' Ashore*

CONCH INN MARINA

Tel: 242-367-4000 • Fax: 242-367-4004 • VHF 16 (VHF 82 for Moorings charter boats) • moorings_conchinn@oii.net

The largest of the marinas in the main harbor, the *Conch Inn Marina* is home to charter boat operations, *Curly Tails Restaurant*, *Concept Boat Rentals*, ***Dive Abaco*** and the *Albury Ferry* that runs to Great Guana Cay. The Conch Inn has 8 rooms on the property. *Curly Tails* is a popular spot that offers live music. The office staff and marina personnel are very helpful and friendly; open from 7:30 a.m. to 6 p.m. daily, with night security.

Slips 80. **Max LOA** 200 ft. **MLW at Dock** 6 ft. Dockage $1.60 per ft. per day (includes water and TV), 35-ft. minimum; long-term rates. **Fuel** Dock open 7:30 a.m. to 6 p.m. daily; diesel and gasoline. **Facilities & Services** Power Metered 100A, 50A, and 30A. Water at the fuel dock $0.20 per gallon, $10 minimum. Water in slips, $12 daily over 50 ft. Showers for marina guests. Laundry service $12. Telephones on docks. Ice $4 bag. Cable TV hookup, $2.50 daily, pool by the hotel, convenience store open daily until 6 p.m. ***Dive Abaco*** with daily dive trips and snorkeling info@diveabaco.com. *Concept Boat rentals*. Mail from home can be held at the office. **Restaurant**

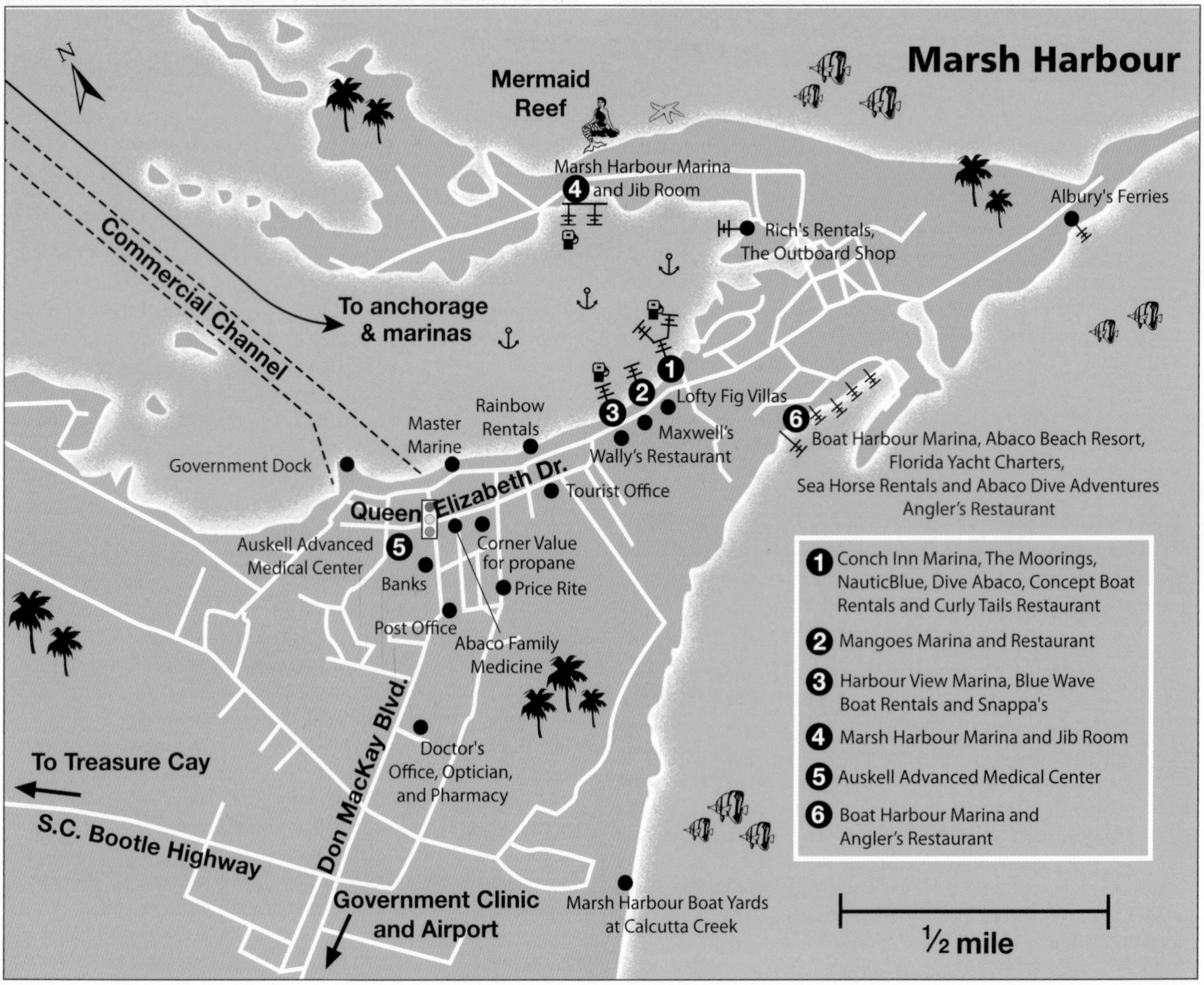

& Bar *Curly Tails* • 367-4444 • VHF 16 • Breakfast, lunch and dinner daily. Live music Thursdays and Sundays. **Accommodations** Conch Inn Hotel Rooms from $120 per night, plus 13% service tax. Discount for marina guests. **Credit Cards** Visa and MasterCard. **Dockmaster** Candice Edmond.

Facing south on the Sea of Abaco:

ABACO BEACH RESORT AT BOAT HARBOUR
Tel: 242-367-2158 • Fax: 242-367-2819 • VHF 16 •
info@AbacoBeachResort.com • www.AbacoBeachResort.com

Boat Harbour is a first-class marina and a favorite with sportfishermen Guest enjoy all the facilities of the Abaco Beach Resort, as well as proximity to town, without being in the busy main harbor. It hosts fishing tournaments throughout the year, and has the added advantages of being kid friendly, with excellent dining and entertainment ashore.

Slips 192. **Max LOA** 200 ft. **MLW at Dock** 10 ft. Dockage $2.75 per ft. per day short term, $1.35 from 31 to 60 days, $0.90 over 61 days. **Fuel** Diesel and gasoline. **Facilities & Services** Power is metered at $0.65 per kWh, all three phase service. Water is metered monthly at $0.15 per gallon. Free showers, token laundry. Complimentary telephone hookup with 50¢ service charge for local calls, $2.50 for long distance. Wireless and Internet access available. Cable TV hookup $5 per day. T-zers logo boutique dockside; Swimming pools, fishing, tennis; golf nearby. *SeaHorse Boat* rentals on property; **Restaurant & Bar** Anglers Restaurant Open for breakfast, lunch and dinner. Sandbar Swim-up bar. **Accommodations** *Abaco Beach Resort* offers 72 oceanfront rooms from $235 per night, 4 suites from $400, and 6 cottages from $550; MAP $60; 17% service charge added. Packages available. Meeting facilities. **Credit Cards** Visa, MasterCard, AMEX, Discover. **Harbourmaster** Chris Higgs **Harbour Services** Howard Pinder.

EMERGENCIES

Ambulance *Trauma One* • VHF 80 • 242-367-2911
Dentist *Greater Abaco Dental Clinic* • 242-367-4070
Marine • VHF 16, Phone 911
Medical *Abaco Family Medicine* • 242-367-2295 during the day, 242-357-6569 in emergency.
Auskell Advanced Medical Center • 242-367-0020 during the day, 242-577-0113 in emergency.
Marsh Harbour Government Clinic • 242-367-2510 after hours.
Police • 242-367-2560
Veterinary *Island Veterinary Clinic* • 242-367-0062

PORT DIRECTORY

Airport 5 miles from town. Taxis charge $12 for two people to the marinas or downtown.

Airlines Serving Marsh Harbour and/or Treasure Cay:

Abaco Air • 242-367-2266 • www.flyabacoair.com To Nassau, North Eleuthera and Moores Island.

American Eagle • 242-367-2231 • To Miami daily.

Bahamasair • Marsh Harbour - 242-367-2095 • To Nassau daily. Treasure Cay Airport - 242-365-8601.

Calypso Air • Marsh Harbour - 242-367-0140 • Treasure Cay - 242-365-8660 To Fort Lauderdale and West Palm Beach, or charters.

Continental Connection • Marsh Harbour - 242-367-3415 • Treasure Cay - 242-365-8615 To Fort Lauderdale, Miami, and West Palm Beach daily.

Cherokee Air • Marsh Harbour • 242-367-2089 • Charters to South Florida and Bahamas.

Craig Air • Marsh Harbour • 904-641-0300 • To Daytona, St. Augustine, Jacksonville.

Locair • 800-205-0730 • www.locair.net • To Ft. Lauderdale from Marsh Harbour and Treasure Cay.

Sky Bahamas • 242-367-0996 • www.skybahamas.net • Marsh Harbour to Nassau, Turks & Caicos.

Yellow Air Taxi • Marsh Harbour • 242-367-0032 • Treasure Cay • 242-365-8522 • To Fort Lauderdale and West Palm Beach, charters throughout the Bahamas.

ATMs and Banks Most banks are on Don MacKay Boulevard and open from 9:30 to 3 weekdays, to 4:30 p.m. Friday. All the banks in Marsh Harbour have ATMs, but only *ScotiaBank* will allow you to use your U.S. bank card to withdraw Bahamian cash with no charge. *Royal Bank of Canada* and *First Caribbean* will give you cash advances on MasterCard or Visa. ATMs give Bahamian dollars.

Churches *Aldersgate Methodist Church, Church of Christ, Presbyterian Church of Abaco, St. John the Baptist Anglican/ Episcopalian Church, St. Francis de Sales Catholic Mission.* Others are listed in Destination Abaco.

Couriers *UPS* - 242-367-2333 - at Frederick Agency Building, *FedEx* - 242-367-4339; *DHL* at 242-367-3710 in B&V Plaza on Don MacKay.

Customs • 242-367-2522/2525 • **Immigration** • 242-367-2536/2675 • Both will come to marinas for check-in. Ask marina staff for details.

Dinghy Dock *Union Jack Dock* Closest to downtown.

Email and Internet Emergency emails can be sent to cruisers@oii.net, or any marina. Make sure that your call sign is in the subject line so you can be identified on the Cruisers Net (VHF 68 at 8:15 a.m.). Keep messages brief. If you are a *Royal Marsh Harbour Yacht Club* member, emails addressed to rmhyc@hotmail.com with your boat name in the subject line will be called on VHF 78 at 8 a.m., Monday, Wednesday and Friday.

Out-Island Internet - 242-367-3006 - www.abacoinet.com.

Many of the marinas offer Internet access in the marina office and will receive regular emails for you.

Bahamas Family Markets • 242-367-3714 • bfm@batelnet.bs • Open from 7 to 9 weekdays, 8 to 5 Sundays, at the traffic light. $2 minimum charge for 1 to 10 minutes, then 20 cents a minute.

Ferries *Albury's Ferry* • 242-367-3147 and 242-365-6010 • VHF 16 • From Crossing Beach to Hope Town at 7:15, 9, 10:30 a.m., 12:15, 2, 4, and 5:45 p.m. and 6:30 p.m. except Sundays and holidays, 20 minute ride. To Man-O-War at 10:30 a.m., 4 and 5:45 p.m.; and at 12:15 and 2:30 p.m. except Sundays. From Conch Inn Marina to Great Guana Cay and Scotland Cay: 6:45, 10:30 a.m., 1:30 p.m., 3:30 p.m. and 5:45 p.m. Fares $15 one-way, $25 open return trip. Charters available.

Green Turtle Ferry • 242-365-4166/4128/4151 • VHF 16 • Leaves from *Treasure Cay Airport* dock at 8:30, 10:30, 11:30 a.m., 1:30, 2:30, 3:30, 4:30 and 5 p.m. for Green Turtle Cay. Round trip fare $12. Taxi from Marsh Harbour to Treasure Cay dock $70.

Pinder's Ferry Service • 242-365-2356 • From Crown Haven to McLeans Town, Grand Bahama, leaves daily at 7 a.m. and 2:30 p.m. Round trip fare $80, $50 one-way. Buses between Freeport and McLeans town. Rental cars at both terminals, book cars in advance. Taxi from Treasure Cay airport to Crown Haven $75.

Bahamas Fast Ferries • 242-367-5250, 242-366-4119, 242-323-2166 • Leaves Sandy Point for Nassau on Tuesdays at 12:30 p.m., on Fridays and Saturdays at 8 p.m. for the 4-hour journey. $90 round trip, $50 one-way. Call for car or cargo rates.

Hotels & Lodging *Abaco Beach Resort* • 242-367-2158 • Hotel, villas, pool, tennis and marina.

Island Breezes Motel • 242-367-3776

Lofty Fig Villas • 367-2681 • 6 villas across from Mangoes.

Pelican Beach Villas • 242-367-3600 • Beachfront villas near Marsh Harbour Marina with small boat dockage.

Regattas of Abaco • 242-367-2227/2221 • www.abacotowns@oii.net Two-bedroom rentals, swimming pool and tennis court. Between *Abaco Beach Resort* and *Conch Inn.*

Liquor *A & K Liquor* • 242-367-2179 • Burns House Duty Free Liquor Store • 242-367-2172 • *Bristol Wine and Spirits* • 242-367-2180 on Queen Elizabeth Drive. *Tupps* • 242-367-2936 across from Mangoes offers a wide selection of wine. Delivery available to marinas.

MEDICAL SERVICES

Air Ambulance *National Air Ambulance* • 954-359-9900 • Cleveland Clinic/Broward General Hospital.

Life Flight-Miami • 305-663-6859 • Pediatric only to Jackson Memorial Hospital Miami.

Clinics *Abaco Family Medicine* • 242-367-2295, 242-357-6569 in emergency • Drs. Frank Boyce, Mark Binard and EJ Downes. Clinic hours 9 to 5 Monday to Friday, to noon on Saturdays.

Auskell Advanced Medical Center • 242-367-0020 • General practioner, food doctor, obstetrician/gynecologist, ultrasound technician, audiology department, neurologist and plastic surgeon. Doctors visit weekly. Walk-ins Welcome.

Marsh Harbour Government Clinic • 242-367-2867 during the day, 242-367-2510 emergency • On Don MacKay Boulevard, out toward the airport. The largest and most comprehensive government clinic in the Abaco islands, two 2-bed wards. 9 to 5 weekdays with 2 doctors and 7 nurses.

Dentists *Diamante Dental Centre* • 242-367-4968 • *Agape Dental Centre* • 242-367-4355 • *Greater Abaco Dental Clinic* • 242-367-4070.

Optician *Abaco Optical Services* • 242-367-3546 • In Lowe's Plaza.

Pharmacy *Lowe's Pharmacy* • 242-367-2667 • *Chemist Shoppe* • 242-367-3106 • *Island Pharmacy* • 242-367-2544. All well-stocked. Prescription refills accepted.

Post Office • 242-367-2571 • Dove Plaza on Don MacKay Boulevard. 9 to 5 weekdays.

Propane *Corner Value* • 242-367-2250 • On Queen Elizabeth Drive. Open weekdays, to 1 p.m. Saturday. Same-day propane tank refill service; leave your tank before 9 a.m., back by 12 p.m.; in by 1 p.m., back by 4 p.m. Please don't be impatient if the tanks are sometimes a little late returning; this is a very generous free service to boaters. Don't leave tanks outside *Corner Value*'s door overnight.

Provisions *Abaco Grocery* • 242-367-0278 • On Don Mackay Blvd. Monday to Saturday 7:30 a.m. to 6 p.m. Fresh vegetables, grocery items and tobacco. Delivery to marinas on bulk orders.

Save-A-Lot • 242-367-2020 • On Don Mackay Blvd. Open 8:30 to 5 Monday to Thursday, 8 a.m. to 6 p.m. Friday and Saturday. Fresh produce, meats, groceries, beverages and supplies. Delivery of bulk orders to marinas.

Bahamas Family Market • 242-367-3714 • bfm@batelnet.bs • Open 7 a.m. to 9 p.m. Monday to Saturday, 8 to 5 Sundays, at the stop light. Small but good, with a deli, bakery and fresh produce. Internet access $2 per minute for 1 to 10 minutes, then $0.20 a minute.

Price Right • 242-367-7283 • On Stratton Drive, open daily 8 to 7, Saturdays till 7:30 p.m. Sundays from 9 a.m. to 3 p.m., with a new butcher shop, expanded fruit and vegetable section.

Mangoes. Marsh Harbour. WATERWAY GUIDE PHOTOGRAPHY.

Long's Landing • 242-367-3079 • Fresh and frozen fish, conch and lobster; dinghy dock across the street.

Maxwell's Super Center • 242-367-2601 • Fax: 242-367-2731 • Nathan Key Drive. Open daily from 8 a.m. to 7 p.m., from 9 a.m. to 2 p.m. on Sundays. High standard of fresh produce and breads, choice meats, deli and dairy products, wholesale and half cases available.

Restaurants *Anglers* at *Boat Harbour Marina* and *Abaco Beach Resort* • 242-367-2158 • Open daily for breakfast, lunch and dinner. Great international food, served in their attractive dining room overlooking the marina, hosting many boaters and frequent special events. Nightly entertainment. $$$

Curly Tails at the *Conch Inn Marina* • 242-367-4444 • Open for breakfast from 7:30 to 11:30, lunch from 11:30 to 4 and dinner from 5 to 9 daily. Live music Thursday and Sunday nights. Daily specials, bar snacks. $$

Golden Grouper • 242-367-2301 • In Dove Plaza. Breakfast and lunch. $

Jamie's Place • 242-367-2880 • Across from entrance to Abaco Beach Resort. Ice cream parlor. Bahamian and American cuisine. Popular with the locals. $$

Java • 242-367-5523 • Between Conch Inn and Boat Harbour. Open for coffees, teas, baked goods and art work.

Jib Room at Marsh Harbour Marina • 242-367-2700 • Open for lunch and dinner Wednesday through Saturday. Rib night on Wednesdays. Steak night with live music and dancing on Saturdays. Closed Sundays. $$

Kentucky Fried Chicken • 242-367-2615 • Open for lunch and dinner. $

Mangoes • 242-367-3266 • VHF 16 • Waterfront dining and patio bar. Open for lunch from 11:30 to 2:30 daily, dinner from 6:30 to 10 p.m. Monday to Saturday, Buffet Grill from 6 to 10 p.m. Sundays. Picnic menu, dinghy dock for customers, bar snacks all day, Internet access, live music, boutique. $$$

Matilda's Snack Shack • 242-367-4005 • Best burgers in Abaco. Takeout breakfast and lunch. $

Snappas Grill and Chill at Harbour View Marina • 242-367-2278 • VHF 16 "Snappas" • Open daily for drinks and grilled foods overlooking the marina from 11 a.m., with happy hour from 5 to 7:30 p.m., Wild Wednesday Happy Hour from 5 to 11 p.m. $

Subway • 242-367-2798 • Open for lunch and happy hour.

Wally's • 242-367-2074 • VHF 16 • Daily lunch. Elegant dinner Friday and Saturday; live music Saturdays. Dinner reservations recommended. Boutique. Closed Sundays. $$$

RENTALS

Bicycles *Rental Wheels* • 242-367-4643 • VHF 16 • Bicycles $8 daily, motor cycles from $25 daily.

Boats *Blue Wave Boat Rentals* • 242-367-3910 • Fax: 242-367-3911 • VHF 16 "Blue Wave Rentals" • At *Harbour View Marina.* Duskys, Ocean Pros, Paramounts.

Concept Boats • 242-367-5570 • Fax: 242-367-5569 • VHF 16 • At *Conch Inn Marina.* 23-ft. and 27-ft. Concepts from $130 daily, special rates available. *Rainbow Rentals* • 242-367-4062 • rainbow@oii-net./go-abacos.com • At Bay Street and Union Jack Dock. Fully equipped 22-ft. CDM White Caps. *Sea Horse Rentals* • 242-367-2513 • VHF 16 • www.seahorseboatrentals.com • At *Boat Harbour Marina* and Hope Town. 30 boats from $130 daily for an 18-ft. Privateer, to $225 daily for a 26-ft. Paramount. Complimentary delivery to Man-O-War, Elbow Cay and Lubbers Quarters.

Cars REMEMBER TO DRIVE ON THE LEFT! There is a 45-mph speed limit throughout the island, 15 mph near schools, 20 mph through the settlements. *A & P Rentals* • 242-367-2655 *Rental Wheels Abaco* • 242-367-4643 • VHF 16 • Closest to *Boat Harbour* and *Conch Inn Marina,* with cars from $65 per day, scooters and bicycles. *Sea Star Car Rentals* • 242-367-4887 • seastar@coralwave.com • www.go-abacos.com/seastar

Taxis At the airport or in town on VHF 06. From the airport to town marinas costs about $12 and each additional person $3, to Treasure Cay Marina $65 to $90. Rates are regulated, but always ask what the fare is before you set off.

Telephones At all the marinas, outside the *BTC* office, and in town. Phone cards from *BTC*, 9–4:30 weekdays.

Tourist Office • 242-367-3067 • In Memorial Plaza, open weekdays, 10 a.m. to 4 p.m.

Travel Agents *A & W Travel Service* • 242-367-2806/2755 • In *Abaco Shopping Centre.*

Travel Spot • 242-367-2817 • On Don Mackay near *Island Bakery.*

Veterinary *Island Veterinary Clinic* • 242-367-0062 • On Don Mackay Blvd, open 9 to 5:30 Monday to Friday, Saturdays by appointment.

Caribbean Veterinary • 242-367-3551 • In *Abaco Shopping Centre,* open Thursdays.

Yacht and Vacation Broker *Terrance Edgecombe* • 242-554-9978 tesail@hotmail.com • Boat sales and vacation packages.

Weather Reports For Abaco and Northern Bahamas and Gulf Stream Crossings • *Cruisers Net* • VHF 68 • At 8:15 a.m. daily. • *Freeport Weather Service* • 242-352-9114 • *Radio Abaco* FM 93.5 Reports at 8 a.m. and between 6 and 6:30 p.m. weekdays • *Waterway Net* 7.268 at 7:45 a.m.

SPORTS & RECREATION

Boat Charters *Florida Yacht Charters* at *Mangoes Marina* • 242-367-4853, 800-537-0050 • Fax: 242-367-4854 • VHF 74 fyc@oii.net • Family-run yacht and motor yacht charters out of Miami Beach, Key West and Marsh Harbour.

The Moorings, Sunsail and NauticBlue at *Conch Inn Marina* • 242-367-4000, 800-535-7289, 727-535-1446 • VHF 82 • www.moorings.com • An extensive fleet of 40 sail and power boats, including catamarans. Ice, fuel, water, linens, snorkeling gear, dinghy, chart briefing and boat check-out provided.

MARINE SERVICES

Abaco Marine Propellers • 242-367-4276 • Fax: 242-367-4259 • VHF 16 • amp@batelnet.bs • Propellers, aluminum, brass, stainless, welding, sand blasting, across the street from *Abaco Outboards.*

Abaco Outboard Engines • 242-367-2452 • Fax: 242-367-2354 • Yamaha agents, repairs, dry storage to 12 tons. Sales, service and parts.

B & D Marine • 242-367-2622 • Fax: 242-367-2395 • VHF 16 • At the traffic light. Best-stocked marine store. Suzuki distributor, generators, marine hardware/supplies, fishing tackle, dive gear and Wavey Line charts. Closed Sundays.

Bodie's Engine Repairs • 242-554-9241 • Diesel engine repairs on Caterpillar, Cumming, Onan, GM, Westerbeak, Yanmar, Volvo, Northern Lights, gas engines, steering and hydraulics and toilet repair.

Browntips • VHF 16 • Does scrubbing below the water line.

CJ's Welding and Machine Shop • 242-367-4011 • At *Marsh Harbour Boat Yards.* Marine items, boat T-tops, water and fuel tanks, shaft and rudder repairs.

Cliffords Pumping Service • 242-367-2071 • Septic tank pumping.

Gratitude Marine Services • 242-367-2480 • VHF 16 • Dennis Dupuch is a certified diesel mechanic and can help with diesel, gas, and electrical repairs and installations.

Marsh Harbour Boat Yards • 242-367-5205 • Fax: 242-367-4018 • VHF 16 • info@mhby.com • www.mhby.com • Full-service boat yard, 1.5 miles south of Boat Harbour and north of Witch Point. Leave the pole at the entrance to starboard as you come in. With an 85-ton lift (the second-largest in the Bahamas), haul, launch, and block prices start at $8 per ft. Bottom cleaning and painting, welding, machine shop and repairs. Well-stocked marine store on site, formerly Triple J Marine. See Lawrence Higgs, Ian Carol or Hilland Albury.

Master Marine • 242-367-4760 • VHF 16 • Terrence Roberts has a good selection of Suzuki outboards and is a Honda marine dealer and four-stroke outboard specialist. Yamaha outboard engine rebuilding and tuning, cylinder boring and honing, with mobile service. Can help with pumps, alternators, etc.

Merlin's Marine Electronic • 242-367-2163 • Located at National Marine. Factory-authorized sales and service. Raymarine, Furono, Garmin, Icom and Simrad.

The Outboard Shop • 242-367-2703 • VHF 16 • At Pelican Shores. Evinrude & Johnson motors and parts with factory-trained mechanics. Dry storage.

National Marine • 242-367-2326 • Mercury & Mariner outboard sales, service and marine accessories.

Precision Marine Repairs • 242-367-2742 • Fax: 242-367-2682 • Mike Davies specializes in fiberglass and gel coat repairs.

Prop Pullers Inc. • VHF16 "Ice Man" • Colin Albury offers yacht maintenance, management and propeller repairs.

Quality Marine Repair • 242-367-5295, 242-357-6832 • Adam Weatherford. Fiberglass, gel coat and Awlgrip.

Ciganka • boatpeople@myexcel.com • www.sailingshipcharter.com • Captain Thomas Owens and Linda charter and captain their 78-ft. steel, gaff-rigged ketch that they built themselves. See their Web site for the construction photographs of this interesting boat, used for Scout Adventure Training during 2004 throughout the Bahamas.

Bonefishing *Justin Sands* • 242-367-3526 • *Edmund Williams* • 242-367-7123 or 242-359-6013 • *Jay Sawyer* • 242-367-3941 • *Buddy Pinder* • 242-366-2163 • *The Delphi Club* • 242-366-2222 • www.delphi-bahamas.com. Luxury bonefishing lodge for the aficionado. Gourmet chef, accommodations and a relaxing atmosphere in Rolling Harbour.

THINGS TO DO IN MARSH HARBOUR

- Take advantage of well-stocked stores to provision.
- Tune in to the Cruiser's Net on VHF 68 at 8:15 a.m. to hear what is going on in Abaco and what the weather prospects are.
- Sort out that pesky electronic problem on board.
- Go over to Great Guana Cay for the Sunday pig roast at *Nippers*, or down to Little Harbour for *Pete's Pub's Pig n' Pea Party* on Saturdays. Listen for their advertisements on the Cruiser's Net. You can always enjoy the ferry ride if you don't want to take your own boat.
- Perhaps you would like to join the *Royal Marsh Harbour Yacht Club*? Listen out for them at 8 a.m. on VHF 78. Social gatherings, small membership fee; email at rmhyc@yahoo.com.
- Go snorkeling off Mermaid Reef or diving with one of the dive operators.

Diving and Snorkeling ***Above and Below Abaco*** • 242-367-0350 • www.aboveandbelowabaco.com. Specializing in custom designed dive trips, small groups with Kay Politino. Outstanding service, scuba and snorkeling tours. Instruction. Rentals and air fills. Located on *Bay Street*. NAUI Certification courses.
Dive Abaco • 242-367-2787, 242-367-4646, 800-247-5338 • dive@diveabaco.com • www.diveabaco.com • With Keith Rogers at the *Conch Inn Marina*. 2-tank dive $80. Full dive center and dive shop, NAUI and PADI certification courses. Night and wreck dives.
Dive Abaco Adventure • 242-367-2963. www.abacodivers.com. Capt. Tim Higgs is a 14th generation Bahamian.
Fishing Guides *Buddy Pinder* 242-366-2163, *Jay Sawyer* 242-367-3941, *Justin Sands* 242-367-3526, *Terrance Davis* 242-367-4464, *Danny Sawyer* 242-367-3577.
Fishing Tournaments • 242-367-2158 • Contact *Boat Harbour Marina* for dates.
Golf 18-hole course at Treasure Cay.
Regattas *Regatta Time in Abaco* • 242-367-2677 • davralph@batelnet.bs • www.rtia.net • Held during the first week in July. Races form at Green Turtle Cay, Guana Cay, Hope Town, Man-O-War and Marsh Harbour. Contact Dave or Kathy Ralph in Marsh Harbour.

LITTLE HARBOR

art gallery • moorings • restaurant & bar

Little Harbour is a very special place. Pick up one of the moorings in the crystal clear waters of the tiny bay. It is surrounded on three sides by hills dotted with private homes. There is an art studio, gallery and museum. It was here that the charismatic and dynamic sculptor Randolph Johnston, and his artist wife Margot, found their escape from the world and a place to work in peace. While they were building their house and studios in the 1950s, the Johnston family lived in a cave and on their boat. Randolph and Margot wouldn't recognize Little Harbour today. Their son, Pete, has turned Pete's Pub into a hub of activity. At least 40 families have houses here, and the 25 mooring balls in the harbour are always filled with visiting cruisers. Perhaps it is such a special place because it lacks the usual amenities of public telephones, fuel, water, groceries, showers or Internet. There is only 3.5 feet of water in the channel if you come in at low tide, but it is well-marked. There is no charge for dinghy dockage for visiting boats on moorings. Ice is available at $3 per bag.
Ferry *Albury's Ferry* • 242-365-6010 • Charter from Marsh Harbour.
Froggies • 242-366-0431 • From Hope Town on full-day dive trips.
Gallery/Museum *Johnston Studios Art Gallery* Open 11:30 to 4. A collection of Randolph Johnston's bronzes are on display, as well as Pete's current collection of dolphin sculptures and jewelry, which are for sale. Woodcarvings, prints, T-shirts, postcards.
Moorings There are 25 moorings offered on a first-come, first-served basis. Call VHF 16 "Pete's Pub" if you have a problem. Someone will come around to collect the $15 later in the day. You can also anchor in Little Harbour if there is room.
Restaurant & Bar *Pete's Pub* • 242-366-3503 • pete@petespub.com • www.petespub.com • Open from 11 a.m. daily, under the able management of the Johnston clan. An open-sided beach bar festooned with funky memorabilia overlooking the harbor serves hamburgers, hot dogs, fresh fish and more, with a Pig n' Pea Party on Saturdays from April to July. Their specialty drink is a lethal Blaster, made with four types of rum and fruit juice. Happy hour on Fridays at 5 p.m. until... Dinner reservations are requested or get there before sundown.
Taxi To Marsh Harbour will cost $80.
Telephone $3 per minute, $10 minimum charge.
Trash Please take your trash away with you. If you really have to leave that 10-gallon bag, it will cost you $5.
Water Rainwater is $2 per gallon.

THINGS TO DO IN LITTLE HARBOUR

- Visit the gallery, and browse through some very attractive artwork by three generations of Johnstons, or admire the Sculpture Garden.
- Walk over to the old lighthouse.
- Take the dinghy around to explore the blue holes and shallow creeks in the Bight of Old Robinson.
- Snorkel the reef at North Beach, on your port side as you enter the channel. It is now even more beautiful since it is protected; no spearing or taking coral or fans is permitted. The whole of the bight may be protected before long.
- Take a picnic across to Lynyard Cay for snorkeling.
- Dive Sandy Cay Reef on your way to Little Harbour.
- Enjoy good company and a Blaster at *Pete's Pub.*

CHEROKEE SOUND

groceries • post office • telephone • water

Cherokee Sound has beautiful, clear water in a sandy bay on the west side of Cherokee Point. The settlement once boasted a flourishing boatbuilding yard and still has the longest dock in Abaco. The settlement is quiet, clean and tidy, with vegetables, fruit and flowers growing inside neatly fenced gardens. There is a good grocery store, but no restaurant or bar.

The Abaco Club on Winding Bay, 242-367-0077, www.theabacoclub.com, is a private, gated resort with ocean views and world class golf. Private homes, cabanas and fractional units, between Cherokee Sound and Little Harbour, has changed the ambience of both settlements. By road, the secured entrance to Winding Bay is the second left past the turn to Little Harbour, before you go around to Cherokee Sound.
Bonefishing Guides *Junior Albury* • 242-366-3058, *Noel Lowe* • 242-366-2107, *Marty Sawyer* • 242-366-2115, *Theodore Sawyer* • 242-366-2111, and *Will Sawyer* • 242-366-2177.
Catering *Wendy Sawyer* - 242-366-2115 and *Darlene Sawyer* • 242-366-2025 will cook meals. Or contact Cherokee Food Fair.
Church *Assembly of God, Epworth Methodist Chapel.*
Groceries *Cherokee Food Fair* • 242-366-2022 (also fax) • Open 7:30 a.m.

to 6 p.m., daily. Closed Sunday. Well stocked with fresh produce, frozen and canned foods, sodas, juices, some hardware and a clothing corner. *Diane Sawyer* • 242-366-2066 • Bakes fresh bread daily.

Marine Supplies, Fuel, Laundry *Cherokee Auto and Boat Haven* • 242-366-2092 • Open 7 to 10 a.m. and 2 to 4 p.m. weekdays, and 7 a.m. to noon and 2 to 5 p.m. on Saturday. Trevor and Jennifer Sawyer • 242-366-2065 • will always open up for you. Diesel in 5-gallon drums, with a hand pump to your boat or fuel can. Gasoline at their fuel dock for shallow draft boats only. A small assortment of fishing tackle, marine supplies, ballyhoo bait, sodas, snacks and ice. Coin-operated washers and dryers ($2) open 7 a.m. to 7 p.m. daily, from 10 a.m. Sundays.

Post Office Open 3 to 4 weekdays except Wednesdays.

Telephone By the tower, outside the old BTC office.

Trash Bins in town.

THINGS TO DO IN CHEROKEE SOUND

- Swim in the glorious clear water.
- Take your dinghy and explore the narrow channel leading up to Mangrove Cay.
- Walk through the quiet settlement, and admire the colorful and prolific gardens.
- Enjoy lunchtime drinks and snacks on the end of the pier at the *Sand Bar* on Saturday or Sunday.

SANDY POINT

airstrip • fuel • groceries • medical • police • restaurant • telephone • water

This small village settlement was once home to a thriving lumber industry. It is about 50 miles south of Marsh Harbour. The settlement is laid out on a neat and tidy grid. The perfect aqua waters and powdery sand offer the adventurous cruiser beautiful surroundings. There is excellent bonefishing and a colorful yearly festival with sailboat races and conch cleaning contests, as well as wonderful food booths. There is a Texaco Starport with dockage and a ferry service to Nassau. A new luxury development, Gilpin Point, has added a new dimension to the Sandy Point ambiance. There is a post office, medical clinic and BTC in the settlement, as well as a pub and hardware and small grocery stores.

MARINAS

LIGHTBOURNE MARINE

Tel: 242-366-4185 • VHF 16

The marina has room for a few boats in the 20- to-40 foot range. Call ahead to ensure they have 5 feet of water at the approach and at the docks. The settlement offers good provisioning, restaurants and air service via Cat Island Air and Flamingo Air. Customs and Immigration can be arranged with 24-hour advance notice. David Lightbourne will look after you. **Slips** 4. **Max LOA** Up to 120 ft. **MLW at Dock** 5 ft. Dockage Varies. **Fuel** Diesel, gasoline and oils. **Services** Electric and Water, Toilet and Shower.

Accommodations *Oeisha's Resort* • 242-366-4139 • *islandlife@oeishasresort.com* • *www.oeishasresort.com*.

Pete & Gay Guest House • 242-366-4119 • peteandgay@batelnet.bs • www.peteandgayguesthouse.com.

Rickmon Bonefish Lodge • 242-366-4477.

Gilpin Point • Private, luxury estates available for rent.

Moores Island • 242-366-6334 • Bonefishing lodge with 8 rooms.

Airlines *Cat Island Air* • 242-377-3318 • Four flights per week • *Flamingo Air* • 242-351-4963

Airport *Sandy Point Airport* • Runway 10/28 is 3,000 feet of packed coral, elevation 8'. It serves private as well as commercial flights and is an airport of entry with 24-hours advance notice • One mile south of settlement.

Bonefishing Guides *Christopher Pinder* • 242-366-2163, *Justin Sands* • 242-367-3526, *Links Adderly* • 242-366-4335, *Anthony Bain* • 242-366-4107, *Ferdinand Burrows* • 242-366-4133, *Floyd Burrow* • 242-366-4175, *Ricky Burrows* • 242-366-4233, *Patrick Roberts* • 242-366-4286.

Churches *Anglican, Baptist and Church of God*

Customs and Immigration 242-366-4150 • Visit four times a week or on special request.

Dinghy Dock Government Dock and *Lightbourne's*.

Ferry *Sea Link Fast Ferry* at the Government Dock to and from Nassau • Stanley White at Pete & Gay's is the ferry booking agent • 242-366-4119 • Leaves Sandy Point for the 3-hour and 45-minute journey to Nassau on Fridays and Sundays at 8 p.m. $90 round trip, $300 with a car and driver.

Fuel *Lightbourne Marine*, Texaco gas and diesel • *Thompson's*, Esso gas and diesel.

Hardware and Lumber *Thompson's*.

Laundry Ask at *Lightbourne's*, various ladies in town do laundry.

Medical Clinic • 242-366-4010 • Nurse and doctor.

Police In the Administration Building, 242-366-4044.

Propane Bring to *Lightbourne's* for refill in Marsh Harbour.

Provisions *E&E Grocery*, on West Bay Street • Fresh baked bread, pastries and produce available in town • *Stop & Shop* • *Clarke's Gift Shoppe*

Restaurants & Bars *Oeisha's Resort* • 242-366-4139 • islandlife@oeishasresort.com • www.oeishasresort.com • Conch salad, stuffed lobster in air-conditioned bar and restaurant • Pool table, card and domino games, satellite TV, dances and karaoke events. *Beach Club Inn* • 242-366-4102. *Big J's Restaurant & Bar* • 242-366-4020. *Enza's Place* • 242-366-4129. *Nancy's Seaside Inn Restaurant* • 242-366-4120 • The lobster plate they serve for lunch alone if worth the long drive from Marsh Harbour. *Pete and Gay Guest House* • 242-366-4119 • peteandgay@batelnet.bs • www.peteandgayguesthouse.com • Restaurant, sports bar (70" projection TV) and game room. *Rickmon Bonefish Lodge* • 242-366-4477

Taxi ***Donna's Taxi Service*** • "Taxi 98" • 242-475-7766 or 242-577-7766 • dbain198@gmail.com; Call Donna if you don't feel like "hoofing it."

Telephone BTC office, 242-366-4000

Trash Bins in settlement.

Volunteer Headquarters *Oeisha's Resort* • 242-366-4139 • Volunteer for four hours to assist the elderly or a special project to receive discounts on meals.

EMERGENCIES

Marine • VHF 16

Medical *Clinic* • 242-366-4010 • Open 9 a.m. to 3 p.m. weekdays. After hours phone 242-475-7737 for on-call nurse.

Chapter 7
Grand Bahama and the Grand Lucayan Waterway

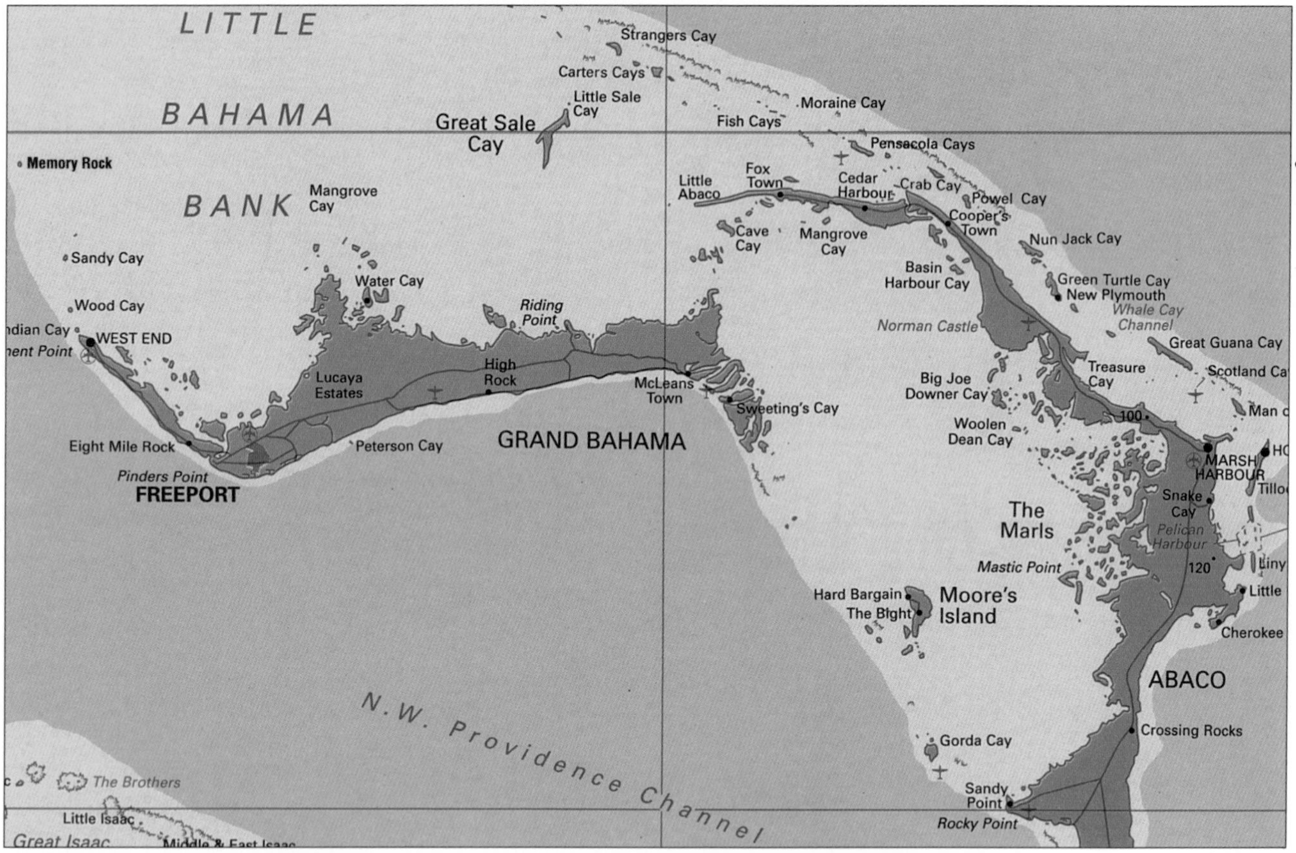

Not to be used for navigation.

Looking At the Charts

Grand Bahama is the fourth largest island in the Bahamas, ranking behind Andros, Eleuthera and Great Abaco. The island runs west to east just above latitude N 26° 30.000'. It is almost 70 miles long, seven miles wide and stretches 16 miles at its widest point. Grand Bahama offers close proximity to Florida, boasts five-star marinas and accommodations, offers numerous and varied restaurants and a vibrant Lucayan nightlife and bar scene. It also provides a myriad of recreational facilities, activities, duty-free shopping and a first-class international airport. For cruisers to whom these things are important, Grand Bahama is a virtual dream come true.

This Guide has already covered West End in Chapter 3, because for many, it is the gateway entry port to the Little Bahama Bank from Florida. In that chapter, we mentioned the northern approach to the Grand Lucayan Waterway. In this chapter, we turn to the south coast of Grand Bahama Island, home to Freeport and Port Lucaya; and we return, in detail, to the Grand Lucayan Waterway.

In the Spotlight. Freeport and Port Lucaya

It is difficult to describe the southern coast of Grand Bahama. It is a vast, narrow track of scrub-covered, almost flat, territory. Tourist facilities and development are quite widespread along the island's perimeter. Although there are still many stretches of barren, open land, in general, the roads on the island are good, and the main arterial routes are well-landscaped and maintained. Grand Bahama International Airport is a first-rate facility with international and domestic terminals. A number of general aviation carriers and charter services offer good connections with the United States, Canada, the United Kingdom and the other islands of the Bahamas.

Freeport Harbour is a vast commercial trans-shipment port; a stopover for super ships to unload their cargoes for transfer to freighters and smaller cargo vessels. The entrance to the harbor is 1,800 feet long by 500 feet wide with a controlling depth of 50 feet. Although the Port Authority does permit smaller vessels to clear Customs and Immigration there, common sense tells you to stay away from this hub of activity. Anchoring in the harbor itself is beyond fool hearty and definitely not allowed.

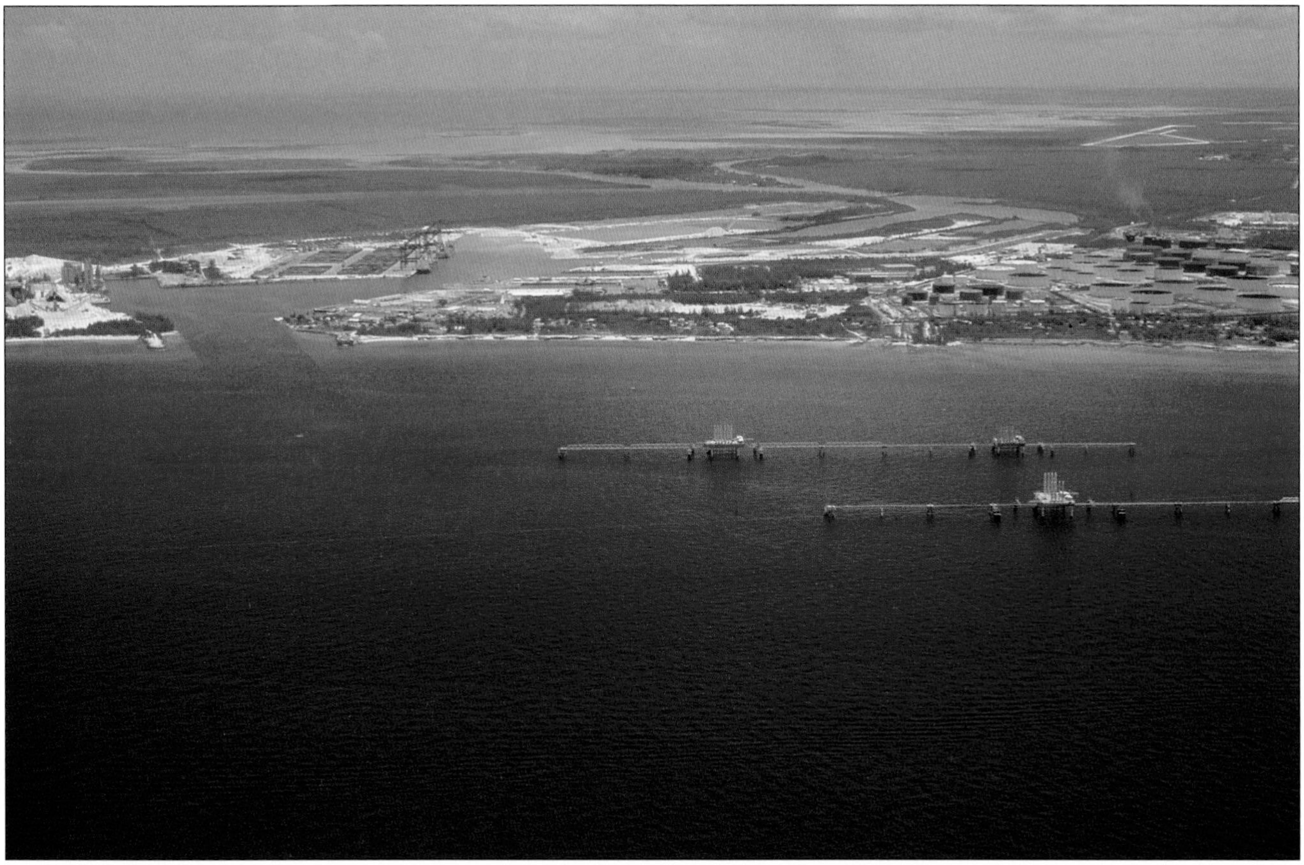

Freeport Harbour, from the south. Commercial Harbor, not for cruisers. (Not to be used for navigation.) WATERWAY GUIDE PHOTOGRAPHY.

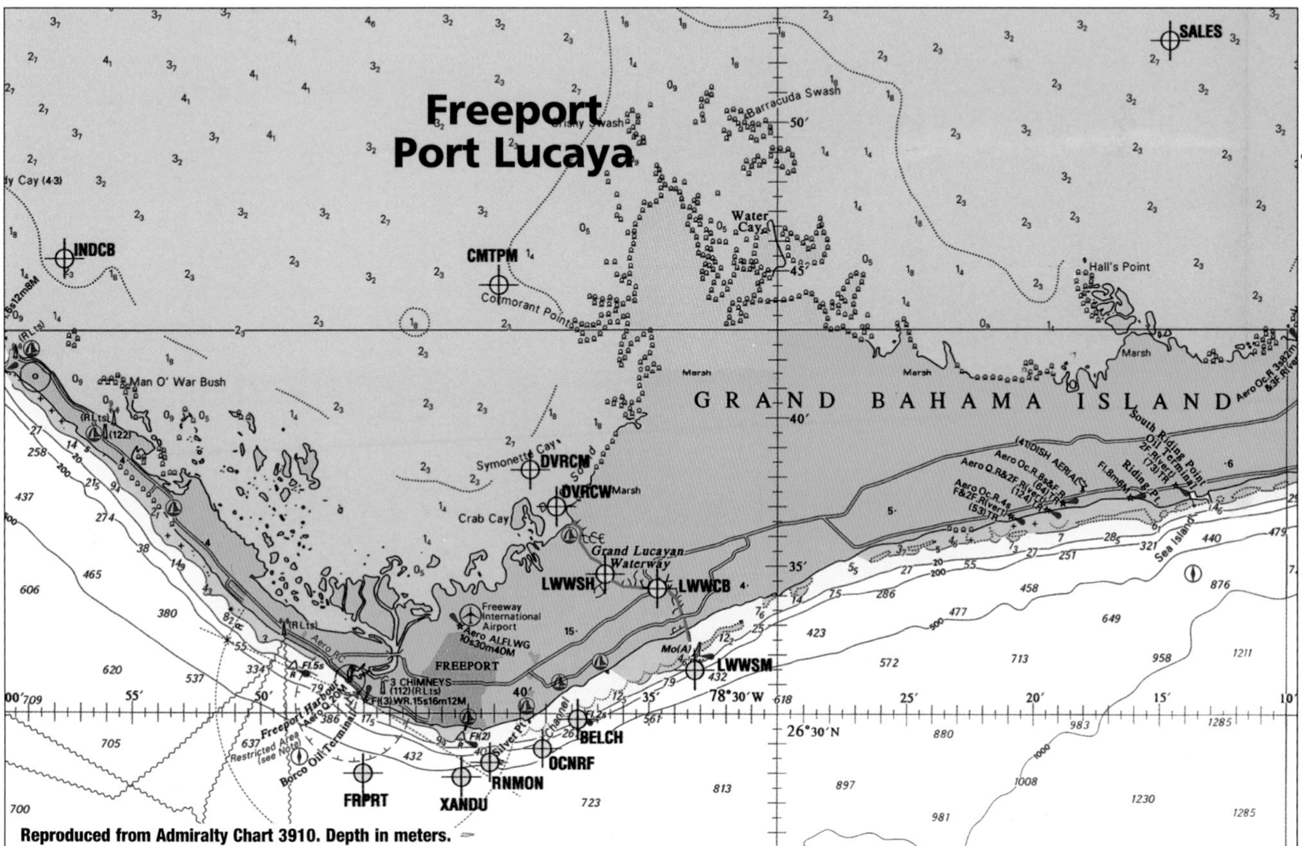

Not to be used for navigation.

Grand Bahama

FREEPORT, XANADU		Largest Vessel Accommodated	VHF Channel Monitored	Transient Berths / Total Berths	Approach / Dockside Depth (reported)	Floating Docks	Gas / Diesel	Groceries, Ice, Marine Supplies, Snacks	Repairs: Hull, Engine, Propeller	Lift (tonnage), Crane, Rail	1=110V, 2=220V, B=Both, Max Amps	Laundry, Pool, Showers	Pump-Out Station	Nearby: Grocery Store, Motel, Restaurant
		Dockage					Supplies		Services					
1. **Bradford Marine Bahamas**	**242-352-7711**	**400**	**16**	**/50**	**35/35**	**F**	**GD**	**IMS**	**HEP**	**L150**	**B/200**	**S**	**P**	**GMR**
2. Bahama Bay Marina (WiFi)	242-351-5063 x223	55		14/	6/10						B/100	LS		GMR
3. Xanadu Beach Resort and Marina	242-352-6783	120		/60	13/6.5									MR
4. Sunrise Resort and Marina (WiFi)	800-932-4959	100	16	/58	8/10	F	GD	I			B/100	LPS		GMR
5. **Knowles Marine Service at Sunrise Resort**	**242-351-2769**	**75**	**16**	**17/**	**12/6**		**GD**		**HEP**	**L75**		**S**		**GR**

Corresponding chart(s) not to be used for navigation. Internet Access (WiFi) Wireless Internet Access

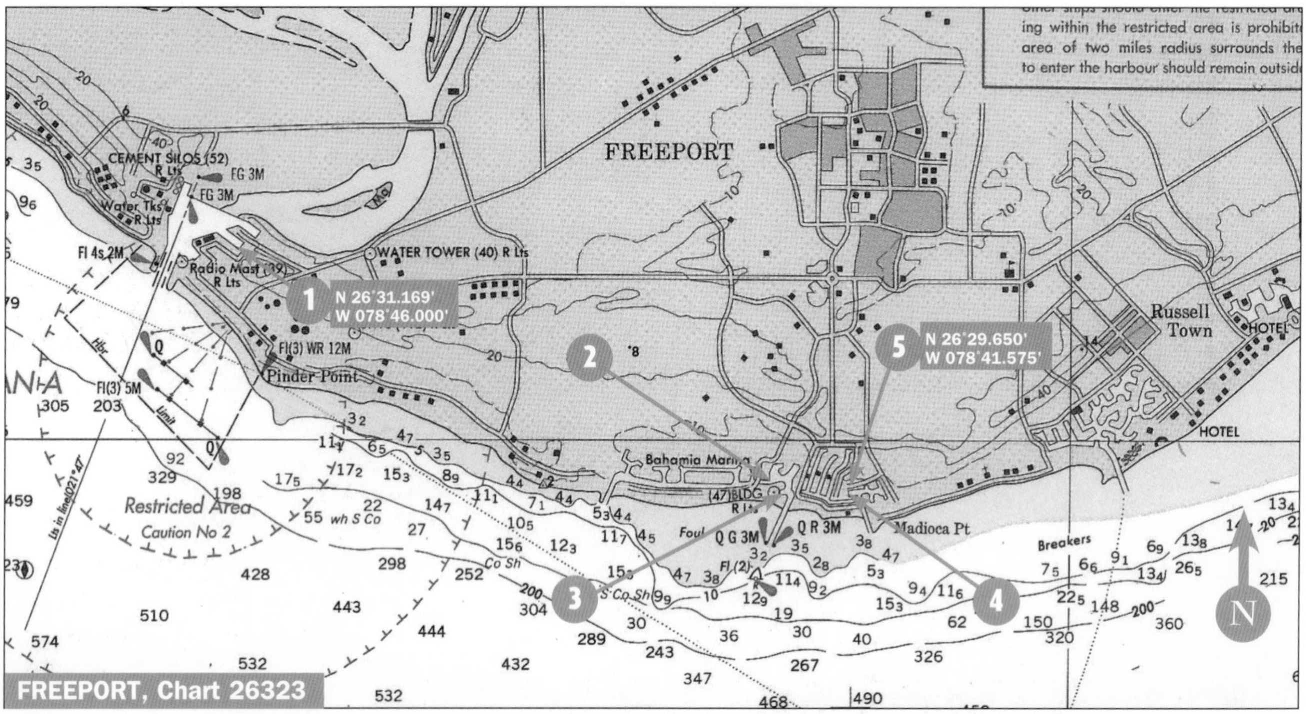

Snorkeling. Photo Courtesy of Peter Mitchell.

Freeport is the island's main city, and everyone and everything on the island has a Freeport mailing address. Downtown Freeport is where locals shop and conduct their business. Here are the doctors, lawyers, business professionals and true commerce on the island. "Downtown" Port Lucaya is the tourist epicenter. Its focus is shopping, restaurants, entertainment, hotel resorts, golf and gaming. Beaches and water sports extend along the front of the resorts and on southern shores of the island. For cruisers, the chief attraction in Port Lucaya is the two first-class marinas—the Grand Bahama Yacht Club and Port Lucaya Marina.

Clearing In—Your Options in Grand Bahama

Old Bahama Bay at West End, Freeport Harbour (for commercial vessels only) and Port Lucaya are the only entry ports in Grand Bahama. Vessels bound for Bahama Bay, Ocean Reef or Flamingo Bay must clear in at one of those locations before landing at their destination. In 2009, fines as high as $2,000 were being assessed for those failing to do so. Xanadu, Sunrise, Port Lucaya Marina and Grand Bahama Yacht Club can arrange Customs and Immigration procedures for their guests.

What's There? Grand Bahama

West End

Simply because of its position, we treated West End as the gateway to the Little Bahama Bank, the first landfall entry port en route to the Abacos. Because West End is virtually isolated from the Grand Bahama south coast and its domi-

Grand Bahama

PORT LUCAYA		Largest Vessel Accommodated	VHF Channel Monitored	Transient Berths / Total Berths	Approach / Dockside Depth (reported)	Floating Docks	Gas / Diesel	Groceries, Ice, Marine Supplies, Snacks	Repairs: Hull, Engine, Propeller	Lift (tonnage), Crane, Rail	1=110V, 2=220V, B=Both, Max Amps	Laundry, Pool, Showers	Pump-Out Station	Nearby: Grocery Store, Motel, Restaurant
		Dockage					Supplies				Services			
1. **Ocean Reef Resort &Yacht Club** (Internet Access, Wireless Internet Access)	**242-373-4662**	**120**	**16**	**54/54**	**8/8**	**F**		**GIMS**	**HEP**		**B/100**	**LPS**		**GMR**
2. **Port Lucaya Marina** (Internet Access)	**242-373-9090**	**190**	**16/17**	**106/106**	**8/12**	**F**	**GD**	**IS**			**B/100**	**LPS**	**P**	**GMR**
3. **Grand Bahama Yacht Club** (Wireless Internet Access)	**242-373-8888**	**175**	**16**	**150/150**	**6.5/10**		**GD**	**GIMS**			**B/200**	**LPS**	**P**	**GMR**
4. Flamingo Bay Hotel & Marina	242-373-5640	100	23	/16	12/12			GIS			B/60	LPS		GMR

Corresponding chart(s) not to be used for navigation. ☐ Internet Access (WiFi) Wireless Internet Access

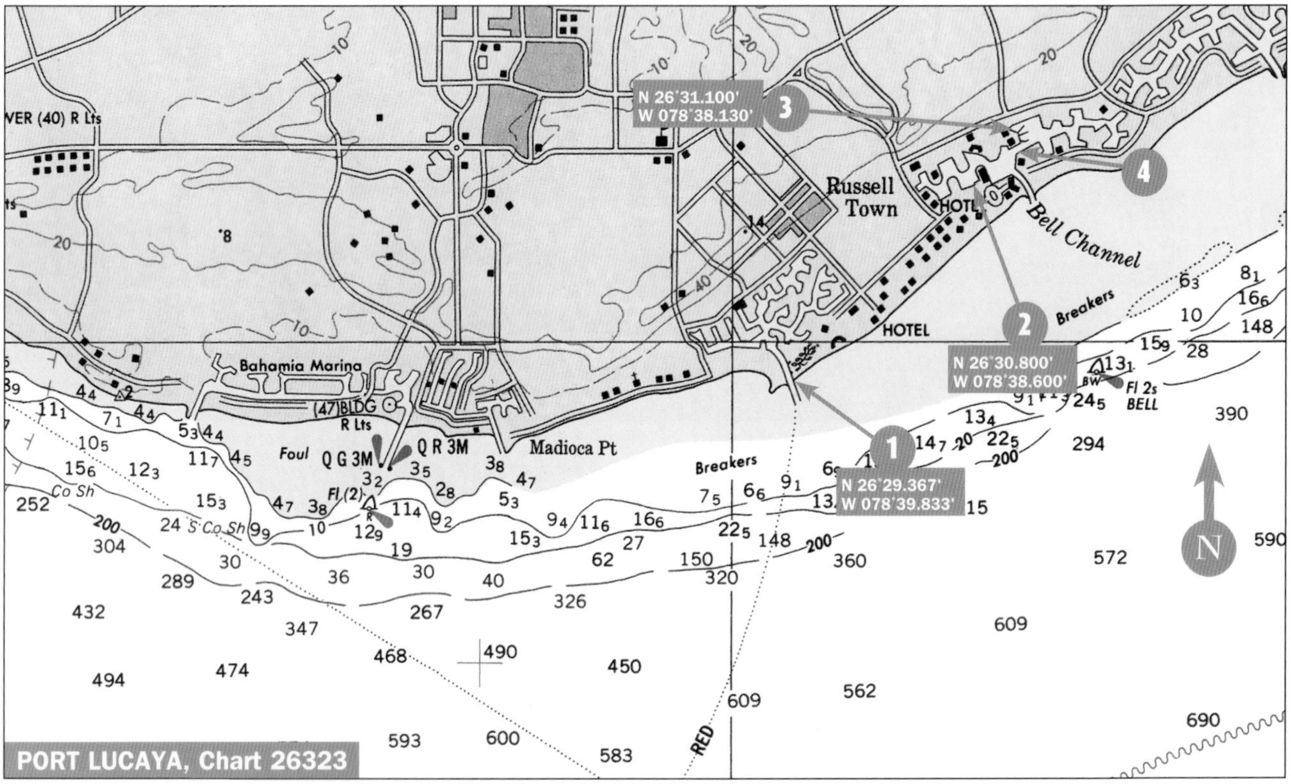

nating Freeport–Port Lucaya complex, we will not repeat our coverage. However, we do describe the route from Freeport to West End in this chapter, and we also detail the alternative access route to the Little Bahama Bank, the Grand Lucayan Waterway.

Freeport Harbour

Located about 20 nautical miles southeast from West End, Freeport Harbour is the most predominant feature on the island. Although the harbor hosts the largest of ocean-going vessels, the inshore coast between West End and Freeport is dangerous water; shoal-prone and reef-strewn. Keep well offshore, at least four nautical miles or so.

Freeport Harbour is a major commercial port and should be avoided by most cruisers unless needing the repair facilities of Bradford Grand Bahama Marine, used by those operating vessels in the megayacht category. Bradford offers the full-service facilities of their Florida parent company including a 150-ton Travelift, 1,200-ton floating dry dock, wet dockage to 315 feet and dry storage for vessels under 150 tons.

When approaching Freeport Harbour, an oil terminal with offshore tanker jetties and shoreside tanks and towers are obvious, as are the gantries of the container terminal. As an offshore fix, airplanes landing and departing Grand Bahama International Airport help you gauge where and how close you are to the harbor. The leading channel marks are there for super ships; they are large and unmistakable.

The Freeport–Port Lucaya Coast

Bell Channel, the entranceway to Port Lucaya, is nine nautical miles east of Freeport Harbour. Between these two significant channels, there are three smaller channels into interior basins. Their dredged entrances are maintained by visible

The Bell Channel and Port Lucaya, from the south. (Not to be used for navigation.) WATERWAY GUIDE PHOTOGRAPHY

jetties and breakwaters. It is imperative to stay in deep blue water, at least two nautical miles offshore, as you make your journey down the coast. When approaching these channels, do so with extreme care. These are shallow coastal waters and the inherent dangers are not to be taken lightly especially in strong easterly through westerly winds. A continuous reef parallels the coast speckled with bobbing buoys marking dive sites. Inside the reef line, the inshore waters shoal rapidly, hence the need for the jetties and breakwaters. And, even with these protectors, many keels bump bottom in the channels. Taken from west to east, the channels provide access to Xanadu Marina, Bahama Bay Marina, Sunrise Resort and Marina and the Ocean Reef Yacht Club.

Xanadu Resort Channel

Xanadu Resort Channel, the first of the smaller channels, is located about five nautical miles east of Freeport Harbour. An offshore landmark is a tower-like building with a white pyramid roof. The entry to Xanadu channel is straightforward. It carries 1.8-meter/6-foot depths at mean low water and is marked by a flashing white lighted buoy.

Bahama Bay Marina offers daily, weekly and monthly transient dockage on short docks with stern-to tie-ups. They also provide complimentary wireless Internet. There are plans to refurbish the Xanadu Resort. Its adjacent marina is in disrepair and not recommended for use.

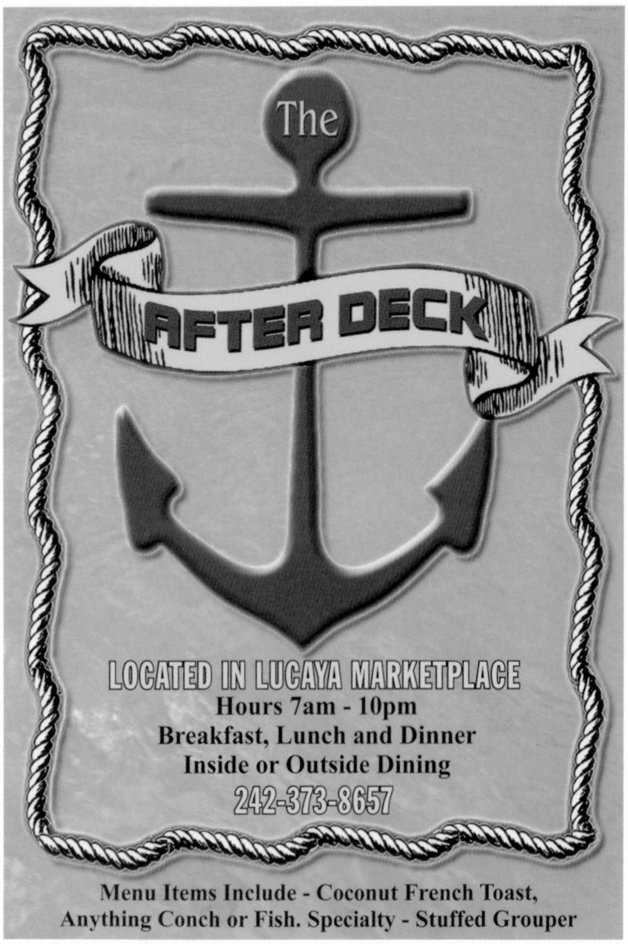

The
AFTER DECK
LOCATED IN LUCAYA MARKETPLACE
Hours 7am - 10pm
Breakfast, Lunch and Dinner
Inside or Outside Dining
242-373-8657
Menu Items Include - Coconut French Toast,
Anything Conch or Fish. Specialty - Stuffed Grouper

Sunrise Resort and Marina

The Sunrise Resort and Marina entry channel is 2.5 nautical miles east of Xanadu Resort's access channel. The channel carries 1.8-meter/6-foot depths at mean low water and is identifiable offshore by a long group of terraced apartments, all with balconies facing south. The Sunrise Resort and Marina offers floating docks to visiting cruisers, along with complimentary television and wireless Internet at the slips, a ship's chandlery and full resort amenities. For those in need of repairs above or below the waterline, Knowles Marine Yacht Services is located in the channel's terminal basin. See the Goin' Ashore section later in this chapter for details.

Ocean Reef Yacht Club

Located about half a nautical mile farther east from Sunrise, you will spot what appears to be a large French chateau, complete with turrets, looming on shore. This was the home of Hayward Cooper, who built his fortune from a humble start, running a small store on the road outside Freeport Harbour. You will see the breakwaters of the Ocean Reef Resort & Yacht Club marked with a red and a green lighted buoy. The channel has 1.8-meter/6-foot depths into the marina. Some shoaling was observed mid-channel late 2009, so mid-tide would be recommended. This gated community invites cruising visitors to tie up for a few nights or a few months to enjoy its beautiful surroundings and facilities. The Resort also serves as the operational base for BASRA. Arriving vessels will need to check-in with Customs and Immigration in West End or Port Lucaya prior to landing here as this is not a Port of Entry.

Port Lucaya (Bell Channel)

Bell Channel is a mile and a half east of Ocean Reef. Stay in blue water one to two nautical miles offshore until you turn to make the entry approach. This keeps you well clear of the inshore reef and dive sites, as well as the parasail and inshore watersports craft.

You will know you are approaching Bell Channel when you see the long stretch of white beach with two, half-moon ripraps in front of a large resort complex. The channel dissects the white beach, and substantial entrance jetties jut out to protect its depth. There are large, yellow cruise ships moorings approximately one-half mile west of Bell Channel's red-and-white striped entrance buoy. There are fixed, lighted markers to guide you into the channel that leads you to the interior bay. Once you are in the bay, Port Lucaya Marina lies to port, just around the Pelican Bay Hotel complex that projects into the lagoon. The Grand Bahama Yacht Club is to starboard. You will see the docks. Hail either marina on VHF Channel 16 for helpful guidance through the channel and into their facilities. Both marinas are on-call ports of entry.

Port Lucaya Marina and Grand Bahama Yacht Club

Port Lucaya Marina and Grand Bahama Yacht Club offer opulent amenities at each facility for guest vessels.

Port Lucaya Marina is a large complex with dockage for megayachts to pocket cruisers. Conventional docks and a fuel dock are both to port as you enter. If you want to partake in all of the action, this long-established marina is the place to be.

Not to be used for navigation.

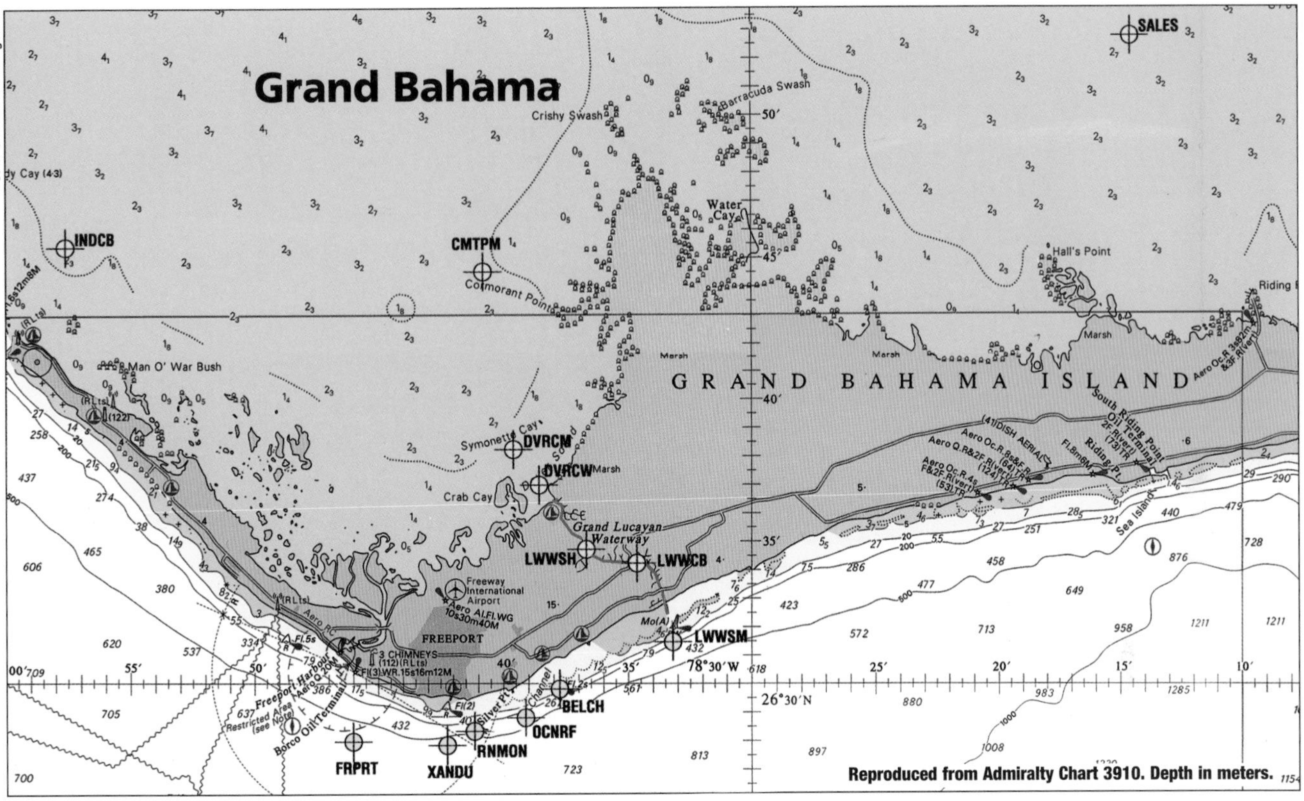

Reproduced from Admiralty Chart 3910. Depth in meters.

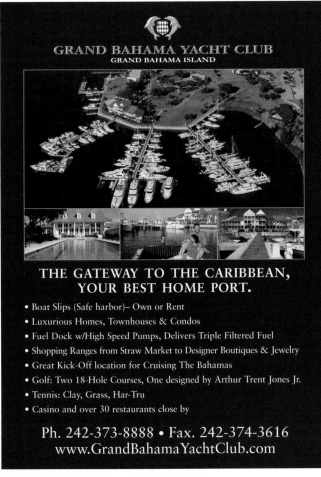

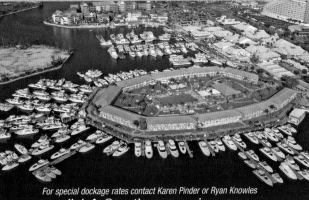

Grand Lucayan Waterway, South Entry. (Not to be used for navigation.) WATERWAY GUIDE PHOTOGRAPHY

Half of the marina's slips are right on the Port Lucaya Marketplace waterfront. From there, you can stroll to the bars, restaurants and shops in the area. There is a wide range of entertainment, right at your gangplank. Snorkeling trips, beach parties, scuba diving and semi-submarine reef tours beckon the adventurous. If duty-free shopping is your gig, a myriad of stores offer everything from the finest cognac to custom jewelry. The other half of the marina's docks circle the peaceful Sea Garden wing of their hotel. The Sea Garden dockage offers easy access to a swimming pool and jetted spa, its adjacent showers and restrooms and a restaurant and al fresco bar.

If you prefer an altogether quieter atmosphere, choose the Grand Bahama Yacht Club. It lies to starboard after you have traversed Bell Channel. This marina is surrounded by a village of multi-hued houses, creating a remarkably Mediterranean flair and a feeling far removed from the East Coast of the United States or the Bahamas. The lush surroundings are particularly serene, and the marina facilities are first class. Visiting marina guests can enjoy a dip in one of two swimming pools, partake

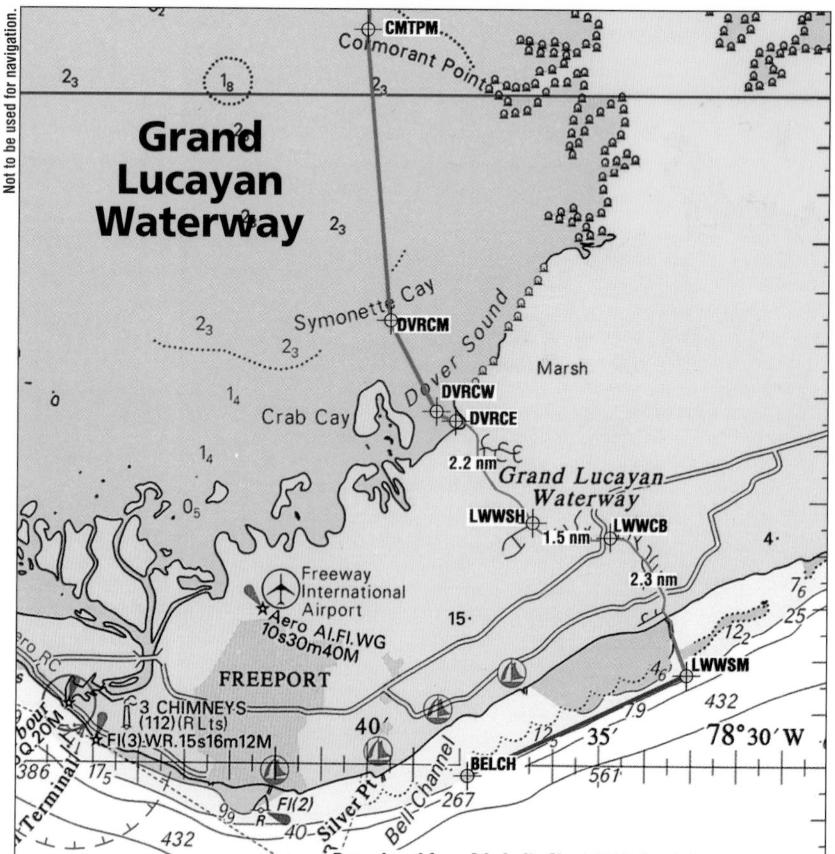

Grand Lucayan Waterway, from the south. (Not to be used for navigation.) WATERWAY GUIDE PHOTOGRAPHY

of libations and snacks at the poolside bar or practice their putts at the Lucayan Golf Club. Complimentary transportation runs between the dockmaster's office to the wonderful Sabor Restaurant at the Pelican Bay Hotel and the Port Lucaya Marketplace.

Flaming Bay Hotel and Marina at Taino Beach Resort features a complete watersports center on-site.

Freeport Marine Coastal and Offshore Weather Service

The Freeport Weather Department issues weather reports at 6 a.m. daily. All the Grand Bahama marinas make copies of these valuable reports to distribute to yachtsmen each morning. Make sure to avail yourself of these reports, and thank them for the service. Weather reports of this quality are difficult to come by in other parts of the Bahamas.

The Grand Lucayan Waterway

If you are heading for the Abacos from the southeast coast of Florida, the Grand Lucayan Waterway, almost five miles east of the Bell Channel, may offer a dandy little shortcut to the Little Bahama Bank. Unfortunately, vessel size, draft and height from the waterline limit its use. The Waterway was the largest engineering feat ever attempted in the Bahamas. This 1960s-era dream of opening the heartland of Grand Bahama to development, as well as providing a direct route between Florida and the Abacos, cost $26 million. The Waterway was envisaged as the Venice of Grand Bahama, or at least a good imitation of Venice, FL. It was supposed to be a hinterland of interconnecting canals and a beatific boating lifestyle. Perhaps it was just poor timing or lousy marketing, but the development failed to achieve takeoff speed. As a canal system, despite some shoaling and bank deterioration, it perseveres.

The southern sector of the Grand Lucayan Waterway is not so much a canal as the winding, 250-foot-wide, walled main artery of a canal system. It runs mostly north with a lean to the west. It has many narrower side basins, turning areas and secondary, branching canals.

The northern sector is less engineered. It is more ditch-like with raw banks, and narrows significantly in some places. Concrete walls appear again, briefly, in its final northern section. You may find fellow travelers partaking of the quiet, protected anchorages here, but often the Grand Lucayan Waterway, although it is used, appears to be deserted. There are few signs of life within its waters and even less on its banks. The area remains a wonderful harborage when caught in an unexpected blow while transiting between Great Sale and West End.

A few new homes are being built in the area south of the 40 year old Casuarina Bridge. Building lots remain available, as most are the result of descendants of the original foreign speculative land owners discovering the land holding papers and making a decision to sell the property.

In July 2009, plans were announced to construct a four lane concrete bridge. The bridge will begin at the intersection of Grand Bahama Highway and Fortune Bay Drive and

Casuarina Bridge. (Not to be used for navigation.) WATERWAY GUIDE PHOTOGRAPHY

will span the channel opening with a 30-foot fixed vertical height. The bridge is expected to spurn rapid development of the housing allotments that line the channels along the Waterway. Like so much of the ongoing development in the Bahamas, only time will tell.

To Take the Waterway or Not?

The Grand Lucayan Waterway is not a difficult route. Before attempting passage, here are the facts to consider:

- Vertical Clearance. About one-third of the way up the canal, one encounters the Casuarina Bridge. It has an 8-meter/27-foot clearance at high water, and the shortsighted planners built it fixed. There are no clearance gauges on its approach pilings. There is a new bridge planned for construction nearer the Waterway's opening. It will have a 30-foot fixed clearance. Authorities investigated building a 65-foot high bridge here, but it was not feasible.
- Draft. Expect 1.5-meter/5-foot depths at mean low water throughout the canal. You may enjoy depths of 2.4 to 3 meters/8 to 10 feet depending upon the wind and tidal state. The channel leading into Dover Sound is critical. At mean low water, you should not expect depths of more than 1.2 meters/4 feet.
- Timing. There is a tidal difference of two hours between the south end and the north end of the Waterway. A further complicating factor is that strong tidal sets affect the choke points in the Waterway—essentially Casuarina Bridge and the first spoil narrows north of the bridge. This suggests that it is wise to avoid a transit of these points in hours three and four after high or low water. Fine in theory, but because the Waterway is a complex water basin linking two entirely different sea areas, it is not quite that predictable. Consequently, it is the tidal state in Dover Sound that is the critical factor. We estimate that Port Lucaya is 30 minutes after Nassau, and Dover Sound is 2 hours 30 minutes after Nassau.

How long will it take you to transit the Waterway at a maximum speed limit of 5 knots? A little over one hour. Whichever way you are traveling, it is going to work out to about half the time it would take to get to West End from Port Lucaya, if you decided to go around that way. On the Little Bahama Bank, the West End to Mangrove Cay and the Dover Channel to Mangrove Cay legs, are just about equal in length—around 20 nautical miles. Is it worth taking the Waterway? It depends entirely on where you came from, where you are heading and whether your boat can transit the canal. We cover the navigation side of the Grand Lucayan Waterway, which you should read before setting out, under Pilotage.

Pilotage. Talking Captain to Captain

West End to Freeport

Keep well offshore, in deep water all the way. Inshore, there are reefs and the island shelf shoals considerably, well off the beach line. Freeport Harbour necessitates a prudent distancing because of its offshore oil jetties and its commercial traffic, largely container ships and cruise ships, none of which has the ability to maneuver in the convergence zone. As the set along this coast is generally onshore, we recommend standing well off (at least four nautical miles) at night and particularly under sail.

Approaches to Freeport Harbour

There is a prominent radio mast to the west of the oil terminal, and the entry to the harbor is just west of the oil tanker jetties. The sea approach around the jetties is a restricted area. You should not transit it, nor anchor there. Don't even try to enter Freeport Harbour without first contacting the Port

Xanadu Entry Channel. (Not to be used for navigation.) WATERWAY GUIDE PHOTOGRAPHY

Authority. Be aware that your charts may be out of date. If you have to enter Freeport Harbour at night, your leading lights are two vertical, white pipe lights both visible out to five nautical miles. Freeport Harbour is changing shape day by day, but the approach (apart from the additional guidance of those two vertical pipe lights) has not changed.

Freeport Harbour to Port Lucaya

Keep well off the reef line running the nine miles from West End to Freeport Harbour. Here you are going around the southern "hump" of Great Bahama Island, so unless you plan to go well offshore, you can't play it as a straight shot. Far better to parallel the reef in a continual gentle curve, keeping sufficiently far out to pass outside any dive boats or their mooring buoys along the drop-off.

Bell Channel

If you are approaching from the west, just short of the Bell Channel, there are four, yellow cruise ship mooring buoys in the area of N 26° 29.600'/W 078° 38.200' that are easily spotted. The Bell Channel Marker Buoy, your primary landfall mark, is at N 26° 29.850'/W 078° 37.720'. Approaching from the east there is a submerged buoy at N 26° 29.930'/ W 078° 37.290'. But if you take the channel marker as your approach point, you should be well clear of this hazard. The waypoint BELCH lies a bit in shore from the channel marker.

From the channel buoy, or the waypoint, the Bell Channel entry stakes and the entry channel should be obvious on a heading of 335/155 degrees true. A shoal area (1.5 meters/5 feet deep at mean low water) lies to port off the west entry breakwater. Channel depth is 1.9 meters/6.5 feet at mean low water.

Grand Lucayan Waterway Southern Approaches

From the Bell Channel entry buoy, head east running parallel to the coast a safe 1.5 nautical miles offshore for 4.4 nautical miles. Stay in the blue water well outside the line of white dive boat mooring buoys marking the edge of the island shelf.

The Lucayan Waterway's south-channel entrance buoy is red and white striped with a red nose on top like a circus clown's and a white light. This is waypoint LWWSM. At this point, you can see the breakwaters clearly. If you see Petersons Cay off your port bow, a tiny islet with four wind-blown trees, you have missed the entrance buoy. You have gone too far. Turn back and get your bearings.

Grand Lucayan Waterway Northern Approaches

See Chapter 3, The Little Bahama Bank.

The Grand Lucayan Waterway from South to North

Once inside the breakwaters, the southern section of the Grand Lucayan Waterway is straightforward. If the tide is right, you will have 4.2-meter/14-foot depths, and 2.4 to 3 meters/8 to 10 feet of depth inside later. A warning sign, which you may not be able to read, tells you to stay at least 20 feet off the sides of the Waterway and to contact BASRA or the police on Channel 16 if you are in trouble. You don't need a map or a chart of the Grand Lucayan Waterway. Despite its many side alleys, you won't get lost.

The Southern Entry Breakwater to Spoil Hill Narrows (3.9 nautical miles)

You will reach the Casuarina Bridge 2.39 nautical miles after entering the south section of the canal. This fixed bridge has a fixed 27-foot clearance above the water at high tide. There are no clearance gauges on its supports to tell you what is really

Spoil Hill Narrows. Site of the future bridge. (Not to be used for navigation.) WATERWAY GUIDE PHOTOGRAPHY

there at the time of your arrival. Expect to feel an appreciable tidal flow. Just keep motoring and don't dawdle.

The Waterway is much the same after Casuarina Bridge as it was before. After 1.51 nautical miles, two conical spoil hills flank the narrow cut (This is the site of the future bridge.) You will be able to pass between them. The Waterway now changes character. Although no real problems lie ahead, be more alert at the helm in the northern part than perhaps the southern section required.

Spoil Hill Narrows to Dover Sound (2.83 nautical miles)

If there is a tidal set, you will really feel it at the Spoil Hill Narrows. You have no room to maneuver or to pass oncoming traffic. The width of the Waterway is reduced briefly to 20 feet or less, as you pass between the Spoil Hills.

- At this point, the concrete embankments disappear, and the main course of the Grand Lucayan Waterway narrows to 100 feet or less and becomes ditch-like in character. Stay in the center. The embankment returns 1.28 nautical miles after passing between the two spoil hills. When you reach the embankment, favor the wall side. Rocks, undredged areas and hidden ledges are in the Waterway itself on the port side.
- In this stretch, on the port side, a wetland wilderness opens up to the west with signs of earlier human activity—a sand mound from some excavation, a radio mast—but none of this must take your eye off the canal. To starboard, the scrub area reveals further mounds of spoil. The concrete walls open into a dead-end basin. And then, on the port side, as the west bank falls away completely, you will come level with the first of two concrete posts.
- You are close to gaining access to the Little Bahama Bank. There are two more concrete posts that must be left to port, and then you are at the end of the Grand Lucayan Waterway and the beginning of a dredged channel leading out onto the Little Bahama Bank. Your entry point, marked by two lighted posts—green to starboard and red to port, when traveling from the south—is ahead of you. You will have traveled 2.25 nautical miles since passing between the two spoil hills and have another 0.58 nautical mile to go before before arriving at the open water of the bank.

Dover Sound. Getting Out on the Little Bahama Bank

The Dover Channel, which leads out onto the Little Bahama Bank, requires a 90-degree turn to port as you exit the Lucayan Waterway. The half-mile-long Dover Channel runs close to east to west (290/110 degrees true). It should be marked by seven pairs of marker poles with the first pair at each end bearing lights—red right returning or incoming from the west. The weather is tough on these aids to navigation, and some of the markers may not be there.

The Dover Channel is narrow and open to wind from the north. It is also shallow (as little as 1.8 meters/6 feet at best and maybe 1.2 meters/4 feet at worst). You can't hammer through it at speed to counter a side wind, for you may dig your stern in too deeply and run yourself aground. Go for the best compromise speed if you have a side wind, but keep moving. You will notice there is a prominent sandy spoil ledge on the south side of the channel. What is the total travel distance you have traveled through the Waterway when you reach the end of the Dover Channel? From the south entry buoy, 7.41 nautical miles. From the south breakwater, 6.73 nautical miles.

From the Dover Channel exit markers, head 324/144 degrees true for 1.8 nautical miles to the Dover Channel approach mark (waypoint DVRCM), which, again, may or may not be there. At this point, you are ready to continue on to Mangrove Cay.

Going On to Mangrove Cay

See Chapter 3, The Little Bahama Bank. Reverse the route, and use the reciprocal headings.

Moving On to the Central Cruising Grounds

Use Port Lucaya and the Bell Channel (BELCH) as your exit waypoint for the Northern Berry Islands, and run 54.5 nautical miles on a course of 138/318 degrees true for Little Stirrup Cay (LSTRP). It is a straightforward bluewater passage across the Northwest Providence Channel.

If you want to get to Chub Cay in the southern Berry Islands or go straight to Nassau, an alternative route from Port Lucaya will save you going east around the Berry Islands. Drop south from BELCH on 170/350 degrees true heading for the Russell Light on the Great Bahama Bank. About one mile north of the light, having traveled about 61 nautical miles, turn to the Northwest Channel Light waypoint (NWCHL) (Note that the Northwest Channel Light itself may or may not be on station, so use the waypoint as a point of reference only.) That will give you about 15 nautical miles to run on a course around 093/273 degrees true. From there, Chub Cay is 15 nautical miles and Nassau 48 nautical miles. See Chapter 9, The Great Bahama Bank.

This route cuts your transit of the Northwest Providence Channel down to 38 nautical miles. The drawback is that shoaling on the Great Bahama Bank, particularly along the projected course line you might take, is fluid. You might find yourself in trouble, and running at cruise speed might be placing too great a trust in just hoping that you will have the depth you need.

We will touch on a third route. Long ago, the Northwest Channel was said to run across the Great Bahama Bank along the line projected, albeit farther to the east. We speculate that the area around the Northwest Channel Light and the approximate run of the old Northwest Channel is difficult due to both changing shoals and reef. We rank it in the exploration category. Even the charts naming this channel describe it as "very intricate."

Finally, while we are touching on Great Bahama Bank navigation, do not rely on seeing the navigation marks shown on the charts. More than once, and often for long periods, these marks have been missing. ■

WATERWAY GUIDE is always open to your observations from the helm. E-mail your comments on any navigation information in the guide to: editor@waterwayguide.com.

Grand Bahama Waypoints

West End	WESTW (B2)	26°42.00N / 79°01.50W
Harbour Hotel Marina Dock	HARBH	26°41.36N / 78°57.96W
Freeport	FRPRT	26°29.72N / 78°47.42W
Xanadu	XANDU (B3)	26°28.50N / 78°42.50W
Sunrise Resort	SNRSR	26°28.66N / 78°41.31W
Ocean Reef	OCNRF	26°29.09N / 78°39.27W
Bell Channel	BELCH	26°29.94N / 78°37.79W
Lucayan Waterway S Mark	LWWSM	26°31.79N / 78°33.23W
Casuarina Bridge	LWWCB	26°34.36N / 78°34.86W
Spoil Hill Narrows	LWWSH	26°34.82N / 78°36.50W
Dover Channel Outer Mark	DVRCM	26°38.27N / 78°39.64W
Dover Channel West	DVRCW	26°36.80N / 78°38.46W
Dover Channel East	DVRCE	26°36.62N / 78°37.90W

Our position format is latitude and longitude in degrees and minutes (hddd°mm.mm). Waypoints in RED are NOT for autopilot navigation. Codes in parenthesis are Wavey Line waypoints marked on the charts. If you have programmed waypoints we listed in a previous edition of this guide, check carefully to ensure the coordinates you have recorded match the list. If a waypoint is no longer on our list we may have changed its code or deleted it.

Blue Skiff. Photo Courtesy of Peter Mitchell.

GOIN' ASHORE:

FREEPORT & PORT LUCAYA

airport • bank • church • customs & immigration • fuel • groceries • marinas • marine services • medical • police • post office • propane • restaurant • telephone • water

The wide, tree-lined boulevards of Grand Bahama, with elegant new homes and upscale shopping in Freeport and Port Lucaya, welcome you to an attractive, independent and prosperous 530-square-mile island. The older, high-rise hotels in Port Lucaya have given way to *Our Lucaya Reef Village* with the upscale *Raddison* and the family oriented *The Reef* resorts along the beach, every possible resort amenity, including golf courses, superb restaurants, infinity pools and a casino. The commercial harbor has a state-of-the-art container port and vastly improved cruise ship facilities, as well as a huge marine repair yard. Grand Bahama is a sophisticated and well-organized island for visiting boats, especially for those with children on board, with interesting places to visit and things to do on shore, together with excellent beaches, diving and watersports. Freeport and Port Lucaya are ports of entry, with Customs on call at the marinas.

MARINAS

Marinas are listed west to east.

XANADU BEACH RESORT AND MARINA
Tel: 242-352-6783, ext 1333 • Fax: 242-352-5799 • VHF 16 •
info@xanadubeachhotel.com

About fifteen minutes west of Freeport, this older marina is sadly in need of updating. The hotel is open, but with no restaurant. It is sparsely inhabited and receiving mixed reviews. The marina facilities are in disrepair and there are no amenities. You may want to call ahead. Plans were being discussed to outsource the marina operations, however as of this writing nothing has changed. If you decide to land there, Customs and Immigration can be called.

BAHAMA BAY MARINA
TEL: 242-351-5063 • FAX: 242-351-5064
info@bahamiaservice.com • www.bahamiaservice.com

Slips 14. **Max LOA** 55 ft. **MLW at Dock** 10 ft. **Dockage** $45/day power included; $175/week power included; $210/month plus power; **Facilities & Services** 100 amps; water; laundry, showers, beach and restaurant. Close to Golf. **Credit Cards** accepted.

SUNRISE RESORT AND MARINA
Tel: 800-932-4959 • Fax: 242-352-6835 • VHF 16
tashar@sunriseresortandmarina.com
www.sunriseresortandmarina.com

Slips 70. **Max LOA** 100 ft. **MLW at Dock** 10 ft. **Dockage** $1 per foot/day; $15 per foot/month; 30 ft. minimum **Fuel** Diesel and gasoline. **Facilities & Services** Floating docks, metered power 100 amps; water $7/day; laundry, showers, beach and fresh water pool, pump-out, wireless Internet; repair yard with 40-ton lift, 24-hour security. **Restaurants** *Mahi-Mahi Seafood Restaurant,* Poolside Sports Bar and cafe. **Accommodations** 31 air-conditioned/heated rooms equipped with cable TV, refrigerator, coffee machine, ironing board. One (1) bedroom suite, beautifully furnished, air-conditioned/heated; with all amenities. **Credit Cards** Visa, MasterCard and AMEX. Port of entry - Customs and Immigration clearance.

OCEAN REEF RESORT & YACHT CLUB
TEL: 242-373-4662 • FAX: 242-373-8261 • VHF 16
www.oryc.com • orycguestservice@coralwave.com

Customs and Immigration must be cleared before arriving as this is not considered a port of entry.

Slips 54 **Max LOA** 120 ft. **MLW at Dock** 8 ft. **Dockage** Up to 50', $45/day; 50'-65'$55/day; over 65', $65/day; monthly rates; **Facilities & Services** Power $0.50 kWh. On-site car and bicycle

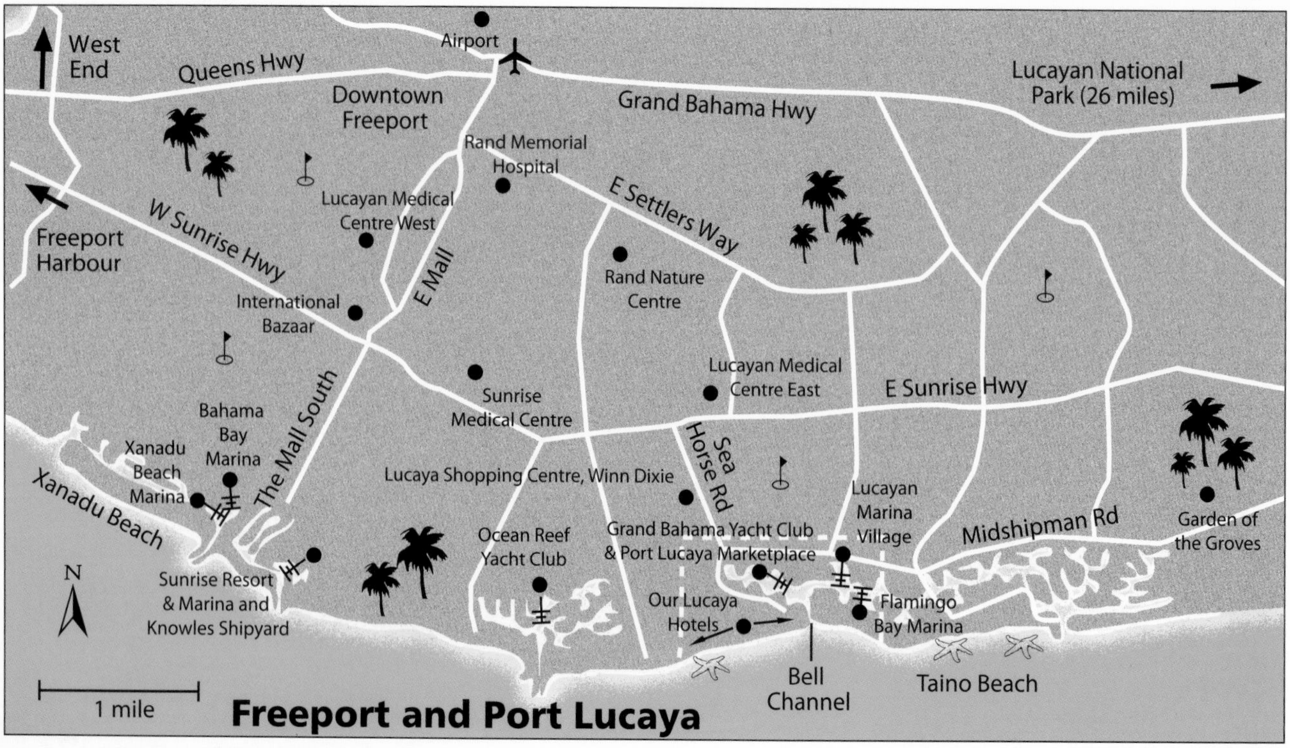

rental, laundry, free wireless Internet, bar & restaurant, pools, free shuttle to beach and grocery store, free water and cable, shower facilities, tennis court, room accommodations, on-site dive shop. **Restaurants** *Groupers Bar & Grill.* Groupers serves breakfast, lunch and dinner in a leisure outdoor setting. **Accommodations** Range from efficiencies to three-bedroom townhouses. Customs and Immigration must be cleared before arriving as this is not considered a port of entry.

CLUB NAUTICA RESORT AND MARINA
Tel: 242-373-1724 • www.clubnautica.com
This marina belongs to the owners of the pink condominiums on the east bank of the channel as you approach the Bell Channel to come in to the marinas in Port Lucaya.

PORT LUCAYA MARINA
Tel: 242-373-9090 • Fax: 242-373-5884 • VHF 16 •
info@portlucayamarina.com • www.portlucaya.com
To port after entering the Bell Channel, the long-established and well-run *Port Lucaya Marina* is the busiest of all the marinas in Freeport and Port Lucaya, with a wide range of activities and facilities. The Central wing is alongside the *Port Lucaya Marketplace* with its bars, shops, restaurants, live music and dancing. For quieter slips, ask for the Sea Garden Wing, which wraps around the *Port Lucaya Resort Hotel.* **Customs and Immigration** in the marina; this is a port of entry.
Slips 106. **Max LOA** 190 ft. **MLW** 12 ft. in marina pool. The Bell Channel carries 6.5 ft. at low water. **Dockage** $2.40 per ft. per day on the T-head or alongside. Long-term dockage rates, with complimentary weekly washdown. **Fuel** Diesel and gasoline, open 7 a.m. to midnight with bait, oils, detergents, pump out. **Facilities & Services** Power $0.25 per kWh for 30A, 50A, 100A and 200A. Water $5 per day charged to all vessels berthed in the marina; showers by the hotel swimming pool and adjacent to the marina office; telephone $5 hookup charge; CATV $2 daily for 53-channel fiber-optic reception. Domestic cleaning, laundry service, babysitting, catering, long-term boat checks and maintenance. *UPS* and *FedEx* delivery through the marina office. Yacht brokerage. Propane refills can be arranged. Fishing tournaments, rendezvous, regattas and special events throughout the year. Jitneys from Sea Horse Road run to Freeport and grocery stores for $1. Courtesy transport to *Freeport International Airport*; to local grocery store at 10 a.m. and 3 p.m. weekdays, Sundays at 9 a.m. **Restaurants** *Tradewinds Cafe at Port Lucaya Resort* • 242-373-6618 • Breakfast and dinner buffets daily. Pool Bar open daily 10 a.m. to 6 p.m. International restaurants in the *Marketplace*; *the Reef Village* at *Our Lucaya* across the street has 14 restaurants and bars to choose from. Live entertainment every evening in Count Basie Square. *Treasure Bay* across the street. **Accommodations** *Port Lucaya Resort and Yacht Club* • 242-373-6618 • vacation@batelnet.bs • Rooms from $100; discount for marina guests. **Credit Cards** All major credit cards, except Diners and Discover.

GRAND BAHAMA YACHT CLUB
Tel: 242-373-8888 • Fax: 242-374-3616
info@grandbahamayc.com • www.grandbahamayachtclub.com
To starboard after you enter through the Bell Channel, *Grand Bahama Yacht Club* is a state-of-the-art marina with excellent facilities and a wonderfully helpful staff. The full-service, deep-water marina offers superior facilities in a classic setting of turn-of-the-century brick and coral walkways, mature shade trees and picturesque piers. *Grand Bahama Yacht Club* offers everything a yachtsman could wish for in an island locale. **Customs and Immigration** are on call; this is a port of entry.
Slips 150. **Max LOA** 175 ft. **MLW at Dock** 10 ft.; 6.5 ft. in the Bell Channel at low water. **Transient dockage** $1.70 per ft. per day April–September with a $0.25 per ft. per day surcharge over U.S. holidays. **Fuel** Diesel and gasoline; open 7 a.m. to 8 p.m. daily. **Facilities & Services** Power $0.45/ kWh, from 30A to 200A; water $5 per day. Excellent clean showers and handicap-accessible toilets; laundry; telephones by the showers. Free telephone and TV hookups (cable TV $2/day). WiFi. Barbecues around the marina, ice, propane same-day refill on weekdays. Fax $4 to send. Two-level pool with Olympic-length lap area and separate children's pool. Bonefishing with guides; fish-cleaning table on the fuel dock. Complimentary ferry runs between 8 a.m. and midnight to *Port Lucaya Marketplace* and *the Pelican Bay Hotel.* Marine repair, services and pump out can be arranged through the dockmaster. **Restaurant and Bar** *Pool Bar & Grill* serves breakfast, lunch, snacks and cocktails poolside. Enjoy an elegant dinner at

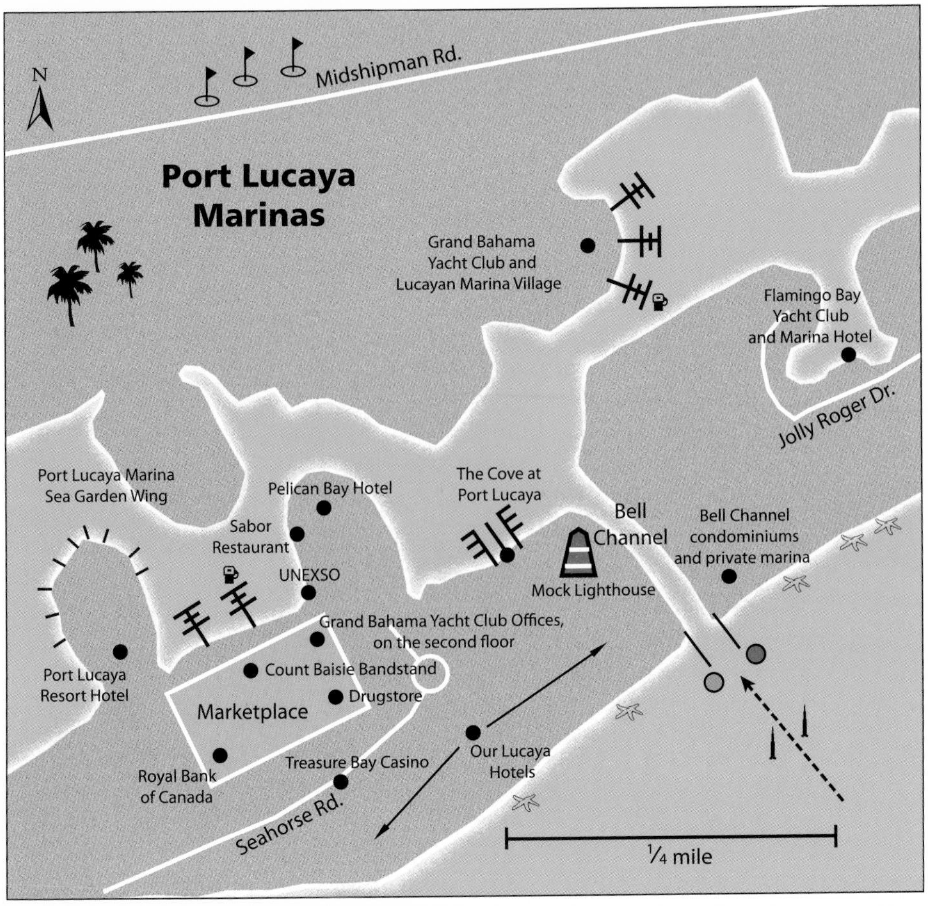

Sabor on the waterfront by the *Pelican Bay Hotel* or at one of the many restaurants in Port Lucaya Marketplace. This gated community has 24-hour security. **Credit Cards** Visa, MasterCard and AMEX. **Dockmaster** Thomas Lockhart.

FLAMINGO BAY HOTEL & MARINA
TEL: 242-373-5640 • FAX: 242-373-4421 • info@flamingobayhotel.com • www.tainobeach.com
Slips 16. **Max LOA** 100ft. **MLW at Dock** 12ft. **Dockage** $1.25/ft/day plus power & water **Facilities & Services** Metered power, water and cable. Lucaya Watersports, Grand Bahama's most complete watersports center, is located right on-site. All boat tours depart from the Flamingo Bay Marina at Taino Beach. **Accommodations** Standard features include king size beds in single occupancy rooms and two full size beds in double occupancy rooms. All rooms have full service kitchenettes, cable televisions, telephones, hair dryers and ironing boards.

PORT DIRECTORY

Airport Taxis charge around $25 for two people from Port Lucaya to the airport.
Airlines *Air Canada* • 888-247-2262, *American Eagle* • 800-433-7300, *Bahamasair* • 242-352-8341, *Continental Connection* • 242-352-6447, *Delta/Comair* • 800-221-1212 , *US Airways* • 800-622-1015, *Major's Air Flies* to Abaco and Bimini, *Spirit Airlines* 800-772-7117.
ATMs *Scotiabank* at *Our Lucaya* and at *Freeport Airport*, the two at the *Treasure Bay Casino* give U.S. dollars, at *Royal Bank of Canada* in *Port Lucaya Market Place* and the *First Caribbean Banks*, give Bahamian dollars.

MARINE SERVICES

Adnil Marine Supplies & Services • 242-352-1856 • Fax: 242-351-6282 • Full-service marine store and fiber glass and repair work, open daily 8 to 5, closed Sundays. On Wimpole Street, behind Dolly Madison.
Bradford Marine Bahamas • 242-352-7711 • Fax: 242-352-7695 • info@bradfordmarinebahamas.com • www.bradfordmarinebahamas.com • Full-service yacht and ship repair facility within Freeport Commercial Harbour, for vessels up to 400 ft., 150-ton travel lift and a 1,000-ft. floating dock for repairs on vessels. 35-ft. depth approach and easy access; no overhead restrictions. General Manager Dan Romence. Call Freeport Harbour Control on VHF 16 before entering the commercial harbor.
OBS Marine • 242-352-9246 • Evinrude, Mercury dealers. Full service engine repair, service and supplies. 8:30 a.m. to 5 p.m. Monday through Friday, 9 a.m. to 12 p.m. Saturday.
Cash Marine Supply Center • 242-352-9154
Knowles Marine Yacht Services • 242-351-2769 (and fax) • cell 242-359-4222 • VHF 16 • knowles_marine@hotmail.com • Charlton Knowles has a 40-ton travel lift, taking boats up to 18-ft. beam on site, and offers boat repairs, rebuilds on gas and diesel engines, prop and shaft repair, Micron 44 paints, at *Sunrise Resort & Marina.* Yard open weekdays 8 to 5, on call 24 hrs. Yard Manager Aron Long Cell 242-375-1610.

Banks Banks are open 9:30 to 3 weekdays; to 4:30 p.m. Friday in downtown Freeport. *Royal Bank of Canada* • 242-352-6631 • in *Port Lucaya Marketplace* and *Western Union* at *British American Bank* • 242-352-6676 • on *The Mall downtown*.
Buses *Jitneys* around/between Freeport and Port Lucaya charge $1.
Car Rentals *Bahama Buggies* 242-352-8750. *Brad's Car Rental* 242-352-7930. *Island Jeep & Car Rentals* 242-373-4001.
Casinos *Treasure Bay* • 242-373-1333 • With 400 slot machines, high-limit table games and slots and restaurants. Open daily 10 a.m. to 2 a.m. All you can eat Sunday buffet at their Cove restaurant 11:00 a.m. to 4:00 p.m. (Formerly Isle of Capri)
Churches There are 16 churches in the Freeport area. See "*What To Do in Freeport*" for locations and outside the churches for times of services.
Customs • 242-352-5827 • **Immigration** • 242-352-5454
Consulates and Embassies In Nassau. *American Embassy* • 242-352-7256, *British High Commission* • 242-325-7471/7472/7473, *Canadian Consulate* • 242-393-2123/2124.

EMERGENCIES

Ambulance • 242-352-2689
Dentist *Bain Dental Office* • 242-352-8492
Freeport Dental Center • 242-352-4552
Emergency Medical Services • 242-352-2689
Emergency Pager • 242-352-6222, ext 8339
Fire • 242-352-8888
Hospital *Rand Memorial Hospital* • 242-352-6735/5101 • 24-hour emergency room.
Hyperbaric Chamber *Lyford Cay Hospital* in Nassau • 242-362-4025
Marine • VHF 16 "BASRA Grand Bahama" • 242-352-2628 or 911 (days)
Police • 911 • 242-352-2628
Search and Rescue • (BASRA) Bahamas Sea Air Rescue Association • 242-325-8864 9 a.m. to 5 p.m. Seven days a week • Emergencies only • 24 hour answering service 242-322-3877 or VHF Channel 16 and 2182 SSB.
Veterinarians *Caribbean Veterinary Health and Healing Centre* • 242-351-6441 • In emergency.
Freeport Animal Care • 242-352-6521 • In emergency.

Ferries *Pinder's* • 242-353-3093 • McLeans Town to Crown Haven, North Abaco, leaves at 8:30 a.m. and 4:30 p.m., $60 one way.
Hotels Freeport and Port Lucaya are changing and improving so fast that we suggest you look in the current edition of *What To Do* for accommodations. All the marinas have good hotels that offer discounts for marina guests.
Liquor Stores in *Port Lucaya Marketplace*, *International Bazaar*, *Lucaya Shopping Centre* and downtown Freeport.
Pharmacy *Oasis* in *Port Lucaya Marketplace* • 242-373-8413, *Chappies Pharmacy* • 242-374-4720.
Post Office • 242-352-9371 • Explorer's Way, Freeport. Stamps from *Crown Drugs* and *Oasis* in the *Port Lucaya Marketplace*.
Provisions *City Market* • 242-373-5500 • *Lucaya Shopping Centre*, Sea Horse Road, closest to Port Lucaya. *City Market* branches in *Freeport Shopping Centre*, Downtown • 242-352-7901 and *Harbour West at Eight Mile Rock* • 242-348-3644. All stores open 7:30 a.m. to 9 p.m. weekdays, 7 a.m. to 10 a.m. Sundays. *Cost Right* and *Solomon's* in *Freeport*. Specialty Foods *Thompson's Family Market*. *Coral Road*. Specialty store with on-site bakery, fresh fruit, vegetables and a butcher serving custom meats and deli foods. Well-stocked wines. In downtown Freeport, the island's open-air fruit market is a fun spot to poke around. There are splendid tables to peruse there, but make sure to find the homemade red pepper sauce that is sold in half-pint liquor bottles or Kalik bottles. The sauce is a "must have" addition for your conch salad or cracked conch and seafood fritter batter. They also make great souvenirs for your landlubber friends.
Restaurants There are many restaurants on Grand Bahama to suit all tastes, with 14 in *Our Lucaya* and about 20 more in the *Port Lucaya Marketplace* and at the *International Bazaar*.
After Deck • *242-373-8657* • in the Lucaya Marketplace. Delicious seafood in a casual environment. Open for breakfast, lunch and dinner, 7 a.m. to 10 p.m. Have coconut French Toast for breakfast, then come back and have Stuffed Grouper for dinner. Dine inside or out. $-$$
Sabor Restaurant and Bar • 242-373-1595 • At *Pelican Bay*. Elegant, waterfront dining for lunch from 12 to 2:30 p.m., and dinner 6 to 9 p.m. daily except Mondays. International food, beautifully presented. Complimentary ferry. Reservations requested for dinner. $$$
Pier One • 242-352-6674 • At Freeport Harbour waterway. Fresh seafood with ocean views and sunsets; shark feeding at 7, 8 and 9 p.m. daily. Reservations recommended. Open daily 10 a.m. to 10 p.m., from 4 p.m. Sundays. $$$

In *Port Lucaya Marketplace*:
East • 242-374-2773 • Fine Asian cuisine, sushi and sashimi. Reservations recommended. $$$
Giovanni's Cafe • 242-373-9107 • Genny and her husband/chef serve some of the best food outside Italy. Reasonable prices in a friendly atmosphere. Open from 4 p.m. to 11 p.m., closed Sundays. $$
La Dolce Vita • 242-373-8652 • Italian restaurant serving regional food, fresh pasta and the best espresso in town. $$$
Santorini Café and Deli • 242-374-5194 • American and Bahamian dishes with a Mediterranean flair. $$
Shenanigan's Irish Pub • 242-373-4734 • A popular meeting place for Dublin Draft Guinness and a full Irish menu. Happy hour 5 to 7 p.m. Closed Sundays. $$
The Pub at Port Lucaya • 242-373-8450 • Hearty pub fare, fresh seafood, and tropical drinks. Open from 11 a.m. daily. $$
Zorba's Greek Cuisine • 242-373-6137 • Authentic Greek dishes, accompanied by Greek music. Indoor and outdoor dining.
Taxis Most drivers charge fixed fares for standard routes. From Port Lucaya to the airport is about $25 for two. *Freeport Taxi Co* • 242-352-6666, and *Grand Bahama Taxi Union* • 242-352-7101. Shuttle vans are inexpensive, alternative means of transportation.
Telephones Ten in the *Port Lucaya Marketplace*; Phone cards available from many stores and the *BTC* offices in the *International Bazaar* and downtown Freeport.
Tourist Information • 242-352-8044 • Pick up a copy of *What To Do* from marina offices, hotel front desks, some stores or the tourist offices at the *Port Lucaya Marketplace*.
Veterinarians *Caribbean Veterinary Health and Healing Centre* • 242-351-2103, 242-352-6222/6441 for emergencies • At the Churchill and Jones Remax Building, Queens Highway.
Community Animal Hospital • 242-351-DOGS or 242-351-CATS, 242-352-6222 Pager #1017 for emergencies • Queens Highway.
Freeport Animal Care • 242-352-6521 emergency, 242-373-3914 for Dr. Alan Bater • Queens Highway. All veterinary office hours 9 a.m. to 6 p.m. Monday to Friday, to 12:30 p.m. Saturdays.
Weather Forecast *Freeport Weather Services* • 242-352-9114 • 915 (automated) - Fax: 242-352-9432 • Local & Gulf Stream forecasts.

MEDICAL SERVICES

Ambulance and Emergency Medical Services • 242-352-2689
Clinics *Lucayan Medical Centre West* • 242-352-7288
Sunrise Medical Centre • 242-373-3333
Dentist *Bain Dental Office* • 242-352-8492
Freeport Dental Center • 242-352-4552
Diving Emergency *Hyperbaric Chamber* at *Lyford Cay Hospital* in Nassau • 242-362-4025
Hospital *Rand Memorial Hospital* • 242-352-6735/5101 • Fully staffed 24-hr emergency room.

SPORTS & RECREATION

Bahamas National Trust Parks *Rand Nature Centre* • 242-352-5438 • Two miles from downtown, with 100 acres of pine forest highlighting native plants and their medicinal uses. Open weekdays 9 to 4, Saturday to 1 p.m. Guided nature, bird and wildflower walks, and tickets for visits to other National Trust properties.

Lucayan National Park • 242-352-5438 • Nature trails and one of the largest underwater cave systems in the world, 26 miles east of Freeport. *Lucayan Burial Mound, Ben's Cave,* M*angrove Trail and Gold Rock Beach.* No swimming in the caverns; *Ben's Cave* is closed to visitors during the summer to protect the bat maternity colonies. Park opens daily 9 to 4, admission $3. Purchase tickets in advance at the *Rand Nature Centre* or take a $40 cave tour with *H. Forbes Charter Services* • 242-353-9311.

Peterson Cay National Park • 242-352-5438 • 15 miles east of Freeport and a mile offshore. Take a half-day tour with *Kayak Nature Tours* • 242-373-2485; kayak over from Barberry Beach to visit the smallest National Park in the Bahamas. If you want to take your own boat, you must buy a ticket first from the *Rand Nature Centre* on East Settlers Way, open Monday throgh Friday, 9 a.m. to 4 p.m. • 242-352-5438; be very careful not to anchor over or damage any coral; park rules apply.

Beaches *Xanadu Beach*, with a mile-long stretch of white sand and watersports; *Williams Town*, where you may meet riders from *Pinetree Stables*; *Taino Beach, Smiths' Point, Fortune Beach* and *Gold Rock Beach*, at the end of the trail from the *Lucayan National Park*. Or join a *Bonfire on the Beach* party at the *Pirates of the Bahamas Beach Theme Park*, 3 days a week; all you can eat and drink for $50. Call 242-352-9311.

Bonefishing *Deep Water Cay Club* • 242-353-3073, *Pelican Bay Hotel* - 242-373-9550, *Sweeting's Cay Beach Resort* • 242-353-3023, phllmel@batelnet.bs.

Bonefishing Guide *Perry Demeritte* • 242-353-3301 • At McLeans Town.

Botanical Gardens *Garden of the Groves* • 242-374-7778 • Winding paths through 12 acres of mature tropical trees, waterfalls, fern gully, hanging gardens and a petting zoo with children's playground. Guided tours 11 a.m. and 2 p.m. Café open 11 a.m. to 9 p.m. $9.95 admission.

Diving *Caribbean Divers* • 242-373-9111 • At *Bell Channel Inn*. Rentals, specialty dives, resort course and snorkeling. NAUI and SSI
Underwater Explorers Society (UNEXSO) • 242-373-1244, 800-992-DIVE • www.unexso.com • Between *Pelican Bay* and *Port Lucaya Marketplace*. One of the oldest and largest dive operations in the Bahamas, UNEXSO offers a wide range of swims and diving with dolphins; specialty *Dolphin Experience*, lightweight scuba kit with shallow water dives for kids, night and wreck dives; 2-tank dive $80. Excellent new dive shop and training pool; *Dive In Bar and Grill* open for breakfast and lunch.

Eco Tours • *Bahamas Eco Ventures* • 242-352-9323 • Outback adventures to view wildlife and blue holes with biologist.

Fishing Charters *Captain Walter Kitchen* • 242-373-2222 • 53-ft. Hatteras Sport Fish; daily fishing or cruising charters for up to 6 people. *Fisherman's Safari* Captain John Roberts • 242-352-7915
Reef Tours Ltd • 242-373-5880 • In *Port Lucaya Marina*. Deep sea, bottom and reef fishing, glass bottom boats.

Fishing Tournaments & Regattas *Port Lucaya Marina* • 242-373-9090 • Billfish, Dolphin/Tuna and Wahoo Championships; Sailing Regatta in June, Rendezvous and Boating Flings. *Annual Bahamas National Bonefishing Championship* • 800-32-SPORT • In July, by invitation only. For other tournaments contact *Grand Bahama Tourist Board* at 242-352-8044.

Golf *Fortune Hills Golf and Country Club* • 242-373-2222 • 9 holes. *Lucaya Golf and Country Club* • 242-373-1066, *The Reef Gold Course* • 242-373-1066, and *The Ruby Golf Course* • 242-373-2002. All have 18 holes.

Horseback Riding *Pinetree Stables* • 242-373-3600/1677 • 2-hour Pine Forest trail and beach rides—"you will get wet!" $85 per person, minimum age 8 years. Visa and MasterCard. Closed Mondays. *Trikk Pony Adventures* • 242-374-4449 • leo@trikkpony.com • Trails and beach ride.

Kayaking and Ecotours *Kayak Nature Tours* • 242-373-2485 • Kayak and snorkeling trips to Peterson Cay and *Lucayan National Park*; biking and sightseeing. *Grand Bahama Nature Tours* • 242-373-2485 • Kayak and land tours.

Skydiving *Skydive Bahamas* • 242-374-2362 • At the airport.

Tennis More than 40 courts, mostly at the hotels.

Watersports On the beaches: personal watercraft, banana boat rides, parasailing, powerboat rides, glass bottom kayaks, paddleboats, center console reef fishing boats, snorkeling and trips to Peterson Cay.

RENTALS

Bicycles and Scooters *Econo Motorbike* • 242-351-6700 • Bicycles $20 per day, plus $50 deposit. Scooters from $50 per day, with a $100 deposit for two people. Helmets supplied.
Boats *Reef Tours* • 242-373-5880 • 17-ft. Boston Whaler, $115 for 3 hours, plus fuel.
Cars Don't forget to drive on the left! The speed limit is 25 mph in town, 45 mph outside built-up areas. *Avis* • 242-352-7666 • *Bahama Buggies* • 242-352-8750 • *Budget* • 242-351-8616 • *Cartwright's* • 242-351-3002, jeeps from $45 a day • *Dollar* • 242-352-9325 • *Hertz* • 242-352-3297 • *Island Jeep and Car Rentals* • 242-373-4004 • *Thrifty* • 242-352-9308 • Cars rent from about $65 a day.

THINGS TO DO IN GRAND BAHAMA

- Pick up your copy of the *Bahamas Trailblazer* map and *"What To Do"* in Freeport and Port Lucaya, to give you suggestions and up-to-the-minute ideas of what is going on here.
- Shop till you drop! Find designer bargains and treasures from all over the world at the *Port Lucaya Marketplace* and the *International Bazaar*.
- Play a round of golf at one of the four courses.
- Spend a day with *Kayak Nature Tours* and paddle through the mangroves at Gold Rock Creek; kayak and snorkel off Peterson Cay; go birdwatching; go for a 19-mile bicycle ride; or visit the botanical garden and have lunch at Banana Bay.
- Dive some of the 36 regularly visited dive sites off the southern shore of Grand Bahama, within easy reach of Port Lucaya.
- For a quick buzz, how about skydiving or parasailing?
- Rent a car for the day and explore the smaller settlements along the coast to West End. Or drive east and explore the *Lucayan National Park*.
- Join in the nightly dancing at the *Port Lucaya Marketplace*. All ages, lots of fun, especially the limbo dancers.

Part II
Central Cruising Grounds

WATERWAY GUIDE PHOTOGRAPHY

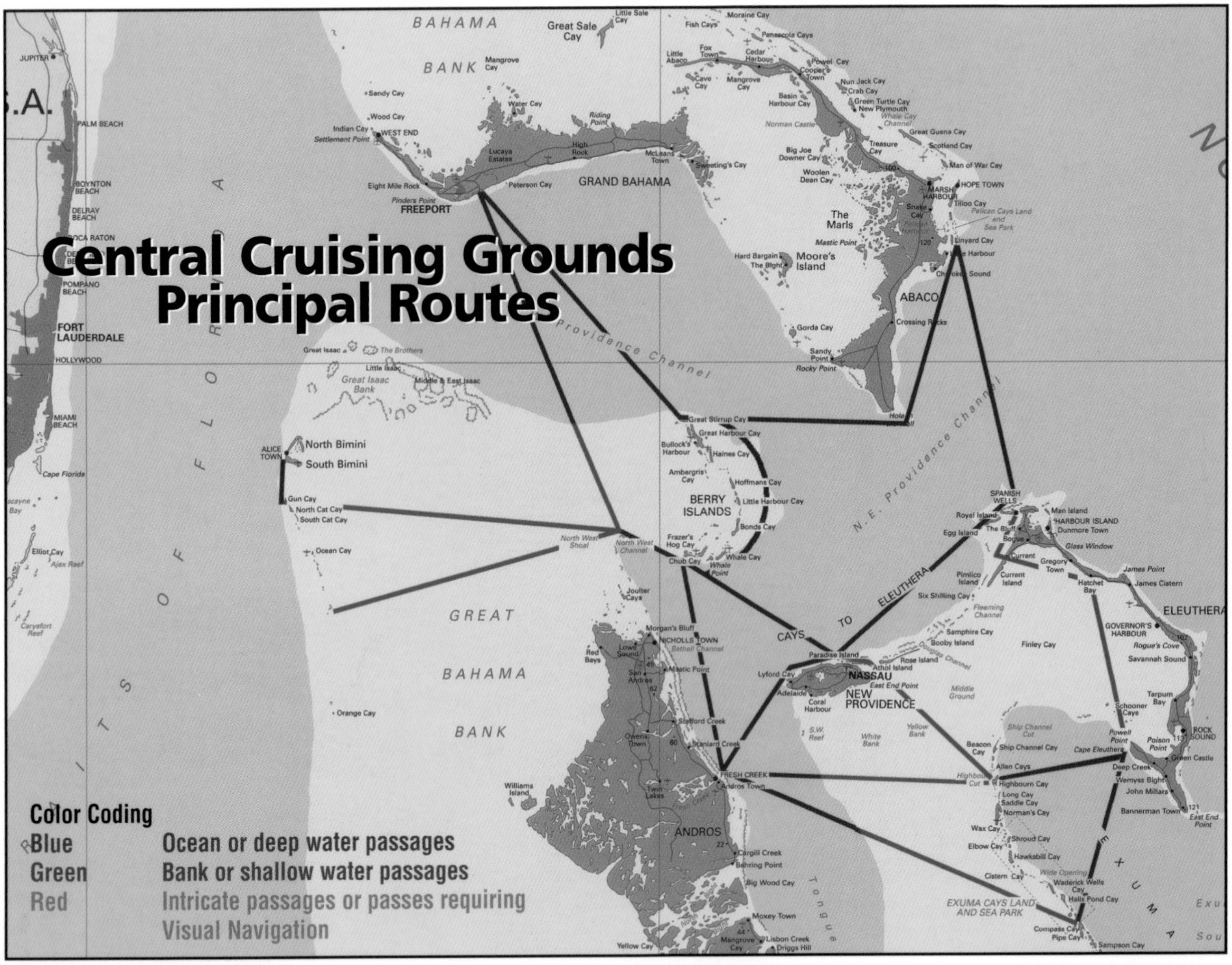

Route From	To	Headings	Distance	Passage
Fort Lauderdale, Florida	Bimini	119/299°T	48 nm	Gulf Stream Crossing
Fort Lauderdale, Florida	Gun Cay Cut	127/307°T	52 nm	Gulf Stream Crossing
Miami, Florida	Bimini	095/275°T	42 nm	Gulf Stream Crossing
Miami, Florida	Gun Cay Cut	106/286°T	43 nm	Gulf Stream Crossing
Bimini	Gun Cay Cut	see text	09 nm	Florida Strait Coastal
Gun Cay Cut	Northwest Channel Light	095/275°T	61 nm	Great Bahama Bank
Northwest Channel Light	Chub Cay, Berry Islands	112/292°T	15 nm	NE Providence Channel
Chub Cay	Nassau	120/300°T	35 nm	NE Providence Channel
Chub Cay	Fresh Creek, Andros	167/347°T	42 nm	Tongue of the Ocean
Little Stirrup Cay	Chub Cay, Berry Islands	see text	40 nm	Atlantic Coastal
Fresh Creek, Andros	Highbourne Cay, Exumas	093/273°T	50 nm	Tongue of the Ocean/Bank
Fresh Creek, Andros	Conch Cut, Exumas	114/294°T	74 nm	Tongue of the Ocean/Bank
Nassau	North Eleuthera	see text	44 nm	NE Providence Channel
Nassau	Allans Cay, Exumas	see text	36 nm	Exuma Bank
Spanish Wells	Harbour Island	see text	14 nm	Devils Backbone
Spanish Wells	Governors Harbour	see text	43 nm	Current Cut/Bank
Governors Harbour	Cape Eleuthera	see text	28 nm	Davis Channel/Bank
Cape Eleuthera	Highbourne Cut, Exumas	256/076°T	25 nm	Exuma Sound
Cape Eleuthera	Conch Cut, Exumas	195/015°T	33 nm	Exuma Sound
South Eleuthera	Little San Salvador	096/276°T	10 nm	Exuma Sound
South Eleuthera	Hawks Nest, Cat Island	129/309°T	43 nm	Exuma Sound

Distances exclude inshore close approaches at the start and end of a passage. The notation "see text" indicates multi-leg passages that are fully covered in the text.

Chapter 8
The Bimini Islands Group

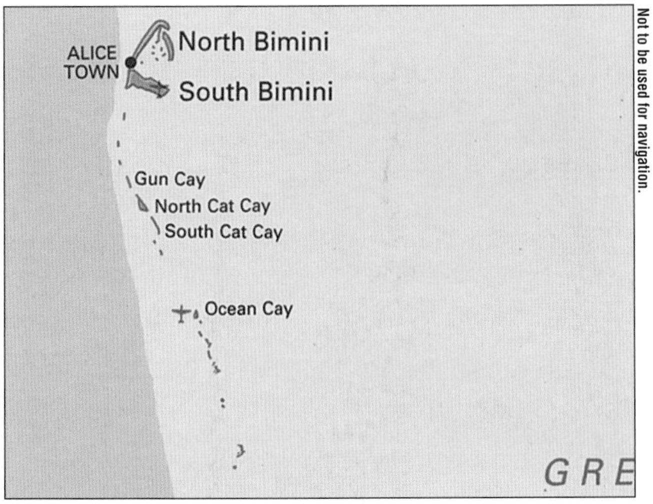

Looking At the Charts

It doesn't take more than a cursory glance at a chart to notice that the shortest routes from the east coast of Florida all converge on the Bimini Islands. Even contending with the Gulf Stream's northern push, most boats with any speed can comfortably leave for these islands at daybreak and reach them before sunset. Hence, their historic and present-day popularity with the rich and famous as well as the foot-loose and fancy-free.

Slower, smaller vessels will want to pay close attention to the NOAA reports on the offshore whereabouts and speed of the Gulf Stream. Its proximity to shore varies widely, and you will want to stage your departure with that in mind. Generally, the farther south one can get, the better, but many boats leave Fort Lauderdale or Miami, and with frequent mini-corrections throughout the day, make landfall in the Biminis right where they planned. Cruisers frequently travel the routes from Fowey Rocks to Alice Town, North Bimini, Nixons Harbour or the Gun Cay lighthouse cut. These are the most popular crossings to the Bahamas, and you will have company to share the adventure or ease your fears.

Because of their popularity, the island chain has a plethora of accommodations, restaurants, bars and marinas from which to choose—from funky to outright fabulous. In addition, Customs and Immigration officials are used to dealing with hoards of busy folks wanting for clearance. Consequently, they are among the most accessible, efficient and friendly officials in the Bahamas. If you have your paperwork together, there is no easier place to clear in than Alice Town.

Tying up to the government dock to go to Customs and Immigration is no longer allowed. Anchoring off the northernmost marina in Alice Town is not recommended now that the channel through Alice Town is regularly dredged to accommodate megayachts winding their way to Bimini Bay Resort. Dockage in North and South Bimini is among the most reason-

Alice Town, North Bimini and South Bimini, looking southeast. (Not to be used for navigation.) WATERWAY GUIDE PHOTOGRAPHY

ably priced that you will find anywhere. Why not treat yourself and the crew to a hassle-free Customs check in and a stay at a nice marina? There are lovely places to drop the hook later as you explore the islands southward.

If you need to push on and bypass the Biminis, most cruisers choose the Gun Cay cut to Northwest Channel route and head straight across the Great Bahama Bank. Although many slower vessels still anchor out on the Great Bahama Bank, please keep in mind that there are more and more island freighters traveling from Florida to the Berry Islands and Nassau. These freighters frequently travel at night without running lights and with inadequate lookouts. Anchor far off the magenta rhumb line routes in very shallow, water and make sure your anchor lights are both very identifiable and visible. Even with these precautions, be very alert at anchor on the Bank. A previous cruising editor was mistaken for the Russell Beacon by a freighter when they weren't anchored even remotely close to Russell Beacon. Only the steady, and increasingly loud, thump, thump, thump of the freighter's engine alerted them to imminent danger. Soon after that incident, they docked along side a large sailboat in Nassau that had miraculously slid down the side of a freighter that sideswiped them in much the same circumstances.

In the Spotlight. Alice Town

Don't miss the museum in Alice Town. The pictures of Hemingway and earlier times tell it all. This was a special place where the only laws were "anything goes, deep-sea fishing rules and rum flows." Today, it is tamed and much more family oriented, but the ghosts of that enchanted era still roam the narrow streets of this historic settlement.

The "Bimini" part of the names of the two largest islands, North Bimini and South Bimini, has become the moniker for the whole string of smaller cays, rocks and reefs that run south from North Bimini Island, fringing the edge of the Gulf Stream and Great Bahama Bank for nearly 30 miles.

The Biminis always held promise. Juan Ponce de León passed this way in 1513, in his pursuit for the Fountain of Youth, but he left disappointed.

In the 1600s, entrepreneurial pirates made wrecking, and subsequent salvaging, a profitable business. Reliable lighthouses were finally built putting an end that heyday. During Prohibition (1920–33), ingenious islanders capitalized on the short hop between Bimini and Florida and created the epicenter of the rum-running trade. When the 18th Amendment forbidding alcohol was repealed, Bimini might have slumped, but the luck of the islands held. By 1935, Ernest Hemingway and others had discovered that the Bimini Islands embraced one of the best ocean fishing grounds in the world. Since then, Alice Town on North Bimini has dominated the scattering of islands that share her last name. Today, the Bimini Islands remain an all-time favorite cruising destination for many reasons:

- The Biminis are the closest Bahamian islands to Florida, less than 50 nautical miles away. It is a two-hour trip at 25 knots and only 10 hours at five knots—well within reach of any weekend visitor.

Atlantis Dive site. WATERWAY GUIDE PHOTOGRAPHY

Atlantis or the Bimini Road Dive Site

You have heard that the Bahamas were the site of Atlantis? The evidence is right there. Want to dive it? There is a marker buoy there, waiting for you. Atlantis, or the Bimini Road rock formation, is on the sea bed in 4.5 meters/15 feet of water off Paradise Point, North Bimini. We said "dive," but all you need is a mask and snorkel.

What is at the Atlantis dive site? A relatively small area of roughly rectangular flat rocks lying almost totally buried in the sand, which look like the paving stones of a ramp or road, or perhaps the cap stones of an ancient harbor wall. Certainly the stones have the appearance of having been fashioned and placed by man rather than a geological freak of nature. If you go for the Atlantis theory, you are into wish fulfillment, for it is impossible to divine any plan in the site and, were it prehistoric, too much (one guesses) lies buried to permit analysis. This site has also been linked with the Moselle Bank, to the northwest of Bimini, which was also wrapped up in the Atlantis theory, as were the "lemon shark" sand mounds discovered in 1977 in the mangroves to the east.

What are the "paving stones?" Beach rock. Ancient reef. You can see much the same in many places.

- Some of the best fishing found anywhere in the islands. It is truly world class.
- Great diving and snorkeling with sites that eclipse Florida's best.
- A place that really is different. There is no mistaking, as you stroll North Bimini's one-car-wide main street—King's Highway—that you are not in the United States.
- These islands literally beckon you to stop after crossing the Gulf Stream. Who can resist spending a few nights here before setting off across the Great Bahama Bank or waiting out a blow to return to the east coast?

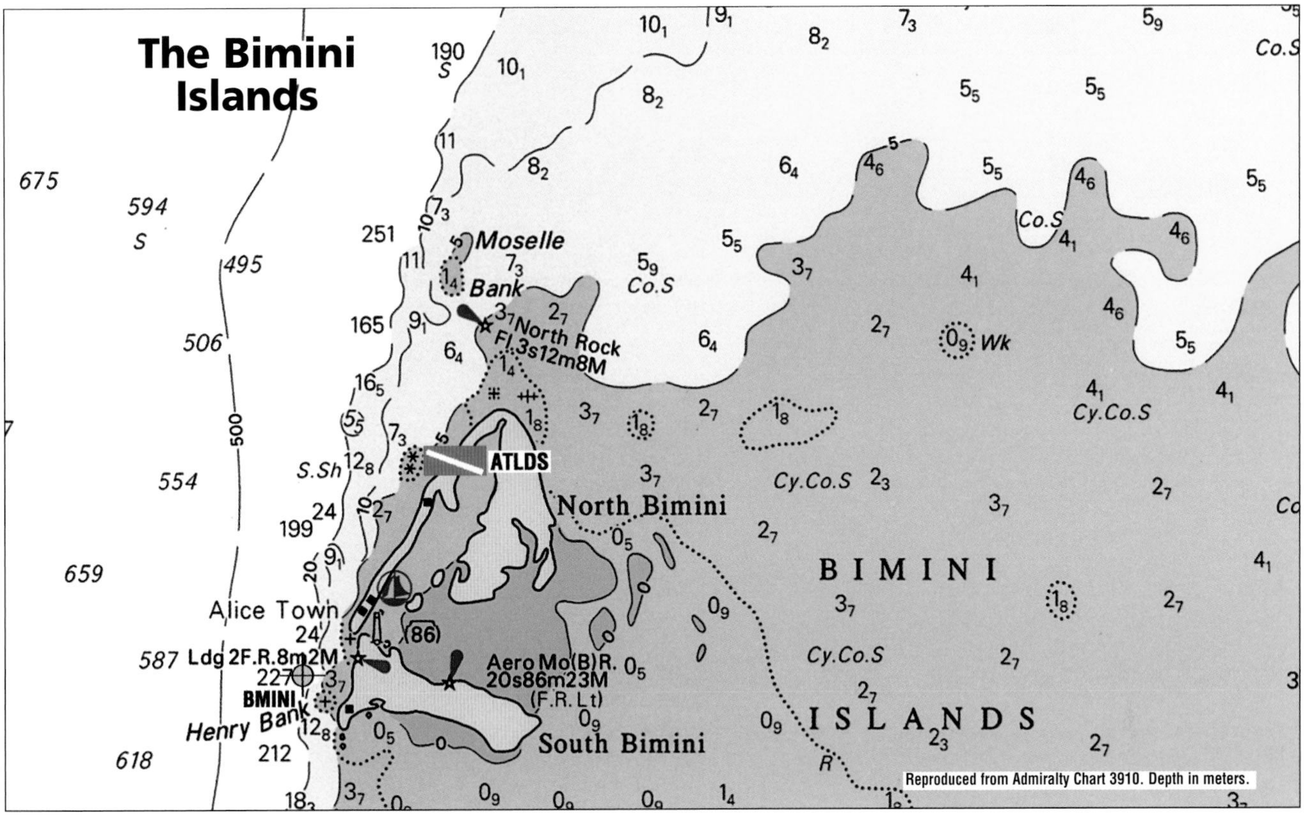

Reproduced from Admiralty Chart 3910. Depth in meters.

Clearing In—Your Options in the Biminis

Ports of entry are Alice Town in North Bimini, Bimini Sands in South Bimini and Cat Cay Yacht Club on North Cat Cay. Be advised that if you do not book dockage at Cat Cay Yacht Club, there is a charge to clear in.

What's There? The Bimini Islands

Alice Town, North Bimini

North Bimini's main settlement, Alice Town is a bustling hub of island activity. Although you can walk everywhere and enjoy the ambience of the town at a slow pace, golf carts are readily available for rent, and the guided trolley tour is not only fun, but also a history lesson in itself.

Alice Town's King's Highway is a busy lane lined with homey restaurants, interesting shops, an art gallery, museum and marinas. You will also find Customs and Immigration offices here, next to the delightful women selling souvenirs and freshly baked coconut bread at the Straw Market. Farther south, there is a lovely beach to comb and a cemetery with tales to tell. To the north, are administration buildings, schools, a war memorial, a laundry, a well-stocked grocery store and some of the largest piles of conch shells to be found in the islands. If you have your walking shoes on, continue to Bailey Town to drink in more local flavor.

As you explore, do find the remains of the Compleat Angler Hotel (Hemingway's old haunt). It used to be Alice Town's centerpiece. It is, sadly, little more than ashes today. Its entry sign still hangs for a poignant picture of your visit. Be sure to ramble up and down the side streets that connect the King's Highway to its parallel road, the Queen's Highway. Queen's runs along the western shoreline and offers an extraordinarily pristine, shell-strewn beach. An absolute "don't miss" along your side street exploration is "The Dolphin House." The dwelling is a work of art. It is covered entirely, inside and out, with seashells, mosaic tiles, found treasures and bits and pieces of flotsam and jetsam. The owner and artist, who lives downstairs and rents the upstairs to tourists, is a local teacher, historian and author. If you are lucky, he will be home to give you a tour.

Alice Town Harbour

The entrance channel into Alice Town is clearly marked with red and green nun buoys lined up directly off the southern-most point of the island. Outdated charts note this passage as a dinghy channel. Although breaking water over nearby shoals can be very disconcerting, the entrance and channel are maintained for megayachts' use. Older charts show another entrance channel hugging the western shore of South Bimini. This is still a viable passage into Alice Town, and it is detailed under Pilotage in this chapter.

After negotiating the entrance and entering the harbor basin, Alice Town marinas line the shoreline, all to port. In order from south to north are Browns Hotel and Marina, Weech's Dock, the government dock (with Customs and Immigration), Sea Crest Hotel and Marina, Bimini Blue Water Marina and Bimini Big Game Club. The Bimini Big Game Club was scheduled to reopen in May 2010, with many amenities and activities. From

Bimini Islands

PETERSON FUEL DELIVERY 1-866-404-FUEL

NORTH BIMINI, ALICETOWN		Largest Vessel Accommodated	VHF Channel Monitored	Transient Berths / Total Berths	Approach / Dockside Depth (reported)	Floating Docks	Gas / Diesel	Groceries, Ice, Marine Supplies, Snacks	Repairs: Hull, Engine, Propeller	Lift (tonnage), Crane, Rail	1=110V, 2=220V, B=Both, Max Amps	Laundry, Pool, Showers	Pump-Out Station	Nearby: Grocery Store, Motel, Restaurant
		Dockage					Supplies				Services			
1. Bimini Bay Resort and Marina 🖳 WiFi	242-347-2900	225	16/68	240/240	12/15	F		GIMS			B/100	PS		GMR
2. Bimini Big Game Club WiFi	242-347-3391	120	16/09	/103	9/9			I			B/50	PS		GMR
3. Bimini Blue Water Resort WiFi	242-347-3166	120	68	27/32	7/5		GD	IMS			B/50	PS		GMR
4. Sea Crest Hotel & Marina WiFi	242-347-3071	105	68	12/18	7/5			GI			B/50	LS		GMR
5. Weech's Bimini Dock	242-347-3028	70	18	/15	/10			I			B/50	S		GMR
6. Browns Hotel & Marina WiFi	305-423-3213	150	68	/20	12/8			I			B/100	S		GMR

Corresponding chart(s) not to be used for navigation. 🖳 Internet Access WiFi Wireless Internet Access

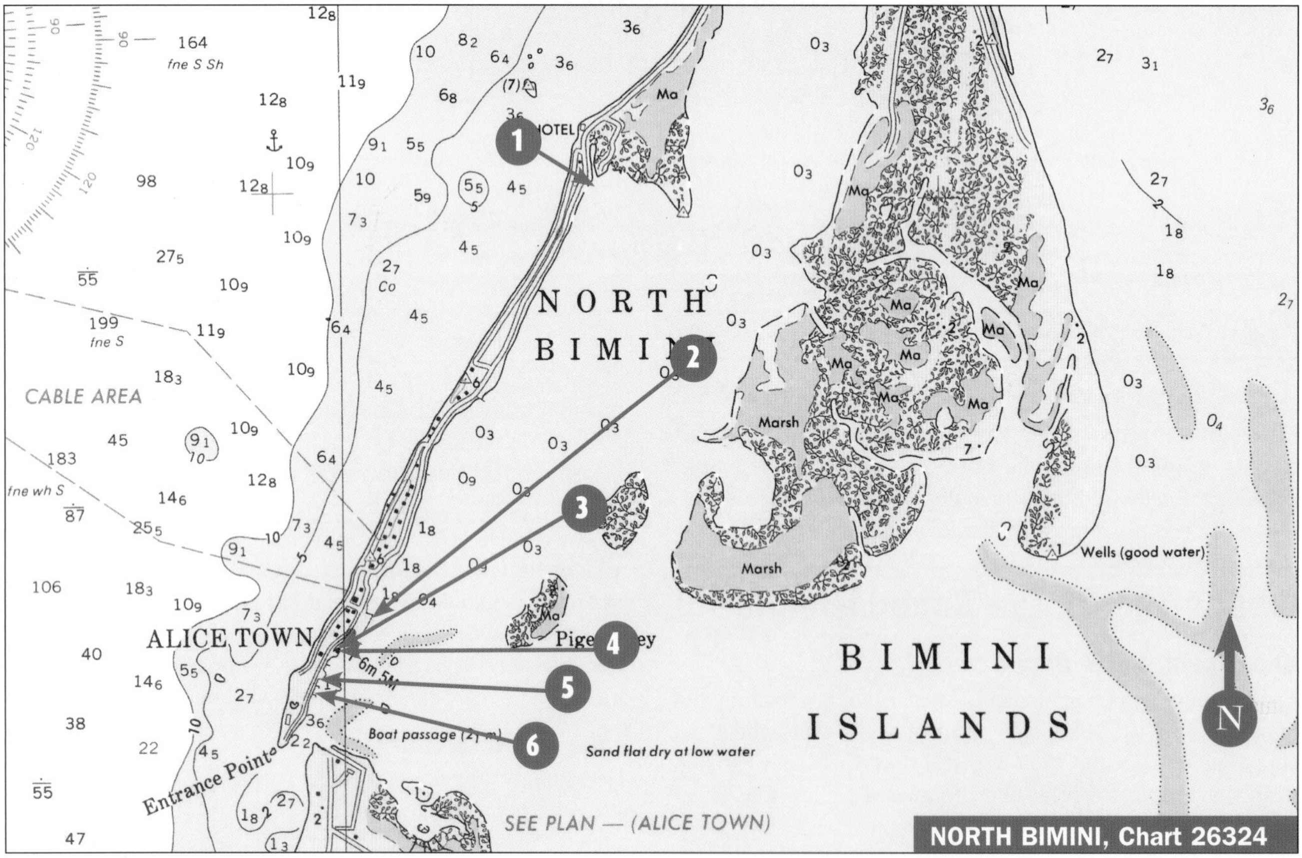

NORTH BIMINI, Chart 26324

there, tall-lighted pilings, like red and green festooned gendarmes, march stalwartly northwards towards Bimini Bay Resort and Marina. Two marinas at this location are equipped with concrete floating docks and complimentary wireless Internet.

South Bimini

South Bimini, always the more tranquil of the Bimini siblings, is connected to Alice Town by a short ferry ride off Buccaneer Point. A bit farther south, Bimini Sands Marina and Bimini Sands Beach Club offer dockage in two fully protected harbors-one midway on the western shore of the island and one off the southern tip in Nixons Harbour. The marinas offer first-class amenities in scenic surroundings. Taxis can bring your guests from the airport to the marinas or their townhouses. Ask the driver to point out South Bimini's legendary site of Ponce de Leon's Fountain of Youth.

South of the Biminis. Gun Cay and Gun Cay Cut

Cruising south from South Bimini, you are in interesting waters. For snorkelers and spear fishermen, there are Turtle Rocks and the spooky, skeleton wreck of the *Sapona*, victim of a 1929 hurricane. Both are great shallow dives. There are also Picquet Rock and Holm Cay to investigate; and then, at the north end of Gun Cay, Honeymoon Harbour, where the sting rays are particularly friendly and looking for a hand out. For scuba divers, Sea Crest Hotel and Bimini Undersea Adventures can arrange

Honeymoon Harbour. (Not to be used for navigation.) Waterway Guide Photography

offshore and shipwreck dives to test your skills including the *Bimini Barge* in depths of 20 to 30 meters/65 to 100 feet and the *Bimini Trader*.

On the south end of Gun Cay, there is the famous landmark, Gun Cay Light. The passage between Gun Cay and Cat Cay, to its south, is the access channel to the Great Bahama Bank known as Gun Cay Cut. It is a very busy route to either Chub Cay in the Southern Berry Islands, Fresh Creek in Andros or Nassau, New Providence Island. Navigation through Gun Cay Cut, which is not difficult, is covered under Pilotage. Gun Cay offers good anchorages on either side and in Honeymoon Harbour itself. Where you anchor depends entirely on the wind. Holding is good in the sandy spots, but carefully set your anchor to make sure it has not just flopped on top of marl or a rocky ledge.

North Cat Cay

North Cat Cay is a private island with a marina/yacht club situated about two-thirds of the way south on its eastern shore. Those who choose to anchor off the airstrip are not welcome ashore. You are invited to partake of their facilities if you dock at the club. North Cat Cay may have *No Wake* buoys running out from the club. While these are not channel markers as such, they serve as a useful entry line. Stay to the east of them (in other words, don't run between the markers and the beach) to safely enter the marina. The marina is a port of entry. The club has a fine restaurant and lovely surroundings.

South of Cat Cay

The cays and reefs that form the "trailing end" of the Bimini chain are particularly picturesque and intriguing. Their very barrenness and unfamiliarity make them little nubs of unexplored wonder. Reefs that fringe the Gulf Stream side team with sea life. There are anchorages on both sides of South Cat Cay and at its southern tip, Cat Point. The anchorages on the eastern side, protected by both the cay and the banks, are movie-set like, half-moon harbors of sugar sand and swaying palm trees. The Victory Cays are noted dive sites. Farther south, there are Sandy Cay, Ocean Cay with its aragonite sea mining operation that is a high-visibility landmark, Browns Cay, Beak Cay and the Riding Rocks. The Riding Rocks lead to South Riding Rock. We deal with the South Riding Rock approach to the Great Bahama Bank in Chapter 9.

The Bimini Marker Buoys

There are sixteen mooring buoys in the Bimini area, all placed to mark dive sites by Bill and Nowdla Keefe who run Bimini Undersea Adventures. They welcome you to make use of these buoys when you go diving, but ask that you call them first on VHF Channel 6 (Bimini Undersea) and check that the buoy you would like to use is not required by them that day.

Pilotage. Talking Captain to Captain

North Bimini and Bimini Sands Marina

There is a dredged channel into Alice Town. Red and green nun buoys safely guide you through the entrance at the southernmost tip of North Bimini. However, if you would like to use the tried and true old way into Alice Town, or if you are headed for Bimini Sands Marina on South Bimini, the waypoint (BIMAP) places you off South Bimini, a tad northwest of the approach range leading you inshore.

With all the changes and dredging that took place here, be sure to get the latest information on using this entry way from one of the local marinas before you attempt it. The range markers lead you straight toward the white sand beach on the western shore of South Bimini. Turn to port after you are safely by the sandbar on port and the rocks and shallows on starboard. You will be close to the beach, but in deeper

Bimini Islands

SOUTH BIMINI		Largest Vessel Accommodated	VHF Channel Monitored	Transient Berths / Total Berths	Approach / Dockside Depth (reported)	Floating Docks	Gas / Diesel	Groceries, Ice, Marine Supplies, Snacks	Repairs: Hull, Engine, Propeller	Lift (tonnage), Crane, Rail	1=110V, 2=220V, B=Both, Max Amps	Laundry, Pool, Showers	Pump-Out Station	Nearby: Grocery Store, Motel, Restaurant
		Dockage					Supplies		Services					
1. Bimini Sands Resort & Marina (Internet Access) (WiFi)	242-347-3500	100	68	/60	8/8	F	GD	GIMS			B/50	LPS		GMR
2. Bimini Sands Beach Club (Internet Access) (WiFi)	242-347-3500	70	68	/45				I			1/30	PS		R

Corresponding chart(s) not to be used for navigation. Internet Access, WiFi Wireless Internet Access

SOUTH BIMINI, Chart 26324

water. Entering Bimini Sands Marina is quite uncomplicated. Simply turn in. You will find 2.4-meter/8-foot depths once you are in their channel.

If you are bound for Alice Town via this route, pass the Bimini Sands entry channel and head away from the beach. It can be shoal between the Bimini Sands channel and the entrance to Alice Town. Read the water carefully. At any state of tide, go cautiously on your final run in, watch your depth and be prepared to abort.

If the wind is from the west and any kind of significant sea is running, either approach is not usable. Don't do it. Your immediate options are to go south to Nixons Harbour and dock at Bimini Sands Beach Club, or utilize Gun Cay cut to anchor in the lee of Gun Cay or North Cat Cay. Shoal draft boats can cautiously plot a course through the protected waters from Nixons Harbour, east of Turtle Rocks, to the anchorages east of Gun Cay or proceed to Cat Cay Yacht Club. Regardless, it is important to remember:

- Conditions. Beware of trying to enter Alice Town or Bimini Sands Marina in southwest through northwest winds, particularly if the sea state is building. In moderate conditions, you should be fine, but you are exposed broadside running along the beach from the range markers. You are very close to the beach as you do the final leg. Do not attempt it in unfavorable weather.
- Approach Markers. The range markers can be hard to locate. If you don't spot them, run slowly up and down parallel to the beach. Stay in safe in deep water until you have them fixed. Don't try to go in by guesswork.

Aragonite

Do you know what aragonite is? We didn't. Aragonite, named after Aragon in Spain, is an orthorhombic mineral made up of calcium carbonate, $CaCO_3$. It resembles calcite, but is heavier and harder, has less cleavage and occurs less frequently. Our source is Webster's New World Dictionary.

Any wiser? Apparently it is a pure limestone, used for cement and fertilizers.

North Cat Cay

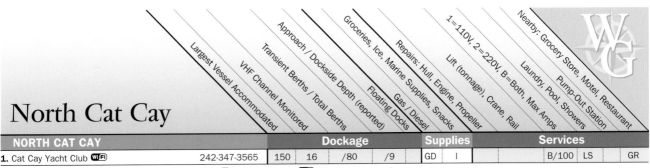

NORTH CAT CAY		Largest Vessel Accommodated	VHF Channel Monitored	Transient Berths / Total Berths	Approach / Dockside Depth (reported)	Floating Docks	Gas / Diesel	Groceries, Ice, Marine Supplies, Snacks	Repairs: Hull, Engine, Propeller	Lift (tonnage), Crane, Rail	1=110V, 2=220V, B=Both, Max Amps	Laundry, Pool, Showers	Pump-Out Station	Nearby: Grocery Store, Motel, Restaurant
		Dockage					Supplies		Services					
1. Cat Cay Yacht Club (WiFi)	242-347-3565	150	16	/80	/9		GD	I			B/100	LS		GR

Corresponding chart(s) not to be used for navigation. Internet Access (WiFi) Wireless Internet Access

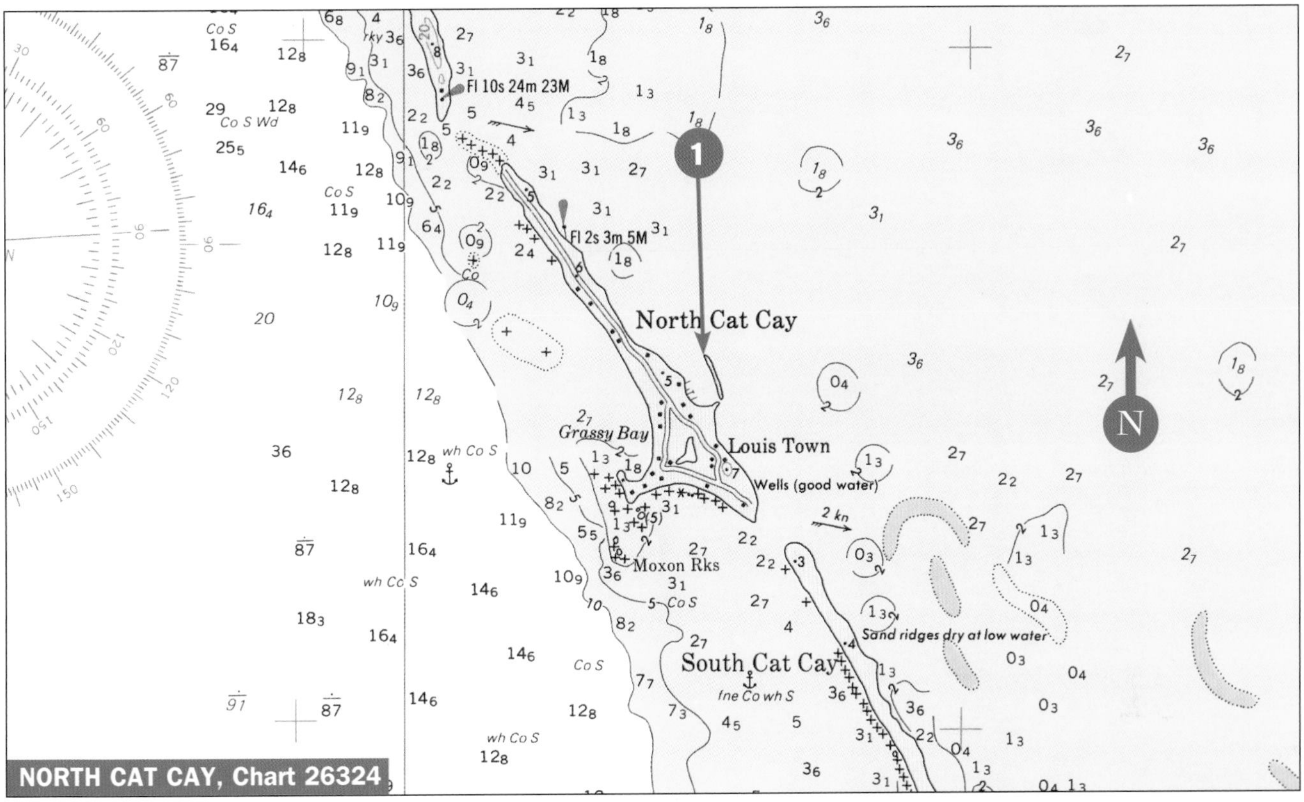

NORTH CAT CAY, Chart 26324

- Chart Accuracy. Your GPS may placed you on the sand by Pigeon Cay by the time you are at your slip in Bimini Blue Water Marina. Remember, the GPS is accurate, but the chart positions may not be. As always, treat every GPS waypoint with caution and the charts with reservation. It is your eyes that count every time when you are close to shore or in shallow water.

South Bimini

Heading to the Bimini Sands Beach Club Marina, use Round Rock, to the south of South Bimini, as your landmark. Go south of Round Rock (the BSAP1/B11 waypoint) and continue almost due east for 0.2 nautical mile to the BSAP2/B58 waypoint. Here, turn northwest back toward South Bimini (around 297 degrees true) and the Beach Club Marina entrance is ahead. It is clearly marked with pilings. Some areas of Nixons Harbour (see the chart) dry at low water. And, as you alter course to head for the Bimini Sands Beach Club, you will have no doubt that you are in skinny water. The approach channel into the marina provides 2-meter/6.5-foot depths at mean low water, which hold into the marina.

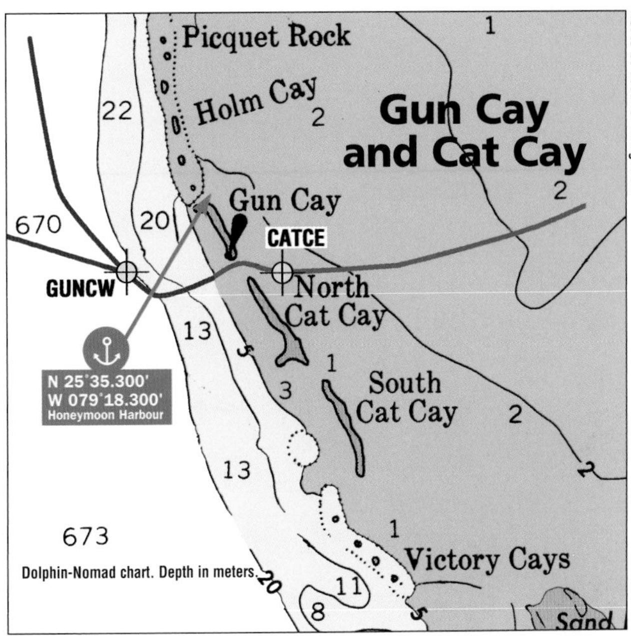

Not to be used for navigation.

Bimini Sands Beach Resort, South Bimini. (Not to be used for navigation.) WATERWAY GUIDE PHOTOGRAPHY

Rafting. Photo Courtesy of Peter Mitchell.

Gun Cay Cut, from the northwest. (Not to be used for navigation.)
WATERWAY GUIDE PHOTOGRAPHY

Gun Cay Cut

Once you are at the Gun Cay West waypoint (GUNCW), turn to pass through Gun Cay Cut. The 2.5 nautical miles or so run through Gun Cay Cut must be taken visually, favoring Gun Cay Point and staying in the deep water parallel to the shoreline until through the cut. There is a hard, rocky bar to the south. Hold course until you can see the entrance to Cat Cay Yacht Club with its dwarf lighthouse. Whether you are bound for a Bank crossing or for North Cat Cay, turn to starboard at that point. Using the two lights, Gun Cay and North Cat Cay as markers, one ahead and one astern, head south. This line will keep you clear of the shoal area close in to North Cat Cay and shoals that lie to the east of Gun Cay Cut. If you are going to North Cat Cay, carry on into the marina. If heading across the Great Bahama Bank, turn east to pick up the departure waypoint Cat Cay East (CATCE) at the line of latitude N 25° 34.000'. For routes across the bank, see Chapter 9.

The Gun Cay Anchorage

Be aware that the holding on either side of Gun Cay is unpredictable. Look for the sandy spots among the grass, set the anchor securely, and dive to double check its hold if any kind of weather is forecast. In some areas, there is marl or a solid ledge underneath your keel. It is worth the jockeying and jostling to get the anchor set properly for a good night's sleep. ■

WATERWAY GUIDE is always open to your observations from the helm. E-mail your comments on any navigation information in the guide to: editor@waterwayguide.com.

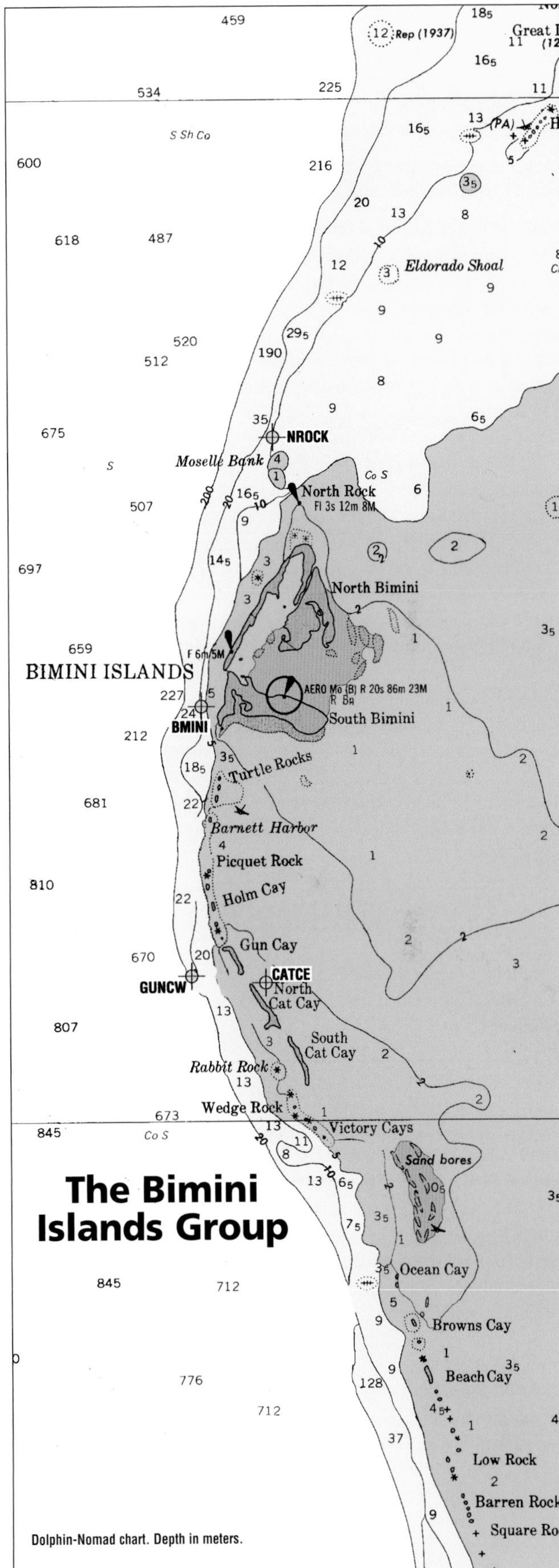

Dolphin-Nomad chart. Depth in meters.

Bimini Islands Waypoints

Bimini	BMINI (B8)	25°42.60N / 79°18.50W
Bimini Approach	BIMAP (B77)	25°42.80N / 79°18.13W
Atlantis Dive Site	ATLDS	25°45.73N / 79°16.73W
Bimini Sands Approach 1	BSAP1 (B11)	25°41.00N / 79°19.00W
Bimini Sands Approach 2	BSAP2 (B58)	25°41.30N / 79°17.70W
Gun Cay West	GUNCW (B13)	25°34.65N / 79°18.50W
Cat Cay East	CATCE (B15)	25°34.00N / 79°17.20W

Our position format is latitude and longitude in degrees and minutes (hddd°mm.mm). Waypoints in RED are NOT for autopilot navigation. Codes in parenthesis are Wavey Line waypoints marked on the charts. If you have programmed waypoints we listed in a previous edition of this guide, check carefully to ensure the coordinates you have recorded match the list. If a waypoint is no longer on our list we may have changed its code or deleted it.

GOIN' ASHORE:

NORTH BIMINI

bank • customs & immigration • fuel • groceries • marinas • medical • police • post office • restaurant • telephone • water

If this is your first taste of the Bahamas, you are off to a great start. North Bimini's main settlement, Alice Town, is a bustling hub of island activity. The main street, the King's Highway, is a busy lane lined with homey restaurants, interesting shops, an art gallery, museum and marinas. Everything is only a minute's walk away from long, sandy Radio Beach running along the west side of Alice Town. The fishing is world renowned, and the diving is excellent. The new Bimini Bay Resort has brought a whole new megayacht element to this once sleepy oasis favored by Ernest Hemingway and his fishing pals.

If this is your port of entry, Customs is in the blue building at the government dock, open 7 a.m. to 7 p.m. daily. Immigration is next door adjacent to the *Straw Market*, open 8 a.m. to 6 p.m. weekdays, 7 a.m. to 6 p.m. weekends. If Customs and Immigration officials are unavailable, take your forms to the government offices at the northern end of town, next door to the school. Forms are available at any marina. Boat captains should take papers and passports to the offices for everyone on board.

While you are in North Bimini, you don't want to miss visiting the Bimini Museum, the Dolphin House and Bonefish Ansil Saunders Bimini Boat Building Shop. The museum is usually open (free will donation). To tour the Dolphin House, visit Ashley Saunders in his shop or give him a call 242-347-3201 (he has wonderful Bimini history books that he wrote for sale, and he gives historical walking tours). The Boat Building Shop is in Bailey Town (a short walk north or hop on the tour bus). Ansil is usually there or give him a call, 242-347-2178 or 242-464-5113.

EMERGENCIES

Marine • VHF 16
Medical *Bimini Community Health Center*
242-347-2210 • Open 9 to 4 weekdays. Doctor • 242-347-2101
Police • 919 • 242-347-3144

MARINAS

On your port side coming into Bimini Harbour:

BROWNS MARINA AT BIG JOHN'S HOTEL AND CONCH BAR - VHF 16
Tel: 305-423-3213 or 242-347-3117
info@bigjohnshotel.com •
www.brownshotelandmarina.com

Browns invites transients to visit its excellent docks, tasty restaurant and lively bar. Browns Hotel offers seven boutique rooms for your guests. You will enjoy their live music in the Conch Bar Thursday through Sunday.

Slips 20 **Max LOA** 150 ft. **MLW at Dock** 9 ft. **Dockage** $1.75 per ft. per day. Includes showers, laundry, restrooms and swimming pool. **Facilities & Services** Power, based on vessel sized, from $15 per day. Ice. Water $0.30 per gallon, Satellite and Cable TV, phone, 24-hour security. **Restaurant & Bar** *Big John's Conch Bar*, live music Thursday through Sunday. **Accommodations** Seven air-conditioned, boutique rooms with LCD televisions and luxury linens, starting from $125 per day.

WEECH'S DOCK
Tel: 242-347-3028 • Fax: 242-347-3508 • VHF 18 (Hail "Stubby")

Weech's offers short-term tie-up to clear customs for a small fee. They also have a decent hardware and marine supply store on site. Not the fanciest facility in Alice Town, but the shower rooms are always spotlessly clean, and the welcome warm and friendly. It is still a favorite with "old-timers." Weech's is the easiest marina from which to walk a dog south on "grass," not asphalt. Please clean up after your pet.

Slips 15. **Max LOA** 70 ft. **MLW at Dock** 10 ft. **Dockage** $0.85 per ft. per day, $30 minimum. Includes showers, restrooms, barbecue grills and a great parrot to talk to. **Facilities & Services** Power $15 per day for 30 amp, $25 for 50 amp. Ice. Water $5 per day or by the gallon (not reverse osmosis). **Accommodations** *Weech's Bay View Rooms Five* rooms from $85; efficiency apartment sleeps four, $170 per night. **Credit Cards** Cash only.

SEA CREST MARINA AND HOTEL
Tel: 242-347-3071 • Fax: 242-347-3495 • VHF 68
www.seacrestbimini.com

No contest here! Sea Crest offers the best wireless Internet connection in Alice Town. The wonderful fare at Cap'n Bob's restaurant directly across the street is legend. Need nice accommodations nearby for guests? The Sea Crest Hotel is a few steps away, across the street and up the hill. Gorgeous Radio Beach is a short walk to the west.

Slips 18. **Max LOA** 100 ft. **MLW at Dock** 8 ft. **Dockage** $1.00 per ft. per day. **Facilities & Services** Power $14–$32 per day depending on boat length, **Water** $0.30 a gallon. Showers, restrooms, barbecue grill, public telephone, complimentary WiFi, scuba tanks refilled. There is on-site security. **Accommodations** *Sea Crest Marina Hotel* Rooms from $99 to $329 per night. **Credit Cards** Visa and MasterCard, 6% surcharge. Pets are welcome at the marina, walk south for grass.

Beach at Alice Town. WATERWAY GUIDE PHOTOGRAPHY

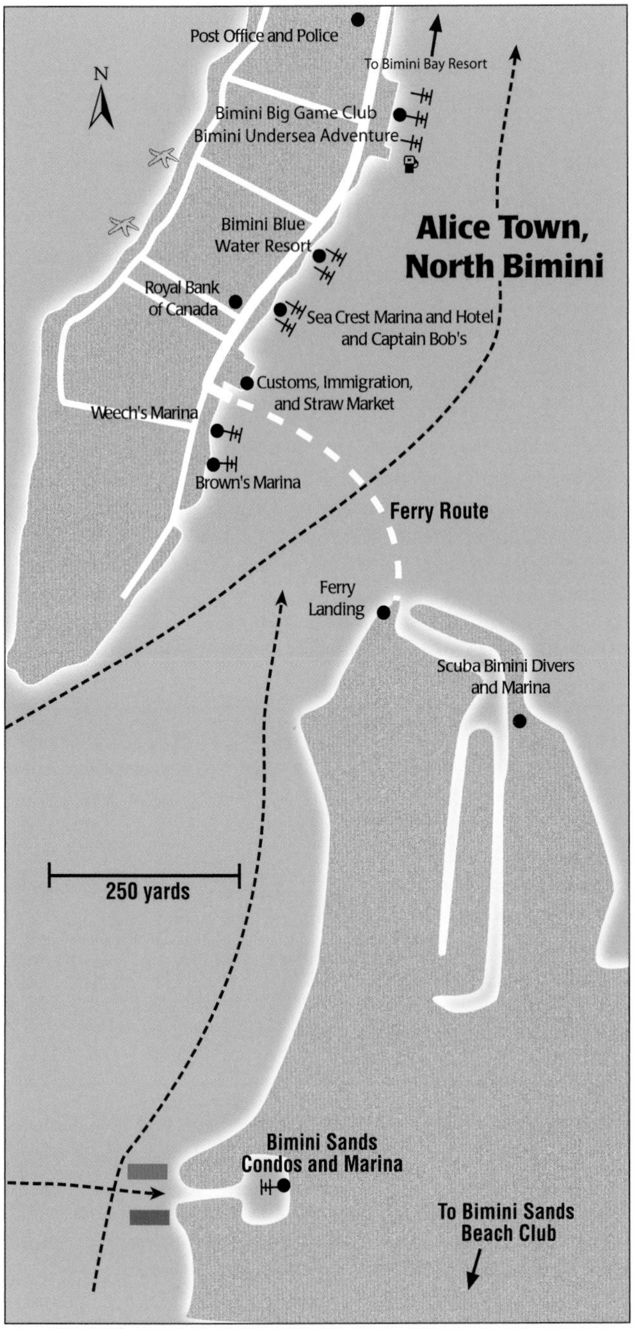

BIMINI BLUE WATER RESORT
Tel: 242-347-3166 • Fax: 242-347-3293 • VHF 68

Bimini Blue Water Marina has the best reverse osmosis (RO) water in Alice Town. This is your source for water if you need it! The marina facility offers gated security after hours. The Bimini Blue Water Resort Hotel is on Radio Beach. If you put up family and guests there, they will not be disappointed. This is Ernest Hemmingway's old haunt. Their restaurant serves excellent island cuisine. Advance reservations are recommended. Let the office know if you would like to receive a "Nassau Punch" newspaper on Tuesday. The office staff can help you with golf carts and places to putt around to on the island.
Slips 32. **Max LOA** 120 ft. **MLW at Dock** 10 ft. **Dockage** $1.00 per ft. per day. **Fuel** Diesel and gasoline; open 7 a.m. to 5 p.m. daily. **Facilities & Services** Power $10 to $25 per day, depending on boat length. **Water** $0.50 a gallon, showers, restrooms, barbecue grill, ice, public telephone, WiFi $10 for 24 hours. **Restaurant** *The Anchorage Restaurant* open 6 p.m. to 10 p.m. for dinner. **Accommodations** *The Anchorage at Blue Water Resort* Rooms from $100. **Credit Cards** Visa, MasterCard, AMEX. Pets are welcome at the marina.

BIMINI BIG GAME CLUB (GUY HARVEY RESORTS)
Tel: 242-347-3391 • Fax: 242-347-3392 • Reservations: 800-867-4764 • VHF 16 and 09 • sales@guyharveyoutpostresorts.com

Bimini Big Game Club underwent $3.5 million in renovations and was scheduled to re-open on May 1, 2010. This marina is legend for sportfishermen and its tournaments. The resort's accommodations and restaurants are favorites for visitors to Alice Town. The Guy Harvey renovations are just the cream on the top of an already wonderful marina. The dive shop offers first-class services for tanks and trips. The guest rooms and pool area will exceed your guest's expectations.
Slips 70. **Max LOA** 180 ft. **MLW at Dock** 8 ft. **Dockage** $1.50 per ft. per day. **Fuel** Future. **Facilities & Services** Power charges depend on boat length. Water charged per gallon. Showers, restroom public telephone, cable TV hookup, WiFi for a fee, barbecue grills, ice, swimming pool, weigh station, 24-hour security, spa and game room. On-site, full-service scuba. Shop with sport fishing and casual island attire. Gourmet market with delicacies and fine wines. **Restaurants & Bars** There are two restaurants. *The Tackle Box* is a casual sports bar open for breakfast, lunch and dinner daily with a live band on weekend late nights. *The Gulf Stream* is a more formal dining option open nightly in season and on weekends out of season. There is a poolside bar as well. **Accommodations** Rooms and cottages with seasonal and promotional rates. **Credit Cards** Visa, MasterCard, AMEX. **Dockmaster** Robbie Smith.

BIMINI BAY RESORT
Tel: 242-347-2900
www.biminibayresort.com/marina • VHF 16 and 68

Bimini Bay Resort is the newest, most luxurious facility on North Bimini. The marina is world-class. The resort is condominium and cottage estate territory. Marina guests are invited to utilize all of the resort's beautiful facilities. The long channel north into the marina if very well marked. You will not be disappointed by the facilities or staff that serves you here. Bimini Undersea operates a full-service dive shop on-site.
Slips 240. **Max LOA** 225 ft. **MLW at Dock** 15 ft. Dockage $2.00-$2.50 per ft. per day. **Facilities & Services** Power $0.60 per kwHr, RO water $0.45 a gallon, showers, restrooms, daily trash pick up, complimentary WiFi, public telephone, weigh-in station, ice, on-site Customs and Immigration. Tennis courts, swimming pool, playground, Bocci ball, fitness center. **Restaurant & Bar** *Casa Lyon's* open daily for breakfast and dinner. **Accommodations** One to four-bedroom suites and villas from $250-$2400 per day, plus tax and resort levy. **Credit Cards** Visa, MasterCard, AMEX.

PORT DIRECTORY FOR ALICE TOWN

Accommodations *Big John's*, 242-347-3117. Seven air-conditioned, boutique rooms with LCD televisions and luxury linens. • *Bimini Bay Resort*, 242-347-2900. One to four-bedroom suites and villas from $250 to $2400 per day, plus tax and resort levy. • *Bimini Big Game Club*, 242-347-3391. Rooms and cottages with seasonal and promotional rates. • *Bimini Blue Water*, 242-347-3166. *The Anchorage at Blue Water Resort* Rooms from $100. • *Bonefish Ebbie's*

The Alice Town cemetery. Waterway Guide Photography

Bimini Sands. Waterway Guide Photography

Bonefish Club, 242-347-2053, www.biminibonefishclub.com. Five air-conditioned kitchenettes, dockage for guests. Club Bar, dinner nightly at 7 p.m. • *Ellis Cottages*, 242-347-2258. • *Dolphin House*, 242-347-3201, ashleysaunders2@yahoo.com. Truly unique, once-in-a lifetime, accommodations, upstairs, above the artist and historian, Ashley Saunder's place. The interior walls are molded from sponges, seashells and sea fans. Crown molding is conch shells and starfish. • *Hemmingville Condos*, 242-554-4377. • *Katt's Kottages Beachside Rentals*, 242-347-3382. • *M & J Town Houses*, 242-347-3184 or 3451. Four, split-level townhouses in the center of Alice Town, just up the hill from Bimini Big Game Club. • *Sea Crest Marina Hotel*, 242-347-3071. Rooms from $105 to $143 per night. • *Weech's Bay View Rooms*, 242-347-3028. From $85; efficiency apartment sleeps four, $170 per night.

Airlines *Bimini Island Air*, 800-444-9904, 954-359-9942, 954-938-8991. Fly into South Bimini airport from Fort Lauderdale, taxi and water taxi across to North Bimini • *Island Air Charters*, 800-444-9904, 954-359-9942, islandaircharters.com • *Western Air*, 242-347-4100 • *Regional Air*, 242-347-4155 • *Continental*, 242-347-4122 • *Lynx Air*, 242-347-4988 • *Ferg's Air*, 242-377-3333, 242-357-3130. Flights to the Out Islands.

Bank *Royal Bank of Canada*, 242-347-3031. Open Monday through Thursday, 9:30 a.m. to 3 p.m.; Friday, 9:30 a.m. to 4:30 p.m. ATM, 24/7.

Boat Tours *Bimini Sands Resort and Marina*, 242-347-3500. Narrated, 40 ft. pontoon boat tours of Bimini's legendary water sites. • *Bonefish Ebbie's Sightseeing Tours*, 242-347-2053.

Bonefishing *Bonefish Ebbie's*, 242-347-2053.

Books and Magazines *Dolphin House*, 242-347-3201 • *Chic Store*, 242-347-3184 • *Sue & Joy's Variety Store*, 242-347-3115.

Churches *Community Church of God, Heavenly Vision Church of God, Holy Name Catholic Church, Mt. Zion Baptist Church, Our Lady and St. Stephen Anglican Church, Wesley Methodist Church.*

Cigars *Sue & Joy's Variety Store*, 242-347-3115.

Customs *North Bimini*, 242-347-3100 • *South Bimini Airport*, 242-347-3101.

Ferry Between North Bimini (Government Dock) and South Bimini (across from Buccaneer Point). Taxis wait at both sides.

Gifts & Souvenirs *Bimini Native Straw and Craft Market*, next to the Government Dock. Many shops, some duty free, up and down the Kings Highway. • More shops and resort fare at *Bimini Bay Resort.*

Hardware and Charts *Brown's Hardware*, 242-347-2620.

Immigration • 242-347-3446.

Laundry Coin Laundromat in *Motel* next to Robert's Groceries. In Bailey Town, *Sparkle Laundromat*, across from the Medical Center. Library Located downstairs, just north of the museum.

Liquor *Beverage Depot* • 242-347-3112; *Butler and Sands*, 242-347-3202 open 9 to 5, to 9 p.m. Sat. • *Sue and Joy's Variety Store*, 242-347-3115.

Marine Supplies *Bimini General Store*, 242-347-3028. Closed at noon on Wednesdays • *Bimini Sands Ship's Store*, 242-347-3500.

Medical *Bimini Community Health Center* • 242-347-2210; 242-347-2210 for a nurse, 347-2660 for the doctor • Open 9 to 4 weekdays with a doctor and nurse full time and an 8-bed overnight facility. Take a taxi from Alice Town to Bailey Town.

RENTALS

Bicycles *Bimini Undersea* • 242-347-3089 • $10/hour, $25/day.

Boats *Seacrest Marina* • 242-347-3477 • See Michael Murphy. *Weech's Bimini Dock* • 242-347-3028 • VHF 18 • Boston Whaler.

Golf Carts *Captain Pat's* at *Sea Crest Marina* • 242-347-3477 • VHF 68 • *Elvis Golf Cart Rental* • 242-347-3055 • *Dolphin Carts* • 242-347-3407, VHF 68.

Kayaks *Bimini Undersea Dive Shop* • 242-347-3089 • VHF 6 • trimmer@batelnet.bs. 2-person kayaks $40 half day, $70 full day, includes lifejacket and safety equipment. Instructional tours.

Scooters *Watson's Supermarket* • 242-347-3089

Museum Across from the *Straw Market*. Open weekdays, with an interesting collection of Hemingway photographs and fishing memorabilia. 242-347-3038. Don't miss it!

Police • 919, 242-347-3144 In the Government Administration building, north of the memorial park and the All Age School on the west side of King's Highway.

Provisions Mailboat comes in on Thursdays. Look for fresh produce, lunch meat and cheese, around 4 p.m. in the stores and markets. *Roberts Market* has a good selection of food in coolers and freezers, as well as fresh produce, deli meats • *Tootsie's Groceries, Inzey's Groceries, Mel Rose Grocery, King Brown Groceries* (In Bailey Town, get a walking map from tourist office; quite a hike).

Restaurants & Bars It is fun to wander along King's Highway and choose one that suits your mood and your pocketbook.

Anchorage Restaurant and Bar at *Bimini Blue Water* • 242-347-3166. Well-cooked food in an old-home setting, with large windows overlooking Radio Beach and ocean. Dinner reservations suggested. $$ • *Bimini Big Game Resort & Marina*, Gulf Stream Restaurant • 242-347-3391 • Dinner reservations recommended, live music. *The Tackle Box* sports bar serves breakfast, lunch and dinner daily. *Barefoot Bar Poolside* from mid-afternoon. Box lunches, order a day in advance. $-$$ • *Captain Bob's* Across from *Sea Crest Marina*, serving the best breakfast in Bimini from 6:30 a.m., conch burgers and grouper fingers and more at lunchtime. Let's not forget the best Bahamian dinners, too. Popular with early-rising fishermen and divers. Legend! $-$$ • *Casa Lyons* at Bimini Bay Resort. Its handmade bar of solid wood and illuminated white onyx is worth going to see. The restaurant is named after George Lyon, known for inventing the stainless steel sink among other things. It is on the site of the original building where Mr. Lyon entertained his personal friends. $$-$$$$

CJ's Deli, Air-conditioned deli serving sandwiches and local fare. $ - *Ena's Take Out*, The best of the best home-cooked food. Lunch only; Breakfast on Saturdays. Just north and a bit behind the Island *House Bar and Chic Store*, 242-347-3349. $ • *Fab's Conch Salad Bar*, in Bailey Town, worth the walk or take the tour bus, 242-347-2474. • *End of the World Sand Bar* Not to be missed! Bring the camera! Funky in all capital letters! $ • *Red Lion Pub Restaurant and Bar* on the waterfront; cheerful, with home-cooked meals. May or may not be open. Cross your fingers. Bar can be very lively scene. $

Street Food Alice Town is one of those few places where entrepreneurial ladies will open their automobile trunks and offer home-cooked and home-baked goodies—from chocolate chip cookies to conch fritters. Never, ever pass up these opportunities! This is the equivalent of fresh tortillas and goat meat tacos sold at the *topes* (speed bumps) in Mexico. It doesn't get better, more local or delicious than this.

Taxis *M & D's Taxi Service*, 242-347-2340 or 242-473-0233 • *Bank's Taxi Service*, 242-347-2104 or 242-473-0526.

Telephones At the marinas • *BTC* office, 242-347-3343.

Tourist Office Tel: 242-347-3529, www.bimini.bahamas.com, www.bahamas.com. Open Monday through Friday, 9 a.m. to 5 p.m. In the Government administration building, north of the memorial park and the All Age School on the west side of King's Highway or at the *Straw Market*, 242-347-3528.

Tours The tourist office has good walking tour maps • *Ashley Saunders*, historian and author, gives guided tours • Ansil Saunders, boatbuilder extraordinaire, 242-347-2178 • *3 B's*, VHF 68 • *TSL Transportion*, VHF 68 • *Bimini Bus 1 or 2*, VHF 68.

Trash Containers around town. Please contain it securely in heavy mil trash bags. No flimsy grocery bags!

Water Best RO water at Bluewater.

Water Taxi Service from airport to Alice Town, one-way, $5 • *3 B's Water Taxi & Bus Service*, VHF 68, Yvette Weech • TSL *Water Taxi & Bus Service*, VHF 68.

Weddings Services are available from the ministers of several denominations or by the Administrator at the Government Offices. Marriage license fee, $100; Notary fee, $20; Wedding performed by Administrator at office, $150; elsewhere, $300. CASH ONLY.

SPORTS & RECREATION

Bonefishing *Ebbie David*, 242-347-2053 or 242-359-8273 • *Benjamin Francis*, 242-347-2630 • *Leo Levarity*, 242-347-2346 • *Raymond Pritchard*, 242-347-2269 • *Mark Rolle*, 242-347-2462 • *Ansil Saunders*, 242-347-2696 • *Tommy Sewell*, 242-347-3234 • *Edward Stuart*, 242-347-2328.

Deep Sea Guides *Capt. Frank Hinzez*, 242-347-3072 • *Capt. Jerome Stuart*, 242-347-2081 • *Capt. Alfred Sweeting*, 242-347-3477.

Dive Sites *Bimini Undersea* has marked a number of sites with their own buoys, which not only make locating the dive sites easier, but also protects the reef. You are welcome to pick up one of their buoys for your dive if they are not using it themselves, but please call them first on VHF 06. A list of GPS coordinates for dive site positions is available from them for $25, which goes to help maintain these buoys.

Diving Bill & Nowdla Keefe's Bimini Undersea • 242-347-3089 and 305-653-5572 • Fax: 242-347-3079 • VHF 6 • info@biminiundersea.com • www.biminiundersea.com • Located at *Bimini Big Game Resort & Bimini Big Game Club.* They offer a full range of dive experiences, snorkeling, wild dolphin excursions, kayaking, rentals, air fills, bicycles and cameras. Two-tank dives and snorkeling trips include rental gear. Tel: 800-348-4644. In the U.S., Chris Keefe • *SCUBA Bimini*, 242-347-4444, www.scubabimini.com. At SCUBA Bimini Dive Resort. 2-tank dive, dive packages, rentals, daily reef and wreck dives.

SOUTH BIMINI

airport • customs & immigration • fuel • groceries • marina • restaurant • telephone • water

Separated by only 150 yards of water from its northern neighbor, South Bimini is an attractive alternative to the activity of Alice Town. There are a few homes, *Big Willie's* Laundromat, liquor, and grocery store on the north end, as well as an automobile and small boat repair shop close to the airport and the SCUBA *Bimini Dive Resort* on a narrow canal catering to divers. The salmon-colored townhouses you see as you approach Alice Town Harbour are *Bimini Sands Condos & Marina* with their own marina entrance clearly marked. This development, along with their *Bimini Sands Beach Club* at the southern tip of the island, are treasured safe harbours for weather weary cruisers. *Bimini Sands Marina* is a Port of Entry.

While staying at South Bimini, don't miss touring the Bimini Biological Field Station where the role of the lemon shark in the tropical-marine ecosystem is researched, hiking the Bimini Nature Trail with a guide who will increase your knowledge of island flora and fauna, visiting Ponce de Leon's Fountain of Youth (you won't regain your youth, but he did visit here in 1513), Bul Peter Well (a natural rock well carved by an ex-slave to water his crops), The Healing Hole (a freshwater spring that percolates inside a saltwater mangrove swamp) and The Sand Mounds (enormous creature shaped mounds thought to be 1,000s of years old that rise above the mangroves).

MARINAS

BIMINI SANDS MARINA and BIMINI BEACH CLUB
Tel: 242-347-3500 • Fax: 242-347-3501 • VHF 68 and 16
www.biminisands.com

Slips 60 floating docks at *Bimini Sands*, 45 slips at the *Beach Club* **Max LOA** 110 ft. **MLW at Dock** 8 ft. **Dockage** $1.10 per ft. per day over 30 ft, up to 30 ft $33 per night at Bimini Sands; $0.70 per ft, per day, up to 30 ft. $27 per night at the Beach Club. **Fuel** Diesel, gas, oils; open 7:30 a.m. to 5:30 p.m. daily at Bimini Sands. **Facilities & Services** Power $10 per night, RO water $0.20 per gallon, showers, restrooms, coin-operated laundry $3 per load, public telephone, complimentary WiFi, grills and Tiki huts on the beach, gas grill by the tennis court, ice, ship's store and commissary, swimming pools on both properties, complete recreational activities department offering rentals and arranging trips to snorkel, feed sharks, swim with dolphins, etc. grant@biminisands.com or katie@biminisands.com. Diving with Bimini Undersea • 242-347-3089 or *SCUBA Bimini* • 242-347-4444; fishing charters, tennis courts lighted until 10 p.m., snorkeling. **Restaurant & Bar** *The Petite Conch*, with its interesting tables made by a local artist, is open 7:30 a.m. to 10 p.m. daily in season. Sushi bar open Wednesday through Saturday. *The Bimini Beach Club*, open 3 p.m. to 10 p.m. daily. **Accommodations** One to three-bedroom condominiums from $250 to $425 per night, minimum 2 nights; well-equipped and spotlessly clean. Promotional rates for marina guests. **Credit Cards** Visa, MasterCard, AMEX. Personal and Travelers Checks. Both marinas welcome pets.

PORT DIRECTORY

Airport and Airlines Fly into South Bimini Airport take taxi to South Bimini facilities or water taxi across to North Bimini. • *Bimini Island Air* • 954-938-8991 800-444-9904, 954-359-9942 • Fly into South Bimini airport from Fort Lauderdale, taxi and water taxi across to North Bimini • *Island Air Charters*, 800-444-9904, 954-359-9942, islandaircharters.com • *Western Air*, 242-347-4100 • *Regional Air*, 242-347-4155 • *Continental*, 242-347-4122 • *Ferg's Air*, 242-377-3333, 242-357-3130. Flights to the Out Islands.

Accommodations *Bonefish Ebbie's Bonefish Club*, 242-347-2053, www.biminibonefishclub.com. Five air-conditioned kitchenettes, dockage for guests. Club Bar, dinner nightly at 7 p.m. • *Bimini Sands Marina*, One-to three-bedroom condominiums from $250 to $425 per night, minimum 2 nights; well-equipped and spotlessly clean. Promotional rates for marina guests • *SCUBA Bimini Dive Resort*, 242-347-4444, www.scubabimini.com.

Bonefishing *Bonefish Ebbie's Bonefish Club*, 242-347-2053, www.biminibonefishclub.com.

Customs and Immigration On site at *Bimini Sands Marina* and the airport.

Diving SCUBA Bimini • 242-347-4444 • www.scubabimini.com • At *Scuba Bimini Dive Resort*. 2-tank dive, dive packages, rentals, daily reef and wreck dives.

Sail boat on island shoreline. Photograph Courtesy of Gavin Spencer

Restaurants *Bimini Sands*, 242-347-3500. *Mackey's Sand Bar*, breakfast, lunch and dinner • *Petite Conch Restaurant*, opens at 3 p.m. for lunch and dinner. Live music, $-$$ CASH ONLY.

Water Best RO water at Bimini Sands.

THINGS TO DO IN NORTH AND SOUTH BIMINI

- Take off your watch and get accustomed to Bahamian time.
- Find the remains of the Compleat Angler and yearn for yesteryears.
- Dive the Bimini Road; maybe discover Atlantis? (not the one in Nassau).
- Visit the Bimini Museum.
- Take your boat and your bride to Honeymoon Cove.
- Sign up for a kayak or snorkeling eco-tour with Bimini Undersea to East Wells, Three Sisters Rock and Rainbow Reef.
- Visit Juan Ponce de León's Fountain of Youth on South Bimini.
- Go fishing!

NORTH CAT CAY

customs & immigration • fuel • marina • medical • restaurant • telephone • water

North Cat Cay is privately owned by the members of the *Cat Cay Yacht Club* with an excellent marina that welcomes visiting boats if space is available. It makes a pleasant overnight stop after crossing the Gulf Stream from Florida or the Bank from Chub Cay. You can clear in with Customs (242-347-5011) and Immigration at Cat Cay from 9:30 a.m. to 4 p.m. weekdays; there is a docking fee unless you stay overnight. Transient guests can enjoy the marina area and facilities including the *Nauticat Restaurant* and *BU's Bar,* the commissary, boutique and clinic.

MARINA

CAT CAY YACHT CLUB
Tel: 242-347-3565 • Fax: 242-347-3564 • VHF 16 • sbain@catcayyachtclub.com

Slips 80. **Max LOA** up 150. **MLW at Dock** 9 ft. **Dockage** $3.25 per ft. per day, for transient guests, less for members. **Fuel** Diesel and gasoline, open 8 a.m. to 5 p.m. daily. **Facilities & Services** Power $0.65 per kwHr for 30 Amp, 50 Amp and 100 Amp, RO water $0.40 per gallon; showers, restrooms, coin-op laundry $1.00 per load, public telephone, cable TV, complimentary WiFi, barbecue grills with picnic tables, bait, tackle and ice. The office will send or receive faxes for you. Medical clinic next to the commissary staffed by Emergency Medical Physicians. Fully-equipped; emergency air evacuation service available. Boutique with logo wear and commissary with a good selection of groceries, produce, dairy products and liquor, open daily 9 to 5, to 2 p.m. Sundays. Daily STOL flights to Fort Lauderdale with Island Air Charters (954-359-9942). Rental accommodations for sponsored guests only. Golf course and tennis for members. **Restaurant & Bar** *The Nauticat Restaurant* open for lunch and dinner to marina guests, with a pleasant veranda bar for drinks; collared shirt and long trousers required for dinner in the dining room. *BU's Bar* dockside. Security Police on island; 24-hr security. **Credit Cards** Visa, MasterCard, AMEX. Pets are welcome at marina.

Chapter 9
The Great Bahama Bank

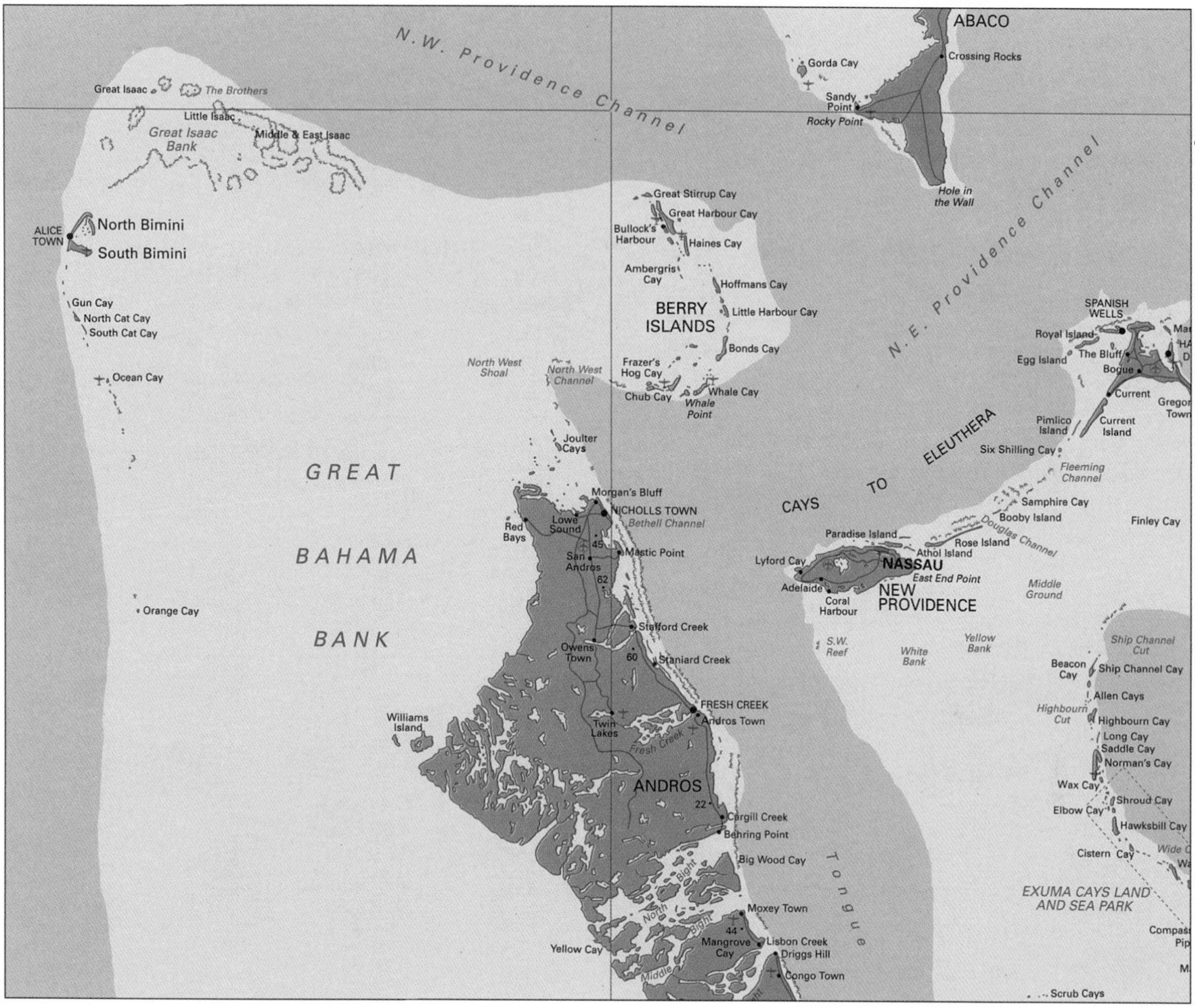

Looking At the Charts

The Great Bahama Bank is, by anyone's standard, a significant sea area. It is a great tableland of shallow water that has a pervasive influence on the tides and currents, wave patterns, navigable routes and marine life of the central Bahamas just as the Little Bahama Bank influences the north.

First, let us mention size. The Great Bahama Bank extends 50 nautical miles across at its widest point and measures about 180 nautical miles from north to south. Its waters are mostly 4.5–5.4 meters/15–18 feet deep, but it spawns far shallower sandbars that are always changing. For this reason, the bank is almost impossible for cartographers to survey accurately. There are navigation aids on the main routes across the bank, but the constantly changing depth contours, and the loss of beacons in storms or through human inattention, make these markers a bonus if they are in place. They are not signposts on which to rely.

The tidal set across the Great Bahama Bank, like the set across its smaller cousin to the north, runs roughly northeast to southwest. The autopilot may compensate for this, or alternatively, you must keep an eye on the cross track error and make continual adjustments, which will be needed for both tide and wind.

For the cruising skipper, the overriding concern is the immense size of the Great Bahama Bank and the consequent length of navigational routes that cross it. Any way you choose, there are 75 nautical miles of bank to cross no matter which way you are heading. This means if you are sailing from North Cat Cay to Chub Cay, the distance to run may be greater than your achievable daytime range. If this is so, and it is impossible to squeeze your Great Bahama Bank passage into every available minute of daylight to complete the course, there is only one answer - anchor out during the night.

Anchoring out on the bank is not difficult, and it is done often. Pick a spot well off the beaten track in shallow water so that a Bahamian freighter doesn't plough you down during the night. Set your anchor well, and use visible and identifiable anchor lighting. As previously mentioned, you do not want to be mistaken at 3 a.m. for Russell Beacon Light. Make sure to use a deck-level light along with a masthead light. Like any shallow sea, be prepared for an unpleasant, short chop if the wind picks up.

In the Spotlight. The Northwest Channel Light

Most eastern routes across the Bank ultimately converge at the Northwest Channel Light. Some vessels enter the western edge of the Great Bahama Bank from the north at Hen and Chickens or North Rock to Mackie Shoal to the Northwest Channel Light (approximately 57 to 59 nautical miles). Others may enter from the south, Riding Rock to Russell Beacon to the Northwest Channel Light (approximately 56 nautical miles). Most cruisers take a straight shot from Gun Cay Cut to the North Cat Cay waypoint to the Northwest Channel Light to the Chub Cay waypoint (approximately 64 nautical miles to the light or 78 nautical miles to Chub Cay). The Northwest Channel Light (NWCHL) waypoint is set a bit to the north of the beacon. This waypoint should serve as a course to plot. Do not plan to see a "light" as it is frequently missing. Whatever you do, don't swing too far north or south of the light tower's position (N 25° 28.200'/W 078° 09.600'). There are reefs and shoals both to the north and to the south. The Northwest Channel Light marks the western finger of the Northwest Channel. It is an area where confused seas are common due to the confluence of tidal flows and the effect of two deep bodies of water—the Northwest Providence Channel and the Tongue of the Ocean—converging at the very shallow bank. The Northwest Channel Light is the jumping off spot to visit Chub Cay, Frazers Hog and the gorgeous Berry Islands, or to head southwest to Andros or southeast to New Providence. The conditions you encounter at the light may well determine which direction you choose to venture. Our editor was caught out at Northwest Channel in a gale about 10 years ago. It came up unexpectedly and produced huge seas coming onto the Banks from the deep waters of the Tongue of the Ocean. Make sure you have enough time to get from the North Cat Cay or Bimini Islands across the Banks to your destination with a generous weather window.

Clearing In—Your Options in the Central Bahamas

If you didn't clear Customs and Immigration in the Bimini Islands or at North Cat Cay, Chub Cay is a good option. Expect to pay dockage to clear in, however. If you choose to wait until you reach Andros or New Providence, you must be prepared to restrain yourself and your crew from going ashore and to keep your Q flag flying.

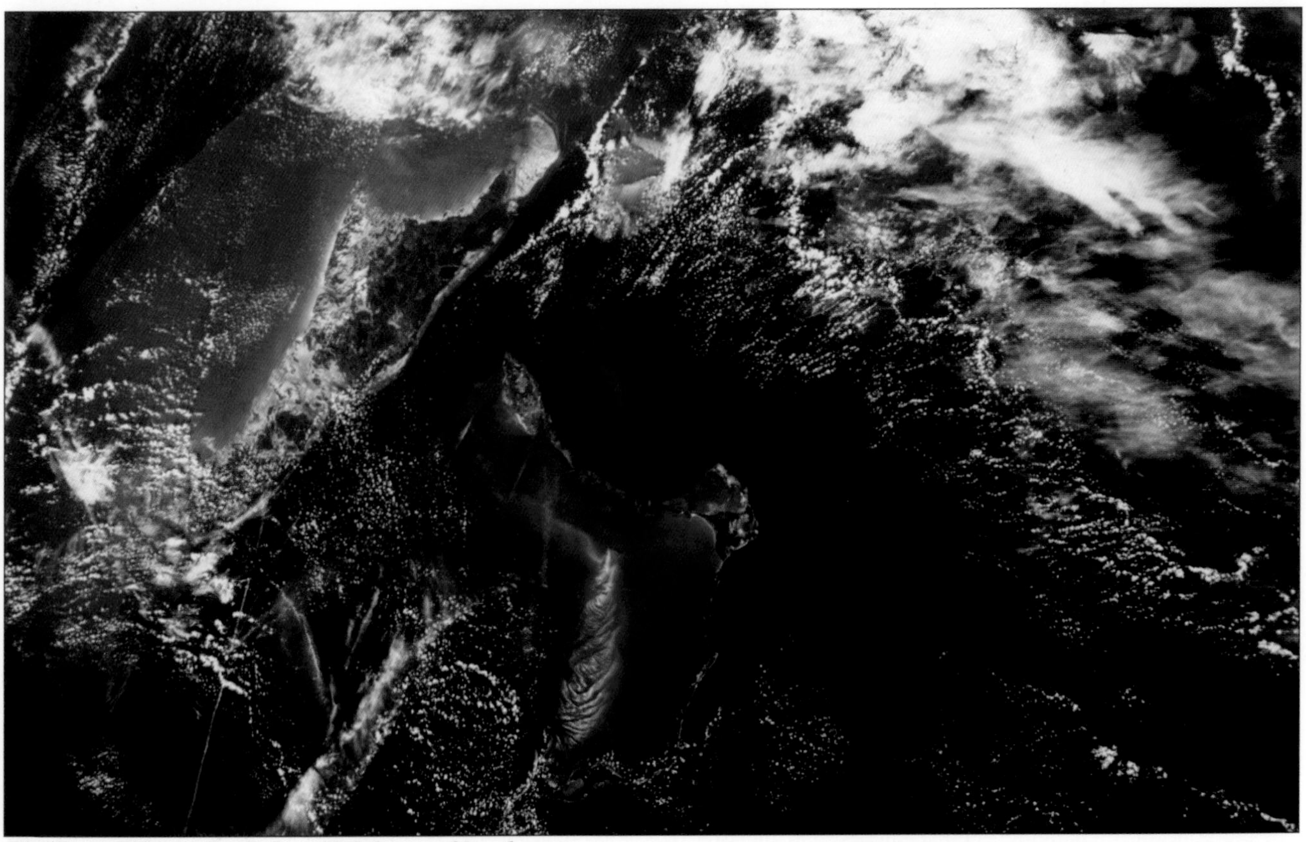

The Great Bahama Bank, from Skylab, seen from the east.

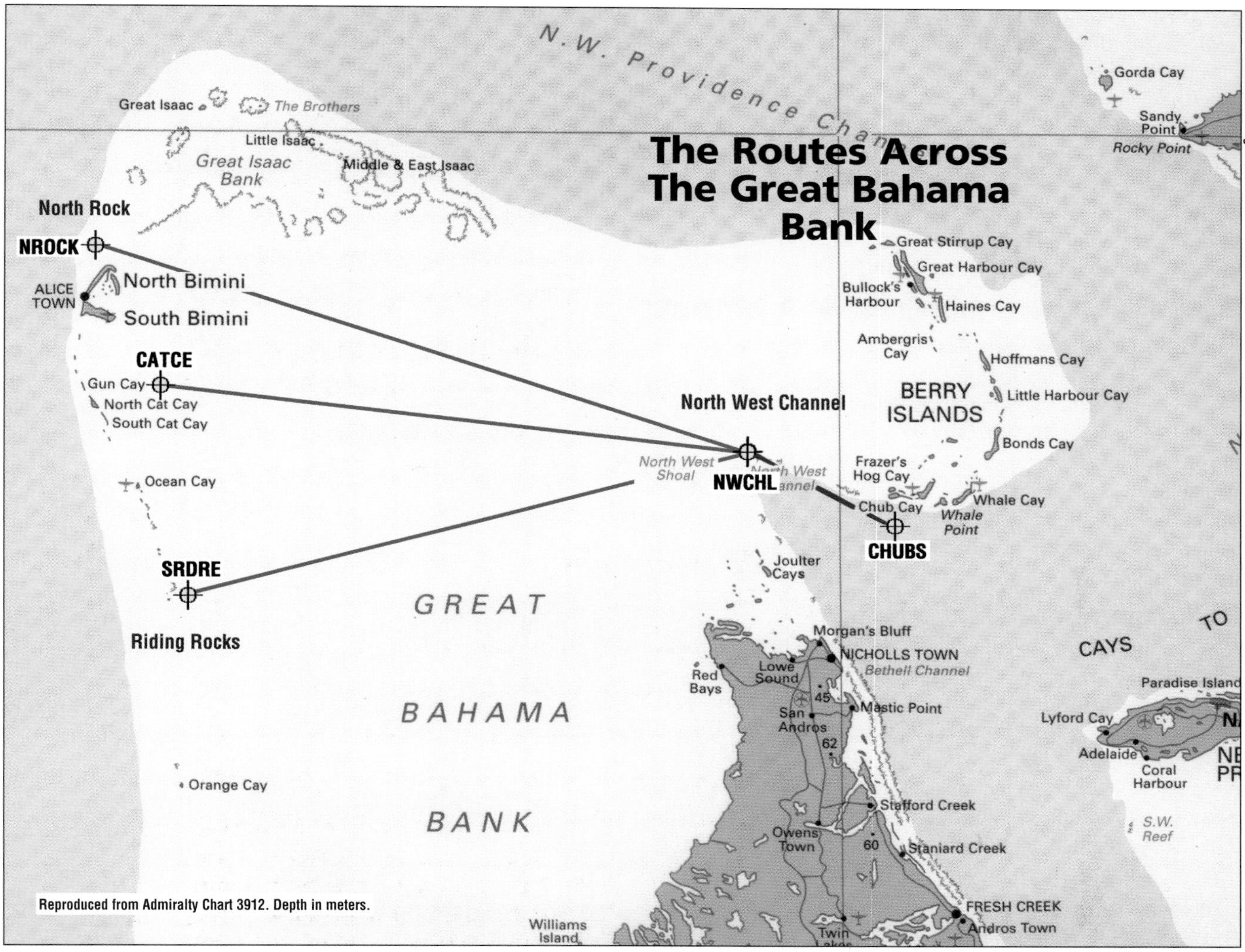

What's There? The Great Bahama Bank

There are several west-to-east routes across the Great Bahama Bank. Let's discuss these first, and then look at the options at the Northwest Channel Light junction.

Northern Departure Points: North Rock, Moselle Bank and Hen & Chickens

If you would like to ride the Gulf Stream beyond North Bimini or have accidentally overshot the island, you can enter the Great Bahama Bank at Moselle Bank (N 25° 50.000'/W 079° 16.000'), North Rock (N 25° 51.000'/ W 079° 16.500') or Hen and Chickens (N 26° 00.600'/W 079° 06.500'). All three are perfectly viable destinations for entering the Bank to make your way east. From Hen and Chickens, you can divert to the Berry Island's Bullocks Harbour area along the Moselle Bank route or continue to Mackie Shoal (N 25°42.000'/W 078° 40.000') and on to the Northwest Channel.

It is a straight shot from Moselle Bank to Bullocks Harbor, or you can also divert to Mackie Shoal when you cross the Hen & Chickens route. Follow the North Rock route to Mackie Shoal. If you would like to sidetrack to Bullocks Harbour, you can do so three-fourths of the way down to the Northwest Channel on the Berrys Bank dogleg (N 25°36.000'/W 078°14.000').

Many cruisers prefer these entry routes onto the Great Bank particularly if they need to depart from a more northern Florida city and can't fight the Gulf Stream. In addition, these waters are less popular with island freighters and mailboats. They provide deeper waters en route and, perhaps, safer options for anchoring on the banks at night in shallower pools.

Gun Cay Cut to Cat Cay Waypoint to the Northwest Channel Light

Once you have passed through Gun Cay Cut and dipped south to avoid the shifting sandbars, you can set a straight course for the Cat Cay waypoint (N 25° 34.000'/W 079° 13.000') and then the Northwest Channel Light (N 25° 28.250'/W 078° 09.500'). Choose an overnight anchoring spot on the Great Bank with care on this route. The Gun Cay Cut to Cat Cay waypoint to the Northwest Channel Light and on to either Chub Cay or Nassau are the most popular and heavily traveled of all the Great Bahama Bank transit routes.

If you like, you can work your way north to cruise south through the Berry Islands on the way to Nassau. Or, if you just want to anchor in some idyllic waters, take the Berrys Bank dogleg north at the Northwest Shoal Light (N 25° 30.000'/W 078° 14.000'). The recommended anchorages are just a wee bit north and then due east of either the Northwest Shoal Light or the Berrys Bank waypoint. There is good conching in the grassy patches here. It is not unusual to see local skiffs piled mountain high with conch shells plying these waters.

South Riding Rock to Russell Beacon to Northwest Channel Light

If you have no interest in the Bimini Islands, and started very south from Florida, you can pass onto the bank just south of South Riding Rock (N 25° 14.400'/W 079° 09.000'). There are no problems gaining the bank here, and you can set a direct course for Russell Beacon (N 25° 28.500'/W 078° 25.500') and on to the Northwest Channel Light. You may encounter more sand ridges and shallower-than-average water along this route, perhaps as little as 1.8 meters/6 feet deep in places.

Routes from Grand Bahama Island

Coming from Port Lucaya, Grand Bahama and bound for either Chub Cay in the Berry Islands, Nassau on New Providence or Fresh Creek on Andros, the transit to and the short trip across the Great Bahama Bank is safest by way of Lucaya to Bullocks Harbour, Bullocks Harbour to Berrys Bank, Berrys Bank to Northwest Shoal Light and then on to the Northwest Channel Light. The more adventuresome can plot a direct route from Port Lucaya to the Berry's Bank waypoint, but this route has not been proven and does not show up in guidebooks and charts as a recommended route.

Options After the Northwest Channel Light

After the Northwest Channel light, you have three options. The first is Chub Cay, nearby (14 nautical miles) and very inviting, in the southern Berry Islands. The second is Nassau, almost 50 nautical miles farther on across the Northwest Providence Channel. The third, southeast approximately 20 nautical miles in extremely deep water, is Morgan's Bluff on North Andros, with other Andros alternatives farther south (Fresh Creek).

Pilotage. Talking Captain to Captain

North Rock to Northwest Channel Light

Two shoal areas, which need to be avoided, lie across what would be the straight-line track from North Rock to the Northwest Channel Light. There is also the wreck of a ship with just 0.9-meter/3-foot depths, shown on the chart at N 25° 47.000'/W 079° 06.750', which lies to the south of the route by 0.75 nautical mile. Watch to correct your cross track error on the first leg. The first of the shoal areas, Mackie Shoal, lies across the path at the 35-nautical-mile point, so one has to head a little more north than they might wish to at the outset. The shoal is marked with a stake and light. The second shoal area is the Northwest Shoal, north of the Northwest Channel Light. It too, is hopefully staked and lighted. This route offers good anchoring options off the Northwest Shoals and lovely alternative destinations to the north if persistent south-southeast winds are predicted on the nose.

South Riding Rock to Northwest Channel Light

The 2.26 nautical miles from the South Riding Rock West (SRDRW) waypoint to the east waypoint (SRDRE) must be visually piloted. The second waypoint is your departure point for the Great Bahama Bank crossing.

Northwest Channel Light to Andros

If you are going to Andros, consider going first to the Chub Cay waypoint (CHUBS), and then set a course for your destination. It is a dogleg, but a safer route that keeps you in deep water and well away from the area of shoal, rocks, small cays and reefs that lie to the north of Andros. ■

Waterway Guide is always open to your observations from the helm. E-mail your comments on any navigation information in the guide to: editor@waterwayguide.com.

Waterway Guide advertising sponsors play a vital role in bringing you the most trusted and well-respected cruising guide in the country. Without our advertising sponsors, we simply couldn't produce the top-notch publication now resting in your hands. Next time you stop in for a peaceful night's rest, let them know where you found them—Waterway Guide, The Cruising Authority.

Great Bahama Bank Waypoints

Great Isaac	ISAAC (B4)	26°06.00N / 79°02.00W
Moselle Bank	MOSEL (B6)	25°50.00N / 79°16.00W
North Rock	NROCK	25°51.00N / 79°16.50W
Mackie Shoal	MCKIE (B9)	25°42.00N / 78°40.00W
Russell Turn Point	RUSSL	25°29.97N / 78°26.47W
Northwest Channel Light	NWCHL (B19)	25°28.25N / 78°09.50W
South Riding Rock West	SRDRW	25°13.50N / 79°11.00W
South Riding Rock East	SRDRE (B73)	25°13.40N / 79°09.00W

Our position format is latitude and longitude in degrees and minutes (hddd°mm.mm). Waypoints in RED are NOT for autopilot navigation. Codes in parenthesis are Wavey Line waypoints marked on the charts. If you have programmed waypoints we listed in a previous edition of this guide, check carefully to ensure the coordinates you have recorded match the list. If a waypoint is no longer on our list we may have changed its code or deleted it.

Sunset over Chub Cay. Waterway Guide Photography.

Chapter 10
The Berry Islands

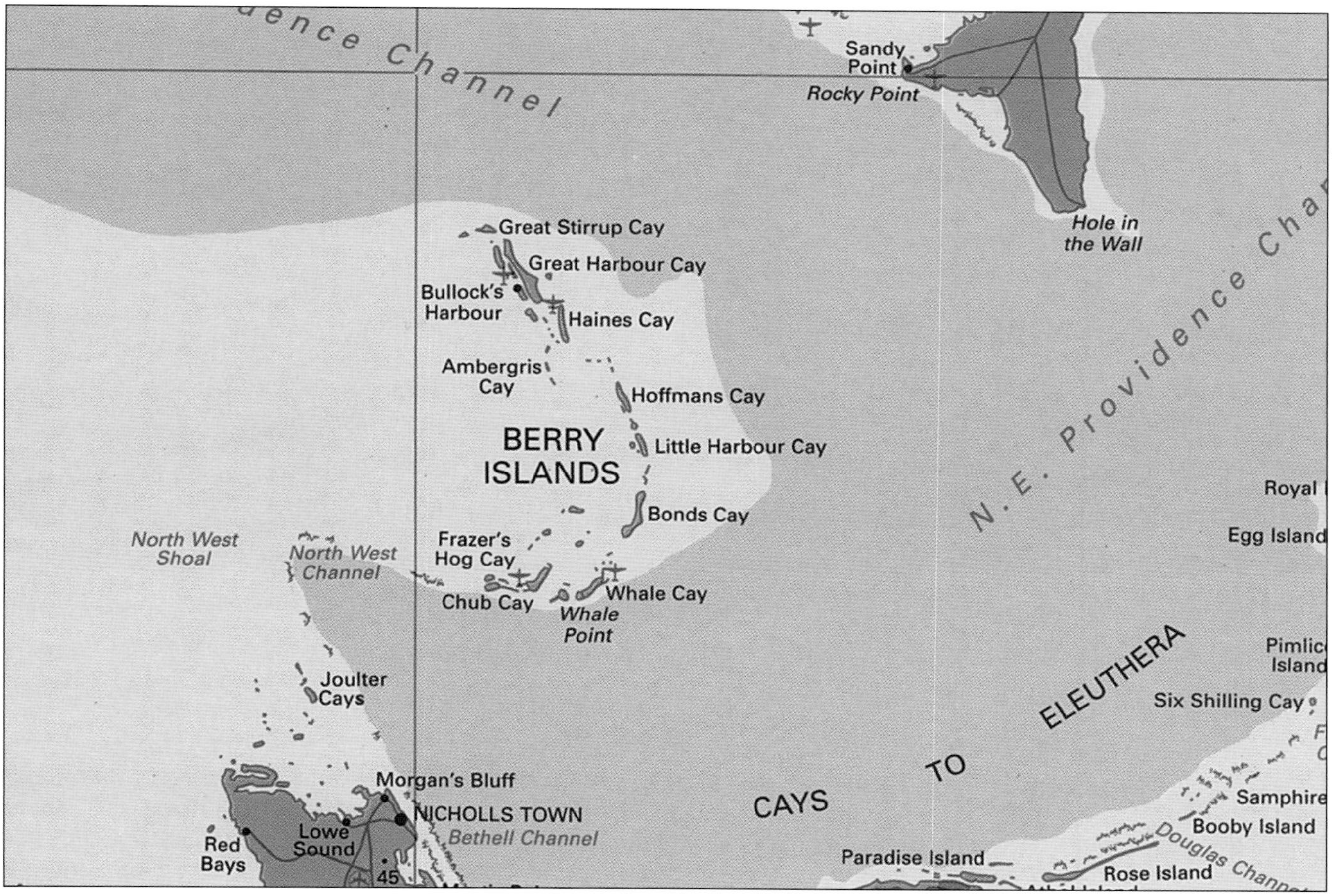

Looking At the Charts

The Berry Islands, an enchanting crescent of small cays lying on the eastern extension of the Great Bahama Bank, skirt the edge of the Atlantic Ocean. The Northwest Providence Channel runs between Grand Bahama Island and the northern cays. The Northwest Channel separates the southern Berrys from Andros. The Northwest Providence Channel separates them from the Abacos. And, the Northeast Providence Channel separates them from New Providence Island.

Shoal-draft boats can hop from cay to cay within the Great Bank watersing of owning your own little bit of paradise is enhanced. The Berry Islands do not usually appear on the cruising itineraries of those who seek crowds or organized activities. For cruisers who do seek unadulterated isolation, the small unfrequented anchorages tucked behind the cays offer great appeal.

The northern Berry Islands, apart from the cruise lines' faux Tiki villages on Little Stirrup and Great Stirrup Cays, have remained largely untouched. Bullocks Harbour settlement on Great Harbour Cay offers everything cruising boats seek—a good selection of funky restaurants and bars, well-stocked grocery and liquor stores and a marina protected enough to ride out a hurricane. Don't miss the unrivaled, fiery conch salad served by local fishermen at the eastern end of the marina pier.

A short walk farther east and up the hill brings visitors to the ghostly remains of the Old Sugar Loaf Lodge; built by the "Rat Pack"—Frank Sinatra, Dean Martin, Sammy Davis Jr., Joey Bishop and Peter Lawford—as their private playground for friends like Judy Garland, Marilyn Monroe, Shirley MacLaine, Lauren Bacall and Angie Dickinson. Musing over what is left of the incredible stone lodge structure, one can only hope that someday it will be brought back to its former grandeur.

Not to be outdone, some of the southern Berrys are owned by equally interesting celebrities. Along with Florida property developers who envision an angler's seventh heaven at Chub Cay, celebrities as unlikely as pop star Shakira and Pink Floyd's Roger Waters own property here. Shakira plans to develop her island with a 14,000-square-foot art museum and an 85,000-square-foot sports center with the capacity to host large-scale events. It may only be a Shakira fantasy,

Chub Cay Marina, from the southwest. (Not to be used for navigation.) WATERWAY GUIDE PHOTOGRAPHY.

but it has paid off for others to dream big in the Bahamas. We lucky cruisers can watch the progress, or not, while enjoying the same beautiful waters and excellent fishing in the Berry Islands.

In the Spotlight. Chub Cay

Chub Cay is perfectly located to serve as a final destination for anglers content to remain in the Berry Islands or as a staging point for boats heading to New Providence, Eleuthera or the Exumas. For anglers, whose goal is to land the big one in the Northwest Providence Channel or the Tongue of the Ocean between Andros and the Exuma Bank, Chub Cay couldn't be better placed. If you are sailing, Chub Cay is at the limit of your daytime cruising range crossing the Great Bahama Bank. If you want to dive in the Bahamas, the Chub Cay area offers a wide a range of dive sites including a wall.

For years, Chub Cay was the Great Bahama Bank's travelers refuge. The anchorage offered decent protection from prevailing winds, and the marina welcomed cruisers into its harbor to use its fuel dock, laundry, showers, grocery store and homey restaurant and transient dockage (when available).

Today, under new ownership, it has transformed from a cruisers haven to an exclusive anglers club. The entrance channel is enlarged, dredged and lighted. The docks are state-of-the-art, concrete floating berths. Customs and Immigration are available for marina guests and club members. Their offices are at the private airport with its 5,000-foot-long asphalt runway. Depending on supply, fuel may be available to marina guests only. The beach, luxurious clubhouse, pool and surrounding grounds are for guests and club members only. Do not dinghy into the beach to run your dog or mosey around. There are resident police on Chub Cay protecting the members villas and facilities.

Clearing In—Your Options in the Berry Islands

You have two choices available: one north and one south. In the north, friendly and reasonable Great Harbour Cay Marina at Bullocks Harbour can arrange for Customs and Immigration officials to come from the public airport to the marina. In the south, private and impeccable Chub Cay Club offers Customs and Immigration clearance to members and guests of its facilities.

What's There? The Berry Islands

Great Stirrup and Little Stirrup Cays

At the western end of Great Stirrup Cay, on the north shore at Bertram Cove, you will spot the Norwegian Cruise Line passengers' faux village. It is not in cruising boat waters, and one hardly knows that it is there. At the eastern end of Great Stirrup, in Great Harbour, you can go ashore and hike up to the old, white lighthouse. There is a panoramic view from the hilltop. Land your dinghy at the small, grassy beach at Panton Cove to make the hike. The anchorages in Great Harbour can be difficult to set an anchor and are subject to current and surge, but when a blow kicks up the Northwest Providence Channel, you will have plenty of company, often for quite awhile.

Little Stirrup Cay, from the southwest. (Not to be used for navigation.) WATERWAY GUIDE PHOTOGRAPHY.

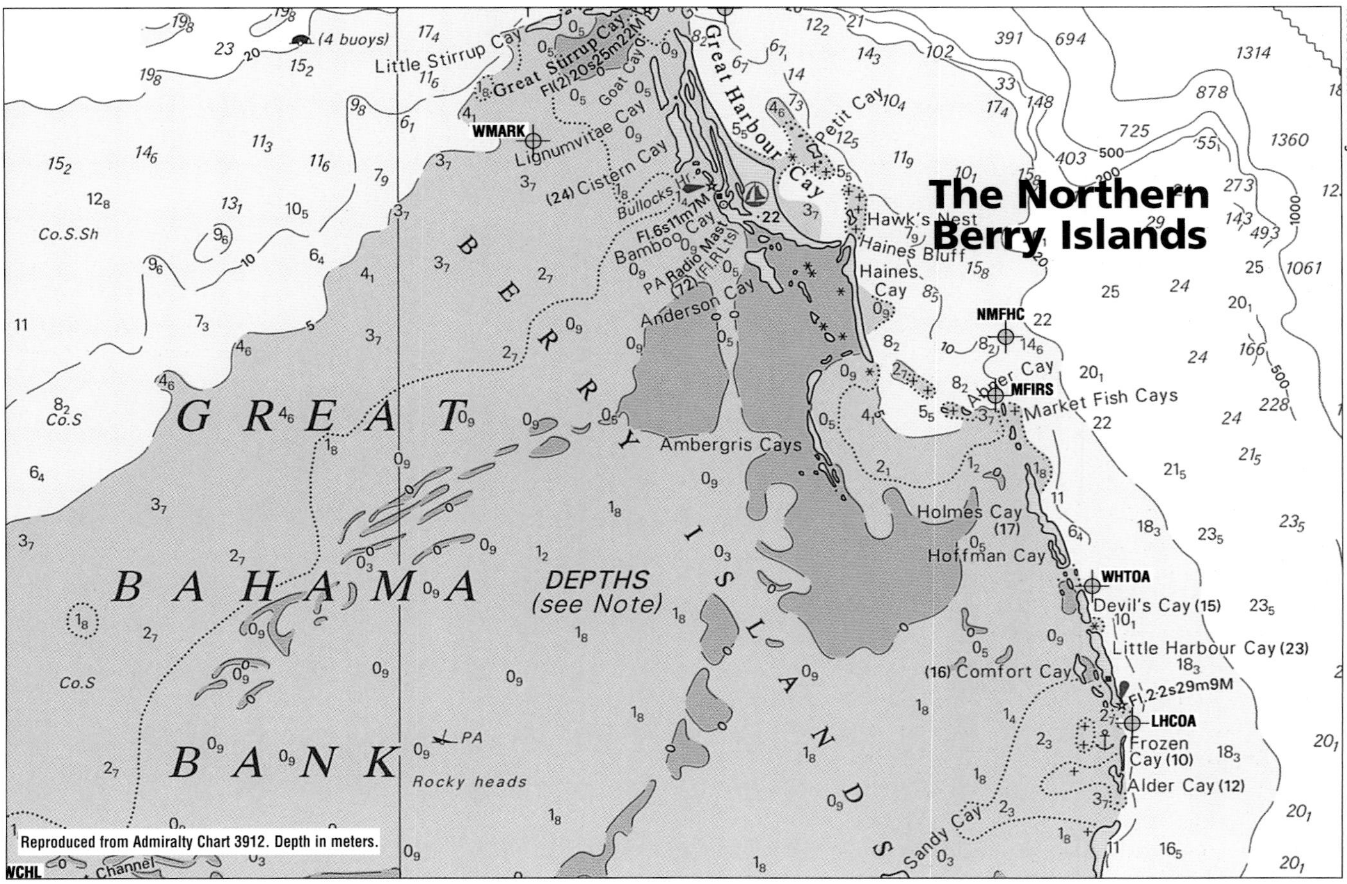

Reproduced from Admiralty Chart 3912. Depth in meters.

Little Stirrup Cay, from the northeast. WATERWAY GUIDE PHOTOGRAPHY.

Great Harbour

At this point, maybe we should make clear that Great Harbour (the sea area between Great Stirrup Cay and the north end of Great Harbour Cay) is no harbor at all. You can anchor there, in one of three anchorages, which we cover below. All of them have some protection. But that is it. If you are after a real harbor in the Northern Berrys, there is only one, and that is Great Harbour Cay Marina on the west side of Great Harbour Cay (just about halfway down).

Great Harbour Anchorages

The best protection and holding is found, tucked up as close as you dare get, to the northwestern shore of Great Harbour Cay, south of its tip, in 1.8 meters/6 feet of water. Although there is more water than charted on the western shore, take care maneuvering south and east. It goes from 6 feet to next-to-nothing quickly.

If you need more water under your keel and don't mind strong current, wiggle as far south as you can into the deep pool of water west of Lignumvitae Cay. You will easily find 2.5 meters/8 feet of water. Be forewarned, however, the workers at the cruise line "villages" blast by here in large skiffs, full-out, early in the morning from Bullocks Harbour.

Panton anchorage is in the cove beneath the Great Stirrup lighthouse. It is shallow (1.8 meters/6 feet deep at best) and restricted by tiny Snake Cay that lies to the east. With shoal draft, a vessel can work its way farther up the shoreline. Otherwise, one is forced to anchor farther out. This can be uncomfortable. There is protection from the north, but not much else. The holding around Panton Cove is not good.

Goat Cay has good water, some 3 meters/10 feet or more in places, off its east-facing side. This will shield you from the west, but otherwise you are in the open, subject to surprisingly strong current and surge, and exposed from all other directions.

Little Stirrup Cay is a Royal Caribbean Cruise Line playground. When anchored off the cay, their tenders land passengers non-stop for swimming, volleyball, water sports and lounging. Everything is waiting for them at the eastern end of the cay, a mini-settlement complete with shops, hundreds of beach chaises, bars, a cafeteria and a first-aid station. The number and size of the water toys available at the southern

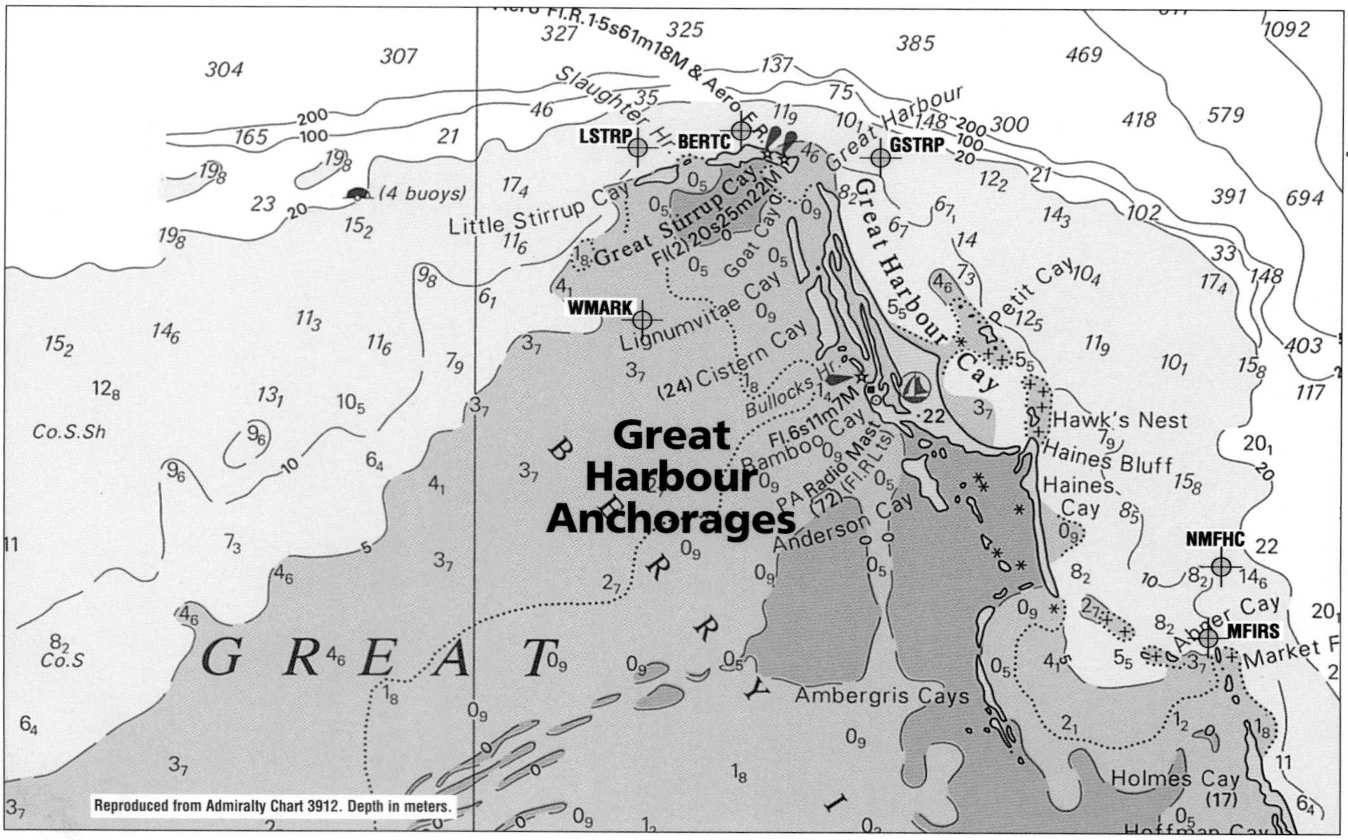

Not to be used for navigation.

Great Harbour Cay Marina, from the southeast. (Not to be used for navigation.) WATERWAY GUIDE PHOTOGRAPHY.

tip of the cay is amazing. You can still enjoy the anchorage at Slaughter Harbour when the cruise ships aren't visiting. With all the activity, it becomes quite chaotic if they are. Take care to avoid the trains of inexperienced personal watercraft operators that circle the cays.

You are part of the scenery here, and the passengers enjoy taking your picture as you cruise on by towards Bullocks Harbour or to the anchorages at Great Harbour. Smile and wave. They can only dream of participating in what you are doing.

Great Harbour Cay

Nearly six nautical miles long, but hardly a mile wide, Great Harbour Cay is by geography and population a key player in the northern Berry Islands. It has a public airstrip, regular service to Nassau and a fine marina—the only marina in the northern Berrys.

The main settlement, Bullocks Harbour, would be its own little isle if not for the isthmus that connects it to Great Harbour Cay. Its government dock is at the northern tip, just in front of the public park with a seawall and cleats to tie up dinghies. The park is a hub of weekend and holiday activity. A fish fry there is not to be missed. The settlement is strung out along the main road going south.

You will pass every aspect of settlement life on the main road from churches to schools to Coolie Mae's Sports Bar and Restaurant. About halfway down the island, the road takes a sharp bend to the east. Along this stretch, there is a good-sized market with fresh produce, plenty of refrigerated foods and a good selection of frozen items. There are also liquor stores, including a Bristol store with a good wine section, a post office, a clinic with the wonderful nurse, "Frenchie" and some interesting side streets to walk about. What you will not find is a way to the marina. The marina channel splits the small isle on which Bullocks Harbour settlement sits. Long ago there was a connecting bridge. The marina is on the other side of the inner lagoon, east and south of the settlement. If Bullocks Harbour seems to have escaped the golden boom and subsequent tourist crowds of other Bahamian destinations, you are correct.

Great Harbour Cay Marina

The approach to Great Harbour Cay Marina lies west from the Great Bank. The route is well-marked by easy-to-spot stakes. We cover the course in some detail under Pilotage. In many ways, the marina is a remarkable, safe harbor. The third of three interlocking basins, it would probably be a superb hurricane hole should one ever decide to veer here. The multi-colored marina, flanked by townhouses, offers all the normal marina conveniences. Maybe not brand new, but certainly clean and functional. What lacks in luxurious facilities is more than compensated by the friendly, helpful personnel and locals who bend over backwards to make your stay enjoyable. The docks are sound. The shorepower is reliable. There is well water for wash downs and reverse osmosis water to fill your tanks. The washer and dryer are convenient, and the fuel dock opens early. The Rock Hill Pool Bar and Grill is picture-postcard pretty and begging for

Berry Islands

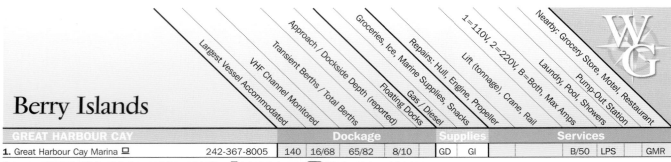

GREAT HARBOUR CAY	Phone	Largest Vessel Accommodated	VHF Channel Monitored	Transient Berths / Total Berths	Approach / Dockside Depth (reported)	Floating Docks	Gas / Diesel	Groceries, Ice, Marine Supplies, Snacks	Repairs: Hull, Engine, Propeller	Lift (tonnage), Crane, Rail	1=110V, 2=220V, B=Both, Max Amps	Laundry, Pool, Showers	Pump-Out Station	Nearby: Grocery Store, Motel, Restaurant
		Dockage					Supplies		Services					
1. Great Harbour Cay Marina 💻	242-367-8005	140	16/68	65/82	8/10		GD	GI			B/50	LPS		GMR

Corresponding chart(s) not to be used for navigation. 💻 Internet Access (WiFi) Wireless Internet Access

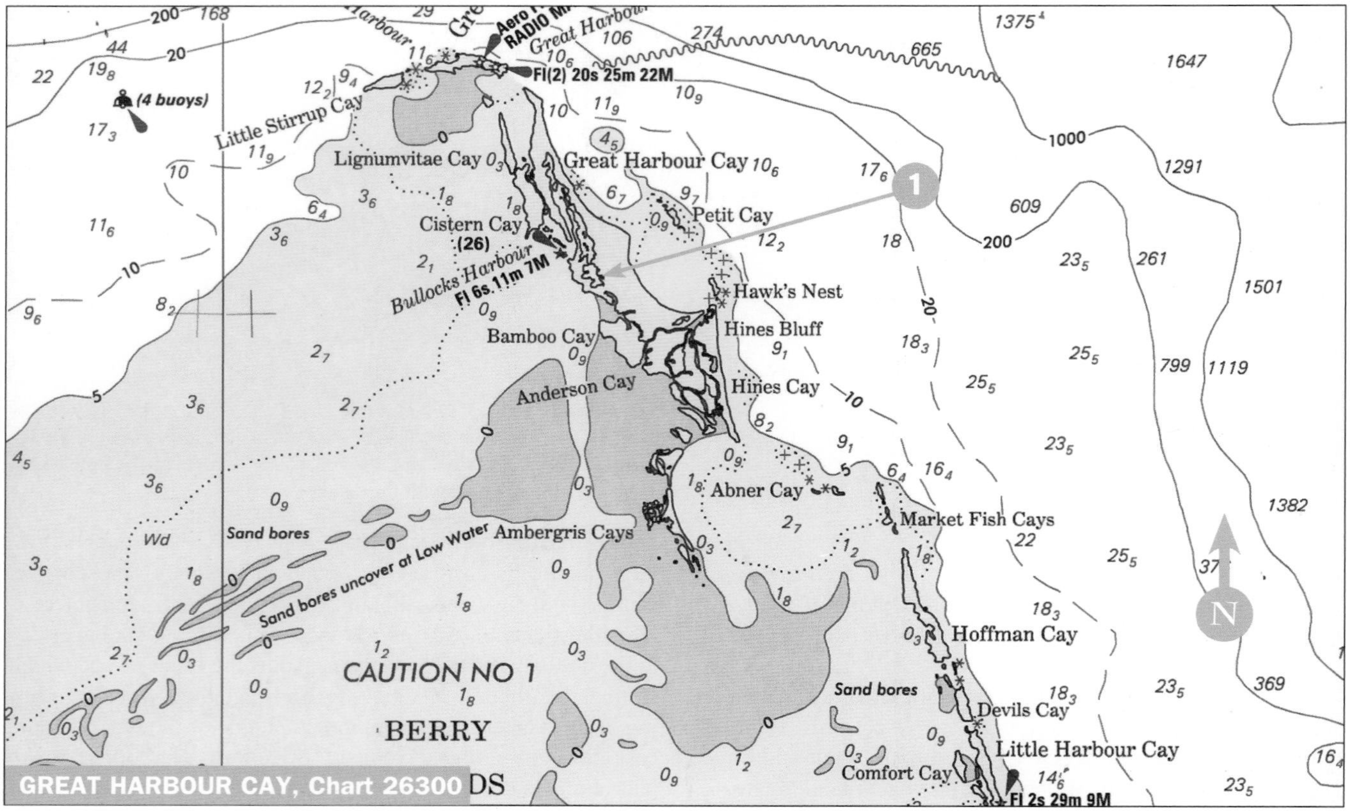

you to take a refreshing dip. If you are looking for a Nikki Beach scene, move on. However, if you seek a tranquil, out-island-like atmosphere without the trip, you have found the place.

Haines, Water and Money Cays

Haines Cay, with a clutch of lesser islets—Anderson, Turner and Kemp Cays, as well as the slightly larger Water and Money Cays—are fine for exploring in an inflatable or skiff, but are not cruising grounds.

Fanny, Ambergris, Pigeon, Abner and High Cays

These cays, despite the attraction of their beaches, fall into the same category as above, good for fair weather exploration, swimming and snorkeling.

Market Fish and Soldier Cays

These cays are the gateway to the inner route linking the Berry Islands. They are the first of many idyllic anchorages from which to choose that offer outstanding spear fishing opportunities on either side of the cays. Although marked on few charts, there is an anchorage with plenty of water close to the beach in the cove on the west side of Market Fish Cay. It is north of, and more protected than, the recommended anchorage off the northern tip of Soldier Cay.

Hoffmans Cay

Hoffmans Cay offers several anchoring possibilities along its western shore. Just follow the distinct blue channel that weaves around the shallow banks and sand bores and throw out the hook where the blue water widens.

If you draw more than 6 feet, ride a rising tide. The most popular anchorages are at the northern tip of the cay, mid-way down the cay just north of a very shallow lagoon and in the next to the last, southern beach cove. This cove and

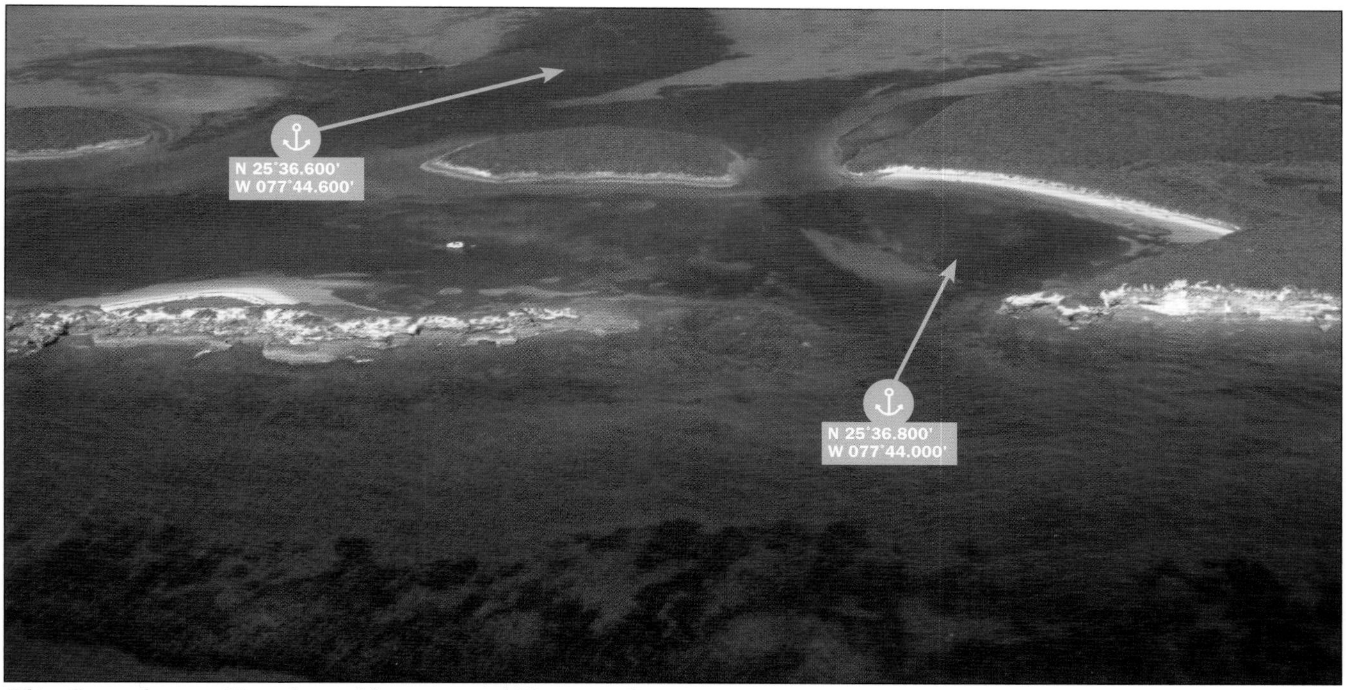

White Cay anchorage. (Not to be used for navigation.) WATERWAY GUIDE PHOTOGRAPHY.

its prominent tree mark the trailhead for the hike to the blue hole. The trail branches to the left and right about halfway up the hill. The branch to the left takes you to the blue hole. There is a thin side trail to the right of the table rock that leads down to the rim of the hole. It is okay to jump in and snorkel the hole. If you are lucky, some friendly grouper will greet you to beg for food. They love minnows, but green peas or dry dog food seems equally as popular. The trail branch to the right leads to the shallow beach at the southern-most cove. You can walk around the rocky coast back to your boat if you have had enough of the mosquitoes on the trail.

The Hoffmans Cay Blue Hole

The trail climbs up over the spine of the headland, and just about the time you are beginning to think you have volunteered for a jungle warfare course, the trail splits. The right fork goes to the first beach, the one you ignored. The left fork leads you almost immediately to the rim of the blue hole.

If you have been to Chichen Itza in Yucatan and seen the Sacred Well, the Hoffmans Cay Blue Hole carries much the same sense of shock when you first come on it. Suddenly you are right on the brim of this great sheer-sided hole, the water far below you, unfathomable but looking deep.

If you take the continuation of the trail that runs to your right along the rim of the hole, you will find that within a few yards it takes you down under an overhang and you can reach the water there—and swim if you wish! Sacrificial virgins apart, it is said that someone once stocked the hole with just one grouper, but no one knows whether the fish found friends, died or has survived in isolation. It could be, it just could be, that there is a world record giant grouper lurking there, if it found its new home agreeable!

The White Cay, Fowl Cay and Little Gaulding Cay Anchorages

These deep anchorages are not accessible from the inside route unless your boat draws only inches. From the outside, in good conditions, vessels can enter these anchorages in between the scattered rocks south of White Cay and Devils Cay. We recommend utilizing an electronic navigation program or The Near Bahamas Explorer Chartbook™ to ascertain waypoints into the cut and to navigate your vessel northward to the anchorages. Although the blue water and the places where you can anchor are obvious once you get there, play it safe! These are some of the loveliest anchorages in the entire Bahamas Islands and worth the careful journey. However, keep in mind the weather forecast and the wind conditions, or you may be anchored there for longer than you intended.

Big Gaulding and Devils Cays

Big Gaulding Cay has an interesting cave and Robinson Crusoe beach on its east side. It is a fun picnic spot and a lovely place to play in the water. In between Devils Cay and Little Harbour Cay, the shelling is particularly good after storms and high seas.

Little Harbour, Comfort, Guano and Cabbage Cays

There is a pretty anchorage with good holding and 2-meter/6.5-foot depths just south of the northern tip of Little Harbour Cay. It is a great base to explore the waters of Devils Cay and to visit the blowhole on White Cay. Another good anchorage lies off Comfort Cay, about one-third of the way down from its northern point. You will spot the remains of a stone cairn on shore as a landmark. The water depth holds to over six feet close to shore here.

Boats drawing up to six feet can safely make the trip around Comfort and Guano Cay to visit Flo's Conch Bar and Restaurant. However, do so on a rising tide, and stay within 100 to 200 feet of the islands for the deepest water. There is a conspicuous underwater rock where you might touch when you veer to avoid it. To put your mind at ease, sound the route in your dinghy with your handheld depth sounder before trying it. There is an alternate, deeper route farther west on the Bank.

Guano and Cabbage Cays shield the southern end of Little Harbour Cay from the west. They form a sheltered harbor, indeed a hurricane hole, along the western shore of Little Harbour Cay. Here, you will find five moorings in 5-foot depths or less. Dredging of the channel and harbor was in the works, so unless it has been completed, one must still pass through the shallower stretch to reach the moorings in the deeper water. However, with a high tide, and Chester Darville's guidance, it can be done.

Chester, his mother Flo and whoever is helping at the conch bar, comprise the entire population of Little Harbour Settlement. Chester is virtually a one-man enterprise. His business, called Flo's Place, is not to be missed. It is the quintessential island bar and restaurant you have been dreaming to visit. Mountains of conch shells line the shore at the Tiki Hut dock, and Chester and Flo's menagerie of chickens, geese, peacocks, sheep, goats, dogs and cats greet you on the meandering pathways around the colorful bar and restaurant up on the hilltop.

Hail Chester before noon on VHF Channels 16 or 68 to order fresh baked bread for breakfast the next morning and to make dinner reservations for that night. The conch, lobster, fish and other tasty things will be cooked especially for you by Chester, himself. Chester's rum punch is the stuff of legend. Sip a few while you peruse the hundreds of pictures papering the walls of fellow cruisers enjoying a night at Flo's.

Make sure you bring dinghy running lights because you will want to stick around to hear Chester's stories about the hurricane that wiped everything off the island except the settlement his grandfather founded, the sting ray that killed one of his dogs (he will show you the stinger) or the hilarious tale about the wily rat onboard a friend's schooner and Chester's famous rat trap.

If you are not anchored west of Comfort Cay, and you draw too much to pick up one of Chester's moorings, there are three other recommended anchorages that appear on charts close to Flo's: first, in between Cabbage and Little Harbour, second, south of Guano and third, west of Cabbage. All three can be perfectly delightful one visit and roly-poly, full of surge and rushing currents the next. A lot depends upon tides and what is going on in the Northwest Providence Channel. Many a cruiser has spent a pleasant night at anchor in the finger of deeper water that extends west into the bank from the cut's entrance. You will be surrounded on three sides by the shallower, bank water. There are also other options a little farther south at Frozen and Alder Cays.

Frozen and Alder Cays

Both Frozen and Alder Cays are private. Although you can not go ashore, the cays are so attractive and the anchorages so secure, who cares? You can work your way towards the cays from the deeper water as close as your draft allows. The waters off Alder Cay affords some shelter from the north and good protection from the east. Swimming from your dinghy in the sandy, shallower waters to the west is sublime.

One warning: A large, red, island-freighter-type boat delivers fuel by hose to Alder Cay. If you are awakened by loud blasts from a boat's horn, weigh anchor and move quickly. The land "hook up" for the incredibly lengthy hose from the boat is behind some oleanders on the northwestern shore of the cay's small harbor. If you are lucky enough to be anchored out of its way, prepare to watch the proceedings, especially the hose handling, with stupefied awe.

Bonds Cay

Bonds Cay joins the majority of the southern Berrys in being privately owned. As we have previously mentioned, Shakira has big plans for Bonds Cay. It will be interesting to watch those plans develop as we hang off our anchors in the two magnificent anchorages along her western shores.

The northernmost anchorage has a nice beach with nearby coral heads for snorkeling, but is a bit short on protection. The second anchorage, midway down the cay, offers near all-round protection with shallow bank waters to the north, west and south and Bonds to the east. Anchor in 1.8 meters/6 feet of water in the sandy spots within the grassy bottom. Exit south on a rising tide to skim over the one shallow section along the route.

Many vessels utilize the cuts here to and from the Northwest Providence Channel. Although there is an inside route to Little Whale Cay in deep water west of Sisters Rocks, it gets mighty shallow off the western end of Little Whale. It is best left to those with very shallow draft or for exploration by dinghy with handheld sonar before attempting the transit.

Little Whale Cay

Little Whale Cay, a private getaway for Wallace Groves, the forward-thinking developer of Freeport Harbour, remains a little pink and white enclave of tranquility floating in the shifting, shallow sand ridges of the Great Bahama Bank. You can anchor not far from its private lighthouse and small boat harbor, but it may take some jockeying around in quick-to-

Whale Cay reefs, from the south. (Not to be used for navigation.) WATERWAY GUIDE PHOTOGRAPHY.

thin water to find good holding here. Some boats drop the hook and hold tight due west of the jetty and cove on the northern tip of Whale Cay. Others have not been that lucky. Take care and make sure that anchor is set before you decide to spend the night.

Whale Cay

Whale Cay is also private. From the number of maple leaf flags seen flying from staffs along the coast here, it appears to be populated by a small legion of proud Canadians. Stand well off Whale Cay's eastern coast when running by it in the Northwest Providence Channel waters. Its coral reefs extend far offshore.

At the southern end of Whale, there are stunning white cliffs and a large white lighthouse that appears to have once been a residence. It just begs investigation. There is a picture-perfect anchorage in between Whale Cay and Bird Cay. There is only room for about one good-sized, shallow-draft boat. If you are the vessel who snags that site for the night, treasure it.

Bird Cay

Bird Cay, also private, often has an interesting looking, ocean-exploration vessel anchored off either side of its western tip. We are not sure what the scientists onboard are researching, but their conversations on the VHF radio and their activities in the water are fascinating to listen to and to observe.

The fishing triangle between the end of Bird Cay towards Diamond Cay and up towards Frazer's Hog channel is always good one. Folks seldom fail to land dinner by trolling off their stern, although sometimes it takes one or two passes. If you are not as lucky, you can always get a nice fish dinner at the Berry Island Club on Frazer's Hog.

Frazers Hog Cay

Frazers Hog Cay is significantly larger than Chub Cay, but it remains virtually undeveloped, perhaps because a great deal of it is low lying and mangrove covered. It is separated from Chub by a narrow creek and connected by a roadway to the airport. If you feel like a long walk or the need to run, there is a road, albeit sometimes awash or quite muddy, that runs north and south and east and west like a dogleg along Frazers Hog.

There is still a neat little beach bar at the southern terminus of the road, but there has not been activity there for some years. It is good for a shady rest, though. About midway up the cay's south to north leg, you will find the Berry Islands Club. The Club offers fuel, dockage, a pleasant restaurant and a mooring field. Holding in the anchorages north of the moorings can be marginal. Things can get downright dicey in strong southerly winds. It is best to pick up one of the Club's moorings. Shoal draft boats can work their way north toward Fish and Cockroach Cays, but the shifting shallow bars are winning the depth wars in these waters.

Berry Islands

FRAZERS HOG CAY, CHUB CAY		Largest Vessel Accommodated	VHF Channel Monitored	Transient Berths / Total Berths	Approach / Dockside Depth (reported)	Floating Docks	Gas / Diesel	Groceries, Ice, Marine Supplies, Snacks	Repairs: Hull, Engine, Propeller	Lift (tonnage), Crane, Rail	1=110V, 2=220V, B=Both, Max Amps	Laundry, Pool, Showers	Pump-Out Station	Nearby: Grocery Store, Motel, Restaurant
		Dockage					Supplies				Services			
1. Chub Cay Club	242-325-1490	150	68	/110	/12		GD	GIS			B/100	LPS		GMR
2. Berry Islands Club (WiFi)	242-357-2229		16	/12	/9		GD	I			B/50	L		MR

Corresponding chart(s) not to be used for navigation. Internet Access (WiFi) Wireless Internet Access

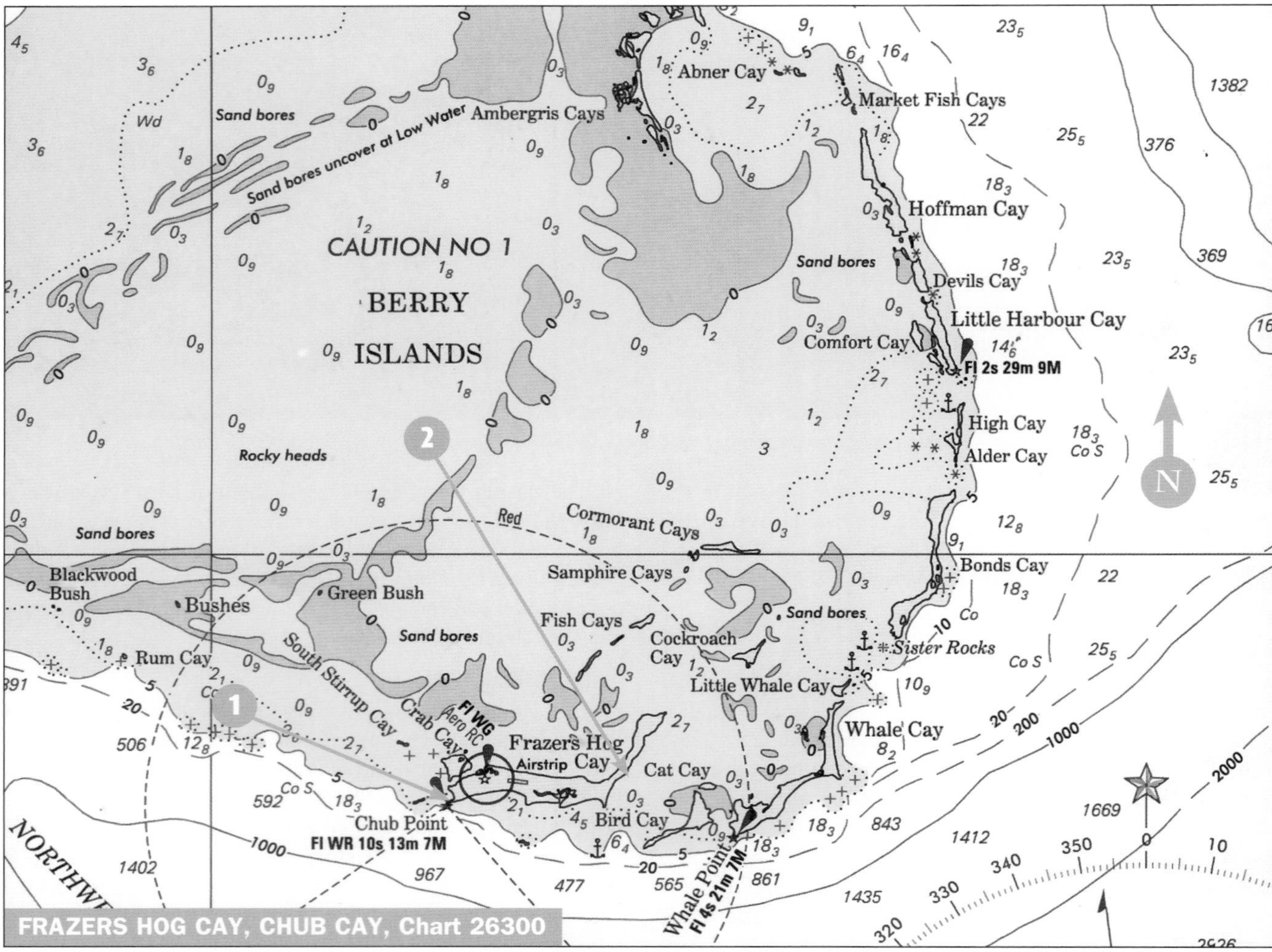

Chub Cay Club Marina

Please read coverage on Chub Cay in our Spotlight feature.

Crab Cay and South Stirrup Cay

Crab Cay and South Stirrup Cay lie lonely and barren to the north and west of busy Chub Cay. Boats do anchor to the west of Crab Cay off the creek, but the holding is reported to be poor there. South Stirrup looks deceivingly close and appears to be surrounded by pretty beaches. Do not waste the dinghy gas. It is not sand, and they are definitely not beaches. There are many more bank cays in the Berry Islands that we have not discussed. Because they are surrounded by barrier shoals and sand bores, they are not cruising grounds. Nevertheless, they are there for you gunkholers to discover and to leave your virgin footprints, if only for a little while.

Visit www.WaterwayGuide.com TODAY for current navigation information, fuel pricing and more!

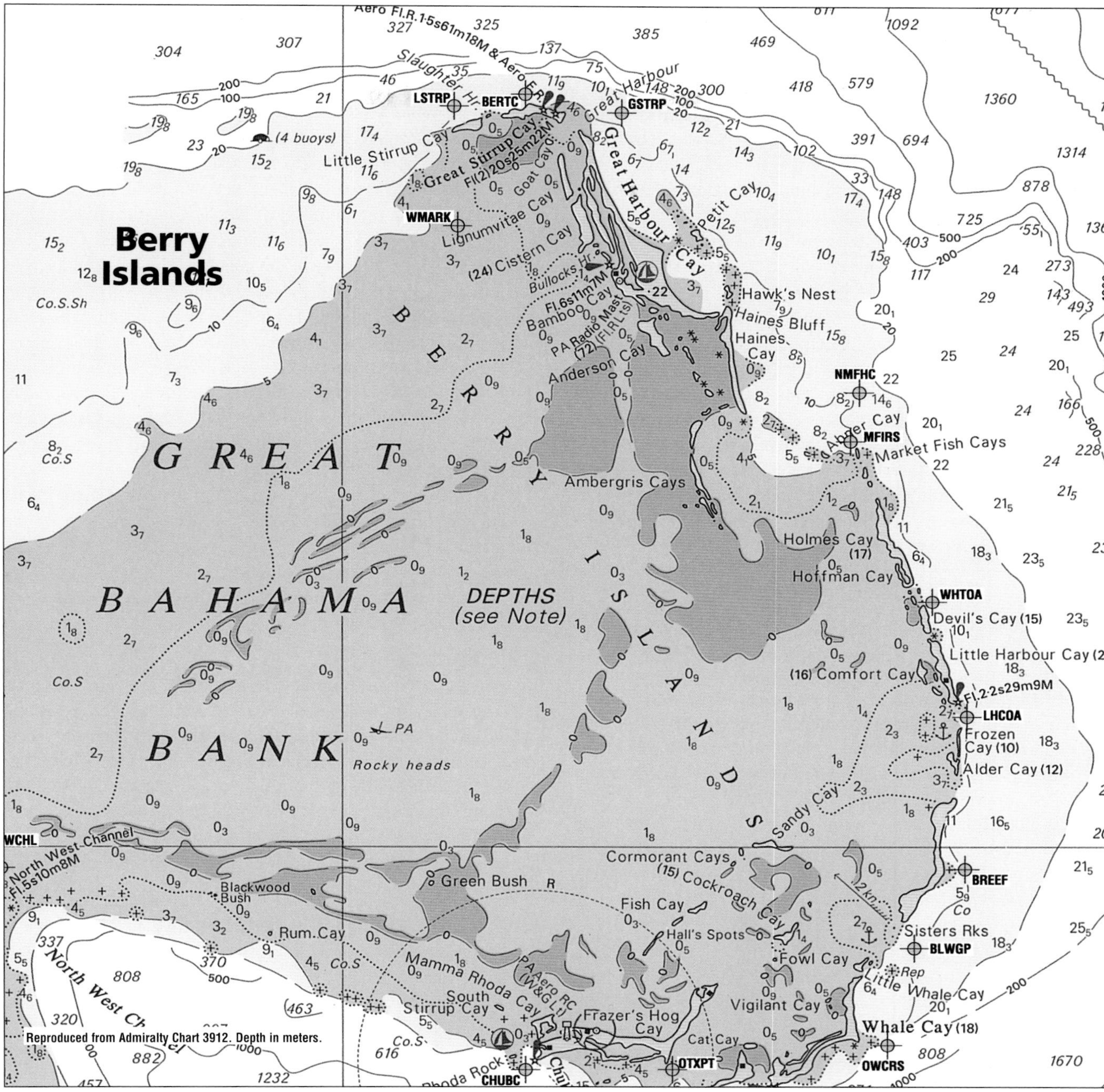

Reproduced from Admiralty Chart 3912. Depth in meters.

Not to be used for navigation.

Pilotage. Talking Captain to Captain

The Approach to Great Harbour Cay Marina

From Little Stirrup Cay to the Great Harbour Marina, the entry cut is about eight nautical miles. You will have some 2.4 meter/8-foot depths at mean low water all the way in. However, don't run on autopilot, and don't rush. Watch the color of the waters and your depth sounder as you work your way in.

Head south from LSTRP for the West Mark (WMARK) waypoint on a course of 180/000 degrees true, a run of 3.5 nautical miles. This track skirts the western edge of extensive flats immediately to the south of the Stirrup Cays. You should see the first Harbour Cay aid to navigation using the WMARK waypoint. From here, you have 4.2 nautical miles to run to Great Harbour. There are well-spaced markers to assist you.

Way back, the entry course markers must have been sequentially numbered all the way to the marina. Today the surviving posts still carry their original numbers, which make little sense. All of these numbers are in parentheses in case you need them for reassurance.

- At WMARK, alter your course to about 131/311 degrees true, roughly lined up with the Great Harbour BTC antenna on shore, and hold that line for just over one nautical mile to mark M2 (#5).
- From M2, the next mark, M3 (#7), is two nautical miles on a heading of 099/279 degrees true. You will start to see houses off to port and the government dock, which may or may not have a mailboat or fishing boats alongside. This is Bullocks Harbour settlement. It is not the way to the marina. The cut into the marina does not reveal itself until you are closer, almost ready to make the 90-degree turn to port to pass through the cut.
- At M3, alter course to 112/292 degrees true to the next mark, M4 (#8), just under one nautical mile farther. The final mark, M5, comes up after a short distance (0.4 nautical miles) on a course of 115/295 degrees true. Look at the headland off your bow. You will see a conspicuous roof. Look carefully below the roof for two red and white, vertically striped, range-mark boards. In front of them, in the water, is a single pole with a red triangle. If you can't see the range marks, don't worry. Just continue south until you see the manmade entry cut through solid rock to port, and make your turn:
- The entry cut has around 3.3-meter/11-foot depths at mean low water and a decent tidal flow. Be prepared for current.
- The first inner basin, named the Bay of the Five Pirates, has a fuel dock to starboard. It is one of the more difficult fuel docks to approach, and is tucked right up into a corner under a small headland with a rocky shoreline. However, friendly helpers will take your lines and guide you to the pumps.
- Your course across this basin, and the continuation of the bay, requires a turn to starboard, marked by a succession of poles—red right returning.
- The second basin has a prominent, white-roofed house with its own dock to starboard and a circular restaurant building with a balcony around it. The entry to the marina lies to port just before this building. You will pass a "No Wake" sign, and turn to port to enter.
- Pass the row of townhouses with their own docks to port, then again, 90-degrees to starboard. The Great Harbour Cay Marina, with its colorful slips, is to starboard. You have arrived.

Moving South from the Northern Berry Islands

Moving north or south outside the Berry Islands, there is only one safe route—stay well east of the chain. From a starting point off Great Stirrup Cay (GSTRP), you will want to be in deep water to clear Petit and Hawksnest Cay. Stay in the 10-meter/30-foot depth contour about one nautical mile offshore to be safe. The entry to the bank-side route for shallower-draft vessels is close to Market Fish Cay (MFIRS).

White Cay Anchorage

First, ignore the gap north of White Cay. You want to go in the south gap, midway between the rocks at the south of White Cay and the north tip of Devils Cay. Your turning point will be around the White Cay ocean approach waypoint (WHTOA). As you turn, you will be on line for the south tip of Saddle Back Cay, which lies immediately behind White Cay. Beyond the southern tip of Saddle Back, there is the southern tip of another island lying behind Saddle Back. If you keep these two southern tips in line as a rough transit, you won't go far wrong.

There will be a good 5.4 to 7.2 meters/18 to 24 feet of water, which will take you well inside. Once you come abeam of the sand of the beach on the north of Devils Cay, turn to starboard to head north between Saddle Back Cay and White Cay. The White Cay beach, roughly in the center of the cay, marks your anchorage. You will find 3.6 to 5.4 meters/12 to 18 feet of water there and surprising depth close to the beach over sand. Otherwise, it is grass all around.

The beach itself, pure white sand backed with sea oats, is something to write home about. The anchorage is reasonably protected, but flanked as it is by two ocean passes, can be uncomfortable if the ocean is kicking up. Under those circumstances, you would not want to attempt running in there anyway. If wind and strong seas are running from the east, do not try it.

The cay beyond Saddle Back Cay, whose southern tip we suggested you might use as a transit, has a pretty beach in the middle. Obviously there are others who think so too, for there is a stone barbecue grill built in the little palm grove and two crude deck chairs.

Little Harbour Cay

If you are coming in from the ocean side, the cut between Little Harbour Cay and Frozen Cay is wide and deep. There is one reef mid-channel, which normally shows with breaking seas. Once you have noted it, you can pass to either side. We favor turning in at the Little Harbour Cay ocean approach (LHCOA) waypoint, for this gives you the chance to check out the anchorage behind the north end of Frozen Cay as well as the Little Harbour Cay anchorage. Depending on the set of the swell, go for the better-protected one.

Anchorages in the Little Harbour Cay Area

At first sight, particularly if you first see it at high water, the Little Harbour Cay anchorage looks like a perfect place. Beware. Unless your vessel is shoal draft, there is only one place you can anchor and that is over the mid-channel sand patches in line with the north end of Cabbage Cay. There is just room for two boats to anchor here. The tidal current is strong, runs north to south and produces a 180-degree swing every six hours. Dive on your anchor to ensure it is set. If in doubt, dig it in by hand.

Depth in the anchorage area is around 3 meters/10 feet at mean low water. On the way to Flo's dock, depths can be close to zero in some patches and around 0.2 meter/1 foot in others. Hence, the moorings require a high tide approach and Chester's assistance. Off the dock, there is good, deeper water around 1.1 to 1.7 meters/3.5 to 5.5 feet deep at mean low water. If all this is too daunting, you can anchor off Comfort Cay or in the deep finger of water on the bank.

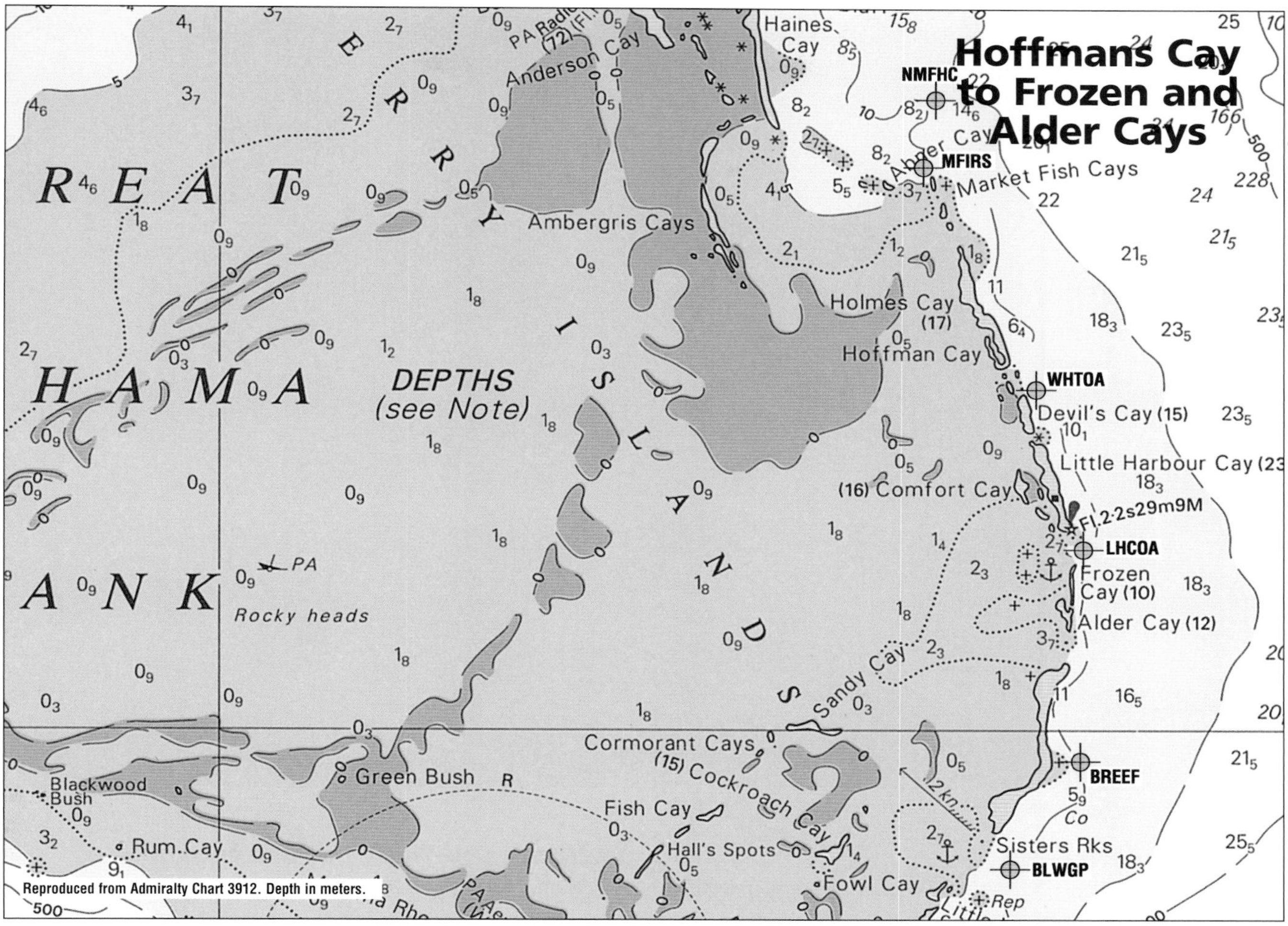

Frozen and Alder Cays. (Not to be used for navigation.) Waterway Guide Photography.

Whale Cay, from the south. (Not to be used for navigation.) WATERWAY GUIDE PHOTOGRAPHY.

Frozen and Alder Cays

If the winds are settled, you can also anchor behind the northern tip of Frozen Cay. There are depths of 6 meters/20 feet and 3.6 meters/12 feet around waypoint FRCAN. Check that anchor. The bottom is hard. Rumor has it there is one rock there, blazed with bottom paint, which in the words of our informant "we never knew existed, and we would never have noticed but for the bottom paint." Our cruising editors were fortunate and never encountered it in all their casting around for the ideal spot to drop the hook. Just be warned. There is a rogue rock somewhere in that area, which others, all too clearly, have found. The other recommended anchorages you see on charts in this area—one west of the bight in between the two cays and one west of the small basin on Alders Cay—offer good protection and good holding and no painted rocks!

Bonds Cay

On the inside route, the anchorages off Bonds Cay are particularly welcoming. The southernmost one, after a 90-degree dogleg to the east, provides good all-round shelter and protection from almost any blow. Search for sandy spots to drop your hook securely. On the outside, almost halfway down Bonds Cay at N 25° 29.000'/W 077° 43.000', an area of reef and shoal juts east, reducing your depth to 4.8 meters/16 feet. Anticipate this, and keep well offshore. Stay at least a mile out, particularly if the set of wind and wave is pushing toward the shore. Use the Bond Cay Reef (BREEF) waypoint.

The Bonds Cay–Whale Cay Gap Anchorage

If you are going to anchor in the Bonds Cay–Little Whale Cay gap, you have the Sisters Rocks of which to take note and a shoal area to the north of Little Whale Cay that extends into the ocean. If you turn in at the Bonds Cay–Whale Cay Gap waypoint (BLWGP), you should be well set for this day anchorage, which is more of a roadstead in the nautical sense than a protected place. It offers the right kind of depth and the sea room to accommodate a small armada, but you will be exposed to wind from every direction, as well as ocean swell. If the weather is kind, the Bonds Cay–Whale Cay gap makes a good place to stop for a swim and lunch. Around the anchorage waypoint (BLWAN), is 3.6 to 5.4 meters/12 to 18 feet of water, but you don't need coordinates to help you decide where to drop your hook. You have all the space you could wish for and the depth to settle anywhere you like.

The Little Whale Cay Anchorage

A protected basin lies tucked between Little Whale Cay and the north tip of Whale Cay. This offers some protection from north and south, little from the other directions, nothing from the east and southeast, and is open to ocean surge. It has a measure of shoal ground and reef to negotiate, whichever way you choose the approach. The ocean way takes you between two reefs, keeping more north than south, holding closer to Little Whale Cay. If there is any kind of wave action or swell coming in from the ocean, you will find breaking seas here and the approach,

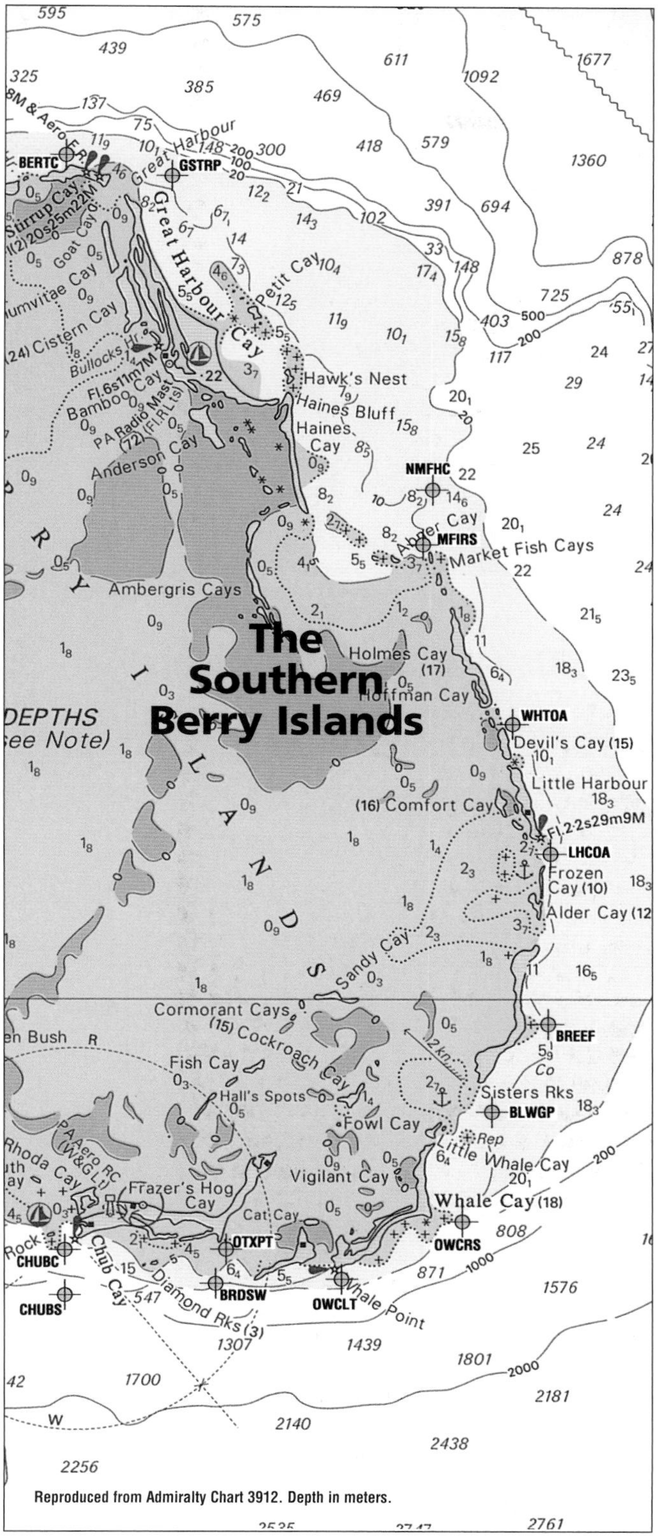

Reproduced from Admiralty Chart 3912. Depth in meters.

Not to be used for navigation.

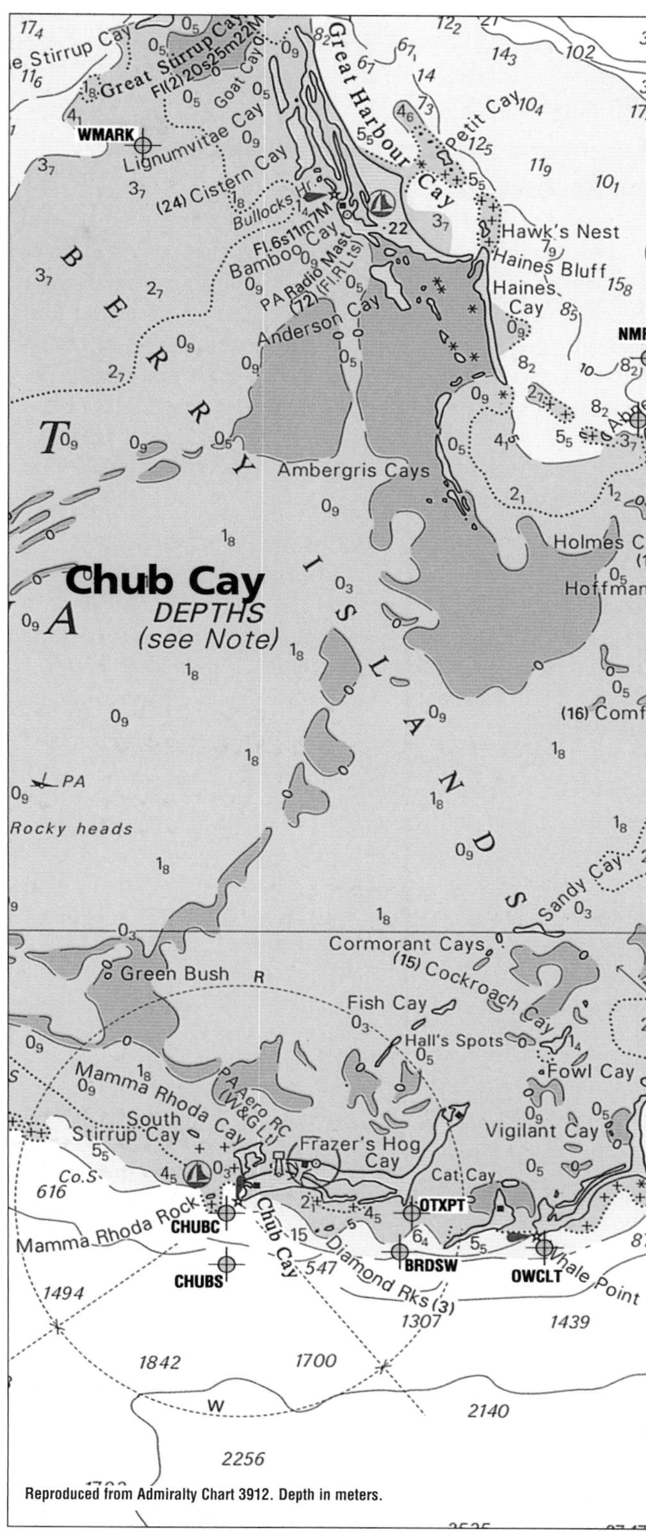

Reproduced from Admiralty Chart 3912. Depth in meters.

Not to be used for navigation.

particularly at low water, is not attractive. Do not consider it. From the bank, you have 1.2 meters/4 feet at the most in some areas, maybe less. Just go slowly. Inside the anchorage, there are depths of 1.8 to 2.7 meters/6 to 9 feet over a hard bottom.

Whale Cay

Unless your vessel draws only inches, you will not be traveling any more inside routes after Little Whale Cay. Here, you will run in the Northwest Providence Channel, far off the coast of Whale Cay. The waypoint (OWCRS) keeps you safely off the coral reefs edging the cay in 18 meters/60 feet of water. When you reach the end of Whale Cay and Whale Cay light with Bird Cay off your starboard bow, your position will be around the OWCLT waypoint.

Frazers Hog Cay, The Berry Islands Club and Anchorages

The approach from the Northwest Channel into Frazers Hog Cay is quite straightforward. From the end of Bird Cay, aim for the southern tip of Frazers Hog (OTXTP) and follow the obvious, deep-blue water channel along the eastern shore to the Berry Islands Club docks or moorings. The recommended anchorages shown on charts just north of the Club offer notoriously poor holding. If there is any kind of weather anticipated, it is best to take a mooring in this picturesque, but exposed, anchorage. The anchorages north of Frazers Hog Cay require good visual piloting and a shoal-draft boat.

Chub Cay Approach, Marina and Anchorages

Going along the southern end of Frazers Hog and the coast of Chub Cay, it is hard to see the creek where Frazers Hog Cay ends and Chub Cay begins. Avoid the very obvious Diamond Cay and its rocks. Momma Rhoda Rock looms off your bow and the Chub Cay light, really just a stake, stands on Chub Cay Point.

The Chub Cay entry waypoint is CHUBC, but you hardly need it because the channel is so well-marked. To the east of the channel, you will see the deeper water in which to anchor, nestled in the cove and close to the sugar-sand beach. There is deeper water than noted on the charts, especially towards the northern end in the cove. Use the older, stone-faced, single-story house as a landmark. It has an easy to spot "Do Not Trespass" sign on its beach. Boats also anchor to the west of the channel, but test the holding on that side carefully. If you want to anchor away from the Chub Cay frontage, the alternative is west of the creek between Crab and Chub Cay. This is shallow, shoal-draft stuff (like for catamarans that draw 0.7 meter/2 feet 6 inches fully laden). Regardless, if the winds switch to the south or west, it can be uncomfortable on the hook here. Move into Chub Cay Marina, try to set an anchor on the eastern side of Frazers Hog Cay, or go to the Berry Islands Club.

Inbound from the Northwest Channel Light, a run of about 15 nautical miles, places you at the Chub Cay South waypoint (CHUBS). Once you have reached the Chub Cay South waypoint, go north on 000/180 degrees true for just one nautical mile. That brings you to CHUBC, ready to enter Chub Cay Marina or to anchor off, as you wish.

The school in Bullocks Harbour settlement.
Waterway Guide Photography.

Little Bahama Bank Waypoints

THE NORTHERN BERRY ISLANDS

Little Stirrup Cay	LSTRP	25°49.50N / 77°57.00W
Bertram Cove	BERTC	25°49.92N / 77°55.02W
NW Stirrup Cay	GSTRP	25°49.45N / 77°52.26W

GREAT HARBOUR APPROACH MARKS

West Mark	WMARK (B7)	25°46.00N / 77°57.00W
Marker Pole 2	M2	25°45.60N / 77°55.97W
Marker Pole 3	M3	25°45.28N / 77°53.69W
Marker Pole 4	M4	25°45.01N / 77°52.95W
Marker Pole 5	M5	25°44.83N / 77°52.53W
North Market Fish Cay	NMFHC	25°42.17N / 77°45.54W
Market Fish Inside Rte Start	MFIRS	25°40.75N / 77°45.75W
White Cay Ocean Approach	WHTOA	25°36.48N / 77°43.48W
Little Harbour Ocean App	LHCOA (B17)	25°34.00N / 77°41.00W
Guana Shoal Pass	GCSHP	25°34.16N / 77°44.08W
SW Comfort Cay	SWCCA	25°34.50N / 77°44.08W

THE SOUTHERN BERRY ISLANDS

Frozen Cay Anchorage	FRCAN	25°32.91N / 77°43.05W
Bond Cay Reef	BREEF	25°29.24N / 77°42.49W
Bond-Little Whale Cay Gap	BLWGP	25°27.17N / 77°44.32W
Bond-Whale Cay Anchorage	BLWAN	25°27.75N / 77°46.50W
Off Whale Cay Reefs	OWCRS	25°24.80N / 77°44.94W
Off Whale Cay Light	OWCLT	25°23.24N / 77°47.62W
Bird Cay SW	BRDSW	25°22.96N / 77°50.78W
Bird Cay Anchorage	BRDAN	25°23.66N / 77°50.16W
Off Texaco Point	OTXPT	25°24.08N / 77°50.83W
Chub Cay Entry	CHUBC (B20)	25°24.00N / 77°55.00W
Chub Cay South	CHUBS	25°23.25N / 77°54.83W

Our position format is latitude and longitude in degrees and minutes (hddd°mm.mm). Waypoints in RED are NOT for autopilot navigation. Codes in parenthesis are Wavey Line waypoints marked on the charts. If you have programmed waypoints we listed in a previous edition of this guide, check carefully to ensure the coordinates you have recorded match the list. If a waypoint is no longer on our list we may have changed its code or deleted it.

GOIN' ASHORE:

GREAT HARBOUR CAY

airport • customs & immigration • fuel • groceries • marina • medical • police • post office • propane • restaurant • telephone • water

The Berry Islands are an idyllic constellation of 30 islands and 100 cays that stretch over 30 miles along the Great Bank. The Islands have well-spaced marinas and some of the most beautiful and secluded anchorages in the entire island nation. In the south, Chub Cay Club and the Berry Islands Club are useful stops on the route between Bimini and Nassau. The northern marina is on Great Harbour Cay, the largest of the Berry Islands. Great Harbour Cay Marina is well located as a transit point between the northern and central cruising grounds. There is a superb seven-mile-long beach a short walk from the marina on the eastern shore with easy accessibility and glorious water colors, as well as some very good shelling. Chub Cay Club and Great Harbour Cay Marina are both entry ports. Customs and Immigration will clear you in upon request from the marinas.

EMERGENCIES

Marine • VHF 16 or 68
Medical *Clinic* • 242-367-8400 • In Bullocks Harbour; nurse is there 9 to 2 weekdays. Doctor comes about once a month.

MARINA

GREAT HARBOUR CAY MARINA at BULLOCKS HARBOUR
Tel: 242-367-8005 • VHF 16 or 68
Slips 82. **Max LOA** 140 ft. **MLW at Dock** 10 ft. **Dockage** $1.20 per ft. per day. **Fuel** Dock open 7:00 a.m. to 4 p.m., to noon on Sundays. **Facilities & Services** Power $0.70 per kwHr. RO water $0.35 per gallon, $10 for well-water wash down, public telephone, coin-op washer and dryer $2.50 per load, showers, restrooms, ice, nearby store with snacks, soda, beer and some provisions. **Restaurant & Bar** *Rock Hill Pool Bar and Grille*, open noon to 11 p.m. daily. **Credit Cards** Visa, MasterCard, AMEX. **Accommodations** *Green Harbour Inn*, suites from $75 to $125 per day. Car or jeep rentals from *Happy People at the Inn*. Pets are welcome at the marina.

PORT DIRECTORY FOR BULLOCKS HARBOUR

Airlines *Cat Island Air* • 242-367-8021, 242-377-3318 • Daily flights from Nassau.
Tropical Diversions • 954-921-9084 • Fax: 242-921-1044 • Charter flights from Florida for people using their rental properties.
Airport 4,536 x 80 ft. runway, 242-367-8566.
Bus Bus stop at end of the sidewalk, at eastern end of the marina.
Church *Church of God Prophecy.*
Clinic and Pharmacy In the administration building, 242-367-8400, "Frenchie" Trincard is the wonderful nurse who seems to be always on call.
Customs • 242-367-8566 • **Immigration** • 242-367-8112.
Diving Private dive trips can be arranged through *Green Harbour Inn*. Bring your own equipment.
Fire 242-367-8344
Fishing Deep-sea and bone fishing guides can be arranged at the marina or the *Green Harbour Inn.*
Golf There is a nine-hole golf course on the island. Ask at the marina or the Inn for information regarding a round of golf.
Police • 242-367-8344
Post Office In the administration building. Open 9 a.m. to 4 p.m. weekdays, 242-367-8293. Will cash certified bank checks.
Provisions Fresh produce, meat and cheese when the mailboat comes in on Wednesday. Several stores and markets in *Bullocks Harbour Settlement*. Walk the main road south and east to visit them all. Many folks bake fresh bread and sell it in the markets. Retail fish and seafood, *Miller's Fish House*, 242-367-8011.
Rental Cars *Dee's* serves the entire island, 242-367-8666.
Restaurants *The Beach Club* is open for breakfast, lunch and dinner daily, on the beach looking out to Petit Cay. $ • *Rock Hill Pool Bar & Grille* at *Great Harbour Cay Marina* is open for lunch and dinner daily. $-$$. *Collie Mae's Sunset Restaurant & Sports Bar*. $-$$. *Conch Salad Mon*, At the end of the marina dock, next to the convenience store. $
Taxi The marina or the Inn will be happy to call you a taxi, or hail one down in front of the marina or in town.
Telephones There are BTC phone card telephones at the marina and in town. Purchase phone cards at the Inn.
Tourist Office 242-367-8344/8291. Very nice, helpful folks in the office.

THINGS TO DO IN GREAT HARBOUR CAY

- Take your inflatable north, up the banks side of Great Harbour Cay, to visit *Great Stirrup Cay Lighthouse*. Wave to the parasailing cruise ship passengers as you go.
- Head south and go fishing off the Market Fish Cays.
- After an exhausting morning of walking, swimming and enjoying the pure white sand and shades of emerald water on the beach at Petit Cove, treat yourself to lunch at the *Beach Bar*.

LITTLE HARBOUR

Flo's Conch Bar and Restaurant bids cruisers, "Welcome," atop the hill on Little Harbour Cay. Chester Darville has mooring buoys for shoal-draft boats right in front of this little island delight ($10 per night). He also cooks the Bahamian specialties at the restaurant and mixes his own celebrated rum punch. Chester's mother, Florence, after whom the restaurant is named, keeps an eye on him as he prepares her famous conch fritters and lobster dinners. Chester is the BASRA representative for Little Harbour. He can be reached on VHF Channel 68 or 16. Call before noon for dinner reservations and next-day, fresh baked bread.

Why have we chosen Little Harbour for one of our Goin' Ashore entries when all that is here is one family and a small island bar and restaurant? We do it to highlight just one small entrepreneur, out of the many in the Bahamas, who have made countless cruising visitors "family" over the years. Of course, they earn their living this way, but the greeting and hospitality are the same, whether you have come to pass the time of day, have just one drink or an evening meal. It is people like the Darvilles who are "the Bahamas" and the reality behind our Goin' Ashore section.

LITTLE WHALE CAY

erica@info.com • www.littlewhalecay.com
A private, 93-acre island, 40 miles from Nassau; with its own airstrip, harbor, lighthouse and chapel for getaway weddings; Ten staff for 12 guests. Available to rent from $9500 to $10,750 per night plus 15%, minimum five nights. All inclusive: meals, drinks, WiFi and phone calls. Air charter from Florida, Nassau, seaplane or boat.

FRAZERS HOG CAY

Frazers Hog Cay is significantly larger than Chub Cay, but is virtually undeveloped. It is separated from Chub by a narrow creek and connected by a roadway to the airport. About midway up the cay on the eastern shore, you will find the Berry Islands Club.

MARINA

BERRY ISLANDS CLUB
Tel: 242-367-2229 • VHF 16 • www.theberryislandsclub.com
Mooring Balls Several in front, $15 night **Slips** 10-12. **Max LOA** depends on availability. **MLW at Dock** 9 ft. **Dockage** $1.50 per ft. per day. **Fuel** Dock hours vary. Gas and diesel available. **Facilities and Services** Power 30 and 50 amp, coin-op washer and dryer, showers, water by the gallon, ice and WiFi. **Restaurant & Bar** In the marina clubhouse, Herbie, the chef, specializes in Cajun and Bahamian dishes • herbie009@yahoo.com. **Accommodations** Private rooms with baths. **Customs & Immigration** $25 trip charge to airport to clear customs.

CHUB CAY

airport • customs & immigration • fuel • groceries •
marina • police • restaurant • telephone • water

The island virtually is the Chub Cay Club, a private guest or members only facility. Impeccable service and attention to detail prevail here. Customs and Immigration (242-325-5788) office at the airport, offers clearance to guests at the marina 9 a.m. to 5 p.m., Monday through Saturday. Private aircraft and charters use the 5,000-foot runway. *Bimini Island Air* (954-938-8991) and *Sky Limo* (954-522-6632) provide air charter service from Fort Lauderdale; Southern Air flies to Nassau.

MARINA

CHUB CAY CLUB
Tel: 242-325-1490, 877-231-CHUB (reservations only)
Fax: 242-325-7086 • VHF 68 and 72 •
reservations@ChubCay.com • www.chubcay.com
Slips 96-110. **Max LOA** 150 ft. **MLW at Dock** 12 ft. **Dockage** $2.50 - $3.50 per ft. per day, 40 ft. minimum. **Fuel** Dock open 7 a.m. to 6 p.m.; diesel, gasoline and oil may be available for members and guests only. Facility will recommend the Berry Islands Club if this is the case. **Facilities & Services** are available to members and guests only, unless permission is granted by the management **Power** from $30 to $120 per day depending on amps required, water $0.40 per gallon; showers, restrooms and coin-op laundry across from the marina near the staff grocery store, coin-op washers and dryers $2.00 per load. Public telephone outside the marina office, complimentary WiFi and trash disposal. The Island Shoppe has groceries, liquor and wine. The Police Station is behind the fish cleaning house (242-322-7359). Mail can be sent from reception. Ice, swimming pool and tennis courts. **Fishing tournaments:** Billfish in April and Wahoo in June. Call the Club for details. **Restaurant & Bars** The Harbour House Restaurant serves breakfast, lunch and dinner. Harry's Bar serves beverages. Accommodations Two and three-bedroom villas are available for $650 to $945 per day, plus 15% hotel tax. **Credit Cards** Visa, MasterCard, AMEX. Pets are welcome on a leash at the marina, but not on the beach. **Customs & Immigration** $100 fee to tie up at slip for non-members. Fee is credited towards the purchase of other goods or services for guests.

THINGS TO DO IN CHUB CAY

• The best diving is around Mamma Rhoda Rock, where you will find wall dives down to 230 feet, as well as canyons and caves. Lots of sharks and rays. The actual Mamma Rhoda Reef is stunning for snorkeling. This is the closest marina to the Tongue of the Ocean, which makes it a very popular fishing center.
• Look for shells between Chub Cay and Crab Cay.
• Fish along the 100-fathom line up to Rum Cay, which lies halfway to the Northwest Channel Light. This is the Berry Islands' Rum Cay, not the Exumas'.
• Snorkel Mamma Rhoda Rock in calm conditions, always aware of the current.
• Take your dinghy on a long trip to explore South Stirrup Cay.
• Relax and enjoy the swimming pool and beach before moving on.

Bougainvillea. WATERWAY GUIDE PHOTOGRAPHY.

Chapter 11
Nassau and New Providence Island

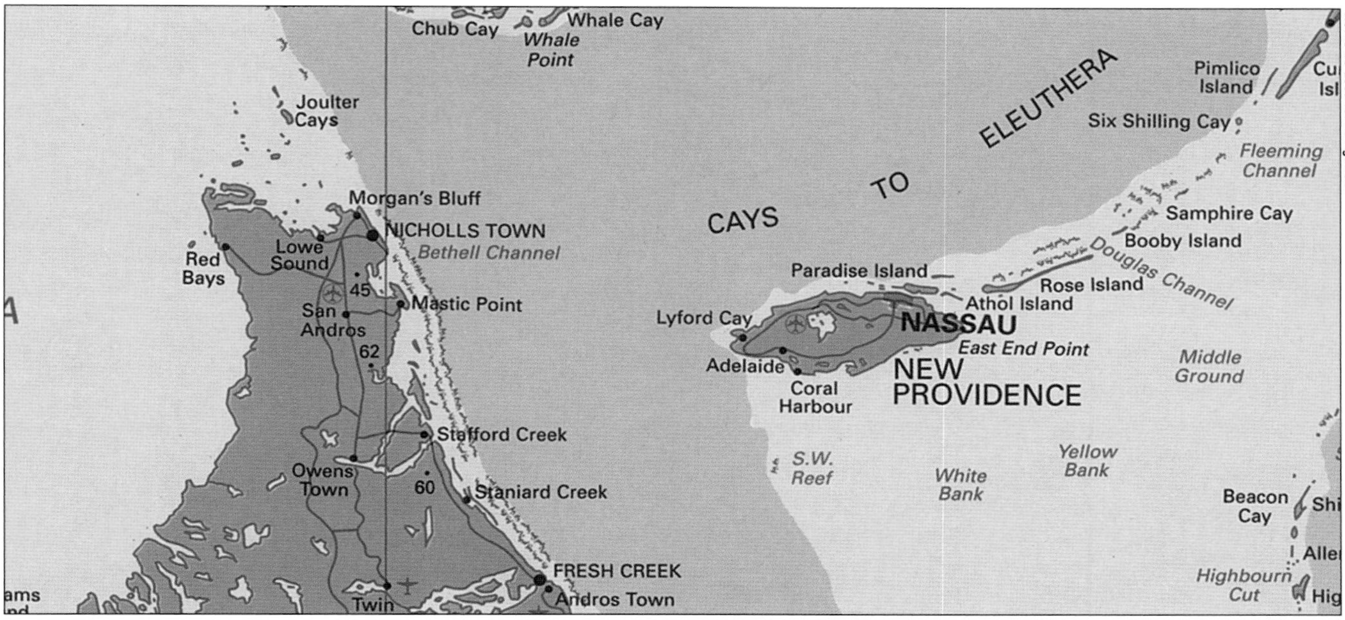

Looking At the Charts

Vessels reach New Providence Island via two deep-ocean thoroughfares that join off its northern coast—the Northwest Providence Channel that connects to the Florida Straits and the Northeast Providence Channel that connects to the open Atlantic Ocean. To its south, the Exumas and the Out Islands serve as rest stops on the maritime highway to the Dominican Republic and beyond. There are essentially no problems approaching Nassau from the north. From other directions, there are bank approaches, shallower but well-charted and frequently traveled.

In the Spotlight. Nassau

Nassau, the capital and most heavily populated city of the Bahamas Islands, dominates New Providence Island to the extent that when visitors speak of Nassau, they mean the whole island. Nassau, despite its smaller neighbors, Paradise Island and Rose Island, is the tourist's singular destination.

Even cruisers are more likely to spend time in Nassau than elsewhere on New Providence. Nassau and Paradise Island have enjoyed an unprecedented development boom in years past, with Rose Island next on the list. The transformation is clearly visible as one nears the islands. The enormous, sunset-hued towers of Atlantis Resort slowly rise on the horizon, like specters of an underwater kingdom, until their sheer size dominates the skyline.

New Providence Island is a little over 20 miles long by seven miles wide, with Nassau dominating the eastern half. Over 250,000 people live on New Providence Island. Thousands of motor vehicles compete for space on its road system. In downtown Nassau, Bay Street and the parallel Shirley Street are designated one-way, as are the two bridges on and off Paradise Island. This arrangement streamlines harborside traffic flow, but trying to cross busy streets on foot can be a challenge! Don't step out into the street without looking at least twice, both ways! It is easy to forget that these commuters are driving on the "other" side of the road.

Locals ride around town to the foot of the Paradise Island bridges and to Cable Beach on public buses called "jitneys." It is only $1.00 to ride them. If you want to go to beyond Cable Beach to Lyford Cay, it will cost you $2.00 on the Western Transportation buses. Before you board a bus, make sure you have plenty of singles. The drivers cannot make change. The clean, 32-seat jitneys run numbered routes until 6 p.m. around Nassau. Buses 6a and 6b pick you up and take you back to the East Bay marinas. To get to Cable Beach, wait at a bus stop, and catch any jitney going west on Marlborough Street. To go beyond Cable Beach to Compass Point, Lyford Cay and farther destinations, catch a Western Transportation bus on the hour. Western buses run until midnight, but that won't help you get back to your marina! These are daylight bus adventures. Make sure that you are well on your way back to the Nassau and the jitneys to return to the boat before 6 p.m.

If you would rather take a more formal tour than a $1.00 jitney bus ride, guided walking tours of historic sites and points of interest in the city start at the Welcome Center on Prince George Wharf. Go on a weekday when there are few (and maybe no) cruise ships in port. The hour-long tours cost $10 per participant and are conducted every day but Sunday. Fancy a surrey ride

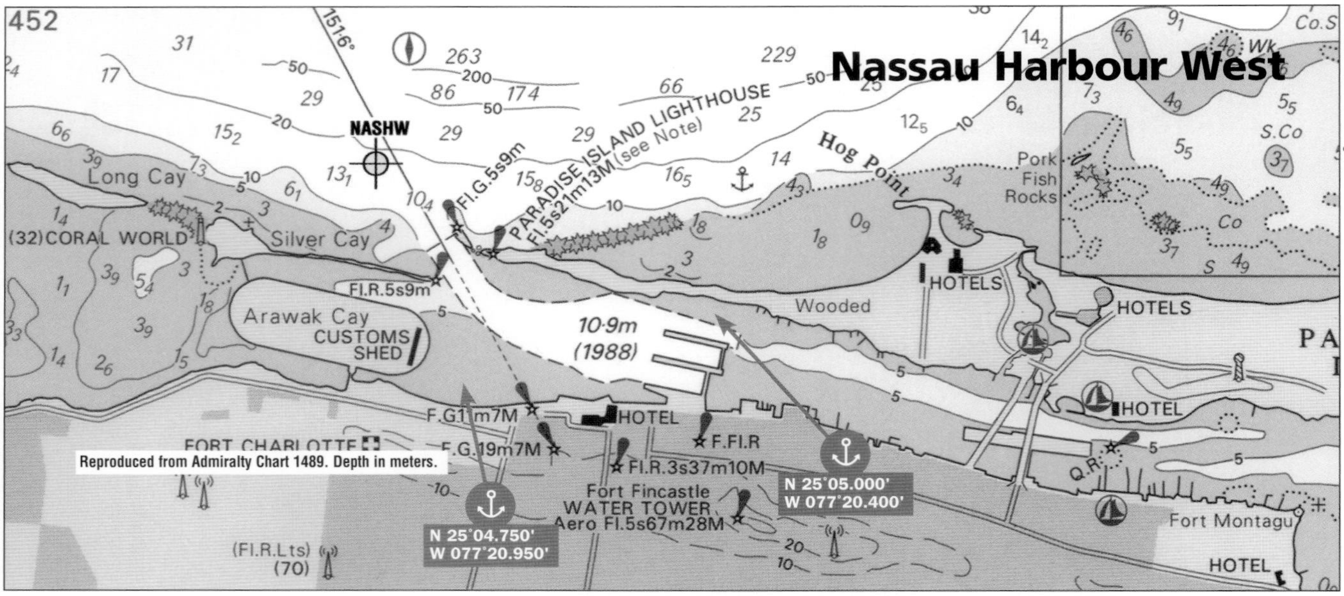

around old downtown Nassau? All the rides start and end at the Prince George Wharf. The short ride takes 15 minutes, the long one, 25 minutes. The surrey travels by the Houses of Parliament, east along Bay St. onto Dowdeswell, then along Deveaux St. onto Shirley and returns to the wharf via Charlotte or East St. You can easily "hoof" that itinerary yourself! You can also take a ferry to Paradise Island from the Straw Market. That will set you back $3.00, but with no place to tie up dinghies, it is a viable way to the island and eliminates the hike across the bridge.

Clearing In—Nassau and New Providence Island

Your principal Nassau entry facilities are The Marina at Atlantis, Hurricane Hole Marina, Nassau Harbour Club, Nassau Yacht Haven and Lyford Cay Club and Yacht Harbour. In each case, dockmasters will arrange for Customs and Immigration to come to your boat at your slip.

Lighthouse at Nassau harbour. Photo Courtesy of Robert Linder.

Nassau Harbor, with Prince George Dock, from the west. (Not to be used for navigation.) WATERWAY GUIDE PHOTOGRAPHY.

What's There? Nassau

Downtown Nassau

The tight confines of downtown Nassau and Paradise Island, with Nassau Harbour sandwiched between them, did not hamper its development. The West Bay Street area's renovation of both the British Colonial Hilton and Prince George Wharf has significantly increased its appeal to tourists. Paradise Island also benefited from a boom of new construction spurred by the success of the landmark Atlantis Resort. The second Paradise Island bridge broke the bottleneck that once kept Paradise Island a place apart, and pedestrian walkways on the bridges provide the much-needed safe paths for foot traffic.

On the Nassau side of the harbor, Bay Street runs west to east, parallel to the harbor. The western end is the epicenter for cruise ships and their passengers. Count the cruise ships as you pass their piers, and you can guess what the crowds are like on West Bay Street. The largest cruise ships have floating populations that rival many a small Florida town. It is clear that many visitors enjoy the offerings of this area. It is certainly worth your time for a look-see and a lot like going to downtown Las Vegas. You might not want to live there, but it is hard to beat the entertainment—lively stalls to peruse local wares, good eats cooked on the street, interesting crowds with fanny packs and foreign accents everywhere.

East Bay Street is of little interest to these folks. It caters to the cruising vessel and its crew. Here you will find plenty of friendly marinas and high-speed fuel docks, shopping centers with pharmacies and Radio Shacks, marine supply stores and repair specialists, dive shops, liquor stores, fast-food joints and cocoa-dusted mocha Joes. Don't forget the wonderful City Market, formerly Winn Dixie, with everything you would find in a supermarket in the United States or Canada. Of course, there are restaurants and bars where the nautical set hangs out to spin a tall tale and throw back a pint or two. Everything of interest to boaters is within an easy walk along East Bay Street.

A word to the wise about walking, don't wander off Bay Street or around the back streets of Nassau at night. Stay close to your marina and fellow boaters. Like any big city, there is crime. Be sensible and street smart. Don't walk around looking like an invitation for a stickup—leave the gold, jewels and Rolex in the safe. When you tie up to a dinghy dock, chain and lock everything that is not attached. Put your outboard's safety-switch cut-off "bracelet" in your pocket. The marinas are secure. Many offer 24-hour guards and locked access to the docks. However, just to be safe, they will advise you to securely lock your tender/dinghy/inflatable and its outboard. If you are at anchor, get them out of the water and locked onboard. Thefts, though rare, are most likely to occur during the wee hours of the night, and your presence on board, at anchor or a marina slip, is not a deterrent. The incidents of night boarding have increased to the point that some cruisers who spend many days or weeks at anchor here have installed motion alarms to alert them to an intruder.

Nassau Harbour

Hardly surprising, Nassau Harbour is crowded and carries a traffic load akin to an international airport. Indeed, all traffic in the harbor area is controlled by the Nassau Port Authority Harbour Control. You are required to contact Nassau Harbour Control on VHF Channel 16 to request permission to enter

Nassau, Paradise Island

NASSAU, PARADISE ISLAND		Largest Vessel Accommodated	VHF Channel Monitored	Transient Berths / Total Berths	Approach / Dockside Depth (reported)	Floating Docks	Gas / Diesel	Groceries, Ice, Marine Supplies, Snacks	Repairs: Hull, Engine, Propeller	Lift (tonnage), Crane, Rail	1=110V, 2=220V, B=Both, Max Amps	Laundry, Pool, Showers	Pump-Out Station	Nearby: Grocery Store, Motel, Restaurant
		Dockage					Supplies		Services					
1. Harbour Central Marina	242-323-2172	100	16	/32	/8		GD	I				LS		R
2. The Marina at Atlantis, Paradise Island 💻 WiFi	242-363-6068	240	10	62/62	11/12			GIMS			B/100	LPS	P	GMR
3. Hurricane Hole Marina 💻 WiFi	242-363-3600	200	16/11	/70	15/10		GD	GI	HEP		B/100	LPS	P	GMR
4. Nassau Yacht Haven WiFi	**242-393-8173**	**150**	**16**	**40/135**	**18/**			**IS**			**B/50**	**LS**		**GMR**
5. Bayshore Marina	242-393-7873	60	16	/200	/6		GD	M						R
6. Brown's Boat Basin	242-393-3331		16		9/9		GD	GI	H	L40				GMR
7. Texaco Harbour View	242-393-4106						GD							GMR
8. Nassau Harbour Club Marina WiFi	242-393-0771	200	16/12	/65	/6		D	IS			B/50	LPS		GMR
9. Paradise Harbour Club & Marina 💻 WiFi	**242-363-2992**	**205**	**16**	**20/23**	**8/**			**IS**			**B/100**	**LPS**		**GMR**

Corresponding chart(s) not to be used for navigation. 💻 Internet Access WiFi Wireless Internet Access

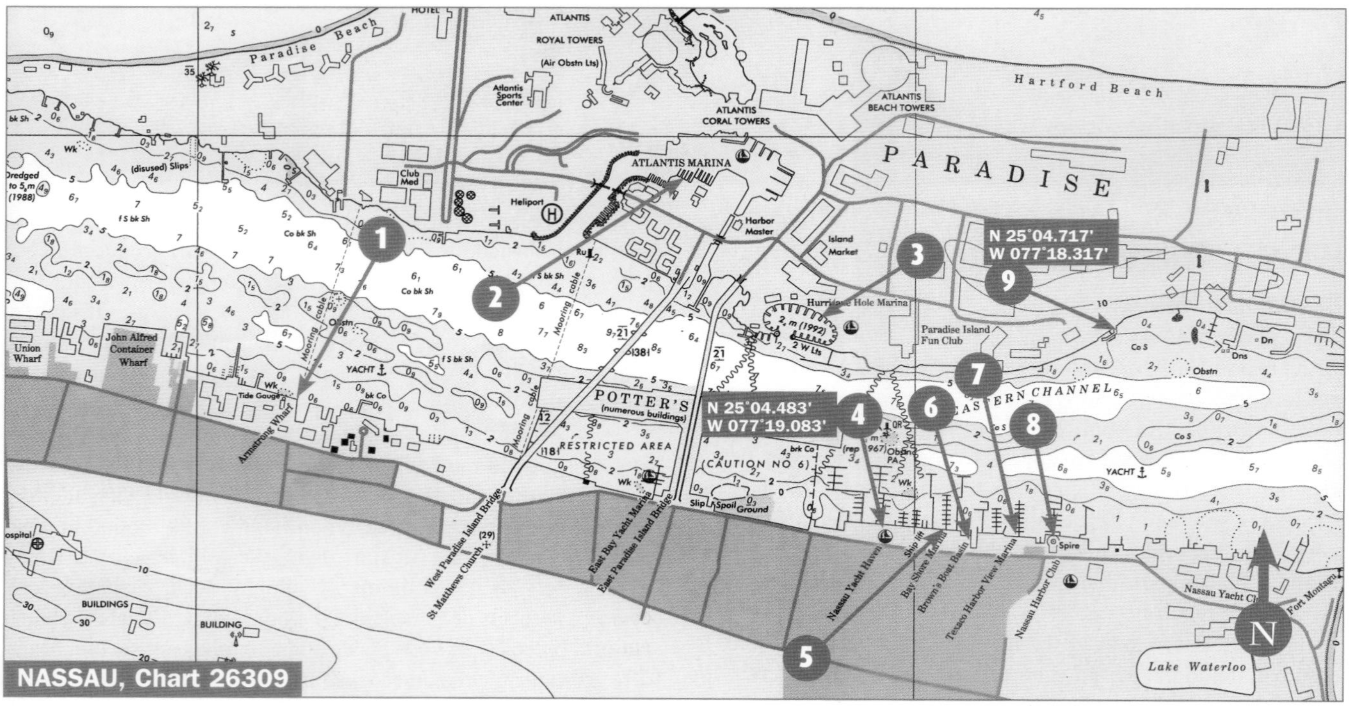

the harbor, report changing your location in the harbor or to inform them before departing the harbor. Harbour Control also records information pertinent to your vessel, so have your papers nearby.

Harbour Control will ask you to stand off the entrance if cruise ships are approaching or departing. Be prepared to do so. When transiting the harbor, pass well off the cruise ship piers, and be vigilant for fellow vessels, from personal watercraft to overloaded Haitian boats, under sail. The number and variety of watercraft running back and forth on these waters at all hours of the day and night can be disconcerting. Take it slowly, and get your bearings. The marinas' dockmasters can be particularly helpful to visiting boaters. Hail them if you need assistance.

Atlantis

From air or sea, the surreal Atlantis Resort dominates Paradise Island and Nassau Harbour. There is no doubt that the sheer mass of Atlantis, with its high-bridged towers, tapered cupolas and leaping sailfish, makes a statement. It is an amazing sight from afar, particularly at night, ablaze with lights. Even if you have no interest in the hotel, the casino, the beaches or its marina, you should go there just to observe a structure of this scale. The aquarium, alone, is worth the visit. There you will marvel at a walk-through tunnel surrounded by a reef, a glass-sided fish domain and the "Atlantis Dig," an archaeological fantasy world surpassed only by your imagination.

VHF Channels in Nassau

In Nassau, VHF Channel 16 takes on its normal international significance as the primary sea traffic contact and distress channel. VHF Channel 16 is not a ship-to-ship contact channel, a standby channel, or ship-to-shore channel, as it is in the greater part of the Bahamas. We underline this by reminding our readers that BASRA has its headquarters in Nassau. Channel 16, kept clear of non-essential traffic, is vital to their task. **The contact channel for common use in Nassau is VHF Channel 68.** Use this channel to make contact. Then switch to another channel of your choice.

Also note that in Nassau the following VHF channels have a reserved use as follows:

08	Paradise Harbour Club and Marina
09	Harbour Control
10	Atlantis
11	Hurricane Hole
12	Nassau Harbour Club
14	Nassau Pilots
72	Nassau Yacht Haven
22A	Remains the U.S. Coast Guard frequency

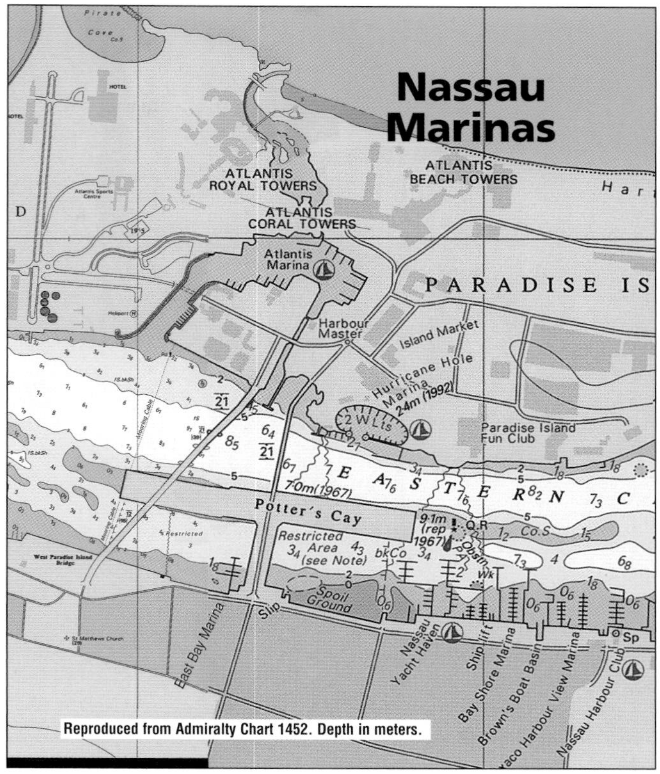

Reproduced from Admiralty Chart 1452. Depth in meters.

Nassau Harbour Marinas – Paradise Island

The Marina at Atlantis on Paradise Island

There is no mistaking that this is a megayacht facility with the capacity to support such vessel's visits. Call ahead for permission to enter The Marina at Atlantis' 30-meter/100-foot-wide entrance channel. From the west, it is just prior to the two Paradise Island bridges. Marina guests enjoy all the Atlantis attractions via a complimentary shuttle bus. Accommodations for you, your crew or your guests are available at the Atlantis Resort from $333 to $25,000 per night.

Hurricane Hole Marina

Hurricane Hole Marina, like Atlantis, is on Paradise Island immediately to port after the second bridge. Its legendary welcome mat is still there for all transient vessels. You will never dock at a more beautifully laid out marina. All berths encircle the Hurricane Hole like an enormous sunflower's petals. It is a photographer's fantasy, and the sort of place where the potential for a dream picture of your boat beckons you to stop and stay awhile. As if that is not enough, Hurricane Hole is within walking distance to the Atlantis Resort, the white-sand Cabbage Beach, the Cloisters and the verdant Versailles Gardens with its strange assortment of statues ranging from gods and goddesses to Franklin Delano Roosevelt.

Paradise Harbour Club & Marina

The Paradise Harbour Club & Marina is located across the harbor from Fort Montague on the eastern end of Paradise Island. This secluded, highly-secured private resort and marina offers dockage to transients and welcomes them to share all on-site

Nassau Harbour, east entrance looking west. (Not to be used for navigation.) WATERWAY GUIDE PHOTOGRAPHY.

facilities. This includes a lagoon-style pool with waterfall as well as a ten-person Jacuzzi. Showers and bathrooms are located beside the pool area. Also on property is Columbus Tavern Restaurant and Bar. Breakfast, lunch and dinner are served daily. There is also a daily happy hour from 5 to 7 p.m. with discounted cocktails and free hors d'oeuvres.

Guests may enjoy day complimentary shuttle service to and from downtown Nassau, the Straw Market and Prince George Whart tourist attractions. Furthermore, a gold car shuttle goes to and from Paradise Harbour Club to Cabbage Beach (where a mini-mart is located) frequently throughout each day. With so many flights available to Nassau from the U.S. and Canada, a special local resort rate is offered to all marina guests. The spacious apartments and suites of Paradise Harbour Club overlook the marina and are perfect accommodations for guests of the marina that choose to stay on property rather than on their vessel.

Nassau Harbour Marinas – New Providence

Nassau Yacht Haven

Nassau Yacht Haven is on New Providence. Pass under the eastern bridge, and past Potters Cay pier and the mailboat dock. To starboard, you will see gaily decorated party boats at rest awaiting their nightly booze cruises. Once past the eastern end of Potters Cay, you will turn to starboard, and there will be Nassau Yacht Haven. The marina office is on shore at the western end of the long yellow building. You will see its big blue letters as you wind your way in and among the transient slips. Nassau Yacht Haven

New Providence

NEW PROVIDENCE, WEST BAY		Largest Vessel Accommodated	VHF Channel Monitored	Transient Berths / Total Berths	Approach / Dockside Depth (reported)	Floating Docks	Gas / Diesel	Groceries, Ice, Marine Supplies, Snacks	Repairs: Hull, Engine, Propeller	Lift (tonnage), Crane, Rail	1=110V, 2=220V, B=Both, Max Amps	Laundry, Pool, Showers	Pump-Out Station	Nearby: Grocery Store, Motel, Restaurant
		Dockage					Supplies		Services					
1. Lyford Cay Club Harbour (WiFi)	242-362-7499	235	16	/74	14/14		GD	GI			B/100	LS		GR

Corresponding chart(s) not to be used for navigation. Internet Access (WiFi) Wireless Internet Access

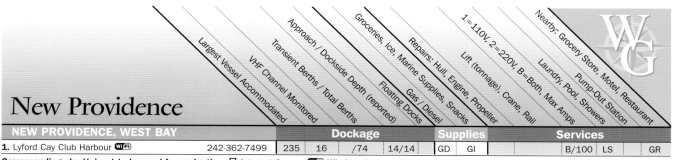

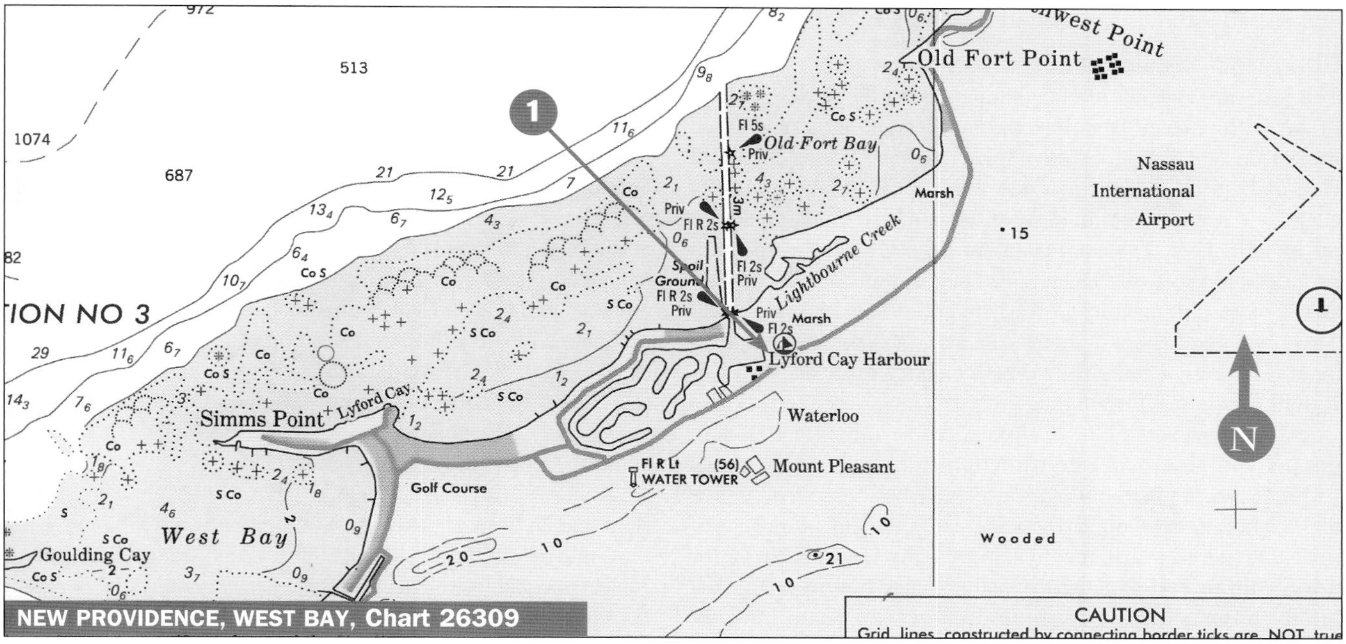

NEW PROVIDENCE, WEST BAY, Chart 26309

is a popular marina for good reason. It includes an adjacent dive shop with an excellent selection of gear, a well-stocked liquor store across the street and the on-site Poop Deck bar and restaurant— a long-time favorite with boaters. The coin-op washers and dryers are among the best you will find in Nassau, and their book and magazine exchange in the marina office is worth a visit to restock your shelves. Marine supply stores are close by, as is the famous Potters Cay market with its marvelous little "island shack" restaurants, fresh produce and just-caught fish stalls. Although the City Market grocery store is a bit of a hike, the market employees will push your overloaded cart all the way to Nassau Yacht Haven for merely a tip and a thank you. Expect tidal current and traffic wake at Nassau Yacht Haven slips. Manage your dock lines and spring lines accordingly, and use fenders generously.

Marinas Between Nassau Yacht Haven and Nassau Harbour Club

The marinas between Nassau Yacht Haven and Nassau Harbour Club provide do-it-yourself to full-service yards. Most have fuel docks and do haul outs, repairs and painting.

Visit www.WaterwayGuide.com TODAY for current navigation information, fuel pricing and more!

They offer short- to long-term storage in their yards. What they don't have is transient dockage. Most, if not all, of their slips are committed to locals. They are wonderful resources for the cruising skipper and certainly worth investigating just in case you need their help in a hurry.

Nassau Harbour Club Marina

Nassau Harbour Club is another very popular marina destination on New Providence. Although the motel rooms are not available, you can still sit in a chaise lounge to laze in the sun next to a sparkling swimming pool. Freshly renovated showers, restrooms and laundry facilities are on the premises, and the City Market shopping center is literally across the street. You can even rent a cell phone for $5 here to call home to say you have arrived, or pay for wireless Internet service. Like Yacht Haven, Nassau Harbour Club is subject to strong current, but lies farther south off the beaten path of harbor traffic and their subsequent wakes and noise.

Nassau Harbour Club is the easternmost marina on New Providence Island and is recognizable by its two T-docks, usually with megayachts on the ends, and a central courtyard of club-like accommodations around the pool. Your host, Peter Attaloglou, has been greeting cruisers to Nassau for over 20 years. He will not only make sure that your stay at his marina is enjoyable; he will see to it that you find everything you want or need on New Providence. Just ask! Peter loves dogs, so bring yours by his office to say, "Hi!"

NOTE: At the time of this writing, Nassau Harbour Club's newly renovated hotel rooms are being used as an embarkation point for managers and developers of the $1 billion Ritz-Carlton Rose Island Marina and Resort. The rooms are not available for the general public until further notice. Future reconstruction of the Harbour Club's landmark round lobby and restaurant building are planned. Keep an eye on this fine marina and resort as renovations progress.

Other New Providence Marinas

The Lyford Cay Club marina entrance is on the northern shore of New Providence Island on the far western end, away from the hustle and bustle of downtown Nassau. Its dredged and well-marked channel begins due west of Old Fort Point. The exclusive, private club invites transients to stay at its docks for up to four days. The marina offers a host of complimentary services and an on-site restaurant, The Captain's Table, as well as the more routine coin-op washers and dryers and fuel dock. There is a good shopping center nearby. Maybe you will meet Sean Connery, or one of the other celebrity residents who call Lyford Cay home, out running errands.

Albany is a new 565-acre luxury resort and with a 15-acre marina complex under construction. It is about five miles from Nassau on the southwestern shores of New Providence and is being developed by Tiger Woods and a group of investors. The 71 slip, megayacht, Albany House Marina for vessels up to 240 feet, will boast a luxury boutique hotel, a family water park and an equestrian center, set to be open at press time. An 18-hole golf course designed by Ernie Els is taking shape and the greens are planted. Construction on the deep-water channel is complete and the concrete floating docks are in place. The center of the community is the historic Albany House. The James Bond movie, Casino Royale, was filmed at the Albany House. This new marina offers berths at an area previously inaccessible on New Providence. Whether there will be room for transient vessels remains a question. If you are in the area and seeking world-class dockage, do contact them for availability.

Cruise ships docked at Nassau. Photo Courtesy of Robert Linder.

All work on the 230-acre resort and marina approved for Rose Island has halted at the time of this writing. No word on when it will resume.

Nassau Harbour Anchorages

Nassau Harbour anchorages are infamous for being less than great. From time to time, Bahamian officials discuss the outright banning of anchoring in the harbor. That is not to say you won't see plenty of boats anchored here. Many have done it when the wallet was thin and necessity outweighed common sense. However, be particularly cautious if you choose to anchor anywhere in the harbor.

There is an officially designated yacht anchorage due south and west of the cruise ship's turning basin, off flashing red "8." Unfortunately, the sandy bottom there that once offered good holding can sometimes leave you fouled with abandoned holding gear and sunken, derelict boats. There is a good deal of street noise and strong current mixed with traffic wakes. There is another officially designated anchorage across the turning basin from this one, on the Paradise Island shore, directly north of the cruise pier. The exceptionally strong current and wash effect of wakes bouncing off the pier make it even less attractive than its southern alternative. Boats "unofficially" anchor all along this shoreline, going east almost to the entrance of The Marina at Atlantis. It cannot be comfortable, and the reason to do so eludes us.

Another unofficial anchorage lies off the New Providence shoreline, in front of BASRA (whose ramp is not a dinghy landing), just before the western Paradise Island bridge. This area is subject to equally strong currents and heavy commercial boat traffic. Green Parrot Restaurant and Bar (with Internet access) will let you use its dinghy dock any time, but City Market and marine supply stores are a very long hike. Boats also anchor farther east, down from Nassau Harbour Club's second T-dock and a bit west of the Nassau Yacht Club. If you drop your hook here, you must allow maneuvering space for the large vessels using Nassau Harbour Club's dock. The waters along this shoreline are dry at low tide, particularly from in front of the dark aqua-blue, one-story house west to Nassau Harbour Club. More than one chagrined skipper has returned to a vessel lying on its side. This anchorage provides close proximity to City Market and marine supply stores, but places to tie up a dinghy are few and far between.

Due north of this anchorage and across the Eastern Channel, just off The Cloisters—a pretty monastery that was bought and brought disassembled from France to the United States by William Randolph Hearst and eventually wound up rebuilt in the most unlikely of locales, Paradise Island—you will find 2.4

Warning

You are required to report your destination to Nassau Harbour Control (VHF Channel 16) and receive permission to transit Nassau Harbour. If you are going to anchor, you must clear your intended anchorage with Harbour Control. They will direct you. If you move from one place to another within the harbor, or are departing Nassau, again you must obtain clearance.

meters/7 feet of water in which to anchor. Drop your hook in the cove area just west of the conspicuous dock in front of what is rumored to be the vacation home of a rock and roll legend's daughter. Again, no place to tie up your dinghy, but nobody will step on your blue suede shoes, either. You can tuck in fairly closely for good northerly wind protection, but you are still subject to strong current and traffic wake.

Regardless of where you choose to anchor in Nassau Harbour, remember that holding is not good even if your hook feels reasonably well set. The tidal wash through the harbor long ago scoured the bottom. That "well-set" anchor might be that you are hooked to old hurricane chains running across the bottom of the harbor, and the captain may have to dive down to release you. Be prepared for reversing tides and ready to endure both unnerving waves in higher winds and the near-continuous wake of passing vessels.

Athol Island and Rose Island Anchorages

These anchorages offer wonderful respite from the harried atmosphere of Nassau Harbour. They are beautiful spots to rest your weary bones before heading to Royal Island, St. George's Cay, Eleuthera Island or south to the Exumas. They are very popular weekend anchorages for locals, so try to plan your stay there during the week. The Athol Island anchorage is reached via the Porgee Rocks to Chub Rock route to Hanover Sound. The anchorage is nestled in between the eastern end of Athol Island and Spruce Cay to the north. You will find 3 meters/10 feet of water entering along the northern coast of Athol and depths of 1.8 meters/6 feet just south of Spruce.

There are two ways to reach the Rose Island anchorage. You can continue on the Hanover Sound route toward Chub Rock and turn due east to transit the deep southern shore of Rose Island (be alert for a stray coral head known to be in the channel) to the anchorage that is protected by a southern barrier island, or you can travel due north towards Rose Island in between Porgee Rocks and Periwinkle Rocks using the waypoint N 25° 03.900'/W 077° 13.400'. The Ritz Carlton development of Rose Island's marina and resort is slated to continue for 10 years and to have substantial impact on this thin, string bean of an island. Enjoy anchoring here while you can, but set your hook carefully. Holding can be tenuous in places.

Pilotage. Talking Captain to Captain

Nassau Harbour (Western Entrance)

The Nassau Harbour West (NASHW) waypoint places you off the entrance to Nassau Harbour, within sight of the first entry buoys. By this point, you will have done your homework and know where you are heading. Keep in mind, the peak cruise ship days are Fridays, Saturdays and Sundays. At this initial waypoint, do not forget to contact Nassau Harbour Control on VHF Channel 16 to obtain permission to enter the harbor.

That NASHW waypoint is the start of the standard western approach into Nassau Harbour. Your primary landmark here is the white lighthouse on the western end of Paradise Island. Long Cay and Silver Cay will be on your starboard side. The entrance is well-marked with entry buoys, and as you move into the harbor, you will see the cruise ship berths ahead to starboard. Also ahead are the unmistakable elliptical spans of the two Paradise Island bridges.

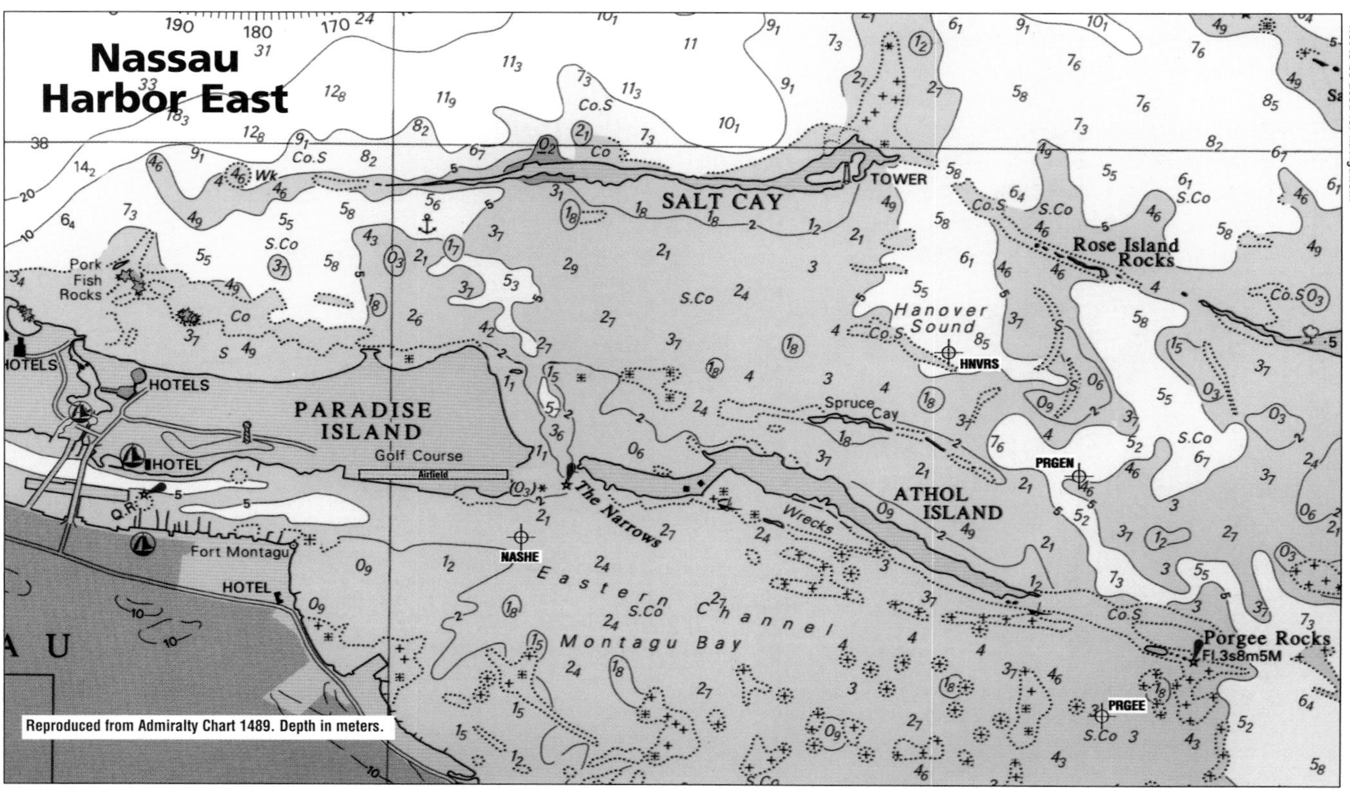

Reproduced from Admiralty Chart 1489. Depth in meters.

Charts and Nassau Harbour

Many of the Nassau Harbour charts currently on the market are out of date, with nothing of the harbor development that has taken place over the last 10 or so years. In particular, Potters Cay may be shown as an island with only the central portion "squared off" as dock (the whole is now developed), the bridge connecting Silver Cay and the commercial Arawak Cay may not be not shown, nor may the Crystal Cay observation tower on Silver Cay (this is one of the most prominent landfall marks, which is far more obvious than Paradise Island lighthouse).

Even the recent British Admiralty charts are already dated as the Paradise Island airport, shown at the east end of the island, no longer exists and has been superceded by a golf course. As you pass this way, the entrance to what appears to be a marina is a boat channel leading into a private canal built to serve docks dedicated to the condominium complex to be built there.

Check your charts carefully, and check any new chart or chart kit you buy. You can still use them if they are outdated, but you should overwrite them with your own corrections while you are in Nassau.

Wavey Line Bahamas 019 is up to date on Nassau Harbour (an October 2002 survey), but does not show the harbor approaches from the east.

Nassau Harbour (Eastern Channel)

Leaving or entering Nassau Harbour East (NASHE) presents no problems as long as you favor the northern shore where the deepest water parallels Paradise Island. Fort Montague's old outer wall runs out into the water, as does a shoal in that area. Farther west, you will note on the charts that there is a shoal area in the middle ground of the Eastern Channel. If you have any significant draft, you should pass either north or south of this area particularly at low water. Aside from this, the eastern entrance is straightforward. Be aware that during peak periods, you will share these waters with a maze of fast ferries, mailboats, dive and day excursion boats and booze cruises.

Porgee Rocks (PRGEE) serve as a visual indicator of your departure waypoint whichever direction you are bound, either northeast to Eleuthera or southeast to the Exumas. Once you have reached Porgee Rocks bound for Eleuthera, you still have four legs to negotiate before you are in ocean water. For the Exumas, you can set a direct course to an Exuma waypoint from Porgee Rocks.

Nassau–Northeast Providence Channel

North Eleuthera Offshore

The normal route is to run to Porgee Rocks (PRGEE), go north to the Porgee North waypoint (PRGEN), transit Hanover Sound (HNVRS–HNVRN) and gain deep water at Chub Rock (CHBRK), a total of 5.7 nautical miles from the Nassau Harbour East waypoint (NASHE). Then it is a straight run of 27.9 nautical miles along the line of the Northeast Providence Channel to the Little Egg Island waypoint (LEGGI). The total distance from NASHE is 33.6 nautical miles.

Nassau–Northeast Providence Channel to North Eleuthera Inshore

If you want to stay closer inshore to poke into the channels on your way to North Eleuthera, from CHBRK, run 8.5 nautical miles to the Douglas Channel waypoint (DGLAS) on 72/252 degrees true, then 5.5 nautical miles to the Samphire Channel (SMPHR) on 57/237 degrees true, 5.8 nautical miles on to Fleeming Channel (FLEMG) on 49/229 degrees true and 11 nautical miles to run to LEGGI on 10/190 degrees true. Total distance from NASHE: 36.5 nautical miles. ■

WATERWAY GUIDE is always open to your observations from the helm. E-mail your comments on any navigation information in the guide to: editor@waterwayguide.com.

Nassau and New Providence Island Waypoints

Goulding Cay	GLDNG (B27)	25°02.00N / 77°35.00W
Nassau Harbour NW	NASNW	25°06.50N / 77°23.00W
Nassau Harbour West	NASHW (B25)	25°05.50N / 77°21.40W
Coral Harbour	COHBR	25°58.46N / 77°28.50W
Nassau Harbour East	NASHE	25°04.50N / 77°17.50W
Porgee Rocks	PRGEE (B26)	25°03.50N / 77°14.50W
Porgee Rocks North	PRGEN	25°04.75N / 77°15.00W
Porgee Rocks SE	PRGSE	25°03.00N / 77°12.00W
Hanover Sound South	HNVRS	25°05.25N / 77°15.66W
Hanover Sound North	HNVRN	25°05.83N / 77°15.75W
Chub Rock	CHBRK	25°06.85N / 77°15.00W
Douglas Channel	DGLAS	25°09.52N / 77°06.04W
Douglas Channel SE	DGLSE	25°05.13N / 77°01.00W
Samphire Cays Channel	SMPHR	25°12.53N / 77°00.86W
Samphire Cays SE	SMPSE	25°10.25N / 76°57.63W
White-Yellow Banks Jct	WYBNK	24°52.00N / 77°12.00W

Our position format is latitude and longitude in degrees and minutes (hddd°mm.mm). Waypoints in RED are NOT for autopilot navigation. Codes in parenthesis are Wavey Line waypoints marked on the charts. If you have programmed waypoints we listed in a previous edition of this guide, check carefully to ensure the coordinates you have recorded match the list. If a waypoint is no longer on our list we may have changed its code or deleted it.

GOIN' ASHORE:

NASSAU

airport • banks • customs & immigration • fuel • groceries • marinas • marine services • medical • police • post office • propane • restaurants • telephone • water

Nassau is the very heart of the Bahamas. As its capital city and center of government, it is full of life and energy, culture and color with lots of places to go and things to do. Cruise ships bring thousands of visitors from all over the world to its shores. Its museums catalog the historical evidence of centuries of change and development. As a tax haven, Nassau attracts international banks and a large, wealthy expatriate community. Island citizens enjoy a high standard of living with improved education and health care. From a boater's perspective, it is not so much a destination as a handy spot to re-provision and ensure ship-safe status for future voyages.

EMERGENCIES

Police, Fire and Ambulance Dial 911 or 919

Diving Emergencies

Lyford Cay Hospital • 242-362-4025 • Contact any of the dive operators or go straight to the hospital where there is a Hyperbaric Chamber. The direct line to the Chamber is 242-362-5765, but you should contact a doctor first through the hospital.

Marine Emergencies

BASRA • 242-325-8864 • VHF 16 • BASRA monitors VHF 16 from 9 a.m. to 5 p.m. daily, except on public holidays.

Nassau Harbour Control • 242-322-1596 • VHF 16 • Monitors VHF 16 the remaining hours each day.

Medical Emergencies

Ambulances *DHHS* • 242-302-4747 • *Med Evac* • 242-322-2881 • *EMS* • 323-2597.

Air Ambulance Services Ltd. • 242-362-1606/1692 • *Advanced Air Ambulance* • 800-633-3590 • *Trauma One* • 242-352-2689.

Clinic *The Walk-In Clinic* • 242-328-0783, 242-326-4026 • Fax: 242-356-9825 • Up the hill on Collins Avenue, between Third and Fourth Terrace, if you just need to see a doctor or nurse for something minor. Open 7 a.m. to 10 p.m. daily, including holidays, with no appointment necessary.

Dentist *The Walk-In Dental Clinic* • 242-393-6588 • Open 11 a.m. to 7 p.m. weekdays, 9 to noon Saturday with Dr. Ellen Strachan Moxey. Visa and MasterCard accepted.

Bayview Dental office • 242-393-9050 • On Bay Street.

Hospitals *Bahamas Heart Center Hospital* • 242-356-6666 - Collins Ave. • *Doctor's Hospital* • 242-322-8411 • Private hospital on Shirley Street with a 24-hr. emergency room and a complete range of medical facilities. • *Princess Margaret Hospital* • 242-322-2861 • Government Hospital on Shirley Street; may involve a wait. • *St. Luke's Medical centre Hospital* • 242-326-6229 • Collins Ave.

Veterinary Emergencies

Animal Clinic • 242-328-5635 • Dr. Dawn Wilson.

Bahamas Humane Society • 242-323-5138 • Emergency after hours.

Central Animal Hospital • 242-382-0392 • Emergency pager for Dr Basil Sands.

MARINAS

On New Providence Island, approaching from the west:

HARBOUR CENTRAL MARINA & TEXACO STARPORT FUEL DOCK

Tel: 242-323-2172 • VHF 16 • harbourcentral@yahoo.com

This marina is just east of the cruise ship docks next to the Tropical Container dock on the southern shore. There are no transient slips available, but the staff is very accommodating to boats at anchor. Look for its Texaco Starport sign and large, tan-colored, dry storage sheds where the large forklift never seems to stop moving boats (up to 28 ft.) back and forth. The fuel dock is open 7 a.m. to 7 p.m. daily with gas and diesel. Water is $0.10 a gallon; $3.00 to dump a large bag of garbage. There is 8 ft. MLW at the dock and okay holding in front of its docks if you have a big anchor (there is truly no "good" holding in Nassau Harbour in a blow). However, if you drop your hook out front, make sure you leave enough maneuvering room for the large boats at the Harbour Central slips.

NASSAU YACHT HAVEN

Tel: 242-393-8173/8174 • Fax: 242-393-3429 • VHF 16

info@nassauyachthaven.com • www.nassauyachthaven.com

Slips 120. **Max LOA** 200 ft. **MLW at Dock** 18 ft. **Dockage** $2.00 per ft. per day. **Facilities & Services** Power 50 amp, $0.60 per kwHr/100 amp may be available. Water barged in from Andros, minimum $10 per day and more depending on boat length, showers restrooms, WiFi for a fee, public telephone in hallway, coin-op washers and dryers with plenty of machines; $2.00 per load, satellite TV included in dockage fees, ice, propane same-day refill, magazine and book exchange in marina office. Bahamas Divers dive shop and rental equipment on-site. Shipwreck Liquor Store across the street will deliver to boats. **Restaurants & Bar** Poop Deck Restaurant and Bar serves lunch and dinner daily from noon to 10:30 p.m. $$-$$$. Bar opens at 11 a.m. and stays open until the last person is standing, usually around midnight. **Credit Cards** Visa, MasterCard, AMEX. **Security** The marina entrance from Bay Street is locked and guarded at night. Pets are welcome like family members at the marina.

TPA Marina

Tel: 242-394-1605 • VHF 11 or 08 "Vince"

TPA may not have room; but if it does, it is a secret gem! It is nestled behind Nassau Yacht Haven. The owner's 150-ft. yacht, Maratani X, acts like a breakwater. It protects you from the mess of wakes coming at the slips from all the activity in Nassau Harbor. The marina is at the southwest end of Nassau Yacht Haven and a bit tricky to enter the first time you do it. Vince will talk you in: First starboard turn is right after the mail dock, this heads you south; second starboard turn, heads you west; then a turn to port into the marina. If you stop at Nassau every year, take the time to meet Vince landside, and get your name on his "list" of welcome vessels. You will find free WiFi and one of the best managers/dockmasters you will ever know, Vince Symonette.

BAYSHORE MARINA
Tel: 242-393-7873 • VHF 16

This is a working boatyard with sporadic slip availability for transient boats and few facilities for visitors.

Fuel Diesel and gasoline 7:30 a.m. to 5 p.m. **Facilities & Services** Ice. Haul-out for bottom painting and repairs. Marine store on site. **Restaurant & Bar** *Sailor's Choice* • 242-393-7910 • Waterfront bar and light meals, at the eastern end of the boatyard. $ **Credit Cards** Visa and MasterCard.

BROWN'S BOAT BASIN
Tel: 242-393-3331• Fax: 242-393-1863 • VHF 16

This boatyard has no slips available for transient boats. It is primarily a working yard specializing in general boat and yacht repairs, hull and boat repairs, and painting is a specialty. Travel hoist up to 35 tons with an 18-ft. beam. Brown's marine supply store opposite on East Bay Street. Fuel dock is open 7:30 a.m. to 5 p.m. daily. **Credit Cards** Visa and MasterCard.

HARBOUR VIEW MARINA

Harbour View Marina offers long-term dockage for smaller craft. It runs from the Texaco Starport fuel dock to the Texaco Starmart filling station on East Bay Street. There is a dock at the Starmart to tie up your dinghy.

NASSAU HARBOUR CLUB MARINA
Tel: 242-393-0771 • Fax: 242-393-5393 • VHF 16 • nhc@bahamas.net.bs

Slips 65. **Max LOA** 200 ft. **MLW at Dock** 6 ft., 15 feet at T-dock pier heads. **Dockage** Charges vary, please call Peter Attaloglou for current charges and availability. **Fuel** High-speed diesel only, open 7 a.m. to 5 p.m. daily. **Facilities & Services** Shore power charges vary for 30 amp, 50 amp and 3-phase; city water, charges vary; showers, restrooms, coin-op laundry open 24 hours daily, satellite television, cell phones for rent daily, weekly and monthly, WiFi for a fee, same day propane tank refills arranged, swimming pool and barbeque area. Courtyard with eating area and chaise lounges. Literally right across the street from the best shopping center on East Bay Street with a bank, pharmacy, liquor warehouse store, Radio Shack, hardware store, several coffee and fast food spots, good book store, clothing stores, dentist, computer shop, DHL, vision center and, of course, the wonderful City Market. **Credit Cards** Visa, MasterCard, AMEX. **Security** The marina is locked at night with a security guard on duty. Pets are very welcome at the marina.

THE NASSAU YACHT CLUB and THE ROYAL NASSAU SAILING CLUB

Both yacht clubs have small marinas near Fort Montague. The Nassau Yacht Club welcomes transients for $2.00 ft. when they have the room. Give them a try by phone, 242-393-5132, or stop in to talk to staff. They are on East Bay Street just west of Fort Montague.

PORT DIRECTORY FOR NASSAU

Accommodations There are so many hotels, resorts and guesthouses in Nassau that it is better to ask for a complete list at a Tourist Information office or log onto the Bahamas Tourist Board Web site. At peak times, such as Spring Break and public holidays, hotel rooms in Nassau are at a premium.

Airlines *Air Canada, Air Jamaica, American Airlines/American Eagle, Bahamasair, British Airways, Cat Island Air, Continental, Delta, Jet Blue, Southern Air Charter, Spirit Airlines, United Airlines, US Air* and *WestJet*. It is best to go online or consult the BTC yellow pages for the current phone numbers, connections and flights that you require. Airport Lynden Pindling International Airport, daily flights to every island and the U.S.

ATMs Widespread throughout Nassau. Many filling stations, most of the banks close to marinas, the tourist areas on Bay Street, the casinos and the airport have ATMs. Most give Bahamian dollars; the casinos and airport give U.S. dollars. *Scotiabank*, 242-356-1400 • *FirstCaribbean Intl. Bank*, 242-322-8455 • *Royal Bank of Canada*, 242-356-8500.

Banks Banking hours in Nassau 9:30 a.m. to 3 p.m., Monday through Thursday, and until 4:30 p.m. Friday. Most of the big banks are in downtown Nassau, many with offices on Bay Street.

BASRA • Tel: 242-325-8864 • Fax: 242-325-2737 • VHF 16 • www.basra.org • BASRA monitors VHF 16 from 9 a.m. to 5 p.m. daily with the help of volunteers. Nassau Harbour Authority monitors VHF 16 the remaining hours each day. BASRA HQ (Bay Street, PO Box SS 6247, Nassau, NP, Bahamas) is open 9 a.m. to 5 p.m. daily, except public holidays. Tie your dinghy up at the Green Parrot to visit BASRA. Are you a BASRA member? You should be. You never know when you might need BASRA's help.

Buses Jitneys run throughout the island, charging $1 (have the correct change). Many of them leave from and run to Bay Street, but there are bus stops and benches. The drivers will stop anywhere to pick up a fare. It is good manners to greet your fellow travelers as you board the bus. Then sit back and enjoy the music, usually played at full blast. Jitneys 9a and 9b, for the East Bay Street marinas, leave from the street outside the ScotiaBank ATM and Rawson Square.

Car Rentals Don't forget to drive on the left! *Avis* • 242-377-7121 (airport), 242-326-6380 (Nassau), 242-363-2061 (Paradise Island) • *Budget* • 242-377-3095 • *Dollar/Thrifty* • 242-377-8300 • *Hertz* • 242-377-6321 • *National/Alamo* • 242-377-0355 • *Virgo Car Rental* • 242-394-2122.

Carriage Tours Surreys line up by the cruise ship dock at Prince George Wharf to take you for a 15- or 25-minute drive around town, usually with a cheerful commentary.

Casinos *Atlantis* • 242-363-3000 • On Paradise Island. More than 800 slot machines and 80 gaming tables.

Crystal Palace Casino • 242-327-6200 • On Cable Beach. More than 400 slot machines and 25 gaming tables.

Churches Nassau has over 25 churches, representing 18 different religions. Most churches give their times of services outside the church.

Couriers *DHL Worldwide Express* • 242-394-4040 • East Bay Street.

FedEx • 242-322-5656 • Fax: 242-322-5659 • 3 Hillside Plaza, Thompson Boulevard. • *UPS* • 242-325-8227 • Fax: 242-328-0014 • Oakes Field Shopping Centre.

Customs • 325-6550; 322-8791 or 242-326-2408 after hours • VHF 16 • **Immigration** • 242-322-7531, 242-323-3330. Can be called from any of the marinas if you need to clear in.

Diving & Snorkeling Gear *Bahama Divers* • 242-393-5644 • In front of Nassau Haven Marina. Everything you could possibly need for diving, spearfishing and snorkeling. Also carries bathing suits and T-shirts. A very nice store. If you don't see what you need, they can get it from their other store on Paradise Island.

Embassies & Consulates *American Embassy* • 242-322-1181/ 1182/1183, *British High Commission* • 242-325-7471/7472/7473, *Canadian Consulate* • 242-393-2123. For other consulates, look in the yellow pages of the BTC telephone directory under Diplomatic and Consular Representation.

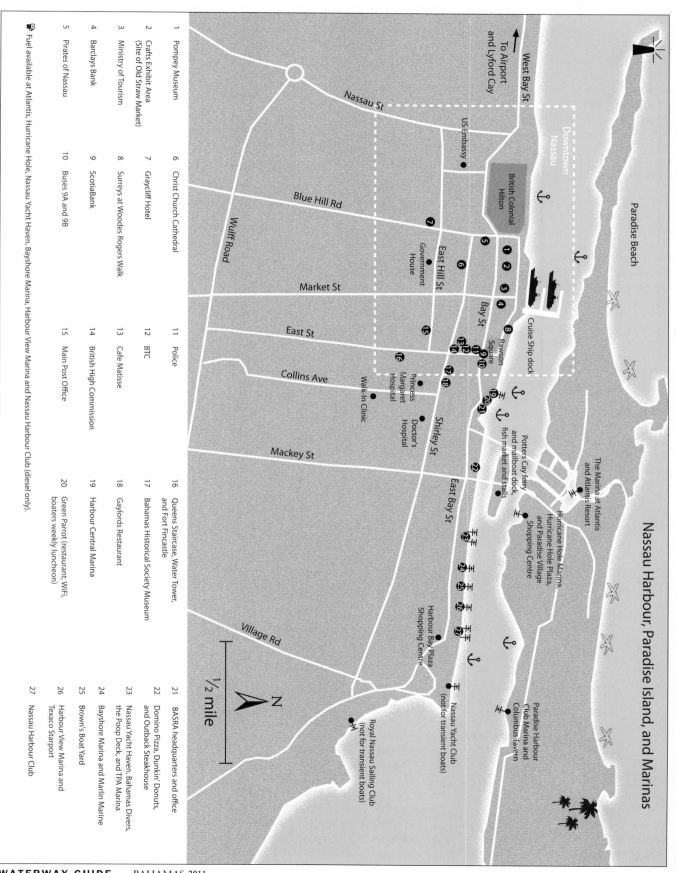

Nassau Harbour, Paradise Island, and Marinas

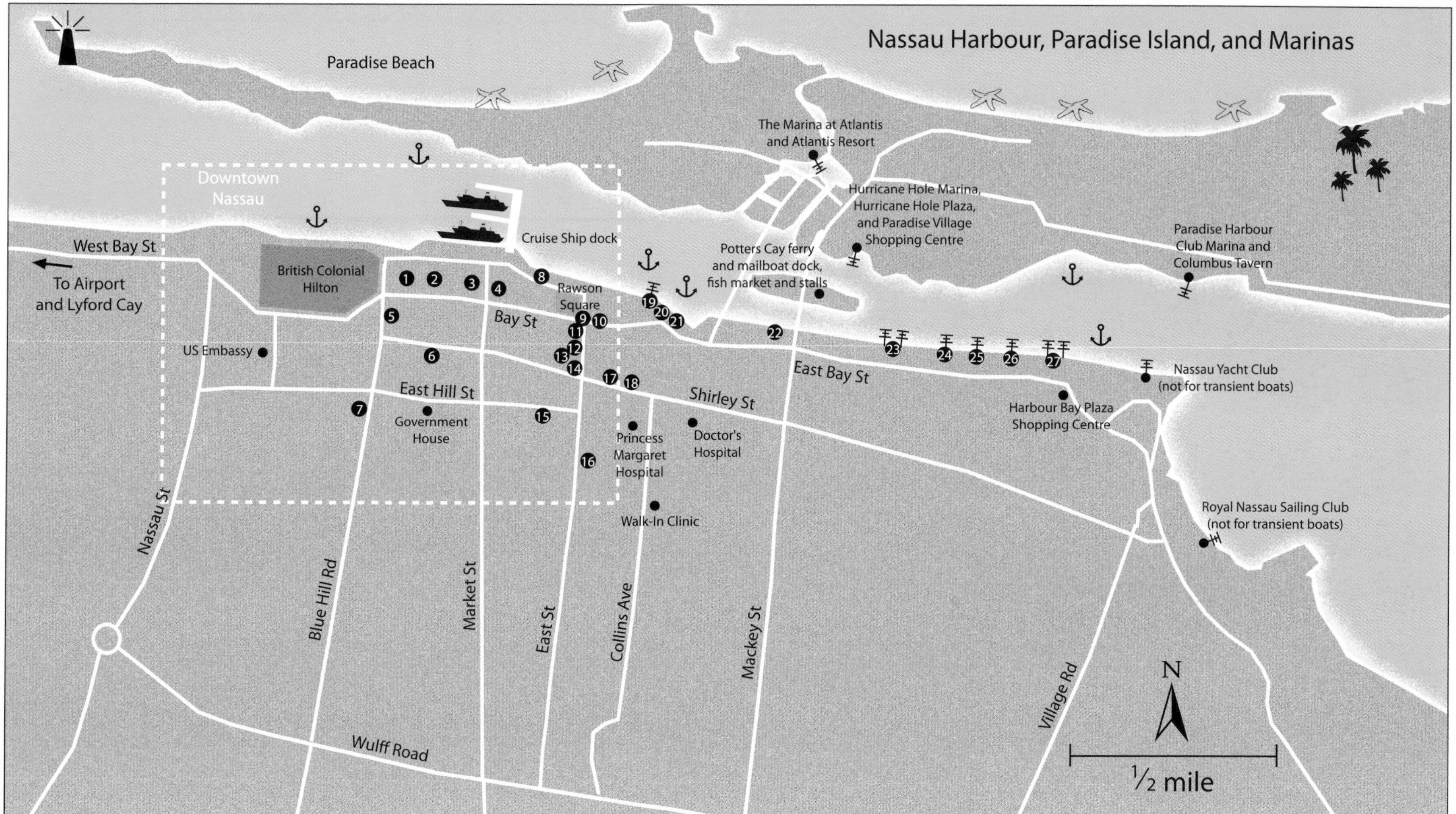

1 Pompey Museum
2 Crafts Exhibit Area (Site of Old Straw Market)
3 Ministry of Tourism
4 Barclays Bank
5 Pirates of Nassau
6 Christ Church Cathedral
7 Graycliff Hotel
8 Surreys at Woodes Rogers Walk
9 ScotiaBank
10 Buses 9A and 9B
11 Police
12 BTC
13 Cafe Matisse
14 British High Commission
15 Main Post Office
16 Queens Staircase, Water Tower, and Fort Fincastle
17 Bahamas Historical Society Museum
18 Gaylords Restaurant
19 Harbour Central Marina
20 Green Parrot (restaurant, WiFi, boaters weekly luncheon)
21 BASRA headquarters and office
22 Domino Pizza, Dunkin' Donuts, and Outback Steakhouse
23 Nassau Yacht Haven, Bahamas Divers, the Poop Deck, and TPA Marina
24 Bayshore Marina and Marlin Marine
25 Brown's Boat Yard
26 Harbour View Marina and Texaco Starport
27 Nassau Harbour Club

Fuel available at Atlantis, Hurricane Hole, Nassau Yacht Haven, Bayshore Marina, Harbour View Marina and Nassau Harbour Club (diesel only).

Ferries *Bahamas Fast Ferries* • 242-323-2166 • Fax: 242-322-8185 *Paradise Island Ferry* Leaves Prince George Wharf/Straw Market every 30 minutes from 9:30 a.m. to 6 p.m. Ferry stops at docks on Paradise Island and returns to cruise ship dock for $3.

Fish Fry Arawak Cay • Over 100 seafood stands with conch, crab, lobster and fresh fish served • Potters Cay, in between the Paradise Island bridges, every assortment of fresh produce and fresh fish stand imaginable, over a dozen seafood stands serving conch every way possible— crab, lobster, fish—you name it! Best on Saturdays.

Liquor *Harbour Bay Wholesale Liquors* (10 to 8 except Sunday). Harbour Bay Plaza across from *Nassau Harbour Club.*

Mail All the marinas will hold mail for you.

Post Offices Open 9 a.m. to 5 p.m. weekdays on East Hill Street or Shirley Street. Stamps often available in the Bay Street stores and at *City Market.*

Propane Take your tank to the BASRA office on Bay Street, close to the Green Parrot. Chris Lloyd is very generous in filling tanks for boaters for a small donation.

Provisions There are many shopping malls on the island with good grocery stores. The closest one to the main marinas on New Providence is the *Harbour Bay Plaza*, with a big *City Markets* supermarket (7:30 a.m. to 9 p.m. daily, 7 a.m. to 10 a.m. Sunday), First Caribbean International Bank and ATM (9:30 a.m. to 3 p.m. weekdays, to 4:30 p.m. Friday), *ACE* hardware store (9:30 a.m. to 6:30 p.m. except Sunday), *Harbour Bay Liquors* (10 a.m. to 8 p.m. except Sunday), *Lowe's Pharmacy* (8 a.m. to 8:30 p.m. daily, 9 a.m. to 5 p.m. Sunday), and *Caffe Caribe* and Logos Bookstore, (8:30 a.m. to 6 p.m. daily).

Restaurants There are so many restaurants in Nassau and on Paradise Island that we suggest you look at the one of the free maps or tourist brochures for ideas. The choice is wide, and the food is generally very good. Check whether your bill already includes service before adding your tip. We list a few that are easily accessible if you are on your own boat in the harbor area, but there are dozens more all over New Providence.

Restaurants On New Providence:

British Colonial Hilton • 242-322-3301 • The refurbished hotel has an elegant *Wedgewood Restaurant, Portofino Italian Café* and a *Patio Grille & Pool Bar* serving snack lunches poolside. From $ to $$$.

Cafe Matisse • 242-356-7012 • On Bank Lane, behind Parliament Square. Open Tuesday through Saturday for lunch and dinner. Matisse prints and delicious homemade Italian food served indoors or outside in a delightful courtyard. Reservations suggested. Smart casual dress for dinner. $$$

Conch Fritters Bar and Grill • 242-323-8778 • On Bay Street, across from British Colonial Hilton. Specializing in Bahamian and American food. Open 10:30 a.m. to midnight daily. $$

Green Parrot • 242-323-3341 • West of Paradise Island bridge on East Bay Street, overlooking Nassau Harbour. Open for lunch and dinner from 11 a.m. daily. Fun, casual island fare at reasonable prices, happy hour daily. Boaters meet here for lunch on Thursdays. WiFi available. $$

East Villa Restaurant • 242-393-3377 • Lunch and dinner. Reservations suggested, resort casual dress. Excellent Chinese food and New York strip steaks. Within walking distance of the Nassau Harbour Club. $$

Gaylords • 242-356-3004 • On Dowdeswell Street, between Bay Street and Shirley Street. Authentic Indian cuisine in a historic Bahamian mansion built in 1871. Open daily for lunch and dinner. Reservations and smart casual attire requested for dinner. $$$

Montagu Gardens • 242-394-6347 • Next to Waterloo, a short walk from the *Nassau Harbour Club.* Lunch and dinner in an old Bahamian home and gardens on Lake Waterloo. Flame-grilled and blackened specialties; catering and delivery service. $$$

The Poop Deck Restaurant & Bar • 242-393-8175 • At the Nassau Yacht Haven, open daily for lunch and dinner. Another *Poop Deck* is located beachside at Sandyport, 242-327-DECK. $$$

Potters Cay Fish Fry stands are open daily. Best day to go is Saturday when every stand is open and the stalls are full. Our cruising editor likes the conch salad at the very first stand that is painted magenta pink (next to the gazebo where all the men are playing dominoes), but walk through all of them to compare. The best "*non-tourist*" tourist attraction in Nassau! Don't forget your camera! $

Restaurants on Paradise Island:

Atlantis has 26 restaurants: choose from burgers and sandwiches to sushi and fine dining. If you go to *Atlantis*, don't miss *Fathoms*, with a raw bar and superb seafood for lunch or dinner, and panoramic windows into the huge aquarium. Smart casual attire required for dinner; reservations 242-363-3000. *Atlantis* restaurant prices range from $ to $$$$$.

Restaurants Outside Atlantis on Paradise Island:

All the hotels have restaurants; reservations preferred. *Anthony's Caribbean Grill* • 242-363-3152 • At the *Paradise Village Shopping Center.* Caribbean/American food, with exotic specials. Lunch and dinner daily. *Breakfast at Anthony's* Express Deli, from 7:30 a.m. $$ Blue Marlin • 242-363-2660 • Bahamian food, open for dinner from 5 p.m. to 10 p.m. daily; floor shows some nights. $$ *Columbus Tavern* at the *Paradise Harbour Club* • 242-363-2992 • Great food and atmosphere. $$$

Shopping The length of Bay Street, from Rawson Square to the *British Colonial Hilton*, is all shops. From fancy designer stores, duty-free shops and glamorously expensive jewelry to souvenirs and T-shirts. There is something for everybody. When there are several cruise ships in port, it can be very crowded. *The Straw Market* is large and colorful, though make sure there is not a MADE IN CHINA tag of the

MARINE SERVICES

Marine Consultant *Captain Helge Menk* • 242-357-4336 • EWASCO@GMX.net

Marine Services Most of the agencies we list are found on Bay Street and East Bay Street, within walking distance of the Nassau Harbour area marinas. There are several more marine stores on New Providence; ask the dockmasters for help, or look in the Nassau telephone book yellow pages.

Albert's Marine • 242-394-6989 • Fax: 242-394-6991 • albertsmarine@hotmail.com. Vacuflush, VDO, Marine parts and accessories.

Bahamas Yacht Management • 242-380-2628 • Fax 242-393-4814. • *info@bahamasyachtmanagement.com* • www.bahamasyacht management.com • Full-service maintenance and provisioning services at Shirley Street and Kemp Road.

Brown's Boat Basin • 242-393-3331 • Fax: 242-393-1868 • Long-established family-run supply store across from their own boatyard; with hoist up to 35 tons, 18-ft. beam. 5-ft. draft boats at high tide. Fuel dock monitors VHF 16; diesel and gas.

Cooper's Marine • 242-393-7475 • 242-328-9228 (pager) • On Abundant Life Road • Fiberglass work, bimini repairs, marine upholstery and boat painting.

Harbourside Marine • 242-393-3461 or 242-394-8360 • 119 Mackey Street. Yamaha sales and service, with marine supplies, lubricants and cleaning materials.

Island Marine Electronics • 242-394-3826 • Near Nassau Stadium. #8 Fowler Street. Furuno, Ray Marine, Garmin, Northern Lights and other parts and accessories.

Lightbourne Marine • 242-393-5285 • Fax 242-393-6236 • Agents for Honda and Mercury outboards, Perkins engines, Honda and Kohler generators. Marine supplies including 3M marine products and complete fiberglass repair supplies. Well-stocked charts, lines, accessories and fishing tackle. Services for diesel engines, outboard engines and generators. The boat yard can haul and launch vessels up to 25 ft. Monday through Friday 8 a.m. to 5 p.m. Saturdays 8 a.m. to noon. Closed Sundays.

Marlin Marine and Bayshore Marina • 242-393-7873 • Fax: 242-393-0066 • VHF 16 • Large store adjacent to the marina and working boatyard. Full service and parts for Johnson and Sea Doo. Agents for Evinrude and Carolina Skiffs; a wide selection of generators, fishing gear and equipment in the store. The boatyard is used primarily for bottom painting. Fuel dock with diesel and gasoline.

Marine Diesel Ltd. • 242-394-2135 • At 5 Shirlea Road. Parts, sales and service for Yanmar, Volvo, Westerbeke, Perkins and Lugger engines.

Phillips Sailmakers • 242-393-4498 • phillipsailmakers@hotmail.com • Sails, bimini tops and marine upholstery on East Shirley Street, Waterloo Lake. Phillips can also provide that marine survey you need updated for your insurance company.

bottom of your "local" souvenir. The temporary *Straw Market* under the white tents is undergoing major renovation and a rebuild. You will want to visit the new facilities once they are completed.

Spa *The Dermal Clinic*, Sandyport Plaza, www.dermal-clinic.com. Face mapping, microzone treatments, skin bar and other "skinny" delights • *Sivananda Ashram Retreat*, www.sivanandabahamas.org. Beachfront meditation and yoga begins at 6 a.m., all levels of yoga enthusiasts welcomed.

Taxis Taxis charge per mile, per the number of people and per the amount of luggage. The fare can vary, so it is a good idea to ask how

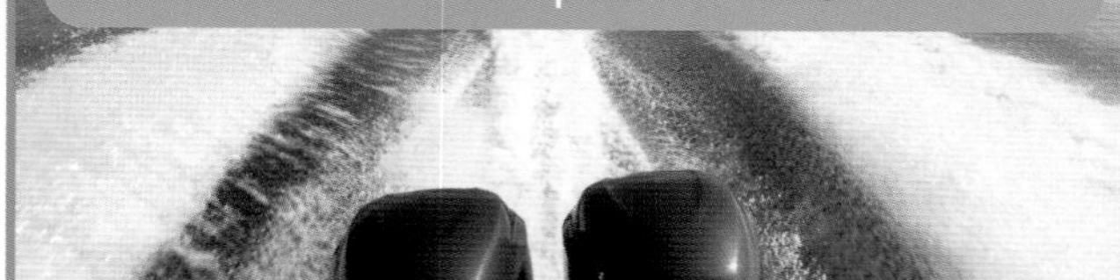

much it will be before you set off. Zone rates are regulated, but you would never know it! Regulated rates for one or two passengers ($3 each additional person): Lynden Pindling Int. Airport to/from Cable Beach, $18; Downtown, $27; Paradise Island, $32 • Cable Beach to/from: Downtown, $15; Paradise Island, $20 • Paradise Island to/from Downtown, $11 • $1 charge to Paradise Island for toll bridge; Up to two pieces of luggage is included. $0.75 per additional piece of luggage • All other destinations are metered. Meter rates are set by the government, and all meters are supposed to be in good working condition. Now you know why most cruisers learn how to ride the buses!

Telephones can be found at all the marinas, hotels and many at the cruise ship dock. Telephones either take BTC prepaid phone cards, available in $5, $10 and $20 denominations from the BTC offices. Many stores and marinas have International Direct Dial phones that use a credit card, but they are very expensive. But most local people have cell phones, using the QuikCell cards that are widely available, too. If you are going to spend a long time in the Bahamas, it is easier to purchase a cell phone with your own number from either from a BTC office or an electronics store. Then buy prepaid QuikCell phone cards as you need them. Some U.S. cell phones will work in the Bahamas if they have reciprocity with BTC. Beware the additional costs.

SPORTS & RECREATION

Beaches There are many to choose from, but a few suggestions on New Providence are *Cable Beach* and *Goodmans Bay, Orange Hill Beach*, *Saunders Beach* and *South Ocean Beach*. On Paradise Island try *Paradise Beach* and *Hartford Beach*.

Cricket At *Haynes Oval* on West Bay Street, Saturday & Sunday at 1 p.m., from March to November.

Diving Bahama Divers • 242-393-5644, 800-398-3483 (reservations) • Fax: 242-393-6078 • bahdiver@coralwave.com • www.bahamadivers.com • PADI five-star facility with exclusive trips to the Lost Blue Hole, intriguing wreck dives and a 3,000-foot living wall on the Tongue of the Ocean; excellent, well-stocked dive shop at Nassau Yacht Haven. *Custom Aquatics* • 242-362-1492 • 242-427-2836 (cell) • young@coralwave.com • 25 years of diving and cruising experience; 3 dive boats. All-day unlimited dive packages, charter only. *Dive Dive Dive* • 242-362-1143/1401 • At Coral Harbour. Shark dives, Dolphin Experience. *Diver's Haven* • 242-363-6707 • At Paradise Island Ferry Terminal. *Nassau Scuba Centre* • 242-362-1964 • At Coral Harbour. Shark Suit adventures. *Oceanus Sail and Dive* • 800-738-2434 • www.oceanus.net • Week-long sailing and diving trips from Nassau to the Abacos and Exumas. Scuba divers must bring proof of certification. *Stuart Cove's Dive Bahamas* • 242-362-4171/5227 • With 24 instructors and guides and 11 dive boats. All-day wilderness trips and wall flying adventures. No Scuba experience needed for Scenic Underwater Bubble (SUB) trips.

Ecotours *Bahamas National Trust Ornithology Group* • 242-362-1574 • Meet on the first Saturday of the month at 7 a.m. for bird watching tours. *Bahamas Outdoors* • 242-362-1574 • cwardle@batelnet.bs • www.bahamasoutdoors.com • Bird watching, nature tours and off-road biking.

Fishing *Born Free Charters* • Captain Philip Pinder, 242-363-2003 • Captain Dudley Smith • 242-322-3202 • 242-457-1731 (cell) • bornfree@batelnet.bs • At *Nassau Yacht Haven*. Deep sea fishing, skin diving, piloting and yacht deliveries. *Chubasco Charters* • Captain Mike Russell • 242-324-FISH • chubasco@100jamz.com • *Orion Charters* • 242-324-7781 • www.orionsportfishing.com • Full- or half-day fishing trips.

Golf *Cable Beach Golf Club* • 242-327-6000 • *Ocean Club Golf Course* (on Paradise Island, open only to members and guests at Atlantis 242-363-6680), *South Ocean Golf Club* at Clarion Resort, New Providence • 242-362-4391 • Members only at Lyford Cay. Coming soon: Ernie Els designed *Albany House* 18-hole Golf Course in the Albany Resort community.

Horseback Riding *Happy Trails* • 242-362-1820 • In Coral Harbour.

Miscellaneous Tennis courts, parasailing, water skiing at all the major hotels and on the beaches.

Regattas *Annual Bahamas Atlantis Superboat Challenge* • 242-302-2006 • Power boat racing held in late September. Call the Ministry of Tourism for more information. Nassau Race Week and the Miami-Nassau Race. Contact the Nassau Yacht Club race committee • jlawrence@coralwave.com.

Squash *The Village Club* • 242-393-1580

PLACES OF INTEREST

Ardastra Gardens and Conservation Centre • 242-323-5806 • Five acres of zoological gardens on Chippingham Road, west of Fort Charlotte. Flamingos, iguanas, monkeys, snakes and rare Bahama parrots. Open daily 9 a.m. to 5 p.m.

Art Gallery of the Bahamas • 242-328-5800 • www.nagh.org.bs • At historic Villa Doyle, opened in 2003, on West Hill and West St. Open Tuesday through Saturday, 11 a.m. to 4 p.m. with paintings, sculpture, textiles, ceramics and exhibitions.

Bahamas Historical Society Museum • 242-322-4231 • On Shirley Street and Elizabeth Avenue. Bahamian history from pre-Columbus to the present day, with Lucayan, Taino and Arawak exhibits. Open 10 a.m. to 4 p.m. weekdays except Wednesdays; to noon Saturdays.

Balcony House • 242-302-2621 • On Market Street, off Bay Street. The oldest wooden house in Nassau, dating from the eighteenth century, now a museum. Open 10 a.m. to 4:30 p.m. daily; to 1 p.m. on Saturdays (closed Sunday).

Botanical Gardens • 242-323-5975 • 600 species of tropical trees and plants on Chippingham Road off West Bay Street. Open 8 a.m. to 4 p.m. weekdays, 9 a.m. to 4 p.m. weekends.

The Cloister and Versailles Garden Features a fourteenth-century arched walkway built by monks and brought in by Huntington Hartford as part of his initial island development. Overlooking the harbor on Paradise Island, this makes a popular wedding site.

Fort Montagu Built in 1741 of local limestone. It guards the eastern entrance to Nassau Harbour and was captured by the Americans during the American War of Independence in 1776.

Fort Charlotte Completed in 1789 to guard the western entrance to Nassau Harbour. Not a shot was fired against an invader by its 42 cannons. Self-guided or tour guides, 8 a.m. to 5 p.m. daily.

Fort Fincastle Completed in 1793, built in the shape of a ship. Nearby is the 126-foot tall Water Tower with a dramatic view of the harbor. Open 8 a.m. to 5 p.m. daily.

Pompey Museum of Slavery and Emancipation This was the old slave market until emancipation in 1834. Features artifacts from the wreck of the "Henrietta Marie."

The Retreat • 242-393-1317/2848 • The headquarters of the *Bahamas National Trust*. Set in 11 acres of lush tropical gardens, with the world's third-largest collection of rare and exotic palm trees. Guided tours, or self-guided tours with a map. Open 9 a.m. to 5 p.m. weekdays. On Village Road, opposite Queen's College.

THINGS TO DO IN NASSAU

- Visit *Atlantis*; take a *Discover Atlantis* tour to the wonders of The Dig and see the fantastic aquariums. Enjoy a meal at one of their many restaurants or try your luck at the slot machines. You have to be docked in the Marina at Atlantis to enjoy the water chutes or sports and swimming facilities. These are reserved for Atlantis' guests.
- Visit one of the museums or forts, on New Providence. Climb the 65 steps of the Queen's Staircase leading up to Fort Fincastle and photograph Nassau from the top.
- Stock up on groceries and fresh provisions, or just window shop along Bay Street.
- Shop the marine supply stores for replacement parts you are sure to need when you least expect it.
- Become a BASRA member—you never know when you may need their help.
- Meet friends at the Cruising Yacht People's lunches at *The Green Parrot* (242-323-3341) on East Bay Street every Thursday at 12:30 pm. Complimentary dinghy dock.

PARADISE ISLAND

MARINAS

On Paradise Island, approaching from the west:

THE MARINA AT ATLANTIS
Tel: 242-363-6068 or 1-800-ATLANTIS • Fax: 242-363-6008
VHF 16 and 10, request permission to enter
www.Atlantis.com • peter.maury@kerzner.com

Slips 62. **Max LOA** 240 ft. **MLW at Docks** 12 ft. **Dockage** $3.00 to $7.00 per ft. per day, 40-ft. minimum. **Fuel** open 7 a.m. to 7 p.m. daily. **Facilities & Services** Power $0.65 per kwHr, single, three-phase and direct 480 volt power, RO water $0.25 per gallon, ice, same-day laundry and dry cleaning service, coin-op washer and dryers $3.00 per load, multiple phone/fax lines at each slip. Complimentary cable television, WiFi and daily newspaper delivery. Propane tanks refilled on request. Full guest privileges at Atlantis extended to marina guests including use of the waterscape, exhibit lagoons, pools, restaurants, entertainment complex and casino, spa and fitness center, golf course and tennis courts. A separate crew lounge has a pool table, drinks center, television, showers and laundry. Tie-up assistance for arrivals and departures. Dock assistance for transfer of luggage and provisions. Courtesy transportation between marina and resort. Private catering and 24-hour room service to vessels. Faxes, UPS and FedEx deliveries can be sent care of the dockmaster's office. Sanitary sewer pump-out facility at each slip. Security 24-hour. **Restaurants & Bars** 26 restaurants and 19 bars at *Atlantis*. $$ to $$$$$ **Accommodations** at *Atlantis Resort*, rooms and suites from $333 to $25,000 per day. **Credit Cards** Visa, MasterCard, AMEX.

HURRICANE HOLE MARINA
Tel: 242-363-3600 • Fax: 242-363-3604 • VHF 16 and 11 •
info@hurricaneholemarina.com •
www.hurricaneholemarina.com

Slips 70 **Max LOA** 200 ft. **MLW at Dock** 10 ft. **Dockage** $4.00 per ft. per day, weekly and monthly rates available. **Fuel** Diesel, gasoline, oils, lubricants; Dock between the two bridges, open daily 7 a.m. to 7 p.m., daily. **Facilities & Services** 30, 50, 100 amp shore power $0.65 per kwHr, RO water $0.25 per gallon, showers, restrooms, coin-op washers and dryers $3.00 per load, public telephone and telephone hook-ups available. Ice, swimming pool, propane tanks refill arranged, concierge service available upon request. **Security** Around the clock. **Restaurant & Bar** Green Parrot Bar and Grill Open 11 a.m. to midnight daily for drinks, lunch and dinner around the pool. $$$ **Credit Cards** Visa, MasterCard, AMEX; no personal checks. Pets are welcome at the marina.

PARADISE HARBOUR CLUB and MARINA
Tel: 242-363-2992 • Fax: 242-363-2840 • VHF 16 •
mrolle@festivaresorts.com • www.phc.bahama.com

Slips 23. **Max LOA** 200 ft. **MLW at Dock** 8 ft. **Dockage** $3.00 to $3.50 per ft. per day, $100 minimum. Monthly rate available. **Facilities & Services** Power $0.75 per kwHr, water $0.10 per gallon, showers, coin-op washers and dryers $1.50 per load, telephone at each slip with public phone outside reception, cable television hookup $5 per day,

WiFi. Complimentary water taxi service to the *Straw Market*. Golf Cart shuttle to *Cabbage Beach* and the *Mini-Mart*. Lagoon style swimming pool with waterfall and spa jets. **Restaurant** The friendly *Columbus Tavern* overlooking the marina serves very good breakfast, lunch and dinner, from 7 a.m. to midnight. Meals can be delivered to your boat, and you can charge your bill at the Tavern to your slip. $$-$$$$ **Accommodations** Apartments and suites from $210 to $410 per day. **Credit Cards** Visa, MasterCard, AMEX, 4% surcharge. Pets are welcome at the marina.

PORT DIRECTORY FOR PARADISE ISLAND

Ferries Run half hourly during the day from Paradise Island to the *Straw Market* and *Cruise Ship dock*.

Shopping & Restaurants *Hurricane Hole Plaza Gift* shops, restaurants and an ATM. *The News Café* serves breakfast, lunch and a light dinner daily with all the newspapers; *Zio Gigi's* has good Italian food for lunch and dinner; and the *Blue Marlin* serves dinner daily from 5 p.m. with floor shows. *Paradise Village Shopping Centre* includes *Paradise Supermarket and Deli* • 242-363-1056 open 8 a.m. to 10 p.m. daily, from 9 a.m. Sundays; *Bristol Cellars* liquor store; ATM at *ScotiaBank*; *Straw Market* and gift shops; and *Anthony's Carib Grill and Deli*, which opens for lunch until late. More restaurants, plenty of choices! 26 at *Atlantis*, *Columbus Tavern* at the *Paradise Harbour Club*, *Ocean Club*, *Sheraton Grand Resort* (with five), *Comfort Suites*, *Holiday Inn Sunspree* and all the hotels on Paradise Island. $ to $$$$$.

Marinas outside the Nassau Harbour area:

LYFORD CAY MARINA

Tel: 242-362-7499 • 242-362-4131 • VHF 16 and 11
harbour@lyfordcay.com

Slips 74. **Max LOA** Over 235 ft. **MLW at Dock** 10 to 12 ft. **Dockage** $5.25 per ft. per day. **Fuel** Dock open 8 a.m. to 10 p.m.; diesel and gasoline. **Facilities & Services** Power $0.65 per kwHr, 50 and 100 amp, RO water $0.25 per gallon, showers, restrooms, coin-op washers and dryers $1.75 per load, complimentary telephone hookup, satellite television, WiFi and trash pick-up. Just outside the Lyford Cay Club, there is a shopping center with a *City Market* supermarket, as well as a bank with ATM, hardware store, liquor store, boutique, public telephone and travel agent. **Restaurant** *The Captain's Table*, open 10 a.m. until midnight, daily. **Credit Cards** Visa, MasterCard, AMEX. Pets are welcome at the marina.

THE ALBANY HOUSE MARINA, GOLF AND BEACH CLUB

Tel: 888-909-7001 • www.albanybahamas.com

Situated on the southwest end of New Providence, this development has had many lives. The marina was dredged years ago, but complications regarding its impact on the nearby aquatic environment continue. Perhaps with Tiger Woods now involved in the development, the 71-slip megayacht marina will be completed as well as the hotel, restaurant, bar, golf course and equestrian center. *The Albany House* was the setting for the James Bond movie, *Casino Royale*. It has yet to be announced if there are slips for transients at the marina. Do call for information if you would like to visit here.

THE RITZ CARLTON ROSE ISLAND MARINA & RESORT

The first phase of the development is on hold in 2010. The master plan and dredging for the marina has been fully approved, but not completed. The island resort will be accessible by boat or helicopter. Plans call for 65 condominium units, 137 resort estate homes and a marina village. No word at this time when work will resume.

Nassau, Eastern Channel, south of mailboat dock. WATERWAY GUIDE PHOTOGRAPHY.

Chapter 12 Eleuthera:

Spanish Wells and Harbour Island, Hatchet Bay and Governors Harbour to Cape Eleuthera

Waterway Guide Photography

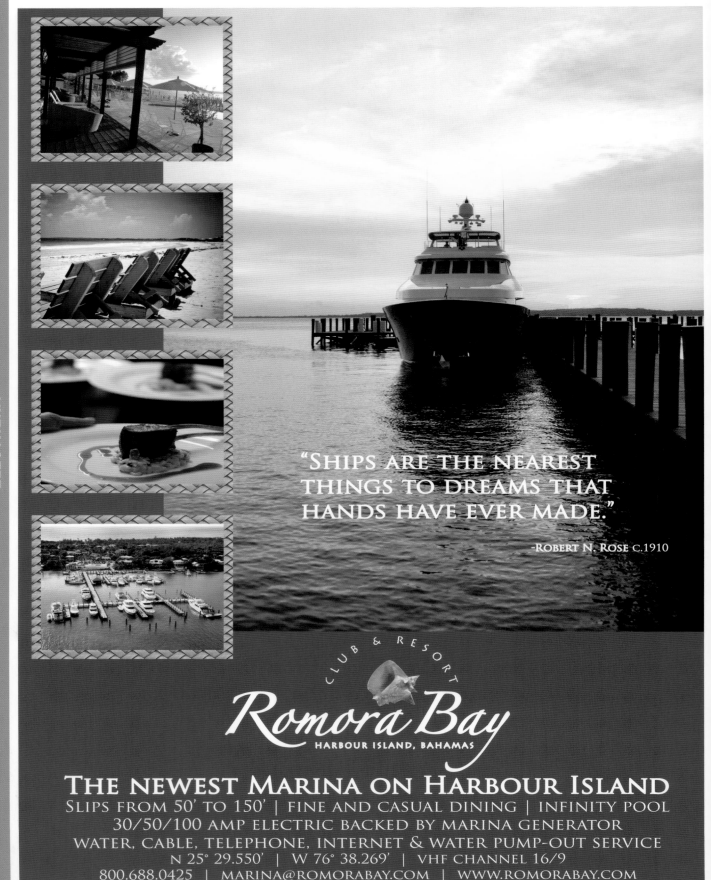

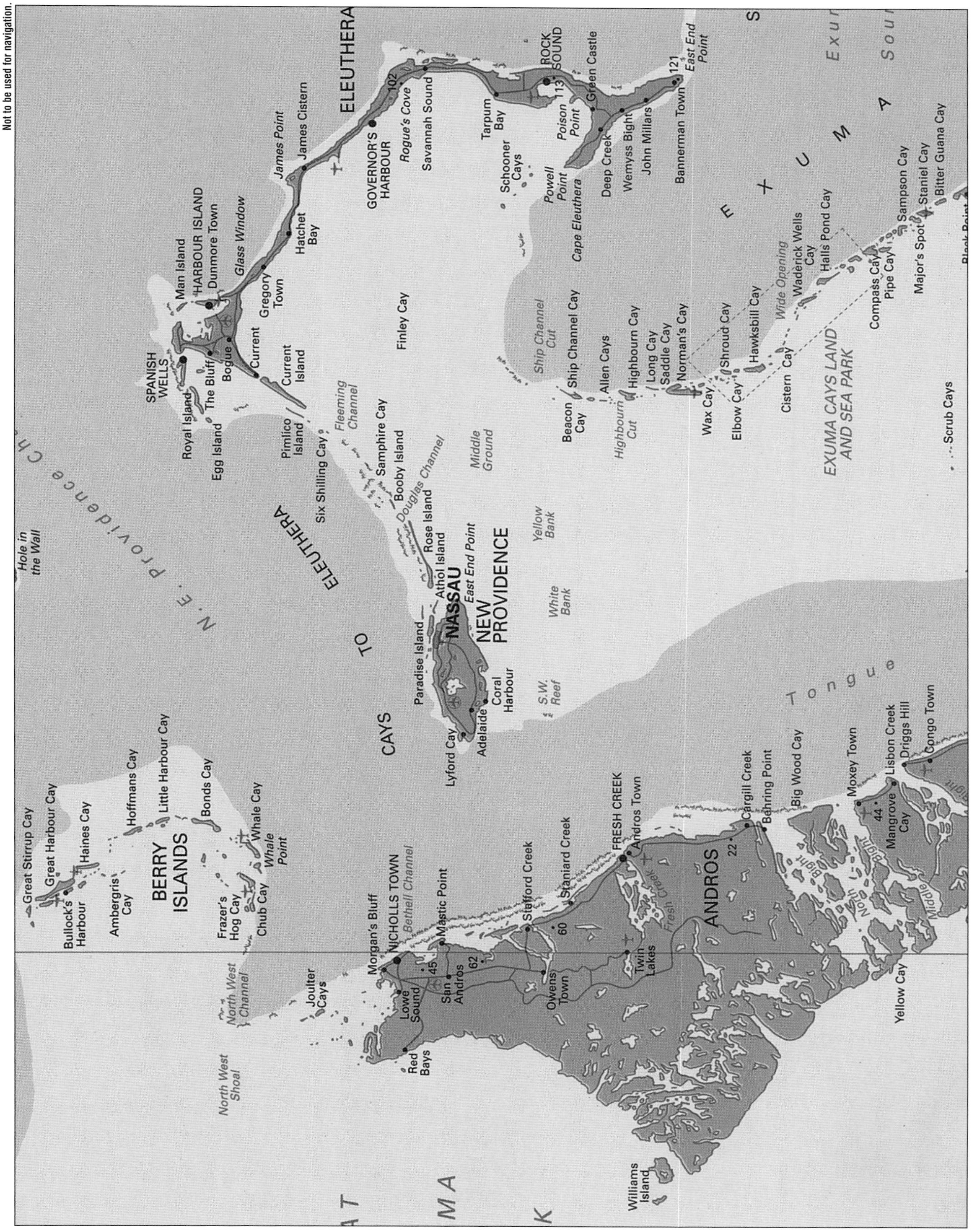
Not to be used for navigation.
ELEUTHERA
HARBOUR ISLAND
Dunmore Town
Man Island
Glass Window
SPANISH WELLS
Royal Island
Egg Island
The Bluff
Bogue
Current
Current Island
Gregory Town
Hatchet Bay
James Point
James Cistern
GOVERNOR'S HARBOUR
Rogue's Cove
Savannah Sound
Tarpum Bay
ROCK SOUND
Green Castle
Poison Point
Powell Point
Schooner Cays
Cape Eleuthera
Deep Creek
Wemyss Bight
John Millars
Bannerman Town
East End Point
Finley Cay
Pimlico Island
Six Shilling Cay
Fleeming Channel
Samphire Cay
Booby Island
Douglas Channel
Rose Island
Athol Island
East End Point
Middle Ground
Yellow Bank
White Bank
NASSAU
NEW PROVIDENCE
Paradise Island
Coral Harbour
Adelaide
Lyford Cay
S.W. Reef
ELEUTHERA
TO
CAYS
N.E. Providence Ch
Hole in the Wall
Ship Channel Cut
Ship Channel Cay
Beacon Cay
Allen Cays
Highbourn Cut
Highbourn Cay
Long Cay
Saddle Cay
Norman's Cay
Wax Cay
Shroud Cay
Elbow Cay
Hawksbill Cay
Cistern Cay
Wide Opening
Waderick Wells Cay
Halls Pond Cay
Compass Cay
Pipe Cay
Major's Spot
Sampson Cay
Staniel Cay
Bitter Guana Cay
EXUMA CAYS LAND AND SEA PARK
Scrub Cays
EXUMA
Exuma Sound
Tongue
BERRY ISLANDS
Great Stirrup Cay
Great Harbour Cay
Bullock's Harbour
Haines Cay
Ambergris Cay
Hoffmans Cay
Little Harbour Cay
Bonds Cay
Whale Cay
Whale Point
Frazer's Hog Cay
Chub Cay
North West Channel
North West Shoal
Joulter Cays
Morgan's Bluff
NICHOLLS TOWN
Bethell Channel
Mastic Point
Lowe Sound
San Andros
Red Bays
Stafford Creek
Staniard Creek
Owens Town
Twin Lakes
FRESH CREEK
Andros Town
Fresh Creek
ANDROS
Cargill Creek
Behring Point
Big Wood Cay
Moxey Town
Mangrove Cay
Lisbon Creek
Driggs Hill
Congo Town
North Bight
Middle Bight
Yellow Cay
Williams Island
AT
MA
K

Chapter 12
Eleuthera
Spanish Wells and Harbour Island
Hatchet Bay and Governors Harbour
to Cape Eleuthera

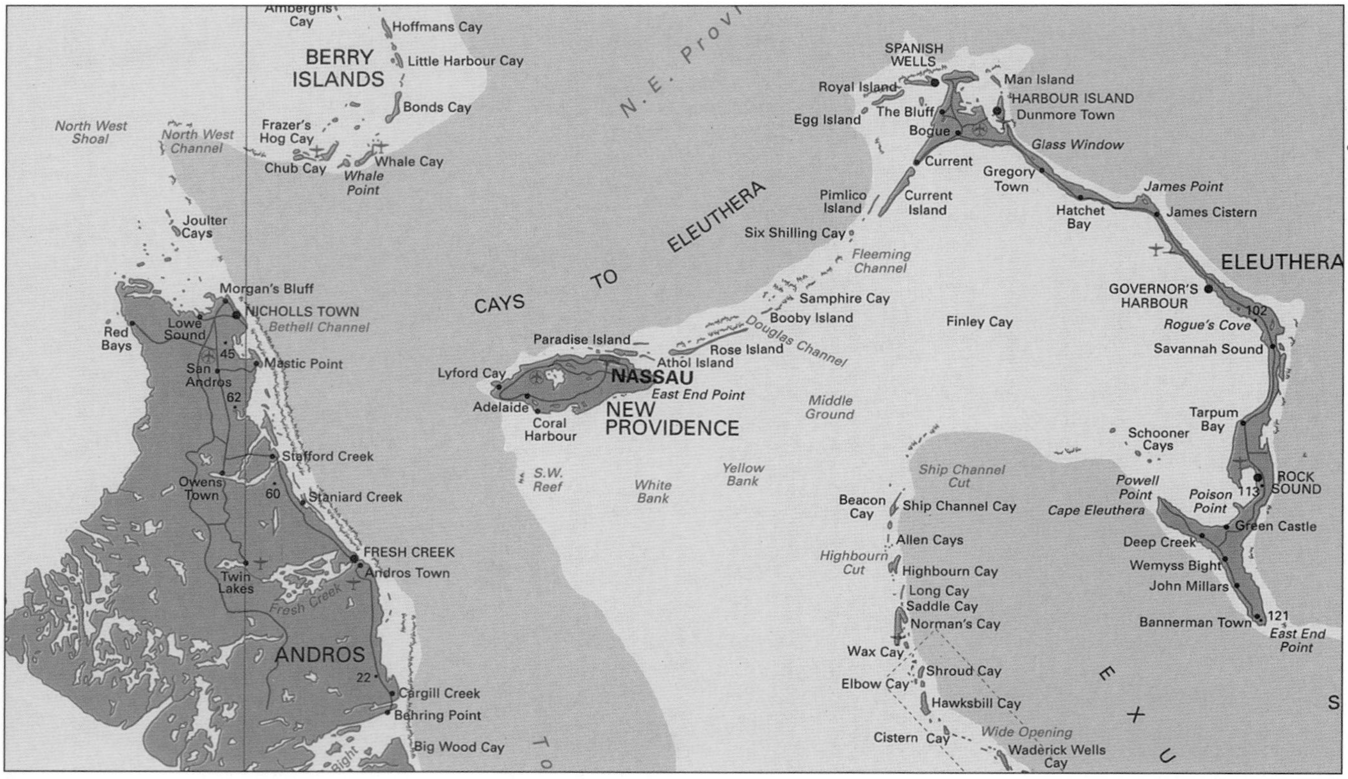

Not to be used for navigation.

Looking At the Charts

The archipelago east of New Providence is erroneously referred to as "Eleuthera" in some guidebooks. Without looking at your charts, you may well think that you are heading for one island. Not true! One glance at the number of "magenta lines" heading from Nassau to the other islands of the archipelago (not to Eleuthera) makes this fact quite apparent. The majority of the vessels headed this way are bound for Royal Island, St. Georges Cay or Harbour Island, and then they head south to the Eleuthera destinations.

Royal Island has long been a welcome sight for sailors making the run south from Great Abaco Island. Its beautiful harbor has provided safety to voyagers and a fabulous picnic spot for Nassau day-trippers for years. St. Georges Cay, usually just called "Spanish Wells," is the epicenter of the Bahamian commercial lobster, conch and fishing industry, supplying over 50 percent of the total gross production. It has two, full-service marinas and a boatyard at which to haul. Many moorings provide safe anchorage here, too. Moreover, it is a handy, and inexpensive, portal to Dunmore Town, Harbour Island by fast ferry.

Harbour Island is most easily reached by that fast ferry, but many skippers want to add a notch to their bow—a trip through the Devils Backbone (with a pilot from Spanish Wells) to Harbour Island. How else to get that photo of your boat at anchor in plush Dunmore Town? Harbour Island's famed pink beaches (pinker than Bermuda, we think) and the historic hillside village of Dunmore Town take you away to a place you have always wanted to be. The town is primarily a resort for the rich and famous, or those who want to vacation like one. You would never know it, however, by the relaxed ambiance and friendly folks you meet here.

Eleuthera Island is almost 90 miles long and narrow, little more than three miles wide, except at its extreme ends. Its topography is a study in contrasts—steep cliffs and productive

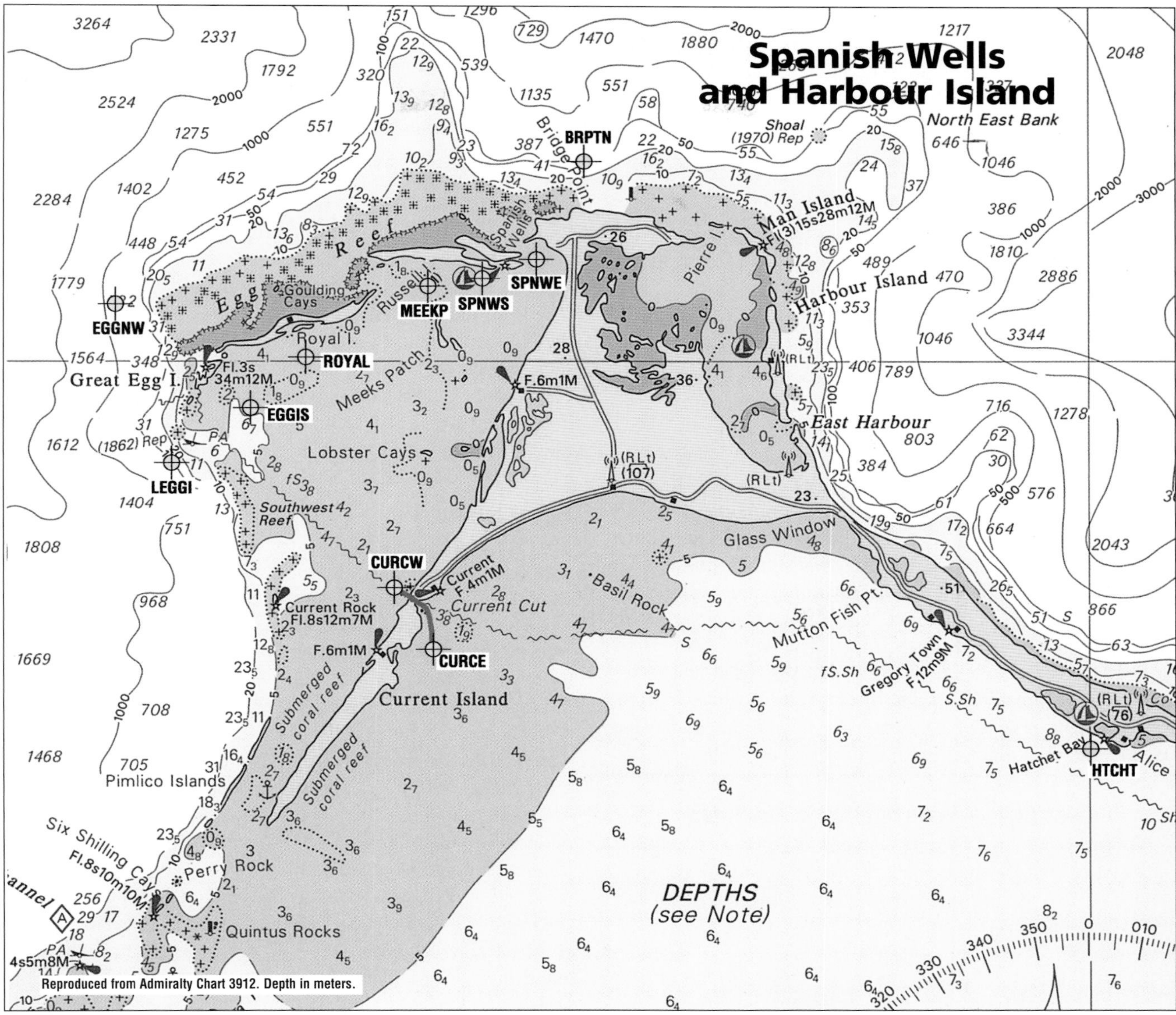

valleys, wooded lands and inland lakes, spectacular beaches and impenetrable reefs. It is those reefs that limit the approaches to Eleuthera. You are going to have to go around one end or the other to access its west coast.

A look at the chart shows the mindboggling number of choices from almost any jumping off point. The approaches from the Abacos inevitably involve avoiding Egg Reef and rounding Egg Island. (You can make first landfall at the northern entrance to Harbour Island, but just because you can, doesn't mean it would be a good idea.) The voyage onward then entails a passage through Current Cut or Fleeming Channel into the Bight of Eleuthera.

Current Cut is a narrow slit of water that runs between Current Island and the Current Settlement, North Eleuthera. The cut is less than 10 nautical miles south of Royal Island and southwest of St. George's Island. Current Cut earned its name for a reason. Tidal currents can be 10 knots or more during strong tides. This makes for challenging navigation not only inside the cut, but also on approach from either the east or west. If conditions look unfavorable, or if your boat is underpowered, go to Fleeming Channel (south of Six Schilling Cay). It is only 10 miles to the south, and much friendlier in terms of tidal current.

As we said at the beginning of this Guide in "Where to Go? A Cruising Ground Analysis," Eleuthera deserves study before hauling up the anchor and setting out for its shores. Eleuthera's east coast offers only Dunmore Town for safe haven. The rest is near continuous offshore reefs and, as we said in the analysis, not a cruising ground.

As for the west coast, it has three, bona fide, all-weather havens: Hatchet Bay, Cape Eleuthera Marina and Davis Harbour Marina. In between, there are places like Pelican Cay, Governors Harbour and Rock Sound where you can find some kind of shelter. If the prevailing southeast winds hold steady, you will have no problems cruising the west coast of Eleuthera, and you can safely anchor off most of the small villages. In unsettled weather, you have the three all-weather options, but make sure you plan carefully in case you have to turn tail to get there.

In the Spotlight. Harbour Island

Harbour Island is roughly 3.5 miles long by 1.5 miles wide. Once the capital of the Bahamas (and its second largest city in the early 1900s), the current population is close to 2,000. Harbour Island's tiny gem is Dunmore Town, a Victorian-style village of narrow streets, pastel-painted cottages with white picket fences and bougainvillea-draped arbors perched on the edge of cotton-candy colored beaches. The friendly people who call Harbour Island home descended from folks who came seeking freedom from religious persecution or from slavery.

Today, Dunmore Town is one of the fabled Bahamian hideaways of celebrities—famous for its seclusion, relaxed lifestyle, friendly atmosphere and glam-dripping accommodations.

Dunmore Town is easily reached by plane. There are direct flights daily from Fort Lauderdale, Miami and Nassau to an airport on North Eleuthera that is only a five-minute water taxi ride away. Yachts can come into one of three marinas. Harbour Island is very popular and can get quite crowded during holidays. In the same area, the new Romora Bay Club and Resort offers upscale amenities. If a norther or strong winds from the west stir up, the Harbour Island marinas can become untenable. Use all your dock line skills, and put out plenty of fenders.

Clearing In—Your Options in Eleuthera

You are well-served by entry options in North and Central Eleuthera, with Spanish Wells, Harbour Island, Governors Harbour and Rock Sound on the list. Only the south of Eleuthera has no entry port.

What's There? North Eleuthera

Little Egg Island and Egg Island

Little Egg Island is barren, and Egg Island, despite a fishing shack, has little to offer but a light that may or may not be working. You might find yourself drawn to the Egg Islands because the Egg Reef is there with good snorkeling, diving and fishing.

The good fishing involves a scientific mystery surrounding a Lebanese freighter, the *Arimoroa MV* (called by local dive operators the Freighter Wreck or the Egg Island Wreck), and its cargo, guano-based fertilizer. In the 1970s, while en route from South America to Europe, this steel-hulled vessel was purposely grounded on Egg Island. For reasons unknown, a fire started in the galley and spread with such speed and intensity that the captain decided the only way to save the crew was to beach the ship on the nearest visible land, Egg Island. All the crew made it to land without injury. The fire smoldered for three months.

During this time, the high-phosphate cargo was flushed out through the ship's cracked keel. For a few years afterwards, the surrounding reef was poisoned by the fertilizer and became devoid of sea life. Today, the rusting remains of the *Arimoroa* sit perfectly upright in 25 feet of water. There is a debris field around the wreckage composed of steel hull plates, deck winches and various other ship fittings. However, the most intriguing aspect of the wreck is the impressive amount of fish that now congregate around her hull. Local dive operators report seeing schools of 50 to 100 gray angels, an amount that is extremely unusual for this species. They keep company with dozens of yellow stingrays, snapper, grouper and enormous parrotfish.

This drastic turnaround of events has been studied by scientists from the University of Miami, the Rosenstiel School and the Florida Institute of Technology. They have so far catalogued over 60 species of fish. There is speculation about the reef's comeback. Could it be due to the after effects of the *Arimoroa's* organic fertilizer? No one knows for sure. Whatever the reason, the number and variety of fish seen here will certainly impress even the most seasoned Caribbean diver.

Royal Island

Royal Island is a string bean of an island, 430 square acres strung out 4.5 nautical miles long and 0.5 nautical miles wide at its widest point. Its central, almost land-locked harbor, is as perfect a natural haven as one could ever hope to find. The harbor is well-protected from everything but the south and southwest. If those winds come, you can tuck yourself up in the ends (beware the east end) even if it blows straight in the entrance.

The construction of the very exclusive, super high-end development, Montage of Royal Island, backed by the former professional football player, Roger Staubach, has been halted. The slips that were in place for the water taxis to shuttle potential investors from The Bluff on North Eleuthera to the Preview Village have been pulled out of the water. Although the Preview Village remains on shore, it is no longer in use.

There were great plans here that have not come to fruition: a 140-acre harbor with over 200 slips from 50 to 400 feet in length and a Marina Village with shops, cafe and club house; an 18-hole, Jack Nicklaus golf course situated amongst 275 homes and villas; 83 five-star hotel rooms and suites; four restaurants, tennis club and spa; and complimentary water shuttles to and from The Bluff, St. Georges Cay and Harbour Island. Perhaps it will be finished in ours, Roger's or Jack's lifetime, perhaps not. Let us hope so for the investor's sake and for the island's, as it has been scraped clean and left denuded. The runoff is deadly to coral and sea life. Nonetheless, in the meantime, we all have a front-row seat to see what happens next, swinging at anchor in this nearly perfect, beautiful harbor.

Russell Island

Russell Island, at three nautical miles in length, is twice the size of its cousin, St. Georges Cay. It is home to the locally owned and run power plant for both islands, an item of utility of which the Spanish Wellsians are immensely proud. In addition to the power plant, off of which there is decent anchorage in 5-foot depths, Russell Island has a considerable amount of agriculture, including citrus trees. On a stroll, in addition to the citrus trees,

St. Georges Cay

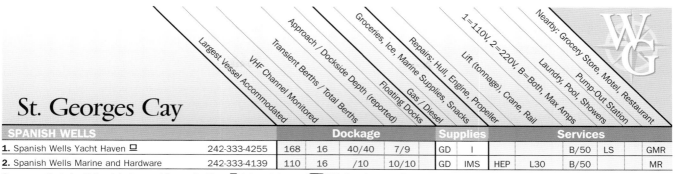

SPANISH WELLS	Phone	Largest Vessel Accommodated	VHF Channel Monitored	Transient Berths / Total Berths	Approach / Dockside Depth (reported)	Floating Docks	Gas / Diesel	Groceries, Ice, Marine Supplies, Snacks	Repairs: Hull, Engine, Propeller	Lift (tonnage), Crane, Rail	1=110V, 2=220V, B=Both, Max Amps	Laundry, Pool, Showers	Pump-Out Station	Nearby: Grocery Store, Motel, Restaurant
		Dockage					Supplies		Services					
1. Spanish Wells Yacht Haven 🖳	242-333-4255	168	16	40/40	7/9		GD	I			B/50	LS		GMR
2. Spanish Wells Marine and Hardware	242-333-4139	110	16	/10	10/10		GD	IMS	HEP	L30	B/50			MR

Corresponding chart(s) not to be used for navigation. 🖳 Internet Access (WiFi) Wireless Internet Access

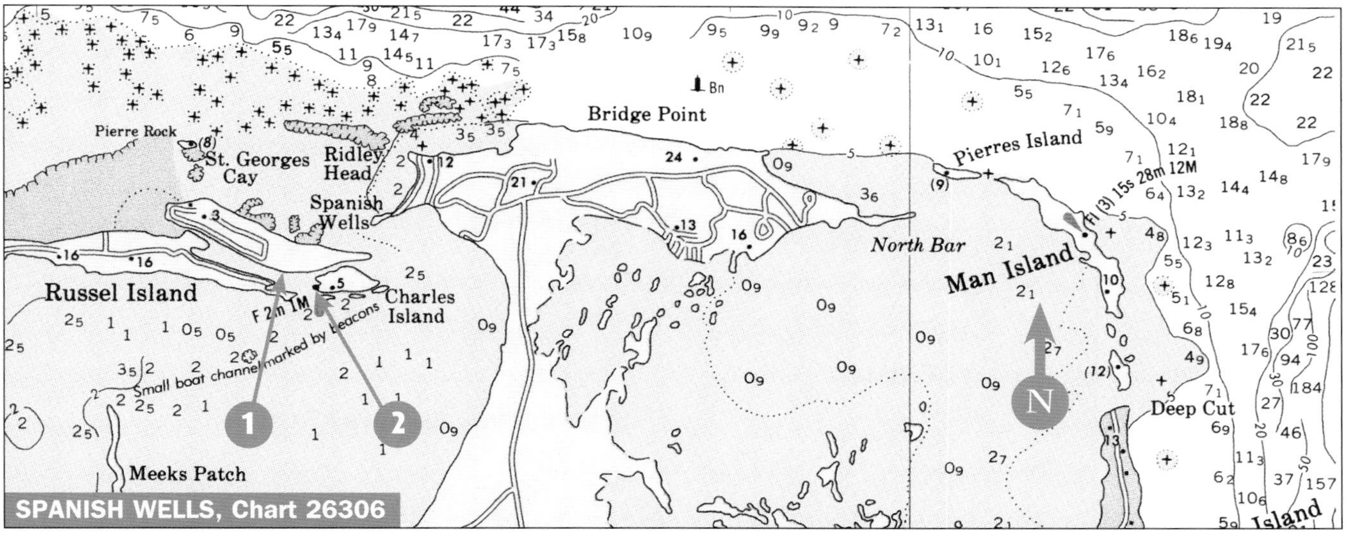

Spanish Wells Harbour, from the southwest. (Not to be used for navigation.)

you will find some very handsome houses, two good beaches on the north side and some fishing shacks.

Spanish Wells (St. Georges Cay and Charles Island)

St. Georges Cay is so totally identified with its settlement, Spanish Wells, that we deal with the island and its settlement (as well as little uninhabited Charles Island, which has no role to play other than to help form Spanish Wells Harbour) under the moniker Spanish Wells.

The name Spanish Wells sounds romantic. Legend says the Spanish filled their water casks from the sweet wells on the island before setting off for Spain. It sounds good, but is it credible? Look at the charts. Look at the reefs. Study the wreck history of the area. If you were a Spanish admiral with your life on the line, would you lead your Fleet to Spanish Wells? Such is the stuff of legends, but if you want to see the real Bahamas, Spanish Wells should be on your list. Go to its tiny museum. It may not seem like much is there, but everything, from the house itself to the story and exhibits, speaks of the area's pride in its history and culture.

Spanish Wells is no tourist resort, although its marinas—Spanish Wells Yacht Haven and Spanish Wells Marine—are both very nice and accommodating. And, half the town folk seem to have a cottage of some sort for rent. But, at the forefront, Spanish Wells is all about fishing. Serious fishing with ocean-going craft and the infrastructure to support them.

These islanders proudly produce close to 75 percent of the nation's annual production of spiny lobster that is exported to markets worldwide. It is an industry built on the grit of the Eleutheran adventurers, who were tough, ornery, independent of mind and not prepared to live by the rules of the day.

If you are looking for luxurious lodging, gourmet dining and celebrities on the beach, take the ferry to Harbour Island. If you enjoy visiting a settlement of sturdy, well-built, well-cared-for houses in Abaco colors (but then weren't they much the same people?) in which real grass, flower beds and trees are tended with meticulous care by inspiring, self-reliant people, stay here.

The Devils Backbone Passage

The Devils Backbone Passage, through the reefs around the north coast of Eleuthera, is an exercise in coastal navigation that should not be undertaken lightly. It is potentially hazardous, but not dangerous. Nonetheless, no matter how good your eyeball navigation, this is one passage where there is only one way to go and that is to have a Spanish Wells pilot on board to take you around to Harbour Island; moreover, to take you back to Spanish Wells when you are ready to return. A pilot's services will cost you at least $70 (up to 70 feet in length, thereafter add $1 per foot), but it is money well-spent. Our ground rules, if you reject the piloting advice, are these:

- Never attempt this passage in bad weather, particularly with wind, wave or ocean swells coming onshore from the north, northwest or northeast.
- Never attempt the passage from Spanish Wells to Harbour Island early in the morning with the sun in your eyes, or the reverse passage in the late afternoon with the sun in your eyes.
- Never attempt it if the light is not good. Any time after 10 a.m., when the sun is reasonably high in the sky, is okay, and around noon is best.
- High water is always an extra safety dividend. It makes sense to have the reassurance of 2 feet or so extra under your keel.
- If you are in trouble, stay in 12 meters/40 feet of water and call for help. (The reason we say 12 meters/40 feet is that the top of the reefs and isolated coral heads in this area rise about 7.5 to 9 meters/25 to 30 feet from the seabed.)
- If you are overtaken by weather, use your best anchor, and wait until it clears. Or alternatively, call for a pilot.

We have more to say about the Devils Backbone Passage under Pilotage, which you should read.

Pierre, Man and Jacobs Islands

The three islands to the north of Harbour Island are not usually on a cruisers itinerary, though anchorages may be found off all three. Beware that there are shallows on the west of all three islands, and that there are no navigable gaps between them out into the Atlantic Ocean.

Dunmore Town, Harbour Island

Harbour Island, as most refer to it, is well-served by its marinas. Valentine's Yacht Club and Inn is well-established and well-known. Its docks, shoreside facilities and accommodations are resort standard.

Farther to the south, the same can be said of Harbour Island Marina with its quality docks, bar and restaurant. The Romora Bay Club & Resort has a 40-slip eco-friendly marina, coffee shop and upscale restaurant. It offers a vibrant social scene. Self-described by the developer as a laid-back, villa-style resort and marina on nearly six acres, he remained committed to building an appropriately sized facility that safeguards the marine environment. The new marina was built without dredging, a big contributor to the death and destruction of Bahamian reefs and sea life. Dockage was designed and built to accommodate the no-dredging rule. Smaller boats with shallower drafts dock closest to the resort; larger vessels use outer docks sunk on pilings in deeper water. Through its unique pump-out system, all liquid waste undergoes primary and secondary treatment that converts it for irrigation purposes. In addition, a special tracing dye is used to detect any discharge into the harbor from its facilities. The Romora Bay Club & Resort has slips available for sale or transient visits. If you want to anchor off Dunmore Town, the best place is somewhere south of Harbour Island Marina, away from all the traffic. Ferries operating between the government dock and the Three Islands Dock (serving North Eleuthera and its airport) run back and forth all day. Other ferries that use the northern harbor entrance and traverse the area, do so at 30-knot speeds.

Harbour Island

DUNMORE TOWN		Largest Vessel Accommodated	VHF Channel Monitored	Transient Berths / Total Berths	Approach / Dockside Depth (reported)	Floating Docks	Gas / Diesel	Groceries, Ice, Marine Supplies, Snacks	Repairs: Hull, Engine, Propeller	Lift (tonnage), Crane, Rail	1=110V, 2=220V, B=Both, Max Amps	Laundry, Pool, Showers	Pump-Out Station	Nearby: Grocery Store, Motel, Restaurant
		Dockage					Supplies		Services					
1. Valentine's Resort & Marina 🖳 WiFi	242-333-2142	200	16	4/4	9/13		D	IMS	HEP		B/100	LPS		GMR
2. Harbour Island Club & Marina WiFi	242-333-2427	200	16	/40	5/8		GD	GI			B/100	LPS	P	GMR
3. Romora Bay Club & Resort 🖳 WiFi	**242-333-2325**	**150**	**16/09**	**40/40**	**10/10**			**IS**			**B/100**	**LPS**	**P**	**GMR**

Corresponding chart(s) not to be used for navigation. 🖳 Internet Access WiFi Wireless Internet Access

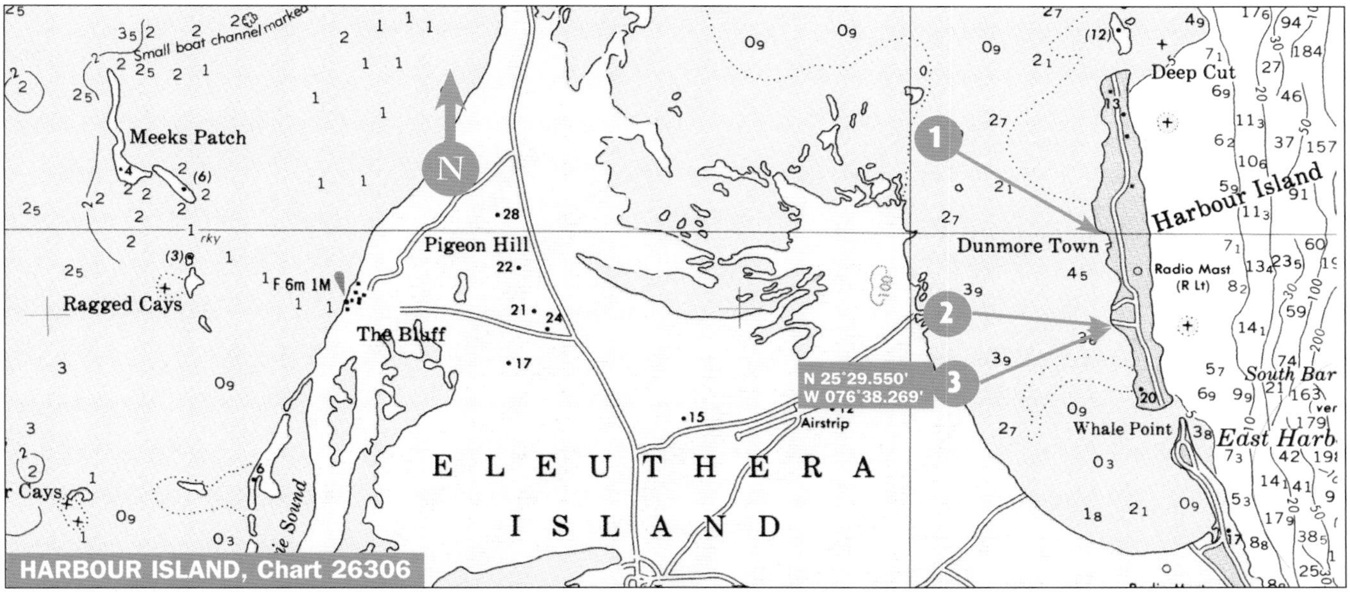

HARBOUR ISLAND, Chart 26306

Harbour Island and Dunmore Town. (Not to be used for navigation.)

The Harbour Mouth Ocean Pass

The ocean pass, known as Harbour Mouth, lies at the south end of Harbour Island. The depth in this pass, though good for 6-meter/20-foot depths in the mouth can, due to shoaling, drop to no more than 1.2-meter/4-foot depths at mean low water. Local marinas recommend passage with a local pilot at all times. Without their knowledge and service, forget it. Nevertheless, we cover this pass in more detail under Pilotage.

A North Eleuthera Inland Tour

There are times when you should leave your boat to take a taxi or a rental car tour of the hinterland, for otherwise you will never get the feel of the place or see all that there is to enjoy. Eleuthera is one of those places. If you are in Spanish Wells, go to Genes Bay ferry landing and take a taxi from there. If you are in Harbour Island, go to Three Islands ferry landing and do the same.

Upper and Lower Bogue

The Bogues take their name from a corruption of the word "bog" or low-lying, nearly useless land. It was unclaimed and unwanted right from the start, and so it was here that the freed slaves staked out their tracts when the chains were cut after Emancipation. Drive through to see a part of the Bahamas that is far removed from either Spanish Wells or Harbour Island's Dunmore Town. Upper Bogue, as the name suggests, is higher; and Lower Bogue, lower. The longevity of the Bogues is testimony to the tenaciousness of its founders. There is a little ice cream parlor here. Stop for a cone and some interesting, first-hand history lessons.

The Current

The tiny settlement of The Current, "POPULATION 131, ESTABLISHED 1648," as its welcoming sign advertises, is slated for changes, to include a $12 million marina and an upscale resort and residential community of 34 condominium hotel units with a restaurant and bar. The Current Club Villas, Restaurant and Marina encompasses six acres. Construction has started. A development of this sort would be a real boast to the folks in Current and The Bogues, and a nice addition to barren marina territory.

Moving On to Central & South Eleuthera

Current Cut is your Eleutheran Panama Canal. It will take you directly (or as directly as you can go) from Spanish Wells to Hatchet Bay. Current Cut looks like a canal when you first see it. It may be broader than you thought it would be and has a well-defined, dark blue channel, which is always reassuring. It can carry a tidal flow of monumental proportions and is well-known in diving circles as the source of the greatest "drift" dive ever. Divers report that it is not uncommon to be rocketed totally out of control through the cut at 6 knots or more, often with an escort of fish who seem in much better control of their moving parts. It is also said that wet suits in the heaviest of millimeters are a necessity if you want to keep all your skin intact.

The Glass Window

The Glass Window is the point in the rock spine of Eleuthera, once no more than a natural arch undermined by the ocean, which became a real break. It was named for the facility to "look through" the window formed by the arch. Today, the road crosses a rock gorge on a new bridge, the last in a series of storm-damaged bridges. Stop, and while your taxi turns around, look about you.

To the east, and right up to the concrete bridge itself (though well below it), you have the deep blue water of the Atlantic Ocean. To the west, it is the turquoise green, far-shallower water of the Bahama Banks. When the Atlantic Ocean rollers come surging in, or the powerful swells of a distant mega-storm, 3,000 miles of ocean fetch hit that rock spine beneath the bridge and can throw walls of water 100 to 120 feet high that will carry away anything on the bridge. It has happened more than once including removing the bridge itself.

Up on the surface, you must contend with the full force of the tidal current and wind, and if you don't have the power to punch through it, you will regret choosing the Current Cut. The best time is slack water, and make it high tide, for there are shallows to cross on the eastern side. The tide at Current Cut should be the same as Nassau (with Spanish Wells running 30 minutes after Nassau), but double check the shore-line water marks. In addition, don't forget that much more forgiving Fleeming Cut is a short 10 miles farther south from here. If the winds and the tides aren't working for you, and Current Cut looks like more than you want to handle, choose Fleeming Cut.

What's There? Central & South Eleuthera

Hatchet Bay

Hatchet Bay, which advertises itself as the safest harbor in the islands, looks as if its claim might well be justified at first sight. The bay is the focal point of that stretch of the coast, and the local settlement, Alice Town, has been virtually lost to the Hatchet Bay name. The narrow entrance into the harbor is hard to pick out from the water, but the settlement's BTC tower is a giveaway, as are some very visible white silos onshore. The silos are the remnants of a failed cattle-raising venture. First, three pairs of silos loom on the horizon, then about two nautical miles from the harbor entrance, another three silos come into view. Soon you will see a light on a mast to port, some scruffy casuarinas to starboard and the BTC tower, briefly. You will lose sight of it as you line up to enter the harbor.

Hatchet Bay is yet another man-made entrance (see Great Harbour in the Berry Islands) into a landlocked pond. It was formed by cutting an entrance through the limestone cliffs. It was supposed to assure success for the Hatchet Bay cat-

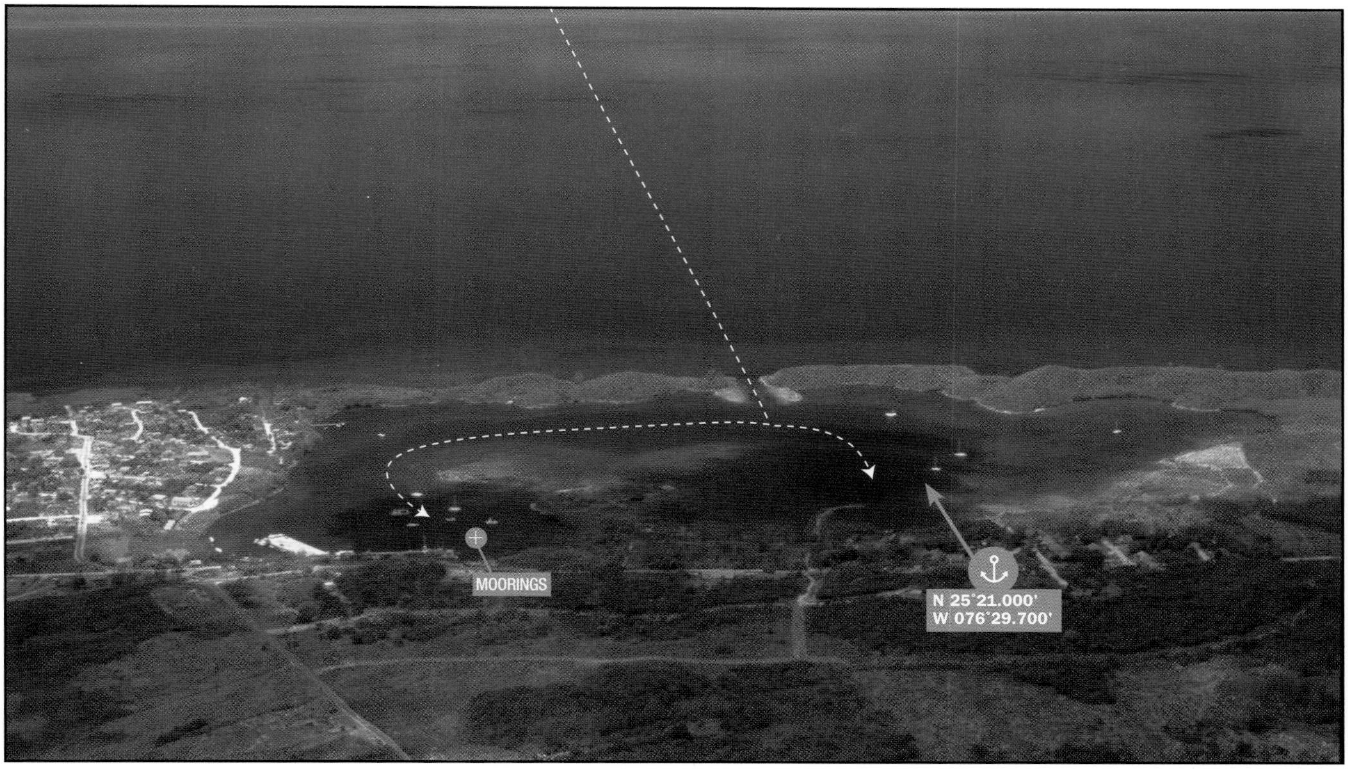

Hatchet Bay. (Not to be used for navigation.) WATERWAY GUIDE PHOTOGRAPHY.

tle-raising project. That lost, it now has appeal to mariners and potential developers.

The entrance to Hatchet Bay looks forbidding at first sight. It appears far too narrow, but actually has good width (27 meters/90 feet) and good depth (3 meters/10 feet).

Once inside, anchorages lie to port and starboard. To starboard, you can head toward two silver-colored propane tanks, favoring the shore side of the harbor, leaving little Olive Island to port. There is complimentary tie-up at the government dock, but the concrete wharf may be hazardous your boat's health. There are also free, government-supplied moorings. Many are taken by local boats, and the maintenance and safety of those that are available should be checked. However, there are finger piers with ladders at which to secure a dinghy. Moorings here have come and gone over the years, and their ground tackle (as well as other debris) fouls the thick grass under your keel. This is what is to port, where there is space and water depth to anchor. Use a trip line in anticipation of the fouled, grassy bottom. In addition, be on the lookout for underwater pilings, especially off the channel entrance and the northern shore.

Locally, in Alice Town, there are some grocery stores, a post office, a medical clinic and some spelunking guides. The nearby caves are very interesting. There may be fresh produce at the packing house—worth a visit just to see the operation. Ice and pure water are available. Trash bins are located around the settlement. Like any town in an out of the way place, there might be opportunistic mischief by local youth. Lock down your boat and your dinghy so you can enjoy walking the settlement with peace of mind. Local police appreciate hearing about the miscreant's behavior or any pan handling by those who might have had a drink or two too many. It is an unlikely and rare occurrence, but it does happen. Keep in mind that the vast majority of islanders know the value of, and appreciate, the patronage of tourists. You are much more likely to be bothered by biting insects (than crime) while anchored in Hatchet Bay.

The Hatchet Bay Hinterland

If you want to see something more of Eleuthera from your Hatchet Bay anchorage, rent a car. Taking the main highway north, you are in cave country. There are extensive caves in the limestone spine of the island, particularly in this area. They are home to many, many bats and their subsequent guano. If they sound interesting to you, and you have guano-proof shoes, have a local guide take you on a tour.

As you travel toward Gregory Town and the Glass Window, you will pass through silo country. The rolling pastures will remind you of Nebraska and Texas cattle land, and you will see why a cattle operation seemed feasible.

In Gregory Town, the island's pineapple center, don't miss The Cove Restaurant with its European ambiance. Not only do many consider it the best place to eat on Eleuthera, management makes four moorings available for cruisers use. If you are looking for something a lot more casual (and you are not in a hurry), "surf's up" at the Surfers Beach Manor, whose grouper in mushroom sauce is worth the wait. The actual surfers are more likely to be hanging out at Elvina's Restaurant & Laundromat. Nearby Surfers Beach is home to the annual Big Wave Surf Classic Pro-

Am. The jam sessions at Elvina's are legendary. Lenny Kravitz is usually there when he is in town. Try Tuesday and Friday nights to get in on the action.

Going south of Hatchet Bay, you will see more abandoned silos and grassland run wild without the attendant munching and tillage of many, hoofed bovines. About three miles south of Hatchet Bay, you will spot the octagonal buildings of the Rainbow Inn, sitting on the low cliffs overlooking a shallow bight and a little island called Rainbow Cay. The restaurant serves only dinner.

Farther south on your journey, James Cistern stretches along the Queens Highway. It offers moorings and a dinghy dock for cruisers and Lee's Cafe in town, home of the best fried chicken and baked snapper on the island. As you approach Governors Harbour, you will notice that is it perched on a high hill. This scenic town that overlooks the sweep of the bay is worth a stop and a walk about. Here you will find Colonial-style houses and businesses swathed in bougainvillea and steeped in history. Because of its beauty and good facilities, most cruisers stop here. There are plenty of choices here to grab a bite to eat from Chinese cuisine at the Cigatoo to the Sunset Inn with its lively clientele and family-cooked food. Every Friday night, cruisers and tourists alike go to the community Fish Fry, whose proceeds support the annual Governors Harbour Homecoming festival.

It is easy to cross to the Atlantic Ocean side from Governors, and although the east coast is not a cruising ground, is highly prized by surfers, as well as being known for its breath-taking eateries perched on the rocks overlooking the crashing waves. Tippy's is the "in" place. You can take a dip and shower off the pink sand before visiting the bar and restaurant. Same at Captain Jack's, where there is the most incredible view of the Atlantic Ocean. If your sweet tooth needs a sugar charge, stop in at the Country Cafe for an ice cream, and drool over the display of candies. Or, make your last stop the only hotel on the Atlantic side of central Eleuthera, the Unique Village Hotel, Restaurant and Bar.

Rainbow Cay, James Cistern, Pelican Cay and Alabaster Bay

Rainbow Cay affords protection in winds from the north to northeast. Stay north of the cay, and anchor close to the beach in 3.5 meters/12 feet of water. Rainbow Inn is a short dinghy ride away. Beautiful Atlantic Ocean beaches, with nearby coral reefs, are a short hike from the Rainbow Cay anchorage.

James Cistern is an attractive spot. There is a new government dock off this settlement with a dinghy landing nearby. You can anchor off town, or inquire about the moorings, if they remain. Beware, it is rocky. You will find places in town where bread is still baked in "Dutch" ovens. (What is the British connection to the Dutch in these very British islands?) The Dutch produced cast iron cooking vessels using dry sand molds. Their process was more advanced than the English system and produced a better pot in which to cook.

An Englishman named Darby decided to do something about that. After observing the Dutch work, he returned to England, patented the process and captured the market for metal cooking vessels in Britain and the colonies. Ironically, to differentiate them from the inferior British products, they became known to this day as "Dutch" ovens, not Darby ovens. In addition to the bread bakers, you will find restaurants, a telephone, gasoline and a place to dump your trash. You can make a circle walking around town and just about see it all, from the school, to the churches and cemetery.

Farther south is Pelican Cay and Alabaster Bay. Between the anchorages off Pelican and in Alabaster Bay, a cruiser can ride out a front hauling up the hook and moving around to follow the protection. The anchorages all lie close to the Governors Harbour Airport, but like so many other island airports, there are no real facilities close by.

Governors Harbour

Governors Harbour is a lovely place to walk about, but not a great place to anchor. We suggest that you anchor north of Levi Island off the jetty by Toms Rocks or to the south, just north of Long Point. Like all of the western shoreline, don't expect protection from blows, particularly from the west. Holding may be less than trustworthy, so anchor with special care.

The settlement of Governors Harbour is a picture postcard in many ways with touches of Harbour Island's Dunmore Town and the more distant Hope Town. While in town, inquire about the government moorings in the harbor. They may or may not be buoyed. The officers at the port authority or at Customs on Cupids Cay should be able to give you some answers.

If anchoring seems untenable, be sure to rent a car from where you settle to visit this photogenic place. Most things you might want are there, and there is even a dive shop, although they don't run a dive boat. Why? They deem that there is nowhere safe locally to keep a boat at anchor. This may all be changing soon, however.

Developers are rebuilding the old Club Med Marina at Governors Harbour. It will require the reconstruction of the breakwater, but when completed, offer safe haven on state-of-the-art docks with accommodations for 120 vessels. It will be part of the $120 million French Leave and Savannah Hill resorts that will embrace 356 acres on both coasts. The developers have stated that first phase buyers are expected to be able to move in soon. Eventually, the resorts will feature 106 residences, a boutique hotel, two marinas, condominiums and oceanfront lots. Cross your fingers that these great plans reach fruition. At press time, the French Leave Marina was open, but with no power or water. Hopefully those things will be available by the time you make your way down the coast of Eleuthera.

Palmetto Shores. Runaway Bay Marina

On the west coast's Palmetto Shores, south of Governors Harbour, Runaway Bay Marina remains closed at press time. Run southeast from the Governors Harbour waypoint, paralleling the coastline. After five nautical miles you reach the Pineapple Cays. Continue past the cays for a mile, and then turn to run east toward the coast for another mile. At that point, you will see a fabulous restaurant, the Dolce Vita, on a headland

Governors Harbour. (Not to be used for navigation.) Waterway Guide Photography.

above the marina, nestled between two headlands in Rogue Cove. If you want to plot the location, it is N 25° 08.550'/ W 076° 10.210'. The restaurant overlooks the marina. The owner of the restaurant says that one can still tie up at the marina slips to visit his restaurant, but there are no slipside facilities. Call the marina owner for permission to be sure.

Tarpum Bay

Tarpum Bay is very shallow and exposed to wind and weather

Governors Harbour. Waterway Guide Photography.

over an arc of 180 degrees. The anchorages off its shore are rocky and not recommended. The government has built the settlement a new dock with dinghy ladder and placed some free moorings awhile ago. Like so many moorings in the islands, you will have to check to see if they are there and ascertain their condition. The Tarpum Bay Settlement is an interesting community of artists and artisans and well worth a look-see, but perhaps you will have to see it by car.

Rock Sound

From the cruiser's perspective, Rock Sound has a lot to offer. It is centrally located, offers good protection and good provisioning—and to welcome boaters, several places to tie up or land a dinghy. You will find the deepest water off the western and eastern shores of the harbor. Avoid the center and northern shore if you have a deep draft. Make your way toward the settlement carefully, and you will find 1.8 to 2 meters/5 to 6 feet of water reliably along the shoreline. There is good holding north of the Little Gully dinghy dock and due west of the old pier ruins. Avoid the blue holes that run south along the shore south of the old pier, as they are over 16 meters/50 feet deep! For shelter from the south and the best holding, anchor off the hammerhead between Poison Point and Starved Creek. For westerly protection, you can find good holding just about anywhere along the shore north of Deucy Rocks. It has more water north than you would expect to find.

Eleuthera

GOVERNORS HARBOUR, PALMETTO SHORES		Largest Vessel Accommodated	VHF Channel Monitored	Transient Berths / Total Berths	Approach / Dockside Depth (reported)	Floating Docks	Gas / Diesel	Groceries, Ice, Marine Supplies, Snacks	Repairs: Hull, Engine, Propeller	Lift (tonnage), Crane, Rail	1=110V, 2=220V, B=Both, Max Amps	Laundry, Pool, Showers	Pump-Out Station	Nearby: Grocery Store, Motel, Restaurant
		Dockage						Supplies		Services				
1. French Leave Marina	242-332-3616	200		/8										M
2. Runaway Bay Marina	242-332-1744	NO SLIPSIDE FACILITIES												R

Corresponding chart(s) not to be used for navigation. Internet Access Wireless Internet Access

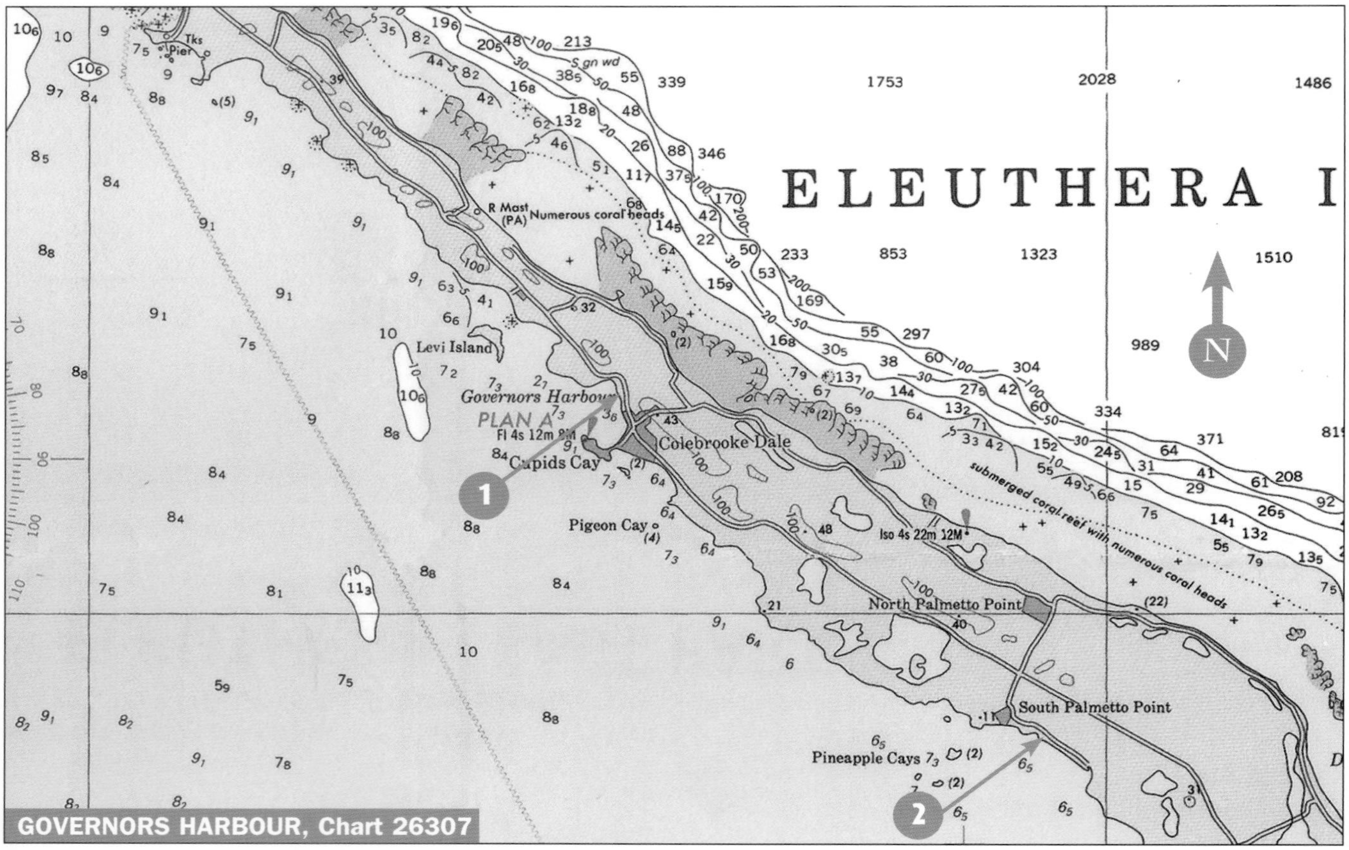

GOVERNORS HARBOUR, Chart 26307

You can dinghy to the Customs and Immigration dock if you want to clear in (which is unlikely) or head for town and tie up to visit the Market Place Shopping Center to find liquor, provisions, a laundry, hardware or gasoline. Or, just walk around town to find local coconut bread, fresh fruit and vegetables, wonderful local handicrafts or stop at a food van for homemade macaroni and cheese, or peas and rice with chicken.

The local ESSO station has a dinghy dock just north of the pilings of the old dock. You can go ashore there to hike to Rock Sound's inland blue hole. And, be sure to attend the cruiser potlucks at Dingle's waterfront gazebo for all the news and goings-on in the floating community.

The Davis Channel

The Davis Channel is your connector from Central to South Eleuthera—the safe route across the mouth of Rock Sound to take you around Powell Point and to Cape Eleuthera Marina. Coming from the north, around the Davis Channel East waypoint (DAVCE), you are in 4.5 meters/15 feet of water with scattered coral heads that are easily seen.

At the start, the Davis Channel seems indeterminate, hardly a visible channel at all, but in time, the sand marking the northern and southern limits becomes more visible, and the color of the water takes on the hues more expected in deeper water. More detail on the Davis Channel is under Pilotage.

Cape Eleuthera and the Cape Eleuthera Resort and Yacht Club

Cape Eleuthera Resort and Yacht Club is a welcome respite from the previous rigors of harbor life, of setting the hook and hauling 'er up again! The marina's channel markers are clearly evident from the busy Powell Point waypoint, a crossroads for

Not to be used for navigation.

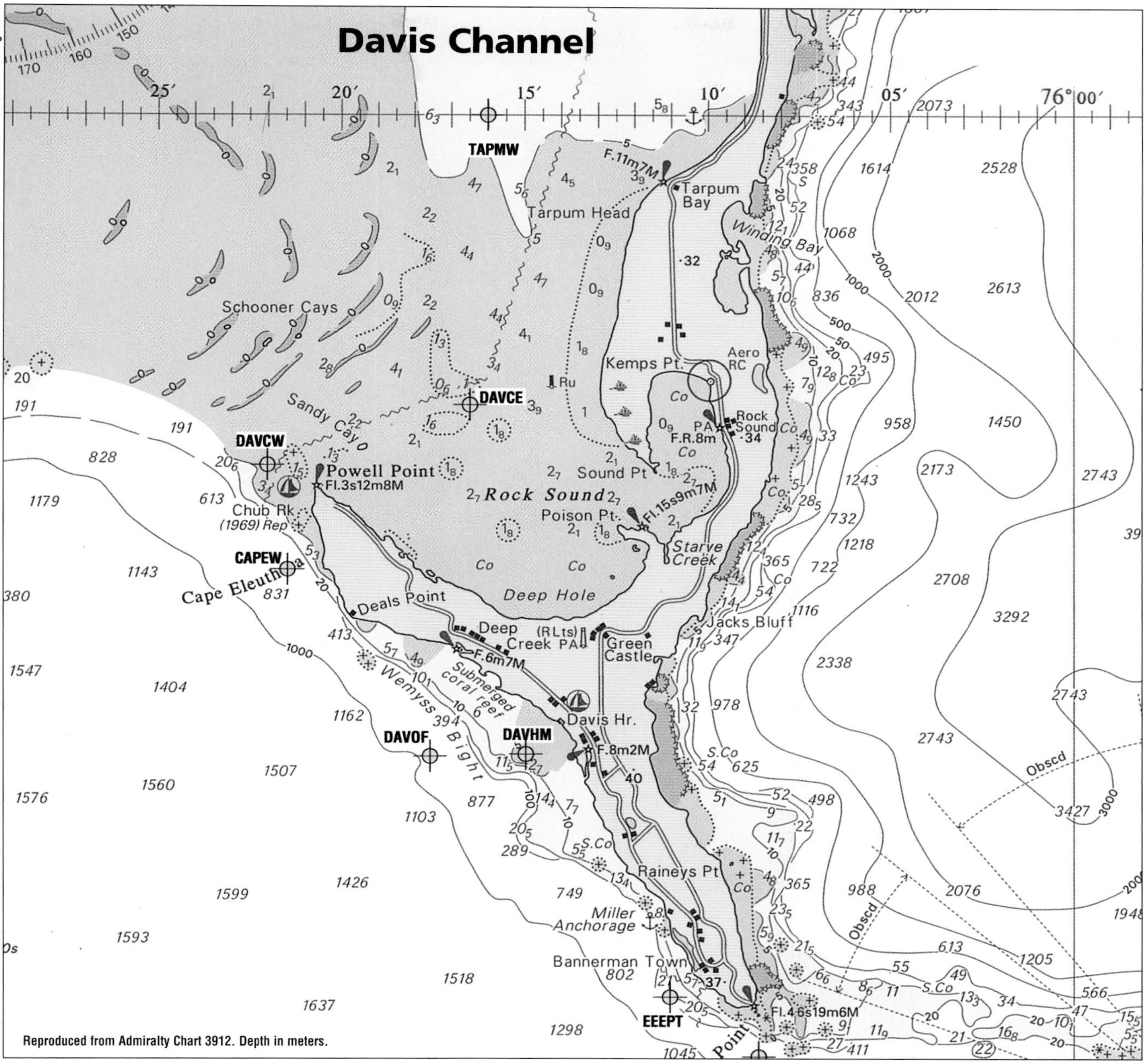

Reproduced from Admiralty Chart 3912. Depth in meters.

vessels coming from or going to Highbourne Cay or Warderick Wells. The entry channel to Cape Eleuthera Resort and Yacht Club carries 3.6-meter/12-foot depths. Upon entering and leaving, be careful of a ledge that extends out from the north entry arm (it is conspicuously marked by a green aid). Line up well out, and run straight in. On leaving, keep going straight until that ledge falls away.

The marina's design is outstanding. It is a well-protected, surge-free, circular harbor within a 4,500-acre nature preserve. It has a tidal through-flow aided by a well-placed canal at one end and the marina entrance at the other. The water is clear and, especially at night, one can watch stingrays, sharks and the occasional grouper frolicking about the bottom. In its deepest section—where you can't see the bottom—there is no telling what may be lurking.

This flow-thru arrangement, along with its state-of- the art facilities, protective seawalls and the owners' commitment to the environment, keeps the resort and the marina's waters pristine. The marina offers the longest dock in the islands (450 feet) and Blue Flag (clean and green) honors.

The marina is owned by Rich DeVos, the Michigan billionaire and owner of the Orlando Magic basketball team. Mr. DeVos' dream for Cape Eleuthera is different from most developers in the islands. You will not find fancy boutique shops, chain restaurants, man-made waterfalls, fake reefs, glass-walled tunnels through pretend oceans, Vegas-style casinos or high

Davis Harbour. *(Marina, not an anchorage) (Not to be used for navigation.)* WATERWAY GUIDE PHOTOGRAPHY.

rises here. Instead, you will catch your own dinner and watch it being cooked over a real barbecue. In five minutes, you can swim from some of the best beaches or dive some of the best reefs in the world.

Davis Harbour

The Davis Harbour entrance channel is well-marked and easily located. After you have gone around Cape Eleuthera, stay out in deep water, and for safety, pass 1.5 to 2 nautical miles off Bamboo Point, as you head south to avoid the rocks lying one nautical mile south of Bamboo Point. After passing the line of Latitude N 24° 45.000', start towards the shore, aiming for the Davis Harbour offshore waypoint (DAVOF). See Pilotage for the entry details.

Davis Harbour Marina, cut square and purposeful, is an attractive, welcome safe haven along a shore devoid of such. Ever popular with anglers, the marina welcomes all vessels and provides every service they may seek, including hauling, and engine and hull repair. If you are fishing or diving, you can't find a better base for those activities.

Davis Harbour Marina has been linked to the Cotton Bay development in past years. The proposed project, a mammoth one, would involve at least $100 million in development and take over 10 years to complete. The first phase of the development would encompass the sale of 114 estate lots, ranging in size from 2/3 acre to 1.5 acres, and the construction of a boutique hotel, based on a villa concept, called, "The Seashells Club at Cotton Bay." The developers promise that Seashells would employ a number of Bahamians, particularly Eleutherans, in a variety of tourist-related and front office jobs.

Eleuthera

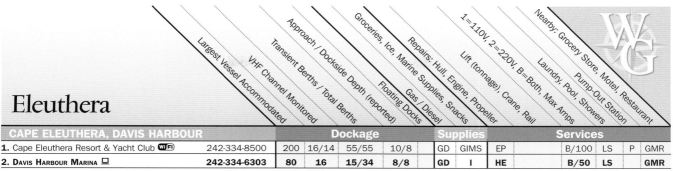

CAPE ELEUTHERA, DAVIS HARBOUR		Largest Vessel Accommodated	VHF Channel Monitored	Transient Berths / Total Berths	Approach / Dockside Depth (reported)	Floating Docks	Gas / Diesel	Groceries, Ice, Marine Supplies, Snacks	Repairs: Hull, Engine, Propeller	Lift (tonnage), Crane, Rail	1=110V, 2=220V, B=Both, Max Amps	Laundry, Pool, Showers	Pump-Out Station	Nearby: Grocery Store, Motel, Restaurant
		Dockage					Supplies		Services					
1. Cape Eleuthera Resort & Yacht Club WiFi	242-334-8500	200	16/14	55/55	10/8		GD	GIMS	EP		B/100	LS	P	GMR
2. **Davis Harbour Marina** 🖳	**242-334-6303**	**80**	**16**	**15/34**	**8/8**		**GD**	**I**	**HE**		**B/50**	**LS**		**GMR**

Corresponding chart(s) not to be used for navigation. 🖳 Internet Access WiFi Wireless Internet Access

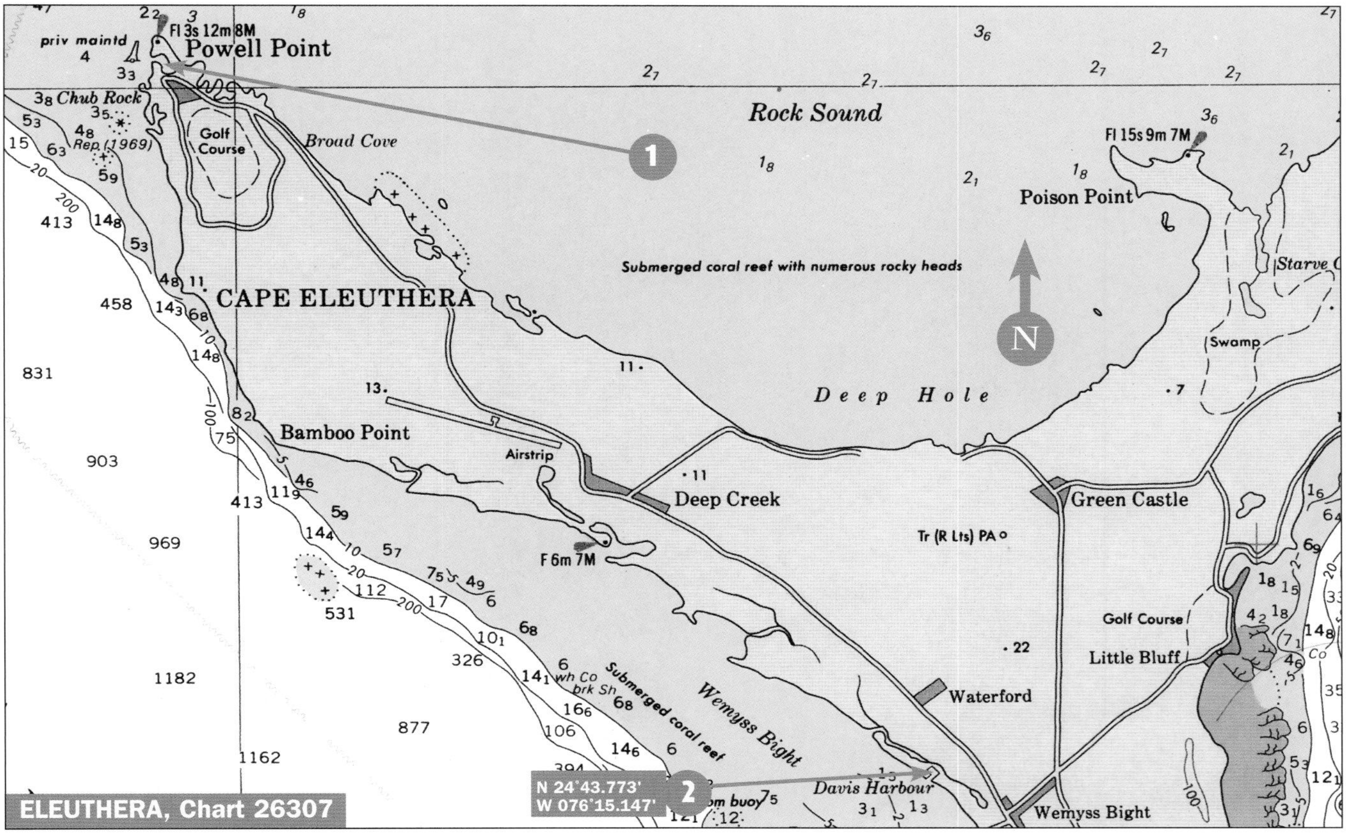

The 1,500-acre development site, situated in South Eleuthera, would include the existing Davis Harbour Marina. For now, we will just have to wait and see what happens.

Bannerman Town and Princess Cay

Eleuthera East End Point (EEEPT) is given as a waypoint to satisfy your curiosity if you are on passage along the western coast of South Eleuthera. Just north of Bannerman Town, you will see a blaze of glowing salmon red roofs, what appears to be two breakwaters, and behind them two blazes of brilliant white sand beach, lined with sun loungers. On the beachfront are three complexes of huts or houses. This is the "desert island" port-of-call of the Princess Cruise Line. Their ships anchor off for a day, ferry their passengers ashore to soak up the sun, and play with every conceivable water toy, eat and drink.

A Central and South Eleuthera Inland Tour

Central and South Eleuthera, like North Eleuthera, present real problems if you want to see the island. Unlike a small cay that can be covered in a day with some walking, Eleuthera's 110-mile length means that even if you carve it up into bite-size chunks, you will still need wheels to get around. Renting a car for an entire day is one solution. Then you can do the island from top to bottom. Having said that, we go for the bite-size chunks, but this increases the cost. Whatever you decide, there are places to see. The Eleutheran landscape, and its small villages, have a character all their own.

Of particular interest is the Unique Village at North Palmetto Point. The nearby hotel (which carries the same name) faces a pink beach that rivals Harbour Island's. It

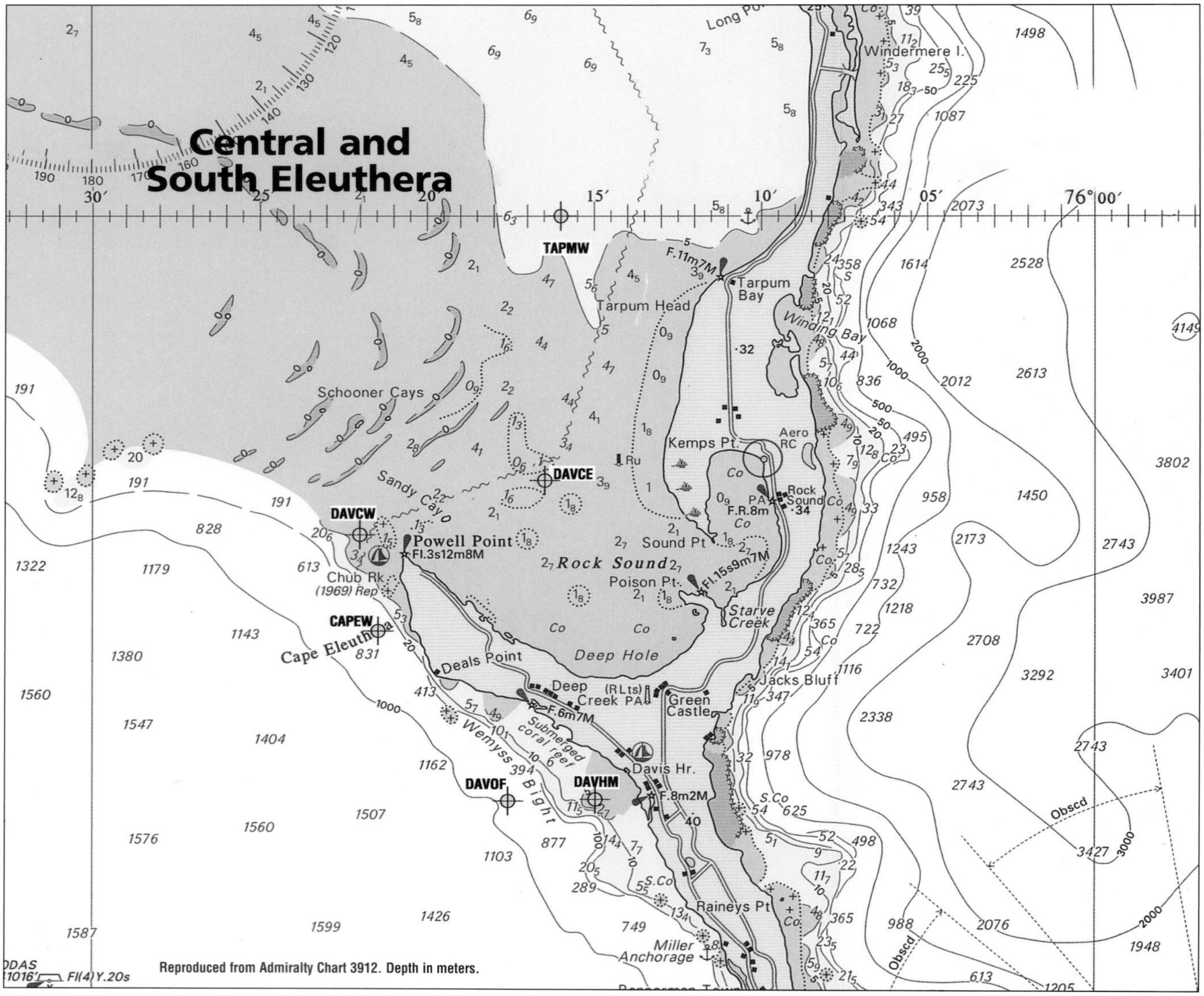

Reproduced from Admiralty Chart 3912. Depth in meters.

Not to be used for navigation.

offers refreshment in a gazebo-like restaurant-bar set high over the Atlantic Ocean beach with a 180-degree view of ocean and reef. Farther south, our cruising editor failed in their objective to reach the lighthouse at Eleuthera Point, the southern tip of the island. The road running south from Bannerman Town gets worse and worse and you soon find yourself driving over limestone ridges through a tunnel of scrub, barely as wide as the car. If they had had no conscience, they might have let the rental car take it, but after a realistic assessment of the car's tires, suspension and steering, they quit.

Pilotage. Talking Captain to Captain

Approaches to Spanish Wells, Harbour Island and North Eleuthera

The Egg Island Northwest waypoint (EGGNW) is the landfall (or departure point) for those arriving from or setting out for the Abacos. The Little Egg Island waypoint (LEGGI) is the landfall if coming in from the west, say Chub Cay or Nassau, taking the Northeast Providence Channel. Running between these waypoints, keep in deep water standing well off the Egg Islands, which are ringed by coral reef. There was at one time a usable cut to the north of Little Egg Island, but this has now shoaled.

If you are coming from Nassau, your heading will be around 043/223 degrees true from the Chub Rock waypoint (CHBRK), with about 28 nautical miles slipping under your keel before you reach the Little Egg Island waypoint. There, you are set up for the pass through the reef to the south of Little Egg Island. At one time, a shipwreck high on the reef was the landmark of this pass, but the wreck has all but disappeared in successive storms. Nonetheless, this deep water inlet (plainly shown on the charts) shows plainly, too. The reef to the north is more easily seen than the reef to the south, but you should have no problems.

The Egg Island approach is not the only route you can take

between Nassau and Spanish Wells. We cover an alternative route, which offers some protection in weather from the north and the east, later in this section.

Little Egg Island to Spanish Wells

From the deep-water inlet, your route to Spanish Wells has few hazards. The bar to the south of Royal Island has depths of 1.2 to 1.5 meters/4 to 5 feet at mean low water. Pass between Royal Island and this bar, keeping about 0.5 to 0.75 nautical miles off Royal Island. The depth over the bank within the Royal Island–Russell Island–Meeks Patch triangle has shoaled to 1.8-meter/6-foot depths at mean low water. Close to Meeks Patch, and to its northwest, this reduces to 1.5 to 1.6 meters/5 to 5.5 feet. On your route in toward Spanish Wells, favor Russell Island rather than Meeks Patch.

Royal Island

To enter the Royal Island anchorage, go in the central, obvious entrance favoring the west side between the little cay with its marker and the headland with its board. There are depths of 2.4 meters/8 feet there at mean low water. Don't take the other side, the east channel. There is a submerged rock there (that is marked).

Farther along the Royal Island coast there is another entrance to the east end of the harbor, but this is small boat stuff. The east end is, in any event, shallow, far too shallow at low tide to serve anything drawing more than 1 foot. You will have 3.6- to 4.2-meter/10- to 14-foot depths at mean low water in the harbor. If you find mooring buoys there, they have deteriorated and are, therefore, unsafe.

The South Entry to Spanish Wells Harbour

By the time you have run 0.5 nautical miles from SPNWS, you should have the skyline water tank plainly in sight, and you will be altering course for the tanks (dark blue with white tops) on a northeast heading. As you get closer, you will see the narrow channel between Russell Island (with a lot of dredging material on your port side as you enter) and Charles Island (shaggy green vegetation). Your best lead marks are the water tank on the skyline and a second larger, but shorter, water tank (also dark blue) slightly below and to the right. The other confirmation of your landfall is the fishing boats (if they are in port, which is mostly April to July) seen to the right of the second, lower-level water tank.

There are two approach markers (both steel I-beams) at the entrance to the channel, which are hard to pick up from a distance. The port marker has heeled over, and the starboard marker (still upright) bears a faded trace of red paint. More obvious is the line of dredged sand and marl on the port side. The spoils define the line of the channel more clearly than the shoreline of Charles Island. First-time visitors have trouble identifying this entry. What confuses folks are the pilings that mark a water pipeline off toward the North Eleuthera coast. Don't let them lead you astray. If you head in that direction, you will run aground.

Once you are in the channel, there is a marker farther to starboard. Then you have two choices. Turn to starboard if you wish to go to Spanish Wells Marine. Also to starboard, you can anchor, or pick up a mooring behind Charles Island. Turn to port (in the obvious channel with a marker piling to be left to starboard) if you wish to go to Spanish Wells Yacht Haven, easily recognized by its large shed. You will have good depths on your approach all the way: well over 1.8 meters/6 feet, and mostly 3 meters/10 feet or more.

If you are going around Spanish Wells, be aware that a water pipeline was laid between Charles Island, Spanish Wells and "mainland" North Eleuthera. The spoil from the trench was never spread or removed; consequently the straight line shoal reduces the depth to 1.2 meters/4 feet at mean low water in some places.

The East Entry to Spanish Wells Harbour

The alternative route into Spanish Wells Harbour is to continue around Charles Island to Spanish Wells East (SPNWE) and pick up the channel, which runs east–west directly into the cut between St. Georges Cay and Charles Island. Beware of the shallows on both sides. Pick up the three channel marks (to be left to port), which will take you in a curve around the shallows to port. Then, you will see two channel entry markers with, as a companion to the starboard one, a leaning telephone pole. When you get close you may see that the starboard entry piling has a single red reflector on it, the kind you use to mark your driveway.

By now you are heading almost due west. There is a line of four single posts to be left to starboard leading straight into Spanish Wells Harbour. You have good depth in this channel, but there is no reason to take this route into the harbor if you have come from the west. Don't be confused by a continuation of these markers leading east from the entry pair. This is the route used by the Spanish Wells boats bound for Genes Bay ferry landing on Eleuthera, directly opposite the channel entrance.

You may prefer to use this entrance if you are going to pick up a mooring ball. The moorings are to port as you proceed up the channel. You can also get to them by running down the length of Spanish Wells Harbour from the south entry.

Spanish Wells Harbour

Spanish Wells Harbour is, in fact, just one long cut running between St. Georges Cay (Spanish Wells) to the north and two islands - little peanut-shaped Charles Island to the southeast and Russell Island to the southwest. It is not a natural harbor in the sense of being a cove or a landlocked bay, but it serves well with adequate protection from virtually all weather other than wind funneling in from the east. The open, free-to-all anchorage that once existed at the eastern end of Charles Island has now been converted into moorings, which is a better, and safer, arrangement. Contact "Cinnabar" on VHF Channel 16 to reserve a mooring, as there is often a few days wait for one. The speed limit is 4 knots in Spanish Wells Harbour.

Spanish Wells Yacht Haven is the only marina, but it is well-found and well-kept. It is a pleasant, agreeable place with every facility you are likely to need, including a circular swimming pool and rooms if you wish to put up shoreside guests. The shorepower outlets are 50 amp. If you require 30 amp, you

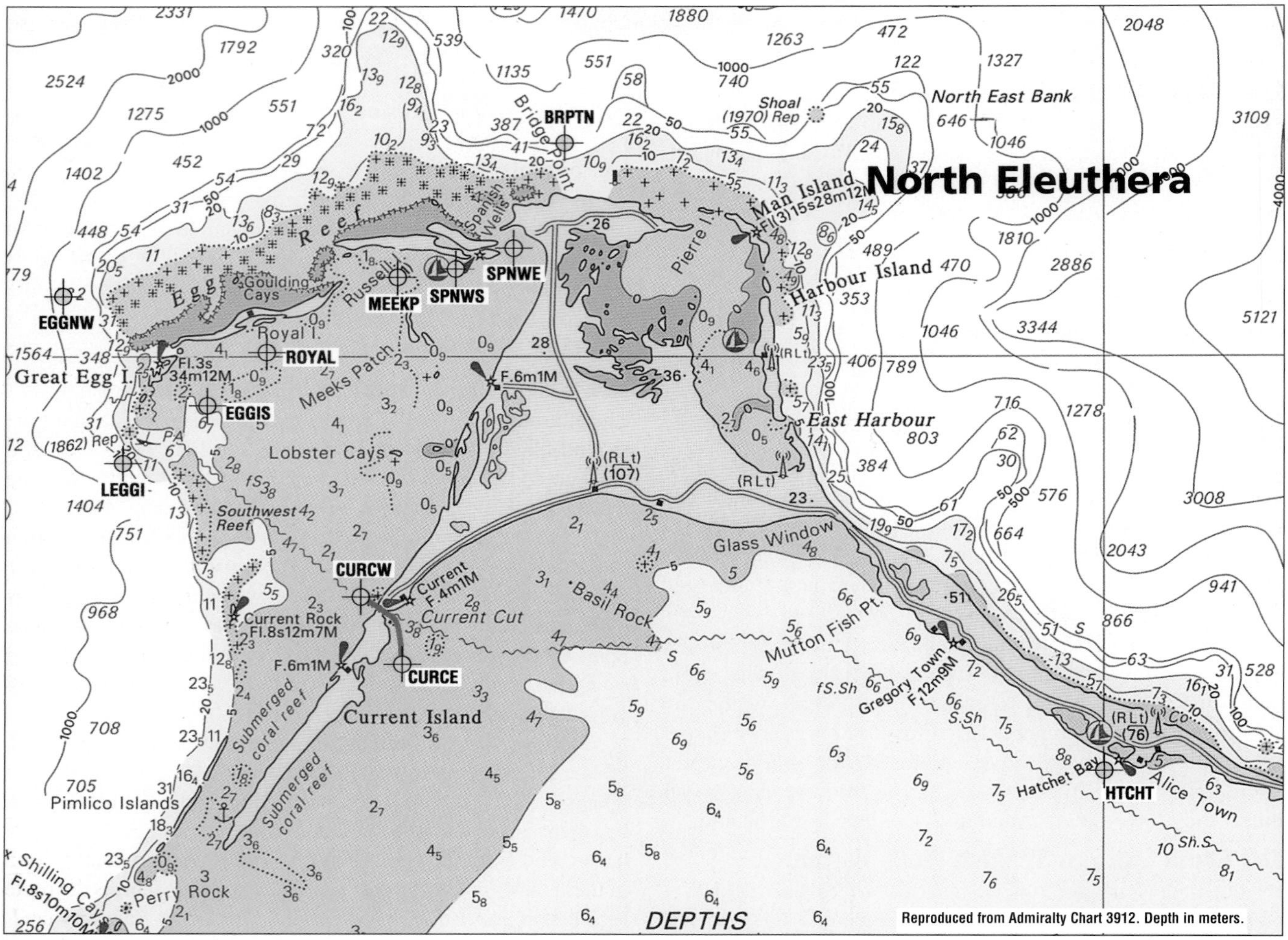

Reproduced from Admiralty Chart 3912. Depth in meters.

Not to be used for navigation.

will need a pigtail adapter. They may be able to lend you one. If you carry on up the cut, between Russell Island and St. Georges Cay, to port there are two openings into the Mud Hole. This is the local hurricane shelter where, when a hurricane threatens, the local boats are laced with a spider's web of lines into the mangroves.

Spanish Wells Harbour, which is entirely weighted in its layout to favor the St. Georges Cay side (the 'butment, as it is called). It is geared toward supporting the fishing fleet. Starting from the eastern end, Ronald's Marine, Anchor Snack Bar, Pinder's Supermarket, Pool's Boatyard with a rail track into the harbor and mini-drawbridge, Texaco Service Center at Spanish Wells Marine and Hardware, and Jack's Outback Snack Bar are the main shoreside facilities on the waterfront. The fishing boat services and docks continue right up the harbor to the St. Georges Cay–Russell Island Bridge, where the two islands have a road link at the west end. You can take a small boat out under this bridge at half tide or better to gain the open water of the bank between Pierre Rock and St. Georges Cay. From there, head west to reach the gap between Russell Island and Royal Island. At less than half tide, the area to the east of the bridge dries. If you go this way, beware of the wreckage of the old bridge lying on the north side of the channel, east of the bridge site.

Spanish Wells to Harbour Island. The Devils Backbone Passage

From the beginning of the settlement of the Bahamas, the Devils Backbone claimed its first victim when a shipload of Eleutheran settlers went on the reef and ended up destitute, holed up in Preachers Cave. It was a discouraging start. Since then, the Devils Backbone and the North Eleuthera reefs have claimed many victims and gained a fearsome reputation.

The passage is best done in flat calm conditions with perfect light. In poor light, a bumpy sea state and a 20-knot wind from the east–northeast, you could get caught by a freak storm, halfway through the passage and have no where to run. On the fast ferry at 30 knots in 5-foot northeast seas and again, 20-knot winds, you might fare a little better. Veterans who have checked it out from the shoreline and have flown over the whole run at low altitude - all the way from Spanish Wells to Harbour Island - know what it looks like and could map it, but would still not go it alone.

If you have done it once, there are some who say that given good conditions you can do it on your own. One boat owner, who had taken a pilot the first time, decided he could go it alone on the return trip. He buckled two propellers and bent his shafts.

The Devils Backbone. (Not to be used for navigation.) Waterway Guide Photography.

Saving that Spanish Wells pilot's fee cost him around $50,000 by the time his boat had been repaired in Florida. A five-trip "veteran," determined to navigate a course he knew well, ran on the Devils Backbone when moving clouds took away the sunlight. Simply put, this is a passage where you are utterly dependent on good weather and perfect visibility. However accurate your reading of the water may be, you still have to factor several parameters into your decision making.

- It is hard to distinguish between coral and grass. If you lose sunlight, even temporarily, you lose your ability to see either reef, grass or sand.
- From a relatively short distance, it is almost impossible to guess the depth accurately over any kind of bottom, be it sand, coral or grass.
- Forward speed, even at 5 knots, will be sufficient (given an average reaction time) to carry you exactly where you don't want to be. Yet in any kind of weather, you need a speed of 8 knots-plus to take you through the choke points quickly enough so that you are not swept sideways.
- There is no room to maneuver on the critical sectors of this passage.
- The obstacle course is never quite the same. The sand between the Devils Backbone and the beach changes with each storm.
- Finally, depth counts. You need the safety of high or mid-tide whatever your draft. The initial leg to Ridley Head and the final run-in to Harbour Island's Dunmore Town have average depths of 1.8 meters/6 feet, so if you draw over 1.2 meters/4 feet, you may not want to attempt it. It can be unnerving at best to run with just half a meter or two feet under the keel. It is too close for comfort, especially in strange or difficult waters, or where you bottom out in the troughs of waves.

Negotiating the Devils Backbone Passage is not supposed to be a test of character. Taking a pilot does not reflect on your competence and seamanship, but not using a pilot says a great deal about your common sense. Of course you can try it alone, if you wish. We do not recommend it. At one stage, as other guides have done, we fixed waypoints over the full run of this passage, but we have now discarded them. Why? Primarily because everything changes after severe storms. Secondly, a waypoint is nothing. Just one safe spot, barely the length of your boat. The critical determination is what happens on each leg. Are you exactly on course regardless of wind, wave and set? The margins on this passage are narrow. There are places where even minimal cross track error can spell disaster.

We offer a commentary on the Devils Backbone Passage so that you can follow the course as you go - taking it in stages. Use the sketch chart to follow the commentary. This, we hope, will make your piloted passage more interesting and make you realize how wise you were to do it that way.

Spanish Wells Harbour to Ridley Head

You will leave Spanish Wells by the eastern entry and, turning north at SPNWE, head for Gun Point (WPT01). You will pass about 50 feet off Gun Point. The next landmark is Ridley Head (WPT02), just over a half-mile run. There will be 1.8-meter/6-foot depths all the way (possibly as little as 1.5 meters/5 feet at

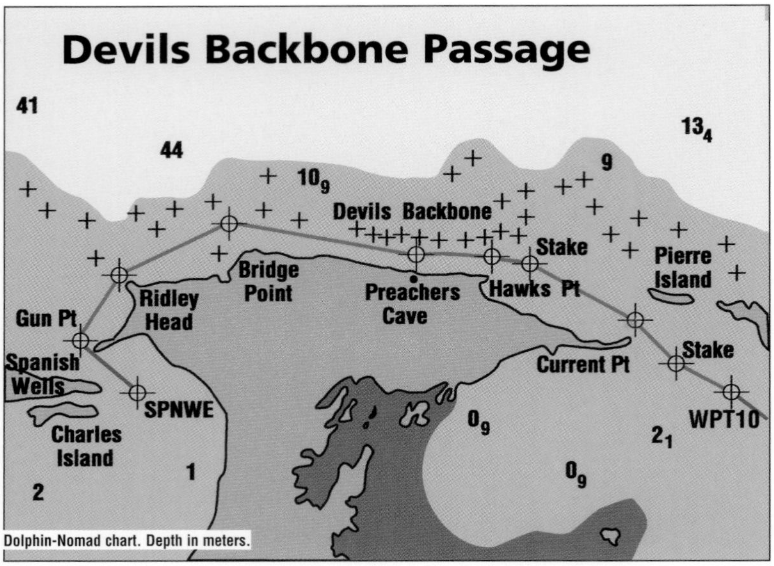

Dolphin-Nomad chart. Depth in meters.

Not to be used for navigation.

astronomical low tide) except off Gun Point, where the bank depth is 0.3 meter/1 foot.

As you cross the small bight between Gun Point and Ridley Head, the dark patches ahead and to starboard are grass; to port they are coral. Pass outside (offshore) Ridley Head stake, leaving it a good boat length or so off to starboard (it stands on an isolated reef). You will have some 9 meters/30 feet of water there. Be warned that if the weather is marginal, and the wind has a northerly element, the worst area for high seas is from Ridley Head to just after the Devils Backbone.

Ridley Head to Bridge Point

Immediately after Ridley Head, you will alter course to pass the next headland, Bridge Point (WPT03), just under a mile away. At the start, you will parallel the beach. The dark patches to port are reef. Favor the beach side. When you run out of beach, there will be four dark patches, which are reef, coming up on your starboard bow. Point slightly out to sea to leave these to starboard. You will find yourself over or close to other dark patches, which are also reef, but you should have sufficient depth on your run to Bridge Point.

Bridge Point

Stand reasonably well off from Bridge Point, as the depth shoals closer in. Bridge Point is not only a landmark on the Devils Backbone Passage, but also a jumping off point for the Abacos (or alternatively an arrival point). The Bridge Point North waypoint, lying outside the reefs, is your actual point of departure. If arriving from the Abacos, you are advised to call Spanish Wells on VHF Channel 16 for a pilot at this point.

The Devils Backbone

You now have just over a mile to run to pass the actual Devils Backbone Reef. After Bridge Point, alter course to starboard (some eight to 10 degrees) and look out for Blowhole Rock, dark and cave-like, which will be off your starboard bow. When you are just about abeam of it, a reef will come up on your port side. Keep inshore of that reef, and head for what appears to be the next headland, but is actually the northern tip of Pierre Island.

You will now run progressively closer to the shoreline to take you safely between the Devils Backbone Reef and the beach. You will see the Devils Backbone, dark on your port side. The reef hooks inward toward the shore, forcing you closer and closer to the beach. At what will be your closest point, you will realize that the beach itself is hooking out toward the reef. Many people, scared of grounding on the sand (around WPT04), alter away from the beach and crunch on the Devils Backbone. You have to keep your cool and hug that beach, about 150 feet out, and don't be afraid of it. (Sand is more forgiving than coral.) After squeezing around the Devils Backbone, you can start easing out away from the beach, and flex your hands to get rid of your white knuckles. You still have potential hazards ahead, but perhaps the worst leg is over.

Preachers Cave Beach to Hawks Point

It is just over half a mile to run to clear the next low point. At WPT05, you are off Preachers Cave Beach, and in the limestone cliff face to starboard you can see the cave entrance. The course then generally heads farther offshore, to pass around the low, rocky Hawks Point (WPT06). After that, you are almost on the home stretch. There is grass underneath you. Then two coral heads appear (which come up about the time you reach the end of Preachers Cave beach), which you leave to starboard. Farther offshore there are plenty of reefs. But you are not out of reef country yet.

Hawks Point to Current Point

After reaching Hawks Point, set a course to pass off the next point of land, Current Point, which is obvious, just over a mile away. Stand off from the shoreline rather than paralleling close to it, for on the way, there is an isolated stake that marks a ledge running out from the coastline. WPT07 is roughly where one aims to be to pass safely around it. Don't shave it too closely, or you will hit the ledge. After passing the stake, alter course to take up a southeasterly heading to pass off Current Point (WPT08). From this point on, there are no particular problems to face. On this leg, you will have grass under you all the way. Pass 200 feet off Current Point.

Current Point to Dunmore Town (Harbour Island)

After Current Point, alter course to about 135/315 to 140/320 degrees true to acquire a lone stake, half a mile away, marking a channel through sands that lie to the north of the Harbour Island "inland sea" area. The stake (WPT09) must be passed on the south side (left to port if inbound from Spanish Wells). Pass reasonably close to it, for you have easily seen shallows to starboard. Your general direction, after passing the stake, should be toward the south beach on Man Island. Hold this heading for about half a mile to WPT10 to

Between Ridley Head and Bridge Point. (Not to be used for navigation.) WATERWAY GUIDE PHOTOGRAPHY.

clear the shallows, and then take up a heading for Dunmore Town. The mean low water depth on the final stretch is 1.8 meters/6 feet.

You have two final hazards to avoid, neither of them difficult. Look out for Eastmost and Westmost Rocks to starboard, and avoid them. Look out for Girls Bank to port (which shows clearly), and skirt around that. Then you are all set to proceed to Valentine's, the Harbour Island Marina or Romora Bay Club & Resort. You can also anchor off, if space permits, wherever you wish.

Harbour Mouth Pass, Harbour Island

A very large shoal (similar to Girls Bank) extends to the west from the southern peninsula of Harbour Island as far as N 25° 27.500'. To reach the ocean, you have to favor the shore of North Eleuthera until you have passed the gap between Harbour Island and Whale Point, then turn to go out into the Atlantic Ocean.

The route through Harbour Mouth carries little more than 1.8-meter/6-foot depths even with a favorable tide, maybe less. It is beset by moving sandbanks, tidal currents and ocean swell. Never try it at less than a half tide, and never when the set comes from the east. Complicating things further, there is an underwater pipeline that creates an irregular sand scar running diagonally across the shoal area from Eleuthera to Harbour Island. The Harbour Mouth Pass may be best left to the locals. If you want to use it, get some local advice, and sound it beforehand in your dinghy. It is the gateway to ocean fishing between the Northeast Bank and the offshore "obstruction" off James Point to the south, as well as good departure point for the Abacos or Cat Island. You would need ideal conditions and prior knowledge to use it as an arrival point.

Spanish Wells to Current Cut

This is a simple two-leg run from waypoint SPNWS to Meeks Patch (MEEKP). From there, it is 7.4 nautical miles on a course of 186/006 degrees true to the west of the Lobster Cays to just off Current Cut. The houses at The Current are good landmarks. Although hidden at this point, Current Cut is just about 0.5 nautical miles south of The Current, at the Current Cut West waypoint (CURCW).

Current Cut

Using the Current Cut West waypoint (CURCW) as your starting point, hold 130/310 degrees true for about 0.3 nautical miles, placing you in a position to negotiate the cut.

The tidal flow runs quickly. It gets stronger as the cut narrows traveling east. A boat with marginal longitudinal stability will have a difficult time staying on course. Ideally, you should time your passage for either slack water or against the tide. With the tide, it is quite a ride! Against the tide, it is very slow going, and requires a lot of power to maintain forward motion. Read the water, both for depth and tide rips, and choose your path. Favor the deepest, least turbulent path. After about 0.75 nautical miles, you will pass the busy government dock (on the North Eleuthera side) and see some marooned boats high and dry along the shoreline.

Taking the deep water line through the cut, you will have held a course of around 099/279 degrees true; but use your eyes as you exit the cut. Then turn, still favoring deep water, on a course of 118/298 degrees true and hold that for just over one nautical mile. You are heading for the Current Cut East waypoint (CURCE). You should have no problems on this leg, other than to keep one eye on the depth sounder and the other on the water. At CURCE, you will have 14.9 nautical miles to run on a course of 102/282 degrees true to Hatchet Bay. You can anchor at Hatchet Bay to visit Alice Town, then you can dinghy ride or bike north to the Glass Window and to visit Gregory Town.

An Alternative to Current Cut heading for Nassau

If you are heading for Nassau from Eleuthera, and don't wish to take the Current Cut to Little Egg Island route to gain the deep water of the Northeast Providence Channel, both the PMLIS and FLMSE waypoints can take you there. You will want to go carefully around the south end of Little Pimlico Island because of the sand bar. Unless the sun is right and conditions are good for eyeball navigation, we would not go this way.

Apart from the sand we have mentioned, there is continuous reef, barely awash at low water, to the south of the deeper water lying immediately south of Little Pimlico. It would be easy to find yourself temporarily trapped in a kind of sand-and-reef-locked swimming pool. With high water, and good visibility, you should have no problems. Just probe forward cautiously, or take the dinghy to explore first.

Current Cut to Hatchet Bay

For a long time, you will have seen the Glass Window bridge off to port. Gregory Town is easily visible with a scattering of houses to its south.

The Davis Channel

From the DAVCE waypoint, it is a 4.7 nautical miles to run on a heading of 253/073 degrees true to bring you to the Davis Channel West (DAVCW) waypoint. This route takes you 0.26 nautical miles north of the obelisk marker on the shoal to the south. By the time you are level with the obelisk, it is obvious that you are in a channel. Gradually, the water will take on a blue coloration, rather than the green of the banks. The Schooner Cays are clearly visible to the north. At DAVCW, swing around gently to the Cape Eleuthera Marina (CAPEM) waypoint, just one nautical mile on a course of about 150/330 degrees true.

If you are coming from the south, after you round the CAPEM waypoint, you will see what appears to be a blue-water channel off your starboard bow, which can be mistaken for the Davis Channel. If you were to turn at this point, you would find yourself running south (rather than north) of the sand with the obelisk marker, and would run into shallows and coral. Heading for the Davis Channel from this direction, make sure you head for the DAVCW waypoint. That southern "look-alike" channel can be deceptive coming up from the south.

Davis Harbour

After you have gone around Cape Eleuthera, use the CAPEW waypoint to stay in deep water. For safety, pass about 1 to 1.5 nautical miles off Bamboo Point, as you head south, to avoid the rocks lying one nautical mile south of Bamboo Point.

Current Cut, looking east. WATERWAY GUIDE PHOTOGRAPHY.

Current Point. (Not to be used for navigation.) WATERWAY GUIDE PHOTOGRAPHY.

Aim for the Davis Harbour offshore waypoint (DAVOF). From there, aim for the outlying Davis Harbour marker (DAVHM), which is hard to see until you are almost on top of it. The first landmarks are the Deep Creek BTC mast (some 2.5 nautical miles north of Davis Harbour), a wrecked boat on a beach to the north of Davis Harbour and a dense clump of casuarinas hiding the harbor. The marker is a small red radar reflector on a white post planted on a large isolated coral head. By then, you will be in 7.5 meters/25 feet of water, shoaling to depths of 4.8 meters/16 feet or less. There are a number of isolated coral heads all around.

The Davis Harbour entrance, which bears 065/245 degrees true about one nautical mile from the marker, should be obvious at this point. There is a double line of stakes marking the entrance and a Shell sign that shows against the trees, as well as a white painted signal mast. At mean low water, the entry channel has 1-meter/3.5-foot depths, but during "moon tides," that can reduce to barely 0.9-meter/3-foot depths. The shallowest point is just before the first two markers. We suggest you check with the dock-master on VHF Channel 16 if you are in any doubt about the state of the tide. Inside are depths of 2.1 meters/7 feet at mean low water.

Greencastle Church. WATERWAY GUIDE PHOTOGRAPHY.

Moving On from Eleuthera

Heading for the Northern Exumas from North Eleuthera

From Spanish Wells, you essentially have two choices. One is to run virtually due south from Egg Island to the Fleeming Channel, pass through it on to the bank and head for Beacon Cay (or your destination), passing over the coral-strewn area of the Middle Ground Bank. The other is to go through Current Cut, parallel the west coast of Eleuthera to the Davis Channel, then set out for the Exumas from Powell Point (or the Cape Eleuthera Marina). This is a straightforward 25-nautical-mile blue water run to Highbourne Cay.

The Fleeming Channel and the Middle Ground Route to the Exuma Cays

From the Little Egg Island waypoint (LEGGI), it is a straight run of 11 nautical miles on a course of 190/010 degrees true to our FLEMG waypoint. The Fleeming Channel (FLEMG to FLMSE) is straightforward; 2.5 nautical miles on a course of 139/319 degrees true, with good depths.

Our chosen route from FLMSE takes you 21.6 nautical miles on a course of 169/349 degrees true across the Middle Ground Bank to a waypoint just northwest of Beacon Cay and the Ship Channel (BCSCW). On the route from the Fleeming Channel to Beacon Cay, the first 10 nautical miles or so is problem free with adequate depth. The final 10 nautical miles are testing, with plenty of coral and depths reduced to 2 meters/7 feet over the reefs and heads. This continues until you are just 1.5 nautical miles off the BCSCW waypoint. You must have good conditions, a quiet sea state and good sunlight in your favor. Do not run on autopilot.

From the waypoint northwest of Beacon Cay, a 2.2 nautical mile run on a course of 140/320 degrees true takes you to another waypoint (BCSCE), which places you in the deep water of Exuma Sound. At Beacon Cay, you are set to run either on the bank side or the Exuma Sound side to Allans Cay, Highbourne Cay or wherever you are bound. Ship Channel itself has no problems. Our only caution is that the Exuma Bank routes require detailed charts or personal knowledge and good, careful eyeball navigation.

Heading to Cat Island or the Exumas

Southeast Eleuthera (waypoint SELEU) is a good jumping-off point for Cat Island. You are closer there than you will be anywhere else, and Little San Salvador makes a good stop on your way. Either Cape Eleuthera Marina or Davis Harbour Marina make ideal departure waypoints for the Exumas, giving you single-leg runs straight across the deep water of Exuma Sound. Your choices in landfall extend virtually the entire length of the Exuma chain. ■

Waterway Guide is always open to your observations from the helm. E-mail your comments on any navigation information in the guide to: editor@waterwayguide.com.

THE DEVILS BACKBONE PASSAGE (WEST TO EAST)

Gun Point	WPT01	25°32.94N / 76°44.71W
Ridley Head Stake	WPT02	25°33.50N / 76°44.40W
Bridge Point	WPT03	25°33.88N / 76°43.43W
Bridge Point North	BRPTN	25°35.00N / 76°43.33W
Devils Backbone	WPT04	25°33.64N / 76°42.04W
Preachers Cave	WPT05	25°33.65N / 76°41.76W
Hawks Point	WPT06	25°33.63N / 76°41.15W
Stake	WPT07	25°33.55N / 76°40.81W
Current Point	WPT08	25°33.09N / 76°39.91W
Stake	WPT09	25°32.74N / 76°39.55W
	WPT10	25°32.51N / 76°39.08W

WARNING

These waypoints are NOT for navigation. They are included purely for interest. Quite apart from all the other navigational hazards of this passage, the sand at the narrowest part and the width of the deeper water between the beach and the Devils Backbone reef, changes.

Eleuthera Waypoints

Egg Island NW	EGGNW (B18)	25°30.00N / 76°54.50W
Little Egg Island	LEGGI	25°27.22N / 76°53.85W
Egg Island South	EGGIS	25°28.47N / 76°51.52W
Royal Island	ROYAL	25°30.16N / 76°50.46W
Meeks Patch	MEEKP	25°31.87N / 76°47.16W
Spanish Wells S Ent	SPNWS	25°32.00N / 76°45.64W
Spanish Wells E Ent	SPNWE	25°32.63N / 76°44.33W
Current Cut West	CURCW	25°24.45N / 76°48.04W
Current Cut East	CURCE	25°23.55N / 76°45.83W
Pimlico Islands North	PMLIN	25°21.60N / 76°50.73W
Pimlico Islands South	PMLIS	25°18.00N / 76°53.10W
Fleeming Channel	FLEMG (B21)	25°16.00N / 76°56.00W
Fleeming Channel SE	FLMSE (B22)	25°14.80N / 76°54.50W
Six Shilling Cay	SSHLG	25°16.35N / 76°54.05W
Hatchet Bay	HTCHT	25°20.53N / 76°29.66W
Governors Harbour	GOVNH	25°12.00N / 76°16.00W
Tarpum Bay	TAPMW	25°00.00N / 76°16.08W
Davis Channel East	DAVCE	24°52.45N / 76°16.75W
Davis Channel Obelisk	OBLSK	24°51.41N / 76°19.61W
Davis Channel West	DAVCW	24°51.10N / 76°21.73W
Cape Eleuthera Marina	CAPEM	24°50.24N / 76°21.20W
Cape Eleuthera West	CAPEW	24°48.22N / 76°21.72W
Off Davis Harbour	DAVOF	24°43.81N / 76°17.83W
Davis Harbour Outer Mark	DAVHM	24°43.81N / 76°15.08W
Eleuthera East End Point	EEEPT	24°37.31N / 76°11.04W
South Eleuthera	SELEU	24°35.61N / 76°08.73W

Position format is latitude and longitude in degrees and minutes (hddd°mm.mm). Waypoints in RED are NOT for autopilot navigation. Codes in parenthesis are Wavey Line waypoints marked on the charts. If you have programmed waypoints we listed in a previous edition of this guide, check carefully to ensure the coordinates you have recorded match the list. If a waypoint is no longer on our list we may have changed its code or deleted it.

Avoid the Pinot Grigio

A wino's guide to 'eyeballing' Bahamian waters

By Peter Swanson

In his *Master and Commander* series, author Patrick O'Brien describes one far-off patch of water as a "wine-dark sea." O'Brien, who himself had borrowed the phrase from the ancient Greek poet Homer, might as well have been describing the Tongue of the Ocean in the Bahamas.

Any boat sliding down The Tongue will find a comfortable 6,000 feet beneath her keel. At the other extreme, if Bahamian water looks like Pinot Grigio, back down on the throttles because you're about to run aground. Those are the extremes of "eyeball navigation" in the Bahamas; dark means very deep while yellowish-white signifies the skinniest of waters. The skill, which comes with experience, is deciphering the blue-green gradations in between—the equivalent of Rose.

You nitpickers out there may be saying, Wait a minute, Bahamian water is not reddish at all. True, but Homer's observation was about saturation of color, not necessarily its hue. Homer, after all, was blind.

Speaking of which, for that 5 percent of the male population that suffers from color blindness, Bahamian cruising will no doubt be angst-filled, requiring extreme conservatism, reliance on the observations of others and a Homeric sense of saturation on the greyscale.

Color sense is important because neither paper charts nor electronics substitute for the human eye when navigating the shifting sands of the Bahamas' shallow banks and inlets. Depth sounders can only tell you the depth at that moment, not which way to turn to remain in safe soundings. And navigational markers are virtually non-existent.

That having been said, learning to associate color with depth doesn't take years of Bahamian cruising experience, or even months. As you have gathered, deep blue means deep water. As the blue lightens it means the sun is reflecting off a rising bottom. Green begins to dominate as the depth shallows to 40 feet. That postcard-perfect green-blue signifies a navigable 6 to 9 feet of depth. Yellow or white: don't go there.

Among the most dangerous hazards are keel-ripping coral heads, which appear as black patches against the green water. Insidiously, some coral heads rise to just a few feet below the surface of what is otherwise deep water. In this situation, the prudent thing to do is avoid any dark spots. To further complicate decision-making, grassy spots also show as dark brown or black. Best avoid them all, as one cruising guide author once wrote, comparing them to mouse droppings in your Jello desert.

Clouds, too, are your enemy because not only do they obscure bottom colors with their shadow, but the shadow itself can be confused with dark coral heads. Best remember, however, that coral heads stay put.

Color differentiation is key, of course, and that ability can be enhanced by three factors: polarization, timing and elevation.

Buy yourself some good polarized sunglasses. If you never have, you'll be amazed how much more vibrant the colors will seem. Shadows and gradations in water color that can easily be missed with ordinary sunglasses become more defined.

Late risers have the edge in Bahamian cruising because the low morning sun doesn't sufficiently illuminate the bottom to bring out the colors, particularly if the sun is ahead of you. Eyeball navigation works best when the sun is high and behind. If depth is a factor at your destination, this dictates a rather short cruising day, say from 10 a.m. to 2:30 p.m., with plenty of daylight left to swim or hunt lobster. Obviously, night cruising on the banks is risky at best.

Another way to give your eyes an edge is to elevate them, particularly if waters are choppy. Sportfish towers and flying bridges, of course, are ideal for this. Standing on the cabin top with an autopilot remote is almost as good. Lacking that, communicate. Some trawler cruisers have wireless headsets for docking; these can be handy as one partner, high up, calls out directional changes to the other at the helm. Otherwise, you'll just have to do it the old-fashioned way—by hollering at one another.

Your reward for successful eyeball navigation will come at the end of the day. You've anchored, the sun is low in the sky and you've poured yourself a chilled glass of fermented fruit juice. It's time to get saturated.

GOIN' ASHORE:

ST. GEORGES CAY SPANISH WELLS

bank • customs & immigration • fuel • groceries • marina • marine services • medical • police • post office • propane • restaurant • telephone • water

Named because Spanish galleons stopped here to take on fresh water, Spanish Wells has a long association with the sea. There are still descendants of the early loyalist settlers among the folks living in this premier Bahamian fishing port. Seventy percent of the annual Bahamian lobster production is harvested by the Spanish Wells' fishing fleet, which has to travel far to sea to catch these creatures. In the settlement, colorful gardens surround pristine houses, many with fruit trees and English roses blooming side by side. Everything here is very virtuous and pious; most shops close on Wednesday afternoons and all day Sunday. Like Man-O-War Cay in the Abacos, there is no liquor store on the island. There is a lovely, long beach on the northeast side of the cay. It is sugar sand and crystal-clear water with good snorkeling off the reef farther out. There are also good beaches on the northern tip of St. Georges Cay and all along the north side of Russell Island. Spanish Wells is a Port of Entry. Customs and Immigration are at freight dock. Clear in at *Spanish Wells Yacht Haven.*

EMERGENCIES

Marine • VHF 16 • Any of the Spanish Wells Pilots.
Marine Repairs • 242-333-4122/4462
Dentist At the clinic on Thursdays.
Medical *Clinic* • 242-333-4064/5145 • Nurses on call after hours; their numbers are posted at the stores.
Pharmacist • 242-333-4675 days; 242-333-5072 in emergency.

MARINAS

SPANISH WELLS YACHT HAVEN
Tel: 242-333-4255/4328 • Fax: 242-333-4649 • VHF 16
yachthaven@gmail.com
Slips 40. **Max LOA** 168 ft. **MLW at Dock** 9 ft. **Dockage** $1.50 per ft. per day. ($1.00 per ft. monthly) **Fuel** Diesel and gasoline, 5% credit card surcharge. **Facilities & Services** Power $0.55 per kwHr, water $0.25 per gallon, ice, showers, washers and dryers for marina guests only, public telephone, satellite television, propane tanks refilled at Pinder's, bicycle rentals, covered storage, small book exchange, weather reports. **Credit Cards** Visa, MasterCard, AMEX.

SPANISH WELLS MARINA AND HARDWARE
Tel: 242-333-4139/4122 • VHF 16
Slips 10. **Max LOA** 110 ft. **MLW at Dock** 10 ft. **Dockage** $1.25 per ft. per day **Fuel** Diesel and gasoline **Facilities & Services** Power, cistern water, ice haul out to 30 feet, fully-stocked marine store, wet and dry storage. **Accommodations** Efficiency apartments above the marine store.

R & B BOAT YARD
Tel: 242-333-4462 • Fax: 242-333-4249 •
mbboatyard@gamail.com
No transient dockage. Full service boat yard specializing in boat bottom maintenance and repair, welding and fabrication, fiberglass construction and repair. Synchrolift for catamarans up to 70 ft. LOA, 28-ft. beam, 40 tons. Railway up to 90 ft. LOA, 22-ft. beam, 120 tons. Marine hardware, paint, filters, cutlass bearings, zincs, in-water prop/shaft/rudder repair, vessel recovery and more.

MOORINGS

There are nine moorings off the east end of the island, owned by Jock Morgan (VHF Channel 16 "Bandit"). They are strong and cost $15 per night. Call ahead to see if there is one vacant. Expect a few days wait for an opening. Someone will come around in the evening to collect your cash.

PILOTS

Due to the very complicated route through the reefs of the Devils Backbone as you go around to Harbour Island, it is imperative to take a pilot with you, at least the first few times. We suggest you contact one on VHF Channel 16. Pilots charge from $70 according to boat length.

MARINE SERVICES

Chris Electronics • 242-333-4638 • splashfm@hotmail.com • www.splashfmradio.com • Jane Forsythe can help arrange electronic problem solving. They also run Splash FM radio on 89.9 with local weather on the hour.
On Site Marine and Auto Service • 242-333-4382 • Fax: 242-333-4772 • VHF 16 • Charlie Pinder and Charlie Sands can help you with diesel engines, generators, autopilots, watermakers, winches, pumps, exhaust systems and marine plumbing.
Ronald's Service Centre • 242-333-4021 • Fax: 242-333-4594 • VHF 16 • Diving and marine supplies, fuel, Johnson outboards, apartments to rent on the beach and fish for sale.
Spanish Wells Marine and Hardware Store • 242-333-4122 • The best-stocked marine store in the Out Islands, on the waterfront. They will stay open late in an emergency. Mercury and Mariner engine repair, hauling facilities for boats up to 30 ft. Four air-conditioned apartments above the store, $60 per day and $400 per week.
R&B Boatyard • 242-333-4462 • Specializing in Micron 44 Original Formula and Petit-Hard Horizons bottom paints, with a marine railway taking 95-ft boats, up to 120 tons.

PORT DIRECTORY

Accommodations *Spanish Wells Harbourside Rentals*, 242-333-5022 • *Spanish Wells Marina and Hardware*, 242-333-4139. Efficiency apartments.
Airport There is no airport on Spanish Wells. Go to North Eleuthera by ferry to Genes Bay, then by taxi to the airport. For airport details, see under North Eleuthera.
Bakery *Kathy's Bakery* • 242-333-4405 • Wonderful fresh bread and baked goods.

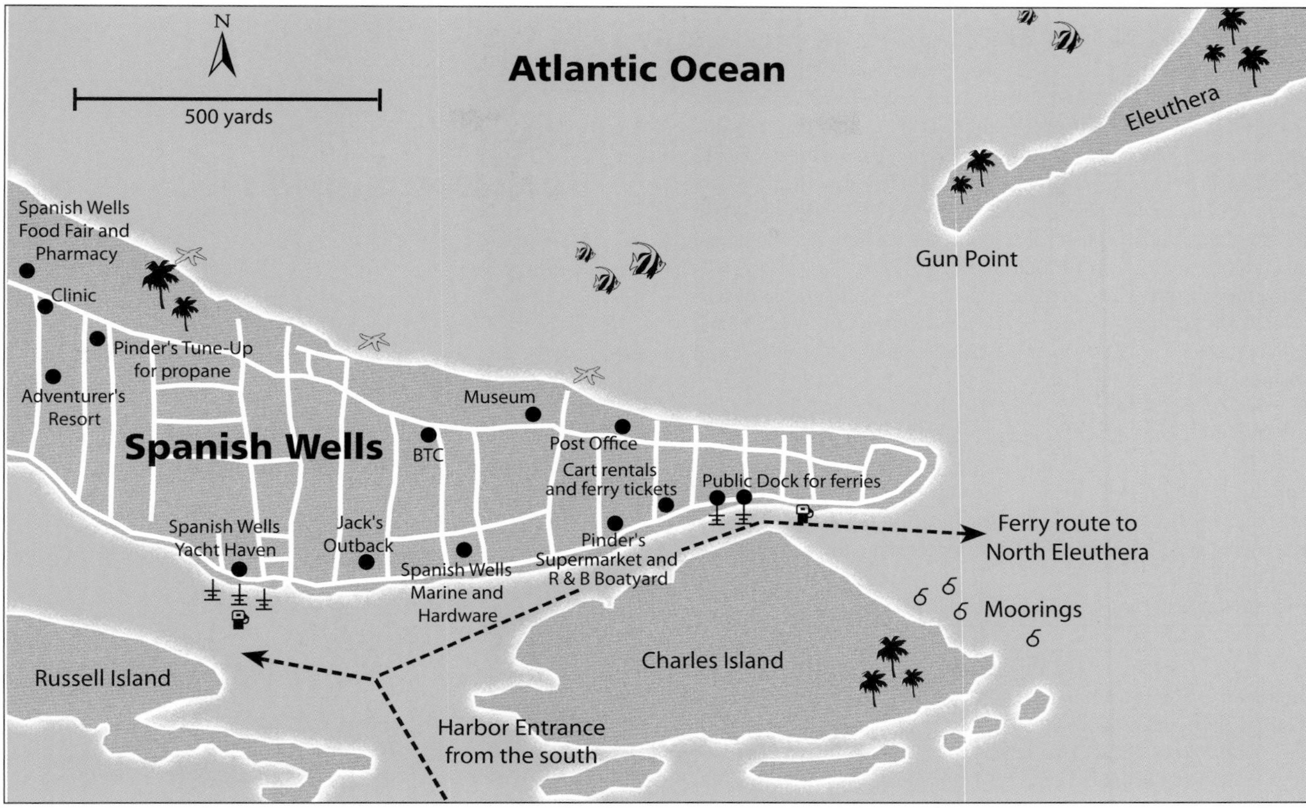

Bank *Royal Bank of Canada* • Open 9 to 3 Monday, 9 to 5 Friday, to 1 p.m. Tuesday, Wednesday, Thursday. Visa accepted for cash.

Boutiques *The Islander Shop* • 242-333-4104 • Clothing, swimsuits, souvenirs, T-shirts, notions, greeting cards, driftwood and charts. *Lynette's* • 242-333-2405 • Jewelry, watches, clothing, accessories. *Three Sisters Variety Store* • 242-333-4618 • Clothes, gifts, swimwear and T-shirts. *Ponderosa Shell Shop, Oliver's Straw Works - The Quilt Shop* • *Idy's Handmade Quilts* • *Sarah's Souvenirs & Straw Work* • *Borden's Shell Tings* • *Julie's Shell Crafts* • *Roddie's Wood Work* • *Theron's Hand Painted Plaques*.

Churches *Gospel Chapel, Methodist Church, People's Church*.

Cinema Opposite the Gap.

Computers *Computer Concepts* • 242-333-4507 • Opposite the *Generation Gap*. Sales, repairs, accessories and printing.

Customs • 242-333-4760.

Ferries • Government ferry to Genes Bay, North Eleuthera; water ferry taxis to North Eleuthera or Royal Island: *Knight Rider* and *Seabird*. Arrange water taxi and taxi trip to airport at *Pinder's Supermarket*. Fast *Ferries "Bo' Hengy" or "Seawind"* • 242-323-2166 • To Nassau and Harbour Island daily. At the government dock.

Hotel *Adventurers Resort* • 242-333-4883 • Fax: 242-333-5073 • Rebuilt on the site of the old Harbour Club at the west end of town. Within walking distance of the beach, this small hotel has nine rooms, four single apartments and three double apartments.

Jewelry *Robert's Jewelry*, 242-333-4102.

Laundromat In the *CW Grocery* building on Central Road.

Marine Repair and Supplies *On-Site Marine*, 242-333-4382. Marine engine, electrical, refrigeration and welding. • *Ronald's Marine*, 242-333-4021. Johnson/Evinrude dealer • *Spanish Wells Marine and Hardware*, 242-333-4122. Mercury/Mariner/Yamaha dealer • *Pinder's Tune Up*. Propane, welding, engine repair and parts.

Medical Clinic • 242-333-4064/5145 • General practice clinic, across the street from Food Fair. Open 9 a.m. to noon and 1 p.m. to 5 p.m. weekdays. There is a nurse full-time, and nurse on-call for after hour's emergencies. Dr. Mark Davies • 242-333-4909 • Dentist comes in once a week on Thursday. • Dr. Stephen Bailey • 242-333-4868/4869 • Medical doctor practices from home, with his own laboratory and EKG.

Mooring Balls *Jock Morgan*, 242-333-4695, VHF 16 "Bandit." Also answers to "Cinnabar."

Museum *Spanish Wells Museum* Next to the *Islander Shop* in a Spanish Wellsian house. Fascinating insight into the life and history of this island. Admission charge.

Nail Salon *Nails R Us*, 242-333-4817.

Pharmacy *Spanish Wells Food Fair and Pharmacy* George is the only pharmacist in Eleuthera, and the pharmacy in the store is open the same hours as the *Food Fair*, except for Wednesdays when he takes a day off. In emergencies, his home number is 242-333-5072.

Photography *Magic Photo*, 242-333-5300.

Pilots *A-1 Broadshad*, 242-333-4427, VHF 16 "A-1" • *Woody Perry*, 242-333-4433, VHF 16 "Little Woody" • *Jock Morgan*, 242-333-4695, VHF 16 "Bandit" • *Captain John Roberts*, 242-333-4171.

Police • 242-333-4030 or 919.

Post Office 242-333-5254. Open 9 a.m. to 4:30 p.m., next to the school.

Propane *Pinder's Tune Up* • 242-333-4262.

Provisions *CW's Groceries* • 242-333-4856. *Pinder's Supermarket* • 242-333-4048 • VHF 16 • On the waterfront. Well-stocked, with some fresh fruit and vegetables; free delivery. *Spanish Wells Food Fair and Pharmacy* • 242-333-4675 • VHF 16 - Open 8 a.m. to 5 p.m. daily, closed Wednesday afternoon and Sunday. Well-stocked with groceries, meats, fresh fruit and vegetables. Free delivery.

Radio Stations ZNS 1540 AM; 104.5 FM; 100.3 jamz FM.
Restaurants *Anchor Snack Bar*, 242-333-4023. On the harbor front. Snacks and entrees. $ • *Eagles Landing Restaurant*, 242-333-4955. Open for breakfast, lunch and dinner, with a drive thru. $ • *Jack's Outback* • 242-333-4219 • Open 9 a.m. to 10 p.m. on the waterfront. Breakfast, lunch and dinner. Jack and Sherry Pinder prepare home-cooked food in simple, friendly surroundings. They have fresh lobster in season. $ • *The Generation Gap*, 242-333-4464 • Open for breakfast, lunch and dinner with a counter that looks like an American diner and a seated dining room. Lots of loud music. $ • *Teen Planet*, 242-333-5551/3. Open for breakfast, lunch and dinner. $ • *Seafood Bandit* sells stone crabs in season • *Spanish Wells Marine and Hardware* sometimes has lobster • *Ronald's Service Centre* • 242-333-4021 • Fresh fish some days.
Taxi *Pinders Transportation and Taxi Service* • 242-333-4068 • Transport between the ferry dock and North Eleuthera Airport, or on to *Three Islands Harbour* for the Harbour Island ferry.
Telephone BTC 242-333-4053 • Telephone outside their office, at marinas and stores around the settlement.
Tours The lobster processing plant offers interesting tours of its facilities and operations.
Travel Agency Adventurer's Resort, 242-333-4882.

RENTALS

Boats *Ronald's Service Centre* • 242-333-4021
Golf Carts • 242-333-4890 • Abner Pinder's, opposite the *Fast Ferry Dock*. Two-seater carts from $40 per day, four-seater from $60. Linda and Rachel in the office also sell the Fast Ferry tickets to Nassau and Harbour Island.
Sea Life 34, Bahamas Ltd. • 242-333-4890

SPORTS & RECREATION

Diving *Manuel's Dive Station* • 242-333-4495 • Masks, fins, compressors, tanks, spears, hooks and wetsuits. There is no recreational dive facility on Spanish Wells.
Fishing Guides *A-1 Broadshad* • 242-333-4427, VHF 16 "A-1", *Woody Perry* • 242-333-4433, VHF 16 "Little Woody", Deep sea fishing with live bait, reef fishing, bone fishing, reef snorkeling trips and beach trips • *Jock Morgan* • 242-333-4695, VHF 16 "Bandit". *Captain John Roberts* • 242-333-4171 • Charters, piloting and deliveries.
Fitness *Eagles Landing Restaurant & Gym*, next to Food Fair, has an exercise room with equipment.
Surfing Sites Egg Island, Atlantic Side, sheltered reef break, best in SE winds and swell direction from the North, reef provides left and right hand breaks.

THINGS TO DO IN SPANISH WELLS

- Go to the museum; it is one of the best town museums in the Bahamas. Stop in at Cecile Dunnam's across the street for quilting supplies.
- Join in and help quilt or just chat with the ladies at the quilting bee held every afternoon opposite the museum.
- Take time to walk around Spanish Wells.
- Find out more about the lobster industry; Spanish Wells is a world leader in the lobster market.
- Ask a Spanish Wells pilot to take you around the Devils Backbone.
- Go snorkeling along the northern reef, anywhere from Spanish Wells to Egg Island in the west. Some of the best elk horn coral you will ever see is here.

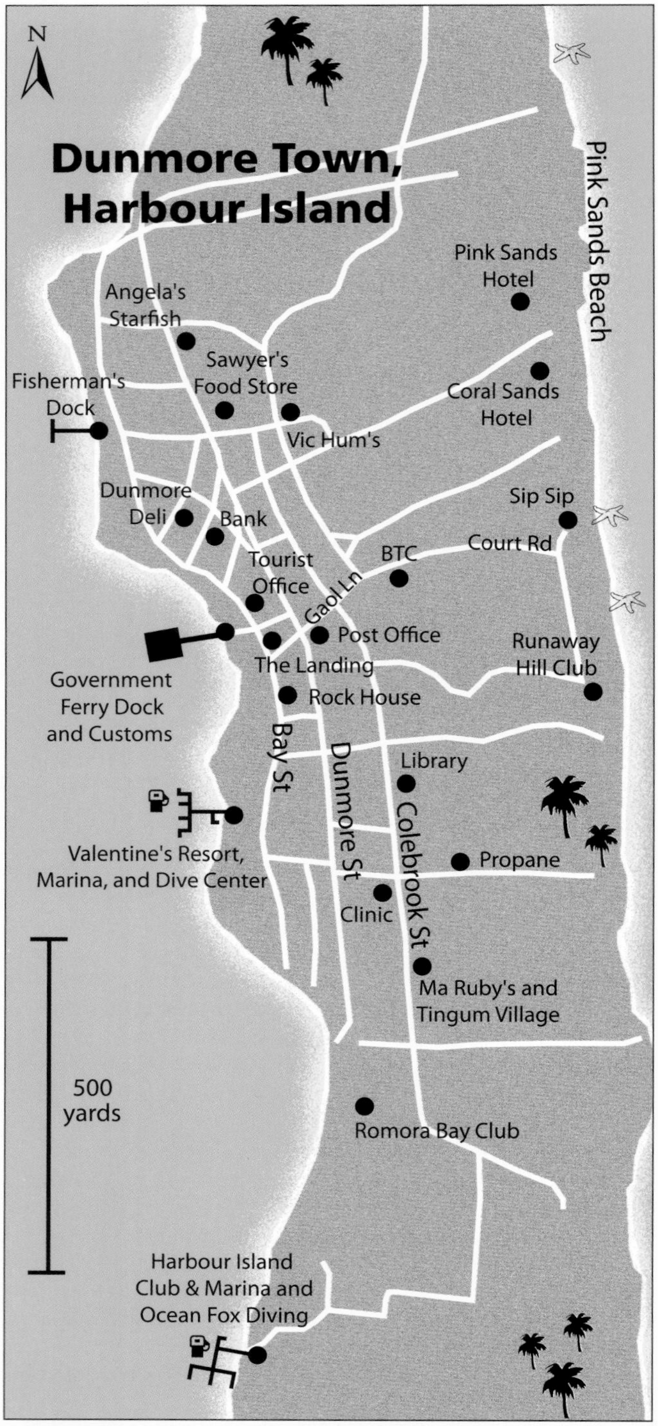

HARBOUR ISLAND DUNMORE TOWN

bank • customs & immigration • fuel • groceries • marinas • medical • police • post office • propane • restaurant • telephone • water

This fabled Bahamian hideaway is known affectionately as "Briland" to several generations of visitors who return each year to their pastel-painted cottages sprinkled like colored Easter eggs throughout the now well-populated island. The already chic image of Harbour Island has been recently polished by all the glossy magazines labeling it as the "new St Barths," while the emergence of the Rock House boutique hotel makes celebrity spotting a daily sport. There is still a wonderfully relaxed feeling here, despite the bumper-to-bumper golf carts during holiday periods on narrow flower-lined streets. Art galleries, restaurants, boutiques and straw work of Dunmore Town give way to the big hotels at the edge of the legendary blush pink sand beach, glowing in the dawn light. For more information, go to www.briland.com or www.myharbourisland.com. Harbour Island is a port of entry. The Customs office is in the administration building on the government pier. Marinas can arrange for Customs and Immigration to come to their facilities for clearance.

EMERGENCIES

Marine VHF 16
Medical *Clinic* or *doctor* • 242-333-2227/3073

MARINAS

VALENTINE'S RESORT AND MARINA
Tel: 242-333-2142 • Fax: 242-333-2135 • VHF 16 and 12
reservations@valentinesresort.com • www.valentinesresort.com
Slips 51. **Max LOA** 187 ft. **MLW at Dock** 12 ft. **Dockage** $3.00 per ft. per day. **Fuel** Dock open 7 a.m. to 11 p.m., daily. Diesel only. **Facilities & Services** Power $0.65 per kwHr, water $20 per day, cable television at slips, complimentary WiFi, ice, showers, restrooms, public telephone, coin-op washer and dryer, fluff and fold services available, propane tanks refilled nearby, mechanic available. Marine store open 8 a.m. to 5 p.m. daily except Sunday. Freshwater pool in the Resort. On-site is Valentine's Dive Center (242-333-2080, VHF 16, dive@valentinesdive.com) on site. Deep sea fishing charters, kayak rentals, bonefishing guides available. **Restaurant and Bar** The Boat House, breakfast 7 a.m. to 10 a.m.; lunch 11 a.m. to 3 p.m.; dinner 6 p.m. to 10 p.m. Bar open 10 a.m. 'til the last person standing. **Credit Cards** AMEX, Visa and MasterCard; Travelers Checks and personal checks with ID. Pets welcome at the marina on a leash.

HARBOUR ISLAND CLUB AND MARINA
Tel: 242-333-2427 • Fax: 242-333-3040 • 800-492-7909 • VHF 16
dockmaster@harbourislandmarina.com •
www.harbourislandmarina.com
Slips 35-40. **Max LOA** Up to 200 ft. with 35-ft. beam in slips. **MLW at Dock** 8 to 10 ft. **Dockage** $3.00 per ft. per day. **Fuel** Dock open 8 a.m. to 6 p.m. daily, diesel and gasoline. **Facilities and Services** Shore power, 30 to 100 amps, single and 3 phase at every slip, $0.65 per kwHr. City water $0.20 per gallon, cable television, WiFi $15/day, fluff and fold laundry service, good restrooms and showers, telephone. Pool overlooking the marina. Diving and private boat charters with *Ocean Fox Diving* • 242-333-2323 • www.oceanfox.com. **Restaurant** Hammerhead's open from 11 a.m. to 10 p.m. daily, with the same menu served all day. Happy hour 5 to 7 p.m. A lovely terrace to sit out and enjoy the sunset. $$ **Credit Cards** Visa, MasterCard with 5% surcharge.

ROMORA BAY CLUB & RESORT
Tel: 242-333-2325 • 800-688-0425 • Fax: 242-333-2500
marina@romorabay.com • www.romorabay.com
Slips 40. **Max LOA** 150 ft.; minimum 30 ft. **MLW at Dock** 10 ft. **Dockage** $3.00 per ft. per day. **Facilities and Services** Shore power, $40 per day. Each slip is equipped with individually metered electric service, pump out, fresh water, telephone, high-speed internet capability and cable television. Gourmet coffee shop serving Starbuck's Coffee while cruisers socialize and peruse USA Today every morning. Casual waterfront bar and grille (stunning sunsets, free of charge). Elegant, fine dining in haute cuisine restaurant, VUE. A complete water sports facility, lower pool (resident members have access to the private upper pool), fitness and spa treatment facilities, beach facility with barbecue grill, member concierge service and on board dining. Underwater habitat for marine life and visitor viewing. Tracing dye used to ensure harbor protection from illegal flushing. Own your own income-producing dock; they will rent it for you. **Accommodations** Villas and resort hotel on six acres.

PORT DIRECTORY

Airport See details under *North Eleuthera Airport*. Water taxi ferry from the town dock across to Three Islands, then taxi to the airport.
Art Galleries specializing in Bahamian and Caribbean art. *Princess Street Gallery* • 242-333 2788 • *Iris Lewis*, 242-333-2839 • *Briland Brush Strokes*, 242-333-3069.
ATM & Bank *Royal Bank of Canada* • 242-333-2250 • On southeast corner of Dunmore and Clarence Streets, one block down. Open weekdays 9:30 a.m. to 3 p.m., Friday to 4:30 p.m.
Bakery *Arthur's Bakery* • 242-333-2285 • Open 8 a.m. to 2 p.m.; closed Sunday. Wonderful fresh bread, European dessert pies and temptations, breakfasts and lunches served in their bakery cafe. • *Sybil's Bakery*, 242-333-3011, Fresh bread and good stuff from local folks.
Bars *Charlie's Bar* • *Daddy D's* • *George's Bar* • *Gusty's Bar* • *Seagrapes Club*, this bar on Colebrook St. is open from 7 p.m. Wednesday through Saturday for music, dancing, snacks, cocktails, beer and wine. Home of "The Funk Gang" band with live music • *South Bar Club* • *Vic Hum's*, Bahamian license plates cover the yellow walls of this bar on Barracks St. where owner Humphrey Percentie "Shabby" will keep you entertained with local stories. These and all the marina bars are much enjoyed by cruisers, tourists and residents.
Beauty Salons and Nails *Creative Fingers*, 242-333-2907 • *Toy'a Beauty Spot*, 242-333-2243 • *Clip & Curl*, 242-333-2712 • *Personal Touch*, 242-333-3233 • *Bay View Concepts*, 242-333-2846 • *Fabulous Design*, 242-333-3232 • *The Island Spa*, 242-333-3326.
Boutiques *Miss Mae's*, 242-333-2003 • *Sand Dollar*, 242-333-2839 • *Valentine's Ship Store*, 242-333-2142 • *Dilly Dally*, 242-333-3109 • *Blue Rooster*, 242-333-2240 • *The Landing Boutique*, 242-333-2707 • *Briland Androsia*, 242-333-2342 • *Daniel's Den*, 242-333-2243 • *Dorris' Dry Goods*, 242-333-2372 • *Lemmie's Secret*, 242-333-3379 • *Bahamian Shells & Tings*, 242-333-2839 • *William's Men and Boy's Shoes*, 242-333-2306 • *Top of the Line*, 242-333-3641.
Churches *Blessed Sacrament Catholic Church, Methodist Church* (built in 1843, the largest Out Island church), *St Johns' Anglican Episcopal Church* (built in 1768: the oldest building on Harbour Island and the oldest church in the Bahamas).
Courier *DHL* • 242-333-2372 • *At Doris's Dry Goods*.
Ferries *"Bo Hengy" or "Seawind"* • 242-323-2166 • *Fast Ferry* to Nassau. *Major's Rental and Taxi* service • 242-333-2043 or 242-359-7867 • Wayne Major provides taxis and golf carts, as well as his boat ferry.
Hardware *Chacara Lumber* • 242-333-2176 • *Thompson's Plumbing*, 242-333-2335 • Carlette's Variety Store, 242-333-3231.
Hotels & Lodging *Coral Sands Hotel* • 242-333-2350 • Fax: 242-333-2368 • 39 rooms overlooking the pink sand beach, 2 restaurants.

Dunmore Beach Club • 242-333-2200 • Fax: 242-333-2429 • 12 cottages.
The Landing • 242-333-2707 • Fax: 242-333-2650 • info@harbourislandlanding.com • www.harbourislandlanding.com • Harbor or garden view rooms.
Pink Sands Hotel • 242-333-2030 • www.pinksandsresort.com • Ocean-view cottages.
Rock House • 242-333-2053 • reservations@rockhousebahamas.com • Pool or garden view rooms overlooking the bay. All rooms have private cabanas poolside. Private gym. No children under 12.
Romora Bay Club • 242-333-2325, 800-688-0425 • Fax: 242-333-2500 • www.romorabay.com • 30 uniquely decorated rooms, with bay views and a fine French restaurant. Weddings a specialty.
Runaway Hill Club • 242-333-2150 • Fax:242-333-2420 • www.spscaribnet.com • 10 rooms and villas on the edge of the pink sand beach.
Tingum Village Hotel • 242-333-2161 • On Colebrook Street. Run by Ma Ruby, with her own restaurant and reasonable room rates.

Jewelry *John Bull Shoppe*, 242-333-2950 • *Valentine's Ship's Store*, 242-333-2142 • *Dilly Dally*, 242-333-3109.

Laundry *Seaside Laundromat* On Bay Street.

Liquor *Bayside Liquor Store* • VHF 16 • On Bay Street. • *Briland Booze Liquors* Next to the *Dunmore Deli*, wines, beers, cigars. Free delivery to boats. • *Bristol Wine & Spirits*, 242-333-2645 • *Burns Wholesale Liquors*, 242-333-2373 • *Cash's Liquor Store*, 242-333-2084 • *Grants Liquor Store*, 242-333-2531.

Medical *Government Clinic* • 242-333-2227/2225/3073 • On Colebrook and South Streets, open 9:30 a.m. to 5 p.m. weekdays, with a doctor and two registered nurses.

Pharmacy *Harbour Pharmacy* • 242-333-2174 • Closed Wednesday afternoons and Sundays. • *Briland Pharmacy*, 242-333-3427.

Photography *Dilly Dally*, 242-333-3109 • *Briland Photo*, 242-333-3496.

Police • 242-333-3111 • In the same building as the post office.

Post Office • 242-333-2315 • On Gaol Street, Monday through Friday 9:30 a.m. to 4:30 p.m

Propane *Eleuthera Petroleum* • 242-388-2726 • Opposite *Sea Grapes* on Colbrook St.

Provisions *Dunmore Deli* • 242-333-2644 • Stock your boat with special treats, which can be delivered to you at the marinas. *Johnson's Grocery* • 242-333-2279 • shop@johnsonsgrocery.com • On Dunmore St., useful and central with a phone outside. Open 8 a.m. to 7 p.m. weekdays, 8 a.m. to 1 p.m. Sunday. Will deliver to boats; email a list to them ahead of arrival. *Patricia's* • 242-333-2289 • Fresh fruits and vegetables, as well as homemade jams, bread, island spices and hot sauce. On Pitt St. No credit cards. *Percenties* • 242-333-2195 • On Dunmore St. Fresh vegetables and a barber shop. Closed Sunday. *Piggly Wiggly*, 242-333-2120 and *Tip Top Convenience Store*, 242-333-2251. Open 8 a.m. to 1 p.m. and 3 a.m. to 5 p.m. weekdays. *Pineapple Fruit 'n Veg* • 242-333-2454. *Sawyer's Food Store* • 242-333-2358 • Good selection of groceries, boat provisions, fresh meat, frozen foods and vegetables; they will deliver to your boat. On Dunmore and Duke Streets, open 8 a.m. to 7 p.m. daily, to 11 a.m. Sundays.

Restaurants With so many to choose from, Harbour Island is an exciting gastronomic experience. All the hotels have good restaurants, which will welcome you for breakfast, lunch and dinner (usually with reservations). Menus range from conch fritters to international gourmet dining. A few restaurant suggestions include:
Angela's Starfish Restaurant • 242-333-2253 • Grant St., at the north end of Dunmore St. Open 8:30 a.m. to 10 p.m. The menu is written up on a blackboard and you order by writing down what you would like to eat. No credit cards. Local favorite. $-$$
Acquapazza Wine Bar & Ristorante, 242-333-3240, lunch and dinner, open 11 a.m. to 5 p.m. for lunch, 5 p.m. to 10 for dinner. Credit cards accepted. $-$$$
Avery's Takeaway, 242-333-3126, Breakfast, lunch and dinner. Credit cards accepted. $
Baretta's Restaurant, 242-333-2361, Breakfast, lunch and dinner. Credit cards accepted. $-$$
Bayside Restaurant, 242-333-2174, Breakfast, lunch and dinner. No credit cards. $-$$
Brian's Grill & Jerk, 242-333-3051, Dinner. No credit cards. $
Coral Sands, The Terrace Restaurant, 242-333-2350. Lunch can be crowded with visitors from Nassau coming over for the day on the Fast Ferry. Dinner overlooking the ocean. Credit cards accepted. $$$
Debbie's Takeaway, 242-333-2626, scrumptious breakfast. No credit cards. $
Dunmore Beach Club, 242-333-2200, Breakfast, lunch and dinner. Credit cards accepted. $-$$
Dunmore Deli, 242-333-2646. Serves light breakfasts and lunches at small tables. Tasty breakfast and lunch boxes. No credit cards. $$
Elsie's Takeaway, 242-333-319, Breakfast lunch and dinner. Good, local, home-cooked food. No credit cards. $
Harbour Lounge Restaurant and Bar, 242-333-2031. On Bay St. Lunch and dinner daily (except for Sunday lunch and all day Monday). Excellent presentation of fresh meats and seafood, distinctive home-made soups and drinks. Served on their cool, breezy veranda. $$-$$$$
Harry O's Takeaway, Breakfast, lunch and dinner. Good, local, home-cooked food. No credit cards. $-$$
Linc's Takeaway, 242-333-3286. Lunch. No credit cards. $
Ma Ruby's at the Tingum Village Hotel, 242-333-2161. Good value Bahamian food in a cheerful setting, famous for *Jimmy Buffet's "Cheeseburgers in Paradise."* Open from 8 a.m. Credit cards accepted. $
Pink Sands, 242-333-2030. Lunch served daily at the *Blue Bar on the Ocean*. Dinner by reservation at *The Garden Restaurant*. Credit cards accepted. $$$
Rock House, 242-333-2053. Breakfast, lunch and dinner. Chic and elegant, good for celebrity spotting. Terrace dining overlooking the harbor, or casual ambience in the courtyard with open grills. Reservations required for dinner. Credit cards accepted. $$$
Romora Bay Club, 242-333-2325. Breakfast, lunch and dinner. Starbucks coffee for breakfast on the waterfront. Lunch at the dockside bar and grille. Dinner at the haute cuisine, elegant restaurant, VUE, reservations suggested. Credit cards accepted. $-$$$$
Runaway Hill Club, 242-333-2150. Open to the public for dinner only, by reservation, at 8 p.m. Jackets required. Credit cards accepted. $$$$
Seaview Takeaway, 242-333-2542. Open daily on Bay St. for breakfast, lunch and dinner from 7:30 a.m. No credit cards. $
Sip Sip, 242-333-3316. Overlooking North Beach at the end of Court Road, which is a continuation of Gaol Lane. Open for lunch daily 11 to 3, except Tuesdays; popular with winter residents and their houseguests. Light, imaginative salads, soups and desserts with interesting

daily specials. Attractive decor. Bar open until late, evening parties catered on request. Credit cards accepted. $$

The Harbour Lounge, 242-333-2031. Open for lunch and dinner. Credit cards accepted. $$

The Landing, 242-333-2707. On Bay St. greeting you as you step off the Government Dock. A traditional 1800s house and garden, beautifully restored. Open daily, except Wednesdays, for breakfast if they have hotel guests, dinner and Sunday brunch. Dine in their elegantly understated dining room or in the charming courtyard garden with an enthusiastic staff running the hotel and the restaurant. Superb food, well worth the wait and fantastic sunsets from the verandas. Call ahead for reservations. Credit cards accepted. $$$$

Tingum Village, 242-333-2161. Breakfast, lunch and dinner. Credit cards accepted. $-$$$

Tropic Hut Restaurant and Ice Cream Parlour, 242-333-3700. Lunch and dinner. No credit cards. $

Valentine's Waterfront Restaurant & Bar, 242-333-2141. Open for breakfast, lunch and dinner. Credit cards accepted. $$-$$$

Shopping *Brilands Androsian Boutique* • 242-333-2342 • Batiks, souvenirs, T-shirts from Andros. *Dilly Dally* • 242-333-3109 • Wide variety of Bahamian-made gifts and books. *Miss Mae's* Beautiful clothes and interesting accessories. *The Landings Boutique* Fine cottons and silks from the Orient and Liberty children's clothes. *Straw Market* Colorful local stalls selling shells and straw work along the waterfront on Bay St.

Taxis *Neville Major Taxi & Car Rental*, 242-333-2361 • *Reggie Major Taxi*, 242-333-2166.

Telephones At the BTC office on the corner of Gaol Lane and Colebrook St. Open weekdays 9 to 4:30. Also on the government dock, at the marinas and outside *Johnson's Grocery* on Dunmore Street.

Tourist Office • 242-322-2621, www.harbourisland.bahamas.com • www.bahamas.com • Above the *Sugar Mill* on Bay St.

Travel Agency *TraverusTravel*, 242-333-3604.

Water Taxis Call on VHF 16. Fares $4 to $8 (some expect a $20 tip; ask beforehand, so they don't ask you for it after the trip).

SPORTS & RECREATION

Beaches The famous blush pink sand beach stretches for three glorious miles along the eastern side of the island. This is a perfect beach for children, well-protected by the reef with some good snorkeling within an easy swim. Although the main hotels border the beach, there is public access. There is also good snorkeling on the shallow side of Jacobs Island and Mann Island, to the north of Harbour Island.

Bonefishing *Patrick Roberts*, 242-333-2213 • *Bone Fish Stuart*, 242-333-2072 • *Herman Higgs*, 242-333-2021/2372 • *Bonefish Jermaine*, 242-464-0760.

Dive Operators *Ocean Fox Diving* • 242-333-2323 • www.oceanfox.com • Rental equipment, PADI SCUBA diving training, expeditions to Current Cut, Cape Eleuthera Wall, and more. Two-tank dives. Deep sea fishing in *Top Cat* with *Jeff Fox*. • *Valentine's Dive Center* • 242-333-2080 • VHF 16 • dive@valentinesdive.com • www.valentinesdive.com • PADI instruction courses, drift dives, underwater scooters, scuba-resort courses and bubble maker classes for kids 8 to 10 years. Two-tank scuba dives. Deep sea fishing charters. Kayak rentals. • *Romora Bay Dive Shop*, 242-333-2325, complete on-site dive operation with dives trips to Blue Holes, Caves, Reefs and Walls. Staff of four, two are instructors that have been in business for more than 20 years. PADI. One and two tank dives.

Dive Sites *Blue Holes:* Grouper Hole, Blow Hole, Tarpon Hole and White Hole • *Caves:* The Cave/Miller's Reef • *Reefs:* Glass Window Bridge, The Arch (Man Island), Cistern Rock, The Devils Backbone, Loreto Reef, Bridge Point, Bamboo Point, Split Reef, The Cave/Millers Reef, Pink House Reef, Tunnel Reef • *Walls:* Current Cut Dive, Plateau, Three Trees, Wrecks, The Cage & Hole in the Wall, Carnavon Wreck, Potato & Onion, Cienfuegos Wreck.

Fishing Guides *Devon Stuart*, 242-422-9343 • *Stuart Cleare*, 242-333-2072 • *Valentine's Deep Sea Charters*, 242-333-2080 • *Joe Cleare*, 242-333-2663 • *Sterling's Fishing Guide*, 242-470-8340.

Horseback Riding *Robert Davis*, 242-333-2337.

Kayaking/Snorkeling *Michael's Cycles*, 242-333-2384 • *Lil Shan's Watersports*, 242-422-9343 • *Valentine's Dive Center*, 242-333-2080.

Regattas *North Eleuthera Sailing Regatta* In October, with 5 days of racing locally built sailing sloops from all over the Bahamas between Harbour Island and Three Island Bay on North Eleuthera.

Surfing Sites On the southern side of the Harbour Mouth cut on the Atlantic, Whale Point Cut is an exposed point break with reliable surf. It is best in SW winds and a swell direction from the N-NE.

THINGS TO DO IN HARBOUR ISLAND

- Walk through the town and take photographs of some of the prettiest streets and houses in the Bahamas. Browse and shop the galleries and boutiques.
- Go to the fabled pink beach to walk or swim. Enjoy a leisurely lunch at Sip Sip or one of the hotels.
- Take a ferry to North Eleuthera. Visit Preachers Cave on the north coast. While you are there, why not make a day of it and head south through Upper and Lower Bogue to see the natural wonder of the Glass Window; drive down to Governors Harbour and explore the attractive, historic town.
- Take advantage of the great dive sites around the island, or try an exhilarating drift dive through Current Cut.
- Ask one of the Spanish Wells pilots to come with you on your boat to teach you the secrets of the Devils Backbone passage as you work your way around to Spanish Wells.
- Enjoy a spectacular sunset drink at one of the waterfront restaurants and bars, and do a bit of celebrity spotting while deciding where to go for dinner.

RENTALS

Golf carts Readily available in town, except at peak holiday times, for around $50 a day.

Johnson's Rentals • 242-333-2376 • johnsonrentals@batelnet.bs.com

Michael's Cycles • 242-333-2384 • 242-464-0994 • VHF 16 • Bicycles and motorbikes, boat rentals, kayaks, golf carts and rooms to rent.

Kayaks *Valentine's Dive Centre* • 242-333-2080 • $65 per day.

ELEUTHERA ISLAND

Mention Eleuthera and most people think of Harbour Island and pink sand. Cruisers think of the dreaded Devils Backbone that claimed its first victims in 1647 - the Eleutheran adventurers who crawled up the beach and took refuge in the very same Preachers Cave that you can tour today. The large cave, site of the Bahamas first Christian service, still has large boulder shaped like a pulpit standing at the end of the cave.

Because of early settlement, the island is rich in history. But, it is also the home to another kind of settler, those whose families, some extremely wealthy, bought land here back in the 1930s and have been returning each year since. Cruise Eleuthera, and you too will think of pink beaches, but more likely you will think of Current Cut that sucks you through like a straw sucks soda pop, then of pineapples and oranges, mangoes and bananas, blue holes and limestone caves, grey sharks and eagle rays, brown groupers and lane snappers, silos and 747s.

Northern, central and southern Eleuthera, may be less frequently visited by tourists than Harbour Island, but they offer the same historic charm of the neighboring islands plus evidence of more modern attempts at industrialized agriculture and tourist development in ensuing years. The length of Eleuthera Island, and the relatively large distances between safe harbors and good anchorages along its western shores, make the land summary a long story. Therefore, we have taken it in one sweep, as if you were driving from north to south.

NORTHERN ELEUTHERA ISLAND

airport • bank • customs & immigration • groceries • medical • police • post office • restaurant • telephone • water

Arriving on northern Eleuthera Island from Spanish Wells, the ferry lands at Genes Bay and only a telephone and the Pinders' taxis await you. The Harbour Island Ferry lands at Three Islands ferry dock with the Pineapple Cafe and a telephone to greet you. Alternatively, you may have flown into North Eleuthera Airport, where a small community of cafes and gift shops welcome you. At the main airport crossroad, you will find the North Eleuthera Service Station. It is a good place to pick up gas if you need it (except on Sundays). There is also a branch of Destinations Travel Agents and a ScotiaBank. Lower Bogue is a thriving community that hosts a very popular annual homecoming. There is a medical clinic in Lower Bogue, as well as a liquor store, laundry, bookstore and beauty salon at Bonnie's Plaza. Get ice at Johnson's grocery store. There is a Post Office in Upper Bogue. To the southwest is the settlement of The Current, close to Current Cut, which you will undoubtedly pass on your boat. It is well worth stopping if you have the time. It is a small, neat settlement with colorful bougainvillea dripping from well-maintained homes. The Current has a glorious beach. Bahamas Sealink Ferries leave The Current on Fridays and Sundays at 8:30 p.m. for the 2.5-hour trip to Nassau from the government dock. The ferries leave Nassau at 5 p.m. for The Current. As you make your way south to Gregory Town and on to Hatchet Bay, stop for a moment to look at the Glass Window. This narrow bridge is the only land link between the north end of this very long, thin island and the southern two thirds of the island. In high seas, the Atlantic waves come crashing through the rocky cliffs under the road necessitating frequent repair. This does not deter the hundreds of bicycle riders who come each year to participate in the Annual Ride for Hope. Riders of all ages and skill levels raise money to support cancer treatment in the Bahamas. So far, the riders have raised over $1 million dollars pedaling distances from six to 100 miles along the beautiful North Eleuthera countryside.

Airlines *Bahamasair*, 800-222-4262 • *Twin Air*, 954-359-8266. *Continental Connections*, 800-992-8532 • *LeeAir*, 242-334-2829 • *Pineapple Air*, 242-377-0140 • *Yellow Air Taxi*, 888YELLOW4 • *Southern Air*, 242-332-3270 • *Major's Air Services*, 242-332-2742.
Airport *North Eleuthera Airport* • 242-335-1241 • With its 4,500-ft. runway, this airport serves the northern part of Eleuthera, Harbour Island and Spanish Wells. Connecting ferries and taxis from both islands are reliable and efficient.
Bank *Scotia Bank*, 242-335-1400. Open 9:30 a.m. to 3 p.m. weekdays; to 4:30 on Fridays. No ATM.
Car Rental Some car rentals do not accept credit cards. *Burch Car Rental* • 242-333-2358 • At the Bluff. *Eleuthera Island Car Rental* • 242-333-1353, 242-335-1582 • Cars, vans and jeeps, MasterCard and Visa. *Shavago Johnson* • 242-335-1077 • will meet you at the Three Islands ferry dock with a car. *J & R Rentals* in Upper Bogue • 242-335-1145 and 242-464-0871 • email • j.r.ward@coralwave.com. *Cash's Taxi & Car Rental* • Lower Bogue, 242-335-1096.

GREGORY TOWN

The brightly painted houses, churches and school surrounding Gregory Town's tiny harbor, Pittman Cove (which is best suited to dinghies), plays host to the annual Eleuthera Pineapple Festival, a cheerful Labor Day event in June that is not to be missed. There is a concrete jetty inside the harbor for dinghy tie-ups, but enter in calm weather only. North of town, you can find some shelter in the bights south of the cove, but absolutely no protection in winds from anywhere out of the south through west. In town, you will find ice, water, groceries, a laundry, liquor store, public telephones and some cool surfer gear.

Gregory Town

Accommodations The Cove Eleuthera, Tel: 242-335-5142, 800-552-5960, Fax: 242-335-5338, Email: george@thecoveeleuthera.com • www.thecoveeleuthera.com • Twenty-six room, 28-acre beachfront resort between Hatchet Bay and Gregory Town. Tennis, kayaking, bicycles, swimming pool, hammocks and their own restaurant. Breakfast, lunch and dinner. $$ Boaters are welcome to anchor off their beach and come up to the hotel for lunch. Four complimentary moorings are available for cruisers: two with 4,800 lb. anchors, two with 2,400 lb. anchors. *Cambridge Villas*, Tel: 242-335-5080, Fax: 242-335-5308. Restaurant serves breakfast, lunch and dinner. A Cousteau Snorkeling Adventure facility.
Bakery *Thompson's Bakery* • 242-335-5053.
Boutiques *Island Made*, 242-335-5369 • *Rebecca's Gift Shop*, 242-335-5436.
Churches *Anglican, Catholic, Church of God, Methodist.*
Clinic • 242-335-5108 • The doctor from Governors Harbour visits on Tuesdays; in addition, the nurse is there on Thursday and Friday.
Gifts *El Caracol* • 242-355-5369 • Pamela Thompson stocks a wide selection of driftwood paintings, Androsia clothing, handcrafted dolls, native straw work, including lots of her own work, as well as books and post cards.
Groceries *Thompson Brothers Supermarket* • 242-335-5009 • Fresh produce, beef, poultry, canned foods, dairy. • Monica's Dis n Dat, 242-335-5664.
Jewelry *Island Made*, 242-335-5369.
Laundromat *Jay's Laundromat* • *Elvina's Restaurant*, 242-335-5032.
Liquor *Mr. Bones*, 242-335-5489.
Police 242-335-5322.
Restaurants *Elvina's Bar & Restaurant*, 242-335-5032, Breakfast, lunch and dinner. Popular with the surfers. Live music on the weekends. Lenny Kravitz often jams with the band. $ • *Cambridge*

Restaurant & Lounge, 242-335-5080. At Cambridge Villas. Breakfast, lunch and dinner. $$ • *Surfer's Beach Manor Restaurant & Bar*, 242-335-5300, Breakfast, lunch and dinner. Accepts credit cards. $-$$ • *Cush's Place*, 242-335-5301. Causal spot for lunch or dinner. $-$$.

HATCHET BAY

"Home of the Country's Safest Harbour," Hatchet Bay is steeped in history (see What's There?), but is not really the safest of harbors in which to anchor. Yes, you can ride out a frontal passage in here, but the best of holding is over heavy grass and a debris field. Fortunately, Marine Services of Eleuthera offers mooring balls, but they fill up fast. There is good dinghy tie-up off finger piers at the government dock (lock it up!), and groceries, hardware, ice, laundry service, a clinic, a post office and UPS delivery at the dock (ask at the hardware store if you need a part). There are trash bins for your garbage and a big park where the Bay Festival is held in August.

Hatchet Bay

Accommodations *The Rainbow Inn*, 242-335-0294 (also fax), 800-688-0047, www.rainbowinn.com. Attractive cottages in a garden setting, 2.5 miles from Hatchet Bay overlooking Rainbow Point with tennis court, bicycles, salt-water pool and a good restaurant that is open daily except Sundays and Mondays in the summer and Sundays in the winter. $$ Rooms from $140 per night, villas for 6 people $200 per night. 10% hotel tax, no additional service charges. A Cousteau Snorkeling Adventure facility.

Boutiques *Constance's Fashion Den*, 242-335-0531.

Churches *Baptist, Catholic, Methodist.*

Clinic • 242-335-0091, in government building.

Hardware *Bethel's Big Rock General Store. Triple TLC.*

Mooring Balls *Marine Services of Eleuthera*, 242-335-0186, VHF "Hatchet Bay Marina". Email: pbell@batel.net. Ten mooring balls on a first-come, first-served basis. Tie-ups with electric and water along the long concrete dock. Use several fenders; the wall is rough. Fax and Email services.

Police 242-335-0086.

Post Office In Alice Town, open Tuesday and Friday.

Provisions *Sawyer's Grocery Store* • 242-335-0417 • Groceries, frozen foods, meats, fresh vegetables. *Big Rock General Store* • 242-335-6008 • At James Cistern, owned and operated by Mr. Bernard Bethel, with a liquor store next door. Open daily 7:30 a.m. to 7:30 p.m. except Sundays • Fresh produce at the packing warehouse.

Restaurants *Rainbow Inn*, 242-335-0294, 2.5 miles from Hatchet Bay. Breakfast, lunch and dinner in gorgeous setting overlooking Rainbow Point. $$ • Front Porch Delights, 242-335-0727. Casual dining for breakfast and lunch. $

Surfing Sites East on Ocean Boulevard about two miles south of Gregory Town on the Atlantic side, *Surfers Beach* is an exposed beach and reef break with reliable surf. Best in wind from the S-SW and swell angle from the NE. Left reef break is best, but there is a right reef, too. Home of the "Big Wave Surf Classic Pro Am." • South of Surfers Beach, on the Atlantic side, *Ledges* is an exposed point break that peels to the left. It is best in S-SW winds with a swell from the N • On Tarpum Bay, directly across from Ledges, *The Dump* is a sheltered break point with reliable surf from winds wells and distant groundswells. Best in winds from the N and swell direction from the SE. • Just north of James Point, on the Atlantic side, *Hidden Beach* is an exposed reef break, best in S wind and swell direction from the N. • South of James Point, on the Atlantic side, *James Point* is an exposed left and right breaking reef. It is best in SW winds with swell direction from the N. All surfing sites are best at mid tide.

Taxi *Hilton Johnson* • 242-335-6241 • At James Cistern. He may be able to help with a rental car too, and accepts Visa and MasterCard.

Telephone BTC Open 9 a.m. to 4:30 p.m., Monday through Friday.

EMERGENCIES

Marine • VHF 16

Medical *Clinic* • 242-335-0071 • VHF Rescue 3 • Open 9 to 3:30 p.m. daily. Or call 242-335-0341 or 242-335-0521 for one of the nurses. Closed weekends except for emergencies.

GOVERNORS HARBOUR

airport • bank • customs & immigration • groceries • medical • moorings • police • post office • propane • restaurant • telephone • water

One of the most attractive, long-established communities in the Bahamas, Governors Harbour has great charm. The holding is not particularly good in the harbor, but there may be some government moorings available on a first-come, first-served basis (inquire at Port Authority office). The best beach is on the Atlantic Ocean side, up and over the hill through town where the French Leave Resort is being built to replace the old Club Med. Well-stocked grocery stores make this a good place to provision, as well as being an interesting place to visit, with everything within easy walking distance. Customs and Immigration are on the government dock.

MARINAS

FRENCH LEAVE MARINA

Tel: 242-332-3616 • info@frenchleaveresort.com • www.frenchleaveresort.com

This new facility is now open in Governors Harbour, capable of hosting megayachts to 200 feet. This "boutique" resort is aiming to provide both a luxury resort and maintain a Bahamian atmosphere. **Slips** 2. **Max LOA** 200 ft.: minimum 40 ft. **MLW at Dock** 8 ft. **Dockage** $3.00 per ft. per day. August 16 through November 16, $4.00 per ft. per day November 16 through August 15. **Facilities and Services** Power $0.65 per KwHr (single and three phase power under construction at press time 2010), water $0.20 per gallon. Tie-up assistance, daily trash pick-up, laundry and dry cleaning, transportation and rental cars available, close to beach.

PORT DIRECTORY

Accommodations *The Buccaneer Club*, Tel: 242-332-2000/800-688-4752, Fax: 242-332-2888. A converted Bahamian farmhouse perched on a hill above Governors Harbour. Restaurant serves breakfast, lunch and dinner. $-$$ • *Cocodimama Resort and Restaurant*, 242-332-3150. Restaurant serves breakfast, lunch and dinner. Accepts credit cards. $-$$ • *The Duck Inn*, Tel: 242-332-2608/800-688-4752, Fax: 242-332-2160, duckin@batelnet.com • Cottages • *Laughing Bird Apartments*, Tel: 242-332-2012/800-688-4752, Fax: 242-332-2358, ddavies@batelnet.bs • Beachfront, garden efficiency apartments overlooking the beach • *Orchid Cottage*, www.discover-eleuthera-bahamas.com • Secluded, two-bedroom cottage on beautiful Banana Beach.

Airlines *Bahamasair* • 242-332-2648 • Twice-daily flights to Nassau. *Twin Air* • 242-335-6079 • To Fort Lauderdale Monday, Wednesday, Friday, Saturday, Sunday. *Southern Air* • 242-332-3270 • Fly three times daily to Nassau.

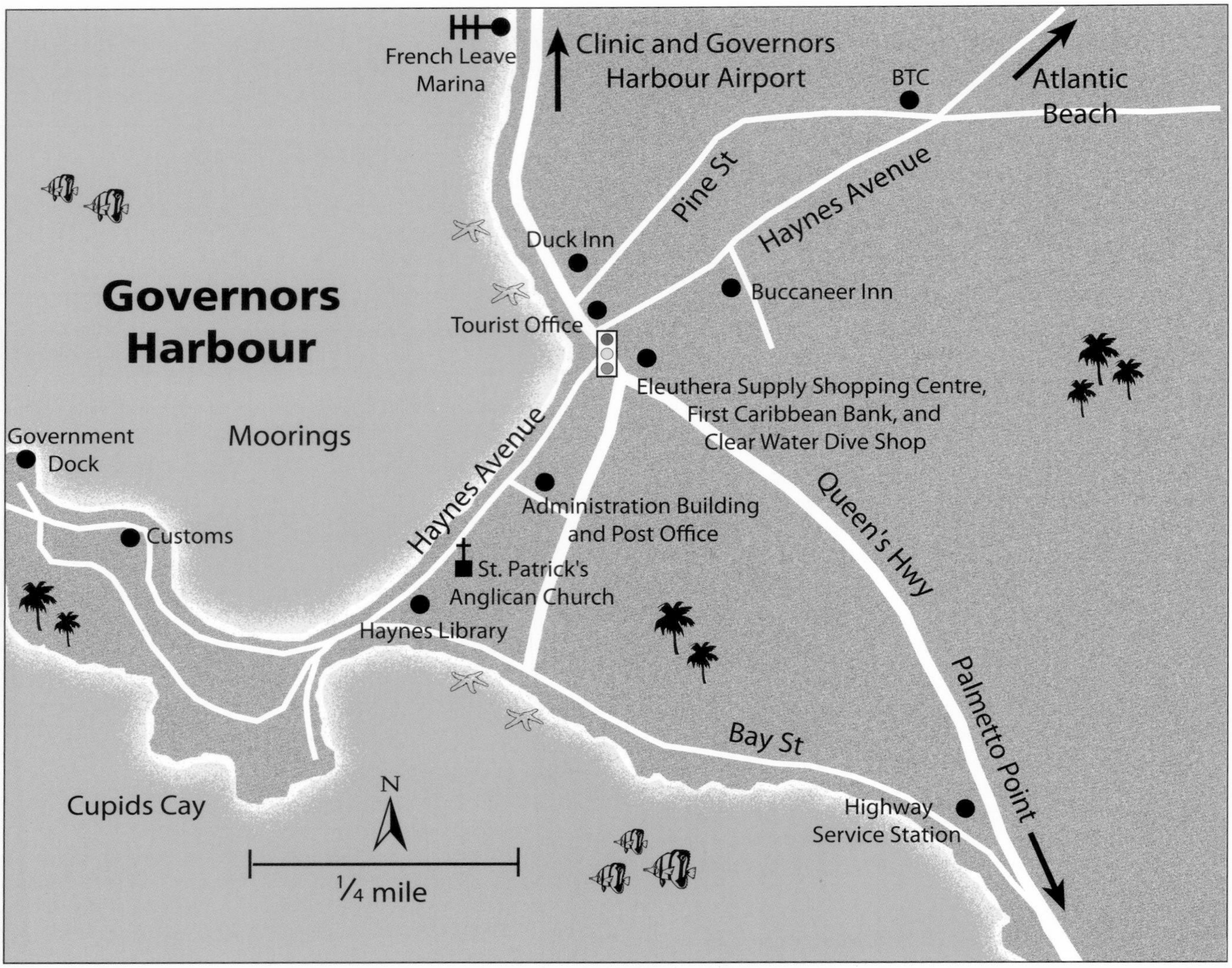

Airport *Governors Harbour Airport* • 242-332-2321.

Art Gallery, Arts & Crafts *Dornell's Treasures*, 242-332-2932. Gifts, crafts, local artwork • If you missed *Karin Goodfellow's "Nantucket Baskets,"* superbly woven Lightship baskets in Harbour Island, visit her studio near Governors Harbour, 242-332-2506.

Bakery *Governors Harbour Bakery* • 242-332-2071 • Cakes, breads and pastries. Opens at 9 a.m., closed Sunday.

Banks *First Caribbean Bank* • 242-332-2300 • with an ATM, and *Royal Bank of Canada* • 242-332-2856. Open 9:30 a.m. to 3 p.m. weekdays, until 4:30 p.m. Fridays.

Bars *Ronnie's Hi-D-Way*, 242-332-2307. Cigars, sports bar and liquor shop.

Beauty Salon *Zovie's Beauty Salon*, 242-332-2505.

Books & Magazines *Living Word Ministries Book Store*, 242-332-2138.

Boutiques *Brenda's Boutique*, 242-332-2089, Nicole's Casual Wear, Norma's Gift Shop, 242-332-2002 • Top of the Line • The Beach House, 242-332-3387.

Car Rentals *Edgar Gardiner* • 242-332-2665, *Highway Service Station and Rental Cars* • 242-332-2077, VHF 9, *Johnson's Car Rental* • 242-332-2226, *Tommy Pinder Taxi & Car Rental* • 242-332-2568 • *Clement Cooper Taxi & Rental*, 242-332-1726 • *Stanton Cooper's Taxi Service*, Car Rental:Mini Vans, Jeeps, SUV's, 242-332-2575/242-359-7007.

Churches *Methodist Church,* the beautiful old *St. Patrick's Anglican Church, St. Paul's Catholic Church, Baptist, Bible Gospel, Church of God.*

Cinema *Globe Princess*, every day except Thursday.

Couriers *DHL* • 242-332-2077 • VHF 9 • At the Highway Station. Will hold deliveries for you, if the package is addressed "Hold for Arrival" with your name and your boat name. Deliveries take 2 working days from the U.S. UPS delivers at Paul Simmon Customs Brokerage three times a week. Try the hotels for FedEx.

Customs and Immigration • 242-332-2714 • Open 9 to 5 Monday through Friday.

Dive Shop *Clear Water Dive Shop* • 242-332-2146 • Fax: 242-332-2546 • Equipment rental and tank refills. There is no dive operation in Governors Harbour, but Charles Sands can put you in touch with people who can guide you. Closed Sunday.

Ferries *Sea Wind Ferry* Leaves Governors Harbour at 2 p.m. on Mondays and Thursdays for the 4-hour trip to Nassau. *"Bo Hengy" Fast Ferry* To Nassau on Fridays at 9:45 p.m., Sundays at 7 p.m.

Fishing Guides *Gladstone Petty*, 242-334-2341 • and *Paul Petty*, 242-332-2963.
Fuel & Propane *Eleuthera Supply* Fuel & Groceries, 242-332-2026.
Hardware *Lord Byron Building Supplies*, 242-332-3476.
Internet *The Beach House*, 242-332-3387. WiFi.
Kayaks *Cocodimama*, 242-332-3150 • *The Beach House*, 242-332-3387.
Laundromat *Sands Laundromat.*
Liquor *Butler and Sands Liquor Store*, 242-332-2328 • *Pyfrom's Liquor Store. Ronnie's Hi-D-Way*, 242-332-2307. Cigars, sports bar and liquor shop. • *Bristol Wines & Spirits*, 242-332-3663 • *Burrows 1 Stop Liquors*, 242-332-2310.
Medical *Governors Harbour Medical Clinic* • 242-332-2774 • Open 9 to 5 weekdays, with their own ambulance.
Pharmacy *Eleuthera Supply Shopping Centre*, 242-332-2026.
Photography *Theresa's Photography*, 242-332-2992.
Police • 242-333-2111.
Post Office In the administration building, open 9 to 4:30 weekdays.
Provisions *Eleuthera Supply Shopping Centre* • 242-332-2026 • Well-stocked with a good selection of canned and fresh goods, as well as a pharmacy section and separate hardware store with propane. Open daily from 7 a.m. to 5 p.m.; to 3 p.m. Sundays. *Burrows 1 Stop Shop Groceries*, 242-332-2310. frozen foods, meats and fresh vegetables.
Restaurants *The Buccaneer Club* • 242-332-2000 • Native and American dishes can be ordered for take-away. $ Dwight Johnson, the owner and operator, can also help you find a bonefishing guide. *The Blue Room* • 242-332-2736, *The Harbour Inn* • 242-332-2686, *Pammy's Snack Bar and Take Away* • 242-332-2843. $ • *Sunset Inn Restaurant and Bar*, 242-332-2487. Open for lunch and dinner. $$ • *Waidie's Outback*, 242-332-3803. Open for breakfast, lunch and dinner. $-$$ • *The Beach House*, 242-332-3387. Open for lunch and dinner. WiFi. Accepts credit cards. $-$$ • *Cocodimama Resort and Restaurant*, 242-332-3150. Restaurant serves breakfast, lunch and dinner. Accepts credit cards. $-$$
Snorkeling *Cocodimama*, 242-332-3150 • *The Beach House*, 242-332-3387.
Taxis *Arthur H. Nixon* • 242-332-2568. *Tommy Pinder* • 242-332-2568. • *Clement Cooper*, 242-332-1726 • *Stanton Cooper*, 242-332-1575/242-359-7007.
Telephones In town, on the government dock and up the hill at BTC, 242-332-2476. Open 9 a.m. to 4 p.m. weekdays.
Tourist Office • 242-332-2142 • Just along from the only traffic light in Eleuthera.
Travel Agent *Destinations* • 242-332-2720 • Next to the dive shop and the bank. *Destinations* has another branch in North Eleuthera, near the service station.
Trash Bins in settlement. Please tie it up in heavy mill bags. This is no place to re-use plastic grocery sacks.
Weddings *Pineapple Fields*, 242-332-2221 • *The Beach House*, 242-332-3387.

EMERGENCIES

Marine • VHF 16
Medical *Clinic* • 242-332-2774 •
Doctor after hours 242-332-2020
Customs • 242-332-2714

PALMETTO POINT & TARPUM BAY

fuel • groceries • marina • propane • restaurant • telephone • water

North Palmetto Point affords great views of the Atlantic Ocean after a rigorous hike from the western shores. It is home to gated communities, which are very much off limits, and some stores that would be a hefty hike back to the boat with the backpack. *The Unique Village* (242-322-1830) is a restaurant offering dinner on the terrace overlooking the Atlantic Ocean. It is lovely, but if you want to arrive dressed and feathered appropriately, you'd better take a taxi (*Winsett Cooper Taxi & Car Rental*, 242-332-1592). If you would like to stay, *Unique Village* has lovely rooms, as does the *Palmetto Shores Villas* (242-332-1305) and the *Paradise Sands* (242-332-3740). All three are popular wedding sites.

Cruisers will have more interest in South Palmetto Point, where one can anchor, utilize the dinghy landing and shop the various stores. There may, or may not be, free government moorings off the government pier. Unfortunately, the wonderful, protected marina that had opened here (*Runaway Bay, 242-332-1744, 10 ft. MLW, Max. LOA 60 ft. - sonia@soniacrisp.com*) has hit upon hard times. The fabulous Italian *Dolce Vita* restaurant (242-332-0220, info@dolcevitabahamas.com) is open 5:30 p.m. to 10 p.m. daily except Wednesdays, with homemade bread, gelato and Italian specialties. Situated above the marina, the owner of the restaurant tells us that the marina has slips, but no services, not even water. You may, however, be able to tie up there for the night to partronize *Dolce Vita*. If you would just like a drink and some fun company, *Tippy's Bar & Beach Tavern* is great (242-332-3331) as is *The Corner Bar* (242-332-1522).

In the settlement itself, you can find fuel at *CS Service Station* and at *Sands Enterprises* (as well as hardware), groceries at *Sands Supermarket* and several other shops, the Internet and computer help at *SPP Computer Center* and some pizza at *Mate & Jenny's Pizza* (242-332-2502). It is a busy place; you might want to call beforehand so you don't have to wait. About one half mile south of Sands, look for *The Island Farm* (open 9 a.m. to 4 p.m.) for fresh fruit and vegetables, herbs, homemade jams, jellies and condiments. For a special treat, grab a loaf of their fresh-from-the-oven Pesto Bread. Plenty of palm groves and palmettos trees make the South Palmetto Point settlement a particularly pretty one to walk around with your camera and get some good shots. There are also some beautiful beaches and caves to explore to the north and south of the settlement.

Tarpum Bay is about 15 miles south of Palmetto Point. It is very shallow, and exposed to wind and weather. The anchorages off its shore are rocky and not recommended. The government has built the settlement a new dock with dinghy ladder and placed some free moorings out front. Like so many moorings in the islands, you will have to check to see if they are there when you are there. The Tarpum Bay Settlement is an interesting community of artists and artisans. If you would like to learn more about their work, visit *MacMillan Hughes Art Gallery* and, two miles south of Tarpum Bay village, *Mal Flanders Art Gallery*. Tarpum Bay's most visible landmark is the remarkable castle-like tower built by artist-sculptor Peter MacMillan Hughes. Its most historic landmark, however, is the *Tarpum Methodist Church*. It is the oldest church in the settlement, erected in 1809. The walls are two-feet thick. The church bell came from a wealthy pineapple baron, who took the bell from his own schooner.

If you are just driving through, and you would like to wet your whistle, try *The Pink Elephant* (242-334-4440). Planning to stay longer? In Tarpum Bay, you can stay at Mary Hilton's *Haven Motel* (242-334-4231), with its own restaurant. *Cartwright's Ocean Front Cottages* (242-334-4215, cartwrights@hotmail.com) are 50 feet from the water. At *Kinky's Corner* in Tarpum Bay, there is a hardware store in the shopping center, *Carey's Groceries* at the *Shell Station*, and *Bayside Liquor*, as well as *Shine's Seafood Restaurant and Bakery*. Getting hungry? Look for *Barbie's Snack Shack, Jackie's* and *Papa George's Pizza & Internet Cafe*. All of them serve lunch and dinner. From Tarpum Bay, the road drops due south to Rock Sound, past the airport.

ROCK SOUND

airport • bank • customs & immigration • fuel • groceries • medical • police • post office • restaurant • telephone • water

Rock Sound is a diverse settlement, rapidly becoming the next "Staniel Cay" or "George Town" of Eleuthera. *Dingle Motors*, "The Rock Sound Welcoming Station" and the other business people in town offer special services for yachtsmen to make your winter stay there especially fun and comfortable. At *Dingle's* alone you can enjoy the Cruisers gazebo for potlucks and happy hours, use the dinghy dock to shop around town, get mail sent to you, or use DHL to get packages, drop off your laundry, exchange some books, pick up a newspaper, *The Eleutheran*, access your e-mail on the Internet, pick up diesel, gasoline or water by jerry can, and get some ice for your sundowner! About one mile north, you will find *The Market Place*, a modern shopping center with a good grocery store, liquor and hardware stores and a *ScotiaBank* with ATM. The South Eleuthera Airport is in Rock Sound and offers easy in and out for guests and crew.

Rock Sound offers great protection when at anchor (you may have to move around some for a frontal passage), beautiful beaches, nice destinations for day trips with guests and neat places to visit right there like the famous Blue Hole. There is Junkanoo on December 26 and the South Eleuthera Homecoming in April. Call the Eleuthera Tourist Office (242-332-2142) for details. For other special occasions, or just for a night out, cruisers enjoy *Sammy's Place* and the *Four Points Restaurant*.

EMERGENCIES

Marine • VHF 16
Medical *Ambulance and Clinic* • 242-334-2225/2115 • VHF 16
Dingle Motor Services • 242-334-2031/2231

Accommodations *Northside Ocean Resort*, 242-334-2573. A couple of miles across from Rock Sound on the Atlantic shore with stunning views and good Bahamian food (lunch and dinner) and five rental cottages • *Edwina's Place*, 242-334-2094.
Art Gallery *Luna of the Sea Gallery*, 242-334-2738. Next door to the tailor. Original artwork.
Airlines *Bahamasair* • 242-334-2125 • Daily flights to Nassau. *Twin Air* • 242-334-2142 • Flights to Fort Lauderdale on Wednesday, Friday and Sunday.
Airport *Rock Sound Airport* • 242-334-2177.
Bank *ScotiaBank* Open 9:30 to 3 weekdays, to 4:30 p.m. Friday, with an ATM, at the Market Place.
Beauty Shop *Ladzia's Hair Care*, 242-334-2565.
Books and Magazines *Eleuthera Stationery*, 242-334-2765.
Churches *Anglican, Catholic, Church of God, Methodist, Seventh Day Adventist.*
Customs At Rock Sound Airport, 242-334-2183.
Dinghy Docks In front of Tiki Hut at *Four Points Restaurant* • Old Town Dock, close to the white church, solid, wooden ladders • *Dingle Motors*, at low tide, very shallow and rocky.
Email and Fax *Dingle Motors* • 242-334-2031. *Eleuthera Stationery and Office Supplies* • 242-334-2494 • Fax: 242-334-2765 • Michelle Gibson-Leary has office, school and business supplies, and can help with email and fax service. Closed Sundays.
Fishing Supplies *Eleuthera Fish and Farm Supplies* • 242-334-2489 • A short way north of town.
Ferry *Sea Wind Ferry* Runs from Governors Harbour to Nassau on Mondays and Thursdays, with space for cars; $65 one way, $110 round trip. *"Bo Hengy" Fast Ferry* For passengers, runs on Fridays and Sundays from Governors Harbour. Tickets from *Dingle's.*
Fuel *Dingle's Motor Services* • 242-334-2031/2231 • This is where it all happens in Rock Sound. Chris Cates, and his father Kermit, can also rent you a car. They also have ice and some groceries, a laundry, propane refills, Internet access for $8, a Sotheby's agency and DHL courier service. They sell *Fast Ferry* tickets to and from Governors Harbour and Nassau. Betsy and Bradley are there most of the time. Find out anything about Rock Sound at the Boaters' happy hour under the gazebo shore side at their dock. *Shell* filling station at the *Market Place*.
Hardware *Automotive and Industrial Distributors* (NAPA) store, 242-334-2060 that is useful for engine spares, etc. • *NAPA* in Rock Sound Shopping Center. *Rock Sound Hardware* • 242-334-2253 • In the Market Place. • *Dingles*, 242-334-2031 • *The Lumber Shed*, 242-334-2031.
Laundry Take laundry to *Dingle Motors*.
Liquor *Burns House Liquor Store*, 242-334-2250, in the Market Place. • *Sturrup Liquor Store*, 242-334-2219.
Marine Services *Dingle Motors* 242-334-2031. *Elite Automotive* • 242-334-2275/2600/2039.
Medical *Rock Sound Medical Clinic* • 242-334-2225/2226 • VHF 16 • In buildings opposite the Government Dock, on the street above, next to the church. With a doctor, nurses and their own ambulance.
Pet Food & Supplies *Eleuthera Fish & Farm*, 242-334-2489.
Police • 242-334-2244.
Post Office At the Administration Building, open 9 to 4:30 weekdays.
Propane *Rock Sound Hardware*, 242-334-2253. In the Market Place.
Provisions *Nat's Produce Store* Fresh vegetables and fruit. *Rock Sound Super Market* in the Market Place. Open 8 to 5 weekdays, 8 to 2 Wednesdays. Very well-stocked with plenty of fresh fruit and vegetables and a good choice of large packs of essentials. Dinghy to the *Tiki hut* at *Four Point's Restaurant* to go to the Market Place. *Sawyer's* Food Stores • 242-334-2123 • Groceries, frozen foods, meats, fresh vegetables. Fresh fish, vegetables and fruit are often available in the late afternoons at the *Dingle Happy Hour* in the pergola.
Restaurants *Northside Restaurant and Bar*, 242-334-2573. A couple of miles across from Rock Sound on the Atlantic shore, with stunning views and good Bahamian food. Lunch and dinner. $ Make reservations in the morning at *Dingle's*. Free transportation to restaurant from there or take your dinghy to their new dinghy dock • *Sammy's Place* • 242-334-2121 • Casual restaurant serving Bahamian food and a wide selection of beer. $ • *Vita's Blue Diamond Restaurant* • 242-334-2425 • $ • *Four Points Restaurant and Tiki Hut*, a favorite with cruisers • Several take-aways in town, look for their signs and crowds.
Surfing Site On the Atlantic Side, Rock Sound is a fairly exposed reef break that provides both lefts and rights. Best in SW winds. Most surf comes from groundswells. Optimum swell angle is from SE.
Taxi *Avian Morley Taxi #160*, 242-334-2962/242-357-3301 • *Wilfred Major Taxi & Car Rental*, 242-334-2156.

Telephone BTC Open 9 to 4:30 weekdays. Other phones around town. **Trash** Bins in settlement and at *Dingle's*. Please use heavy mil trash bags. This is not the place to reuse plastic grocery bags that break apart and let your garbage fly all over the village. NO WASTE OIL!

SOUTH ELEUTHERA

POWELL POINT TO WEMYSS BIGHT

This is about as far south as civilization goes on Eleuthera. This is serious angler and diving territory. There is not much here in the way of settlements or population; most of the people who live here and all of the people who visit here would like to keep it that way. This doesn't mean that it is not a wonderful place to end your magical water tour of Eleuthera. Quite the contrary, the beaches, reefs, fishing and facilities at the two marinas are extraordinary. You wouldn't want to miss what might be an experience left only for our generation (Princess Cruise Lines has already carved out a landing basin with faux island village nearby)—truly pristine waters and rugged terrain, both above and below water to explore. There is nowhere to anchor, so you will need your marina to meet all your needs. Enjoy the service and savor the opportunity. In the unlikely event this is your first port of call in the Bahamas, Cape Eleuthera is served by the Rock Sound Airport. Customs charges $200 to clear you in here. Contact Rock Sound Customs at 242-334-2183.

MARINAS

CAPE ELEUTHERA RESORT AND YACHT CLUB
Tel: 242-334-8500 • Fax: 616-825-6188 • VHF 16
info@capeelueuthera.com • www.capeeleuthera.com/marina
Slips 60. **Max LOA** 220 ft. **MLW at Dock** 8 ft to 35 ft. **Dockage** 25 ft. minimum; 100 ft. or less, $2.25 per ft. per day; over 100 ft., $2.50 per ft. Fire protection at slips. **Moorings** Med-style off seawalls **Fuel** Dock open from 7 a.m. to 8 p.m., daily. Gasoline and diesel. Pump out at fuel dock. $20 per gallon charge for waste oil removal. **Facilities & Services** Shore power, 30-100 amp plus 3-phase at six slip, 200+ ft. megayacht dock, $0.50 per kwHr; RO water $0.45 per gallon, trash disposal, marina guests only, $2.50/bag. High-speed Internet throughout the marina, $15/day. Public telephone and cell phone rental available. Showers, $3.00 for seven minutes. Restrooms. Licensed and trained mechanic available. Two fish cleaning stations w/solar salt water wash down. Covered lanai for festivities. 24-hour security. **Store** *Island Outfitters*: Internet kiosk available, $10 for 30 minutes; propane tanks refilled; coin-op washer and dryer w/ironing board; DVD rentals; book exchange; gifts, fine liquors and wine, beer, groceries, produce, ice cream, cigars, fishing supplies, ice and water sports. **Restaurant and Bar** *Barracuda's Beach Bar & Grill at Sunrise Beach*; *Bahamas Coffee Company*, deli and bakery. **Accommodations** 4,500-acre nature preserve and beaches; special rates and packages at resort townhomes and estates for marina guests. **Credit Cards** Visa, MasterCard and AMEX.

DAVIS HARBOUR MARINA
Tel: 242-334-6303 • Fax: 242-334-6520 • VHF 16
info@davisharbourmarina.com
Slips 34. **Max LOA** 80 ft. **MLW at Dock** 8 ft. **Dockage** $1.25 per ft. per day. **Fuel** Dock open 7 a.m. until dark. Diesel and gasoline. **Facilities & Services** Power $15 to $25 per day, depending on boat length. RO water $8 to $15 per day. Showers, restrooms, complimentary trash bag disposal, coin-op washer and dryer, Internet access at the dive shop (*Ocean Fox*, www.oceanfox.com), use of telephone in marina office, cable television, ice. Propane tank refills can be arranged through *Rock Sound Hardware.* Hauling, engine repair, hull and electronic repairs at *Pinder's Marine* in Deep Creek. **Credit Cards** Visa MasterCard and AMEX **Security** This is a gated marina, security guard at night. Pets are welcome on a leash.

THINGS TO DO IN ELEUTHERA

• Take photographs of the Glass Window, but not in bad weather. It can be dangerous there if heavy swells and high seas are coming in from the Atlantic Ocean.
• Drive out on the sand road to Preachers Cave and see where it all started in 1648. Swim off the beach. Snorkel on the Devils Backbone!
• Visit the Bogues and see real Bahamian villages.
• Go to The Current at low water and search the long beach for sand dollars. A short way farther south, check Current Cut before you run it in your own boat.
• Wade and swim off white-sand Ten Bay Beach at low tide, on the west coast at Savannah Sound; good bonefishing nearby.
• If you are in Gregory Town in June during the Pineapple Festival, join in the fun.
• Enjoy the flower-lined, narrow hillside streets of Governors Harbour; visit the historical Haynes Library that has weekly social events, and an internet café.
• Meet with other boaters at the informal happy hour under the gazebo at Dingle's Dock in Rock Sound; the Blue Hole in town is popularly believed to be bottomless!

BEACHES IN ELEUTHERA

Preachers Cave There is a pretty beach opposite the entrance to the cave, which overlooks the Devils Backbone.
Gauldin Bay Continue north of Gregory Town until you pass the salt ponds and look for a pasture on the second dirt road. Follow the road around to the right looking for the overhead power lines until you come to the beach.
Rainbow Bay Drive east on Hidden Beach Drive from Queen's Highway, which dead ends at the beach. There is good snorkeling close in, or below the tennis court at the Rainbow Inn. Go in at the boat ramp and swim to the left, about fifty yards around the point. Stay close to the cliff, unless the waves are too big.
James Point If you turn east on Johnson St. in James Cistern, go to the top of the hill and then follow the dirt road to the right. You will find a wonderful beach. Coming in from the Governors Harbour direction, this would be after the first speed bump.
Ten Bay Beach Between Savannah Sound and Palmetto Point.
Ocean Side South from the airport at Governors Harbour. Take the first dirt road on the left at the end of the runway where you will find miles of beach in both directions.
Surfer's Beach East on Ocean Boulevard about 2 miles south of Gregory Town. A rocky track leads you over to a long, sandy Atlantic beach. Challenging pipeline curls, comparable with Hawaiian surfing, given the right conditions.

EMERGENCIES

Marine • VHF 16
Medical Nurse in Wemyss Bight, and a doctor and nurses on duty in Rock Sound, monitoring VHF 16 or call
242-334-2225/2115.

Chapter 13
North Andros

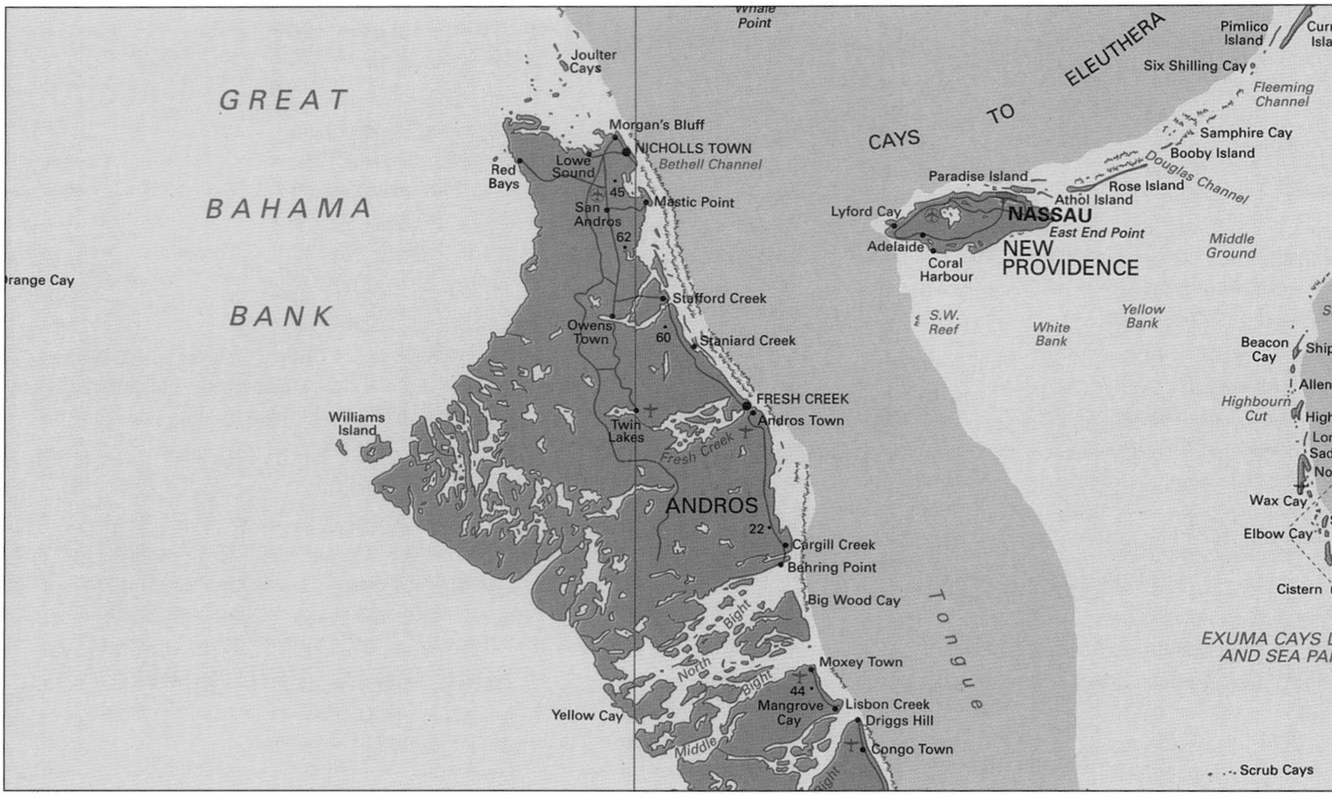

Looking At the Charts

Andros Island, over 100 miles in length and 40 miles wide (close in size to Puerto Rico, but without the mountains), is the largest island in the Bahamas. It has about 9,000 people living in scattered, isolated villages on the east coast. Together, they work to sustain the largest citrus groves and produce farms in all of the Bahamas. Andros has four small airfields, one marina, a few small resorts and some of the finest bonefishing on the planet. In the interior of the island, hardwood forests (home to rare birds such as the Kirtland Warbler, the Wood Star Hummingbird and the West Indian Whistling Duck) abut expanses of freshwater marshes and imperiled pine rock land where giant land crabs and the nearly extinct, Northern Bahamian Rock Iguana roam (albeit, slowly). The interior is hot, rife with insects and challenging to explore.

The west coast, a maze of wetland and mud flats, is uninhabited, but often ablaze with the blooms of widespread orchids and hibiscus. The east coast has the cooling winds and the ocean—the link that connects the people and sustains the island.

Looking at a chart of Andros, you will see three, lateral, physical divisions, where distinct bights of water cut right across the island from east to west. These bights make connection between land and people more complex and significant settlement more difficult. Effectively, the land below the North Bight from Behring Point to the south is more remote than the Everglades, and both Central Andros and South Andros are reached only by boat and air.

It is the water, ultimately, that makes Andros special. Its corner of the ocean contains the third-largest continuous barrier reef in the world, lying less than a mile off its east coast and running over 140 miles long. The reef has significant geological and marine value. Its long platform contains low cays, massive coral, lagoons, coastal estuaries, legendary "blue hole" karsts and supports diverse fauna and flora. Andros attracts divers and marine biologists from all over the world.

Outside the reef, a singular and unique piece of deep ocean water, known as the Tongue of the Ocean, separates Andros from the shallow Exuma Bank. The Tongue of the Ocean is a shelf that begins around 70 feet deep and plunges down over 6,000 feet. Divers are surprised by its sudden appearance; the change from the multi-hued reef to suspension in water space, surrounded by sheer walls that plummet into the depths of darkness. Swimming, swarming and surviving in the Tongue's waters are every kind of pelagic fish on this good earth. It is Mother Nature's aquarium for sports and commercial fishermen. This phenomenally deep water has also brought the U.S. Navy and the Royal Navy, jointly interested in undersea testing and evaluation programs. For purposes of security, their work is secret. However, their presence helps Andros prosper.

As if the treasures of the ocean are not enough, water—fresh water—also provides for this island. Andros supplies New Providence Island with over 50 percent of its fresh water requirements. It is shipped by tanker (most locals say "barged") from North Andros. Androsians grumble that both the naval testing and the export of fresh water barely benefit them "because the rental monies for the naval bases are paid to the government, and the water is downright taken as a Bahamian birthright." Perhaps the "trickle down" effect never trickles fast enough for anyone, regardless of national origin. Or, perhaps, it is just as well. Wealth would probably be the root of all evil for a heavenly spot called Andros.

Andros is an ethereal place. It is an island where ghosts roam and chickcharnies—tiny, short-tempered, feathered creatures with enormous eyes who hang bat-like, upside down from trees—wield powerful psychic influence and create mischief.

Andros was a base for pirates attracted here by Mariner's Well, a freshwater natural spring well purported to have been used by pirates as far back as the early 17th century. Pirates like Henry Morgan, whose treasure, so legend has it, remains buried in Andros.

Seminole Indians, who did not take kindly to their enslavement in the United States, ran away and sought refuge here. Their descendants survive in Red Bay.

Andros Lighthouse stands at the southern entrance to Fresh Creek where the entire community stood helplessly on the shoreline and watched the seas swallow four of its sloops and crew under the glow of its revolving light during a 1929 hurricane.

Moreover, of course, there are the famous blue holes of which Andros has more than any place else on earth. Even noted scientists are fascinated by the mysteries and mischief associated with the blue holes. None can yet explain why Indian skulls were found lying at the bottom of the deep blue waters of Star Gate Blue Hole during a National Geographic scuba diving expedition.

In the Spotlight. Andros as a Cruising Ground

It is not surprising that Andros has remained a land apart in the Bahamas, and that the name Andros doesn't come up too often in cruising circle's conversations. It is hard trying to figure out the nature of the place. A newcomer to Andros might well be forgiven for believing that chickcharnies built the ominous looking, square offshore towers called autecs (see the next section What's There? North Andros). Maybe little feathered creatures do haunt the mahogany forests! Taking a cool, dispassionate look at navigation in Andros is as difficult as trying to explain an autecs' architecture.

Andros certainly falls into the big island category. What is the cruising analysis? The whole east coast of Andros offers superb fishing and diving. Central and South Andros offer tiny remote settlements where one can tuck in, feel like a native, and just be one with nature (do not forget bug spray that truly works.) Catamarans with a 0.7-meter/2.5-foot draft and no compelling requirement for amenities, shouldn't hesitate to explore these unfrequented waters.

We analyze "cruising territory" with a critical eye and the weight of sending others there on our shoulders. We see an approachable east coast; and maybe, a shoal-draft, trans-Andros passage through the South Bight. Even that one coastline, with its barrier reef, presents challenges. There are very few places to enter through the reef and very few places to run for safety once inside the reef. The inside route is teeming with coral heads and crawling with sand bars. The overall depth is shoal-draft territory. Support facilities for cruisers are minimal, in some areas, nonexistent. Fresh Creek offers the most for cruisers in terms of facilities and supplies, but don't expect a lot. Fortunately, Nassau is nearby (15 minutes by air, flights twice daily). With this in mind, we will focus on the Fresh Creek area first and then on the Bethel Channel area.

Clearing In—Your Options in North Andros

Your principal port of entry is Fresh Creek, Andros Town. The Customs and Immigration officials at San Andros Airport will, however, clear you in at Nicholls Town or Morgans Bluff, on request.

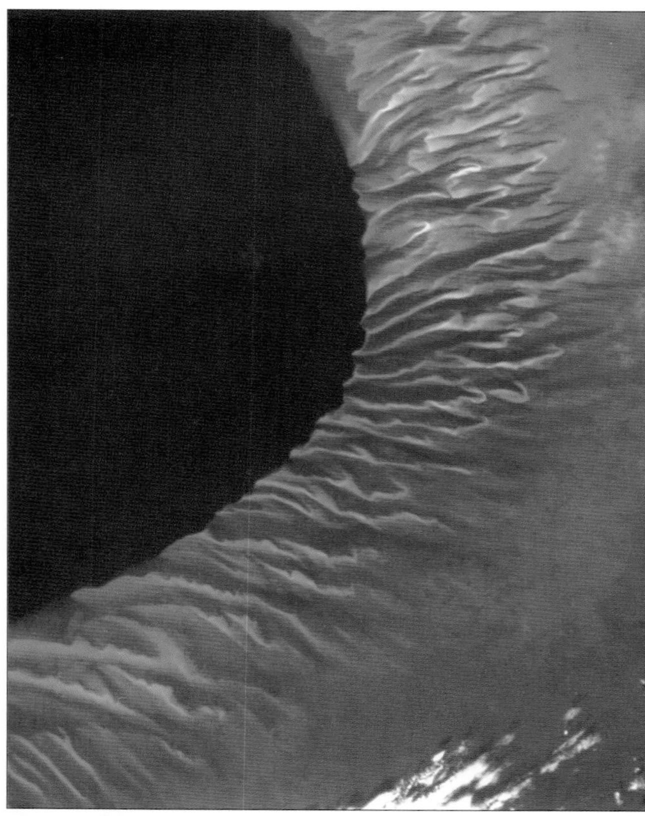

NASA

Tongue of the Ocean, southeastern end.

North Andros

FRESH CREEK, STANIARD CREEK		Largest Vessel Accommodated	VHF Channel Monitored	Transient Berths / Total Berths	Approach / Dockside Depth (reported)	Floating Docks	Gas / Diesel	Groceries, Ice, Marine Supplies, Snacks	Repairs: Hull, Engine, Propeller	Lift (tonnage), Crane, Rail	1=110V, 2=220V, B=Both, Max Amps	Laundry, Pool, Showers	Pump-Out Station	Nearby: Grocery Store, Motel, Restaurant
		Dockage					Supplies				Services			
1. Kamalame Cay Marina (Internet Access) (Wireless Internet Access)	800-790-7971	50		/8			GD	I			/50	S		MR
2. Lighthouse Yacht Club & Marina (Wireless Internet Access)	242-368-2305	100	16	/34	/12		GD	IS			B/50	LPS		GMR

Corresponding chart(s) not to be used for navigation. Internet Access, Wireless Internet Access

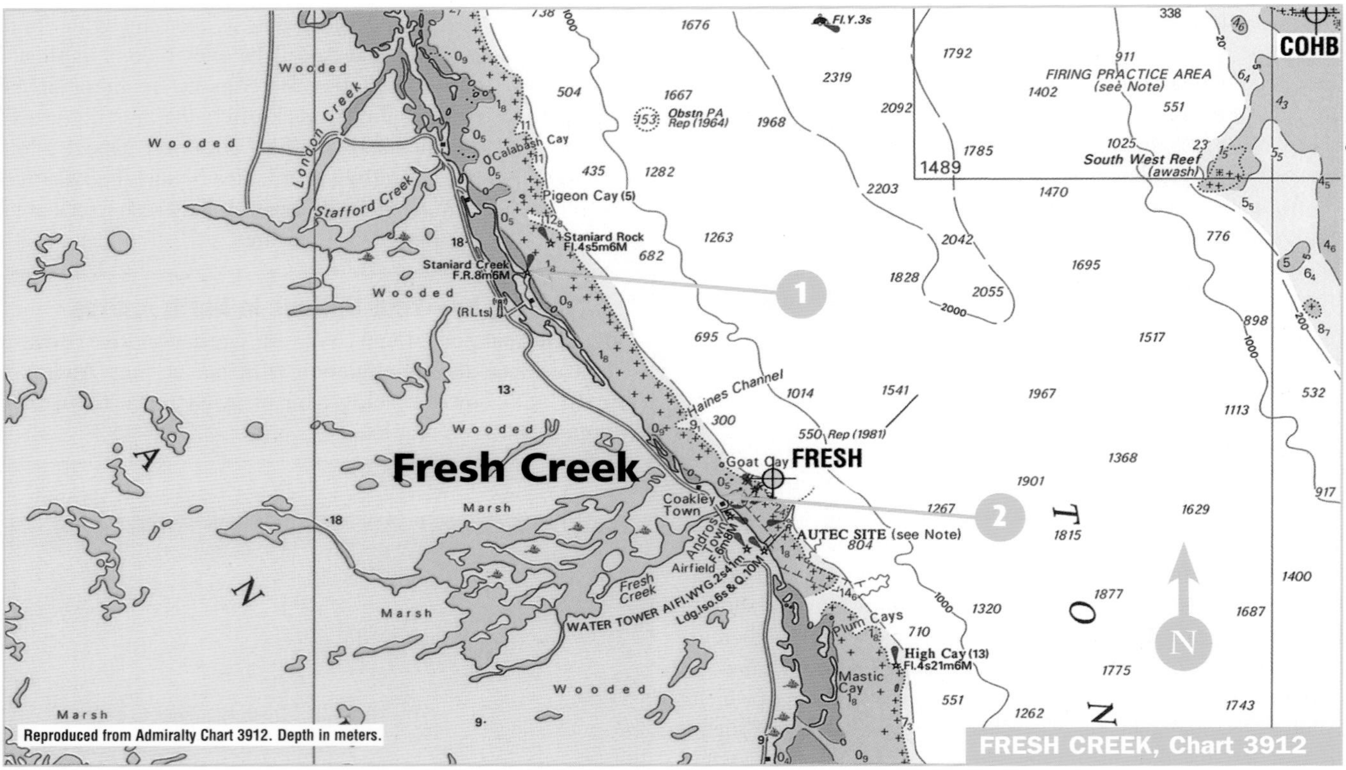

Reproduced from Admiralty Chart 3912. Depth in meters.

FRESH CREEK, Chart 3912

What's There? North Andros

Tongue of the Ocean and Andros Barrier Reef

The Tongue of the Ocean, whether you approach it from the shallow green waters of the Exuma Bank or directly from Andros, is extraordinary! The color changes range from green to ultramarine to ink blue, almost in sync with the depth sounder. Incidentally, yours may go "Bermuda Triangle" on you and then give up.

As for the top-secret testing, if you are around Andros Town, you will soon learn that AUTEC (Atlantic Underwater Test and Evaluation Center) is everywhere and manifests itself in an array of buoys (that attract dolphins), strange towers, forbidden harbors and communication masts. Other than using AUTEC facilities as landmarks, treat them like top-secret, and stay away. You are likely to fall short of a welcome if you take an AUTEC harbor as a storm refuge.

The barrier reef has to be seen to be believed. We are talking visibility (30 meters/100 feet is minimal), coral formations, drop-offs and walls, blue holes, marine life—the whole essence of the diving world. You can dive the reef without guides, but the wise go guided so nothing is missed. Anchoring depths off the reef are deep (13 to 15 meters/45 to 50 feet). Dive depths can be deep, too (36 to 55 meters/120 to 185 feet). The blue holes can be hazardous, sucking in water and expelling water with the tide like "a boiling pot." You could be stuck in one until the tide changes. Don't mess in one without professional dive partners!

In April 2002, the Bahamian government created the Central Andros National Park. Encompassing more than 300,000 acres, the sanctuary protects major terrestrial and marine habitats. The combination of a relatively small population of islanders and local support for conserving natural resources means protection efforts can be advanced. The Kerzner (as in Atlantis, Paradise Island) Marine Foundation has established a private, nonprofit

Fresh Creek Lighthouse Marina. WATERWAY GUIDE PHOTOGRAPHY.

foundation that fosters the preservation and enhancement of global marine ecosystems through scientific research, education and community outreach. In 2005, the Foundation awarded its first grant to the long-term protection of Andros Island. Since then, the Kerzner Marine Foundation and The Nature Conservancy, in collaboration with the Bahamas National Trust (BNT), the Bahamas Sportfishing Conservation Association (BSCA) and other partners, has worked with the Bahamian government toward the creation of a new marine, ocean and coastal protected area. It enjoys similar safeguards to other national parks under the BNT flagship.

Fresh Creek (Andros and Coakley Towns)

The lighthouse on the south entrance to the Creek was built in 1892. It still stands to welcome visitors to its harbor and is the hallmark for all of Andros. You may well feel that you have reached your dream destination when you put in to the Lighthouse Yacht Club and Marina here. The marina, on the south bank of Fresh Creek facing Coakley Town, is an oasis in the desert. The docks, which front a hotel with a lively bar (known for its Rum Punch, fine restaurant and on-site dive shop), are well-designed and well-built.

There is a bank and a Tourist Office just behind the marina and hotel. Moreover, just a five-minute walk up the road, tucked behind the trees, is the birthplace of the cottage industry, now famous in the islands, the Androsian Batik Fabrics factory with an outlet shop. A bridge links Andros Town and Coakley Town over Fresh Creek. And, although there are lots of many places to see and things to do in both towns, most cruisers refer to the duet as "Fresh Creek."

Across the bridge in Coakley Town, don't miss a visit to Papa Gay's Chickcharney Hotel, and its bar and restaurant. Be wary of tying up to its small concrete wall, however. The strong tidal flow makes it untenable. Nearby, visit Hank and Eva Roberts at Hank's Place for a Hanky Panky, their specialty drink. Hank and Eva serve exceptionally good Bahamian food along with fun and frivolity that make for a laugh-filled evening. There are also supermarkets and a liquor store here, plus a number of small specialty shops in which to poke around.

Small Hope Bay

To the north, some three miles out of Coakley Town, you will come to the mini-settlement of Small Hope Bay. There, on a beach promontory, a Canadian, Dick Birch, opened the Small Hope Bay Club in the 1960s. Devoted primarily to diving and the pursuit of a simple life, that could be summed up as wearing sarongs and running in bare feet, the Birchs built a business that has a 60 percent repeat rate. His son, Peter Birch, now runs the little resort, and life there continues unchanged. It is small, family-oriented, totally informal and communal in its lifestyle.

Staniard Creek. Kamalame Cay

Farther north, just offshore at Staniard Creek, lays the plush spa and resort built on Kamalame Cay. The small marina there has eight slips that can accommodate vessels requiring less than 4 feet at mean low water to enter their channel. And,

Approach to Fresh Creek. (Not to be used for navigation.) WATERWAY GUIDE PHOTOGRAPHY.

even then, you want to enter on a rising tide. Surprisingly, if you can float in here, their T-dock can accept a 15-meter/50-foot yacht or greater. The docks have 2.4 meters/8 feet of water at mean low water. The entry channel is well-marked, and the friendly staff will help talk you through it. Dockage is generally reserved for guests, but you can never tell. You might get lucky! Expect to pay $3 to $5 per foot per night as a transient.

For cruisers, Kamalame Cay is the only North Andros alternative to Fresh Creek, other than anchoring off Morgans Bluff or working through a pass to find another coastal hole inside the barrier reef. There is a green channel marker just north of Staniard Rock at N 24° 50.820'/W 077° 53.330'. Pass north of this marker. A red channel marker comes up at N 24° 51.810'/ W 077° 52.930'. You are just north of Kamalame Cove House at this marker, which you keep to starboard incoming and pass between the marker and the cove. Exercise extreme caution using this channel as our cruising editor was not able to verify this information.

The Bethel Channel. Nicholls Town

Places seem to come and go faster in Nicholls Town than a chickcharney can cause mischief. There is a resort there called The Bahama Coconut Farm. The town's dock has never been for cruisers, so in that sense, you have lost nothing. Nevertheless, it is always worth a visit to see what was there, what is there and what is supposed to be coming.

The San Andros airport is still there, although many people who land there are at the wrong airport. With an airport, something should be there, right? You will find groceries, hardware, laundry service, the police, restaurants, shops and telephones. What you won't find is a safe channel through the reef, anchorages or a marina. You can throw out the hook in front of the old, unusable dock of the shuttered Andros Beach Hotel and Dive Shop, but don't spend the night there.

The North of Andros. Morgans Bluff

If you were printing a travel brochure, you would probably advertise Morgans Bluff as the home of Henry Morgans Cave, the source of Nassau's tasty, clean water (with a special dock built for the water tankers to fill 'er up) and the site of the Morgans Bluff Regatta held in June. Maybe not a lengthy list for a travel brochure, but certainly enough to make cruisers interested.

Morgans Bluff Bay faces north, tucked inside a great spine of limestone (an aquifer). That is the source of its water and a notable landmark. If your draft can handle it, the anchorage, south of the water dock along the sandy shore, offers some protection from the northeast, south and west, but plenty of surge. There is a small inner harbor where you can dinghy in to get some fuel at the ESSO, or visit Willie's Water Bar—where there is a lot more served up than water. Apart from that, and Henry Morgans Cave, which lies off the main road in the limestone strata about 200 yards from the beach, there is little else to do here except meet the nice locals, chat and enjoy the beauty of the bay. Why would you need anything more?

If you are looking for action, wait until Independence Day, when beach stalls brimming with food and drink transform the area. Residents are aching for lots of fun and good Bahamian

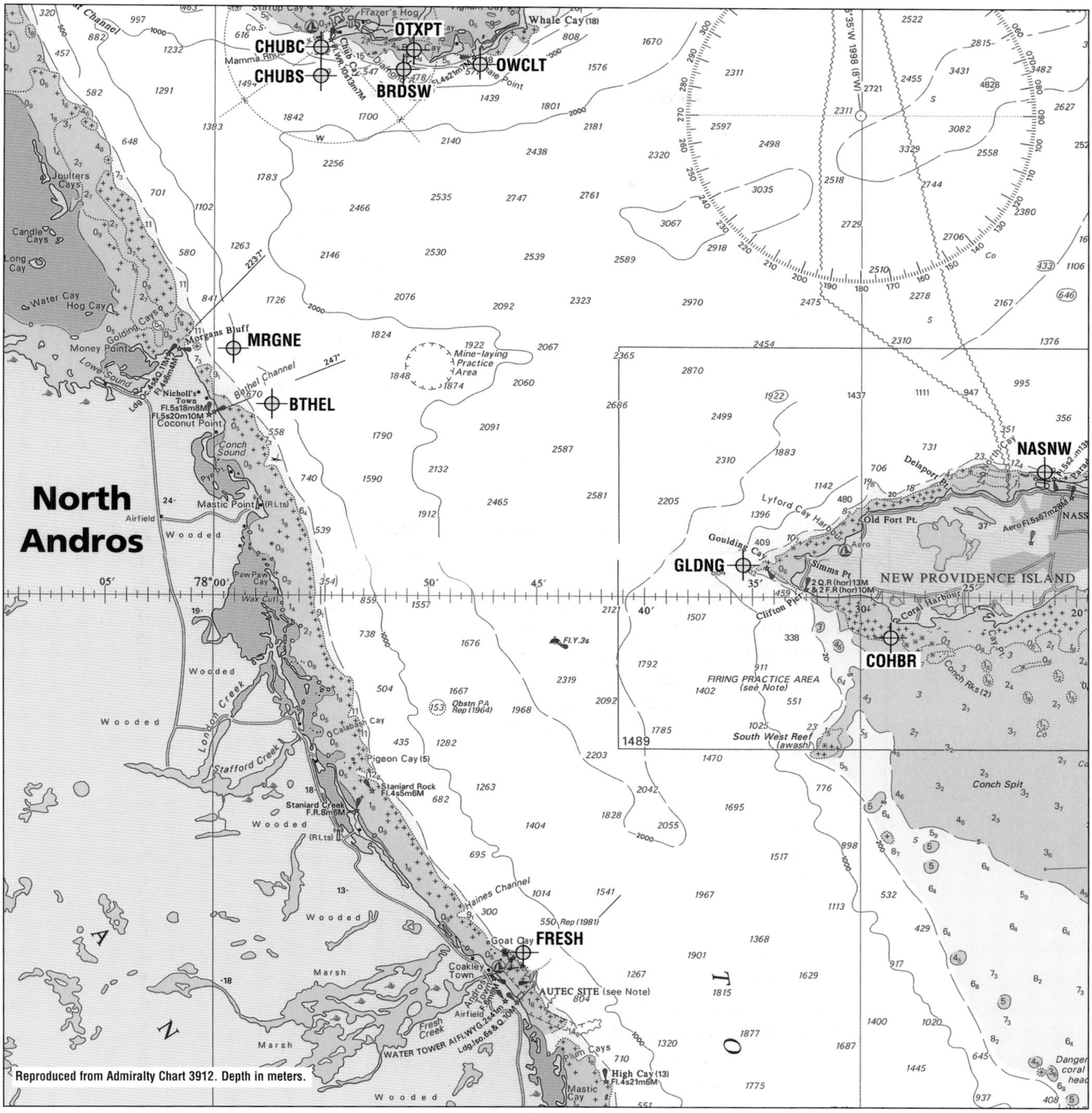

sloop racing. Read our Goin' Ashore to discover all the other anchoring opportunities in the Morgans Bluff area.

Pilotage. Talking Captain to Captain

Approach to Fresh Creek

The approach to Fresh Creek is simple. From the approach waypoint FRESH, the first landmarks are two radio towers. One is at the AUTEC base south of Fresh Creek, the other a BTC mast in Coakley Town north of Fresh Creek. On the southern side, there is an orange-and-white-checkered water tower in addition to the radio tower at the entrance to the AUTEC harbor. On the north side, a string of seven low-lying rock islets (some with a little green on them) run north to south paralleling the line of the barrier reef. The entry run is about 1.8 nautical miles on a course of around 244/064 degrees true. Two posts mark the channel at the south end of this chain of rock. The reef continues to port, but it is not so obvious. Favor the better-marked north side. Two AUTEC towers (square huts on stilts) mark the channel, one to the

Joulter Cays. (Not to be used for navigation.) WATERWAY GUIDE PHOTOGRAPHY.

south and the other to the north, right on the edge of the entry channel. Favor the AUTEC tower to the north (but don't get closer to it than 60 meters/200 feet).

As you get closer to the entry to the Creek, you will see a rock promontory running out a little way from the north point. There is shallow water to the south (a ledge, about 30 meters/100 feet out into the narrows). Just swing around the clearly visible rock, staying safely off the ledge, then make your way up Fresh Creek, holding to the center of the channel.

Fresh Creek Anchorage and the Lighthouse Marina

The Lighthouse Marina is immediately on your port side. The tidal flow is formidable (over 6 knots during extreme tides). Heading into the Lighthouse Yacht Club and Marina at any time other than slack tide demands well-applied power and a degree of seamanship not normally called for at most marinas. Two mailboats have gotten into trouble here; one swept ashore at the entrance to Fresh Creek and one coming very close to demolishing a Lighthouse Marina dock. If you have not achieved a slack water entry, it is worth holding off to call for extra help and to check the direction and force of the stream before committing yourself to an approach.

Once you are there and tied up, you are fine. The marina offers safe berths, nice hotel accommodations with a lively bar and restaurant, showers, laundry and fuel. There is no other marina in Andros. If you are using your boat day-to-day for fishing or diving, make sure to listen to AUTEC broadcast warnings over VHF Channel 16 each day for the areas they have declared off limits.

The Bethel Channel

The Bethel Channel is a marginally viable boat channel through the Andros barrier reef between Fresh Creek and Morgans Bluff. It had importance in the past when the mailboat used the channel to serve the Conch Sound settlement to the south and Nicholls Town to the north. Now the Bethel Channel is a route for local, shallow-draft boats. It is not an entryway to anchorages, docks, shoreside facilities or anything else of importance to a visiting boat. Why do we mention it? Because the Bethel Channel is identified on the charts, and if we ignore it, you are going to wonder why.

The channel has an entry range (lighted, with white lights) that will bring you in through the passage (1.2 meters/4 feet at mean low water but the locals claim a greater depth) toward inshore water. Keep going until you are about 30 meters/100 feet from the shore, but use your eyes, judging the water depth rather than measuring that distance off so precisely. Then turn north if you want Nicholls Town, or turn south for Conch Sound, staying inshore (30 to 45 meters/100 to 150 feet) all the while. Exercise extreme caution if you decide to take a chance on this shallow entrance.

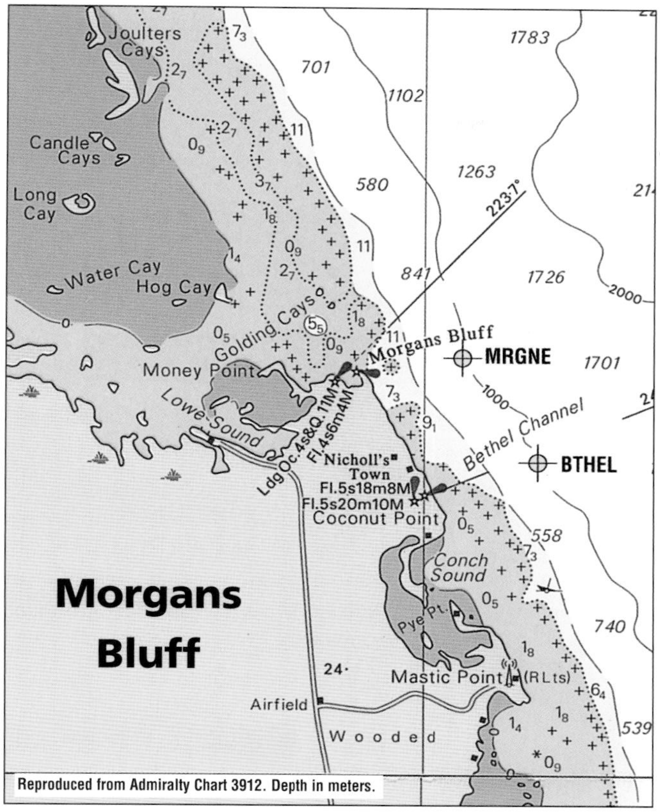

Reproduced from Admiralty Chart 3912. Depth in meters.

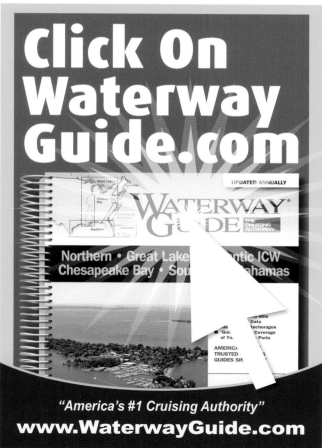

Conch Sound

Only the old concrete government dock, with a survey mark embedded in it, remains to remind Conch Sound of its mailboat days. Even then, the mailboat couldn't get to the dock, and passengers and goods had to be tendered ashore. If anyone tells you that Conch Sound is a good place to anchor, they are either pulling your leg or think you live on a Jon boat. There is, however, great diving farther south around the sunken wreck of the *Potomac* and a cave in which a world-record dive was scored.

Morgans Bluff

You can not miss Morgans Bluff. The Bluff is a 12-meter/40-foot-high spine of limestone that is the northern marker of Andros Island. North of here is the water maze of the Golding and Joulter Cays. Andros starts (or ends) in style with this one long, gray, jagged headland. The entry channel to Morgans Bluff is well-marked with conventional buoys, and you will have no problems. The outer buoys lie at N 25° 11.1500'/W 078° 01.030' and are easy to pick up.

Around the corner behind the bluff, to port you have the long government dock, off limits to all but mailboats, traders and the water tankers. The anchorage lies off the curve of sand beach. It offers around 2.4 meters/8 feet of depth or more at mean low water, but is completely exposed to the north. If you get caught there in a norther, unless you have a shoal-draft boat and can work your way behind one of the cays to the north, or farther around to the west into Lowe Sound, you are going to be uncomfortable. The anchorage is large, so you are unlikely to be crowded.

The Inside Reef Passage

We have always defined a cruising territory as an area where no unusual hazards exist. The vagaries of weather, for most, are quite enough to deal with whether there is 300 meters/1,000 feet under the keel or 4.5 meters/15 feet. For this reason, we do not recommend traveling behind the Andros Barrier Reef as a "cruising" territory.

Andros Waypoints

Morgans Bluff	MRGNE	25°11.00N / 77°59.00W
Morgans Bluff Entry Buoy	MRGNB	25°11.15N / 78°01.03W
Bethel Channel	BTHEL	25°08.50N / 77°57.50W
Fresh Creek	FRESH (B46A)	24°44.25N / 77°45.50W

Position format is latitude and longitude in degrees and minutes (hddd°mm.mm). Waypoints in RED are NOT for autopilot navigation. Codes in parenthesis are Wavey Line waypoints marked on the charts. If you have programmed waypoints listed in a previous edition of this guide, check carefully to ensure the coordinates you have recorded match the list. If a waypoint is no longer on the list we may have changed its code or deleted it.

GOIN' ASHORE:

ANDROS

Andros is the largest island in the Bahamas. It offers some of the best diving in the world off the third largest barrier reef on this planet. The sportfishing in the Tongue of the Ocean, as well as superb bonefishing, draws serious anglers from all points of the globe. With more than 50 varieties of orchids and a large and varied bird population, there are more attractions than just watersports to entice visitors.

Largely unexplored by cruisers, Andros is still a mysterious and beckoning island. Our Goin' Ashore cover the areas that are easily accessible to cruising boats from the north to as far south as Fresh Creek. There are an increasing number of bonefishing lodges, but they are difficult to reach in a cruising boat. The only public marina on Andros, Fresh Creek, attracts true adventurers—those who like to cruise, explore, fish and dive independently.

EMERGENCIES

Police • Fresh Creek 242-368-2626; Kemps Bay 242-369-4733; Nicholls Town 242-329-2353; Mangrove Cay 242-369-0083; The Bluff 242-369-4733.
Medical • North Andros, *Nicholls Town Clinic*, 242-329-2055, *Mastic Point Clinic,* 242-329-3055.
Central Andros, *Fresh Creek Clinic,* 242-368-2038, 242-368-2060; *Mangrove Cay Clinic*, 242-369-0089.
South Andros, *Kemps Bay Clinic,* 242-369-4849, *The Bluff Clinic*, 242-369-4849, 242-369-4620.
Customs • Central Andros 242-368-2031. Congo Town 242-369-2640, 242-369-2641.

MORGANS BLUFF

Willy's Water Lounge, at the commercial harbor, is a good source for local news and information. The good folks at Willy's will cook you a meal, direct you to the grocery store, send you off in a taxi and put you in touch with guides for fishing, diving or island sight-seeing. Diesel and gasoline are available at the ESSO on the commercial dock. This is the only fuel available until Fresh Creek. The pirate's hideout, Henry Morgans Cave, is near Morgans Bluff. If you decide to see it, wear hiking shoes, lots of insect repellent and take a flashlight with you. The settlement of Red Bay, home to the descendants of Seminole Indians, is 40 minutes away by vehicle.

ANCHORAGES

The channel into Morgans Bluff is well-marked for commercial traffic. It is deep and wide. The commercial harbor could offer emergency shelter, but in general it is not available for tying up or for anchorage. The best anchorages are east of the commercial harbor, tucked up as close to the cove shore as you can safely get; to the west of Joanne Point off the second cove; and to the north of Joanne Point, around Money Cay to its western shore. None of these anchorages provides much shelter from strong winds and holding varies. They are pleasant in calm weather with west, east or south winds.

If you are going to get caught in northerly wind conditions, talk to locals about navigation to potential anchorages in Lowe Sound Harbour, in the lee of Hog Cay or south of Joulter Cays. There are always knowledgeable locals to guide you, so take advantage of their skills. Customs and Immigration will come to Morgans Bluff from the airport for clearances. Police, in the unlikely event you would need them, are in Morgans Bluff, 242-329-2718.

NICHOLLS TOWN

In Nicholls Town, there is a Customs office, a police station and Andromed Medical Centre and The Nicholls Town Government Clinic. You will also find a BTC office with telephones, a post office and ScotiaBank. There are several restaurants with wonderful local food. Rental cars usually run from $60 to $85 daily; vans, $125.

Accommodations *Beneby's Bayside Motel*, Tel: 242-329-3074, Fax: 242-329-3035, beneb2003@yahoo.com. • *G J's Resort & Fishing Lodge*, Tel: 242-329-2005. *The Green Windows Inn* • *West Side Fishing Resort*. Tel 242-329-4026.
Airlines *San Andros Airport. Bahamasair*, 800-222-4262. To and from Nassau • *Major's Air Service*, 242-368-2766 Flights to and from Marsh Harbour • *Western Air*, daily flights to and from Nassau, 242-369-4000.
Bank & ATM *ScotiaBank*, 242-329-2700.
Boutiques *Farieba's Dry Goods & Fashion* • *Seashell Nook* • *The Big Shop*.
Car Rental *Executive Car Rental*, 242-329-2636 • *A&H Car Rental*, 242-329-2685 • *GJ"s Car Rental*, 242-329-2055.
Customs 242-329-2278. **Immigration** 242-329-4466. At the airport.
Laundry Drop off at *Pratt's Laundry*.
Medical Clinics *Andromed* Private Medical Centre, 242-329-2171. Open Fridays • *Nicholls Town Government Clinic*, 242-329-2055/2399. Open 9 a.m. to 4 p.m. weekdays. Has a doctor and nurses.
Police Tel: 242-329-2353.
Propane Sent on mailboat to Nassau.
Restaurants *Grizzly's* • *The Green Windows Inn* • *Rumours* • *Picaroon Restaurant* • *Rolle's Takeaway* • *New Eagle Rock Restaurant & Bar* • *Angus Poop Deck* • *Lan' Crab* • *Barbies* at the airport.
Taxi Ask at lodgings or restaurants.
Telephone *BTC*, Tel: 242-329-2131.
Trash Bins in the settlement.

ANCHORAGES

A recommended anchorage shows up on charts off Nicholls Town, just off the old Andros Beach Hotel dock. There is no protection there, and holding is poor. It can be used as a quick day anchorage or in dead calms.

STANIARD CREEK

Kamalame Cay • 242-368-6281/800-790-7971 • Fax: 242-368-6279 • info@kamalame.com • www.kamalame.com
Kamalame Cay is an exclusive resort on a 100-acre private island at the mouth of Staniard Creek, with its own 8-slip marina. The docks

Andros reef. Waterway Guide Photography.

have 8 feet at mean low water, however, the channel has 2 feet; 5.5 ft. at the highest tides. There is a marker north of Staniard Rock to guide you through the reef.

Accommodations *Kamalame Cay Resort & Marina*, Tel: 242-368-6281/800-790-7971, Fax: 242-368-6279, info@kamalame.com, www.kamalame.com. Rooms from $400 per person; suites from $760 per person; 4-bedroom villa from $3,840 per night. Diving, bonefishing and adventure tours for guests.
Bakery *Kamalame Cay Resort*, the local ladies bring baked goods to be sold at the resort.
Car Rental *Enterprise Renta' Car*, ask at Kamalame Cay Resort.
Provisions *Staniard Creek Grocery • Kamalame Resort & Marina*
Restaurants *Helen's • Kamalame Resort.*

FRESH CREEK, ANDROS AND COAKLEY TOWNS

airport • bank • customs & immigration • fuel • groceries • marina • medical • police • post office • restaurant • telephone • water

MARINA

LIGHTHOUSE YACHT CLUB ON FRESH CREEK
Tel: 242-368-2305 • Fax: 242-368-2300 • VHF 16
relax@androslighthouse.com • www.androslighthouse.com
Slips 34. **MLW at Dock** 12 ft. **Max LOA** 100 + ft. **Dockage** $1.30 per ft. per day. **Moorings** $10 per day. **Facilities & Services** Power $13 to $34 per day and water $6 to $14 per day depending on boat length. Cable television, ice, showers and restrooms. Coin-op washers and dryers $2.00 per load. WiFi in lobby, public telephone, propane truck stops by to refill tanks and swimming pool. **Restaurant & Bar** *Beacon Restaurant and Bar*, open 7 a.m. to 9:30 p.m. for breakfast, lunch and dinner. Bar with good rum punch and great dining on terrace overlooking the marina. $$ **Credit Cards** Visa, MasterCard, AMEX and Discover. Travelers checks accepted. Pets are welcome at the marina.

PORT DIRECTORY

Accommodations *Lighthouse Yacht Club* 20 spacious rooms with private baths from $115 to $145 per night, overlooking the gardens or the marina • *Chickcharnies Hotel*, Tel: 242-368-2025. Across the creek from *Lighthouse Yacht Club*. The concrete dock outside has space where you can tie up alongside, but you will need extra-fat fenders to hold you off against the tidal creek flow • *Coakley House*, Tel: 242-368-2013/800-223-6961, Fax: 242-368-2015. Three air-conditioned bedrooms in the former *Commander of the Royal Navy's* house at the entrance to Fresh Creek. Reservations through *Small Hope Bay Lodge* • *Point of View Villas & Lodge*, Tel: 242-368-2750 • *Small Hope Bay Lodge*, Tel: 242-368-2013, Fax: 242-368-2015.
Airport and Airlines *Andros Town Airport* is three miles south of town. *Bahamasair* has daily flights to and from Nassau. *Small Hope Bay Lodge* and *Kamalame Cay* have their own charter flights. • *Gulfstream*, 800-231-0856, flights to and from Ft. Lauderdale • *Majors Air Service*, 242-368-2766, flights to and from Marsh Harbour • *Western Air*, 242-368-2579, flights to and from Nassau.
Bank *Royal Bank of Canada* • 242-368-2071/2072 • Behind the hotel, open 9 a.m. to 3 p.m. Monday through Thursday; Friday to 4:30 p.m.
Boutique *Small Hope Bay Lodge Boutique*.
Car Rental Ask at *Lighthouse Marina* for *Rolle's Auto Rental* • *Adderley's Car Rental*, 242-357-2149 • *Roney's Car Rental*, 242-368-2255. Cars usually cost $60 to $85 daily; vans, $125.
Ferry *Bahamas SeaWind* Ferries • 242-368-2886 • Leave from Fresh Creek for Nassau.

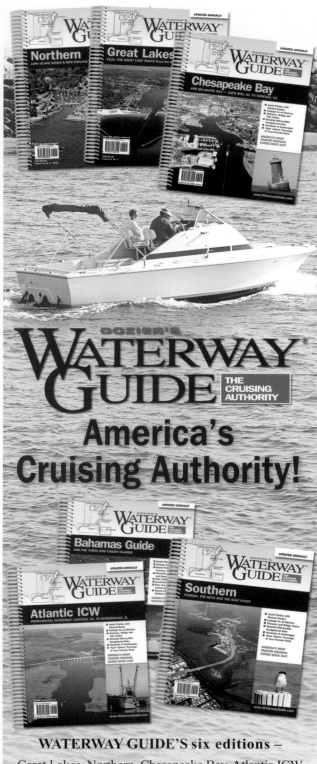

Laundry *Adderley's Washerette* • 242-368-2201.
Medical Clinic • 242-368-2000 • In Fresh Creek on the first road left after you cross the bridge into town from the *Lighthouse Marina.* Doctor and a nurse on-site.
Police • 242-368-2626.
Post Office In the administration building, a short walk out of town. Open 9:30 to 4 weekdays.
Propane *KC Investments*, 2 miles north of Fresh Creek.
Provisions *Adderley's Bargain Mart.* • *Andros Market* • Bottled water, canned and dried goods, and some fresh vegetables and fruit. • *Chickcharnie Hotel* • A general store carrying a surprising assortment, but no fixed opening hours. • *Gaitor's Market* • Open 8 a.m. to 10 p.m. daily, to 10 a.m. Sunday. A limited selection of food, but very helpful. • *Mable's Meat Market and Convenience Store* Frozen meats and a few groceries, open 8 a.m. daily, to 1 p.m. Sunday. • *Skinny's Wholesale Liquor* Open weekdays. Vegetable Stand Some mornings, Magnolia, or Maggie as she likes her friends to call her, brings fresh fruit and vegetables to sell from the back of a pickup behind the *Lighthouse Yacht Club.*
Restaurants & Bars *Lighthouse Yacht Club* $$ • *Chickcharnie Hotel* $ • *Golden Conch Restaurant* • *Skinny's Landmark Hotel and Bar* and *Treat's Bar* Both noisy and well frequented. $ • *Small Hope Bay Lodge* • Three miles north of Fresh Creek, dine family style. Call ahead for dinner reservations. $$ • *Hank's Place*, home of the Hanky Panky specialty drink. Excellent Bahamian food and frequent special events draw a fun, friendly local crowd. $-$$. • *Gaitors* • *Oasis* • *Square Deal* at Coakley Town.
Shopping *Androsia Factory Outlet Store* • Near the Lighthouse Marina. Interesting hand-screened batik that is exported worldwide; tours available. Open 8 a.m. to 5 p.m., Monday through Friday, 9 a.m. to 5 p.m. on Saturdays. • *Small Hope Bay Lodge Boutique.*
Tourist Office • 242-368-2286 • Open weekdays next to the bank, behind the marina.
Taxis Ask at the hotel.
Telephones BTC opposite *Skinny's Landmark Hotel and Bar*, Open 9 a.m. to 4:30 p.m. weekdays. No U.S. or Canadian $50 or $100 bills accepted.
Trash In bins in town.
Water *Lighthouse Marina* • Town water at town dock.

SPORTS

Diving *Small Hope Bay Lodge* • Shark observation dives, blue holes and NITROX diving. They are also the dive operators for George Town. Exuma at the Club Peace and *Plenty Beach Lodge.* • *Andros Undersea Adventures.*

THINGS TO DO IN ANDROS

- Dive and snorkel the world's third-largest barrier reef.
- Take advantage of the brilliant bonefishing.
- Go crabbing, fish for sharks from piers, collect shells, visit the blue holes, meet the local herbalists, explore the mangroves and maybe catch a glimpse of the chickcharnee?
- Join in "Andros Nights" on Friday evenings in Fresh Creek, at the brightly painted booths next to the school. Local stalls, lots of noise, food and drinks.

Part III
Southern Cruising Grounds

WATERWAY GUIDE PHOTOGRAPHY

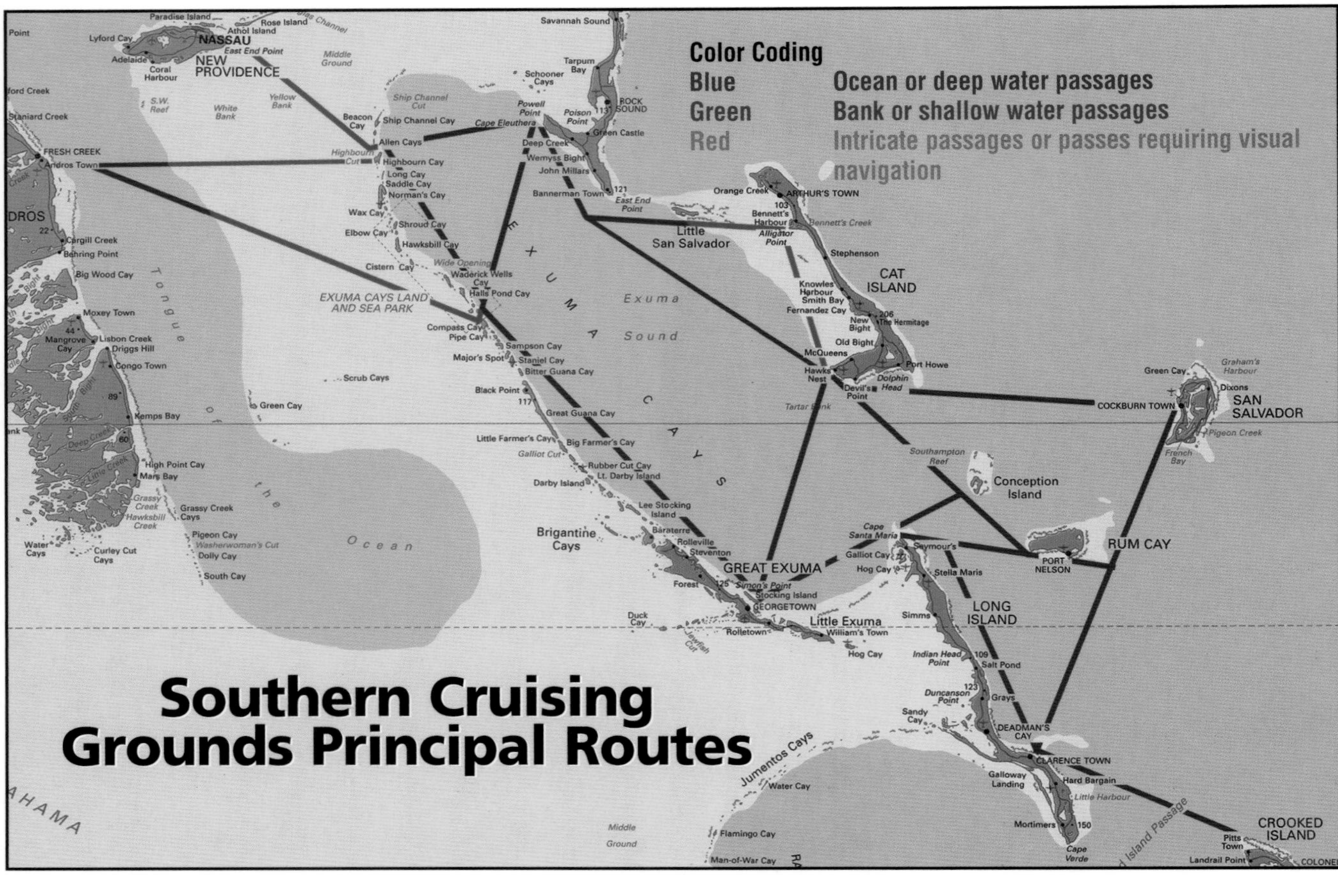

Not to be used for navigation.

Route From	To	Headings	Distance	Passage
Fresh Creek, Andros	Highbourne Cay, Exumas	093/273°T	50	Tongue of the Ocean/Bank
Fresh Creek, Andros	Conch Cut, Exumas	114°/294°T	74	Tongue of the Ocean/Bank
Nassau	Allans Cay, Exumas	see text	38	Exuma Bank
Cape Eleuthera	Highbourne Cut, Exumas	256/076°T	25	Exuma Sound
Cape Eleuthera	Conch Cut, Exumas	195/015°T	33	Exuma Sound
South Eleuthera	Little San Salvador	096/276°T	10	Exuma Sound
South Eleuthera	Hawks Nest, Cat Island	129/309°T	43	Exuma Sound
Allans Cay, Exumas	Warderick Wells, Exumas	see text	36	Exuma Bank
Highbourne Cay, Exumas	Conch Cut, Exumas	147°/327°T	30	Exuma Sound
Warderick Wells, Exumas	Staniel Cay, Exumas	see text	18	Exuma Bank
Dotham Cut, Exumas	George Town	136/316°T	46	Exuma Sound
Staniel Cay, Exumas	Farmers Cut, Exumas	see text	19	Exuma Bank
Farmers Cut, Exumas	George Town	130/310°T	37	Exuma Sound
George Town	Cape Santa Maria, Long Island	054/234°T	23	Exuma Sound
George Town	Hawks Nest, Cat Island	023/203°T	37	Exuma Sound
Little San Salvador	Hawks Nest, Cat Island	138/318°T	35	Exuma Sound
Hawks Nest, Cat Island	Conception Island	131/311°T	32	Atlantic Open
Hawks Nest, Cat Island	San Salvador	see text	58	Atlantic Open
Cape Santa Maria, Long Island	Conception Island	068/248°T	14	Atlantic Open
Conception Island	Rum Cay	see text	14	Atlantic Open
Rum Cay	San Salvador	026/206°T	30	Atlantic Open
Rum Cay	Clarence Town, Long Island	191/011°T	31	Atlantic Open
Cape Santa Maria, Long Island	Clarence Town, Long Island	152/332°T	40	Atlantic Coastal
Clarence Town, Long Island	Bird Rock, Crooked Island	115/295°T	35	Crooked Island Passage

Distances exclude inshore close approaches at the start and end of a passage. The notation "see text" indicates multi-leg passages that are fully covered in the text.

Chapter 14
The Northern Exuma Cays

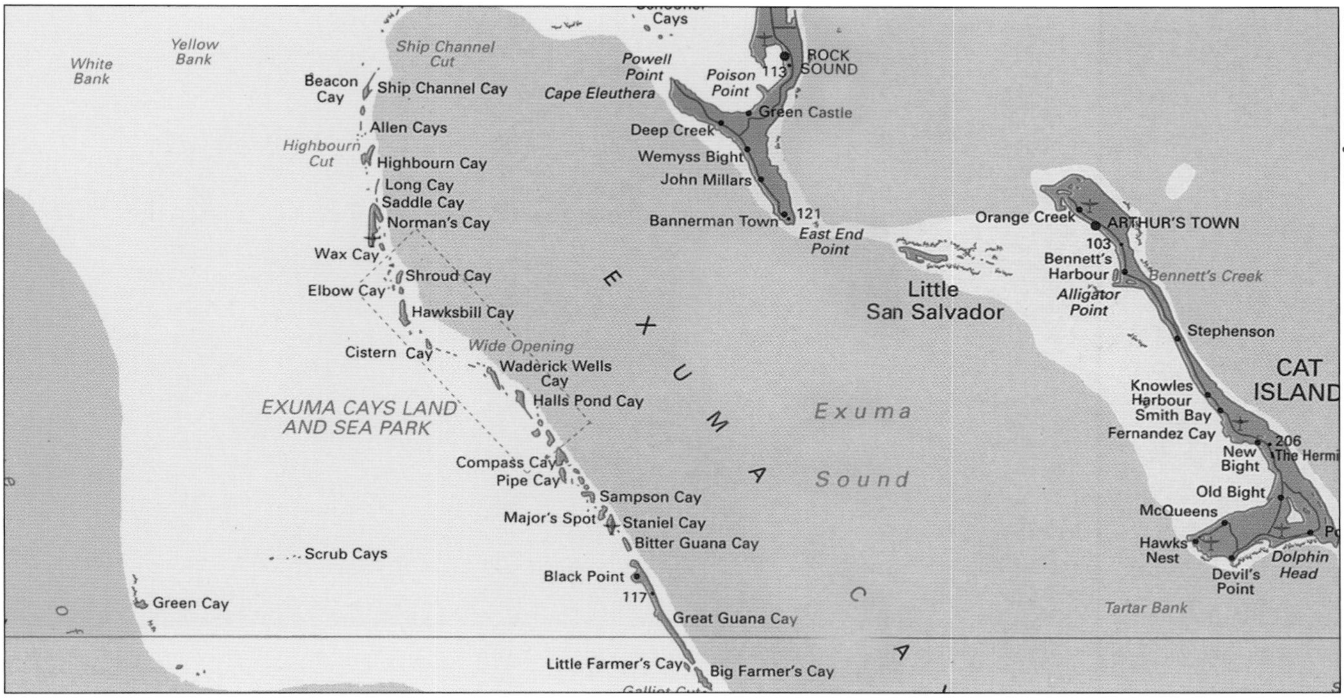

Looking At the Charts

The Exuma Cays rate with the Abacos as some of the most popular islands for cruising in the Bahamas. Both, as it happens, are roughly the same length measured as a chain. And, both offer many of the same attractions to the cruising boater—Bahamian water at its best, an apparently endless succession of small cays where, if you feel escapist, you can be on your own and way stations where you can find fuel, food and the rest of the cruising world if you want company.

The Exumas run northwest to southeast from N 25° 00.000' to N 23° 25.000'. The chain starts south and east of New Providence Island and ends where the Out Islands, the truly remote southern Out Islands, begin. In some ways, the Exumas are a lot like the Florida Keys as a cruising ground. There are two navigable sides, an east and west coast, and a number of cuts between the islands that allow you to switch sides depending upon the wind.

In the Exumas, the east side—the Exuma Sound side—is deep, blue water. In the sound, there may be swells, and in strong winds some pretty good-sized waves; but you get a break from the myopic look-out for coral heads, sand banks and shoals.

The west side—the Exuma Bank side—is protected from prevailing winds; but like any bank, it is shallow in spots and tests your visual navigation skills. None of these cuts, back and forth from bank to sound, have a particularly good or bad reputation. They all deserve careful chart examination before an attempt and extreme caution during their passage. Each cut presents its own unique set of considerations depending on which way it faces and the wind and tide conditions present. Because the prevailing weather in the winter is from the northern quadrant and in the summer from the southern quadrant, leaving the Exuma Bank often offers less of a challenge than reentering it from the sound unless the wind and tide are opposing. Then, you will find standing walls of water at most cuts. You might even encounter a "rage."

Our advice is simple. If you are in a big hurry to reach George Town, travel in the Exuma Sound unless the weather is adverse. If you want to cruise the Exumas in the time-honored fashion, island-by-island and cay-by-cay, tour the Exuma Sound. Make your initial choice to fit weather conditions, and keep in mind that you can switch from side to side through the cuts as you wish. Just one glance at a chart shows you that the primary approach routes to the Exumas are from New Providence Island to the northwest, from Andros to the west, from Eleuthera to the east and from the open ocean to the south.

In the Exumas, you will find so many places to go and so much to do that you will wonder how you can see it all in a few years, let alone a few weeks or months. For snorkeling, fishing and diving, as well as shoal-water gunkholing, one could go on almost forever without exhausting new places to discover. Mindful that we are writing a cruising guide on all of the Bahamas, we must be selective. We have narrowed the Exumas down to four areas in this northern section. All of them should

Exuma Land & Sea Park. Photo Courtesy of Peter Mitchell.

feature high on your "visit wish list." Taken in geographic order from north to south, the first is the Allans Cay to Highbourne Cay area. The second is Normans Cay. The third is Warderick Wells and the Exuma Land and Sea Park, and the fourth is the Compass Cay to Staniel Cay area.

In the Spotlight. Exuma Land & Sea Park

In 1958, the Bahamian government set aside the 176-square-mile area known as the Exuma Cays Land and Sea Park as a land and marine protected area. Parliament also established the Bahamas National Trust as a non-profit, non-governmental organization to oversee national parks. Today, the Bahamas National Trust manages 25 national parks and protected areas within the Bahamas.

The Exuma Cays Land and Sea Park stretches north from Wax Cay Cut and south to Conch Cut. The park is 22 miles long and extends nearly four nautical miles on either side of the cays. It includes 15 cays and many more tiny ones. The park's purpose is to provide a safe haven and replenishment area for native species and to educate the public to save this beautiful environment for future generations. The park is a complete "No Take" zone. Fishing, conching, lobstering, shelling and hunting are strictly prohibited throughout the boundaries of the park. Some of the cays here were privately owned before the park was created, and the rights of private landholders have been maintained. Landing on these privately owned cays is by invitation only. The park controls the seabed throughout its boundaries.

Allans Cay Iguanas

What about these iguanas? One guesses that once they existed Bahamas-wide, but sometime post-Columbus that was it—curtains for most of them. As it is, if you wonder at the name, it is Spanish, and they took it from the Arawak word for the animal, "iwana." So in the end, the creatures you see on the beach carry the dignity of *iguana iguana* as their scientific name, which seems a mouthful for a small scaly creature about the size of a dachshund, and with no more ground clearance than a few inches. The iguanas you will see upon landing may well come out to meet you, looking for handouts and appear tame. They are not. Treat them with caution.

Janet Wilson

Warderick Wells Cay is home to park headquarters and the famous Boo Boo Hill and spectacular blowhole nearby. Throughout the park, there are beautiful reefs and underwater life for snorkelers and lookie-bucketeers.

Shroud Cay offers outstanding exploration through mangrove creeks to a gorgeous ocean beach. You can find loyalist ruins on the southwest side of Warderick Wells and Hawksbill Cay and spectacular stalactites and stalagmites at Rocky Dundas. If you are out and about at dawn or sunset, you might spot a hutia, the only land mammal native to the Bahamas. Regardless of the cays you visit or the waters you swim, there is something for everyone to enjoy and too little time to discover it all at the Exuma Cays Land and Sea Park.

We cover the park in more detail in our Goin' Ashore. Suffice it to say, "It is a must visit." We know of no anchorage more beautiful, anywhere, than that in front of the headquarters. The stately crescent of boats hanging at attention to the wind on their moorings in shimmering, almost otherworldly, opalescent waters paints a mental picture that will stay with you for life.

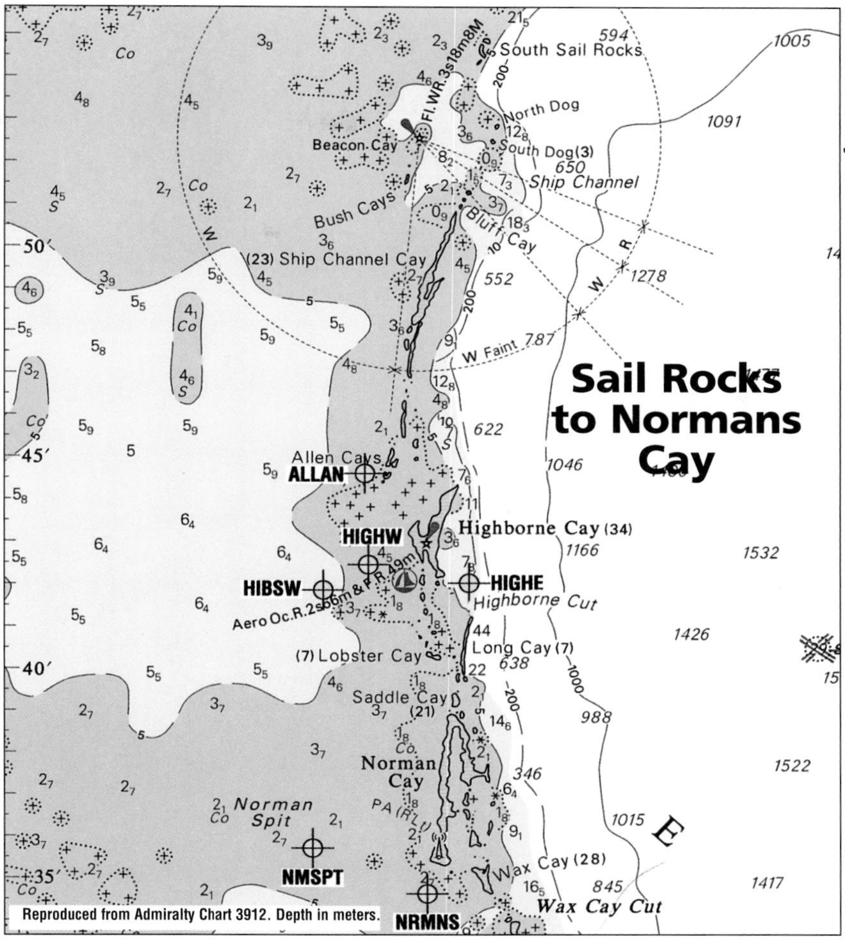

Reproduced from Admiralty Chart 3912. Depth in meters.

What's There? The Northern Exumas

Sail Rocks

Despite the name, Sail Rocks is not an area hospitable to sailors. It is a maze of bare rock, reefs, coral heads and rip tides. The only folks who do frequent the area are Bahamian commercial fishermen. In settled weather and calm winds, if you are looking for waters untouched by other cruisers for exploring, snorkeling and fishing, you can dinghy up from anchorages farther south and poke around.

So, on the face of it, you might well declare it as a sea reserve. It is unlikely to happen, for the only people who do frequent the area are Bahamian fishermen, and they might well object. More seriously, in settled weather if you want an area for exploring, snorkeling and fishing that has little been touched by visiting boaters, you might decide to anchor off and dinghy in to look around.

Ship Channel

Ship Channel is a genuine pass. The light on Beacon Cay, if it is working, is there for guidance. However, do not risk this passage at night, even if the light is working. The cut offers a 26-mile-long, straightforward route to Powell Point, Eleuthera, however, getting to this cut from New Providence is so convoluted, who would bother? We cover the cut at Highbourne Cay later. That is the better way to travel to Eleuthera.

Ship Channel Cay, Pimlico Cay and Roberts Cay

Just south of Ship Channel, and a mere three miles north of Allans Cay, are Ship Channel, Pimlico and Roberts Cays. The knolls of Ship Channel Cay usually produce the first excited shouts of "Land, ho!" from the crew after crossing the Yellow Bank bound for the Exumas. If you decide to make the side trip north to visit these cays, you will find a good anchorage in settled winds at the northern-most tip of Ship Channel Cay in between the island and the shallow sand bar to the west. There is great shelling on the sandbar when it is dry at low water.

Farther south, there is good holding on the western shore, with nice protection from easterlies in the lee of the high hills. Look for good holding and some protection from easterly winds off the western shores of Little Ship Channel Cay and Roberts Cay. For very shoal-draft boats, there is all-around protection, but less than ideal holding, in between Roberts Cay and Pimlico Cay (sound your way in by dinghy before trying the entrance).

Allans Cay, Leaf Cay and Southwest Allans Cay

This group of cays is generally just referred to as "Allans Cay." The area is often crowded with first-time cruisers keyed up after crossing the Yellow Bank and finally making it to the Exumas. At first glance, one might think that Allans Cay offers all-

Northern Exumas

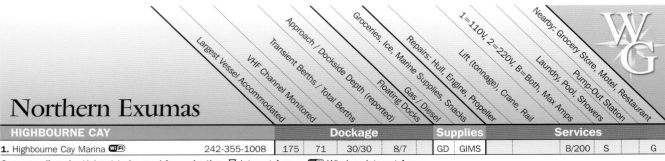

HIGHBOURNE CAY		Largest Vessel Accommodated	VHF Channel Monitored	Transient Berths / Total Berths	Approach / Dockside Depth (reported)	Floating Docks	Gas / Diesel	Groceries, Ice, Marine Supplies, Snacks	Repairs: Hull, Engine, Propeller	Lift (tonnage), Crane, Rail	1=110V, 2=220V, B=Both, Max Amps	Laundry, Pool, Showers	Pump-Out Station	Nearby: Grocery Store, Motel, Restaurant
		Dockage					Supplies		Services					
1. Highbourne Cay Marina WiFi	242-355-1008	175	71	30/30	8/7		GD	GIMS			B/200	S		G

Corresponding chart(s) not to be used for navigation. Internet Access WiFi Wireless Internet Access

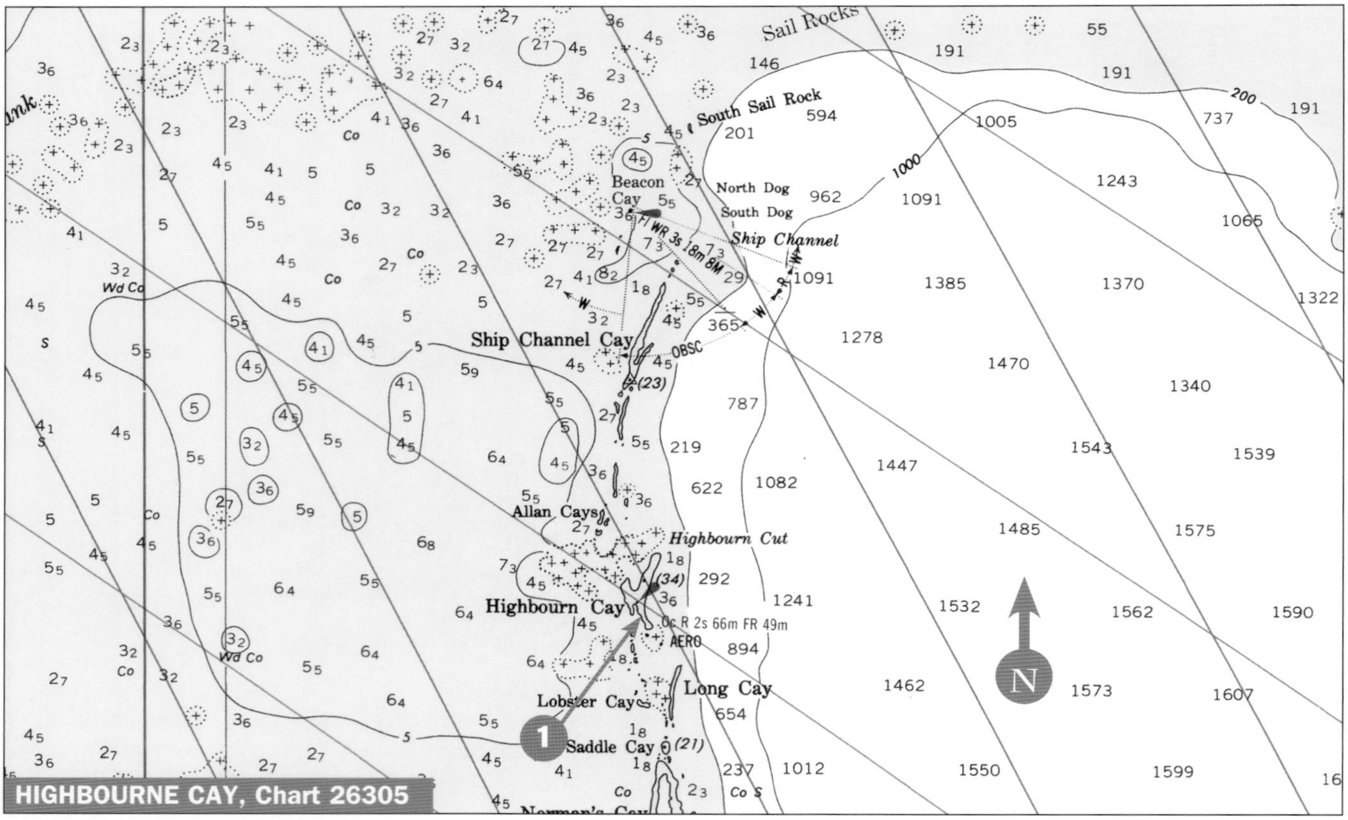

HIGHBOURNE CAY, Chart 26305

around protection in deep water with good holding. In actuality, the bottom varies from hard-scour to small patches of good sand. Large swells roll through the anchorage in windy conditions, and strong tidal currents course through the area.

If you have your choice of spots, there is good holding and sandbar protection on the western shore of Leaf Cay about three-quarters of the way north up the island, across from the ruins. There are similar conditions, with deeper water, on the eastern shore of Allans Cay, tucked up as close as you dare to the sandbar. One, maybe two, shoal-draft boats can anchor in the bay at Southwest Allans Cay in 1.5 meters/3 to 6 feet of water—the closer to the beach, the lesser the surge and the shallower the water. Although you may see boats anchored off the southern end of Leaf Cay, the holding, currents and surge there are truly terrible. In addition, powerboats often approach that beach to feed the iguanas. Sometimes they pay little heed to the bad mix of propellers and anchor lines.

The once-curious iguanas that used to stealthily blink and wink at visitors are now quite well-trained to hide out in the brush until the "go-fast" boats from Nassau arrive with their loads of tourists complete with iguana kibble. If you want pictures, time your photo opportunity for the tourist's arrival, and bring a companion to throw the critters goodies. They will bite, however, so use caution. There are also many iguanas on Southwest Allans Cay that are not fed and not quite as aggressive.

You will meet lesser numbers, but friendlier iguanas on other cays (there is a particularly nice, pinkish one on the northern end of Leaf Cay). If you must see the Allans Cay iguanas, and the anchorages are untenable, it is a short, two-mile-long dinghy ride from Highbourne Cay back to Allans. Allans Cay is a Bahamas National Trust Preserve, and pets are prohibited onshore.

Immediately north of Allans and Leaf Cays, there is a navigable cut between the Bank and Exuma Sound. There are many reefs and coral heads in that pass, so we don't favor it.

Immediately south of Allans and Leaf, there is a route through a tricky narrow cut in a reef to Highbourne Cay. It is not really a "shortcut," because you will be going very slowly looking for the rocks and coral heads to find the cut. Head west to the bank from Allans, and make your way around to Highbourne safely.

Highbourne Cay

Highbourne Cay, home to the northernmost marina in the Exumas, offers dockage, fuel, water and a small store. But above all, it offers a strategic location for that first stopover after Nassau or the only place to tie up securely in a big northeastern blow. The anchorages around Highbourne Cay are subject to strong tidal currents and surge due to their proximity to Highbourne Cut. There is good holding, easterly protection and some surge along the western shore, north of the conspicuous 300-foot-high BTC tower. Tuck in as far north and east as possible in 2 meters/6 to 9 feet of water for best protection. Keep the Highbourne Rocks and coral reefs in mind. For short trips into the marina, you can find fair holding south of the marina in 3.6 meters/12 to 15 feet of water north of the private houses on the southeastern tip of the island. You will have some protection from the north and east, but lots of surge.

Highbourne Cay is private, but limited privileges and the use of the store are extended to visiting boaters. If you are at anchor, request permission to land on the beach, but respect the privacy of the island as a whole.

Long Cay and Saddle Cay

In settled easterly winds, you can venture south of Highbourne and anchor off the western shores of Oyster Cay and its two southern sister islands in 2 meters/6 to 9 feet of water. If you would really like to be away from it all, follow the visual navigation route along the eastern side of Oyster Cay around Lobster Cay to an unspoiled anchorage with good holding to the west of Long Cay. Use this anchorage as a base to explore the Saddle Cay/Island World area, which offers some of the most spectacular turquoise waters in the islands. You can re-enter the Exuma Bank on a rising tide from the Long Cay anchorage.

Highbourne Cut

Highbourne Cut, just south of Highbourne Cay, is a relatively straightforward, "read-the-water-as-you-go" pass between the Exuma Bank and Exuma Sound. Look at the chart, and then use your eyes. You should have no problems. Just remember that wind against tide produces turbulence, and that like all passes, the current can run fast.

Normans Cay

Normans Cay won fame, or rather infamy, as the base of Colombian drug runner, Carlos Leder, during the bad old days of Bahamian drug trading. Leder's operation was eventually infiltrated by "the feds," but not before there were (supposedly) a bevy of murders when cruising boaters came too close to his operation. Today, haphazard development on the southern tip of Normans Cay (once the heart of Lederland) with a large dock (now deteriorating) and some houses (still there and bullet ridden) and the remains of a "Berlin" wall, which once guarded Leder's territory, are just north of the airstrip. A ditched aircraft in the southern anchorage (now

Normans Cay anchorage, from the south. (Not to be used for navigation.) Waterway Guide Photography.

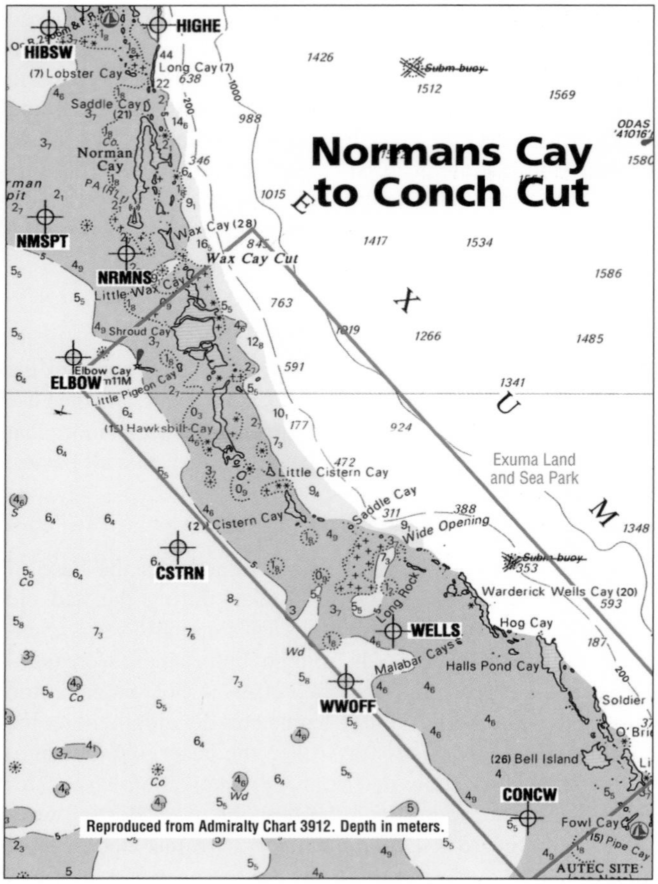

Reproduced from Admiralty Chart 3912. Depth in meters.

almost completely obscured) and a BTC-type mast on the southwest tip of the cay (still used as a landmark) are all that is left of Leder's domain.

Today, the visible signs of the bad old days are disappearing as new owners bring about revitalization and development. Normans Cay has always been at the top of the list of boater's favorite cruising destinations because of its beautiful beaches, good gunkholing, nice hiking and great anchoring options. If we cruisers wish to remain welcome here, please don't even consider burning your trash on the beach by the dock or leaving it at the old dump. Better yet, come to shore with an empty bucket, and help remove the remnants of previous trash transgressions! There is good easterly protection along the entire western shore of the cay, but there are also coral heads and shifting sand bars. Negotiate this shore with good light, and use your sunglasses. You will find good holding and protection from surge south of Galleon Point in at least 1.8 meters/6 feet of water. Explore the area around Galleon Point and Saddle Cay by dinghy. The colors of the waters here are extraordinary.

Farther south down the island, there is good holding north and south of Skipjack Point in 1.5 to 2.4 meters/5 to 8 feet of water. The sandbar off Skipjack Point continues to move west, so give it wide berth. It is best to anchor south of Skipjack Point to visit Normans Cay Beach Club, the pocket-sized resort that serves remarkable hamburgers and offers Internet access to cruisers. There are rocks and coral heads off the club, and it gets quite shallow quickly, south of there.

In westerly winds, head for the popular anchorages in between Normans and Boot Cay. Larger vessels with deeper drafts that can better handle the surge anchor in the deep-water channel between Battery Point and Normans Cut. Smaller, shallower-draft vessels can tuck closer to Boot Cay, or feel their way in to the 1.5- to 1.8-meter/5- to 6-foot-deep water just north and south of the dilapidated pier in front of the beach club ruins. There is a hurricane hole, or at the very least a bad weather hole, in North Harbour that is accessed from the sound. Once inside, there is plenty of water and room to swing, but the entrance is extremely difficult. It deserves exploration in calm weather by dinghy with handheld sonar before attempting it.

Normans Cay to Warderick Wells

The Wax Cays, Wax Cay Cut, Shroud Cay, Elbow Cay, Hawksbill Cay, the Cistern Cays and the gap known as the Wide Opening, lie on your route south from Normans Cay to Warderick Wells, and the Exuma Cays Land and Sea Park Headquarters.

Wax Cay is a magnificent private-island resort, complete with thatched-roofed accommodations supported by carved beams and poles shipped in from Bali. Guests fly in by private plane into the airport on Normans and go by boat to the island's private marina. The custodians don't mind if you beach your dinghy on their beaches, and they may give you a tour of the facilities. They are breathtaking! Please do not abuse their island hospitality by bringing your dog there to run on the beaches.

Wax Cay Cut looks better on the charts than in person. The surrounding little bitty cays and reefs are a fun place to poke around, but we would not use the cut to gain entry to the sound either coming or going. The cut does mark the northern boundary of Exuma Cays Land and Sea Park. South of here, pack your fishing gear away. The first significant island in the park area is Shroud Cay, a curious three-mile-long isle fringed by coral reefs with a heartland of mangroves and creeks. The northern creek can be explored by motorized vessel at idle speed all the way to the lovely beach at the eastern terminus on the sound. Other creeks here are strictly off-limits to all but hand propulsion. The area is great for sea kayaking or poling your dinghy like a gondolier—the water is certainly clearer (and cleaner) than in Venice.

Inshore Bank Route to Warderick Wells

If you elect to hug the bank cays, what will you find? We mentioned Shroud Cay. If you are there in March or April, the acrobatic tropicbirds, recognizable by their long white tails, will be swooping, courting and nesting. Hawksbill Cay has great beaches and popular settled weather anchorages. You will locate one midway down, and the other just north of the southern tip.

Little Hawksbill Cay is osprey nesting territory. Listen for their unique calls. Get too close, they will dive bomb you.

Cistern Cay is private, but there is a secluded, very shoal-draft anchorage along the southwestern shore of its northern-most cove. If you hug the shoreline, you will be rewarded with 1.5-meter/ 5-foot depths all the way in. Just don't forget, all of these cays are within Exuma Cays Park. Unless you want to thread the needle of coral heads, reefs and rocks southeast of Cistern, you will skirt the sand bars and head back onto Exuma Bank from there. That large gap projecting out into Exuma Sound is called the Wide Opening. It is a dream world for experienced divers, but strong currents dictate that this is no territory for the inexperienced.

Folks have done this inshore route to Warderick Wells in a shoal-draft boat and even then, sand bores, areas of shoal and reefs, oblige you to detour out to the west. Much of the shoreline, such as the Hawksbill Cay anchorages, are accessible to vessels with "normal" draft, but you are wise to take the state of the tide, as well as the angle of the sun, into consideration before choosing this as a path to Warderick Wells.

The Wide Opening

This is a viable route between the bank and the sound, and in many ways, the easiest approach to Warderick Wells Headquarters and the mooring field there. The cut back in (know as Warderick Cut), lies at the northern end of Warderick Wells Cay. It is wide, deep and easily identifiable.

The Offshore Bank Route to Warderick Wells

If you are southbound on the bank route from Normans Cay to Warderick Wells, it is rather like the route out onto the Bank from Highbourne. In this case, the route to the west of Elbow Cay is the most direct and least prone to sanding paint off your keel. There is a lighted stake on Elbow Cay, but it would be more helpful placed on the rocks one needs to skirt west of there. This route on the Bank side takes you well off Shroud, Hawksbill and the Cistern cays to the south. That doesn't prevent you from making turns to wiggle eastward to avail yourself of their anchorages, however. The Cistern Cays have spawned sand bores that run far out to the west, and there is no point in attempting to work any closer to land than three to four nautical miles along this route. The track we take is probably farther out than you need to go, but most cruisers like the sea room and passage legs where you can relax to some extent.

Poachers

Visiting yachtsmen have been caught taking fish, lobster and souvenirs from the Exuma Land and Sea Park. Apart from the mandatory $500 fine per person on board per incident (a single fish, lobster or shell counts as one incident), your boat can be confiscated. The park wardens take action against cruising visitors and will continue to patrol, make arrests and impound vessels for violations, regardless of the flag they fly. The rules are absolute. Enjoy everything that is there, but leave it as you found it.

Warderick Wells

We have already featured Warderick Wells in our Spotlight, and other than encouraging you to go there, we will wait to give you more details in the Goin' Ashore. It is really everyone's park, the sort of place other cruisers from around the world can only dream of; and like any good stewards, we must take care of it.

Warderick Wells to Sampson and Staniel Cays

After leaving Warderick Wells, you have some choices to make. If the weather is calm, you can cut back and forth in between the cays and throw out your hook at anchorages off Little Halls Pond Cay (owned by Johnny Depp), O'Briens Cay or Bell Island. You can even access the next mooring field at Cambridge Cay from the sound. Alternatively, take a cast west from Warderick Wells, back onto the Exuma Bank, and set your route for the moorings off Cambridge Cay. Regardless of your course, don't miss snorkeling in the coral gardens off the southern end of Cambridge Cay or at the Rocky Dundas underwater caves. After your visits to Cambridge Cay moorings and Rocky Dundas caves, you will have reached Conch Cut, the southern boundary of the Exuma Cays Land and Sea Park.

Conch Cut

Conch Cut is one of the best Exuma cuts, lying between Cambridge Cay and Compass Cay. It has strong tidal flows. Its one hazard is a rock that is barely awash in the middle of the cut.

New wireless Internet antennae are being installed on many of the islands from Conch Cut to Black Point all the way down to Cave Cay. Do try your computer when you are at anchor in this cruiser's paradise—you might just get connected to the whole wide world from your cockpit!

Compass Cay

Compass Cay Marina is an excellent, if not the best, example of just how great a pocket marina can be. The site is a sound, all-weather haven, proved by the unscathed survival of six boats there during Hurricane Floyd. The dock space has been expanded, power and water are on tap, and careful attention is paid to the entrance so all feel not only welcome, but also comfortable coming here.

The owner and custodians are role models for implementing and executing concerns for the environment. There is no trash, no spoil. Fishing is banned. As far as it is humanly possible to ensure (given that property rights end at the high water mark), Compass Cay is a nature reserve. Your peace of mind is protected here, too. For those who don't need or want a crowd scene, this is your dream marina. Don't miss a visit to their eastern beach. It is one of the most pristine in the Bahamas.

Pipe Cay Alley

The cays between Compass Cay and Sampson Cay enclose a protected inner passage that is known as Pipe Creek Alley, or more simply, The Pipes. Although much of the enclosed water is shallow or dries at low tide, there are deeper channels on both inner sides. It is an area of almost unbelievable water color, everything from white to turquoise to sapphire blue, with a clarity that can only be described as gin clear. Roaming this area by dinghy is an experience not to be missed.

The easiest way to reach Pipe Creek Alley from the sound is to enter through Thomas Cay Cut, in between Joe Cay and Thomas Cay, and turn south. You can exit back to the bank by following the blue water path along the western shore of Thomas Cay, taking a wide curve to the western shore of

Northern Exumas

COMPASS CAY, SAMPSON CAY, STANIEL CAY		Largest Vessel Accommodated	VHF Channel Monitored	Transient Berths / Total Berths	Approach / Dockside Depth (reported)	Floating Docks	Gas / Diesel	Groceries, Ice, Marine Supplies, Snacks	Repairs: Hull, Engine, Propeller	Lift (tonnage), Crane, Rail	1=110V, 2=220V, B=Both, Max Amps	Laundry, Pool, Showers	Pump-Out Station	Nearby: Grocery Store, Motel, Restaurant
		Dockage					Supplies		Services					
1. Compass Cay Marina (Internet Access, Wireless Internet Access)	242-355-2137	165	16	20/20	6/12			GIMS			B/50	L		GMR
2. Sampson Cay Club (Wireless Internet Access)	242-355-2034	150	16	24/24	8/8		GD	GIS			B/100	LS	P	GMR
3. Staniel Cay Yacht Club (Internet Access, Wireless Internet Access)	242-355-2024	170	16	18/18	6.5/8		GD	IS			B/100	L		GMR

Corresponding chart(s) not to be used for navigation. Internet Access; Wireless Internet Access

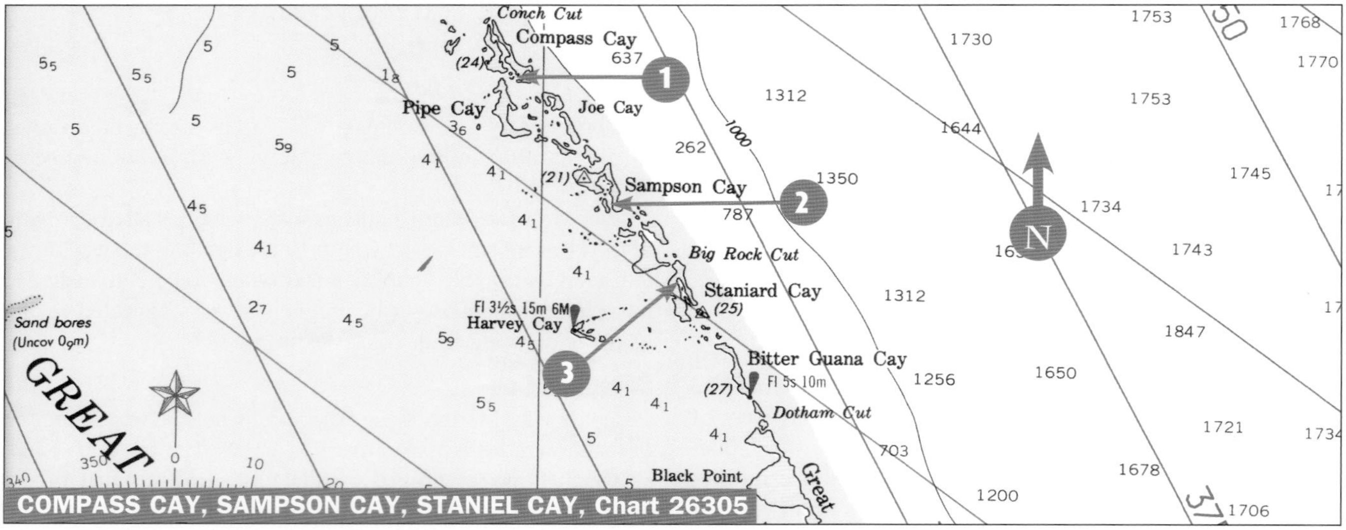

COMPASS CAY, SAMPSON CAY, STANIEL CAY, Chart 26305

Compass Cay Marina, from the south. (Not to be used for navigation.) Waterway Guide Photography.

Overyonder Cay, then rounding Rat Cay and lining up on the light off Little Pipe Cay. The dogleg west from the Little Pipe Cay light is an obvious blue path onto the bank. From the bank side, just reverse the previous route. There is room for one boat to anchor in between Rat Cay and The Mice. There is also protection and good holding in the channel running along the west coast of Thomas Cay. Expect to hang off the current, not the wind, here.

There is quite a bit of construction activity on Overyonder Cay. A very attentive security person will ensure that you no longer land a dinghy there. However, the decorative cruisers "yacht club," constructed on the beach on Thomas Cay, still welcomes you. It is frequently the site of spur of the moment potlucks and sundowner "get togethers." Lately, more and more cruisers have taken to burning their garbage in a fire ring on the beach. This leaves behind the debris of unburned paper, cans and bottles—tantamount to creating a garbage dump on a pristine Bahamian island. Please do not follow this practice. For a small fee, garbage bags can be deposited at the Yacht Club or Isles General Store on Staniel Cay.

Sampson Cay

Sampson Cay has two small anchorages on either side of the entrance to its marina, but essentially, it is a marina destination—and a luxurious one. It has all the facilities you need: all-around protection at well-maintained docks with reliable power, showers, laundry, bar, charming restaurant, a nice little market with fresh produce, frozen meats, liquor and wine and attractive villas for guests to come visit. The inner harbor has almost total protection from wind, waves and surge. Many vessels call Sampson their second home. Visitors who come by dinghy are welcomed warmly and are free to stroll the many paths on this beautiful island. Bring your camera for great shark pictures at the docks!

Little and Big Majors Spots

The large anchorage to the west of Big Majors Spot rivals any in the Exumas for popularity, for many reasons: the holding is excellent; protection is fine except from the west (and you can run to the other side if it gets too bad), the airport, marina facilities and settlement of Staniel Cay are an easy dinghy ride

Staniel Cay Yacht Club. Waterway Guide Photography.

Waterway Guide Photography.

The entrance to Thunderball Cave, Staniel Cay.

away; the snorkeling and diving are as good as they get, especially with Thunderball Cave just around the corner; the beach is clean, white and wide; and, of course, there are the pigs! No one fails to get a good laugh (and great pictures) from the freckled pigs swimming out to beg for handouts off the beach. They particularly enjoy carrots. Watch your fingers! They may accidentally bite.

In between Little and Big Majors Spots there is another "alley," similar to Pipe Creek Alley, but with more potential for surge and current. Big, solid boats that aren't bothered by the surge often spend the entire winter in this alley.

The blue hole off Fowl Cay (a private resort favored by celebrities), at the entrance of the alley, is teeming with fish. Do stop with your "lookie bucket" or glass bottom dinghy for an underwater show. The alley is a good short cut to Club Thunderball and Staniel Cay Yacht Club. It usually affords a much drier trip as well.

Staniel Cay

Staniel Cay is a bustling little settlement with a lot more to offer than its size suggests. On Wednesday (mailboat day), you will not believe such a tiny place can be home to so many big pick-up trucks. Perhaps the variety of offerings here—from three, well-stocked, Easter-egg colored markets, to artisans selling items as diverse as slow-rise, whole grain breads, to oil paintings—explains the traffic jam. Staniel Cay is populated by particularly entrepreneurial and industrious natives and is second home to a good-sized community of folks from all over the globe. From wake-up call weather reports, to large birthday party celebrations at the Yacht Club's restaurant, it is clear that everyone who calls this magical place home enjoys each other's company as much as they do the company of their visitors.

Swimming pig off Big Majors Spot. ©Peter Swanson

Wonderful additions to Staniel Cay are a very popular dive operation—look for their dive shop next to the Yacht Club. A new bakery is in the bright yellow building named "Titta Emil's," where you will find freshly baked goods and homemade fritter batter loaded with conch in their freezer. Club Thunderball is back! Listen to VHF Channel 16 for their announcements. The new owners stage "pizza & a movie" nights, barbeques and other special activities.

Because Staniel Cay is home to many rental properties, it offers the easiest connections and best flights for friends and family to meet you in paradise. Watermaker's airplanes regularly fly from Ft. Lauderdale to the island. This is as hassle free as entertaining gets! Arrivals are met at the airport by Staniel Cay Yacht Club's tram (no expensive taxi rides here). Your guests and their duffle bags are brought right to the dock. There is no airport building, per se, so contact the Yacht Club for arrival and departure information.

The Staniel Cay Yacht Club is the hub of boating activity. Like many of the "yacht clubs" in the Bahamas, it is not an elitist club, nor does it cater only to yachts. On the contrary, Chubby greets every single boat with the same welcoming smile and offer of assistance. The Yacht Club's hospitality at its restaurant and bar is legendary, from posting print outs of Chris Parker's latest weather forecast, to providing dozens of places for cruisers to sip, sit and access the Internet. Come sun down, the bar is the epicenter of social life. Just remember running lights for the dinghy if you are returning to a nearby anchorage. Although this is a wonderful spot to tie up, the docks are untenable in strong west through north winds.

Thunderball Grotto

Thunderball! As in the James Bond movie, Thunderball (be sure to have a DVD of this classic on board for all to watch). This is no Universal Studio pseudo-cave, constructed of plaster and stucco. It is the real thing, sans the cameras and Sean Connery. No real "diving" skills are necessary to snorkel this attraction, but you do need good, overhead sunlight to get the full, magical effect. The cave has two entrances, both just barely lapped by water at the right tide—one on the western side (the primary entry) and one on the east. At high tide, the lintels of both entries are underwater, in effect forming what a spelunker would call "sumps," and you have to duck underwater to clear them.

Once inside, you will be dazzled by the overhead dome pierced with dramatic shafts of sunlight slicing down into the water. You will see the ledge where James Bond sought cover. Put your mask back on, and look below you. Here is the live show. The shafts of sunlight illuminate the depths, creating a blaze of neon blue that contrasts the outer blackness of the surrounding walls. Here is where you will find the real movie stars, the "Nemos" of this world and friends. They are a curious, multi-hued, rag-tag family of fins waiting for handouts, or should we say demanding handouts. They are a fearless lot who will bump your mask and nibble your gloves to get at the goodies in your baggie. Green peas or niblets corn are particularly favored snacks, and they are okay for a fish-digestive system. Alfalfa fish pellets are even better for them, but you likely do not have room for a store of alfalfa pellets onboard.

What is the easiest time to enter Thunderball Grotto? At low slack water, especially for weak swimmers and children. The tidal current can be very strong inside the cave. Humor the folks who brag that they dove Thunderball. All anybody really needs is a mask. Fins aren't necessary unless you are swimming a long way from your boat for exercise. Don't forget an underwater camera. If the mooring buoy outside the entrance is clogged with dinghies, the cave will be more snorkels and fins than magic. No one stays too long, and the fish are continuously hungry. Hang back, take your time, and wait until the crowds clear to make your "descent."

Bitter Guana Cay

As you make your way south from Staniel Cay, we suggest that you initially head west and go all the way around Harvey Cay like the rest of the "big boys." Unless you can assuredly navigate through 4-foot-deep waters (more likely less), don't try the route in between the shoals off Harvey Cay and South Staniel Cay.

Once you have cleared Harvey Cay, this warning shouldn't deter you from heading back east toward the anchorage in the pretty cove off Bitter Guana Cay, however. Bitter Guana is a protected iguana preserve, so no pets ashore, with lots of critter-picture opportunities. As we said, you will find friendlier iguanas than the ill-mannered beasts on Allans Cay. There are interesting caves farther south at Gaulin Cay. Stay anchored at Bitter Guana to visit these by dinghy. Holding is poor there for bigger vessels, and if the wind swings north, you may drag onto a rocky bar. The route along the western shore of Bitter Guana Cay is a deep, viable time-saver to Dotham Cut or to the Black Point Settlement anchorages.

Dotham Cut

Dotham Cut is a wide, clear opening that is visible as you run south on the bank side of Gaulin Cay. The suggested course places you just off Dotham Point, a touch farther south than you might think necessary. The reason is a sand bore running out to the west from the southern point of Gaulin Cay that you must avoid. Dotham Cut offers the simplest, most direct route to George Town south of Conch Cut. It presents no navigational problems. If you choose Dotham Cut to enter the sound, be sure to look to starboard for the White Horse Cliffs as you pass.

Black Point Settlement, Great Guana Cay

Black Point is the second most-populated settlement in the Exumas after George Town. There is no particular industry, commerce nor agricultural production to make this so. Perhaps the reason for its size and lack of population attrition was best explained to us by locals, "It's good here. None of our children want to go to Nassau. They hear bad stories of what it is like there. So, they stay. You may not think that there is much here; but it is enough for us, and it's better than Nassau. We go to church, support our schools and watch out for each other. We fish a bit. We catch the conch. We work. We rest. We love. We know the people to trust, and the places where to go. It's all good, you know?" Those that have been here would agree.

The attractive Black Point settlement is perched on a wide, west-facing bight formed by Dotham Point to the north and Black Point to the south. You can anchor virtually anywhere you wish, but the best holding and protection is north and east of the government dock in sand with 2.1 meters/7 feet of water surprisingly close to shore. If you anchor in front of the government dock, avoid the fairway unless you want to meet a mail boat intimately.

The laundry on Black Point is on par with U.S. and Canadian facilities. There is a good dinghy dock for you to conveniently tie up and lug up the laundry. Next door, everyone meets at Lorraine's Cafe for lunch and wireless Internet. The blue grocery store up the street has a nice selection of meats in its freezer and a good produce selection. There is a free waterspout across from the commercial dock from which you can jerry can water. You can also get wireless Internet from the nearby church while the skipper totes the jugs. Walk towards the sound, and look for the little sign that points to a blowhole (it is before the cemetery). On windy, wavy days, its "Old Faithful-like" plumes will not disappoint!

An alternative anchorage lies off the community dock, the smaller dock to the west and tucked off a knob of land called Adams Point. If you draw 1.2 meters/4 feet or less, you can come alongside the dock; but anchoring off in 3.6 to 4.5 meters/12 to 15 feet of water is probably better. The little bay itself shoals past the dock. Other than an open shelter built for local partying, there are no facilities here, but it is a pleasant, well-shaded and quiet place (and great for the yoga mat) no farther from the center of the settlement than the government dock. Wherever you choose to go, you are exposed to winds from any westerly quadrant in that bight. In the summer's prevailing southeast winds, Black Point is a good choice. In any time of year, it is a wonderful settlement to visit.

WATERWAY GUIDE PHOTOGRAPHY.

Small boats at Black Point settlement.

The Utility of the Exumas Cuts

The more we look at the geography of the bank side and the real utility of the Exumas cuts, the more we are led to three conclusions.

- The primary passage-making cuts listed are vital to you whether you are on the Exuma Bank or in Exuma Sound. Other than the dubious importance of Rat Cay Cut, these passes are your best way of switching from one side to the other.
- The real utility of the secondary cuts is to open up anchorages on the bank side if you are out in the sound, or, if you have worked your way far enough south on the bank, to give you your last opportunities to get out into the sound. But the more difficult eyeball navigation needed on the west side, in many cases, reduces their attractiveness for spur-of-the-moment changes in route.
- The Exuma Bank is no cruising ground south of Rudder Cut. In truth, the practical limit to relatively straightforward Exuma Bank cruising comes at Cave Cay Cut. From then on, making your way south is a slow business. It is fine if you want to take your time and poke around wherever you fancy, but it is time consuming and best avoided if you have dates to keep.

In the waypoint list, we have listed only one east waypoint (incoming from Exuma Sound) and one west (bank-side) waypoint for each cut. A single waypoint works well in the sound, but on the bank side, the channels threading between reef and sand often demand a succession of waypoints. But channels can change as the sand changes. Rather than list an endless stream of directions, you will be eyeballing your way in. In any event, we give you just one fix for reassurance.

The Principal Navigable Cuts

There are almost as many cuts or passes between the Exuma Bank and Exuma Sound as there are cays and islands in the Exumas. Some are navigable given the right conditions. Others are more difficult passes that you may explore in your dinghy, but are not transits that we would recommend. Even the navigable ones, as we have said, are subject to weather, and by that we mean the state of the tide, wind direction, wind strength and the angle of the sun. Wind against tide will inevitably set up adverse seas, which at best are uncomfortable, and at the worst, something approaching a "Rage" meaning dangerous seas that could, particularly in some passes, be life threatening.

Listed below are the principal cuts to use. Other passes, which you may bring into use once you have gained the knowledge and confidence to negotiate them, are mentioned in our sections dealing with each geographic area. To help you in your route planning, we give the approximate latitude of each cut.

Highbourne Cut (24°42N) At the south end of Highbourne Cay. At least 1.8 meters/6 feet at mean low water and straightforward, but you need good light in your favor. As with almost all the Exuma cuts, it can develop a short chop with wind against tide.

Warderick Wells Cut (24°24N) At the north end of Warderick Wells Cay. Apart from strong currents, it is a fine, wide pass.

Conch Cut (24°17N) Between Cambridge Cay and Compass Cay. Again, a strong current, and in this case, a rock awash in the middle (stay to its north), but there is plenty of room, no other hazards and good depth.

Dotham Cut (24°07N) At the north end of Great Guana Cay (named after Dotham Point). Sand bores on the Bank side dictate swinging north or south almost as soon as you are clear of the pass and the reef that extends west from the south tip of Gaulin Cay/ Bitter Guana Cay.

Farmers Cut (23°57N) and Galliot Cut (23°55N) Narrow, but good depth. Both used by the mailboats.

Cave Cay Cut (23°54N) Deep (over 6 meters/20 feet), but strong currents.

Rudder Cut (23°52N) Straightforward. While a muddle of small cays and reef clutter the southeast on the Bank side, they present no problem.

Rat Cay Cut (23°44N) An unusual north–south pass between Rat Cay and Boysie Cay. If the wind gets up from the east, this is the best cut.

Conch Cay Cut (23°34N) This pass is the west (and best) entrance into George Town Harbour.

Farmers, Galliot, Cave and Rat Cay Cuts

When you move south of Dotham Cut, you must think seriously about which cut you will use to gain access to the Exuma Sound. Consider Farmers, Galliot, Cave and Rat Cay cuts. None of these cuts pose any particular navigation problems; but like all the Exuma Cuts, they are subject to strong reversing tidal flows which, when running against wind, wave and swell, can portend extremely turbulent, choppy and potentially hazardous conditions. The effect of this kickback can be felt as far as a mile or more off a cut. With enough energy, walls develop that are not necessarily readily apparent. These conditions can affect wide or narrow cuts; usually the narrower, the more affected.

Sensible boaters do not force the issue, nor try to punch their way through. They hold off, wait for the wind and tide "window of opportunity," and then make their move. It seems that this should be understood, but every year you hear of vessels that wouldn't and didn't - wouldn't wait and didn't make it, that is. They capsize, turtle or go up on the rocks. Frenzied and desperate, they "MAY DAY," abandon ship half-dressed themselves, with kids barely tied into inadequate life jackets, while the family pets are left onboard to perish. It sounds melodramatic, but unfortunately true. These stories should not scare you; they should make you prudent and wise.

Great Guana Cay

Over 10 nautical miles in length, Great Guana Cay dominates the central Exumas. Pleasant Black Point is its only settlement, so far. Developers come and go on Great Guana. They dream of luxury estates and condominiums surrounding megayacht marinas, but years pass with little to show for their dreams. There is a pretty "castle" on Little Bay, off which you can anchor. The castle is privately owned, but listen to VHF Channel 16. The owners just might have a barbecue planned on the beach while you are there. Next door, the one completed condominium and forest of rebar poking up through the sand still hopes to turn into a resort and marina. For now, just enjoy the quiet anchorage and beautiful surroundings. As you hug the shore from the sand castle towards White Point, get your camera ready. There is a wonderful rock off the first point that you will swear is a real Atlantic bottlenose porpoise leaping out of the water. Depending on the wind, either side of White Point offers good holding and exquisite beaches. The rocky point is an osprey nursery. Please enjoy them from a distance, and leave your pets in the cockpit.

The western coast of Great Guana is dotted with spectacular coves and bays in which to drop the hook. Some have sugar-sand beaches and others, easy table-rock paths to the sound coast offering virgin territory for shelling and sea bean hunts. As you travel south along the coastline to pick your next anchorage, do keep an eye out for coral heads. They are prolific off Great Guana, and as you might guess, so are the fish. The free diving here is good, but there are many territorial eels and sharks on these heads. Don't stray too far from the dinghy!

Little Farmers Cay and Cut, from the northwest. (Not to be used for navigation.) WATERWAY GUIDE PHOTOGRAPHY.

Farmers Cay Cut

The 260-foot-tall BTC tower on Little Farmers Cay clearly indicates the proximity of both the cay itself and Farmers Cay Cut. The entrance to the cut from the east is well-defined. Stay south of the small cay in the center and avoid the patch of shoal and reef that extends southwest of it by passing to starboard or port. Past that, there are no hazards. The water is clear and easy to read. Taking the cut from west to east is just the reverse. The deeper water is obvious. That said, approach this cut under ideal and favorable conditions, particularly from the bank. Currents here can be very strong and require a firm hand at the helm.

Little Farmers Cay

Little Farmers Cay could be the ideal, archetypal Bahamian settlement; or maybe it is just everyone's dream vision of what a small Bahamian settlement should look like. It is situated superbly with two attractive, if not viable, harbors (both are very shallow), enough land elevation to add interest and attractive houses in a cornucopia of colors set among swaying palms and flowering shrubs.

You have a number of choices. Anchor off the southwest tip of Great Guana Cay, where a narrow tongue of deeper water places you just off the beach, but the holding is not good. Slightly better holding may be found to the west side of the sand bar enclosing that tongue of deeper water.

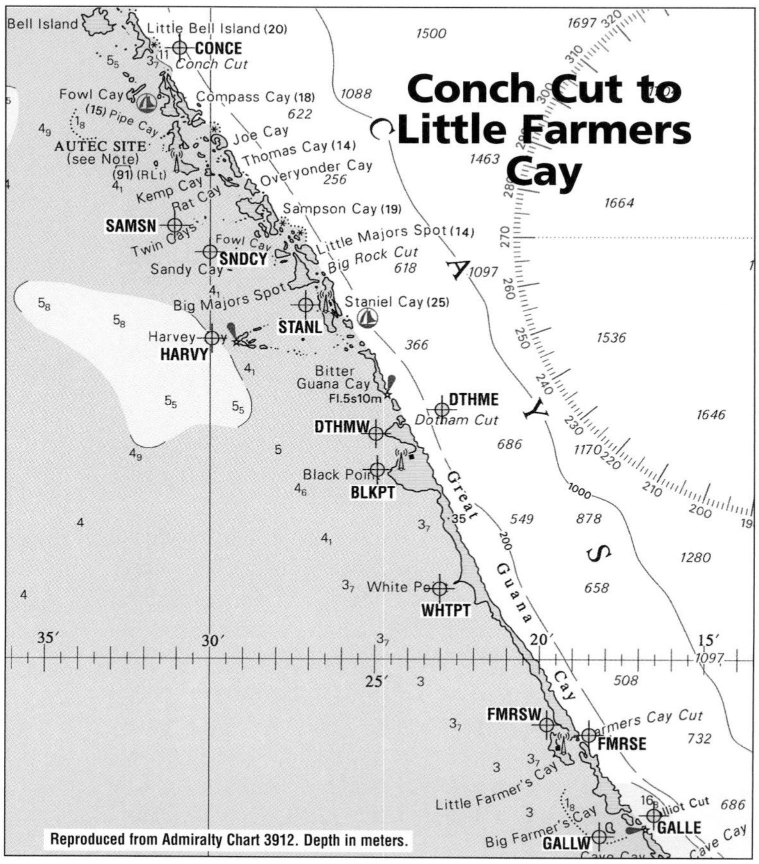

Not to be used for navigation.

Northern Exumas

LITTLE FARMERS CAY		Largest Vessel Accommodated	VHF Channel Monitored	Transient Berths / Total Berths	Approach / Dockside Depth (reported)	Floating Docks	Gas / Diesel	Groceries, Ice, Marine Supplies, Snacks	Repairs: Hull, Engine, Propeller	Lift (tonnage), Crane, Rail	1=110V, 2=220V, B=Both, Max Amps	Laundry, Pool, Showers	Pump-Out Station	Nearby: Grocery Store, Motel, Restaurant
		Dockage					Supplies		Services					
1. Farmers Cay Yacht Club (WiFi)	242-355-4017	140	16	8/	9/9		GD	IMS			B/50	LS		MR
2. Ocean Cabin (WiFi)	242-355-4006	44	16	8/	/10			IS	E			LS		R

Corresponding chart(s) not to be used for navigation. Internet Access (WiFi) Wireless Internet Access

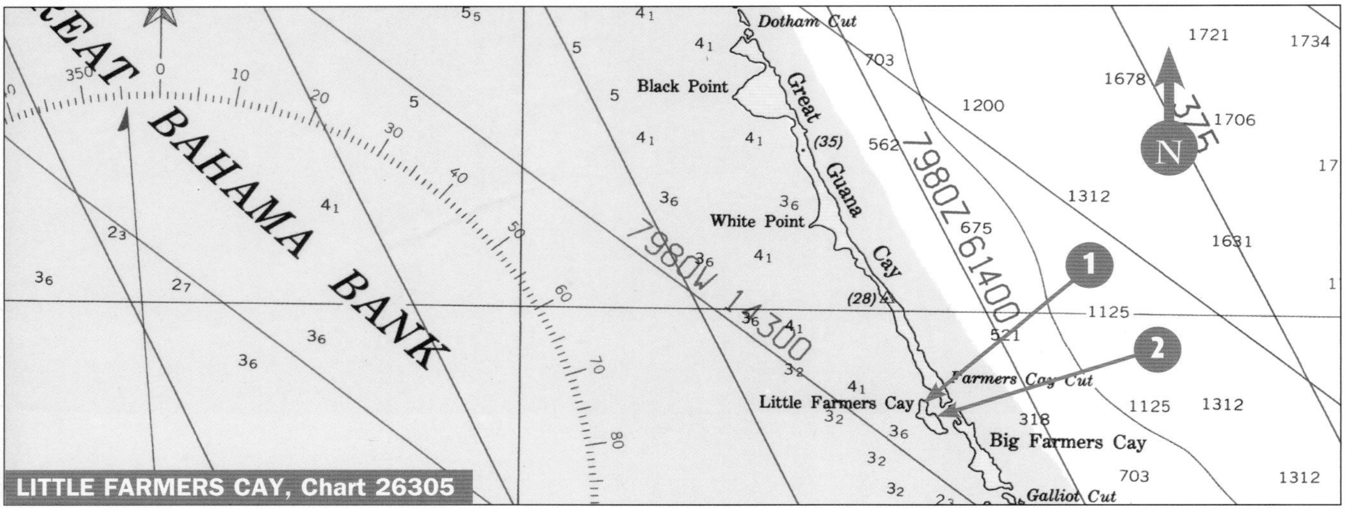

LITTLE FARMERS CAY, Chart 26305

You can drop south to the northwest cove of Big Farmers Cay, but this places you the full width of the cut away from the settlement, and you are exposed to surge. Neither of the two harbors, Little Harbour nor Big Harbour, is an option. Both shoal rapidly, and what anchoring space is there belongs to local boats. The government dock off Little Harbour is used by fishing boats and the mailboat on Wednesdays. However, 10 moorings in this area are available for transient use. One of these is suitable for larger vessels with deeper draft.

For those who prefer a slip, the Farmers Cay Yacht Club and Marina awaits your visit. The approach to the marina is straightforward, and the depths are good at 2.4 meters/8 feet at mean low water. There is everything a cruising boat could want here including a little market and a great restaurant and bar with complimentary wireless Internet.

Within the settlement itself, don't miss a visit to Ocean Cabin Restaurant and Bar and its owner, Terry Bain. Terry started the Five F's celebration (for Little Farmer's First Friday in February Festival) in 1986 and has been the driving force behind it, and several other reasons to celebrate, ever since. During the Five F's, Roosevelt Nixon, Terry's cousin, sponsors "C" Class sailboat races, a 15-stage event on Friday and Saturday. As often happens in the islands, some cruisers have decided to stay awhile and made Little Farmers Cay their winter home. When you are ready to put away the charts and laze on the decks, you may well choose to join them in this little corner of Bahamian heaven. Want to have guests visit paradise, too? Talk to Terry about his own little island available for rental complete with a new cottage and the makings of dreams of a lifetime.

See more information about the happenings at Little Farmers Cay in our Goin' Ashore section at the end of this chapter.

Pilotage. Talking Captain to Captain

From North Eleuthera and the Fleeming Channel

The area of bank to the immediate north of Exuma Sound in the Middle Ground/Finley Cay/Schooner Cay triangle is more shoal, and more hazardous, than the charts suggest. We do not recommend this route.

New Providence to Allans Cay or Highbourne Cay

As you leave Nassau Harbour for the Exumas, there are many choices for landfall, but a waypoint off the Allans Cay area is a sound choice. You can anchor off Allans Cay or continue to Highbourne Cay. You can access Exuma Sound via Highbourne Cut or continue south along the bank.

Although just one waypoint off Allans Cay could serve all these options, we list two waypoints—the first for Allans Cay and the second for Highbourne Cay and Highbourne Cut. On this approach, you will transit the Yellow Bank. There are many coral heads in this area, the shallowest of

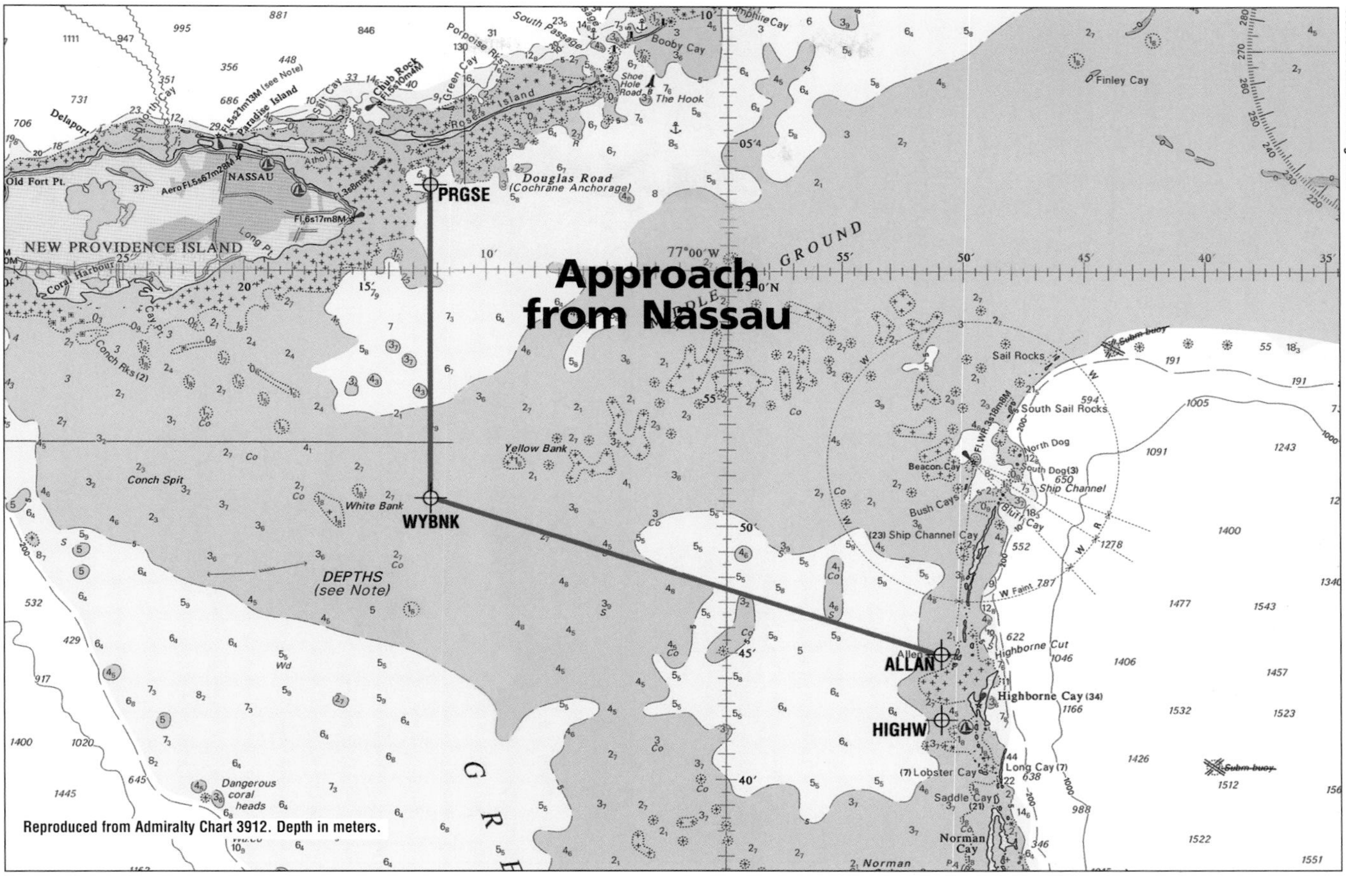

Reproduced from Admiralty Chart 3912. Depth in meters.

Not to be used for navigation.

which lie 0.9 meter/ 3 feet below the surface at mean low water. The average depth on the Yellow Bank at mean low water is 1.8 meters/ 6 feet. Do not run the Yellow Bank on autopilot. You must keep careful watch, and you need the sun in the right position. Also, you will need favorable weather, and you must be prepared to thread your way around the coral heads as you cross the Yellow Bank. Plan that the tide on the Yellow Bank will be one hour behind Nassau. Your optimum time to gain the Yellow Bank is around 11 a.m., so that the sun is to your advantage (high so you can see the heads). Finally, if the wind is going to be on your nose at 20 knots or more, expect steep, nasty seas. Anchor at Rose Island, and wait for favorable weather.

Avoiding the Yellow Bank

Set a dogleg course directly south from the Porgee Rocks Southeast waypoint (PRGSE) (N 25° 03.000'/W 077° 12.000') for a run of 11 nautical miles due south. You will reach a point midway between the Yellow and White banks (WYBNK). From this waypoint, you can alter course, and head for your chosen landfall.

Although this route is generally believed to be clear of keel-threatening coral heads and rock ledges, there are isolated coral heads here. From the time you reach the bank (about N 25° 55.580'/W 077° 12.000'), go slowly, and keep a lookout until you are well past the junction between the Yellow and White banks on your new heading (111/291 degrees true for Allans; 116/296 degrees true for Highbourne) and safely southeast of the Yellow Bank. Read the chart, and use your eyes. The depth of water is a good indicator, perhaps 2.7 to 3.6 meters/9 to 12 feet at mean low water, where you should take it slowly, and 1.5 meters/5 feet more than the depths we have quoted elsewhere. Take it slowly, once again, on the approach to your final waypoint.

Andros to Conch Cut

From Andros, Fresh Creek is your most likely departure point, and Conch Cut the most useful arrival waypoint. This provides the option of turning north for Warderick Wells, south for Sampson or Staniel Cays, or going through Conch Cut to get into Exuma Sound.

On this approach route, there is one area where you will find reefs and coral heads. Go slowly, and keep a sharp lookout. That is the point where you leave the deep water of the Tongue of the Ocean and come on to the bank. This is marked as waypoint (EBNKN) to remind you. A second area where you must go carefully is after reaching the Conch Cut West waypoint. Here there are sand bores to north and south as you visually navigate to Conch Cut itself.

Conch Cut from the west, just south of the main Pass. Rocky Dundas and Fowl Cay are in the foreground. (Not to be used for navigation.) WATERWAY GUIDE PHOTOGRAPHY.

Allans Cays, from the west. (Not to be used for navigation.) WATERWAY GUIDE PHOTOGRAPHY.

Highbourne Cut, from the south. (Not to be used for navigation.) Waterway Guide Photography.

Cape Eleuthera to Highbourne/Conch Cuts

From Eleuthera, the best departure points are either just off Cape Eleuthera or Davis Harbour. Use either Highbourne Cut or Conch Cut as your arrival waypoints. You then have the choice of staying in Exuma Sound or making your way on to the bank.

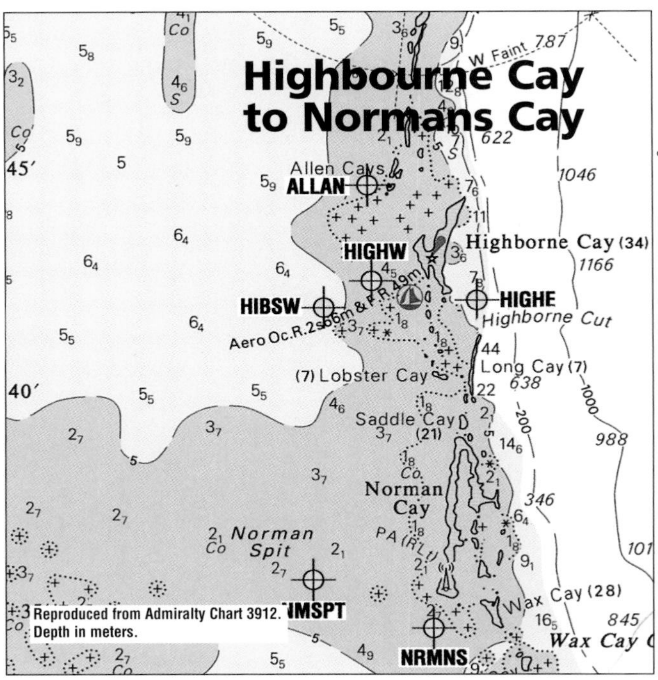

Approach to Allans Cay

Your approach to the Allans Cay group, bank or sound, is not difficult, because when you are still some distance off, the higher ground of Highbourne Cay to the south becomes visible, together with Highbourne's 260-foot-tall BTC tower. If you are coming in from Exuma Sound, take Highbourne Cut, swing out into the deeper water of the bank to avoid the shoals and reefs to the northwest of Highbourne Cay, and then make your way in to the Allans Cays from the Allans waypoint. From the bank side, simply make for that Allans waypoint. If there are other boats in the Allans Cay anchorage, you will see their masts showing above the cay.

Take the obvious way in between Allans Cay and Southwest Allans Cay, south of the little rock to the south of Allans Cay. Then turn to anchor either in the bight of Southwest Allans Cay to starboard or between Allans Cay and Leaf Cay to port. Don't go farther up the channel than the final part of Leaf Cay for it shoals rapidly. Check your anchor, as anchors drag here, and make sure it is well-bedded. Then launch your dinghy, and go meet the iguanas. Remember do not take a pet ashore and no garbage. The islands are a protected reserve.

Allans Cay to Highbourne Cay

To make for Highbourne Cay from the Allans group, the safest way is to head out southwest onto the bank, and swing around to avoid the reefs and shoals that lie to the west of the Allans Cay Cut. There is a direct route that shoal-draft vessels can take at high tide, but there is no point in trying to prove it. Save that for exploration later in your dinghy.

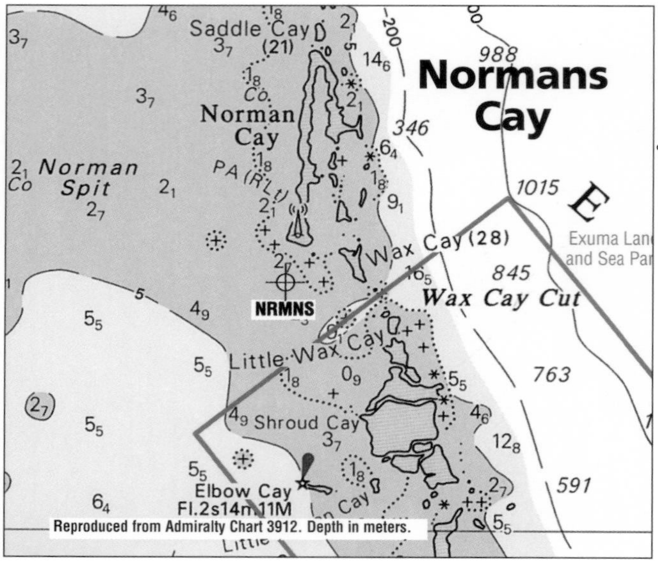

Reproduced from Admiralty Chart 3912. Depth in meters.

Not to be used for navigation.

Approach to Highbourne Cay

Lining up to enter Highbourne Cay is not difficult. Highbourne has a long, white beach on the west side, the irregular high ground we have already mentioned, a white house and trees on one of the humps and the 260-foot BTC tower. The anchorage and the Highbourne Marina are to the south of the tower, and as you get closer, you will see boats at the dock. Ahead, there are two rocks, one with a white stake on its north tip. Leave that stake to starboard as you enter. Beyond these rocks, on the shore of Highbourne itself, you will see two orange range marks. Once you have your bearings, there are no problems. Go in reading the water, particularly at low tide, and swing easily north toward the marina once you are safely past that stake. Stay in the deep water (there is a sand bar to port), and go on past the end of the concrete dock to where you plan to secure. The fuel dock is hard to starboard past the concrete dock. The personnel at Highbourne Cay are very professional and helpful. Don't hesitate to call them if you have any concerns about entry. If you are visiting by dinghy, request permission to land beforehand.

Highbourne Cay to Normans Cay

A shoal-draft boat, with the right tide and light, can work their way south on the bank side from Highbourne Cay to the north tip of Normans Cay, by way of Oyster Cay, Long (a.k.a. Spirit) Cay, Lobster Cay and Saddle Cay. Once there, the shoals to the west of Normans Cay will, most likely, require a detour into deeper water to the west before working your way inshore again to the Normans Cay anchorage under its south end.

The safe route from Highbourne to Normans involves getting well out on to the bank and staying out until you have cleared the shoal area called Normans Spit, which runs westward from the southeast tip of Normans Cay. From here, you visually navigate into Normans Cay's southern anchorage. It sounds like a lot of zigzagging around, but the plain truth is all you have to do is take one easy loop out on to the bank to get to Normans from Highbourne, keeping about three nautical miles offshore.

Normans Cay Southern Anchorage

The approach to the southern anchorage is easy from either Exuma Sound or the bank. On the sound side, the channel is narrow, carries depths of about 2.1 meters/7 feet, but is straightforward. Coming in from the west, keep slightly to the south as you go in, following the obvious deep-water channel. Then, you can follow a branch of this channel that runs roughly between the ruined dock and the ditched aircraft, or stay in the main stream that runs just north of a pretty little cay with white sand and a hillock with three smaller palm trees. The depth overall in the anchorage is 1.8 to 2.4 meters/6 to 8 feet at mean low water. You are well-protected there, other than from the southwest. If you are in the main tidal flow, expect reversing current and 180-degree swings as the tide changes, but the holding is good. Don't go farther up the apparent anchorage than the line running between the dock and the ditched aircraft, because it shoals.

Normans Cay North Harbour or Normans Pond

If you want to try it, the entrance to Normans Pond lies at the break in Normans Cay's east shore just to the north of latitude N 24° 37.000'. The entry channel lies between two large rocks or islets. Each has a fallen marker on it, both looking rather like cannons facing inward at the pass. On the far shore, there is a conspicuous white house. (After one visitor spent longer than he intended in Normans Pond, he determined to set up, once and for all, markers to guide other cruisers safely in and out of the pond.) When you are between the two "cannons" (in fact angled pipe), immediately look to your right, and you will see two markers. If you don't look to your right immediately, you will fail to see both markers, they will merge as one, and you will run in too far and ground waiting to pick up the second marker.

- The bottom one is float-shaped and white. The second is a white pole with a circle on the top. Use them as leading marks and turn to starboard.

At anchor in Normans Cay. WATERWAY GUIDE PHOTOGRAPHY.

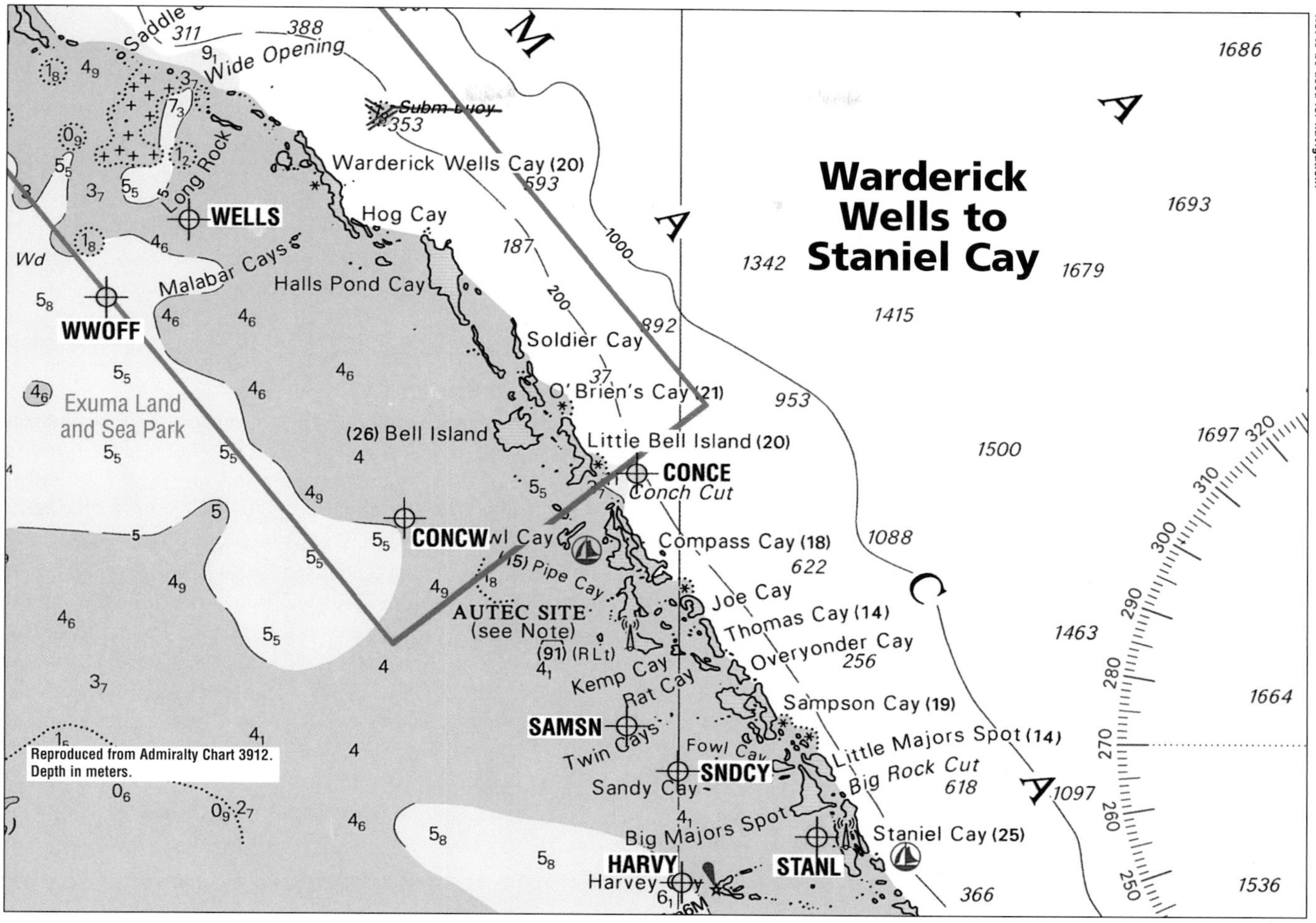

• Bear to starboard almost immediately after passing through the entry, and feel your way over a shoal (the 1.3 meter/4-feet-6-inch depth covered earlier), working your way closer to the shoreline to starboard. As you do this, you will enter deeper water and notice a pronounced shallow water contour running parallel to the shore. Stay in the deep water, keep going parallel to the shore, and you will soon be in the basin of the North Harbour. The first of two caves that will come up to starboard is the signal that you have made it. Thereafter, you are free to roam.

When departing, at the "cannon" point, there are two markers on the rock to the right of the "cannon." The lower marker has a black aircraft tire on the top, and the upper one is white.

Normans Cay Western Beach Anchorage

A third option for anchoring at Normans Cay is to make your way in north of Normans Spit to anchor off the airstrip beach, where you will see the Normans Cay Beach Club development, or anchor farther up the coast north off Skipjack Point.

Warderick Wells Main Anchorage

The approach into Warderick Wells anchorage from the approach waypoint (WWOFF) is simple. There is a very obvious sand bore to starboard. Keep it that way. To port, you will soon have another sand bore. Favor the first one. Your heading will be around 047/227 to 049/229 degrees true by way of the WELLS waypoint. More importantly, there are two rocks in the wide opening ahead. The left one looks flat like a table top, the right one rounded, a bit like an upturned salad bowl. Once you have them identified, head toward the northern tip of Warderick Wells just south of the salad bowl rock. As you get closer, a small, highly visible sand beach just south of Warderick Wells' northern point, makes a good lead-in mark. Head toward it. You will have deep water all the way. Don't go in the first entrance you see to starboard. Take the last one, where you see a line of marker buoys - white, red, blue - then the line of white mooring buoys with boats already on them. Upon turning in, there are first two white floats, then two floating post channel marks - a red and a green (red right returning). Call Exuma Park on VHF Channel 09, and declare yourself as you enter. You must have already been assigned a mooring buoy by number to enter. As you enter the harbor the darker, deep-water blue channel that curves ahead of you is as obvious as the Yellow Brick road leading to Oz. Just stay in the channel, and pick up your allotted buoy. They are numbered from your entry point, the colored ones included. Then take your dinghy and check in at the Park headquarters.

The Malabar Cays

There is a sunken boat around N 24° 21.500'/W 076° 38.500', which startles cruisers when they pass over it, but it is not believed to present any hazard to navigation. Just before the Malabar Cays, turn northeast, and head toward the Park Headquarters on Warderick Wells. Gradually turn more toward Emerald Rock, and anchor where water depth permits. This is a good alternative to the mooring field if a mooring is not available. The holding is excellent in 2 meters/7 feet.

Conch Cut

The three legs of the Conch Cut course, from west to east, are:

1. CONCW to CONC1 is 2 nautical miles on 057/237 degrees true.
2. CONC1 to CONC2 is 1.4 nautical miles on 088/268 degrees true.
3. CONC2 to CONCE is 1.5 nautical miles on 054/234 degrees true.

All three legs should be piloted visually. The mostly awash rock in the center of Conch Cut should be left to starboard when going out into Exuma Sound.

Related courses and distances to run are:

1. Conch Cut West (CONCW) to offshore Warderick Wells (WWOFF) is 7.7 nautical miles on 311/131 degrees true.
2. Conch Cut West (CONCW) to Edge of Bank North (EBNKN), heading for Andros, is 41 nautical miles on 295/115 degrees true (with another 28.4 nautical miles to run to Fresh Creek (FRESH) on 294/114 degrees true).
3. Conch Cut West (CONCW) to Sampson (SAMSN) is 5.7 nautical miles on 129/309 degrees true (running in to Sampson Cay Marina from the SAMSN waypoint is about 2 nautical miles on 081/261 degrees true).
4. Sampson (SAMSN) to Sandy Cay (SNDCY) is 1.1 nautical miles on 150/330 degrees true (for Staniel Cay).
5. Conch Cut East (CONCE) for Cape Eleuthera West (CAPEW) is 31.4 nautical miles on 015/195 degrees true, heading for Cape Eleuthera Marina or the Davis Channel.
6. Conch Cut East (CONCE) for Highbourne Cay East (HIGHE) is 28.7 nautical miles on 327/147 degrees true.

Conch Cut to Staniel Cay

Both Conch Cut West and the Sampson Cay waypoint provide access to the whole area lying between Compass Cay and Staniel Cay. In fact, the waypoint might be better described as Twin Cays, for it is just west of these landmark cays. From the Conch Cut West waypoint on the bank side, run six nautical miles on a heading of 134/314 degrees true to get to the Sampson/Twin Cays waypoint (SAMSN). If bound for Sampson Cay, turn east to pass south of Twin Cays. The Sampson Cay Club buildings will be ahead of you. If you are going on to Staniel Cay, Sandy Cay serves as a waypoint in the same manner as Twin Cays. You have another 1.4 nautical miles to run on a course of 140/320 degrees true to get to the Sandy Cay waypoint from Twin Cays. Then go around Sandy Cay to the west, and navigate visually for three nautical miles toward Staniel Cay and its 260-foot-tall BTC tower.

Staniel Cay, from the southwest. (Not to be used for navigation.) WATERWAY GUIDE PHOTOGRAPHY.

Compass Cay Approaches

The entry route to Compass Cay Marina from the bank side is well-marked and easily navigated. Just take it slowly. You can utilize Conch Cut to enter the channel to Compass Cay with a dogleg south soon after you pass the rock awash. Leave reds to starboard, and favor the Compass Cay shoreline as you point towards Pipe Cay. The channel into the marina is dredged, deep and well-marked. We do not recommend entering Compass Cay from Joe Cay Cut without local knowledge and piloting help from Compass Cay. The marker buoys are faded and confusing. The sand bars and shoal waters are prone to shifting, and the deep-water channel in is not obvious.

Approaches to Staniel Cay

Either Sandy Cay (SNDCY to the northwest) or Harvey Cay (HARVY to the southwest) are your lead marks to gaining Staniel Cay (STANL). From either of these, you should be able to pick up the BTC tower and steer for it. Go easy once you pass longitude W 076° 27.500', and pay attention to the color of the water, particularly on your port side, as a sandbar bulges down from the north as you get closer in. Your heading now should be fixed on the larger of the low-lying rocks ahead, which has a hard-to-define stake on it. Short of this rock, you will become aware that deeper-water channels fork off to the north and south.

The north channel leads toward the Staniel Cay Yacht Club. To reach Staniel Cay Yacht Club, you must parallel the line of rocks heading up the deep-water channel, then round a reef that extends north from the last visible rock. In effect, you go past the docks, then make a 180-degree turn to come back to them. If you wish to anchor off, the southwest edge of the bulging sandbank (to port side on the way in to Staniel Cay Yacht Club) is good, because it is just off the Yacht Club (but there is little room here for more than two boats).

If you are coming from the north, the approach, reduced to its simplest form, is this: Round Sandy Cay safely off, then turn directly for the Staniel Cay marker stake on the southern rock. If you are coming up from the south, stand safely off Harvey Cay, and continue northward, gradually turning northeastward in a gentle curve until you intersect the course line running in from Sandy Cay. Then head in on that line. The waypoints show you the way.

Staniel Cay to Farmers Cays

Harvey Cay, a short run from STANL of 2.7 nautical miles on 248/068 degrees true, is rather like Elbow Cay, an outlying cay that makes staying out to the west necessary if you are passage-making on the Bank side. Harvey Cay to Dotham Cut West is a short run of 5.3 nautical miles on a heading of 121/301 degrees true.

Dotham Cut

With wind and tide fighting over this shoal, Dotham Cut can produce untenable conditions on the Bank side. The cut itself is fine, deep and holds no other hazards. Recognition of Dotham Cut is aided by a light stake on Gaulin, as well as by the white cliffs. As with all passes, go through it piloting visually.

Dotham Cut to George Town

Dotham Cut East, to the northwest entrance of George Town Harbour, is a straight offshore Exuma Sound run of 45.2 nautical miles on 136/316 degrees true.

Dotham Cut to Black Point Settlement

To go to Black Point settlement from the north, visually pilot and head southeast on the Bank side to ease around Dotham Point. Then run parallel to the shore to anchor in the bay. Black Point's 100-foot BTC tower is a good marker if you can't pick up buildings immediately. If you veer off toward Black Point, you will find yourself in another shoal area. Favor Dotham Point and the coastline, then head straight for the Government Dock. ■

The Northern Exuma Cays Waypoints

Beacon Cay Ship Channel W	BCSCW (X57)	24°52.30N / 76°49.30W
Beacon Cay Ship Channel E	BCSCE (X71)	24°51.25N / 76°48.00W
Allans Cay	ALLAN	24°44.83N / 76°51.00W
Highbourne Cay West	HIGHW (X58)	24°42.40N / 76°51.00W
Highbourne Cay East	HIGHE (X59)	24°42.05N / 76°48.00W
Highbourne Stake	HSTKW	24°42.50N / 76°50.00W
Highbourne SW	HIBSW	24°42.00N / 76°52.00W
Normans Spit	NMSPT	24°35.75N / 76°52.00W
Normans Cay	NRMNS	24°34.66N / 76°49.50W
Elbow Cay	ELBOW (X60)	24°31.00N / 76°49.60W
Cistern Cay	CSTRN (X61)	24°25.00N / 76°47.00W
Warderick Wells West	WWOFF	24°21.00N / 76°42.00W
Warderick Wells SW	WELLS	24°22.50N / 76°40.25W
Conch Cut West	CONCW	24°15.85N / 76°35.58W
Conch Cut 1	CONC1	24°16.96N / 76°33.71W
Conch Cut 2	CONC2	24°17.02N / 76°32.09W
Conch Cut East	CONCE	24°17.90N / 76°30.74W
Sampson Cay	SAMSN	24°12.23N / 76°30.62W
Sandy Cay	SNDCY	24°11.25N / 76°30.00W
Staniel Cay	STANL	24°10.25N / 76°27.25W
Harvey Cay	HARVY (X62)	24°09.20N / 76°29.50W
Dotham Cut East	DTHME (X63)	24°07.35N / 76°23.80W
Dotham Cut West	DTHMW (X64)	24°06.00N / 76°25.20W
Black Point	BLKPT	24°05.41N / 76°25.00W
White Point	WHTPT	24°02.00N / 76°23.00W
Farmers Cut East	FMRSE	23°57.83N / 76°18.50W
Farmers Cut West	FMRSW	23°58.08N / 76°19.66W

Exuma Bank Routes

HEADING FOR ALLANS CAY AND HIGHBOURNE CAY

White-Yellow Banks Jct	WYBNK	24°52.00N / 77°12.00W

HEADING FOR ANDROS

Edge of Bank North	EBNKN	24°32.91N / 77°16.55W

Position format is latitude and longitude in degrees and minutes (hddd°mm.mm). Waypoints in RED are NOT for autopilot navigation. Codes in parenthesis are Wavey Line waypoints marked on the charts. If you have programmed waypoints listed in a previous edition of this guide, check carefully to ensure the coordinates you have recorded match the list. If a waypoint is no longer on the list we may have changed its code or deleted it.

GOIN' ASHORE:

HIGHBOURNE CAY

fuel • groceries • marina • telephone • water

Located about 42 miles southeast of Nassau, this 500-acre private cay offers good anchorages, great snorkeling and a small, but popular marina (make reservations). It is a petite, but beautiful, Exuma gem. From mini-megayachts to the smallest cruiser, all are welcome here. Marina guests can explore the paths and trails to discover pristine beaches and secluded hideaways. For boats at anchor, hail the marina on VHF Channel 71 for permission to land a tender at the beach in front of the office. Island exploration is restricted, but you can take advantage of the marina's well-stocked store, purchase fuel or RO water, arrange to have your laundry done, or drop off trash bags for a fee.

THINGS TO DO IN HIGHBOURNE CAY

- Swim off one of the beaches.
- Snorkel the *Octopus's Garden*.
- Dive the 230-foot Highbourne Cay Wall or the sixteenth-century Highbourne Cay Wreck.
- Take the dinghy up to Allans Cay, and introduce yourself to an iguana, but please don't feed them.

MARINA

HIGHBOURNE CAY
Tel: 242-355-1008 • Fax: 242-355-1003 • VHF 71
Slips 26. **Max LOA** 240 ft. along the 750-ft. face dock **MLW** 8 ft. **Dockage** $2.10 to $2.75 per ft. per night Tenders charged dock space according to length. **Fuel** Dock Open 8 a.m. to 5 p.m. daily. **Facilities & Services** Power $20 to $125 per day for 30 amp to 3-phase. Water $0.50 per gallon, laundry service available $10 per load, shower for marina guests only, public telephone, WiFi $10 per day, barbecue and outdoor dining area on shore; fish cleaning station. Trash bags: non-marina guests $5 per bag to dispose up to 2 bags of garbage, $25 per bag each additional. Store open 8 a.m. to 5 p.m., daily. Well-stocked with canned foods, produce, ice, snacks, frozen meat, liquor, gifts, books and T-shirts. Please use holding tanks in the marina. *Cool Runner's Catering Service* 242-355-1010, VHF 16 "Cool Runner" delivers homemade bread and delicious appetizers, fresh lobster salad, entrees, cakes and a choice of desserts to your boat. Brilliant snorkeling and deep sea fishing five minutes away. Every morning at 7:30 a.m. Highbourne Cay gives the weather report from NOAA and from Nassau for the Bahamas. Listen on VHF 16 and switch to channel announced. **Credit Cards** Visa, MasterCard, 4% surcharge. Accepts personal checks and Travelers checks. Dogs welcome at the marina on a leash. Please pick up after them!

The anchorages around Highbourne Cay are subject to strong tidal currents and surge, due to their proximity to Highbourne Cut. There is good holding, easterly protection and some surge along the western shore, north of the conspicuous 300-foot BTC tower. Tuck in as far north and east as possible in 2 meters/6 to 9 feet of water for best protection. Keep the Highbourne Rocks and coral reefs in mind. For short trips into the marina, you can find fair holding south of the marina in 3.6 meters/12 to 15 feet of water north of the private houses on the southeastern tip of the island. You will have some protection from the north and east, but lots of surge. In settled easterly winds, you can venture south of Highbourne, and anchor off the western shores of Oyster Cay and its two southern sister islands in 2 meters/6 to 9 feet of water and still reach the marina easily by dinghy.

Deck at Normans Cay Beach Club. WATERWAY GUIDE PHOTOGRAPHY.

NORMANS CAY

Normans Cay is slated for big changes. The containers with supplies and some construction equipment have already arrived. When exactly all the plans will come to fruition is under discussion. Reportedly, the Exuma Resort Developers Limited group will forfeit a $40 million bond to the Bahamas government if the initially proposed 40-unit Aman Resort Hotel, and its supportive infrastructure including roads, power, water and sewer, new airport runway and Customs and Immigration office, is not substantially constructed by 2012. After that, plans call for another $80 million in restaurants, bars, villas, a pool, spa, fitness center and beach club all within the 250-acre site. We continue to take a wait-and-see attitude about this planned development much like owners of Normans Cay Beach Club have done. In the meantime, sit back, relax, and enjoy what you have while you can!

Normans Cay is a favorite place to anchor and stay awhile. There is good easterly protection along the entire western shore of the cay, but there are coral heads and shifting sand bars. Negotiate this shore with good light, and use your polarized sunglasses. In between Normans and Boot Cay, you will find an almost totally submerged aircraft, a legacy from drug-running days, in four feet of water in the lagoon.

NORMANS CAY BEACH CLUB
VHF 16 • 242-357-8846 • normascaybc@yahoo.com
Situated on one of the most beautiful beaches you have ever envisioned, Normans Cay Beach Club offers welcome respite to the weary cruiser. Here you can get ice for your boat and cheeseburgers for your soul - along with great conversation and a cool drink - right on the water's edge. Also, you will find, of all the unexpected things, a high-speed Internet connection. If you have family or

Waterway Guide Photography.

Boo Boo Hill boat signs above Warderick Wells.

guests who want to visit the islands, here they will find the ultimate sugar-sand experience. Normans Cay Beach Club has four colorful, bougainvillea covered villas that can be rented individually or packaged for a group. Discounts are available for extended stays. There are kayaks and a Hobie Cat sailboat for guests to enjoy. The Beach Bar is open daily from noon to 8 p.m. The restaurant opens Tuesday through Sunday from noon to 3 p.m., and 5 p.m. to 8 p.m. Please make reservations. The restaurant is also available for private functions from birthday parties to wedding receptions. Contact Stephan or Chris for arrangements.

WARDERICK WELLS

The Exuma Cays Land and Sea Park covers 176 protected square miles of spectacular subtropical waters, coral reefs and fish-breeding grounds from Little Wax Cay at the northern end to Conch Cut in the south. The Park was established in 1958 largely due to the dedication of Peggy Hall. It is the flagship of the Bahamas National Trust and a model for preservation areas throughout the Caribbean. Check in at the headquarters building to pick up park information and rules (of which there are many.) In addition, there are bird lists, walking trails maps and snorkeling site charts. Office hours are 9 a.m. to noon and 1 p.m. to 4 p.m. Monday through Saturday; Sunday, 9 a.m. to noon. The park monitors VHF 09. Inquire at the Park office about joining the Exuma Cays Land and Sea Park Support Fleet. Support Fleet members receive two complimentary mooring nights at the North Moorings, Emerald Rock Moorings and/or South Moorings as well as priority on the waiting list.

EXUMA CAYS LAND AND SEA PARK –
"Take Only Photographs, Leave Only Footprints"
VHF 09 • 242-225-1791 or 242-225-3281
exumapark@bnt.bs.com • www.exumapark.info

The Park makes a general announcement each morning at 9 a.m. on VHF Channel 16 and switches to VHF 09. At this time, cruisers request a mooring based on location, vessel length and draft. Shortly thereafter, the Park responds on VHF 09 to announce that day's mooring assignments. Being wait-listed is common during the winter months. Vessels use the Park's moorings entirely at their own risk. Mooring fees are subject to change. **Facilities and Services** The park office includes a small gift shop featuring exhibits and specimens of shells and other items collected in the park. Items offered for sale include t-shirts, hats/visors, postcards, books, charts and maps, ice, DVD rental, sunscreen and other miscellaneous items. Provisions and fuel are not available in the park. Wireless Internet is available at park headquarters. Purchase access at the office, or register and pay on-line. There are very specific rules for pets. Please obtain the guidelines from the park office.

Moorings that are assigned include:
North Mooring Field - 22 moorings in front of Park Headquarters. One can accommodate a 180 ft. yacht.
Emerald Rock Mooring Field – 26 moorings placed around Emerald Rock. Buoys marking "No Anchorage" zone are obvious.
South Mooring Field – 6 moorings in between Warderick Wells Cay and Hog Cay. Fees for assigned moorings are payable at Park Headquarters.

First-come, first-served moorings include:
Shroud Cay Mooring Field – 12 moorings. All can accommodate yachts to 65 ft. and 6-ft. draft. Pay box is located on the trail at the north end of the beach.
Hawksbill Cay Mooring Field – 14 moorings. Four are on the west side of the cay. Ten are at the southern tip. All can accommodate yachts to 65 ft. and 6-ft. draft. Two can accommodate yachts up to 150 ft. and are marked "150 MAX." Please use standard-size balls first. Pay box is located behind the large green Bahamas National Trust, Exuma Cays Land & Sea Park sign.
Cambridge Cay Mooring Field – 14 moorings. All can accommodate yachts to 65 ft. and 6 ft. draft. Two can accommodate yachts up to 150 ft. and are marked "150 MAX." Please use standard-size balls first. Pay box is the mailbox behind the large green Bahamas National Trust, Exuma Cays Land & Sea Park sign.

FEES Fees range from $20 per night for a boat up to 40 ft. to $100 per night for a boat over 90 ft. Please inquire at park for fees applicable to your vessel.
ANCHORING Anchoring is not allowed in the North Mooring Field, Emerald Rock Mooring Field or the South Mooring Field. Vessels may anchor between the "No Anchoring" buoys near Emerald Rock and the Malabar Cays. There is room to anchor outside the mooring fields at Shroud Cay, Hawksbill Cay, Emerald Rock and Cambridge Cay. You may anchor in any other area that does not interfere with a mooring field, coral, sea life or seabed.

SNORKELING & DIVE SITES

Hawksbill Cay has good anchorages off the central west coast and an excellent freshwater well near the anchorage. There are white-tailed Tropicbirds nesting here in March and April, providing spectacular flying displays. Between *Little Cistern* and *Cistern Cay*. *Brad's Cay* on the east side of *Long Cay*, has a cave on the northeast side. Between *South Halls Pond*, *O'Briens* and *Pasture Cay*, where there is a sunken drug-smuggling plane. *Cambridge* and *Little Bell Cay* are private, but have good reefs to the east and south. *Rocky Dundas*, except in north through east winds, with its caves and reef. And the Park's own *Sea Aquarium*, which you can locate by the sign on a small rock and a dinghy mooring. Some of the cays within the Park are privately owned, so please respect their privacy. *Don't touch, harm or remove anything you see; take only photographs, leave only bubbles!*

THINGS TO DO IN WARDERICK WELLS

- Swim off your boat in some of the clearest water in the world; you may see Bubba, a 4-foot barracuda, or one of the seven or eight lemon sharks who live around the north moorings.
- Snorkel or dive the unbelievably beautiful, diverse reefs.
- See how many birds you can hear in the total peace and quiet of Warderick Wells, and spot them from the bird check list given out at the headquarters.
- Visit Pirate's Lair off Capture Beach. Hike the Conch Shell Trail, where there is a well in a large clearing and interesting non-indigenous plants growing.
- Discover the ruins of an eighteenth-century Loyalist settlement off Rendezvous Beach or another on Hawksbill Cay. All trails are marked, and you can find them from the water in your dinghy if you look for the green netting or white floats off a beach, indicating a trail on shore.
- Beryl's Beach offers wonderfully sheltered, shallow water swimming, especially good if you have younger children with you, with a marked trail across to the east coast.
- Walk to the top of Boo Boo Hill and leave your boat's name as a memento. Keep to the marked Shaggy Dog Trail, and wear sturdy shoes to protect your feet across the "moonscape." Maybe you will meet a hutia on the way. Don't forget to take a camera; the views from the top are glorious, and you have to be photographed nailing your boat name to the great collection up there...
- Ask how you can help with volunteering in the park.
- Listen for the ghosts of Warderick Wells singing hymns on moonlit nights!

COMPASS CAY

accommodation • beach • marina • moorings • nature trails • water

This small island is a tiny corner of paradise, beautifully tended by its owner and your host Tucker Rolle. Tucker's thoughtful stewardship of the land and surrounding waters are an example of the highest ideals in ecological conservancy. The sheltered harbor offers good hurricane protection and is popular for long-term boat storage. The approach channels have been well-marked by Tucker. The channel in from the bank or via Conch Cut is well-marked with pilings and buoys. On a rising tide, you will see no less than 2 meters/6 feet of water. The entrance channel is dredged to 7 feet. It is wider than it looks on the charts. A lighted piling and a day marker, both with red triangles, guide you in to the docks. With piloting help from the staff at Compass Cay, you may be able to bring a deep draft boat on a high tide from Joe Cay Cut. The buoys there are confusing and the sands constantly shifting. Well-marked trails guide you over the walking paths that crisscross the cay, and "the prettiest beach in the Bahamas" is no false claim to their idyllic crescent beach. Family and friends can fly into Staniel Cay on Watermakers Air and enjoy a stay in the cottages on Compass Cay.

COMPASS CAY MARINA
Tel & fax: 242-355-2064, 242-355-2137 in the dockmaster's office
VHF 16 • compasscaymarina@gmail.com • www compasscay.com

Slips 20. **Max LOA** 165 ft. **MLW at Dock** 10 ft. **Dockage** $2.50 per ft. per night, 70 ft. and under; $2.75 per ft. per night, over 71 ft. **Facilities & Services** Power $40 to $100 per night for 30 to 100 amps. RO water $0.50 per gal. Showers for guests only. Coin-op washer and dryer $10 per load. Public telephone, complimentary WiFi. Recycling is practiced here! Trash disposal for guests only. It is separated into glass/metal and burnable. Store has ice, water, soft drinks, some provisions, beer, wine, as well as T-shirts, caps and charming maps of the island. **Restaurant** Hamburgers and hot dogs for lunch. No breakfast or dinner. Beach parties and potluck suppers on the beach and dockside with other guests. This beach is superb, with good snorkeling on reefs that you can swim to. Marked walking trails on the island. **Accommodations** Two villas and two apartments that can accommodate up to six guests from $2,100 to $5,500. Include the use of a Boston Whaler. Sea kayaks for rent. **Credit cards** Visa and MasterCard, 5% surcharge. Pets are welcome at the marina on a leash.

THINGS TO DO IN COMPASS CAY

- Enjoy lazy days on that gorgeous beach. Snorkel out to introduce yourself to colonies of fish living on the reefs.
- Make new friends at a dockside potluck supper.
- Take the dinghy to explore some of the little bays and inlets among the neighboring islands.
- Feed the pet sharks and fish from the docks.

SAMPSON CAY

accommodation • fuel • marina • provisions • restaurant
telephone • water

With its sheltered marina, nicely maintained docks and shoreside facilities, Sampson Cay is a favorite Exuma destination. It is first-class, luxurious and, at the same time, maintains an Out Island's friendly atmosphere. The cut into the inner harbor has been widened and dredged. Gorgeous landscaping surrounds the marina and villas. There are trails to all seven beaches on the cay. Opportunistic sharks and stingrays that circle in the channel and harbor provide mesmerizing entertainment. Provisioning at the marina store is good. The freezer is stocked with a good variety of poultry and meat. Produce is kept refrigerated for freshness. Visitors are warmly welcomed here whether you come from an anchorage by dinghy, or arrive onboard a megayacht. Don't miss the Saturday beach party buffet!

SAMPSON CAY CLUB AND MARINA
Tel 242-355-2034, Fax 242-355-2038 U.S.: 954-703-6015
Cell: 242-457-3683 • VHF 16 "Sampson Cay"
info@sampsoncayclub.com • www.sampsoncayclub.com

Slips 2,200 ft. linear feet of dockage **Max LOA** N/A **MLW** 7 ft. **Dockage** $2.75 per ft per night. Monthly and yearly dockage available. Boat checkout time is 12 noon, and late fees are charged. **Fuel** Dock open 7 a.m. to 5 p.m.; diesel and gasoline. **Facilities & Services** Shore power $0.85 per kwHr, 30 amp to 3-phase, Water $0.50 per gallon. Showers and restrooms, coin-op washer and dryer, $4 per load; 2 public telephones, complimentary WiFi. Trash and recycling stations marina guests only. Grocery store well-stocked, open 8 a.m. to 5 p.m. daily, to noon on Sunday. Fresh fruit, vegetables, dairy products, meat, fish, poultry, lunch meats, spices, canned goods, cookies, ice cream and candy. Ice. Daily weather fax. **Restaurant & Bar** Opens 8 a.m. to 10 p.m. daily, for breakfast (8 a.m. until 11 a.m.), lunch (12 noon until 3 p.m.) and dinner (6 p.m. until 10 p.m.). Bar open noon until 10 p.m. **Accommodations** Five guest houses and villas with accommodations for 2 to 6 persons from $190 to $2,100 per night/$1,200 to $8,000 per week. Kayak, Sunfish and Hobie Cat are for guests use.

Sampson Cay Yacht Club. Photo Courtesy of Peter Mitchell.

Shuttle service runs from Staniel Cay, $50 one-way, per passenger. Other boats are available for rent. Reservations@samsoncayclub.com or 877-633-0305. **Credit Cards** Visa and MasterCard with a 5% surcharge. Travelers Checks and Bahamian dollars.

THINGS TO DO IN SAMPSON CAY

- Snorkel and dive the many reefs within easy reach of Sampson Cay; explore Pipe Creek in your dinghy.
- Swim from one of the glorious beaches. Take lots of photographs, especially of the sunsets.
- Take the dinghy over to Staniel Cay or Fowl Cay for dinner.
- Leave your boat in complete safety if you have to return to the U.S. or Canada for a while.

FOWL CAY

Fowl Cay not only offers great accommodations from $10,150 to $19,250 for an island home hide-away, but also a fine dining experience for vessels anchored in the area. At the *Harbour Club*, enjoy some of the most creative cocktails, chic company and appealing cuisine to be found for hundreds of miles in any direction at their enchanting restaurant high atop Fowl Cay's highest point. Call *The Harbour Club* for dinner reservations before noon (242-524-8114, VHF 16 "Fowl Cay" or reservations@fowlcay.com) to ensure your spot in an elegantly sculptured period chair awaiting you at your finely set table. Your sumptuous meal might include an appetizer such as grilled scallops on crispy wontons with avocado salsa, followed by a spinach salad with candied pecans and goat cheese tossed with a chipotle vinaigrette, and a grilled pork loin topped with mango chutney, served with smashed sweet potatoes, only to end with a rum laced bread pudding topped with caramel sauce.

STANIEL CAY

airport • fuel • groceries • marina • medical • post office • propane • restaurant • telephone • water

With its good anchorages, first-class marina and a central position in some of the most spectacular waters in the world, Staniel Cay is a favorite Exuma destination. The cheery people, good shops and lots of services just make you want to stay. Everything you want or need is within easy walking distance on the cay. *Watermaker Air flights* from Ft. Lauderdale land your guests and loved ones almost at the dinghy dock. No lengthy, expensive taxi rides from this airport! Hoist that duffle bag on your back and stroll, or hitch a ride on the tram to the Yacht Club. Stay in touch with what is going on by listening to the Boaters Net (VHF 16, switching to 14) at 8 a.m. for weather and local information, or get on the Internet at one of the many hot spots around the island. *Exumas WiFi* continues to add hot spots around all the islands. Need something from the U.S.? Have it sent to you care of *Watermakers Air*. They will put your package on the next plane for your pick up at *Staniel Cay Yacht Club*.

If you have always wanted to be photographed like a swimsuit model, visit the site of their shoots at Kayu Maya on Ocean Ridge. With 40-foot elevations, the vistas from up there are remarkable. If you would like to park your yacht in the harbor east of the airstrip, 50-foot docks with 5-foot depths come with a $2 million Kayu Maya lot purchase. Provisioning on mailboat day is superb in the cay's three grocery stores. And, everyday is fresh bread day at the bright yellow bakery, *Titta Emil's*. Treat yourself to ice cream from *Isles General Store* and enjoy it (and WiFi) in the gazebo. Miss Vivian will even do your laundry for you. For real good time times and local color, the school's fundraiser, a Food Festival, is usually held in February or March, and the annual Staniel Cay Homecoming festival is held in August.

Rent a golf cart to see little visited South Staniel Cay. There are some very pretty beaches in the shallow waters on either side. In particular, visit Ho Tai Cay, South Beach and Pigeon Cay Beach. From Pigeon Cay, you can snorkel or swim-walk at low tide over to Lumber Cay Beach. After your circle tour of South Staniel, head back across the bridge to North Staniel. Follow the arrows to the golf cart parking lot to access the ocean beaches. Shelling and sea beaning are particularly good along these shorelines. You can hike the trail down to Pirate Trap Beach from the parking lot. Pirate Trap is decorated like any good "Cruisers Yacht Club," with painted conch shells commemorating cruiser visits, and every variety of flotsam and jetsam hanging and dangling around. The best map to use for golf carting and beach hunting is, of all things, the placemat at the Yacht Club's restaurant! Go get yourself one, and have a good time.

EMERGENCIES

Marine • VHF 16
Medical *Clinic* • 242-355-2010 • VHF 16 "St Luke's Clinic" or "Nana 2" • Resident nurse, doctor visits once a month. Open 9 to noon and 2:30 to 5 p.m.; closed Sundays, and Wednesday and Saturday afternoons.

MARINAS

Facilities at marinas just don't get any nicer than this. The docks, shorepower and fuel pumps are superbly maintained. The help and assistance from Chubby and his staff are unparalleled. The restaurant and bar is just the sort of place you dreamed of hanging out at in the islands. The conch burgers on fresh baked bread are worth a picture if you can ever get one to sit around on a plate that long. Everyone seems to be happy to work here, happy to live here, happy to be staying at the cottages here, happy to be going to Thunderball Grotto from here, and happy that you are here, too. The only people who are unhappy are those that are leaving here!

STANIEL CAY YACHT CLUB

Tel: 242-355-2024 • Fax: 242-355-2044 U.S.: 954-467-8920 • VHF 16 • info@stanielcay.com • www.stanielcay.com

Slips 18. **Max LOA** 170 ft. **MLW at Dock** 9 ft. **Dockage** $2.00 per ft. per day under 100 ft.; $2.50 per ft over 100 ft. Late checkout fees apply. Dinghy dockage free for bar and restaurant guests. **Fuel** Dock open 8 a.m. to 5 p.m. daily with diesel and gasoline (look for new, more convenient fuel dock with high-speed diesel). **Facilities & Services** Power $30 to $100 per day for 30 amps to 3-phase. RO water $0.40 per gallon. Public telephones by the restaurant. WiFi and a spot to sit and enjoy the experience for a fee. Trash $2.50 for a small bag, $5 for a large bag. Ice. Laundry fluff and fold for $10. No showers. Restrooms in the restaurant. Small store inside the clubhouse has liquor, unique souvenirs and 'tings, nice logo items. Golf cart rentals, kayaks, snorkel & SCUBA gear, air fills available. On-site PADI dive operators and shop. Propane tanks refilled at Isles General Store. Fresh baked bread delivered to your slip or cottage, "Titta Emil's" VHF 16, 242-464-1248. **Restaurant & Bar** Open Monday through Saturday at 8 a.m. to 10 a.m. for breakfast, 11:30 a.m. to 3 p.m. for lunch and 7 p.m. to 9:30 p.m. for dinner. Sunday open 8 a.m. to 9 p.m. The bar is open 11:30 a.m. to 9:30 p.m. daily. It is very popular and lots of fun, elbow to elbow with locals and cruisers and cottage guests. It has a pool table and satellite TV. **Accommodations** Lovely waterfront and water view island-style cottages from 1 bedroom to 3 bedrooms from $145 to $255 per night. Weekly rates available. **Credit Cards** Visa and MasterCard, with a 5% surcharge. Travelers checks accepted. Pets are welcome at the marina, but not inside the bar!

CLUB THUNDERBALL

Tel: 242-355-2125 • VHF 16

Club Thunderball is a lively bar and restaurant with moorings out in front. Listen every morning for the event of the day at Club Thunderball. The young owners offer movie nights, barbeque nights and pizza nights. You can also grab a nice lunch, and access WiFi from their club.

Moorings Five mooring balls in front of Thunderball Grotto. VESSELS USE MOORINGS ENTIRELY AT THEIR OWN RISK. **Max LOA** 50 ft. **Fee** $20 per night.

PORT DIRECTORY

Accommodations *Staniel Cay Yacht Club*. See details under marina • *Chamberlain's Staniel Cay Cottages & "DATT" Art Gallery*, 242-357-0936, five truly unique rental cottages, owned and decorated by local artist, across the street from community beach and anchorage • *Isles General Store*, 242-355-2007, Pretty efficiencies above the grocery store, right across the street from the airport, easy dinghy access at their good dock up the Dinghy Channel.

Airlines *Watermakers Air*, 954-467-8920, www.watermakersair.com. Have packages sent to your vessel "Care Of" Watermakers Air, 2233 S. Andrews Ave., Ft. Lauderdale, FL 33316 ($2 a pound charge). Flights from Fort Lauderdale and Nassau to Staniel Cay twice daily • *Flamingo Air*, daily flights to Nassau, 242-377-0364.

Airport Well-maintained, paved 3,000-ft. runway.

Artwork *"DATT" Art Gallery*, 242-357-0936, studio across from Chamberlain's purple and pink cottages on the beach. You can also find the artist's work for sale at *Staniel Cay Yacht Club, Nikki's 3Ns Golf Cart Rental & Snack Shack and Isle's General Store*.

Bakery *Titta Emil's*, bright yellow house across from the library. Fresh baked goods daily. Homemade conch batter, frozen by the quart, ready for you to fry in the galley.

Boutique *Lindsay's Boutique* • 242-355-2050 • T-shirts, bags, resort wear and straw work.

Church *Mt. Olivet Baptist Church*.

Deep Sea Fishing *Staniel Cay Yacht Club*, 242-355-2024.

Dive Shop *Staniel Cay Divers*, 242-355-2101. www.stanielcaydivers.com • located next door to Staniel Cay Yacht Club. PADI certification. Wall dives. Spearfishing trips. Snorkeling trips, too.

Golf Cart Rentals *TC's Golf Carts*, behind the Yacht Club • *3Ns Golf Carts*, next door to the Post Office and at the Airport.

Internet WiFi available from *Exuma WiFi*, 242-524-4398, Steve will help if you are having trouble connecting. Hot Spots at Staniel Cay Yacht Club, Isles General, Club Thunderball, Compass Cay and Sampson Cay. New antennas being placed along the Pipes. Turn on your computer, and see what happens. WiFi antenna will significantly increase your chances of getting connected.

Laundry New facility being built next to Staniel Cay Yacht Club in Spring 2010.

Library Built in 1776. 11 a.m. to noon and 4 p.m. to 5 p.m. on Mondays and Fridays; 4 to 6 p.m. Wednesdays. Across from Titta Emil's bright yellow house. The library welcomes donations and volunteers.

Medical *St. Luke's Clinic* • 242-355-2010 • VHF 16 "St Luke's Clinic" or "Nana 2" • Open Monday, Tuesday, Thursday and Friday, 9 to noon and 2:30 to 5 p.m.; closed Sundays, and on Wednesday and Saturday afternoons. A resident nurse and a doctor who visits once a month. St Luke's is funded by private donations. Please support their fundraising activities.

Post Office Open 9 a.m. to 4 p.m. weekdays north of *Blue Wing Grocery Store.*

Propane *Isles General Store.* Dinghy up the Dinghy Channel to their store side dock.

Provisions Turn east at *Titta Emil's* yellow bakery and walk to the top of the hill for blue and pink grocery stores • *Blue Wing Grocery Store* • 242-355-2014 • Open 7:30 a.m. to 7:30 p.m. daily except Sunday. Burke Smith has a good selection of groceries, liquor, vegetables, household supplies and fresh bread. Let him know if you need laundry done or special orders. *Isles General Store* • 242-355-2007 • VHF 16 "Isles General" • Open 7:30 a.m. to noon and 1:30 to 7 p.m., Monday to Saturday. Burkie Rolle has a well-stocked store across the creek selling everything from hardware, marine supplies, groceries, ice, propane and homemade bread. Miss Vivian does wash and fold for $10 per load. WiFi in the gazebo out front. There is a customer dinghy dock inside the creek where you can tie up. *Pink Pearl Supermarket* • 242-355-2040 • VHF 16 "Pink Pearl" • Hugh Smith's store is open 7:30 a.m. to 7:30 p.m. Monday to Saturday, with bread, groceries, household items and frozen goods. Hugh also has a mooring for boats up to 50 ft., $10 per day.

Restaurants 2 new restaurants under construction in Spring 2010 near the Staniel Cay public beach.

School *Staniel Cay All Age School* welcomes visits from cruising children. Just stop by the office to make arrangements.

Taxis Golf Carts and *Staniel Cay Yacht Club* tram to and from the airport.

Telephones BTC • 242-355-2060 • Fax: 242-355-2063 • Open weekdays 9 a.m. to 4:30 p.m. Phone cards at *Staniel Cay Yacht Club*, which has Internet access, too.

Trash May only be disposed of at the *Yacht Club* or at the *Isles General Store*; for $2.50/$5 per bag, depending on size. Use heavy mill trash bags. No lightweight plastic grocery bags, please!

Water Taxi *Island Shuttle*, www.stanielcayshuttle.com • a new service available for trips within 10 miles of Staniel.

THINGS TO DO IN STANIEL CAY

- Dive *Thunderball Grotto*, the spectacular underwater cave where shafts of sunlight illuminate the fish inside the cavern. Famous in the James Bond movie, "*Thunderball*," and best visited at slack water, since the currents are strong here. At low slack water, you can swim straight in. Take a bag of frozen peas or corn, and watch the fish flock toward you, almost nibbling your fingers in excitement; schools of fish will greet you outside. Tie up to the mooring buoy on the northwest side of the cave, or small boats can anchor.
- Enjoy dinner at the *Staniel Cay Yacht Club*, or dust off the dinner jacket and make a reservation at the *Harbour Club* at Fowl Cay.
- Meet the pigs on Big Majors Cay.
- Explore the inside route to Compass Cay in your dinghy.

BLACK POINT

groceries • medical • post office • restaurants • telephone • water

This friendly settlement on Great Guana Cay has the second-largest population in the Exumas, after George Town. Anchor off, come in with your dinghy, and tie up to the government pier to explore this friendly settlement. Highlights of the year are the Black Point Homecoming in April and the Black Point Regatta in August. Turn right at the head of the pier to stroll the main street into town. You can find out just about everything you need to know and everywhere you need to go at *Adderley's Friendly Grocery*, *Lorraine's Cafe* or *Scorpio's Bar & Restaurant*. Catch football frenzy at *Lorraine's* or *Scorpio's* while enjoying great food and surfing the Internet. *Rockside Inn and Laundry* offers the best coin-operated washer and dryer facility in the islands. It is also a great place to meet other cruisers!

The lovely ladies of Black Point still plait palms in the shade of the big tree next to *DeShamon's*. They will be happy to show you how to plait. (They will also have a good laugh!) Black Point men take sailboat racing very seriously. You will see their boats under construction in the front yards. The hand construction without the use of power tools is fascinating to behold. If you continue walking south, you pass the Regatta Point community pavilion and *Susan's Bonefish Lodge*. Keep going until you reach the "Garden of Eden" on the left. This rock and driftwood sculpture garden takes a little imagination to "see" it through the artist's eye, but it is one of those i'land tings you don't want to miss.

Walking north from the government pier, you pass the *Bible Mission Church*, where sitting on a bench in the shade affords a WiFi connection. Keep walking past *Lorraine's* pink *Long Bay Cottage* until you see the sign to the Blow Hole (if you reach the cemetery, you missed it). If the surf's up, it blows magnificently! A little farther up the road, there is a pretty beach, albeit covered with flotsam and jetsam. Bring a trash bag, and pick some up as a "thank you" to this lovely community. If you would like to repay the folks here for the RO water spigot and trash disposal trailer in something more than cash, bring the school some gym equipment - basketballs, hula hoops, volley balls, soccer balls, softballs and bats—or art supplies. Bibles are always appreciated at the churches.

The All-Age School Fair is usually held in March. Cruisers turn out in droves to partake of the local goodies; fried, baked and served up by the kid's Moms. Go early to buy your ticket inside the school. The line gets long very quickly under the hot sun! There is DJ music, games for kids and cruisers alike, and the Police patrol the festivities in their formal, red-wool jacket uniforms. A very special picture for your scrapbook, particularly if you stand in front of the barred windows on the jail across the street.

EMERGENCIES

Marine • VHF 16
Medical *Clinic* • 242-355-4015 • Near the BTC office. Open weekdays, 9 to1. Shirley Nixon, wife of Roosevelt Nixon at the FCYC, is the nurse, so call FCYC in an emergency. The doctor from Steventon calls in once a month and a dentist, twice a year.

Accommodations *Rockside Inn*, Tel: 242-355-3113, Fax 242-355-3113, rocksideinn@yahoo.com.
Lorraine's Long Bay Cottage, 242-355-3064/3012, lorrainerolle@yahoo.com, www.mwpr.com/longbaycottages.html. Two-bedroom cottage, ocean side, sleeps up to 4 people, $1,200 per week.
Susan's Bonefish Lodge, 242-355-3116/3010. Fully-equipped rooms and apartments. Bonefishing, trolling and hand-lining guides. Catching fish is guaranteed!
Scorpio's Cottages, 242-355-3003, VHF 16 "Scorpio." Five cottages across the street from the Scorpio Bar and Restaurant.
Bakery Call *Lorraine's Café* on VHF 16 a day in advance or get there early in the morning! It goes fast!
Churches *St. Luke's and Gethsemany Baptist Churches • Bible Mission Church*. Church services can last a very long time. You might want to sit in the back in case you need to quietly leave. You are welcomed warmly at the churches, even in your cruising attire. Try not to wear shorts, however. The ladies in town will be dressed in their very best finery and highest-heeled shoes for Sunday services. It is an uplifting experience just to sit outside and listen to the singing. Worship times are posted in front of the churches.
Fishing Guides • Ask about guides at *Adderley's Friendly Market*, *Susan's Bonefish Lodge* or *Lorraine's Café* for bonefishing, snorkeling and sightseeing tours in the Exuma Cays.
Golf Carts *Adderley's Friendly Market*, 242-355-3016.
Laundry *Rockside Inn and Laundry*, Good dinghy dock in back on harbor. Machines use $3.50 tokens. Clean, modern restroom. Coffee, cake and scintillating conversation with cruisers.
Post Office • 242-355-3043 • Yellow building, facing the head of the pier, open 9 a.m. to 5 p.m. weekdays. Mail comes in on the boat, weekly.
Provisions *Adderley's Friendly Store* • 242-355-3016 • Where "a smile awaits you." Open from 9 a.m. to 6 p.m. daily, and after church on Sunday. Well-stocked with groceries, fruit and vegetables, fresh milk, ice cream and outboard engine oil. Adderley's can get you fresh fish or conch. They will special order from Nassau anything that will fit on the mailboat. The tree out front is a Sappodilla Tree. When the ugly brownish fruit is ripe, ask to taste one. It is a cross between an overripe banana and soft pear with brown sugar undertones. Locals seem to either love them or hate them.
Restaurants *De Shamon's Restaurant* Stop by Simon and Diane Smith's place for current information about hours, menus, etc. Reservations are a must for dinner. Good Bahamian food. *Lorraine's Café* • 242-355-3012 • VHF 16 • lorrainerolle@yahoo.com Opens at 8 am, serves breakfast, lunch, and dinner in a pleasant dining room complete with satellite television and a book exchange. Ice. Fresh baked breads and pastries on the bakery table—grab your bread when you come in. The coconut bread is exceptionally good for French toast! Coffee and soft drink bar (just go behind the bar and help yourself in the coolers). Lorraine will also cater take-away for you on board. Superbowl party in January. Separate computer room with high-speed connections or use your own laptop for WiFi. Free-will donation "can" in the computer room (be generous!). Travelers checks accepted.
Scorpio's Restaurant and Bar • 242-355-3003 • VHF 16 "Scorpio's" • Bar and restaurant serving Bahamian food with real cold bottled Kalik's. Open daily from 9 am, Sundays after church. Look for posters announcing special parties or events. Visa accepted.
Sculpture Garden *Willie Rolle's Garden of Eden*, past Regatta Point on the left-hand side of the street shouldn't be missed. Willie is happy to let you wander through his garden and admire his rock and driftwood "sculptures," though a small token of appreciation for a guided tour is always accepted; some of his work, which ranges from animals to humans, is in the eye of the beholder. His decapitated woman and ballet dancer exposing herself will change the way you look at driftwood forever! You will also enjoy his green garden of self-sufficiency and marvel at the variety of trees and plants that he has planted and cultivated by himself with so little, on so little.
Straw Market *J and D's* have straw goods and souvenirs. Eunice Wright lives in the little green painted house, fourth along on the left-hand side as you leave the pier and turn right into town. Eunice is getting on in years. She no longer sells her creations, but she will greet you sweetly on the street and try to carry on a conversation. Be kind. There are many ladies weaving and plaiting throughout the settlement; you will marvel at their artistry and speed.
Telephone BTC • 242-355-3060 • Fax: 242-355-3063 • Open weekdays 9 to 5, card telephone outside the office. Phone cards for sale in office and at Adderley's.
Trash Leave it tightly tied in heavy mill trash bags on the trailer at the end of the pier. The free-will donation box is on the tongue of the trailer.
Water RO water spigot across from the pier. This is good, clean water; bring your own containers to fill. Make a donation to the school to thank the community for the free RO water.

LITTLE FARMERS CAY

airstrip • fuel • groceries • marina • medical • post office • propane • restaurant • telephone • water

Famous for its *Five F's Festival*, Little Farmers Cay boasts its own flag, too. There are approximately 55 residents on this three-and-a-half-mile-long island, which is the quintessential Bahamian cay, largely undeveloped so far. A particularly lovely and lively cay surviving on spunk and an independent, self-sufficient populace. You don't want to miss getting your picture taken in front of Ocean Cabin's "open hours" sign, nor miss a conversation with its proprietor, Terry Bain, the creator of the Five F's Festival on the first Friday in February. The Five F's attracts visitors from all over and has food booths, live music, dancing, contests and Class-C sailboat racing. Another "don't miss" All-Age School Fair is held here on the last Saturday in March. The Moms cook fabulous local fare, games are played, music is blasted and the cruisers cue up for an incredible feast that helps support the school and the community. Terry always finds an excuse for a good party, so in July you can celebrate the Full Moon Beer Festival. The last hurrah is in October when Terry and his followers celebrate "Camo" Day. If you run into any funky camouflage wear back home, here is the time and the place you get to wear it. This may be your only opportunity to look cool in that hot pink camo baseball cap studded with rhinestones!

EMERGENCIES

Marine • VHF 16
Medical *Clinic* • 242-355-0007 • Nurse at the clinic, just across from the school, open weekdays 9 a.m. to 1:30 p.m. The doctor comes in from Steventon once a month.

MARINA

FARMERS CAY YACHT CLUB
Tel: 242-355-4017 • Fax: 242-355-4030 • VHF 16
Slips 8. **Moorings** 3 **Max LOA** 140 ft. **MLW** at Dock 9 ft. **Dockage** $1.50 per ft. per day and up. **Fuel** Dock open 7 a.m. to 7 p.m. daily, diesel and gasoline. **Facilities & Services** Power $15 per day for 30 amp; $30 per day for 50 amp. RO water $0.50 per gallon. Showers, restrooms. Coin-op washer and dryer, $4 per load. Public telephone, WiFi complimentary to marina, bar and restaurant guests. Satellite television in lounge. Propane from Hallan Rolle. Mail will be held for your arrival. Small repairs done. Trash bag disposal for a small fee. Store carries ice, soft drinks, confectionaries, marine supplies and is open from 7 a.m. to 7 p.m daily. **Restaurant and Bar** Le Bleu Seaside Restaurant and Lounge open for breakfast, lunch and dinner from 7 a.m. until guests leave. Gazebo Bar & Grill, same hours as Le Bleu. **Accommodations** Pretty guest rooms with outside patios and arbors. Rooms from $150 per night. **Credit Cards** Visa, MasterCard, and AMEX with 5% surcharge, travelers checks or cash. Your hosts: Roosevelt Nixon and his wife Shirley, who is also the nurse for Farmers Cay.

OCEAN CABIN
Tel: 242-355-4006 • Fax: 242-355-4011• Cell: 242-524-3744 • VHF 16 "Ocean Cabin"
oceancbn@batelnet.bs • www.oceancbn.com
Moorings 8. **MAX LOA** 44 ft. **MLW** 10 ft. **Mooring Fee** $10 per night; Deluxe Harbour Master mooring for mini-megayacht, $20. **Facilities & Services** Showers, free to guests, restrooms, laundry fluff and fold, $10. Washer only $1 per load. Trash bag disposal, $2 per bag. Propane tanks refilled by Hollan Rolle and Lil' Jeff. Public telephone, Internet access complimentary for bar and restaurant patrons. Satellite television at the bar. Oasis Convenience Store stocked with food, vegetables, bread, toiletries, dry goods and ice. Hiking, caves, shelling and fishing guides available. Ask Terry. **Restaurant and Bar** Ocean Cabin Bar & Restaurant, Earnestine, the chef, specializes in lobster dishes. Let her surprise you with something delicious. Festivals and special events hosted by Ocean Cabin in February, May, July and October.

PORT DIRECTORY

Accommodations One bedroom kitchenette, $100 per night, below *Ocean Cabin* on the hill. Rent your own island, Hattie Cay, complete with 3 bedroom hide-away house with kitchenette, $500 per night. Terry and Earnestine Bain. *Addison Cottages* Five cottages; ask locally.
Airline *Flamingo Air*, with two scheduled flights from Nassau.
Artwork *Tinker's Woodcarving Gallery*.
Bakery Call Earnestine Bain at *Ocean Cabin* or Shirley Nixon at *Farmer's Cay Yacht Club*. Fresh bread and also cakes and desserts.
Church *St. Mary's Baptist Church.*
Dinghy Dock At Government Pier • Dock at *Farmers Cay Yacht Club* • Beach it in Big or Little Harbour.
Fishing Guides Ask Terry Bain or Roosevelt Nixon.
Laundry at marinas.
Medical Nurse at government clinic.
Moorings under Marinas.
Post Office Near the government dock by *Corene's Grocery Store*. Open on Wednesday, handling incoming mail off the mailboat, and on Thursday, handling outgoing mail for the Friday mailboat.
Propane *Hallan Rolle* • 242-355-4003 • VHF 16 "Little Jeff" • Take tanks in early for a same-day fill; available 9 to 5, weekdays.
Provisions Most islanders have their supplies delivered by the weekly mailboat, so the stores do not carry large stocks. Both *FCYC* and *Ocean Cabin* have nice stores, or they can arrange to order for you *Little Harbour Supermarket* • 242-355-4019 • Open 8 a.m. to 7:30 p.m. *Corene's Grocery Store* up the hill toward Ocean Cabin. Terry or Earnestine Bain will open up for you. *Little Harbour Liquor Store* • 242-355-4019 • Open 9 to 5, except Sunday. Ask Eugenia Nixon Percentie at *Little Harbour Supermarket* to open it up for you.
Restaurants under Marinas.
Telephones BTC • 242-355-4060 • Fax: 242-355-4063 • Open 9 to 5 weekdays; also sells BTC phone cards.
Trash Leave trash in heavy mil trash bags by the pink building at the government dock, or dispose of it at the *Yacht Club* or *Ocean Cabin* for a small fee.
Water Taxis *Hallan Rolle* • 242-355-4003 • VHF 16 "Little Jeff" To Barraterre or to explore the surrounding islands. *Cecil Smith* • VHF 16 "Lamonde" • Will also take you to Barraterre to pick up a taxi at *Fisherman's Inn*, 242-255-5016, to take you down to *George Town Airport*. Cecil is a superb free-diver and spearfisherman. Nearest tank air fill is on Staniel Cay.

THINGS TO DO IN LITTLE FARMERS CAY

- Join the fun for The First Friday in February Farmers Cay Festival, also known as the Five Fs party, held the first weekend in February. For more information, call Terry at 242-355-4006 or 242-524-3744.
- Take the Great Guana Cay cave tour with Stanley Rolle, and explore the 90-foot land cave.
- Visit JR's Woodcarving shop; take home a memento of Little Farmers Cay with one of his carvings from the Ocean Cabin.

Air Drying in the Exumas. Photo Courtesy of Peter Mitchell.

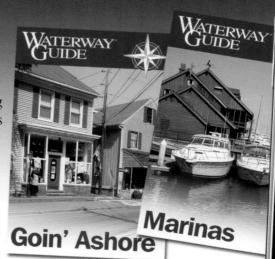

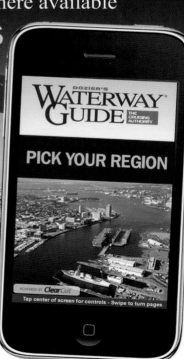

Chapter 15
The Southern Exuma Cays and Great Exuma Island

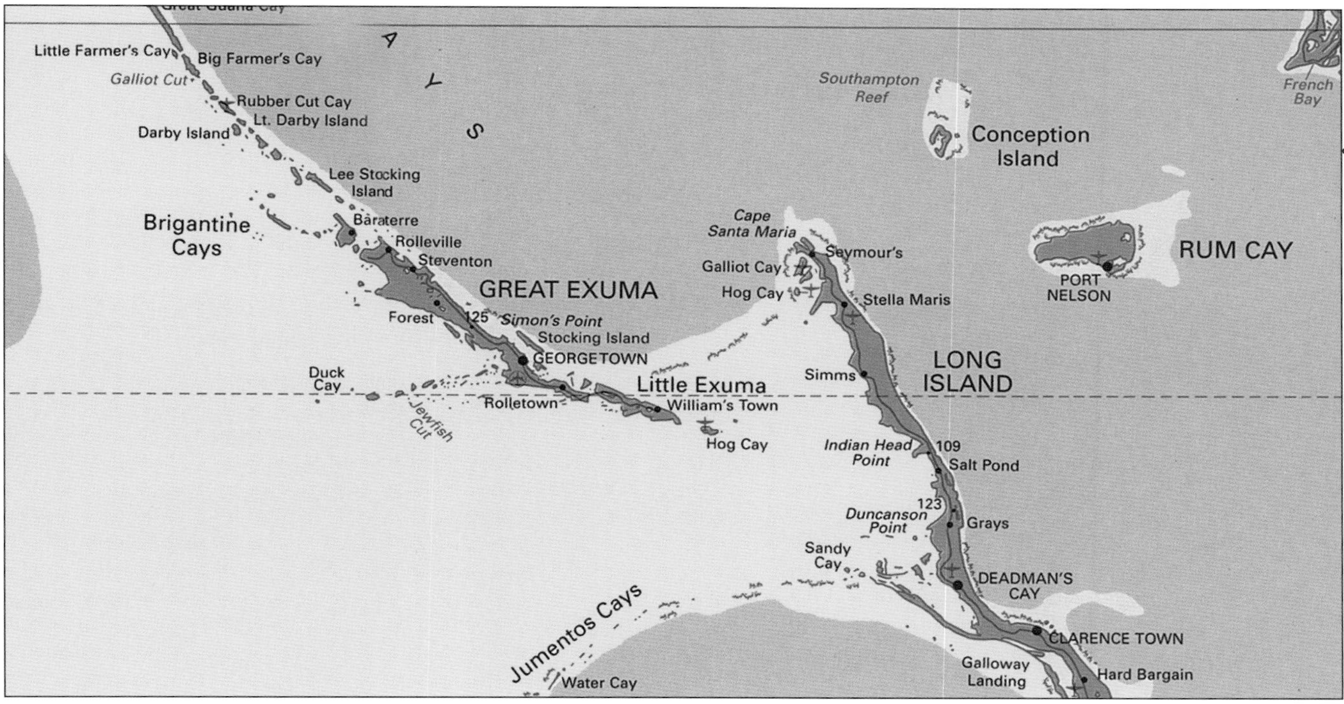

Looking At the Charts

The southern Exumas continue the northwest to southeast line of the Exuma chain from Galliot Cut to Hog Cay and White Cay, just off the southeast tip of Little Exuma Island at N 23° 23.000'/W 076° 25.000'. South of Rat Cay on the bank side, sand bores and shoal water set limits on cruising territory. Rat Cay Cut is the last chance to switch to Exuma Sound to enter George Town. The cays and islands extending south from Rat Cay to Great Exuma Island on the bank side offer a good area for shoal-draft exploration, but if you carry any kind of draft, it is a nightmare ground of deceptive channels, shoals, sand and reef. Leave it to the locals.

The west coast of the two Exuma Islands is shoal-draft territory, strewn with sandbars and mangroves. For most vessels, this is no cruising territory, but it is good for dinghy exploration and bonefishing. Take heart, for most cruisers, everything pales in significance compared to George Town and Stocking Island, the Shangri-La of the Bahamas. Little Exuma Island itself is so diminished by its larger twin that it hardly features on the itinerary of any cruising boat except by rental car.

George Town is either the end stop and turnaround point on a cruise south from Florida, or the launching pad for a voyage to the Caribbean. Whatever your plans, cruising or passage-making, everyone stops at George Town.

Continuing south of Long Island, voyagers commit to serious bluewater passages with Atlantic swells and waves, few safe havens and little, if any, resources available until the Turks and Caicos. Perhaps unfairly, George Town is known as "Chicken Harbor." Many who were bound for the Caribbean found their first passage after George Town less than pleasant and returned to venture no farther. As in all outdoor adventures, weather and timing make the difference. The span of Out Islands running south from Long Island to the Turks and Caicos form one of the tamest tropic transits in the Western Hemisphere. Almost every vessel passing between the Virgin Islands and the East Coast of the United States, and vice versa, stops at George Town, Great Exuma Island.

VHF–HF in George Town

George Town, like the Abacos, has its own conventions:

16	**Distress and calling, Harbormaster**
12–14	**Local business and taxis**
68	**Cruisers Net at 8:10 a.m. until completion**
70	**Digital transmission**

Use low power in Elizabeth Harbour. High frequency transmission is banned 7 to 9 a.m. and 5 to 7 p.m. to prevent interference with weather acquisition for the Cruisers Net in the morning, and the recording of Herb Hilgenberg's broadcasts in the early evening.

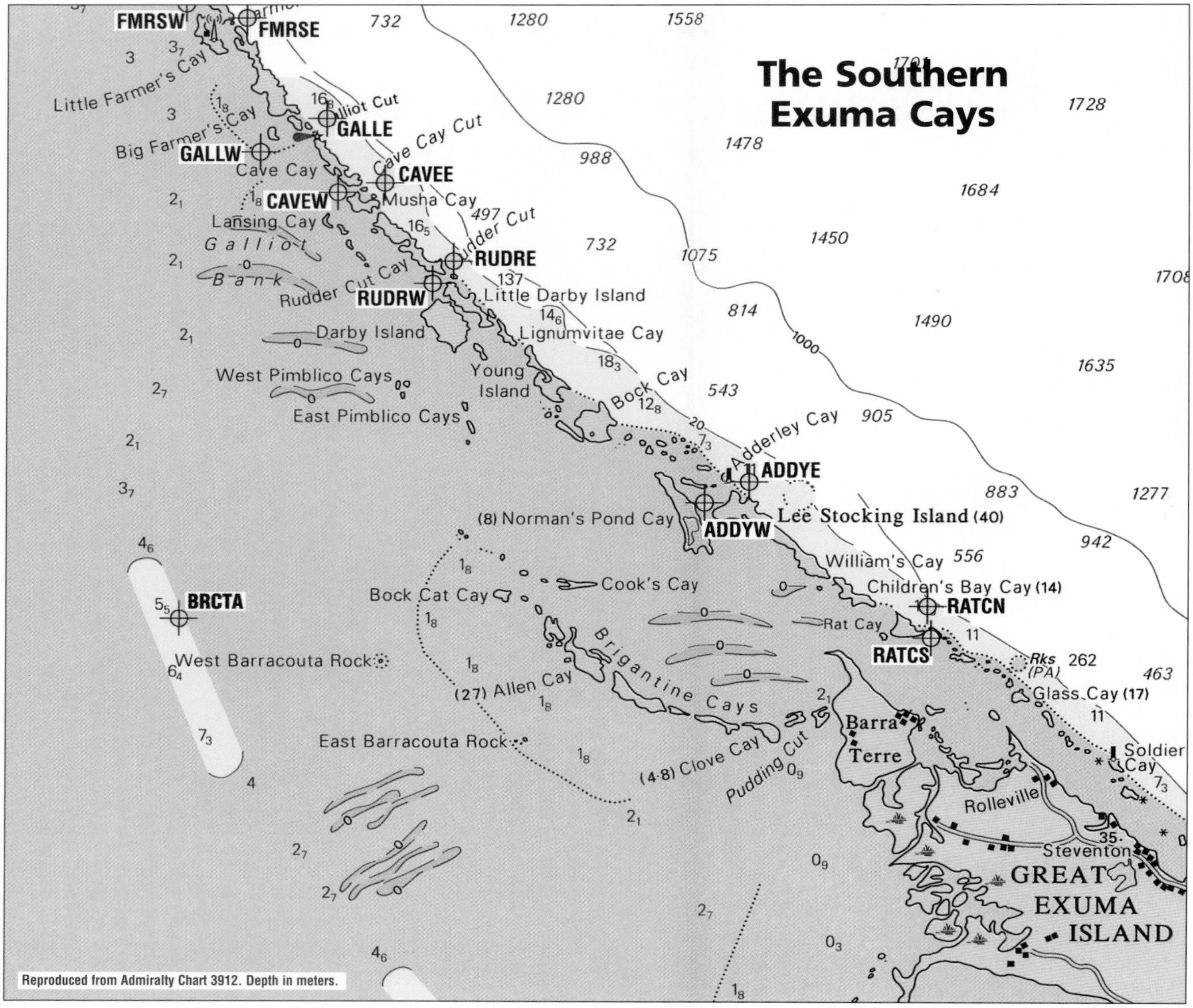

Reproduced from Admiralty Chart 3912. Depth in meters.

Not to be used for navigation.

In the Spotlight. George Town

George Town's claim to fame is having the highest annual cruising visitor totals in the Bahamas. Despite this, some guidebooks caution that it is a difficult harbor to enter. Perhaps this is because George Town does not have a conventional harbor. The "harbor" is nine-nautical-miles long by one-nautical-miles wide and lies between the mainland of Great Exuma Island and barrier islands, Stocking Island to the north and Elizabeth Island to the south. Within these waters, there is shelter. One side or the other, whichever way the winds blow, there is some protection. Not all places are sheltered all the time. In some, you are even exposed to the prevailing northeast or southeast wind. In old-fashioned terms, the harbor would be called a roadstead—a place where a large number of vessels anchor to find better shelter than they would outside.

Most cruisers call the harbor, "Elizabeth Harbour." Others just call the whole place "George Town." The good news is everybody knows what you are talking about regardless of what you call it. There has never been any reason to get fancy with the name or improve on what nature offered here. Back in 1942, George Town became a U.S. Naval patrol base, and the harbor was dredged. The dredging slowly filled in, and the bottom profile of George Town Harbour is much as it was beforehand—shoal areas here and there, rocks and reefs scattered around, dredged hollows and scoured flats.

Still, there is no doubt that George Town is one of the best way stops in the southern Bahamas. For those heading a lot farther south, it is nothing short of a compulsory stop. (Exuma Markets is stocked with every good thing to eat imaginable and has generous, free RO water at its dinghy dock.) Past here, except for the occasional settlement, you are in the Bahamian boondocks, on your own.

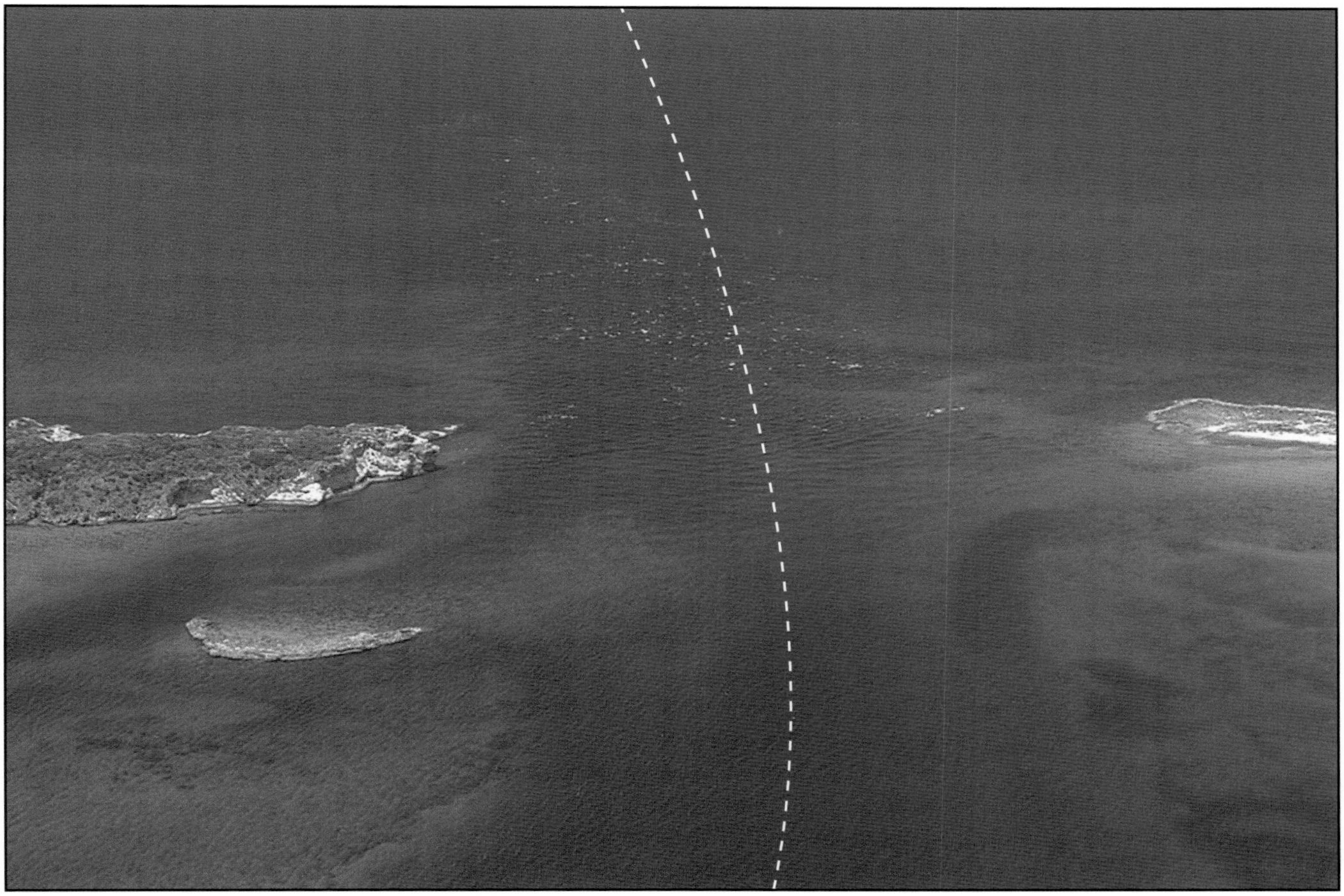

Galliot Cut, from the west. (Not to be used for navigation.) WATERWAY GUIDE PHOTOGRAPHY.

George Town is also an extraordinary place. Year after year, Great Exuma and Stocking Island play host to a seasonal floating population equivalent to a small town. Each fall, the first armada of George Town–bound winter residents sets out from Florida. They make their return passage in the spring or early summer. By midwinter, hundreds of visiting yachts are anchored off Stocking Island, in the Stocking Island basins, off the Peace and Plenty Hotel and in Kidd Cove off George Town itself. In Regatta weeks, add another hundred boats to this total. The highlight of the season for cruisers is the Cruising Regatta and Talent Show in March.

There are so many activities in which you can participate, we can't list them all here. Suffice it to say, that plans for next year's Cruising Regatta and Talent Show starts the day the current activities end. If you would like to compete in next year's "Best Bread Baked Onboard During the Long Distance Race" or "Biggest Fish Caught Trolling During the Long Distance Race," you had better start practicing now. The cruising community is diverse with many talented folks. Artists work all year long to win the contest for next year's T-shirt design. These are no "amateur" designs, either! Entertainers in the talent show are versatile and very good. A special treat each year are performances by "Sonny and Cher." "Elvis" shows up, too. Of course, nowadays, Sonny and Elvis are escorted to the stage by heavenly bodyguards.

The majority of the boats, once they have dropped their anchors, never move until it is time to migrate northward for the summer. George Town has both fans and critics, but the critics are few. It is a good harbor in prevailing winds, particularly on the Stocking Island side. It is a good place to restock, fill your tanks, get in touch with the world and take long hikes along breathtaking, beautiful Atlantic beaches. The airport is excellent, and you can get crew out, friends in and yourself home in a hurry if needed.

What's There? The Southern Exumas

Big Farmers Cay and Galliot Cays

Big Farmers Cay has some beautiful beaches to explore by dinghy, but you will likely not spend much time there. Hattie Cay, nestled in shallow waters, is available for rent from Terry Bain of Ocean Cabin. There is a useful anchorage off its southern end, between it and Big Galliot Cay. Folks wait here and on the western side of Big Galliot to exit through Galliot Cut. Little Galliot Cay is a familiar landmark to pass on your way to Big Galliot Cay and the cuts that lie south of there. You can anchor quite close to shore in the cove off Galliot Cay in easterly winds and will usually have a lot of company here.

Southern Exumas

		Largest Vessel Accommodated	VHF Channel Monitored	Transient Berths / Total Berths	Approach / Dockside Depth (reported)	Floating Docks	Gas / Diesel	Groceries, Ice, Marine Supplies, Snacks	Repairs: Hull, Engine, Propeller	Lift (tonnage), Crane, Rail	1=110V, 2=220V, B=Both, Max Amps	Laundry, Pool, Showers	Pump-Out Station	Nearby: Grocery Store, Motel, Restaurant
CAVE CAY		Dockage					Supplies		Services					
1. Safe Harbour Marina at Cave Cay	242-357-0143		16/14	/25	5.5/11	F	GD				B/50	LS		
SOUTHERN EXUMAS														
2. Marina at Emerald Bay	**242-336-6100**	**240**	**16/11**	**40/150**	**14**	**F**	**GD**	**GIMS**			**B/100**	**LS**		**R**
3. St. Francis Resort (WiFi)	242-557-9629		16		/5			IS						R
4. Exuma Docking Services (WiFi)	242-336-2578	120	16	40/52	7/6.5		GD	GIMS	E	L6.5	B/50	LS		GM
5. George Town Marina and Repair	242-345-5116		16						H	L50			P	

Corresponding chart(s) not to be used for navigation. Internet Access (WiFi) Wireless Internet Access

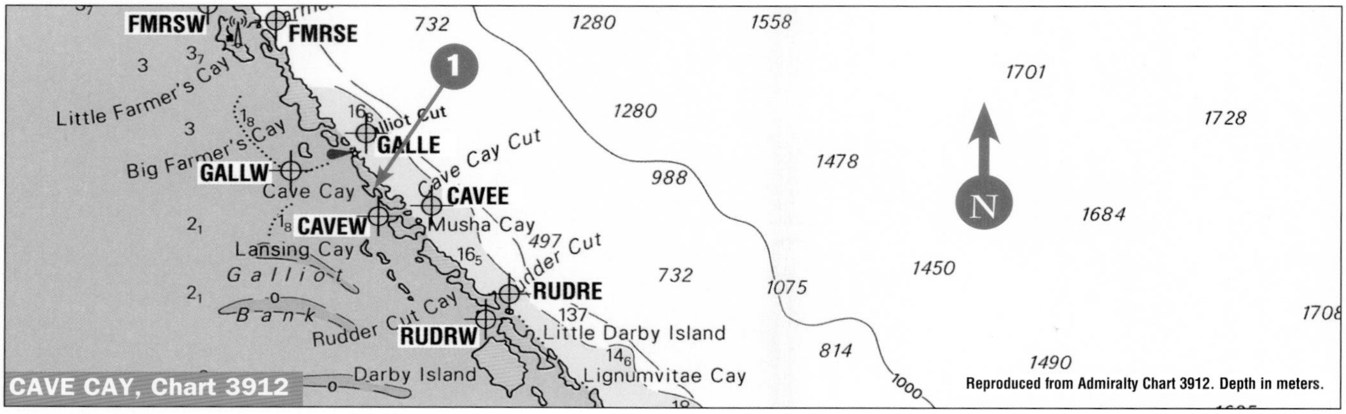

CAVE CAY, Chart 3912

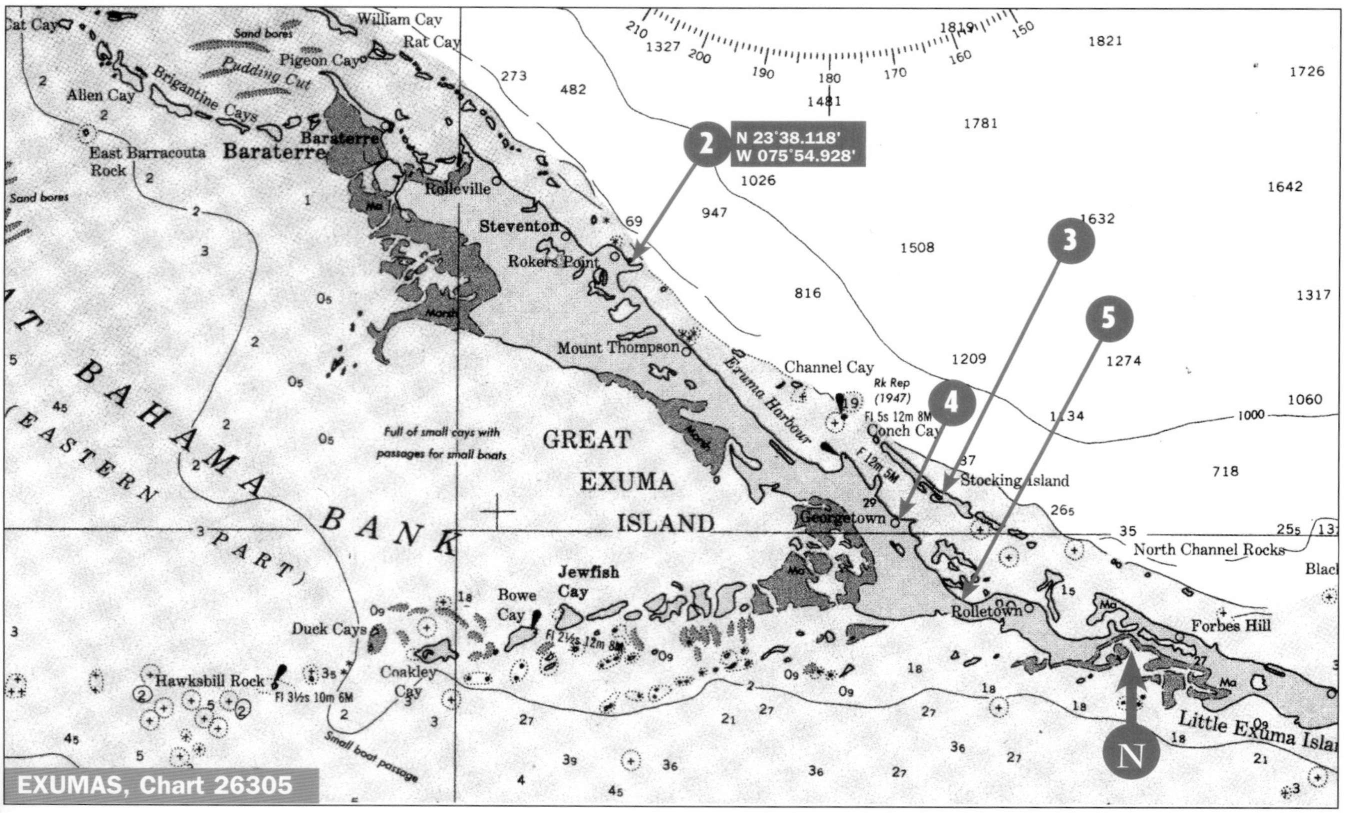

EXUMAS, Chart 26305

Cave Cay Cut, from the west. (Not to be used for navigation.) WATERWAY GUIDE PHOTOGRAPHY.

Galliot Cut

Galliot Cut is easy to identify from the east. High Cay stands immediately north, like an aircraft carrier, and there is a highly visible light on the northern tip of Cave Cay. A shoal contours around the south of Cave Cay, so stay well clear of it. Once you are through the cut, there is a deep water turn to starboard to head for the bank. From the bank side, Galliot Cut is heavily used. You will witness many boats anchored off Galliot Cay waiting for the right wind and tide to pass through onto the sound. Ebb tide flows can build a wall of water here, rather like a standstill tsunami. Boats have been seen almost standing on their fantails. In the wrong conditions, it is just too fast running for comfort. Even the mailboats choose to avoid this cut. In the right conditions, it is quick and painless, but seems to offer no particular advantage over its neighboring cuts. Check them out on your charts.

Cave Cay

Cave Cay, off limits during construction of its marina, now bids welcome to all. In this natural hurricane hole, now dredged, you will find dockage, fuel, water and safe harbor. The bank approach to Safe Harbour Marina and Cave Cay Cut involves one dogleg, but it is deep and obvious. If in doubt when reading the water, favor the Cave Cay side.

Cave Cay Cut

Cave Cay Cut it is deep and uncomplicated. Favor the Cave Cay side when traversing from either the bank or sound side. Watch for current rips outside the cut in the sound. They are obvious and avoidable.

Musha Cay

Musha Cay is a private island resort owned by the magician David Copperfield. It is available for rent. There are two docks here that accommodate guest's yachts. You can anchor well off of them in deep water. It is a good spot to spend the evening before making your way through Cave Cay Cut for George Town. Alternatively, shoal-draft boats can use it as a good jumping off spot to journey farther south on the bank side.

Rudder Cut Cay

Rudder Cut Cay is private and is the site of Musha Cay's airstrip. There are nice anchorages all along the western shore, with the best holding found north of the inland lagoon, however, it is shallow territory. The inland lagoon might have a chain across it prohibiting exploration, but it is muddy and not particularly attractive, so don't pine. The next two anchorages farther south are more popular and have an interesting cave to explore by dinghy or snorkel. They also have pretty beaches to look at (not stroll) with the southernmost offering depths of 3.5 meters/10 to 12 feet in which to set the hook. The deep waters along these shores are frequented by seaplanes. Anchor as close to shore as you can to accommodate them. They usually beach themselves on shore and only stay for a short while, but it sure gives you something neat to photograph and makes a great email story for back home.

Rudder Cut, from the west. (Not to be used for navigation.) WATERWAY GUIDE PHOTOGRAPHY.

Rudder Cut

Rudder Cut is not used as much as some of the more northern cuts, but it is deep and uncomplicated. Favor the Rudder Cut Cay shore to make the passage in 20 feet of water or more. For most boats, except those of very shoal-draft, this is your last viable cut out onto the sound. All the others are "ins and outs," there is no more traveling south down the bank side.

If you seek the cut from the sound side, don't be misled by the unnamed cay that lies off the northern end of Little Darby Island. The actual cut lies between Rudder Cut Cay to the north and that little cay. From this vantage point, it appears to sit in the middle of the cut. Go north of this cay before you make your entry. Deeper inside the cut, turn to starboard well before the massive whale look-a-like rock (the whale is swimming north). You can anchor off Rudder Cut Cay, or continue north towards Galliot if your draft permits it. Although there are two enticing anchorages in between Little Darby Island and Darby Island, the routes to them are intricate, and the islands are private.

Entering Rudder Cut from the sound or exiting to the Sound, look out for the reefs around the southeast hammerhead of Rudder Cut Cay. Rudder Cut really is a pass to nowhere if you draw much more than 5 feet, for every route north or south on the bank side is shallow, and tide becomes critical. South of Rudder Cut Cay on the Exuma Bank side, unless you have the right draft and a passion for shoal water exploration or bonefishing, it is really a no-go as a cruising ground.

The Darby Islands, Goat, Lignumvitae, Prime, Melvin and Bock Cays

The Darby Islands are private and other than the anchorages between them, there is little for the cruising visitor there. Goat Cay and Lignumvitae Cays are private. As you go farther south, Prime Cay is private, as are Neighbor Cay and Melvin Cay. Bock Cay (the 100-foot radio mast is not a BTC tower) is also private and under development. This area is basically out of bounds. There are few anchorages worth marking the effort, and the whole area is such a maze of shoal draft channels that we can see little point in attempting to thread your way around the shallows. The next reasonable point from which you can access the bank side from Exuma Sound with purpose is Adderley Cut.

Adderley Cut

Adderley Cut is your access to Normans Pond Cay, Leaf Cay and Lee Stocking Island, home to the Caribbean Marine Research Center. There is a prominent stone beacon on Adderley Cay marking the cut. One can't miss the entrance. There are the reefs to avoid. They extend north from Lee Stocking Island, but they mercifully put on a display of ebb and flow wash. Simply favor the northern part of the entrance to avoid them. You will choose which way to pass around the central sand bore depending on your chosen destination, north or south. North there are anchorages. South there are mooring balls.

Stocking Island, the end of the day. (Not to be used for navigation.) WATERWAY GUIDE PHOTOGRAPHY.

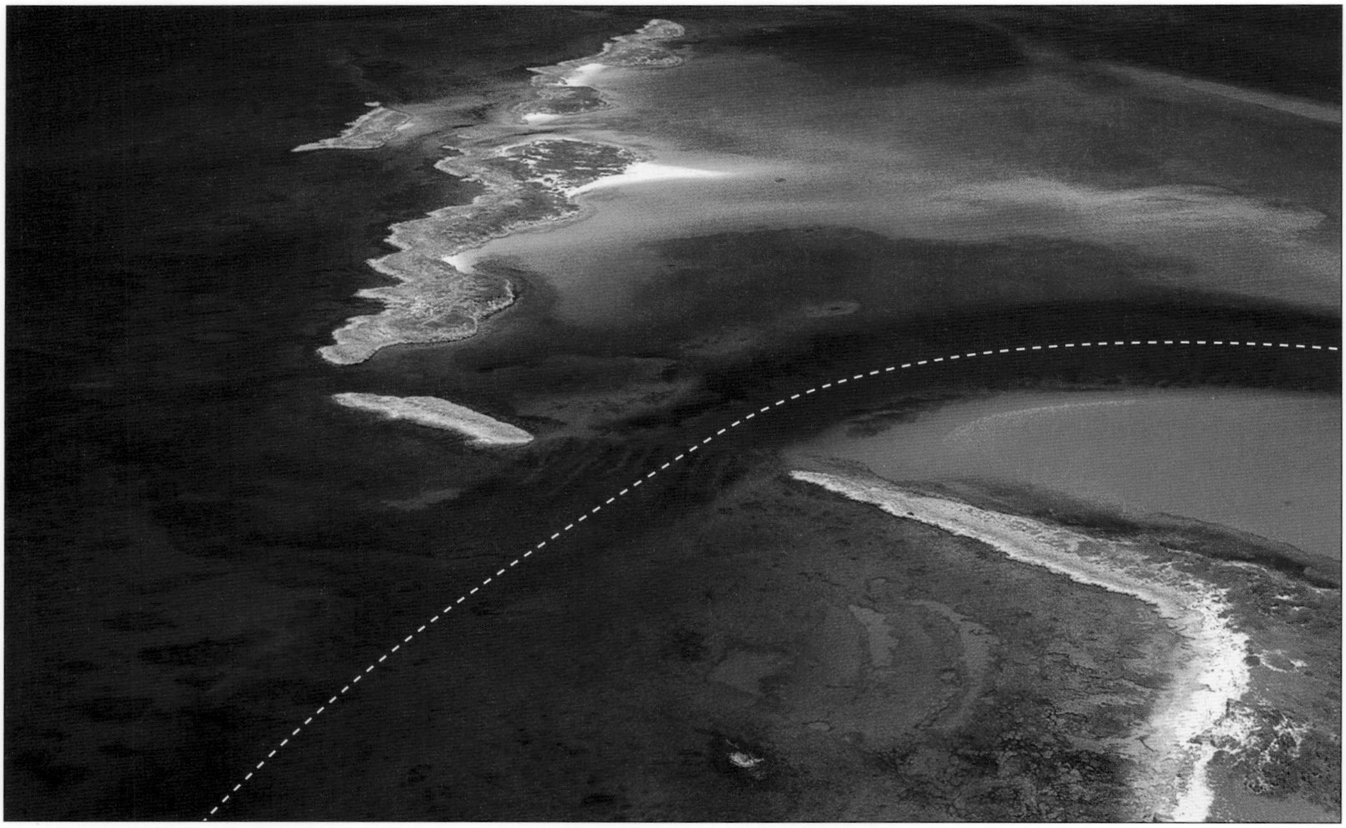

Rat Cay Cut, from the northwest. (Not to be used for navigation.) WATERWAY GUIDE PHOTOGRAPHY.

Normans Pond Cay, Leaf Cay, Lee Stocking Island

Normans Pond Cay was once was home to a productive salt industry. The abandoned ponds remain. The cay has shy, native iguanas. If you land there, leave the pets onboard. The anchorage around the northern tip, off the western shore, can be subject to surge and difficult holding. Cruisers who have worked their way south, in the finger of deeper water between the shoals, find much satisfaction.

Leaf Cay is shoal to the east, but has a useful anchorage to the west. Pink iguanas will peep out from the brush to investigate you. There is a protected little beach on the northwest shore, just made for tots to splash and adults to shell. Take a hike from the beach along the eastern shore. You can find an amazing array of sea beans here. There is an inland lake near the anchorage that is literally alive with butterflies. Poke around in the bushes to reveal the amazing display.

Lee Stocking Island, running south from Normans Pond Cay, is important as the base of the Caribbean Marine Research Center, one of NOAA's National Undersea Research agencies. Located on the northwest tip of the island, just under the anvil head of its northern promontory, is the anchorage where the moorings used to be. To schedule a visit to the center are made by hailing "Research Center" on VHF Channel 16, Monday through Friday from 9 a.m. to 4 p.m. You are asked not to go on shore without permission. Childrens Bay Cay, to the south of Lee Stocking Island, is private. Shoal draft boats can find 2.1-meter/7-foot depths in an anchorage off its southern most dock.

Rat Cay Cut

Immediately south of Childrens Bay Cay lies Rat Cay. South of Rat Cay is Rat Cay Cut, the only cut in the Exumas that runs almost north-south. Although narrow, it offers better conditions with an easterly wind and ebb tide than most other Exuma Sound cuts. There is also some protection from the prevailing winds. There is plenty of water on the western and northern shores of Rat Cay in which to anchor. You can also go north to the anchorages off Childrens Bay Cay or south to Square Rock Cay. If you run into trouble out on the sound, it is a good cut to remember, but it probably won't make your list of destinations.

The Brigantine Cays

The Brigantine Cays, some 40 in total, typify the bank side at this point in the Exuma chain. A confusion of islets, banks, mangroves and channels that are tidal to a degree, they are great for bonefishing, but not for cruising.

Childrens Bay Cay, Rat Cay, Square Rock Cay and Square Rock Cut

As we have said, Childrens Bay Cay is private, and Rat Cay offers anchorages near a one-of-a-kind cut, but little more. Other handy anchorages in this area can be found behind Square Rock Cay. Square Rock Cut is narrow, but deep. It requires skillful handling in easterly winds to maneuver the almost due north turn through the rocky bars on either side. If they have dared go even this far south on the inside passage,

Your Winter Resort – Their Home

A permanent "transient" population of the size that now winters in George Town is bound to generate its own dynamic. If you are new to George Town, listen to the Cruisers Net that opens on VHF Channel 16 (later switching to VHF Channel 68) at 8:10 a.m. each morning. You will discover a whole new world of boat people with a lifestyle that has evolved over the years into a community with its own social events, recreational programs, a safety net of mutual assistance and what almost amounts to a territorial stake on the beaches of Stocking Island. Almost unnoticed, the cruising boats inbound from the Caribbean, or on their way there, come and go. To a lesser extent, much the same migration takes place in the summer months, and there are those who reckon the summer there is the best season.

We are concerned about the environmental and social impact of this temporary floating village, whose numbers equate to about 30 percent of the native population of the entire Exuma chain. On the environmental side, pollution, the discharge of raw sewage into a four-square-mile area, part of which (the Stocking Island basins) is almost landlocked, is at the top of our list. Does every cruising visitor follow the international conventions governing discharge and dumping at sea? Even if the Bahamian government fails to enforce discharge legislation, we, the visitors, ought to follow the rules that apply in our own countries. Use your holding tank in harbor. When it is full, take a day trip out into the ocean. Three miles or more out, flush your tanks. If we fail to take preventive action, George Town will become a marine Chernobyl within our lifetime. The bottom line is that it is not ours to trash. Perhaps, one day, an Elizabeth Harbour marina might offer a pump-out service as part of their facilities. But for now, let's be good environmental stewards.

most boats go no farther than Square Rock Cay toward Great Exuma Island on the bank side. However, shoal-draft boats and adventuresome skippers can visit Barraterre Settlement via the east-west channel of deep water that runs from Square Rock Cut to the northern end of Barraterre Island and then by a long run south along the eastern shore. **Plan for tides one to two hours after Nassau time.**

For those who enjoy isolation and large areas of mangroves to explore, you can find six feet of water or more on a rising tide to anchor in between Jimmy Cay and False Cay on the bank immediately west of Barraterre Settlement. At low tide, you almost feel like you are on the moon—the surrounding sands are that white and the isolation that complete.

Enter the bank through Square Rock Cut in good conditions. After clearing the reefs, make the 90 degree turn west and follow the deep, blue-water channel to Pudding Point. At Pudding Point, turn slightly southwest and continue southward in the obvious blue water. The waters in between Jimmy Cay and False Cay are surprisingly deep, but current and surge free. You will probably not see another living soul while anchored here except maybe a bonefisherman or two. If you have a good outboard, the dinghy ride to Barraterre Settlement for water and provisions is doable.

Barraterre Island and Settlement

Barraterre (bar ah terry) Island is joined to Great Exuma Island by two bridges. Sandwiched in between the two bridges is Madame Dau's Cay. We know that you are begging to hear the origin of that cay's name, but we leave it for you to break the ice when talking to the locals. You can purchase fresh fish from the locals, or stop and chat with the local boatbuilder. It sounds worthy of a rental car trip just to learn about the produce being raised with pothole farming techniques. Onions, cabbage and peppers we can imagine. But, mangoes, bananas and grapefruit? These we would like to see. We bet you would, too.

Rat Cay Cut to Great Exuma Island

Heading for George Town, your arrival waypoint will be the George Town Harbour West (GTAW1) entry waypoint. A scattered line of minor cays leads south from Rat Cay Cut to Rokers Point on Great Exuma Island. Inside these cays, there is a shoal draft channel, but it is primarily of interest to local fishermen.

On your way south, stand well offshore, at least one nautical mile, from the line of barrier cays and reefs along the east coast of Barraterre and Great Exuma Island. Watch out for the Three Sisters Rocks (N 23° 43.000'/W 076° 00.000'). At Channel Cay, you can inch closer to within a third of a mile of land, and then pick up the waypoint between Channel Cay and Conch Cay. To track your progress along the shore as you sail down the sound, look for these landmarks: Barraterre's BTC tower, Rolleville's BTC tower, Soldier Cay's stone beacon, Steventon's water tank, the cut into the Marina at Emerald Bay south of Rokers Point and Farmers Hill's BTC tower, Duck Cay and Channel Cay. From here, if you look carefully, you can spot Stocking Island's "monument" stone beacon (or at least its hill), and know you are almost there.

NOTE: You may see vessels with local knowledge round Salt Pond Point to travel south to Elizabeth Harbour along the western coastline of Great Exuma. The waters are strewn with rocks, coral heads and hard bars. If you decide to do it, make sure you have full insurance coverage. On this route, you may lose your boat.

George Town, Great Exuma Island

We have already featured George Town in the Spotlight. The George Town Harbour area has two principal entrances. The west entrance serves you when you are coming south down the Exuma chain. The east entrance is better if you are coming from the south or heading out toward Long Island. Both have reefs and rocks, deserve caution and require a seaworthy vessel with good auxiliary power. In bad weather - high winds, high seas and limited visibility - they are not to be attempted. To be safe, you must be able to read your way in and have absolute control over your boat. It is also be prudent to take advantage of a favorable tide.

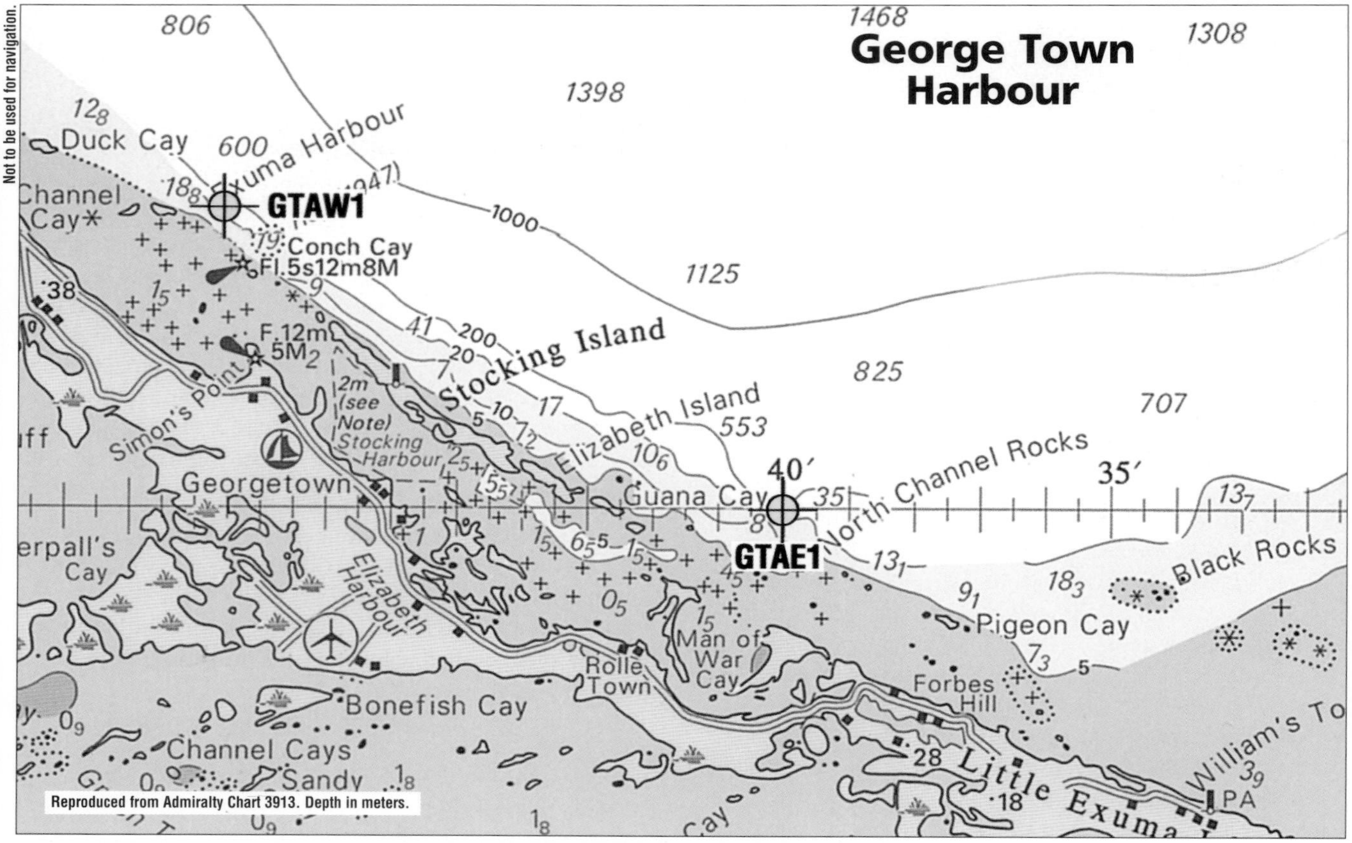

Reproduced from Admiralty Chart 3913. Depth in meters.

George Town, from the west. (Not to be used for navigation.) Waterway Guide Photography.

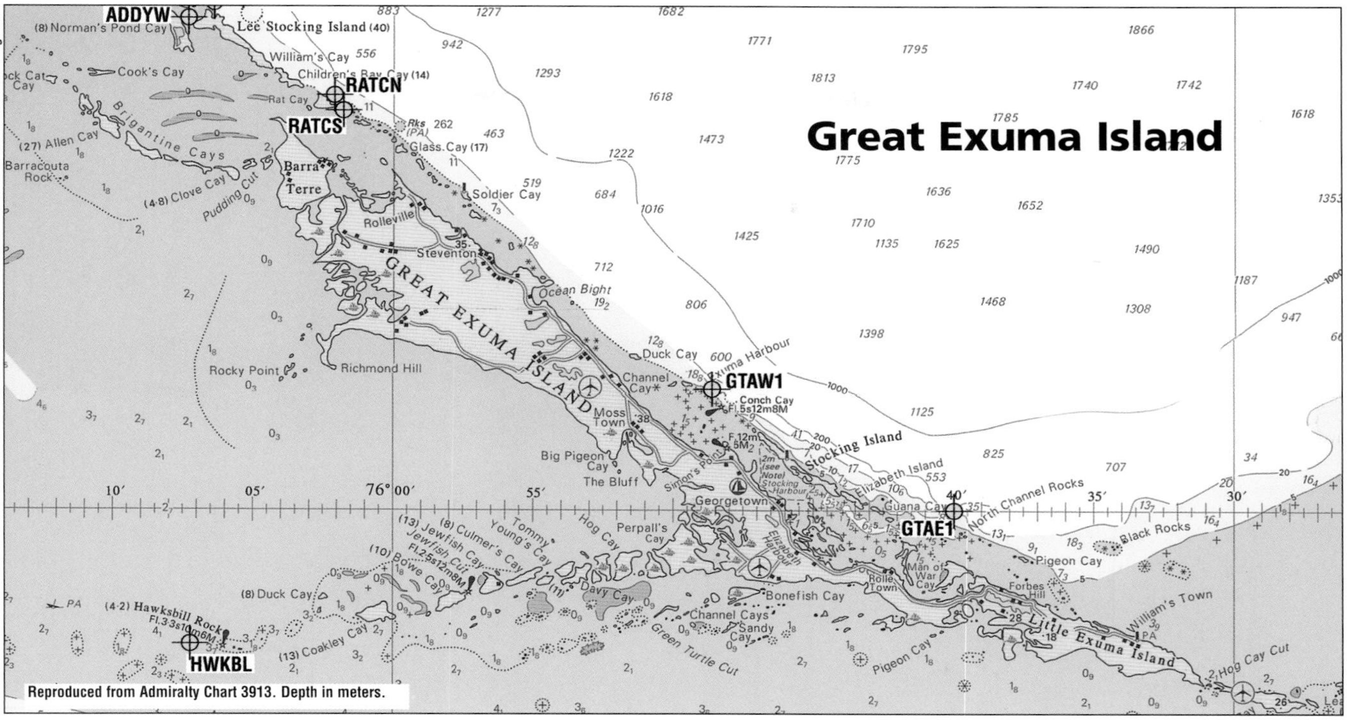

Reproduced from Admiralty Chart 3913. Depth in meters.

Not to be used for navigation.

Given its popularity and traffic, it is puzzling that there are no government installed or maintained aids to navigation into George Town. Where are the buoys? Some blame this circumstance on hurricanes, which take out markers. Others say it is an "i'land 'ting." Why bother when everyone has done so well for so long without them. Every year, good Samaritans, usually by private initiative, check and ensure the marks. Don't sweat it; there are always marks there to guide you.

Along with magenta lines on your electronic plotter and GPS waypoints, you do have two, easy-to-distinguish, distant landmarks to guide you. The stone beacon on Stocking Island that looks like a shorn-off mini-lighthouse and the BTC tower, 180 feet tall with two large satellite dishes, looms on the ridge to the south of George Town. Harbor depths prevent you from steering directly for either of these except on certain legs. Because of the absence of marks, the only way to enter is by a series of legs following your plotter's magenta line or from GPS waypoint to GPS waypoint. The deep water that first veers south abeam Conch Cay towards Simons Point is obvious. (You can proceed along the barrier islands to anchor between Conch Cay and the western end of Stocking Island. To proceed farther southeast, you will eventually have to divert due south to avoid the shoal waters off Lily Cay.) The passage then turns east towards the stone beacon. It is dark blue and easy to follow. The hundreds of masts rocking in the harbor are evidence that it can be done. Both approaches are covered in detail under Pilotage.

Apparently, at one point, official memorandums existed stating that upon entering the harbor, boats are asked to contact the Harbour Control and Harbourmaster's Office on VHF Channel 16 ("George Town Harbour Control") and give your vessel name, registration number and last port of call. Upon leaving, you were requested to call again notifying them of your departure and next destination as in Nassau. If there is a Harbourmaster logging calls and controlling harbor traffic, there is no evidence of such. Perhaps at Family Island Regatta time, when the race areas and all approach channels must be kept free of traffic, there is a George Town Harbour Control? Of course putting "control" in the same sentence with "Family Island Regatta" is an oxymoron. We will leave the decision to hail or not to hail "George Town Harbour Control" to your discretion.

George Town Dockage and Elizabeth Harbour Anchorage

George Town's facilities are best described as popular and crowded. If you can not take close quarters and are not keen on the crowd scene, stay away from George Town until the forest of masts has thinned out.

Transient dockage is limited to Exuma Docking Services; and try as they may to keep up with maintenance and the pressure of ever-increasing numbers of guests, expect only adequate facilities while you are there. George Town Marina and Repair in Master's Harbour (south of the Red Shank Cays) has, alas, folded its business. Work has stopped on the luxurious Crab Cay Marina. If completed, it will offer 11,000 linear feet of floating dock space for vessels 50 to 200 feet with up to a 14-foot draft. Plans include a restaurant and a spa in this new estate community.

Your choices for anchoring are only limited to your patience to find room and your intelligence to stay out of the paths of mailboats, fuel delivery ships and megayachts that need the depth of the designated channel ways to travel. Take note of where the mailboats and delivery ships travel when they enter

Black Rocks, George Town Harbour, east entrance. (Not to be used for navigation.) WATERWAY GUIDE PHOTOGRAPHY.

the harbor, and stay out of that path unless you want their search lights illuminating the inside of your boat in the middle of the night, accompanied by a loud horn.

Anchoring? Take your choice! You have many anchoring options; all depend on wind, depth and desire:

1. Anywhere along the southern shore of Stocking Island; e.g., Hamburger, Monument, Honeymoon, St. Francis Channel, Volleyball, Black Rock, Rocky Point or Sand Dollar. South of Elizabeth Island (midway) and Guana Cay (midway, far off the cay).
2. Moorings in one of the Holes or Turtle Lagoon.
3. Off Goat Cay, Peace and Plenty Hotel or the Administration Building.
4. In Kidds Cove, outside of Kidds Cove or anywhere around Kidds Cove out past Moss Cays and Rolle Cay.
5. South and east of Red Shanks Cays.
6. South and along the shoreline in the blue holes of Crab Cay.
7. North and east of Isaac Cay or North of Rolle Town.

If you choose the more remote reaches of Stocking Island or the Red Shank area, you are in for a long dinghy ride to George Town to get provisions or enjoy time ashore. In good weather, this may be fine. In protracted bad weather, it may be too bumpy, too wet and too uncomfortable to be worth attempting. Off Stocking Island, take care not to anchor in the fairway. Off Peace and Plenty, you must keep clear of the government dock (on the north side of Regatta Point) and the turning basin. In Kidds Cove, you must not obstruct the harbor fairway.

The three Stocking Island basins are well-protected. If you are anchored off Stocking Island, you will feel anything from the western quadrant. On the George Town side, it is almost exactly the reverse, where anything from the eastern quadrant may cause discomfort. To navigate south to the distant, but well-protected, Red Shanks and Crab Cay areas, there are markers off Elizabeth Island to guide you through the narrow cut in between the reefs. From there, follow your plotter's magenta line, or turn almost due southwest abeam Fowl Cay, and visually work your way towards Isaac Cay. The one coral head that you need to avoid is black and obvious. From Isaac Cay, turn northwest to follow the blue deep waters into the anchorages. Visual navigation rules apply to access the anchorages around Rolle Cay and into the north bight of Crab Cay. Much depends on your curiosity and your skill at maneuvering around coral heads or getting off of sand bores. There is a bridge connecting Crab Cay with "mainland" Great Exuma that offers plenty of air draft for dinghies to "short cut" to Kidds Cove and George Town.

Great Exuma Island and Little Exuma Island

The next time you get a stretch of bad weather in Georgetown, and everybody has cabin fever, get together with friends and take a taxi tour, or rent a car and go explore. There are the ruins of abandoned plantations to find, historic cemeteries to discover, magnificent vistas (notably so at the top of Rolle Town), bonefish lodges, salt ponds and salinas close to Williams Town. Stop by Santana's Grill Pit—a favorite of Johnny Depp and celebrities when filming movies in the area. Don't forget to see the pothole agriculture in Barraterre when you go north. You can wrap up your tour there with a stop to see Hughrie Lloyd's latest sailboats and have one of Norman Lloyd's fabulous, fresh seafood dinners. There is so much to see, and you will have so much fun getting there, you will wish for rotten weather more often. ("The Exuma Guide" by Stephan Pavlidis expands on the history and lore of the Exuma Cays making a great car-tour companion.)

The Remaining Southern Exuma Cays

Hog and White Cays, lying south of Little Exuma Island, are the last two cays in the Exuma chain. Difficult to access on either the Exuma Sound or the bank sides because of shoal water and coral, they are best left unvisited unless you elect to anchor off and take your dinghy to explore. If you do decide to feel your way along the coast, the Williams Town BTC tower is a useful mark, but we would be very wary of going this way were it not for the day anchorages off the Pelican Cays and directly off the stone beacon at Williams Town. Once clear of the eastern entrance to George Town Harbour, you are bound for the Out Islands.

Pilotage. Talking Captain to Captain

George Town is an easy place, between Nassau and Providenciales, to touch base with the outside world. Here one finds telephones, fax, email, FedEx, UPS and air delivery. There is good provisioning and whatever backup facilities one may need. George Town would not have developed into the focal point it has become were there not good reasons for it, although Long Island and Thompson Bay is challenging this outpost's claim to fame.

George Town Harbour West Entrance

The list of waypoints makes the approach look like a potential nightmare, but it is not difficult. Just take it easy, in bite-size chunks; and have your first mate call it out as you go. You will have at least 1.8 meters/6 feet on this route. Do not go in on autopilot!

- **Stage 1. Conch Cay Cut.** Two simple half-mile legs take you through Conch Cay Cut (don't confuse this with the Conch Cut already discussed farther to the north). GTAW1 places you about 0.5 nautical miles north of Conch Cay Cut. From there, steer 190/010 degrees true for 0.8 nautical miles to clear the reef (on your port side), that runs northwest from Conch Cay. Conch Cay (or rather its outlier) has a light on it. The Smith Cays, right on your nose on Leg 1, are easily identifiable. There are houses on the hill behind the Smith Cays. At GTAW2, you will be safely past that first reef. Turn to port on a heading of 132/312 degrees true, and run parallel to Conch Cay and its reefs on the port side and off the reefs that will be to starboard. There is a red marker on the reef on the starboard side. Hold this course for 0.6 nautical miles to GTAW3.
- **Stage 2. The Simons Point Legs.** Two easy legs around Simons Point set you up to enter the George Town Harbour area. From GTAW3, turn to starboard and head 163/343 degrees true for Simons Point, on which there are two visible pink houses. Run for 0.5 nautical miles on this leg to reach GTAW4. At GTAW4, turn to port on a heading of 142/322 degrees true, and run parallel to the Great Exuma coast for 0.7 nautical miles to reach GTAW5.
- **Stage 3. Crossing to Stocking Island.** At GTAW5, turn to port. Identify the Stocking Island beacon. Head for it for about one nautical mile on about 105/285 degrees true. This takes you across to the deep-water channel to GTAW6. Once you are there, turn to starboard and parallel Stocking Island on a course of 135/315 degrees true to the anchorage area where there will be other boats. You can hardly go wrong. It is safe where everyone else has gone.

If bound for the George Town side, turn to starboard when you are abeam of the entrance to the Stocking Island basins, then aim for the BTC tower.

George Town Harbour East Entrance

The east entrance also has a list of waypoints, but these are not daunting if you take them in stages. Be alert for the reefs through which you will visually navigate. You should find at least 3.6 meters/12 feet the whole way.

- Stage 1. The Initial Entry. As you approach the east entrance, identify the prominent fort ruins on Man-O-War Cay, visible from some distance out off your starboard bow, and North Channel Rocks off your port bow, showing plainly and black. From GTAE1, a course of 199/019 degrees true held for 0.8 nautical miles, takes you safely in through a wide, 6-meter/20-foot deep cut to GTAE2.
- Stage 2. Running Up to Red Shank Corner. At GTAE2, turn to starboard on 278/098 degrees true for 1.5 nautical miles to reach GTAE3, which lies just short of a coral reef to port and patches of isolated heads to starboard. At GTAE3, alter course a bit to 270/090 degrees true, and eyeball your way for 0.5 nautical miles to reach GTAE4, which we call Red Shank Corner. From this waypoint, if you want Red Shank Cays, work your way southwest around the coral to tuck yourself in behind the Red Shank Cays or Crab Cay.
- Stage 3. The Final Run In. From GTAE4, you have a comparatively long run of almost 1.5 nautical miles on a heading of 297/117 degrees true to reach GTAE5. When you are almost at GTAE5, you pass close between two reefs (about N 23°30.830'/W 075°44.000') that lie midway between Elizabeth Island and Crab Cay. The passage between these reefs is marked by two buoys - red/white to starboard, green/white to port as you enter. A barrel marks the reef to the north just short of GTAE5. At GTAE5, you are still between Elizabeth Island and Crab Cay. You have one last half-mile leg to go on a course of 295/115 degrees true to reach GTAE6, which lies between Stocking Island and Rolle Cay. From here, you can carry on to the Stocking Island anchorages, or swing around Rolle Cay and the little Moss Cays for Kidds Cove, the Exuma Docking Services or the Peace and Plenty anchorage.

Masters Harbour Approach

Whether you have come from the west or east, when you are in the area of the waypoint GTAE4, look for the white house on Elizabeth Island. When you have that house bearing due north, head due south to pass off the east end of Red Shank Cay. There is good depth, but there are five coral heads that should be avoided in the last part of this run. Then head toward Isaac Cay, about half a mile off. You will see two white buoys. Stay close to them, passing to starboard incoming. The shallowest water is around the first buoy, and there is a sandbar that is easily seen.

The Great Exuma Island Cuts

We caution you about using the routes on the banks south of Great Exuma Island to exit into the sound at Comer Channel. This is beautiful cruising territory for shoal-draft boats and a great short cut to the Jumentos and Ragged Islands if the sound is acting up, but the routes require good visual piloting and a rising tide to traverse Comer Channel. ■

Waterway Guide is always open to your observations from the helm. E-mail your comments on any navigation information in the guide to: editor@waterwayguide.com.

The Southern Exuma Cays Waypoints

Galliott Cut East	GALLE	23°55.66N / 76°16.58W
Galliot Cut West	GALLW	23°55.00N / 76°18.00W
Cave Cut East	CAVEE	23°54.16N / 76°15.16W
Cave Cut West	CAVEW	23°53.91N / 76°16.08W
Rudder Cut East	RUDRE	23°52.25N / 76°13.41W
Rudder Cut West	RUDRW	23°51.83N / 76°13.66W
Adderley Cut East	ADDYE	23°47.25N / 76°06.41W
Adderley Cut West	ADDYW	23°46.75N / 76°07.41W
Rat Cay Cut North	RATCN	23°44.08N / 76°02.08W
Rat Cay Cut South	RATCS	23°43.75N / 76°01.91W

Great Exuma Island

WEST ENTRANCE TO GEORGE TOWN HARBOUR

Approach Waypoint	GTAW1 (X8)	23°34.30N / 75°48.50W
West Channel	GTAW2	23°33.66N / 75°48.66W
Conch Cay	GTAW3	23°33.25N / 75°48.16W
Simons Point	GTAW4	23°32.75N / 75°48.00W
Simons SW	GTAW5	23°32.16N / 75°47.50W
Stockling Island Beacon	GTAW6	23°31.91N / 75°46.50W

EAST ENTRANCE TO GEORGE TOWN HARBOUR

Approach Waypoint	GTAE1 (X21)	23°29.70N / 75°40.00W
Middle Channel Rocks	GTAE2 (X20)	23°29.20N / 75°40.37W
Flat Cay	GTAE3	23°29.41N / 75°42.00W
Red Shank Corner	GTAE4 (X19)	23°29.55N / 75°42.93W
Coral Narrows	GTAE5	23°30.10N / 75°44.02W
Red/White Mark	GTAE6	23°30.35N / 75°44.61W

Western Route South

HEADING FOR THE WINDWARD PASSAGE

Barracoutta Sandbores	BRCTA	23°44.00N / 76°20.00W
Hawksbill Rocks	HWKBL (X44)	23°25.25N / 76°06.25W

Position format is latitude and longitude in degrees and minutes (hddd°mm.mm). Waypoints in RED are NOT for autopilot navigation. Codes in parenthesis are Wavey Line waypoints marked on the charts. If you have programmed waypoints listed in a previous edition of this guide, check carefully to ensure the coordinates you have recorded match the list. If a waypoint is no longer on the list we may have changed its code or deleted it.

View from Shroud Cay. Photo Courtesy of Peter Mitchell.

GOIN' ASHORE:

CAVE CAY

Cave Cay Cut has always been one of the favored passages out to the sound. The anchorages in front of Cave Cay provide safe and beautiful spots for vessels who need to lay low and wait for a good opportunity to depart the bank side. For protection from poor weather conditions, take advantage of the good, safe harbor carved into Cave Cay.

SAFE HARBOUR MARINA
VHF 16 and 14 • Tel: 242-357-0143
sejc@aol.com • www.cavecay.com
Slips 25. **MLW at Docks** 11 ft., channel 5.5 ft. MLW **Dockage** $1.50 to $2.50 per foot, per night. Minimum 35 ft. rate. All floating docks. **Fuel** Dock open 9 a.m. to 4 p.m., daily (closed for lunch noon to 1 p.m.) **Services and Facilities** Shore power $0.55 per kwHr, 30 amp and 50 amp, daily minimums $20 and $40 per day. Showers, restrooms, complimentary washing machine, RO water, $0.50 per gallon. Garbage bag disposal, complimentary for guests. $30 per bag for transients. Battery charger available, $12 per day. Packed coral, 2,800 ft. runway, no landing charge for guests. **Accommodations** Motel rooms by the marina are slated to be built in next phase of development **Credit Cards** None. Cash, personal checks or Travelers Checks.

MUSHA CAY

www.mushacay.com
A pristine, private cay owned by the magician, David Copperfield. The whole island is available for rent from $325,000 per week. Maximum number of guests in five villas, 20. Good anchorages off the north end to wait for safe passage through Cave Cay Cut.

BOCK CAY ARCHIPELAGO

16 miles north of Barraterre is a collection of private islands consisting of Bock Cay, Prime Cay, Lignumvitae Cay, Melvin Cay, Neighbour Cay, Wooby Cay and two Rock Islands. From time to time, one or all are for sale.

BARRATERRE & ROLLEVILLE

fuel • groceries • ice • restaurants • telephone • water

Although Barraterre is a separate island at the northwestern tip of Great Exuma, it is joined by two causeways to the mainland. The small community of Rolleville lies to the south. Both offer shallow water anchorages and a few facilities for visiting boats. You can dinghy to both settlements to enjoy an Out Island-style welcome and warm hospitality just a few miles north of the glitz and ritz at Emerald Bay. In Barraterre, there is a small boat fuel pier, a jetty and a Government pier. Beach your dinghy, or tie up at the Shell fuel dock. You will discover an unusual variety of locally grown fresh produce and unequalled Bahamian fare at the *Fisherman's Inn*. The entire community gathers at the *Fisherman's Inn* for Boxing Day festivities. Rolleville is surrounded by pothole farms that grow bananas, tomatoes, onions and peppers. It hosts an annual regatta, usually the first weekend in August. You can dinghy to Kermit's Tavern at Exuma Point. Kermit runs the Snack Bar at the airport, too. There is a convenience store that you can walk to from the Rolleville jetty. The beaches both north and south of Rolleville are pristine and all your own.

PORT DIRECTORY

Accommodations *Barraterre Bonefish Lodge*, 242-355-5052 • *Norman Lloyd's Fisherman's Inn*, 242-355-5017/5016, Two rooms for rent, telephone, bar and restaurant overlooking the water.
Arts & Crafts Wonderful straw work at *Valerie Taylor's*.
Bonefishing Guides *Barraterre Bonefish Lodge*, 242-355-5052. Incredible bonefishing in these waters!
Church *Ebenezer Baptist Church*, an especially joyful place to worship. The singing is sincere and heaven meant. Sit outside and gaze at the incredible array of blues in the waters.
Fuel Gasoline at the *Shell* dock.
Ice Try the *Bonefish Lodge* or the *Fisherman's Inn*. Both keep sporadic hours, and sometimes it is hard to find a living soul.
Laundry *L & D* at Roker's Point, 242-358-0130. Coin-op, wash and fold.
Medical Clinic There is a nurse at the *Steventon Clinic*, south of Rolleville. Doctor and dentist in George Town.
Provisions In season, you can find locally grown avocados, bananas, cabbage, grapefruit, mangoes, onions, peppers and tomatoes. *Ray Ann's Variety Store & Produce*, fresh produce, canned goods, ice cream and basic needs • *McKenzie's Store & Fuel*, fresh produce, soda pop, liquor, fresh fish and conch • At Rolleville, *Heaven Sent Convenience Store*, fresh produce and sundry items.
Restaurants & Bars *Fisherman's Inn at Barraterre*, 242-355-5017. Breakfast, lunch and dinner. Special seafood grill on Saturdays, noon until 7 p.m. $ • *Barraterre's Same Ole Place*, 242-355-5050, VHF 16. Delicious local fare for lunch or dinner. $ • *Barraterre Bonefish Lodge*, 242-355-5052, VHF 16 $ • *Kermit's Tavern*, just south of Exuma Point, north of Rolleville • *Runaway Bay Beach Bar & Restaurant*, south of Rolleville, 242-345-6279. Lunch and dinner. $ • *Coco Plum Beach Bar & Grill*, south of Runaway, 242-554-3358. Breakfast, lunch and dinner. $
Taxi *Norman Lloyd*, 242-355-5016 to George Town Airport and points south.
Telephones Card phones in front of *Fisherman's Inn* and *Same Ole Place*.
Water *Fisherman's Inn* • *McKenzie's Fuel & Produce*.

GEORGE TOWN

airport • bank • customs & immigration • fuel • groceries • marina • marine services • medical • police • post office • propane • restaurants • telephone • water

One of the greatest cruising destinations in the Bahamas, hosting between 400 and 700 boats at Regatta times, George Town has a charm that equals Shangri La for boaters. Some people stay for months at a time to escape the northern winter and meet up with cruising friends year after year. Others stay only a few days as they stop in for provisions en route from the Caribbean. This is a boater-friendly town with good anchorages, easy access to Customs and Immigration, a convenient international airport and some of the best-stocked stores in the southern Bahamas.

Over the years, tiny, remote George Town has seen much develop-

Exuma Markets dinghy dock, Lake Victoria.
Waterway Guide Photography.

ment and is no longer so "tiny" anymore. Stocking Island is home to friendly St. Francis Marina. Crab Cay hopes to be crawling some day with million dollar homes. February Point continues to expand, and Marina at Emerald Bay, a Sandals Resort, offers new growth on the "other" end of the island. All this means better jobs for the good folks of George Town and a little more traffic going "roun' de pond" for which you have to watch out. Despite the changes, George Town folks still devote themselves to the cruisers fall, winter and spring invasion and cater to the floating visitors every need and want. The school children are still polite, the local women still devout, and the restaurants, bars and shops are still a delight.

After years and years of holding tank abuse by hundreds and hundreds of vessels, plus too many showers, dishes and wash-downs with non-biodegradable, petroleum and glycol ether based products, and the advent and popularity of anti-bacterial soaps, George Town anchorage waters are showing the toll. Please do your part to reinvigorate this paradise. Pump out at Emerald Bay, or take the "3-Mile Cruise." Only use biodegradable, non-petroleum and non-glycol ether based products. Look at the labels. You will be surprised to see how many soaps, shampoos and dish detergents contain petroleum-based products. There is a wide variety of products available everywhere. There is no excuse for using the harmful ones. In addition, anti-bacterial products are destroying the "good bacteria," coral heads and reefs. This includes hand and bath soaps and detergents. If you are worried about "bacteria," keep an alcohol-based gel at each sink, and give your dishes a vinegar rinse.

ANCHORAGES

(1) Off Hamburger Beach, on the lee side of Stocking Island. Northwest of the Monument. Look for the Beach Club's taxi pier and short dinghy dock. Hike trails to ocean side or to John's Flip Flop Beach, harbor side, almost to Lily Cay. (2) Monument Beach, directly below the monument. Hike trail to the top of the island and stone beacon. (3) Honeymoon Beach, just southeast of Monument. (4) In front of and behind Chat 'n Chill. Stay out of channel to St. Francis and mooring ball holes. There are a few new berths for long-term dockage in the Cleaning Hole. Ask at St. Francis for local information on mooring balls and berths. (5) Off Volleyball Beach to Black Rock. (6) All along Sand Dollar Beach. (7) Off Elizabeth Island, watch for coral heads. (8) Off Guana Cay, can be rolly there. (9) Off Rolle Town, but you have to negotiate the coral heads from Point Cay and along the shoreline to Rolle Town visually. View from the top of hill in Rolle Town will take your breath away. Actress Esther Rolle from the television show "Good Times" was born here and her relatives remain. You can also hike to the tombs of the Scottish settlers, the Kay family. The tombs have withstood the course of time since 1792. (10) Masters Harbour, tuck around Isaac Cay. (11) Red Shanks, anchor in 5 feet right off the Shanks. (12) Work your way into the anchorages in the protected waters between the Devine Cays, Crab Cay and Moss Cay, gorgeous beach on east side of Moss, Sundowners Cruisers Yacht Club off eastern tip of Crab, turtles frequent these waters, careful in the dinghy, spectacular diving in grotto on shoreline across from the blue hole. (13) In calm weather, you can anchor anywhere along the eastern shoreline of Crab Cay, be mindful of coral heads and un-surveyed waters. There is protection in the eastern Crab Cay cove; a marina is under construction in western cove. (14) From Rolle Cay west all the way into Kidds Cove. (15) In Kidds Cove and surrounding waters off the town. Kidds Cove is named for Captain Kidd, a U.S. Navy officer who visited the cove to pursue pirates. When using the aforementioned anchorages, don't anchor in the commercial shipping channels that lead to the government dock or Exuma Docking Services. (16) In front of the Administration Bldg. or off Peace & Plenty. (17) In front of Fish Fry Village. (18) Either side of Goat Cay, you can go very close to the beautiful beach on the west side of Goat Cay. Land your dinghy at the beach. (Tell Emma in the house across the street from the beach that you have beached your dinghy there. Her daughter owns the little, turquoise beach hut. Emma sells wonderful straw work in her stand). It is a short walk to the veterinarian. The NAPA store is just yards north. Dinghy around Simons Point, beach the dinghy to access Hoopers Bay shopping.

CUSTOMS AND IMMIGRATION

George Town is a port of entry. Incoming captains can clear Customs and Immigration in the two-story building north of the Shell Station between 9 a.m. and 5 p.m., Monday through Friday. Overtime charges apply weekends, public holidays or outside office hours. Customs numbers are 242-336-2072 or 242-336-0071 at the airport. Immigration is 242-336-2569 or 242-336-0073 at the airport. There is a $20 fee if the officer has to come into town outside business hours. There is no duty on engine, transmission or prop parts for your vessel or outboard motor (make sure it is listed on your cruising permit). No brokerage agent is required to fill out the necessary paperwork. A $10 stamp tax is charged. The Chief Customs Officer requires the use of a Customs Broker to fill out the paperwork on all other imports. Duty is 45%.

DINGHY DOCKS

(1) At the government dock across from Kidds Cove, but avoid the mailboat dock. Take trash to the dumpster by the mailboat dock. On Lake Victoria, a.k.a. The Pond, under the bridge. (2) You can tie up at the long Exuma Markets dinghy dock on your port side as you come in under the bridge. They are generous to boaters and provide free RO water at the dinghy dock. (3) There is also a dock across the street from Shop Rite, on the other side of the pond. It is used by local contractors to load building supplies on to boats bound for Stocking Island, but there is no problem tying up off to the side and out of their way. (4) You can land anywhere on the sand from Perez's WiFi (the bright yellow house) to in front of Sam Gray's service station next door to Exuma Docking Services, but you might want to leave someone behind with the dinghy. Wear sturdy shoes. There is lots of broken glass in the shallow water there. Although very rare, theft can occur anywhere, even in George Town. Lock your outboard and its gas cans to your dinghy. Lock your dinghy to something sturdy. Carry anything not locked down with you.

On Stocking Island, St. Francis offers a beautiful dock to tie up dinghies. If you are going for a long walk on the beach, though, beach your dinghy on the sand. At times, there will be hundreds of dinghies on Volleyball Beach. It is smart to stand off shore a bit and throw out an anchor. It is certainly better on the inflatable's bottom. It is no fun to search for wayward dinghies that floated off the beach at high tide.

MARINAS

ST. FRANCIS HOTEL & MARINA
TEL: 242-557-9629 FAX: 242 336 2416 • VHF 16 •
www.stfrancisresort.com
Your gracious hosts at St. Francis are George and Gillian Godfrey. Nina's really the boss, though, so bring her a bone.
Slips 1, permanently leased. T-dock with slips planned. **Moorings** 15 in Hurricane Hole #2; 20' depth on the moorings; 5 ft. in the marked channel to the moorings. $15 per day. **Max LOA** N/A **MLW at dock** 5 ft. **Dockage** Free dockage for dinghies and tenders. **Facilities and Services** Restroom, coin-op washer and dryer, $4 per load. Satellite television at the bar. WiFi available for a small fee. **Restaurant and Bar** Open at 11 a.m. daily. Creative, frosty bar drinks and delicious island specialties in the restaurant. George and Gillian Godfrey roll out the welcome mat to cruisers and have the friendliest place to hang out on Stocking Island, as well as the nicest place! St. Francis is the main sponsor of the Cruising Regatta. **Accommodations** Beautiful suites with breakfast in bed, daily. Protected dune beach walk to spectacular Stocking Island Beach. Eight rooms from $235 per night includes breakfast in bed for two, use of sea kayaks and Hobie Cat, transport to and from George Town. **Credit cards** Visa, MasterCard. Pets are welcome on the deck upon Nina's approval. (Here is where you want to bring out the bone.)

EXUMA DOCKING SERVICES
TEL: 242-336-2578 • FAX: 242-336-2023 • VHF 16 "Sugar One"
Slips 52. **Max LOA** 120 ft. **MLW at Dock** 6.5 ft. **Dockage** $1.00 per ft. per day. **Fuel** Dock is open 8 a.m. to 5 p.m., Monday through Saturday; Sunday, 11 a.m. to 1 p.m., diesel and gasoline. Facilities & Services Shore power metered with minimums based on length. **(Double check the pedestal before hooking up.)** RO Water $0.20 per gallon. Shower, restrooms and coin-op laundry, $1.50 per load. BTC card phone and U.S.-direct phone. WiFi available. Trash in bins, free. Ice. Taxis outside the marina. Mom's fresh bread and pastries, in the van under the tree next to the service station. There is a good selection of marine lubricants and some supplies at the service station. **Liquor** at *Sam Gray's Liquor Store*. **Cars** from *Sam Gray's Car Rentals*. *Scentuous Perfumes* has a small selection of perfumes and cosmetics on the first floor of *Sam's Place Restaurant*. **Restaurant** *Sam's Place Upstairs* Overlooking the docks. Plans to renovate and update the entire facility are in the future. Keep an eye out for bigger and better things here. **Credit Cards** Visa, MasterCard and AMEX, with a 5% surcharge.

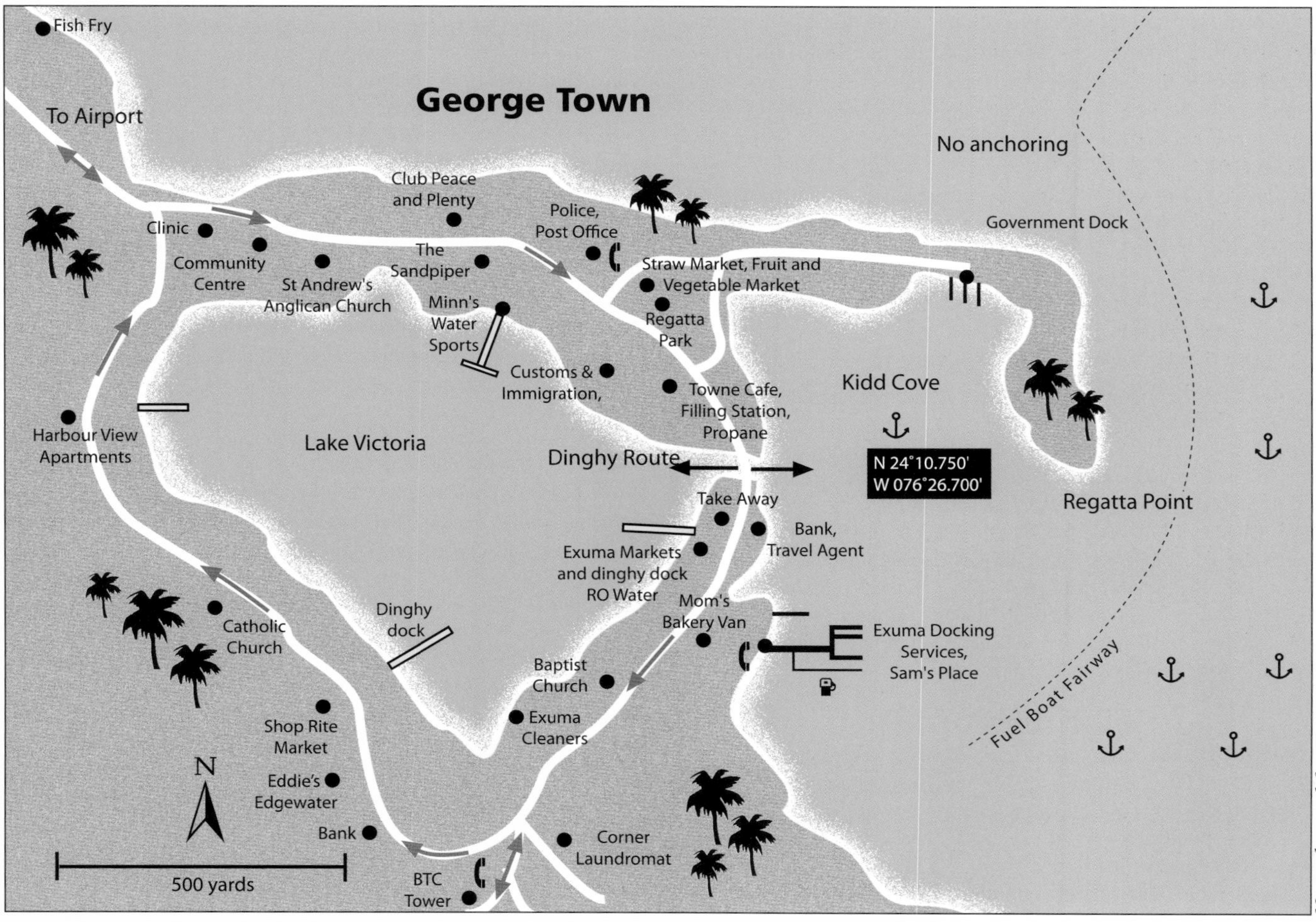

Not to be used for navigaiton.

EMERGENCIES

BASRA • 242-325-8864 • VHF 16
Customs • 242-336-2072
Immigration• 242-336-2569
Medical *Clinic* • 242-336-2088 • During the day; after hours call 242-336-2606 for the doctor; 242-336-2985 for a nurse.
Marine • 242-336-2312 • VHF 16
Police • 919
Veterinarian • 242-336-2806

SANDALS RESORT AND MARINA AT EMERALD BAY
Tel: 242-336-6100 • Fax: 242-336-6101 • VHF 16 and 11 •
Dockmaster Tel: 242-357-0895 • glenroy.smith@grp.sandals.com
(Note: This marina is actually located about 10 miles north of George Town Harbour near Rokers Point Settlement.)
The manager at Sandals Marina at Emerald Bay is Douglas K. Black. **Slips** 150. **Max LOA** 240 ft. **MLW at dock** 14 ft. **Dockage** 40 ft. minimum. $3.75, 40 to 59 ft., $4.00; 60 to 99 ft., $4.50; +100 ft. With no services, $1.50 for cruisers. **Fuel** Dock Open 7:30 a.m. to 5 p.m., daily. Shell gas and diesel. Pump-out, $25. **Facilities and Services** Power $0.85 per kwHr, 30, 50, 100, 3-phase. RO water, $0.30 per gallon. Restrooms, showers, coin-op washer and dryer. Satellite TV, WiFi. Ice. **Restaurant and Bar** At the marina, but also access to all facilities and services at Sandals Resort. Free shuttle service to the spa, golf course, beaches, market, liquor store, bank, gift shops, pools. On-site Customs and Immigration service. **Accommodations:** 183-room resort with 3 restaurants, Spa and Wellness Center, 3 swimming pools, tennis courts and Greg Norman designed 18-hole golf course.

CRAB CAY
The development on Crab Cay includes home sites, an airstrip, a spa and a restaurant in the old plantation house. A bridge links Crab Cay to Great Exuma. The marina has 11,000 linear feet of floating dock space to accommodate vessels from 50 ft. to 200 ft. with a 14 ft. draft.

FEBRUARY POINT
Tel: 242-336-2661/2400 (restaurant) • VHF 16
bamboobistro@februarypoint.com • www.februarypoint.com
February Point plans to add more slips to their private marina. They have little water into and around their facility, but perhaps it may offer slips to those of you who draw less than 3 feet. It is certainly worth a call to find out about transient space availability.
Slips 80. **Max LOA** N/A. **MLW at dock** 3 ft. or less. **Dockage** N/A **Fuel** Gasoline. **Facilities and Services** Power, RO water, Showers, WiFi. Ice. **Restaurant and Bar** *J.P.'s Bamboo Bistro*, intimate dockside dining, lunch and dinner Monday through Saturday, dinner only Sunday. Fresh local seafood, gourmet pizza, Tapas bar menu. Available for parties, events and catering.

PORT DIRECTORY

Accommodations *Club Peace and Plenty* • 242-336-2551, 800-525-2210 • Fax: 242-336-2093 • ppclub@batelnet.bs • www.peaceandplenty.com • Charming, historic downtown location with 32 rooms, three 2-room suites. Serves breakfast, lunch and dinner poolside and in the dining room. The hotel was built in 1958 by hotelier Lawrence Lewis, grandnephew of Henry Flagler. The original hotel is the lounge area. The club is named for the English trading ship, *Peace & Plenty*, that Lord Denys Rolle sailed into the harbor in 1783. There is a water taxi to the *Beach Club on Stocking Island* for swimming and snorkeling during the day and to *Chat 'n Chill*. Restaurant, swimming pool and bar at the hotel. *St. Francis Resort* • 242-557-9629 • stfrancismarine.com • Open to the cruising community with Internet services, moorings, water, laundry, bar, restaurant and villas. Located on Stocking Island, George Town. *Coconut Cove Hotel* • 242-336-2659 • Fax: 242-336-2658 • 11 beachside and garden rooms, from $120 per night, with gourmet dining, just north of George Town. *Sandals Resort* at Emerald Bay • 242-336-6800 • www.sandals.com • 10 miles north of Georgetown, with a 183-room hotel, spa, Greg Norman–designed golf course. Garden view rooms and beachfront suites. *Hotel Higgins Landing* • 242-336-2460 • Accommodates 10 guests in cottages with spacious verandas. Room rate includes breakfast and dinner. *Master Harbour Village* • 242-345-5076 • Fax: 242-345-5140 • Capt. Jerry Lewis has 1-, 2-, and 4-bedroom cottages. *Mount Pleasant Suites* • 242-336-2960 • Double occupancy suites at Hoopers Bay. • *Exuma Palms Hotel*, 242-358-4040, www.exumapalms.com. 12 rooms on the beach with mini-kitchenettes. Restaurant serves breakfast, lunch and dinner. Bar has lively happy hour and 2 plasma televisions. • *La Shante Beach Club and Resort* • 242-345-4190 • At Forbes Hill, 12 miles east of George Town. This small hotel has its own private beach, open-air bar and restaurant. Boat charters, deep sea fishing and bonefishing. *Palm Bay Beach Club* • 242-336-2787 • info@palmbaybeachclub.com • www.palmbaybeachclub.com • 17 brightly painted, 1- and 2-bedroom unpretentious cottages on the beach, 1.5 miles west of George Town. *Regatta Point* • 242-336-2206 • Fax: 242-336-2046 • 6 rooms and 2-bedroom suites, surrounded by water, overlooking the harbor and Kidds Cove; much sought after, especially at Regatta times. Ask at the Tourist Office for an up-to-date list of apartments to rent, especially during Regatta Weeks when accommodation is at a premium. The tourist office is located at Turnquest Star Plaza, second floor.
Airlines *American Eagle* • 800-433-7300 • Daily flights from George Town to Miami. *Bahamasair* • 242-345-0035 • Daily flights to Nassau. *Continental* • 800-231-0856 • Three daily flights from Ft. Lauderdale. *Reggie Express Services* • 954-761-3131 • Freight service from Fort Lauderdale, good for getting most anything you need from the States to George Town. Very helpful personnel will hold your hand through the whole process. • *Strachan's Aviation Service*, 242-345-0641. Office at the airport, where they can be contacted for charter flights.
Airport *Exuma International Airport* with a paved 8,000-ft. runway, is 9 miles from George Town at Moss Town. Listen for taxi shares on the Cruiser's Net. *Kermit's Airport Lounge* serves drinks and meals across from the terminal building. $. Construction and renovation seems never-ending here, but taxi drivers know the way around, and it is not big enough to truly get lost.
Banks and ATMs *ScotiaBank* • 242-336-2651/2652 • Opposite *Exuma Markets*, open 9:30 a.m. to 3 p.m. weekdays, to 4:30 p.m. on Fridays. *Royal Bank of Canada*, 242-336-3255, across from the basketball courts, open 9:30 a.m. to 3 p.m. weekdays. • Bank of the Bahamas, 242-336-3000 • *ScotiaBank*, 242-336-4651. In Emerald Isle Shopping Centre.
Bakery *Mom's Bakery* • 242-345-4062 • Mom arrives daily from Williams Town with a van full of homemade breads, cakes, doughnuts and pastries. She parks outside *Exuma Docking Services* and will greet you with a big hug. • *Towne Cafe & Bakery*, behind the Shell Station • *Straw Market*, at Regatta Park, the ladies sometimes have baked goods.

Beauty Salon *Brianne's Unisex Salon*, 242-336-2330.
Book & Magazines *Sandpiper*, 242-336-2084, across from Peace & Plenty • *Mailboxes, Etc.* 242-336-4100, in Emerald Isles Shopping Center.
Boutique *Sandpiper*, 242-336-2084, across from Peace & Plenty, resort wear and souvenirs • *Simply Beautiful*, 242-336-3314 • *Peace and Plenty Boutique* Open 8:30 a.m. to 5 p.m, except Sundays. Androsia clothes, T-shirts, post cards and guidebooks.
Bus George Town to Emerald Isles and Rolleville at 6:10 a.m., 11 a.m. and 3 p.m. daily for the two-hour trip.
Car Rental *Exuma Transport*, 242-336-2101, George Town • *Joey's Car Rental*, 242-336-4400, wallacewhitfield@hotmail.com. In Emerald Isle Shopping Centre • *Sure to Shore*, 242-336-3466, George Town.
Churches *St. Andrew's Anglican Church* Built in 1802, painted white and blue, like a pretty delft tile. A landmark on the hill above the *Club Peace and Plenty*. Chris Parker gives weather seminars in the Community Center when he is in George Town • *St. John's Baptist Church, St. Theresa's Catholic Church, The Church of God Prophecy, Seventh Day Adventist Church*.
Couriers *FedEx* • 242-336-2857 • VHF 16 • Outgoing packages can be sent from the office at the back of *Turks Island Shipping*. Incoming packages should be addressed c/o *Exuma Markets*, who will hold it for your arrival. Give your name and boat name so that they can call you over the Net in the morning, and remember to keep a tracking number of items sent. Items take about 3 days to or from the United States. *UPS* • Packages can be sent c/o *Seaside Real Estate* (242-336-2091) in George Town, who will hold them for you; packages are dispatched on Tuesdays, Wednesdays and Thursdays. • *Mailboxes, Etc.* 242-336-4100, in Emerald Isles Shopping Center.
Diving *Dive Exuma*, 242-336-2893, 242-357-0313, diveexuma@hotmail.com, www.dive-exuma.com. Specializing in SCUBA diving, snorkeling and sightseeing trips. Air fills and PADI certification available. Dive wrecks, walls, reefs and blue holes.
Diving & Snorkeling Gear *Top II Bottom*, 242-336-2200 • *Minn's Water Sports*, 242-336-3483.
Dry Cleaners *Exuma Cleaners*, 242-336-2038.
Electronics *Bal Sound's Electronics* • 242-336-2375 • DVDs, CDs, electronic repairs, cell phones and quick cell cards.
FAX *Exuma Markets* • Tel: 242-336-2033, Fax: 242-336-2645. Will accept incoming faxes for boats. Check at the market. Faxes can also be sent from here. *Exuma Business Centre* • 242-336-3271 • Fax: 242-336-3272 • ebc@batelnet.bs • Internet access, copiers, printing and fax machines. *BTC*, 242-336-2011. Open 9 a.m. to 4:30 p.m. weekdays, with two card phones outside, Internet access using your own laptop inside. • *Mail Boxes, Etc.* Tel: 242-336-4100, Fax: 242-336-4101, in the Emerald Isles Shopping Centre.
Ferry *Bahamas SeaLink Ferries*, 242-323-2166. Leave Georgetown for Nassau on Tuesdays, Wednesdays and Thursdays at 12 p.m. for the 10-hour trip.
Fuel *Exuma Docking Services* at dock and service station next door. *Shell Station*, 242-336-2738, next to *Exuma Market*.
Hardware *Darville Lumber* • 242-336-2114 • At Hoopers Bay, about three miles out of town. Open 9 a.m. to 5 p.m. weekdays. Builders supplies with a good range of plumbing, electrical, hardware, fishing equipment, cleaning fluids, oils and some marine supplies. • *Top II Bottom*, 242-336-2200. Across from Regatta Park. Good range of hardware, plumbing, electrical, fishing and other supplies.
Internet *St. Francis Resort*, Stocking Island • *Exuma Markets*, sit on curb in front of the bank or on the bridge. FREE! • *Exuma Business Centre*, your computer or theirs • *BTC*, sit in their office • *Blue Shack Communications*, little wooden blue establishment across from the basketball courts on the corner where you turn for the Corner Laundromat and B&M Bulk Goods • Anywhere in Kidds Cove, *Harbour WiFi*. This is Perez's WiFi, sometimes you have to go to his bright yellow house/pet store to pay and get password, Perez wears a Rasta hat on his dreads, easy to recognize • *Eddie's Edgewater* • *Club Peace and Plenty*, 242-336-2551. Their computer or yours.
Jewelry *Tropical Accents & Gifts*, 242-336-2396, by the bridge.
Laundry *Corner Laundromat* • 242-335-2094 • Open 7 a.m. to 11 p.m. daily; Excellent washers and dryers, 2 extra-large dryers. Detergents, snacks and drink machine. Restroom. Attendants will check your machine to ensure it is not overloaded. They sell tokens. They will not take change or coins. Bring bills • *Exuma Cleaners* • 242-336-2038 • VHF 16 • Behind Regatta Park. Open 8 to 5 except Sunday. Take your laundry in before 8:30 a.m., they will wash, dry and fold it for you by 4:30 p.m. the same day. Dry cleaning. *Exuma Docking Services* washers and dryers. Pay close attention to "Out of Order" signs. Open during dock hours.

MEDICAL

Ambulance • 242-357-0610
Dentist At the Government Clinic.
Doctors *Government Clinic* • 242-336-2088 • Staffed by a doctor, a dentist, and nurses. General clinics 9 to 1 weekdays, and a children's clinic on Thursday. Two, 2-bed wards. For nonresidents, the standard consultation charge is $30. In an emergency, call 242-336-2606 for the doctor, 242-336-2985 for a nurse.
Island Med Medical Clinic • 242-336-2220 • Private clinic just past the *NAPA* store out of town, on the left. Dr. Fox comes in once a week from Nassau on Thursdays from 9 a.m. to 4 p.m. Dr. Thompson is there on Mondays from 9 a.m. to 3 p.m., and a pediatrician visits twice a month on Saturdays. Secretary Erica is at the *Clinic* Monday through Thursday, 10 a.m. to 1 p.m. to make appointments. The doctors have their own pharmacy at the clinic, open Monday through Thursday, 10 a.m. to 1 p.m.

MARINE SERVICES

Brown's Auto and *Brown's Marine* • 242-336-2883/2928 • Call Perry Brown for marine and fiberglass repairs, painting and engine work.
George Town Marina and Repair Ltd • 242-345-5116 • phone and fax • gtmarine@hotmail.com • In Masters Harbour, 5 miles southeast of George Town. Ask for Mark Turnquest. 50-ton Acme marine hoist for a maximum draft of 7 ft., and a maximum beam of 22 ft. General, fiberglass, refrigeration, diesel, electrical and outboard repairs; bottom painting, rental tools and equipment; spare parts and dry storage for short or long-term stays. Pump-out facility on site. Cargo flights in every Tuesday. 24-hr security.
Minn's Water Sports • 242-336-2604 • Fax: 242-336-3483 • info@mwsboats.com • www.mwsboats.com • On Lake Victoria opposite *Peace and Plenty*. Kent Polley has Boston Whalers; Carolina Skiffs; Johnson, Evinrude and Yamaha engines; sales and service; rentals, dockage and storage.
NAPA • 242-336-2780 • North of town, has some marine parts and supplies.
Top II Bottom • 242-336-2200/2114 • Open 8 to 5 Monday through Friday, 9 to 3 Saturdays, with a selection of marine supplies and household goods. Agents for *DHL*.

Liquor *BGS Liquor Store*, 242-336-2900 • John Marshall's Liquor Store, 242-336-2771 • *Sam Gray's Liquor Store* at Exuma Docking. All closed on Sundays. • *CNK Liquor Store*, 242-336-2145 fine wines, beer and spirits, Hoopers Bay next to Smitty's. • *Bristol Wines & Spirits*, 242-336-2834, Emerald Isle Shopping Centre.

Mail *Exuma Markets* will hold mail for you. Have it addressed to: your name, c/o your boat name, *Exuma Markets*, George Town, Exuma, Bahamas and mark it HOLD FOR ARRIVAL. There are boxes with incoming mail addressed to boaters inside the store.

Marine Supplies *NAPA Auto Parts*, ride the bus, hitchhike or anchor west of Goat Cay and cross the street. Can order just about anything • *Top II Bottom*, sometimes surprises you with their selection of marine goods.

Moorings Kevalli Cove Moorings are located in Cleaning Hole (a.k.a. Hole 3) on Stocking Island in Elizabeth Harbour. It is one of the best hurricane holes in the Bahamas. The have 12 helix-style moorings and 9 slips for boat storage. Kevalli House has two guest cottages available for rent. Contact Bob at kevallihouse@gmail.com for more information.

Police 242-336-2666, emergency 919 • Office is in the administration building.

Post Office 242-336-2636. In the administration building, open 8 a.m. to 4:30 p.m. weekdays.

Propane From the *Shell* filling station in town. From *Clarence* on Wednesday's across the street from *Eddie's Edgewater*, 242-357-0245. *Clarence* will refill your tank.

Provisions Local fruit and vegetables from the *Straw Market* ladies. *Exuma Markets* • 242-336-2033 • Fax: 242-336-2645 • With their own dinghy dock under the bridge and behind the store on the pond, free RO water at the dinghy dock. Open 8 a.m. to 6 p.m. daily, to 10 a.m. on Sundays. This is the best-stocked store in the Exumas. Fresh fruit and vegetables, dairy and cheeses, imported meats, canned and dried goods, bottled and canned juices and sodas, water, batteries, film, household cleaners, some pharmacy, daily newspapers and more. They are extremely generous to boaters. *Shop Rite Mart* • 242-336-2670 • Open 7:30 a.m. to 7 p.m. daily, to 10 a.m. on Sundays. *Smitty's Convenience Store and CNK Liquor* • 242-336-2144 • At Hoopers Bay, open 8 a.m. to 6 p.m. daily and to 10 a.m. on Sundays. Prescription service • *Emerald Isle Supermarket & Deli*, Tel: 242-336-4002, FAX: 242-336-4006. 25,000 square foot store, meat, poultry, fresh produce and fruits, household goods, deli serves breakfast and lunch. Open Monday through Wednesday, 8 a.m. to 7 p.m. Thursday through Saturday, 8 a.m. to 8 p.m. Sunday, 8 a.m. to noon. Deli open 8 a.m. to 2 p.m.

Restaurants & Bars There is something for everybody here, from souse and hot dogs to elegant dining at the hotels. Several of the out-of-town restaurants will send transport on request.

Chat 'n Chill Beach Club • 242-358-5010 • VHF 16 • www.chatnchill.com • Open daily for lunch and dinner on the beach on Stocking Island, with sandwiches, salads, grill menu, ice, drinks and party catering. Pig roast on Sundays. Water available at their beachside pump. Friday night music. Water sport rentals and their own water taxi, VHF 16 "Georgetown Water Taxi". $-$$

Cheaters • 242-336-2535 • 2.5 miles east of town on the Queen's Highway. Fun, Bahamian food. Friday night barbeques $10. $

Club Peace and Plenty • 242-336-2551 • Serves breakfast, lunch and dinner poolside and in the dining room. Bar is located in the original, 18th century slave kitchen. Johnny Depp accepted his People's Choice award by satellite in the bar. Snacks available at the *Stocking Island Beach Club.* Breakfast, lunch and dinner (reservations requested). $-$$$

Coconut Cove Hotel • 242-336-2659 • VHF 16 • Elegant food in delightful surroundings, 1.5 miles west of George Town. Open for breakfast, lunch and dinner, with *The Sandbar* open 3 p.m. to 9 p.m., and their own dinghy dock. Call ahead for dinner reservations and complimentary transport to and from George Town. $-$$$

Come 'N Get It, Look for the truck under the trees in town. Has fresh bread. Serves pizza, hot dogs, guava duff.

Eddie's Edgewater Bahamian cuisine and local color on the edge of the pond, with a bar and restaurant, open for breakfast, lunch and dinner. Monday rake and scrape party. Free WiFi. Don't miss their snack fish! Barbeques on Fridays, $10. $-$$

Emerald Isle Deli, 242-336-4002. Open 8 a.m. to noon. Serves breakfast, lunch sandwiches and salads. Emerald Isles Shopping Centre. $$-$$$

Exuma Palms Restaurant & Bar, 242-358-4040. Overlooking Three Sister's Beach. Daily specials. Children's menu. Breakfast, lunch and dinner. Happy Hour at Bar. $$-$$$

February Point Bistro and Bar • 242-336-2400 • VHF 16 • Serves the February Point homes; dinghy dock, call ahead for dinner from 6 p.m. to 9 p.m., Monday to Saturday. $$-$$$

Fish Fry Village South of the Tropical Port commercial landing, on the beach. Almost directly across from Hamburger Beach. Look for the lively colored Fish Shacks and Take-Aways. Always a fun and active place. Never know what you might find, spontaneous rake and scrape, live music, special events or parties. $

Gemelli's Pizza • 242-336-3023 • On the edge of the pond. Serving pizza, fried chicken and fish. Open 5 to 11 p.m. $

Jean's Dog House • 242-345-5055 • A social place to meet and enjoy hot dogs and daily specials from the back of the white truck, parked outside the library from early morning. $

Kermits Airport Lounge • 242-345-0002 • Open all day at the airport. $

Mariella's Pizza & Ice Cream, 242-336-4400. In Emerald Isles Shopping Center. Will deliver. $$

St. Francis Resort Tel: 242-557-9629, Fax: 242-336-2416, VHF 16, www.stfrancisresort.com. Restaurant and Bar opens at 11 a.m. daily. Creative, frosty bar drinks and delicious island specialties served in the restaurant. Don't miss the pizza parties, Texas Hold 'Em poker parties on Monday, Thursdays Trivia Team nights, Karaoke and surprise guest bands, Cheeseburger in Paradise Parrothead parties and the Super Bowl Extravaganza. The "in" spot for Cruisers! WiFi. $-$$

Sandals Resort and Marina at Emerald Bay, Tel: 242-336-6100 • Fax: 242-336-6101 • VHF 16 and 11. Restaurant and Bar at marina. Three restaurants in resort: By the pool, breakfast, lunch and dinner. Beachfront, lunch and dinner. Main building, dinner. $$-$$$$

Splash • 242-336-2787, www.palmbaybeachclub.com, The bar and grill at Palm Beach Bay Beach Club are open daily for breakfast, lunch and dinner from 7 a.m. Daily specials, Fettuccini Fridays, Seafood Saturdays. Catch the big games on their wide screen televisions. $$-$$$

Silver Dollar Restaurant and Bar • 242-336-2939 • East of BTC in town, serving native dishes with rake and scrape on Wednesdays. $

The Palappa Bar & Grill • 242-353-5000. At Grand Isla Resort & Spa, Emerald Bay. Overlooking gorgeous crescent beach. Open daily for lunch and dinner. Seafood, steaks and vegetarian dishes. $$-$$$$

Towne Cafe • 242-336-2194 • Behind Shop Rite grocery store. Open for breakfast and lunch from 7:30 a.m. Ice cream, sandwiches, salads and Bahamian entrees. $

Shipping Company G & G Shipping, 242-336-2359, George Town.

Shopping *Peace and Plenty Boutique* Open 8:30 a.m. to 5 p.m., except Sundays. Androsia clothes, T-shirts, post cards and guidebooks. *The Sandpiper* A wide selection of books, gifts, pottery, art work, fashions, post cards and much more. Louise will help you in this well-stocked, attractive store. Open 8:30 to 5 daily, except Sundays. • *Tropical Accents*, 242-336-2396. Open 8:30 a.m. to 5 p.m. Monday through Saturday. Accessories, Italian, Asian, Greek and Mexican pottery, perfume, jewelry, gifts, cards, table linens and kitchen ware • *Straw Market T-shirts*, locally woven baskets, shell jewelry, fresh vegetables and fruit in season. Monday through Saturday, under the trees in Regatta Park • Top II Bottom, good place to poke around for souvenirs and unexpected finds.

Taxis Call one on VHF 14. Some wait under the trees at *Exuma Docking Services*, in front of *Exuma Markets*, and *Club Peace and Plenty*. Taxi #12, Leslie Dames Taxi Service, 242-524-0015; Taxi # 29, 242-357-0662; Taxi # 43, 242-357-0400; Taxi # 49, 242-357-2375; Taxi #52 & Livery #11, Ken Nixon, 242-422-7399; *Bal Sound Taxi*, 242-336-2375; *Junior Taxi Service*, 242-336-2509; *Luther Rolle Taxi Service*, 242-345-5003; *Exuma Transit Services*, 242-345-0232. Listen for "Taxi Share" on Cruisers Net.

Telephones There are many telephones in town, though not always working. Two reliable card phones outside the BTC office. Find others outside *Club Peace and Plenty*, at *Exuma Docking Services*, outside *Exuma Markets* and in the Administration building.

Tourist Office • 242-336-2430 • 242-336-2457. Tourist Office is located in Turnquest Star Plaza on the 2nd floor.

Trash If you are in a slip at *Exuma Docking Services*, leave trash in their bins. If you are at anchor, use the bins at the mail boat dock. Contain your trash in heavy mil trash bags! If cruisers continue to dump trash in flimsy grocery bags, we will lose our free trash privileges. Do your part!

Travel Agent HL Young • 242-336-2705 • Above the *ScotiaBank*.

Veterinarian *Howard Deyoung* • 242-336-2806 • VHF 16, "Peach House Vet." Anchor off Goat Cay, dinghy to his boat ramp. Also does x-rays for the medical clinic. Superb veterinarian and facilities. Has heartworm medication for your dog in case you didn't anticipate the flesh-eating mosquitoes!

Water Taxis • 242-357-0724 • VHF 16 "Water Taxi" • To and from Stocking Island and the Fish Fry.

Weddings *February Point*, 242-336-2661 • *Sandals Resort*, 242-336-6800 • *Peace & Plenty*, 242-336-2251 • *St. Francis Resort*, Tel: 242-557-9629, Fax: 242 336 2416. Photographer: *Personal Touch Studio*, 242-336-3478.

Wedding Consultants *A Wedding Breeze*, 242-336-2700, www.aweddingbreeze.com. Mrs. Kwanza Bowe, CWS, Stocking Island • *Sunrise*, 242-336-2055, sheilamoss@batelnet.bs. Mrs. Sheila Moss, CWS, George Town • *Creative Avenues Wedding & Event Planning*, 242-336-2423, creativeavenues@hotmail.com. Mrs. Victoria McKenzie, CWS, George Town • *Unique Etiquette Weddings*, 242-336-2711, shavonnemckenzie@yahoo.com. Mrs. Shavonne McKenzie, George Town.

RENTALS

Bicycles *Starfish* • 242-336-3033 • VHF 16 • With map and helmet, from $20 per day.

Boats *Minn's Water Sports* • 242-336-3483 • 17-ft., 18-ft. and 22-ft. Boston Whalers, Carolina Skiffs and Glacier Bays. Dockage and storage, ice, gasoline and repairs at their dock on Lake Victoria, across from *Club Peace and Plenty*. Security deposit required. Visa and MasterCard accepted. Open 8 to 5 weekdays, to noon on Saturday, and to 11 a.m. on Sunday.

Starfish • 242-336-3033 • VHF 16 • Hobies and Sea Pearls from $85 per day, kayaks from $40 per day. PFD, gear and map included in rentals.

Cars DRIVE ON THE LEFT! There is a one-way system around the pond. Valid driver's license and security deposit required. Average rental $70 per day. Book in advance during *Regatta* weeks.

Airport Rentals, 242-345-0090 • *Sam Gray's Car Rentals* at *Exuma Docking Services*, 242-336-2101 • *Don Smith Rentals*, 242-345-0112 • *Thompsons Rentals*, 242-336-2442 or thompsonrental@hotmail.com, or see Kim Thompson above the bank • *Uptown Rent-a-car*, 242-336-2822.

Houseboats *Bahama Houseboats* • 242-336-2628 • VHF 16 info@bahamahouseboats.com • Michael and Godfrey Minns have fully-equipped 35-ft., 43-ft. and 46-ft. luxury houseboats for weekly rental from their dock in Kidds Cove, starting at $1,750 per week, depending on length and season. They occasionally have dock space for $0.60 per ft. per day.

SPORTS & RECREATION

Beaches *Hamburger Beach* and *Volleyball Beach* are popular with boats at anchor off Stocking Island. There are literally dozens of glorious beaches the whole length of the Exuma chain.

Bonefishing *La Shante Beach Club* • 242-345-4136 • At Forbes Hill. Call Marvin or Trevor Bethel for snorkeling, trolling, spinfishing, and sightseeing. *Peace and Plenty Bonefish Lodge* • 242-345-5555 • Fax: 242-345-5556 • ppbone@batelnet.bs • www.ppbonefishlodge.com • Complete bonefishing packages and vacations, with guide Bob Hyde, from $845 for 3 nights per person at the Bonefish Lodge, with a new pool, waterfall and pergola.

Bonefish and Fishing Guides The Tourist Office will be glad to recommend Certified Bonefishing Guides.

Diving *Exuma Scuba Adventures* at *Peace and Plenty Beach Inn* • 242-336-2893, 242-357-2259 • VHF 16 • www.exumascuba.com • Owned and operated by Small Hope Bay Lodge, from Andros, managed by Tom Sutton. Rental equipment, certification courses and all-day adventures.

EcoTours *Starfish Exuma Adventure Tours* • 242-336-3033 • VHF 16 • kayak@starfishexuma.com • www.kayakbahamas.com • Snorkeling adventures, ecotours, Castaway Getaways and bicycling. Twenty-five-foot, 12 passenger Starship picks you up at Peace & Plenty.

Regattas *George Town Cruising Regatta* Attracts over 500 yachts for a week of racing and festivities in March. For information, contact St. Francis Marina, the Exuma Tourist Office, 242-336-2430 or www.georgetowncruising.com. *Annual Family Island Regatta* Hosts scores of locally built sloops, representing each of the major islands, for four days of fierce racing in April for the coveted "Best in the Bahamas" title. This is when George Town comes alive, with a carnival atmosphere in town; beauty pageants, fashion shows, volleyball, weightlifting and the village of "shacks" that spring up along the Government Dock, serving food and drinks all day and most of the night. Contact the Exuma Tourist Office 242-336-2430 for more information.

Tennis Courts At *Island Club House* and *February Point.*

THINGS TO DO IN GEORGE TOWN

- Provision your boat with fresh island breads and produce.
- Enter your own sailboat in the early March Cruiser's Regatta. Or share the excitement of Family Island Regatta week in late April.
- Rent a car for a day and explore Great Exuma all the way up to Barraterre. Or head southeast to see the Cotton House at Williams Town and the ancient tombs at Rolletown in Little Exuma.
- Dinghy to *The Ferry,* and visit *St. Christopher's Anglican Church*, the smallest church in the Bahamas.
- Go bonefishing in the flats on the south side.
- Take your dinghy in to Volleyball Beach; games every afternoon include backgammon, dominoes and bridge at the picnic tables—or just socialize and meet friends at *Chat 'n Chill.*
- Make a contribution to the Exuma Foundation, a nonprofit community foundation set up to support education on Exuma and to enhance the quality of life here. Exuma Foundation, PO Box 29111, George Town. 242-336-2790, exumafoundation2@hotmail.com.

LITTLE EXUMA

Southeast of George Town, Little Exuma is a charming, smaller edition of its larger namesake, and well worth a visit. It is joined to Great Exuma by a narrow bridge at The Ferry, so named because for years that was the way you crossed between the two islands. You can still see the remains of the old haulover ferry alongside the bridge.

If you can't take your boat down to Little Exuma, rent a car or minivan with friends. Take a taxi ($$$) or, if you are feeling energetic, you could make it a real adventure by bicycle. Don't miss going on to Williams Town, home of *Mom's Bakery* and the church that you support when you buy her goodies - the very pretty *St. Mary Magdalene* Anglican church. There you can see the remains of an old Loyalist cotton plantation and the impressive, Roman Column stone beacon built as a Salt Marker to guide schooners in to load salt from the salinas. The restaurant overlooking the water in Williams Town is *Santana's Grill Pit* - 242-345-4102, open every day but Monday. Here, Johnny Depp, and other stars of *Pirates of the Caribbean*, ate and partied like the locals. On the way back to George Town, stop by the *Bonefish Lodge* to learn about bonefishing. Look for goats and long-legged sheep that still wander among what remains of stonewalled pastures, a poignant reminder that this island has been farmed since the 1700s. Stop by Rolle Town if you haven't visited it by dinghy. The vistas from the top of the hill are spectacular. It is the birthplace of the "Good Time" television show star Esther Rolle. Her relatives are everywhere. Go down the hill to see the tombs of the Scottish McKay family, dated 1792. If you haven't had lunch, stop by the *Haulover Bay Cafe* by the tombs for good, home-cooked fare.

A pile of conch shells sit on the beach. ©IstockPhoto/Wildrozea

Chapter 16
The Out Islands North of the Tropic of Cancer
Little San Salvador, Cat Island, Conception Island, Rum Cay and San Salvador

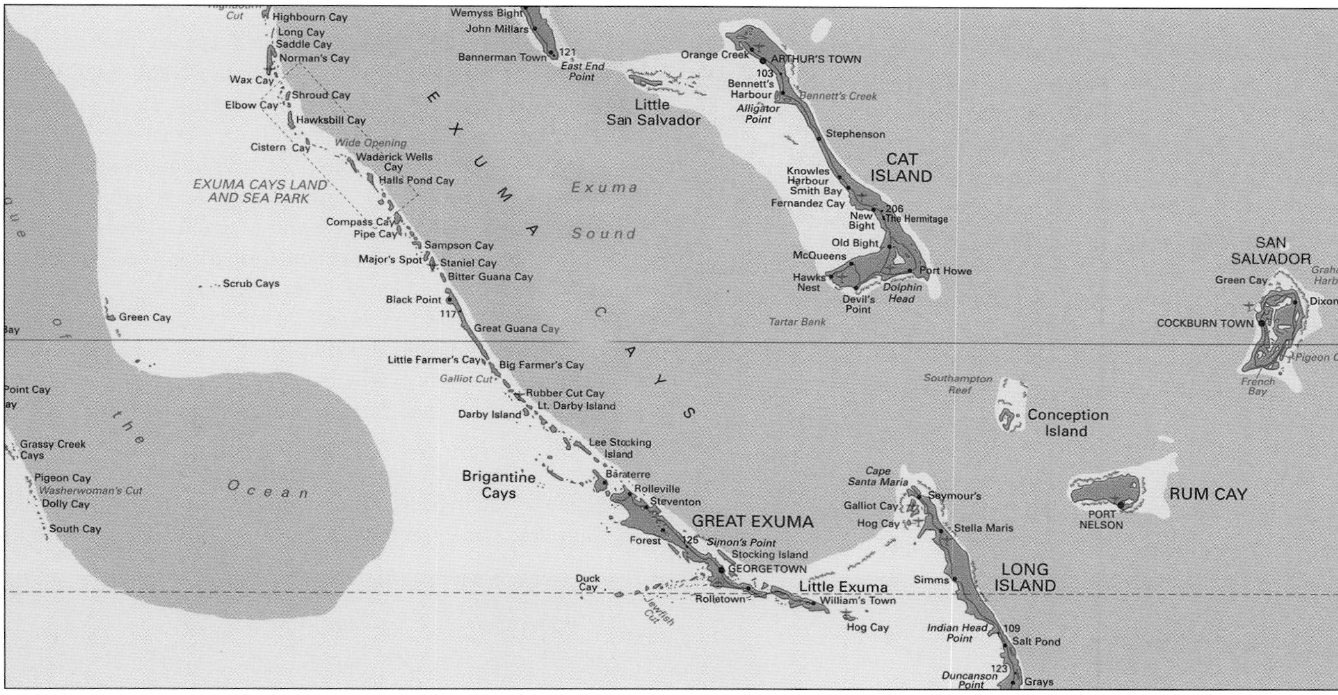

Looking At the Charts

Traveling from Eleuthera to Cat Island requires a long leg along the southern whale tale of Eleuthera. Departing from Davis Harbour, rather than Powell Point, shortens your journey significantly. It is about an eight nautical mile trip from Davis Harbour to the jumping off spot, East End Point. From there, it is almost eleven nautical miles in open ocean to Little San Salvador. So, plan your departure with a keen ear to the weather report and sea conditions. Although a cruise ship claims ownership of Half Moon Bay Beach on Little San Salvador, it is a magnificent anchorage and large enough to share with the flower-shirted, straw hat bedecked tourists on the southern end. Once they depart, you are free to stroll the beach to search for shells and sea beans. There is good free-diving and spearfishing on the nearby reefs. If you plan to explore Cat Island from north to south, you will still have to take a leg well south of Little San Salvador before pointing your bow towards Cat Island. This is an area of widely scattered coral heads. The waters are in the 6 meter/20-foot depth range, and most of the heads are deeper than 3 meters/10 feet, but you will still want to maintain a good look out.

Fifty-mile-long Cat Island starts out high and mighty to the north and runs down to low, slippery ironstone straddling the sandy shores to the south. This is a remote island with exquisite beaches and excellent snorkeling and diving along its Atlantic coast. Most anchorages, however, are relatively exposed and will require some moving around to find protection when winds shift. There are friendly, industrious people in the settlements. The folks in Arthurs Town are justly proud of being home to the second high school started in the Bahamas as well as being the birthplace of the prodigious actor, Sidney Poitier.

Up to this point, passages, in terms of exposure to the open Atlantic Ocean, are reasonably protected. However, south of Cat Island, there are open-water passages to navigate to San Salvador, Conception Island and Rum Cay. Looking at the chart, note that the island and sea area south of Cat Island form an interlocking series of five triangles, all of them close to equilateral. There are the Hawks Nest–George Town–Cape Santa Maria triangle; the Hawks Nest–Cape Santa Maria–Conception Island triangle; the Cape Santa Maria–Conception–Rum Cay triangle; the Conception Island–San Salvador–Rum Cay triangle and lastly the Cat Island-San Salvador-Conception Island triangle. The average length of the legs of these interlocking triangles is 27 nautical miles. What to deduce from all this geometry and rhetoric? You may well be in open, deep-blue water in the Out Island area, but you have plenty of options given any wind or set and no great distance to run in any direction. Use your charts, and read the sky. In addition, the diving and snorkeling off San Salvador, Conception Island and Rum Cay are world class.

In the Spotlight. Cat Island

At fifty miles long and sometimes a skinny one mile wide, Cat Island fits the archetypal mold of the Bahamian Atlantic Ocean barrier island. It is so much like its kindred neighbors, Eleuthera to the north and Long Island to the south. Their primary characteristics are identical: long and thin, hostile east coasts, sandy, beautiful west coasts that are just about completely devoid of natural harbors. At first glance, one might say that Cat Island should not rate high as a cruising destination. However, let us reconsider that notion.

Cat Island is part of the stepping-stones to destinations farther south. Starting north, the hops are Abacos to Eleuthera, Eleuthera to Cat Island and Cat Island to Conception Island, Rum Cay or Long Island. Cat Island is an alternative to the Exumas and also a side step to San Salvador (the real outlier when in the Out Islands). Good geography, but is Cat Island worth a visit? The answer is, "Yes!"

Why? Because it has a mood and an ambiance you will not find elsewhere. Up until ground was broken for the Cat Island Golf & Beach Club, there was little disruption of the environment. It is an island with small settlements running along its west coast in which the ruins of abandoned houses often seem to outnumber the inhabited. Clusters of limestone spines produce the highest land in the Bahamas and divide the island into three parts: the north, with Arthurs Town as its administrative center; the central, with New Bight, the seat of government; and the south itself, a low-lying hammerhead running west, marked by desolation. To reinforce this triad, Cat Island has three airfields: Arthurs Town, the Bight and Hawks Nest.

The cruising geography of Cat Island is simple. Its western coastal waters are shallow, averaging 3.6 meters/12 feet deep. It is largely free of reefs and coral heads, except in the north. Anchorages are pretty, but the holding can be problematic. Anchor beds are frequently hard sand over coral. Sand bores extend westward in the Orange Creek area, from Bennetts Harbour (Alligator Point) to just south of Fernandez Bay and just north of Hawks Nest Creek. At this point, a steep drop off comes within a half mile of the shore. Although the south coast has long been considered un-navigable, locals encourage cruisers to ride out the winter northers in Reef Harbour, on the far eastern end. There is an entrance through the reef at N 24° 08.773'/W 075° 21.347'. One inside, turn east into the spacious anchorage, and pick your spot. You are safely protected, as no swell makes it over the reef. One mile east, enjoy the day anchorage the locals call Winding Bay, created by Columbus Point.

Like Eleuthera and Long Island, the only way to see all of Cat Island is with wheels. Bikers can get good exercise on the long shoreline road, but for the rest of us, a rental car fits the

Little San Salvador. (Not to be used for navigation.) WATERWAY GUIDE PHOTOGRAPHY.

Not to be used for navigation.

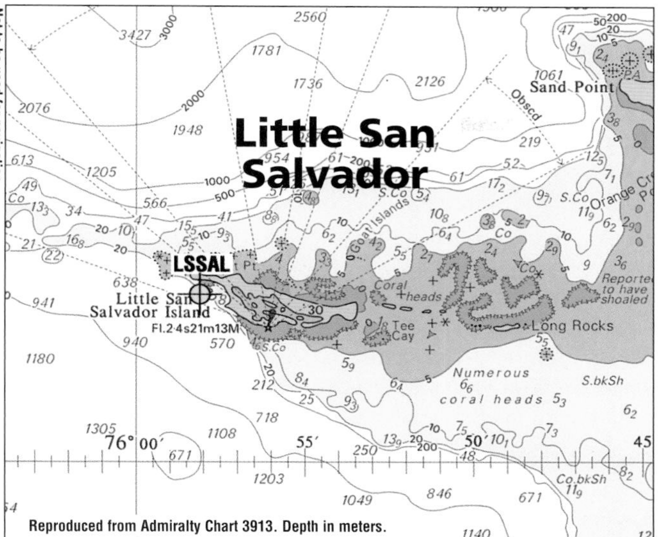

Reproduced from Admiralty Chart 3913. Depth in meters.

bill. To gain mobility, your landing spots are critical. Weather is bound to dictate the length of your stay in the exposed anchorages. Winds, southwest through west to northwest to north, rule. Except for one all-weather haven, Hawks Nest, you must keep an eye on the weather.

What's There? The Out Islands North of the Tropic of Cancer

Little San Salvador

At one time uninhabited, Little San Salvador is a five-nautical-mile-long ridge of limestone, lagoon and reef. It lies almost midway between Eleuthera and Cat Island. It is surrounded by a maze of coral heads and reefs; and in weather less than gentle, smart boaters keep well out in Exuma Sound. Long Rocks, a line of rocks and reef lying 4.5 nautical miles east of Little San Salvador, is a good reminder to keep south on your Cat Island passage. Little San Salvador has long been a favorite fair-

Not to be used for navigation.

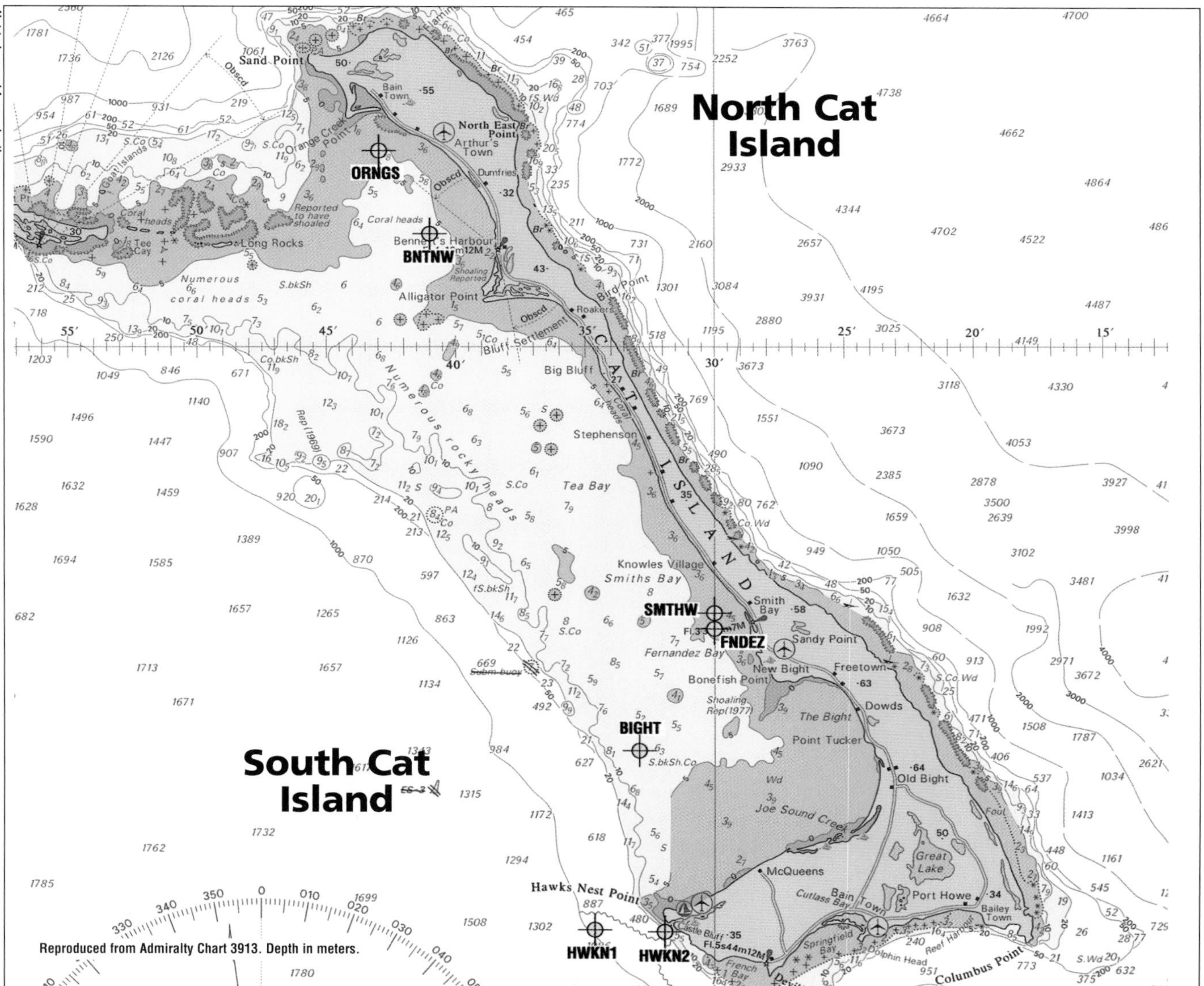

Reproduced from Admiralty Chart 3913. Depth in meters.

weather picnic stop for fast boats from Nassau. The only viable anchorage is in Half Moon Bay. It provides protection from the north and east, and marginal protection from the southeast. The beach is picture perfect with patches of good sand to hold an anchor and patches of coral that are easily avoided. Once the cruise ship is gone, the entire area is your little piece of paradise. The reefs lying to the north and east of the island, extending out toward Long Rocks, are superb snorkeling and shallow-dive territory. The inland lagoon is great gunkholing territory, but bring the bug spray, and don't forget the camera. The birding can be spectacular.

The North of Cat Island. Orange Creek

Start your northern exploration of Cat Island anchored in front of Orange Creek Settlement. The settlement has everything you need on a small scale. There are a food store that offers laundry service and a hardware store that handles propane refills. If you are under the weather, there is a medical clinic. You can rent a car to explore the southlands, too. There is also the newly opened Shannas Cove Resort with its beachfront bungalows and restaurant. This resort is a welcome addition to the north end of Cat Island.

Arthurs Town

The next stop south is Arthurs Town, where there is an airport served by Bahamasair and a BTC office. You will find plenty of good places to grab a bite to eat and four-wheel drive roads to Atlantic beaches. Arthurs Town has gas and diesel, too. If you are lucky enough to be there in June, don't miss the Rake 'n Scrape Festival! The elevation decline starts in Arthurs Town. If you are on a bike from Orange Creek, remember that the return trip is going to be uphill. Although you can anchor anywhere in between Orange Creek and Arthurs Town, the best protection is tucked in off Orange Creek.

Bennetts Harbour

Bennetts Harbour is a misnomer. There is no harbor at all. You can anchor off the harbor in front of Pompey Rocks Villas to run into Ducky's for some conch fritters or fresh bread, but that is about it. In an absolute emergency, you could temporarily tie up to the new Government Dock, but use lots of fenders. There are bathrooms there and a concrete ramp to land your dinghy. South of Bennetts Harbour, you can find some protection from the southeast north of Pigeon Creek. Farther south, the shoal waters off Alligator Point extend well west. Give them wide berth. The good news is, when you round them, there is good protection from northerly winds. From Roakers south to Smith Bay Settlement, there are some bluffs that offer shelter from easterly winds and caves to explore by dinghy. There are also scattered heads on which to dive and to avoid hitting with the big boat.

Central Cat Island. Smith Bay

If you need to clear in at Cat Island, the port of entry is Smith Bay. A cut into Culbert's Creek, marked by a light, serves a government dock that accommodates mailboats and the exportation of Cat Island produce. Smith Bay seems a like good harbor, but its usable depth extends only from the entry channel to parallel the dock. The remainder shoals rapidly, and you are not protected from surge or from the west. Nevertheless, it is here that Customs will clear you in. In addition, you can get diesel and gasoline delivered by truck from the Shell service station in New Bight.

Fernandez Bay

To the south of Smith Bay, set in a cove-like hook of land, is the Fernandez Bay Resort. Upscale and attractive, Fernandez Bay welcomes cruisers to land on its beach (sans dogs) and, properly attired, to join their guests in the restaurant. The anchorage in front of the resort is beautiful, but small. There is room for only one or two vessels. Please read more about Fernandez Bay in our Goin' Ashore.

Father Jerome (A.K.A. John Hawes) 1876–1956

The builder of the Hermitage on Comer Hill at New Bight in Cat Island, the place he called Mount Alvernia, was by any measure, an extraordinary man. English by birth, born of a comfortably affluent family, he studied architecture and suddenly switched to theology. He was ordained in the Church of England early in the 20th century. In 1908, he arrived in the Bahamas, where he combined his architectural expertise with bare-hands skills and his Anglican faith, and devoted himself to traveling the islands and repairing storm-devastated churches.

A John Hawes (as he was know then) church had unmistakable characteristics. It was always stone built, thick-walled, often Romanesque in style. His approach to religion was modeled on St. Francis of Assisi, a barefoot simplicity, which, among other tenets of his faith, had no time for distinctions between black and white, poor and affluent, and he undoubtedly challenged the status quo of the Bahamian social order at that time. Perhaps it was social rejection or dissatisfaction that took him out into a wider world, both as a sailor and into virtually any employment that came his way. There was time spent in Canada. In 1911, he made a second abrupt move in his vocation. He went to Rome, studied Catholicism, became a priest and adopted a new name.

As Father Jerome, he went to Australia as a bush priest and remained there for almost a quarter of a century. Then, perhaps sensing his own mortality after a heart attack, he returned to the Bahamas in 1939. He settled in New Bight, chose Comer Hill, the highest point in the Bahamas, as the site of a hermitage and started to build the place you see today. He died, and was buried there, barefoot in a bare grave, 17 years later.

His memorials are not only the Hermitage. There are four other Father Jerome churches in Cat Island and five churches in Long Island, which include the two highly visible Clarence Town churches—the Anglican St. Paul's and, in an extraordinary marriage of Greek Island, Celtic and Romanesque architecture, the Roman Catholic church of Saints Peter and Paul.

Cat Island

CAT ISLAND		Largest Vessel Accommodated	VHF Channel Monitored	Transient Berths / Total Berths	Approach / Dockside Depth (reported)	Floating Docks	Gas / Diesel	Groceries, Ice, Marine Supplies, Snacks	Repairs: Hull, Engine, Propeller	Lift (tonnage), Crane, Rail	1=110V, 2=220V, B=Both, Max Amps	Laundry, Pool, Showers	Pump-Out Station	Nearby: Grocery Store, Motel, Restaurant
		Dockage					Supplies				Services			
1 Hawk's Nest Resort & Marina (WiFi)	242-342-7050	115	16	/28	/7	F	GD	IM			B/100	LS		MR

Corresponding chart(s) not to be used for navigation. Internet Access (WiFi) Wireless Internet Access

New Bight and Mount Alvernia (The Hermitage)

When you anchor off the 230-foot-tall BTC tower, you are right in the heart of the settlement. Everything you need is within walking range. Ignore the small concrete dock, which has rocks around it, and anchor your dinghy right off the beach. You can walk from there to Mount Alvernia, the extraordinary hilltop hermitage of Father Jerome (206-foot climb), famed architect and builder of the two Clarence Town churches on Long Island. The hilltop is the highest point in the Bahamas. Regardless of your religion and your interest in Jerome churches, that should make Mount Alvernia a place to visit. We cover Mount Alvernia more completely in our Goin' Ashore. Some repair work and care have reversed what was a steady deterioration of the site. Although not yet restored to pristine condition, Father Jerome's memorial is in good hands and should yet endure. See if you can volunteer while you are visiting, or make a donation to ensure that this is so.

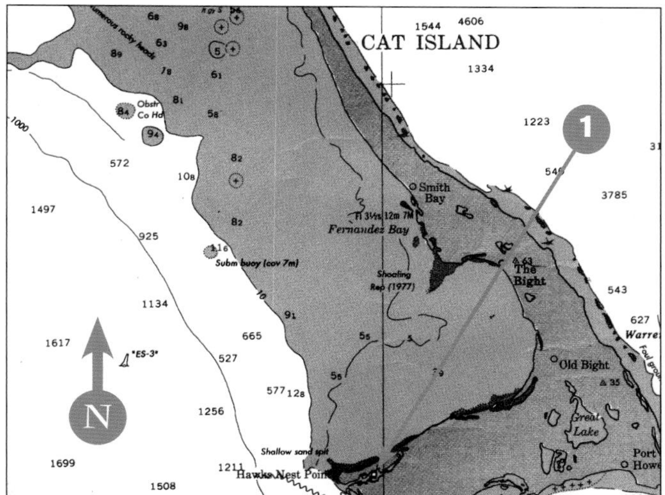

CAT ISLAND, Chart 26280

The South of Cat Island. Hawks Nest

Hawks Nest is perhaps the best single reason to choose Cat Island as a destination. It wins on just about every count. The first plus is location. Hawks Nest is one of the key points in the Greater Exuma Sound cruising area. Take a map. Draw a line, and connect Powell Point in South Eleuthera with Highbourne Cay in the Exumas. Draw that Exuma line down to George Town, then across to Cape Santa Maria in Long Island and on to Rum Cay. Now complete the box back to Eleuthera. Hawks Nest is right there, on the line. Location counts. In addition, it

Hawks Nest Creek, from the west. (Not to be used for navigation.) WATERWAY GUIDE PHOTOGRAPHY.

is on the doorstep of the Tartar Bank, one of the best fishing grounds in the southern Bahamas. Although no one can forecast the effects of a direct hit by a hurricane, Hawks Nest Marina is as safe for severe weather as they get. These factors aside, what is here? A small well-run resort, restaurant and marina complex. There is access by air (charter or private aircraft only) or sea. A rental car is available for Cat Island exploration as are golf carts, if you find it tiresome walking between marina and resort. There are good beaches, snorkeling and diving, boats to rent or charter if you wish, and bonefishing too. There is fuel and water, rooms for crew changes and a rental house. To access the Reef Harbour anchorage with excellent, all-round protection, go due south of Hawks Nest, and respect the coral reefs off French Bay and Devils Point. Then, sail due east to the gap through the reef at N24° 08.773'/W075° 21.347'. Once inside, turn east and drop the hook. It is about a 10-nautical-mile trip from Devils Point in open water.

Moving On from Cat Island

Hawks Nest is well-placed for moving on to the other Out Islands or making your way to George Town. It lies at the apex of a triangle whose base runs from George Town through Cape Santa Maria (the northern point of Long Island) to Conception Island, all of which are just about equidistant from Hawks Nest. If you want to head directly for San Salvador from Hawks Nest, we suggest that you create a waypoint north of Conception Island to accommodate your turn to run east somewhere above the line of N 24° 00.000'. The "standard" route to San Salvador goes from Rum Cay, by way of Conception, but there is no reason not to make your own tracks.

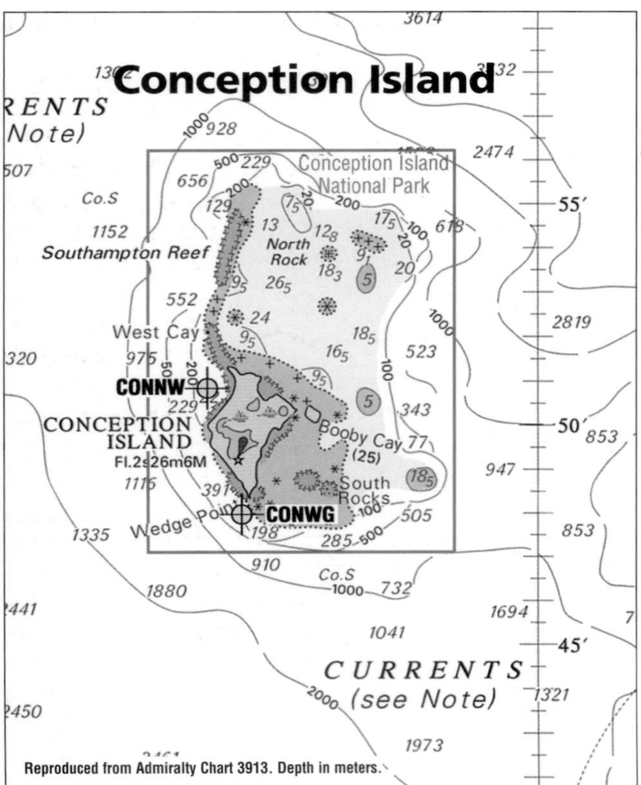

Reproduced from Admiralty Chart 3913. Depth in meters.

Not to be used for navigation.

Conception Island

Conception Island itself is barely six square miles in land area, but sits in a surrounding shield of reef that extends 4.5 nautical miles to the north, four nautical miles to the east and just over one nautical mile to the south. The island itself rises to 60 feet. Don't be deceived into thinking that this high land is your aiming point. It may be, but rather like the bull's eye being just the center of a target, you must be acutely aware of those rings of surrounding reef, and go cautiously as you draw close to the island.

The whole island, including the reef, is a marine park, protected under the same terms as the Exuma Land and Sea Park, and is uninhabited. You are welcome to visit, anchor and land there and dive its reefs, but take nothing from this pristine and beautiful site, and leave only footprints. This remote and quiet place, with its beautiful crescent beach, makes this island a favorite.

The most-often-used anchorage lies on the northwest tip of the island proper, shielded in part by West Cay. You are exposed there from the northwest through west to the south, and you may find surge from easterly ocean swell, particularly if the set is from the northeast. The depth is 9 meters/30 feet running to 2.4 meters/8 feet just off the beach. There are isolated reefs and coral heads in the area, which can be easily seen. Enter with the light in your favor. Just to the north of this anchorage, there is the four-mile run of Southampton Reef, which is a prime destination for divers. Snorkeling or diving on any reef or coral head will be equally rewarding. The creek halfway down the west coast of Conception Island is shoal-draft and not a viable anchorage, but is great for dinghy exploration. You will see numerous small sharks and turtles there.

It is possible to work up along the east coast of the island, eyeballing around Wedge Point (you will note the wedge-shaped rock formation that led to the name) and pick your way up toward Booby Cay. In calm weather, with nothing threatening, this presents no problems other than the need for careful navigation. This east anchorage should not be used for an extended stay unless there are stable, calm conditions, simply because you can not cut and run from there.

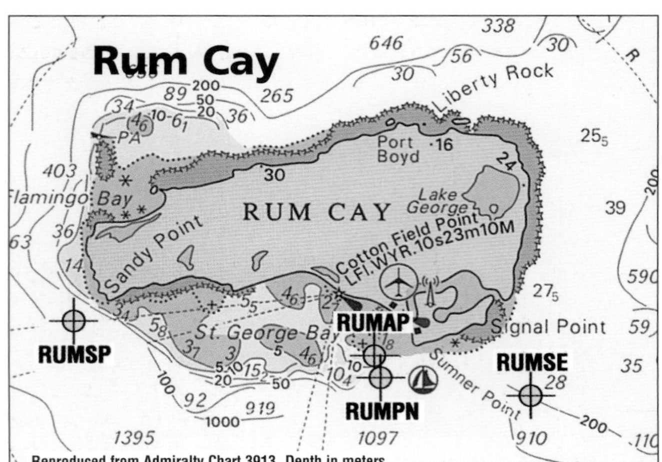

Reproduced from Admiralty Chart 3913. Depth in meters.

Not to be used for navigation.

Rum Cay

RUM CAY		Largest Vessel Accommodated	VHF Channel Monitored	Transient Berths / Total Berths	Approach / Dockside Depth (reported)	Floating Docks	Gas / Diesel	Groceries, Ice, Marine Supplies, Snacks	Repairs: Hull, Engine, Propeller	Lift (tonnage), Crane, Rail	1=110V, 2=220V, B=Both, Max Amps	Laundry, Pool, Showers	Pump-Out Station	Nearby: Grocery Store, Motel, Restaurant
			Dockage				Supplies				Services			
1. Sumner Point Marina (Internet Access) (Wireless Internet Access)	242-331-2823	180	16	/30	/6.5		GD	IS			B/50	L		GMR

Corresponding chart(s) not to be used for navigation. (Internet Access icon) Internet Access (WiFi icon) Wireless Internet Access

Rum Cay

Rum Cay, a nine- by five-nautical-mile chunk of an island, has a reassuringly solid appearance from the ocean. Its surrounding reefs are tucked close to its shoreline. Only one reef, extending two nautical miles north from the northwest tip, is a significant offshore hazard. One of its victims was a Haitian boat that foundered there years back. However, the inshore reefs have claimed many vessels over the years, including the one-time pride of the Royal Navy. The landfall waypoints are chosen to set up two approaches to St. George Bay and the Port Nelson–Sumner Point area, which will be your destination if you are calling in at Rum Cay.

For boaters, the location of Rum Cay marks it as a prime waypoint on the route to and from the Caribbean. It also holds the fishing grounds of the Diana Bank and the drop-offs of the deep-water Atlantic passages between Long Island and Providenciales. For years, Rum Cay was rarely visited because its only anchorage was open to prevailing winds, and its surrounding reefs were feared. When Sumner Point Marina opened, just a ten-minute walk from Port Nelson, Rum Cay was added to cruisers lists as both a transit stop and a destination in its own right. We cover the broad island details first, and turn to inshore navigation, which requires some homework, under Pilotage.

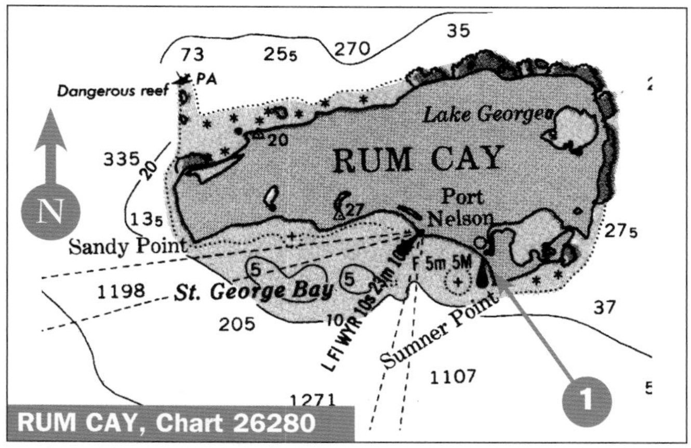

RUM CAY, Chart 26280

Port Nelson Anchorage

Port Nelson anchorage is the bight of St. George Bay running along the frontage of the Port Nelson settlement from the "town" dock westward toward Cotton Field Point. You may anchor wherever you fancy in suitable depth anywhere along the beach. There are two pockets of slightly deeper water that will become apparent. Don't go west of Cotton Field Point. You are exposed from southeast through south to west in St. George Bay, and you can get thrown around if the wind comes from these quadrants in any strength. Even in relatively calm conditions, some surge works it way into the anchorage, but it fine in lighter winds.

Sumner Point Anchorage and Marina

Sumner Point Marina is a surprise and a delight. With friendly owners, fuel, water and power, Sumner Point has all the basics, plus a clubhouse-like restaurant and bar, meals that have won well-deserved praise and shoreside accommodations. The fuel dock (at the entry) has been extended, and a second inner basin, with 15- to 20-foot walls cut back into the hill behind it, could

Summer Point Marina. (Not to be used for navigation.) WATERWAY GUIDE PHOTOGRAPHY.

HMS Conqueror

In 1860, *HMS Conqueror* was one of the Royal Navy's latest ships and took pride of place in the British line of battle in that day. She was a 101-gun battleship, capable of throwing a prodigious weight of metal from a broadside. Still very much a three-decker with the masts and full rig of a ship of the 18th century, she had the incongruous addition of a smokestack amidships and a vast, primitive, coal-burning engine driving one great screw. Still virtually on her maiden voyage, she was lost on Sumner Point Reef, Rum Cay, on December 13, 1861. Her crew of 1,400 all survived.

She was 20 nautical miles out, in estimating her position and, after making her landfall, cut rounding the southeast point of Rum Cay too closely and went hard on the reef. Her captain, fearing that his crew (most of whom could not swim in those days) would drink themselves senseless when it became obvious the ship was lost, ordered all ale, wine and spirit casks to be broken and their contents ditched. He then sent the two largest ship's boats, rigged with sail as well as oars, to Nassau and Jamaica requesting help. For the next two days, the ship's company unloaded everything they could salvage, and set about making a camp on the island. The captain remained on board with one midshipman and ten seamen until the ship broke up. Then all of them, less the boat parties, were marooned on Rum Cay. They were rescued soon after the news of the disaster was known.

well set the seal on Sumner Point Marina's already proven reputation as a hurricane hole. There are 30 slips in the marina, with 2.1-meter/7-foot depths at the docks. They can accommodate vessels up to 180 feet in length. The entry channel has 1.9-meter/6.5-foot depths at mean low water.

Port Nelson

Port Nelson has spread itself along a loosely aligned grid of sand roads. Two small stores, three bars and two restaurants are distanced as if proximity were forbidden by local zoning. You can find most staples in Port Nelson. There is a BTC office, along with the far spread bars and restaurants. Rum Cay suffered when its salt pond operation shut down, precipitating a population drop from 5,000 to 60. Although it has suffered from isolation and from hurricanes, residents are self-sufficient and incredibly warm and friendly. What Rum Cay does have to offer is superb snorkeling, diving and fishing and perhaps some of the largest lobsters you will ever lay eyes upon. (Think about one lobster feeding three to four people.) In addition to reefs is the wreck of the ill-fated *HMS Conqueror*, the Royal Navy's first propeller-driven warship, which came to an untimely end on the reef off Sumner Point. *HMS Conqueror* is still there. You can dive her, in some 9 meters/30 feet of water.

San Salvador

San Salvador, roughly 12 by six nautical miles, is a strange mix of elevation, hills and bumps (140 feet at the highest). Saline creeks and lakes make up most of the interior land area. It

San Salvador

SAN SALVADOR		Largest Vessel Accommodated	VHF Channel Monitored	Transient Berths / Total Berths	Approach / Dockside Depth (reported)	Floating Docks	Gas / Diesel	Groceries, Ice, Marine Supplies, Snacks	Repairs: Hull, Engine, Propeller	Lift (tonnage), Crane, Rail	1=110V, 2=220V, B=Both, Max Amps	Laundry, Pool, Showers	Pump-Out Station	Nearby: Grocery Store, Motel, Restaurant
		Dockage					Supplies		Services					
1. Riding Rock Inn Resort & Marina (WiFi)	242-331-2631	140	6	/25	/8		GD	I			B/50	LPS		MR

Corresponding chart(s) not to be used for navigation. Internet Access (WiFi) Wireless Internet Access

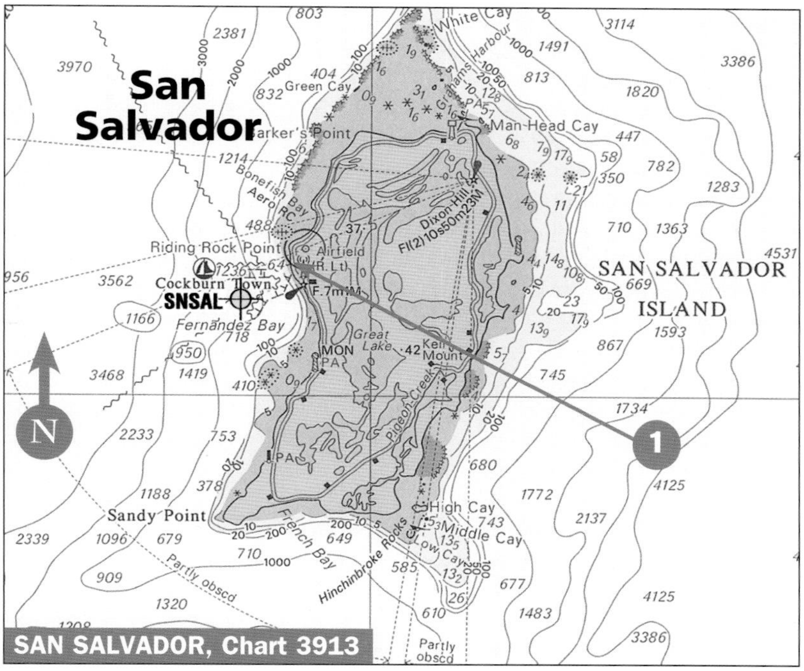

Reproduced from Admiralty Chart 3913. Depth in meters.

might well be just another Out Island clinging to subsistence but for two strokes of fortune. The first was the alleged first landing of Christopher Columbus after his 1492 Atlantic voyage. Many now dispute this claim (see the Green Pages under The Columbus Controversy). However, those that do ignore the fact that San Salvador is the only island with archeological evidence of Columbus' landing. The long-established official Bahamian endorsement is that San Salvador was indeed his first stop. Consequently, the island was given a star role in a set of Bahamian Quincentennial postage stamps.

San Salvador, exceptionally, has always had an island VHF net on Channel 06. You may get no response on 16 if you use it. We suggest, while you are in San Salvador waters, using VHF Channel 06 as your hailing channel.

The second benefit dealt by fortune is simply the spinoff of fame. With the aura of being the "Columbus Island" has come four commemorative memorials (one of these to the landing of a Santa Maria replica in 1991), and selection as the offshore transit site of the Olympic flame on its way from Greece to Mexico. Add two resorts, the Riding Rock Inn and a Club Méditerranée, an 8,000-foot airstrip with international service, and the unique distinction of having a paved circle-island road, and you have a destination.

Tightly bound by fringing reefs, except in the north where the coastal reefs extend out for three nautical miles, San Salvador is famous in the diving world. Its legendary diving comes from the most incredible drop-offs, where the bottom contour hits 180 meters/600 feet within a hand span and 1,800 meters/6,000 feet within a second hand span. Only five nautical miles out from the fringing reef, you will have 7,200 meters/24,000 feet under your keel. Relative isolation and geographic location, well off the beaten track between Florida and the Caribbean, has meant that San Salvador is not a popular cruising destination. This is reinforced by the absence of natural harbors and the presence of one small marina, which, given weather from the westerly quadrants, presents entry and exit problems, and surge.

We will discuss anchoring off here, for you should keep this in mind, simply because there is only that one small marina, which itself is exposed to the west. There is no all-weather anchorage. Grahams Harbour (an exaggeration in name) in the northeast is shoal, exposed to the north and has no real protection. On the west coast, anchoring off Cockburn Town, Fernandez Bay or Long Bay, are options in prevailing southeast weather. In the south, French Bay (with a decent entry cut) is open from southeast through south to the west. It is an option in a norther.

Riding Rock Inn Marina

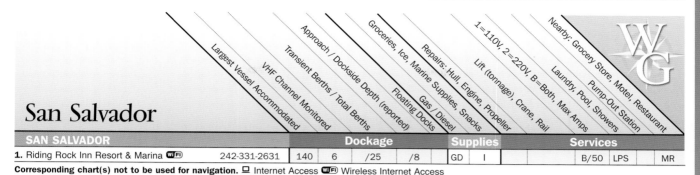

Part of the Riding Rock Inn complex north of Cockburn Town, San Salvador's only marina has 17 slips plus space for a number of boats lying alongside the south basin wall. The marina is divided into two basins that open up each side of the entry channel. The north basin wall is used by their dive boats. The resort, marina and their diving programs are active and popular. The marina suffers from surge problems that its breakwater on the northern side has not solved. If there is any significant swell, particularly from the west and southwest, be aware that entry or exit through the 15-meter/50-foot cut carries a risk of grounding in the troughs of waves. The channel has range markers and is not difficult in calm conditions.

Government Dock

The government dock is midway between the Riding Rock Marina and Cockburn Town. You could enter and secure there, and we doubt that anyone would turn you away. This said, it can be manic in that basin on mailboat days when two boats may come in at the same time, one of which needs to turn and reverse in to offload vehicles and containers over its stern ramp. The government dock also serves as the base of the Club Med dive boat. If you put in there, you will find yourself with high walls, no pilings, some surge in westerly weather and no shoreside facilities. In an emergency, however, it could serve as a refuge. The local Shell station is on the doorstep and has gasoline and diesel fuel.

Cockburn Town

Cockburn (pronounced "Coburn") Town is recognizable offshore by its 200-foot-tall BTC tower and large satellite dish, and the ruins of its old government dock. Cockburn is an entry port (Immigration and Customs are at the airport). You can anchor off the old government dock to clear in, or put in at the Riding Rock Marina. The town itself has the range of facilities you would expect to find in the main out islands: a BTC office, a relocated and much-improved clinic north of the airport, a bank, small stores and Internet access. See our Goin' Ashore for our suggestions on what you might want to see in San Salvador. If you take a circle island tour, at Sugar Loaf (on the west coast just south of Long Bay) you will see the two dredged basins of a failed attempt to construct a marina. The project appears doomed, for the site will always fill with sand.

The color of the water all around San Salvador is outstanding. The ocean drop-off runs so close to the land that it brings deep, ultramarine blue water virtually within swimming distance of the beaches. You have three bands of vivid color almost wherever you look: the white sand, the aquamarine of the shallows and the deep, deep blue. Despite this gem-like water, and quality fishing and diving, the cruising visitor, unless taken up with big-game fishing or diving the walls, is unlikely to rate San Salvador high on their visit list, simply because of its offshore isolation.

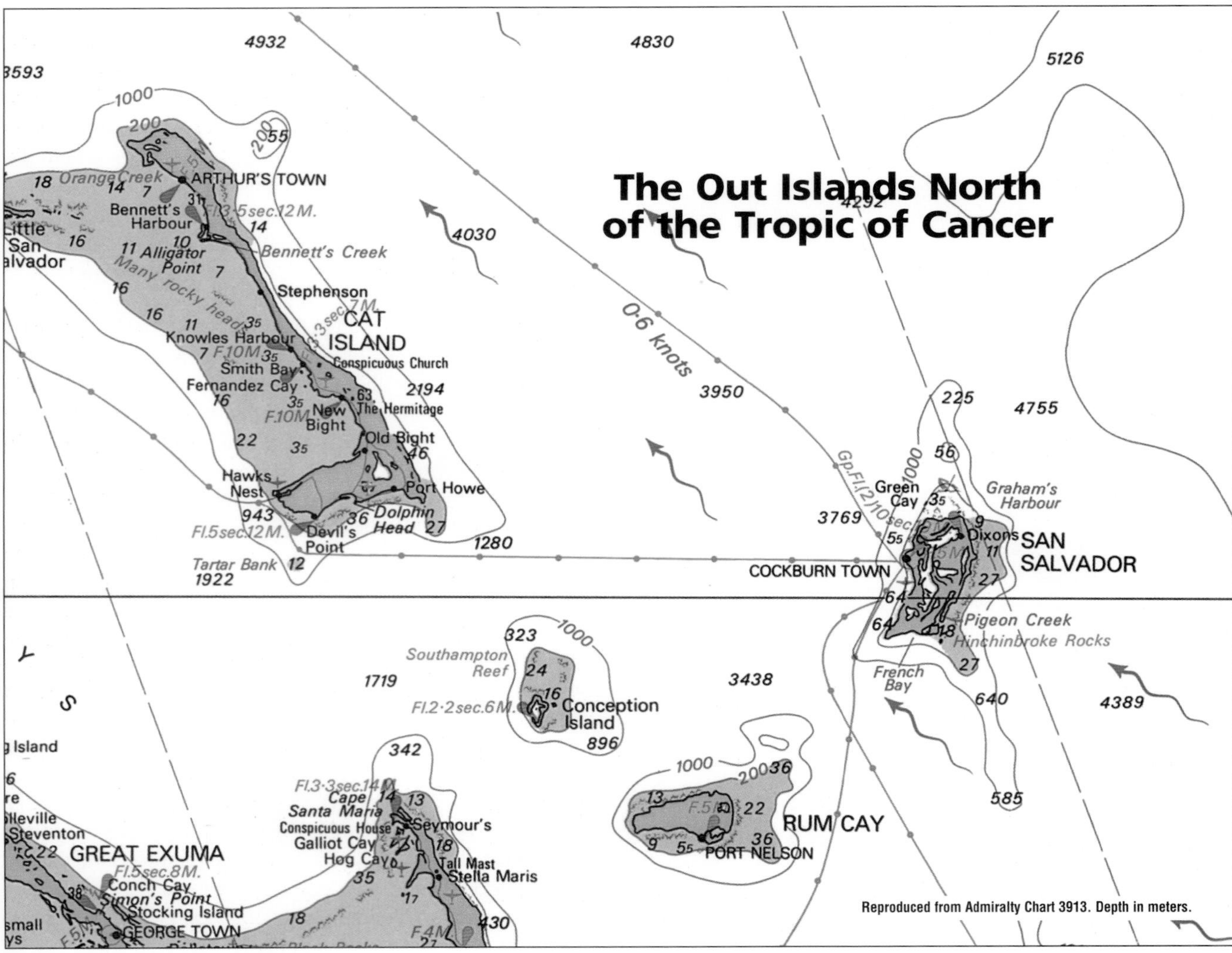

Reproduced from Admiralty Chart 3913. Depth in meters.

Not to be used for navigation.

Pilotage. Talking Captain to Captain

Approach to Hawks Nest Marina, Cat Island

Hawks Nest offers 28 slips, a bar and restaurant, showers, laundry facilities and a dive shop. The one shallow spot on the approach route is dredged to 1.8-meter/6-foot depths at mean low water. Hawks Nest Creek itself was "improved" by Hurricane Floyd, broadened by some 6 meters/20 feet, and is a vastly better anchorage as the result. There are two mooring buoys there (with a 10.5-meter/35-foot length overall limit), but there is ample space to anchor safely farther up the creek.

The HWKN1 waypoint is probably redundant, but it is given as a safe offshore waypoint for approaches made in poor visibility. From there, the critical waypoint, HWKN2, lies 0.5 nautical miles on a course of 75/255 degrees true just past the drop-off line, which runs close to the shore at Hawks Nest. At HWKN2, you can see exactly what lies ahead. You have another 0.5 nautical miles to run to the marina, three red buoys to lead you in and a red marker on a rock spine to starboard. On the port side, your principal landmarks are a yellow house (Point House) and a shallow bay (which partially dries at low water). Right on the nose, you have Hawks Nest Creek.

From HWKN2, navigate visually on a course of 075/255 degrees true. Leave the three red buoys close to starboard. Go straight on—the fuel dock (diesel and gas) will be on your port side. Just after the fuel dock, swing to port to enter the marina (which up to that point has remained concealed). The fuel dock has 2.1-meter/7-foot depths at mean low water, and the slips in the marina have 2.3-meter/7.5-foot depths.

Ahead of you, farther up the creek, are the Hawks Nest mooring buoys, with 1.8-meter/6-foot depths at mean low water. Farther in, you will find 1.7-meter/5.5-foot depths at mean low water. We suggest you explore by dinghy first and take soundings. It is quite possible to work yourself surprisingly far in, and in severe weather, the surrounding mangroves can serve as "air bags" if you get carried by wind or surge.

Cat Island to San Salvador

Leave Hawks Nest, as if you were going to Conception Island, on a course of 132 degrees true. Run for six nautical miles until you are two nautical miles due south of Cat Island's Devils Point. Then, turn east on a course of 092 degrees true, and run for 49 nautical miles to San Salvador.

Rum Cay

We cover approaches in detail, but two factors are vital for your safe arrival or departure: the first is good weather, and the second is the sun, which must be in your favor. If it turns out that you can add the advantage of a high tide, you have a winning combination.

Approach to Rum Cay from the Southwest

Sandy Point, the southwest tip of Rum Cay, can be rounded reasonably close in, between a quarter and half a mile offshore. From there, set a course to Sumner Point, which will be the southernmost tip of land you see. There is deep water all the way until you are level with Cotton Field Point, on which there

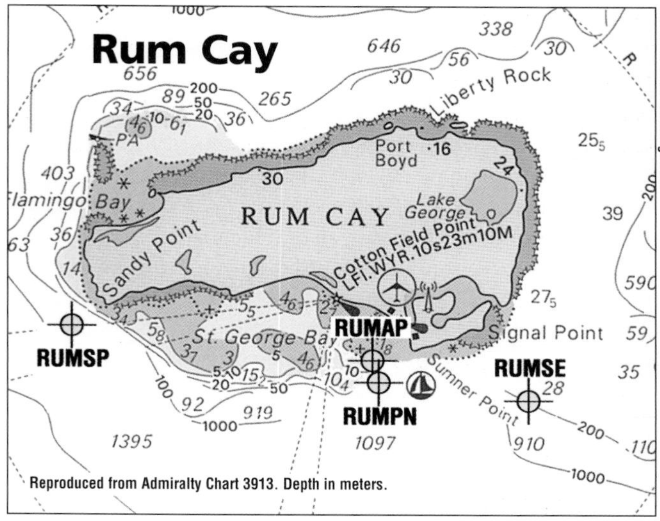

Reproduced from Admiralty Chart 3913. Depth in meters.

is a prominent house. Ahead of you, about a half a mile away, you will see a red buoy, which is the outer marker for the route into Sumner Point Marina, and the point at which you turn to port toward the anchorage. Adjust your heading to approach this outer buoy, as if to leave it to starboard. Your position should be around N 23° 38.160'/W 074° 51.000', standing safely clear of the buoy in around 6 meters/20 feet of water.

Wherever you are bound, whether it is to anchor off or go into Sumner Point Marina, check your orientation. Cotton Field Point is at 345 degrees true. Sumner Point bears 100 degrees true, and the marina is just to its north. Use the TEXACO sign and the oil tanks ashore as landmarks. Port Nelson is barely visible. There are a few houses, some palm trees and a 200-foot-tall BTC tower. The settlement dock is lost against its background.

To anchor, turn for Cotton Field Point, favoring the house to the east with the shiny tin roof bearing at around 005 degrees true. The anchorage lies between the house with the shiny roof and the dock at Port Nelson, which will become apparent as you get closer. Make your way in, eyeballing as you go, then turn toward the beach if you want to be closer to Port Nelson.

If you are bound for Sumner Point Marina, a series of red entry markers will lead you in from the outer reef. It is vital that you identify the outer marker accurately, for if you mistake an inner marker for the first one, you will end up on the reef. In effect, you have three legs from that outer marker, then you are at the entry channel. You will have plenty of sea room as you go in, although you have coral on both sides. Your depth will go from 6 meters/20 feet to 3 meters/10 feet, and then to 2.4 meters/8 feet at mean low water.

If you cannot identify the marker buoys, or if it appears that one is missing, call Sumner Point Marina to guide you in. The Sumner Point Marina entry channel has 1.9-meter/6.5-foot depths. Moving sand is known to clog the channel, so if you are entering at low water, and depth is critical, try calling them on VHF Channel 16 and check. If it is too shallow for you, there is a good place just off the entry channel to anchor and wait for the tide.

Approach to Rum Cay from the Southeast

Coming into St. George Bay from the southeast, you must avoid the reefs that run west for just over one nautical mile from Sumner Point. The only safe approach is to run on an east–west line almost 1.5 nautical miles south of Sumner Point straight to the Port Nelson waypoint. Don't be tempted to turn in sooner than longitude W 074° 51.000', even if you see what you take to be the entry buoys leading you into the marina.

At the Port Nelson waypoint, turn to run due north on longitude W 074° 51.000'. Contact Sumner Point Marina on VHF Channel 16 at the Port Nelson approach waypoint. About one nautical mile past the approach waypoint, you should be able to pick up, off your starboard bow, the first of the red buoys marking the route in to the Sumner Point Marina. Don't run too close to this first buoy, which you must leave to starboard. It marks the outer limit of the reef. Once you are at that mark, follow the instructions we have already given in the last section. ■

Waterway Guide is always open to your observations from the helm. E-mail your comments on any navigation information in the guide to: editor@waterwayguide.com.

Out Islands Waypoints

LITTLE SAN SALVADOR

Little San Salvador	LSSAL	24°34.64N / 75°58.00W

CAT ISLAND

Orange Creek	ORNGS	24°37.00N / 75°43.00W
Orange Creek Dock	ORNGE	24°38.78N / 75°42.75W
Bennetts Harbour	BNTNW	24°34.00N / 75°41.00W
Bennetts Harbour Dock	BNNTS	24°33.54N / 75°38.42W
Smith Bay	SMTHW	24°20.00N / 75°30.00W
Smith Bay Govt Dock	SMITH	24°19.96N / 75°28.53W
Fernandez Bay	FNDEZ	24°19.50N / 75°30.00W
The Bight	BIGHT	24°15.00N / 75°33.00W
New Bight Dock	NBGHT	24°17.26N / 75°24.91W
Hawks Nest 1	HWKN1	24°08.53N / 75°32.47W
Hawks Nest 2	HWKN2	24°08.66N / 75°31.94W
Hawks Nest Marina	HWKNM	24°08.85N / 75°31.44W
Hawks Nest Beach	HWKNB	24°09.31N / 75°31.41W

CONCEPTION ISLAND

Conception NW Anch	CONNW (B44)	23°51.00N / 75°07.75W
Conception Wedge Point	CONWG (B45)	23°47.80N / 75°07.00W

RUM CAY

Rum Cay Sandy Point	RUMSP (B47)	23°38.35N / 74°57.50W
Rum Cay SE	RUMSE (B48)	23°37.50N / 74°47.50W
Sumner Pt Marina App	RUMAP (B49)	23°37.80N / 74°51.80W

LITTLE SAN SALVADOR

San Salvador	SNSAL (B75)	24°03.40N / 74°32.50W

Position format is latitude and longitude in degrees and minutes (hddd°mm.mm). Waypoints in RED are NOT for autopilot navigation. Codes in parenthesis are Wavey Line waypoints marked on the charts. If you have programmed waypoints listed in a previous edition of this guide, check carefully to ensure the coordinates you have recorded match the list. If a waypoint is no longer on the list we may have changed its code or deleted it.

Beach House on San Salvador, Bahamas. ©IstockPhoto/ CaraMaria

GOIN' ASHORE:

CAT ISLAND

Plantation houses still stand as a reminder of the historical significance of this enchanting island, when cotton, pineapple and sisal used to grow in such abundance that ships called at the Cat Island ports from New England and Europe. And, the railroad at Old Bight—the only one ever constructed in the Bahamas—was very busy. It is one of the most beautiful islands in the Bahamas, still largely unspoiled. The west coast is lined with narrow beaches, and if you drive north or south down the main road, you will be delighted by the attractive coastline and small village settlements, some with derelict slave cabins among the hardscrabble farms. Don't miss Father Jerome's Hermitage on Mt. Alvernia, the highest point in the Bahamas. The snorkeling and diving off Cat Island, as well as the deep sea angling and bonefishing, make this a fascinating island to visit. Anchor off New Bight in good weather or take a slip in Hawks Nest Marina, and take time to explore.

LITTLE SAN SALVADOR

Half-Moon Bay Little San Salvador, and its idyllic west-end beach, is a short, nine-mile hop from Eleuthera Point or a mere 13-mile journey from Cat Island. This cruisers dream destination is now the playground of cruise ships and their accompanying frenzied "watersports" take on a day in paradise. You can still anchor here (even the cruise lines don't own the water) in moderate winds from the north to east, but you will want to avoid the southern end if a cruise ship is visiting. If you have made the trip and just want to see the island, you can day anchor off the eastern end, off the northern beach at Eastern Bay. The interior is largely a shallow lagoon adored by a variety of birds. Bring your binoculars to fully appreciate the avian show.

NORTHERN CAT ISLAND

airport • fuel • groceries • medical • police • post office • restaurant • telephone • water

Orange Creek is the northernmost settlement on Cat Island and home to the attractive *Orange Creek Inn*. There is a well-stocked food market and large coin-operated laundry. The anchorage, with northerly and easterly protection, is in front of the *Orange Creek Inn*, the large white, two-story building. You will find 2.2 meters/7 feet of water. This anchorage is unsafe in southeast, south or westerly winds. There is a dinghy landing at the mouth of Orange Creek and a wall a short way up the creek.

The Hermitage. WATERWAY GUIDE PHOTOGRAPHY.

Accommodations *Orange Creek Inn* Tel: 242-354-4110 • Fax 242-354-4042 • VHF 74
Here you will find 16 mini-suites from $80 per night.
The *Sea Spray Hotel* Tel: 242-354-4116 has a restaurant and bar ($) and pleasant rooms from $65 per night.
Shannas Cove Resort Tel: 242-354-4249 • Fax: 242-354-4250 • shannascove@gmail.com • www.shannas-cove.com
5 beachfront bungalows from $170 per night. Additional taxes of 10%. On-site restaurant, and dive school and boat.
Bakery *Club Crystal Service Station,* south of town in The Lot Settlement.
Car Rentals *Sea Spray,* 242-354-4116.
Church *Seventh Day Adventist.*
Fuel Gas and Diesel at *Club Crystal Service Station,* south of town in The Lot Settlement.
Hardware *Target Hardware,* south of town in The Lot Settlement.
Laundry Coin-operated laundry at *Orange Creek Food Store.*
Medical *Government Clinic*, 242-354-4050.
Provisions *Orange Creek Food Store.* Well-stocked store with fresh produce.
Propane *Orange Creek Food Store*. Sent to Nassau, comes back on mailboat.
Restaurants *Club Crystal Service Station Restaurant & Bar,* south of town in The Lot Settlement.
Shannas Cove Restaurant serving continental breakfast from 8 a.m. to 10:30 a.m. ($15 per person), small snacks (hamburgers, salads, etc.) from noon to 2 p.m. ($8 to $14 per person) and dinner, which includes hors d'oeuvres, then a 3-course meal starting at 7 p.m. ($35 per person).

Arthurs Town is the center of government on Cat Island. You can anchor anywhere along its western shore with good holding and easterly protection. You can land a dinghy near the police station by the jetty. Arthurs Town has an airport served by *Bahamasair*, a BTC office with a card phone outside, police, a post office, food stores including *Island Mart Meats*, a straw market, a liquor store and a superb bakery and restaurant called *Cookie House*. Pat Rolle, who owns Cookie House, serves delicious Bahamian bread and other delights and is an encyclopedia of local knowledge, including boyhood stories of Sidney Poitier, the actor and activist who hails from this island. He will also rent you a motor scooter to "scoot" around town. RO water, gasoline and diesel are all available in Arthurs Town. Ask locals for help in procuring these essentials if you can't find them.

EMERGENCIES

Orange Creek Clinic, Tel 242-354-4050
Police, 242-354-3039

⚓ *Goin' Ashore*

Accommodations *Boogie Pond Lodge*, Tel: 242-354-4110 • *Cookies Cabanas*, 242-354-2027.
Airport & Airlines *Bahamasair,* 242-354-2049, Tuesday, Friday and Sunday flights.
Arts & Crafts *Larimore Straw Works.*
Bakery *Cookie House* • *Club Crystal Service Station,* north of town in The Lot Settlement.
Car Rentals *Sea Spray,* 242-354-4116.
Fuel Gas & Diesel *at Club Crystal Service Station,* north of town in The Lot Settlement • Gasoline at *Boggie Pond Station.*
Hardware *Target Hardware* in The Lot Settlement.
Laundry Coin-operated laundry at *Orange Creek Food Store*.
Medical *Government Clinic*, 242-354-4050 in Orange Creek Settlement.
Police Tel: 242-354-3039. In the Government Building.
Post Office In the Government Building.
Provisions *Big Bulls Food Store* • *Campbell's Food Store* • *Island Mart Meat.*
Propane *Orange Creek Food Store*. Sent to Nassau, comes back on mailboat.
Restaurants *Cookie House* • *Boggie Pond* • *Gossip Restaurant* • *Nancy's Takeaway* • *E&K Takeaway* • *Periwinkle's* • *Rita's Fruits & Drinks* in Zion Hill.
Taxis & Tours At the airport.
Telephone *BTC*, 242-354-2060. Office with a card phone outside.
Water *Oasis Springs*, 5-gallon bottles of RO water.

Traveling south from Arthurs Town, you will pass Zion Hill, home to a very nice fruit stand in season, Bonamy Town and Dumfries. There is a good anchorage outside Dumfries and a dinghy landing by the road down to the beach. A short walk north takes you to *C&S* pharmacy and a hardware store. Farther south, you will come to Bennetts Harbour, which is really more of a shallow lagoon, but the settlement has a good government dock and a ramp for dinghy landing. There are groceries here at *Better Value* and seafood at *Tito's*. *Ducky's Restaurant* serves up great Bahamian fare along with news and local information. There is another good anchorage, again with easterly protection, south of Bennetts Settlement and north of Alligator Point. Do not try to short cut Alligator Point, however!

The shoal area extends significantly to the west off the point. Once past the point, you can continue your travels closer to the island's shoreline. There is an anchorage with good northerly protection off Pigeon Cay Club at the eastern end of the long beach. There is a round house to starboard marking rocks and heads to avoid. Pigeon Cay Club is secluded and private, but the same beach their members walk and shell hunt is available for you, too. If you want to shop at *Roaker's Island General Shopping Center*, haul anchor and move to just south of the jetty off *The Bluff*. It is a shorter walk to the road from there. If you need a bite to eat after all this moving and walking, try *Apple Tree Inn's* restaurant. There is a telephone in *The Bluff*, too. Farther south, you can anchor with real good easterly protection in the shadow of Big Bluff, 27 meters/90 feet high or off Ben Bluff. There are many caves to explore along the stretch of coastline from The Bluff to The Cove. The settlements of Gaitors, Industrious Hill, Stevenson and Knowles were once thriving. You will see Loyalist ruins as you hike the roads, but today there are sparsely populated by friendly folks who will welcome your wave and "Good Day."

SMITH BAY SETTLEMENT

airport • customs & immigration • fuel • groceries • medical • police • post office • restaurant • telephone • water

EMERGENCIES

Medical *Smith Bay Clinic*, 242-342-3026

Smith Bay Settlement has a government dock that hosts the big event of the week: the mailboat's arrival. There is also a commercial center that packs produce grown on the island for shipment to New Providence. You can anchor to the north of Culbert's Creek for easy access to the settlement (watch for the rocks north and south). A heavenly anchorage, with protection from the north, east and southeast, awaits you a bit farther south in Fernandez Bay. The anchorage is in the cove on which the Fernandez Bay Village Resort fronts, so consider their needs when anchoring here. Considerate cruisers are welcome to land their dinghies on the beach (please, no dogs), and visit the resort for lunch and dinner (appropriate dress required).

Accommodations: *Fernandez Bay Village,* Tel: 242-342-3043, Fax: 242-342-3051 • fernandezbayvillage@fernandezbayvillage.com • www.fernandezbayvillage.com
A remote, luxury resort with a crescent-shaped white sand beach, and villas and cottages with garden baths as well as private baths inside. Sportfishing, SCUBA and bonefishing guides available, as are boat, bicycle and kayak rentals. Excellent restaurant & bar • *Haulover Hotel, Restaurant & Bar*, 242-342-2028 • *Little Bay Inn*, 242-342-2004 • *Island Hopp Inn*, 242-342-2100.
Airport & Airlines *New Bight International Airport*. Midway between Smith Bay and New Bight. Daily flights to or from some where you could make connections. Port of entry. *Bahamasair,* 800-222-4262 • *Cat Island Air,* 242-342-2125 • *Continental Connection (Gulfstream)*, 800-231-0856 • *Major's Air Service*, 242-352-5778.
Boutique *Fernandez Bay Boutique & Gifts*.
Car Rentals *Fernandez Bay, 242-342-3043* • *New Bight Car Rental,* 242-342-3514.
Clinic *Smith Bay Community Clinic*, 242-342-3026. Open 9 a.m. to 4 p.m. weekdays and 24-hr emergency service. Main clinic for Cat Island with a resident doctor and full-time nurse.
Customs & Immigration Tel: 242-342-2016. At airport. Will come to the Government Dock.
Fuel *The New Bight Service Station*, 242-342-3014 will truck in fuel to the Government Dock. Determine charges beforehand.
Laundry Ask around for local ladies who wash and hang dry • *Dorsett's*, 242-342-2158.
Hardware *MLR Hardware & Building Supplies.* South of the airport, a long hike.
Provisions *Government Packing House*, 242-342-3087. Fresh produce on mailboat day • *Alvernia Foods* • *Heritage Convenience Mart* • *Vanny's Convenience Stop.*
Restaurants *Hallover's Inn and Restaurant* & Bar, 242-342-2028. Open 11 a.m. to 6 p.m. with good local food. Opposite the Government Dock. $ *Fernandez Bay Village.* $$$ • *Island Hopp Inn.*
Trash In settlement bins and dumpsters.
Water At Government Dock and Government Packing House.

NEW BIGHT, DOUDS, MOSSTOWN, OLD BIGHT, MCQUEENS AND HAWKS NEST POINT

airport • fuel • groceries • police • post office • propane
estaurant • telephone • water

If you plan to anchor in The Bight, your best bet is to position off New Bight where everything is within walking distance, although the anchorage east of the shallows off Bonefish Point affords better westerly wind protection and wonderful snorkeling. If you have not cleared in, remember that Smith Bay is a Port of Entry. New Bight offers the cruising boater a good dinghy landing within close proximity to many stores and services, while in the shadow of Mount Alvernia, the highest hill in the Bahamas, at 206 feet above sea level. It is the site of The Hermitage, a particularly noteworthy church built by a priest, Father Jerome. Father Jerome was schooled as an architect and then decided to become a missionary. In 1908, he arrived in the Bahamas to save souls and rebuild local wooden churches that could not withstand hurricane-force winds, redesigning them in mortar and stone construction. At the unlikely age of many cruisers, 62-years old, he built The Hermitage, a scaled-down model of European monastic buildings. Here, he remained cloistered in monastic quarters next to his beloved chapel with its pretty bell tower and lived peacefully until his death at age 80 in the late 1950s. The views from the top of the hill are well worth the climb, past his Stations of the Cross. Also, locate the replica of Jesus' tomb that he recreated, rolled-away stone, et. al. It is a remarkable tribute to his Godly devotion. Other examples of Father Jerome's work are the St. Francis of Assisi Catholic Church at Old Bight and two churches of different faiths in Clarence Town on Long Island.

There are good anchorages with easterly protection just off Moss Town and Old Bight. At Old Bight, you will find St. Mary's Church, donated by Governor Balfour, who read the Bahamian Emancipation Proclamation. The church stands as a monument to emancipation. There are still ruins of former plantations east of the settlement and the St. Francis of Assisi Catholic Church. Stop by to see Maud or Winifred Rolle, who have some of the best straw work in the islands. You will also find the *Pass Me Not Bar, Peter Hill Bar and Restaurant, Dawkins Food Store, Hart's Convenience* and *BJ's Payless*. On the remote eastern coast, *The Greenwood Inn Beach Resort* has 20 beachfront rooms on an 8-mile-long beach with good elkhorn coral for snorkeling and full dive facilities.

From McQueens to Hawks Nest Point, there is good anchoring in sand with protection from the east and south. Watch out for coral heads as you travel south and toward shore and head for other safer locations if the winds turn west, north or northeast.

Accommodations *Bridge Inn Hotel and Restaurant*, Tel: 242-342-3013, Fax: 242-342-3041 • *Gilbert's Inn*, 242-342-3011 • *Twin Palm Beach Resort,* 242-342-3108 • *Two Corner Inn*, 242-342-3130.
Airport *New Bight International Airport*. Midway between Smith Bay and New Bight. Daily flights to or from someplace. Port of entry. *Bahamasair,* 242-342-2107 • *Cat Island Air,* 242-342-2125 • *Continental Connection (Gulfstream)*, 800-231-0856 • *Major's Air Service*, 242-352-5778.
Bakery Find *Olive King's* place near the Administration Office.
Car Rental *New Bight Service Station,* 242-342-3014, VHF 16 • *Gilbert's Car Rentals,* 242-342-3011 • *3J's*, 242-342-4010 • *Friendly Taxi & Tour,* 242-342-3134.
Customs 242-342-2016. At the airport. Officers will come to Smith Bay Government Dock.
Fuel *New Bight Service Station* • 242-342-3014 • VHF 16 • Open 8 a.m. to 6 p.m., Monday through Saturday. They will truck diesel for boats to Smith Bay. They have diesel and gasoline, as well as batteries and outboard oils. Parts can be ordered from the U.S.
Gift Shop *Charmaine's Fashions* • *Gina's Variety* 242-342-3017 • *Irene's Straw Shop* • *Iva's Jewelry & Straw.*
Hardware *MLR Hardware*. South of the airport. A good hike north of town • *New Bight Food Market.*
Police Tel: 242-342-3039. In the Government Administration Building.
Post Office In the administration building.
Propane Propane goes on mailboat to Nassau.
Provisions *New Bight Food Market* and *Liquor Store,* Open 8 a.m. to 7 p.m. Groceries, bread, fruit, vegetables, pasta, sodas and small pharmacy. • *Friendly Proprietor's Sodas* • *Sancheas's Convenience Store.*
Liquor *Harry Bethel's Wholesale Liquor Store*; *Butler and Sands Liquor Store, New Bight Market & Liquor, Two Ladies Liquors.*
Restaurants *Blue Bird Restaurant and Bar,* 242-342-3095/3023 $ *Bridge Inn Motel and Restaurant,* 242-342-3013 $ • *DDD* • *Two Corners Restaurant.*
Telephone BTC, Card phone at the office behind the police station.
Trash Bins and dumpsters in the settlement.

HAWKS NEST

airstrip • fuel • marina • restaurant • telephone • water

Reached by a bumpy road from McQueens, Hawks Nest is another small Bahamian resort that offers both a private airfield and a full-service marina. It has the advantages of a large, dramatic site with tranquil, secluded beaches and dazzling snorkeling and diving off the point, plus the amenities of a full-service resort. Whether you arrive by sea or by air, you are bound to enjoy your stay. The anchorage near Hawks Nest Creek requires great care for holding if anchoring, has strong currents and no-can-see-ums that take out big chunks when they bite. Get the screens out or go to Hawks Nest Marina.

MARINA

HAWK'S NEST RESORT AND MARINA
Tel: 242-342-7050 • Fax: 342-7051 • 1-800-688-4752 •
VHF 16 • info@hawks-nest.com • www.hawks-nest.com

Slips 28 + floating dock. **Max LOA** 115 ft. **MLW at Dock** 5 to 7 ft. **Dockage** Slips, $2.50 per ft. per day, seven-day minimum, $500 fee for early departure. Floating dock: $10 per day, 25' or less, including dinghies; $20 per day, 26' or greater. **Fuel** Dock open 7:30 a.m. to dark, daily. Diesel and gasoline. **Facilities & Services** Power $15 to $60 per day for 30 to 100 amp. Filtered well water $0.50 per gallon; Showers, restrooms, coin-op washer and dryers, $6 per load. BTC card telephone, complimentary WiFi and satellite television available. Trash disposal. Ice. Marina store is stocked with boat essentials. **Restaurant & Bar** *Hawk's Nest Dining* open daily for breakfast, 8 a.m. to 10 a.m.; lunch, noon to 2 p.m.; dinner, 7 p.m. to 10 p.m. *Sharkey's Bar* and *The*

Sandy Point, Rum Cay, looking southeast. (Not to be used for navigation.) WATERWAY GUIDE PHOTOGRAPHY.

Club Bar are open for guest's enjoyment. Tennis, badminton, basketball courts and swimming pool at the hotel; secluded beaches. Two air-conditioned fish cleaning houses. SCUBA, two-tank dives. Recently resurfaced airport runway. **Credit Cards** Visa and MasterCard. Travelers checks accepted. Pets are welcome at the marina.

Accommodations *Hawk's Nest Resort,* 242-342-7050. Ten rooms and a two-bedroom beach cottage. Hotel rooms, $211 to $218 per night. *Point House* with two bedrooms and baths, $488 per night. Luxury villas, $5,000 w/seven night minimum.

Airfield *Hawk's Nest Resort* 4,600-ft. hard-surfaced air strip for private and charter aircraft, with aviation fuel. *Hawks Nest* is not a Port of Entry. The nearest public airport with Customs and Immigration is at New Bight.

Boutique Straw work, caps, shirts at the marina.

Churches *Baptist • Catholic • Ruins of Anglican Church.*

Dive Sites Most of the favorite dive sites are off Port Howe. Many of these are drop-offs, going down to 230 feet. *Tartar Bank* is absolutely spectacular, about 16 miles offshore from Devils Point, but you need calm seas. The Devils Point itself is a brilliant site, closer in shore, where the wall drops off very quickly, and there are masses of fish and sea fans.

Diving *Hawk's Nest* Full-service PADI dive center. Open-water dives, night dives, equipment rental, walls, wrecks and blue holes. Equipment rental and tank refills avai able. Three guided dives daily and shore diving from beach. • *Cat Island Dive Center, Greenwood Beach Resort, Port Howe* • info@greenwoodbeachresort.com • www.greenwoodbeachresort.com • Two dive boats, rental equipment and instruction in both German and English.

Fishing Guides Excellent bonefishing on the west side of Cat Island. Inquire at *Hawk's Nest Marina.* • *Top Cat's Fishing Service,* 242-342-7003.

Fishing Charters Inquire at *Hawk's Nest Marina* for full- or half-day charters.

Fuel Diesel and gasoline at the marina.

Laundry Wash and fold services at the marina. Ask for charges before you drop off.

Restaurants & Bar *Hawk's Nest Resort.* Breakfast, lunch and dinner. Happy hour at the Sports Bar on the docks.

Taxis George's Taxi Service, VHF Channel 16.

Telephone Card phone at the restaurant. BTC cards for sale at the marina.

THINGS TO DO IN CAT ISLAND

- Make time to climb the rough track leading out of New Bight up Comer Hill (Mount Alvernia) to see the Hermitage built by Father Jerome. There are steep steps as you approach, with hand-carved Stations of the Cross, but the 360-degree view from the top is well worth the short climb, especially at sunset.
- Attend the annual Cat Island Regatta in August, with sailboat races at The Bight, and lots of rake and scrape, festivities and fun.
- Drive to Port Howe and Bailey Town, the most historic areas on the island. In pirate days, it was ringed by fortresses against such infamous brigands as Augustino Black, Blackbeard, Black Caesar, Josephus and other privateers. Visit the Deveaux Plantation ruins.
- Enjoy some of the best fishing and diving in the Islands.

RUM CAY

airstrip • fuel • groceries • marina • post office
restaurant • telephone • water

At one time way, Rum Cay was considered way off the beaten track. Sumner Point Marina changed cruisers minds about that. Sumner Point Marina is open for business under Bobby Little whose family first developed it. The residents here are stalwart, industrious and self-sufficient folks. They hope you will visit their beautiful cay and its surrounding, unspoiled wonders. The diving off its reefs, which are largely unexplored, defines Rum Cay as

The colors of San Salvador, Sandy Point. (Not to be used for navigation.) WATERWAY GUIDE PHOTOGRAPHY.

one of the premier dive destinations in the Bahamas. However, you must come with your own equipment and experience to dive without guidance. There are no dive facilities on the cay. You may find a local willing to take you to some of the areas prime lobstering locations. The tamer, inshore snorkeling is some of the best in the islands. For sportfishermen, there are blue marlin, tuna and record-size wahoo waiting to be caught offshore. Anchorages in the Rum Cay area can be unsafe in south and west winds, and are subject to surge and poor holding. Anchor with care! This may be marina dockage territory for you.

EMERGENCIES

Marine • VHF 14

MARINA

SUMNER POINT MARINA
TEL: 242-331-2823, 954-281-8281 • FAX: 242-331-2824
sumnerpointmarina@rumcay.com • www.rumcaymarina.com

Slips 30. **Max LOA** 180 ft. **MLW at Dock** 6.5 ft. **Dockage** $1.45 per ft. **Fuel** Gasoline and diesel. **Facilities & Services** 30 amps, $20 per day. 50 amps, $30 per day. RO water, WiFi and laundry. Restaurant and bar. **Accommodations** Four beachfront cottages, a guesthouse and Inn. All major credit cards accepted.

PORT DIRECTORY

It is a short walk to Port Nelson from the dinghy landing in front of the government dock.

Accommodations *Sumner Point Marina* handles lodging.

Airstrip/Airline Charter and private pilots use the 4,500 x 100 foot runway.

Bakery *Kaye's Restaurant* • *Ocean View Restaurant* • *Two Sisters Take Away* • *Sumner Point Marina.*

Churches *St. Christopher's Anglican Church, St. John's Baptist Church.*

Fuel Diesel and gasoline at the marina.

Medical *Government Clinic*, 242-331-2104 with full-time nurse.

Provisions *Kaye's Last Chance Market* Open 9 a.m. to 4 p.m. daily. Canned goods, staples, frozen meats and fresh produce. • Terry *Strachan's One Stop Shop* Open 9 a.m. to 5 p.m. except Sunday. Canned goods, staples, frozen meats and ice cream.

Police Tel: 242-331-2870.

Post Office In the government building.

Propane Sent to Nassau on the mailboat.

Restaurants *Kayes Restaurant & Bar*, 242-331-2816, VHF 16. Open daily, but call ahead for dinner, served at 8 p.m. Bar stays open. Kaye's is the gathering spot on Rum Cay. • *Ocean View Restaurant* • VHF 16 • Ruby and Ted Bain open daily, but call ahead for dinner reservations. • *Two Sisters' Take-Away*. Will deliver to the marina and the Government Dock • *Out of the Blue* and *Green Flash* at Sumner Point Marina.

Telephone BTC office at the foot of the BTC tower.

Trash Dumpster at Government Dock. Bins in the settlement.

Water At the marina $.

THINGS TO DO IN RUM CAY

- Dive or snorkel some of the best—and least-known—reefs in the islands.
- Go for a walk around the settlement of Port Nelson. Its sand roads are attractive, and you are seeing the real Bahamas as every island once was.
- Explore the wreck of the Royal Navy's first steam-powered ship, *HMS Conqueror*, which sank in 1861 in 30 feet of water off Sumner Point.

SAN SALVADOR

airport • bank • customs & immigration • fuel • groceries
marina • medical • police • post office • propane
restaurant • telephone • water

San Salvador holds claim to the first landfall of Columbus in the New World, with monuments and a museum to prove it. The east coast is almost deserted, just two houses sharing a generator. Much of inland area is covered by lakes. The island is home to 16 of the world's 23 varieties of sea birds and the rarest iguana species in the world. If you are a diver, this is the place for you. The spectacular wall dives offer some of the finest diving in the Bahamas, year round, with normal visibility between 100 and 200 feet. The sportfishing for marlin (catch and release) and wahoo in particular is superb. Cockburn Town (pronounced coe-burn town), is a Port of Entry, but call *Riding Rock Marina* on VHF 06 as you come in to arrange clearance. Customs and Immigration, 242-331-2100, are based at the airport and will come to the marina. Anchoring is not a good option off San Salvador due to surge, swell and holding.

EMERGENCIES

Marine • VHF 6 (not VHF 16)
Medical *Clinic* • 242-331-2105 • Open from 9 a.m. to 5:30 p.m. weekdays. Doctor in emergency at 242-331-2033. Nurse in emergency 242-331-2109.
Police • 242-331-2010, or 242-331-2919 in emergency.

MARINA

RIDING ROCK INN RESORT AND MARINA
Tel: 242-331-2633/2631, 800-272-1492 • VHF 6
reservations@ridingrock.com • www.ridingrock.com

Slips 25. **Max LOA** 140 ft. **MLW** 8 ft. **Dockage** $1.25 per ft. per day. **Fuel** Dock open 8 a.m. to 5 p.m. daily, except Saturday. Diesel and gasoline. **Facilities & Services** Power 30 amp, $20 per day; 50 amp, $40 per day. Water $15 to $30 per day depending on boat length. Showers, restrooms, coin-op washers and dryers, $2 per load. Public telephone, WiFi, satellite television, ice, picnic area, weigh station and lighted fish cleaning table. Freshwater swimming pool at the hotel. Sand beach west of the marina. *Riding Rock Divers* on site. **Restaurant** *Seaview Restaurant* open for breakfast, 7:30 a.m. to 9 a.m.; lunch, 12:30 to 2 p.m.; and dinner, 6:30 p.m. to 8:30 p.m. *Driftwood Bar* open 11 a.m. to midnight. **Accommodations** *Riding Rock Inn Oceanfront* and poolside room. **Credit Cards** MasterCard and Visa. Pets are welcome at the marina.

PORT DIRECTORY FOR COCKBURN TOWN

Accommodations *Bougainvillea Apartments*, 242-331-2750. Above *J's Pharmacy*. $125 a night for the one-bedroom apartment, $150 for two bedrooms. • *Club Med*, 242-331-2000. Caters mainly to guests on packages from France and Europe, but with 286 rooms can sometimes offer accommodation for a few nights. $155 per person includes meals, drinks and entertainment. Diving extra • *Riding Rock Inn*, 242-331-2631.

Airport & Airlines 8,000 x 150 ft. paved runway, with *Avgas* and *Jet A* fuel usually available. • *Bahamasair,* 242-331-2920 • *USAirways,* 800-428-4322.

Bank *Bank of the Bahamas,* 242-331-2237, open 10 a.m. to 2 p.m., Monday through Friday, between town and Riding Rock. Credit card cash advance given.

Car Rental *Walkers*, 242-331-2368 • *D&W*, 242-331-2184 • *Hosanna*, 242-331-2688.

Churches *Holy Saviour Catholic Church, Church of God Prophecy, St. Augustine of Canterbury Anglican Church, Seventh Day Adventist Church.*

Gifts *Laramore's,* 242-331-2282, open Monday through Saturday, 9 a.m. to 5:30 p.m., household goods and clothing. • *Straw Market Waterfront.*

Laundry *Dutch Laundromat*, 242-331-2324, open weekdays, 8 a.m. to 5 p.m., a short walk from the marina toward town. $2 a load, $3 to dry.

Liquor *Harlem Square Bar* Opposite the T*hree Ships Restaurant.* • *Juice Sports Bar* Past the graveyard on the waterfront.

Medical *Clinic*, 242-331-2105, open 9 a.m. to 5:30 p.m. weekdays, with two nurses and a doctor. Delivery room, 3-bed male and female wards, an x-ray machine, morgue and their own ambulance. A dentist comes to the island every two months.

Museum *The Columbus Museum* with Columbian and Lucayan artifacts.

Pharmacy *J's Pharmacy*, 242-331-2750, well-stocked with over-the-counter medications. Open 9 a.m. to 5 p.m. Monday and Tuesday, 9 a.m. to 8 p.m. Wednesday through Saturday, with two rental efficiencies above. The clinic also has a small dispensary.

Police 242-331-2010.

Propane Available from *Shell* in Cockburn Town.

Provisions *Dorette's Food Store* Open 8 a.m. to 7 p.m., Monday through Saturday. Closed Sunday • *Jake Jones Food Store*, 242-331-2688, open 7 a.m. to 5 p.m., closed Sundays. Well-stocked with frozen foods and meats, and fresh produce when the mail boat comes in. • *Island Distributors One Stop Shop*, 242-331-2331 on the waterfront, opposite the *Straw Market.*

Restaurants & Bars *Club Med Columbus Isle* • 242-331-2000 • Day pass costs $64 and includes lunch. Call ahead for dinner reservations, $79 per person, all drinks and entertainment included. *Riding Rock Inn Restaurant and Driftwood Bar* • 242-272-1492 • Bar open from 11 a.m. daily, beside the waterfront dining room at the hotel. Breakfast from 7:30 a.m. to 9 a.m.; lunch from 12:30 to 2 p.m. includes soup, homemade bread, entree, dessert and coffee or tea for $15 plus service. Dinner, from 6:30 to 8:30 p.m., includes a glass of wine, soup, salad, entree, homemade Bahamian bread, dessert and coffee or tea for $30. Complimentary Rum Punch and Conch Fritters in the bar on Monday and Saturday. *The Three Ships Restaurant and Bar* • 242-331-2787 • Faith still cooks a good Bahamian lunch and dinner on request.

Taxis At *Riding Rock Inn* and the airport. VHF 06.

A great view of the bay of Little San Salvador Island. Tourists enjoy the great weather and beautiful beach. ©IstockPhoto/jrtb

Telephones *BTC*, 242-331-2571. Open 9 a.m. to 4:30 p.m. weekdays. Phone cards for sale • Telephones at the dock, *Riding Rock Marina.*

Tour Guide *Fernander Tours* • 242-331-2676 or 242-427-8198 • Clifford Fernander will take you round this 63-square-mile island, with some wonderfully remote areas, deserted beaches, inland lakes and fascinating history. Ask him about bush medicine; much of it is still in use today.

VHF Radio The whole island monitors VHF 6.

RENTALS

Bicycles *Riding Rock* • 242-331-2631/2638 • $10 a day.

Cars *C and S Car Rentals* • 242-331-2631/2714 • At *Riding Rock Inn*. $85 a day.

Scooters *K's Scooters* • 242-331-2125/2651 • At the airport. Visa, MasterCard and AMEX.

SPORTS

Dive Sites There are 40 white mooring buoys off San Salvador, some with the site name on them. Dinghies and boats under 30 feet are welcome to pick one up if they are not being used by the dive operators. Snapshot Reef, at 20 feet, is good for snorkelers. The walls are fantastic, starting at 35 feet and dropping down to 200 feet, in waters with 100- to 200-foot visibility year-round. Hammerhead sharks are a frequent winter sight. Wild dolphins, turtles even a grouper or two might socialize with you. This is truly world-class diving. Check with *Riding Rock Marina*.

Diving *Club Med Divers* • 242-331-2000 • Daily dive trips, using their catamaran dive boat. *Riding Rock Divers* • 242-331-2631/2922.

Fishing *Island Venture Fishing Trips*, 242-331-2306.

THINGS TO DO IN SAN SALVADOR

- Walk the Long Bay beach where Columbus and his sailors are believed to have landed in their longboat more than five centuries ago. You can swim and snorkel, and there is a monument placed on the floor of the ocean in Long Bay marking the exact spot where it is believed Columbus dropped anchor on October 12, 1492. Or photograph the simple white Columbus Cross, the Japanese memorial and the Mexican Olympic Monument only three miles out of Cockburn Town.
- Visit Watling's Castle, the ruins of an eighteenth-century Loyalist plantation and the lookout tower at Sandy Point Estate, built to spot any unfortunate ship that ran aground on the reefs below.
- Farther north, the Chicago Herald Monument poses the question as to how Columbus could possibly have anchored off in the maze of reefs there and planted his cross in honor of Spain?
- Visit the famous lighthouse at Dixon Hill. This is one of only three remaining lighthouses in the world that are hand wound by the lighthouse keepers every two hours during the night, using a vapour burner and unique Fresnel "bull's eyes" lenses, which concentrate the light so that it is visible for 19 miles. There are stunning views, and it is well worth climbing the 81 steps to the top if only to learn how the lighthouse works. Why not leave a small donation for the Bahamas Lighthouse Preservation Society while you are there to help maintain this historic landmark and the similar lighthouses at Hope Town, on Elbow Cay in Abaco and farther south on Great Inagua?
- Dive, dive and dive again!

Chapter 17
Long Island

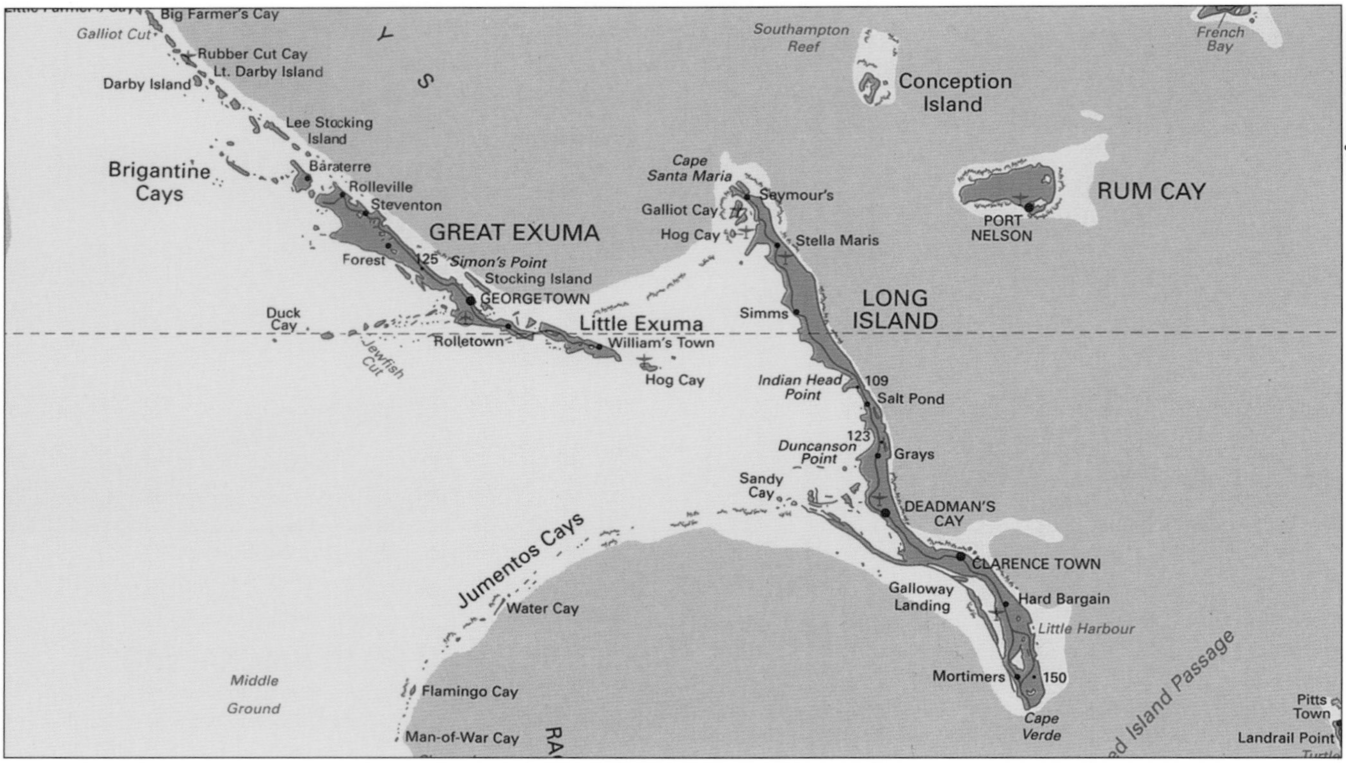

Not to be used for navigation.

Looking At the Charts

At nearly 80 nautical miles north to south, Long Island is aptly named. Its narrow geography, rarely more than four nautical miles in width, seems to accentuate its length. Rather like some stretches of interstate highways across Wyoming or Nebraska, Long Island seems to go on forever, even more so if you are on passage south (or north), when its eastern coastline drags on interminably. If your first sight of Long Island is from the Atlantic side, take heart, the good beaches are coming! Up north, Cape Santa Maria presents stunning white cliffs with a "to-die-for" beach tucked on the eastern corner. Once around Cape Santa Maria, Calabash Bay is dream-world material. In addition, if you are a diver, the diving offered by Stella Maris is legendary. If your boat needs work, the facilities and skills of Stella Maris Marina are ranked highly. The northwestern side is bonefishing territory, and the bonefishing on the western flats is unequalled. Moving farther south, there are pretty beaches and secluded coves with historical sites to hike to, caves to explore and blue holes at which to marvel. Often there are hike-able roads leading to the Atlantic Ocean side with fantastic shelling, snorkeling and reef diving or spear fishing.

If you are making your way from the south, the east coast is rocky, steep and weather beaten. It is best held at a wide berth, well-offshore. Fortunately, there are two places of refuge, Clarence Town, a safe haven, and Little Harbour. Just as it sounds, it is a little harbor. Navigation around the northern tip of Long Island, Cape Santa Maria, requires some caution. Cruisers returning north or heading south to the Caribbean are almost certainly going to make Clarence Town a port-of-call. At the northern and the southern ends of the island, vessels can play east and west coast options to their advantage. However, if you need to find real protection, the west coast is a no-go for the long-haul passage-maker. Most readers of this Guide will be crossing to Long Island from George Town's eastern cut.

Long Island's northernmost point is Cape Santa Maria. It is a mere 22 miles northeast from North Channel Rocks. Unless you are heading directly to Conception Island, there is no reason to aim for Cape Santa Maria. Some cruisers choose to first go south to Thompson Bay and work their way north along Long Island's coast. The trip from North Channel Rocks to Indian Hole Point is about 30 miles. Folks who plan to cruise south along Long Island aim for Cape Reef or Joes Sound. If you start at Cape Reef, there is good trolling and free-diving off the coral reefs all the way to Joes Sound. The first anchorages are close to the shoreline off Galliot Cay in Calabash Bay and south of Rocky Point. From there, cruisers move to the anchorages off Hog Cay or up Joes Sound to explore the blue holes, mangroves and shallow waters. From Hog Cay, it is about a six-mile dinghy ride to Stella Maris Marina and a short walk to a coin laundry, bank, liquor store and the Stella Maris Resort's excellent restaurant.

The next anchorages south are off Simms. Holding can be tough here, so check your anchor. There are some stores in Simms with produce and food basics. The Alligator Bay Marina you see on charts has never realized its dream. There is a beautiful, one boat anchorage, flanked by a high bluff and sugar-sand beach, just before the Dilda Rocks. A bigger, crescent shaped beach offers good anchorages for several boats in between the Dilda and Whale Head. There is a pretty beach off Millers Bay, but if you anchor there, respect the guests of the resort whose cabins line the sand. You will find good holding in the waters in front of McKanns and some supplies in town there, too. Not far from McKanns, Salt Pond settlement is working hard, like Rock Sound, to be the next "George Town." And, the friendly merchants and wonderful resort, The Long Island Breeze, are doing a good job of it! Like George Town, Salt Pond hosts an annual regatta, caters to the cruisers every need (including showers) and offers funky to lovely accommodations and restaurants. The walk to the Atlantic Ocean and fabulous coral reefs is just up and over the hill from Long Island Breeze. Unless you make the trip to anchor off Pratts Hill, Salt Pond is probably as far as you will venture on the west coast of Long Island by big boat. South of Upper and Lower Channel Cays is dinghy territory.

Long Island is a little greener than some of the other islands you have been to. Its gentle, self-reliant people depend on agriculture not only as sustenance, but also as a major export to the rest of the Bahamas. Their environment is better tended out of necessity and good stewardship. Their friendliness (everyone will wave at you as you hike along Queen's Highway) is something, even in the generally jovial Bahamas, that you will not have encountered elsewhere. Long Island has always done well, primarily through agriculture, but lately there is a new feeling of optimism here. Power lines, telephone services and tax breaks for new construction are producing not a boom, but a well-planned growth spurt—a managed renaissance.

In Long Island, the popularity of bonefishing has encouraged new growth of small inns and kitchenette accommodations, small restaurants, car and van rentals, and fishing guides. Those who discover Long Island express surprise and delight at the tranquility, peacefulness and honest "Golden Rule" life of Long Island communities, where doors are left unlocked, keys are left in trucks, and neighbors take care of neighbors.

Like visiting any large Bahamian island with a good road system and many settlements, you will want to rent a car or van for a road trip. The settlements on Long Island, each named for a one-time plantation-owning family, are spread out along the Queen's Highway, each with a unique story and special something for you to discover. You will find cabbage, citrus fruit, mango, pineapple and tomato "pothole farms" in many of the communities. The churches all along the way are stunning, usually white with proud red or blue shutters, ranging from the wayside chapel to full parish church fit for a major wedding. Each one is special and the pride of the community. Photos of the churches, with the dramatic turquoise sky and cotton candy clouds behind their edifices, make stunning souvenirs of your trip. Don't miss the two Father Jerome churches in Clarence Town.

In the Spotlight. Thompson Bay and Salt Pond

Thompson Bay/Salt Pond is the best-known anchorage on the west coast of Long Island. The clutch of small cays off the settlement offer some shelter if the wind works to the west. Cruising boats usually migrate from one side to another, playing the shelter to advantage, although most huddle as close as they can to Long Island Breeze. Salt Pond is homeport to a sizeable fishing fleet that anchors off Evas Cay. They aren't troubled by the influx of cruising boats into their anchoring area. Just north of the Salt Pond bight, Indian Hole Point runs virtually east to west out into the bank forming Thompson Bay. The choice of anchoring either side of the headland offers protection from either the southwest or northeast. Many cruisers prefer to anchor here. Nearby, The Parrots of the Caribbean at The Bahamian Village offers pretty beach cottages and an outdoor bar that serves tasty conch salad. Morning joggers and yoga enthusiasts land their dinghies east of Parrots on the beach just west of the McKies Jetty. You can jog the entire dirt road to Indian Hole Point. Bring your yoga mat to the cruisers "yacht club." For an interesting side trip, follow the signs and markers to an old fresh-water well. The "yacht club" is also the site of evening Sundowner get-togethers. Don't wait for an invitation. Just grab something to share, and enjoy the camaraderie. Folks going to the Anglican Church services tie up to the abandoned McKies Jettey walls to keep their feet dry. Please don't leave

Beach view of the Bahamas. Photo courtesy of Robert Wilson.

your trash at the corner of the dirt road and Queen's Highway (there is a sign there telling you so). There are trash dumpsters at the Government dock where you can deposit all the trash you want to for no charge.

Salt Pond is enjoying its increase in cruising visitors and working to fulfill their needs. Long Island Breeze Marina and Resort is the "in" spot for cruisers. The Breeze offers a daily Cruisers Net in the mornings, free wireless Internet and a dinghy dock. There are showers and a tidy coin laundry downstairs. Upstairs you will find all the action. The bar and restaurant serve tasty i'land-style drinks and cuisine. You can even sip your soda in their swimming pool, and sunbathe on their deck. Special events, dances and live bands are announced on the Cruisers Net. Bahamasair has daily flights from Nassau, so getting crew and guests to Long Island is easy. Your guests will love the pretty accommodations at The Breeze, too. There, settlement's grocery stores are just steps away from The Breeze's dinghy dock. You will find fresh frozen seafood at Atlantic Fisheries, up the hill on the way to the Post Office. Or, go spear your own off the shallow coral reefs that line the Atlantic coast, just a short walk away. If you would like to venture out farther into the Atlantic with professionals, Reel Divers provides diving lessons, tours, equipment and air-fills.

For snowbirds who want to stay awhile, there is fuel, propane and water at the Long Island Petroleum ESSO fuel dock, approachable at high water, but easily jerry-canned back to the boat. There is an excellent marine store farther up the road. The grocery stores are well-stocked and staffed by friendly, knowledgeable folks. If a marina slip is important to you, you will want to move on (or at least wait until Long Island Breeze gets theirs completed). But, for scores of cruisers who enjoy small settlement life on the hook, in safe, uncrowded anchorages with pretty beaches nearby and warm, welcoming onshore residents, this is the place!

In the Spotlight. Clarence Town

Clarence Town has long had the reputation of being one of the best-kept settlements in the Bahamas, as well as the site of two Father Jerome churches—each as interesting and as different as his Cat Island Mount Alvernia Hermitage. Clarence Town itself sits on a spectacular site with twin hills and limestone ridges fronting an Atlantic Ocean harbor dotted with cays and rocks. Clarence Town is blessed with great location, close to the halfway mark on Long Island's Atlantic Ocean coast.

The Clarence Town anchorage is in between Strachan Cay and and Salt Pond Cay (watch out for the cable!). At best, it offers scant shelter from winds and surge. Even southeast weather will bring surge into the anchorage. Remember that you are on the Atlantic coast, and even distant Atlantic storms can bring heavy ground swell a day or two later into Clarence Town Harbour, with rollers carrying right through the anchorage onto the beach. The other charted anchorages require navigation around coral heads and shallow waters with shifting sand bars. Expect getting to them and surge to be problematic.

Saints Peter and Paul Church, Clarence Town.
WATERWAY GUIDE PHOTOGRAPHY.

With this in mind, Flying Fish Marina, tucked behind Harbour Point with its own breakwater, should look immensely appealing. The approach to the marina is straightforward. Make the normal entry run into Clarence Town Harbour, then dog-leg into the marina. Flying Fish Marina offers good dockage shielded by a wonderful breakwater with many services and amenities.

Near the marina, Rowdy Boys Bar & Grill offers accommodations and a fun spot for cruisers to congregate. If you walk to the government dock or take your dinghy there, you will find the Harbour View Restaurant nearby. In the settlement, you will enjoy a bakery, grocery stores, a medical clinic, fresh produce, prescription service, a BTC and, of course, the two Father Jerome churches with twin spires. They dominate the settlement much as medieval cathedrals do in Europe. The Anglican Church, St. Paul's, is older, somewhat ornate and certainly shows the kind of adornment more normally associated with cathedrals. The Roman Catholic Church, St. Peter and Paul's, is newer, built when Father Jerome returned to the islands after converting to Catholicism. It has round towers, white paint and blue windows. It looks like it was transplanted from the Greek Cycladic Islands. Inside it is monastically plain and quite unadorned.

Clearing In—Your Options on Long Island

Stella Maris Airport has the only Customs and Immigration office on Long Island. Both marinas can arrange for officials to clear you in at your slip, but Flying Fish Marina needs at least 24-hours notice.

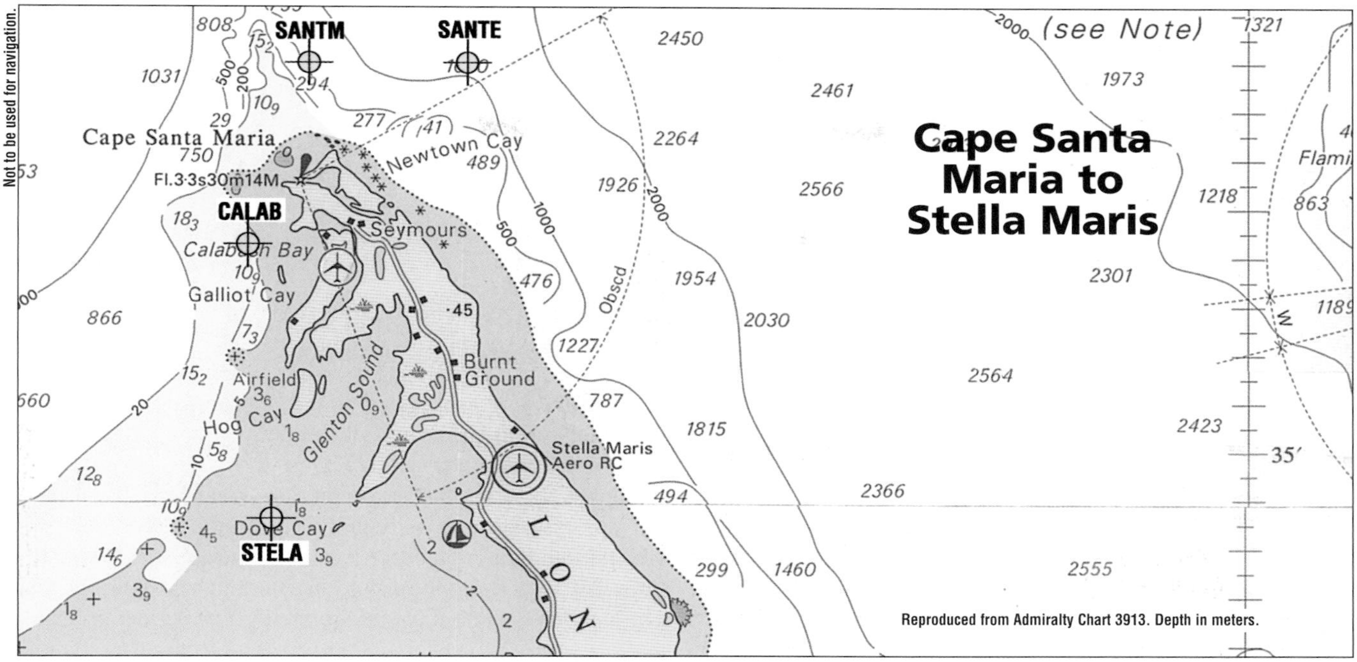

What's There? Long Island

The North of Long Island. Cape Santa Maria

The northern point of Long Island, Cape Santa Maria, is dangerous. Reefs surround the cape and run out for a mile north of it, and a bank with barely 15 meters/50 feet of water extends an additional two miles offshore. As the surrounding ocean has depths averaging 1,800 meters/6,000 feet, you can understand that breaking seas can develop around this cape even under conditions of moderate swell. For this reason, the Cape Santa Maria waypoint is 1.5 nautical miles north of the reefs, close to the northern limit of this bank. In bad weather, we would add another mile north to this, and for a night passage, for prudence, an additional mile.

If you are turning south down the east coast of Long Island, it is practical to take the Cape Santa Maria East waypoint as your turning point. This will give you a two-nautical-mile cushion at the outset as you run down the Long Island coastline. Your actual course depends on your destination. If you are coming up from the south and heading for George Town or the shelter of

Cape Santa Maria. Waterway Gudie Photography.

Calabash Bay, the natural temptation to round the cape within a mile or so is hard to resist, but don't do it. Stand well out. The Cape Santa Maria East waypoint is a good one to use to keep well off the reefs and the Santa Maria shoal.

Cape Santa Maria itself is easily recognizable (it is, after all, the only land in sight), and the light stands on the top of a prominent white cliff. It is around this cape, if you are outward bound, that you will meet ocean swells and waves for the first time. You will also experience a strong set to the northwest, particularly if you are heading for Conception Island or Rum Cay, and your cross track error can build up rapidly unless you consider this early in the passage.

Cape Santa Maria and the Columbus Monument

To find the Columbus Monument, drive along Queen's Highway until you reach the hilltop settlement of Seymours. Look for the sign, "Columbus Monument," and turn there. It is a rough track, only for trucks with four-wheel drive. If you have rented a car, walk. The Columbus Monument, built in 1989, is high and in front of you along with the Cape Santa Maria Light. Walk the lagoon beach around to your right to get a better view of the cliff and the memorial before you climb up there.

The memorial's inscription is worn away. It dedicated the site to Columbus and offered a belated apology to the indigenous people of Long Island for killing them all within fifty years of their first contact with the European world. Since there is much dispute about where Columbus actually first landed, the dedication seems a little unnecessary, and the apology a moot point. If the entire thing seems too contrived, that beach we first mentioned is a great swimming and picnic spot, and well worth the drive.

If you want to continue to the north end of the Queen's Highway, you will find the road ends at the eastern mouth of a lagoon, a narrow neck of mangrove swamp crossed by a small footbridge. This is it by vehicle. If you walk on, there will be an apparent harbor on the Atlantic side, partially protected. It is called Columbus Harbour. Despite the appeal of its name, it is too open to prevailing winds and ocean fetch to offer any utility to the visiting cruiser.

Calabash Bay

Calabash Bay is about two nautical miles southwest of Cape Santa Maria. It is an attractive, temporary haven from prevailing winds, but has to be entered through fringing reefs. The entry passage is not difficult, but requires care and attention. The Calabash Bay waypoint serves as a midpoint between two alternative close approaches into the bay. Once through the reef, you can anchor where it looks good, but don't crowd other boats that are anchored there. There are good depths, with 4.5-meter/15-foot depths going down to 2.7-meter/9-foot depths as you move in toward the beach. By the lighthouse (to port as you as approach the beach), a high water channel leads into Seymours Lagoon, where there is both all-round protection and deep water if you want a secure anchorage, but it is not a place for staying on board. Slightly farther south, following much the same "feel-your-way-in" technique, you can find some good places to tuck yourself up close to Hog Cay.

Cape Santa Maria Beach Resort

The Canadian-built and operated Cape Santa Maria Beach Resort (on Galliot Cay at Calabash Bay) welcomes cruisers anchored in Calabash Bay to enjoy meals there, frequent the bar and use the lobby telephones. Their guest services—fishing and diving trips, dive tank refills, rental cars and accommodations—are available. If you were considering crew changes, the resort has a 2,600-foot-long airstrip, and Stella Maris airport, with Bahamasair service, is about a half-hour down the road to the south. The resort is one small development in a remote, unspoiled area that still welcomes cruisers. We should ensure that we do not intrude on their space nor degrade their environment.

Stella Maris

The Stella Maris Marina, an adjunct of the Stella Maris Resort, lies under a protective hook of shoal water just south of Dove Cay. The resort's specialty has long been diving, and in a sense, the marina is both the child of this specialization and a vital support facility for it. They have a compressor there, but more importantly, a marine railway haul-out that can take boats up to 22.5 to 24 meters/75 to 80 feet in length and a beam of 7 meters/23.5 feet (which counts for most catamarans). Above this, their boat shops carry out virtually any task, and replacement parts can be ordered and flown in to Stella Maris from Florida within 48 hours. The entry channel, which is marked, carries 1.5-meter/5-foot depths at mean low water. The marina itself has dockside depths of

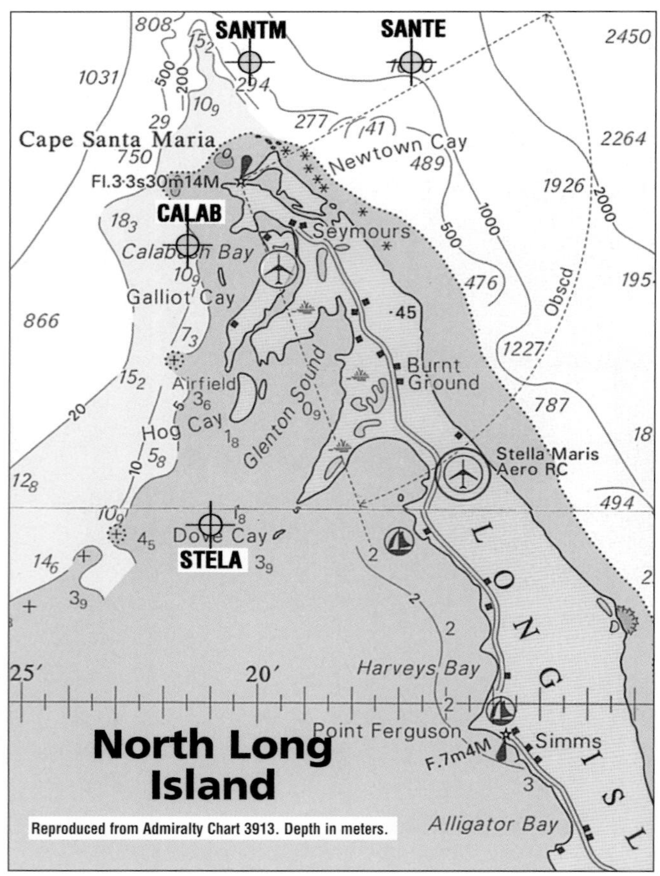

North Long Island

Reproduced from Admiralty Chart 3913. Depth in meters.

Not to be used for navigation.

Long Island

NORTH LONG ISLAND	Phone	Largest Vessel Accommodated	VHF Channel Monitored	Transient Berths / Total Berths	Approach / Dockside Depth (reported)	Floating Docks	Gas / Diesel	Groceries, Ice, Marine Supplies, Snacks	Repairs: Hull, Engine, Propeller	Lift (tonnage), Crane, Rail	1=110V, 2=220V, B=Both, Max Amps	Laundry, Pool, Showers	Pump-Out Station	Nearby: Grocery Store, Motel, Restaurant
		Dockage					**Supplies**		**Services**					
1. Stella Maris Marina & Resort Club (WiFi)	242-338-2051	100	16	/12	4/8		GD		HE		B/50	LPS		MR

Corresponding chart(s) not to be used for navigation. □ Internet Access (WiFi) Wireless Internet Access

1.5 meters/5 feet at mean low water. Just about everything you might require is there if you wish to make use of the Stella Maris Resort facilities—rooms, restaurant, bar, rental cars, rental scooters, activities and an airport with scheduled and charter air services. The airport has Customs and Immigrations officials and is a Port of Entry.

Simms and the Tropic of Cancer

If you are touring Long Island by road or anchoring out in front, visit Simms, a tiny settlement south of Stella Maris, for two reasons: the first is the tropic of Cancer, the N 23° 30.000' line of latitude that marks the northern limit of the sun's summer migration in the Northern Hemisphere. It passes right through there. South of that line, you are in the real Tropics, not the subtropics. The second reason for stopping in Simms is to see the administrative center of this tiny settlement. This example of design efficiency has to be seen to be believed. It is a neat quadrangle of one-story buildings: the administrator's office, the post office, the police station and the magistrate's court. And right next door? Her Majesty's Prison. The two Simms churches, one active and one ruins, are also interesting. A new government dock is to the south of Simms, by the clinic. Both are visible from offshore.

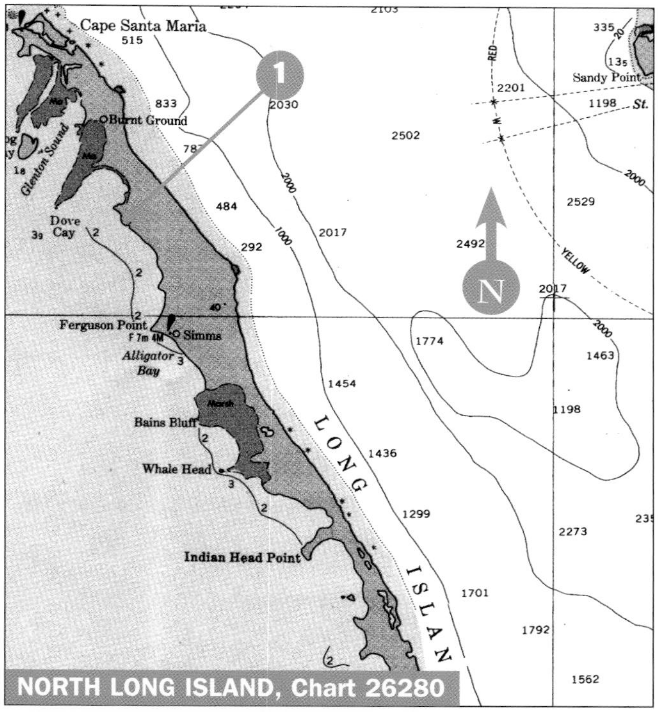

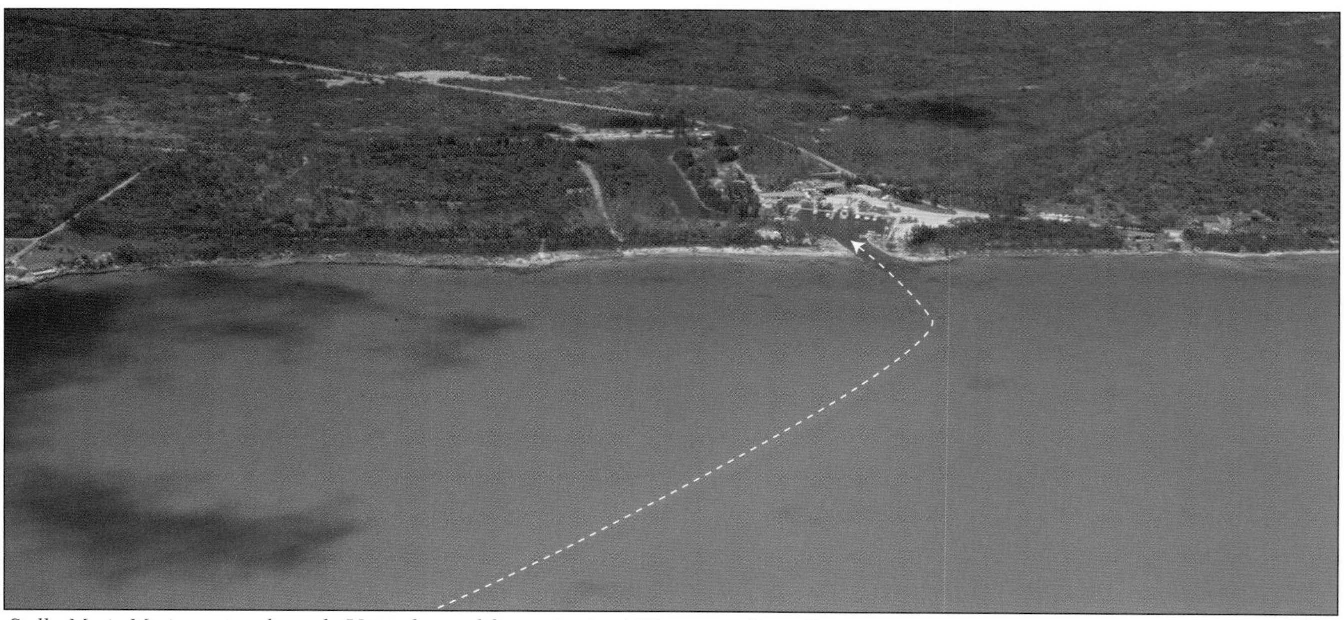

Stella Maris Marina entry channel. (Not to be used for navigation.) WATERWAY GUIDE PHOTOGRAPHY.

Thompson Bay and Salt Pond

The Thompson Bay and Salt Pond area was previously covered in the Spotlight at the beginning of this chapter. For navigation instructions, see Pilotage.

Deadmans Cay

Deadmans Cay, still mainland Long Island despite that name, is so spread out that it is hard to define its start and finish. If you want banks, Bahamasair, BTC or general provisioning, most things are there. You will need wheels or your dinghy to get there (bring your chart with you the first couple of times to find the dinghy docks). Be sure to wear good walking shoes. Take a break at the Seaside Cafe where you will find free wireless Internet, and pick up some fresh coconut bread at Ritchie's Bakery for back on the boat.

Hamiltons

On the west side of the road in Hamilton, a small sign outside a house advertises cave tours for Hamilton's Cave. Caves served as important ceremonial settings in Lucayan life. And, tours with local residents as guides are always a special treat. Don't miss this one. Need a cold one after the tour? Stop in to meet the nice proprietors of Alexis Deli or Coco's. If Ritchie's was out of bread in Deadmans, try Barbara Well's place here.

Turtle Cove

Turtle Cove, the next bight in the coast north of Clarence Town (on the east coast), is a beautiful spot for the few houses that have been lucky enough to build there. The Cove itself is shallow, virtually open to the ocean and shielded only at its southern end by a spine of rock. The photo opportunities from atop the high cliffs are endless.

Deans Blue Hole

Just south of Turtle Cove, there is a blue hole in the northern curve of rock in the cliff along the beach. At one time accessible to all by land, this blue hole was and remains a "must see." In 1992, Jim King and a team of four explored it. They discovered that the blue hole opened up into a vast 4,000-foot-deep, underwater cavern, ranking it as the largest yet discovered in the world. Today, it is the site of the AIDA Free Diving World Championships and other free diving competitions. From land, the road is barred to the blue hole unless there are scheduled events. The blue hole is at N 23° 06.360'/W 075° 00.520'.

Clarence Town

The Clarence Town area was previously covered in the Spotlight at the beginning of this chapter. For navigation instructions, see Pilotage.

Long Island South of Clarence Town

South of Clarence Town, Lochabar Bay (a blue hole) is a fantastic beach, known for the stunning water color and pinkish sand. Continuing south by road, there are several small settlements and three more Father Jerome churches. You can turn east at Roses settlement to go see Little Harbour, another photographic

Deans Blue Hole. WATERWAY GUIDE PHOTOGRAPHY.

Long Island

CLARENCE TOWN		Largest Vessel Accommodated	VHF Channel Monitored	Transient Berths / Total Berths	Approach / Dockside Depth (reported)	Floating Docks	Gas / Diesel	Groceries, Ice, Marine Supplies, Snacks	Repairs: Hull, Engine, Propeller	Lift (tonnage), Crane, Rail	1=110V, 2=220V, B=Both, Max Amps	Laundry, Pool, Showers	Pump-Out Station	Nearby: Grocery Store, Motel, Restaurant
		Dockage					Supplies		Services					
1. Flying Fish Marina (WiFi)	242-337-3430	130	16	/18	/12		GD	GIMS			B/50	LS		R

Corresponding chart(s) not to be used for navigation. Internet Access (WiFi) Wireless Internet Access

paradise. If you intend to go all the way down to Gordons, the last settlement, you will find quaint little bars and restaurants, but no gasoline. Remember your only source of gasoline is Clarence Town.

Little Harbour

About 11 nautical miles south of Clarence Town, there is the Little Harbour anchorage, good in an emergency or if daylight is not going to hold out until Clarence Town. The only usable entrance into Little Harbour is the southernmost. Favor the north side on entering, and dip due south to anchor in the deeper water, well off the beach. It shoals rapidly. To the north, anchor off the beach as far away from the coral reefs as you can get. Expect surge, and bear in mind that even if you entered Little Harbour under ideal conditions, a change of weather could keep you there for much longer than you would like.

The Keel Print of Columbus

The Long Island area south of Clarence Town holds voyaging waters of great interest. The indigenous Arawaks and Lucayans were competent interisland voyagers, and the Lucayans (according to Columbus) frequently journeyed to Crooked Island (to the southeast) and Cuba (to the southwest).

Arcing away from mid-Long Island on the western side, one finds the Jumentos Cays and the Ragged Islands, which head south toward Cuba. Nuevitas Rocks, at the start of the chain, offer a safe pass between Great Bahama Bank waters and the ocean on that side for a straight run to Cuba. On the eastern side, a chain of larger islands - Crooked, Acklins, Mayaguana and the Turks and Caicos - serve as stepping stones to and from the Dominican Republic, Puerto Rico, the Virgin Islands and the Caribbean. Columbus sailed these waters on his First "Discovery" Voyage in 1492. Did he sail to the east or the west of Long Island? The experts are certain about his route, but none agrees with each other. See our Green Pages for "The Columbus Controversy."

Pilotage. Talking Captain to Captain

The Entries to Calabash Bay

There are two approach routes through the barrier reef. The first, about 0.5 nautical miles north of the CALAB waypoint, is to round the northern headland with the old lighthouse on its inner point. Just read your way in, but don't go close to the lighthouse or the creek-like opening (Seymours

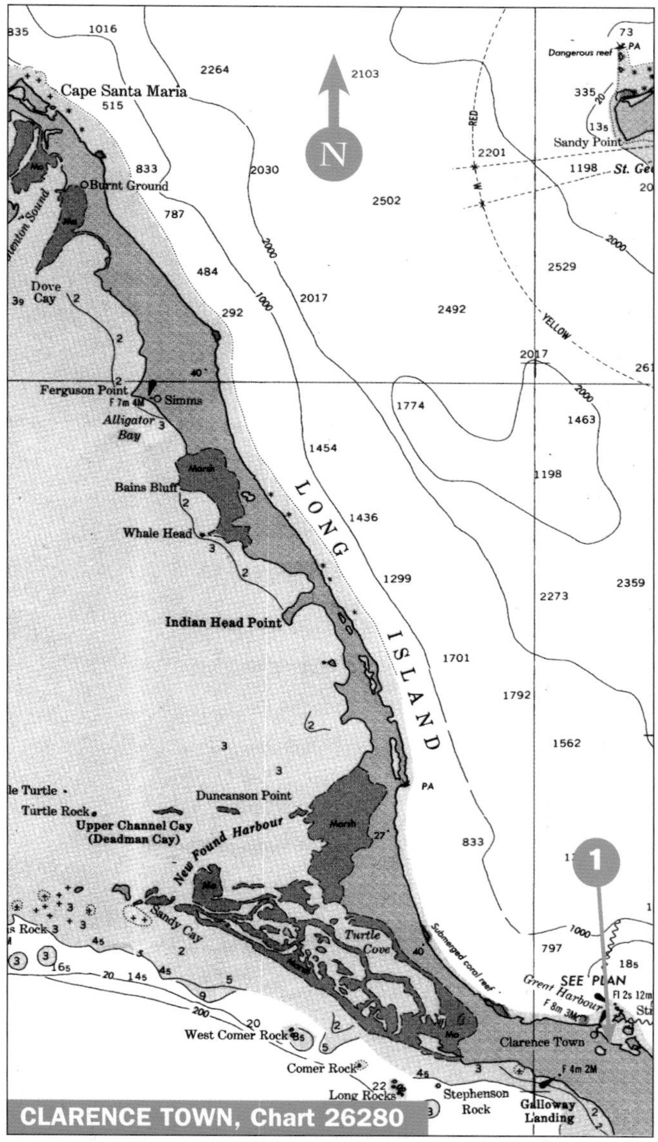

CLARENCE TOWN, Chart 26280

Little Harbour south entrance, from the east. (Not to be used for navigation.) Waterway Guide Photography.

Lagoon) that shoals to 0.6-meter/2-foot depths or less at mean low water.

The second, about 0.5 nautical miles south of the CALAB waypoint, is to pick up the house with the white roof to the south of the Cape Santa Maria Beach Resort (obvious with its club house, a mast of flags, highly colored umbrellas on a frontal terrace and its flanking cottages). Fix on the house with the white roof, and go in on a course of 090/270 degrees true. This will take you through another gap in the reef. Don't make this compass course serve as a rigid leg. Remember, this is eyeball navigation, not a straight-line guaranteed safe course.

Seymours Lagoon, Calabash Bay

The entry channel to Seymours Lagoon is barred at low water by a sandbar that runs from the lighthouse to the Cape Santa Maria Resort beach. At high water, you have perhaps 1.2-meter/4-foot depths over the bar, 3.6-meter/12-foot depths in the channel by the lighthouse and 1.2-meter/4-foot depths in the sound, increasing to 1.5- to 1.8-meter/5- to 6-foot depths farther in. These depths hold virtually all the way past the fuel dock (to starboard) up to the Cape Santa Maria Resort fishing boat docks at the far end. But, if you want to put in here, call and clear it with them first, as there is not much space. It is not an anchorage, and they operate their boats from there. We list it as a refuge, just in case you need it.

Approach to Stella Maris Marina

The STELA waypoint places you in the channel just over one nautical mile northwest of Dove Cay. Swing gently southeastward around Dove Cay. Stay in deep water (you have both Dove Cay itself and sand reaching out there), aiming to end up on the N 23° 33.000' line of latitude south of Dove Cay. Now run due east to pick up the dredged entry channel that leads in, with some three nautical miles to go from south of Dove Cay. At the end, you will turn northeastward into the marked channel to enter the marina.

Approach to Thompson Bay/Salt Pond

Cruisers who now make Salt Pond their winter destination depart from George Town through the east cut and travel the recommended route eastward from Pigeon Cay to Hog Cay for a little less than 10 nautical miles. At the Hog Cay waypoint, commonly notated in navigation programs as N 23° 25.200'/W 075° 29.500', turn east, and stay well north of the White Cay Bank for approximately eight nautical miles to the White Cay Bank waypoint (N 23° 25.000'/W 075° 21.000'). From there, sail 112 to 114 degrees true for approximately 11 nautical miles to Indian Hole Point (N 23° 20.700'/W 075° 09.600'). This is a nice sail on a safe course of less than 30 nautical miles in any wind except easterly. It also facilitates the exploration of the western shore of Long Island.

Clarence Town approach. (Not to be used for navigation.) Waterway Guide Photography.

Approaches to Clarence Town

As you approach Clarence Town from a mile out, it is almost impossible to pick up your bearings. It becomes clearer when you pass Booby Rock. Initially, head to leave Booby Rock well to port, and pick up your bearings when you draw level with Booby Rock (bearing 085 degrees true). Steer for the apparent middle of the open channel on a course of about 180/000 degrees true for about 0.5 nautical miles. Simply head for the center of this wide opening. Use caution, as there is breaking surf on your starboard bow. Favor that side if you cannot see the reef to port that runs out to the west from the north of Strachan Cay. Treat Lighthouse Point and Lark Point as the entry arms to the harbor, and stay between them. There are buoys there to guide you into the harbor. Keep an eye on the church with the twin white towers. When it is bearing 220/040 degrees true, you are clear to turn in to the Flying Fish Marina. The anchorages are ill-defined and not safe, as they lie off a northern entrance that is nearly a mile wide and peppered with reefs and coral heads. The only option is in between Strachan Cay and Salt Pond Cay, but there are anchor trapping submarine cables there.

The Clarence Town Flying Fish Marina

A 60-meter/200-foot-long breakwater protects the marina from light surge and easterly weather, but in heavy weather, you would still feel its effects. However, the docks are strongly constructed, and with well-rigged dock lines and fenders, you can lie there with confidence in all but a major storm. ■

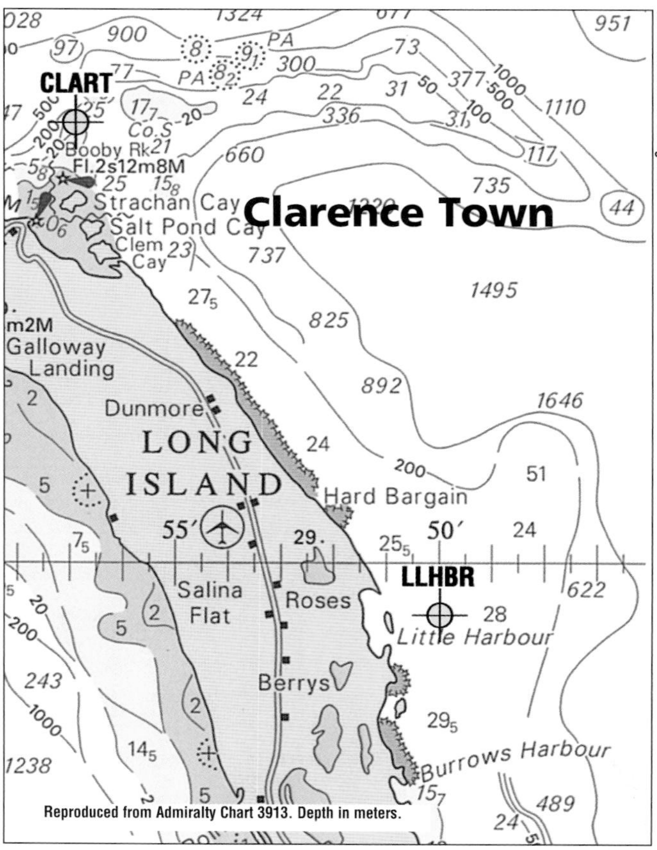

Reproduced from Admiralty Chart 3913. Depth in meters.

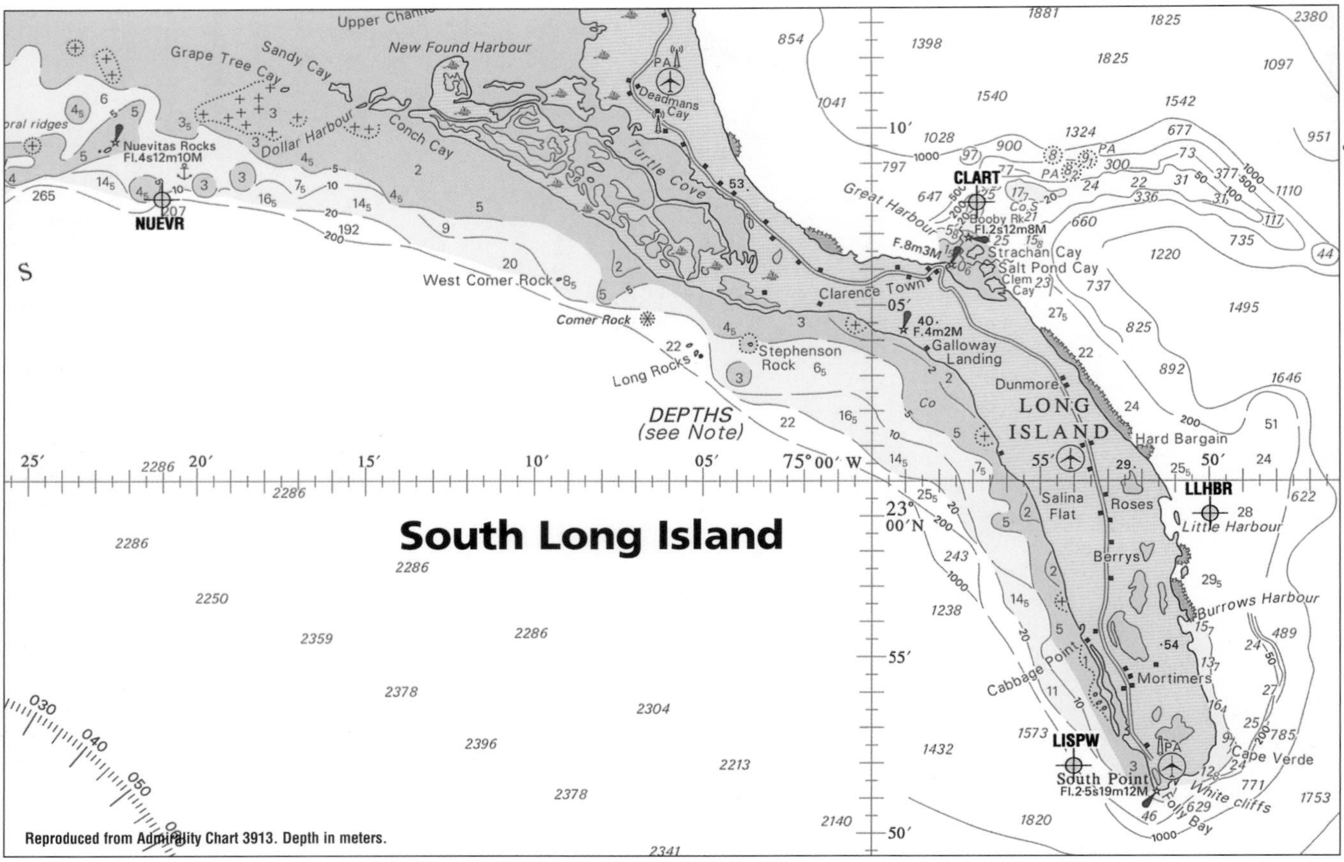

Waterway Guide advertising sponsors play a vital role in bringing you the most trusted and well-respected cruising guide in the country. Without our advertising sponsors, we simply couldn't produce the top-notch publication now resting in your hands. Next time you stop in for a peaceful night's rest, let them know where you found them—Waterway Guide, The Cruising Authority.

Long Island Waypoints

Cape Santa Maria	SANTM (L1)	23°42.50N / 75°20.50W
Cape Santa Maria East	SANTE	23°43.00N / 75°17.00W
Calabash Bay	CALAB	23°39.25N / 75°21.65W
Stella Maris	STELA	23°33.50N / 75°21.00W
Alligator Bay Marina	ALIBM	23°27.00N / 75°14.00W
Salt Pond	SALTP	23°21.00N / 75°11.00W
Clarence Town (2 nm N)	CLART (L2)	23°07.50N / 74°57.00W
Little Harbour (1 nm NE)	LLHBR	22°59.00N / 74°50.00W
Long Island South Point E	LISPE	22°51.00N / 74°45.00W
Nuevitas Rocks	NUEVR	23°08.00N / 75°21.00W
Long Island South Point W	LISPW	22°52.00N / 74°54.00W

Position format is latitude and longitude in degrees and minutes (hddd°mm.mm). Waypoints in RED are NOT for autopilot navigation. Codes in parenthesis are Wavey Line waypoints marked on the charts. If you have programmed waypoints listed in a previous edition of this guide, check carefully to ensure the coordinates you have recorded match the list. If a waypoint is no longer on the list we may have changed its code or deleted it.

GOIN' ASHORE:

NORTH LONG ISLAND CAPE SANTA MARIA, STELLA MARIS, SIMMS, MCKANN'S

airport • bank • customs & immigration • fuel • groceries • marina marine services • medical • police • post office • restaurant telephone • water

Long Island was called Yuma by the Indians and Fernandina by Columbus, who described this still largely undeveloped island as "the world's most beautiful island." It stretches for more than 80 miles, with farming communities, steep cliffs and shallow bays, and represents the best of the old, Out Island traditions with its historic churches and long-established family villages. The beaches of Cape Santa Maria at the northern tip are captivating, perfect for beachcombing and exploration. It is such a very long island that it is fun to explore by renting a car; so much of it is not readily accessible from the water. Customs and Immigrations can be called on request from Stella Maris Marina on VHF 16, switching to VHF 6, if you need to clear in here when you arrive.

The south of Long Island is rarely visited by cruising boats. The west coast waters are too shallow, and Salt Pond is as far as you can go on this side. Perhaps the Long Island Regatta held there each year will attract you? The east coast may feature in your plans if you are bound for the Turks and Caicos or the Caribbean, especially since you can stop at the Flying Fish Marina in Clarence Town. We give information for Long Island north to south.

At the far north, Cape Santa Maria with the Cape Santa Maria Beach Resort (242-338-5273, 800-663-7090, Fax: 242-338-6013, capesm@batelnet.bs, www.capesantamaria.com), is highly praised by guests who have vacationed there. The resort is welcomes those who anchor off the island and like to go for a drive, for a drink or a meal. Stella Maris Resort, with its marina, haul-out facilities and nearby airport, is of more interest to cruisers. Just about everything a boater could want is within easy walking distance or at the marina.

EMERGENCIES

Marine • VHF 16

Medical *Clinic* • 242-338-8488 • At Simms, open 9 to 5 on Mondays and Wednesdays, 9 to 12 on Thursdays, with a doctor and 3 nurses. The doctor is at Glinton/Seymours on Tuesdays and Fridays. To contact the Long Island (North End) government doctor, or in emergency, call the front desks at *Stella Maris Resort* or *Cape Santa Maria Beach Resort* on VHF 16.

MARINA

STELLA MARIS MARINA AND RESORT CLUB

Tel: 242-338-2051 • 800-426-0466 • Fax: 242-338-2052 • VHF 16

info@stellamarisresort.com • www.stellamarisresort.com

Slips 12. **Max LOA** 100 ft. **MLW** 4 to 4.5 ft. in the approach channel, 7 to 8 ft. at the docks. **Dockage** $1.20 per ft. per day. **Fuel** Dock open 7 a.m. to 5 p.m., Monday through Saturday. Diesel and gasoline. **Facilities & Services** Power $0.58 per kwHr, minimums apply. RO water is trucked to the marina, so please use accordingly. *Speed Queen* coin laundry opposite the marina open 8 a.m. to 6:30 p.m. Full-service laundry at the hotel. Public telephone dockside. Phone cards from marina office. Propane available, ask at the marina office. Complimentary WiFi at hotel. Hotel facilities open to marina guests, who are encouraged to take part in the activities and entertainment. Three swimming pools, private beaches, complimentary shuttle to beaches, bicycles, tennis courts, table tennis and volleyball, scuba diving, fishing, island tours, videos and evening entertainment. For transportation, call Stella Maris Taxi on VHF 16, going to VHF 6. Bicycle, moped and car rental. Dive instructors, rental equipment and a compressor tank for refills. Bone, bottom, reef and deep sea fishing. Marine services include boat hauling and launching on marine railway up to 100 ft. long, 6-ft. draft and 70 tons. Can handle catamarans. Full-service marine repairs including carpentry, electrical, fiberglass, painting, power plants/gearboxes. **Restaurant & Bar** At the hotel. Open for breakfast, 8 a.m. to 10 a.m.; lunch, noon to 2 p.m.; and dinner, 7 p.m. to 9 p.m. Excellent Bahamian and European cuisine, with cave parties, lunch boxes to order, Rum Punch parties on Wednesday evenings and a Saturday dance. Reservations requested. $$ **Credit Cards** Visa, MasterCard, AMEX, 4% surcharge.

PORT DIRECTORY

Accommodations Galliot Cay: *Cape Santa Maria Beach Resort,* Tel: 242-338-5273, 800-663-7090, Fax: 242-338-6013, capesm@batelnet.bs, www.capesantamaria.com.
Stella Maris: *Stella Maris Resort,* Tel: 242-338-2055, 800-426-0466, Fax: 242-338-2052, VHF 16, info@stellamarisresort.com, www.stellamarisresort.com. Thirty rooms and apartments; 24 bungalows and villas from $125 to $630 per night.
Salt Pond: *Long Island Breeze Resort at Salt Pond,* Tel: 242-338-0170, 800-763-4654, VHF 16, www.longislandbreezeresort.com. Four bedroom, 4.5 bath luxurious, two-story cottage available for rent. Restaurant, bar, swimming pool, sun deck, sandy Thompson Bay-side beach. The newest resort on Long Island with all the modern conveniences. WiFi, dinghy dock, nearby shopping and short walk to Atlantic beaches and Salt Pond. Full diving services from nearby *Reel Divers.*
Seymours: *Atlantic View Villas,* Tel: 242-338-6027.
Millers: *Chez Pierre Villas,* 242-388-8809. Restaurant, bar. Bonefishing guides, kayaks and snorkeling trips. Gorgeous crescent beach with the lounge chairs waiting for you.

Airlines *Bahamasair*, 242-377-8451 • *Pineapple Air*, 242-337-0370 • *Southern Air*, 242-377-2014 • *Air Sunshine*, 800-435-8900 (from Ft. Lauderdale).

Airport *Stella Maris Airport (SML)*, 242-338-2050/2015, 4,000 x 75 ft. paved runway, avgas, light ground services, snack bar and air charter office. • *Deadmans Cay Airport (LGI)*, 242-337-0877.

Art, Crafts & Straw Work *Knowles Straw Work,* Millerton • *Elsie's Quality Straw*, north of Simms • *Alecia Knowles Straw Work*, Simms.

Banks & ATM *ScotiaBank* • 242-338-2057, Stella Maris. Open 9:30 a.m. to 3 p.m., Monday through Thursday; to 4 p.m. Friday.

⚓ Goin' Ashore

Bait & Tackle *Bonafide Fly Shop*, Stella Maris.
Bakery *Murleen's*, McKann's.
Beauty Supplies *Four Wings Drugs,* Burnt Ground • *Nel's Unisex Beauty Salon*, Sam McKennons.
Bonefishing *Guide Eagle Eye's Bonefishing*, 242-338-7075, Burnt Ground.
Boutiques & Shopping *Cape Santa Maria Boutique*, Galliot Cay • *Stella Maris Boutique, S&M Variety Store,* Stella Maris • *Atlantic View Gifts, Barbie's Boutique,* Seymours • *Burt's Dry Goods & Straw work, Four Wings Drugs, KD Linen Store*, Burnt Ground • *Da' Culture Shoppe, Gift Box*, Glentons • *DNA Gift Shop, Shoes City*, Simms • *Oralee's Fashions*, Doctors Creek • *Charlene's Fashions*, Sam McKennons.
Car Rentals *Shaneas Car Rental,* 242-338-7020, Stella Maris • *William's Auto*, 242-338-5002, Glentons • *Wellie's Car Rental,* 242-338-7065, Glentons • *Taylor's Garage*, 242-338-7001, Burnt Ground • *Pratt's Bus Service*, Burnt Ground. • *Allie's Car Rental,* 242-338-6036, Seymour • *Adderley's Car Rental,* 242-338-8925, Millers • *Stan's Car Rental*, 242-338-8987, Millers • *Swift Car Rental,* 242-338-8533, Doctors Creek.
Customs & Immigration Tel: 242-338-2012, Stella Maris International Airport.
Fuel Diesel and Gasoline at *Stella Maris Marina* • Gasoline at *Adderley Supply,* Burnt Ground • Gasoline at *Jameson Service Station*, Simms.
Hardware *MGS*, Burnt Ground.
Internet *Stella Maris Resort Club* • *Bonafide Fly Shop*, Stella Maris.
Laundry *Speed Queen Coin Laundry*, 242-388-2016. Open 8 a.m. to 6:30 p.m. Across from Stella Maris Marina.
Liquor *The Watering Hole, Stella Maris General Food & Liquor Store.*
Police 242-338-8555.
Post Office Simms, 242-338-8423.
Provisions *Pratts Convenience Store*, Seymours • *Adderley Produce, Rose Haven Meat Mart*, Glentons • *MGS Food Store*, Burnt Ground • *Pratts Produce*, Burnt Ground • *J's Allmart*, Scrub Hill • *Rose Haven Food Fair,* Bains • *C&M Total Mart, Gardiners*, Simms • *L&H Supermarket, S&R Fruit and Vegetable Market*, Millers • *Knowles Supply*, McKanns.
Regatta *Long Island Regatta* The *Stella Maris Marina* hosts the vessels that come from George Town in late May/early June.
Restaurants *Cape Santa Maria,* Galliot Cay • *Sunset*, Seymours • *A&A* • *Alfred's* • *Ice Cream Shoppe & Restaurant,* Glentons • *Pratt's Restaurant & Bar* • *Zia's Take Away* • *Two Sisters*, Burnt Ground • *Stella Maris Resort*, Stella Maris • *Crossroads*, O'Neils • *Anita's Take-Away*, 242-338-8277 • *Blue Chip Restaurant & Bar,* Simms • *Vindell's Take-Away*, Sam McKennons • *Chez Pierre at Chez Pierre Villas*, Millers • *Club Washington*, McKanns.
Telephone and FAX *BTC*, 242-338-8044, O'Neils • 242-338-8012, Simms.
Taxis VHF 16 • *#10,* "Smithy's," 242-357-1408, Seymours • *#11*, Omar Daley, 242-357-1043, Stella Maris • *# 2*, Vernonica Knowles, 242-338-8842.
Tennis Two hard surface courts with lighting at the Stella Maris Resort.
Trash Bins and dumpsters in the settlements and at the marina.
Water Available at the marina for guests and in 5-gallon bottles at the shops and stores.
Weddings *Cape Santa Maria Beach Resort* • *Stella Maris Resort* • *Chez Pierre*, Millers.

CENTRAL AND SOUTH LONG ISLAND: THOMPSONS BAY TO DEADMANS CAY

EMERGENCIES

Marine • VHF 16
Medical *Deadmans Cay Health Centre* • 242-337-1222/1224 • At Cartwright, with a doctor and nurses. After hours, call the doctor at 242-337-0555 or the nurses at 242-337-0666.

The northern headland that creates **Thompson Bay** provides many attractive spots to drop your hook with good holding, little swell and nearly all-round wind protection. From this anchorage, it is about a 2-mile dinghy trip to Salt Pond. The area here is very popular with cruisers and fills up quickly. If you are on a smaller, lighter vessel, any winds with from a southerly quadrant can be uncomfortable. In those conditions, you will want to move to the waters off Salt Pond Cay, into the lee of Evas Cay or snuggle into Line Bay. If your depth sounder seems to suddenly malfunction in Line Bay, you have wandered over a blue hole.

Cruisers land their dinghies on the beach in front of *Parrots of the Caribbean* to enjoy drinks and conch salad at their bar and grill. Farther east, there is a cruisers "yacht club" for Sundowner drinks and potlucks. Land your dinghy on the beach to join in the fun. In the morning, after the Long Island Breeze Cruisers Net on VHF Channel 68 at 8:15 a.m., you can join the joggers who run the dirt road to Indian Hole Point or the yoga enthusiasts who line up their mats on this beach. If you walk your dog here, please be kind, and clean up after you pet. In the far eastern corner, there is an abandoned, walled mini-harbor. It is marked on charts as "McKies Jetty." You can tie your dinghy up to the walls there. It is crowded with dinghies on Sundays when cruisers attend services at the nearby Anglican Church. *Parrots of the Caribbean at the Bahamian Village* and *The Long Island Breeze* offer nearby lodging. *The Long Island Breeze* has brought fine-dining to Thompson Bay cruisers as well as showers, a modern coin laundry with four washers and dryers, a sunny deck and swimming pool and a lively nightlife scene at the bar with special events and dances.

Salt Pond has become a Snowbird's "destination" that many boaters would like to keep secret. The settlement offers all the things the snow escapists desire for a few month's stay, including the ambiance of George Town *before* 600 boats dropped their anchors in front of *Chat n' Chill Bar & Grill.* There are enough good anchorages in Thompson Bay to give each other space, to move around from time to time for a change of scenery and to escape the occasional westerly blow.

The settlement itself offers everything cruisers need. *The Long Island Breeze* has made sure of that! *Long Island Petroleum* not only has gasoline, diesel, lubricants and batteries, with 5 ft. at its dock at mean low water, but also offers water by the gallon and propane tank refills. *Harding Supply Center* is well-stocked with groceries, produce, some pharmacy, BTC phone cards, lumber, marine supplies and paint. If you can't find what you need at Harding's, try *Hillside Grocery*, too. Time your shopping excursions late in the afternoon on Wednesday's after the mailboat visits. Fresh, frozen seafood is available at *Atlantic Fisheries*. Medical clinics are nearby in Simms or Deadmans Cay—the dentist visits Salt Pond regularly. As you learn your way around, you will find mechanics, machine shops, fishing guides, diving pros, the post office, household and dry goods stores, a beauty shop with plants and flowers, a bank, car rentals and free trash disposal in dumpsters in town. There are also nice churches of many denominations.

Salt Pond hosts the famous *Long Island Sailing Regatta* complete with Junkanoo parade and rake n' scrape music contests. The regatta is held yearly over the Whitsun Holiday in late May/early June. Bake sales and other tasty fundraisers are held throughout the year to support the regatta. Do go to the fundraisers, and enjoy the good food, and try to stay for the race at least one year. You won't be sorry!

There are a few more opportunities to anchor along the western coast of Long Island south of Salt Pond, particularly in The Bight. However, you are nearing the end of the cruising grounds for all but those who need just inches to anchor. A road trip farther south is certainly worth the effort, and you will discover some truly amazing people, places and things.

PORT DIRECTORY

Accommodations Salt Pond: *The Long Island Breeze Resort,* Tel: 242-338-0170, 800-763-4654, VHF Channel 16, www.longislandbreezeresort.com. Four bedroom, 4.5 bath luxurious cottage available for rent. Restaurant open for lunch and dinner. Bar open for lunch until the party ends. Swimming pool, sunny deck, sandy beach, dinghy dock, coin laundry. Diving adventures from nearby *Reel Diving* • *Parrots of the Caribbean*, Tel: 242-338-0828, Fax: 242-338-0103, tbvl@hotmail.com, www.thebahamianvillage.com. Bayside cottages on a sandy beach. Bar & Grill under a thatched roof. Internet connection and shuttle to area attractions and restaurants • *Reel Divers,* Tel: 242-338-0011, Reeldivers@aol.com, www.reeldivers.com. Bayfront rental units on a beautiful sandy beach. Full diving services. A diver's dream • *Sea Shells Apartments*, 242-338-0103, short and long-term rentals for Snowbirds. **Millers**: *Chez Pierre Villas,* 242-388-8809. Restaurant, bar. Bonefishing guides, kayaks and snorkeling trips. Gorgeous crescent beach with the lounge chairs waiting for you.

The Bight: *Midway Inn, 242-337-7345.*

Airlines *Bahamasair*, 242-377-8451 • *Pineapple Air*, 242-337-0370 • *Southern Air*, 242-377-2014 • *Air Sunshine*, 800-435-8900 (from Ft. Lauderdale).

Airports *Stella Maris International Airport (SML)*, 242-338-2050/2015. 4,000 x 75ft. Paved runway, avgas, light ground services, snack bar, air charter office • *Deadmans Cay Airport (LGI)*, 242-337-0877.

Art, Crafts & Straw Work *Sea Babies,* straw work and shells at Thompson Bay Inn (ask locals if it is still open; proprietorship has changed here) • *Fox Hill Gift Shop*, up the hill by the Post Office in Salt Pond.

Banks & ATM *ScotiaBank*, 242-338-2057, Stella Maris. Open 9:30 a.m. to 3 p.m., Monday through Thursday; to 4 p.m. Friday • *Royal Bank of Canada* at Grays Settlement, 242-337-0100. Open Tuesday, 9:30 a.m. to 3 p.m. and Friday, 9:30 a.m. to 4:30 p.m. (may be open more days seasonally. Ask Michael, Jackie or John at *The Long Island Breeze* for current information).

Bakery *Murleen's*, McKann's • Look for fresh baked goods to show up on the cash register counters at *Harding's Supply* and *Hillside Grocery*, especially on mailboat day.

Beauty Supplies *Marcie's Beauty Spot,* Salt Pond.

Bonefishing Guide *Eagle Eye's Bonefishing*, 242-338-7075, Burnt Ground.

Boutiques & Shopping *Fox Gift Shop,* Salt Pond • *Moree's Supply,* The Bight • *Archie's Supply, Bonnie's Dry Goods,* Grays.

Car Rentals *Seaside Car Rental,* 242-338-0041, *Fox Auto,* 242-338-0042, Salt Pond.

Canvas Work *Reel Divers,* 242-338-0011, Salt Pond.

Churches *St. Joseph's Anglican Church*, *Assembly of God*, Salt Pond • *St. Mary's Church*, built by the Spanish in the 17th century, oldest church on Long Island, The Bight.

Customs & Immigration Tel: 242-338-2012, Stella Maris International Airport.

Diving *Reel Divers*, 242-338-0011, reeldivers@aol.com, www.reeldivers.com. Full diving services, sales, rentals, repairs, tours, lessons and air-fills, Salt Pond.

Fuel ESSO diesel and gasoline and water at *Long Island Petroleum,* Salt Pond.

Hardware *Harding's Supply Center,* Salt Pond • *Archies Supply*, Grays.

Internet *Long Island Breeze Resort,* free WiFi, Salt Pond.

Kayak Rentals *Reel Divers,* Salt Pond.

Laundry *Long Island Breeze Resort,* $4 wash or dry, tokens at bar upstairs, Salt Pond.

Lumber *Harding's Supply Center,* Salt Pond.

Liquor *The Watering Hole* • *Stella Maris General Food & Liquor Store* • *Long Island Breeze.*

Machine Shop, Welding & Metal Fabrication *Reel Divers*, Salt Pond.

Pharmacy *D'Island Drug Store,* McKanns.

Post Office Up the hill near *Hillside Grocery*, Salt Pond.

Provisions *Hardings Supply Center*, *Hillside Grocery*, *Atlantic Fisheries*, Salt Pond • *Midway Mini-Market,* The Bight.

Propane *Long Island Petroleum*, Salt Pond.

Regatta *Long Island Regatta*, in late May/early June, *Regatta Park* festivities next to *Long Island Petroleum*, Salt Pond.

Restaurants *Long Island Breeze Resort, Restaurant & Bar, Parrots of the Caribbean,* Salt Pond • *Midway Inn Restaurant & Bar,* The Bight.

Telephone *Harding's* sells BTC phone cards. Card phones around the settlement.

Trash Dumpster at the Government Dock.

Water *Long Island Petroleum* at the dock and available in 5-gallon bottles at the shops and stores.

Weddings *Long Island Breeze Resort.* Photographer: *Eyes of Love,* Grays.

Deadmans Cay is the largest town on Long Island with shops, schools, churches and the big clinic for the island (242-337-1222). On the way to Deadmans, you can stop in **Grays** at the *Royal Bank of Canada* (242-337-1044) open 9 a.m. to 3 p.m., Monday through Thursday, to 4:30 p.m. on Fridays, 24/7 ATM. At the Deadmans Cay Airport, *Bahamasair* flies daily to Nassau (242-337-0877). Other airlines that service the airport are *Pineapple Air* (242-337-0411) and *Southern Air* (242-337-1722). You can get a bite to eat at *Sierra's Club Airport Restaurant*. The best Bahamian food on the island is at *Max's Conch Bar* ($) alongside the road just south of the turn for the airport with the line of flags outside. If you are having laptop troubles, *Fox Tech Computer Sales and Service* can help you out. You can rent a car through *Mr. T* (242-337-1054) at the airport or *Ophelia's Rent-a-Car* (242-337-1042). *J.B. Caroll*'s has snacks, soft drinks, groceries and some household items. *Deadmans Cay Supermarket* stocks some clothing, as well as groceries and cleaning supplies. Don't forget to pick up some fresh bread at *Ritchie's Bakery* before you return to the boat.

Gathering Spot. Photo Courtesy of Peter Mitchell.

Be sure to stop at **Buckleys** to visit the *Long Island Museum* (242-337-0500). Open from 9 a.m. to 5 p.m., Monday through Friday, it is well worth the contribution to the museum to see their collection of beautiful straw and shell work, and to learn more about the traditions and heritage of this unique island. The gift shop is stocked with "i'*land tings*." In season, you will get a real treat—fresh, local pineapple. If you want to stay awhile, try the *Atlantic Hideaway Inn* (242-337-1055), or just enjoy their restaurant or *The Dew Drop Inn* for lunch or dinner. *ScotiaBank* is in **Buckleys** (242-337-1029). It is open 9:30 a.m. to 3 p.m., Monday through Thursday, 9:30 a.m. to 4:30 p.m. Fridays with a 24/7 ATM. A bit farther south, you can get a meal at *Cartwright's Snack Bar*, the *Hot Spot Restaurant* or the *Greenwich Creek Lodge* in **Cartwrights.** Look for unique souvenirs and gifts in the towns and settlements you pass from here on down to Deadmans Cay. Need more cash? *Royal Bank of Canada* has a branch in Cartwrights (242-337-0001) open 9:30 a.m. to 3 p.m. Tuesday, 9:30 a.m. to 4:30 p.m. Friday with a 24/7 ATM. These are the last banks as you make your way south until you reach Great Inagua or Providenciales.

At **Mangrove Bush**, *Under the Sea Marine Supplies* and *Chamcem Boat Building* (242-337-0199, Fax: 242-337-0341) are run by Francis & Cathy Darville. Open 7:30 a.m. to 6 p.m., Monday through Saturday. They provide Yamaha sales and service, general marine supplies, diving equipment and boatbuilding. If you need sail repairs, contact sailmaker, Mark Knowles. If you are looking for everything under the sun, try *It's All Under The Sun* department store and deli.

Legend has it that the Arawak Indians once inhabited the Hamilton caves north of Clarence Town, which were more recently used to mine bat guano for fertilizer. An authenticated Arawak chair from here resides in a Minnesota museum, thanks to a traveling clergyman who took it back to his home town. All of this you will learn if you take the hour-long cave tour with Leonard Cartwright. You can call him on VHF 16 "Cave Man," or stop by his house in Hamilton, which has a sign Cave Tours outside. In Hamilton, *Long Island Wholesale Groceries* (242-337-0249) is a very well-stocked and friendly store. For marine supplies, visit Violet Cartwright at *Fisherman's Marine Center* (242-337-6226, Fax: 242-337-6234, VHF 16, fmc@batelnet.bs), an Evinrude/Johnson parts and service center, as well as a source for diving equipment, Racor filters, fiberglass repair supplies, anchors and chains and anything else a boater may need. This ever-expanding marine store is open 7 a.m. to 6 p.m., Monday through Saturday.

CLARENCE TOWN

customs & immigration • fuel • groceries • marina • marine services • medical • police • post office • propane • restaurant • telephone • water

On the east coast, Clarence Town is famous for its two skyline churches designed by Father Jerome. If you have visited Cat Island, his name will be familiar to you. Father Jerome was a priest, trained as an architect at the end of the last century, who became a missionary. In 1908, he arrived in the Bahamas to rebuild the local, wooden churches that could not withstand hurricane winds and reconstructed them in stone. Here in Clarence Town, you find two examples of his work, one Anglican and the other Roman Catholic.

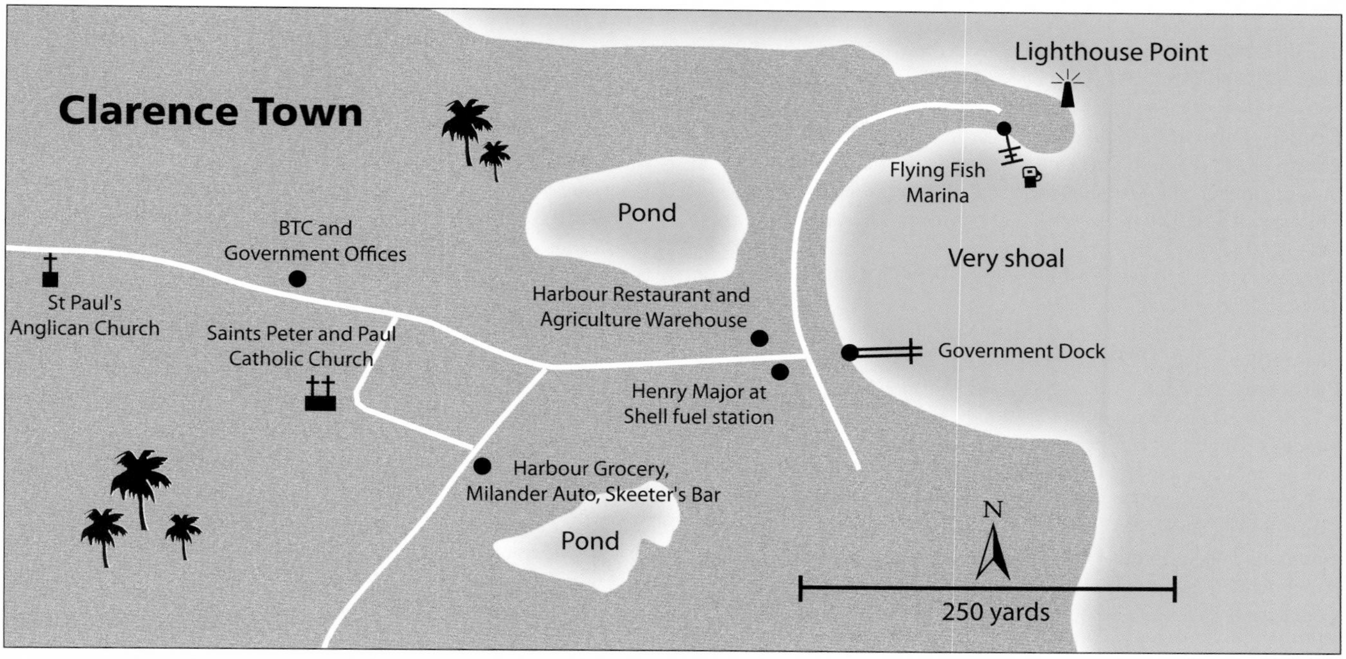

MARINA

FLYING FISH MARINA
Tel: 242-337-3430 • Fax: 242-337-3429 • VHF 16
flyfishmarina@batelnet.bs • www.flyingfishmarina.com

This is a recent development in cruising terms if you are on passage between the Bahamas and the Turks and Caicos. It is a little oasis where you can take shelter and replenish your stores. While Clarence Town is designated as a port of entry, Customs and Immigration do not occupy an office in Clarence Town. Their office is located 50 miles north at the *Stella Maris Airport*. Please advise the marina of your arrival 24 hours in advance, and they will request a Customs and Immigration officer on your behalf. Occasionally, the Customs and Immigration officer will instruct yachtsmen to clear in at their next stop in the Bahamas. Clarence Town is a five-minute walk from *Flying Fish Marina*.

Slips 18. **Max LOA** 130 ft. **MLW** 12 ft. **Dockage** $1.40 per ft. per day. **Fuel** Dock open 8 a.m. to 6 p.m., daily. Diesel, gasoline and lubricants. **Facilities & Services** Power $15 to $58 for 30 to 100 amp. RO water $0.30 per gallon. Clean showers free to marina guests. Restrooms, coin-op washers and dryers, $4 per load. Card telephone on dock, WiFi at office. Convenience store with ice, soft drinks, bottled water, confectionaries, t-shirts, caps, souvenirs, Cuban cigars, marine hardware, lures and fishing gear. Car rental available on site. **Restaurant** *Outer Edge Grill*, lunch and dinner, Thursday through Sunday, 10:30 a.m. to 9:30 p.m. **Credit Cards** Visa, MasterCard, AMEX; 5% surcharge on fuel. Travelers checks accepted with ID. Marina guest's pets are welcome at the marina. Pets on vessels anchored off their marina are not permitted on the grounds or shoreline.

EMERGENCIES

Marine • VHF 16 • 242-337-3936/3047 (Henry Major)
Medical *Clinic* • 242-337-3333 • Nurse available, nearest doctor at *Deadmans Cay Clinic*. 242-337-1222, or 242-337-0555 in emergency.

PORT DIRECTORY

Accommodations *Gems at Paradise*, Tel: 242-337-3016/3019, Fax: 242-337-3021, gemsatparadise@batelnet.bs, www.gemsat-paradise.com. Small resort with 450 ft. of beachfront in Lochabar Estates. Saltwater swimming pool, deep sea fishing. 1-bedroom condominiums • *Greenwich Creek Lodge*, Tel: 242-337-6278, info@greenwichcreek.com, www.greenwichcreek.com. Family-run fishing lodge, 10 minutes from Clarence Town with courtesy shuttle bus, restaurant and bar on the edge of a salina • *Rowdy Boys,* Tel: 242-337-3062, Fax: 242-337-6131, info@winterhavenbahamas.com, www.winterhavenbahamas.com. Next door to *Flying Fish Marina.* Rental cars for guests and non-guests • *Milander's Auto,* 242-337-3227, VHF 16. Carlos Milander has apartments to rent.

Bakery *Oasis Bakery and Restaurant* • 242-337-3003 • One mile north of town on the Queen's Highway.

Car Rental *Phils Car Rental*, 242-337-3249 • *Flying Fish Marina*, 242-337-3430. • *Rowdy Boys*, 242-337-3062.

Churches *St. Paul's Anglican Church, Saints Peter* and *Paul Catholic Church* with the twin towers.

Diving & Snorkeling Blue holes nearby are just north at Deans, between Clarence Town and Hamilton. Another, farther south is in Lochabar Bay.

Fuel Henry Major at the *Shell* station • 242-337-3936/3047 • by the government dock has diesel and gasoline on the dock, where there is 10 feet at MLW. *Flying Fish Marina* also has fuel.

Guided Island Tours *See It All Fun Tours,* 242-337-2031.

Liquor Skeeter's *OK Bar and Liquor Store* next door to *Ena's Harbour Grocery*, with limited supplies, but can usually bring in more. Mailboat comes in on Wednesday.

Marine Services For any marine problems in Clarence Town, see Henry Major, the Harbourmaster, at the *Shell* filling station by the *Government Dock.* Henry, 242-337-3936/3047, is a local encyclopedia and will give you valuable advice. *Milander's Auto* • 242-337-3227 • VHF 16 • Open 8 a.m. to 5 p.m., Monday through Saturday. Carlos Milander is very helpful and also has apartments to rent. He has limited spare parts in the store, but can help with marine repairs. Red Major is a diesel mechanic who can be contacted at *Oasis*

Bakery, 242-338-3003; his wife runs the bakery. *Andrew Cartwright,* 242-337-2424, who is well-recommended, will come out to your boat. *Rudolph Pratt,* 242-338-2378, lives in Cabbage Point, but will come to Clarence Town. He also runs a mobile diesel fuel operation if Clarence Town dock is out of diesel. Extra charge for delivery.

Music If you feel like throwing a party in Clarence Town with live music, contact *The Originals*, an enthusiastic group of musicians. Call either *Paul Darville,* 242-337-0116, or *Orlando Turnquest,* 242-337-1334.

Pharmacy *Prescription Parlour*, 242-337-3903, 48-hr. prescription service at *True Value Food Store.*

Police • 242-338-3919 • Open 9 a.m. to 5:30 p.m. weekdays.

Post Office • 242-337-3030 • Open 9 a.m. to 4 p.m. weekdays.

Provisions *Harbour Grocery* • 242-337-3934 • Fax: 242-337-3935 • VHF 16 • Ena Major opens 8:30 a.m. to 7:30 p.m., 8 to 10 a.m. Sundays. Well-stocked with meats, vegetables, canned and dry goods, cold drinks, local straw work and insect repellent (a must in Clarence Town). *Department of Agriculture Warehouse* on the Government Dock, has locally grown bananas, limes, peppers, pumpkins and watermelons almost all year. Tomatoes, onions and sweet peppers in spring; mangoes and pineapples in summer. Open weekdays 8:30 a.m. to 4:30 p.m., but you can call ahead at 242-337-3276 to check. Stocks are best on Tuesday before the Wednesday mailboat arrives to collect them, but almost nonexistent after prolonged winter droughts. • T*rue Value Food Store and Pharmacy.*

Restaurants *Harbour Restaurant and Bar* • 242-337-3247 • From 10:30 a.m. to 8 p.m., daily. Annie Minnis specializes in Bahamian dishes, cakes, pies, pastries and guava duff. $ *Le Pon Restaurant & Grill* on the corner walking up into town from the government dock. *Oasis Restaurant* • breakfast and lunch with fresh baked bread, 8 a.m. to 5 p.m., Monday through Friday; 7:30 a.m. to 5 p.m. on Saturday. *Rowdy Boys Bar & Grill at Winter Haven,* • open daily from 8 a.m. until...

Taxi Inquire at marina, hotels and restaurants. Depending on where you need to go, it could be cheaper to rent a car.

Telephones BTC • 242-337-3000/3001 • Fax: 242-337-3100 • Open 9 a.m. to 4:30 p.m. weekdays, with phone cards for sale.

Trash Bins at Government Dock.

Water Flying Fish Marina.

THINGS TO DO IN LONG ISLAND

- Hike up to the Columbus Monument at Cape Santa Maria.
- Swim in Calabash Bay.
- Go diving at some of the incredible Long Island sites.
- Have your boat repairs done in Stella Maris; their catamaran facility is a plus.
- Photograph the many pretty Long Island churches, and visit the two in Clarence Town built by Father Jerome. Contrast them with the Hermitage on Cat Island.
- Explore Hamilton's Cave with Leonard Cartwright.
- Visit the Long Island Museum in Buckleys. See how the Long Island folk lived before modern conveniences came to the island, what Junkanoo means, and what makes up a Rake 'n' Scrape band. Take home some locally made straw work and small gifts from their museum shop.
- In good weather, swim across to Guana Cay, south of Salt Pond (ask for directions) and visit the iguanas. There is an old freighter wreck on the ocean side, worth snorkeling if it is very calm.

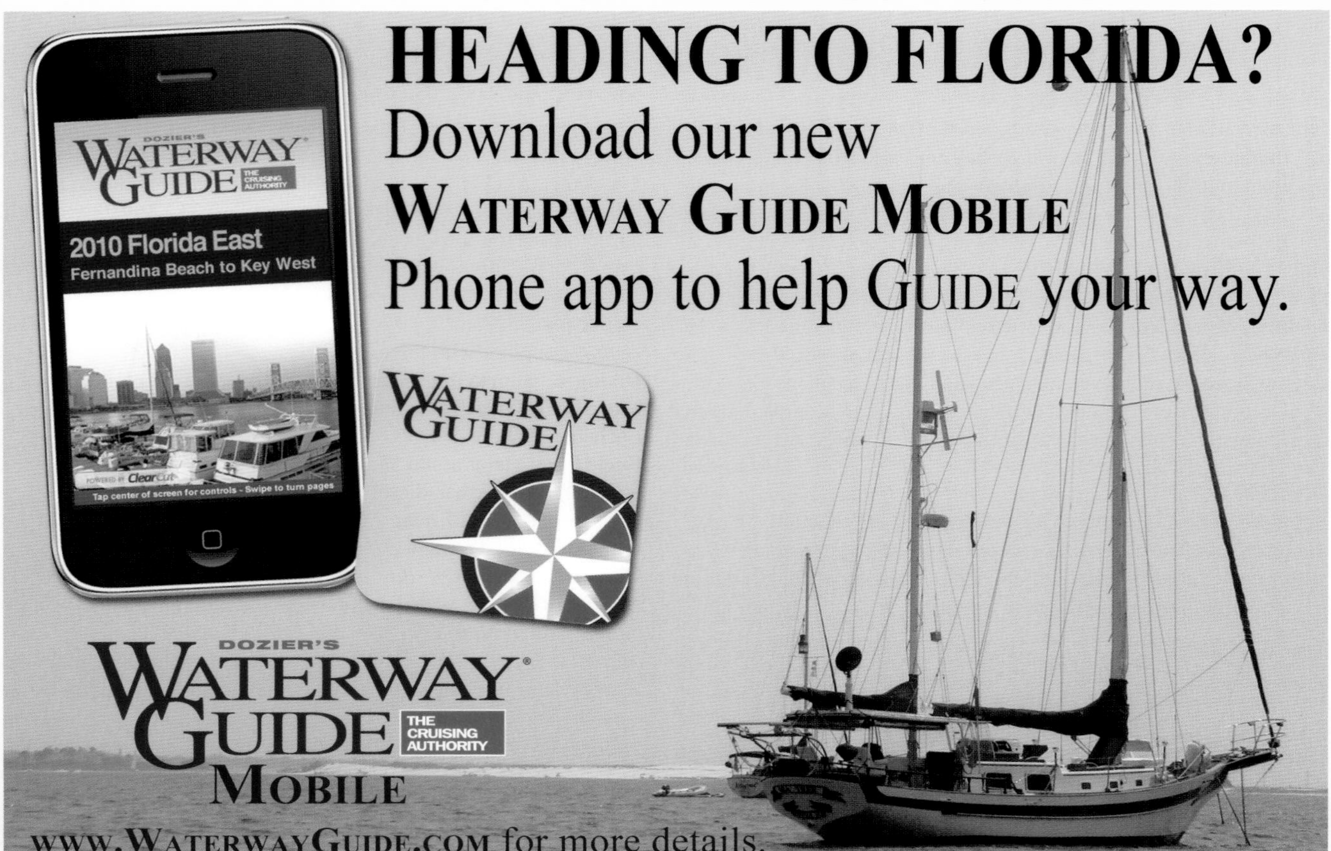

Part IV
Far Horizons

Photography Courtesy of Leslie Taylor and Waterway Guide

Not to be used for navigation.

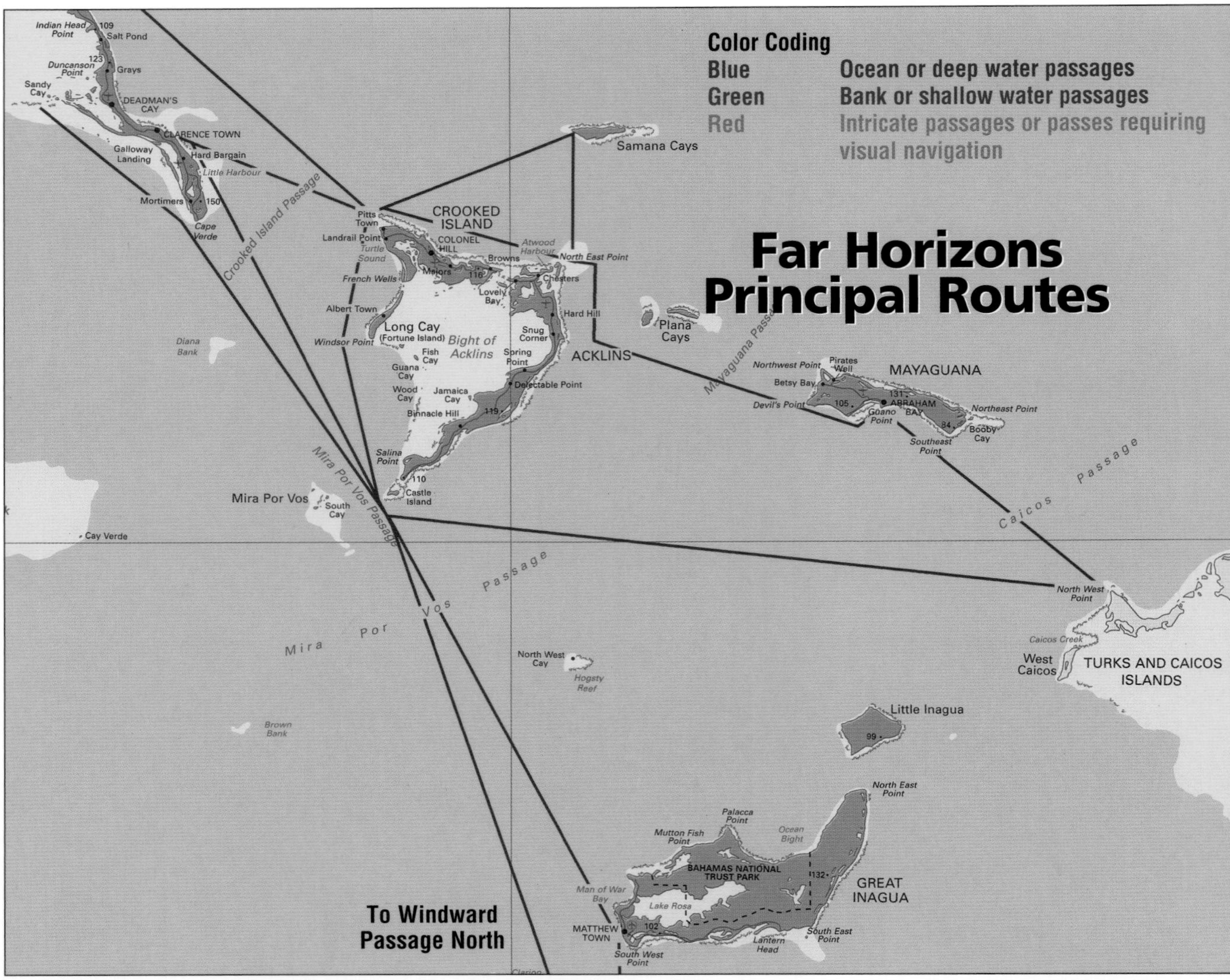

Route From	To	Headings	Distance NM	Passage
Cape Santa Maria, Long Island	Bird Rock, Crooked Island	135/315°T	71	Atlantic Open
Clarence Town, Long Island	Bird Rock, Crooked Island	115/295°T	35	Crooked Island Passage
Bird Rock, Crooked Island	Acklins Northeast	104/284°T	29	Atlantic Open
Bird Rock, Crooked Island	Samana Cay	075/255°T	36	Atlantic Open
Samana Cay	Acklins Northeast	170/350°T	17	Atlantic Open
Acklins Northeast	Plana Cays South	180/000°T	16	Atlantic Open
Plana Cays South	Mayaguana West	106/286°T	39	Mayaguana Passage
Mayaguana West	Providenciales North	121/301°T	47	Caicos Passage
Mayaguana West	Sandbore Approach	136/316°T	47	Caicos Passage
Long Island South Point East	Mira Por Vos Passage	157/337°T	49	Crooked Island Passage
Bird Rock, Crooked Island	Long Cay	185/005°T	21	Crooked Island Passage
Long Cay	Mira Por Vos Passage	180/000°T	26	Crooked Island Passage
Nuevitas Rocks	Mira Por Vos Passage	140/320°T	81	Crooked Island Passage
Nuevitas Rocks	Long Island, South Point West	123/303°T	30	Atlantic Pocket
Long Island, South Point West	Mira Por Vos Passage	149/329°T	53	Crooked Island Passage
Long Island, South Point West	Long Cay	126/306°T	34	Crooked Island Passage
Mira Por Vos Passage	Matthew Town, Great Inagua	151/331°T	80	Atlantic Open
Matthew Town, Great Inagua	Windward Passage North	192/012°T	28	Atlantic Open

Distances exclude inshore close approaches at the start and end of a passage.

Chapter 18
The Bahamas South of the Tropic of Cancer

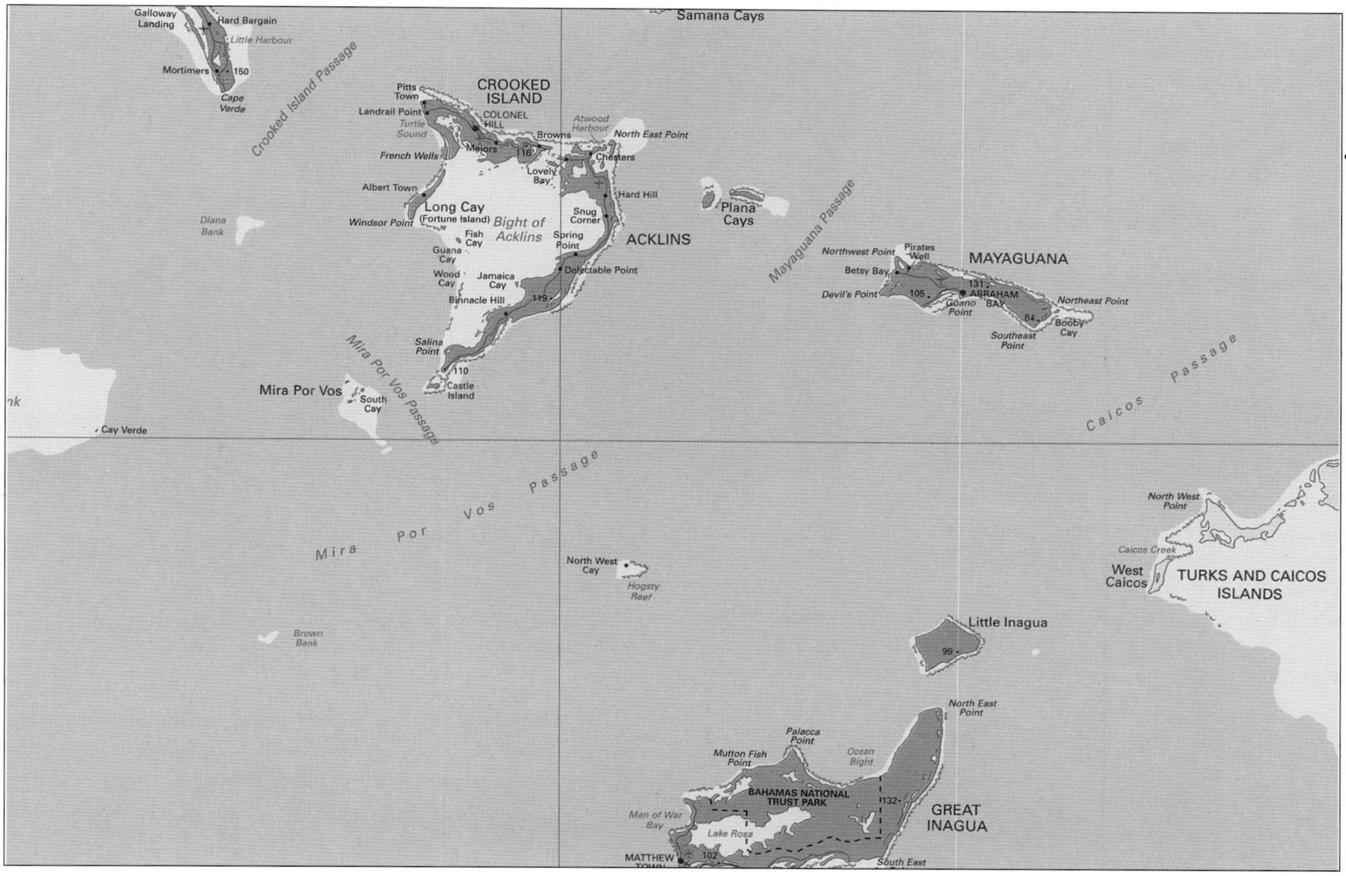

Looking At the Charts

South of Latitude N 23°30.000'

The generally perceived wisdom that "it is different south of George Town" is true. For good reason, we draw the bottom line of the southern cruising grounds along latitude N 23° 30.000'. So what about this line? Why is it so special? Well, perhaps it is academic that it happens to be the Tropic of Cancer (that is as far north as the sun travels above the equator during the Northern Hemisphere's summer). Below the line, you are in the Tropics. The real Tropics. Not the subtropics. The difference on the ground? Not much, not immediately. What about the marine side?

Once you head south of the N 23° 30.000' line, you are in a different game. You are exposed to the Atlantic Ocean. You have legendary passages to negotiate (all of which carry a weather factor rather like crossing the Gulf Stream). There are almost no all-weather anchorages, few settlements and over much of the area, no sources of fuel. It is understood that you shouldn't venture into these waters in a craft that isn't well-founded and well-equipped. The sailboat really comes into its own here, for it is not completely fuel dependent. The powerboat must calculate fuel and endurance, and keep a 20 percent reserve in hand.

This area lies across the direct path to and from the Caribbean. If you are going that way (or returning), then fine. Choose the best route suited to you, and do it. If you have no purpose other than poking around to see what it is like down there, think twice about it, particularly if passagemaking or cruising in an area like this lies outside your experience. Let us look at two basic considerations.

Fuel

Between George Town or Rum Cay and Providenciales (Provo) in the Turks and Caicos Islands, the only sources of fuel are Long Island (Clarence Town), Crooked Island (Landrail Point), Mayaguana (the government dock) and Great Inagua (Matthew Town). The first three run out of fuel repeatedly. Check ahead if you hope to acquire what they have. They may be waiting for resupply.

Air Links

There is another consideration above fuel that may be worth taking into account, and that is air links with the outside world. You are unlikely to schedule crew changes during your transit from George Town to Provo, but you might have to fly someone out in an emergency. Where can you do it? Bahamasair serves Crooked Island, Acklins Island, Mayaguana and Great Inagua. Just keep that in the back of your mind.

Passages to the Caribbean

A quick glance at the chart tells you that the obvious direct route is to parallel Long Island's east coast, leave Crooked and Acklins to starboard and Semana to port, leave the Plana Cays to port, maybe stop in Mayaguana, and go on to Providenciales. Of course, if you are heading for the Windward Passage, you would drop south down to the Crooked Island Passage and wouldn't want to fool around in the Turks and Caicos. Maybe you would stop in Great Inagua. Every route has options at every waypoint.

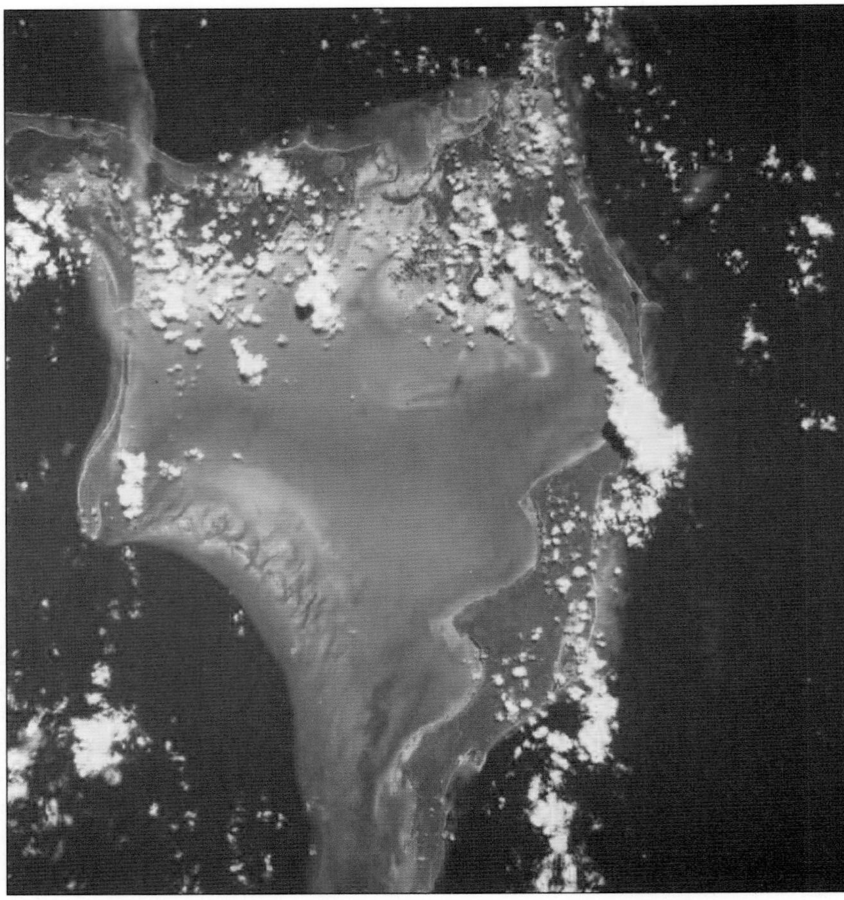

The Crooked–Acklins–Long Cay archipelago from Skylab.

On the face of it, the Crooked–Acklins–Long Cay Archipelago looks like a definitive route-setter. If you are going to or coming from Provo or the Turks and Caicos, you would pass to the east. If you are bound for, or coming from, the Inaguas and the Windward Passage, you would pass to the west. However, in truth, that is not so.

The archipelago is best seen as a traffic circle, and this is why: the weather factor. Generally, the weather is incoming from the Atlantic Ocean, from east to west. The east coast of Long Island offers no shelter, although there are two places where, in a last resort, you might find refuge if you entered before the onset of bad weather. The north coasts of Acklins and Crooked islands offer nothing. There are not only wind, wave and swell to consider. Other hurdles on that route that make it seem like the endless hazards in Homer's Odyssey: the tide-rips and seas off Cape Santa Maria and a mean current running through the Mayaguana Passage.

We are not trying to cause panic. In settled weather, the eastern route bound to or from Provo, and the western route bound to or from the Inaguas and the Windward Passage, will work just fine. But, destined for Provo or heading north from there, if the weather kicked up, you would switch to the west of the archipelago, taking the Crooked Island Passage. The reason? To use the land mass and the Bight of Acklins as a shield from weather and current, and to tuck up behind the southwest tip of Long Cay, in French Wells (Crooked Island) and around Salina Point (the south of Acklins Island) to find shelter (read the detailed notes). You still have the east coast of Long Island to face, but is there an alternative?

An Alternative Route?

Many captains look at charts and ponder, is it possible to gain the deep pocket of ocean water to the northwest of the Crooked Island Passage by a transit from the Southern Exumas or Salt Pond in Long Island? It is unlikely. This is not to say that local captains do not safely cross the southeast corner of the Great Bahama Bank. Underline that word "local." It requires an encyclopedia of local knowledge. Add un-surveyed waters to storms that constantly alter the whole lay of the sand, and it is not possible for a cruising guide to offer waypoints that say, "go this way."

However, we have identified one longer route that, in theory, will take you on the bank side from west of Harvey Cay in the mid-Exumas to the deep water south of Nuevitas Rocks. This could be attractive as an alternative to the east coast of Long Island. We will outline the traditional Eastern Route, and turn to this option later when we cover the Crooked Island Passage and the route to the Inaguas, and the Windward Passage lying to the west of the Crooked–Acklins–Long Cay archipelago.

Eastern Route: George Town to the Turks & Caicos

You will see by the route and waypoints that your starting point is probably George Town, and the route takes you by way of Cape Santa Maria down the east coast of Long Island. Because we have covered Long Island in detail under the Southern Cruising Grounds, we won't repeat it here. Your pick-up point lies somewhere around the Long Island Southeast waypoint (LISPE), which, in all probability, you won't use. It is just a point on the chart. We will pick up the route after you have made your 30-nautical-mile transit across the Crooked Island Passage in the Crooked–Acklins–Long Cay Triangle.

In the Spotlight. Crooked–Acklins–Long Cay Triangle

Seen from outer space, the triangular atoll formed by Crooked Island, Acklin's Island and Long Cay is spectacular. All around is the dark blue of deep ocean. A thin-line of breaking white seas defines the fringing barrier reefs that are almost continuous around the archipelago.

Next, there is a narrow band of brilliant light blue shallow water and the green of the land. Inside this frame are the turquoise waters of the Bight of Acklins, forming a virtual lagoon. (One snippet to add to your trivia file if you are a Campari drinker, these islands are the world's source of cascarilla bark, the ingredient that gives Campari its bitter, astringent taste.)

As you make your way south of Long Island, you meet the first of the West Indian Passages, ancient deep-water channels, all of which slant in from the Atlantic. Ocean swells, together with high seas in unsettled weather, can produce surprising and less-than-welcome bumpy rides as you cross each passage.

Counting the passages as you go south, the Crooked Island Passage is the first, then the Mayaguana Passage and the Caicos Passage. Farther to the southwest is the closest entry point to the Caribbean, the Windward Passage. Heading for Providenciales, one way or another, you are going to cut across the first three passages. As for the land, watch out for the barrier reefs, and stand well offshore everywhere unless you are definitely closing for a specific destination. Our advice is to stand five nautical miles off any coastline, and add more miles to that if you are passing the southeast point of Great Inagua Island.

Nature, in a sense, has ill-served the passage maker. In a perfect world, the Crooked–Acklins–Long Cay archipelago should offer havens if you want to rest or wait out the onset of unfavorable weather. In reality, your choices there are very limited and, as is true with most of the Bahamas, all-weather anchorages do not exist. The one exception lies with true shoal-draft craft that can play the Bight of Acklins to their advantage.

Clearing In—Your Options in the South Bahamas

Mathew Town in Great Inagua is the entry port for the area, although it lies far off your route coming north from the Caribbean via the Turks and Caicos. A second clearance option exists in Abrahams Bay, Mayaguana, where there is a Customs and Immigration office. The post is "double-staffed" from Inagua. The officers may not be there, but the commissioner has the power to act in their absence.

What's There? South of the Tropic of Cancer

Bird Rock, Crooked Island

Bird Rock, the northern of the two Crooked Island Passage lighthouses, is dated 1876. It is not only a fine landmark, but also a triumph of construction, built from Crooked Island stone quarried from nearby Gun Bluff. At one time, its mechanism and lenses were a match to Hope Town Lighthouse in the Abacos. However, when the Bird Rock Lighthouse was electrified, its 19th century machinery and museum-quality Fresnel lenses were destroyed. Having survived for over a century, the lighthouse most recently was deteriorating rapidly and no longer

Bird Rock Lighthouse. (Not to be used for navigation.) WATERWAY GUIDE PHOTOGRAPHY.

working. The Bahamas Defence Force tried to get Bird Rock Light working, but despite initial success, failed. The owners of Crooked Island Lodge at Pittstown Point are working on renovations of the lighthouse to use for accommodations. You may soon be able to stay in the Bird Rock Lighthouse, certainly one of the most romantic settings in the Bahamas.

Portland Harbour, Crooked Island

Portland Harbour, at the northwest tip of Crooked Island, is, in truth, the perpetuation of mistaken identification. There is no harbor, just a ring of circling reef where, if the wind is from the south, one can find a pleasant anchorage off the beach just to the east of Pittstown Point. You will be uneasy there at any other time and crazy to think of it when the wind is either west or north.

Pittstown Point Landings, Crooked Island

Pittstown Point is the location of a secluded, relaxed, low-rise resort, Crooked Island Lodge at Pittstown Point, just two miles north of Landrail Point. The 12-room hotel is centered on its 2,000-foot-long paved airstrip, and guests arrive piloting their own aircraft or fly Bahamasair to Colonel Hill, the Crooked Island airport with a 4,000-foot-long runway. Crooked Lodge (extraordinarily the site of the first post office in the Bahamas) is a delight. Certainly, on the short list of the more remote places that, for setting and ambiance, win instant stars as an island retreat. Portland Harbour and Landrail Point offer two exposed anchorages to consider.

Landrail Point, Crooked Island

Landrail Point, about four nautical miles south of Bird Rock, appears the most unlikely place to construct a government dock to serve a mailboat, but it is there with a small settlement behind it. There is a drop-off on the Crooked Island Passage that runs close to and parallel with the shore at Landrail.

Farther south, the margin of offshore shallows gradually increases until you are held well off the coast by a shallow shelf. There is no protecting reef off Landrail, and both the mailboat and you can make your way in from deep water to within a stone's throw of the shoreline.

The government dock is not a tie-up option, because of surge, except for a short visit to take on fuel. Your landmark for the dock, which doesn't stand out clearly from the shore, is the group of fuel tanks (three large and one small) just to the north of the dock and a yellow building with blue shutters just by the dock. If you want fuel, call "Early Bird" on VHF Channel 16. You can fill your cans at the nearby gas station. If you need more than can be handled can by can, they will send the fuel truck (carrying both diesel and gasoline) to the dock to meet you.

Landrail Point is a small, compact settlement designed around a short triangle of roads, one marked Pittstown and the others Inland and Airport. There is a clinic, a one-room school, a Seventh Day Adventist church, the gas station and the Lunch Room. You will find a BTC card phone by the government dock. Guides can take you fishing and diving. The people of Landrail, mostly Seventh Day Adventist, are friendly and approachable. Just remember that Saturday is their Sabbath Day, and alcohol is not part of their lifestyle.

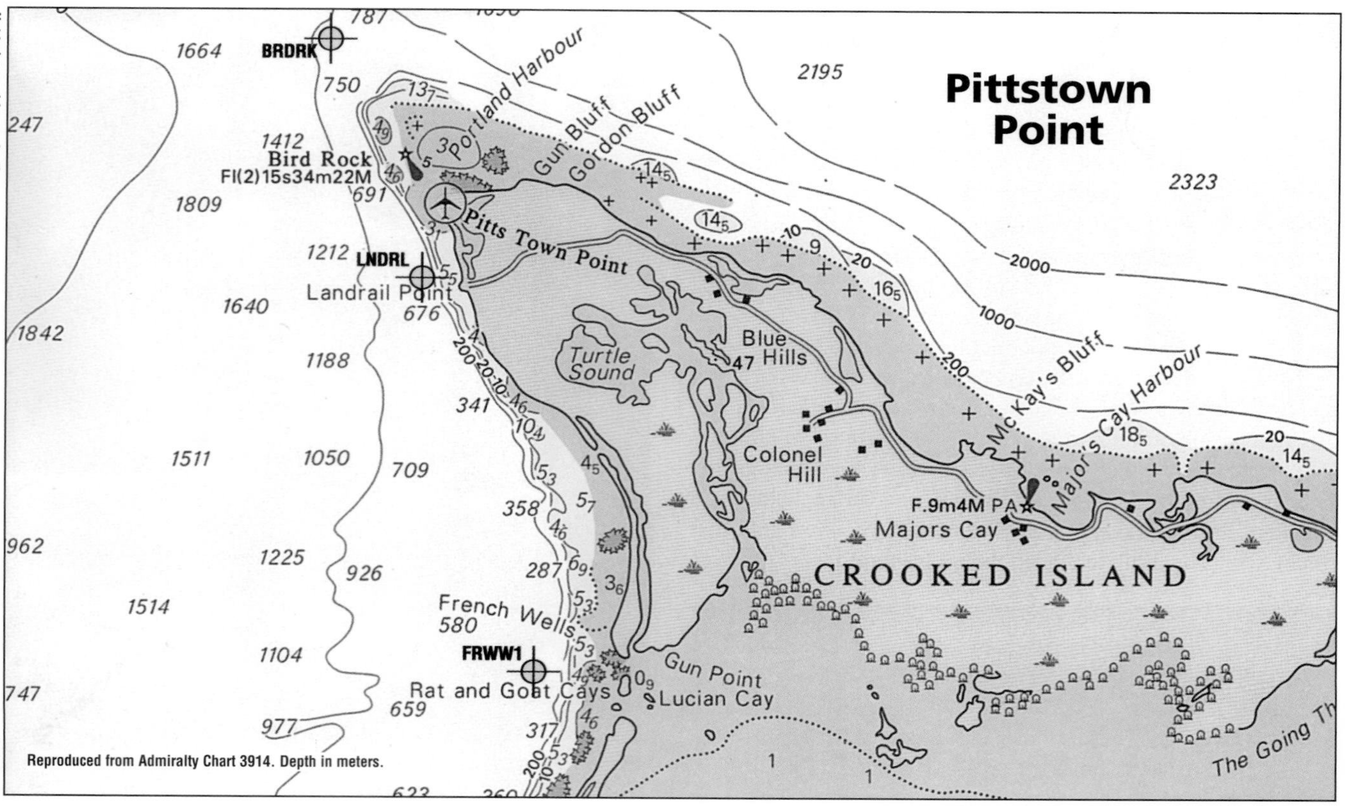

Reproduced from Admiralty Chart 3914. Depth in meters.

Not to be used for navigation.

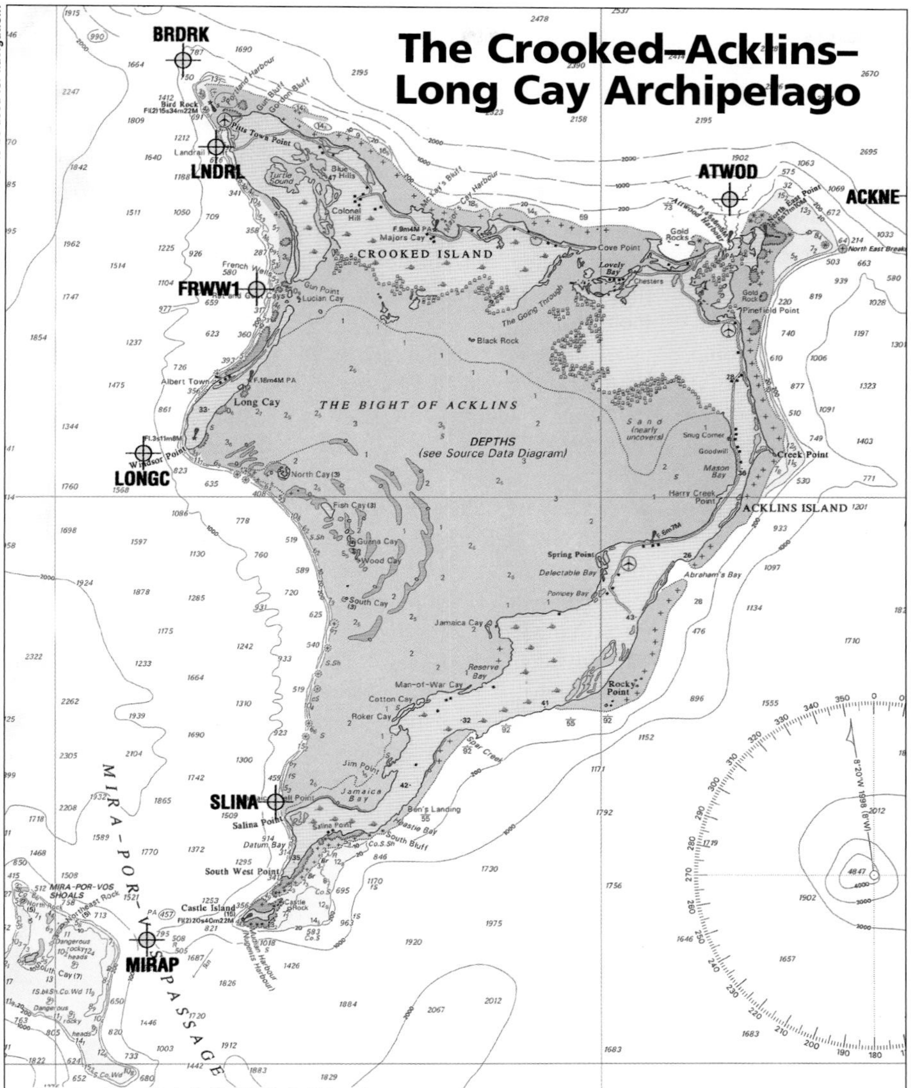

Reproduced from Admiralty Chart 3914. Depth in meters.

Not to be used for navigation.

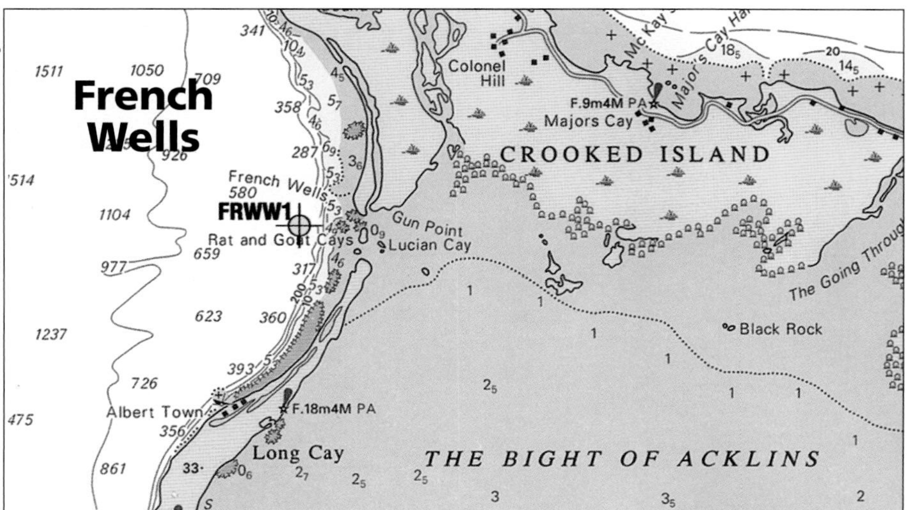

Reproduced from Admiralty Chart 3914. Depth in meters.

French Wells, Crooked Island

Although not directly on the eastern route, weather, or simply the desire to take a break from passagemaking, may prompt you to divert to French Wells at the southern tip of Crooked Island. French Wells, despite its alluring name, long ago lost its population. Nevertheless, it offers the best all-weather anchorage in the Crooked–Acklins–Long Cay archipelago.

Follow the deep water along the Crooked Island Passage drop-off and then, when you are off French Wells, turn in between Crooked Island and Goat Cay (north of Long Cay), and head almost due east on a course of 090/270 degrees true. Port and starboard you have sandbars reaching out toward the drop-off, and you have a shoal area to cross with just 3.6-meter/12-foot depths at mean low water.

Passing the southern point of Crooked Island, you will find yourself in a deeper channel bordered by shoal on both sides. We add one caution: Feel your way in. Sand is the governing factor; and, as we all know, sand moves. French Wells, in the words of one Bahamian captain, "comes and goes." Much of the time, you can get in there. Sometimes it is a no-go. However, it worked for Columbus in 1492.

Work your way in to anchor in 4.5- to 6-meter/15- to 20-foot depths over sand. The farther you go, within reason, the more protected you will be and the better the sand underneath you.

You are shielded by sand virtually on all sides, and only vicious west weather could rock you. The locals say it "never gets really bad in there." If you are lucky, flamingos will join you at dusk. At the turn of the tide, the bottom fishing is good. On the west side of Crooked Island, running north from its tip for just over three nautical miles is one of the most fabulous continuous runs of pure white sand beach facing pure white sand–bottomed turquoise water there is in the islands.

The Rest of Crooked Island

Colonel Hill, a settlement resting securely notched into its north coast spine of limestone, is (a proud schoolteacher says) the capital of Crooked Island. The center of the island's population of 300 souls is spread along on the Colonel Hill–Cabbage Hill ridgeline. To the east, in the low ground, is the airport and to the west, high on that spine, a BTC tower with three great dish antennae. Crooked Island may well be set for significant change. Together with road improvement, the age of centrally generated electricity has arrived (every generator in the island is now relegated to stand-by status), and it is ready for progress.

Long Cay

Logic would dictate that we cover Long Cay, running south from French Wells and the southern tip of Crooked Island at this point in our text. However, since it is not part of the eastern route from George Town to Providenciales, we will address it later. If you elect to take the Crooked Island Passage, making for the Windward Passage, continue south, paralleling Long Cay (for this see coverage on the western route).

The North of Acklins Island

Acklins Island, with a population of around 500 spread over 150 square miles, has a look of depopulation. The center of Acklins is Spring Point, which is located on the Bight of Acklins, almost exactly halfway down the west coast. This places it out of reach of any cruising boat. The east coast has a virtually continuous inshore reef, and there is no place into which you could safely bring a boat. If you are taking the Eastern Route between George Town and Providenciales, the only place in Acklins that you can use is Atwood Harbour in the northeast. The south of Acklins Island is only relevant to those taking the western route. We will cover it under that heading.

Atwood Harbour and Northeast Point, Acklins Island

Atwood Harbour, a cup-shaped bay behind the reef two nautical miles southwest of Acklins Northeast Point, is the only anchorage worth that name in the Crooked–Acklins area. It has good protection, except from the north, when it should not be attempted. Getting in requires care and attention. It is unfortunate that Atwood lies at the far limit of a passage length in either direction, because it means that many people reach Atwood just too late to have good light and are, most probably, tired. Dozen of boats have run into trouble entering Atwood. Be warned, but don't be put off.

Samana Cay

Samana Cay, 35 nautical miles from Bird Rock and 20 nautical miles from Acklins Northeast Point, is not on your route; but we include it as you may wish to divert there purely out of interest. No longer populated, Samana Cay lies 30 nautical miles northeast of Crooked Island and is nine by two nautical miles in land area with a sibling mini-cay to the east. Its surrounding reefs extend the sea area of the whole Samana Cay landmass to approximately 16 by four nautical miles. Despite apparently protected bays on both the north and the south coasts, there is no easy-to-enter anchorage. The problem is simply those surrounding reefs that have no breaks or cuts through the coral.

Why go there? Perhaps you are a maritime history buff interested in the Columbus voyages and a member of the "It Wasn't San Salvador" school? (See "The Columbus Controversy" in the Green Pages). There is a compelling case to believe that Samana Cay was Columbus' first transatlantic landfall. Alternatively, you might elect to go there simply because it is there, or because it is remote and largely unvisited except occasionally by fishermen from Acklins Island.

The Plana Cays

West Plana Cay offers a good anchorage on the west side in northeast to east winds, but you will feel swell there. Expect to roll. Avoid it in northwest and southwest winds. In favorable weather, West Plana is a good place for beachcombing, but you are unlikely to want to stay there long. By reputation, its sibling, East Plana Cay, has poor anchoring. We suspect there could be a fantastic drift dive site between the two cays. Be cautious if

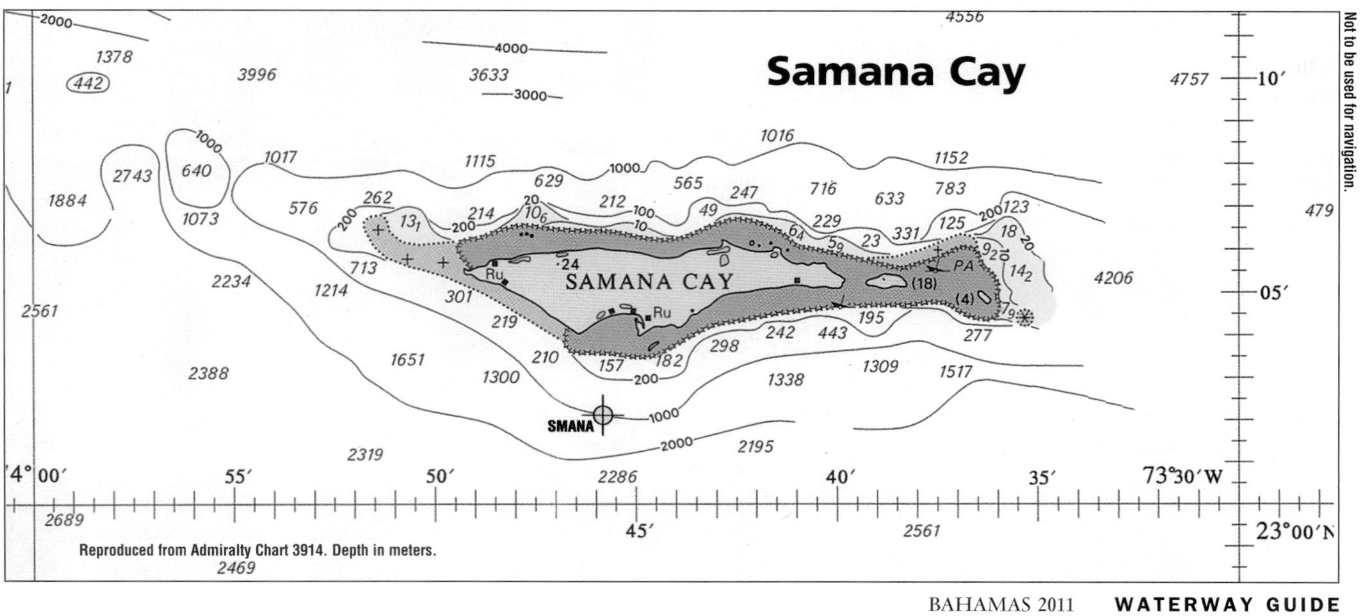

Reproduced from Admiralty Chart 3914. Depth in meters.

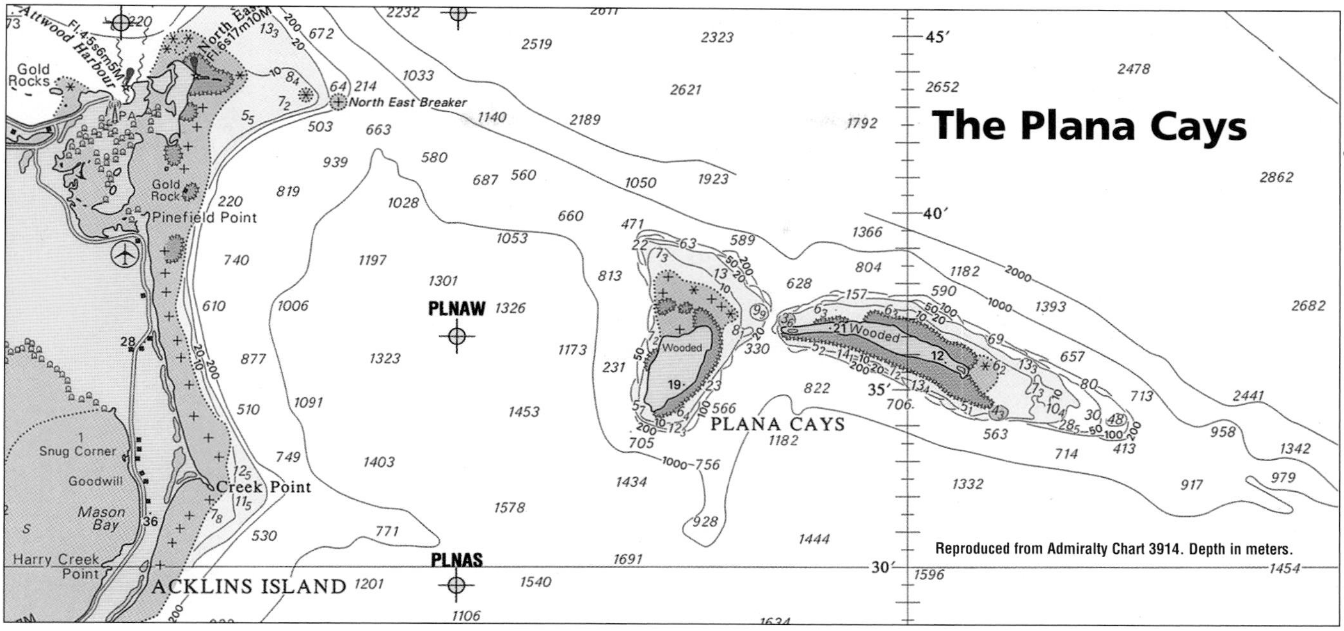

you do. The current there can be strong. East Plana is the only undisturbed habitat of the hutia, a small, native, Bahamian, cat-size rodent. How did they get there? One can only guess that way back in time, the hutias were great swimmers. By all accounts, the Arawaks rated hutia as gourmet fare, so perhaps it is hardly surprising that the unfortunate hutias learned to swim and made a last ditch stand in East Plana Cay. A more likely scenario is that they were transported there as a food source and outlived their captors.

Mayaguana

Mayaguana marks the midway point between Acklins Island and Providenciales. It is sizable, 24 nautical miles in length and six miles in width. The island is mostly a low-lying tangle of scrub and trees and offers the cruising visitor good shelter. Its population of 500 is spread between three settlements: Pirates Well on the northwest coast, Betsy Bay on the west coast and Abrahams Bay, the largest settlement. Mayaguana was once part of the U.S. missile-tracking network. They left an 11,000-foot-long runway, 7,700 feet of which are still usable. It is located five miles west of Abrahams Bay. Once used by the mailboat, a U.S. Air Force (USAF) dock is now in a state of advanced decay. Little else of this period remains. Four stripped-out aircraft, that you can see on the apron if you visit the airfield, were seized from drug-runners.

Were Mayaguana anywhere else other than right on the main cruising path to and from the Caribbean, it would probably remain unvisited. However, it is there, right on your route; and you may wish to call in. Its isolation is broken by the weekly mailboat calls and twice-weekly Bahamasair visits. Mayaguana has the good fortune to be a brief stop on the scheduled Nassau–Inagua service. Add these together with centrally generated power, re-graded and surfaced roads, a BTC station, a police post and government clinic, and Mayaguana wins status as a refuge. Therefore, we cover it in some detail.

Turning to navigation, the chart of Mayaguana can be frightening at first sight. The island is surrounded by an almost continuous reef that forms great bights at the northwest tip, the east and at Abrahams Bay to the south. Look at the chart, and you will see no less than eight shipwrecks marked on the reef, but the Mayaguana total is far higher than this. You have a few options. The first is to anchor off the west coast, where from Northwest Point down to the first sand beach south of Betsy Bay, there is no barrier reef. The depths are good, and you are protected from the prevailing winds, east and southeast. However, it is a real no-go in northwest and southwest weather. The second option is to go into Abrahams Bay. The third, if the weather is mild and the breezes are light and out of the northwest through east, is Southeast Point.

Northwest Point to Betsy Bay, Mayaguana

Northwest Point is low-lying, but marked by a light pole close to its tip and shows even more prominently by the breaking seas on its barrier reef. If you have a shoal-draft boat, you can work your way inside the reef close to Northwest Point, and anchor somewhere off the shore running east to Pirates Well. The downside is that it is shallow there, and open and exposed to the north.

Pirates Well has one small store and a small, low-rise beach hotel. A new government dock one nautical mile south of Northwest Point is reached via a cut through the beach rock and coral to provide a square basin with one concrete wall for the mailboat. The beach reef on the north side was not completely cut away and remains a hazard; but there are range marks—two triangles on stakes behind the dock. The depth at the dock is good, 1.8 to 2.4 meters/6 to 8 feet deep at mean low water, but there is surge. The dock is the best place to take on fuel (either diesel or gasoline) if the island has fuel in stock. The fuel is brought to the dock in drums. There is no filtration. You either come alongside or bring your fuel cans ashore having anchored off (remember there is no offshore reef there).

Start Point Pass, Mayaguana, from the west. (Not to be used for navigation.) Waterway Guide Photography

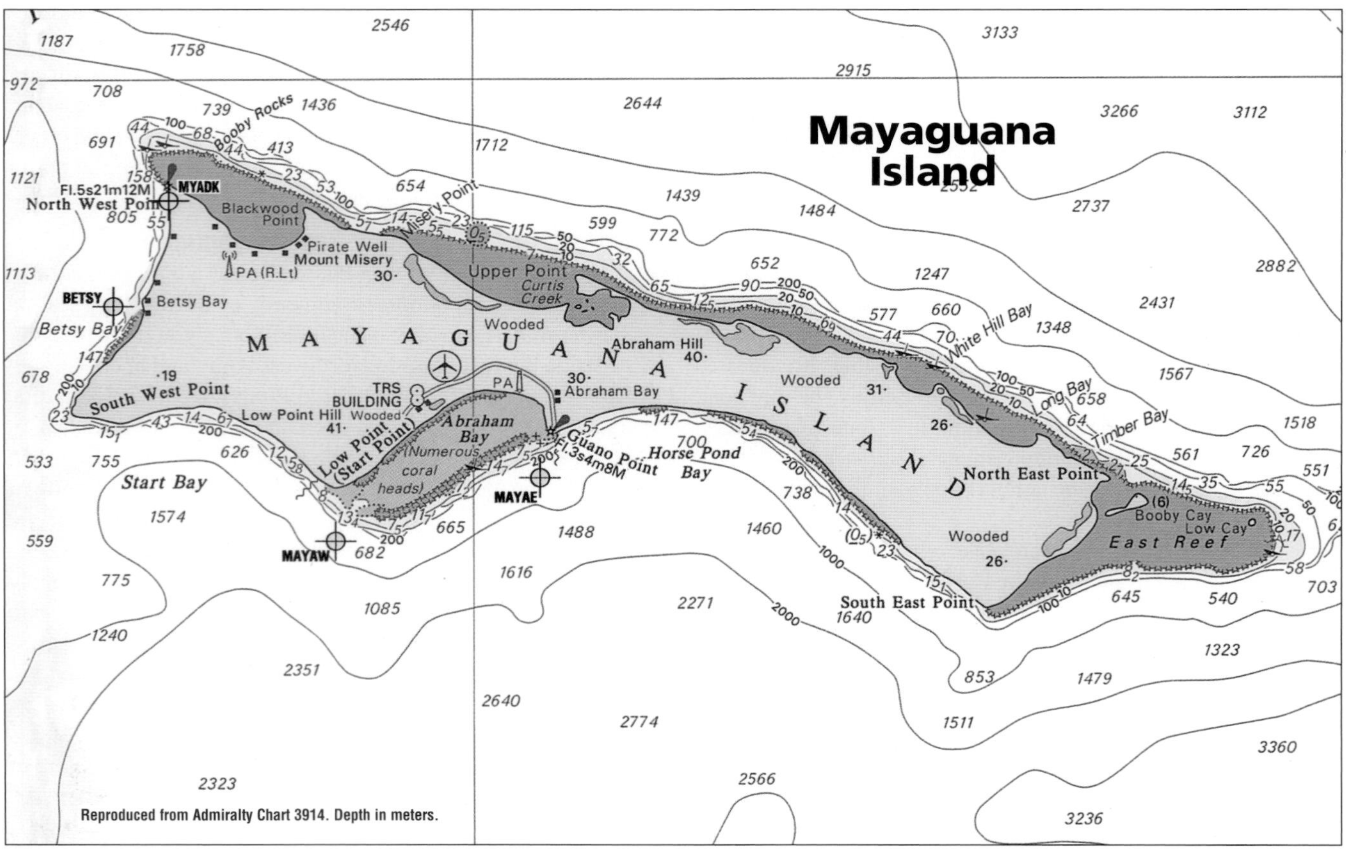

Reproduced from Admiralty Chart 3914. Depth in meters.

Not to be used for navigation.

Guano Point Pass, Mayaguana, from the south. (Not to be used for navigation.) WATERWAY GUIDE PHOTOGRAPHY

The government dock is untenable, even for the mailboat, in southwest and northwest winds of any strength, and under these conditions, the mailboat diverts to Abrahams Bay where whatever can be easily offloaded is cross-decked into small boats. The best way to call for fuel, or indeed for anything in Mayaguana, is to contact BTC on VHF Channel 16, and they will help you. If for some reason you get no response, try the police, who also monitor VHF Channel 16.

Betsy Bay, Mayaguana

Betsy Bay is recognizable by its 104-foot-tall BTC tower with a dish antenna coupled to it. The settlement parallels the beach, which has an inshore reef about 100 feet out. Betsy Bay offers a fair-weather anchorage and a new government dock, just two miles north. The new dock is useful to take on fuel by jerry can. Surge there makes coming along side in a vessel larger than a skiff perilous.

Abrahams Bay, Mayaguana

Abrahams Bay, just over five nautical miles in length and two nautical miles wide, is an all-weather anchorage accessed by two passes through the barrier reef. Apart from its obvious reef, two landmarks are useful in defining each end of Abrahams Bay. In the west, you will see two towers - actually the still-standing buttress walls of what were once part of the USAF missile-tracking complex and the remains of two water tanks. In the east, there is a 175-foot-tall BTC tower in Abrahams Bay settlement.

The bay itself virtually dries along its shoreline. It has an inner, near-continuous run of beach reef just offshore and a generous scattering of random coral. Its navigable waters have depths from 3.6 meters/11 feet to 2.2 meters/7 feet, plus the benefit of a broad band of shielding coral on the ocean side. You must visually navigate through the reef pass and not rely solely on your GPS waypoint. Distracted skippers have run their vessels up onto the reef while attempting to enter the harbor and not posting a look-out on the bow or up the mast. The closer you are to the beach, the more quickly it shoals. Anchored there, you are open to wind from southeast through to southwest, however, the reef breaks up some of the wave action.

A 10-minute walk from the Abrahams Bay dock brings you to the settlement by the BTC tower and the government offices. Abrahams Bay is an official port of entry, but Customs and Immigration may be absent. They commute from Great Inagua. Should you be in a hurry, the Commissioner has powers to act in their absence. The BTC office is open seven days a week. Farther into the settlement, there is the police station, the government clinic (staffed by a nurse—a doctor from Inagua visits once a month), two small stores and two shops where you can purchase food or a drink. The BTC office will guide you.

Southeast Point, Mayaguana

If you are not planning to stop in Mayaguana, but want an easy place to anchor for the night coming from or going to the Turks and Caicos, there is a convenient spot at Southeast Point. Although deep nearly up to the beach, one can anchor very close to shore in 3.7 meters/12 feet of water over isolated coral heads. The holding is good, but there is some surge. As always, do not anchor on the coral to avoid harming this fragile ecosystem.

Cruisers heading south have spent a few days here waiting for a good window to make the relatively short 40-nautical-mile passage to the Sandbore Channel across the Caicos Passage.

Elsewhere in Mayaguana

In settled conditions, you can work your way through cuts in the reef around Northwest Point, as already mentioned. In addition, you can enter almost due south of Booby Cay in the Eastern Bight. The charts show a fairly wide break in the reef with good depths at about N 22 17.80'/W 072 43.20'. A U.S. development on North Beach (N 22° 24.360'/W 072° 58.830'), launched under the curious cover title of the Mayaguana Ecological Group, has yet to produce more than the frame of one half-completed Italianate house and some foundations. There was talk of a cut in the reef, some dredging and a marina. The bight is shallow there, and idea of constructing anything approaching a marina, quite apart from the exposure of the northern coast to weather, seems unlikely to achieve reality.

The Western Route South to the Windward Passage

If you are heading for the Windward Passage, you have a choice at the start. The "standard" route is to go by way of George Town and the east coast of Long Island, then turn to take the Crooked Island Passage south. When you reach the Crooked Island Passage, head for the Mira Por Vos Passage. We covered this route as far as French Wells in Crooked Island under the Eastern Route, "George Town to the Turks and Caicos." We won't duplicate the Long Island port information and the first stage notes on the Eastern Route south to the Turks and Caicos. If you are setting out from George Town or heading that way, the information you need is there.

We have fixed a Long Island South Point East waypoint (LISPE), at which you can turn to take the Crooked Island Passage and make for the Mira Por Vos Passage. Crooked Island lies to port for much of your way after you have taken up the new heading. In addition, the Crooked Island landfalls, particularly French Wells, offer places where you may wish to stop for the day. If you choose to fish as you are going south, try trolling along the line of the Crooked Island–Long Cay drop-off. You may be rewarded with dinner. Just remember that your potential stops are, as ever, weather dependent. The entry to French Wells is sand-governed and can change from year to year.

The alternative, if you are heading for the Windward Passage or coming north from it, is to transit the southeast corner of the Great Bahama Bank. The bank side route was and is used by Bahamian captains when unfavorable weather makes exposure to the Atlantic a real danger. In continued heavy Atlantic Ocean weather, a bank transit may prove attractive.

Let us be clear at the start about the downside of going the bank way. First, it dictates that you bypass George Town, the best stop for fuel, provisions and spares (or traveling north, your entry port). Going west of the Exumas and Long Island, you have nothing. Nothing at all. Secondly, it is not a straight, obstacle-clear run. Your route crosses snake-like sand bores in the area of the Barracouta Rocks that may or may not bar your passage, coral scattered like coarse-ground black pepper in the area of Hawksbill Rock, and reefs and isolated coral heads around the Nuevitas Rocks. In short, it is no playground. Nevertheless, it has been navigable in the past; and depending largely on whether the Barracouta sand has moved as the result of storms, may still be navigable at the time you read this. (See Pilotage later in this chapter for more information.) We pick up this route now in deep water at Nuevitas Rocks. The Long Island east coast transit is the standard, safe route to follow. However, whichever way you go, either going south or coming north, both routes are the same from the Mira Por Vos Passage to the Windward Passage.

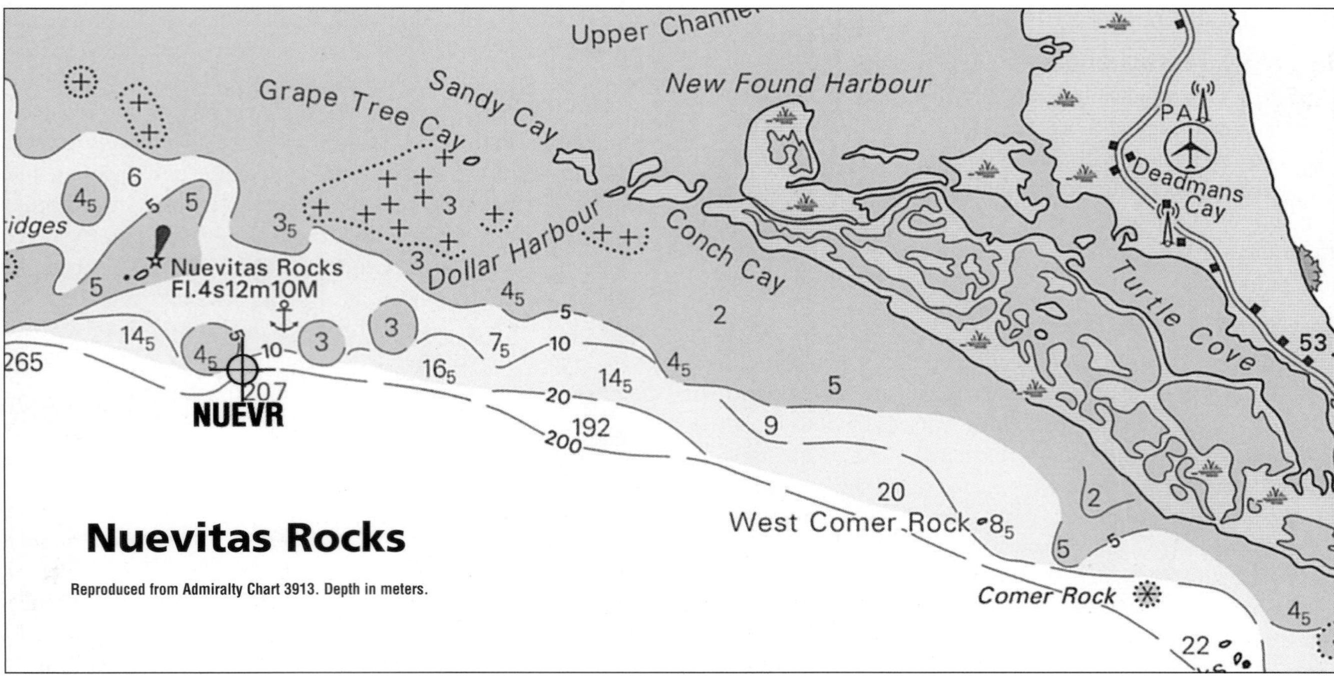

Nuevitas Rocks

Reproduced from Admiralty Chart 3913. Depth in meters.

Not to be used for navigation.

Nuevitas Rocks to the Mira Por Vos Passage

Once you are in deep water, you are free to set course to take you past the southern tip of Long Island, across the Crooked Island Passage, past the southwest point of Long Cay, through the Mira Por Vos Passage, leaving Castle Island and Acklins Island to port. The first leg takes you safely to the east of the Diana Bank, the only shallow area in this deep pocket of ocean water. If conditions are right, you might wish to visit the Diana Bank area, for it is a fishing ground good enough to be the target of both Long Island and Crooked Island fishermen. If you need to seek shelter, there are two options open to you. The first is anchoring off the west coast of Long Island about one nautical mile north of South Point, and the second is French Wells, although it lies off your direct course.

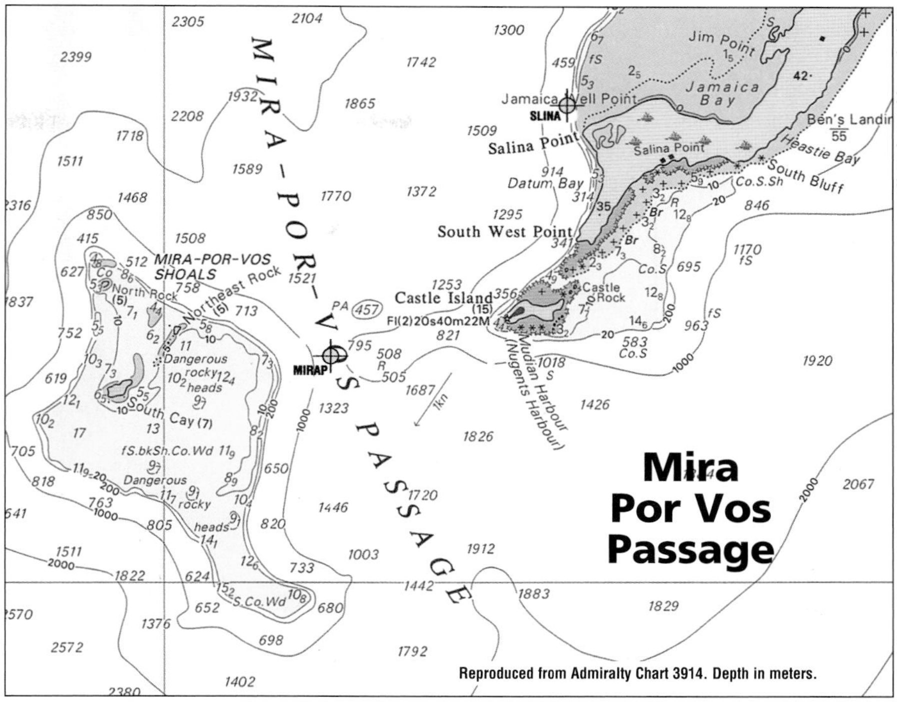

Reproduced from Admiralty Chart 3914. Depth in meters.

Not to be used for navigation.

Farther south, there is not much shelter. However, on the east coast of Long Cay, the area about one nautical mile north of Windsor Point (the southern point), has long been regarded as a potential anchorage. In theory, you are protected from the west there and the shoal water of the Bight of Acklins offers some protection from most other directions; but in practice it doesn't work out so well. As one local fisherman put it, "the ocean is too close there." The shallow bights on the west side of the southern end of Acklins Island on each side of Salina Point offer another option, but like so many potential anchorages, are weather dependent.

Long Cay

Long Cay, with a population of around 25, is yet another once-prosperous Bahamian island that has fallen on hard times. Its large, nearly empty church is sad evidence of this decline. In the past, Long Cay was a rest stop for sailing vessels taking the Crooked Island Passage, a sponging center, and like so many islands, a salt production site. Albert Town on the west coast is protected from the east, but is open to surge and has no clear anchorage.

North Cay, Fish Cay and Guana Cay

To the southeast of Long Cay on the edge of the Bight of Acklins lie North Cay, Fish Cay and Guana Cay. These cays are the last refuge of the local species of iguana, which for reasons yet unknown, have suffered a devastating decline in population. The iguanas are the subject of scientific study hoping to determine the cause for this reversal. If you visit there, tread carefully. Land no animals, and leave no garbage.

The Bight of Acklins

Spectacular as it may be from outer space, unless you are bent on shoal-draft exploration, the Bight of Acklins is not a cruising ground for everyone. You will find charted routes from Long Cay across to Spring Point then down to Rokers Cay in Jamaica Bay, but depths are only from 5 to 8 feet.

South Acklins Island

North Acklins was covered under the eastern route. The south of Acklins is not tourist territory and even in Spring Point, the local inhabitants admit they rarely venture down that way.

This leaves the one southern settlement of Salina Point in near total isolation. Confusingly, Salina Point itself is the headland projecting to the northwest while Salina settlement lies on the opposite (Mayaguana Passage) shore. The shallow bights on each side of the point have both been, at one time or another, labeled Jamaica Bay on charts, but it hardly matters which one is the original.

It is entirely possible to work yourself into the first one, and you can probe farther, moving around Salina Point, but if you carry any kind of draft, local advice is against it. A clear route is not easy to find, and if the weather turns, you may have a tough time getting out and away. If you anchor off this coast, you can make contact with the Salina settlement. You will find fresh bread and a telephone, and folks happy to see you. How do you get there? Not by dinghy. Walk up the beach heading northeast. You will come to a straight road crossing the width of that Acklins promontory. It runs right into the settlement. It is a long walk, and it could be hot. Maybe someone will give you a lift back.

The Mira Por Vos Passage

Mira Por Vos! Look Out for Yourself! The Spanish must have been terrified by this area—a nightmare of coral and sand almost smack in the middle of the southern entrance to the Crooked Island Passage. If they couldn't slip between the Mira Por Vos Cays and Castle Island, a tough shot for the captain of a lumbering galleon to call, they had to go to the west of the Mira Por Vos Cays. But, if the current set and the wind forced them too far west, they would have been on the Columbus Bank. If they clawed their way off that, but were taken too far to the northwest, they would have ended up in the deep-water trap, ringed from the west to the northeast by the Jumentos Cays and Long Island. One could regret the day he won the captaincy of a galleon, or even worse, the command of a fleet of treasure ships.

An alternative translation is *Look Out For Us!* In other words, a prayer for safety. The end effect of both messages is one of total accord and could be summed up as "Keep Away!" Small wonder that the Spanish decided to take the Gulf Stream route from Havana, settled on St. Augustine as a take-off point into the Atlantic Ocean, and quit trying to play it as a straight shot through the Bahamas.

Castle Island

The Castle Island Lighthouse, the southern complement to Bird Rock in the north, marks the southern exit of the Crooked Island Passage. Sadly, this lighthouse, in its conversion to power, suffered the same demise as Bird Rock. Beware of the currents around Castle Island. As is the norm at a place that is the focal point of a deep-water passage—here compounded by the shallows of the Mira Por Vos reefs, shoals and cays—the currents are strong and unpredictable. Expect anything from southwest to northeast.

There are charts showing an anchorage to the south of Castle Island in Mudian Harbour. Unfortunately, the shallow bay there is chock full of coral. You might get in, but you would lie uneasily there. It should only be considered as an emergency anchorage in winds out of the north. If it blew, or you suffered surge, you could be in serious trouble. As for the east or ocean coast of Acklins, it is forbidden territory. A long run of nothing but reef and coral heads. Keep well clear of it.

South of the Mira Por Vos Passage

At this point on the western route, your only sensible course, if you are heading south, is to make a straight run for the Windward Passage, standing well to the west of Hogsty Reef and well off Great Inagua. You will be setting off on a course of 160/340 degrees true with around 100-plus nautical miles to go—a run that can be broken with no great cost in diversionary miles at Great Inagua.

If you are bound for the Turks and Caicos, you have already gone out of your way. A straight run to Sandbore Channel, passing well north of Hogsty Reef and, of course, well north of the two Inagua Islands, is possible. Your course of 100/280 degrees true, and a run of 110 nautical miles or so, will place you at the Sandbore approach waypoint. It is not an efficient way to reach Providenciales, when you compare it to the eastern route, and more times than not, you will be heading into the prevailing winds. However, on a reverse course, it could be a different story, and the Crooked Island Passage, and indeed the bank route, could be an attractive option using the protection of the Crooked–Acklins–Long Cay group and Long Island to advantage. We will conclude this section on the Western Route with brief coverage of the remaining two Bahamian territories that lie in this area of ocean, but are not on your direct track whichever heading you follow.

Hogsty Reef

About as remote as you can get in Bahamian waters (over 30 nautical miles from land in any direction), Hogsty Reef is a one-off in the Western Hemisphere. It is a nearly perfect atoll, barely five nautical miles east to west and three nautical miles north to south. In its time, it has also been a mean ship-cruncher, and no one knows how many vessels have fixed the exact position of

Castle Island Lighthouse. (Not to be used for navigation.) Waterway Guide Photography.

Hogsty Reef more accurately than they may have wished. Two long-abandoned, rust-red wrecks remain there, high and dry on the reef. It is one of the fabled remote Bahamian dive sites, visited occasionally by live-aboard dive boats, but otherwise, you might want to give it a pass.

If you do elect to go there, it is entirely possible to make your way into the lagoon through a pass on the west side to the south of Northwest Cay, and anchor wherever the depth suits you. You will find anything from 5.4-meter/18-foot to 1.8-meter/6-foot depths. Being caught there in bad weather is not the stuff of pleasant dreams. Hogsty is dangerous in southwest and northwest weather.

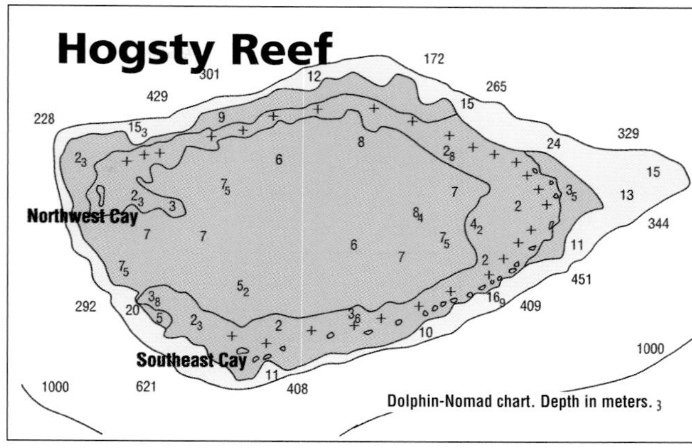

The Inagua Islands

Great Inagua, which dwarfs its smaller sibling to the northeast, Little Inagua, also dominates the southern Bahamas by land mass alone. It is almost 40 nautical miles wide running east to west, by 26 nautical miles north to south. Its little sibling, just five nautical miles away across a strait, is a stout 10 nautical miles wide, by eight nautical miles running north to south. Despite the total land mass, perhaps it is a blessing that the two islands lay on no direct track, for there is little there, and both islands are almost completely surrounded by reefs. There are possible anchorages off Little Inagua's northwest and southwest points, but not much else to attract the cruising or passage-making visitor.

Great Inagua has far more to offer than its sibling. Its only settlement, Matthew Town on the southwest tip, has an airstrip and small harbor. The island is the source of raw product for Morton Salt, and over a million tons of it are exported each year, 99.4 to 99.6 percent pure. This good fortune means a salt-loading dock at Man-of-War Bay on the west coast to the north of Matthew Town, where the backdrop of stockpiles of salt gives the disorienting appearance of snow-covered peaks. Matthew Town has the stamp of a company town and the

The *Lady Mathilda*

You could say that Hogsty Reef is (1) so remote and (2) such a well-known hazard that the probability these days that anyone should run onto the reef was close to zero. On the night of December 9, 1998, the mailboat *Lady Mathilda* was bound from Mayaguana to Great Inagua on her regular run in the southern Bahamas. She was carrying her normal load; vehicles as deck cargo, drums of fuel and frozen food, as well as whatever had been requested for delivery from Nassau. It was a routine trip she had done time and time again. She ran straight on to the southeastern circle of the reef.

The weather was okay. It was five days after a full moon. There was good visibility, scattered clouds, moderate southeasterly winds and a sea state that was within her limits. But none of this would have helped if she came within sight and hearing of the surf breaking on Hogsty's barrier reef at passage speed. Our immediate reaction was to wonder about the course steered, and more particularly, the compensation made for a relatively strong set to the northwest.

Hogsty Reef. (Not to be used for navigation.)
WATERWAY GUIDE PHOTOGRAPHY.

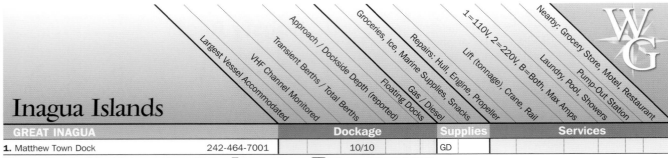

Inagua Islands

GREAT INAGUA		Largest Vessel Accommodated	VHF Channel Monitored	Transient Berths / Total Berths	Approach / Dockside Depth (reported)	Floating Docks	Gas / Diesel	Groceries, Ice, Marine Supplies, Snacks	Repairs: Hull, Engine, Propeller	Lift (tonnage), Crane, Rail	1=110V, 2=220V, B=Both, Max Amps	Laundry, Pool, Showers	Pump-Out Station	Nearby: Grocery Store, Motel, Restaurant
		Dockage					Supplies		Services					
1. Matthew Town Dock	242-464-7001			10/10			GD							

Corresponding chart(s) not to be used for navigation. Internet Access Wireless Internet Access

Not to be used for navigation.

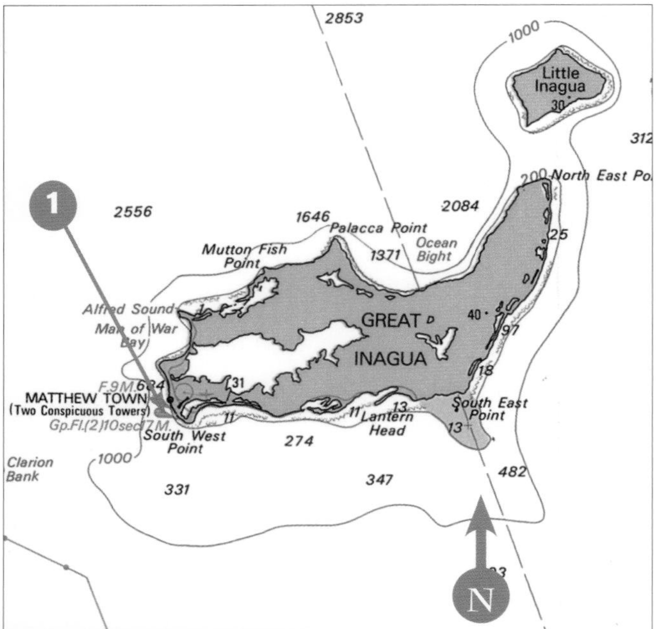

GREAT INAGUA, Chart 3914

Reproduced from Admiralty Chart 3914. Depth in meters.

A Second Hogsty Reef Story

A trimaran, with four on board, ran on the reef attempting to enter the lagoon some time back. There was no one else there. Hogsty Reef was deserted. Five days later, a small Bahamian fishing boat passed and stopped. They could take no more than one person on board. Three of the trimaran crew were left to trust that their companion would reach some place where he could make contact with the outside world. It must have been an unnerving period. They were lucky. Their crewman reached safety and a telephone. They were rescued by the U.S. Coast Guard.

advantages that brings: better-stocked stores than most Out Islands, a regular air service, better back-up facilities and a U.S. Coast Guard station.

For the visiting yachtsman, there are few attractions. The reefs around the island are formidable, particularly at Southeast Point where they run out for five nautical miles. There are no anchorages anywhere, save off Matthew Town where there are no reefs, but wind and ocean swell could make any extended visit uncomfortable, to say the least.

Matthew Town Harbour

If you are going to enter the harbor, go carefully. The slanted entry into this small concrete and rock basin has a single leading mark at its southeast corner. Watch out for the reef to starboard that runs out from the shore as you approach. Once inside, you will have 3-meter/10-foot depths at mean low water, however the entrance channel is reported to have as little as 1.5 meters/5 feet. To starboard, you have the concrete dock used by the mail-boat, which has a short arm on the seaward side and a longer run on the land side. Aside from the fuel facility near the range marker in the southeast corner, there is the Bahamas Defence Force office, a BTC telephone box and a restaurant and bar, Topps, in town. This is essentially a government dock used by a mailboat. It is not intended to be a facility for cruising boats. The U.S. Coast Guard has a presence in Matthew Town, but they are there as "guests." If you run into trouble, the responsibility for monitoring VHF Channel 16 lies in the hands of the Bahamas Defence Force.

What may get you to Matthew Town? Crew changes and air-delivered spares or maybe fuel, and possibly back-up engineering from the workshops of the Morton Salt Company. You would also have access to their grocery and hardware stores. Maybe medical help (there is a small hospital there) and air evacuation is always possible. That alone may be worth an entry in your "What If?" file. If you do need to visit, remember that your coastal landmarks are the lighthouse on the coast to the south of Matthew Town and the two BTC dishes to the north of Matthew Town and Matthew Town Harbour. Surge into the harbor, especially in any strong winds out of the west, would make this an uncomfortable landing, but in any winds from an easterly quadrant, anchoring off of town or even up under Northwest Point in Man of War Bay could be viable options.

Inagua National Park

If none of this sounds particularly encouraging, perhaps in settled weather, there is a good reason for visiting Great Inagua: the Inagua National Park. The park, given a boost by the Audubon Society, is now home to the largest colony of West Indian flamingos in the world, about 50,000 birds, narrowly saved from extinction. The pink birds share their habitat with a number of other native birds, also virtually extinct, not the least of which is the cute little Bahamian parrot. An early cruising visitor, a Genoese sailor working for Spain, reported that the parrots circled them in flocks as they approached each island. His name? It doesn't often feature in works on wildlife,

Morton Salt. WATERWAY GUIDE PHOTOGRAPHY.

but you may have heard of him for other reasons—Columbus. Christopher Columbus. For all these reasons, we have covered Great Inagua in our Goin' Ashore.

Pilotage. Talking Captain to Captain

George Town to Long Island East Coast

The initial legs of the eastern route south from George Town down the Atlantic coast of Long Island are covered in Chapter 17, Long Island. We will not repeat the navigation data, warnings and port/harbor detail here. The run across the Crooked Island Passage is straightforward and starts after your arrival at Bird Rock (BDRCK).

Portland "Harbour" Anchorage (Pittstown Point), Crooked Island

The entry point lies to the south of Bird Rock. Working your way in, you have 6 meters/20 feet of water, and keeping the obvious coral to starboard, once you are "inside" Bird Rock, turn to starboard toward the center of the first white sand beach. It is eyeball navigation territory, the coral easily seen and easily avoided, with the main reef lying to starboard. Anchor over sand as close in as you desire, comfortably off the beach, about midway between Pittstown Point and the next mini-point to the east (N 22° 49.980'/W 074° 20.530'). There will always be some motion inside Portland Harbour, but with south winds and no significant ocean swell, it is fine.

Landrail Point Anchorage, Crooked Island

The best place to anchor lies north of Landrail Point (LNDRL), halfway to Pittstown Point, off the white sand beach just opposite the only mid-beach stand of casuarinas. However, the absence of a reef doesn't mean that there is no coral there, and you must read your way in. You will anchor in 6- to 9-meter/20- to 30-foot depths over good sand. Here you will be fine in east to northeast winds, and wind from the south of no significant strength. Anything from the north is out of the question. Don't be tempted to move closer to Landrail Point. The bottom there looks good, sand in part, but it is thin sand over rock. A grapnel might eventually hold, but you are likely to drag. In Landrail Point, there is a small-craft basin cut into the rock at the north end of the settlement that you can use, but you may prefer to run your dinghy right up on the beach.

Samana Cay

If you wish to visit Samana Cay, either Bird Rock or the Acklins northeast waypoint (ACKNE) is a logical departure/return waypoint. If you want to anchor off Samana Cay, forget the bay in the north. The only place to attempt anchoring is the shallow bight in the south, just north of the SMANA waypoint.

From here, you have to find your way in to the bay through the coral. Hopefully, you can anchor off and scout the area by dinghy first, and will also have the dividend of the extra 0.6-meter/2-foot depths that a high tide will give you. Mark your way in with temporary buoys. Even the Acklins fishermen do this, and if you find other people's markers there, be wary of using them. Check the whole thing out yourself. Once in, you will be safe if the wind is from the north. Forget Samana Cay if the wind is northwest or southwest, and forget it whenever high seas are running.

Atwood Harbour, North Acklins

From the waypoint ATWOD, the break in the Atwood barrier reef normally shows, but you have no particular leading mark as you enter the "harbor" (which is no more than a crescent-shaped bay) other than to steer almost due south leaving Umbrella Rock and the white light on the headland to port. Look out for the coral inside the harbor area, and once inside the curve of the anchorage, turn to port and find your chosen place to drop your hook. There are two houses there, on the foreshore.

There is a small settlement, Chester's, about two miles to the west, with one small store and a telephone. A second small settlement, Pinefield Point, on the east coast about four miles south of Northeast Point, is primarily a fishing village. If you wish to find a local guide try Newton Williamson answering on VHF Channel 16 as *Holiday Inn* or use BTC and call 242-344-3210.

Northeast Breaker, North Acklins

A reef known as the Northeast Breaker lies four nautical miles east of Northeast Point. It is marked on the chart, and it shows, hence its name, as breaking seas. Take note that a continuous spine of reef runs between Northeast Point and the Northeast Breaker. Stay well clear, and round the Northeast Breaker to the east. The ACKNE and PLNAW (Plana West) waypoints will keep you clear.

Crooked/Acklins Islands to Mayaguana

Your legs from BRDRK to the Mayaguana West (MAYAW) waypoint pose no problems. The two Plana Cays waypoints, PLNAW and the south waypoint PLNAS, are set to keep you clear of the Plana Cays, but you may well wish to visit them. Just eyeball your way in to wherever you want to go. Be aware that there is often a rip between the two cays. The final leg of this section takes you across the Mayaguana Passage.

Abrahams Bay West (Low Point Pass), Mayaguana

The entry at the west end of Abrahams Bay is just under a mile slightly southeast of Low Point. If you choose to put in here, it places you farthest away from the Abrahams Bay settlement, but it is certainly the easier of the two cuts to negotiate and carries some 3.6-meter/12-foot depths at mean low water. The break in the reef is easily defined, and it is this entry that is used by the mailboat if it has to divert to Abrahams Bay.

Your primary coastline landmark, just to the west of Low Point, is the remains of the U.S. missile station dock (N 22° 20.100'/W 073° 03.850') with a tank farm behind it. The range marks still stand, but the dock is unusable. Nonetheless, this docking facility, partly kept in use, is the island's source of fuel. The fuel tanker anchors off, and runs its discharge hoses over the sea to the dock, where they are connected to working pipelines running back to two in-use fuel tanks in the farm. Low Point itself, by no means a well-defined feature, is your second landmark.

The Mayaguana West (MAYAW) waypoint lies just over one nautical mile from the Start Point dock, which bears 330/150 degrees true from the waypoint, and 0.7 nautical miles from Low Point, which lies on a bearing of 342/162 degrees true. The pass through the reef is wide and clearly defined by its blue color, and, even as it shoals, gives you 4-meter/13-foot depths. There is plenty of sea room and good depth for the first half mile, which you take on a heading of about 052/232 degrees true, and then you will be in around 3.6 meters/12 feet of water. At this point, alter slightly to a course of 076/256 degrees true, and carry on to give yourself shelter behind the barrier reef. Just another half-mile or so should do it.

Atwood Harbour, from the north. (Not to be used for navigation.) Waterway Guide Photography.

Atwood Harbour, from the south. (Not to be used for navigation.) Waterway Guide Photography.

North Acklins, from the east. (Not to be used for navigation.) Waterway Guide Photography.

North Acklins, from the northwest. (Not to be used for navigation.) WATERWAY GUIDE PHOTOGRAPHY.

The downside of this anchorage is that if you want to take your dinghy to the Abrahams Bay settlement dock, you have a long haul (just over two miles) to get there. Don't attempt it at low tide. You could be walking long before you get anywhere near the dock. You might consider working your way eastward to anchor closer to the Abrahams Bay dock, but we see little advantage in it. If you really need the settlement, choose the Guano Point Pass anchorage.

Abrahams Bay East (Guano Point Pass), Mayaguana

At the east end of Abrahams Bay, under Guano Point, where there is a light that may or may not be lit, you have another well-defined break in the reef but less water, only 2.4-meter/8-foot depths at mean low water, and the opening turns out to be deceptive. At first sight, it seems wide and fairly well-defined, but after the initial pass through the outer barrier reef, there is a secondary reef, known as Middle Reef, lying right in the middle. There appears to be the option at this point of passing Middle Reef on either side, for apparent deeper water seems to run each way, but under no circumstances should you choose to pass between Middle Reef and Guano Point. You will wreck as others have done. That way runs right into a coral trap.

From the Mayaguana East (MAYAE) waypoint, which lies one nautical mile due south of Guano Light, take a heading of around 315/135 degrees true and follow the deeper water that runs in a northwesterly direction, leaving Middle Reef to starboard. You will have 2.7-meter/8-foot depths at mean low water, but go carefully. Just short of a mile in, there are two shallow shelves or steps where the water depth will reduce by half, but both are avoidable. Navigate visually as you go in. At this point, you are just about abeam of Middle Reef, and Guano Light will bear about 090/270 degrees true. Start heading more

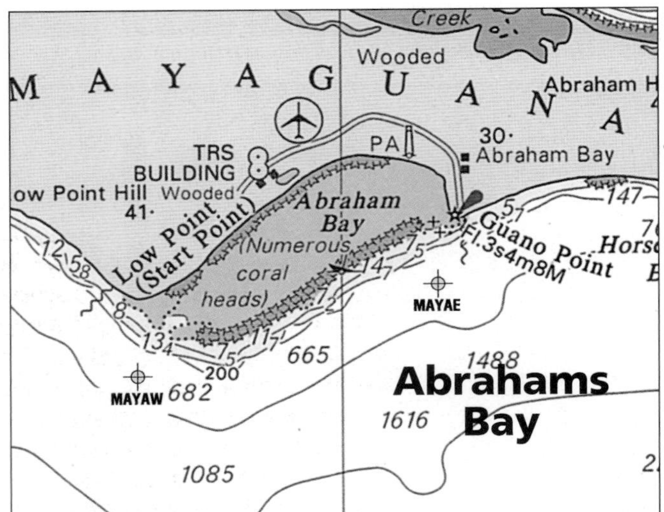

Reproduced from Admiralty Chart 3914. Depth in meters.

Not to be used for navigation.

An Abrahams Bay Cautionary Tale

A small sailboat was wrecked on the reef leaving Abrahams Bay through the Guano Point Pass. Her captain sailed late in the day, despite heavy surf breaking along the reef, and realized too late that the seas were too much for him. He turned back, but had lost his light by then, and with it, his ability to read the water. It hardly mattered, for in turning he was swept sideways. He hit Middle Reef. The state of the surf at the Guano Pass entry tells you everything. If there is a lather of white water there, forget it.

to the west, following the deeper water, and run in behind the barrier reef to drop anchor wherever you fancy. Your depth on this curve should hold at 2 meters/6.5 feet at mean low water.

Don't head toward the Abrahams Bay concrete dock that lies to the northeast, nearly a mile off. In no time at all, you would be in is 0.9 meter/3 feet of water. Despite a scar with the semblance of a channel carved by a local fishing boat, the dock is only approachable by dinghy, and as was said earlier, don't even try it at low tide. You will find barely a foot of water there. Don't be fooled by the fishing boat if it is at the dock.

Southeast Point, Mayaguana

From the Mayaguana Southeast waypoint (MAYSE), head due north for about 1.5 miles, and anchor off the sandy beach. You have to practically be on shore to find shallow enough water in which to anchor. Southeast Point makes for an easy early morning departure without having to have good light to negotiate the reef pass out Abrahams Bay. Its crystal clear waters are teeming with fish and may provide you with dinner.

Mayaguana to Turks and Caicos Approaches

You are set up to head across the Caicos Passage, and make your landfall in the Turks and Caicos Islands from MAYAW, MAYAE or MAYSE.

Western Route South. Harvey Cay to Nuevitas Rocks

The first leg is a 27-nautical mile straight shot from a position safely to the west of Harvey Cay (HARVY) to the area of the Great Bahama Bank lying off the Brigantine Cays, and by extension, East and West Barracouta Rocks. In this first part of your transit, the critical parameter is that you should be running along a general line to pass no closer than eight nautical miles to the west of Darby Island, and for that matter, the rest of the coastline

Approaches to Providenciales, Turks and Caicos

Whether the Turks and Caicos Islands are your turnaround point or just a waypoint on an extended passage, makes little difference to the geography of your approaches in the early stages, unless you are going to bypass the Turks and Caicos completely as do those who don't want to transit the Caicos Bank. If you elect to stop in the Turks and Caicos, you are bound to make Providenciales (known as Provo) your first stop and your port of entry. Why? Because it is, right on your path. And Provo has everything. Nowhere else in the Turks and Caicos has as much to offer the transient boater.

You have two landfall options, as Provo is a barrier island, one of the circlet of islands bordering the Caicos Bank starting at West Caicos in the west and continuing around to South Caicos in the southeast. If you elect to stay outside the Caicos Bank initially, PROVN off Northwest Point will be the approach waypoint after crossing the Caicos Passage. If you want to get on the Caicos Bank at the outset, you must pass between Provo and West Caicos, through the Sandbore Channel (a.k.a. Caicos Creek). Here the Sandbore Channel Approach mark (SBORA) is the waypoint.

For details, turn to the section on the Turks and Caicos Islands, in which we also give the location of an anchorage that may be found in darkness if, arriving early, you wish to drop your hook rather than stand off waiting for daylight. However this option is weather dependent. Your cruise planning should call for a daylight landfall.

Guano Point Pass from the east. (Not to be used with navigation.) WATERWAY GUIDE PHOTOGRAPHY.

as you proceed south. Keep your eyes open for sand, but you should have 1.8- to 2.1-meter/6- to 7-foot depths all the way.

In the Barracouta Rocks area (BRCTA), you will come across a wide band of sand that has worked its way in from the west. At first it appears Sahara-like (albeit an underwater Sahara), a broken pattern of dunes and ridges that gives way to a snake pattern of sand ridges, yellow-white against an electric blue background. It is some of the most extraordinary water you will see in the Bahamas. The sand continues to advance, but with any luck, you should have 1.8-meter/6-foot depths or more at mean low water. It is a continually changing area.

The next target is to pass to the west of Hawksbill Rock (HWKBL), some 22 nautical miles farther south. Coral reefs and isolated coral heads lie both east and west of Hawksbill Rock. Aim to pass to the west of Hawksbill Rock, fairly close to it without hugging the rock, and there will be a channel there relatively clear of coral in which you will have 1.8- to 2.1-meter/6- to 7-foot depths at mean low water.

The final bank leg is 46 nautical miles to pass east of Nuevitas Light (NUEVR). You will have no problems there, for the Nuevitas Rocks are obvious, and you have a well-defined blue-water pass to take you out into deep ocean water.

It is understood, but we will say it anyway. You must have good light to do this transit south from Harvey Cay or northbound from Nuevitas Rocks. You must use your eyes, for the underwater pattern is constantly changing, and if you can't read the water, you must stop, anchor, and go no farther until you have useful light.

Nuevitas Rocks to Windward Passage

If you are heading directly for the Windward Passage, a 30-nautical-mile straight shot to the Long Island South Point West (LISPW) waypoint sets you up to head 53 nautical miles on to the Mira Por Vos waypoint (MIRAP). From here, 102 nautical miles on a course of 161/341 degrees true will take you to the Windward Passage North (WINDN) waypoint. This is blue water all the way, with the only relatively shallow areas being the Diana Bank, that you pass on the first leg, and the Mira Por Vos reefs, but you have a deep-water pass there.

Alternatively you may well wish to visit Crooked Island, Long Cay and Acklins. Or, farther to the south, stop at Hogsty Reef or in Great Inagua. These places were commented on earlier in the chapter. Wherever you go in these Far Horizons, you will be one of the few vessels that ventures this far afield. ■

WATERWAY GUIDE is always open to your observations from the helm. E-mail your comments on any navigation information in the guide to: editor@waterwayguide.com.

The Bahamas South of the Tropic of Cancer. Far Horizons Waypoints

CROOKED ISLAND

Mid-Crooked Island Passage	MIDCP	22°51.00N / 74°35.50W
Bird Rock NW	BRDRK	22°53.00N / 74°23.00W
Bird Rock	BRDRE	22°50.70N / 74°21.56W
Portland Harbour Entry	PTLNH	22°50.40N / 74°21.25W
Portland Anchorage	PTLNA	22°50.20N / 74°20.78W
Landrail Anchorage	LNDAN	22°49.16N / 74°20.80W
Landrail Point	LNDRL (B59)	22°48.50N / 74°21.00W
Landrail Small Boat Basin	LNDSB	22°48.30N / 74°20.48W
Landrail Government Dock	LNDGD	22°48.11N / 74°20.36W
French Wells West 1	FRWW1	22°41.00N / 74°19.00W
French Wells West 2	FRWW2	22°41.08N / 74°18.00W
French Wells Anchorage	FRWAN	22°41.07N / 74°16.48W

LONG CAY

Long Cay Windsor Point	LONGC	22°32.50N / 74°25.00W

SAMANA CAY

Samana Cay	SMANA (B54)	23°03.30N / 73°47.00W

ACKLINS ISLAND

Atwood Harbour North	ATWOD (B61)	22°44.00N / 73°53.15W
Atwood Harbour	ATHBR	22°43.90N / 73°53.20W
Acklins NE Point	ACKNE	22°46.00N / 73°43.00W
Salina Point	SLINA	22°14.00N / 74°18.00W
Mira Por Vos Passage	MIRAP (B31A)	22°06.00N / 74°21.00W

PLANA CAYS

Plana Cays West	PLNAW	22°37.00N / 73°43.00W
Plana Cays South	PLNAS	22°30.00N / 73°43.00W

MAYAGUANA

Government Dock	MYADK (B62)	22°27.00N / 73°08.00W
Betsy Bay	BETSY	22°25.00N / 73°09.00W
Mayaguana West	MAYAW (B65)	22°19.30N / 73°03.30W
Mayaguana East	MAYAE (B63)	22°20.80N / 72°58.05W
Mayaguana Southeast	MAYSE	22°16.800N / 72°47.00W

HOGSTY REEF

Hogsty Reef	HGSTY	21°41.00N / 73°54.00W

GREAT INAGUA ISLAND

Mathew Town	INAGA (B34)	20°57.00N / 73°44.00W

WINDWARD PASSAGE

Windward Passage North	WINDN	20°30.00N / 73°50.00W

Position format is latitude and longitude in degrees and minutes (hddd°mm.mm). Waypoints in RED are NOT for autopilot navigation. Codes in parenthesis are Wavey Line waypoints marked on the charts. If you have programmed waypoints listed in a previous edition of this guide, check carefully to ensure the coordinates you have recorded match the list. If a waypoint is no longer on the list we may have changed its code or deleted it.

GOIN' ASHORE:

CROOKED ISLAND

The Landrail Point area still has the only settlement for boaters on Crooked Island. There is a small boat harbor through a narrow cut, (suitable only for dinghies) that will bring you into Landrail settlement with a small government dock, filling station and BTC office. You will also find groceries, restaurants and the Gibson and Scavella families, who are delighted to meet visitors and will help in any way they can.

About two and one half miles north of Landrail Point, on a superb site, is the renamed *Crooked Island Lodge at Pittstown Point* (formerly Pittstown Point Landings), one of the best-kept secrets in the Bahamas. Crooked Island Lodge offers its own 2,300-foot paved landing strip. New home sites and a marina are planned. This would make a significant difference to cruising between Clarence Town and Providenciales. If you call in, you will find a warm welcome.

In the settlements, there is usually water, fuel in drums or cans, and basic food stores. But the lack of all-weather anchorages probably dictates that you will soon move on, and your ability to move around the islands or from one settlement to the other is limited to the endurance of your dinghy or success at hitching a ride. A sporadic ferry runs between the southeast tip of Crooked Island and Lovely Bay on Acklins Island. Other than private aircraft into Pittstown Point, both Crooked and Acklins Islands are served by Bahamasair if you need to fly in or out. There is always BTC if you need to contact the outside world. There are medical clinics in the larger settlements. There is no bank on either island, so make sure you have enough cash.

We don't cover the island exhaustively, but give a brief review of "what's there" in the place you are most likely to make a landfall—Landrail Point.

EMERGENCIES

Marine • VHF 16

Medical *Clinic* • 242-344-2676 • Nurse Blanche, the nurse practitioner, can be contacted through *BTC* at Landrail Point. Doctor from Acklins comes over every two weeks.

LANDRAIL POINT

Accommodations *Gibson's House*, 242-344-2676. At Landrail Point. A two-bedroom cottage with a shared bathroom • *Crooked Island Lodge at Pittstown Point*, Tel: 242-344-2507, Fax: 242-344-2573, info@pittstownpoint.com, www.pittstownpoint.com. Twelve rooms from $240 per day. This small resort is greatly dependent on its own airfield and pilot loyalty, but welcomes visiting boaters. If you anchor off their beaches in a favorable wind, come ashore at the end of the runway for dinner. If you are at anchor off Landrail Point, call VHF 16 "Pittstown Point" ahead of time. You can be picked up from the town's small boat harbor • *Scavella's Guest House* Four rooms to rent. Ask at the gas station or the grocery store.

Airstrip & Airline *Pittstown Point Landings* private airstrip. Charter flights arranged at hotel• *Bahamasair,* 242-344-2357. Flights into Colonel Hill on Wednesday and Saturday • *Over and Under, 305-852-8015.*

Bakery *Chez Willie.*

Bonefishing Guide *Willis McKinney*, VHF 16 "Ocean View."

Church *Seventh Day Adventist Church, Anglican Church, Baptist Church, Church of God, Pentecostal Church.*

Fuel *Scavella's Fuel Service* • 242-344-2598, VHF 16 "Early Bird." • Usually has diesel and gasoline. Carry it out to your boat in jerry cans.

Hardware *Scavella's Fuel Service*, 242-344-2598, VHF 16 "Early Bird."

Mailboat Calls every 10 days.

Medical *Government Clinic*, 242-344-2166.

Propane Sent to Nassau on mailboat that comes into Government Dock.

Provisions *Scavella's Grocery Store,* Next to their filling station. Canned and dried goods. Occasionally fresh fruit and vegetables • *Green Valley Grocery Store* • Local residents will sell you their citrus and produce right off their trees and out of their gardens.

Restaurants *Chez Willie*, open for lunch and dinner daily. • *Seaside Cafe* • *Lunch Room #2* • *Crooked Island Lodge at Pittstown Point.*

Telephone *BTC*, 242-344-2423.

Water RO at *Scavella's*.

THINGS TO DO ON CROOKED ISLAND

- Go to French Wells for gunkholing and fishing; maybe anchor there for a couple of days in a blow.
- Take your dinghy out to Bird Rock Lighthouse. You can snorkel around it.
- Find someone to guide you across the lagoon to see ruins and the few old cannons at the Marine Farm, a one-time British fortification.
- Visit the bat caves about four miles east of Pittstown Point, or dive the 1,500-foot wall that is only 200 feet offshore.
- Snorkel along the unlimited barrier reef.

ACKLINS ISLAND

Until the cotton crops were wiped out by blight in the last century, large, working plantations covered this island. Beautiful and undeveloped, and no longer heavily populated, Acklins offers some of the most pristine and highest land in the islands. The local tarpon and bonefishing is some of the best in the Bahamas. There are a few onshore facilities, and the ones listed are sprinkled throughout the island.

You can access Acklins at Atwood Harbour in the north or anchoring off Jamaica Bay in the south. Chesters settlement is your northern point of contact and Salina Point is the southern one. The center of the island is Spring Point, reached only by road. The ocean side offers no viable anchorage, and the bight side is accessible only by very shoal-draft craft. Spring Point is a *Bahamasair* stop and offers some facilities.

EMERGENCIES

Marine • VHF 16
Medical *Main Island Clinic* • 242-344-3615/3550/3536 • At Spring Point. *BTC* will contact a doctor during working hours. In an emergency or on weekends, the number is transferred to the doctor's home phone. Nurse 242-344-3139 after hours. The clinic is open 9 a.m. to 5:30 p.m., weekdays.
Clinic at Masons Bay • 242-344-3165, 242-344-3628 after hours and on weekends.
Clinic at Chesters Not staffed, but a doctor visits twice a month.
Med-Evac Handled through *Spring Point Airport.*

Accommodations *Greys Point Bonefishing Inn*, 1-800-99-FLATS, At Pinefield Point • *Nai's Guest House*, 242-344-3173 • *Acklin's Island Flyfishing Camp*, 242-334-3500 • *Top Choice Bonefishing Lodge*, 242-344-3628 • *Airport Inn & Restaurant*, 242-344-3600, VHF 16, "Red Devil."
Airstrip & Airline Spring Point airstrip • *Bahamasair,* 242-344-2357. Flights into Spring Point.
Bonefishing *Joe Deleveaux* • VHF 16 "Lovely Bay" or call Elijah Beneby, 242-344-3087 to pass a message. *Newton Williamson* • 242-344-3210 • VHF "Holiday Inn."
Churches *Anglican, Church of God, Seventh Day Adventist.*
Contacts These people can be very helpful in the various settlements: **Chesters** *Edmund Johnson,* 242-344-3108, **Hard Hill** *Leonard Collie*, 242-344-3613, **Lovely Bay** *Elijah Beneby,* 242-344-3087, **Pinefield Point** *Newton Williamson,* 242-344-3210, VHF 16 "Holiday Inn", **Salina Point** *George Emmanuel,* 242-344-3671.
Ferry A ferry runs between Lovely Bay and Crooked Island at about 8 a.m. and 4 p.m.
Fuel Diesel and gasoline are available at the government dock. Call VHF 16 "Central," or contact Felix at BTC at Spring Point at 242-344-3536. • Gasoline in Chesters.
Guides *Scully Cartwright,* 242-464-9524 • Fishing, snorkeling and sightseeing.
Medical *Governments Clinics* at Spring Point and Chesters.
Police • 242-344-3666 • In Spring Point. Open 9 a.m. to 5:30 p.m., weekdays. The office at the airport keeps the same hours, 242-344-3541.
Post Office • 242-344-3169 • In Masons Bay.
Propane *Nai's Service Station* in Spring Point.
Provisions *McKinney's Grocery and Meats (a.k.a. Bigmac's)* • 242-344-3625 • Open 7 a.m. to 9 .pm. weekdays; 7 a.m. to 10 a.m. and 2 p.m. to 9 p.m. on Sundays.
Restaurants & Bars *Nai's* • 242-344-3089 • VHF 16 "Nai's Place" In Spring Point. Call ahead for serving time and menu selection of Bahamian dishes. A bar, with satellite TV & pool table, has music most nights. *Bluebird Bar and Restaurant* Serves drinks, can provide lunch and dinner. Located at Salina Point.
Telephone BTC • 242-344-3550/3536 • VHF 16 • At Spring Point, open 9 a.m. to 5 p.m., weekdays.
Water RO at *Acklins Blue* • 242-344-3252. *McKinney's* • 242-344-3614.

THINGS TO DO ON ACKLINS ISLAND

- Go bonefishing.
- Visit the caves in Hard Hill. Leonard Collie (242-344-3613) can put you in touch with guides.

MAYAGUANA

As far as Goin' Ashore information is concerned, Mayaguana falls into the same category as the islands in the Crooked–Acklins–Long Cay archipelago. Mayaguana is large, 110 square miles, but with only 400 inhabitants. As you pass along its coast, it seems to go on forever. There are only a few reasonable access points. The first on the west coast where the small settlement of Betsy Bay offers a fair-weather anchorage and a new government dock, just two miles north. The new dock is useful to take on fuel by jerry can. Surge there makes coming along side in a vessel larger than a skiff perilous. Another access point on Mayaguana is Abrahams Bay, offering good anchorages behind its barrier reef. Its dock is also suitable for dinghies. There are no taxis or buses here. You will have an adventure hitching rides with the friendly locals. The Southeast Point anchorage is just that, an anchorage. There is no access to any services.

At Mayaguana, you can take advantage of the Abrahams Bay anchorages, which are as close as you can get to all-weather anchorages in these waters. It is a port of entry so you can clear in here. There is a clinic, BTC, basic food stores, fuel in drums, an airport and a mailboat every two weeks. There are no banks, so have cash on hand. Most importantly, there are wonderfully friendly and kind people who will do everything they can to help you, and make you feel welcome on their own special island.

EMERGENCIES

Marine • VHF 16
Medical *Clinic* • 242-339-3109 • Open weekdays 9 to 5, two nurses on-call.

Accommodations *Sheraton Guest House*, Tel: 242-339-3131. Two guest rooms in his own home • *Baycaner Beach Resort*, Tel: 242-339-3726, Fax: 242-339-3727, info@baycanerbeach.com, www.baycanerbeach.com. Sixteen rooms on the beach from $122 per night, with air-conditioning, satellite TV and private baths. There is a restaurant and bar on the premises. Bonefishing, diving and snorkeling available, but bring your own gear. 6% surcharge for credit cards. Accept Visa, MasterCard and Travelers checks • *Mayaguana Inn*, Tel: 242-339-3067/3116 • *Paradise Villas,* 242-339-3059 • *Reggie's Guesthouse*, 242-339-3749.
Airport & Airline *Mayaguana Airport.* No facilities • *Bahamasair,* 242-339-3020, flies in from Nassau three times a week.
Bonefishing Inquire at the *Baycaner Beach Resort* • *Scully Cartwright*, 242-464-9524.
Churches *Zion Baptist Church* • *Jehovah's Witness.*
Customs and Immigration 242-339-3100. Open weekdays 9 a.m. to 5 p.m. at the Administrator's Office, next to BTC in Abrahams Bay, a ten-minute walk up from the jetty.
Fuel Diesel and gasoline at Mayaguana Petroleum, 242-339-3321.
Laundry Several local ladies will do your laundry and hang dry. Ask at *Lorraine's*.
Medical *Government Clinic,* 242-339-3209 with a 24-hour nurse.
Post Office Tel: 242-339-3100. Open 9 a.m. to 5 p.m. weekdays.
Propane *Gulf Gas*, VHF 16.
Provisions *Brook's Dry Goods* and *Lorraine's Variety & Fresh Produce* in Abrahams Bay • *Brown's Convenience Store* in Pirates Well • *L & L* in Betsy Bay.

Restaurants & Bars *Paradise Villas Restaurant* Open for breakfast and lunch by arrangement, and for dinner most nights. Good Bahamian home cooking. *Reggie's Bar* Open daily for drinks and Bahamian meals. *Baycaner Beach Resort* Call ahead for reservations.
Telephone *BTC* • 242-339-3203 (in Abrahams Bay); 242-339-3709 (at Betsy Bay) • VHF 16 • Phone cards. Open 8 a.m. to 5 p.m. weekdays. If you need to talk to anyone in the settlement, *BTC* will pass a message to them or they can be called to the phone in the office.
Trash Bins in settlements.
Water Public RO water in settlements.

THINGS TO DO IN MAYAGUANA

- Go fishing, or better still, go crabbing with new friends from Abrahams Bay, any time between March and August.
- Snorkel the reef surrounding Abrahams Bay in still weather. Bird watch and star gaze.
- Find someone to give you a ride up to Baycaner Beach Resort at Pirates Wells. Check it out. Maybe you could have lunch or dinner in their large dining room, along with a bonefishing group.
- Finish that good book you have been meaning to read.

GREAT INAGUA

airport • bank • customs & immigration • fuel • groceries • marina medical • police • post office • propane • restaurant • telephone water

Famous for salt and flamingos, Great Inagua is one of the largest islands in the Bahamas at 596 square miles. For the cruising visitor, it lies almost directly on the Windward Passage route between the Bahamas and the Caribbean. This said, few marina support facilities have yet to be developed. Great Inagua owes its continuing prosperity to the Morton Salt Company, which exports around a million and a half tons of salt each year. Morton Salt has its own company houses, backup facilities and dock here. Matthew Town, founded in 1847 and named after Governor George Matthew, is very much a satellite to the salt activity. In Great Inagua, despite the presence of the U.S. Coast Guard, the Royal Bahamas Defence Force has responsibility for monitoring VHF 16 and responding to emergency messages. Vessels can find anchoring with protection from easterlies, north of the salt pier, in 15 ft. of water in front of the church ruins. Although the Matthew Town Harbour looks good, it is not recommended for use in anything but your dinghy. Even then, make sure you enter only in calm conditions.

EMERGENCIES

Marine • VHF16 "Royal Bahamas Defence Force"
Medical *Hospital* • 242-339-1444 • In Matthew Town; clinics held 9 to 5:30 weekdays. Doctor's residence • 242-339-1226 • nurse's residence • 242-339-1540.
Police • 919

MARINA

MATTHEW TOWN HARBOUR
Tel: 242-339-1550, cell 242-464-7001 • VHF 16 "Harbour Pilot"
This is not a marina. The little harbor offers some protection from wind and a friendly welcome from its dockmaster. Plans to upgrade this facility to a marina are not yet in the works.

PORT DIRECTORY

Accommodations *Morton Apartments Main House*, 242-339-1267. Six rooms, four with a bathroom; reservations necessary • *Walkine's Guest House*, 242-339-1612 • *Enrica's Inn*, 242-339-2127 • *GAGA's Nest*, 242-339-2140. Five fully-equipped suites. Cash only.
Airport & Airlines *Matthew Town Airport*, 242-339-2680 • *Bahamasair* • 242-339-1415 • flights to Nassau on Monday, Wednesday and Friday • *Sunshine Air*, 800-327-8900.
Bank *Bank of the Bahamas* • 242-339-1264 • Open 9 a.m. to 2 p.m. on Monday and Thursday; 10 a.m. to 4 p.m. Fridays.
Bakery *Major's Bakery & Meat Market*, 242-339-1421.
Car Rentals *Ingrahams Rent-a-Car*, 242-339-1677 • *AB Rent-a-Car and Service Center*, 242-339-2224, ab_rentalcar@hotmail.com.
Churches *St. Philip's Anglican Church, Wesley Methodist Church, Zion Baptist Church, Greater Bethel Temple Mission Church, Seventh Day Adventist.*
Customs • 242-339-1254 (Matthew Town), 242-339-1605 (at the airport) • **Immigration** • 242-339-1234 (Matthew Town), 242-339-1602 (at the airport) • Both open 9 a.m. to 5 p.m. weekdays.
Fuel *Crystal Service Station* • 242-339-1427 • at the harbor. *Winston Burrows Gas Station* and *Ingrahams Service Station* in Matthew Town.
Internet *BTC*, WiFi.
Island Administrator Mr Rolle • 242-339-1271/1521 • Office open 9 a.m. to 5:30 p.m. weekdays.
Laundry Local ladies in town will do your laundry. Ask at *Ingrahams Variety*.
Library & Museum *Erickson's Public Library and Museum* • 242-339-1683.
Liquor *Ingrahams Liquor Store* Open 8 a.m. to 8 p.m. daily, after church on Sundays. This store is owned jointly with *Ingrahams Variety Store*, so check both if one is not open.
Photo Shop *Abby's Photo Shop* • 242-339-1750 • Film and developing.
Police • 242-339-1444 (in Matthew Town), 242-339-1604 (at the airport).
Post Office • 242-339-1248 • Open 9 a.m. to 4 p.m. weekdays.
Provisions & Propane *Inagua General Store* • 242-339-1460 • Open 9:30 a.m. to 5:30 p.m. This is a well-stocked and good-sized store. • *Ingrahams Variety Store* Carries food and household goods.
Propane *Inagua General Store*, 242-339-1460. Open 9:30 a.m. to 5:30 p.m.
Medical Hospital with doctor and nurse, 242-339-1249. Open 9 a.m. to 2:30 p.m. daily. Medevac can be arranged.
Repairs In an emergency, the *Morton Salt Company* machine shop may help. Call 242-339-1300 or 242-339-1849.
Restaurants & Bars *Cozy Corner Restaurant and Bar* • 242-339-1440 • Opens at 10 a.m. daily, and 1:30 p.m. on Sundays. Bahamian food, snacks, pool table, satellite TV and weekend DJ. • *Snake Pit Bar* Open from 10 a.m. daily, from 2 p.m. on Sundays. Weekend music, large, local crowd. Snacks. • *Topp's Restaurant and Bar* • 242-339-1465 • VHF 16 • Open 9 a.m. to 10 p.m. daily,

Fishermens Dock. Photo Courtesy of Peter Mitchell.

6 p.m. to 10 p.m. Sundays. Bahamian dishes and fantastic cracked conch. Call ahead for reservations and to check menu availability. • *Last Stop Take Away* • *Hide Out Cafe.*

Telephone BTC • 242-339-1000/1007 • Fax: 242-339-1323 • Office open 9 a.m. to 5:30 p.m. weekdays, with phone cards for sale.

Tours *Great Inagua Tours* • 242-339-1862/242-339-1336 • VHF 16 "Park Ranger" • Organized tours to the Inagua National Park, where huge numbers of flamingos and many types of birds can be seen, as well as donkeys and ducks, and maybe even wild boar. All-day tours include the lighthouse on the southwest coast to Arawak Indian sites and noisy bat caves.

Water RO water at the government dock.

INAGUA NATIONAL PARK

The *Bahamas National Trust,* with help from the Audubon Society, maintains the Inagua National Park. It is home to more than 50,000 flamingos, the largest nesting colony of West Indian Flamingos in the western hemisphere, as well as many other birds such as roseate spoonbills, rare reddish egrets, hummingbirds, blue herons, tree ducks and Bahamian parrots. More than 250 species of plants and animals live on Great Inagua. You can also visit the Caves, the Bonsai Forest and the inland Blue Hole. The road leading to the park is open to the public, but you will need a guide. Contact Bahamas National Trust, 242-339-2123, for tours.

THINGS TO DO IN GREAT INAGUA

- Photograph the massive salt piles; could it be snowing in the Bahamas?
- Dive the wall sites, at the edge of the Great Bahama Wall. Devils Point, in particular, has a pure sand drop-off with giant coral heads that tumble toward a vast abyss.
- Visit the famous Great Inagua Lighthouse, which became necessary after 65 boats met their final destination on the reef in one year, 1859. Built in 1870, this is one of only three remaining lighthouses in the Bahamas that are hand wound by the lighthouse keepers every two hours during the night, using a vapour burner and unique Fresnel "bull's eyes" lenses that concentrate the light so that it is visible for 15 miles. There are stunning views, and it is well worth the climb to the top, if only to learn how the lighthouse works. Why not leave a small donation to the Bahamas Lighthouse Preservation Society while you are there to help maintain this historic landmark and the similar lighthouses at Hope Town, on Elbow Cay in Abaco and at Dixons Point on San Salvador?
- Take a tour through the Inagua National Park. Day passes to the park are available from the *Bahamas National Trust.*

Chapter 19
The Unexplored Bahamas
South Andros, the Jumentos Cays, the Cay Sal Bank and the Route to Cuba

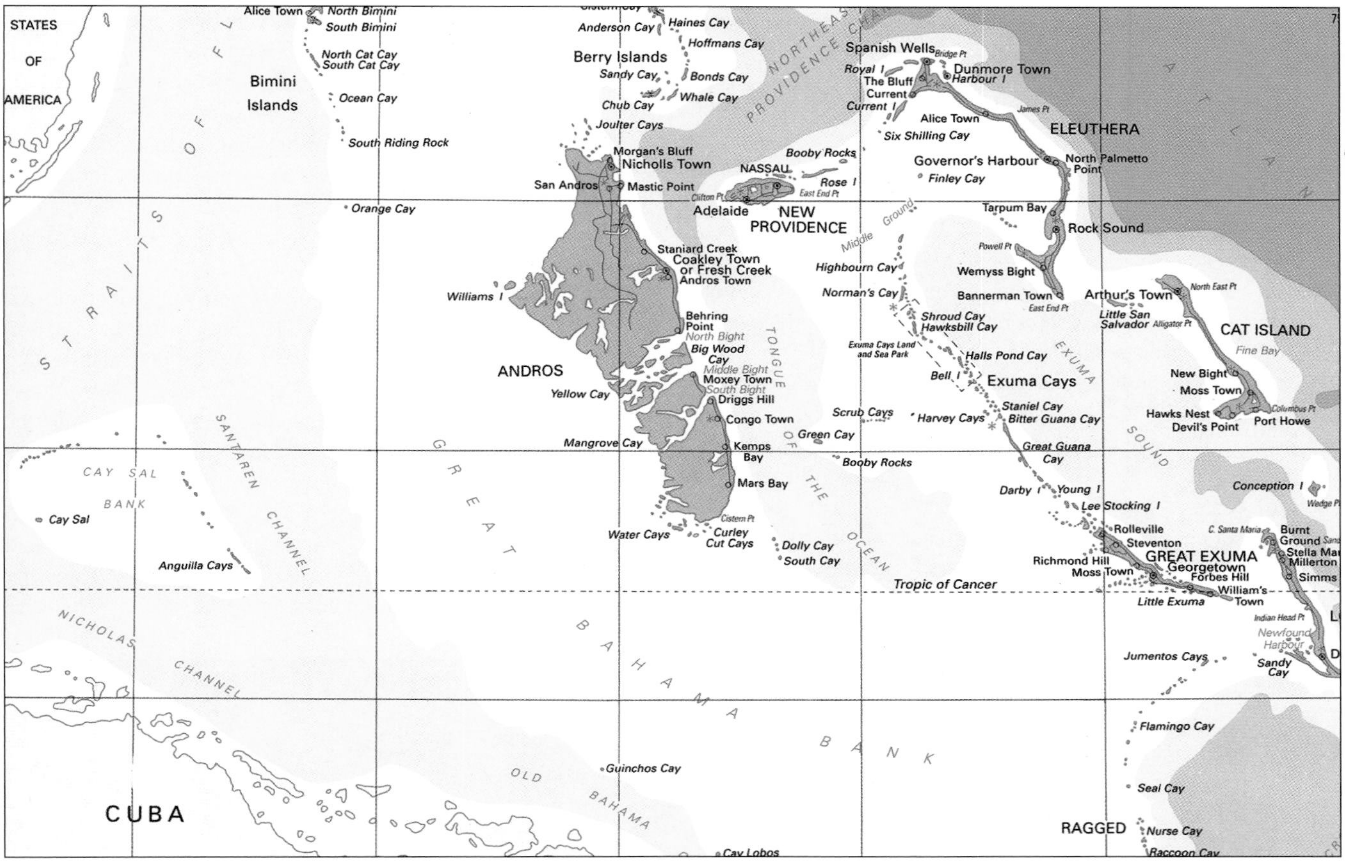

Looking At the Charts

If you look at the charts for details of these places, we think you will appreciate why they don't feature on "must-visit lists" of some pleasure cruisers to the Bahamas. South Andros attracts bonefishermen and divers. A number of isolated fishing camps, some accessible only by seaplane, keep the fishermen happy and the camps in business. The divers, often scientists, make their way there any way they can. After all, it is the third largest barrier reef in the world. Farther to the south, the Jumentos Cays are a much sought after notch on the bow for extreme sailing adventurers and a dream destination for those who want to spearfish in waters more reminiscent of yesteryear. The Cay Sal Bank seems closer and closer as more and more cruisers discover this uninhabited wonderland so close to so many Floridian's homeland, Cuba. They may just end up on your wish list.

What's There? South Andros

From the air, South Andros looks like a maze of shallows, deeper-water channels, tidal inlets, coral heads, shoals and mangrove swamps. What land is there is barren, for the most part tangled low-growth forest, scrub, sinkholes and shallow ponds. Nevertheless, winding through all this confusion, there are channels that offer transit ways across, up and down the interior and along both the coasts. It is unlikely that you will make this area a cruising destination, but it is there if you want to try it.

What's There? The Jumentos Cays

The Jumentos Cays are a great 50-nautical-mile arc of cays that start just north of the Ragged Islands at latitude N 22° 30.000' and swing northeast toward Long Island, ending 18 nautical miles south of Little Exuma. They are bordered on the east by a pocket of deep water, north of the Columbus Bank; and on the west, by the southeast edge of the Great Bahama Bank. The Jumentos form an area for real exploration, shelling, fishing and diving that remains largely untouched (although the fishing pressure there has been increasing, as Bahamians must venture farther and farther in their skiffs). Largely unvisited, except by fishermen, you are on your own there. Take note of your weather before you set out, and watch the sky while you are there. As more cruisers seek more remote areas to throw out the hook, you can expect to have company here. But, plan to take care of yourself.

The Cay Sal Bank, Cay Lobos and the Route to Cuba

Looking at the Straits of Florida chart, you can see that the straits drop almost due south to Cuba and split at the last moment into two channels by the Cay Sal Bank. The western channel keeps the Florida Straits name, but the eastern channel, called the Santaren Channel along the Bank, changes its name to the Old Bahama Channel as it runs southeastward to parallel the coast of Cuba. Where the channel narrows to barely 10 nautical miles wide, you will see Cay Lobos on the north side and the reefs of Cuba on the south.

Both Cay Sal and Cay Lobos are Bahamian territory. Both have Bahamian lighthouses built in the last century. The Cay Sal Bank Lighthouse (1839) is on Elbow Cay. The Cay Lobos Lighthouse (1860) is on the cay, hardly a stone's throw away from the coast of Cuba. The Cay Sal Bank is one great circular collection of cays and rock, about 142 nautical miles in circumference, with the closest cays about 56 nautical miles from Boot Key in the Florida Keys. There are eight named island groups in the Cay Sal Bank, 96 cays total. Of these, about 55 show up as cays on electronic charts. The named cays include Elbow Cay (with the lighthouse you can explore), Double Headed Shot Cays, Deadman Cays, Muertos Cays (which has two under water tunnels that lead to a pool in the center, cenote-like), Dog Rocks, Damas Cays, Anguilla Cays and Cay Sal.

The largest island is Cay Sal, in the southwest corner. There is a beautiful, horseshoe shaped harbor in the center of Cay Sal accessed from the southwest coast. There are unprotected anchorages, as well, off the western shores of Damas Cays and Anguilla Cays. Until recent years, the Cay Sal Bank was of little interest to anyone but Bahamian fishermen, primarily Spanish Wells lobster boats. In recent years, more and more cruisers have discovered these cays and pristine waters.

The Cay Sal Bank has one of the highest concentrations of blue holes in the world and spectacular vertical walls for diving. The cays also offer great snorkeling and diving, and is a popular fishing spot for U.S. anglers making day trips to the banks from the Keys.

Getting to the Cay Sal Bank requires bucking a lot of current. In addition, once you are on the bank, it is 6 to 10 meters/20 to 30 feet deep, and still subject to current. Do not anchor near blue holes. If going to the Cay Sal Bank or Cay Lobos, please remember that you are in Bahamian territory, and you must be cleared in and permitted beforehand by a Bahamian Customs and Immigration official (make sure you have your papers on hand). For most cruisers, these are uncharted and unexplored waters, perfect for those who want a quiet corner of the planet all to themselves. From here, you are a stone's throw across the Nicholas Channel to the north coast of Cuba.

A South Andros bonefish. ©IstockPhoto/jsafanda

Part V
The Turks and Caicos Islands

WATERWAY GUIDE PHOTOGRAPHY

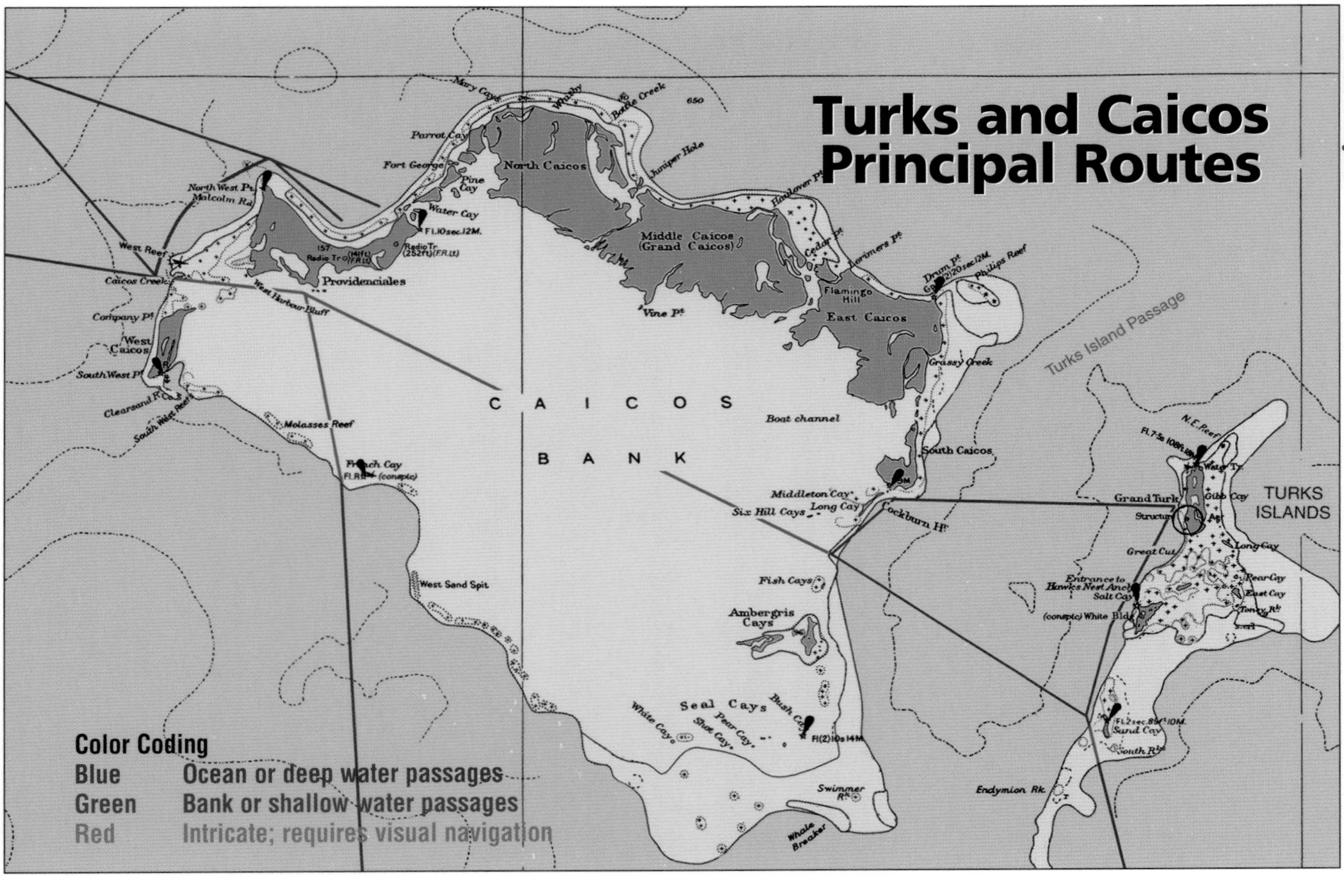

Route From	To	Headings	Distance	Passage
Mayaguana West	Providenciales North	121/301°T	47	Caicos Passage
Mayaguana West	Sandbore Channel Approach	136/316°T	47	Caicos Passage
Mira Por Vos Passage	Providenciales North	095/275°T	117	Caicos Passage
Mira Por Vos Passage	Sandbore Channel Approach	100/280°T	110	Caicos Passage
Providenciales North	Sellars Cut Approach	133/313°T	10	Atlantic Coastal
Providenciales North	Leeward Cut Approach	117/297°T	10	Atlantic Coastal
Providenciales North	Sandbore Channel Approach	221/041°T	12	Atlantic Coastal
Sandbore Channel	South Dock	see text	10	Caicos Bank
West Caicos	South Dock	see text	13	Caicos Bank
South Dock	French Cay	see text	15	Caicos Bank
South Dock	Fish Cay Channel	see text	44	Caicos Bank
West Caicos	Luperón, DR	Not covered in this Guide	133	Atlantic Open
French Cay	Luperón, DR	Not covered in this Guide	118	Atlantic Open
Fish Cay Channel	South Caicos	046/226°T	6	Turks Passage
Fish Cay Channel	Big Sand Cay	125/305°T	23	Turks Passage
South Caicos	Grand Turk	091/271°T	21	Turks Passage
Grand Turk	Big Sand Cay	see text	19	Turks Passage
Big Sand Cay	Luperón, DR	Not covered in this Guide	80	Atlantic Open
Big Sand Cay	Puerto Plata, DR	Not covered in this Guide	90	Atlantic Open
Big Sand Cay	Mona Passage	Not covered in this Guide	270	Atlantic Open
Big Sand Cay	San Juan, PR	Not covered in this Guide	360	Atlantic Open
Big Sand Cay	St Thomas, USVI	Not covered in this Guide	390	Atlantic Open

Distances exclude inshore close approaches at the start and end of a passage. The notation "see text" indicates multi-leg passages that are fully covered in the text.

Chapter 20
Introduction to the Turks and Caicos

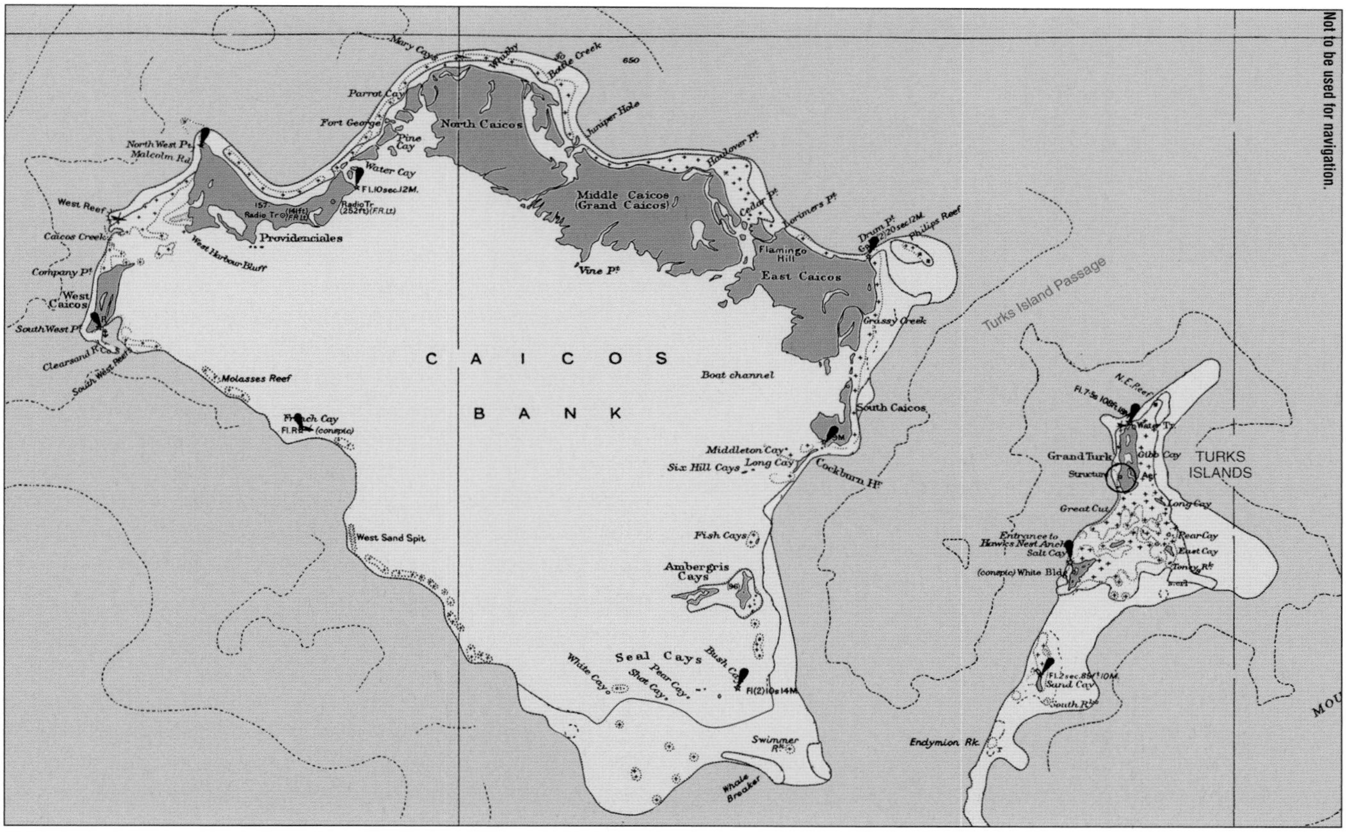

Looking At the Charts

If you open an atlas, take a straight edge and lay it on the map to connect Fort Lauderdale or Miami with the Virgin Islands, the straight edge line will pass Long Island's Cape Santa Maria, between Samana Cay and Crooked Island, then past Mayaguana. Then, it will cross over North Caicos in the Turks and Caicos and continue across open water to the Virgins.

The Turks and Caicos Islands lie between N 21 and 22° and W 71 and 72°30. There are two groups of islands, the greater part forming a crescent around the northern edge of the Caicos Bank. To the east, separated from the Caicos Bank by the deep water of the Turks Passage, is Grand Turk, Salt Cay and a number of smaller cays. With the Turks and Caicos combined, the island count numbers about 40 islands and cays spread over 193 square miles.

In the Caicos group, only Providenciales, North, Middle, South Caicos and two cays, Pine and Parrot, are inhabited. In the Turks group, the count drops down to two: Grand Turk Island and Salt Cay. The land is low lying (coral and limestone), and barely shows beyond sea-level sight range. The highest elevation in Providenciales is 163 feet. Native vegetation is scrub, savanna and marsh swamp. Native wildlife is essentially Caribbean with iguanas and flamingos as exotic extras. The islands are a main stop on the route of many migrating birds.

Think of the Caicos Bank as a 60-nautical-mile-wide, near-circular, reef-fringed atoll. Water depths on the bank run from around 6 meters/20 feet to zero at mean low water. Proven transit routes carry about 2.4 meters/8 feet. Much of the bank remains unsurveyed. For navigation, you need your eyes and good light, with the sun high in the sky. For this reason, a boat crossing the bank under sail may well choose to anchor for one night in transit.

The Turks Bank is lozenge-shaped, running from northeast to southwest for roughly 36 nautical miles. Navigable in part, it has much the same characteristics as the Caicos Bank. Both areas, like the Bahamas, have claimed many ships as victims since Juan Ponce de León discovered the islands for the European World in 1512. As always, safety lies in keeping an

Turtle Cove Marina. WATERWAY GUIDE PHOTOGRAPHY.

eye on the weather, never attempting a night passage and using the sun to advantage. Yes, you can run on autopilot on a bank transit, but you need eyes on deck as well. Otherwise, your boat's name may join the list of Turks and Caicos wrecks.

The ocean waters around the Turks and Caicos are seriously deep, plunging to 3,600 meters/12,000 feet between the Dominican Republic and these islands, then to 2,700 meters/9,000 feet in the Caicos Passage to the northwest and 4,500 meters/15,000 feet in the open Atlantic Ocean. To the southeast, three banks, the Mouchoir, Silver and Navidad banks, shoal to 18 meters/60 feet or less and have coral that is awash at mean low water. These banks are the winter breeding ground for the Atlantic Humpback Whale population. The adults and calves migrate from here every year to the New England coast for the summer. The Turks Passage, 22 nautical miles wide and 2,100 meters/7,000 feet deep, is part of their long-established ocean highway.

The Turks and Caicos claim to fame is the water world. The colors, clarity and warmth of the ocean and bank waters are unbelievable. The reefs are pristine. The diving is world-class, from shallow reef dives to breathtaking wall dives. The fishing is excellent. Turn shoreward, and Turks and Caicos beaches are "to die for"-gently shoaling water and soft white sand.

The main reason the islands are important to the voyaging mariner is their geographic location, midway between Florida and the Caribbean. Providenciales provides just about everything you are likely to require, short of a major shipyard. Three islands, Providenciales (commonly called "Provo"), South Caicos and Grand Turk, currently offer shoreside facilities and shelter. Two others, West Caicos and Big Ambergris Cay, have private marinas planned. The other islands and cays are best left for the very shoal-drafted vessels to explore.

Some cruising sailors may think that the Turks and Caicos are just too far and too remote to be attractive as a destination. But, think again. So much depends on who you are, what your level of experience is and how you choose to tackle this cruising business. In short, if you want to push the envelope a little bit, to voyage out and find new places, you might well decide to visit the Turks and Caicos. There is a very good likelihood that you will stop here if you are destined for the Virgin Islands or the Dominican Republic. It certainly means blue-water passages, but none of them are overly long. They are George Town to Long Island, to Crooked and Acklins islands and to Mayaguana and Providenciales across the Crooked Island, Mayaguana and Caicos Passages. None of these ocean trenches is significantly greater in width than the Gulf Stream. If you only have two or three weeks, forget it. But, for those who have the luxury of time, why not?

In the Spotlight. Turks and Caicos

Let us eliminate one misconception right now. Some believe that the Turks and Caicos are part of the Bahamas. There is no geological connection. Just like the Bahamas, the Turks and Caicos consist of shallow, sub-sea platforms and some isolated, sub-sea mountain peaks, separated by deep ocean troughs. The two areas share this physical similarity, but they have no physical linkage.

The same holds true socially and politically. The islands share a common ancestry as British Colonies. Nevertheless, historically, they are very different. A different settlement pattern, a different development and a different personality today. As for political status, the Turks and Caicos remain a part of the United Kingdom. On a day-to-day basis, they are semi-autonomous. However, the link with Britain is strong, and with it comes tangible assistance, as well as membership in the European Union and the financial support derived from this relationship.

Climate and Weather

The climate is tropical with temperatures averaging 24–27°C/ 75–80°F in winter (November to April) and 29–32°C/85–90°F in summer (May to October). The prevailing winds are the Trades - easterly to southeasterly - but these winds, which do much to moderate temperature and humidity, rarely bring rain. The annual average rainfall is only around 29 inches. The islands have no underlying aquifers and cannot survive on rainfall. Desalinization is vital to the local population and the tourist industry.

During the winter, the islands are affected by northers. Cold fronts from the northwest are heralded by a period of calm, invariably followed by the standard wind switch to the southwest, then to the northwest as the front moves through. It brings disturbed skies and disturbed seas, making reef passes temporarily impassable and anchorages unpleasant and, depending on

Turks and Caicos Coat of Arms, Cockburn Town. WATERWAY GUIDE PHOTOGRAPHY.

their location, untenable. A day or longer may elapse before the weather returns to normal.

As with the Bahamas, the hurricane season runs from June through November. Statistically, the Turks and Caicos seem well-favored by nature. They are hit by a hurricane, on average, only every 10 years.

The People

The Taino Indians, whose traces date back a thousand years, never survived their "discovery" by the European world. The ones who weren't sold off as slaves died from the diseases brought from the settlers. Ninety percent of the islanders are the descendants of former slaves, and the centers of population of any significance are Providenciales and Grand Turk. Strange as it now may seem, Grand Turk, the outlier, is the capital. It is one of those rare places that appears to have been bypassed by the political genesis and pressures of the Southwest Atlantic–Caribbean region. It is, perhaps, a quarter of a century behind in time. Providenciales is where the action is. The spot where all the tourist development, and much of the accompanying money, is targeted. The decision to accept the increasing isolation of the central government from its greatest concentration of population and its financial center could be questioned, but so far, there seems to be no move to reconsider the arrangement.

The Turks and Caicos Islanders call themselves "Belongers," a self-protective definition, perhaps necessary in Providenciales, as flight after flight of tourists arrive at Providenciales International Airport. Along the northern sweep of Grace Bay Beach, the resort hotels dominate the entire coastline. Elsewhere, the entire island appears to be subdivided into building lots or new houses, built for winter visitors, tax exiles and offshore bankers who crowd the most desirable sites.

Long ago, the Turks and Caicos population depended on fishing (mostly conch and lobster), boatbuilding and salt for its income. Today their livelihood depends almost entirely on tourism and tax-free status that has attracted thousands of foreign financial institutions to nail up corporate signs in Providenciales. It is different in Grand Turk. If you go to South Caicos, you will be even more removed from the glitter, glitz, drive and dust of Providenciales and its ever-expanding Gold Coast.

The Turks and Caicos National Marine Parks

The Turks and Caicos are world leaders in the field of marine conservation. To date, six marine parks have been established, as well as another 50 sites designated as land parks, reserves, sanctuaries and historical sites. The marine parks cover most of the western and the northern waters of Providenciales, West Caicos, Chalk Sound, the Pine Cay area (between Providenciales and North Caicos), South Caicos and Grand Turk. Three marine sanctuaries are of particular interest to boaters because they are definitive transit waypoints. They are French Cay, Big Sand Cay and the Seal Cays with Bush Cay Light. Protected areas are covered in the Skipper's Handbook Green Pages under Parks and Wildlife Preserves.

For the cruising visitor, conservation legislation significantly affects where you can go and what you are able to do there. In the conservation areas, except in designated anchorages, vessels over 18 meters/60 feet in length overall are prohibited. Anchoring is allowed over sand, but not within 300 feet of a dive site or within 400 feet of the low water mark. The penalties for damaging coral by grounding or anchoring are severe. The highest fine on record, levied against a U.S. yacht for damaging coral with an anchor, is $40,000. This subject is covered more fully in the Skipper's Handbook Buff Pages under Boating Regulations.

South Caicos Harbour. WATERWAY GUIDE PHOTOGRAPHY.

The Names, Turks and Caicos

Why Turks? The answer lies in a cactus plant that grows on Grand Turk Island. It looks pretty normal - green, fattish and prickly most of the time. But in flower, it produces a red top that looks just like a Turkish fez, those round red hats with a tassel that Atatürk banned when he took Turkey into the twentieth century. The plants clearly impressed the early Western European navigators. So Grand Turk got its name.

What about Caicos? It was derived from a Lucayan term "cayo hico" or "string of island."

Clearing In—Options in the Turks and Caicos

GRAND TURK: Freighter dock and anchorage at government pier.
PROVIDENCIALES: At all Marinas or dinghy to shore.
SOUTH CAICOS: Government dock, SHELL dock at the Seaview Marina.
SALT CAY: the duty police officer has the authority to clear you in.

Charts and Lights

Current Wavey Line charts are vital. TC001 covers the whole of the Turks and Caicos, and includes the approaches to the Caicos Bank, West Caicos, the Grand Turk Freighter Dock and Big Sand Cay on the Turks Bank. The more detailed TC002 covers Providenciales, Water Cay, Pine Cay and the Fort George Land and Sea Park. TC003 covers East Caicos, South Caicos, the Ambergris Cays, the Seal Cays, Grand Turk and the Turks Bank, with Salt Cay in detail.

British Admiralty and DMA charts, primarily concerned with bluewater passages, should not be used for coastal navigation in the Turks and Caicos Islands (the current DMA chart misplaces Endymion Reef on the Turks Bank by a mile).

Turks and Caicos Islands lights are gradually being repaired and brought back into operation. Do not rely on any light. It may have not been restored, or it may have failed. You should not transit these waters at night, in poor visibility or without the ability to read depths visually and accurately.

Pilotage. Talking Captain to Captain

Landfall and Departure Points

Three of the inhabited cays offer facilities to the cruising visitor. Providenciales, with several ports of call, is the most important and where you are most likely to go. South Caicos may serve as short-term shelter and Grand Turk, pleasant though it is, lacks any significant marina facilities. Grand Turk's North Creek could be listed as a hurricane hole, but don't consider it if you can't get there before the onset of severe weather.

There are a handful of other cays - one sparsely populated, the others uninhabited - that can offer you shelter in reasonably good weather and a chance to get some sleep before you continue on passage. They also offer the chance to swim, snorkel, dive and go beachcombing. French Cay, the Fish or Ambergris cays on the rim of the Caicos Bank are the most obvious choices. Salt Cay and Big Sand Cay may be your best bets on the Turks Bank.

From Big Sand Cay, Luperón is 80 nautical miles away, Puerto Plata 90 nautical miles and the Mona Passage, between the Dominican Republic and Puerto Rico (if you want to take it as a straight shot), is a 270 nautical mile trip. As you leave the Turks Bank, don't share *HMS Endymion's* 1790 misfortune (a fate shared by at least two other vessels at a later date) and hit the reef that bears the ill-fated frigate's name.

As always, weather and your endurance will dictate the way you choose to go. If you are sailing, you may be trying to ride northers to get south or running with the Trades to reach the Bahamas. Be aware that the Turks Island Passage can be a millrace, with the current taking you northward on a faster track than you desire. Additionally, the edges of the banks, like all deep-water/shallow-water interfaces, can kick up like mad when wind against current piles the water the wrong way and stacks it up against the tide. One thing is for sure, this is deep-water trolling territory at its best. ■

The Columbus Landfall

Did Columbus make his first landfall on Grand Turk Island? A plaque in the Plaza of Cockburn Town (the Government Square) will tell you so. The sea area off the western coast of Grand Turk Island has been designated the Columbus Landfall Marine National Park. Yet many maritime historians, interested in fixing the exact location of the Columbus landfall for all time, don't subscribe to the Grand Turk Island claim.

And yet, The Grand Turk Island theory has one extraordinary premise. The island he named *San Salvador* was said, in its overall shape, to resemble a bean pod. In Spanish, a *haba*. Now in a 1636 book titled *Herbal*, written by a biologist called Gerard, there is an illustration of the "wild Greeke beane" which, if you are into wish fulfillment, could be said to look like the outline of Grand Turk Island. A fluke? The rest of the supposition starts to become more tenuous as we move on from beans to the later sequence of the Columbus log.

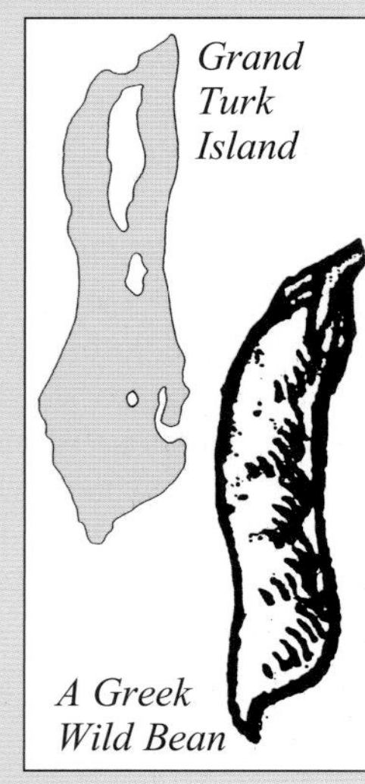

Waterway Guide is always open to your observations from the helm. E-mail your comments on any navigation information in the guide to: editor@waterwayguide.com.

Chapter 21
Providenciales

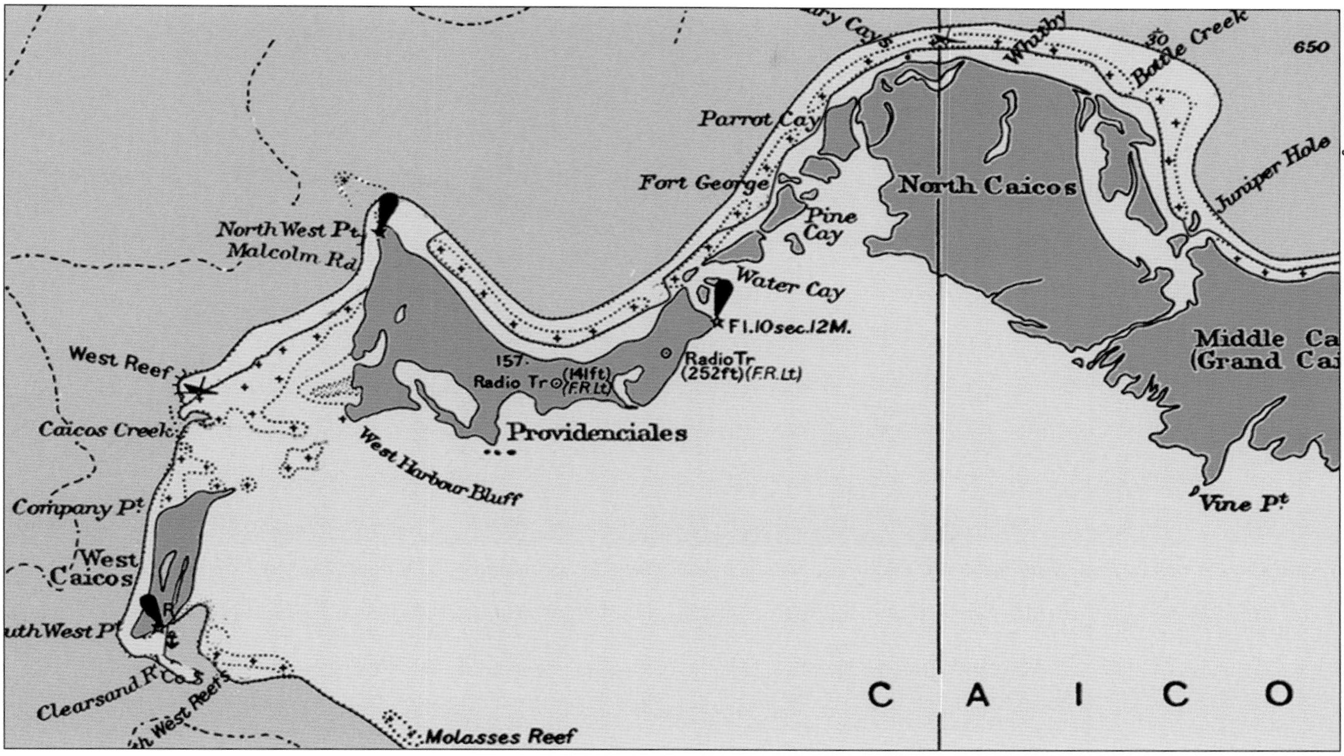

Not to be used for navigation.

Looking At the Charts

Whether you are making a passage or just cruising, Providenciales, better known as "Provo," is bound to be on your list of destinations in the Turks and Caicos. Because Provo is a barrier island, you have a choice to make. Will you approach Provo from the north (the ocean side) or approach it from the south, over the Caicos Bank? If you are making a passage, you may wish to maximize your time in blue water, and avoid the bank. With this in mind, one of the area's first marinas, Turtle Cove, was built on the north coast of Provo. For years, the south coast was the most visited by cruisers, but had the least marina facilities. That has changed.

To the north and northeast, Turtle Cove Marina is one of Provo's first-class marinas that has the appearance, facilities and "feel" of a larger stateside marina. Turtle Cove is not far north of downtown Provo. The marina can be challenging to enter. We recommend using a pilot the first time you traverse Turtle Cove's well-marked, but coral head-strewn channel.

Leeward Cut to the Leeward Marina is difficult to run in anything but moderate conditions, but especially with winds from the north. The marked channel runs between sandbars off the southwest tip of Little Water Cay and Provo's northeast tip, Pelican Point. Leeward Marina is not currently operational, although the docks remain. Hopefully the resort will decide to re-open. Consider entering from Fort George Cay.

There are no sheltered north coast anchorages. There is an anchorage in Leeward Going Through, between Mangrove Cay and Provo, but it is narrow, busy, at the mercy of current and tidal flow, and best suited for small boats or short-term stays.

The south coast offers a few more choices. Sapodilla Bay at Gussy Point is the well-known and fairly well-protected anchorage west of the government dock, also known as South Dock. Just to the east, the Five Cays offers an alternative anchorage. Fuel and lubricants are available at the government dock and town is about four miles away.

When you are looking for a lot more than a place to set the hook and only a nice marina will do, you have choices—The South Side Marina and the Caicos Marina and Shipyard. Southside is a marina managed by cruisers and works to be the most cruiser-friendly marina in the Turks and Caicos Islands. Caicos Marina and Shipyard not only offers a do-it-yourself yard, but full-service facilities as well. It is a renovated marina that caters to cruisers on a budget.

You can, of course, have both worlds. Put in to the north, then backtrack into ocean waters, and make your way around to the Caicos Bank from the west or the east, as one would in a direct ocean approach. There is no navigable connector that will

Turtle Cove Marina, from the southwest. (Not to be used for navigation.) Waterway Guide Photography.

serve most cruisers between the northern and southern coastal waters of Provo, but with a local pilot, you may be able to enter the Caicos Banks via Leeward Going Through. This shoal channel is said to only carry 4 feet at mean low water. Your decision on which approach to take and where to go will most certainly depend on whether you are just dropping by on passage or spending time in the islands. They are so incredibly lovely; you may want to make the time to visit.

In the Spotlight. Provo

Provo, 14 miles long, one to four miles wide, with an ever-growing population, is the pacesetter in the Turks and Caicos. The island is marketed as a "dream destination," and rightly so. Just look at the colors of the sand, the water and the coral of Grace Bay. Hotels, beachfront resorts and villa estates are mushrooming.

Elsewhere on the island, development is less tourism oriented, but continuous. Provo, as a town, rather than an island (for the name serves both), appears to have no grand master plan. Serendipity seems to guide its growth. Handy mini-malls, investment banks, gas stations and liquor stores have sprung up where needed for over three miles along the Leeward Highway, the island's main artery. The island appears to be one great never-ending site of entrepreneurial opportunity.

What does Provo offer the incoming cruiser? Almost everything they may require. Once you have decided where to put in, you will soon be asking, "How do I get around?" A lot depends on where you are and what you want to do. From the anchorage in Sapodilla Bay, most of the provisioning requires a ride to the main shopping areas. They are much closer to the marinas on the north coast. The distances between the shopping areas are not that great in terms of miles, but the Leeward Highway is not hiker friendly. There may, or may not be bus service. Ask, as taxis can be expensive. It may be cheaper to rent a car for a day than it is to take two taxi rides. The rental car agencies will bring the car to you and deliver you back to your boat upon its return. But be aware that driving conditions are less than comfortable; some visitors would describe them as downright dangerous.

The Leeward Highway is the only paved road. If you are lucky, you can find someone heading in the direction you need to go, and they will give you a lift. The semi-permanent cruisers at anchor in Sapodilla Bay can help you with their favorite places to tie up dinghies and procure needs on shore. If you call a store first, don't forget to ask if they deliver.

Sellars Cut, from the south. (Not to be used for navigation.) Waterway Guide Photography.

Providenciales

PROVIDENCIALES		Largest Vessel Accommodated	VHF Channel Monitored	Transient Berths / Total Berths	Approach / Dockside Depth (reported)	Floating Docks	Gas / Diesel	Groceries, Ice, Marine Supplies, Snacks	Repairs: Hull, Engine, Propeller	Lift (tonnage), Crane, Rail	1=110V, 2=220V, B=Both, Max Amps	Laundry, Pool, Showers	Pump-Out Station	Nearby: Grocery Store, Motel, Restaurant
		Dockage					**Supplies**		**Services**					
1. **Turtle Cove Marina** 💻 WiFi	**649-941-3781**	**140**	**16**	**/106**	**7.5/7.5**		**GD**	**I**			**B/100**	**S**	**P**	**MR**
2. Leeward Resort Marina WiFi	877-7745486	CLOSED AT PRESS TIME												
3. Caicos Marina and Shipyard WiFi	649-946-5600	125	16	/25	13/4.5	F	GD	I	HEP	L75	B/50	LS		
4. South Side Marina WiFi	649-241-2439	65	16	/19	6.5/10		GD	IM			B/50	LS		G

Corresponding chart(s) not to be used for navigation. 💻 Internet Access WiFi Wireless Internet Access

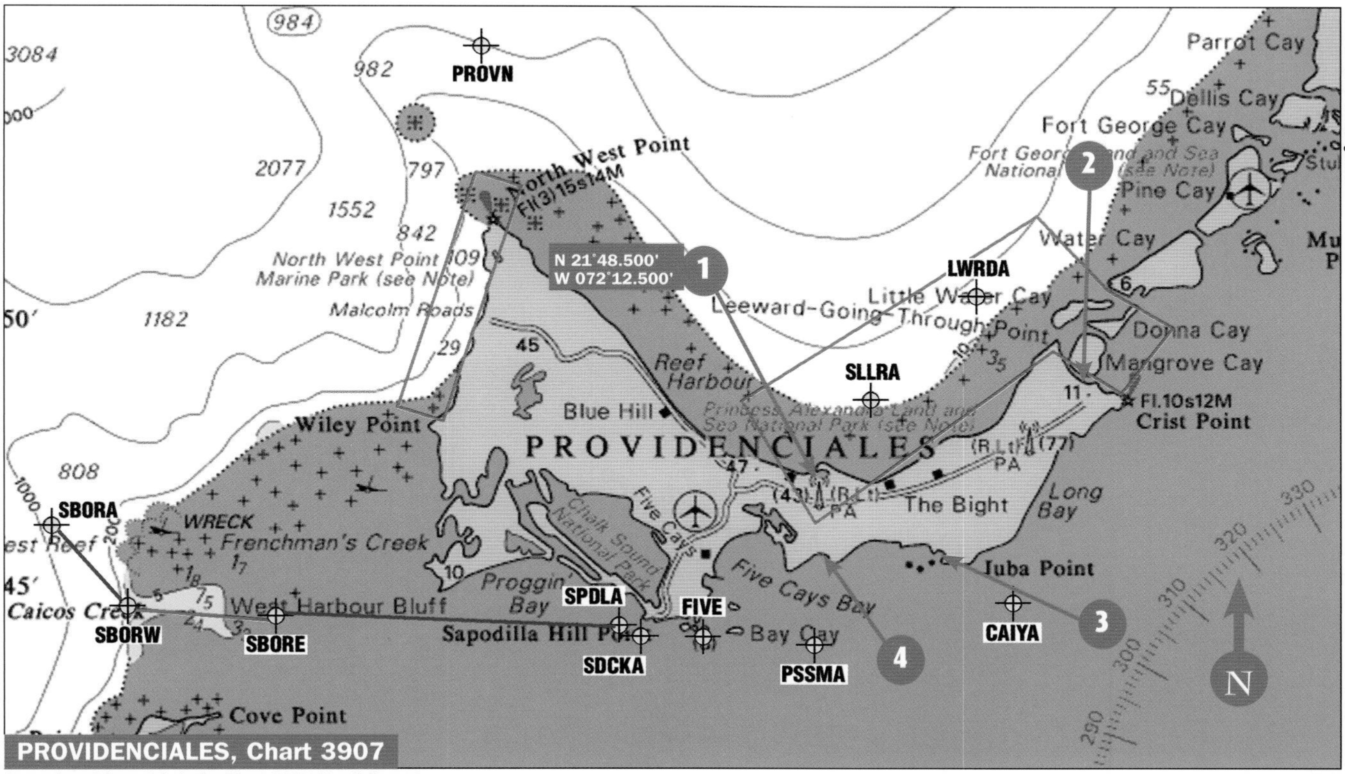

PROVIDENCIALES, Chart 3907

Reproduced from Admiralty Chart 3907. Depth in meters.

Clearing In—Your Options in Provo

All marinas in Provo are recognized entry ports. You can also clear in at Sapodilla Bay if the government dockmaster is available to contact an officer, and an officer is available to clear you in. Please contact the tourist office on Provo (649-946-4970) for the latest Customs and Immigration information for cruisers. At the time of this writing, officers have the authority to grant a seven-day stay, during which time visiting vessels, yachtsman and passengers can apply for a 90-day cruising permit. Additional permits are required to visit other islands.

What's There? Provo

Provo North Coast Approach

From the Provo north waypoint (PROVN) you have 9.5 nautical miles to run to the Sellars Cut Approach waypoint (SLLRA for Turtle Cove) on a course of 133/313 degrees true. It is a 9.8-nautical-mile run to the approach waypoint for the Leeward Going Through (LWRDA for the Leeward Marina) on a course of 117/297 degrees true. Both approach legs are in deep blue water.

Sellars Cut and the Turtle Cove Marina

On the north coast, Turtle Cove Marina, accessed through Sellars Cut, meets all that is implied in the word marina. As a matter of prudence in any weather, we recommend calling Turtle Cove Marina for complimentary guidance before entering its channel. The route to the marina is very well-marked with six-foot-tall vertical floating posts, but it is a two-mile-long, multi-leg approach with a cut through a finger reef. From the Sellars Cut waypoint (SLLRA), you can follow these marks (red right returning) using the large white house as a range. Once through the cut, turn to 240 degrees magnetic, and follow the channel. Stay to the center of the channel that cuts through the finger reef. If in doubt, don't take the risk! Turtle Cove will gladly lead you in.

Turtle Cove offers the most slips of any marina on Provo. They have room for 100 vessels in stern-to berths. Here you can enjoy cable television and wireless Internet, refuel the tanks and feed the crew at the many restaurants and bars within easy walking distance. Or, better yet, treat them to breakfast, lunch or dinner at the Aqua Bar and Terrace Restaurant—right by your slip.

The marina is home to many watersports companies, dive boats and shops, glass-bottom boats, glow-worm and sunset tour boats as well as the Undersea Explorer "submarine" tour. Turtle Cove also offers a wonderful affordable hotel, The Turtle Cove Inn, the closest waterfront hotel to "downtown" Provo. Still need something else to do? A casino and golf course are located nearby, and a brief walk will take you to the beach.

The Leeward Cut

The channel serving the Leeward Marina is 1.5 miles long at the Leeward Cut, lighted, marked from the Atlantic Ocean to the marina with the international buoy system and offers 24-hour direct entry into the marina. At the approach waypoint (LWRDA), if any kind of sea is breaking on the reef, you will be able to identify the cut. Inside the main reef, there is some scattered coral. It is not coral but sand that may be your main concern. In any event, check the state of the tide. It can be critical. You should have 5.4-meter/18-foot depths in the channel and 2.7-meter/10-foot depths all the way in, but this may be shallower, due to moving sand.

The Leeward Marina is located on the Leeward Going Through channel and is within a short tender ride to the Fort George National Park and Historical Site, the Princess Alexandra Nature Reserve and the protected area centered on Water Cays. NOTE: At press time, the marina was closed due to foreclosure. Hopefully a facility of this quality will not be dormant too long and will have reopened by the time you transit the area. The adjacent Leeward Resort, however, is open.

The Leeward Going Through

The Leeward Going Through channel offers a narrow anchorage with good holding—much needed, as the tidal flow peaks at 8 knots. The "Going Through" part of the chan-

Tiki Huts Anchorage, from the south. (Not to be used for navigation.) WATERWAY GUIDE PHOTOGRAPHY.

nel title is misleading. It is not a viable route on to or from the Caicos Bank unless you have a very shoal draft.

At mean low water, one has no more than 0.6-meter/2-foot depths in the deepest channel. At high water, shoal-draft powerboats take this route, but only with local knowledge. The Caicos Bank is a maze of shoals and coral in this area.

Malcolm Roadstead and the Tiki Huts Anchorage

There is one anchorage off the west coast that you may wish to note. Running south from North West Point, the western shore of Provo is shielded by reef until latitude N 21° 50.000'. There, the reef disappears for about 0.5 nautical miles and then builds up again, continuing south to the northern edge of the Sandbore Channel. The offshore water between N 21° 50.000' and N 21° 49.000' is known as Malcolm Roadstead. This anchorage may serve in northwest through southeast weather, and can be approached (with caution) at night if you are waiting for high sun to negotiate the Sandbore or the Pony Channel (see below). The 100-meter/320-foot drop-off contour in this area has five dive site buoys (rated for vessels up to 50 feet length overall). It is legal to secure to one of these, if you want to, on a temporary basis. You must move off if a dive operator requires it. Use your own bridle to secure to the buoy. You can, of course, move closer in to the beach and drop your own hook.

The beach here, a prized picnic target on weekends, was inaccessible by land until a French TV company built a mock-Polynesian village, improbably called Atlantis, on a small headland just east of the waypoint TIKIA. The enterprise failed, but the Tiki Huts remain to provide shade. It is a short ride from the Blue Hills area by four-wheel drive. The unspoiled Malcolm's Beach is just adjacent to the magnificent Amanyara Resort Pavilions. For some reason, the television company left a dive cage just off the beach, and it is a popular site for snorkelers and divers to locate.

The South Coast. Sandbore Channel

The Sandbore Channel is a good, relatively straight, 3- to 4.5-meter/10- to 15-foot deep, half-mile-wide cut through the reef about two nautical miles north of the northwest point of West Caicos. Sandbore has a bad reputation with some, but it has been incorrectly labeled a difficult pass. It can be hard to spot. If entered by daylight, with the sun high, you will find yourself tripping along a broad blue highway running almost due east.

The Pony Channel (an alternative to the Sandbore Channel)

Pony Cut is clearly marked on Wavey Line chart TC 001. Because coral and sand are on each side of the route, you must have the chart and use it. It offers an alternative route to Sapodilla Bay and destinations farther east.

Silly Creek

Silly Creek, just over one nautical mile west of Sapodilla Bay, may be a possible storm shelter. It runs parallel to the inland Chalk Sound and can offer protection from every direction. The downside is that there are barely 0.6-meter/2-foot depths in the entry channel at mean low water, and it is shallow inside. You have to seek and find an adequately deep spot.

Sapodilla Bay, from the southeast. (Not to be used for navigation.) WATERWAY GUIDE PHOTOGRAPHY.

This counts it out for "panic" use. If there is any possibility that you may want to go there, take your dinghy, do your survey, and mark your spot.

Sapodilla Bay Anchorage

The Sapodilla Bay anchorage remains ever popular. The anchorage is easily fixed, even if no one else is there (an unlikely occurrence). Sapodilla has reasonable holding in 1.8- to 2-meter/6- to 7-foot depths, however it is open from south-southeast to west, and one may suffer the fetch of short seas built up over the Caicos Bank. The Five Cays offer alternative anchorages where you can ride this out. Fuel and lubricants are available at the government dock, and town is about four miles away by road.

While you are at anchor here, take time to explore and climb Sapodilla Hill behind the old Mariner Hotel. Find the trail that leads up the hill from the hotel. On the top, there are flat rocks carved with the names, vessels and dates of mariners who, legend says, were shipwrecked on that coast. The earliest we noted was in the 18th century. You get a good view of the Bay and of Chalk Sound from the top of the hill and South Dock, too.

South Dock

South Dock is Provo's one commercial dock. It is devoted to fuel and general cargo. You will see the fuel tanks, cranes and containers ashore. It is an interesting, productive place. Occasionally, South Dock will accept the temporary presence of private craft. South Dock currently handles ships up to 225 feet with a draft of 12 feet. The sea area off South Dock is used as an anchorage by commercial vessels waiting their turn to lie alongside one of the two wharves.

Five Cays

The Five Cays—William Dean, Pussey, Sim, Bay and Middle—are about one mile east of South Dock and just over one mile north of the waypoint named FIVE. Sometimes marked on charts as Bermudian or Mudjon Harbour, the cays offer alternative protection if Sapodilla Bay becomes uncomfortable. They offer beautiful, isolated anchorage. Take a trip there first in your dinghy to determine where you can work yourself in between Pussey and Sim Cays or behind the northeast tip of Middle Cay. There is plenty of coral around here. Move only in good light.

Proposed Shelter ("South Side Annex")

Farther east is the entry channel, basin and seawalls for the never completed facility, Cooperjack Marina. The basin is a popular anchorage. It offers over six feet of water and is only a 10-minute dinghy ride away from South Side Marina. For $5 a day, South Side provides dinghy tie-up and all of its marina amenities to those who anchor in the "Annex." Of course, when a buyer is found for Cooperjack Marina, this great anchorage will disappear.

Marinas on the South Side of Provo

To locate the marina from some distance, look for the terracotta red house that covers an entire hilltop. It is due east of the marina. As you get closer, you can see a radio mast above the marine police station, whose office is in the marina. In addition, your eyes are not tricking you; there is a reproduction ship's mast with a crow's nest right there in the marina. The approach route and entry channel are well-marked. The entry channel is narrow and subject to a 6-knot tidal runoff. The mean low water depth

South Side Marina, from the south. (Not to be used for navigation.) WATERWAY GUIDE PHOTOGRAPHY.

through the approach and entry route is 1.3 meters/4.5 feet. However, at slack high water there is plenty of depth (around 6 feet), and no problems. Contact the marina on approach to check tide and actual depth. There are 6-foot depths at the docks at mean low water.

South Side Marina always has some slips available for transients. It is a marina managed by cruisers for cruisers and works to be the most cruiser-friendly marina in the Turks and Caicos Islands (and it has testimonials from guests attesting to that very fact). South Side broadcasts a Cruisers Net and weather forecast daily on VHF Channel 18 at 7:30 a.m. Surrounded by lush landscaping and beautiful grounds, the marina offers every amenity a cruiser looks for including wireless Internet, laundry, next-day propane tank refills, fuel 24/7, cell phone rental, a library, trash disposal, monthly rates and weekly barbecues to get together with all the other cruisers. The marina will even take trash from those who anchor out for only $2 per bag. Cruisers can look forward to a new bar and restaurant at South Side Marina in the not too distant future. Maybe some new slips opposite them, too.

To the east of Juba Point, the Caicos Marina and Boatyard offers a wide range of facilities and is the only repair yard in the Turks and Caicos—both do-it-yourself and full service. Its excellent facilities cater to the cruiser on a budget. The entry channel is marked and carries 13 feet of water, but you are welcome to call for guidance. The CAIYA waypoint places you just about one mile south of the Caicos Marina and Shipyard entrance, where you should find a marker buoy. The entry channel is marked with green and red markers.

Once there, you will find a floating dock and main fixed dock at which to secure dockage. The marina has recently updated all facilities, including showers, restrooms and a laundry. Wireless Internet and trash disposal are complimentary. The shipyard offers on-site diesel and transmission repair with its own mechanics shop. Although you are welcome to do-it-yourself, the yard has a fiberglass shop, metal fabrication department and a repair shop that performs cutlass bearing and general boat repairs. Other services include pressure washing, bottom sanding and painting, topside spray-painting and osmosis repair. The marina offers haul-out to 75 tons with 24-foot beam. In addition to nightly and monthly dockage, hurricane-proof dry storage is available. If you are looking for helpful and friendly service next to none, you have found the right place.

Pilotage. Talking Captain to Captain

Sellars Cut for the Turtle Cove Marina

The cut itself has mid-pass coral, which shows clearly. It sounds forbidding, but for reassurance, a 110-foot Aggressor fleet dive boat, with a 6-foot draft and a single screw, is based in Turtle Cove, and a large visitor, 145 feet in length with a 28-foot beam and a 7-foot draft, made it in safely. Turtle Cove itself, built in the natural lagoon called Sellars Pond, offers total protection from wave and surge, and protection from all wind, save that coming from the northern sectors.

Leeward Cut

The suggested hold-off position of N 21° 50.370'/W 072° 10.120', keeps you in 12 meters/40 feet of blue water off the

Leeward Going Through, from the south. (Not to be used for navigation.) WATERWAY GUIDE PHOTOGRAPHY.

Leeward Going Through, from the north. (Not to be used for navigation.) WATERWAY GUIDE PHOTOGRAPHY.

Providenciales South Dock. Waterway Guide Photography.

Sapodilla Bay. Waterway Guide Photography.

Leeward Cut. If it is rough, stay farther out, in 18-meters/60-foot depths, as wave action will push you toward the reef while you are standing by. Be aware that if it is near flat calm, the outer reef will not show, and if it is early in the day, you will have the sun in your eyes and will not be able to read the color of the water, which is critical. Your approach heading will be around 158/338 degrees true, but this will change as you follow the apparent and well-marked channel. Expect a peak tidal flow of 8 knots. Note that with the marina closed you won't have someone there to lead you in.

The Sandbore Channel

The waypoint SBORW, at the western entrance of the channel, is two nautical miles southeast of the initial approach waypoint SBORA on a course of 136/316 degrees true. You will want to favor the north side of the channel, for it is better defined, with the blue of your deep-water road and the white of the sandbore. The distance to run through Sandbore Channel (waypoints SBORW–SBORE) is 2.7 nautical miles, and your general heading is around 094/274 degrees true. Don't wander off toward the south; it is harder to pick up your course there. Do not attempt the Sandbore Channel with the sun in your eyes. Those who have tried it would never do it again.

The east entry waypoint SBORE, lies 2.5 nautical miles southwest of West Harbour, but marks no recognizable feature. The Sandbore Channel loses its color and peters out, and suddenly you realize that you are there. You have made it, and you are on the Caicos Bank.

Sandbore Channel to Sapodilla Bay and South Dock

From SBORE, head about 092/272 degrees true to run to

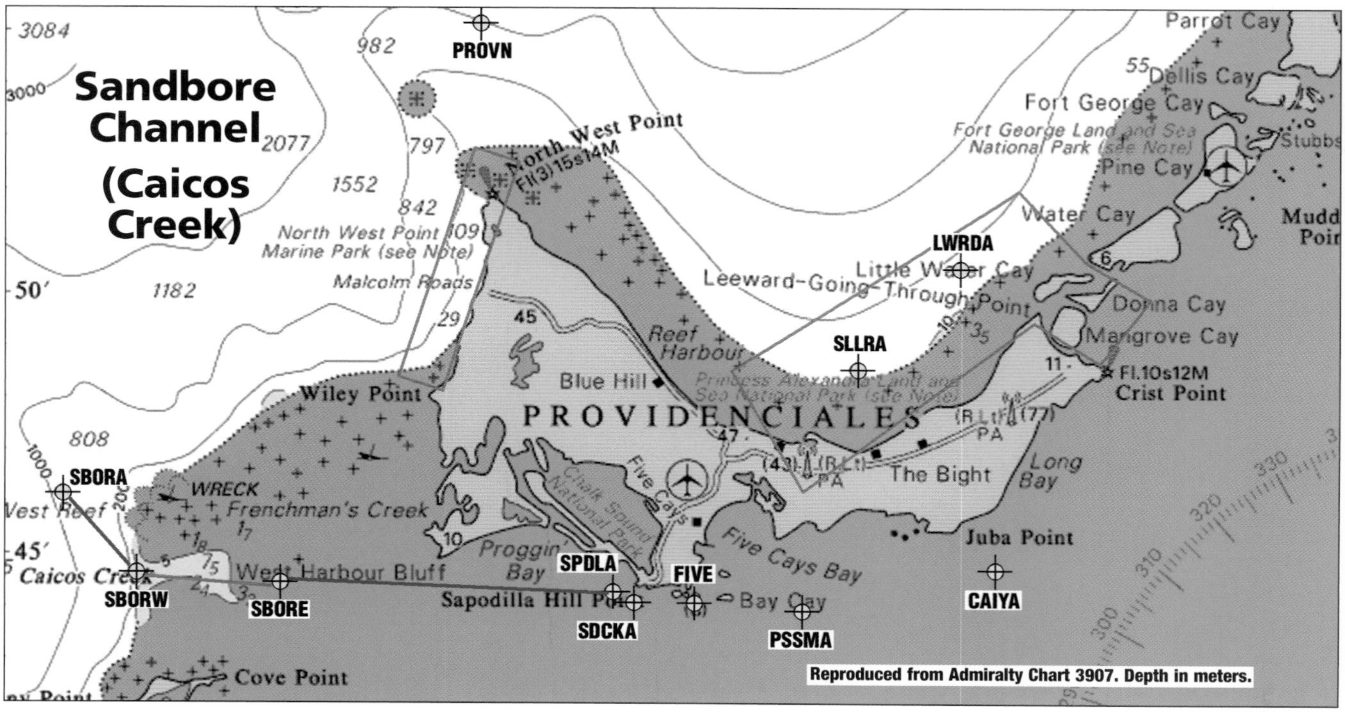

Sapodilla Bay (SPDLA) or on to South Dock (SDCKA), although South Dock itself is unlikely to be your destination. You have about 6.5 nautical miles to run, depending on where you are going.

The Caicos Bank courses are not for running on autopilot (unless someone is always on deck with an eye out for coral heads), as the Caicos Bank is largely uncharted. Few, if any, straight-line courses are safe. The bearings are an indication of heading, not fail-safe courses to steer. Your aim on this run is to hold off at least one nautical mile south of West Harbour Bluff, being conscious of Bluff Shoal, which extends for nearly a mile to the southwest from this point. Stay at least one-quarter mile south of Turtle Rock, which is clearly visible. In general, you should not edge toward the coastline more than one-quarter mile north of the N 21° 44.000' line, and if you hold this track, you should have 2.7- to 3-meter/9- to 10-foot depths along your route. The Sapodilla headland and Mariner Hill, and some of the Five Cays, show clearly off your port bow, and Turtle Rock is a good marker.

Marinas

The route given by the South Side Marina starts at N 21° 43.500'/W 072° 14.650'. From there, head 030 degrees true for 1.88 nautical miles to N 21° 45.260'/W 072° 13.930', in line with a house on the background hill with a round tree behind it and a distant antenna, toward a red marker buoy. Then turn 20 degrees to starboard, and ahead you will see a second red buoy. Go red right returning in to the marina, leaving a green buoy, which comes up later, to port. The marina will provide guidance if you call.

The entry channel to Caicos Marina and Shipyard is marked and carries 13-foot depths, but you are welcome to call for guidance. The CAIYA waypoint places you just about one mile south of the Caicos Marina and Shipyard entrance, where you should find a marker buoy. The entry channel is marked with green and red markers. Enjoy your stay in Provo! ■

Providenciales Waypoints

PROVIDENCIALES NORTH AND WEST COAST WAYPOINTS

Northwest Point	PROVN	21°55.00N / 72°20.00W
Sellars Cut Approach	SLLRA (8)	21°48.50N / 72°12.50W
Leeward Cut Approach	LWRDA (9)	21°50.50N / 72°10.50W
Tiki Huts Anchorage	TIKIA (89)	21°50.00N / 72°21.00W

PROVIDENCIALES SOUTH COAST WAYPOINTS

Sandbore Channel App	SBORA (1)	21°46.00N / 72°28.00W
Sandbore Channel West	SBORW (3)	21°44.55N / 72°27.00W
Sandbore Channel East	SBORE	21°44.50N / 72°24.00W
Sapodilla Bay Approach	SPDLA	21°44.25N / 72°17.50W
South Dock Approach	SDCKA (10)	21°44.21N / 72°17.00W
Five Cays Anchorage	FIVE	21°44.08N / 72°16.00W
South Side Marina App	SSMAP	21°43.85N / 72°13.85W
South Side Turn In Pt	SSMTP	21°45.40N / 72°13.86W
Caicos Boatyard App	CAIYA(12)	21°44.66N / 72°10.07W
Caicos Boatyard Entry	CAIYE	21°45.65N / 72°10.05W

Position format is latitude and longitude in degrees and minutes (hddd°mm.mm). Waypoints in RED are NOT for autopilot navigation. Codes in parenthesis are Wavey Line waypoints marked on the charts. If you have programmed waypoints listed in a previous edition of this guide, check carefully to ensure the coordinates you have recorded match the list. If a waypoint is no longer on the list we may have changed its code or deleted it.

North Beach, Salt Cay, Turks Islands. WATERWAY GUIDE PHOTOGRAPHY.

GOIN' ASHORE:

PROVIDENCIALES

airport • banks • customs & immigration • fuel • groceries • marinas marine services • medical • police • post office • propane • restaurants telephone • water

If this is your first visit to the Turks and Caicos Islands, Providenciales (Provo, as it is called), will delight you with its brilliant waters and wide variety of amenities. If this is a return visit, after several years absence, the up-market building and development will amaze you. Pick up a copy of *Where, When, How* to find out what is going on. Lacking an island center, downtown, Ports of Call and Salt Mills are the three main shopping areas. Everything else is sprinkled along or off the Leeward Highway. You may need wheels to get around. The hotels and shops along Grace Bay accommodate tourists from all over the world, many of whom come specifically to dive. The Turks and Caicos have legislated more protected areas per square mile than any other place in the world, with 33 areas separated into national parks, nature reserves, areas of historical interest and sanctuaries. There are miles of pristine beaches, healthy reefs, migrant and wading birds and crystal-clear seas to enjoy. See the National Parks section in the Green Pages for more information. For Customs and Immigration procedures, cruising and fishing permits and regulations, see the Buff Pages.

MARINAS

TURTLE COVE MARINA
Tel: 649-941-3781 • Fax: 649-946-4350 • VHF 16 •
tcmarina@tciway.tc • www.turtlecovemarina.com
Slips 100. **Max LOA** 145 ft. **MLW** 7.5 ft. at docks and 7.5 ft. in the channel. **Dockage** $1.00 per ft. per day. **Fuel** Dock open 7 a.m. to 5 p.m. daily, with diesel and gasoline. **Facilities & Services** Shore power 110 & 220, $20 daily minimum, $0.50 per kWh. RO water $0.20 per gallon. New showers, laundry service available. Two telephones dockside with phone cards available. WiFi cards available at marina office. Office open 8 a.m. to 5 pm. Cable TV, $5 per night, 11 premium channels. Trash bag disposal complimentary. $5.00 per bag for non-marina guests. *Quality Supermarket* on Leeward Highway is the closest for provisions, about a 10-minute walk away. Propane tank refills can be arranged or ask for directions to *T.C. Gas*. A fabulous beach is within a few minutes' walk. *Provo Turtle Divers, Dive Provo* and *Ocean Vibes* for diving. Several fishing boat charters within the marina. Fishing tournaments held in June, July. FedEx delivers to the office. A mechanic can be arranged. Pump-out facility on site. Please use holding tanks. **Accommodations** *The Turtle Cove Inn* • 649-946-4203 and 800-528-1905 • 800-887-0477 • info@turtlecoveinn.com • www.turtlecoveinn.com. **Credit Cards** Visa, MasterCard, AMEX or Travelers Checks. Pets are welcome at marina. Please clean up after your dog.

THE LEEWARD RESORT (MARINA)
Toll Free: 877-774-5486 or 877-407-6197 • VHF 16
(NOTE: At press time, the marina was closed, but the resort is open. There was no indication given about when or if the marina will reopen. The docks are still present and folks are said to tie up there.) **Slips** 110. **Max LOA** 200 ft. **MLW** 10 ft. in the channel; 13-15 ft. at the dock **Dockage** Contact resort **Facilities & Services** No services currently. **Restaurant and Bar** None currently **Accommodations** *Leeward Resort* **Credit Cards** Visa, MasterCard and AMEX.

SOUTH SIDE MARINA
Tel: 649-241-2439/649-946-4747 • VHF 16
southsidemarina@gmail.com • www.southsidemarina-tci.com
Slips 19. **Max LOA** 65 ft. **MLW** 6.5 ft. in channel, 10 ft. at docks **Dockage** $50 per slip per night or $750 per month. **Moorings** Installed in Cooper Jack Bay, planned **Fuel** Dock is open 24 hours a day, 7 days a week. Diesel and gasoline. **Facilities & Services** Shore power 30 and 50 amp, 110 $0.52 per kwHr plus fuel surcharge. Showers, coin-op laundry, $5 per wash or dry. WiFi available, $5 connection fee only. Trash disposal complimentary; $2 per bag for non-marina guests. Cell phones for rent. Rental cars delivered to the marina. Grocery store within walking distance. Cruisers library. Weekly barbeque cookout. Propane tanks refilled, next day service. Mechanic available by appointment. Cruisers Net and weather forecasts daily at 7:30 a.m. on VHF 18. Marina Store with ice, bottled water, 2 stroke oil and lubricants. **On-site Dive Operators** *Caicos Adventures, Flamingo Divers, Provo Turtle Divers* **Accommodations** *Harbour Villas* next door Restaurant and Bar/2010 completion date **Credit Cards** Visa, MasterCard, AMEX, no surcharge. Travelers checks and local banks personal checks. Pets are welcome at the marina.

CAICOS MARINA AND SHIPYARD
Tel: 649-946-5600 • Fax: 649-946-5390 • VHF 16 •
caicosmarinashp@tciway.tc • www.caicosmarina.com
Slips 20 under 35 ft. on floating docks; Main fixed dock depends on length of boats. **Max LOA** 125 ft. **MLW** 4.5 to 6.5 at docks; 13 ft. in channel. **Dockage** $1.00 per ft. per night; monthly rates available. **Fuel** Dock open 8 a.m. to 5 p.m., daily, diesel and gasoline. **Facilities & Services** Shore power 30 and 50 amp, $15 minimum plus metered at $0.70 per kwHr. City water $0.15 per gallon. Showers, restrooms, coin-op laundry $4.50 per wash and dry. Card phone dockside; cards available from the office. Propane tanks refilled with compatible universal fitting. Ice. Mail, FedEx, DHL and UPS. Write *"Boat in Transit"* on packages containing spare parts to avoid paying customs duty. Marine services include a diesel shop with full-service facilities, Yanmar and Caterpillar agents. Honda Outboard dealer, repair facilities for all outboards and stern drives in the yard. Fiberglass repairs and bottom painting, 2,000-lb. forklift and a 75-ton sling lift with 24-ft. beam. Covered rack storage for boats up to 36 ft. Incinerator recently installed for safe disposal of fuels/oils. See Web site for complete information on services and rates. **Restaurant & Bar** Licensed bar and bistro coming soon. **Credit Cards** Visa, MasterCard, AMEX, with a 4.5% surcharge.

SAPODILLA BAY ANCHORAGE
This beautiful crescent bay, long chosen by visiting yachts and larger boats as their corner of paradise on the island, saw a spectacular housing boom during the 1990s. It is still magnificent. Taxis answer VHF channel 6. Make certain to call Customs on VHF Channel 16 "Harbourmaster" at South Dock for clearance information.

"SOUTH SIDE ANNEX" ANCHORAGE

The entry channel, basin and seawalls of the never completed facility, Cooperjack Marina, is called the "South Side Annex." The basin is a popular anchorage for cruisers who chose not to stay at South Side Marina or draw too much water. South Side Marina is the cruisers "Mecca." The Annex Anchorage offers over six feet of water and is only a 10-minute dinghy ride away from South Side Marina. For $5 a day, South Side provides dinghy tie-up and all of its marina amenities to those who anchor in the "Annex." Of course, when a buyer is found for Cooperjack Marina, this great anchorage will disappear. Enjoy it (and South Side Marina's hospitality) while you can. And, don't miss the weekly lunch pilgrimage from South Side to Da' Conch Bar—free transportation in the marina's "Stretch Limo" (the back of their pickup truck!) or the ridiculously popular barbeque they throw for cruisers at the Marina.

EMERGENCIES

Dentist • 649-946 4321
Diving *Recompression Chamber* • 649-946-4242 • VHF 81 • At *Associated Medical Practices.*
Emergency • 999 or 911
Fire • 649-946-4444
Marine • VHF 16 and 68 TACRA
Medical *Associated Medical Practices* • 649-946-4242
Grace Bay Medical Centre • 649-941-5252 or 649-231-0525 after hours.
Pharmacy *Island Pharmacy* • 649-946-4150
Grace Bay Dispensary • 649-946-8242
Police • 911 or 649-946-4259
Veterinary *Dr. Mark Woodring* • 649-231-0685 or 649-946-5578

PORT DIRECTORY

Accommodations A wide variety of resorts and hotels cater to all tastes and pocketbooks. *Lee Ingham* at the Tourist Board (lingham@turksandcaocostourism.com) will be happy to give you a complete list. Also read *Where, When, How* • *Leeward Resort,* www.leewardresorttci.com • 877-407-6197 • Oceanfront or ocean view luxury suite accommodations starting at $299 per night. VISA, MasterCard and AMEX accepted. 11% tax and surcharge additional. No dining facilities on-site at present. ***The Turtle Cove Inn***, 649-946-4203 and 800-528-1905/800-887-0477, info@turtlecoveinn.com, www.turtlecoveinn.com. With the *Aqua Restaurant* and rooms overlooking the marina or pool, from $85 per night • *Blue Villa*, www.bluevillatci.com, a private accommodation within a short walk to Turtle Cove Marina, suitable for family groups.

Airlines *American* 800-433-7300 • *Air Canada* 800-247-2262 • *Air Turks & Caicos* 649-946-4999 • *Bahamasair* 800-222-4262 • *British Airways* 649-941-5464 • *Continental* 800-231-0586 • *Delta* 800-221-1212 • *US Airways* 800-433-7300.

Airport *Providenciales International Airport*, 649-941-5670.

ATMs *First Caribbean International Bank* in Butterfield Square, with a drive-thru branch on Leeward Highway, *ScotiaBank,* Main Branch, Leeward Highway and Cherokee Rd., *Ocean Club Plaza*, Grace Bay Rd., *Ports of Call*, Grace Bay Rd., *Graceway IGA*, Leeward Highway, *Petro Plus*, Millennium Highway, *Ocean Club Plaza*, Grace Bay Rd., Ports of Call, Grace Bay Rd., Graceway IGA, Leeward Highway, Petro Plus, Millennium Highway, Ocean Club Plaza, Grace Bay Rd.

Banks Offshore banking plays a large part in the economy of the islands, so there are many banks here. First, *Caribbean International Bank,* 649-946-4007, in Butterfield Square is open Monday through Thursday, 8:30 a.m. to 2:30 p.m., until 4:30 p.m. on Friday. *ScotiaBank*, 649-946-4750, on Leeward Highway is open 9:00 a.m. to 3 p.m. weekdays, to 4:30 p.m. on Fridays and in Grace Bay at the *Ocean Club Plaza*, 10:00 a.m. to 6:00 p.m., Tuesday through Friday; Saturday, 9:30 a.m. to 3:00 p.m.

Bookstore *Unicorn Bookstore* • 649-941-5458 • Fax: 649-941-5510 • unicorn@tciway.tc • Books, magazines, newspapers and nautical charts. Any book can be ordered. Open 10 a.m. to 5:30 p.m., Monday through Saturday. In the *IGA Plaza* on Leeward Highway.

Churches S*t. Monica's Anglican Episcopal Church, Our Lady of Divine Providence, Faith Tabernacle Church of God.*

Couriers *DHL Worldwide Express,* 649-946-4352, Butterfield Square; *Federal Express,* 649-946-4682, The Centre, *Atlas House* on Leeward Highway; *UPS* Only available for incoming package delivery.

Ferries *North Caicos Ferry Service* • 649-231-3018 (days) or 649-946-7029 (evenings).

Gaming *The American Casino* at *Allegro Resort* • 649-946-5508/5555 • On Grace Bay.

MEDICAL

Air Ambulance *AAA-Air Ambulance America* • 800-222-3564 or call collect 512-479-8000.

Clinics *Associated Medical Practices* • 649-946-4242 or 649-231-0642 (Dr. Euan Menzies) • 649-946-4222 or 649-231-0000 (Dr. Steve Bourne) • www.doctor.tc • On Leeward Highway, with a Red Cross on the building. With five doctors, CAT scan, mammography, decompression chamber, full-service general practice, emergency room, ambulance and air ambulance, dentist, chiropractor, optometrist, pharmacy, ultrasound and X-ray.
Carolina Medical Clinic • 649-946-4367 • In *Town Centre Mall.* Dr. Hugh Malcolm. Walk-ins welcome.
Grace Bay Medical Centre • 649-941-5252 (649-231-0525 after hours) • In *Neptune Plaza* on Allegro Road at Grace Bay. With Dr Sam Slattery. Emergency and evacuation to the U.S., family and pediatrics, X-ray, ultrasound, pharmacy and diving and aviation medicine.

Recompression Chamber • 649-946-4242 • VHF 81 • At *Associated Medical Practices*, with the Red Cross on the building, on Leeward Highway. Hyperbaric chamber with fully trained staff.

Dentists *Dr. Johann Pretorius and Dr. Roxanne Jeffries* • 649-946-4321 • At the *Associated Medical Practices* building on Leeward Highway.

Pharmacies *Grace Bay Dispensary* • 649-946-8242 • In *Neptune Plaza,* Allegro Road.
Island Pharmacy • 649-946-4150 • At *Associated Medical Practices* on Leeward Highway.
Provo Discount • 649-946-4844 • In *Central Square.*
Sunset Pharmacy Plus • 649-941-3751 • In *Times Square.*
Super Value Pharmacy • 649-941-3779 • Open 7 days a week at *South Winds Plaza* on Leeward Highway.

Laundry Many of the marinas have coin-op laundry. For boats at anchor in Sapodilla Bay, the nearest is at Five Cays or on Airport Road. There is also one next to the *Medical Centre* on Leeward Highway.

Liquor *Carib West* • 649-946-4215 • at the corner of Airport Road. *Discount Liquor* • 649-941-5600 • Open from 8:30 a.m. to 5:30 p.m., closed Sundays, on Leeward Highway. *I.G.A. Supermarket* • 649-941-5000 • Open daily, on Leeward Highway. The Wine Cellar & Discount Liquor • 649-946-4536 • centrally located on Leeward Highway, open 8:30 a.m. to 5 p.m., Monday through Saturday.

Marine Services Caicos Shipyard See under MARINAS. Caribbean Marine and Diesel Ltd. • 649-941-5903 • Fax: 649-941-5902 at Long Bay. S Walkin and Sons • 649-946-4411 • Fax: 649-946-4945 • walkinmarine@tciway.tc • Off Blue Hills Road. Marine mechanical repairs. Large range of marine products, boat cleaners and coolers, spare parts and oil, fishing line and tackle, paints and varnish, Marine batteries, and Sperry and Topsider shoes. walkinmarine@tciway.tc. *Provo Building Supply* • 649-946-4441 • Leeward Highway. *Do It Center* • 649-946-4131 • Leeward Highway. *NAPA* • 649-946-4224 • Suzie Turn at Leeward Highway • Large selection of marine parts. *Caribbean Marine & Diesel* • 649-941-5903 • Long Bay Highway. *Osprey Marine Service* • 649-946-5122 • *Turtle Cove Marina.*

Post Office At the corner of Airport Road, downtown. Open 8 a.m. to 4 p.m. weekdays, to 3:30 p.m. on Fridays.

Propane *TC Gas* • 649-941-3585 • Marinas can arrange refills.

Provisions *IGA Supermarket* • 649-941-5000 • www.gracewayiga.com • Open every day 7 a.m. to 10 p.m. on Leeward Highway. The most comprehensive market in the islands, with excellent fresh produce and bakery, meats and fish, liquor and wines. ATM, MasterCard, AMEX, Discover/Novus, Visa. *Island Pride Supermarket* • 649-941-3329 • *Town Centre Mall,* downtown. Open 7:30 a.m. to 9 p.m., Monday through Saturday, 8 a.m. to 1 p.m., Sundays and holidays. Well-stocked with a good range of meats, deli, dairy, bakery, fresh produce, house wares and pharmacy. *Quality Supermarket* • 649-946-4600/4644 • On Leeward Highway, open 7 a.m. to 9 p.m., Monday through Thursday, to 10 p.m. on Fridays and Saturdays. Open on holidays until 5 p.m.

Restaurants The imaginative use of fresh, locally caught fish and the high standard of international cuisine throughout the island is an unexpected delight. Restaurants close slightly earlier, and the cost of your meal will be higher than stateside. But, it is fun to try different ones, and there are plenty of choices. Pick up a copy of *Where, When, How* to give you ideas. You will need wheels to get to most restaurants, unless you happen to be in the *Turtle Cove Marina* where there are several within walking distance. We have grouped them geographically to make it easier, and have not covered the restaurants at all the hotels. A government tax is added to meal bills. A 15 to 20% tip is appreciated.

GRACE BAY AREA

Anacaona • 649-946-5050/5757 • Elegant dining at the *Grace Bay Club*. Reservations recommended. $$$

Barefoot Café • 649-946-JAVA • Open from 7 a.m. to 6 p.m. for breakfast and deli lunches, and dinners nightly, except Sundays. Live music 8 to 10 p.m. on Fridays.

Bay Bistro at Sibonné Boutique Hotel • 649-946-5396 • Open daily for breakfast, lunch, and dinner; brunch on weekends. Closed from 3 p.m. Mondays. Creative, international cuisine, beachfront dining. $$

Bella Luna Ristorante • 649-946-5214 • The glass house on Governor's Road. Open for dinner with Italian and Continental specials. $$

Caicos Café • 649-946-5278 • Terrace dining for breakfast, lunch and dinner in the French fashion. Tuesday to Saturday, and nightly dinner with grilled fresh local seafood and meats; choose from their daily chalkboard specials. A favorite with both residents and visitors. $$$

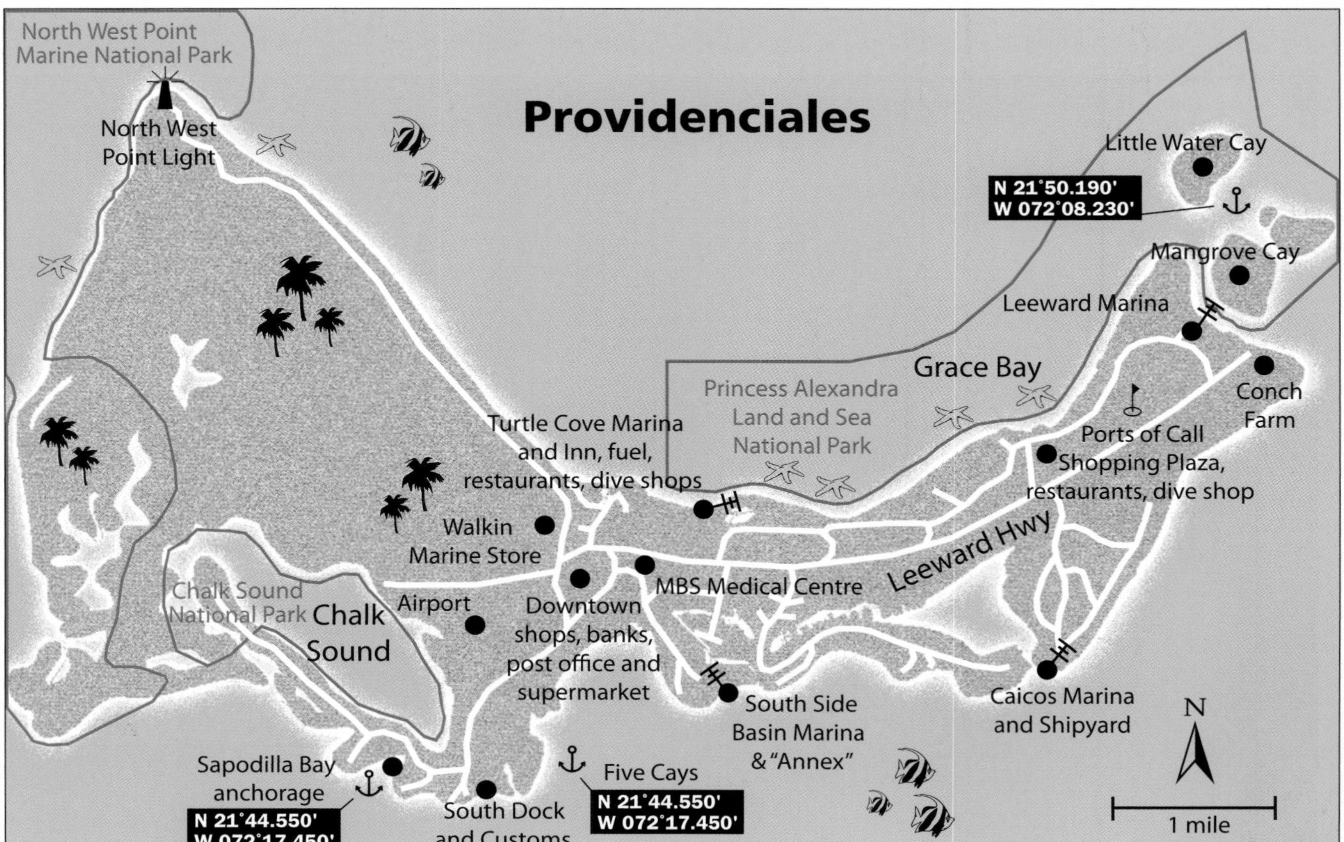

Calico Jack's • 649-946-5129 • On the upper level at *Ports of Call.* Pizza and local cuisine. Open daily. $$
Coco Bistro • 649-946-5369 • In Provo's only coconut grove on Grace Bay Road. Serving elegant Mediterranean food under the palm trees, reservations suggested, closed Mondays. $$$.
Danny Buoy's • 649-946-5921 • On Grace Bay Road. Open for lunch and dinner daily. Traditional Irish cuisine with imported draught beers. $$
Grace's Cottage • 649-946-8147 • At Point Grace Resort. Open for elegant dining nightly in a Caribbean gingerbread cottage atmosphere. Reservations recommended. $$$
Hemingway's on the Beach • 649-941-8408 • At The Sands. Casual beachfront restaurant, open for breakfast, lunch and dinner daily, music on Tuesday and Thursday. $$
Saltmills Café • 649-941-8148 • At *The Saltmills* on Grace Bay Road. Full-service deli for breakfast and lunch. *Jasmin Asian Cuisine* next door for dinner nightly except Sundays. Open 6 to 10 p.m. *Bambooz Bar* next door for casual dining. Open from 3 p.m. Monday through Friday, dinner from 5:30 p.m. Pool tables and draught beer. $$

ON THE LEEWARD HIGHWAY
Hey Jose's • 649-946-4812 • Central Square. Mexican-American restaurant, open daily from noon for pizzas and world's best margaritas; half-price on Fridays. Video poker and large screen TV, with NFL Football on Mondays. $
Pizza Pizza • 649-941-3577 • *Provo Plaza.* Fresh pizzas baked to your instructions, eat in or carry out, with Tuesday lasagna special, closed Mondays. $
Tasty Temptations • 649-946-4049 • Butterfield Square. *The Downtown* cafe for coffee and breakfasts, with homemade sandwiches and fresh salads at lunchtime.
Top of the Cove Deli • 649-946-4694 • Open for breakfast and lunch, daily. Fresh baked bread, cappuccino, bagels, over-stuffed subs, soups, salads, wines and picnic lunches, plus dinner-to-go specials. $

TURTLE COVE
Aqua Bar and Terrace • 649-946-4763 • aqua@tciway.tc • At *Turtle Cove Inn.* Specializing in food from the sea, overlooking the marina. Open from 7 a.m. to 11 p.m., daily. Big breakfasts, fast lunches and great happy hour. Saturday night sushi and many favorite recipes from *The Terrace.* Childrens menu. $$
Baci Ristorante • 649-941-3044 • At Turtle Cove, on the water. Fine Italian dining, specializing in veal and fresh fish, with brick oven pizzas. Serving dinner nightly. Open for lunch, noon to 2 p.m., Monday through Friday. Open for dinner, 6 p.m. to 10 p.m., Monday through Saturday. Closed Sunday. Reservations recommended. Visa, MasterCard, Travelers Checks. $$$
Magnolia Wine Bar and Restaurant • 649-941-5108/649-946-4240. Spectacular sunsets overlooking Turtle Cove with excellent international food at the Miramar Resort. Open for breakfast and dinner daily except Monday. Reservations recommended. $$$
Sharkbite Bar and Grill • 649-941-5090 • Waterfront at *Turtle Cove.* Happy hour daily 5 to 7 p.m. on the deck. Sports bar and games room. Family-friendly lunch and dinner menu seven days a week. $.
Tiki Hut Bar and Grill • 649-941-5341 • Dockside at *Turtle Cove Marina,* serving breakfast at weekends, lunch and dinner daily. Popular with locals and boaters, childrens menu, a popular happy hour, special curry, and chicken or ribs nights, pizza. $$

VENETIAN ROAD
Back of Beyond • 649-941-4555 • South of Leeward Highway, closest to *South Side Marina.* Call ahead for opening times. $$

Shopping There is no shortage of shops on the island, but they are very spread out in small shopping plazas. You really do need a car to get around. Grocery stores are well-stocked, and people are very helpful. Most stores close at 5 p.m., though the supermarkets and small local stores will be open later. Almost everything except food stores close on Sundays.
Taxis VHF 6. Taxis are expensive, but friendly. It is easy to find your way around the island. Rental car companies will pick you up from Sapodilla Bay or the marinas. There are jitneys that run around the main tourist areas on the island; timing is erratic, fares are cheap. Ask local advice.
Telephones The area code for the entire Turks and Caicos is 649 and calling within the islands, you only dial 7 digits, e.g. 946-2200. Most public telephones need phone cards, available in $5, $10 and $20 denominations. Buy them from stores or restaurants near a telephone, or from the LIME office on Leeward Highway, which is open 8:30 a.m. to 4 p.m. weekdays, to 3 p.m. on Fridays. SIM cards for cell phones are available at the LIME office.
Tourist Office • 649-946-4970, 649-941-5494, provo@turksandcaicos.com.
Veterinarians *Woodring Veterinary Services* • 649-231-0685 or 649-946-5578 • Mark Woodring at *Animal House, Neptune Plaza.* • *Turks and Caicos Veterinary Associates Ltd* • 649-946-4353 • Fax: 649-941-4046.

RENTALS

Bicycles and Scooters *Provo Fun Cycles and Autos* • 649-946-5868 • At *Ports of Call Plaza.*
Scooter Bob's • 649-946-4684 • VHF 22 • Next to *Turtle Cove Inn*; open 9 to 5 daily, to noon on Sundays. Also has Jeeps, SUVs, bicycles and fishing bait and tackle.
Cars DRIVE ON THE LEFT! Maximum speed limit is 40 mph and 20 mph through the settlements, though most cars show kph on the speedometers. Government Stamp Duty of $15 payable on each agreement; liability insurance $4 per day, collision damage waiver from $12 per day and a 9% airport fee if you pick up a car at the airport. You will need to show a valid driver's license. Jeeps rent from about $50 a day, cars from $65.
Avis • 649-946-4705 • At the airport and on Leeward Highway. Free unlimited mileage.
Budget • 649-946-5400/4079 • *Town Centre Mall.* Free pickup and dropoff.
Provo Fun Cycles and Autos • 649-946-5868 • At *Ports of Call Plaza.* Jeeps, Honda and motorcycles.
Provo Rent-a-Car • 649-946-4404 • At *Grace Bay Plaza,* across from *Allegro.* Free pickup and return.
Rent-a-Buggy • 649-946-4158 • Leeward Highway. Free pickup and delivery.
Scooter Bob's • 649-946-4684, 649-941-0262 • VHF 22 • See bicycle rentals.

SPORTS

Beaches With more than 12 miles of some of the most beautiful beaches in the world to choose from, there is plenty of room for everyone to enjoy themselves. As in any other part of the world, don't leave valuables in your beach bag while you go off for an hour's snorkeling. Sapodilla Bay Beach is the gentle crescent of almond sand when you come in from the anchorage. Taylor Bay Beach, northwest of Sapodilla Bay, is secluded and shallow. Long Bay Beach is nearest to the *Caicos Marina and Boatyard*. Malcolm Roads has 2 miles of white sand, south of North West Point, with some tiki huts on the beach and good snorkeling, though the approach road is rough. From Turtle Cove, walk over to Long Point, with Smiths Reef just off the point for snorkeling. There is a marked underwater trail. This beach leads northeast to the 7-mile stretch of beach, including Grace Bay and the hotels, which ends at Leeward Going Through.

Diving *Caicos Adventures* • 649-941-3346 • divucrzy@tciway.tc • www.caicosadventures.com • Fun, professional, small groups, flexibility, and attention to detail with "dive you crazy" as their catch phrase. 2-tank dives including lunch and drinks. Rentals and packages. *Dive Provo* • 649-946-5029 • diving@diveprovo.com • At Ports of Call. Daily 2-tank dives to West Caicos, North West Point, Grace Bay, French Cay or Pine Cay. Continuing diver education is encouraged, with advanced open water classes conducted on the dive boats. Gratuities not included. www.diveprovo.com. *Ocean Vibes* • 649-941-3141 and 649-231-6636 • oceanvibes@tciway.tc • www.oceanvibes.com • At Turtle Cove. Small group diving, dive propulsion vehicles. 2-tank including water and snacks. *Provo Turtle Divers* • 649-946-4232, 800-833-1341 • www.ProvoTurtleDivers.com • At *Turtle Cove Marina and Ocean Club*. Dive shop, equipment rental, tank fills, and still and video cameras available. Private dive courses and charters, and hotel dive packages.

Eco-tours and Kayaking *Big Blue Unlimited* • 649-946-5034 • bigblue@tciway.tc • www.bigblue.tc • Half-day kayak and snorkeling trips; full-day trips to North Caicos by airplane for nature hikes, biking, kayaking, native sailing sloops and cave safaris; to Middle Caicos for mountain biking, nature walks, kayaking, bird watching, cave exploring, and historic sites. Lunch at *Daniel's Café,* in a local home or on the beach. Race model sailboats, explore the caves and watch a handcraft demonstration.

Fishing *Bonefish Unlimited* • 649-946-4874/649-941-0133 • Bonefish@Provo.net • Fish with Captain Barr Gardner. *Gwendolyn* • 649-946-5321 • At *Turtle Cove Marina*. *Good Phrienz Sportsfishing Charters* • 649-231-0341/649-946-4342 • At *Turtle Cove Marina*. *J & B Tours* • 649-946-5047 • jill@jbtours.com • www.jbtours.com • At *Leeward Marina*. Bone and bottom fishing, snorkeling, water skiing. *Silver Deep* • 649-946-5612 • www.silverdeep.com • info@silverdeep.com • Fishing, snorkeling, waterskiing. • *Bite Me Sportfishing,* 649-946-4398/649-231-0366 • biteme@tciway.tc • www.lfishingTCI.com • At Turtle Cove Marina, 28' custom Blackfin fishing boat. Fish with the top angler in the Caicos Classic Billfish Tournament and winner of the Biggest Fish in the Heineken Grand Turk Tournament, Captain FineLine.

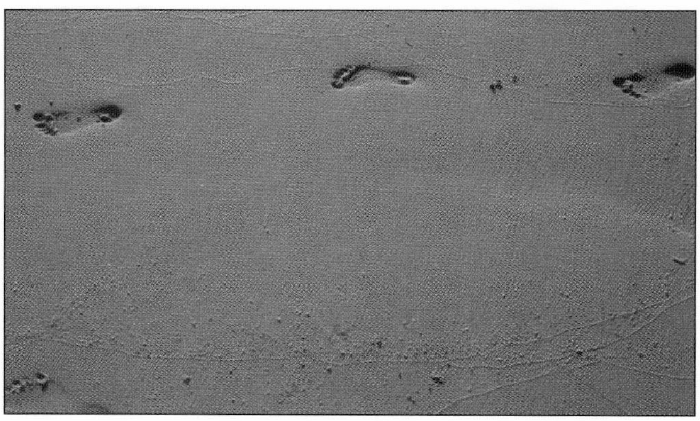

Leave only footprints, Sapodilla Bay. Waterway Guide Photography.

THINGS TO DO IN PROVIDENCIALES

- Dive, dive and dive again. Some of the best diving in the world is here!
- Climb Sapodilla Hill where flat slabs of rock lie. They are carved with an assortment of names and initials, it is thought, by sailors who had the misfortune to be shipwrecked on Providenciales. You will find them atop a rugged hill leading up the track to your right between the gates to South Dock and the old Mariner Hotel. 360-degree views from the site make it well worth the climb for the view out over Sapodilla Bay, South Dock and Chalk Sound, quite apart from the interest of the carvings themselves.
- Explore the Cheshire Hall Ruins. A short walk from the Leeward Highway are the ruins of an early Loyalist Plantation. Their crops of Sea Island cotton and, later, sisal were wiped out by a combination of depleted soils, devastating insects and the 1813 hurricane. The Planters were forced to move on, leaving behind many of their slaves who became the settlers and developers of the Caicos Islands. What remains of the 1790s construction are an interesting reminder of an earlier, pioneering lifestyle and some of the hardships they had to endure.
- You have heard of conch, but have you ever heard of Island Princess, Ocean Escargot and Pacific Rim? To learn more about these new members of the mollusk family that are being developed by Chuck Hesse, and to visit the only successful conch hatchery under its geodesic dome, take a trip to the Conch Farm at the eastern end of the Leeward Highway on Leeward Going Through. Open 9 to 4, weekdays and Saturday.
- Within the Princess Alexandra National Park lies Little Water Cay with its Rock Iguana nature trails. This little gem of a cay is given over entirely for the benefit of some 1,500 to 2,000 of these threatened Cyclura carinata, or Rock Iguanas. Walkways thread through the 150-acre cay from beach to mangrove estuary, through native palms and shrubs, with viewing towers on both the North and South Shore Trails to highlight osprey nests and the surrounding reef. Do keep to the boardwalks, so as not to disturb the iguanas' many burrows and underground nesting chambers. You need an access pass before visiting this nature reserve, from the National Trust office (649-941-5494), open during daylight hours. Any of the tour operators will take you over to Little Water Cay, or you can visit it with your own dinghy, but get a pass first.
- Kayak in the mangrove channels; snorkel the shallow reefs and lagoons; explore Middle Caicos with its caves and trails; visit the glow worms a few days after full moon; take an eco-adventure with *Big Blue* (649-946-5034) at Leeward Going Through.

⚓ *Goin' Ashore*

Golf *Provo Golf and Country Club* • 649-946-5991 • On Grace Bay Road. 18 holes with a pro shop, driving range and professional instruction. Casual dining served daily at the *Fairways Bar and Grill.*

Horseback Riding *Provo Ponies* • 649-241-6350 or 649-946-5252 • camille@tciway.tc • In Long Bay Hills. 1.5-hour trail rides with up to 20 horses, Monday through Friday, along secluded beaches of Long Bay. Protective headgear provided.

National Parks, Nature Reserves, Sanctuaries and Historical Sites For details, Park Rules and Regulations, see our Green Pages.

Submarine Exploration *Undersea Explorer at Turtle Cove Marina* • 649-231-0006/0007 • caicostours@tciway.tc • www.caicostours@tciway.tc • Australian-built viewing submarine. Three sailings daily.

Little Water Cay sign. WATERWAY GUIDE PHOTOGRAPHY.

WEST CAICOS

West Caicos is a pretty little island, a mere 6,000 acres peeking out of the water only 60 feet high. Most of West Caicos is a National Park. Because there are no designated Park anchorages, only vessels under 60 feet can anchor here. If you meet the 60-foot and under restriction, there is a recommended anchorage on the west side of the island, at the midpoint. Look for sand, of course, to drop your hook. Scope out your charts and electronic navigation carefully as you navigate these waters, for there are reefs and a wreck for which to watch out. The snorkeling and diving off the west of West Caicos is superb. Beaches on the east coast are picture perfect. There is an interior salt lake on the island, Lake Catherine, in which there are small blue holes to dive. So take a hike and jump in! Along the way, look for ruins of an old community, the "ghost town," *Yankee Town*. It is said that the 70 residents who used to work the saltpans still roam the old plantation. There is construction on the north shore of the island. A large resort and marina community called Molasses Reef is a work in progress. Construction has started on some buildings. The last we heard, the marina channel and basin had been dredged, bulkheaded and then put on hold. Supposedly, cruisers could anchor in the basin. It might be worth the dinghy adventure to check it out.

PARROT CAY and **PINE CAY** are both private islands; *Parrot Cay Resort and Spa* is reached from Provo by water; Pine Cay is home to seasonal residents and the Meridian Club.

MIDDLE CAICOS is linked by a 15-minute plane ride from Provo or by weekend ferry service to North Caicos. Nature trails, flamingos, the *Rocks of Dragon Cay*, and *Mudjin Harbour* offer spectacular photo ops. Just 271 people live on this island with 15 miles of above-water caverns and quaint villages.

NORTH CAICOS is home to *Wades Green* plantation ruins and is the greenest of the islands with more rainfall than any other. There are almost no cars. But, it has the largest flock of flamingos in the islands. Come and see more flamingos and ospreys than you have ever imagined, or visit the crab farm on Greenich Creek. Accommodations include a couple of hotels and eco-lodges. Explore on land by bicycle on land or in the water with a mask and snorkel off Three Marys Cay.

An inhabitant of Little Water Cay. WATERWAY GUIDE PHOTOGRAPHY.

Chapter 22
The Caicos Bank and South Caicos

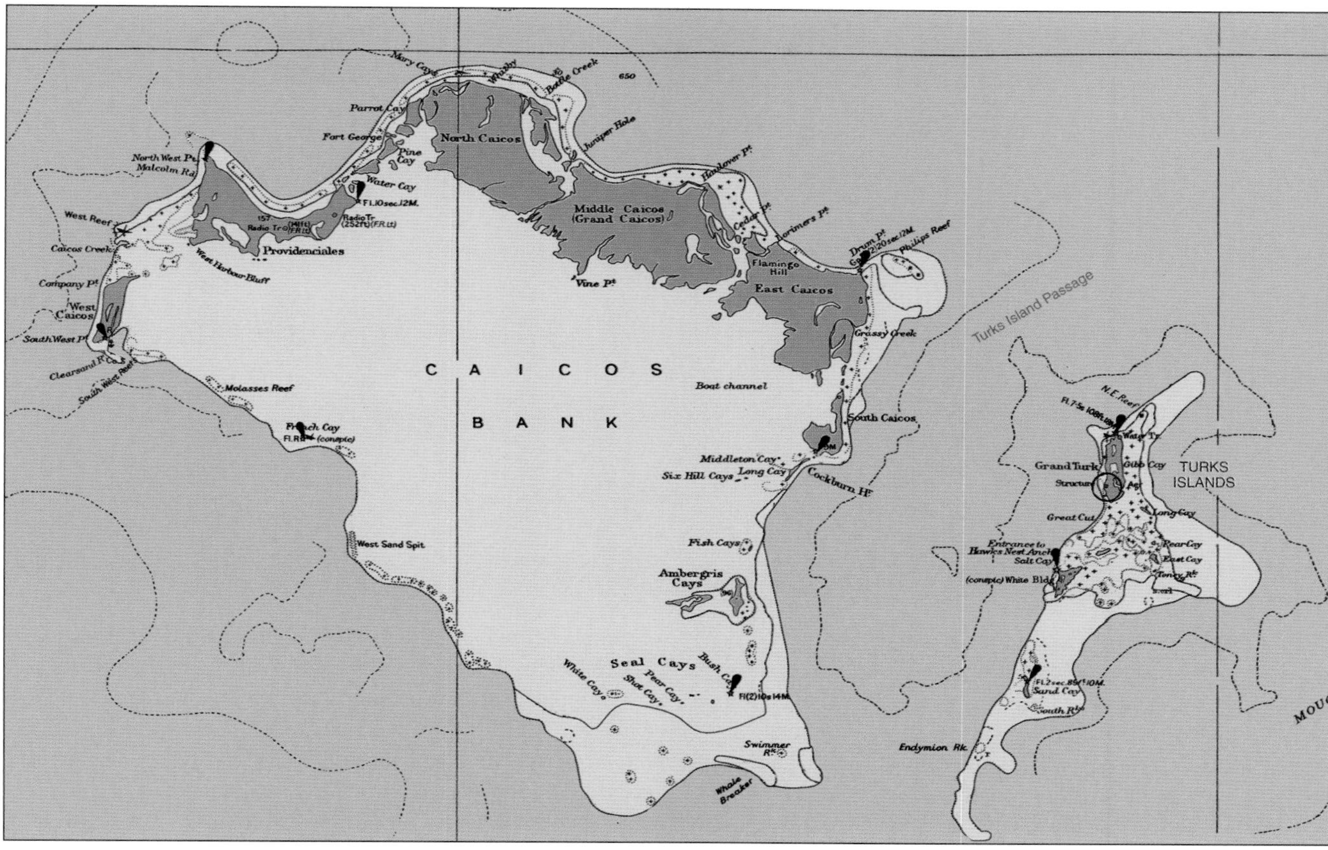

Not to be used for navigation.

Looking At the Charts

Astronauts tell us that given clear skies, two natural creations and one man-made formation head the list of the most stunning sights from space. Taken in reverse order, the man-made category wins with the Great Wall of China. It is incredible, because of its length and duration. The two natural features may be difficult to guess. One is the stark terracotta vastness of Saharan Africa. The other is the stunning sight of the Turks and Caicos Islands and their surrounding waters—brilliant turquoise set in the indigo blue of the deep North Atlantic. The gem in this extraordinary piece of natural jewelry is the aquamarine waters of the Caicos Bank.

The Caicos Bank is an almost circular atoll, 60 nautical miles across at its widest point, approximately 1.8 to 3.8 meters/6 to 12 feet in depth and peppered with reefs and coral heads. For this reason, you must cross in good daylight. Don't tempt fate by heading straight into the sun, particularly when it is low in the sky. Slower vessels may not be able to cross the Caicos Bank in a single day. There is no particular problem in that. Just anchor out. It is a weird and wonderful feeling to anchor for the night out of land sight, far from the glow of shore lights on the water. If you have no moon, the stars are fantastic.

Strangely enough, some people refuse to undertake a Caicos Bank crossing, but it is one of those memorable experiences of passagemaking. If you want to see what the Caicos Bank looks like from above, and you are not enrolled in the NASA astronaut training program, try it another way. Fly from Miami to San Juan, Puerto Rico or the reverse. Your flight will pass directly over the Caicos Bank. A much less expensive look is through Google Earth. You will see the deep indigo ocean with a pocket of bright turquoise in its center.

Looking at the Caicos Bank chart, notice that French Cay is a good starting point for Luperón, Dominican Republic, about 120 nautical miles away. Unfortunately, you can't plot a straight-line course from there because the Caicos Bank extends to the southeast for another 30 nautical miles. You have to run south-southeast for about 10 nautical miles before taking up your blue-water heading.

South Caicos

COCKBURN HARBOUR		Largest Vessel Accommodated	VHF Channel Monitored	Transient Berths / Total Berths	Approach / Dockside Depth (reported)	Floating Docks	Gas / Diesel	Groceries, Ice, Marine Supplies, Snacks	Repairs: Hull, Engine, Propeller	Lift (tonnage), Crane, Rail	1=110V, 2=220V, B=Both, Max Amps	Laundry, Pool, Showers	Pump-Out Station	Nearby: Grocery Store, Motel, Restaurant
		Dockage					Supplies		Services					
1. SeaView Marina	649-946-3219		16	/3	/6.5		GD	GM	E		B/50	LS		R

Corresponding chart(s) not to be used for navigation. Internet Access Wireless Internet Access

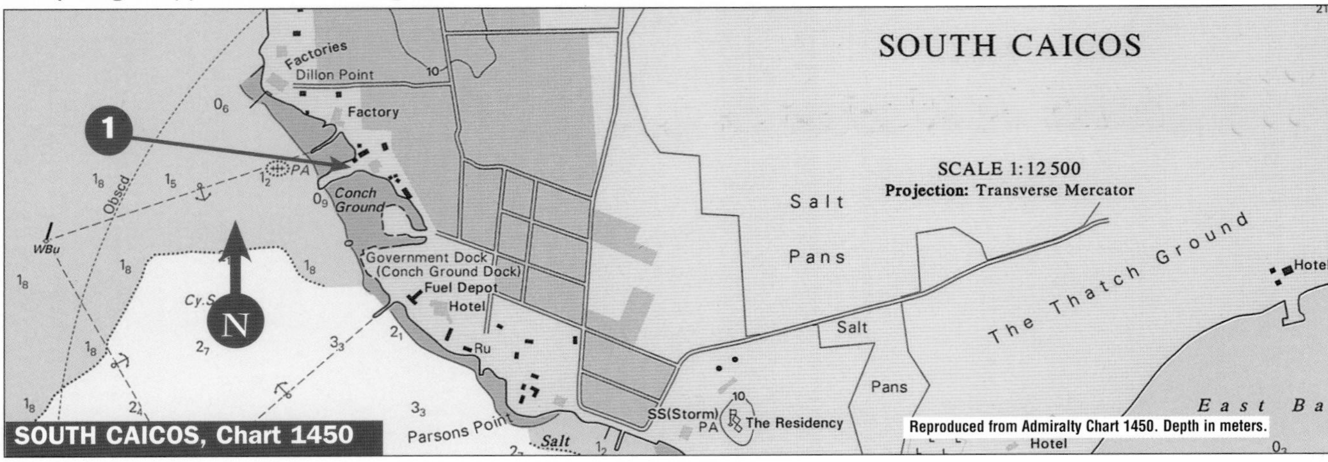

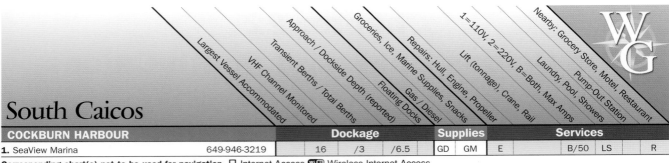

SOUTH CAICOS, Chart 1450

You might think of splitting the distance between French Cay and West Caicos and exiting somewhere there. Look carefully at the charts. There are reefs along that stretch (including Molasses Reef, the site of the oldest discovered shipwreck in the Turks and Caicos). South Caicos is a good starting point for the Dominican Republic, Puerto Rico and the Virgin Islands, but it is short on facilities. Northbound from the Caribbean, unless you particularly want to put in to South Caicos or decide to clear in there (which you can do), you will probably join the majority of cruisers who continue on to Providenciales.

In the Spotlight. South Caicos

South Caicos, in the salt-trade days, was the Gold Rush port of the Turks and Caicos. Not only did the island have salt-pans, it also had the finest, and largest, natural harbor right on the edge of the Turks Island Passage. In the days of sail, proximity counted. Today, the islanders make a seasonal living from fishing, conch, lobster and some tourist trade.

Taking a 360-degree look around South Caicos, to the north lies East Caicos, almost linked to South Caicos by a string of small cays. There is a nice anchorage at the west end of East Caicos, but it requires local knowledge or extremely careful visual piloting under very good conditions. To the east is the Turks Island Passage, very important in the days of salt trade. To the south, little Dove Cay and Long Cay lend Cockburn Harbour its protection. To the west, is the Caicos Bank—with its sands, coral heads and shoals. Part of the bank is the Admiral Cockburn Land and Sea National Park, a protected zone along with three other nature reserves in the South Caicos sea and land area and one historical site.

In looking at South Caicos as a town, one sees Cockburn Harbour, a bit of an open roadstead. There is glorious diving nearby. There are two docks of interest—the government dock and the Shell dock. The small boat harbor, just past the government dock, is still in use, but mostly by small outboard craft. There are an unfortunate number of derelict boats abandoned there that, much like Florida, the island doesn't have the means or the resources with which to cope. In the same area, the SeaView Marina Shell dock and its welcoming berths and facilities offers more than one would expect on such a small island, from fresh produce to a haul out.

There are not a lot of facilities for cruising boats here, but you will find what you need. There is a surprisingly good supermarket, a few restaurants serving real island dishes, a divers guest house and bed and breakfast to rest your weary bones, and an interesting boarding school in an old hotel that conducts research in marine biology. The School for Field Studies offers classes to high school and college students in resource management. It is the perfect place to send a child for study abroad. The town itself is charming and very quiet. Don't be surprised if you see horses wandering the streets. The townsfolk are unassuming, delightful and pious. Keep South Caicos on your list as a staging point to visit Grand Turk, or as a place to put in after passing to the north of Navidad, Silver and Mouchoir Banks, as you make your way north from the Caribbean.

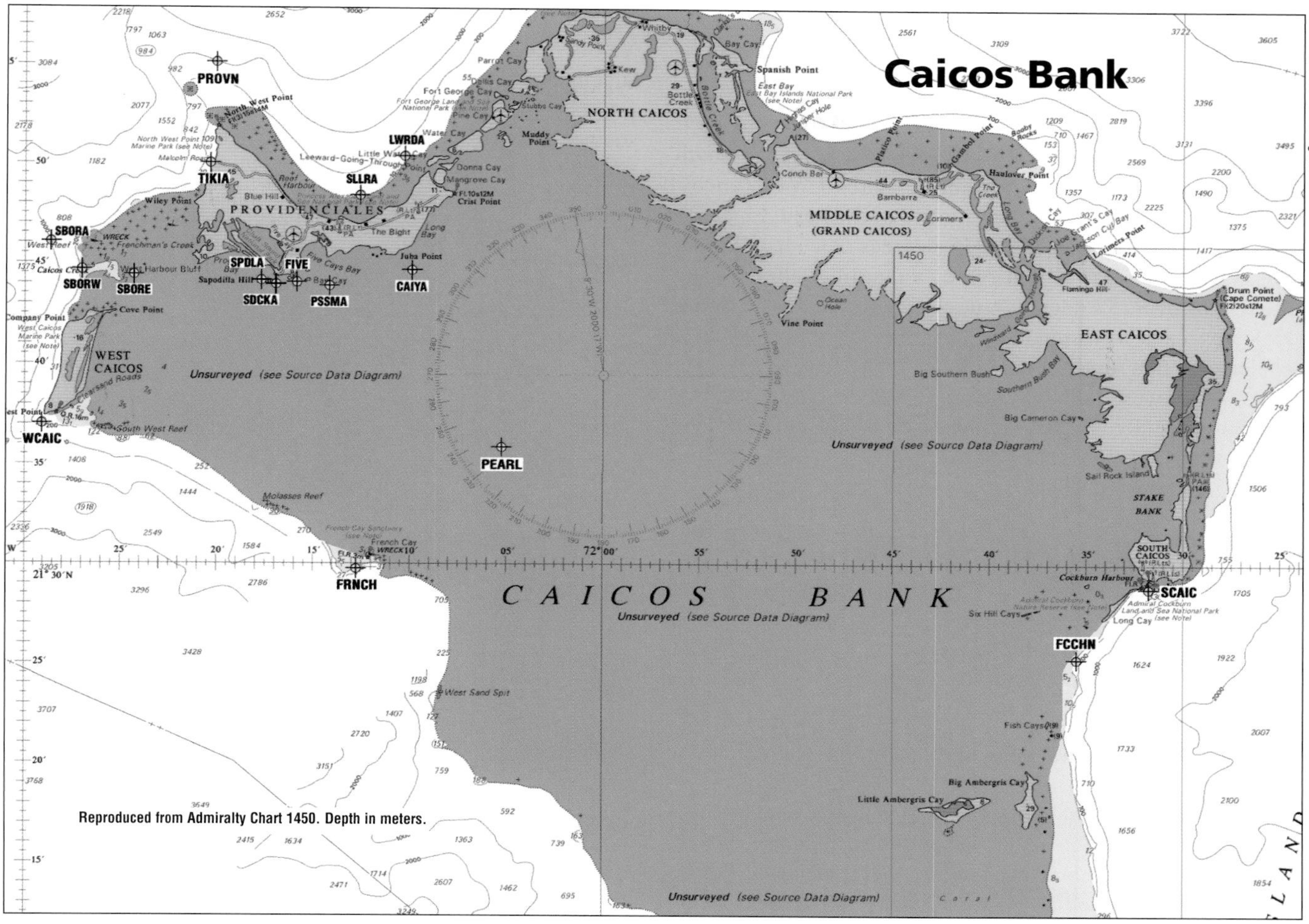

What's There? The Caicos Bank and South Caicos

The Sandbore and Pony Channels

These routes on to the Caicos Bank were covered in Chapter 21, as they are the main approach routes to the south coast of Providenciales from the north.

West Caicos

Most of West Caicos is a national park. Because there are no designated park anchorages, only vessels under 60 feet can anchor here. If you meet the 60 feet and under restriction, there is a recommended anchorage on the west side of the island, at the midpoint. Look for sand, of course, to drop your hook. Scope out your charts and electronic navigation carefully as you navigate these waters, for there are reefs and a wreck for which to watch out.

The snorkeling and diving off the west of West Caicos is superb. Beaches on the east coast are picture perfect. There is an interior lake on the island, Lake Catherine. So take a hike! Along the way look for ruins of an old community. There is construction on the north shore of the island. A Ritz Carlton-backed resort and marina community, called Molasses Reef, has been struggling to be completed. The last we heard, the marina

Clearing In—Your Options in South Caicos

The one Caicos Bank entry port, other than the options we have listed in Providenciales, is Cockburn Harbour on South Caicos. You can clear in at either the government dock or SeaView Marina.

Small boat dock, South Caicos. WATERWAY GUIDE PHOTOGRAPHY.

channel and basin had been dredged, bulkheaded, then put on hold. Supposedly, cruisers can anchor in the basin. It might be worth the dinghy adventure to check it out.

West Caicos to Sapodilla or South Dock

The entry route on to the Caicos Bank, serving the south coast of Providenciales, runs from the south of West Caicos. From the West Caicos waypoint (WCAIC), head 13 nautical miles on a course of 055/235 degrees true. It will take you to Sapodilla Bay (SPDLA), or a marginal alteration to a course of 057/237 degrees true will take you to the South Dock Approach waypoint (SDCKA). There are no particular problems on this route. Don't hug the coast close to the West Caicos Southwest Point at the start, and be conscious that the Southwest Reefs are to starboard as you enter Caicos Bank water.

Molasses Reef

Molasses Reef is about half way between West Caicos and French Cay, at approximately N 21° 35.000'/W 072° 20.000'. You are unlikely to pass this way, but we mention the reef simply because it is the site of the oldest shipwreck discovered in the Turks and Caicos. Go to the National Museum in Grand Turk to see what was recovered from the site.

French Cay

French Cay is a good departure waypoint for Luperón, Dominican Republic, and offers a staging anchorage if you want to overnight there rather than carry on directly. Remember that French Cay is a wildlife sanctuary, which governs your activities while you are there. From the South Dock Approach waypoint (SDCKA), set a course of 164/344 degrees true for 14.7 nautical miles for French Cay (FRNCH). Bear in mind the warnings about Caicos Bank charting and the depths on the Caicos Bank. You cannot run this course as a straight shot because the Caicos Bank extends to the southeast for another 30 nautical miles. Run south-southeast for about 10 nautical miles to N 21° 20.000'/W 072° 10.000' before taking up your bluewater heading.

The Caicos Bank No-Go Areas

There are three areas that are only for exploration in a shoal-draft vessel. The first is the full run of the northeastern segment—the Caicos Bank bordering North Caicos, Middle Caicos and East Caicos all the way to South Caicos. There is a shoal-draft route from the Leeward Going Through to South Caicos used by local craft, but it has no utility to the cruising yacht. One would probably regret the attemp. The second area is the whole sector south of the Ambergris Cays, centered on the Seal Cays. Yes, explore it if you wish and are prepared for it, but don't go straight through the middle of it heading from the Caicos Yard to Luperón. The third area is the edge of the Caicos Bank running southeast from French Cay. It is largely unsurveyed. It may offer superb routes on and off the Bank, brilliant fishing and diving, even fair-weather anchorages. Air reconnaissance over the area to get some idea what was there has been done in a light aircraft at low altitude, and it seemed that "all the above" could be true.

We should mention one final area. That is the shoals and coral in the center of the Caicos Bank around N 21° 35.000'/W 072° 05.000'. It is not a no-go area, but it is an area where, if you don't take the Pearl Channel and try to work your way around the shallower water, you could find trouble. You can bypass it, but we think the simplest and best transit route is to take one central waypoint right in the channel, and go that way.

Center Bank

Crossing the Caicos Bank from Providenciales to the Turks Island Passage or the reverse, the Pearl Channel (the PEARL waypoint) through the shallows and reef lying in the middle of the Caicos Bank around N 21° 35.000'/W 072° 05.000' is the best way to go. It is a rather grand name for water that is average Caicos Bank depth and runs between two unattractive shallower and more hazardous areas. One way or another, this effectively dictates that your bank transit will be taken as two or more legs, because the alignment of this channel fails to match up neatly with every bank transit course.

We suggest no courses here, for our chart would look like a spider's web if we were to start plotting every option. Other than your projected route, the only other decision to take make is, are you going to have to spend the night on the Caicos bank, and where will you be at the time you want to anchor? Cruisers have spent comfortable nights in 3.7 meters/12.5 feet of water close to N 21° 30.000'/W 072° 00.000'. The downside is that the only fish you may catch through here are barracuda, so you may be dining on canned tuna.

When the sun sets over the wide, unbroken, open waters of the Caicos Bank, you may see a green flash. You will see stars as you have never seen them before, or if there are no stars, the moon—so close you can count the craters. If you have never gone swimming under a full moon in tropic waters 30 miles from the nearest land, this may be your opportunity.

West to East Caicos Bank Transits. Providenciales to Fish Cay Channel

From the South Dock waypoint (SDCKA), run a course of 126/306 degrees true for 13.6 nautical miles to the Caicos Mid-Bank channel waypoint (PEARL). Remember, this is no channel, just an area where your track gives slightly greater depths than the more shoal and reef-strewn areas on each side of the line you are taking. At this point, alter to a course of 112/292 degrees true, and the Fish Cays Channel (FCCHN) lies 29.4 nautical miles ahead. Again, this is hardly a channel, but a place where you gain largely reef-clear access to the deep water of the Turks Island Passage. These transits need to be navigated visually all the way.

The Fish Cays

Fish Cay Channel (FCCHN), is your exit to the Turks Island Passage. The point at which you move off the bank into the deep water need not be quite as exact as that, and there are other equally good crossing places between Long Cay and the Fish Cays. You are about 30 nautical miles from the PEARL waypoint in this area and about 23 nautical miles from the anchorage coordinates. Working backward, PEARL to Providenciales is roughly 15 nautical miles to Sapodilla (the anchorage stop is almost exactly at the halfway point). The Fish Cays may well be a place you want to go for swimming, diving or fishing. Or rest before setting out again.

Fish Cay Channel to South Caicos

Heading for South Caicos, the preferred route from Providenciales is to go to the Fish Cays, and then head north in the deep water of the Turks Island Passage for the last five miles or so. The reason is that the Caicos Bank side of South Caicos becomes progressively more shoal, and there is no reason to spend hours crawling along there in fear of being stuck. From FCCHN, just run in the deep, blue water on a course of 046/226 degrees true along the western edge of the Turks Passage for 4.6 nautical miles, and then turn in toward South Caicos.

Fish Cay Channel to Big Sand Cay

A run of 21.5 nautical miles on a course of 125/305 degrees true across the Turks Island Passage takes you to a point 2.5 nautical miles to the northwest of Big Sand Cay. If you want to anchor off, the best area lies some 0.3 nautical miles east-southeast of this point. Once you are clear of Big Sand Cay, you are set to take off for Luperón or Puerto Plata in the Dominican Republic or to Puerto Rico. Alternatively, you can set out directly for any of these destinations from the Fish Cay area.

The Ambergris Cays

Big Ambergris Cay has been sold to a development company. Promises have been made to leave Little Ambergris Cay as it is now, and all development will take place on Big Ambergris Cay, which already has an airstrip. The cay's native iguana population has been evacuated to Long Cay, south of South Caicos. Ambergris development plans follow much the same pattern as West Caicos.

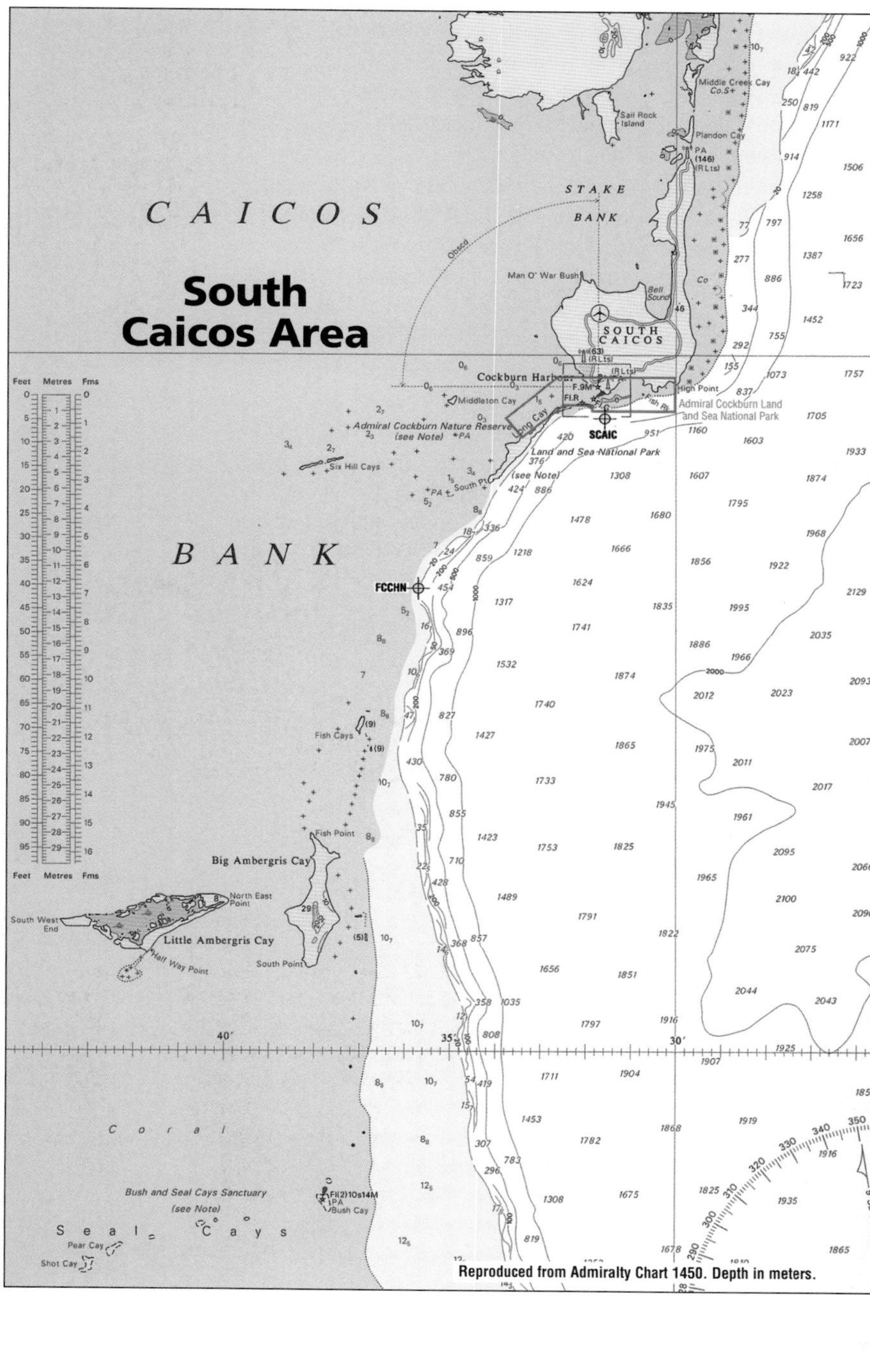

Pilotage. Talking Captain to Captain

South Caicos. Cockburn Harbour

The entry lights on Dove Cay and Long Cay are red right returning. The underwater contours passing beneath your keel as you turn to enter Cockburn Harbour are sensational. Within half a mile, one passes depths from 900 meters/3,000 feet to 15 meters/50 feet, and then 6 meters/20 feet. From the South Caicos waypoint (SCAIC), your close approach into Cockburn Harbour is on a course of about 327/147 degrees true, a line that takes you between Long Cay to port and Dove Cay to starboard.

The 6-meter/20-foot depths gradually reduce to 3.6 meters/12 feet, and then 2.4 to 2.7 meters/8 to 9 feet off the town. The government dock has 2.4-meter/8-foot depths. There is an anchorage behind the northern end of Long Cay, where you will find 1.8-meter/6-foot depths. To the west, the Caicos Bank shoals to depths of 0.9 meters/3 feet, with a lot of sand running northwest from South Caicos itself, and the southern half of Long Cay where the main sandbar hugs Middleton Cay.

The holding in the Cockburn anchorage is questionable. Find a pocket of sand to drop your hook, but be aware it is hard limestone down there, and it probably won't dig in very far. Why this reputation as the finest harbor around? Because South Caicos has protection from high seas from all directions. What you don't have is protection from wind from the southwest through the northwest. Unless there is a storm, winds from these sectors are unlikely to cause concern.

If you don't want to go to Cockburn Harbour, you can also anchor behind Six Hill Cays or Long Cay. Cruising boats headed for Luperon have found safe, overnight anchorage behind these cays in prevailing east to southeast winds. There are sufficient depths to accommodate boats drawing 6 feet. This is a great jumping off point for the Dominican Republic. ■

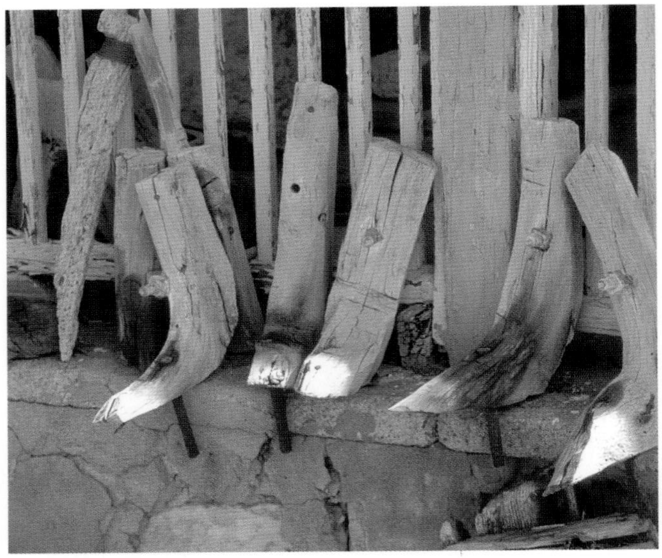

The bones of those who didn't make it.
WATERWAY GUIDE PHOTOGRAPHY.

Caicos Bank and South Caicos Waypoints

Sandbore Channel App	SBORA (1)	21°46.00N / 72°28.00W
Sandbore Channel West	SBORW (3)	21°44.55N / 72°27.00W
Sandbore Channel East	SBORE	21°44.50N / 72°24.00W
Sapodilla Bay App	SPDLA	21°44.25N / 72°17.50W
South Dock App	SDCKA (10)	21°44.21N / 72°17.00W
Five Cays Anchorage	FIVE	21°44.08N / 72°16.00W
South Side Marina App	SSMAP	21°43.85N / 72°13.85W
South Side Turn In Pt	SSMTP	21°45.40N / 72°13.86W
Caicos Boatyard App	CAIYA (12)	21°44.66N / 72°10.07W
Caicos Boatyard Entry	CAIYE	21°45.65N / 72°10.05W
West Caicos	WCAIC (2)	21°36.50N / 72°29.40W
French Cay	FRNCH (11)	21°30.00N / 72°12.50W
Pearl Channel	PEARL (18)	21°36.00N / 72°05.00W
South Caicos	SCAIC (24)	21°28.80N / 71°31.80W
Fish Cay Channel	FCCHN (81)	21°23.80N / 71°35.30W

Position format is latitude and longitude in degrees and minutes (hddd°mm.mm). Waypoints in RED are NOT for autopilot navigation. Codes in parenthesis are Wavey Line waypoints marked on the charts. If you have programmed waypoints listed in a previous edition of this guide, check carefully to ensure the coordinates you have recorded match the list. If a waypoint is no longer on the list we may have changed its code or deleted it.

Turks and Caicos Islands where the rocks lead out to the sea. ©IstockPhoto/e_skop

GOIN' ASHORE:

SOUTH CAICOS

airport • bank • customs & immigration • fuel • groceries • marine services • medical • police • post office • propane • restaurant telephone • water

South Caicos boasts the best harbor (Cockburn Harbour) in the Turks and Caicos Islands, with very good diving close by. The South Caicos harbor is primarily a commercial harbor, handling fresh conch and lobster, and bringing in fuel and supplies to the island via the government dock. Fourteen congregations attend the many churches. South Caicos is an entry port, but you will not likely encounter a long line waiting to clear in at SeaView Marina, an old-world sort of facility that may not look like Turtle Cove, but means every bit as much to the island's citizens. In addition, *SeaView's* helpfulness and service is on par with the very best. For Customs and Immigration procedures and Cruising and Fishing Permits see the Buff Pages. You can anchor in the harbor, but if south-southwesterly winds become uncomfortable, move to the northern side of Long Cay, mindful of the wreck off its shoreline.

MARINA

SEAVIEW MARINA IN COCKBURN HARBOUR
TEL: 649-946-3219/3245 • FAX: 649-946-3508 • VHF 16
SEAVIEWM@TCIWAY.TC

Your hosts at SeaView Marina are Captain Lewis Cox, Norman and Velma.

Slips 3. **Max LOA** 120 ft. **MLW at Dock** 6.5 ft. **Dockage** Free overnight **Fuel** Gas and diesel, Shell fuel, 5000+ gallon fuel truck, open 24/7. **Facilities & Services** Groceries, transportation, restaurant, telephone, experienced mechanic on site, lubricants, oils and spare parts, distributors for OMC products. Haul out to 100', engine and electric repair, propane, water, electric, showers and laundry. Vessels unable to come to the Shell dock are serviced at the government dock. Port of entry. **Credit Cards** Visa, MasterCard, AMEX and Discover.

PORT DIRECTORY

Accommodations *South Caicos Ocean Haven* • 649-946-3444 • divesouth@tciwaytc • www.oceanhaven.tc • room, restaurant and bar, dive operation. *Miss May's Bed & Breakfast*, in the old Commissioner's house.

Airport *South Caicos Airport* • 649-946-3267 • is serviced by charter airlines.

Bank *First Caribbean International Bank*, 649-946-3268, open Wednesday 9 a.m. to 1 p.m.

Dive Operator *South Caicos Ocean Haven* • 649-946-3444 • divesouth@tciwaytc • www.oceanhaven.tc

Customs and Immigration • 649-946-3214/3281 • Will come to SeaView • The most helpful officers in the islands.

Fuel *SeaView Marina Shell* Fuel dock with diesel, gasoline and water. *Pinnacle Fuel Suppliers* • 649-946-3283/3417 • VHF 16 "Charlie Alpha" • *Ken Lightbourne or Norman Saunders.* No 2 diesel, unleaded gas and oils. Will deliver groceries and water too if you are at anchor.

Medical *South Caicos Clinic*, 649-946-6970.

National Parks See our *National Parks, Nature Reserves, Sanctuaries and Historical Sites* section in the Green Pages for more details.

Post Office In town, 649-946-3211. Open Monday through Thursday, 8 a.m. to 4 p.m., Friday until 3:30 p.m.

Provisions *Sea View Market* • 649-944-3245/3508 • Open 6:30 a.m. to 11 p.m. Well-stocked, fresh produce, ice, charts and car rental. Fresh fish, lobster and conch often available.

Regatta Last week in May.

Repairs *SeaView Marina* • *Bayside Autoparts* Ask for Dwain.

Restaurants *SeaView Marina* • *Ocean Haven* • 649-946-3444 • Generous and delicious portions of fish, local conch and lobster in season. $$ • *Pond View Restaurant. Love's,* on the Airport Road. *Miss Muriel's* in the middle of town. *Eastern Inn* in town. *Miss May's Bed & Breakfast.*

Taxi *SeaView Marina.*

Telephone *SeaView Marina.*

THINGS TO DO IN SOUTH CAICOS

- Photograph fish in 100-foot underwater visibility.
- Hike for miles without seeing another person.
- Swim in the shallow, reef-protected water on the east coast.
- Photograph Sassy Sam, the sea serpent turned to stone at the harbor entrance. Or, walk over to the Boiling Hole. You might see some pink flamingoes.
- Perhaps you will find the pirate treasure if you search between Blackbeard and Treasure Islands.

Caicos Bank sunset. WATERWAY GUIDE PHOTOGRAPHY.

Chapter 23
Grand Turk Island and the Turks Bank

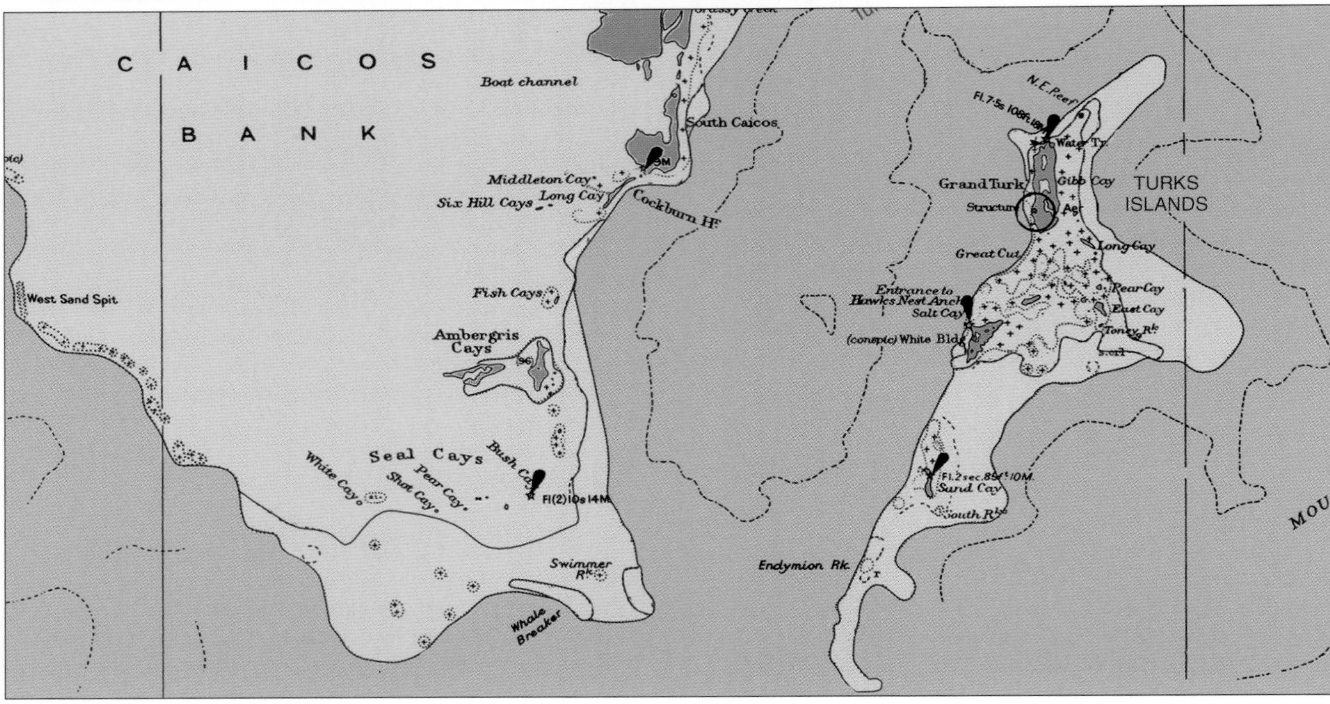

Not to be used for navigation.

Looking At the Charts

Historic and charming, Grand Turk is the long-established center of government for the Turks and Caicos Islands. It is the largest of the Turks islands and a principal port. However, even as the largest, it is less than seven miles long, and one and a half miles wide, so you can walk or golf cart to just about everything. It is much warmer here than even in the southernmost Bahamas. The average year-round temperature is 83 degrees, but the steady, easterly trade winds temper the heat and keep the island pleasant.

The island is almost encircled by off-lying reefs. Some are very close to the western shore and others, one to ten miles off, on the eastern side. There are no natural harbors on Grand Turk, but there are designated national park anchorages along the western shore. The salt lake to the north, named North Creek, looks so promising for protection. But its northern exposure and constant shoaling make it inaccessible to all but the shallowest draft boats in the most placid conditions.

In the Spotlight. Cockburn Town, Grand Turk Island

Cockburn Town is the seat of government for the Turks and Caicos Islands. The government and the governor are here, as are the ceremonial mansions and offices. However, much of government work happens at South Base, just to the south of the airport. An unusual name? South Base was once a United States Air Force (USAF) center built to support the initial orbital flights of the U.S. Space Program. Their mission was to recover space capsules after splashdown in the adjacent ocean waters. From space monkeys to astronauts like John Glenn, they returned from space to this paradise.

North Base, a second USAF station on the northeast corner of the island is home to the Turks and Caicos Community College campus. Near North Base, there is an 1852 lighthouse worth visiting. It is a rare one indeed, constructed of ship plate sent to Grand Turk from England in do-it-yourself kit form, but that is not its only unusual feature. Four massive steel springs support its tower to flex and right it under storm stress, and to serve as lightning conductors. A chain dropped into a cistern dug deep into its supporting platform grounds each spring. The lighthouse is still in service.

The only thing that picturesque Cockburn Town is missing are horse-drawn coaches with Dalmatians running at their

All Those Cockburns

What about all these Cockburns. Cockburn Harbour in South Caicos, just across the road, and now Cockburn Town, with those 22 miles of fast-running deep ocean passage between them?

Admiral Cockburn is the man. Just one "Go Everywhere" 18th-century Admiral, with a passion for property acquisition. The naming seems a touch of overkill, but then think of all the (Admiral of the Ocean Seas) Columbuses. These namings just happen. Maybe as favors, maybe to keep the legend alive.

wheels to take you back in time. Some buildings are new, but most are vintage, with a charm you will not find anywhere else in these islands. The town is planned along the simple pattern of two narrow roads leading through the town, connected by lateral lanes or "streets."

Behind the town, still-flooded saltpans or salinas give a curious Venetian look to the whole area - lagoon on one side, ocean on the other. The town's buildings are of the Bermudian style with steep-pitched red roofs, wide verandas and attractively painted shutters to match the gates of their surrounding yard walls.

Curiously, with all this historic beauty to tour on the island, the busy $60 million Grand Turk Cruise Center ship dock is home to the largest Margaritaville bar and restaurant in the Caribbean. The restaurant is 17,000 square feet of cheeseburger- and fry-eating cruise ship passengers, who, when they aren't eating, can shop duty-free at the Trading Post shopping complex or dip their toes in a 500,000 gallon, 3-foot-deep swimming pool. With 50,000 passengers per month dropping by during the high season, clearly they are looking for just this sort of entertainment on Grand Turks Island.

Clearing In—Your Options in Grand Turk

Your one entry port in Grand Turk Island and in the Turks Bank sea area is South Dock, the government wharf off South Base on the west coast, just south of Grand Turk Airport.

Grand Turk Island

North Creek

We said Grand Turk has no natural harbors. Now we will counter our assertion. Look at the north end of the island. The inland lagoon that connects to the ocean through a narrow channel is known as North Creek. Long ago, before a hurricane or two, that connecting channel was wider and navigable. Two problems prevent North Creek's viability as a harbor.

The first is the close approach offshore. The full force of the Atlantic Ocean can hit you on the run in. The second is the coral reef a quarter of a mile off the entrance. Much of it lies deep enough to pass under your keel, but some not. (Unfortunately, part of the reef was blasted with dynamite back when Rothschild was working on the entry channel.) As if those aren't enough obstacles, the main problem is depth in the entry channel. Given the right tide, beam and draft, one can get into North Creek, and it could well serve as a storm refuge, but not for most of us.

South Dock

To clear in at Grand Turk Island, report to South Dock (GTDCK), two nautical miles to the south of the GTURK waypoint. The dock is prominent and stands out from the coast. If you have any landfall ID problems, the airport—Grand Turk International—lies just about halfway between the town (the waypoint) and South Dock. Its runway is aligned east-west. The approach path of incoming aircraft can lead you. On shore, in the inherited buildings of the one-time USAF South Base, the Turks and Caicos government carries out much of its business. Immediately to the north is Governors Beach, named because it fronts Waterloo, the residence of the UK-appointed Governor of the Turks and Caicos. Governors Beach, despite its name, is in the public domain, open to all. After clearing in at South Dock, you may want to move and anchor off Cockburn Town so you can tour the town and visit the museum.

The North Creek Story

Looking at Grand Turk Island, you don't need anyone to tell you that North Creek would make a superb all-weather harbor and no bad choice as a hurricane hole. Some 15 years ago, a Rothschild from New Jersey held this view. At that time, the run-off between the lagoon and the ocean was no more than a trickle of water, and clearly what amounted to the excavation of a canal had to be set in motion. He had money at his disposal and extraordinary mechanical aptitude. He was hooked on heavy machinery, and enjoyed nothing better than putting it to work, hands on, himself. He proposed opening up North Creek to make it a harbor, and wanted no more in return than the title to the land each side of the entry channel he would excavate. The proposal was accepted.

The equipment needed was shipped to Grand Turk at his own expense. He started work, and took the channel down to 2.4 to 3 meters/8 to 10 feet, using the spoil to build a breakwater extending out into the ocean on the western side of the entrance to the creek. At the lagoon end, a continuation of the entry channel for three-eighths of a mile took the channel through the northern shallows to reach the deeper interior water. At last, North Creek was open to boats, but Rothschild quit at that point.

Perhaps the effort had been too great. Perhaps it had become evident that the new channel was already threatened. At the ocean end, wind and waves eroded the spoil bank and silted the entrance. The coral remained an unsolved problem. All the length of the channel, the banks were collapsing, and the water depth achieved was short lived. Later, in a desperate move to halt this continual erosion, every derelict vehicle in the island was taken and dumped along the spoil bank to reinforce it. The rusted frames are there to this day, together with the rusting hulks of the abandoned Rothschild plant. At the ocean end, the flamingos now take advantage of sand flats that at one time were never there.

North Creek approach. *(Not to be used for navigation.)* WATERWAY GUIDE PHOTOGRAPHY.

Grand Turk's South Dock. *(Not to be used for navigation.)* WATERWAY GUIDE PHOTOGRAPHY.

Grand Turk Island

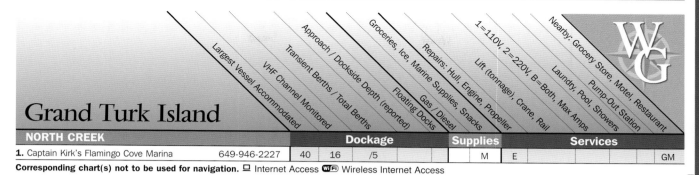

NORTH CREEK	Phone	Largest Vessel Accommodated	VHF Channel Monitored	Transient Berths / Total Berths	Approach / Dockside Depth (reported)	Floating Docks	Gas / Diesel	Groceries, Ice, Marine Supplies, Snacks	Repairs: Hull, Engine, Propeller	Lift (tonnage), Crane, Rail	1=110V, 2=220V, B=Both, Max Amps	Laundry, Pool, Showers	Pump-Out Station	Nearby: Grocery Store, Motel, Restaurant
		Dockage					Supplies		Services					
1. Captain Kirk's Flamingo Cove Marina	649-946-2227	40	16	/5				M	E					GM

Corresponding chart(s) not to be used for navigation. Internet Access Wireless Internet Access

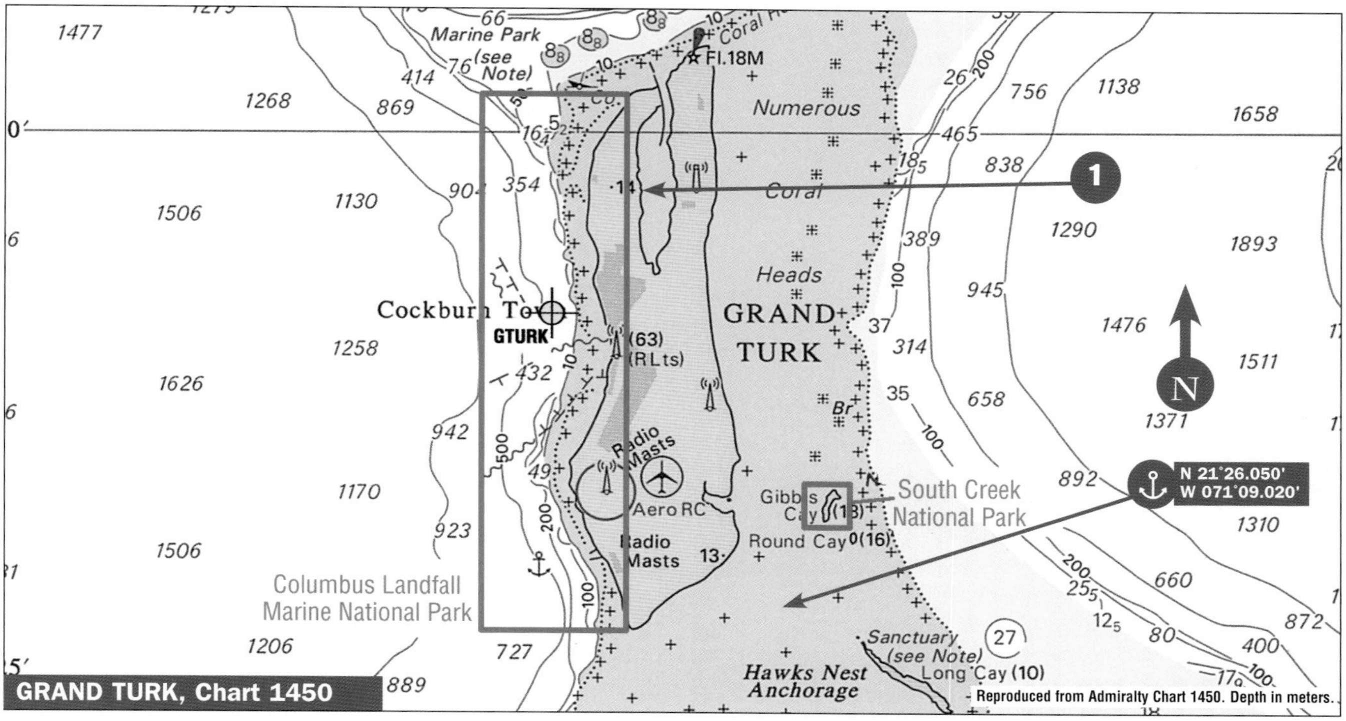

GRAND TURK, Chart 1450

- Reproduced from Admiralty Chart 1450. Depth in meters.

The Turks Bank

The Turks Bank, though significantly smaller in area than the Caicos Bank, is nonetheless a significant feature. Roughly 36 miles in length and 15 miles across at the widest point, it runs from 15 meters/50 feet deep to the near-zero of shipwrecking reefs, of which there are many. Grand Turk Island, Salt Cay and Big Sand Cay farther south, are the principal land features.

The Turks Bank is not a cruising ground, as it is exposed to the Atlantic Ocean. There are virtually no marine backup facilities, and other than North Creek in Grand Turk Island, no place to even consider in severe weather. What the Turks Bank does offer is Grand Turk as an entry port, with communications facilities, including its air services and a hospital. Big Sand Cay is fine springboard waypoint for passagemakers heading for the Caribbean. Those coming from the Caribbean are more likely to come around the north of Grand Turk Island passing on the northern side of the Navidad, Silver and Mouchoir Banks.

Count on superb fishing and diving on the Turks Bank and around its drop-offs, but for diving, it is best to go with Grand Turk and Salt Cay local operators who know their home territory. For these reasons, our navigational offering on the Turks Bank is minimal. We have no desire to tempt you into trouble.

Hawks Nest Anchorage

The Hawks Nest anchorage is the broad area of deeper water about one nautical mile southeast of the southern point of Grand Turk. It is protected from the open Atlantic Ocean by the reefs and Long Cay, Pear Cay and East Cay. If you tuck yourself close in to the Grand Turk shore, you can gain protection from the north. Nevertheless, you are going to be exposed to wind from just about every direction. In truth, it is not rated highly as an anchorage.

Salt Cay

Barely three miles in length and just 2.5 square miles in area, Salt Cay, has a maximum elevation of 25 feet. It was at one time nothing but salt ponds and a world leader in salt production. Much of the salt went straight up north to pack the cod of the Grand Bahama Banks fishing fleets. Today, picturesque windmills still pump salt ponds that are hundreds of years old. The salt business did not end here until 1964.

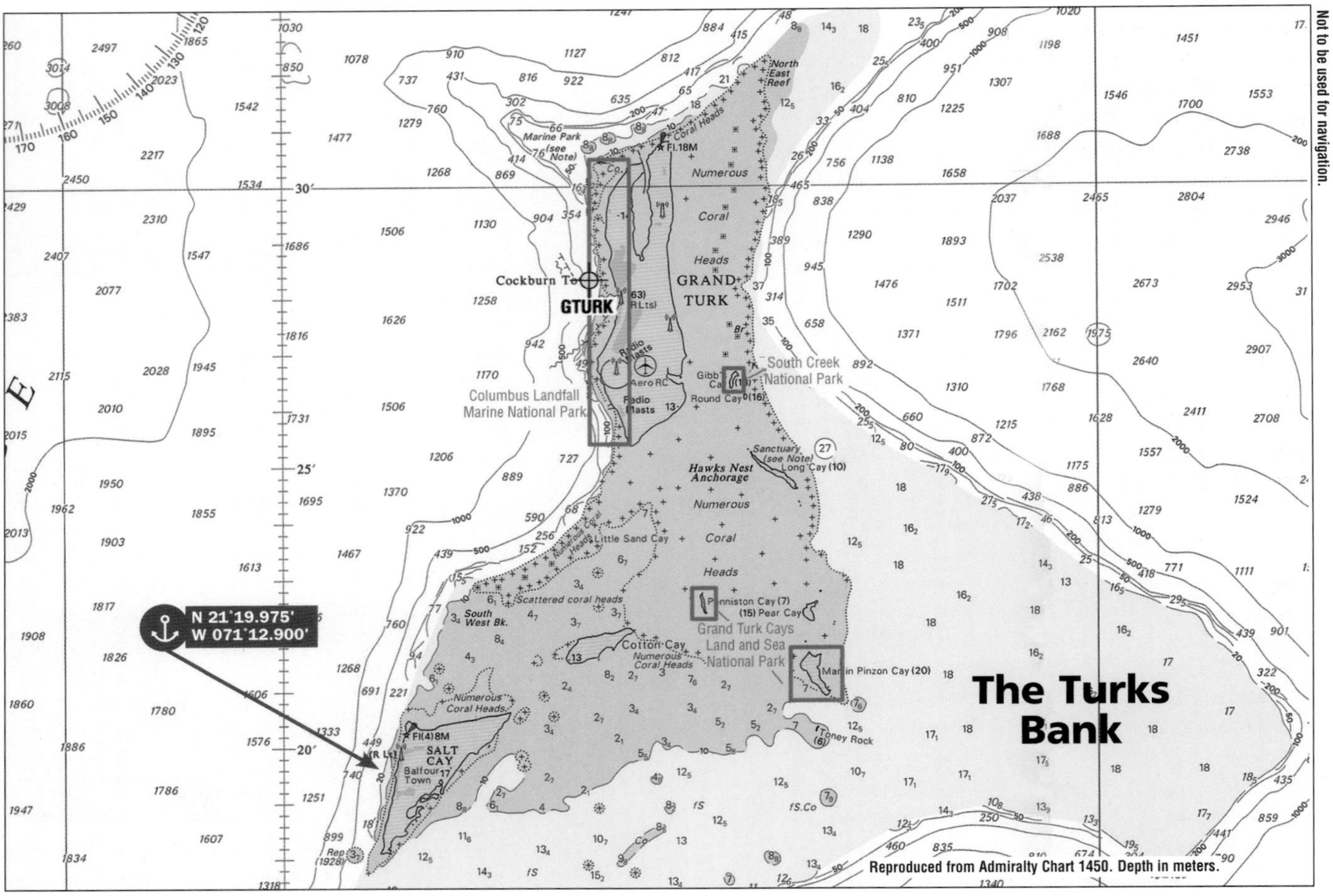

Reproduced from Admiralty Chart 1450. Depth in meters.

About 125 people live on the island, which has now become fashionable with Non-Belongers—refugees from harsher, more northern climates. They find the isolation of Salt Cay and its lack of any of the trappings of the outside world refreshing and agreeable.

Big Sand Cay

The cay, just over 1.25 miles in length, is uninhabited. Its navigation light, shared with Grand Turk Island, has the distinction of being the only working light in the Turks and Caicos at the time of this writing. A popular anchorage is over sand just to the southwest of the light, where you will find 3.6 to 4.5 meters/12 to 15 feet of water, just about 0.3 nautical miles southeast of our approach waypoint.

Protected Areas

The Columbus Landfall Marine Park off Grand Turk Island, the South Creek National Park and the Grand Turk Cays National Land and Sea Park protects the Turks Bank. Long Cay, to the southeast of Grand Turk Island, is a Sanctuary, as is Big Sand Cay. Salt Cay itself and the *Endymion* wreck are listed as Historical Sites.

Pilotage. Talking Captain to Captain

Cockburn Town Anchorage

The largely coral-free area to the immediate north of South Dock is the anchorage used by freighters. We suggest that if you have cleared in, move farther north and anchor off Cockburn Town if you want to stay. There is a near continuous belt of coral along the west coast between the wall and the beach. A relatively coral-free area comes up just south of the N 21° 29.000' line. Be aware that anchoring is prohibited under the approach path to the airport.

North Creek

North Creek extends for two nautical miles running almost due north-south, from the coral at the entry point to its southern limit. The entry channel is three-quarters of a mile in length, narrow (no more than 6 meters/20 feet at one point), but able to take most craft under 15 meters/50 feet in length. It has 0.9-meter/3-foot depths at mean low water, reduced to around 0.7-meters/2.5-foot depths at the southern end by a sand hump. Locals try to maintain two white poles as markers to the channel.

We hesitate to be specific about the draft that can be taken into North Creek because one sandbar (the hump we mentioned), by a little beach about one-quarter of the way in on the port side, is encroaching into the channel. That mean low water depth dictates use of the channel at high water, which will give you another 0.6 meters/2 feet of depth. It should be slack high water, because the tidal flow runs quickly, about 5 to 7 knots at peak. This flow certainly scours the channel and helps keep it clean, but contributes to shoaling.

Inside, North Creek has 4.5-meter/15-foot depths in the middle, its western half shoaling rapidly to 0.6- to 0.9-meter/2- to 3-foot depths. Don't be fooled by the fact that the marine police have their base on that side, about half-way down, and that a clutch of boats may be clustered around their dock, which extends into the deeper water. The median line is as far as you want to go toward the western side.

The eastern side is a far better choice. There are 1.8-meter/6-foot depths almost up to the shoreline (3-meter/10-foot depths under the "White Cliffs") and are protected from the prevailing wind by the limestone ridge that runs northward to Northeast Point. The bottom is soft muck and sand, and your anchor will dig in easily. Maybe too easily. If you don't get it into anything with some hold, you could drag. You would have to have strong winds in there for that to happen and in truth, if you did drag, unless you hit another boat (or the police dock), you would come to little harm in North Creek. Now for our cautions:

- You must enter before the onset of severe weather. Anticipate. Even the swell from a storm in the southern Bahamas can make the entry impassable. Don't wait for the sky to tell you that bad weather is coming your way. If the wind and set are already northerly, forget it.
- Go in only at slack high water (inside North Creek the highs and lows run about twenty minutes after ocean times).
- Watch out for the coral. You should have enough water at high tide, but use your eyes. Even after the blasting, there may still be rogue heads out there.
- Be prepared for a longer stay than you might expect. You cannot exit until the ocean has settled down. This may be as long as two to three days after the storm has passed.

Salt Cay

Salt Cay mooring buoys may or may not be in place for visitors parallel to the shoreline off the west coast. The anchorage, roughly at the latitude of the salinas, is fair and safe in settled weather, but no more than that. Both north and south of this point, coral starts to work out from the coast, markedly at North West Point and at South Point, where the reef extends southward for a good half mile.

Big Sand Cay

Getting to Big Sand Cay from Grand Turk, run south in the deep water along the eastern edge of the Turks Island Passage. From waypoint GTURK, this bluewater route gives you just over 17 nautical miles to run on a course of about 203/023 degrees true to N 21° 12.540'/ W 071° 16.770'. At that point, you will be nearly 2.5 nautical miles northwest of Big Sand Cay, ready to feel your way in to where you want to anchor. A popular anchorage is over sand just to the southwest of the light, where there are 3.6- to 4.5-meter/12- to 15-foot depths, about 0.3 nautical miles southeast of the SANDC waypoint.

The east coast of Big Sand Cay is riddled with too much coral to encourage blind exploration. Three Marys Rocks to the south are visible, as is the line-up of rocks and cays running to

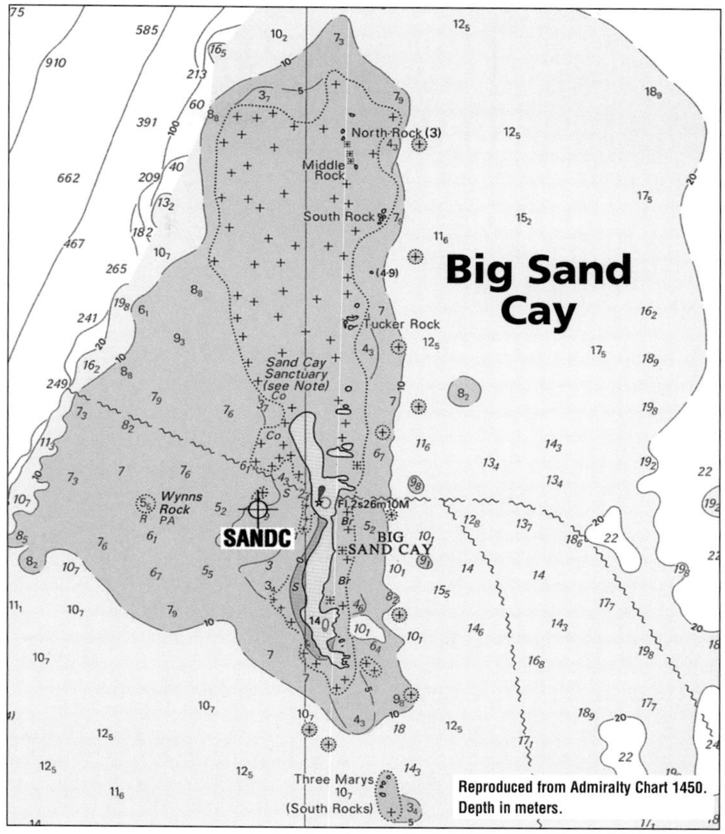

Reproduced from Admiralty Chart 1450. Depth in meters.

the north of Big Sand Cay. What is not so obvious is Endymion Reef, five nautical miles to the southwest. Unless you are going to the reef deliberately to dive, your safest course is to draw a two-nautical-mile radius circle around N 21° 07.000'/ W 071° 18.000', and stay out of this area. If you wish to dive the *Endymion* wreck, Salt Cay Divers, who operate out of the Mount Pleasant Guest House on Salt Cay, can take you there.

If you are on your way to Luperon and points south, be sure to drag a fishing line behind your boat. Even a slow-moving vessel can be rewarded with an exciting bout with a sailfish or marlin in this deep stretch of water. Also, do not be surprised if you encounter a whale on your passage north or south. Get plenty of rest, and set out in the afternoon from Big Sand Cay for an overnight passage to arrive at the entrance to Luperon in early morning, before the onshore breeze kicks in. Then you can rest up and start out on your next adventure on Hispaniola. ■

Grand Turk and Turks Bank Waypoints

North Creek	NCREK (T70)	21°30.96N / 71°08.48W
Grand Turk	GTURK	21°28.15N / 71°09.15W
Grand Turk So Dock	GTDCK (T35)	21°26.00N / 71°09.50W
Salt Cay	GTSLT (T38)	21°20.00N / 71°13.00W
Big Sand Cay	SANDC (T41)	21°11.75N / 71°15.25W

Position format is latitude and longitude in degrees and minutes (hddd°mm.mm). Waypoints in RED are NOT for autopilot navigation. Codes in parenthesis are Wavey Line waypoints marked on the charts. If you have programmed waypoints listed in a previous edition of this guide, check carefully to ensure the coordinates you have recorded match the list. If a waypoint is no longer on the list we may have changed its code or deleted it.

GOIN' ASHORE:

GRAND TURK

airport • bank • customs & immigration • fuel • groceries • medical police • post office • propane • restaurant • telephone • water

Historic and charming, Grand Turk is the long-established center of government for the Turks and Caicos Islands. It is the largest of the Turks Islands and a principal port. Picturesque Cockburn Town homes are bounded by stone walled courtyards and streets lighted with quaint iron street lamps. Be sure to take your camera to Duke and Front Streets. It is a photographer's dream. You will not want to miss the national museum on Front Street, either. It features shipwreck displays, to remind you of the perilous waters in which you journey, and a natural history room with fascinating exhibits on the ecology, geology and topography of these beautiful islands.

There are designated National Park anchorages off Cockburn Town. Consult your charts and electronic navigation aids for details. In the designated park anchorages, regulations apply. There may or may not be park anchorage markers. Do not confuse dive buoys with park markers. The entire west coast of Grand Turk is part of the park system.

The Grand Turk Cruise Center ship dock is off Cockburn Town. The facility is for cruise ship guests only.

Customs and Immigration are at the South Dock on the southwest end of the island. The officers are busy on cruise ship days or if several freighters are anchored off and unloading. All vessels must clear customs before entering the town anchorage. Hail the Harbourmaster on VHF Channel 16 to summons a customs officer to receive instructions.

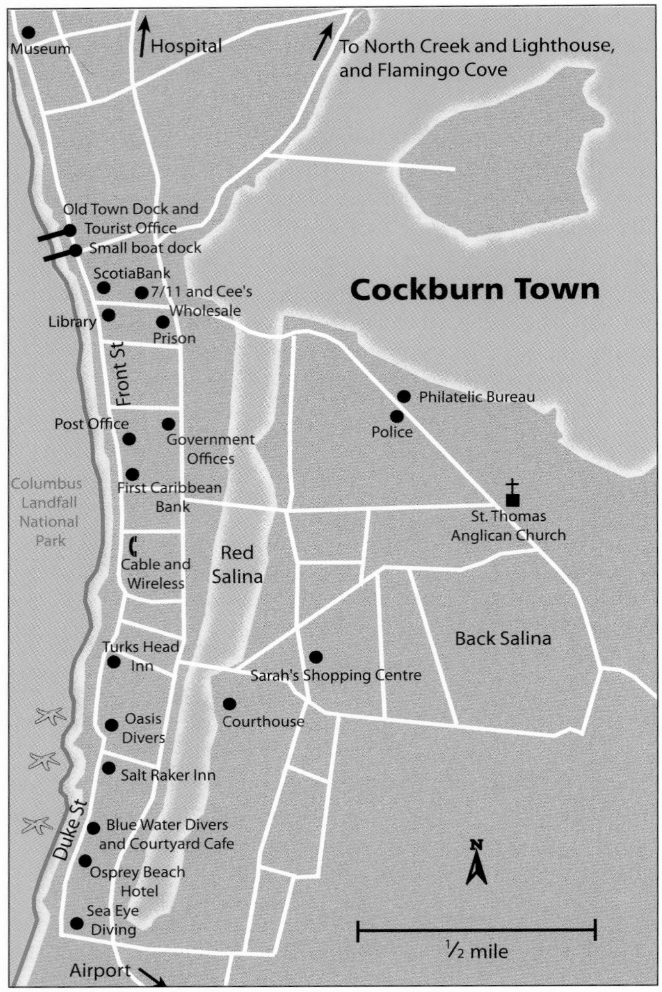

EMERGENCIES

Marine • VHF 16
Medical *Grand Turk Hospital* • 649-946-2040, 649-943-1212, 649-946-2333 (in emergency).
Police • 999 or 911

MARINA

FLAMINGO COVE MARINA IN NORTH CREEK
TEL: 649-946-2227 • FAX: 649-946-2227• CELL: 946-231-0376
captain@tciway.tc • mpl@tciway.tc • www.yamaha.tyc www.captnkirks.com

No transient dockage. They do welcome visitors as best they can to their shallow service dock. **Max LOA** 40 ft. **MLW at Dock** 5 ft.; 3 to 4 feet in channel with as little as 2.5 ft. in some places. **Facilities & Services** Water, engine and hull repairs. Transportation to town can be arranged. The owner of *Flamingo Cove*, Kirk Graff, also runs *MPL Enterprises* that sells and services Yamaha outboard motors and generators.

Accommodations *Arches of Grand Turk*, 649-946-2941, www.grandturkarches.com. Four townhouses.
Island House, 649-946-1519, www.ishousetci.com, ishouse@tciway.tc. Mediterranean-style villa with 8 suites. WiFi, dive packages, golf carts, bicycles, laundry, swimming pool • *Osprey Beach Hotel*, Tel: 649-946-2666, Fax: 649-946-2817, www.ospreybeachhotel.com. Twenty-seven beachfront rooms, 12 atrium rooms. WiFi • *Salt Raker Inn*, 649-946-2260, saltraker@tciway.tc. Twelve rooms. Internet access • *Bohio Dive Resort & Spa,* 649-946-2135, www.bohioresort.com. Twelve rooms, 4 suites with kitchenettes. Fronts a deserted beach. Yoga sessions. Thursday night fire pit parties with roasts and music. Restaurant, bars, pool, spa, WiFi, diving.
White Sands Resort, 649-946-1065, info@whitesandsbeachresorttci.com. Sixteen beachfront condominiums overlooking the cruise port.
Airport & Airlines Cockburn Town Airport, 649-946-2138 • *Air Turks & Caicos*, 649-946-4999 • res@flyairtc.com.
Banks *First Caribbean International Bank*, 649-946-2831. Open Monday through Thursday 8:30 a.m. to 2:30 p.m.; Friday 4:30 p.m. ATM, 24/7. • *ScotiaBank*, 649-946-2506. Open Monday through Thursday 9 a.m. to 3 p.m.; Friday 4:30 p.m. Both banks are on Front Street.

Northeast Point Lighthouse. WATERWAY GUIDE PHOTOGRAPHY.

Churches *St. Mary's Anglican Cathedral Church* built in 1900 • *St Thomas's Anglican Church a*cross the salina. The oldest church on the island, though used infrequently, is well worth visiting to see the old headstones in its cemetery • *Grand Turk Methodist Church* built in 1930.

Couriers FedEx • 649-946-2542/4682 • At *Harbour House*, Front Street. DHL • 649-946-4352 • Daily service from Providenciales. UPS has incoming package delivery only.

Fuel *Texaco Caribbean, Inc*., 649-946-1062.

Library Victoria Public Library, since in 1887. On Front Street.

Liquor *Timco*, 649-946-2044. On Front Street, in *Sarah's Shopping Centre,* an old salt warehouse • *Dot's Liquor*, across the salina. On Pond St.

Marine Supplies & Repairs *MPL Enterprises* • 649-946-2227/649-231-0376 • mpl@tciway.tc • www.yamaha.tc • In North Creek. Distributor for Yamaha products, outboard motors, generators, Carolina Skiffs, Century, Cobia and Eduardono Boats, pumps and accessories • *Do It Yourself* • 649-946-2095. On Airport Rd.

Medical *Downtown Clinic* • 649-946-2328 • Open 8 a.m. to 12:30 p.m. and 2 p.m. to 4:30 p.m. • *Grand Turk Hospital* • 649-946-2040. One mile north of Cockburn Town. Doctors and full-time nurses, surgery, X-ray, laboratory and general medicine • *Philatelic Bureau* • 649-946-1534. Open 8 a.m. to 4:30 p.m. weekdays; to 4 p.m. Fridays. At Church Folly.

Post Office In the blue building on Front Street • 649-946-1331. Open Monday through Thursday, 8 a.m. to 4 p.m.; Fri, 3:30 p.m.

Propane *Grand Turk Gas Depot* • 649-946-2532/649-231-6289. On South Dock.

Provisions *Cee's Wholesale Grocery and Sundries,* 649-946-2030, On Pond Street • *Dot's Food Fair & D&G Wholesale*, 649-946-2324. On Pond Street • *7-Eleven Grocery* around the corner form Cee's and Dot's • *Sarah's Shopping Centre & Sunset Pharmacy*, 649-946-2370. On Frith Street across the Salina. A good selection of canned and dried goods, as well as fresh fruit and vegetables, liquor and pharmacy section • *Robinson Food*, 649-946-1773. On West Rd • *Halls Groceries & Variety Store*, 649-946-2938 • *K's Drugs*, 649-946-2799.

Restaurants Government tax added to all meals, 15 to 20% tip is appreciated.

Courtyard Café Opposite Osprey Beach Hotel. Phyllis serves delicious home-cooked breakfasts and lunches. $

Delany's On Airport Road, serving Caribbean food with a Jamaican flavor. $

Michael's Atrium Restaurant at *Osprey Beach Hotel*, 649-946-2878. Jamaican dishes are the specialty. $

Mookie Pookie on Hospital Road for the best pizza on the island. $

Regal Begal, 649-946-2274 on Hospital Road. Specializing in seafood and Caribbean dishes. $

Secret Garden Restaurant, 649-946-2260. At the *Salt Raker Inn* on Duke Street. Courtyard setting for breakfast, lunch and dinner. $

Water's Edge, 649-946-1680. Very laid-back on the beach on Duke Street. Open for lunch and dinner overlooking the ocean with music from 5:30 p.m. Bar and snacks all day. Happy hour on Fridays. A favorite with divers. $

Taxi *Jackie Williams*, 649-231-6769 • *Omaind Been*, 649-231-0934.

Telephones *LIME* on Front Street. Open 8:30 a.m. to 4 p.m. weekdays; Friday, 3 p.m. $5, $10 and $20 phone cards for sale.

Tourist Office Tel: 649-946-2321. On Front Street.

Travel Agent *T and C Travel*, 649-946-2592. Next to the *Courtyard Café*.

RENTALS

Bicycles Hotels and dive shops have bicycles to rent.

Cars Don't forget to drive on the left, and watch for one-way streets in Cockburn Town. *Dickenson Car Rental*, 649-241-1549 • *Dutchie's Car Rental*, 649-946-2244 or 649-231-1684 • *Yellowman Car Rentals*, 649-231-0167.

Scooters *Val's Scooters* • 649-946-1022 • At the *Triangle Garage*.

SPORTS & RECREATION

Diving All Grand Turk dive operators charge the same amount and have packages with local hotels.

Blue Water Divers, 649-946-2432, rollingmitch32@gmail.com, www.grandturkscuba.com. The only Gold Palm 5 star PADI center on Grand Turk with daily dives over the Grand Turk Wall. Dive trips to South Caicos, cay trips and picnics. Dive shop next to the *Courtyard Café* opposite the *Osprey Beach Hotel*. Mitch Rolling has been leading dive trips since 1983 as well as singing at the Osprey Beach a couple of evenings a week. Visit their web site and quarterly newsletter for dive information.

Oasis Divers, 649-946-1128, oasisdiv@tciway.tc, www.oasisdivers.com. Captains Everette Freites and Dale Barker will show you some of the best dive sites and teach you about migrating patterns of humpback whales. PADI open watercourse, advanced open water-course, rescue, first-aid and dive master courses offered. Equipment rental from their dive shop on Duke Street including Nitrox. Picnic trip to Gibbs Cay for snorkelers and dive trips to Salt Cay.

Sea Eye Diving, 649-946-1407/1408, ci@tciway.tc. Cecil Ingham and his team have been diving the Grand Turk Wall for over a combined 35 years. They specialize in Nitrox diving, teaching underwater photography and video, and extended range diving with picnic trips on Gibbs Cay for everyone.

Fishing *Kel and Meat* at *Bohio Dive Resort*, 649-946-2135 • *White Man's Boat*, 649-946-2244/649-231-1684. Call Dutchie.

Golf *Grand Turk Golf Club*, 649-946-2308/649-231-2514. At the *Governor's Residence* at Waterloo. Nine holes.

National Parks, Sanctuaries, Nature Reserves & Historical Sites For more information on sites and Park Regulations, see the Green Pages.

THINGS TO DO IN GRAND TURK

- Visit the 160-year-old Guinep House, home to the Turks and Caicos National Museum (649-946-2160), on the north end of Front Street. Did you know that the oldest shipwreck in the Americas was found on the rim of the Caicos Bank? You can see the remains of the ship's hull and rigging, as well as cannons, tools and personal possessions of the crew in the museum's central exhibit. Did you know that the highest mountain in the Turks and Caicos is more than 8,000-feet tall? Only 140 feet of it is above sea level—the reason for the breathtaking wall dives. The natural history room in the museum explains and re-creates reef formation. In addition, did you know that the first human inhabitants, the Lucayan Tainos, arrived here by boat more than 1,000 years ago? Find out about pirates and salt rakers, cotton planters, Yankee traders, sisal farmers, ship wreckers and even astronauts by visiting this gem of a museum. Open 10 a.m. to 4 p.m., Monday through Friday, 10 a.m. to 1 p.m. on Saturdays. Admission is donation. Small gift shop with a good selection of books, maps, postcards and island handicrafts.
- Dive the wall! Moreover, dive as many of the fantastic sites as you have time for. Try Nitrox diving, or take a course and improve your dive qualifications. This is world-class diving.
- Return home with a set of the unusual and attractive island stamps, from the Philatelic Bureau at Church Folly.
- Perched on the cliff at Northeast Point, the light from the Grand Turk Lighthouse used to shine out for 20 miles. Built in 1852 of cast iron shipped from England, the original eight small burners produced such a dim light that ships continued to wreck until 1894, when kerosene lamps and a Fresnel lens were installed. Today, the restored lighthouse keeper's quarters, interpretive signs and magnificent ocean views make this national trust site well worth a visit, even if the lighthouse isn't working.
- Watch the whales on their annual migration north, from January through March, or join in the fun of the Conch Carnival in June, Iron Man free-dive competition, barbecue and Junkanoo. For information go to the dive Web site, www.grandturkscuba.com.
- Take a picnic over to Gibbs Cay to ride the horses, meet the rays and snorkel the reef. Take a mini-sub ride, or go on a dive helmet walk.

SALT CAY

diving • medical • restaurant • telephone

The island that time forgot, Salt Cay. Only four square miles and home to three-score people, wandering cows and donkeys. It is only about six miles south of Great Turk, but light years away in modern diversions. Picturesque windmills still pump salt ponds that are hundreds of years old. The salt business did not end here until 1964. One can see evidence of Bermudan influence in some of the older homes, built while the salt trade was flourishing. Salt Cay offers some of the best diving in the region from its shores. It is a mere 40 minutes from the famous *Endymion* wreck dive. The guesthouses and the welcome you will find here are warm and friendly. Salt Cay is a proposed nature reserve. The anchorage off the cay's western shore is unsafe in anything but settled weather. Hopefully when you visit, the plans to have mooring buoys installed off tiny *Deane's Dock* will have materialized. Salt Cay is now a Port of Entry. If this is your arrival in the Turks and Caicos Islands, find the local police officer to obtain clearance.

PORT DIRECTORY

Accommodations *Mount Pleasant Guest House*, 649-946-6901/6927, enquiries@mountpleasantguesthouse.com, www.mountpleasantsalt-cay.com. The oldest guesthouse on Salt Cay. Restaurant, bar and six rooms • *Pirate's Hideaway*, 649-946-6909, piratequeen3@hotmail.com, www.pirateshideaway.com. Two en-suite rooms in the main house and a self-efficient cottage with four bedrooms • *Villa Frangipani, Tradewinds & Compass Rose Cottage & Tradewinds Guest Suites*, 649-946-6906, www.saltcay.us, www.saltcayvilla.com, info@saltcay.us, tradewinds@tciway.tc. Contact Debbie & Ollie • *Genesis Beach House,* 649-946-6906, www.genesisbeachhouse.com. Two, 2-bedroom oceanfront villas adjacent to the dive shop and *Coral Reef Cafe*.

The Vistas of Salt Cay, Two, 2-bedroom suites. Contact Salt Cay divers, 649-946-6906, scdivers@tciway.tc, www.saltcaydivers.tc.

Airlines *Air Turks & Caicos*, 649-946-4181 • *InterIsland Airways* Fly from Grand Turk to Salt Cay on Monday, Wednesday and Friday at 9 a.m. and 4:50 p.m.; returning at 9:20 a.m. and 5 p.m. Daily flights to Provo at 11:40 a.m. and 2:25 p.m.

Diving *Salt Cay Divers*, 649-946-6906, scdivers@tciway.tc, www.saltcaydivers.tc. Full service PADI dive operation. Whales, walls and wrecks. Arches, caves, corals, sponges, sharks and porpoises. Daily dive trips including the *Endymion* wreck. Dive shop and their own accommodations at *Genesis Guest Suites* next to *Deane's Dock*.

Ferry Tel: 649-946-6913. To and from Grand Turk daily. Departs Salt Cay 7 a.m. Departs Grand Turk 2:30 p.m.

Fishing *Lionel Talbot*, 649-946-6929/6909. Fishing guide for wahoo, tuna, marlin and snapper. 700-ft. fishing by hand line and trolling. 18-ft. Boston whaler.

Groceries *H & P Mercantile • Ship to Shore Groceries • Smith's Groceries • Pat's Groceries • Nettie's Groceries.*

Medical *Government Clinic,* 649-946-6968. Open every weekday morning with a resident nurse on the island. For anything major, go to Grand Turk or Provo.

Restaurants Reservations are suggested at all the restaurants, especially for dinner.

Island Thyme Bistro & Internet Cafe, 649-946-6977, pwiii@aol.com. Open for breakfast, 7 a.m. to 9 a.m.; lunch, noon to 2:30 p.m.; dinner, 5 p.m. to 9 p.m. Closed Wednesday. Creative dining with a full bar. $$

Mount Pleasant Guest House, 649-946-6901. Open for breakfast, lunch and dinner. Patio restaurant with bar. $

Pat's Place, 649-946-6919. In the South District. Enjoy *Pat's* native Salt Cay food served in a garden setting. Breakfast at 7:30 a.m., lunch at 12:30 p.m. and dinner at 7:30 p.m. daily. Please call in advance. $

Smuggler's Tavern at *Pirate's Hideaway*, 649-946-6909. By reservation only. Specializing in cheesy fish bake. $

Coral Reef Cafe at the *Salt Cay Dive Shop*, 649-946-6906. Free WiFi.

Green Flash Cafe, 649-946-6904, greenflashwhales@gmail.com. Breakfast, lunch and dinner right on the dock. Fresh fish, lobster, conch and specialty of the house--chicken wings. Wing Night Wednesdays. Come for Rum Punch and watch the sunset. Glow Worm night monthly to watch the sea light up right from the dock. Also, conducts whale-watching trips.

RENTALS

Golf Carts *Nathan Smith* • 649-946-6928 • Charges $40 for a day's rental, carts outside his house to the left of *Mount Pleasant Guest House*. Nathan also has a taxi.

Kayaks *Salt Cay Tours* • 649-946-6904 • At *Deane's Dock.* Visits to surrounding cays, picnics and snorkeling; also ferry service to Grand Turk and babysitting!

THINGS TO DO ON SALT CAY

Don't pass this island by; it is worth a visit, and you can always rent a golf cart for the morning and explore on your own—you can't get lost, and the north beach is glorious. The salinas are interesting, and take a look at the big old White House with its sail lofts and docks. There is another yet unidentified wreck dive, near the site of *HMS Endymion*, which SCUBA Diving Magazine has rated as one of the ten outstanding wreck dives in the world.

BIG AMBERGRIS CAY

The Turks and Caicos Sporting Club on Ambergris Cay is developing the entire cay. Its 5,700-foot jet strip is operational, and a new welcome center is open. The marina is still on the planning books. But, when completed, is expected to offer moorings for yachts greater than 200 feet, as well as a dive shop and marina village accommodations.

Waterway Guide advertising sponsors play a vital role in bringing you the most trusted and well-respected cruising guide in the country. Without our advertising sponsors, we simply couldn't produce the top-notch publication now resting in your hands. Next time you stop in for a peaceful night's rest, let them know where you found them—Waterway Guide, The Cruising Authority.

Subject Index

H

I

J

K

L

M

N

O

P

T

U

V

W

X

Y

Z

Skippers Notes

Advertising Sponsor/Marina Index

ATLANTIC HURRICANE TRACKING CHART

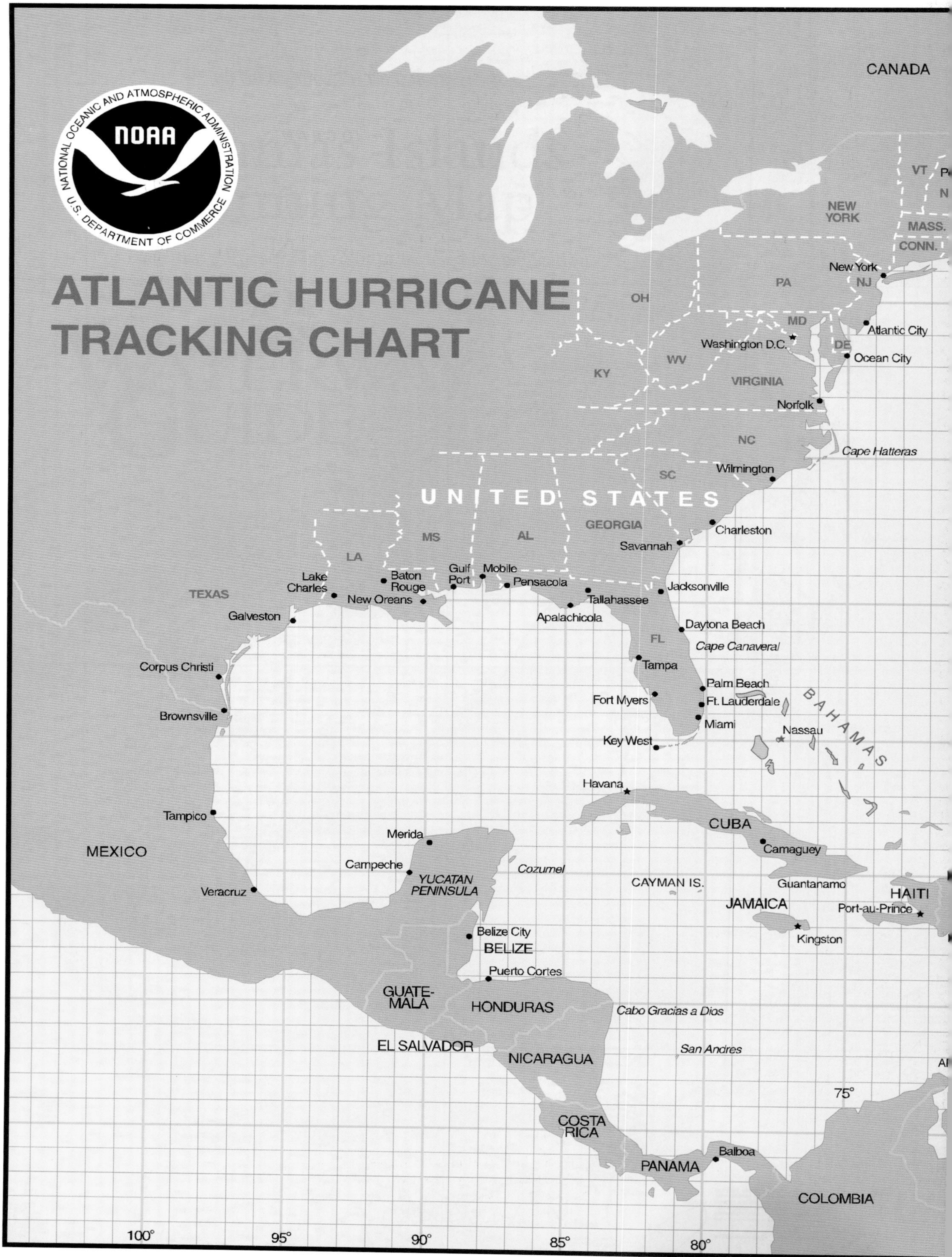

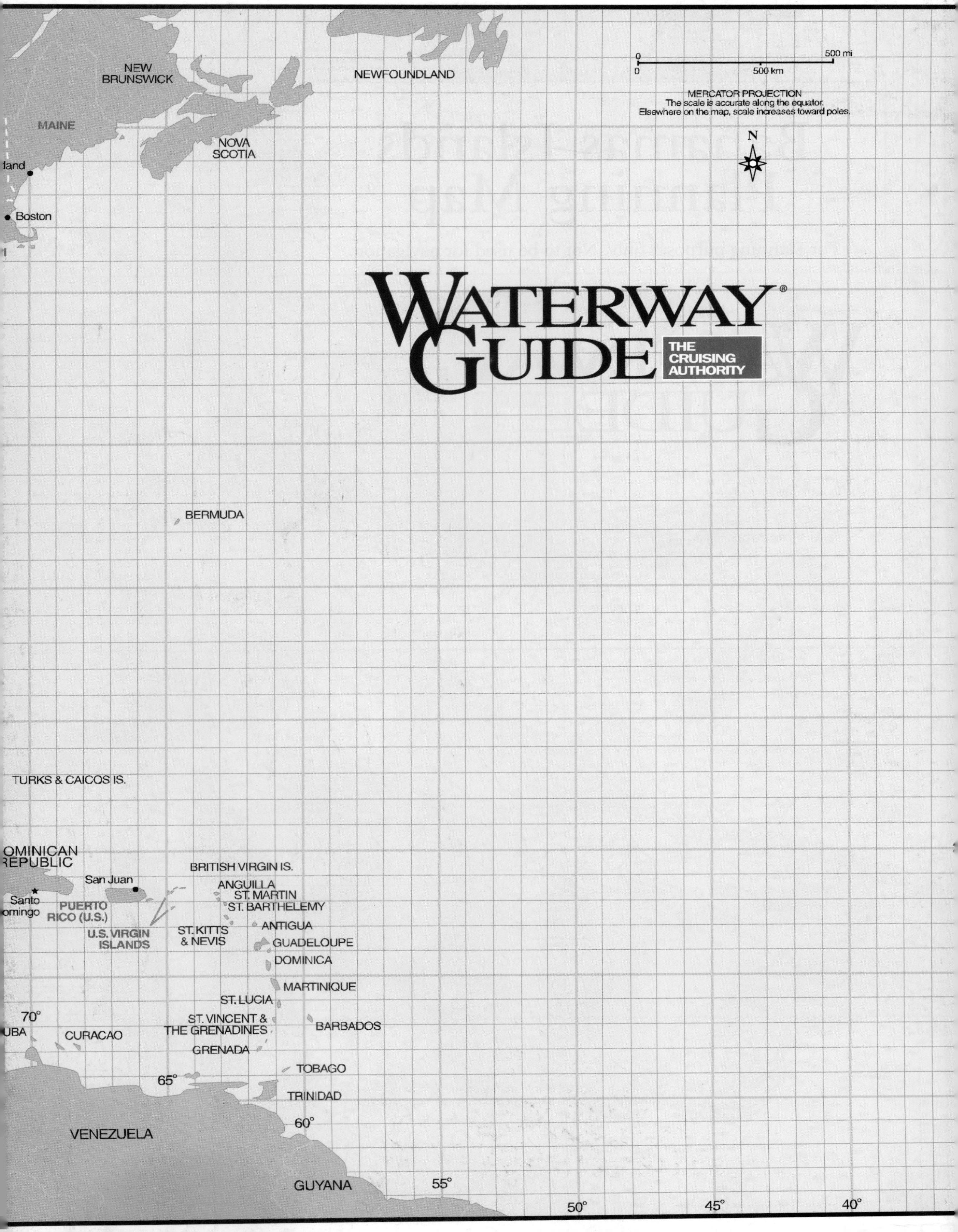
NEW BRUNSWICK
NEWFOUNDLAND
MAINE
NOVA SCOTIA
land
Boston
0 500 mi
0 500 km
MERCATOR PROJECTION
The scale is accurate along the equator.
Elsewhere on the map, scale increases toward poles.
N
WATERWAY® GUIDE
THE CRUISING AUTHORITY
BERMUDA
TURKS & CAICOS IS.
OMINICAN REPUBLIC
San Juan
Santo omingo
PUERTO RICO (U.S.)
U.S. VIRGIN ISLANDS
BRITISH VIRGIN IS.
ANGUILLA
ST. MARTIN
ST. BARTHELEMY
ST. KITTS & NEVIS
ANTIGUA
GUADELOUPE
DOMINICA
MARTINIQUE
ST. LUCIA
ST. VINCENT & THE GRENADINES
BARBADOS
GRENADA
70°
UBA
CURACAO
TOBAGO
65°
TRINIDAD
60°
VENEZUELA
GUYANA
55°
50°
45°
40°